An Exposition of

THE THIRTY-NINE
ARTICLES
OF RELIGION

Historical and Doctrinal

Edward Harold Browne

Reprinted, 1998
Classical Anglican Press
ISBN: 1-893293-50-5

AN EXPOSITION

OF THE

THIRTY-NINE ARTICLES,

HISTORICAL AND DOCTRINAL.

BY

EDWARD HAROLD BROWNE, D.D.

LORD BISHOP OF ELY.

First American, from the Fifth English Edition.

EDITED, WITH NOTES, BY

J. WILLIAMS, D.D.

BISHOP OF CONNECTICUT.

NEW YORK:

H. B. DURAND, 49 WHITE STREET.

1865.

AN EXPOSITION

OF THE

THIRTY-NINE ARTICLES.

HISTORICAL AND DOCTRINAL.

BY

EDWARD HAROLD BROWNE, D. D.

LORD BISHOP OF WINCHESTER.

EDITED, WITH NOTES, BY THE

RT. REV. J. WILLIAMS, D. D.

BISHOP OF CONNECTICUT.

NEW YORK

E. P. DUTTON & COMPANY

39 WEST TWENTY-THIRD ST.

1887

TO

THE RIGHT REVEREND FATHER IN GOD,

CONNOP,

Lord Bishop of St. David's, and Visitor of St. David's College,

IN AFFECTIONATE GRATITUDE FOR UNSOUGHT AND UNEXPECTED KINDNESS, AND
WITH DEEP RESPECT FOR PROFOUND INTELLECT AND HIGH CHRISTIAN
INTEGRITY, THE FOLLOWING PAGES

Are Dedicated

BY HIS LORDSHIP'S ATTACHED AND FAITHFUL SERVANT,

THE AUTHOR.

PREFATORY NOTE TO THE AMERICAN EDITION.

———◆———

THE BISHOP OF ELY having kindly given his assent to the proposal for a reprint of his admirable Lectures on the Articles, it has fallen to the lot of the American Editor to add a few notes, which, it is hoped, may prove useful. These are all placed in brackets, with the Editor's initials; not because they are deemed to possess any special value, but, simply, to relieve the Author from any responsibility for them.

The volume thus presented to American Students of Theology needs no words of commendation. The Editor has employed it, in instruction, for many years, with an ever-growing sense of its value.

J. W.

BERKELEY DIVINITY SCHOOL,
    February, 1864.

INTRODUCTION.

THE Reformation was not the work, either of a year, or of a generation. Its foundation was laid both in the good and in the evil qualities of our nature. Love of truth, reverence for sacred things, a sense of personal responsibility, a desire for the possession of full spiritual privileges, coöperated with the pride of human reason, the natural impatience of restraint, and the envy and hatred inspired among the nobles by a rich and powerful hierarchy, to make the world weary of the Papal domination, and desirous of reform in things spiritual and ecclesiastical.

Wickliffe in England, and Huss and Jerome of Prague in Germany, had long ago given utterance to a feeling which lay deep in the hearts and spread wide among the ranks of thinking men. It was said of Wickliffe, that half of the secular priests in England agreed with him ; and his followers long gave serious trouble both to Church and State. On the Continent, the Bohemian Church was rent by faction ; and even open war was the result of an obstinate denial of the Cup in the Lord's Supper to the lay-members of Christ's Church. The two great Councils of Constance (A. D. 1415) and Basle (A. D. 1431) were the results of the general call for a reformation of abuses ; and they left them where they were, or aggravated and strengthened them.

But there was a leaven which could not be prevented from working. The revival of letters and the art of printing taught men how to think, and how to communicate their thoughts. Men, whose character was almost purely literary, contributed not a little to pull down the system which threatened to stifle learning by confounding it with heresy. Amongst these, on every account, the most important and influential was Erasmus. It is thought by many that his Biblical criticism and his learned wit did more to rouse men to reform, than the honest but headlong zeal of Luther. At least, if there had been no Erasmus to precede him, Luther's voice, if it could not have been stilled, might soon have been stifled. He might not have found both learning and power

zealous to protect him, so that he could defy and prove superior to
the allied forces of the Emperor and the Pope.   But Erasmus was
himself alarmed at the spirit he had raised.   He had been zealous
for reformation ; but he dreaded destruction.   And he was the
type of many, more in earnest than himself.   On both sides of
the great controversy, which soon divided Europe into two hostile
communities, were many who wished to have abuses eradicated,
but who feared to see the fabric of ages shaken to its centre.
Some, like Erasmus, remained in communion with Rome ; others,
like Melancthon, joined the Reformation.   The distance in point
of sentiment between the more moderate men, thus by force of
circumstances arrayed in opposition to each other, was probably
but very small.   But in the ranks of both parties there were
many of a more impetuous and less compromising spirit ; and, as
the voice of a community is generally expressed in the tones of
its loudest speakers, we are apt to look on all the reformers as
actuated by a violent animosity to all that was Roman, and on the
adherents of Rome as unrelentingly bent to destroy and extermi-
nate all that was Protestant.

While this state of things was pending, and whilst the spirit of
inquiry was at least as much alive in England as on the Continent,
Henry VIII. was drawn into a difference with the Papal see on
the subject of his divorce with Catharine of Aragon.   The merits
of the question may be debated elsewhere.   This much alone we
may observe, that Henry, if he acted from principle, not from
passion, might have suffered his scruples to weigh with him when
his wife was young and well-favoured, not when she had grown
old and care-worn ; when she brought him a rich dowry, not when
he had absorbed and spent it ; when he had hopes of a male heir
to his throne, not when those hopes had been disappointed, the
lady Mary being the sole issue of his alliance.   But, whatever
the moving cause, he was in hostility to the see of Rome ; and his
only chance of making head against it was to call up and give
strength to the spirit of reformation.

Cranmer had been introduced to him by some casual observations on the best way of settling the question of the divorce ; and
Cranmer from that time forth Henry steadily favoured and protected.   In 1533, the king threw off the supremacy of the Bishop
of Rome, and declared the independence of his kingdom and of its
Church.   But it has been said that he rejected the Pope, not the
Papacy.   The Church was to be independent of Rome, but not
independent absolutely.   For a spiritual, he substituted a temporal

head, and wished to confer on that temporal head — himself — all the ecclesiastical authority which had been enjoyed by the spiritual. Cranmer was now Archbishop of Canterbury. His character has been differently described by those who have taken their views of it from different sides of the question. His greatest enemies can scarcely deny him the virtues of mildness, moderation, and patience, nor the praise of learning and candor.[1] His greatest admirers can hardly affirm that he was free from weakness and timidity, and a too ready compliance with the whims and wishes of those in power. But he had a hard post to fill. Henry had thrown off the power of the Pope, and so had thrown himself into the party of the reformers; but he had no mind to throw off all the errors of Popery, and to go all lengths with the Reformation. Cranmer had often to steer his course warily, lest his bark should make shipwreck altogether; and over-zeal for his cause might provoke the hostility of one whose word was law, and whose will would brook no restraint from an archbishop, when it had dethroned a Pope.

During Henry's reign, several documents were put forth, varying in their complexion, according as Cranmer had more or less influence with him. The *Six Articles* nearly swamped the Reformation, and endangered even the archbishop. The *Bishops' Book*, or *the Institution of a Christian Man*, was a confession of faith set forth when Cranmer and Ridley were in the ascendant. But it was succeeded by the *King's Book*, the *Necessary Doctrine*, which was the king's modification of the *Bishops' Book*, in which Gardiner had greater influence, and which restored some of those doctrines of the Roman communion which the *Bishops' Book* had discarded.[2]

Cranmer was himself not as yet fully settled in his views. He had early split with the Papacy, and convinced himself of the

---

[1] His first Protestant successor in the archiepiscopal see has thus described him: Ut theologiam a barbarie vindicaret, adjecit literas Græcas et Hebraicas; quarum sane post susceptum doctoratus gradum constat eum perstudiosum fuisse. Quibus perceptis antiquissimos tam Græcos quam Latinos patres evolvit: concilia omnia et antiquitatem ad ipsa Apostolorum tempora investigavit; theologiam totam, detracta illa quam sophistæ obduxerant vitiata cute, ad vivum resecavit: quam tamen non doctrina magis quam moribus et vita expressit. Mira enim temperantia, mira animi lenitate atque placabilitate fuit; ut nulla injuria aut contumelia ad iram aut vindictam provocari possit; inimicissimosque, quorum vim ac potentiam etsi despexit ac leviter tulit, ab offensione tamen ad inimicitias deponendas atque gratiam ineundam sæpe humanitate duxit. Eam præterea constantiam, gravitatem ac moderationem præ se tulit, ut in omni varietate rebusque, sive secundis, sive adversis, nunquam turbari animum ex fronte vultuque colligeres. — Matt. Parker, *De Antiq. Britann. Eccles.* p. 495. Lond. 1729.

[2] See Cardwell's *Synodalia*, p. 34, note

2

need of reformation, and of the general defection from the faith of the Scriptures and the primitive Church. But he was some time before he gave up the doctrine of Transubstantiation, and other opinions in which he had been educated.[1] The bishops and clergy in general were far less disposed to reformation than the king or the archbishop. It was rather by an exercise of regal prerogative than by the force of persuasion, that changes were effected, even to the extent which took place in Henry's reign. It was also not much to the taste of the clergy, that they should be forced to pay the same obedience to a temporal which they had hitherto paid to a spiritual head: especially when Henry seemed to claim, and Cranmer, at least for a time, to sanction, spiritual obedience to such a temporal authority; and most of all when Henry had given marked indications, that, instead of making lighter the yoke which the Pope had put upon them, his little finger would be thicker than the Pope's loins. But neither clergy nor people were allowed to speak louder than the king chose to suffer. Convocation, both in this reign and the next, had little weight, and was not often consulted.

However, in Henry's reign many important steps were taken. The Church was declared independent of Rome. The Bible was translated into English. So also were many portions of the Church service. Negotiations were opened with the German Reformers, especially with Melancthon, whom Henry and Cranmer besought in vain to come over and help them.[2] And in 1538, in consequence of conferences between Cranmer and the German divines, a body of thirteen articles was drawn up, in great measure agreeing with the Confession of Augsburg.[3]

On the accession of Edward VI., who was himself a zealous partisan of the Reformation, greater changes were speedily made. In 1547 the first book of Homilies was put forth. In 1548 " The Archbishop of Canterbury with other learned and discreet bishops and divines " were appointed " by the king to draw an order of divine worship, having respect to the pure religion of Christ taught in the Scripture, and to the practice of the primitive

---

[1] Ridley was converted from a belief in Transubstantiation to believe in the Spiritual Presence by reading Ratramn's book, and he was the means of bringing over Cranmer, who in time brought Latimer to the same conviction. See Ridley's *Life of Ridley*, p. 162. The date assigned to Ridley's conviction is 1545. See also Soames's *Hist. of Reformation*, III. ch. II. p. 177

[2] Melancthon seems to have known Henry's character too well to wish to become his counsellor. See Laurence, *Bampton Lectures*, p. 198, third edition, London, 1838; and Dr. Cardwell's *Preface to the two Liturgies of King Edward VI.* Oxf. 1838, p. iv. note 6.

[3] See Cranmer's *Works*, by Jenkyns, IV. p. 273.

Church." This commission is said to have consisted of Cranmer, Archbishop of Canterbury; Day, Bishop of Chichester; Goodrich, Bishop of Ely; Skip, Bishop of Hereford; Holbeach, of Lincoln; Ridley, of Rochester; Thirlby, of Westminster; May, Dean of St. Paul's; Taylor, Dean of Lincoln; Haynes, Dean of Exeter; Robertson, Archdeacon of Leicester; Redmayne, Master of Trinity College, Cambridge; Cox, almoner to the king and Dean of Westminster and Christ Church.[1] These commissioners, or a portion of them,[2] drew up the first Service Book of Edward VI., which was approved by Convocation, and confirmed by both Houses of Parliament. The principal sources from which it was derived were the ancient offices of the Church of England, and with them very probably the Liturgy drawn up by Melancthon and Bucer, at the request of Herman, Archbishop of Cologne, for the use of his diocese, which had been principally derived from the ancient liturgy of Nuremberg.[3]

The same year, Cranmer translated a Catechism written by Justus Jonas, which he put forth with his own authority, and which is commonly called Cranmer's Catechism. The Calvinistic reformers of the Continent made many objections to the Liturgy as drawn up in 1548; and many English divines entertained similar scruples. It is probable that the clergy at large were not desirous of farther reformation. But the king and the archbishop were both anxious for a revision, which should do away with any appearance of giving sanction to Roman superstitions. Accordingly an order was given to prepare a new Service Book. The king and his council were most zealous in favor of the change, and it is even said that the king declared, in a spirit like his father's, that, if the bishops would make the desired change, he would interpose his own supreme authority to enforce its acceptance.

The new Service Book was put forth in 1552, and, with few exceptions, although these few are very important, it is the same as that we now possess under the name of the Book of Common Prayer.

[1] See Strype's *Cranmer*, p. 193. Ridley's *Life of Ridley*, p. 221. Collier's *Eccl. Hist.* II. p. 252, &c. Downes's *Lives of the Compilers of the Liturgy*, prefixed to Sparrow's *Rationale*. Soames's *Hist. Ref.* III. p. 352. The first Service Book was attributed by his contemporary Bale to Cranmer. On Cranmer's approbation of it, see Jenkyns's *Cranmer*, I. pp. liii. liv.

[2] Soames seems satisfied that the parties actually engaged were Cranmer, Ridley, Goodrich, Holbeach, May, Taylor, Haynes, and Cox. "If," he says, "it be true that Dr. Redmayn did not cordially approve the new Liturgy, that circumstance is to be regretted, for his age could boast of few men more erudite and honest."— III. p. 256. This wit ness is true.

[3] See Cardwell's *Preface to the two Liturgies of Edward VI.*, p. xiii., and the authorities there referred to.

The Convocation was not permitted to pass its judgment on it, because it would, in all probability, have thrown all possible difficulties in the way of its publication. It came forth with the authority of Parliament; though the act which enjoined its acceptance declared that the objections to the former book were rather curious than reasonable.[1]

The same year saw the publication of the forty-two " Articles of Religion." They were framed by the archbishop at the king's command, and committed to certain bishops to be inspected and approved by them. They were then returned to the archbishop and amended by him; he then sent them to Sir William Cecil and Sir John Cheke, who agreed that the archbishop should offer them to the king, which accordingly he did. They were then communicated to some other divines, and returned once more to the archbishop. The archbishop made his last remarks upon them, and so returned them again in three days to the council, beseeching them to prevail with the king to give authority to the bishops to cause their respective clergy to subscribe them.[2]

It has been doubted whether these articles, thus drawn up, were ever sanctioned by Convocation. Dr. Cardwell, in his *Synodalia*, has given good reason to think that they received full synodical authority.

It has been shown by Archbishop Laurence [3] and others, that the Lutheran Confessions of Faith, especially the Confession of Augsburg, were the chief sources to which Cranmer was indebted for the Articles of 1552. He did not servilely follow, but yet made copious use of them.

The chief assistant to Cranmer, both in this labor and in the

---

[1] Strype's *Cranmer*, pp. 210, 266, 289. Ridley's *Life of Ridley*, p. 333. Collier's *Eccl. Hist.* II. 309. Soames, III. ch. VI. p. 592. " The prelates themselves appear to have considered the existing Liturgy as sufficiently unexceptionable, for in the act authorizing the new one it was declared that the former book contained nothing but what was agreeable to the word of God, and the primitive Church; and that such doubts as had been raised in the use and exercise thereof proceeded rather from the curiosity of the ministers and mistakers, than of any other worthy cause." — Soames, III. p. 595.

[2] Wake's *State of the Church*, &c., p. 599. quoted by Cardwell, *Synodalia*, I. p. 3. See also Jenkyns's *Cranmer*, I. p. 357. It is asserted by Strype, in his *Life of Cranmer*, and repeated by Glouces-

ter Ridley, that of these Articles " the archbishop was the penner, or at least the great director, with the assistance, as is very probable, of Bishop Ridley." *Ridley's Life*, p. 343.

Mr. Soames says," Of the Articles now framed Abp. Cranmer must be considered as the sole compiler. . . . It seems likely that he consulted his friend Ridley, and that he obtained from him many notes. It is however certain, that the Bishop of London was not actually concerned in preparing the Articles, as Cranmer, when examined at Oxford, took upon himself the whole responsibility of that work:" for which he quotes Foxe, 1704. Soames's *Hist. Ref.* III. p. 648.

[3] *Bampton Lectures*, *passim*, especially p. 230.

translations and revisions of the Liturgy, was unquestionably his great friend and counsellor, Ridley. It is well known that he had material influence in inducing the archbishop to renounce the doctrine of Transubstantiation and to embrace that of the Spiritual Presence;[1] and the Romanist party of the day asserted that Cranmer derived all his learning from Ridley. However untrue this may be, it is pretty certain that they always acted in concert. In the drawing up of the first Service Book, Ridley was one of the commissioners; and no doubt, next to Cranmer, had a principal hand in compiling and afterwards revising it. Some of the commissioners protested against the passing the act for authorizing the first book, inasmuch as it went beyond their views of liturgical reform. But Ridley showed the greatest zeal to induce conformity both to it, and to the Second Service Book, which was far more extensively reformed. And indeed throughout, Cranmer and he appear to have walked in the same course, and acted on the same principles.

It is of consequence to remember these facts. For, if Cranmer and Ridley were the chief compilers both of the Prayer Book and of the Articles, although the Church is in no degree bound by their private opinions, yet, when there is a difficulty in understanding a clause either in the Articles or the Liturgy, which are the two standards of authority as regards the doctrine of the English Church, it cannot but be desirable to elucidate such difficulties by appealing to the writings and otherwise expressed opinions of these two reformers. It is true, both Liturgy and Articles have been altered since their time. Yet by far the larger portion of both remains just as they left them. The Convocation appears to have made little alteration in the Articles, and none in the Liturgy in Edward's reign; for the Second Service Book was not submitted to it, and it has been even doubted whether the Articles were passed by it.

The event which seemed to crush the Reformation in the bud, in fact gave it life. Neither clergy nor people appear to have been very hearty in its cause, when it came commended to them by the tyranny of Henry, or even by the somewhat arbitrary authority of Edward and the Protector Somerset. But when its martyrs bled at the stake, and when the royal prerogative was arrayed against it, it then became doubly endeared to the people, as the cause of liberty as well as of religion.

Elizabeth, though not less a Tudor than her predecessors, was

[1] Ridley's *Life of Ridley*, p. 162, referred to above

wiser, if not better than they. She at once disclaimed the title of Supreme Head of the Church in such a sense as might make it appear that her authority was spiritual, or trenching on the prerogative and rights of the clergy.[1] She allowed the Convocation to be consulted, both on the Liturgy and the Articles.

And now both clergy and laity were more prepared to adopt the tenets and the worship of the Reformers. Men who did not wish to change their creed at the will of Henry, had learned to dread the despotism of Rome, as exhibited in the reign of Mary. There were yet many different sets of opinion in the country. A large number of clergy and laity were still for ·communion with Rome and for retaining the mass; others had imbibed a love of the doctrine and discipline of Geneva, and viewed a surplice with horror and aversion; others again leant to what were called Lutheran sentiments, and were viewed by one extreme as papists, by the other as heretics. Happily the leading divines in the Church, and especially Parker, the new archbishop, were imbued with moderate sentiments, and succeeded for a time in steering the Ark of the Church skilfully amid the fury of the contending elements. Their wise conduct and the gradual progress of opinions in the course of time appeased the vehemence of the Romanist party; though it is painful to add, that measures of a most cruel character were too often adopted by the friends of the Reformation, against the leading propagators of Romish doctrine: measures which stain the memory of Elizabeth's reign almost as deeply, and not so excusably, as the fires of Smithfield do that of Mary's.[2] But, though Romanism was then decaying, the opposite extreme party was gradually advancing; and it advanced, till in the end it overthrew the altar and the throne. Its influence, however, was not great on the formularies of the Church. The Second Service Book of Edward VI. was restored in the beginning of the reign of Elizabeth, with some alterations, principally the insertion of a few rubrics and passages from the First Service Book, and partly the omission of one or two sentences, which were thought needlessly offensive, or doubtful in their orthodoxy. The Prayer Book underwent subsequent revisions in the reigns of James I. and Charles II., which reduced it to its present form.

The alterations in the Articles have been fewer, and perhaps less important. Soon after his appointment to the primacy, which

---

[1] In her Injunctions set forth in the year 1559, referred to and confirmed in the XXXVIIth Article of the Church.

[2] See Soames's *Elizabethan Religious History*, ch. v.

took place in 1559, Archbishop Parker set on foot various measures for the regulation and government of the Church, now again under the care of a reforming sovereign, and with a reforming archbishop at its head. It appears that one of Parker's earliest labors was directed towards a recasting of the "Articles of Religion." He expunged some parts of the original Articles, and added some others. In this work he was guided, like Cranmer, in a great degree by Lutheran formularies. As Cranmer had derived much from the Confession of Augsburg, so he took several clauses from the Confession of Wurtemberg.[1] Both Houses of Convocation considered the draught of the Articles thus made by the archbishop, and by him committed to their inspection and revision. The Convocation, as appears from an original document in the Library of Corpus Christi College, Cambridge, made several farther alterations, besides those which the archbishop had made. Especially, they erased the latter part of the original 3d Article, concerning the preaching to the spirits in prison, the whole of the 39th, 40th, and 42d, the archbishop having previously erased the 41st, thus reducing the whole number to 38. There was some little difference between the copy of the Articles thus submitted to and approved by the Convocation in 1562 and the copy afterwards published by the queen's command, and with her royal approbation. The latter omitted the 29th Article, whose title was " Impii non manducant Corpus Christi in usu cœnæ," and added the famous clause in the 20th Article, " Habet Ecclesia ritus statuendi jus et ·in fidei controversiis auctoritatem." Both alterations are believed to be due to the queen herself, in the exercise of what she considered her undoubted right.

An English translation of these Articles was put forth soon after by the authority of Convocation, not apparently of the queen. This translation does not contain the famous clause on Church authority, which the queen or her council had inserted, nor yet the Article " Impii non manducant," which the Convocation had authorized, but which the council had expunged.[2]

In the year 1571 the Articles were again subscribed by both Houses of Convocation, and committed to the editorship of Bishop Jewell. They were then put forth in their present form, both in Latin and English; and received, not only the sanction of Convocation, but also of Parliament. The Latin Articles, as published at this period, omitted the famous clause concerning Church authority;

---

[1] Laurence's *Bampton Lectures,* p. 233.
[2] See Cardwell's *Synodalia,* p. 34.

the English retained it. Both contained the 29th Article, concerning the wicked not eating the Body of Christ.

The Articles, which were now 39 in number, making, with the Confirmation, 40, were thus set forth with the authority of the Queen, of the Convocation, and of the Parliament. The clause concerning Church authority was still, however, in a measure doubtful; it being even to this day uncertain whether it received fully the sanction of Convocation. The bishops of both provinces soon after enacted canons, by which all members were bound to subscribe the Articles approved in the synod.[1]

The mode in which the Articles, thus reduced to their present form, were drawn up and imposed upon the Church is a subject which may well admit of question and debate. The exercise of State authority, in the whole course of the Reformation, corresponds more with the notions of prerogative suited to those days, than with the feelings of modern times.[2] But whatever may be said on this head, one fact is plain, namely, that the Articles thus drawn up, subscribed, and authorized, have ever since been signed and assented to by all the clergy of the Church, and by every graduate of both Universities; and have hence an authority far beyond that of any single Convocation or Parliament, namely, the unanimous and solemn assent of all the bishops and clergy of the Church, and of the two Universities for well-nigh three hundred years.

In the interpretation of them, our best guides must be, first, their own natural, literal, grammatical meaning; next to this, a knowledge of the controversies which had prevailed in the Church, and made such Articles necessary; then, the other authorized formularies of the Church; after them, the writings and known opinions of such men as Cranmer, Ridley, and Parker, who drew them up; then, the doctrines of the primitive Church, which they professed to follow; and, lastly, the general sentiments of the distinguished English divines, who have been content to subscribe the Articles, and have professed their agreement with them for now three hundred years. These are our best guides for their interpretation. Their authority is derivable from Scripture alone.

On the subject of subscription, of late so painfully agitated,

[1] Cardwell's *Synodalia*, i. p. 127.

[2] It will be remembered, that in the reigns of Henry VIII. and Edward VI. the whole nation, and therefore, of course, the king and the Parliament, considered themselves as members of the national Church. Hence their interference in the reformation of the Church was a very different thing from the interference of a Parliament not consisting exclusively of churchmen. The question, as to how far the laity ought to be consulted in drawing up formularies or services, may be considered as open to discussion.

very few words may be sufficient. To sign any document in a non-natural sense seems hardly consistent with Christian integrity or common manliness. But, on the other hand, a national Church should never be needlessly exclusive. It should, we can hardly doubt, be ready to embrace, if possible, all who truly believe in God, and in Jesus Christ whom He hath sent. Accordingly, our own Church requires of its *lay* members no confession of their faith, except that contained in the Apostles' Creed.[1]

In the following pages an attempt is made to interpret and explain the Articles of the Church, which bind the consciences of her clergy, according to their natural and genuine meaning; and to prove that meaning to be both Scriptural and Catholic. None can feel so satisfied, nor act so straightforwardly, as those who subscribe them in such a sense. But, if we consider, how much variety of sentiment may prevail amongst persons, who are, in the main, sound in the faith; we can never wish that a national Church, which ought to have all the marks of catholicity, should enforce too rigid and uniform an interpretation of its formularies and terms of union. The Church should be not only Holy and Apostolic, but as well, One and Catholic. Unity and universality are scarcely attainable, where a greater rigor of subscription is required, than such as shall insure an adherence and conformity to those great catholic truths, which the primitive Christians lived by, and died for.

---

[1] See the Baptismal Service and the Visitation of the Sick.

[The Articles were not adopted in the United States of America till September 12th, 1801, although a body of twenty Articles appears in the PROPOSED BOOK. Bishop White states that the subject had been seriously considered and discussed by the bishops, both in 1789 and 1792. In 1789, Bishop Seabury, the only bishop present besides Bishop White, "*doubted* of the need of Articles." In 1792, Bishops White and Claggett were in favour of adopting them, while Bishops Provoost and Madison were "directly against" them. Bishop Seabury still doubted, but was disposed to consider their adoption more favourably than in 1789. The latitudinarian objections of Bishops Provoost and Madison might well startle any man who found himself, even though on very different grounds, occupying the same position with them.

In the General Convention of 1799, the subject was taken up "at the pressing instance of the deputies from Connecticut," and in consequence of instructions to them "from the Convention of their Diocese." The only action, however, was that of the House of Clerical and Lay Deputies. They appear to have appointed a committee who reported "a proposed body of Articles wholly new in form," which were printed in the Journal. These articles were never voted on in the House in which they were reported, were never acted on by the bishops, and, indeed, were never seen by them till they appeared in print. The measure was, in every aspect of it, injudicious, and even absurd. But, after all, it worked towards a good result, by "showing the impossibility of agreement in a new form," and exhibiting the inherent folly of the proposal. The feeling of opposition against any such attempt was a continually growing one; and at last — with some alterations, which will be specified in their proper places — the English Articles were adopted, in 1801.

See Bishop White's *Memoirs*, &c., notes K and N. — *J. W.*]

3

ARTICLE I.

Of Faith in the Holy Trinity.

De fide in Sacrosanctam Trinitatem.

There is but one living and true God, everlasting, without body, parts, or passions ; of infinite power, wisdom, and goodness ; the Maker and Preserver of all things, both visible and invisible. And in the unity of this Godhead there be three Persons, of one substance, power, and eternity : the Father, the Son, and the Holy Ghost.

Unus est vivus et verus Deus, æternus, incorporeus, impartibilis, impassibilis ; immensæ potentiæ, sapientiæ, ac boni· tatis ; Creator et Conservator omnium, tum visibilium, tum invisibilium. Et in unitate hujus divinæ naturæ tres sunt Personæ, ejusdem essentiæ, potentiæ, ac æternitatis : Pater, Filius, et Spiritus Sanctus.

Section I. — HISTORY.

THIS Article is evidently concerned with two somewhat distinct subjects.

First. The Nature and Essential Attributes of God in the general.

Secondly. The Doctrine of the Trinity in Unity.

The First part is common to natural and revealed religion, and requires less either of illustration from history or demonstration from Scripture ; it having been the universal creed, both of Jews and Christians, " God is one, living and true, everlasting, without body, parts, or passions ; of infinite power, wisdom, and goodness, the Maker and Preserver of all things, both visible and invisible."

There have, however, been two classes of speculators, against whom we may suppose these words to be directed.

1. The obscure sect of the *Anthropomorphites* is reckoned as a heresy of the fourth century, and is said to have reappeared in the tenth, in the district of Vicenza in Italy.[1] Their opinion, as

---

[1] See Suicer, s. v. ἀνϑρωπομορφῖται, and Mosheim, *Ecclesiast. Hist.* Cent. x. pt. ii. ch. v. § 4.

[This error has been revived by the *Mormons.* In the *Latter-Day Saints' Catechism, or Child's Ladder*, by Elder David Moffat, God is described as an "intelligent, material personage, possessing both body and parts," possessing " passions,"

and unable to "occupy two distinct places at once." The same statement occurs in the *Millennial Star.* On the Divine attributes, the profound work of Dean Jackson, and the fourth chapter of Mr. Owen's *Introduction to the Study of Dogmatic Theology*, should be studied. — *J. W.*]

expressed by their name, was that God was in form as a man,
material, and with body and members like our own.

2. The more important and dangerous error of the *Pantheists*
may not be directly alluded to in the Article, but is plainly
opposed by it.

Pantheism has been the prevailing Esoteric doctrine of all
Paganism, and, with various modifications, the source of a great
part of ancient philosophy.[1] The Orphic Hymns have evident
traces of it. Thales and the Eleatic School expressed it distinctly,
and in the definite language of philosophy.[2] There can be little
doubt, that it was the great doctrine revealed in the mysteries.
The Egyptian theology was plainly based upon it.[3] It was at the
root of the Polytheism of the Greeks and Romans; and their
gross idolatry was probably but an outward expression of its more
mystic refinements.[4] The Brahmins and Buddhists, whose religious systems still prevail amongst nearly half the human race,
though also, exoterically, gross Polytheists, are yet, in their philosophy, undisguised Pantheists.[5] The Jewish Cabala is thought
to have drunk deep of the same fountain.[6]

When the Christian faith came in contact with Eastern philosophy, it is probable that Pantheistic notions found their way
into its corruptions. Gnostics and Manichees, and possibly some
of the later heretics, such as the Paulicians, had some admixture
of Pantheism in their creeds. Simon Magus himself may possibly
have used its language, when he gave himself out as "the great
power of God."

Its leading idea is, that God is everything, and everything is
God.[7] Though all mind, whether of men or animals, is God, yet
no individual mind is God; and so all distinct personality of the
Godhead is lost. The supreme being of the Hindoos is therefore
neither male nor female, but neuter.[8] All the numberless forms
of matter are but different appearances of God; and though he is

[1] Cudworth, *Int. Syst.* ch. IV. *passim,*
especially §§ 29, 32, 33, 34.

[2] Cudworth, B. I. ch. IV. §§ 30, 31.
Tennemann's *Manual of Philosophy,* pp.
59, 70. (Oxf. 1832.)

[3] Ἐγώ εἰμι πᾶν τὸ γεγονὸς, καὶ ὂν, καὶ
ἐσόμενον· καὶ τὸν ἐμὸν πέπλον οὐδείς πω
θνητὸς ἀπεκάλυψεν: "I am all that hath
been, is, and shall be, and my veil hath
no mortal ever uncovered." Inscription
on the Temple of Saïs, ap. Plutarch. *De
Iside.* Again, τὸν πρῶτον Θεὸν τῷ παντὶ
τὸν αὐτὸν νομίζουσιν. Plutarch, from Hec-
atæus, *De Iside et Osiri.* See Cudworth,
II. ch. IV. pp. 170, 175. All that Cud-

worth adduces, and it is well worth
reading, shows that the Egyptians were
genuine Pantheists.

[4] See Faber, *Pagan Idolatry,* B. I. ch.
III.

[5] See Sir W. Jones's *Works,* I. p. 252;
Maurice's *History of Hindostan* and *Indian
Antiquities, passim;* Faber, as above,
Mill's *Pantheistic Theory.*

[6] Burton's *Bampton Lectures,* note 16.

[7] "Jupiter est quodcumque vides, quo-
cumque moveris." Lucan. IX. 580. See
also Virg. *Eclog.* III. 60, *Georg.* IV. 219,
Æn. VI. 724; Lucret. II. 61.

[8] Sir W. Jones's *Works,* I. p. 249.

invisible, yet everything you see is God.[1] Accordingly, the Deity himself becomes identified with the worshipper. " He, who knows that Deity, is the Deity itself."[2] Hence, as all living beings are manifestations of, and emanations from the Deity, the devout Brahmin or Buddhist, while he believes that by piety man may become more and more truly God, looks forward, as his final consummation and bliss, to *Nirwana*, or absorption in the Deity.

This system of religion or philosophy, which has prevailed so extensively in heathendom, and found favour with the early philosophic heretics, and probably with the brethren of the free spirit in the twelfth century,[3] was taught in the seventeenth century by Benedict de Spinoza, a Portuguese Jew,[4] and has been called from him Spinozism. Some of the philosophic divines of Germany have revived it of late, and have taught it as the solution of all the Christian mysteries ; so that with them the Christ or God-man is not the individual personal Jesus : but *mankind* is God made man, the miracle-worker, the sinless one ; who dies and rises, and ascends into heaven, and through faith in whom man is justified.

The history of the SECOND part of this Article, that is, of the doctrine of the Trinity, may be considered as almost equivalent to the history of Christianity.

I. What degree of knowledge of it there may have been previously to the coming of Christ, is a question of great interest, but of great difficulty. This question, as regards Scripture, must be deferred to the next section ; here it is considered by the light of history alone.

It has been thought, with considerable reason, that there are distinct intimations of it (1) in the Jewish writings, (2) in the mythology of most ancient nations, (3) in the works of Plato and other philosophers.

1. The Jewish Targums and Philo-Judæus both speak frequently of the *Word of the Lord*. The latter may possibly have been indebted to philosophic sources. This can hardly be conjectured with probability of the former ; and, although none of them are much earlier than the Christian era, there is no doubt

---

[1] Sir W. Jones's *Works*, I. p. 252. Ward's *Religion of the Hindoos*, IV. 274.
[2] Mill's *Pantheistic Theory*, p. 159.
[3] Mosheim, Cent. XII. pt. II. ch. v. § 10.
[4] Mosheim, Cent. XVII. §§ 1, 24; Tennemann, p. 324. Giordano Bruno, in the sixteenth century, a Dominican, was burnt at Rome as a heretic, A. D. 1600, for holding opinions very similar to Pantheism. See Tennemann, p. 283.

that they speak the language and contain the tradition of former ages. Passages, such as that in the Targum, in Psalm cx., where "the Lord said unto my Lord" is rendered "the Lord said unto His Word," and many like it, seem, at first sight at least, very clearly to indicate a notion of Personal plurality in the Divine Unity.[1] Yet, of late, a different opinion has prevailed concerning the signification of the term *Memra* or *Word* (מִימְרָא דיי) used in the Targums; it being contended, that the phrase means not a distinct and separate Person, but is, in fact, only another form of the pronoun "Himself."[2] Both views have found able advocates, and may be supported by considerable arguments; and therefore the question concerning the Jewish opinions on the Trinity must be considered as one which is not fully decided.

2. In the mythology of almost all nations, it is plain that the number three has been a sacred number. The triads of classical mythology (*e. g.* Zeus, Poseidon, and Hades; or again, Jupiter, Juno, and Minerva in the Capitol) are well known.[3] More remarkable by far is the Trimourti of Hindostan. Christians have frequently believed that the Trimourti originated in some patriarchal tradition, whilst unbelievers have found in it an argument against the Christian Faith, as being merely one development of the many speculations concerning God which have prevailed in India and elsewhere. In answer to the latter, it may be enough to say, that the whole significance of the Trimourti is utterly unlike that of the Trinity, the likeness being in number only. Brahma, Vishnu, and Siva, were no tripersonal unity, but three distinct, created divinities, embodiments of the various powers of nature; though subsequently both Vishnu and Siva were, by their respective votaries, identified with the Great Supreme. And, on the other hand, it is now well ascertained that the gods of the Trimourti were unknown to the Vedas and more ancient books of the Hindoos;[4] so that the origin of a belief in them cannot be traced to primitive tradition, but must

---

[1] See Allix's *Testimony of the Ancient Jewish Church against the Unitarians;* Bryant's *Opinions of Philo-Judæus;* Bull, *Fid. Nic. Def.* i. i. 16–19.

[See also Oxlee, *On the Trinity*, &c., a laborious, curious, and valuable work. — *J. W.*]

[2] Burton's *Bampton Lectures,* Lect. VII. p. 221, and note 93.

[3] Cudworth, B. i. ch. iv. § 27, p. 319, § 32, p. 470. The Jupiter, Juno, and Minerva of the Capitol were the same as the three great Gods, Tinia, Cupra, and

Menrva, who had temples in every Etruscan city.

[4] See especially Professor Wilson's translation of the *Rig Veda.* The legend of Crishna, which seemed peculiarly to resemble some portions of Christian history, occurs first in the *Bhagavat Gita,* a work of about the third century A. D. Some part of it has probably been directly borrowed from the Gospels, or Apocryphal Gospels. The student may consult Rev. C. Hardwick's *Christ and other Masters,* Part II.

more probably be ascribed to the speculations of later Indian Theosophists.[1]

3. Plato and some other Greek Philosophers are generally considered as having expounded a doctrine which bears some resemblance to the doctrine of the Gospels.[2] If it be so, we may, probably enough, trace his sentiments to some like source of patriarchal tradition or Jewish creed. Some think Plato had it of Pherecydes of Syros, who may perhaps have learned it from some Eastern source. Others, that, according to the testimony of Numenius, Plato gained a knowledge of Hebrew doctrine during his thirteen years' residence in Egypt.[3] But, on the other hand, it has been argued, that Plato's view of the Logos was utterly unlike the Christian belief in the Trinity. It is said, he never spoke of the Word or " Reason of God as a distinctly existing person ; it was only a mode or relation in which the operations of the Deity might be contemplated."[4] After the Christian Revelation, indeed, philosophic Christians, and still more philosophic heretics, early used Platonic terms to express Christian doctrine. Hence the language of philosophy became tinged with the language of Christianity : hence, too, at a very early period, the heretics, using the language of Platonism, corrupted Christianity with Platonic philosophy. Hence, again, St. John, who wrote after the rise of such heretics, uses language which they had introduced ; yet not in their sense of such language, but with the very object of correcting their errors.[5] It is clear then, that, in more ways than one, we may account for the fact that St. John used terms which had been used before the Christian Revelation ; and the sneer of the infidel, which hints that he learned his doctrine from Plato, becomes harmless and unmeaning.[6]

II. When once the mystery of the Trinity had been revealed in the Gospel, it became the fundamental doctrine of the Christian faith. Yet we must not expect to find the first Christian writers using the same technical language to express their belief in it, which afterwards became necessary, when heresy sprang up, and controversy gave rise to definite controversial terms. Unitarian writers have charged Justin Martyr (A. D. 150) with being the first

[1] On the Trinity of Zoroaster and the Magi, see Cudworth, *Intell. Syst.* B. I. ch. IV. § 16, &c. On the appearance of a Trinity in the Egyptian Pantheism, see § 18, II. p. 194.

[2] On Plato's *Trinity*, see Cudworth, B. I. ch. IV. § 24. II. p. 300. § 34. III. pp. 54, 82, &c.

[3] On the statement of Numenius, who asks, " What is Plato, but Moses in Attic ?" see Lardner's *Test. of Anc. Heathens,* ch. XXXV. Allix's *Judgment of the Jewish Church,* ch. XXIII. p. 286.

[4] See Burton, *Bampton Lect.* p. 213.

[5] Burton's *Bampton Lect.* Lect. VII. and note 90.

[6] Gibbon's *Decline and Fall,* ch. XV.

to introduce "the Platonic doctrine of a second God" into Christianity; that is to say, they have admitted that Justin Martyr speaks of Christ as God, but deny that the Apostolic fathers held the doctrines of Trinitarianism. Such assertions, however unfounded, render the doctrines of the Apostolical fathers not a little important; as it could hardly fail to puzzle us, if we found the earliest Christians and their most famous pastors ignorant of what we have learned to esteem the groundwork of the faith.

There is certainly nothing in the subjects treated of by any of the Apostolical fathers, to lead them naturally to set forth a distinct acknowledgment of the doctrine of the Trinity, or of the Divinity of Jesus Christ; and many expressions might occur of love to Christ and reverence for Him, without a distinct enunciation of the doctrine of His Godhead. It is therefore the more remarkable and satisfactory, when we find, as we do, in all the works ascribed to those fathers commonly called Apostolical, passages which seem distinctly to assert the Deity of Jesus Christ, and so, at least by implication, the doctrine of the Trinity. Ignatius, especially, is so clear on this point, that the only possible way of evading the force of his testimony is to deny the genuineness of his epistles. A majority of learned men are of opinion that this question has been well nigh set at rest by Bp. Pearson in his *Vindiciæ Ignatianæ*.[1]

---

[1] The following passages exhibit some of the testimonies of the Apostolic fathers to the Divinity of Christ, and, by implication, to the doctrine of the Trinity : —

Clemens Romanus. " The Sceptre of the Majesty of God, our Lord Jesus Christ, came not in the show of pride and arrogance, though he might have done so." (1 *Cor.* xvi.) " Being content with the portion GOD had dispensed to you; and hearkening diligently to His word, ye were enlarged in your bowels, having HIS SUFFERINGS always before your eyes." (1 *Cor.* ii. See also chapters xxxii. xxxvi. xlv. &c.)

Ignatius calls our Saviour " Jesus Christ our God," (in the Inscription to the Epistles to the Ephesians and Romans, also in *Trall.* 7, *Rom.* iii.) speaks of " the blood of God," (*Eph.* i.) "the passion of my God," (*Rom.* vi.) says, " I glorify God, even Jesus Christ." (*Smyrn.* i.) " When God was manifested in human form (ἀν- θρωπίνως) for newness of eternal life." (*Eph.* xix.) " There is one Physician, both fleshly and spiritual, made and not made, God incarnate : true life in death ; both of Mary and of God ; first passible,

then impassible ; even Jesus Christ our Lord." (*Eph.* vii.) " Expect Him, who is above all time, eternal, invisible, though for our sakes made visible, who was intangible, impassible ; yet for our sakes became subject to suffering, enduring all manner of ways for us." (*Ign. to Polyc.* iii.) " God, who was manifested by His Son Jesus Christ, who is the Eternal Word, not coming forth from silence." (*Magn.* viii.)

The Trinity of Persons in the Godhead is plainly referred to in such passages as these : —

" Study that so . . . . ye may prosper in body and spirit, in faith and charity — in the Son, and in the Father, and in the Spirit — in the beginning and in the end ; " and again, " Be subject to your bishop and to one another, as Jesus Christ to the Father, according to the flesh, and as the Apostles both to Christ and the Father, and the Holy Ghost." (*Magn.* xiii.)

Polycarp speaks most clearly in the doxology ascribed to him, as some of his last words, in the *Circular Epistle of the Church of Smyrna on the Martyrdom of Polycarp.*

Justin Martyr, A. D. 150, is the first early Christian writer of whom we have any considerable remains. If he does not state the doctrine of the Trinity in the form of the Nicene or Athanasian Creeds, he yet clearly and constantly asserts that the Son is God, of one substance and nature with the Father, and yet numerically distinct from Him.[1] The word *Trinity* occurs in a treatise attributed to Justin Martyr (*De Expositione Fidei*) ; but this work is generally allowed to be spurious. The first use of this term is therefore commonly ascribed to Theophilus, Bishop of Antioch, A. D. 181, who speaks of the three days of creation, which preceded the creation of the sun and moon, as " types of the Trinity, namely, of God, His Word, and His Wisdom." [2]

" For this, and for all things else, I praise Thee, I bless Thee, I glorify Thee, by the eternal and heavenly High Priest, Jesus Christ, Thy beloved Son, with whom, to Thee and the Holy Ghost, be glory both now and to all succeeding ages, Amen." *Martyrdom of Polyc.* XIV. On this passage see Waterland, II. p. 232.

A vindication of Clement of Rome and Polycarp from the imputation of Arianism may be found in Bull, *F. D.* II. 3, 2.

Barnabas, whose Epistle, though perhaps not the work of the Apostle of that name, is doubtless the work of one who lived nearly contemporaneously with the other Apostolical fathers, writes : " For this cause the Lord was content to suffer for our souls, although He be the Lord of the whole earth ; to whom God said before the beginning of the world, ' Let us make man in our image.' " (*Barnab.* c. V.) Again, " You have in this, also, the glory of Jesus, that by Him and for Him are all things." ὅτι ἐν Αὐτῷ πάντα, καὶ εἰς Αὐτόν (c. XII. See Bull, *F. D.* I. 2, 2.)

Hermas, who is reckoned an Apostolical father, and was certainly a writer not later than the middle of the second century, has the following : " The Son is indeed more ancient than any creature, inasmuch as He was in counsel with the Father at the creation of all things." (*Simil.* IX. 12.) " The Name of the Son of God is great, and without bounds, and the whole world is supported by it." (*Simil.* IX. 14.)

Concerning the genuineness of the seven shorter Epistles of Ignatius, see Pearson's *Vindiciæ Ignat.* in the second volume of Cotelerii *Patres Apostolici.* A Synopsis of his Arguments is given in Dupin's *Eccles. Hist*, in the Life of Ignatius. See also Bp. Horsley's *Works*, IV. p. 133. Dr. Burton (*Testimonies of the Ante-Nicene Fathers,* p. 14) enumerates the following, as great names to be ranked on the same side with Bp. Pearson in holding that the genuineness of these Epistles has been fully proved. I. Vossius, Ussher, Hammond, Petavius, Grotius, Bull, Cave, Wake, Cotelerius, Grabe. Dupin, Tillemont, Le Clerc, Lardner, Horsley, &c. On the opposite side he reckons Salmasius, Blondel, Dallæus, Priestley.

Since the discovery of the Syriac Version of the Epistles of Ignatius, and their publication by Mr. Cureton, a new controversy has arisen ; namely, whether the three Epistles in the Syriac be the only genuine, and the seven shorter Greek Epistles deserving of acceptance only so far as they agree with the Syriac. Whatever may be the ultimate fate of this controversy, it is most satisfactory to know that even the three Syriac Epistles contain some of the strongest of those passages, in the Seven Greek Epistles, which prove the writer's belief in the true Deity of Christ.

[1] An example of his mode of speaking may be seen in the following short passage from *Apol.* I. c. 63 : " They, who say that the Son is the Father, are convicted of neither knowing the Father, nor of understanding, that the God of the universe has a Son, who, being the First-born Word of God, is also God." Of Justin's sentiments on the Logos and the Trinity, see Bull, *F. D.* II. 4 ; Waterland, III. pp. 157, 246 ; Burton's *Testimonies of Ante-Nicene Fathers,* p. 30 ; Bp. Kaye's *Just. Mart.* ch. II. where also, in the Appendix, is an account of the opinions of Tatian, Athenagoras, and Theophilus of Antioch.

[2] *Ad Autolycum,* Lib. II. p 106. τύποι

Irenæus, A. D. 185, gives something like regular forms of creeds, greatly resembling the Apostles' Creed (see I. 9, IV. 33). His statements of the Deity of Christ are singularly clear, and he expressly tells us that the Scriptures would never have given to any one absolutely the name of God, unless he were truly God.[1]

There is a well-known passage in a heathen author, somewhat earlier than Irenæus, (the *Philopatris* of Lucian,) which shows the received doctrine of the Church, at which he sneers, more plainly perhaps than if the words had been those of a Christian. There is a doubt whether the work is Lucian's or not; but its genuineness is not of much consequence, if, as is generally admitted, it was either his writing, or that of some contemporary of his.[2]

Tertullian, A. D. 200, both distinctly propounds the doctrine of the Trinity, and is the first *Latin* who uses the term *Trinitas*.[3]

We might trace the chain onwards through Clement of Alexandria, Origen, Hippolytus, Cyprian, Dionysius, and so down to the Council of Nice. Some may see in the bold speculations of Origen the germ of heresy even on the important doctrine of the Trinity; and Dionysius of Alexandria, in his zeal against Sabellius, appears to have been led into some heedless expressions. There is, however, little doubt that Origen was a firm believer in the Trinity; and the expressions of Dionysius, which called forth the censure of his brethren, were afterwards fully and satisfactorily explained. Thus all the early fathers who continued in the communion of the Catholic Church, are unanimous in their testimony to the faith of that Church in one God and three Persons in the Godhead.

Some, even, who were charged with schism or heresy, as Montanus and Novatian, were yet clear and decided in their language on

τῆς Τριάδος, τοῦ Θεοῦ, καὶ τοῦ Λόγου αὐτοῦ, καὶ τῆς Σοφίας αὐτοῦ. On his doctrine, consult Bull, *F. D.* II. 4, 10.

[1] Iren. III. c. VI. § 1 ; Burton, *Ante-Nicene Fathers*, p. 68, where see the testimony of Irenæus at length; also in Bull, *F. D.* I. 5, and Beaven's *Account of Irenæus*, ch. IV.

[2] The passage is — Κρι. Καὶ τίνα ἐπομόσωμαί γε ; Τοι. Ὑψιμέδοντα Θεὸν, μέγαν, ἄμβροτον, οὐρανίωνα, υἱὸν πατρὸς, πνεῦμα ἐκ πατρὸς ἐκπορευόμενον, ἓν ἐκ τριῶν, καὶ ἐξ ἑνὸς τρία.

[3] *E. g. Adv. Praxeam*, c. III. "Itaque duos et tres jam jactitant a nobis prædicari, se vero unius Dei cultores præsumunt, quasi non et unitas irrationaliter collecta hæresim faciat, et Trinitas rationaliter expensa veritatem constituat."

Dr. Hey, in his lectures on the First Article, observes that the charge, which the heretics made against the Catholics, of holding three Gods, is to him the strongest evidence that the Catholics held the doctrine of the Trinity.

Tertullian distinctly illustrates the consubstantiality of the Persons in the Godhead, by introducing the comparison of the sun, and a ray from the sun, or light kindled from light. As the substance of the light remains the same, though a ray has been sent forth, or another light kindled, "so what proceeds from God is both God and the Son of God, and both are one." *Apol.* c. XXI. See Bull, *F. D.* II. 7 ; Burton, p. 162 ; and Bp. Kaye's *Tertullian*, p. 553, where the ambiguity of some of Tertullian's language is fully considered

this head. Bingham[1] has collected abundant proof, that the devotions of the ancient Church were paid to every Person of the Blessed Trinity.

Bishop Bull, in his *Fidei Nicænæ Defensio*, and Dr. Burton, in his *Testimonies of the Ante-Nicene Fathers*, have given fully the testimonies of the fathers to the Godhead of Christ before the Council of Nice. To their works the student may refer for farther evidence that the doctrine of the Trinity was firmly and fully maintained by the early Christian writers from the first.[2]

But, though the Church was thus sound at heart, it had been declared by the Apostle that " there must needs be heresies, that the approved might be made manifest;" and we find, that, even during the lifetimes and labours of the Apostles themselves, " the mystery of iniquity did already work," which soon after was revealed in the monstrous forms of Gnosticism and other Antichristian heresies.

It is plain from St. Paul's Epistles, that there were two evil elements, even then, at work, to corrupt the faith and divide the Church. Those elements were Judaism and Eastern Philosophy. The Epistles to the Galatians, Ephesians, Colossians, and Timothy, and the writings of St. John, abound with allusions to these dangers. The " Philosophy falsely so called " ($\gamma\nu\tilde{\omega}\sigma\iota\varsigma$ $\psi\epsilon\upsilon\delta\dot{\omega}\nu\upsilon\mu\sigma\varsigma$), and the seeking justification by the Jewish Law, are the constant topics of the Apostle's warning. There are also two points deserving of particular notice : first, that these warnings are especially given to the Churches of Proconsular Asia ;[3] secondly, that St. Paul evidently connects with his warnings against both these errors earnest enforcement of the doctrine of Christ's Divinity.[4]

Accordingly, in the early history of the Church, we find two classes of false opinions, the one derived from a mixture of the Gospel with Judaism, the other from a like mixture with Oriental or Platonic philosophy, and both tending to a denial of the mystery of the Trinity, and of the supreme Godhead of Jesus Christ. As was most probable, the Eastern rather than the Western Church, and especially, in the first instance, the Churches of Asia Minor,

The use of the word *Trinity*, first to be found in Greek in Theophilus, and in Latin in Tertullian, received synodical authority in the Council of Alexandria, A. D. 317.

[1] *Eccl. Antiq.* Book XIII. ch. II.

[2] See also Bull's *Primitiva Traditio;* Waterland, *On the Trinity;* Faber's *Apostolicity of Trinitarianism.*

[3] St. John lived latterly at Ephesus, and especially addresses the Churches of Asia. Timothy was Bishop of Ephesus, and St. Paul's most marked allusions to philosophical heresy are in the Epistles to Timothy, the Ephesians, and the Colossians.

[4] This may be especially seen in such passages as Eph. i. 23 ; Col. i. 15, 19 ; ii. 9 ; 1 Tim. iii. 16, compared with iv. 1, 2, 3.

and afterwards the Church of Antioch, were the birthplaces of the
heresiarchs and of their heresies.   These Churches exhibited, independently of distinct heresy, a considerable tendency to Judaism.
The celebrated controversy about Easter first arose from the
Churches of Proconsular Asia adopting the Jewish computation,
in which they were followed by the Church of Antioch.[1]   Again,
in the East it was that the Judaical observance of the Sabbath, or
seventh day of the week, prevailed; which is first condemned by
St. Paul,[2] then by Ignatius,[3] and afterwards by the Council of
Laodicea.[4]

The earliest heretics of whom we read are Simon Magus and
the Nicolaitans, both mentioned in Scripture; who adopted, according to Ecclesiastical history, the Gnostic philosophy, and
endeavoured to combine it with the Gospel.   Gnosticism, in its
more developed form, seems to have taught, that the one Supreme
Intelligence, dwelling in darkness unapproachable, gave existence
to a line of Æons, or heavenly spirits, who were all, more or less,
partakers of His nature, (*i. e.* of a nature specifically the same,)
and included in His glory ($\pi\lambda\eta\rho\omega\mu\alpha$), though individually separate
from the Sovereign Deity.[5]   Of these Æons, Christ or the Logos
was the chief, — an emanation from God, therefore, but not God
Himself, although dwelling in the *Pleroma*, the special habitation,
and probably the Bosom of God.   Here then we see, that the
philosophic sects were likely to make our Lord but an emanation
from God, not one with Him.

Cerinthus,[6] a heretic of the first century, is by some considered
more as a Judaizer, by others more as a Gnostic or philosophic
heretic.   It is probable that he combined both errors in one.
But early in the second century we meet with the Nazarenes and
Ebionites, who undoubtedly owed their origin to Judaism, although,
like others, they may have introduced some admixture of philosophy into their creed.[7]   All these held low opinions of the
Person and nature of Christ.   The Cerinthians are said to have
held the common Gnostic doctrine, that Jesus was a mere man,
with whom the Æon Christ was united at baptism.   The Nazarenes
are supposed to have held the birth of a Virgin, and to have
admitted that Jesus was in a certain manner united to the Divine
Nature.   The Ebionites, on the other hand, are accused of esteem-

---

[1] See Newman's *Arians*, ch. I. § 1.
[2] Col. ii. 16.
[3] Ignat. *Ad Magnes.* xviii.
[4] *Can.* xxix. See Suicer, ii. p. 922.
[5] Newman's *Arians*, ch. ii. § 4, p. 206.

[6] See Mosheim, Cent. i. pt. ii. ch. v.
§ 16.
[7] Mosheim, Cent. ii. pt. ii. ch. v.
§§ 2, 3. See also Burton's *Bampton Lectures*, p. 217.

ing Christ the son of Joseph and Mary, though with a heavenly mission and some portion of Divinity.[1]

Here we have almost, if not quite, in Apostolic times, the germ at least of all false doctrine on the subject of the Trinity. Such heretics, indeed, as have been mentioned were at once looked on as enemies to, not professors of, the Gospel; and were esteemed, according to the strong language of St. John, not Christians but Antichrists.

In the latter part of the second century, the Church of Rome, which had been peculiarly free from heresy, was troubled by the errors of Theodotus and Artemon. They are generally looked on as mere humanitarians; but they probably held that Christ was a man endued with a certain Divine energy, or some portion of the Divine nature.[2]

The end of the same century witnessed the rise of another heresy of no small consequence. Praxeas, of whose opinions we can form a more definite notion from Tertullian's treatise against him, asserted the doctrine that there was but one Person in the Godhead. That one Person he considered to be both Father and Son; and was therefore charged with holding that the Father suffered, whence his followers were called Patripassians.[3]

Noetus (A. D. 220) of Smyrna, and after him Sabellius of Pentapolis in Africa (A. D. 255), held a similar doctrine; which has since acquired the name of Sabellianism. Its characteristic peculiarity is a denial of the three Persons in the Trinity, and the belief that the Person of the Father, who is one with the Son, was incarnate in Christ. But a more heretical and dangerous form of the doctrine made, not the Godhead, but an emanation only from the Godhead, to have dwelt in Jesus; and thus what we may call the *low* Sabellians bordered on mere humanitarians, and also nearly symbolized on this important subject with Valentinus and other Gnostics, who looked on the supreme Æon, Christ or the Logos, as an emanation from God, which dwelt in Jesus, and returned from Jesus to the Pleroma of God.

Beryllus, Bishop of Bozrah, seems to have taken up this form

[1] Mosheim, Cent. ii. pt. ii. ch. v. § 21.

[2] Theodotus, having denied his faith in persecution, excused himself by saying, that he had not denied God, but man; he, according to Eusebius, being the first who asserted that Jesus Christ was a mere man; for all former heretics had admitted at least some Divinity in Jesus. (See Burton's *Bampton Lectures*, p. 247.) This should seem to show that Theodotus was a mere humanitarian.

[3] See Tertullian, *Adv. Praxeam*; also Bp. Kaye's *Tertullian*, p. 526; Mosheim, Cent. ii. pt. ii. ch. v. § 20. Praxeas is placed A. D. 200. He propagated his opinions at Rome.

of Sabellianism.   He was converted by the arguments of Origen. But, not long after, Paul of Samosata, Bishop of Antioch, the most important see in Asia, a man supported by the influence of the famous Zenobia, professed a creed which some have considered pure humanitarianism ; but which was evidently, more or less, what has been called the Emanative, in contradistinction to the Patripassian, form of Sabellianism.   He held, " that the Son and the Holy Ghost exist in God, in the same manner as the faculties of reason and activity do in man ; [1] that Christ was a mere man ; but that the Reason or Wisdom of the Father descended into him, and by him wrought miracles upon earth, and instructed the nations ; and finally, that, on account of this union of the Divine Word with the man Jesus, Christ might, though improperly, be called God." Several councils were called in consequence of this spiritual wickedness in high places ; and although the rhetoric and sophistry of Paulus for a time baffled his opponents, he was finally condemned by the Council of Antioch (A. D. 264), and dispossessed of his bishopric by Aurelian (A. D. 272), after having held it, in spite of condemnation, by the aid of Zenobia.[2]

The controversies which these various errors gave rise to, naturally tended to unsettle men's minds, and to introduce strife about words ; and so paved the way for the most formidable heresy that has probably ever disturbed the Christian Church.   Arius, a native of Antioch, but a presbyter of Alexandria, began by charging his bishop, Alexander, with Sabellianism.   It is most probable, that, as his predecessor Dionysius, in his zeal against Sabellianism, had been betrayed into incautious expressions, seeming to derogate from the dignity of Christ's Divine nature ; so Alexander, in his zeal to maintain that dignity, may have used language not unlike the language of the Patripassians.   There is no doubt, however, that he was a sound believer in the Trinity.   Arius was, from this beginning, led on to propound, and mould into shape, his own dangerous heresy.

It was unlike the heresy of any of his predecessors.   For, though some of them may have been mere humanitarians, those who held that the Logos dwelt in Christ, held that Logos to be either God, or an emanation from God, and so in some sense co-

---

[1] He spoke of the Son of God, as being an *unsubsisting knowledge* or *energy*, ἐπιστήμη ἀνυπόστατος.   In opposition to which, the fathers of the Council of Antioch speak of Him as ζῶσαν ἐνέργειαν καὶ ἐνυπόστατον, *a living and subsisting energy*.

Routh, *Reliq. Sac.* Tom. II. pp. 468, 469. Bull, *Fid. Nic. Def.* Lib. III. c. IV.

[2] See Mosheim, Cent. III. pt. II. ch. V. § 15 ; Newman's *Arians ;* Burton's *Bampton Lectures,* note 103.

eternal and consubstantial. Arius and his followers, on the contrary, held that there was a period[1] when the Son of God was not (ἦν πότε ὅτε οὐκ ἦν), and that He was created by God, of a substance which once was not (ἐξ οὐκ ὄντων). They called Him by the name of God, and allowed to Him, in terms, all the attributes of God, but denied that He was *homo-ousios*, of one Substance with the Father,[2] or in any sense one with Him. The true Logos they esteemed to be merely the Wisdom, an attribute of God; but the Son they held to have been *created* before all worlds, and so far enlightened by the Wisdom of God, that He might, though improperly, be called the Logos, and that by Him God made the world. They said of Him, that, before He was created or begotten, He did not exist (πρὶν γεννηθῇ, οὐκ ἦν), and they explained the title of μονογενής, Only-Begotten, as though it meant Begotten by God alone, γεννηθεὶς παρὰ μόνου.[3]

Here we see a second and created God introduced into the Christian Theology. The Patripassians, on the one hand, had denied the Trinity of Persons; the Valentinians and Manichees, on the contrary, are accused of saying that there were three unconnected, independent Beings in the Godhead.[4] But Arianism taught distinctly the existence of one, or two beings, who were to be worshipped as God, and yet were neither one nor of the same nature with the Father. The inevitable tendency of this was either to direct Polytheism, or more probably and naturally to Humanitarianism.[5]

The Council of Nice, consisting of 318 bishops, was summoned in 325 by Constantine the Great; which condemned Arianism, established the doctrine of the homo-ousion (*i. e.* that the Son was consubstantial with the Father), and drew up the Creed which now bears the name of Nicene, with the exception of the clauses which follow the words "I believe in the Holy Ghost." Arianism, thus checked for a time, soon revived again. Constantine was convinced that Arius had been unjustly banished, and recalled him. His son Constantius, who ruled first in the East, and then over the whole empire, and afterwards Valens, who

---

[1] He avoided saying "time" (χρόνος); because he appears to have admitted that the production of the Logos was before all time. See Neander, *Church History*, IV. p. 4. London, Bohn, 1851.

[2] Pearson, *On the Creed*, Art. I. p. 135. (fol. Lond. 1723.)

[3] This was the fallacy of Eunomius. See Pearson, *On the Creed*, Art. II. p. 138.

[4] The Apostolical Canons mention and condemn certain persons, who baptized in the name of three unoriginated principles, τρεῖς ἀνάρχους. *Can. Apost.* c. 49. And the first Council of Bracara says that the Gnostics and Priscillianists introduced a Trinity of Trinities. See Bingham, B. XI. ch. III. § 4.

[5] See Newman's *Arians*, ch. II. § 5.

ruled also in the East, favoured the Arians. Partly by this powerful patronage, partly by subtilty of argument, and partly in
consequence of the prevalence of Judaizing or philosophic doctrine,
this dangerous heresy, or some modification of it, spread extensively, especially in the Eastern Churches. The famous Athanasius, Bishop of Alexandria, exhibited unbounded zeal and courage
in defending the Catholic faith, and suffered greatly from the
persecution of the Arians. There then arose a variety of sects,
with more or less of the Arian tenets ; such as the Eusebians,
Anomœans, Semi-Arians. The latter adopted as their symbol
the term *homoi-ousios*, of like substance, instead of *homo-ousios*,
of one substance. From among the latter sprang *Macedonius*.
The pure Arians, and those who symbolized with them, — the
Anomœans, and Eunomians, and Semi-Arians, — appear to have
held that the Holy Ghost, like the Son, was a created being.
Macedonius, Bishop of Constantinople, whose followers were called
Macedonians, or Pneumatomachi, seems to have been more orthodox on the Person of the Son, but to have esteemed, like the
Arians, that the Holy Ghost was a creature.[1] This heresy was
condemned at the second General Council at Constantinople, A.D.
381; which added to the Nicene Creed the clauses which follow
" I believe in the Holy Ghost." [2] With this Council the struggles
between the Catholics and the Arians ended. Arianism thenceforth became a heresy excommunicated and detached from the
Church.[3] It found refuge for some time with the Gothic invaders
of the Empire, who persecuted the Catholics ; but at length
declined and became extinct.

After this, we hear of a sect of Tritheists in the sixth century,
the principal defender of whose doctrine was Philoponus of
Alexandria.[4]

The discussions between the Nominalists and Realists of the
Middle Ages often led to something like erroneous statements
of the Trinitarian question. The Nominalists were charged with
teaching Tritheism, and their founder, Roscellinus, was con-

---

[1] " Macedoniani sunt a Macedonio Con-
stantinopolitanæ ecclesiæ episcopo, quos
et Πνευματομάχους Græci dicunt, eo quod
de Spiritu Sancto litigent. Nam de
Patre et Filio recte sentiunt, quod unius
sint ejusdemque substantiæ, vel essentiæ :
sed de Spiritu Sancto hoc nolunt credere,
creaturam Eum esse dicentes."— S. August. *Hæres.* 52. See Pearson, *On the
Creed*, p. 316, note, Art. VIII.

[2] With the exception of course of the
famous " Filioque."

[3] Much information on the terms of
the controversy may be found by turning to the words Τριάς, ὑπόστασις, οὐσία,
ὁμοούσιος, Ἄρειος, Ἡμάρειοι, Πνεῦμα (c),
πνευματομάχος, &c., in Suicer's *Thesaurus.*
See also Bp. Kaye's *History of the Council
of Nicæa.*

[4] See Suicer, s. v. Τριθεῖται, and Mosheim, Cent. VI. pt. II ch. v. § 10.

demned by the Council of Soissons, A. D. 1092. A subsequent
synod at the same place, A. D. 1121, condemned Abelard, another
famous reasoner of the same school, for errors on the subject of
the Trinity; though what his errors were is a question of some
difficulty. His great opponent, St. Bernard, charged him with
nothing short of Arianism.[1]

After the Reformation, when freedom of opinion was introduced, and an unsettled state of mind naturally sprang from violent changes, several heretics arose, who denied the doctrine of
the Trinity. Servetus, a Spaniard, in 1531, taught a doctrine
like that of the low or emanative Sabellians; that Christ, who
was born of the Virgin, was united to one of the two *personal
representaions* or *modes of existence,* which God, before the world,
had produced within Himself. He was apprehended by Calvin,
on his way through Geneva, and put to death.[2]

Several other sects of Arians and Anti-Trinitarians arose about
this time; some of which took refuge in Poland, as the country
of most religious liberty. They called themselves Unitarians. In
the Cracow Catechism, which they published as their confession
of faith, they plainly deny the Divinity of the Son and of the
Spirit, making Jesus Christ but a prophet of God.

In the mean time, Lælius and Faustus Socinus constructed the
system which bears their name. They were natives of Tuscany,
which they left from hatred to Romanism; and Faustus after his
uncle's death joined the Unitarians of Poland, and there taught
his doctrines, which soon spread into Hungary, Holland, and
England. He professed that Luther had begun, but that he
would perfect the Reformation; which was incomplete whilst
any doctrine which Rome had held remained to be believed.
His fundamental error was, that Scripture should be received as
truth, but be made to bend to reason. He taught, that Jesus
was born of a virgin, and, having been translated to heaven, was
instructed in God's will, and endued with that portion of the
Divine power called the Holy Ghost. He then came down as
a teacher of righteousness. Those who obey him shall be saved.
The disobedient shall be tormented for a time, and then annihilated. In a certain sense, Socinus allowed Christ to be called
God, and worshipped. But his followers have generally looked

---

[1] " Cum de Trinitate loquitur, sapit
Arium; cum de Gratiâ, sapit Pela-
gium; cum de Personâ Christi, sapit
Nestorium."—Bernard. *Ad Guidon. Car-*
in. Epist. 192; apud Cave, *Hist. Lit.* p.
652.

[2] Mosheim, Cent. XVI. pt. II. ch. IV.
§ 3.

on Him as a mere man ; following herein that sect of Socinians whose first leader was Budnæus.[1]

In the Reformed Church of England, in the beginning of the eighteenth century, Mr. Whiston, Professor of Mathematics at Cambridge, adopted and maintained the Arian doctrine, or a slight modification of it.[2] And Dr. Samuel Clarke, a man of learning and unblemished character, maintained the subordination of the Persons in the Godhead in so objectionable a form as to lay himself open to the charge of Arianism, or semi-Arianism. The masterly works of Waterland on the Trinity were many of them called forth by the unsound views of Dr. Clarke.

Later in the century, Priestley advocated with learning and skill, though without accuracy or caution, the far more heretical doctrines of the Socinians, or rather of the pure humanitarians. Those writings of Bishop Horsley are considered as of most value which are directed against Priestley.

It has been observed, that the various bodies of Presbyterian Christians, both in Great Britain and on the Continent, have had a considerable tendency to lapse into Socinianism, with the exception of the Kirk of Scotland, which has maintained a most honourable superiority to all other Presbyterians, partly, no doubt, because — unlike the generality of them — she strictly guards the Creeds of the Church, and other formularies of the faith.

In Germany and Switzerland the rationalism which so generally prevails among foreign Protestants has been favourable to Unitarian views of the Godhead, and humanitarian doctrines concerning Christ.

Section II. — SCRIPTURAL PROOF.

HAVING thus far given a history of the doctrine contained in this Article, I proceed to the proof from Scripture.

So much of the subject may seem to belong to natural religion that we might easily be tempted to begin with proofs from reason alone. It appears to me, however, that, as a Christian Church presupposes acceptance of the Christian revelation, the proper way of treating the symbols and articles of a church is to prove them

---

[1] Mosheim, Cent. XVI. pt. II. ch. IV.   [2] [See Johnson Grant's *History of the* § 3; also Cent. XVII. pt. II. ch. VI. § 2.   *Church of England*, III. c. XVII. — *J. W.*]

from the authentic records of that revelation. The proofs from reason belong rather to the department of Christian evidences. Yet thus much perhaps it may be necessary to premise: that the mystery of the doctrines contained in this Article should be considered as no argument against their truth. For, as, with all our study, we can scarce attain to any clear understanding of the mode in which we exist ourselves; reason alone should teach us to look upon it as hardly likely, that, with any searching, we could find out God. The mode of His subsistence who is infinitely above us may probably enough be infinitely above our powers to comprehend.

According, then, to the division of the subject proposed above, we have to show, —

FIRST, in opposition to Anthropomorphites, that "God is a Spirit, without body, parts, or passions."

SECONDLY, in opposition to Pantheists, that God is a personal, living Being,— "living and true, of infinite power, wisdom, and goodness, Maker and Preserver of all things, visible and invisible," "everlasting."

THIRDLY, in opposition to Tritheists, Arians, and every kind of Polytheists, that God is One.

FOURTHLY, in opposition to Arians, Sabellians, Macedonians, Socinians, &c., that, "in the Unity of the Godhead there are three Persons, of one substance, power, and eternity, — the Father, the Son, and the Holy Ghost."

I shall consider it sufficient to establish the doctrines contained in the first three of the foregoing propositions by simply referring to some of the many texts of Scripture by which they may be proved; reserving for the fourth and last any more extended arguments.

FIRST, then, "God is a Spirit, without body, parts, or passions." Joh. iv. 24. Comp. Isai. xl. 18, 25. Deut. iv. 15. Luk. xxiv. 39. Joh. i. 18; v. 37. Acts xvii. 24, 28, 29. Rom. i. 20, 21. 1 Tim. i. 17; vi. 16.

"Without passions" may be inferred from Num. xxiii. 19. Mal. iii. 6. Heb. vi. 17, 18. James i. 13, 17.

It is perhaps hardly necessary to add, that, whereas God is often spoken of in terms which express bodily relations, it is that the Infinite may in some degree be made intelligible to the finite; the Almighty having been pleased to condescend to our infirmities, and to deal with us, as parents do with their children, teaching them by such figures and modes of instruction as their tender minds will bear.

SECONDLY. God is

1. "Living and true." Exod. iii. 6, 14, 15 ; vi. 2, 3. Num. xxvii. 16. Deut. v. 26. Josh. iii. 10. 1 Sam. xvii. 26. Ps. xlii. 2; lxxxiv. 2. Isai. xlii. 8. Jer. x. 10. Dan. vi. 26. Matt. xvi. 16. Joh. xvii. 3. Acts xiv. 15. Rom. ix. 26. 2 Cor. vi. 16. 1 Thess. i. 9. 1 Tim. iv. 10 ; vi. 17. Heb. x. 31. Rev. iv. 8 ; x. 5, 6.

2. "Of infinite power." Gen. xvii. 1; xviii. 14. Job xlii. 2. Jer. xxxii. 17, 27. Matt. xix. 26. Eph. iii. 20. Rev. iv. 11; xix. 6.

3. "Wisdom." Gen. xvi. 13. 1 Sam. ii. 3. 1 Kings viii. 39. Job xxvi. 6 ; xxviii. 10, 23, 24 ; xxxiv. 21. Psal. xliv. 21 ; xciv. 9 ; cxxxix. 4. Prov. xv. 3. Jer. xxiii. 23, 24. Dan. ii. 22, 28. Acts xv. 18. Rom. xi. 33 ; xvi. 27. Heb. iv. 13. 1 Joh. i. 5. Jude 25.

4. "Goodness." Ex. xv. 11 ; xxxiv. 6. Lev. xi. 44. Deut. iv. 31. 1 Sam. ii. 2. Psal. lxxxvi. 15 ; cxviii. 1 ; cxlv. 8. Isai. vi. 3. Dan. ix. 9. Joel ii. 13. Jonah iv. 2. Mic. vii. 18. Luke i. 77, 78. Rom. ii. 4. 2 Cor. i. 3. Eph. ii. 4. Heb. vi. 10. 2 Pet. iii. 15. 1 Joh. iv. 8. Rev. xv. 3.

5. "Maker of all things, visible and invisible." Gen. i. ii. 2 Kings xix. 15. Neh. ix. 6. Psal. xxxiii. 6 ; c. 3 ; cxxxv. 6. Acts xvii. 24. Eph. iii. 9. **Col.** i. 16. Heb. iii. 4. Rev. iv. 11 ; x. 6.

6. "Preserver of all things." Deut. xxxii. 39, &c. 1 Sam. ii. 6. 1 Chron. xxix. 11, 12. Job xii. 9. Psal. xxii. 28 ; lxxv. 6, 7 ; xc. 3 ; xcv. 3, 4, 5, 7. Isai. xiv. 27 ; xl. 11, 12, 13, 15, 22. Jer. v. 24 ; xviii. 6–9. Dan. v. 23. Matt. vi. 25–30 ; x. 29, 30. Rom. xi. 36.

7. "Everlasting." Gen. xxi. 33. Deut. xxxiii. 27. Psal. ix. 7 ; xc. 2, 4 ; cii. 12, 26, 27. Isai. xliv. 6 ; lvii. 15. Lam. v. 19. Rom. i. 20 ; xvi. 26. 1 Tim. i. 17. Rev. i. 8 ; v. 14 ; x. 6.

THIRDLY. We have to show, in opposition to Tritheists, Arians, and every kind of Polytheists, that "God is One." "Hear, O Israel, the Lord our God is one Lord" (Deut. vi. 4). "The Lord, He is God, there is none else beside Him" (Deut. iv. 35). "Thus saith the Lord . . . Beside Me there is no God" (Is. xliv. 6 ; comp. v. 8). "There is one God, and there is none other but He" (Mark xii. 32). "The only true God" (Joh. xvii. 3). "We know that there is none other God but One" (1 Cor. viii. 4). "God is One" (Gal. iii. 20). "There is One God, and one Mediator between God and man, the Man Christ Jesus" (1 Tim.

ii. 5). "Thou believest that there is one God; thou doest well" (Jam. ii. 19). "Denying the only Lord God" (Jude 4). "The only wise God, our Saviour" (Jude 25).

See also Ex. xx. 3. 2 Sam. xxii. 32. Psal. lxxxvi. 10. Isai. xxxvii. 16; xlii. 8. Mark xii. 29. 1 Cor. viii. 6. Eph. iv. 6.

FOURTHLY. We have to show, in opposition to Sabellians, Arians, Macedonians, Socinians, &c., that "In the Unity of the Godhead there be three Persons, of one substance, power, and eternity,—the Father, the Son, and the Holy Ghost."

As regards this doctrine of the Trinity in Unity, we must not expect to find the same express declarations in Scripture that we find, for instance, of the facts, that "God is a Spirit," "God is a righteous God," or the like. But it by no means therefore follows, that the one is less true than the other. It appears to have been far from the design of the Author of Holy Scripture to set down every article of Christian truth in the form of a distinct enunciation. Scripture is not a system of catechetical instruction, designed to lead us, step by step, to the knowledge of religious verities, and to place everything so clearly before us, that, if we will, we cannot mistake it. On the contrary, it is plainly intended, that, if we do not fear the Lord, we shall not be able to penetrate His secret, and that, unless our hearts are set to do His will, we shall not be able to know of His doctrine. If there were no other reason than this, we might see why many things in Scripture require to be sought out.

But, again, God has appointed various instruments for instruction in His Church; all, of course, in subordination to the teaching of His Holy Spirit. He has bestowed upon us, first, reason; secondly, Scripture; thirdly, the ministry of His word and Sacraments. If Scripture were a regular course of catechetical teaching, so plain that it could not be mistaken, the prophetic or didactic office of the Church and the ministry would be altogether superseded. Again, it is evidently desirable that our reason, enlightened by God's Spirit, should be exercised to the understanding of His word; and one great blessing derived from this appointment is, that so, whilst the ignorant may find enough to guide them safe, the most profound and acutest intellect may find abundance to employ its meditations, and exercise its thoughts. Else, what was suited for the one might pall upon the taste of the other.

Believing, then, that we are not only permitted, but called upon, in humble dependence on the Divine guidance, to use our reason, dispassionately but reverently, in order to understand what God has delivered to us, I shall endeavour to class together the various facts which Scripture has recorded concerning the nature of God, so far as they bear on this part of our subject; and then, by the common process of induction, shall hope to arrive at a just conclusion from a general view of them all.

Now these different facts of Scripture may be classed under four heads.

I. Scripture teaches, that there is One God.

II. There is, nevertheless, clear *intimation* of some kind of plurality in the Godhead, even in the old Testament; but in the new Testament there is a clear *declaration* that

> The Father is God, — the Son is God, — the Holy Ghost is God.

III. This fact of the plurality is not in express terms a contradiction of the Unity; such as would be the case, if in one passage it were said, " There is one God," and in another passage, " There are three Gods;" for it appears from Scripture, that the Father, the Son, and the Holy Ghost are but one and the same God.

IV. Still, though Father, Son, and Holy Ghost are but one God, there is plain evidence from Scripture, that the Father is not the Son, nor is either of them the Holy Ghost; but that they are clearly distinguished from one another, and distinguished, too, as *Personal* Agents, not merely as modes, operations, or attributes.

If I find these four propositions clearly established in Scripture, I do not know what more can be required to prove the doctrine of this Article, that " in the Unity of the Godhead there be three Persons, the Father, the Son, and the Holy Ghost;" and that these three Persons are " of one substance, power, and eternity."

I. In the first place, then, Scripture teaches us, that there is but one God. This has been already shown in the THIRD principal division of the subject. It is revealed as the fundamental truth of all religion. Whatever contradicts this truth is evident falsehood. Therefore Tritheism, which speaks of the Father, Son, and Spirit as three Gods, is false. Therefore Arianism, which speaks of the Father as the supreme God, and of the Son as another inferior, subordinate God, is false. Therefore every kind of Polytheism is false; for " there is one God, and there is none other but He." Mark xii. 32.

II. But next, plain as is this doctrine of the Unity of the Godhead, there are (1) in the old Testament decided *intimations* of a plurality in the Godhead, and (2) in the new Testament express *declarations*, that

> The Father is God, — the Son is God, — and the Holy Ghost is God.

(1) In the old Testament there are decided intimations of a plurality in the Godhead.

The Jews indeed were placed in the midst of idolaters, themselves easily tempted to idolatry; and, being subjects of a carnal dispensation, were but little capable of embracing spiritual truth. It may therefore probably have been in mercy, to prevent the danger of Tritheism, that the doctrine of the Unity was so strongly insisted on, and so little said of a Trinity or plurality of Persons. Yet *intimations* are not wanting.

I do not insist on the plural form of the name of God, because the Hebrews used plurals at times to express greatness or intensity; and such may have been the force of the plural in the name *Elohim*.

But, in the history of the Creation (Gen. i. 26, 27), it is certainly remarkable, that God said, " Let *us* make man in *our* image;" and then it is added, " So God created man in *His* own image." This is the more remarkable, if we compare with it what is said by St. Paul (Col. i. 16; Heb. i. 2, &c.), namely, that God made all things *by His Son*. The same plural expression occurs after the fall, when God says, " The man is become as one of *us*;" and at the confusion of Babel, " Let *us* go down and confound their language." We cannot conceive the infinite Creator of all things thus coupling any finite creature with Himself.

Again, in the old Testament there are various manifestations of God, which at one time are spoken of as manifestations of God Himself, at another as manifestations of a Messenger or Angel sent by God: as though God were at once the Sender and the Sent, — the God of Angels and the Angel of God.

This may be observed of the wrestling of Jacob with the Angel (Gen. xxxii. 24). In Genesis it is said Jacob wrestled with a *man;* but he called the place, " Peniel, because he had seen *God* face to face "— (ver. 30); and where the same is referred to by Hosea (xii. 3, 4), it is first said, " He had power with *God*," and then in the next verse, " He had power over the *Angel*, and prevailed."

In Joshua (v. 14), one appears to Joshua, who calls Himself

"the Captain of the Lord's host." Yet three verses further (ch. vi. 2), when the Captain of the Lord's host speaks to Joshua, the name by which He is called is the LORD (*i. e.* JEHOVAH). From this we infer, that He, who came as the Captain of JEHOVAH's host, was also Himself JEHOVAH.[1]

In the second chapter of Judges, the *Angel* of the LORD appears to speak with full authority, as if He were the LORD *Himself.* "I made you go out of Egypt." "I said, I will never break *My* covenant with you." Ver. 1.

The history of Manoah and the Angel (Judg. xiii. comp. vv 20, 21, 22, 23) seems to teach the same thing.

But not only is One, who is sent by the Lord as His Angel, called by the highest name of God, namely, JEHOVAH; but also there is indication of the clearest kind in the old Testament, that One, who should be sent on earth by God, as a man, to suffer, and to deliver, is also the Fellow of God, and God Himself. Thus, in Jeremiah (xxiii. 6), the Messiah's name is called "JEHOVAH our Righteousness." In Isaiah (vii. 14), it is called "God with us." In Malachi (iii. 1), we are told, "The LORD whom ye seek, shall suddenly come to His temple, even the Messenger of the Cove- nant whom ye delight in,"— language clearly used of the Messiah, but as clearly most suitable to God. In Isaiah (ix. 6), the Child, who is to be born as a Redeemer, is expressly called "The Mighty God." In Zechariah (xiii. 7), in a prophecy of salvation by the Christ, we read, "Awake, O sword, against My Shepherd, and against the Man that is My Fellow (or Companion, עֲמִיתִי), saith the Lord of hosts."

I forbear to adduce such passages as those where the Wisdom, or the Word of God are spoken of with personal attributes (*e. g.* Prov. viii. ver. 22, 23, 24, 30, 31. Psal. xxxiii. 6. Isai. xlviii. 16); because we cannot be certain that in these cases personal attributes are not ascribed by the figure called Prosopopœia. But it is hard to explain how God in creation can use the plural num- ber, speaking as to another, with whom He was, as it were, acting in concert, — how the same Person can be both JEHOVAH, and sent as JEHOVAH's Angel, Captain, or Messenger, — how the same person can be sent on earth as Messiah, and yet be the mighty God, — how God can speak of the Man, that is His Fellow, — without supposing, that some sort of plurality in the Godhead is implied.

---

[1] Compare Ex. xxiii. 20, 21, where the Angel, whom God sends before the Israelites, seems plainly by ver. 21, to be God.

I conclude, therefore, that in the old Testament there are distinct *intimations* of a plurality in the Godhead.

(2) But next, in the new Testament, there are not only intimations of a plurality (such as the very use of the names, Father, Son, and Holy Spirit, and their conjunction in numerous passages plainly imply), but farther, it is *distinctly taught* us

1. That the FATHER is GOD, — 2. That the SON is GOD, — 3. That the HOLY GHOST is GOD.

1. That we are taught the FATHER is GOD, no one can doubt. So strong indeed are the expressions concerning the Father as God, that, if they stood alone, we should naturally conclude, that the Father alone was God, and that, as there is but One God, so there was but one Person in the Godhead. Thus our Lord says (John viii. 54), "My Father, of whom ye say that He is your God." Again, addressing the Father, He says, "This is Life eternal, to know Thee, the only true God" (John xvii. 3). St. Paul speaks (Eph. iv. 6) of "One God and Father of all." And again, "To us there is one God, the Father, and one Lord Jesus Christ." (1 Cor. viii. 6.)[1]

2. We learn also from the teaching of the new Testament that the SON is God. And this fact we deduce both from *reasonable inference*, and from *direct statement*.

Our *reasonable inference* is of the following kind.

We often meet with passages in the old Testament, which speak plainly of the Most High God, applied as plainly in the new Testament to Jesus Christ, the Son of God. For example, in Isaiah xl. 3, it is said, that "the voice of one crying in the wilderness shall prepare the way of JEHOVAH, and make straight in the desert a highway for our God." But in each one of the Evangelists this passage is quoted. The "Voice" is said to be John the Baptist; and He for whom he prepares the way is said to be Christ.[2] Is not the natural and necessary inference, that Christ is as much "our God" and "JEHOVAH," as John was the voice in the wilderness?

Again, in Zech. xii. 4, 10, if we compare the one verse with the other, we shall see that it is written, "In that day, saith JE-HOVAH . . . they shall look on *Me* whom they have pierced." But

---

[1] The apparently exclusive appropriation of the name of God to God the Father must be accounted for by the consideration that the Father is ever represented to us as the Fountain and Source of Life, the Ἀρχή, or Πηγὴ θεότη-τος, from whom eternally both the Son and Spirit derive the same Life and Godhead. See below, pp. 65, 67.

[2] Matt. iii. 3; Mark i. 3; Luke iii. 4; John i. 23.

St. John (xix. 37) tells us, that this prophecy was concerning the piercing of *Christ.* Therefore we must conclude, that Christ is JEHOVAH.

Once more, in Isaiah vi. the prophet sees the Lord sitting upon His throne, even "the King, JEHOVAH of hosts" (ver. 5). But St. John (compare xii. 37–41) says, that the LORD, whose glory Isaiah then saw, was *Jesus Christ.*

Another reason why we *infer* that the Son is God, is that the worship due to God is offered to Him, the peculiar attributes of God are ascribed to Him, and the power of God is exerted by Him.

(1)   He receives worship as God, and is prayed to.

See Matt. ii. 11; viii. 2; ix. 18; xiv. 33; xv. 25; xx. 20; xxviii. 9.   Mark v. 6;   ix. 24.   Luke xxiii. 42.   John ix. 38. Acts vii. 59.   2 Cor. viii. 8, 9.   1 Thess. iii. 11.   Heb. i. 6. Rev. v. 8, 12, 13.

Whereas saints and angels universally refuse worship offered to them, and bid us worship none but God.   Acts x. 26; xiv. 14, 15. Rev. xix. 10; xxii. 9.

(2)   The peculiar attributes of God are ascribed to Him.

a.   He is eternal, existing from everlasting to everlasting. Micah v. 2.   John i. 1, 3; viii. 58.   Col. i. 16, 17.   Heb. i. 8, 10, 11, 12; vii. 3; xiii. ·8.   Rev. i. comp. vv. 8, 11, 12, 13, 18 (which comparison will show that the language is all used of Jesus Christ); xxii. 13.

It may be added, that several of the above passages show, that He is not only eternal, but unchangeable, *e. g.* Heb. i. 10, 11; xiii. 8.

β.   He knows the thoughts, yea, all things.   Matt. ix. 4; xii. 25.   Luke vi. 8; ix. 47; xi. 17.   John i. 48; xvi. 30; xxi. 17. Col. ii. 3.   Rev. ii. 23.

Those of the above passages which show that Jesus Christ knew the thoughts of the heart, should be compared with such as the following: Jer. xvii. 10, "I the Lord search the heart." Acts xv. 8, "God, which knoweth the hearts" (ὁ καρδιογνώστης Θεός), and 1 Kings viii. 39, "Thou, even Thou ONLY knowest the hearts of all the children of men."[1]

γ.   He is everywhere present.   Matt. xviii. 20; xxviii. 20. John i. 48; iii. 13.

---

[1] The objections to Christ's omniscience, taken from John viii. 28; Rev. i. 1; Mark xiii. 32; are answered by Waterland, *Moyer's Lecture,* Serm. VII., *Works,* II. p. 160. See the latter passage considered below, under Art. IV.

The last passage especially shows that, whilst He was on earth, He was still in Heaven.

δ. He is self-existent, like the Father, having derived from the Father the same eternal nature with Himself. John v. 26. Compare John xi. 25; xiv. 6. See also John i. 4; x. 30; xiv. 10. Phil. ii. 6.[1]

(3) The power of God is exerted by Him.

α. He is Lord of the Sabbath, which God ordained, and none but God can change. Comp. Gen. ii. 2, 3, with Mark ii. 28. Luke vi. 5.

β. He sends His Angels, as God. Matt. xiii. 41. Rev. i. 1; xxii. 6.

γ. He has power to forgive sins as God. Matt. ix. 2–6. Mark ii. 5, 7, 10. Luke v. 20–24; vii. 48.

Whereas, when forgiveness is merely ministerial or ecclesiastical, the power is conferred by Him, and exercised in His name. Comp. John xx. 23 with 2 Cor. ii. 10.

δ. He shall judge the world. Job xix. 25. Matt. xiii. 41 xvi. 27; xxv. 31. John v. 22, 23. Acts x. 42. 2 Cor. v. 10.

ε. He created and preserves all things.[2] John i. 3, 10. Eph. iii. 9. Col. i. 16. Heb. i. 2, 3, 10, 11, 12.

With these passages compare Isaiah xliv. 24, " Thus saith the LORD (i. e. JEHOVAH), I am the LORD that maketh all things; that stretcheth forth the heavens *alone;* that spreadeth abroad the earth by MYSELF."

ζ. He has all power in Heaven and earth. Matt. xxviii. 18. Mark i. 27. John iii. 31, 35; v. 19, 21; xvi. 15. Acts x. 36. Rom. xiv. 9. Eph. i. 20–23. Phil. ii. 10; iii. 21. Heb. vii. 25. 1 Pet. iii. 21, 22. Rev. i. 5, 8.

Thus far, then, we have seen, that passages in the old Testament, spoken of God, are in the new Testament applied to Christ, the Son of God: that the worship due to God is offered to the Son: that the peculiar attributes of God are ascribed to the Son: that the power of God is exerted by the Son. If we had nothing more than this, surely our natural and necessary *inference* must be, that the Son is God.

But we are not left to the *inference* of our reason only on this

---

[1] On Phil. ii. 6, see Pearson, *On the Creed*, fol. p. 121.

[2] On the proof of Christ's proper Deity from creation, see Pearson, *On the Creed,* p. 113; Waterland, *Works* (Oxf. 1823), II. 2d and 3d Sermons at Lady Moyer's Lecture

momentous subject.   We have also *direct statement*, and that many times repeated, that Christ, the Son of God, is God.

And here we may recur, for a moment, to what was said concerning intimations of a plurality in the Godhead in the old Testament.   Some of the passages there referred to, when seen in the light cast upon them by the new Testament, become direct assertions of the Godhead of Christ.

The prophecy in the seventh chapter of Isaiah, that a Virgin should bear a Son, whose name should be called Immanuel, *i. e.* God with us, is, in the first chapter of St. Matthew, distinctly interpreted of the birth of Jesus Christ.   Therefore St. Matthew distinctly declares to us, that Jesus Christ is Emmanuel, God with us.   Again, in the ninth chapter of Isaiah, which is a continuation of the prophecy in the seventh chapter, the child that was to be born is called " Wonderful, Counsellor, *the Mighty God*, the Everlasting Father."   This prophecy, too, is by St. Matthew expressly interpreted of the Lord Jesus.   (See Matt. iv. 16, which compare with Isai. ix. 1, 2.)   We have then the express assurance of the Evangelist, that Jesus Christ was called in the old Testament, Immanuel, and the Mighty God.

We might add to these examples the language of Zechariah (xiii. 7), where the Lord's " Shepherd " is called his " Fellow ; " and that of Jeremiah (xxiii. 6), where the " Branch," that should be raised to David, is called " JEHOVAH our Righteousness ; " [1] because both these passages are unquestionable prophecies of Christ, though not so distinctly referred to by the Evangelists.

The first chapter of St. John begins with a declaration of the Divinity of the Son of God.   From whatever source St. John derived the use of the term " the Word of God ; " whether he used language already familiar to the Jews, or, as is perhaps more probable, adopted the phrase of Platonizing heretics ; [2] it is quite plain, that by the " Word " he means the Son of God, who was incarnate in Jesus Christ.   That is proved by Rev. xix. 13, where it is said of Jesus Christ that " His name is called the Word of God ; " and again, by the 14th verse of the first chapter of St. John's Gospel, where we read, " The Word was made flesh and dwelt among us, and we beheld His glory, the glory as of the Only-begotten of the Father."   Of this Word of God then, who was the Only-begotten of the Father, and, when made flesh, was called Jesus Christ, we are told (John i. 1), " In the beginning

[1] On this passage see Pearson, *On the Creed*, fol. p. 148, note.
[2] See Sect. I. *Historical View.*

was the Word, and the Word was with God, and the Word was God." Language cannot more strongly express the Deity of the Son of God, the Word of God. Yet, lest mistake should occur, the Evangelist adds a sentence which at once declares that the Word was uncreated, and was Himself the Creator of all things, exercising that, the highest act of Almighty power. " All things were made by Him, and without Him was not anything made that was made." If no created thing was made but by Him; then was He Himself uncreated, and so He must be the eternal, uncreated Maker of the universe.

In the eighth chapter of the same Gospel, we find our Lord taking to Himself one of the most special names of God. God had first revealed Himself to Moses by the name " I AM." Here, then, Christ having declared Himself the Son of God, having assured the Jews that Abraham had seen His day and rejoiced; when they doubted the possibility of His having seen Abraham, He adds, " Verily, verily, I say unto you, before Abraham was, I AM." Had He merely spoken of His preëxistence, the past tense would have seemed more natural. But He uses that tense which expresses the existence of none but God, — an unchanging present, which has no future nor past, — and so adopts, as His own, the name of the self-existent JEHOVAH. That the Jews so understood Him is apparent from the fact, that, though they bore with Him whilst He called Himself God's Son, as soon as he had uttered the words " Before Abraham was, I am," they took up stones to cast at Him.

Again, (John xx. 28,) when Thomas is convinced of Christ's resurrection, he is therewith, though not till then, convinced of Christ's Divinity; for he immediately " said unto Him, My Lord and My God." [1]

Another important passage is that in the ninth chapter of Romans, ver. 5; where St. Paul, speaking of the Jews, says that of them, " as concerning the flesh Christ came, who is over all, God, blessed forever." In this verse there is, as it were, proof upon proof, that Christ is God. First, the expression " as concerning the flesh," indicates that, according to something higher than the flesh, He had His Being elsewhere. Next He is said to be ἐπὶ πάντων, " over all; " as John the Baptist said of Him (John iii. 31), " He that cometh from above is above all." The very same epi

---

[1] The objections which have been made to the plain sense of this passage may be seen fully replied to, Pearson, *On the Creed*, p. 131; and Middleton, *On the Article*, in loc.

thet (ἐπὶ πάντων) is applied, Eph. iv. 6, to God the Father; nor
can we conceive it to be of less significance than that similar title
of God (עֶלְיוֹן, ὕψιστος) " the *Most High.*" Next comes the name
(Θεός) God, which is in every manuscript and every version.
Lastly, the whole is concluded by the words " Blessed forever: "
a phrase which is a translation, or paraphrase of a well-known
Jewish form used only in speaking of the Almighty: (הַקָּדוֹשׁ
בָּרוּךְ הוּא).[1]

Again, in the second chapter of the Epistle to the Colossians,
ver. 9, St. Paul says of Christ, that " in Him dwelt all the fulness
of the Godhead bodily." The Gnostics made a fulness (pleroma)
of numerous Æons, or emanations from God, and one of these
emanations they believed to dwell in Jesus. The Apostle says,
however, that it was no single Æon, no mere emanation from
God: but that the whole Pleroma, the fulness of God, dwelt in
Him bodily.[2]

The first chapter of the Epistle to the Hebrews, besides
ascribing Creation and Providence to the Son of God, besides
saying that all the Angels should worship Him, distinctly applies
to Him the name of God. It is thus the Apostle quotes the
Psalms: " To the Son He saith, Thy Throne, O God, is for ever
and ever." And again, " Thou, Lord, in the beginning, hast laid
the foundation of the earth."

Let us next take the important passage in the Epistle to the
Philippians (ii. 5–9). The Apostle exhorts the Philippians to
humility by the example of the incarnate Son of God. " Let this
mind be in you, which was also in Christ Jesus, who being in the
form of God, thought it not robbery to be equal with God, but
made Himself of no reputation, and took upon Him the form of a
servant, and was made in the likeness of men; and being found in
fashion as a man, He humbled Himself, and became obedient unto
death, even the death of the cross." There are two ways in which
this passage, or at least one phrase of it (οὐχ ἁρπαγμὸν ἡγήσατο),
may be translated: one, as in our version; the other (as Origen,
Novatian, and many after them have interpreted it), " did not

---

[1] All MSS. all VSS. have the verse
entire. All the Fathers have it, except
that in Cyprian, Hilary, and Leo it is
referred to without Θεός. Such an exception will be very far from invalidat-
ing the reading; but Erasmus observes
that without Θεός, the verse would still
prove the Divinity. See the passage
fully considered, Pearson, p. 132; Waterland, II. p. 133; Middleton, *On the Article,* in loc.; Magee, *On Atonement,* III. p.
91. The Arian interpretation, which
would make the latter part of the verse a
doxology to the Father, is considered and
refuted very fully by Bp. Middleton. See
also Tholuck and Alford on this passage.

[2] See Whitby on this passage. His
Notes on the Colossians are very good.

pique Himself on this His dignity," or, " did not covet and earnestly desire to be so honoured."[1] It does not appear that one of these renderings is more calculated to weaken the force of the passage than the other. Both of them are intelligible, if we admit that St. Paul is speaking of Christ as God: both unintelligible on every other hypothesis.

The Arians indeed interpret the " being in the form of God," not as though it meant being in the " nature of God," but as though it were intended to signify, that Christ, before His incarnation, acted under the old Testament as God's Angel and Messenger, *represented* and *personated* God ; and so might be *said* to be in the form of God. They would therefore explain it, " that Christ, having been sent as God's messenger, and permitted to personate and represent God, yet did not arrogate to Himself to be equal with God." But it must be observed, that, if this were the right sense of the passage, then also the phrase " taking the form of a servant" should mean, not the *becoming really* man, but merely personating or *appearing in the semblance* of a man ; which sense of the passage might be correct, if the writer had been a Gnostic ; not, as it was St. Paul. But as the " taking on Him the form of a servant" must mean that He was *truly* man ; so the " being in the form of God" must mean that He was *truly* God. It must be observed again, that, as the Apostle distinctly tells us that Christ took the form of a servant by being made in the likeness of men, it is therefore quite plain that,

---

[1] Ὅς ἐν μορφῇ Θεοῦ ὑπάρχων, οὐχ ἁρπαγμὸν ἡγήσατο τὸ εἶναι ἴσα Θεῷ, ἀλλ' ἑαυτὸν ἐκένωσε, μορφὴν δούλου λαβὼν, ἐν ὁμοιώματι ἀνθρώπων γενόμενος, καὶ σχήματι εὑρεθεὶς ὡς ἄνθρωπος, ἐταπείνωσεν ἑαυτὸν, γενόμενος ὑπήκοος μέχρι θανάτου, θανάτου δὲ σταυροῦ. " Who, being in the form of God, thought it not robbery to be equal with God (or, did not parade, covet, or pique Himself on the being equal with God) ; but emptied Himself (of his glory) by taking the form of a servant, (and that) by being made in the likeness of men ; and being found in fashion as a man, He humbled Himself by becoming obedient unto death, even the death of the cross." The participles express the manner in which the actions of the verbs were effected. He, being in the form of God, emptied Himself of His divine glory. How ? Why, by taking the form of a servant. And how did He take the form of a servant? By being made in the likeness of men. And then, being no longer in the glory of God, but in fashion as a man, He humbled Himself. How ? By becoming obedient unto death.

Hence it appears, that, as He humbled Himself by becoming obedient to death, so He emptied Himself by taking the form of a servant, and He took the form of a servant by being made man. The taking the form of a servant, then, was the becoming man, the assuming human nature : " the form of a servant" was the nature of man. It follows that the " form of God " was the nature of God.

It must be admitted that οὐχ ἁρπαγμὸν ἡγήσατο is an unusual expression ; but to the interpretation " did not make a parade of, or pique Himself on the being equal with God," the few parallel expressions which are to be found seem most favourable.

On the whole passage see Grotius, Hammond, Whitby, Macknight, Rosenmüller, Middleton, in loc., Suicer, s. v. ἁρπαγμός; Pearson, *On the Creed*, p. 122, fol. ; Waterland, II. Serm. v. p. 89.

before He was made in the likeness of men, He was *not* in the
form of a servant. But who of all created beings is not in the
form of a servant? Who, but the uncreated God, is not a servant
of God? If therefore Christ was, before His incarnation, not a
servant, nor in the form of a servant, then, before His incarnation, He must have been God.

The passage then requires us to interpret it as follows: " Take,
for your example of humility, Jesus Christ. He, being in the
form and nature of God, thought it not robbery to be (or, piqued
not Himself on being) equal with God; but emptied Himself of
His Divine glory, inasmuch, as He, being Lord of all, yet assumed
the form of a servant, by being made in likeness of men; and
when He was thus found in fashion no longer as God, but as man,
He humbled Himself yet further, by becoming obedient unto
death, even the death of the cross."

In the famous passage in 1 Tim. iii. 16, we read, " God was
manifest in the flesh, justified in the Spirit, seen of angels, preached
unto the Gentiles, believed on in the world, received up into
glory." It is indeed true that there are three readings of the
first word, which is in our version *God*. Yet whichever reading
may be the true, the whole drift of the passage and its context
clearly express the Deity of Him of whom the Apostle writes,
that is of Jesus Christ.[1]

There is another passage, in Acts xx. 28, which I couple with
the last, because here too the reading is in doubt. St. Paul exhorts the elders of Ephesus " to feed the Church of God, which
He hath purchased with His own blood."[2] So strongly does this

---

[1] The state of the question is nearly
this : —

ὅς is the reading of C*F.G. 17. 73.
181. —— ὁ of D*. —— Θεός of D*** J. K.
and of nearly all cursive MSS.

B. E. H. are defective in this place,
and supply no evidence at all.

The reading of A has been very much
disputed. At present A reads Θεός, but
the lines which distinguish Θ͞Ϲ from OC
are in a newer and coarser ink than the
original. The MS. is greatly defaced in
this passage : and it is now extremely difficult to decide what the reading originally was. There is no trace now of a line
either in or over the O written in the original ink ; and from close inspection I am
satisfied, that the tongue of the Ϲ in the
page on the other side of the leaf might
have been seen through, and have appeared like the stroke of the middle of Θ.
But it is difficult to say how far this set-

tles the question concerning the reading
of A.

The reading of VSS. is in favour of a
relative, the Latin reading *quod*, the other
ὅς, except the Arabic (Polygl.) and
Slavonic, which have Θεός.

The Latin fathers followed the Vulgate
in reading *quod*, except Hieron. *In Esai*
liii. 2, who reads ὅς.

Of the Greek fathers, some are doubtful. Ignat. *Ad Eph.* 19, Chrysost.
Theodoret, Damasc.,Œcum.,Theophyl.,
read Θεός. Cyril. Alex., Theodor. Mop-
suest., Epiphan., Gelas. (Cyzic.). read ὅς.

[2] Θεοῦ is the reading of Cod. Vat. and
seventeen other MSS., two of the Pe-
shito, Vulg., Æthiop., Athanasius, Tertullian, &c. Κυρίου is the reading of Cod.
Alex., Bezæ, and fourteen others ; Copt.,
Sahid., Armen., Eusebius, &c. The fathers' authority is greatly for the first.
The three readings Θεοῦ, Κυρίου, and Κυ-

speak, and so plainly assert the Deity of Christ, that the fathers, as early as Ignatius, who was a contemporary of the Apostles, considered themselves sanctioned by these words to use the remarkable expressions, " the Blood of God," and " the passion of God."[1]

St. Peter (2 Pet. i. 1) speaks of " our God and Saviour Jesus Christ ; " St. Jude, of " our only Lord God, even our Lord Jesus Christ," Jude 4. Compare Eph. v. 5 ; 2 Thess. i. 12 ; Tit. ii. 13.[2]

Lastly, St. John (1 John v. 20) distinctly calls Jesus Christ " the true God." " We are in Him that is true, even in His Son Jesus Christ. This (οὗτος) is the true God, and eternal life." The pronoun " this " (οὗτος), in all propriety of speech, should refer to the last antecedent, Jesus Christ. Hence, literally and grammatically, the passage teaches, that Christ is the true God. But also the context shows that it is of Him, and not of the Father, that St. John makes this statement. Our Lord is called by Himself, and by His Apostle St. John, " the Life," " the Life of men." Throughout the chapter, the Apostle has been urging, that eternal *life* is in the Son of God. Hence, when he has said all he has to say on the subject, he concludes with once more assuring us, that Jesus Christ is both " the true God and eternal Life." So cogent has this argument appeared, that some Arians have admitted that eternal life was meant of the Son, whilst the true God was meant of the Father. But it can never be denied that οὗτος, *this*, is equally the subject of both the predicates, *true God*, and *eternal life*. Therefore, if it be said, that *Christ* is *eternal life*, it is equally said, *Christ* is the *true God*. Lastly, there is no instance of the contrary interpretation in all antiquity, the objections being all modern, and of no weight in themselves.[3]

We may now then fairly conclude, that Scripture furnishes us, both *by reasonable inference* and by *direct statement*, with proof that the SON is GOD.

3. In the third place we learn also from Scripture that the HOLY GHOST is GOD.

Having found from the Scriptures that the Father is God, and that the Son is God, we shall need the less proof that He whose

---

ρίου καὶ Θεοῦ, are nearly equally supported by MSS. The VSS. in number are nearly equal for Θεοῦ and Κυρίου ; those of greater authority favour Θεοῦ.

The phrase Ἐκκλησία τοῦ Θεοῦ occurs eleven times in St. Paul's writings ; Ἐκκλησία τοῦ Κυρίου, never. See also Bp. Middleton in loc. ; Burton's *Testimonies of the Ante-Nicene Fathers*, p. 15.

[1] Ignat. *Ad Ephes.* 1. μιμηταὶ ὄντες Θεοῦ,

ἀναζωπυρήσαντες ἐν αἵματι Θεοῦ. This passage is in Syriac.

[2] This is, of course, assuming Mr. Granville Sharp's Canon on the Article to be established. See Middleton, pt. I. ch. III. Sect. IV. § 2 ; and upon the five passages quoted and referred to in the text ; also Waterland, II. p. 128.

[3] See Waterland, II. p. 123

name is constantly joined with them is also God. Indeed, but few will deny the Divinity, though they may doubt the Personality of the Holy Ghost. Yet, since in old times Arians, Macedonians, and others appear to have held the strange notion that the Holy Spirit was a creature, it may be well to show briefly that Scripture does speak of Him as God.

As is the case as regards the Son, so to the Spirit are ascribed the power and the attributes of God.

(1) He is the great Worker of Miracles. Matt. i. 20; xii. 28. Luke iv. 1, 14. Acts ii. 4; x. 45. Rom. xv. 19. 1 Cor. xii. 4, 8. Heb. ii. 4.

(2) He is the Inspirer of Prophets, and can teach all things. Mark xii. 36; xiii. 11. Luke i. 15–41; xii. 12. John xiv. 26; xvi. 13. Acts i. 8; viii. 29; x. 19, 20; xiii. 2; xxviii. 25. 1 Cor. ii. 13; xii. 11. Eph. iii. 5. Heb. iii. 7. 1 Pet. i. 11, 12. 2 Pet. i. 21.

(3) He dwells in temples as God. 1 Cor. iii. 16; vi. 19.

(4) He is the Source of all holiness. John iii. 5. Rom. i. 4, 5; viii. 9, 14. 1 Cor. vi. 11. Gal. v. 16, &c. Compare Matt. xix. 17.

(5) He is Omnipresent and Omniscient. Ps. cxxxix. 7. 1 Cor. ii. 10.

(6) He is represented as the Creator. Gen. i. 2. Job xxvi. 13; xxxiii. 4. Ps. civ. 30, with which compare Is. xliv. 24. Mal. ii. 10.

(7) He is everlasting. Heb. ix. 14.

(8) Sin against Him is so great, that, though blasphemy of all other kinds is pardonable, blasphemy against the Holy Ghost is unpardonable. Matt. xii. 31. Mark iii. 29. Luke xii. 10.

Thus are attributes and powers ascribed to the Holy Ghost which can only be ascribed to God.

But, moreover, He is expressly called God.
In 2 Sam. xxiii. 2, 3, we read,

> " The Spirit of the Lord spake by me,
> And His Word was in my tongue,
> The God of Israel said,
> The Rock of Israel spake to me."

According to the usage of Hebrew poetry, it is unquestionable that " the Spirit of the Lord " in the first verse is the same as " the God of Israel " in the third.

In Matt. xii. 28, our Lord says, " If I with the Spirit of God cast out devils." The parallel passage, Luke xi. 20, has, "If I with the finger of God cast out devils;" where the word "finger," like "hand" in the old Testament, simply signifies *by* or *by means of*.[1] So that here *God* and *the Spirit of God* are synonymous.

In Acts xxviii. 25, St. Paul quotes a passage thus, "Well spake the *Holy Ghost* by the prophet Esaias." The passage is from Isaiah vi. 9 : which, if we refer to it in Isaiah, we shall find to have been unquestionably spoken by *God*.

In 1 Cor. iii. 16, we read, "Ye are the temple of *God*." In 1 Cor. vi. 19, the parallel passage, we find, "Your body is the temple of the *Holy Ghost*."

In Exod. xxxiv., it is related that, when Moses had gone up to talk with the Lord on Mount Sinai, the skin of his face shone so brightly, that, when he had spoken to the people, he put a veil over his face, so that they were not able to look upon him; but, "when he went in before the Lord," (*i. e.* JEHOVAH,) "to speak with Him, he took the veil off until he came out," ver. 34. Now in 2 Cor. iii. 16, 17, St. Paul alludes to this history, and plainly referring to this very verse, he says, When the heart of the Israelites "shall turn to the Lord, the veil shall be taken away." He then adds, "Now *the Lord*" (*i. e.* the Lord, before whom Moses stood, and to whom the Israelites were to turn, *i. e.* JEHOVAH) "is that Spirit."

In Acts v. 3, 4, when Ananias had denied the truth before the Apostles, Peter said to Ananias, "Why hath Satan filled thine heart to lie to *the Holy Ghost?*" And immediately after he adds, "Thou hast not lied unto men, but unto God." Plainly, therefore, the Holy Ghost is God.

Such are some of the passages of Scripture from which we may infallibly conclude, that,

As the FATHER is GOD, — And the SON is GOD, — So the HOLY GHOST is GOD.

III. Having shown that God is One, and yet, that, as regards the Father, the Son, and the Holy Ghost, it is said of each that He is God; I propose next to show that these two truths are not direct contradictions to each other, as though it were said in one place, "there is One God," and in another, "there are three Gods;" for it appears from Scripture that the Father, the Son, and the Holy Ghost are but one and the same God.

1. It appears from Scripture, that the Father is One with the

---

[1] Thus תְּיַד מֹשֶׁה "By the hand of Moses," means merely "by Moses."

Son. This is expressly declared by our Lord (John x. 30), " I
and My Father are One." Again, He addresses the Father as
being One with Him; and prays that His Church may be one
Church in God, as He and His Father are One: " that they all
may be One, as Thou, Father, art in Me, and I in Thee, that they
also may be one in us." Again, that " they may be one, even as
we are one " (John xvii. 21, 22). Therefore it is, that the Lord
Jesus says of Himself, " He that seeth Me, seeth Him that sent
Me," and in like manner He reproves His Apostle for asking to
be shown the Father, saying, " Have I been so long time with you,
and yet hast thou not known Me, Philip ? he that hath seen Me,
hath seen the Father: and how sayest thou then, Shew us the
Father ? "[1]

2. That the Spirit of God is one with God the Father is shown
by St. Paul, who compares the Spirit of God in God, to the spirit
of man in man (1 Cor. ii. 10, 11): " What man knoweth the
things of a man, save the spirit of man which is in him? Even
so the things of God knoweth no man, but the Spirit of God."

The passage in 2 Sam. xxiii. 2, 3, quoted above, where " the
Spirit of God spake by me " is synonymous with " the God of
Israel said," is to the same effect.

3. That the Son and the Spirit are One may appear from the
fact that St. John says (xii. 37, 41), that the Lord, whose glory
Isaiah saw in the vision recorded in the sixth chapter, was *the Son*,
Jesus Christ; but St. Paul says (Acts xxviii. 25), that the Lord,
who then spoke to Isaiah, was *the Holy Ghost*.

Again (in Matt. xi. 27) we read, " No one knoweth the Father,
but the *Son*." Whereas, in 1 Cor. ii. 11, we are told that " the
things of God knoweth no man, but the *Spirit* of God."

4. Accordingly we find, that what the Father does, that the Son
does, and that the Holy Ghost does; where the Father is, there
the Son is, and there the Holy Ghost is, *e.g.*

> The Father made the world. Heb. i. 2. 1 Cor. viii. 6.
> The Son made the world. John i. 3. Col. i. 16. Heb. i. 2.
> The Spirit made the world. Job xxvi. 13 ; xxxiii. 4.

Again,

> The Father quickeneth. John v. 21.
> The Son quickeneth whom he will. John v. 21.
> It is the Spirit that quickeneth. John vi. 63.

Again,

> God the Father spake by the prophets. Heb. i. 1.

[1] John xiv. 9; see also Matt. x. 40; Mark ix. 37.

God the Son spake by the prophets. 2 Cor. xiii. 3. 1 Pet. i. 11.

God the Holy Ghost spake by the prophets. Mark xiii. 11. 2 Pet. i. 21.

Again, sanctification is ascribed

To the Father. Jude 1.

To the Son. Heb. ii. 11.

To the Holy Ghost. Rom. xv. 16.[1]

Ordination is ascribed

To the Father. 2 Cor. iii. 5, 6.

To the Son. 1 Tim. i. 12.

To the Holy Ghost. Acts xx. 28.

Indwelling and presence in every Christian are ascribed

To the Father. John xiv. 23. 1 Cor. xiv. 25.

To the Son. John xiv. 23. 2 Cor. xiii. 5.

To the Holy Ghost. John xiv. 17.

From these considerations, and others like them, we naturally conclude, that, though the Father is God, the Son is God, and the Holy Ghost is God, yet are they not three different Gods, but one and the same God.

Those, indeed, who take the Arian view of the Scriptures, maintain that there is but one God, even the Father; but they add, that the Son also is God, yet not the same God, but an inferior God to the Father, and so not of the same nature and substance with the Father. This is both self-contradictory and contradictory to Holy Scripture. First, it is self-contradictory, for it teaches that there is but one God, and yet that there are two Gods. Secondly, it is contradictory to Scripture; for it is opposed to the passages, which, as we have just seen, prove the Son to be one with the Father; and it is opposed most distinctly to such passages as teach that there is no God but the One Supreme Creator of the Universe. For example, we read, Isai. xliv. 8, " Is there a God beside Me ? Yea, there is no God, I know not any ; " and, Isai. xlv. 5, " I am the Lord, there is none else ; there is no God beside me." (So Deut. iv. 35, 39; xxxii. 39. 2 Sam. xxii. 32.) Now, if the Arian hypothesis be true, there is another God, besides God the Father, even His Son Jesus Christ, who is not only another, but an inferior God to the Father. The only way, then, in which we can reconcile the two apparently contradictory truths, (1) that God is one, and (2) that the Father, the Son, and the Holy Ghost are each said to be God, is by admitting, as the

---

[1] See Jones's *Catholic Doctrine of the Trinity.*

Scriptures also teach us, that "they are not three Gods, but One God." [1]

Thus far, then, we have proved, — I. The Unity of the Godhead, — II. That the Father is God, the Son is God, and the Holy Ghost is God, — III. That these two truths are not direct contradictions to each other; for that the Father, the Son, and the Holy Ghost are but One God, not three Gods.

But if this were all that we could learn from Scripture, we might naturally conclude that the Sabellian was the correct hypothesis, and that the names of Father, Son, and Spirit were the names but of different modes, operations, or characters of the Deity: so that, perhaps, God might be called Father, when viewed as Creator and Governor; Son, when viewed as Redeemer and Saviour; Spirit, when considered as Sanctifier and Teacher. Or perhaps we might suppose, that the Son and the Spirit were mere attributes of, or influences from God; as, for instance, the Son, the Logos, might be esteemed but as the Reason of God; the Spirit, as that Divine Influence by which He teaches the minds, and sanctifies the hearts of His servants.

IV. It is therefore necessary to show that there is plain evidence from Scripture that the Father is not the Son, and that neither of them is the Holy Ghost; but that they are plainly distinguished from one another, and distinguished, too, as Personal Agents, not merely as modes, operations, or attributes.

That there is some kind of distinction, must appear from the fact that the three, Father, Son, and Spirit, are so frequently mentioned together in the same sentence; especially in the forms of blessing and of baptism. (2 Cor. xiii. 14. Matt. xxviii. 19.) This alone might be sufficient to prove that these three sacred names were not names merely of different characters assumed by God at various times; for it seems scarcely reasonable to suppose that the Apostles prayed for blessing from three characters assumed by God, instead of praying for blessing from the One God to whom all such characters belonged; nor yet can we well believe that they should invoke blessing from the attributes of God, or baptize converts into a form of faith not in God alone, but in God, His attributes, and His influences.

But, in order to establish more clearly the fact that the Father,

---

[1] It may be observed, that, if this is true, then the doctrine of the *homo-ousion*, the consubstantiality of the Son and the Spirit is proved; for if the Father, the Son, and the Holy Ghost be but one God, the Son and the Spirit must be of one nature and substance with the Father.

the Son, and the Holy Ghost are distinguished as personal Agents, it will be necessary to bring passages from Scripture, in which they are represented to us as acting personal parts, and even in which all three are represented as acting three distinct parts.

1. The Father and the Son act distinct personal parts, and are therefore distinct Personal Agents.

(1) The Father sends the Son; whereas no one can be said to send himself. John v. 36, 37; vi. 38, 39. Acts iii. 20. Gal. iv. 4. 1 John iv. 9, &c.

(2) The Son leaves the Father and returns to Him again. John viii. 42; ix. 4; xii. 49; xvi. 5, 28; xvii. 3. 1 John iv. 14.

(3) The Son offers Himself to the Father. Heb. ix. 14.

(4) The Father loves the Son, and the Son loves the Father. John iii. 35; v. 20; xiv. 31; xv. 9; xvii. 24, 26.

(5) The Son is said to make intercession with the Father. Heb. vii. 25. 1 John ii. 1. Comp. Heb. ix. 24.

(6) The Son in His human nature prays to the Father. Luke xxii. 42; xxiii. 34. John xvii.

(7) The Father hears and speaks to the Son. John xi. 42. Heb. v. 7. Matt. iii. 17; xvii. 5. Luke ix. 35. John xii. 28.

2. The Spirit acts distinct parts from either the Father or the Son.

(1) The Father and the Son both send the Spirit. John xiv. 16, 26; xv. 26; xx. 22. Acts ii. 33. Gal. iv. 6.

(2) The Spirit makes intercession with the Father, whereas no one can intercede with Himself. Rom. viii. 26.

(3) The Son offers Himself to the Father through the Eternal Spirit. Heb. ix. 14.

(4) Christ tells His disciples, that He must go away from them, and that then the Holy Spirit should come in His place; that He would go to the Father; and from the Father send the Comforter. John xiv. 16, 26; xvi. 7.

(5) Christ says, that the Holy Spirit should not speak of Himself, but should receive of Christ's, and show to the Church. John xvi. 13, 14, 15.

3. We not only have the names of the Father, the Son, and the Spirit joined in blessing, and in the form of baptism, but we are told of a scene in which they all three acted jointly, yet separate parts. At the baptism of Christ, the Son was in the Man Christ Jesus baptized; the Spirit in the shape of a dove descended on Him; the Father, out of Heaven, pronounced Him His beloved Son.

All these facts, put together, sufficiently demonstrate that there is a distinction between the Father, the Son, and the Holy Ghost, and that a distinction of Personal Agents. Yet still, that we may leave no room for objection, it may, perhaps, appear necessary to consider separately, and more at length, the Personality (i) of the Son, (ii) of the Spirit.

(i) The general tone of Scripture so clearly indicates that God the Son is a Person, that, at first, it might appear that the Arian hypothesis, which makes the Son an inferior God to the Father, was the only one which could be at all maintained on Scriptural grounds; except, of course, the Catholic doctrine of the Trinity. But as the Sabellian hypothesis is not without its advocates and its arguments, it deserves and requires to be considered.

The view which Sabellianism takes of the Son of God, is, as has been said before, twofold. Some Sabellians considered God the Son as *altogether* the same as God the Father, and as having no proper distinction from Him. These were, in the early ages, called Patripassians. Others, again, looked on God the Son as but an *Emanation* from the Father, not as a Person distinct, in any sense, from Him. These have been called Emanative Sabellians. Both forms have found advocates in some degree in later times. Patripassianism has been virtually held by some divines, who, in the main orthodox, have endeavoured too boldly to make the doctrine of the Trinity square exactly with human reason and philosophy. The emanative theory has been adopted, more or less, by some, who are in fact Socinians, to elude the force or explain the difficulty of such passages as John i. 1.

Now, against both these hypotheses, the marked distinction which our Lord makes between Himself and the Father must be carefully noted. For example (John viii. 17, 18): "It is written in your Law that the testimony of two men is true. I am one that bear witness of Myself, and the Father that sent Me beareth witness of Me." Here is a distinct appeal to two distinct witnesses. As the Jewish Law required the evidence of two men; so here the Lord Jesus appeals to the evidence first of Himself, secondly of His Father. Would this be much unlike equivocation, if the Father and the Son had no personal distinction? Again (John v. 17), our Lord says: "My Father worketh hitherto, and I work." And when the Jews accused Him of blasphemy, for making God His Father, and so claiming equality with God, He does not deny the charge of making Himself equal with God, but still goes on to declare to them, that, notwithstanding His unity of nature with the Father, He, the Son, had a personal subordination to Him. " The Son can do nothing of Himself, but what He seeth the Father do : for what things soever He doeth, these also doeth the Son likewise. For the Father loveth the Son, and showeth Him all things that Himself doeth." In this passage surely, where the Son claims, as the Jews rightly interpreted Him, to be the true Son of God, and so equal with God, He yet plainly sets forth the doctrine, that in His Person, though not in His Nature, He was subordinate to the Father, receiving of the Father, and doing the same things as the Father doeth. And so He goes on, " As the Father raiseth up the dead and quickeneth them, even so the Son quickeneth whom He will. For the Father judgeth no man, but hath committed all judgment to the Son." Again, " As the Father hath life in Himself, so hath He given to the Son to have life in Himself : " that is, " the Father," unlike any creature, is self-existent, having " life in Himself," and so He hath given to the Son to be self-existent, and to " have life in Himself,"— (language clearly spoken of the eternal Son, not merely of the Man Christ Jesus,) — " And hath given Him authority to execute judgment also ; because He is the Son of Man," i. e. because He is not only Son of God, but Son of man also, incarnate, and so the fitter agent to execute the wrath, as well as to show the mercy of God. But again, our Lord goes on, " I can of Mine own Self do nothing : as I hear I judge : and My judgment is just : because I seek not Mine own will, but the will of the Father, which hath sent Me."[1] Again, in the forty-third verse, " I am come in My Father's name, and ye receive Me not : if another shall come in his own name, him ye will receive."

The whole of this passage is one in which our Lord clearly spoke of Himself in His Divine nature, and of His relation to His Father in that nature, which He had in common with Him ; yet no language can more expressly mark a distinction of personal action, and personal attribute.

Again, some of the passages which seem to have as their special object to set forth the glory of the Divine Being of the Son, are so worded as specially to show His distinction of Person from the Father. Thus in Coloss. i. 15, 16, where creation and providence are ascribed to Him in terms of peculiar grandeur, He is called " the Image of the Invisible God, the First Born of," or " Begotten before, every creature." Here He is both repre-

---

[1] See John v. 17–30.

8

sented as the *Image* of the Father, and as having before all creation been *begotten* as *His Son;* both expressions markedly denoting
personal difference.

The same thing is even more remarkable in the beginning of
the Epistle to the Hebrews. It is plain, from the language of the
whole of the first chapter, that the subject is the Divine nature of
the Son. Yet nothing can be more clear than the distinction
which is made between the Father and the Son. First of all, God
is said to have spoken in old times by the *prophets*, but in the
latter days by His *Son*, "whom he hath appointed *heir* of all
things, by whom also He made the worlds. Who being the
brightness (the shining forth) of His glory, and the *express Image*
of His *Person*, and upholding all things by the word of His power,
when He had by Himself purged our sins, sat down on the right
Hand of the Majesty on High" (vv. 1, 2, 3). Now here God is
said to have spoken by His Son, as He did by the prophets; He
is said to have appointed Him heir of all things; (both marking
distinctions of Person); then the Son is said to be "the *express
Image* of the Person" of the Father. It may be a question, what
is meant by the word ὑπόστασις, translated *Person;* but there can
be no question that the word χαρακτήρ, translated *express Image*,
means that *the ὑπόστασις of the Son answers to that of the Father,
as the impression on wax answers to the seal which made the impression.* Whether then ὑπόστασις means "*Person*," or whether it
means "*Mode of existence*," we learn that, as the Son is the
shining forth of the Father's glory, so His Person, or His mode
of being, corresponds to that of the Father, (not only as a Son's
to a Father's, but) as an impression on wax to the engraving on
a seal. This indeed teaches us clearly, that the Son is of one
glory, and so of one eternal essence with the Father; but as the
image on the wax is distinct from that upon the seal, so must
there be a distinction between the Father and the Son, of which
the distinction of the seal and the wax is a figure and similitude.

The prayer of our Lord to His Father, in the seventeenth
chapter of St. John, is another striking proof that the Son is
indeed of one nature and substance, but not of one Person with
the Father. No one can attentively peruse that prayer without
seeing that our Lord speaks of Himself and His glory, as the
Eternal Son, not merely as the Man Christ Jesus; so that whatever diversity we observe is not merely incident to our Lord's
incarnation, but is also characteristic of Him in His uncreated
nature. When, therefore, He says (ver. 1), "Father, glorify Thy

Son, that Thy Son also may glorify Thee," we may inquire, what sense the passage could bear, if the Father and the Son were personally identical ?　Again, the same question is suggested by the following : " And now, O Father, glorify Thou Me with Thine own self with the glory that I had with Thee before the world was" (ver. 5).　And "I have given unto them the words which Thou gavest Me, and they have received them, and have known surely that I came out from Thee, and they have believed that Thou didst send Me " (ver. 8).　And again, "Thou lovedst Me before the foundation of the world" (ver. 24).　Does not all this necessarily prove that, before the world was created, the Person of the Son was different from the Person of the Father ?

Perhaps the passage which most favours the Sabellian notions concerning the Person of the Son, is the important first chapter of St. John.　That passage indeed distinctly asserts the *Divinity* of the Son; but language is used which may be supposed to mean that He is, as regards His Divine nature, not to be distinguished from the Father, or at least to be distinguished only as an emanation or attribute.　Plato had used the term Λόγος ; but he did not probably intend to distinguish, by any *personal* distinction, the Λόγος from God.　The early heretics had mixed up the philosophy of Plato with the religion of Christ ; and they used of the Son of God the language which the Platonists had used of the Λόγος. When, therefore, St. John came to use the same expression (adopted, as some think, on purpose to refute heretical teachers whilst using their own terms), it might be supposed that by the Λόγος he meant no more than the *Thought* or *Reason* of God, which, whilst it remained in the bosom of God, was the Λόγος ἐνδιάθετος, *the inward Reason* or *Thought ;* when it was exerted to create the world or reveal the will of God, it became the Λόγος προφορικός, or, as it were, *the outward Speech* of God.

This view of the passage may seem supported by the eighth chapter of Proverbs ; where the Wisdom of God is spoken of in terms so like St. John's language concerning the Logos, that the fathers, and many after them, have considered that Solomon must there have been writing of Christ.　If this be the meaning of the Logos in St. John, we may paraphrase his words somewhat as follows : In the beginning was the Reason or Wisdom of God. That Wisdom was in God, nay, it was God (for as God is Love, so God is Wisdom).　All things were made by the Reason or Wisdom of God, and without it was nothing made that was made. . . . . It was the true light, that lighteth every man that cometh into the world. . . . . And this wisdom was incarnate, or manifested in Christ, and so dwelt among us.

I have endeavoured to put this argument in its strongest form, that I may give it all the weight which it deserves. I proceed to show wherein it is defective and unsound.

In the first place, the later Platonists, and still more, the Platonizing and Gnostic heretics, had a notion of the Logos very different from Plato's, and far more personal. Again, the Gnostics, against whose opinions in all probability St. John directs many of his statements, considered the Pleroma or fulness of God to be made up of many Æons or Emanations from God, to which they gave the various names of Nus, Sophia, Dynamis, &c. The chief of these was the Logos, whom they believed to have descended on the man Jesus. It is probable that in the first chapter of his Gospel St. John uses the names of other Æons besides the Logos. For example, whereas he first calls the Son of God the Logos, he also tells us, that in Him was Zoe (life), and the Zoe was the Phos (light); by which he has been supposed to mean, that the Logos, the Zoe, the Phos, were not different Æons, but that, as St. Paul informed the Colossians (ii. 9), the whole Pleroma of Godhead dwelt in Christ, bodily. Again, St. John tells us that by the Logos, who is also the Phos and the Zoe, the world was created. The Gnostics taught that the world was created by a fallen Æon, who was an enemy to God, and that the Logos came down to destroy his dominion among men. But St. John teaches that the Logos was Himself the Creator of the Universe, and that without Him nothing was made that was made. Once more, he explains (ver. 14), that the Logos was really made flesh and dwelt among us. The Gnostics did not believe the Logos to be really made flesh; but they supposed, either that He only assumed the *appearance* of humanity, or that He descended, for a time, on the man Jesus, and then left him at his crucifixion. Therefore St. John uses the strong expression ὁ Λόγος σὰρξ ἐγένετο, "The Word was *made flesh*." Lastly, he says that "we beheld His glory, the glory of the *Monogenes* (the Only-begotten) of the Father; full of grace and truth." *Monogenes* (only-begotten) was the name of another Æon in the Gnostic Pleroma. St. John therefore adds to the other titles of the Son this title of *Monogenes*, to show still farther, that the Lord Jesus, the Son of the Father, combined in His own Person all the attributes which the Gnostics assigned to these various Æons, and was therefore not simply a single emanation from God, but, as St. Paul says, had in Him a fulness of

Deity, and was moreover the Creator of the universe, and not, as the Gnostics had it, one who was sent to overthrow the power of the Creator.

Now, if this be the true explanation of St. John's language, it is vastly unlike the language assigned to him by the Sabellian hypothesis. For whilst St. John is ascribing to the Son supreme Divinity, he does so in a manner which essentially implies Personality too.

But there are many other reasons why the word *Logos* in the first chapter of St. John must be interpreted of a Person, not of an attribute or quality, like Reason, or Wisdom.

(1) The Word is said to be God. It is not said that the Word is θεῖος, *divine*, but Θεός, *God*. Now it may be possible improperly to say " God is wisdom," as the Apostle says, " God is love." But we cannot say, " God's wisdom is God," any more than " Man's wisdom or reason is man."

(2) The Word is said to be " with God," not *in* God ; which implies personality. God's *wisdom* is *in* Him, not, properly speaking, *with* Him.

(3) In ver. 11, the Word is said to have " come to His own ; " meaning, no doubt, His own creatures ; which again is personal.

(4) In verse 14, He is called the Μονογενής, *the Only-begotten.* But the idea of Sonship is personal. We cannot conceive of the *Son* of God, but as one in some personal sense distinct from him : just as the term *son* amongst men indicates one distinct from his father. And no doubt, as the term Logos is used to indicate that the Son from all eternity dwelt in the bosom of the Father, as the reason or wisdom dwells in the bosom of one endowed with such faculties ; so the word *Son* is used to indicate to our finite understandings, that, notwithstanding such an intimate union, yet there is a distinction, such, in some degree, as the distinction of father and son.

(5) He is said to have been " made flesh, and to have dwelt among us ; " and that, in opposition to the fancy of the Gnostics or Docetæ, that the Christ or Logos only took a *phantastic* body. Accordingly, in Rev. xix. 13, St. John sees a vision of a Person, who is evidently Jesus Christ, and whose name, written on His thigh, is King of kings, and Lord of lords ; and he tells us that this *Person* is called " The Word of God."

(6) In the eighth verse, John the Baptist is contrasted with Him, and declared *not* to be the Light or the Logos. Now, John the Baptist was undoubtedly a *person*. We must therefore con-

clude that He, with whom he is contrasted, and of whom the
Evangelist had been speaking before, was a *Person* also.

Thus, I trust, we may conclude that the testimony borne by
St. John, in the first chapter of his Gospel, is a testimony to the
doctrine of the distinct personality of the Son, not to Sabellianism.[1]
And with this we may venture to leave the question of the Personality of God the Son.

(ii) We have next to show the Personality of the Spirit of God.

Now, as we are baptized " in the Name of the Father, and of the
Son, and of the Holy Ghost: " as the Apostles bless in the name
of Jesus Christ, God the Father, and the Holy Ghost: and as on
many occasions the Holy Spirit is joined with the Father and the
Son; we cannot but think it probable, at least, that as the Father
is a Person, and the Son has just been shown to be a Person distinct from the Father, so the Holy Ghost is a Person also distinct
from either of them.

But beyond this, we find distinctly that, in Holy Scripture,
personal actions are ascribed to the Holy Ghost.

(1) He makes intercession with God the Father, Rom. viii. 26.
Now to make intercession is a personal act.

(2) He testifies. John xv. 26.

(3) He teaches. John xiv. 26.

(4) He hears and speaks. John xvi. 13.

(5) He gives spiritual gifts, dividing them according to His
will. 1 Cor. xii. 8, 11.

(6) He inhabits a temple, 1 Cor. iii. 16; vi. 19. This is the
act of a Person, not of an attribute or influence.

(7) He not only is represented as speaking generally, but we
have speeches set down in Scripture, which the Holy Spirit is said
to have uttered to peculiar persons, *e. g.* Acts x. 28: " The Spirit
said unto Peter, Behold, three men seek thee . . . . I have sent
them." Acts xiii. 2: " The Holy Spirit said, Separate me Barnabas and Saul, for the work whereunto I have called them."

(8) He is put in direct opposition to evil spirits, who are
doubtless *persons.* 1 Sam. xvi. 14. 2 Chron. xviii. 20, 21.

It has, however, been argued that these and·similar personal
actions, when ascribed to the Spirit, are the actions of the Father,
who, when He does them Himself, is said to do them by His
Spirit. In answer to this, it can plainly be shown that there are
many personal actions ascribed to the Spirit which cannot be

---

[1] On this subject see Waterland's first Sermon at Lady Moyer's Lecture, **on**
John i. 1, ii. p. 1.

ascribed to the Father. For instance, in Rom. viii. 26, as we have just seen, the Spirit intercedes with the Father for the saints. But it cannot be said that the Father intercedes with Himself. Here then we.have an instance of the performance of a personal action by the Spirit, which cannot be performed by the Father. Again, Christ is said to send the Spirit (John xvi. 7). But it is never said of God the Father, that He is sent. He sends both the Son and the Spirit, but is never sent Himself. Moreover (in John xv. 26), our Lord promises " to send the Spirit from the Father." If the Spirit means here the Father, then Christ must send the Father from the Father.[1] Again (in chapter xvi. 13, 14), when our Lord promises to send the Paraclete, He says, that " He," the Paraclete, " shall not speak of Himself, but whatsoever He shall hear, that shall He speak." " He shall glorify Me ; for He shall receive of Mine, and shall show it unto you." Now, it certainly cannot be said of God the Father (from whom eternally both Son and Spirit are derived), that He should not speak of Himself, but should speak what He heard only. Nothing which implies *subordination* is ever spoken of God the Father. We conclude, therefore, that the Spirit (who is here represented as acting personal parts, and parts which cannot belong to the Person of the Father) is both a Person, and a Person distinct from the Father.

The fact that the Spirit is called *Paraclete*, which means either *Comforter* or, more probably, *Advocate*,[2] seems to imply distinct personality.

The use of the masculine pronoun *He*, ἐκεῖνος, to designate the Holy Ghost, surely indicates, that reference is made to a personal Agent, not to an influence or attribute. This is observable especially in John xvi. 13, where we have in immediate connection, " When He the Spirit of truth is come," ἐκεῖνος, τὸ Πνεῦμα τῆς ἀληθείας, a masculine pronoun, whilst τὸ Πνεῦμα is neuter.[3]

From these, then, and similar reasons, we conclude that the Spirit is a distinct Person from the Father and the Son.

Thus we have reached the conclusion of our reasoning on the subject of Personality, and so we believe our Fourth Proposition to be established: that although the Father, the Son, and the Holy Ghost are but one God, yet are they clearly distinguished from One another, and distinguished as Personal Agents.

Now this is the doctrine of the Trinity in Unity, as held by the

---

[1] See Hey, ii. p. 443.

[2] See Pearson, *On the Creed*, Art. viii. p. 329, note, fol. ; and Suicer, s. v. Παράκλη ·ος.

[3] The Personality of the Holy Ghost is fully and admirably treated by Bp. Pearson, Art. viii. p. 308, fol.

Catholic fathers, expressed in the Creeds of the Church, and exhibited in this first Article of the Reformed Church of England,
namely, that "There is but one God," yet that "in the Unity of
that Godhead there be three Persons, of one substance, power,
and eternity, the Father, the Son, and the Holy Ghost."

This conclusion we deduce from the statements of Scripture.
We do not pretend to explain the mystery, for it is, of course,
above the reach of finite understanding. Yet we cannot doubt
that, in the substance of it at least, our conclusions are legitimate.
To explain the subject philosophically would be inconsistent with
the purpose in hand, inconsistent with the assertion that it is a
mystery (that is, a thing which human reason cannot fathom), and
therefore impossible. It may not even be altogether possible to
mark out accurately the exact distinctions between Tritheism and
Trinitarianism on the one hand, between Trinitarianism and Sabellianism on the other. This, by the way, should make us not the
less earnest to maintain the truth, nay! the more earnest, because
of the greater danger of error; but yet the more tender, the more
ready in meekness to instruct those who from the difficulty of
apprehending have been led to doubt this great article of the faith.
But, though all this is true, yet, thoughtfully considered, this doctrine of the Trinity, though above our understanding, does not necessarily appear contrary to our reason. That reason may well teach
us that it is likely God should subsist in a manner above what we
can apprehend. That reason may teach us, that, though God's
nature is infinite, and therefore cannot be multiplied; yet, seeing
that he has shown himself to be essentially loving, and loving to
have partakers of His love, it is not impossible that there might
exist, even in the divine Essence, something like a Personal diversity, that so He, who, as regards the creature, dwells in light
which is unapproachable, might have within Himself that which
would be capable of receiving and imparting the love which can be
perfect in God alone. Yet such a diversity existing in the Godhead, which from its very perfection can admit neither multiplication nor division, could not constitute a distinction of Deity, though
it would constitute what, in the language of Theology, has been
called a distinct Personality.

The Fathers, who used the language which has been inserted
in the Creeds and generally adopted in the Church, never thought,
when they used to speak of three Persons in one God, of speaking
of such three Persons as they would speak of *persons* and *personality* among created beings. They did not consider, for example,

the persons of the Father and the Son as they would have done the persons of Abraham and Isaac, — the Persons of the Holy Trinity as they would have done the persons of Peter, Paul, and John, which are separate from one another, and do not in any way depend on each other for their essence. They held, that the Father is the Head and Fountain of Deity (Πηγὴ Θεότητος), from whom the Son and Holy Spirit are from all eternity derived, but so derived as not to be divided from the Father; but they are in the Father and the Father in them, by a certain περιχώρησις or *inhabitation*. So then, though they acknowledged the Father, the Son, and the Holy Ghost to be really three Persons, yet they held " them to have no divided or separate existence, as three different men have, but to be intimately united and conjoined one to another, and to exist in each other, and by the said ineffable περιχώρησις or *inhabitation* to pervade or permeate one another." [1]

---

[1] Bull, *Posth. Works*, p. 1004, quoted by Waterland, *Works*, II. p. 211. " Patrem, Filium, et Spiritum Sanctum, cum revera tres sint Personæ, nequaquam tamen ut tres homines seorsum et separatim existere, sed intime sibi invicem cohærere et conjunctos esse ; adeoque alterum in altero existere, atque, ut ita loquar, immeare invicem et penetrare per ineffabilem quandam περιχώρησιν, quam *circuminsessionem* Scholastici vocant." — Bull, *Def. Fid. Nic.* II. 9, 23 ; *Works*, IV. p. 363 ; see also Lib. IV. § 4 ; also Pearson, *On the Creed*, Art. II. p. 138, fol.
On the meaning of the word *Person*, see Waterland, *Works*, III. p. 338.

The term by which to designate what we call *person*, was early a subject of dispute. The Greeks mostly used the word ὑπόστασις, the Latins *Persona*. Yet among the Greeks it was not uniformly agreed to speak of τρεῖς Ὑποστάσεις and μία Οὐσία. Some, on the contrary, identified ὑπόστασις with οὐσία, and spoke of μία Ὑπόστασις. These differences in language led to the Council of Alexandria, A. D. 362, at which Athanasius was present, and at which this λογομαχία was condemned.
See Athanasius, *Dial.* II. Tom. II. p. 159 ; Suicer, s. v. ὑπόστασις ; and Newman's *Hist. of Arians*, ch. V. § 2.

[NOTE. It may not be useless to the student in Theology, to become familiar with the following analysis of the Scriptural argument for the Doctrine of the Holy Trinity in Unity. I. God is one. II. The Old Testament contains intimations of a plurality in this One Godhead. III. The New Testament affords proof by (a) necessary inferences, and (b) express declarations : (1) that the Father is God ; (2) that the Son is God ; (3) that the Holy Ghost is God. IV. How are these phenomena to be reconciled ? There are but three modes : (1) Tritheism ; (2) Sabellianism ; (3) the Catholic Doctrine of the Trinity. The first of these modes destroys the Divine Unity. The second ignores all the personal characteristics and agencies attributed to the Father, the Son, and the Holy Ghost. Logically, then, the third remains.

By bringing together the Scripture passages which belong to each of the above heads, and then, by studying out the exact way in which the Catholic Doctrine of the Trinity harmonizes what the other two schemes reject, the student may thoroughly appropriate and make his own the very valuable collections and arguments of the preceding pages.

The fifth, sixth, and seventh chapters of Owen's *Introduction*, may be profitably read. — *J. W.*]

ARTICLE II.

Of the Word or Son of God which was made very Man.

THE Son, which is the Word of the Father, begotten from everlasting of the Father, the very and eternal GOD, and of one substance with the Father, took man's nature in the womb of the blessed Virgin, of her substance: so that two whole and perfect natures, that is to say, the Godhead and Manhood, were joined together in one Person, never to be divided, whereof is one Christ, very God and very man; who truly suffered, was crucified, dead, and buried, to reconcile His Father to us, and to be a sacrifice, not only for original guilt, but also for all actual sins of men.

Verbum Dei verum hominem esse facturi

FILIUS, qui est Verbum Patris, ab æterno a Patre genitus, verus et æternus Deus, ac Patri consubstantialis, in utero beatæ Virginis, ex illius substantia naturam humanam assumpsit: ita ut duæ naturæ, divina et humana, integre atque perfecte in unitate personæ fuerint inseparabiliter conjunctæ: ex quibus est unus Christus, verus Deus, et verus homo, qui vere passus est, crucifixus, mortuus, et sepultus, ut Patrem nobis reconciliaret, essetque hostia, non tantum pro culpa originis, verum etiam pro omnibus actualibus hominum peccatis.

SECTION I. — HISTORY.

THIS Article evidently treats of three distinct points. I. The Divine nature of the Son of God; II. His incarnation; III. His sufferings, sacrifice, and propitiation.

I. First, as regards the Divine nature of the Son of God: as it was shown under the first Article that He was of one substance and coeternal with the Father, so the history of the different opinions concerning His consubstantiality and co-eternity formed part of the history of that Article. It is not necessary to repeat either those arguments or that history here.

I shall consider that I have said enough concerning the Divine nature of our blessed Lord, when, in addition to His consubstantiality and co-eternity before treated of, I have spoken concerning His generation from the Father, whereby He is the Begotten or Only-begotten Son of God.

It has already been shown that the Arians and Eunomians held that the Son might be called μονογενής, not as being the only-begotten of the Father, by a true and proper generation, but as

having been begotten or created by the Father alone;[1] and the
Socinians have endeavoured to explain the word as though it
meant no more than *beloved*, as Isaac was called the *only son* of
Abraham, though Ishmael was his son also.

It is hardly necessary to observe that the orthodox fathers held
that the Son was begotten of the Father from all eternity, so before all time deriving His Divine Essence from His Father (μόνος
ἐκ μόνου γεγέννηται τοῦ Πατρός. Cyril. Alexandr. *in Act. Concil.
Ephes.*) This eternal generation they held to be a proof that
He was of one substance and eternity with the Father ; but the relation of Father to Son they held to constitute a priority of *order*,
though not of *nature* or *power*. They held, that is, not that the
Son was, in His nature as God, in any degree different from, or inferior to the Father; but that, as the Father alone was the source
and fountain (πηγή, ἀρχή, αἰτία) of Deity, the Son having been begotten, and the Spirit proceeding, so there was a subordination,
without diversity, of the Son to the Father, and of the Spirit to the
Father and the Son.[2] It may be difficult to conceive of priority of
order, without being led to believe in superiority of nature. This
seems to have been the cause why Dr. Clarke and other high Arians, perceiving the truth of the doctrine that there was a certain
priority of order among the Persons of the undivided Trinity, and
unable to distinguish between priority of order and superiority of
nature, were led into an assertion of the heretical doctrine of the
inferiority of the nature of the Son.

II. The second part of the Article contains the doctrine of the
Incarnation.

Errors upon this doctrine were held by the Gnostics, or *Docetæ*,
and the Manichees, who taught that our Lord's Body was but a
phantom, and that He came not in the flesh, but in appearance
only (οὐκ ἐν σαρκὶ, ἀλλὰ δοκήσει) ; by those heretics, who denied the
Divinity of our Lord, and therefore, of course, the union of the two
natures in one Person ; and in short by all the Oriental and Judaizing sects. But the most important controversies on this mystery
arose from the errors of, 1, the Arians and Apollinarians ; 2, the
Nestorians ; 3, the Eutychians ; 4, the Monothelites.

1. Arius taught that the Son of God did not take human nature,

---

[1] Οἱ Ἀρειανοὶ λέγουσιν, ὅτι μονογενὴς
λέγεται, διότι αὐτὸς μόνος γέγονε καὶ ἐκτίσθη
ὑπὸ Θεοῦ, τὰ δ' ἄλλα πάντα ὑπ' αὐτοῦ. —
Theophyl. *in Joh.* cap. iii. See Pearson,
On the Creed, p. 138; Suicer, ii. p. 375.

[2] The statements of the Ante-Nicene
fathers on this subject are fully investigated by Bp. Bull, *F. D.* Sect. iv. *De Sub-
ordinatione Filii.* See also Suicer, s. vv.
αἰτία, ἀρχή, πηγή.

but a human body only, and that the Divine Word was in the place of the soul.[1]

Apollinaris, who maintained against Arius the consubstantiality of the Son, agreed with him in a great measure concerning the mode of His incarnation, teaching that our Lord took a human body, and a sensitive or *animal* soul, but that the place of the *rational* soul was supplied by God the Word, thus distinguishing, according to a common notion of those times, between the νοῦς, or *mens*, and the ψυχή, or *anima*.[2]

2. The Nestorian controversy arose as follows: The Greek fathers, justly esteeming that our Lord, from the moment that He was conceived in the womb of His mother, was not only man but God also, and maintaining that the union between His two natures was so perfect that it was right, for example, to say " God suffered," went so far as to call the Virgin Mary by the title Θεοτόκος, or *Deipara*. Nestorius declaimed strongly against this title, as indicating, according to his view of the subject, that God was liable to change, whereas God can neither be born nor die. He held that the *Man* Christ Jesus only could derive His birth from His earthly parent; and that therefore the Virgin might be called Χριστοτόκος, but not Θεοτόκος. These statements were considered to involve a denial of the union of the two natures of God and man in the one Person of Christ.[3] Nestorius was accused of teaching that there were not only two natures, but two persons in Christ, namely, the Person of God the Son, and the person of the man Christ Jesus. For this doctrine (though he appears to have denied the inferences drawn from his statements) he was condemned in the Council of Ephesus, A. D. 431, summoned by Theodosius the younger, and at which Cyril of Alexandria presided. This council determined that the true doctrine was that " Christ was but one Person, in whom two natures are intimately united, but not confounded." [4]

The tenets of the Nestorians, however, spread rapidly and widely in the East. They were embraced by the school of Edessa, were eagerly propagated by Barsumas, who became Bishop of

---

[1] See Pearson, *On the Creed*, p. 160. " In eo autem quod Christum sine anima soʌam carnem suscepisse arbitrantur minus noti sunt: . . . sed hoc verum esse et Epiphanius non tacuit, et ego ex eorum quibusdam scriptis et collocutionibus certissime comperi." — Augustin. *Hæres.* 49, Tom. VIII. p. 18.

[2] Pearson, as above. Mosheim, Cent. IV. pt. II. ch. V. § 17. Neander, *C. H.* IV. pp. 98–106. " Apollinaristas Apollinaris instituit, qui de anima Christi

a Catholica dissenserunt, dicentes, sicut Ariani, Deum Christum carnem sine anima suscepisse. In qua quæstione testimoniis Evangelicis victi, mentem, qua rationalis est anima hominis, defuisse animæ Christi, sed pro hac ipsum Verbum in eo fuisse dixerunt."—Augustin. *Hæres.* 55, Tom. VIII. p. 19.

[3] The technical term for this union was the ἕνωσις καθ᾽ ὑπόστασιν — hypostatic union.

[4] Neander, IV. pp. 123–152.

Nisibis in 435, and by his influence took such root in Persia that a Nestorian Patriarch was established at Seleucia, to whose authority, even to modern times, the Nestorian churches have been subjected. Nestorianism took deep root in many soils ; and the Nestorians proved themselves zealous missionaries.   Their opinions spread rapidly into Armenia, Chaldæa, Syria, Arabia, and India.[1]   They afterwards extended the Christian faith among the Tartar tribes of Scythia ; and, in the thirteenth century, established their bishops and clergy even among the Chinese.   In the eighth century, the sect called Adoptionists revived unconsciously a form of Nestorianism in Spain.[2]   And, in the twelfth century, the Nominalists were accused of Nestorianism, as well as Tritheism, by their adversaries.[3]

3.   Eutyches, an abbot at Constantinople, from opposition to Nestorianism, was led into the other extreme.   He asserted that the Divine and human natures of Christ were originally distinct, but that, after their union, they became but one nature, the human nature being transubstantiated into the Divine.   Before the hypostatic union, he acknowledged two natures; but after that union he acknowledged 'but one.   The Council of Chalcedon, which was summoned by Marcian in 451, and is reckoned the fourth general Council, condemned Eutyches, and declared the Catholic doctrine to be, that " in Christ two distinct natures are united in one Person, without any change, mixture, or confusion."[4]

The Eutychian, or Monophysite doctrine, notwithstanding this condemnation, rapidly gained ground, principally through the zeal of Jacob Baradæus, Bishop of Edessa, from whom the sect of the Eutychians are called Jacobites.   It was established in Syria, Mesopotamia, Armenia, Egypt, Abyssinia.   The Eutychians became united under the patriarchs of Antioch and Alexandria, and so continue to this day.   They are now divided into three principal societies : the Oriental Monophysites, subject to the patriarch of Antioch ; the African Monophysites, subject to the patriarch of Alexandria, embracing the Copts and Abyssinians ; and thirdly, the Armenians, who, though agreeing with the other Monophysites concerning the natures of Christ, are not united with them in other points of faith and discipline, and are subject to patriarchs of their own.[5]

---

[1] Suicer, s. vv. Θεοτόκος and Χριστοτόκος. Pearson, *On the Creed*, pp. 178, 163. Mosheim, Cent. v. pt. ii. ch. v. Neander, *C. H.* iv. pp. 269–271.

[2] Neander, v. pp. 216, *seq.*

[3] See p. 33, note 1.

[4] Suicer. s. v. ἀκέφαλοι. Pearson, p. 162. Mosheim, Cent. v. pt. ii. ch. v. Neander, iv. pp. 203–231.

[5] Mosheim, Cent. iv. pt. ii. ch. v. Cent. xvi. pt. i. § 3. Neander, iv. pp. 271–278.

4. In the seventh century a new controversy on this important subject arose; and a more subtle question was mooted. This question was, whether in Christ there were two distinct *wills*, the Divine and the human, or but one, the Divine. Those who adopted the opinion that there was but one will in Christ, among whom was Honorius, Bishop of Rome, were called Monothelites, Μονοθελῆται, and were condemned in 680 by the sixth general Council, the third Constantinopolitan. Their doctrine was supposed to border too closely on that of the Monophysites. It appears, however, that they entirely disclaimed Monophysite errors; and from the ambiguous manner in which their views were expressed, it has been questioned whether they held that the human will in Christ was wholly swallowed up in the Divine will, or only that it was so completely subservient to the Divine will as always to move in unison with it.[1]

III. As to the third division of this Article, the terms of it probably had reference to the error of the Docetæ, who denied that our Lord "*truly*" suffered, teaching either that He suffered only in appearance, or, as Basilides would have it, that Simon the Cyrenian was crucified in His place.

Of course it may be added, that the propitiatory sacrifice of Christ is necessarily denied by all humanitarian heretics, and others, who nearly symbolize with them. The Swedenborgians also of late times, though in some sense admitting the Atonement, appear to deny anything of the nature of a vicarious sacrifice, maintaining that redemption consists in the subduing of the powers of evil within the Christian, by virtue of union with the Redeemer in His human nature.

Section II.—SCRIPTURAL PROOF.

I. THE division of the subjects treated of in this Article, which has been suggested above, leads us to consider in the first place the eternal generation of the Son of God.

That the nature and being of the Son were from all eternity, and that He was of one substance with the Father, having been shown in the First Article, it is only necessary to prove here, that

---

[1] Mosheim, Cent. VII. pt. II. ch. v.

that nature, though eternal, is yet derived from the Father in such a manner that the relationship of the Father to the Son is best expressed to our understandings by the term, and under the notion of generation.

In order to represent to us the mode of existence of the Second Person in the Trinity, and His relation to the First, Holy Scripture has used various terms, drawn from human relations. The most common and important are the terms "Word" and "Son." The term "Word," or "Logos," is probably used to exhibit the intimate connection of the one Person with the other ; that, as reason dwells in man, so the Logos dwells in God, and that, as the word goeth forth from the heart and lips of man, so the Word is sent forth from God the Father.

In like manner, we must conceive the term "Son" to indicate something definite concerning the relation of the Son to the Father ; the variety of terms being adopted, probably because no one term could sufficiently convey to our understanding just notions of the nature and of the connection of the Persons in the Godhead.

That God the Son is not the same Person with God the Father has already been shown. That He is called the "Word" and the "Son" of the Father, seems sufficiently to declare that He derives in some manner His Being from the Father, even as the word springs from him who thinks and speaks, as the son is derived from him who begets him. This is farther evident from express statements in Holy Scripture. For example, our Lord is distinctly said to be *begotten* of the Father. He is called the Begotten and "Only-begotten of the Father," John i. 14. The Psalmist, as explained by St. Paul, tells us that God said to our Saviour, "Thou art My Son, this day have I begotten Thee," Ps. ii. 7. Acts xiii. 33. Heb. i. 5. And so He is spoken of as having been "begotten before every creature." (Πρωτότοκος πάσης κτίσεως, Col. i. 15.)

In correspondence with this notion of Sonship, our Lord is constantly called "Heir of all things," and said to be Possessor of all things, by right of Sonship. (See Heb. i. 2, 3, 4 ; iii. 6. John xvi. 15.) Again, our Lord speaks of Himself as deriving His own eternal Being from God the Father.[1] "As the living Father hath sent Me, and I live by the Father" (John vi. 57),

---

[1] In John v. 18, our Lord speaks of God as His *true* and *proper* Father, ἀλλὰ καὶ πατέρα ἴδιον ἔλεγε τὸν Θεόν. Compare John vi. 46, ὁ ὢν παρὰ τοῦ Θεοῦ, He that hath His being from God.

and again, "As the Father hath life in Himself, so hath He given to the Son to have life in Himself" (John v. 26). From which we learn that the mode of existence which the Father possessed from all eternity, He communicated to the Son. All created beings have their existence from, and their life in, God. But the Son, who is uncreated, derives indeed His Being from the Father, but it is a Being of the same kind as the Father's, and therefore not dependent, like a creature's, but independent, self-existent, having life in itself.

Accordingly the Son is farther called "the Brightness of His Father's glory, the express Image of His Person," Heb. i. 3; words which in the Greek indicate a relation of the Son to His Father, like that of brightness to light, like that of the impression of a seal on wax to the seal, to which it answers.[1]

Now the communication of the nature of God, thus made by the Father to the Son, may be called a proper generation. Nay! it is more proper than any earthly generation. For, in human generation, the son indeed derives his nature from his father, but it is in a manner according with the imperfection of humanity. Man's generation is in time, and, as connected with that which is material, results, in part at least, from that property of matter called divisibility. The son too, in human beings, when derived from the father, becomes separate from him.

But this is not so with God. God's eternal perfections He, from all eternity, communicated to His Son. "So also the Divine Essence, being by reason of its simplicity not subject to division, and in respect of its infinity incapable of multiplication, is so communicated as not to be multiplied, insomuch that He, which proceedeth by that communication, hath not only the same nature, but is also the same God. The Father God, and the Word God; Abraham man, and Isaac man : but Abraham one man, Isaac another man ; not so the Father one God, and the Word another ; but the Father and the Word both the same God. Being then the propriety of generation is founded in the essential similitude of the son unto the father, by reason of the same which he receiveth from him ; being the full, perfect nature of God is communicated unto the Word, and that more intimately, and with a greater unity or identity than can be found in human generation; it followeth, that this communication of the Divine nature is the proper

---

[1] Origen, commenting on these words of the Apostle, *Splendor est gloriæ Dei,* says : "*Deus lux est,* secundum Joannem. Splendor ergo hujus Lucis est Unigenitus Filius, ex ipso inseparabiliter velut splendor ex luce procedens, et illuminans universam creaturam." — *De Principiis,* Lib. I. ch. II. n. 7.

generation, by which Christ is, and is called the true and proper Son of God."[1]

This peculiar relation of the Father to the Son is that which has authorized the Church, while she confesses an equality of nature, to admit also a priority of order in the Persons of the Trinity. The Father hath this preëminence, that He is not only uncreated, but unbegotten, too. He derives His essence from none, being Himself the Fountain of life and the Source of being. The Son, too, is uncreated, deriving His being, not by creation but by generation, from the Father. Yet in this He is subordinate to the Father; not that His attributes are lower, or His nature inferior, but that both are derived. The Father begat; the Son is begotten. The Father is Life, Christ too is Life; but He confesses that He has life from the Father (John vii. 29), and that "He liveth by the Father" (John vi. 57). "The Father hath life in Himself:" so too has the Son. But the Father not only in Himself but from Himself. The Son in Himself, but from the Father (John v. 26).[2] On this account, therefore, and in this sense, "the Father is greater than the Son" (John xiv. 28); greater as regards priority of order, not greater as regards infinity of nature.[3]

II. The second part of the Article concerns the true doctrine of the Incarnation of the Son of God. It is thus expressed: "The Son . . . . took man's nature in the womb of the blessed Virgin, of her substance, so that two whole and perfect natures, that is to say, the Godhead and manhood, were joined together in one Person, never to be divided, whereof is one Christ, very God, and very man."

1. The wording of this is very important. "The Son of God took man's nature in the womb of the blessed Virgin." It appears directly from Holy Scripture, that the Being conceived by the

---

[1] Pearson, *On the Creed*, Art. ii. p. 138, fol. So Hooker, *Eccl. Pol.* Bk. v. ch. liv. 2. "By the gift of eternal generation, Christ hath received of the Father one and in number the self-same substance, which the Father hath of Himself unreceived from any other. For every 'beginning' (Eph. iii. 15) is a father unto that which cometh of it, and every 'offspring' is a son to that out of which it groweth. Seeing therefore that the Father alone is originally that Deity, which Christ originally is not, (for Christ is God by being of God; light by issuing

out of light); it followeth hereupon, that whatsoever Christ hath common unto Him with His heavenly Father, the same of necessity must be given Him, but naturally and eternally given; not bestowed by way of benevolence and favour, as the other gifts" (*i. e.* those of union and of unction) "both are."

[2] "Pater vita in Semetipso, non a Filio: Filius vita in Semetipso, sed a Patre." — Augustin. *In Johan. Tract.* xix. Tom. iii. par. ii. p. 443.

[3] See Pearson, *On the Creed*, Art. i. p. 34; Bull, *F. D.* § 4.

10

Virgin was, from the moment of His conception, the Son of God
(Luke i. 35, 43. Matt. i. 20, 23). Had the human nature of our
Lord been conceived in the womb of the Virgin, and then united
to the Divine nature ; it is clear that Christ would have consisted
of two distinct persons: one person, the Son of God, the other
person, that human being who had been conceived of the Virgin
Mary. For if a human being had been first conceived of the
Virgin, and then united to God, it is clear that that human being
must have been a human *person*, previously to the union with the
Divine Person ; and so the incarnation would have been the union
of two persons, not the union of two natures.[1] It was from want
of attention to this, that Nestorius was led into error. He denied
that the Person, who was born of the Virgin, was God ; and said
that He was only man. Hence he was obliged to divide Christ
into two persons. "If," says Hooker, "the Son of God had taken
to himself a man now made and already perfected, it would of
necessity follow that there are in Christ two persons, the one
assuming, the other assumed ; whereas the Son of God did not
assume a man's person to His own, but a man's nature to His
own Person ; and therefore took *semen*, the seed of Abraham, the
very first original element of our nature, before it was come to have
any personal human subsistence. The flesh, and the conjunction
of the flesh with God, began both at one instant; His making and
taking to Him our flesh was but one act; so that in Christ there
is no personal subsistence but one, and that from everlasting. By
taking only the nature of man, He still continueth one Person,
and changeth but the manner of His subsisting, which was before
in the mere glory of the Son of God, and is now in the habit of
our flesh."[2]

Thus it is said by St. John, "The Word was made flesh"
(John i. 14) ; by St. Paul, "Forasmuch as the children are partakers of flesh and blood, He also took part of the same" (Heb. ii.
14). "He took not the nature of angels, but He took the seed of
Abraham" (Heb. ii. 16). It was "Emmanuel, God with us,"
who was born of the Virgin (Isai. vii. 14. Matt. i. 23) ; yea, "the
Son of God" (Luke i. 32, 35).[3]

---

[1] "Primo illud nos oportet scire, quod
aliud est in Christo Deitatis ejus natura,
quod est Unigenitus Filius Patris ; et alia
humana natura quam in novissimis temporibus pro dispensatione suscepit." —
Origen. *De Principiis*, Lib. i. ch. ii. n. 1.

[2] Hooker, *Eccl. Pol*. Bk. v. lii.

[3] The Scriptures clearly indicate this
to have been the case. See Luke i. 39-

44 ; ii. 11. The former passage is especially clear, showing that Elisabeth by
the Holy Ghost, and even the yet unborn
"prophet of the Highest," acknowledged
the presence of their "Lord," when He
was yet in the womb of His mother. The
earliest fathers speak as plainly on the
subject as if they had foreseen the heresy
of Nestorius : *e. g.* ὁ γὰρ Θεὸς ἡμῶν Ἰησοῦς ὁ

The fact, thus exhibited, that the Son of God took in the womb of the Virgin the nature of man, explains some of the most remarkable passages in the new Testament. As there is but one Person in Christ, and *that* the Person of the Son of God, it naturally follows, that even the actions proper to man will at times be attributed to God, and the actions proper to God will be attributed to the man Jesus.[1] Thus we understand the Scripture, when it says that men "crucified the Lord of glory" (1 Cor. ii. 8); when it says that "God purchased the Church with His own Blood" (Acts xx. 28); because, though God in His Divine Nature cannot be crucified, and has no blood to shed; yet the Son of God, the Lord of Glory, took into His Person the nature of man, in which nature he could suffer, could shed his Blood, could be crucified, could die. Thus again, we understand the Scripture, when it attributes to a man powers and attributes which belong only to God. Our Lord (John iii. 13) speaks of none having gone up to Heaven "but the Son of man, which is in Heaven" : yet the Son of man was then on earth. Omnipresence is an attribute of none but God. But the Son of man here spoken of was God, God having taken into His own Person man's nature.[2] And so "as oft as we attribute to God what the manhood of Christ claimeth, or to man what his Deity hath right unto, we understand by the name of God and the name of Man, neither the one nor the other *nature,* but the whole *Person* of Christ, in which both natures are."[3] Of that Person, then, we may say, that He reigns as God, that He was subject as man. Of that Person we may say, that He liveth forever, and yet that He suffered and died. Of that Person we may say, that He "was crucified through weakness," and yet that He hath "the Power of God." Of that Person we may say, that whilst He was bound down to live on earth, He yet filled Heaven with His presence and glory.[4]

Χριστὸς ἐκυοφορήθη ὑπὸ Μαρίας κατ' οἰκονομίαν Θεοῦ, ἐκ σπέρματος μὲν Δαβὶδ, Πνεύματος δὲ ἁγίου. — Ignat. *Ad Ephes.* 18.

[1] " Cum ergo in eo quædam ita videamus humana ut nihil a communi mortalium fragilitate distare videamur, quædam ita divina ut nulli alii nisi illi primæ et ineffabili naturæ conveniant Deitatis, hæret humani intellectus angustia, et tantæ admirationis stupore percussa quò declinet, quid teneat, quo se convertat, ignorat. Si Deum sentiat, mortalem videt : si hominem putet, devicto mortis imperio cum spoliis redeuntem a mortuis cernit. . . . Nam et Filius Dei mortuus **esse** dicitur, pro ea scilicet natura quæ

mortem utique recipere poterat : et filius hominis appellatur, qui venturus in Dei Patris gloria cum sanctis angelis prædicatur." — Origen. *De Principiis,* Lib. II. ch. VI. n. 2, 3.

[2] Compare John i. 48.

[3] Hooker, *Eccl. Pol.* v. LIII. 4.

[4] Ἐπὶ γῆς μὲν γὰρ ὁ Υἱὸς καὶ ὁ Θεὸς Λόγος βεβήκει, οὐρανοῦ δὲ ἥπτετο, καὶ πάντες ἐχθροὶ ἐπληροῦντο τῆς αὐτοῦ δόξης· καὶ ἐν Μαρίᾳ ἐτύγχανε, καὶ ἄνθρωπος ἐγένετο, ἀλλὰ τῇ δυνάμει αὐτοῦ ἐπλήρου τὰ σύμπαντα.—Epiphan. *Hæres.* LXIX. Tom. I. p. 788. Colon.

Hooker does not scruple to say : " The union of the flesh with Deity is to that

2. The Article, having expressed the truth that the Son of God took man's nature in the womb of the blessed Virgin, of her substance, adds, " So that two whole and perfect natures, that is to say, the Godhead, and Manhood, were joined together in one Person." Having already shown that there was but one Person with two natures, it is necessary farther to observe, that those two natures continued perfect and entire ; for though the Person was but one, the Person of the eternal Son of God, yet we must not suppose that the verity of either of His natures was lost or absorbed.

(1) That He was perfect God appears by what was proved under the first Article ; and indeed His Divine nature could not cease to be Divine by his taking to Him the nature of man ; for God is not liable to change or to diminution. And though, by taking human nature, the Son of God was enabled to suffer, which to God simply would have been impossible, yet by taking human nature He did not change the nature of God. And this appears from plain passages of Scripture ; for where the Son of God is spoken of as God, it is constantly in those very passages where He is called by the name of Christ or of Jesus or of the Son of Man, or is spoken of as incarnate, e. g. John i. 14 ; iii. 13 ; viii. 58 ; x. 30. Acts xx. 28. Rom. ix. 5. Phil. ii. 5, 6. Col. i. 14, 15, &c.

(2) That He was perfect Man will appear, if we can show that He had a human Body and a human Soul, both subject to human infirmities and invested with human attributes.

That he had a human Body appears from His birth of the Virgin (Matt. i. 25. Luke i. 35 ; ii. 7) ; from His growth like other children (Luke ii. 52) ; from His liability to hunger (Luke iv. 2) ; to weariness (John iv. 6) ; to pain (Luke xxii. 44) ; to bleeding and bloody sweat (John xix. 34. Luke xxii. 44) ; to wounds and laceration (John xx. 27) ; from His possessing flesh and bones (Luke xxiv. 39, 40) ; from His crucifixion, death, burial, and resurrection.

That he had a perfect human Soul appears from His " increasing in wisdom " (Luke ii. 52) ; from the possibility of His being ignorant (Mark xiii. 32), (which could not be true of Him con-

---

flesh a gift of principal grace and favour : for by virtue of this grace, *man is really made God*, a creature is exalted above the dignity of all creatures, and hath all creatures else under it." And again, " Since God hath deified our nature, though not by turning it into Himself, yet by making it His own inseparable habitation, we cannot now conceive, how God should without man either exercise Divine power, or receive the glory of Divine praise ; for man is in both the associate of Deity." — *Eccl. Pol.* Bk. v. LIV

sidered only in His Divine nature) ; from His being liable to temptation (Matt. iv. 1. Heb. iv. 15) ; from His feeling sorrow and sympathy (Luke xix. 41. John xi. 35. Matt. xxiii. 37, 38, &c.) ; from the separation of His Soul from His Body at death, the Soul descending to Hades, whilst the Body was laid in the grave (Acts ii. 27, 31).

And as the nature of His Godhead was not changed (God not being capable of change) by union with His manhood ; so also the nature of His manhood was not changed by being taken into His Godhead, farther than that it was thereby exalted, ennobled, glorified. For the object of God's taking flesh was that He might take to Himself a nature like our own, in which He might be tempted with our temptations, liable to our sorrows and infirmities, and subject to our sufferings and death. The properties therefore of His human nature were not sunk nor absorbed in His Divine nature, any more than His Divine nature was altered or corrupted by His human nature.

3. That these two natures, thus united in the one Person of Christ, shall "never be divided," appears from the nature of the union, the object of that union, and the declaration of Scripture.[1] The nature of the union being that the Person of the Eternal Son took to Himself human *nature*, not a human *person*, it follows, that, if the two natures were divided at any time, either a new person would be brought into being, or else the human nature of Christ would utterly cease to exist. According to the latter supposition, instead of being highly exalted and set above all His fellows, Christ's human Body and Soul would be annihilated and

[1] One of the errors of the Photinians was that they believed the kingdom of Christ would wholly cease at the end of the world, and that the Word would be wholly resolved into the Father, and as a separate Person cease to exist. See Pearson, Art. VI. p. 284, note. The only text which can appear even for a moment to favour the notion that Christ shall ever cease to be both perfect God and perfect Man, is the remarkable passage 1 Cor. xv. 24, 28, where it is said that Christ shall deliver up the kingdom to the Father, and " the Son Himself shall be subject to Him that did put all things under Him, that God may be all in all." We cannot, however, from this infer, that the Son of God shall leave His human nature and be absorbed into the Person of the Father, and that then the human nature of Christ divested of the Divine shall be subject to God ; for, if no other passage in Scripture opposed that notion, this very passage would of itself refute it. It is the *Son* who is to be subject to the Father ; but the human nature of Christ, separated (if that were possible) from His Divine nature, would not be the Son of God. The true interpretation of the passage is, that the Son, who, in His human nature and touching His manhood, is inferior to the Father, yet now seated on the throne of His mediatorial kingdom, reigns supreme over men, angels, and devils. But at the end, when the need of that mediatorial reign has passed away, then the mediatorial sceptre shall be laid down, Christ shall reign with God, upon His right hand ; but as κατ οἰκονομίαν, and in His human nature, He is inferior to the Father, so then He shall be subject to the Father ; God shall be all in all. — See Pearson, *On the Creed*, Art. VI. p. 283.

perish. Surely neither of these hypotheses is tenable. Again, the end and purpose of the union, whereby the Son of God took the nature of man, being that He might join together God and men, Himself both God and man, and the necessity of such conjunction never ceasing, it follows that the union of the natures shall never cease. It is through the instrumentality of Christ's humanity that man is united to God. When the union has been effected, we cannot suppose that the bond will be destroyed, the link annihilated. It is by virtue of incorporation into Christ's Body, that the saints shall rise and reign ; and we cannot suppose that Christ's Body shall cease to be one with the Son of God, when the saints, incorporated into It, reign because of It.

And this farther appears from Scripture ; where we read, that " Christ *ever* liveth to make intercession for us " (Heb. vii. 25) ; that " He is a Priest *forever* "(Heb. vi. 20 ; vii. 21, 24), " consecrated for *evermore* " (Heb. vii. 28) ; that " He is set down at the right hand of God *forever* " (Heb. x. 12) ; that " His kingdom is an everlasting kingdom, and that He shall reign for ever and ever " (Dan. ii. 44 ; vii. 14, 18, 27. Luke i. 32, 33. Rev. xi. 15).

III. The Article, thirdly, asserts that the Son of God, having thus taken man's nature, " truly suffered, was crucified, dead, and buried, to reconcile His Father to us, and to be a sacrifice, not only for original guilt, but also for all actual sins of men."

To enter at full length into each portion of this clause of the Article, would necessarily exceed our present limits. The student may be referred to the Fourth Article of Pearson, *On the Creed*, for a most able exposition of the doctrine of Scripture concerning our Lord's sufferings, crucifixion, death, and burial.

1. To show the *reality* of our Lord's sufferings and death, it is only necessary to read the last chapters of the four Gospels, which require no comment. If they did, such comment would be found in the prophecies of Christ's sufferings (*e. g.* Ps. xxii. Isai. liii.), and in the letters and discourses of the Apostles on them (*e. g.* Acts ii. 22, 23 ; iii. 15 ; x. 39 ; xiii. 29. Rom. v. 10 ; vi. 8. 1 Cor. xv. 16. 2 Cor. i. 5 ; iv. 10. Phil. ii. 8. Heb. ii. 9, 10 ; v. 7, 8 ; ix. 17–28 ; x. 10 ; xii. 2 ; xiii. 12. 1 Pet. ii. 21 ; iii. 18). The reality of the death, indeed, is a subject immediately connected with the reality of the human nature of Christ. The Docetæ, who denied the one, naturally and necessarily denied the other. It was against them that St. John appears to have written many passages both in his Gospel and Epistles, as for example,

John xix. 34, 35. 1 John iv. 3; v. 6. 2 John 7. Errors,
against which the words of Scripture are specially directed, cannot
lightly be disregarded by the Church. But as such errors are not
likely to prevail extensively now, it may be unnecessary to dwell
at length upon their refutation.

2. One subject connected with the death and sufferings of
our Saviour requires to be a little further considered. The Son cf
God by taking on Him human nature became truly man; and one
of the chief ends of His thus becoming man was, that He might
die. But it may be asked still, Wherein did His death consist,
and how did He suffer? Man dies, when His soul leaves his
body. Man suffers, because his whole nature is passible. But
Jesus Christ was man; yet not mere man. His Person consisted
of the Eternal Son united to a human Body and a human Soul.
How then did He suffer, and how die?

He suffered in His human nature, which, being a perfect
human nature, was capable of suffering both in Soul and Body.
We may not imagine, as has already been shown, that His human
nature ceased to be human nature when it was taken by His Godhead; "that the properties of the weaker nature have vanished with
the presence of the more glorious, and have been therein swallowed
up as in a gulf." It is true, then, that the Son of God suffered;
but not in the Godhead. His Godhead could no more suffer than
the Godhead of the Father. But He took human nature, that He
might suffer, and in His manhood the Son of God was crucified,
and suffered and died.

And His death consisted, not in the separation of His Divine
Being from either Body or Soul. Then would not the Son of
God have died at all. Then Christ would have been divided into
two separate Persons, by the Godhead leaving the manhood; and
the mystery and the blessing of the Incarnation would have been
lost. The soul does not die by leaving the body, neither would
the Son of God have died by leaving either Body or Soul. It was
the Person of Christ that suffered death; and as that Person was
invested with the nature of man, death was to Him what death is
to other men, namely, the separation of the human soul from the
human body. The union of the Godhead with the manhood was
not disturbed; but the human Soul of Christ left His human Body.
But even when the Soul forsook the Body, the Godhead forsook
neither Body, nor Soul.[1] "If it had, then could we not truly hold

---

[1] Ὥστε οὐκ ἄνθρωπος Θεοῦ ἐχωρίζετο,   γεῖτο· οὔτε ἡ νέκρωσις ἀποχώρησις Θεοῦ, ἢ
οὔτε Θεὸς πρὸς ἄνθρωπον ἐγκατάλειψιν διη-   ἀπὸ σώματος ἦν μετάστασις, ἀλλὰ ψυχῆς ἀπὸ

either that the Person of Christ was buried, or that the Person of Christ did raise up itself from the dead. For the Body separated from the Word can in no true sense be termed the Person of Christ, nor is it true to say that the Son of God, in raising up that Body, did raise up Himself, if the Body were not both with Him and of Him, even during the time it lay in the sepulchre. The like is also to be said of the Soul; otherwise we are plainly and inevitably Nestorians. The very Person of Christ therefore, forever one and the self-same, was, only touching bodily substance, concluded within the grave ; His soul only from thence severed, but by personal union His Deity still inseparably joined with both." [1]

3. The conclusion of the Article concerns the end and object of our blessed Saviour's sufferings.

The Socinians deny that there was any necessity for a propitiatory sacrifice, or that God had need to be reconciled to man. Man, say they, was at enmity with God, not God with man. Man therefore needed to be reconciled, and so Christ came to call men to repentance and to move them to it by His precept and example, and so committed to his disciples the ministry of reconciliation. But to say that God needed to have blood shed, and *that* the blood of an innocent and holy Victim, in order to appease His wrath, is to make God a vindictive and implacable Being, not a God of love.

The answer to this is twofold.

(1) " A God all mercy is a God unjust: " Justice is an attribute of God as well as mercy. Justice therefore calling for wrath on man, and the love of God calling for mercy, it was necessary, in order to reconcile both these attributes of God, that some means should be devised for satisfying both. We do not say that God was tied to the means which He ordained ; but we learn, that His wisdom ordained the sacrifice of His Son, and in that sacrifice we perceive a manifestation of infinite justice and infinite love.

σώματος χωρισμός. — Athanasius, *De Salut. Advent. Jesu Christ.* Tom. i. pp. 645, 646.

Compare the passage from Fulgentius quoted in the exposition of the next Article : " Secundum Divinitatem suam, quæ nec loco tenetur, nec fine concluditur, totus fuit in sepulchro cum carne, totus in inferno cum anima." — Fulgent. *Ad Trasimund.* Lib. iii. ch. 34.

This is well expressed in some of the Calvinistic Confessions : *e. g. Confessio Belgica,* Art. xix. : " Cæterum duæ istæ naturæ ita sunt simul unitæ et conjunctæ

in unam Personam, ut ne morte quidem ipsius separari potuerint. Quod igitur Patri suo moriendo commendavit, id vere erat spiritus humanus a corpore ipsius egrediens ; at interim divina natura semper humanæ (etiam in sepulchro jacenti) conjuncta remansit : adeo ut Deitas ipsa non minus in ipso tunc fuerit, quam cum adhuc infans esset, etsi exiguum ad tempus non sese exerceret." — *Sylloge*, p. 338.

[1] Hooker, v. lii. 4. The whole subject is admirably treated by Hooker ; and by Pearson, Art. iv. " Suffered," " Dead."

(2) But the same thing appears, too, from many passages in Scripture. There is some ambiguity in the words used in the new Testament for "reconciliation." The most learned critics have observed, that those words are used in a somewhat different sense from that in which the classical authors use them. But it is quite clear from the contexts that in some passages God is spoken of as needing to be reconciled to man. For example, in 2 Cor. v. 19, where it is said that "God was in Christ reconciling the world unto Himself," there might be some ambiguity, if it were not added, "not imputing their trespasses unto them;" but these words clear up the doubt. Indeed the whole context speaks as of two offended parties, God and man. God is represented as giving up His wrath and being reconciled through Christ, and then as sending to man, to invite him to give up his enmity and be reconciled to God.[1]

That the wrath of God is revealed from Heaven against sinful man seems hardly necessary to be proved. The Article on Original Sin is the more proper place for proving it. It may be sufficient now to refer to such passages as the following: Rom. v. 9. Eph. ii. 3. 1 Thess. i. 10. Heb. x. 26, 27. Rev. vi. 16, 17.

The Jewish sacrifices were expressly appointed to deliver from the wrath of God.[2] The Passover was appointed, that the wrath of God might be averted, when the first-born of Egypt were slain. In the 4th and 5th chapters of Leviticus, directions are given for the mode in which those who have sinned shall make atonement for their transgression. Whether it were priest, prince, or people, they were to bring a victim, to confess the sin upon the head of the victim, and then slay it as a sin-offering. The same is observable of the offerings on the day of expiation; when the high-priest made atonement, first for himself, and then for the people ; and also of the scape-goat, which was offered at the same time, the sins of the people being confessed on his head (Lev. xvi.) The Jews looked on these sacrifices as strictly propitiatory.[3] The Gentiles, who imitated them, evidently had a similar notion of

---

[1] See, at length, Magee, *On Atonement*, I. p. 202, fifth edition, and the authors referred to there ; especially Hammond and Whitby on Rom. v. 10, xi. 15; 2 Cor. v. 18, 19, 20; Ephes. ii. 16 ; and Col. i. 20, 21.

[2] It is quite unnecessary to consider the question whether sacrifice was a rite in the first instance divinely instituted, or devised by man. If the latter be, as some learned and pious authors have be- lieved, the truth, still it sprang from a natural feeling of guilt, and the need of atonement, and was sanctioned by Almighty God and made a type of Christ, and rules were given for its observance, that the type might be more clear and express. The argument in the text therefore would not be invalidated, even if the divine institution of sacrifice be denied.

[3] Magee, as above, *Illustrations*, No XXXIII.

their offerings; and those especially, who, in times of peculiar
danger, had recourse to human sacrifice, appear to have entertained a strong feeling of the necessity of propitiating the gods with
the noblest victims.   That the legal sacrifices were types of the
death of Christ, and therefore that Christ's death was a propitiatory
sacrifice for the sins of men, appears plainly from the fact that the
terms taken from the Jewish sacrifices are applied in Scripture
to describe the death of Christ.   Thus He is said to have been
"led as a lamb to the slaughter" (see Isai. liii. 5–8).   He is
called "the Lamb slain" (Rev. v. 6, 12; xiii. 8).   "A Lamb without blemish and spot "(1 Pet. i. 19); " the Lamb of God which
taketh away the sins of the world" (John i. 29).   St. Paul expressly compares the priesthood of Aaron with the priesthood of
Christ; explaining to us that whereas the priest of old offered the
blood of bulls and goats which could not take away sin, but availed
only to a carnal purifying (Heb. ix. 13), so Christ offered, not
the blood of others, but His own Blood — offered Himself to bear
the sins of many ; and so put away sin by the sacrifice of Himself.
As under the Law, without shedding of blood was no remission, and
as the patterns of heavenly things were purified with the blood of
sacrificed victims, so the heavenly things themselves were purified
with better sacrifices, even Christ.   (See Heb. ix. x.) [1]

4.   It may be well to observe one more expression, which occurs
at the very end of the Article, namely, " to be a sacrifice, *not only
for original guilt, but also for all actual sins of men.*" It seems as
if the reformers were anxious to meet a possible, perhaps an actual
error, which, admitting the sacrifice of Christ for original sin, either
denied remission to actual sins, or looked for pardon of them to
something beside the propitiation offered on the cross.   That actual,
and not only original sin is pardoned for the sake of Christ, is
taught repeatedly in the old Testament, as well as the new.

Isaiah, besides saying that Christ " was wounded for our transgressions, and bruised for our iniquities," adds a passage expressly
indicating actual sin: " All we like sheep have gone astray, we
have turned every one to his own way, and the Lord hath laid on
Him the iniquity of us all" (Isai. liii. 6).   It is from "*all* iniquity"
that " He gave Himself to redeem us " (Tit. ii. 14).   It was when
we were not only "alienated " by original guilt, but " enemies
through *wicked works*," too, that Christ reconciled us (Col. i. 21).
The persons whom the Apostle speaks of as not capable of being

---

[1] On the whole subject consult Magee,   the *Illustrations* at the end of Vol. I., and
On Atonement and Sacrifice;   especially   the authors there referred to.

saved by the law, but "justified freely by God's grace through the redemption that is in Christ Jesus," are described in the strongest terms as *actual* sinners (see Rom. iii. 12–26). And again (in 1 Cor. vi. 9, 10, 11) he paints the characters of some who had been "justified in the name of the Lord Jesus," as having been stained with the foulest vices and the deadliest sins. St. John (1 John ii. 1, 2) distinctly assures us that "if any man sin we have an Advocate with the Father, Jesus Christ the righteous; and He is the propitiation for our sins." And that he meant actual sins is most apparent, because he begins the sentence with "My little children, these things I write unto you that ye sin not."

We conclude, therefore, that the sacrifice of Christ, the Son of God, offered by Him upon the cross, whereon in His human nature He suffered and died, is a propitiation, not only for original guilt, but also for actual sins of men.

[The following passage is worthy of consideration in more aspects than one. It is from the pen of the Abbé Guettée. " The existing Roman Church attacks [the doctrine of the Incarnation] indirectly, by the worship which it renders to the *sacred heart of Jesus*. In truth, worship is due only to the divine *person* of Jesus Christ; the human nature in Him shares in it only because of its hypostatical union with the divine nature. It is not permissible to offer worship to the human nature of Jesus Christ, in itself and separately considered, much less to a single organ of His body. The Roman Church excuses this worship by saying that it has relation to the person of Jesus Christ. But the greater part of its writers at this day teach, authoritatively, that the heart of Jesus is adorable by itself." *Exp. de la Doctrine*, p. 64.—*J. W.*]

ARTICLE III.

———◆———

Of the going down of Christ into Hell.

As Christ died for us, and was buried; so also it is to be believed that He went down into Hell.

De descensu Christi ad Inferos.

QUEMADMODUM Christus pro nobis mortuus est, et sepultus, ita est etiam credendus ad inferos descendisse.

———————

TO the understanding of this Article it seems desirable to investigate, historically and from Scripture, FIRST, What is meant by "*Hell;*" SECONDLY, What is meant by Christ's descending into hell; THIRDLY, What was the purpose or object of that descent.

I propose, therefore, to depart from the arrangement adopted in the two former Articles, and to examine the meaning of the word "Hell," first historically, and then scripturally, — and next to proceed in the same manner with the doctrine of our Lord's descent into hell; and thirdly, with the reason or object of his going thither.

FIRST. The word "Hell," as used in the Article, is plainly borrowed from the Apostles' Creed; for it appears that the first five Articles of the Church are little more than an amplification of the Articles of the Creed, intended to set forth, that the Church of England continued truly Catholic in its doctrines, whilst it was constrained to protest against the corruptions of some branches of the Church. In the Latin, the word used is either "*inferi*" or "*inferna.*" The Greek corresponding to this was either τὰ κατώτατα or ᾅδης; the former referring to Eph. iv. 9, the latter to Acts ii. 27. It has, however, generally been admitted, and may fairly be assumed, that the Greek word ᾅδης is the word of Scripture, which both the Creed and the Article render *inferi* and *hell;* and it has been observed, that, according to their derivations, these words answer to one another. ῎Αδης is something unseen, from ἀ and εἶδον. *Inferi* is the Latin from the Greek word ἔνεροι or ἔνϜεροι, *i. e.* those beneath the earth, the Manes or Spirits of the dead.[1] *Hell* is from the same root as *hole* and *hellier* (*i. e.* a roofer, a coverer), and signifies *the covered* or *hidden place*, the Saxon root being *helan*, to cover.

There is indeed another word in the new Testament often rendered in the English by *hell*. That word is γέεννα; and some confusion arises from this indiscriminate translation. As, however, neither the Creeds nor the Church have been wont to use γέεννα, to express the place to which our Lord went after His death, we may lay aside the consideration of the word at present; merely observing that it is the proper term in the new Testament for the state or place of damned souls and apostate spirits.

As regards, then, the signification of the word *Hades*, it will be well to consider the subject: —

I. Historically.   II. Scripturally.

I. The history may be divided into

(1)   The use of the word among the Greeks; (2) among the Jews; (3) among the Christians.

1. It may be true that the Greeks sometimes used Hades to signify no more than the Grave; but if so, it was by an improper and less common use of the word. According to them, Hades, or the abode of Hades, was that place to which the Ghosts or Manes of the dead went after their burial. The unburied were detained on this side the Styx; the buried passed over, and mingled with the souls of men, which were there detained apart from the bodies they had left (εἴδωλα καμόντων). Hades himself was the deity who presided over these lower realms. In the abode of these disembodied souls were placed, on the one hand the happy fields of Elysium, on the other the gloomy realms of Tartarus. In the former, the souls of the virtuous enjoyed themselves, not however without regret for the loss of the body and the light of day. In the latter, the wicked, such as Ixion, Tantalus, the Danaids, and others, were tormented with various sorrows. This is known to every one who has read the Odyssey and the Æneid.[2]

---

[1] This seems a doubtful derivation. *Infer, Infra, Inferus, Inferior*, are obviously all connected. Though this connection does not make the derivation given in the text impossible. The Greek ἔρα is the same as the Hebrew אֶרֶץ, in Chaldee and Syriac אַרְעָא, in Arabic أرض The latter is the same as the German *Erde*, English *earth*. The Chal-

dee and Syriac אַרְעָ is, in sound as well as in its radical letters, the same as the Greek ἔρα. And it is remarkable that it is used as a preposition to designate below, אֲרַע, *Infra*. So אֲרַע מִנָּךְ, *Infra te.* This may account for the force of the preposition *infra*, on the hypothesis that the derivation given in the text is correct.

[2] See Hom. *Od.* xi. Virg. *Æn.* vi

2. The Jews in like manner believed in a state of being after
death, in which the soul existed previously to the final Resurrection, apart from the body, yet in a state of consciousness, either
of happiness or of misery. This state or place they called in
Hebrew, Sheol (שְׁאוֹל), in Greek, Hades (ᾅδης). Its position,
according to their notions and language, was underground. Thus
Josephus says that the soul of Samuel, when he appeared to Saul,
came up (ἐξ ᾅδου) from Hades.[1] He tells us that the Sadducees
" took away the rewards and punishments of the Soul in Hades." [2]
Whereas he says of the Pharisees, that " they held the immortality
of the Soul, and that men were punished or rewarded under the
earth, according to their practice of virtue or wickedness in life." [3]
Lightfoot has shown that the Jewish schools dispose of the souls
of the righteous till the Resurrection, under the threefold phrase :
(1) " the Garden of Eden," answering to the " Paradise " of the
new Testament (Luke xxiii. 43). (2) " Under the throne of
glory," being nearly parallel with the expression (in Rev. vi. 9) of
souls crying " under the altar ; " for the Jews conceived the altar
to be the throne of the Divine Majesty.   (3) " In Abraham's
bosom," which is the expression adopted by our Lord in the parable
of Dives and Lazarus (Luke xvi. 22).[4] He shows that the abode
of the wicked before the Judgment is placed by the same Rabbins
within sight of the abode of the just, and so that the one can con-
verse with the other, as Dives is by our Lord represented as con-
versing with Abraham.[5] From these, and similar authorities, we
may conclude that the Jews, like the heathens, looked for a state
immediately after death, which in their popular language was said
to be under ground, and in their ordinary phraseology was called

The latter describes the two sides of
Hades thus : —

Hic locus est partes ubi se via findit in am-
bas:
Dextera, quæ Ditis magni sub mœnia ten-
dit;
Hac iter Elysium nobis: at læva malorum
Exercet pœnas, et ad impia Tartara mittit.

Æn. VI. 540-543.

[1] Joseph. *Ant.* Lib. VI. c. XV. See
Pearson, *On the Creed,* Art. v. p. 239.
[2] *De Bell. Jud.* Lib. II. c. vii. Ψυχῆς
τε τὴν διαμονὴν καὶ τὰς καθ᾽ ᾅδου τιμωρίας
καὶ τιμὰς ἀναιροῦσι. — Pearson, as above ;
King, *On the Creed,* p. 189.
[3] *Ant.* Lib. XVIII. c. ii. Ἀθάνατόν τε
ἰσχὺν ταῖς ψυχαῖς πίστις αὐτοῖς εἶναι, καὶ
ὑπὸ χθονὸς δικαιώσεις τε καὶ τιμὰς οἷς

ἀρετῆς ἢ κακίας ἐπιτηδεύσοις ἐν τῷ βίῳ γέγονε.
— See Pearson and King, as above.
[4] See Lightfoot. *Horæ Hebraicæ* on
Luke xvi. 22 ; and Luke xxiii. 43.
[5] *Horæ Hebr.* on Luke xvi. 23, 26.
See also Bp. Bull, *Works,* I. Disc. III.
p. 59. Bp. Bull, p. 61, quotes from the
Chaldee Paraphrast on Cant. iv. 12. who,
speaking of the Garden of Eden (that is
Paradise), says that " thereinto no man
hath the power of entering but the just,
whose souls are carried thither by the
hands of angels." "If this," adds the
learned writer, "had been an erroneous
opinion of the Jews, doubtless our Saviour would never have given any the
least countenance to it, much less would
He have plainly confirmed it, by teaching the same thing in the parable of
Dives and Lazarus."

Sheol, Hades, Hell; that in this state were both the just and the unjust : the latter in a state of misery, the former in blissful enjoyment, called sometimes " Paradise, the Garden of Eden," sometimes " beneath the throne of glory," sometimes " in Abraham's bosom."

3. It is well known that the early Christians believed in an intermediate state of the soul between death and Judgment; and this intermediate state they, too, like the Jews, called " Hades." Justin Martyr, speaking against some of the Gnostics who denied the Resurrection, and by consequence the intermediate state of the soul, says, " those who say that there is no Resurrection, but that immediately after death their souls are taken up to Heaven, these are not to be accounted either Christians or Jews." [1] He himself distinctly asserts that " no souls die (that would be a Godsend to the wicked) ; but the souls of good men remain in a better, of bad men in a worse place, awaiting the time of the Judgment." [2] Tertullian distinctly states his belief, that the souls of all men go to Hades (*inferi*) until the Resurrection, the souls of the just being in that part of Hades called the bosom of Abraham, or Paradise.[3] Irenæus says, that the souls of Christ's disciples " go into the invisible place prepared for them, and there remain awaiting the Resurrection ; after which they shall receive their bodies again, and rise complete, that is, in the body, as the Lord arose, and so shall come to the vision of God." [4]

Origen declares his belief, that " not even the Apostles have received their perfect bliss ; for the saints at their departure out of this life do not attain the full rewards of their labors ; but are

---

[1] Οἳ καὶ λέγουσι μὴ εἶναι νεκρῶν ἀνάστασιν, ἀλλὰ ἅμα τῷ ἀποθνῄσκειν τὰς ψυχὰς αὐτῶν ἀναλαμβάνεσθαι εἰς τὸν οὐρανόν,
μὴ ὑπολάβητε αὐτοὺς Χριστιανούς · ὥσπερ
οὐδὲ ᾿Ιουδαίους. — *Dial.* p. 307. Paris,
1615. That the still earlier apostolical
fathers held the same sentiments concerning an intermediate state may be
seen from Clem. 1 Corinth. c. 50. Herm.
III. *Simil.* IX. 16. On the former passage see Bull, *Works*, I. Serm. III. p. 63.
Both his Sermons on this subject are deserving of all attention.

[2] ᾿Αλλὰ μὴν οὐδὲ ἀποθνῄσκειν φημὶ πάσας
τὰς ψυχὰς ἐγώ · ἔρμαιον γὰρ ἦν ὡς ἀληθῶς
τοῖς κακοῖς. ᾿Αλλὰ τί ; τὰς μὲν τῶν εὐσεβῶν
ἐν κρείττονί ποι χώρῳ μένειν, τὰς δὲ ἀδίκους
καὶ πονηρὰς ἐν χείρονι, τὸν τῆς κρίσεως ἐκ-
δεχομένας χρόνον τότε. — *Dialog.* p. 222.

[3] " Nobis inferi non nuda cavositas, nec
subdivalis aliqua mundi sentina credun-
tur; sed in fossa terræ, et in alto vastitas,

et in ipsis visceribus ejus abstrusa pro-
funditas." He then says, Christ went
there, and his servants must not expect
to be above their Lord, but will have to
wait in Abraham's bosom for the resurrection. " Nulli patet cœlum, terra adhuc
salva, ne dixerim clausa. Cum transac-
tione enim mundi reserabuntur regna
cœlorum. . . . Habes etiam *de Paradiso*
a nobis libellum, quo constituimus omnem animam apud inferos sequestrari in
diem Domini." — Tertull. *De Anima,* cap.
55.

[4] Αἱ ψυχαὶ ἀπέρχονται εἰς τὸν [ἀόρατον]
τόπον τὸν ὡρισμένον αὐταῖς ἀπὸ τοῦ Θεοῦ,
κἀκεῖ μέχρι τῆς ἀναστάσεως φοιτῶσι, περιμέ-
νουσαι τὴν ἀνάστασιν · ἔπειτα ἀπολαβοῦσαι
τὰ σώματα, καὶ ὁλοκλήρως ἀναστᾶσαι, τουτέστι σωματικῶς, καθὼς καὶ ὁ Κύριος ἀνέστη,
οὕτως ἐλεύσονται εἰς τὴν ὄψιν τοῦ Θεοῦ. —
Irenæ. v. 31. See also Beaven's *Account of Irenæus*, ch. XVIII.

awaiting us, who still remain on earth, loitering though we be, and slack." [1]

Lactantius is very express upon the same point. "Let no one," says he, "think that souls are judged immediately after death; for they are all detained in the same common place of keeping, until the time come when the Supreme Judge shall inquire into their good or evil deeds." [2]

Hilary says, that it is the "law of human necessity, that bodies should be buried, and souls descend to hell or Hades." And again, that "the faithful, who depart out of the body, are reserved in the safe keeping of the Lord for an entrance to the kingdom of Heaven, being in the mean time placed in Abraham's bosom, whither the wicked cannot enter on account of the great gulf fixed between them, until the time comes when they shall enter into the kingdom of Heaven." [3]

Ambrose still more fully says, that, "while the fulness of time is expected, the souls await the reward which is in store for them. Some pain awaits, others glory. But in the mean time the former are not without trouble, nor are the latter without enjoyment." [4]

Augustine writes, "The time between death and final resurrection holds the souls in hidden receptacles, according as each soul is meet for rest or punishment." [5]

II. We have now to consider what we learn from *Scripture* of the state of the departed, and of the meaning of Hades.

1. The soul, after it has left the body, is not represented as passing directly to its final reward. This will appear from the following considerations: —

Our Lord distinctly assures us, that "no one hath ascended up

[1] "Nondum receperunt lætitiam suam ne Apostoli quidem, sed et ipsi exspectant, ut et ego lætitiæ eorum particeps fiam. Neque enim decedentes hinc sancti continuo integra meritorum suorum præmia consequuntur, sed exspectant etiam nos, licet morantes, licet desides." — Origen. *Hom.* VII. in Lev. num. ii.; Usher's *Answer to a Jesuit*, ch. VII.

[2] "Nec tamen quisquam putet animas post mortem protinus judicari: omnes in una communique custodia detinentur, donec tempus adveniat quo maximus Judex meritorum faciat examen." — Lactant. *Institut. Divin.* Lib. VII. c. 21; Usher, as above; King, p. 202.

[3] "Humanæ ista lex necessitatis est, ut consepultis corporibus ad inferos animæ descendant." — Hilar. *In Ps.* cxxxviii. Edit. Benedict. col. 514.

"Futuri boni exspectatio est, cùm exe-

untes de corpore ad introitum illum regni cœlestis per custodiam Domini fideles omnes reservabuntur, in sinu scilicet interim Abrahæ collocati, quò adire impios interjectum chaos inhibet, quò usque introeundi rursum in regnum cœlorum tempus adveniat." — Hilar. *In Ps.* cxx. Edit. Benedict. col. 383. See Usher, and King, as above.

[4] "Ergo dum exspectatur plenitudo temporis, exspectant animæ remunerationem debitam. Alias manet pœna, alias gloria: et tamen nec illæ interim sine injuria, nec istæ sine fructu sunt." — Ambros. *De Bono Mortis*, c. x. Usher, as above.

[5] "Tempus, quod inter hominis mortem et ultimam resurrectionem interpositum est, animas abditis receptaculis continet, sicut unaquæque digna est vel requie vel ærumna." — Augustin. *Enchirid. ad Laurent.* c. cix. Tom VI. p. 236.

to Heaven but He that came down from Heaven, even the Son of Man which is in Heaven" (John iii. 13). If then no one had then ascended up to Heaven, except the Lord Jesus, the saints departed could not have gone to their place of final and eternal bliss, which is always called Heaven.

Again, our Lord promised the thief on the cross "that he should be with Him that day in Paradise" (Luke xxiii. 43). Now Christ did not go from the cross to Heaven, but, as will appear hereafter, He went to hell or Hades, and did not go to Heaven till after His resurrection. Therefore Paradise, to which the thief went with Him that very day, was not Heaven.[1]

Again, in the Revelation (vi. 9), "the souls of them that were slain for the word of God" are not represented as in Heaven, but they cry from under the altar; and, though white robes are given them, they are bid "to rest for a little season, till their fellow-servants and their brethren should be fulfilled."

Again, our Lord and His Apostles never comfort the Church concerning those who are asleep with the assurance that their souls are in Heaven, nor do they alarm the wicked with the fear that at the instant of death their souls will pass into a state of final punishment. It is ever to the Resurrection of the dead and the Judgment of the great day that the hopes of the pious and the fears of the ungodly are directed. This may be seen most plainly by referring to such passages as the following: Matt. xiii. 40; xvi. 27; xxv. 31–33. Mark viii. 38. Luke xiv. 14. John v. 28, 29. Acts xvii. 31. 1 Cor. xv. passim. 2 Cor. iv. 14; v. 10, 11. Phil. iii. 20, 21. Col. iii. 4. 1 Thess. iv. 13–17; v. 2, 3, 23. 2 Thess. i. 6–10. 2 Tim. iv. 1, 8. Heb. ix. 27, 28. Jas. v. 7, 8. 1 Pet. iv. 5; v. 4. 2 Pet. iii. 10–12. Rev. xx. 13–15.

2. But though the soul does not receive its final reward until the Resurrection and the Judgment, when it shall be united to the body, and receive the sentence of the Judge; yet the soul does not die with the body, nor sleep in unconsciousness between death and Judgment.[2] This appears from the following.

---

[1] "Si ergo secundum hominem quem Verbum Deus suscepit, putamus dictum esse, *Hodie mecum eris in paradiso,* non ex his verbis in cœlo existimandus est esse paradisus: neque enim ipso die in cœlo futurus erat homo Christus Jesus; sed in inferno secundum animam, in sepulchro autem secundum carnem." — August. *Epist.* LVII. *ad Dardanum.* Edit. Benedict. *Ep.* CLXXXVII. Tom. II. p. 679.

[2] The reformers of the Church of England were so strongly of this opinion that they put forth the following in the reign of Edward VI., as one of the Articles of the Church: it is the 40th of the 42 Articles of 1552:—

"*The souls of them that depart this life do neither die with the bodies nor sleep idly.*

"They which say that the souls of such as depart hence do sleep, being without all sense, feeling, or perceiving,

12

The soul of Samuel returned to earth after his body was in the grave (1 Sam. xxviii. 11, 14). This took place four years after Samuel's death. In the parable or history in Luke xvi., both Lazarus and Dives are represented as alive, one in torments and the other in Abraham's bosom; and that all this took place before the Resurrection and the Judgment appears from this, that in vv. 27, 28, the brothers of the rich man were then alive on earth and in their state of probation, and Dives wished that Lazarus should be sent to them to bring them to repent. It is therefore quite clear that the present world was still in existence, and therefore Judgment yet future. The same observations apply in all particulars to the account given of the souls beneath the altar, so often referred to in Rev. vi. 9–11. The promise also to the thief upon the cross, that he should be that day with Christ in Paradise (Luke xxiii. 43), must show that his soul would not be in a state of insensibility, but of bliss.

The same may be inferred from the words of our Lord, " Fear not them which kill the body, but are not able to kill the soul " (Matt. x. 28). If death be, not only corruption of the body, but insensibility of the soul, then men *can* kill the soul, as much as they can kill the body; for they cannot kill the body eternally, nor prevent its rising again. They can kill the body and reduce it to corruption now; but the soul they cannot kill, neither now, nor ever.

Again, the language used by our Lord and St. Stephen at the instant of death shows that the spirit would live: " Father, into Thy hands I commend My Spirit," said Christ (xxiii. 46). " Lord Jesus, receive my spirit," said Stephen (Acts vii. 59).

St. Paul speaks of the Church as, among other companies, having in it " the spirits of just men made perfect " (Heb. xii. 23); where the whole context shows that he refers to the present, not to the future state of Christian privilege and blessing. He declares of himself that he is in a strait between two, " having a desire to 'epart and to be with Christ, which is far better." But if death be annihilation, until the Resurrection wakes both body and soul, he could hardly have called death better than life, nor have spoken of it as " being with Christ " (Phil. i. 23). And again, the same Apostle, speaking of death, and calling the body a tabernacle of the soul (2 Cor. v. 1, 2), says, " Whilst we are at home in the

until the day of Judgment, or affirm that the souls die with the bodies, and at the last day shall be raised up with the same, do utterly dissent from the right belief declared to us in Holy Scripture. '

body, we are absent from the Lord;" and then adds, "we are willing rather to be absent from the body and to be present with the Lord" (vv. 6–8).

From all this we must conclude that the spirit still lives, when it has left the body, and that, though it loses the benefit of having a bodily tabernacle, yet, in the case of pious men, it is very vastly a gainer by death, inasmuch as, though absent from the body, it enjoys the presence of Christ.

3. Having thus seen that the disembodied soul neither sleeps nor enters into its final reward, we have only farther to show that the soul is in an intermediate state, called Sheol or Hades ; and that that state is a state of partial and expectant bliss to the righteous, of partial and expectant misery to the wicked, preparatory to the final consummation of bliss or misery, to be assigned to each at the resurrection of the last day.

It has been seen that this was the opinion of the Jews, and also that our Lord and the Apostles use the very expressions which Lightfoot has shown that the Jews used concerning the state of the departed, namely, "Paradise," "Abraham's bosom," and "beneath the altar," answering to "beneath the throne of glory." This would of itself imply that our Lord and His Apostles sanctioned the sentiments of the Jews upon the subject. The same has appeared concerning the Jewish use of the term Hades, which is a term frequently adopted by the writers of the new Testament.

The various passages of Scripture already referred to fully confirm this view of the case. For example, the souls beneath the altar (in Rev. vi.) are clothed in white robes, and comforted with hope, but plainly not in perfect consummation and bliss. St. Paul (in 2 Cor. v. 1–8), when looking forward to the hope of resurrection, distinctly describes the state of the disembodied soul as imperfect ; and though he says, it is "better to be absent from the body, and present with the Lord" (ver. 8), he still says, that our earnest desire is for the resurrection of the body, which he calls being "clothed upon" (ver. 4). Again (Rom. viii. 19–23), he represents the whole creation as longing to be delivered from bondage, and waiting for the redemption of the body. In Heb. xi. 40 he represents the saints departed as not "made perfect," until those who should succeed them were added to the number of the redeemed.

To these passages we must add the promise to the thief upon the cross, that he should be in Paradise, a place evidently of bliss, yet, as has already been seen, not the same as Heaven. Lazarus is spoken of as *comforted* in Abraham's bosom; an expression by no means answering to the glowing descriptions of the eternal Kingdom of God, though corresponding with the Jewish and early Christian ideas of the state of intermediate bliss. Dives, too, is represented as being in the same place with Lazarus, though separated by a great gulf from him, and, unlike him, suffering torment; and that place is expressly called Hades (Luke xvi. 23). In correspondence with all this, we find, in the old Testament, that Jacob expected " to go down to Sheol (*i. e.* Hades) unto his son" (Gen. xxxvii. 35). Korah, Dathan, and Abiram are said to go down "quick into Sheol" (Num. xvi. 30); and when the king of Babylon's fate is foretold by Isaiah, it is said that " Hades (or Sheol) from beneath shall be moved to meet him;" which is explained by what follows, that the "mighty dead shall be stirred up" at his approach (Isai. xiv.) I think it hardly necessary to add more to show that on this point the opinion of the ancients is more correct than that of the modern popular creeds; and that the Roman Catholic notions of purgatory, the common opinion that the soul at once passes to its final reward, and the belief that the soul sleeps from death to Judgment, are all without support from the Scriptures of God. Those Scriptures plainly speak of the final reward to be attained only at the Resurrection; yet they show, too, that the soul is in a state of consciousness between death and Judgment. That state of consciousness is evidently a happy, though not a perfect state to the good, a suffering, though not a fully miserable state to the wicked. This state also is called at times by various names; but its general designation, whether as regards the just or the unjust, is in the Hebrew *Sheol*, in the Greek *Hades*, and both these words (as well as others of a different signification) are generally rendered by our English translators *hell*.

Our SECOND consideration is, What is meant by our Lord's descent to hell, — and what authority there is for the doctrine.

I. Historically.

The article, "He descended into hell," was not very anciently in the Creeds. The first place we find it used in, was the church of Aquileia,[1] about A. D. 400. Yet it is contained in a sort of exposition of the Christian faith given by Eusebius, which he translated from the Syriac, and which he states to have been given by Thaddæus, the brother of the Apostle Thomas, to the people of

[1] Pearson, p. 225.

Edessa.[1] It is not, however, in the Creeds of Irenæus, Origen, Tertullian, Cyprian, in the Creed of the Council of Nice, nor in the more ancient draughts of the Roman or Apostles' Creed. Still there can be no question of its very general acceptance, as an article of faith, by all the earlier fathers of the Church. Ignatius, Hermas, Justin M., Irenæus, Tertullian, Clement of Alexandria, Origen, Cyprian, have all spoken clearly on this subject; besides later fathers, such as Cyril, Ambrose, Jerome, Augustine, Chrysostom. It will be necessary to refer more particularly to the sentiments of some of these fathers, when we come to our THIRD division, concerning the object of Christ's descent. At present let it suffice to quote a few of the more striking, as well as the best-known passages, from some of the earliest Christian writers. Irenæus says, that " our Lord was in the middle of the shadow of death, where are the souls of the dead, and after that rose again with His body."[2] Tertullian, in a chapter before quoted, says that " Christ, who is God, yet being man too, died according to the Scriptures, was buried, and went through the form of human death in Hades ; nor did He ascend into Heaven till He had gone down to the lower parts of the earth."[3] Cyprian shows that our Lord " was not to be overcome by death, nor to remain in hell."[4] Lord King says that in sundry places Athanasius shows,[5] " that, whilst Christ's Body lay buried in the grave, His Soul went into hell, to perform in that place those several actions, and operations, which were necessary for the complete redemption and salvation of mankind ; that He performed after His death different actions by His two essential parts: by His Body He lay in the grave, by His Soul He went into hell and vanquished death."

One principal reason why the fathers laid great stress on the belief in Christ's descent to Hades was this. The Arians and

---

[1] Euseb. i. 13; Bingham, x. 4, 18; Hey, Bk. iv. Art. iii. § 1; Hammond's *Pract. Catech.* Bk. v. § 2.

[2] Irenæ. v. 31. " Cum enim Dominus *in medio umbræ mortis abierit*, ubi animæ mortuorum erant, post deinde corporaliter resurrexit."—See Pearson, p. 237; and Beaven's *Account of Irenæus*, ch. xviii.

[3] *De Anima*, c. lv. " Quod si Christus Deus, quia et homo, mortuus secundum Scripturas, et sepultus secundum easdem, hic quoque legi satisfecit, forma humanæ mortis apud inferos functus, nec ante ascendit in sublimiora cœlorum, quam descendit in inferiora terrarum," &c.

[4] " Quod a morte non vinceretur, nec

apud inferos remansurus esset." — Cyp. *Test. adv. Judæ.* lib. 2. c. 24.

[5] King, p. 179. The words are Lord King's, not Athanasius's. Nevertheless, Athanasius's language may justify Lord King's statement : . . . μήτε τῆς θεότητος τοῦ σώματος ἐν τῷ τάφῳ ἀπολιμπανομένης, μήτε τῆς ψυχῆς ἐν τῷ ᾅδῃ χωριζομένης. Τοῦτο γὰρ ἔτι τὸ ῥηθὲν διὰ τῶν προφητῶν · Οὐκ ἐγκαταλείψεις τὴν ψυχήν μου εἰς ᾅδην, οὐδὲ δώσεις τὸν ὅσιόν σου ἰδεῖν διαφθοράν. . . . Διὰ τοῦτο ἐν μὲν ψυχῇ Θεοῦ ἡ κράτησις τοῦ θανάτου ἐλύετο, καὶ ἐξ ᾅδου ἀνάστασις ἐγίνετο, καὶ ταῖς ψυχαῖς εὐηγγελίζετο · ἐν δὲ σώματι Χριστοῦ ἡ φθορὰ κατηργεῖτο, κ. τ. λ. — Athanas. *De Salut. Advent. Jes. Christ. et adv. Apollinarium.* Tom. i. p. 645.

Apollinarians denied the existence of a natural human soul in Jesus Christ.[1] Now the true doctrine of our Lord's humanity, namely, that "He was perfect man, of a reasonable soul and human flesh subsisting," was most strongly maintained by asserting the Article of His descent to Hades. For whereas His Body was laid in the grave, and His Soul went down to Hades, He must have had both Body and Soul.[2] Accordingly, the fathers with one consent maintain the descent of Christ's Soul to Hell.

II. The Scriptural proof of our Lord's descent to Hades rests chiefly on three passages. One is the difficult verse, 1 Pet. iii. 19, which was generally esteemed by the fathers to apply to this subject, and was thought conclusive by the reformers of the reign of Edward VI. Yet, as many of our most learned divines have denied its application, I shall defer the consideration of the question till we come to speak of the *object* of Christ's descent.

Another passage is Eph. iv. 9: "Now that He ascended, what is it but that He also descended first into the lower parts of the earth ?"

It is undoubted, that both Jews and Greeks placed Hades, according to their popular notions, beneath the earth, or in the lower parts of the earth; and it is not improbable that the Apostle may have used this popular language to express our Lord's descent or passage to the place of disembodied souls. It is undoubted, too, that some of the fathers and creeds adopted these words, or words similar to them ($\tau\grave{a}$ $\kappa\alpha\tau\acute{\omega}\tau\epsilon\rho\alpha$),[3] to express the doctrine of the descent to Hades. And Bishop Pearson has truly observed, that this exposition of the passage "must be confessed so probable that there can be no argument to disprove it." Yet there is also no question, that the Apostle's language might be used to express merely the fact of the incarnation, or of the burial of Christ. The "lower parts of the earth" may mean only the place beneath, *i. e.* the earth itself, in contradistinction to the heights of Heaven.

Although, then, both these passages may, and we may not be far

---

[1] See an account of their doctrines under Art. II. § I.

[2] Most pertinent is the passage of Fulgentius, *Ad Trasimund.* Lib. III. c. 34, quoted by Pearson, p. 238: "Humanitas vera Filii Dei nec tota in sepulchro fuit, nec tota in inferno; sed in sepulchro secundum veram carnem Christus mortuus jacuit, et secundum animam ad infernum Christus descendit : . . . secundum divinitatem vero suam, quæ nec loco tenetur, nec fine concluditur, totus fuit in sepul-chro cum carne, totus in inferno cum anima ; ac per hoc plenus fuit ubique Christus, quia non est Deus ab humanitate quam susceperat separatus," &c.

So Hilary, *In Ps.* cxxxviii. "Quam descensionem Dominus ad consummationem veri hominis non recusavit."

[3] See Pearson, pp. 226, 228. Irenæus. Origen, Athanasius, Jerome, all quote this passage to prove or express the descent into hell.

wrong in saying that they both very probably do, refer to our Lord's descent to the place or state of departed souls; yet, seeing this application is open to doubt, it may be well to rest the doctrine on a passage the force of which can hardly be evaded. The passage is Acts ii. 27–31. St. Peter there quotes the sixteenth Psalm, "Thou wilt not leave my soul in Hades (εἰς ᾅδου), neither wilt Thou suffer Thine Holy One to see corruption;" and he explains it, that the Psalmist "spake of the resurrection of Christ, that His Soul was not left in Hades, neither His Flesh did see corruption." [1] In which explanation by the Apostle it is plain that the *soul* is ·in antithesis to the *flesh*, and *Hades* to *corruption;* so that the miracle of our Lord's resurrection was the consequence of His Flesh not being suffered to be corrupted in the grave, and His Soul not being suffered to remain in Hades. That is to say, our Lord had a human nature like our own. When human beings die, the soul leaves the body; the latter is laid in the grave, the former passes to the intermediate state of souls. With ordinary men, the body sees corruption, the soul is left in Hades till the Judgment. But with Christ, though He fully passed into the state of death, yet death did not retain dominion over Him. Although, therefore, His Body was laid in the sepulchre, it saw not corruption; although His Soul went to Hades, where other souls go, yet God did not leave it there, but it was on the third day reunited to the Body, and so the Body was raised from the grave.

If it be necessary to add anything to this passage, we may further remark, that, as it has already been shown that Paradise is the state of the departed souls of the redeemed, so our Lord's promise to the thief upon the cross, that he should be with Him that day in Paradise, proves clearly that our Lord, and with Him the repentant thief, passed from the cross into the state of the souls of the dead, which, as has been shown, is called Hades or hell. It was, indeed, into the happy division of Hades called Paradise, or Abraham's bosom; but still it was to part of Hades. [2]

We now come to the THIRD division of our subject, to consider what was the *object* of our Lord's descent to Hades.

---

[1] "Et Dominum quidem carne mortificatum venisse in infernum satis constat. Neque enim contradici potest vel prophetiæ quæ dixit, *Quoniam non derelinques animam meam in inferno;* quod ne aliter quisquam sapere auderet, in Actibus Apostolorum idem Petrus exponit." — Augustin. *Epist.* CLXIV. Tom. II. p. 574.

[2] So the author of the Homily on Dives and Lazarus, attributed to Chrysostom: "Dicat mihi aliquis, in inferno est Paradisus? Ego hoc dico, quia sinus Abrahæ Paradisi veritas est; sed et sanctissimum Paradisum fateor." — *Homil. in Luc.* **xvi.** *De Divite.* Tom. II. Oper. Chrysost. Latin. Usher, *Answer to a Jesuit,* ch. **VIII.**

I. Historically, we must consider this subject as briefly as we can.

1. It has already been seen, that many of the fathers looked on the belief in our Lord's passage to Hades as necessary for the acknowledgment of the verity of His manhood and of His death. This indeed appears to have been the universal sentiment of the primitive Church ; and, accordingly, the descent to Hades was urged by the fathers against the Apollinarian heresy.[1]

2. But, though this may be said to have been the universal sentiment of the early Christians, there were also various opinions current among them, as to what our Lord did during His stay among the souls of the dead.

Almost universal appears to have been the belief, that the Spirit or Soul of Christ preached the Gospel to the souls of the dead.[2] Hermas, who is reckoned apostolical, has set forth the doctrine, that not only Christ preached to the spirits in Hades, but that the Apostles too preached, to those who had died before them, the name of the Son of God.[3] In this he is followed and quoted by Clement of Alexandria.[4]

Irenæus, again, says that he heard from a certain presbyter, who heard it from those who had seen the Apostles, that our Lord descended to the places beneath the earth, and preached His Gospel to those who were there ; and all believed in Him who had foretold His advent, — the just, the prophets, the patriarchs ; whose sins He forgave, as He does ours.[5]

The passage of Scripture on which this general belief of the early Christians was founded is 1 Pet. iii. 19. Justin Martyr and Irenæus also quote a passage from Isaiah or Jeremiah, which is not extant in any copies of the Bible. The passage is this, "The Lord God remembered His dead, who slept in the sepulchral earth, and descended to them to preach His salvation."[6] Justin charges the Jews with having erased it from the LXX. Of the spuriousness of the text there can be no doubt; but it sufficiently shows the judgment of those fathers who quoted it, concerning the doctrine which it was adduced to prove.

Thus far then the early Christians appear almost unanimous.

---

[1] See under the second division of this Article passages from Irenæus, Tertullian, Athanasius, Fulgentius. See also Pearson, p. 238.

[2] Καθικόμενος ἐν τοῖς κατωτάτοις τοῦ ᾅδου μυχοῖς, καὶ διακηρύξας τοῖς ἐκεῖσε πνεύμασιν. — Cyril. Alex. *Hom. Paschal.* xx. Usher, *Answer to a Jesuit*, ch. viii.

[3] Lib. iii. *Simil.* ix. c. xvi. Coteler. i. p. 117.

[4] *Stromat.* vi. Potter, pp. 763, 764. See Bp. Kaye's *Clement of Alexandria*, p. 189.

[5] Iren. Lib. iv. c. 45.

[6] Justin. M. *Dial.* § 72, p. 398. **Iren.** iii. 23. iv. 39. v. 31.

On the purpose or end of Christ's preaching, however, there existed no small difference.

(1) The earlier fathers seem generally to have held, that no change took place in the condition of souls after our Lord's descent among them, and in consequence of His preaching to them. Justin Martyr held, that all souls still remain in Hades: the just in a happy, the unjust in a wretched place, and so shall remain to the Judgment.[1] Irenæus and Tertullian are clearly of the same opinion. The former says,[2] that "no disciple is above his master," and thence infers that, as our Lord went to Hades, so all His servants shall go thither. Tertullian asserts that "Heaven is not open until the end of the world,"[3] and that all men are in Hades, either comforted or tormented.[4] Accordingly, he says that our Lord's descent to Hades was, that the patriarchs might be made partakers of Him.[5]

(2) But, on the other hand, many of the early Christians were of opinion that our Lord, when He descended to Hades, delivered some who were there, and carried them thence to some better place.

Some thought that the prophets and patriarchs were in Hades till the coming of Christ, and that after that they were translated to a better place, called Paradise; whilst others again believed that our Lord preached His Gospel to the souls of the dead, and that those who believed in Him were saved and delivered from Hades, those who rejected Him were condemned.

There seem traces of this opinion in the above-noticed passage of Hermas, commonly called an apostolical father, and in Clement of Alexandria, who followed him. Origen, however, appears to be the first who distinctly propounded the opinion, that, after the coming of Christ, the souls of the just, instead of going to Hades, pass at once to some better place, called Paradise.[6]

---

[1] See the passages quoted in the note under the First head, i. 3, p. 87, note 1.

[2] "Nunc autem [Dominus] tribus diebus conversatus est ubi erant mortui. . . Cum enim Dominus *in medio umbræ mortis abierit,* ubi animæ mortuorum erant, . . . manifestum est quia et discipulorum ejus, propter quos et hæc operatus est Dominus, *αἱ ψυχαὶ ἀπέρχονται εἰς τὸν* [ἀόρατον] *τόπον τὸν ὡρισμένον αὐταῖς. . . . Nemo enim est discipulus super magistrum: perfectus autem omnis erit sicut magister ejus.* Quomodo ergo magister noster non statim evolans abiit, sed sustinens definitum a Patre resurrectionis suæ tempus, . . . post triduum resurgens assumptus est; sic et nos sustinere debemus definitum a Deo resurrectionis nostræ tempus, prænuntiatum a prophetis, et sic resurgentes assumi." — Irenæ. v. 31.

[3] *De Anima,* c. lv., quoted above.

[4] *De Anima,* c. lviii.

[5] "Descendit in inferiora terrarum, ut illic patriarchas et prophetas compotes sui faceret." — *De Anima,* c. lv.

See also *Adv. Marcion.* Lib. iv. c. xxxiv. Also Bp. Kaye's *Tertullian,* p. 262.

[6] This is apparent, as the opinion of Origen, in the whole of the 2d Homily on the 1st Book of Kings, known as the Homily *De Engastrimytho.* There he argues that the soul of Samuel, which

Accordingly, the later fathers generally adopted the notion, that, till Christ's death, the patriarchs and prophets were in Hades, but afterwards (from the time that Christ promised to the thief on the cross that he should be with Him in Paradise) they passed into Paradise, which therefore they distinguished from Hades.[1] Hades indeed they looked on as a place of rest to the just, but Paradise as far better.[2]

Here, of course, we begin to perceive the germ of the doctrine of the *Limbus Patrum*. Yet that the notion entertained by the fathers was vastly different from that of the mediæval Church, will be sufficiently apparent to any one who will read the passages which have been thrown into the notes.

Another opinion, however, grew up also in the early ages, namely, that Christ not only translated the pious from Hades to more joyous abodes, but that even some of those who in old times had been disobedient, yet, on hearing Christ's preaching, believed, and so were saved and delivered from torment and hell.[3] This

was called up by the witch of Endor, was in Hades; so were the souls of Abraham, Isaac, Jacob, and the prophets; none of them could pass the flaming sword, till Christ came to set them free. Therefore it was that Lazarus, though in Abraham's bosom, could see Dives, who was in torments. But after Christ is come, Christians can pass the flaming sword into Paradise without harm. Paradise, however, was not in Heaven, according to Origen, but still an intermediate state, though better than Hades. This appears from the following, if Rufinus has rightly translated him: " Puto enim quod sancti quique discedentes de hac vita permanebunt in loco aliquo in terra posito, quem Paradisum dicit Scriptura divina, velut in quodam eruditionis loco, et, ut ita dixerim, auditorio vel schola animarum, in quo de omnibus his quæ in terris viderant doceantur, indicia quoque quædam accipiant etiam de consequentibus et futuris," &c. — *De Principiis*, Lib. II. cap. XI. num. 6.

Bp. Beveridge, on this Article, quotes a passage from Ignatius, which should show that that ancient father took the same view as Origen and others after him. The passage, however, is from an interpolated Epistle, and therefore proves nothing. *Ad Trall.* IX. Coteler. II. p. 64.

[1] " Dominus resurrectionis suæ pignore vincula solvit inferni, et piorum animas elevavit."—Ambros. *De Fide ad Gratian.* Lib. IV. c. 1.

" Ante adventum Christi omnia ad inferos pariter ducerentur. Unde et Jacob ad inferos descensurum se dicit. Et Job

pios et impios in inferno queritur retentari. Et Evangelium, chaos magnum interpositum apud inferos, et Abraham cum Lazaro, et divitem in suppliciis, esse testatur. Et revera antequam flammeam illam rotam, et igneam romphæam, et Paradisi fores Christus cum latrone reseraret, clausa erant cœlestia."—Hieron. *Com. in Eccles.* c. III. Tom. II. col. 736. Edit. Bened. Quoted in part by King, p. 209 See also Pearson, p. 250.

[2] " Si enim non absurde credi videtur, antiquos etiam sanctos, qui venturi Christi tenuerunt fidem, locis quidem a tormentis impiorum remotissimis, sed apud inferos fuisse, donec eos inde sanguis Christi et ad ea loca descensus erueret, profecto deinceps boni fideles effuso illo pretio jam redempti, prorsus inferos nesciunt, donec etiam receptis corporibus, bona recipiant quæ merentur."—August. *De Civit. Dei*, Lib. XX. c. XV. Tom. VII. p. 593. Quoted in part by King, p. 212. See also *Epist.* CLXIV. Tom. II. p. 575; *Epist.* CLXXXVII. p. 679.

[3] " Expers peccati Christus, cum ad Tartari ima descenderet, seras inferni januasque confringens, vinctas peccato animas, mortis dominatione destructa, e diaboli faucibus revocavit ad vitam." — Ambros. *De Mysterio Paschæ*, c. 4.

" Dominum nostrum Jesum Christum, qui ad fornacem descendit inferni, in quo clausæ et peccatorum et justorum animæ tenebantur, ut absque exustione et noxa sui eos, qui tenebantur inclusi, mortis vinculis liberaret." — Hieron. *In Daniel.* c. iii. Tom. III. col. 1086.

" Invocavit ergo redemptor noster no-

appears to have been the opinion of Augustine. He was evidently puzzled as to the meaning of the word Hades, and doubted whether it ever meant a place of rest and happiness (although at times he appears to have admitted that it did) ; and thinking it a place of torment, he thought Christ went thither to save some souls, which were in torment, from thence.[1] Some indeed went so far as to think that hell was cleared of all the souls that were there in torment, and that all were taken up with Christ, when He arose from the dead, and ascended into Heaven. But this was reckoned as a heresy.[2]

Such were the principal varieties of opinion in early ages touching the end of Christ's descent to hell.[3]

In more modern times, many other sentiments have been adopted. Among the rest, the opinion held by Calvin[4] appears to have been, that our Lord's descent to hell means not His going to the place of spirits, but His suffering upon earth, in Gethsemane and on the cross, all the torments of hell, and the sufferings of damned souls. Dr. Hey thinks that the growing popularity of Calvin's views induced the reformers of Elizabeth's reign to omit the latter part of the Third Article as put forth in Edward's reign, because it was not acceptable to those who followed Calvin on this head.

Others again have supposed that our Lord went down to hell, (taking hell in the sense of Gehenna, the place of the damned,) and that He went there in order to meet and confront Satan in his own abode, and as He had conquered him on earth, so finally to subdue him in hell.[5]

---

men Domini de lacu novissimo, cum in virtute divinitatis descendit ad inferos, et destructis claustris Tartari, suos quos ibi reperit eruens, victor ad superos ascendit." — Id. Lib. II. *In Lamentat.* c. iii. Tom. v. col. 829. The genuineness of this commentary is doubtful.

" Nec ipsam tamen rerum partem noster salvator mortuus pro nobis visitare contempsit, ut inde solveret quos esse solvendos secundum divinam secretamque justitiam ignorare non potuit." — Augustin. *De Genesi ad literam.* Lib. XII. c. 66. Tom. III. p. 322.

Κατελθὼν γὰρ εἰς ᾅδου, καὶ τοῖς ἐκεῖσε διακηρύξας πνεύμασιν, ἀνείς τε τοῖς κάτω τὰς κεκλεισμένας πύλας, καὶ τὸν ἀπλησστον τοῦ θανάτου κενώσας μυχὸν, ἀνεβίω τριήμερος. — Cyril. Alex. *Hom. Paschal.* XI.

σεσύλητο τῶν πνευμάτων ὁ ᾅδης. — Id. *Hom.* VI.

See most of these and some other passages referred to in Usher's *Answer to a Jesuit,* ch. VIII.

[1] See Augustin. *Epist.* CLXIV. Tom. II. p. 573.   Pearson, p. 241, refers to it as *Epist.* XCIX. Concerning Augustine's doubts on the nature of Hades, see Pearson, p. 239 ; King, p. 210 ; and the places referred to *supra* note 3, pp. 124, 5.

[2] Augustine, in his book *De Hæresibus,* reckons this as the seventy-ninth heresy. " Alia, descendente ad inferos Christo, credidisse incredulos, et omnes exinde existimat liberatos." — Tom. VIII. p. 23. See Pearson, p. 241, note.

[3] Tertullian mentions, but does not approve of, an opinion in his day, that Christ went to Hades that we should not go thither : " Sed in hoc, inquiunt, Christus inferos adiit, ne nos adiremus." — *De Anima,* c. 55.

[4] See Calvin. *Institut.* Lib. II. c. 16, § 10 : quoted by Pearson, p. 230, where see Pearson's own observations on this notion.

[5] On the other hand, Mede (Disc. IV. *Works,* p. 23, Lond. 1677) has made it

II. To pass from the *Historical* to the *Scriptural* consideration of the end of Christ's descent to Hades, we may observe : —

1. That it is plain He went thither that He might fulfil the conditions of death proper to human nature. When man dies, the spirit leaves the body, the body is buried, the spirit goes to the abode of the departed, where the souls of men await the Resurrection of the dead. Christ fulfilled this twofold condition. His Body was buried, and His Soul passed into Hades or Paradise. This it is unnecessary to dwell upon, as it seems evident, that, as our Lord was perfect man, so it was His will, and the will of His Father, that He should undergo all the conditions of human nature, and especially that He should truly suffer death. Now death cannot be truly suffered, unless the soul leaves the body, and goes to the abode of departed spirits.

2. But it becomes necessary here to consider, whether the text 1 Pet. iii. 18, 19, (which was so applied by all the fathers, and by the English reformers of the reign of Edward the Sixth,) gives us any farther account of the end and object of Christ's descent to Hades. Many divines of the English Church deny altogether its applicability to this question. Writers of no less name than Hammond, Pearson, Barrow, &c. contend that the only meaning of St. Peter's words is, that our Lord by His Holy Spirit, inspiring Noah, preached to the disobedient antediluvians, who are now for their disobedience imprisoned in hell.[1]

This interpretation of the passage depends on the accuracy of the English version. That version reads in the eighteenth verse " quickened by the Spirit." It is to be noted, however, that all the ancient versions except one (the Ethiopic) seem to have understood it " quickened in spirit ; " and it is scarcely possible, upon any correct principles of interpretation, to give any other translation to the words.[2] If, therefore, we follow the original, in preference to the

---

most probable, if not certain, that Satan is not yet cast into hell, but that evil spirits are allowed to walk to and fro on the earth. So Satan is called the prince of the powers of the air, and it is not till the Judgment that he is to be cast into hell. This, like most of J. Mede's learned discourses, is well worth reading.

See also this view of the end and character of our Lord's descent into hell considered and disproved by Bp. Pearson, p. 248.

[1] A question as to whether this might be the meaning of the passage had been proposed by St. Jerome and St. Augustine. Hieron. Lib. xv. *In Esai.* cap. liv.

August. *Epist.* CLXIV. See Usher's *Answer to a Jesuit*, ch. VIII.

[2] The words in the Greek are θανατωθεὶς μὲν σαρκὶ, ζωοποιηθεὶς δὲ τῷ πνεύματι. The article τῷ before πνεύματι is of so little authority, that Wetstein, Griesbach, and Matthäi have rejected it from the text. Bishop Middleton has observed, that in order to admit of the rendering of the English version, or to allow us to understand by " spirit " here the Holy Spirit of God, it would be absolutely necessary that there should be not only an article, but a preposition also before πνεύματι. If the article be not authentic, **we** must render " dead carnally, but alive

English version, we must read the passage thus : " Christ suffered for us, the Just for the unjust, that He might bring us to God; being put to death in the flesh, but quick in His Spirit ; by which (or in which) He went and preached (or proclaimed) to the spirits in safe keeping," &c.   There is, it will be observed, a marked antithesis between " flesh " and " spirit."   In Christ's Flesh or Body He was put to death.   Men were " able to kill the body," but they could not kill His soul.   He was therefore alive in His Soul,[1] and *in* or *by* that He went to the souls who were in safe custody (ἐν φυλακῇ) ; His Body was dead, but His Spirit, or Soul, went to their spirits or souls.   This is the natural interpretation of the passage ; and if it ended here, it would contain no difficulty, and its sense would never have been doubted.   It would have contained a simple assertion of our Lord's descent to the spirits of the dead.[2]

But it is added, that He not only went to the spirits in safe keeping, but that He went and *preached* to them.   Hence it has been inferred, that, if He preached, they had need of, and He offered to them, repentance.   Hence the passage has appeared to savour of false doctrine, and hence its force has been explained away.   But the word " preached," or " proclaimed," by no means necessarily infers that He preached either faith or repentance. Christ had just finished the work of salvation, had made an end of sin, and conquered hell.   Even the angels seem not to be fully enlightened as to all the work of grace which God performs for man.   It is not likely, then, that the souls of the departed patriarchs should have fully understood or known all that Christ had just accomplished for them.   They indeed may have known, and no doubt did know, the great truth, that redemption was to be wrought for all men by the sufferings and death of the Messiah. But before the accomplishment of this great work, neither angels nor devils seem fully to have understood the mystery of it.   If this be true, when the blessed Soul of our crucified Redeemer went among the souls of those whom He had just redeemed, what

---

spiritually." If we admit the article, we must then translate, "dead in body, but alive in His Spirit," *i. e.* in His soul. The ancient versions support this rendering, and Michaelis and Rosenmüller give a similar interpretation.   Bp. Middleton refers with full approbation to Bp. Horsley's Sermon mentioned below. See Middleton, *On the Article*, in loc.

[1] ζωοποιηθείς corresponds with the Hiphil of חיה, which means " to *keep* alive," as much as " to make alive."

[2] The expression ἐν φυλακῇ by no means necessarily signifies a place of punishment.   It may mean a place of protection.   It is simply *in ward, in guardianship*.   The rendering of the Syriac, which from its antiquity is so important, is ܒܫܝܘܠ, *in Hades*.   The following is its rendering of the whole passage : " He was dead in body, but alive in spirit : and he preached to those souls which were kept in Hades."

can be more probable than that He should have "proclaimed" (ἐκήρυξεν) to them, that their redemption had been fully effected, that Satan had been conquered, that the great sacrifice had been offered up? If angels joy over one sinner that repenteth, may we not suppose Paradise filled with rapture when the Soul of Jesus came among the souls of His redeemed, Himself the herald (κήρυξ) of His own victory?

This is the view propounded by Bp. Horsley in his admirable sermon on this text.[1] It is perfectly unnecessary to suppose that the consequence of Christ's preaching in Hades, or Paradise, was similar to His or His Apostles' preaching on earth. Both indeed were preachings of glad tidings. But in this was the difference. Preaching on earth is to men, who need repentance, and whose repentance is acceptable. Preaching to the souls of the departed was a mere proclaiming of blessedness to men who had already repented when on earth, and had no need of repentance after death, when it never comes, and could not avail, even if it did come.

The only difficulty in this interpretation of this difficult passage is in the fact that the preaching is specially said to have been addressed to those " who had once been disobedient in the days of Noah." That many who died in the flood may yet have been saved from final damnation seems highly probable, and has been the opinion of many learned divines. The flood was a great temporal judgment, and it follows not that " all who perished in the flood are to perish everlastingly in the lake of fire." But the real difficulty consists in the fact that the proclamation of the finishing of the great work of salvation is represented by St. Peter as having been addressed to these antediluvian penitents, and no mention is made of the penitents of later ages, who are equally interested in the tidings.

It must be confessed that this is a knot which cannot easily be untied. Yet should not this induce us to reject the literal and grammatical interpretation of the passage, and to fall back upon those forced glosses which have been devised in order to avoid, instead of fairly meeting and endeavouring to solve, an acknowledged difficulty. Bishop Horsley says that he thinks he has " observed, in some parts of Scripture, an anxiety, if the expression may be allowed, of the sacred writers, to convey distinct intimations that the antediluvian race is not uninterested in the redemption and the final retribution." It may be conceived, too, he thinks,

---

[1] Vol. I. Serm. xx.

that those who perished in the most awful of God's temporal judgments would, more than any, need and look for the comfort of Christ's presence, and that consolation which His preaching in the regions of the departed would afford " to those prisoners of hope." Whether or not such ideas give any clue to the solution of this difficulty it may be hard to say. But in the same author's words, " Is any difficulty that may present itself to the human mind, upon the circumstances of that preaching, of sufficient weight to make the thing unfit to be believed upon the word of the Apostle ? — or are we justified, if, for such difficulties, we abandon the plain sense of the Apostle's words, and impose upon them another meaning, not easily adapted to the words, though more proportioned to the capacity of our own understanding, especially when it is confirmed by other Scriptures that He went to that place ? In that place He could not but find the souls that are in it in safe keeping ; and in some way or other, it cannot but be supposed, He would hold conference with them ; and a particular conference with one class might be the means, and certainly could be no obstruction to a general communication with all. If the clear assertions of Holy Writ are to be discredited, on account of difficulties which may seem to the human mind to arise out of them, little will remain to be believed in revealed or even in what is called natural religion : we must immediately part with the doctrine of atonement, — of gratuitous redemption, — of justification by faith without the works of the law, — of sanctification by the influence of the Holy Spirit ; and we must part at once with the hope of the Resurrection." [1]

---

[1] P. 436. The whole Sermon deserves careful attention, and should be compared with Bishop Middleton, on 1 Pet. iii. 18. It is to be lamented that Bishop Pearson, in his most learned and elaborate article on the Descent into Hell, should have written less lucidly than is his wont. In more passages than one, unless I greatly misunderstand him, he has contradicted himself. At one time he defines hell as the place of departed spirits, and makes our Lord's descent thither no more than a passing into the state of the dead. At another time he argues as if hell meant the place of torment, and says that Christ went there to save us from going thither, for which he quotes Tertullian, who, however, mentions the opinion only to condemn it. See especially p. 251.

[See also Bishop Hobart, *On the State of the Departed*; and Bishop Seabury's Sermon, *The Descent of Christ into Hell.* — *J. W.*]

ARTICLE IV.

———◆———

Of the Resurrection of Christ.	*De Resurrectione Christi.*
CHRIST did truly rise again from death, and took again His body, with flesh, bones, and all things appertaining to the perfection of man's nature, wherewith He ascended into Heaven, and there sitteth, until He return to judge all men at the last day.	CHRISTUS vere a mortuis resurrexit, suumque corpus cum carne, ossibus, omnibusque ad integritatem humanæ naturæ pertinentibus recepit: cum quibus in cœlum ascendit, ibique residet, quoad extremo die ad judicandos homines reversurus sit.

Section I. — HISTORY.

THE subjects treated of in this Article may be divided as follows: —

FIRST, We must consider Christ's Resurrection with His human Body; SECONDLY, His Ascension, and Session at God's Right Hand; THIRDLY, His Return to Judgment.

I–II. The first and second of these divisions may historically be considered together.

Christ's Resurrection forms a part of all the ancient Creeds, and is followed by the Ascension, Session, and Judgment, as in this Article.

The Sadducees, who denied all resurrection, of course would deny the resurrection of Christ. The Essenes also, though they believed the immortality of the soul, yet did not believe that the body would rise. We find, as early as Apostolic times, that some heretics had crept into the Christian Church, who said that "there was no resurrection of the dead" (1 Cor. xv. 12), and that "the resurrection was past already" (2 Tim. ii. 18). Whoever these heretics may have been, not long after them the Docetæ, denying the reality of Christ's flesh, and holding the doctrine of the general malignity of matter, of necessity disbelieved the truth of the resurrection and ascension of Christ. Augustine tells us that the Cerinthians held that Jesus, whom they took to be a mere man, had not risen, but was yet to rise.[1] Apelles, a disciple of Marcion's, held that, when Christ came down from Heaven, He formed for Himself as He descended an airy and sidereal flesh, but when He arose and ascended into Heaven, He restored this body to its pristine elements, which being thus dispersed, His Spirit alone returned to Heaven.[2]

Some of the earlier heretics, though otherwise connected with the Gnostics, did not absolutely deny either a body or a resurrection to Christ, but invented strange fables concerning it. Thus, according to Theodoret, Hermogenes believed our Lord's Body to be placed in the Sun.[3] And Tertullian mentions certain heretics who taught, " that the flesh of Christ was in the heavens devoid of sense, as a scabbard or sheath, Christ being withdrawn from it."[4] The Manichees, like the Gnostics or Docetæ, denying the reality of Christ's flesh, and believing matter to be evil, denied Christ's resurrection ; but as they seem to have identified Christ with Mithras (æthereal Light, the Sun), there may have been some connection between their belief and that of Hermogenes mentioned above.[5] The doctrine of Eutyches concerning the Person of Christ, as it was opposed to the verity of His Manhood, so it by implication opposed the verity of His resurrection ; and so Theodoret accuses him of considering that the Godhead only rose from the grave.[6]

In later ages, when the controversies arose concerning the presence of Christ in the Eucharist, it has been thought that divines of the Roman and Lutheran communions were led to use language concerning the glorified Body of our blessed Lord, and its ubiquity, which almost savoured of Eutychianism ; as though, after His ascension, His human nature had become so deified as to have lost the attributes of humanity, and have been transubstantiated into His Divinity. There is little doubt that the strong language of this Article was designed to oppose so exaggerated an opinion,

[1] "Jesum hominem tantummodo fuisse, nec resurrexisse, sed resurrecturum asseverantes." — August. *Hæres.* VIII. Tom. VIII. p. 7.

[2] Tertullian. *De Præscript. adv. Hær.* c. 33. *De Resurr. Carnis,* c. 5. Epiphan. *Hær.* XLIV. August. *Hæres.* XXIII. Pearson, *On the Creed,* p. 272. Lardner, *Hist. of Heretics,* Book II. chap. XII. sect. X. King, *On Creed,* p. 261.

[3] Theodoret. *Hæret. Fab.* Lib. I. c. 19. Pearson, *On the Creed,* p. 273. King, p. 263.

Philaster and Augustine ascribe the same opinion to the followers of Seleucus

and Hermias. See Lardner, *Hist. of Heretics,* Book II. ch. XVIII. sect. VIII.

[4] "Adfirmant carnem in cœlis vacuam sensu, ut vaginam, exempto Christo, sedere."— *De Carne Christi,* c. 24. Pearson, p. 272. King, p. 269.

[5] Μέχρι σήμερον Μανιχαῖοι λέγουσι φαντασιώδη καὶ οὐκ ἀληθῆ τοῦ Σωτῆρος τὴν ἀνάστασιν γεγονέναι.— Cyril. Hierosol. *Catech.* XIV. Suicer, I. col. 311.

[6] Theodoret (*Hæret. Fab.* Lib. IV. cap. XIII.) says he asserted τὴν θεότητα τῷ τάφῳ παραδοθεῖσαν τετυχηκέναι τῆς ἀναστάσεως. — See Suicer, I. col. 311.

if such really existed; which may be the better seen by comparing the words of the Article with the rubric at the end of the
Communion Service.[1]

It is not to be concealed, that in later times some persons, of
very sound opinions in the main, have been offended by the statement that our Lord took into Heaven "flesh, bones, and all things
pertaining to man's nature;" whereas they contend that our
Lord's Body at His ascension, if not before, became a spiritual
body, and a spiritual body cannot be said to have "flesh and bones,"
which pertain only to a natural body. This objection must be
considered hereafter; and in the mean time we have only to add,
that the language of the Article corresponds with that of the early
fathers. Ignatius says that " he knew and believed Him to be in
the flesh after His resurrection."[2] Irenæus, in one of his creeds,
confesses his belief in "the reception of Jesus Christ into Heaven
in the flesh."[3] In the Epistle of Damasus to Paulinus, the following anathema occurs amongst others, "If any one shall not acknowledge that Christ is set down at the right hand of the Father,
in the same flesh which He took here, let him be anathema."[4]
Augustine meets the objection which may be made to this doctrine: "It offends some," he says, "that we believe an earthly
Body to have been taken into Heaven; they understand not how
it is said in Scripture, It is sown a natural, it is raised a spiritual
body."[5] To the like purpose writes Epiphanius: "He ascended
into Heaven, not divesting Himself of His holy Body, but uniting
it to a spiritual one."[6]

The fathers indeed held that Christ's Body, after His resurrection, remained truly a human Body, and was not changed into a

---

[1] The rubric, after explaining that by
kneeling at the Communion no adoration
is intended either to the "Sacramental
Bread and Wine, or unto any Corporal
Presence of Christ's natural Flesh and
Blood," adds, "The natural Body and
Blood of our Saviour Christ are in Heav-
en, and not here; it being against the
truth of Christ's natural Body to be at one
time in more places than one." This rubric was first inserted in the Second Ser-
vice-Book of Edward VI. It was omitted in the Prayer-Book in Elizabeth's
reign, probably from a wish not to offend
the many persons of Lutheran sentiments
then in communion with the Church.
It was restored in the last revision in the
reign of Charles II., at the request of the
Puritan Divines.

[2] Ἐγὼ γὰρ καὶ μετὰ τὴν ἀνάστασιν ἐν σαρκὶ αὐτὸν οἶδα, καὶ πιστεύω ὄντα.— Epist. ad

Smyrn. c. 3. Pearson, p. 255. Suicer,
i. col. 307.

[3] τὴν ἔνσαρκον εἰς τοὺς οὐρανοὺς ἀνάληψιν
τοῦ ἠγαπημένου Χριστοῦ Ἰησοῦ.—Lib. i. c. 2.

[4] Theodoret. Eccl. Hist. Lib. v. c. xi.
King, On Creed, p. 268.

[5] " Solet autem quosdam offendere, vel
impios Gentiles vel hæreticos, quod credamus assumptum terrenum corpus in cœlum. Sed Gentiles plerumque philosopho-
rum argumentis nobiscum agere student,
ut dicant terrenum aliquid in cœlo esse
non posse. Nostras enim Scripturas non
noverunt, nec sciunt quomodo dictum sit,
Seminatur corpus animale, surgit corpus spirituale." — August. De Fide et Symbolo,
c. vi. Tom. vi. p. 157.

[6] Ἀνελθὼν εἰς οὐρανοὺς, ἐκάθισεν ἐν δεξιᾷ τοῦ Πατρὸς ἐν δόξῃ, οὐκ ἀποθέμενος τὸ ἅγιον
σῶμα, ἀλλὰ συνενώσας εἰς πνευματικόν.—An-
ac(ph. Tom. ii. p. 156. Colon. King, p. 2(2

spirit, or absorbed into God.[1] Yet they held, that it was divested
of all that was mortal, carnal, and corruptible, and became a spiritual Body, incorruptible, unchangeable, impassible.   So Theophylact, " Did He lay aside His flesh?   God forbid; for as He was
taken up, so shall He come.   But He was taken up in the flesh,
and with a Body.   Now Christ is said to have lived after the flesh,
when He lived subject to natural and blameless affections and
feelings, — hungering, thirsting, sleeping, working.   But now He
is no longer after the flesh, that is, He is freed from all such natural and blameless affections, having a body impassible and incorruptible." [2]

III.   The third head concerns our Lord's return to Judgment.

The Marcionites and other Gnostics are supposed to have denied
a future Judgment.   Their creed was, that God was of infinite
grace and mercy;   that the Creator, whom they distinguished
from God, was just; not so God, or His Son Jesus Christ.   They
were also accused of holding that the actions of men in the body
were indifferent;   and this tenet, by implication, is a denial of the
Judgment.[3]   The Manichees are charged, in like manner, with
denying a Judgment, as they, no doubt, did deny a resurrection
of the body.[4]

One of the peculiar views of Emmanuel Swedenborg in modern
times, and of his followers, who call themselves the Church of the
New Jerusalem, was that the passages of Scripture concerning the
Judgment are not to be literally interpreted.   Swedenborg taught
that all men are subject to two opposite influences, one from God
and good spirits, the other from evil angels; that according as they
yield to one or the other influence, the soul rises or falls.   Heaven
and hell then are not the result of a Divine appointment, or of a

---

[1] Οὐκοῦν οὐκ εἰς θεότητος μετεβλήθη
φύσιν, ἀλλὰ καὶ μετὰ τὴν ἀνάστασιν ἀθάνατον μένει καὶ ἄφθαρτον, καὶ θείας δόξης
μεστόν· σῶμα δὲ ὅμως, τὴν οἰκείαν ἔχον πε-
ριγραφήν. — Theodoret. Demonstr. per Syllog. Ὅτι ἀσύγχυτος ἡ ἕνωσις, Syl. ix.

Again : Οὐ μετεβλήθη εἰς πνεῦμα τὸ
σῶμα· σὰρξ γὰρ ἦν, καὶ ὀστέα, καὶ χεῖρες, καὶ
πόδες· τοιγαροῦν καὶ μετὰ τὴν ἀνάστασιν
σῶμα τὸ σῶμα μεμένηκεν. — Ibid. Syl. x.
See Suicer, i. coll. 307, 308.

[2] Theophyl. ad 2 Cor. v. 16.

Τὴν σάρκα ἀπέθετο; μὴ γένοιτο· ὡς γὰρ
ἀνελήφθη, οὕτω καὶ ἐλεύσεται· ἀνελήφθη δὲ
ἐν σαρκὶ καὶ μετὰ ι ῦ σώματος. . . . Ὁ δὲ

Χριστὸς κατὰ σάρκα λέγεται ζῆσαι, ὅτε κι17 ι
τὰ φυσικὰ καὶ ἀδιάβλητα πάθη ἔζη, πεινῶν,
διψῶν, ὑπνῶν, κοπιῶν· νῦν δὲ, οὐκέτι κατὰ
σάρκα· τουτέστι, τούτων τῶν φυσικῶν καὶ
ἀδιαβλήτων ἀπηλλάγη, ἀπαθὲς καὶ ἀκήριτον
σῶμα ἔχων.

So Theodoret on the same passage :
Εἰ γὰρ καὶ αὐτὸς ὁ δεσπότης Χριστὸς παθη-
τὸν εἶχε τὸ σῶμα, ἀλλὰ μετὰ τὸ πάθος ἄφθαρτον τοῦτο πεποίηκε καὶ ἀθάνατον. — See
Suicer as above.

[3] See King, On the Creed, p. 274.

[4] Hey's Lectures, ii. p. 390; and Lardner as referred to there.

future Judgment, but the necessary conditions of a man, according as he is good or evil. The passages of Scripture concerning the last Judgment are to be understood of the end and consummation of the Church which now is, and the establishment of a purer and better Church, which is called the descent " of the New Jerusalem from God out of Heaven."

Section II. — SCRIPTURAL PROOF.

I. A S regards the resurrection of the Lord Jesus, it requires very little argument to prove that Scripture teaches the *fact*. The truth of such teaching must be here, as usual, assumed; all argument on such subjects being referred to the head of evidence.

The concluding chapters of the four Gospels, and the fifteenth chapter of the first Epistle to the Corinthians, contain the fullest account of that miraculous event. They should be studied together, and with such aids as have been furnished by writers on the harmony of the Gospels.[1]

It is to be observed, however, that the Resurrection is in many respects the key-stone of the Christian Faith. On the truth of it depends the truth of the Gospel; for it was to this great fact especially that the Apostles bore witness, and on its veracity they rested their claims to be heard and believed. Our Lord Himself continually foretold it, and so its occurrence became essential to the establishment of His truth. Accordingly we find, both before and after the event, most numerous allusions to it in the writings of the new Testament. For example, Matt. xvii. 9, 23. Mark viii. 31; ix. 31. John ii. 19; x. 17, 18. Acts i. 22; ii. 24, 36; xiii. 30–37. Rom. iv. 25; vi. 4. Eph. i. 20. Col. ii. 12; iii. 1, &c. &c.

Yet the historical is scarcely greater than the doctrinal importance of the Resurrection. In Scripture, the life of the Christian and of the Christian Church is represented as connected with, and depending on the life of Christ, who is the Head of the

---

[1] Those most approved of in our own language are Lightfoot, Macknight, Greswell, &c. Greswell's *Harmonia Evan-* *gelica,* and his five volumes of *Dissertations* on the subject, should be in every student's library.

Church and the Saviour of the Body.[1] The Christian therefore is said to die with Christ, and to rise again with Him.[2] And this connection of the Redeemer and His redeemed is spiritual here, and bodily and spiritual both hereafter. For here the union of the Christian with Christ is the cause of spiritual life ; hereafter the same union shall be the cause of resurrection to life eternal. The Apostle speaks of the power of Christ's resurrection as having been shown already, thus: " God who is rich in mercy . . . when we were dead in sins, hath quickened us together with Christ, and hath raised us up together, and made us to sit together in heavenly places in Christ Jesus," Eph. ii. 4, 5, 6 ; and again : " If ye be risen with Christ, seek those things which are above," Col. iii. 1. But he also speaks of the power of the same resurrection as to be shown hereafter, not only in raising the soul from sin, but the body also from corruption. " If the Spirit of Him that raised up Jesus from the dead dwell in you, He that raised up Christ from the dead shall also quicken your mortal bodies by His Spirit which dwelleth in you," Rom. viii. 11. And again, " He which raised up the Lord Jesus shall raise up us also by Jesus," 2 Cor. iv. 14. And thus it is that by virtue of His own resurrection, or, as St. Paul calls it, " the power of His resurrection " (Phil. iii. 10), the Lord Jesus is to His disciples " the Resurrection and the Life " (John xi. 25).

II. The second head of this article concerns the Ascension, and Session at God's Right Hand.

1. The Ascension into Heaven is related in Mark xvi. 19. Luke xxiv. 51. Acts i. 1–12.

It had been predicted in the old Testament (especially Ps. lxviii. 18, which is explained by the Apostle, Eph. iv. 8) ; it had been foretold by our Lord Himself (John vi. 62; xx. 17) ; and it finally took place in the presence of His chosen disciples.

The importance of it to us was typified on the great day of atonement, when the High Priest entered into the Holy of Holies once every year. The tabernacle, as is familiarly known, consisted of two principal parts. The first was called the Sanctuary or holy place, which typified the world, or more properly the Church on earth ; where daily the priesthood ministered, offering sacrifices for the people, and sending up incense, the symbol of prayer and

---

[1] John xv. 1–7 ; xvii. 23. Rom. xii. 5. 1 Cor. vi. 15 ; xii. 27. Eph. i. 22, 23; iv. 15, 16; v. 23. Col. i. 18, &c.

[2] Rom. vi. 8. Eph. ii. 5, 6. Col. ii. 12; iii. 1. 1 Pet. i. 3. 2 Cor. iv. 10, 11, 14. Rom. viii. 11. 1 Cor. vi. 14, &c.

praise. But within the veil, whither no common priest had access, was the Holy of Holies, or the Holiest of all. Into this, once every year, on the tenth day of Tisri, the Fast, or day of atonement, the High Priest alone entered. He had made atonement for himself, for the sanctuary, and for the people, by sacrificing a bullock, a ram, and a goat; and dressed in the white robes common to the priesthood, he went with blood of the victims into the most holy place, and sprinkled seven times before the mercy-seat the blood of the bullock and the goat (Levit. xvi.) That this all prefigured the entrance of Christ "into Heaven itself, now to appear in the presence of God for us," we have the word of the Apostle in the ninth chapter of the Hebrews. As the High Priest was in the common white garments, not in the gorgeous robe of his high priesthood, so Christ went up in the likeness of sinful humanity, carrying our nature with Him, though pure from the sin of humanity, as the garment of the priest was holy and white (Lev. xvi. 4). As the priest took with him the blood of the sacrifice, so Christ offered His own Blood, and before the mercy-seat of God pleaded, and forever pleads, the merits of His Sacrifice, "seeing that He ever liveth to make intercession for us." [1]

2. The Session at the Right Hand of God, foretold Ps. cx. 1 (comp. Luke xx. 42), and by our Lord, Matt. xxvi. 64, Mark xiv. 62, Luke xxii. 69, is recorded, Mark xvi. 19, Acts ii. 34, Rom. viii. 34, Eph. i. 20, Col. iii. 1, Heb. i. 3, 13, 1 Pet. iii. 22. It is hardly necessary to observe, that, when the Scriptures speak of the Right Hand of God, they mean thereby, not that God has hands like a man, but that as the right hand among men is the place of honour, of power, and of joy,[2] so to be by the Right Hand of God is to have the place of highest glory, power, and pleasure in the presence of God in Heaven; and *to sit* has no reference to posture, but implies dignity, sovereignty, and judgment.

Christ has ascended into Heaven, and there He abides. He now occupies that Mediatorial throne, where He is to sit, till all enemies be made His footstool (Ps. cx. 1. 1 Cor. xv. 25). He had been anointed to His kingly office, when the Holy Ghost descended on Him at His baptism (Matt. iii. 16. Acts x. 38). He vindicated His title to the throne, when by "death He overcame him who had the power of death, even the devil." He made a farther advance to the assumption of His dominion, when

---

[1] Heb. viii. ix. x. *passim.*
[2] 1 Kings ii. 19.   Matt. xxvi. 64.   Ps. xvi. 11

He rose victorious from the grave, and thereupon declared to His disciples, that "all power was given Him in Heaven and earth" (Matt. xxviii. 18). But it was not until His final exaltation, when God, having "raised Him from the dead, set Him at His own right hand in heavenly places, far above all principality, and power, and might, and dominion, and every name that is named, not only in this world, but also in that which is to come," that "all things having been put under His feet," He was "given to be Head over all things to the Church" (Eph. i. 20, 21, 22); "set upon the throne of His father David" (Luke i. 32); and "there was given to Him dominion and glory and a kingdom," "an everlasting dominion which shall not pass away, and a kingdom which shall not be destroyed" (Dan. vii. 14).

3. The next point for our consideration is, that Christ is said "to have taken again His Body, with flesh, bones, and all things belonging to the perfection of man's nature, wherewith He ascended into Heaven."

It has been seen, in the former Section, what the fathers appear to have taught on this subject. That our Lord arose from the grave in the same Body in which He was buried, that the same Body, with flesh and bones, which was laid in the sepulchre a lifeless corpse, was reanimated and rose again to life on the third day, is plainly and unquestionably the statement of the Evangelists. It was on this fact that their preaching and their faith rested. It was the assurance of this fact that convinced St. Thomas of the Divinity of Christ. He had declared that he would not believe the resurrection until he had seen in our Lord's hands the print of the nails, and had thrust his hand into His side (John xx. 25). That is to say, he required proof that our Lord's Body, which had risen, was the same Body which had been crucified; and when our Lord vouchsafed him this proof, then, and not till then, he exclaimed, "My Lord and my God!" (John xx. 25–28).

But farther, when, on one occasion, the disciples were assembled, and our Lord suddenly appeared among them, "they were terrified and affrighted, and supposed that they had seen a spirit; but He said unto them, Why are ye troubled? and why do thoughts arise in your hearts? Behold my hands and my feet, that it is I myself: handle Me and see; for a spirit hath not flesh and bones, as ye see Me have. And when He had thus spoken, He showed them His hands and His feet" (Luke xxiv. 36–40). Thus it is clear that our Lord's Body, after He rose from the

grave, was that Body in which He was buried, having hands and
feet, and flesh and bones, capable of being handled, and in which
He spoke and ate and drank (Luke xxiv. 42, 43).   Moreover, it
appears that our Lord thus showed His hands and feet to His
disciples at that very interview with them in which He was
parted from them and received up into Heaven.   This will be
seen by reading the last chapter of St. Luke, from verse 36 to the
end, and comparing it with the first chapter of the Acts, ver. 4–9;
especially comparing Luke xxiv. 49, 50, with Acts i. 4, 8, 9.   In
that Body, then, which the disciples felt and handled, and which
was proved to them to have flesh and bones, these disciples saw our
Lord ascend into Heaven; and immediately after His ascent, angels
came and declared to them, that that " same Jesus whom they had
seen taken up into Heaven, should so come in like manner as they
had seen Him go into Heaven " (Acts i. 11).   All this connected
together seems to prove the identity of our Lord's Body after His
resurrection, at His ascension, and so on, even till His coming to
Judgment, with the Body in which He suffered, and in which He
was buried; and so fully justifies the language used in the Article
of our Church.

But because we maintain that the Body of Christ, even after
His resurrection and ascension, is a true human Body, with all
things pertaining to the perfection of man's nature (to deny which
would be to deny the important truth that Christ is still perfect
Man as well as perfect God); it by no means therefore follows
that we should deny that His risen Body is now a glorified, and
as St. Paul calls it, a *spiritual* Body.   Nay! we have the strongest
proofs that so it is.

Even before His ascension, He is said to have come and stood in
the midst of His disciples, where the doors were shut for fear of
the Jews (John xx. 19).   On another occasion, He is said to have
vanished out of their sight (Luke xxiv. 31).   Again, His appearing to them " in another form " (Mark xvi. 12), and the disciples
going to Emmaus not at once knowing Him (Luke xxiv. 16), seem
to show that there was some change in the appearance, as well as
in the properties of His Body.   Though His Body had not ceased
to be the same Body which it was before His death, it yet appears
to have received some degree of glorification, and to have been invested with some supernatural qualities.

But, after His ascension, we have St. Paul's distinct assurance
that the Body of Christ is a glorious, is a spiritual Body.   In 1 Cor.
xv. we have St. Paul's assertion, that, in the resurrection of **all**

men, the body shall rise again, but that it shall no longer be a natural body, but a spiritual body; no longer a corruptible and vile, but an incorruptible and glorious body. "It is sown in corruption; it is raised in incorruption: it is sown in weakness; it is raised in power: it is sown a natural body; it is raised a spiritual body. There is a natural body, and there is a spiritual body." "Flesh and blood cannot inherit the kingdom of God, neither doth corruption inherit incorruption. Behold, I shew you a mystery; we shall not all sleep, but we shall all be changed." "For this corruptible must put on incorruption, and this mortal must put on immortality" (1 Cor. xv. 42-53). And this change of our bodies, from natural to spiritual, is expressly stated to be bearing the image of our glorified Lord, — the image of that heavenly man, the Lord from Heaven (vv. 47–49).

So again, the glorified state of the saints' bodies after the Resurrection, which in 1 Cor. xv. had been called the receiving a spiritual body, is, in Phil. iii. 21, said to be a fashioning of their bodies to the likeness of Christ's glorious Body; "who shall change our vile body, that it may be fashioned like unto His glorious Body."[1]

We must therefore conclude, that, though Christ rose with the same Body in which He died, and that Body neither did, nor shall cease to be a human Body, still it acquired, either at His Resurrection or at His Ascension, the qualities and attributes of a spiritual, as distinguished by the Apostle from a natural body, of an incorruptible as distinguished from a corruptible body.

It is not perhaps given us to know the exact meaning of the term "a spiritual body." "We know not yet what we shall be;" and so we do not exactly know what He is, whom we shall be like. It may be better to leave in the obscurity in which Scripture has left it, this great and glorious mystery. And we shall err on neither side, if we maintain that our blessed Saviour still continues our Mediator in Heaven, perfect in His nature of God, and perfect in His nature of Man; but with His human nature, which on earth, though sinless, was mortal and corruptible, now raised to glory and immortality and incorruptibility; His natural having become a spiritual, His corruptible an incorruptible body.[2]

---

[1] "Non ita dictum est, quasi corpus vertatur in spiritum, et spiritus fiat; quia et nunc corpus nostrum, quod animale dicitur, non in animam versum est et anima factum. Sed spirituale corpus intelligitur, quod ita spiritui subditum est, ut cœlesti habitationi conveniat, omni fragilitate ac labe terrena in cœlestem puritatem et stabilitatem mutata atque conversa."—August. De Fide et Symbolo, c. vi. Tom. vi. p. 157.

[2] There may be a difficulty in reconciling this doctrine, which is the plain doctrine of Scripture and the primitive

III. The third head of the Article is on the Judgment; in which we may consider, —

1. The Agent or Person who shall judge, Christ.
2. The object to be judged, namely, all men.
3. The action, judgment.
4. The time, the last day.

1. As regards the Agent; it is, in the first place, clear that *God* shall be "the Judge of all the earth" (Gen. xviii. 25. Ps. lviii. 11). Hence the day of Judgment is called "the day of God" (2 Peter iii. 12), — "the great day of Almighty God" (Rev. xvi. 14). Daniel saw "the thrones cast down, and the Ancient of days did sit" (Dan. vii. 9); and St. John saw "the dead great and small stand before God," for judgment (Rev. xx. 12).

Now, when God is thus generally spoken of, we must either understand God the Father, or the whole blessed Trinity. And in the general, it is true to say that God shall judge the earth, or, that God the Father shall judge the earth. But then, as God made the worlds, but it was by God the Son; as God hath purchased the Church, but it was by the death of His Son; so the Father Himself "judgeth no man, but hath committed all judgment unto the Son" (John v. 22). "He hath given Him authority to execute judgment, because He is the Son of Man" (John v. 27); "He hath appointed a day, in the which He will judge the world in righteousness by that man whom He hath ordained" (Acts xvii. 31); "He will judge the secrets of all men by Jesus Christ" (Rom. ii. 16).

Accordingly, the Judgment, when fully described, is ever represented as the coming of the Lord Jesus. It is called the "day of Christ" (2 Thess. ii. 2). "We must all appear before the judgment-seat of Christ" (2 Cor. v. 10). "The Son of Man shall come in the glory of His Father, with His angels" (Matt. xvi. 27; xxiv. 37; xxv. 31; xxvi. 64). The "same Jesus which was taken up into Heaven, shall come again in like manner as he went

Christians, with the language of the rubric at the end of the Communion Service quoted above. If they be at variance, the language of a not very carefully worded rubric, adopted not without some hesitation by the reformers, ought not to be pressed; but it is plain, that the writers of the rubric did not mean by the words "natural body" to convey the same idea as St. Paul attaches to the term in 1 Cor. xv. The doctrine which they meant to teach was only, that we must not consider the manhood of Christ changed into His Godhead. So St. Augustine: "Noli itaque dubitare ibi nunc esse hominem Christum Jesum, unde venturus est; .... in eadem carnis forma atque substantia; cui profecto immortalitatem dedit, naturam non abstulit. Secundum hanc formam non est putandus ubique diffusus. Cavendum est enim, ne ita divinitatem astruamus hominis, ut veritatem corporis auferamus." — *Ad Dard Epist.* 187. Tom. ii. p. 681.

into Heaven" (Acts i. 11). "He has been ordained of God to be Judge of quick and dead" (Acts x. 42). He says of Himself, "Behold! I come quickly, and my reward is with me" (Rev. xxii. 12).

2. The objects of the Judgment are all men, whether those living at the time of Christ's coming, or those already fallen asleep,—"the quick and the dead."

In the first Epistle to the Thessalonians (iv. 15–17), the Apostle describes the awful scene of our Lord's coming to save His people : "The Lord Himself shall descend from Heaven with a shout, with the voice of the Archangel and the trump of God, and the dead in Christ shall rise first. Then we which are alive and remain" (*i. e.*, whoever of Christ's servants may then remain alive on the earth) "shall be caught up together with them in the clouds, to meet the Lord in the air." In the like manner, he says (1 Cor. xv. 51, 52), "We shall not all sleep, but we shall all be changed, in a moment, in the twinkling of an eye, at the last trump. For the trumpet shall sound, and the dead shall be raised incorruptible, and we shall be changed." Accordingly it is said (2 Tim. iv. 1) that "the Lord Jesus Christ shall judge the quick and the dead at His appearing ;" that He "was ordained of God to be the Judge of quick and dead" (Acts x. 42. Compare Matt. xxv. throughout, John v. 25, 28, &c.)

3. The Judgment itself, which is the action the great Judge is to perform, is fully described in several of the passages already quoted or referred to. The twenty-fifth chapter of St. Matthew especially, under a variety of images, sets forth the terrors of the great day of the Lord : the ten virgins that meet the Bridegroom — the servants with their various talents — the Lord with all nations brought before Him, dividing them as a Shepherd the sheep from the goats.

In all these passages, and many besides, it is expressly said that the Judgment itself shall be "*according to works.*" On this subject the following references may be consulted, and will be found full and express. Job xxxiv. 11. Ps. lxii. 12. Prov. xxiv. 12. Jer. xvii. 10 ; xxxii. 19. Matt. xvi. 27 ; xxv. 31–46. John v. 29. Rom. ii. 6. 2 Cor. v. 10. Col. iii. 24, 25. Rev. xx. 12 ; xxii. 12.

It need only be added, that Judgment according to works is a doctrine of Scripture not opposed to justification by faith. That we cannot be justified by the merits of our own works is a plain statement of St. Paul (Rom. iii. 20; viii. 3. Gal. ii. 16. Eph. ii. 9, &c.) But if we be renewed by the Spirit of God, and transformed in the spirit of our minds; if Christ be in us, and the Spirit of God dwell in our hearts; then, being dead to sin, we can no longer live therein (Rom. vi. 2). Sin will not reign in our mortal bodies (Rom. vi. 12); but "the law of the Spirit of life in Christ Jesus will have made us free from that law of sin" (Rom. viii. 2) which would naturally reign in us; and so "the righteousness of the law will be fulfilled in all who walk not after the flesh, but after the Spirit" (Rom. viii. 4). We are specially warned not to be deceived on this head; for "he that doeth righteousness is righteous;" and "he who committeth sin is of the devil." "He that doeth not righteousness is not of God" (1 John iii. 7–10). Thus, then, the mark of distinction between the children of God and the children of the devil is this,—that righteousness is practised by the one party, sin by the other. And hence it is but likely that Judgment, which is to distinguish Christ's servants from His enemies, should be conducted according to the works of every man, which shall "be brought to light, whether they be good or evil." The just indeed shall be rewarded, not because of the merit of their works, but because of the atonement and righteousness of Christ. Yet still their own good works will be the test of their sanctification, and the proof before men and angels that they are living members of Christ and regenerated by His Spirit; whereas the wicked works of wicked men will justly consign them to death and damnation.

4. It remains but to speak of the time of Christ's coming to Judgment,—the last day.

The general descriptions of the Judgment already referred to (e. g. Matt. xxv. Rev. xx. 11–13, &c.) sufficiently show that it will not take place until the time when all present things shall pass away. All mankind, quick and dead, are represented as brought before the judgment-seat, and the just are sent to an everlasting reward, the wicked to an everlasting punishment. Accordingly, St. Paul says it shall be "at the last trump" (1 Cor. xv. 52), and St. Peter represents "the heavens and the earth which are now," as "reserved unto fire against the day of Judgment." The heavens shall be dissolved, and the elements shall "melt with fervent heat;" yet there shall be for the redeemed "a new heaven and a new earth, wherein dwelleth righteousness" (2 Pet. iii. 7–13).

But though the time is thus accurately marked, as "the last day," the close and consummation of the present state of things, yet we are continually told that it is utterly impossible for us to know how soon that day may come or how long it may tarry. It was not for our Lord's most favoured disciples "to know the times or the seasons which the Father hath put in His own power" (Acts i. 7). They and we are bid to "watch, for we know not what hour our Lord cometh" (Matt. xxiv. 42 : compare also Matt. xxv. 13. Mark xiii. 33. Luke xii. 40. 2 Pet. iii. 9–10). The disciples were taught to be constantly expecting our Lord ; and accordingly they spoke and wrote as though they thought that He might come at any time. (See Rom. xiii. 11. Phil. iv. 5. 1 Thess. iv. 15, 17. Heb. x. 25. James v. 7, 8, &c.) Yet still they were fully aware that He might delay His coming, they knew not how long ; and the importance of this uncertainty St. Paul earnestly impresses on the Thessalonians (2 Thess. ii. 1–3) ; and St. Peter still more fully inculcates on all men (2 Pet. iii. 4, 8–10).

There is one passage, however, especially remarkable on this subject. After our Lord had foretold the destruction of Jerusalem, and assured His disciples that the generation then alive should not pass away till that His prediction was accomplished (Matt. xxiv. 34. Mark xiii. 30), He goes on to tell them that though He thus gave them to know the time when He would execute His judgment on Jerusalem, yet the day of His final judgment (which they had confounded with the destruction of Jerusalem, Matt. xxiv. 36), was unknown to men and angels. Nay, according to the record of St. Mark, our Lord said, " Of that day and that hour knoweth no man, no, not the angels which are in Heaven, *neither the Son*, but the Father " (Mark xiii. 32).

It has been seen that in His human nature our Lord was capable of knowledge and of ignorance. He was perfect Man, as well as perfect God, and He grew in wisdom, as well as in stature (Luke ii. 52). In that nature, then, in which He was capable of ignorance, He, when He was on earth, knew not the coming of the day of God. Though He is Himself to come, yet as Man He knew not the day of His own coming. This is indeed a great mystery, that that Manhood, which is taken into one Person with the Godhead of the Son, should be capable of not knowing everything, seeing that God the Son is omniscient. But it is scarcely more inexplicable than that God the Son in His Manhood should

be weak, passible, and mortal, who in His Godhead is omnipotent,
impassible, and immortal.[1] If we believe the one, we can admit
the other.

[1] The explanation of Mark xiii. 32,
given in the text, is both consonant with
sound principles of interpretation and
with sound theology, and has been the
explanation of the most ancient Christian
fathers.
'Ανθρωπίνως εἴρηκε· καὶ τὸ αἴτιον τοῦ οὕτως εἰρηκέναι ἔχει τὸ εὔλογον· ἐπειδὰν γὰρ ἄνθρωπος γέγονεν, ὡς γέγραπται, ἀνθρώπων δὲ
ἴδιον τὸ ἀγνοεῖν, ὥσπερ καὶ τὸ πεινᾷν, καὶ τὰ
ἄλλα· διὰ τοῦτο καὶ τὴν ἄγνοιαν τῶν ἀνθρώπων, ὡς ἄνθρωπος γεγονὼς, ἐπιδείκνυται·
πρῶτον μὲν, ἵνα δείξῃ, ὅτι ἀληθῶς ἀνθρώπινον ἔχει σῶμα, κ. τ. λ. — Athanas. Epist. ii.
ad Serapion. Tom. i. p. 172. See Suicer,
s. v. κρίσις. v. 4, f.

[It seems desirable to add a few words concerning the difficulty spoken of in note 2,
p. 113. The word used by St. Paul, in 1 Cor. xv. is ψυχικόν (soul-ish), and this can
hard'y be supposed to be the meaning of "natural," in the rubric at the end of the
Communion Service. Had this latter word been written in Greek, it would have
been φυσικόν.

It does so read in a Greek translation of the Book of Common Prayer, printed at
Cambridge in 1665, and published with the Apocrypha and New Testament. The
concluding words of the rubric are καὶ τὸ φ υ σ ι κ ὸ ν τοῦ Σωτῆρος ἡμῶν Χριστοῦ σῶμα καὶ
αἷμα ἐν τῷ οὐρανῷ καὶ οὐκ ἐνθάδε εἰσὶ· τῇ τοῦ φ υ σ ι κ ο ῦ Χριστοῦ σώματος ἀληθείᾳ ἐνάν-
τιον ὂν, ἐν ἑνὶ χρόνῳ ἐν πλείοσι τόποις πλὴν ἑνός ὑπάρχον.

There can, therefore, be no contradiction between St. Paul's words and the rubric,
unless it can be proved that ψυχή and φυσίς are synonymes. I am indebted for the
above extract to the Rev. Mr. Hart, of Trinity College. — J. W.]

[It seems impossible to understand St. Luke xxiv. 36–49, of any other time than
the evening after the Resurrection, consequently not immediately before the Ascension. The argument on page 112, though becoming in consequence less striking, is
not materially weakened. — J. W.]

ARTICLE V.

———◆———

Of the Holy Ghost.	*De Spiritu Sancto.*
THE Holy Ghost, proceeding from the Father and the Son, is of one substance, majesty, and glory with the Father and the Son, very and eternal God.	SPIRITUS Sanctus, a Patre et Filio procedens, ejusdem est cum Patre et Filio essentiæ, majestatis et gloriæ, verus et æternus Deus.

———————————

SECTION I.—HISTORY.

THE subjects of this Article to be treated on are—I. The Divinity; II. The Personality; III. The Procession, of the Holy Ghost.

Those early heretics who denied the Divinity of the Son of God, seem generally to have disbelieved the Personality of the Holy Spirit, and to have looked on Him not as a Person, but as an efficacy, power, or emanation from God.

This heresy appears to have been as early as Simon Magus himself, and his immediate followers, the Gnostics. The like opinion would, of course, naturally prevail among those speculators who afterwards acquired the name of Sabellians, such as Praxeas, Noetus, Sabellius, Beryllus, Paulus Samosatenus.[1]

The Arians, on the contrary, appear to have taught that the Spirit was a separate Person from the Father and the Son, but that He was, as they held the Son to be, but a creature. Nay, as they held the Son to be a creature created by the Father, so they are said to have taught that the Spirit was created by the Son, and hence called Him κτίσμα κτίσματος, the creature of a creature.[2]

---

[1] See the account of these heretics, Art. I. § I.; and the authorities referred to in the notes. See also Pearson, *On the Creed*, Art. VIII. p. 322, note. Suicer, II. p. 774.

[2] Τὸ ἅγιον Πνεῦμα κτίσμα κτίσματος φάσιν εἶναι. Epiphan. *Hær.* LXIX. 56, p. 778, Colon.; Suicer, II. p. 775. A synod held under Damasus at Rome decreed εἴ τις εἴποι τὸ Πνεῦμα τὸ ἅγιον ποίημα ἢ διὰ τοῦ Ὑιοῦ γεγενῆσθαι ἀνάθεμα ἔστω. Apud Theodor. I. v. c. 11. See Pearson, *On the Creed*, p. 316, note. Suicer, as above; and the account given, Art. I. § I. See also Lardner's *Works*, IV. pp. 113, 114.

Macedonius especially was considered the head of the Pneumatomachi, or impugners of the Divinity of the Spirit, being reckoned
among the semi-Arians, orthodox about the person of the Son, but
a believer in the creation of the Holy Ghost.   He is said to have
called the Holy Spirit the servant or minister of God.[1]   This heresy of Macedonius was condemned by the second general council
held at Constantinople, A. D. 381, which added to the Nicene Creed
after the words, "And in the Holy Ghost," the following, viz. :
"The Lord, and Giver of life, who proceedeth from the Father,
who with the Father and the Son together is worshipped and glorified, who spake by the prophets."

Of the fathers, Origen and Lactantius have been charged with
unsound doctrines concerning the Holy Ghost.

It is not easy to arrive at a just conclusion concerning the
statements of Origen, owing to the fierce disputes which arose
concerning them, the obscurity, and the mutilated condition of his
writings.   He has been accused of questioning whether, as "all
things were made by " the Son, so the Holy Spirit may have been
included in "all things," and therefore created by the Son.   The
accusation, however, appears to be unjust, and to have been
grounded on some inaccuracy of language and obscurity of reasoning, not on really heretical statements.[2]

Jerome more than once charges Lactantius with virtually denying the Personality of the Holy Spirit by referring His operation,
through a Jewish error, to the Person of the Father or of the
Son ;[3] an heretical belief, which, he says, prevailed among many.

[1] Suicer, ii. p. 774.

[2] The book in which Origen is especially accused of having spoken blasphemy concerning the Spirit of God is
the first book of the Περὶ Ἀρχῶν (De
Principiis), ἐν ᾧ πλεῖστα βλασφημεῖ, τὸν
μὲν Υἱὸν ὑπὸ τοῦ Πατρὸς πεποιῆσθαι λέγων,
τὸ δὲ Πνεῦμα ὑπὸ τοῦ Υἱοῦ. Photius, Bib-
lioth. cod. viij.   We have this book only
in the translation of Rufinus, who in his
prologue to it says that he has omitted
parts of the book, which had been foisted
into it by heretics, and supplied the omissions from other portions of the genuine
works of Origen.   Jerome (Lib. i. Adv.
Rufinum) accuses Rufinus of having mis-
translated Origen, and he himself undertook to give a new translation.   All but
fragments of the latter are lost.   If Ruf-
finus has given at all a fair representation of his author, the following would
show that Origen cannot have been
very heretical concerning the Holy
Ghost: "Ne quis sane existimet nos ex
eo quod diximus Spiritum Sanctum solis
sanctis præstari, Patris vero et Filii bene-

ficia vel inoperationes pervenire ad bonos
et malos, justos et injustos, prætulisse
per hoc Patri et Filio Spiritum Sanctum,
vel majorem ejus per hoc asserere dignitatem : quod utique valde inconsequens
est.   Proprietatem namque gratiæ ejus
operisque descripsimus.   Porro autem
nihil in Trinitate majus minusve dicendum est, quum unius Divinitatis Fons
Verbo ac Ratione sua teneat universa,
Spiritu vero oris sui quæ digna sunt
sanctificatione sanctificet, sicut in Psal-
mo Scriptum est *Verbo Domini cœli firmati
sunt et Spiritu Oris Ejus omnis virtus eorum.*"
— Origen. *De Principiis*, Lib. i. cap. 3,
num. 7. Comp. num. 2.

[3] "Hoc ideo quia multi per imperitiam
Scripturarum, quod et Firmilianus in oc-
tavo ad Demetrianum epistolarum libro
facit, asserunt Spiritum Sanctum sæpe
Patrem sæpe Filium nominari ; et cum
perspicue in Trinitate credamus, tertiam
Personam auferentes non substantiam
Ejus esse volunt, sed nomen." — Hieron.
In Epist. ad Galatas, cap. iv. Tom. iv. part
i. p. 268.   See also Lardner, iv. p. 60.

One of the strange forms which heresy is said to have assumed was that which is attributed to Montanus, namely, that he gave himself out to be the Paraclete, *i. e.* the Spirit of God. Nay, it is even said that he had his disciples baptized in his own name, as the third Person of the blessed Trinity;[1] though it appears to be doubtful whether Montanus really meant that he was an incarnation of the Spirit, or only that the Spirit dwelt more fully in him than in any former man.[2] Indeed, to some it appears that the Montanists were in their creed Sabellians, and that they thought that the Spirit which animated Montanus was but an emanation from God.[3]

A denial of the Personality of the Holy Ghost, and a belief that He was but an influence or energy, seem to have been general in later times with the Socinians, and may be considered as a necessary consequence of a denial of the doctrine of the Trinity in general.

But the most celebrated controversy which has ever arisen concerning the Holy Ghost was that which had reference to His Procession, and which led to the famous schism between the Eastern and Western churches.

The Council of Constantinople (A. D. 381) had inserted in the Creed of the Council of Nice (A. D. 325) the words "proceeding from the Father" (τὸ ἐκ τοῦ Πατρὸς ἐκπορευόμενον) ; and the Council of Ephesus (A. D. 431) had decreed that no addition should be made to that creed thenceforth. Accordingly, the Greek fathers uniformly declared their belief in the procession of the Holy Ghost from the Father.

The Latin Fathers, on the other hand, having regard to those passages of Scripture which speak of the Spirit of Christ, and of the Spirit as sent by the Son, continually spoke of the Holy Ghost as proceeding from the Father and the Son.[4] The Greek fathers, indeed, were willing to use language approximating to the words of

---

[1] See Bingham, *E. A.* Book XI. ch. III. § 7.

[2] Mosheim, Cent. II. pt. II. ch. v. § 23 ; also, *De Rebus ante Constantinum M.* Sec. II. § 67 ; Bp. Kaye's *Tertullian*, 2d Edit. p. 22; Lardner's *Heretics*, Book II. ch. 19.

Manes, Mohammed, and others beside them, have professed to be the Paraclete promised by Christ to His disciples. Whether by the Paraclete they meant the Holy Ghost is questionable.

[3] See Bingham, as above.

[4] " Spiritus quoque Sanctus cum pro-cedit a Patre et Filio, non separatur a Patre, non separatur a Filio." —Ambros. *De Sp. S.* c. x. " Non possumus dicere quod Spiritus Sanctus et a Filio non procedat, neque enim frustra Spiritus et Patris et Filii Spiritus dicitur."—August. *De Trin.* Lib. IV. cap. 20. See Pearson, p. 324, note. St. Augustine, more clearly and fully than any before him, asserted the procession from the Son. Hence the modern Greeks charge him with having invented it. See Waterland, *Works*, IV. p. 246. Oxf. 1823.

the Latin Fathers, but shrank from directly asserting the procession from the Son. Thus they spoke of the Holy Ghost as "the Spirit of Christ, proceeding from the Father, and receiving of the Son."[1] And it has been inferred that many of the earlier Greek writers held, as did the Latins, a real procession from both the Father and the Son, although they were not willing to express themselves otherwise than in the words of the Creed.

Theodoret, in the fifth century, appears to have been the first of the Greeks who brought the question out into bold relief ; for, taking offence at some expressions of Cyril, who speaking of the Spirit had used the words ἴδιον τὸ Πνεῦμα τοῦ Χριστοῦ, he declares, that, if by such an expression he meant "that the Spirit derived His Being either from or through the Son, then the saying was to be rejected as blasphemous and profane ; for we believe the Lord when He saith, 'the Spirit which proceedeth from the Father,' and we believe St. Paul in like manner saying, 'we have not received the Spirit of the world, but the Spirit which is of God.'"[2] St. Cyril, not directly replying to Theodoret, at least not entering fully upon the doctrine of the Procession, there appears to have been little controversy about it in the East, until attention was roused to the subject by the conduct of some portions of the Western Church. The question having been for some time discussed, whether or not the Spirit proceeded from the Son as well as from the Father, the Churches of France and Spain not only asserted such to be the case, but actually added to the Creed of Constantinople the words *Filioque* ("and the Son"), and so chanted the Creed in their Liturgies with the clause *Credimus et in Spiritum Sanctum Dominum et vivificatorem, ex Patre Filioque procedentem*.[3] In the early part of the ninth century Pope Leo III. was appealed to, and decreed in a Synod held at Aquisgranum, that no

---

[1] Πνεῦμα Χριστοῦ, Πνεῦμα Πατρὸς ἐκπορευόμενον. καὶ τοῦ Υἱοῦ λάμβανον. Epiphan. *Hœres.* LXIX. Tom. I. p. 788. Colon. 1682. See Suicer, I. 1070; Pearson, p. 324, note. Similar or stronger language used on this subject may be seen in the following : Εἰ τοίνυν παρὰ τοῦ Πατρὸς ἐκπορεύεται καὶ ἐκ τοῦ ἐμοῦ, φησι ὁ Κύριος, λήψεται, ὃν τρόπον οὐδεὶς ἔγνω τὸν Πατέρα εἰ μὴ ὁ Υἱὸς, οὐδὲ τὸν Υἱὸν εἰ μὴ ὁ Πατὴρ· οὕτως τολμῶσι λέγειν (f. τολμῶ συλλέγειν) οὐδὲ τὸ Πνεῦμα εἰ μὴ ὁ Υἱὸς ἐξ οὗ λαμβάνει, καὶ ὁ Πατὴρ ἐξ οὗ ἐκπορεύεται. Epiph. *Hœres.* LXXIV. 10, Tom. I. p. 898. Colon. — ζωῆ δὲ ὅλος ὁ Θεὸς, οὐκοῦν ζωὴ ἐκ ζωῆς ὁ Υἱὸς, ἐγὼ γάρ εἰμι ἡ ἀλήθεια καὶ ἡ ζωὴ, τὸ δὲ ἅγιον Πνεῦμα παρ' ἀμφοτέρων, Πνεῦμα ἐκ Πνεύματος. *Hœres.* LXXIV. 7, Tom. I. p. 895.

[2] Pearson, *On the Creed*, p. 325, note. Suicer, I. 1070.

[3] In very early Latin Councils this addition of the *Filioque* is made : as in the first Council of Bracara, A. D. 411, and in the third Council of Toledo, A. D. 589, where the Constantinopolitan Creed is recited. (Bingham, Bk. X. ch. IV. § 16.) The Council of Toledo was that which first ordered the Constantinopolitan Creed to be used in the Liturgy of the Spanish Church. (Bingham, ibid. § 7.) With regard to the insertion of the words *Filioque* in the Confession of the Council of Bracara, it now appears that they are not genuine, but foisted into it in later times. See Waterland, *Hist. of Athan. Creed, Works*, IV. p. 133, note.

such addition ought to be made to the creeds of the Church. Nay, so important did he deem a strict adherence to the symbols in their original form, that he caused the Constantinopolitan Creed, in the very words in which it had been penned at the council, to be graven on silver plates, both in Latin and Greek, and so to be publicly set forth in the Church.[1]

Afterwards, however, Pope Nicolas the First had a violent controversy with Photius, patriarch of Constantinople. Ignatius, who had been deposed from that see, and succeeded by Photius, appealed to Pope Nicolas, who took the part of Ignatius, and excommunicated Photius; who in his turn assembled a council at Constantinople, in 866, and excommunicated Nicolas. Subsequently Ignatius having been recalled by Basilius the Macedonian, and Photius degraded, a council was held at Constantinople (A. D. 869), which is called by the Latins the eighth Œcumenical Council, in which the controversies between the Eastern and Western Churches were hushed for the time. Among the subjects which had been introduced into this unhappy discussion, the most prominent was the question concerning the Procession of the Holy Ghost; Photius charging the Latins with having adulterated the Creed of Constantinople by the addition of *Filioque*, and the Latins vigorously defending themselves concerning this and other charges.[2]

On the death of Ignatius, A. D. 878, Photius was again restored to the patriarchal see, when John the Eighth was Bishop of Rome. On his accession he again renewed the controversies with the West; and in a council held at Constantinople, A. D. 879 (owned by the Greeks as the eighth Œcumenical), it was declared that the addition of *Filioque* should be taken away. Leo the Philosopher afterwards again deposed Photius, and confined him in an Armenian convent, where he died in the year 891.[3]

The contest between the Churches, now suspended for a time, was revived in the year 1053, by Michael Cerularius, patriarch of Constantinople. Between him and Leo IX., Bishop of Rome, a violent contest arose, both on the subject of their respective jurisdictions and concerning the doctrines in dispute between the two great branches of the Church. Cerularius wrote, in his own name and that of Leo Bishop of Achrida, a strong letter to John Bishop of Trani in Apulia, charging the Latins with various errors. Leo

---

[1] Pearson, *On the Creed*, p. 325; Mosheim, Cent. IX. pt. II. ch. III. § 18.

[2] The famous Ratramn, whose book on the Eucharist exercised so important an influence on the English Reformation, was a principal champion of the Latins in this dispute.

[3] Mosheim, Cent. IX. pt. II. ch. III. §§ 27–32; Pearson, as above.

therefore summoned a Council at Rome, and excommunicated the Greek Churches. Constantine Monomachus, the emperor, in vain strove to quench the flame of discord; and though legates were sent from Rome to Constantinople, instead of endeavouring to allay the strife, they solemnly excommunicated Cerularius, Leo of Achrida, and their adherents, who, in their turn, in a public council excommunicated them.[1] Thus arose the schism between the Eastern and Western Churches, which has never since been healed.

Section II. — SCRIPTURAL PROOF.

THE first I. and second II. heads of this Article concern the Divinity and the Personality of the Holy Ghost.

Both these were treated under the First Article, and it is not necessary to repeat the arguments here. It may be enough to add that among the strongest passages of Scripture in proof of these doctrines will be found the following: —

Divinity. Matt. xii. 32. Acts v. 3, 4. 1 Cor. iii. 16; compare 1 Cor. vi. 19.

Personality. Matt. xii. 32; xxviii. 19. John xiv. 16, 26; xvi. 8, 13. Acts v. 3, 4. Rom. viii. 26. 1 Cor. xii. 11. Eph. iv. 30. 1 John v. 7.

III. The third division of the subject is concerning the Procession of the Holy Ghost; the Article, after the Latin versions of the Constantinopolitan Creed, and the Creed of St. Athanasius, asserting that the Holy Ghost proceeds from the Father and the Son.

The distinction between the three Persons in the Godhead was set forth in treating on the First Article. The relation of God the Son to God the Father, how that from all eternity God the Son derived His being from God the Father, by a proper but ineffable generation, was set forth in the FIRST part of the Second Article.

Now, whereas it is certain that the Scriptures ever speak of the Second Person of the Trinity as the Son of God, and as *begotten* of the Father, so it is equally certain that they speak of the Spirit as *coming* forth or *proceeding* from the Father, but never **as** *begotten* of Him. The early Christians, observing this distinc-

[1] Mosheim, Cent. XI. pt. II. ch. III. §§ 9–11.

tion, cautiously adhering to the language of inspiration, and striving to imbibe the notions conveyed by it, ever taught that it was
peculiar to the Father to be underived and unbegotten; to the
Son, to be begotten; to the Holy Ghost, to be proceeding.[1]

1. That the Holy Ghost proceedeth from the Father scarcely
needs to be proved.

In Matt. x. 20, He is called "the Spirit of the Father." In
Rom. viii. 11, He is called "the Spirit of Him that raised up Jesus
from the dead." In John xiv. 26, "the Comforter, which is the
Holy Ghost," is promised, as to be sent "by the Father in Christ's
name." In John xv. 26, we read of the "Comforter . . . even
the Spirit of truth which proceedeth from the Father." Compare
also Matt. iii. 16. Acts v. 9. 1 Cor. ii. 10, 11, 14; iii. 16; vi. 19,
&c. Accordingly, there never has been any doubt, among those
who admit the doctrine of the Trinity, that as the Son is begotten
of the Father, so the Spirit proceeds from the Father.

2. But though the doctrine of the procession of the Spirit from
the Father is thus unquestionable, it has been seen, that the
Greeks doubted the propriety of saying that the Holy Spirit proceedeth from the Son as well as from the Father. They doubted
it, as it seems, merely because in John xv. 26, it is said "that the
Spirit of truth proceedeth from the Father," and there is no passage
of Scripture, which, in the same express terms, says that the Spirit
proceedeth from the Son.

Yet if we except this one expression of John xv. 26, every other
expression whatsoever, from which we infer that the Spirit proceedeth from the Father, is used in like manner concerning His
relation to the Son. For example : —

(1) Is He called "the Spirit of God," "the Spirit of the Father," "the Spirit of Him that raised up Jesus?" In like manner
He is called "the Spirit of Christ," "the Spirit of the Son," "the
Spirit of Jesus Christ." Thus we read, Rom. viii. 9, "If any man
have not the Spirit of Christ;" where it is evident the Apostle
means the Holy Spirit of God spoken of in the preceding sentence.
Gal. iv. 6, "God hath sent forth the Spirit of His Son." Phil. i.
19, "The supply of the Spirit of Jesus Christ." 1 Pet. i. 11,
"The Spirit of Christ," which was in the prophets.

And so surely is this the case, that the Greeks themselves were
even willing to call the Holy Ghost the Spirit of the Son; confessing that "He proceedeth from the Father, and is the Spirit of

---

[1] Ἴδιον Πατρὸς μὲν ἡ ἀγεννησία, Υἱοῦ δὲ   Greg. Naz. Orat. XXIII. Tom. I. p. 422
γέννησις, Πνεύματος δὲ ἡ ἐκπεμψις. — Colon. Suicer, I. p. 1069.

the Son." And hence many of our divines, and even divines of
the Church of Rome, have concluded that their difference on this
point from the Western Church was but *in modo loquendi,* in manner of speech, not in fundamental truth.[1]

(2) But, again, do we infer that the Spirit proceedeth from
the Father, because He is sent by the Father, and is breathed
forth into the prophets by the Father? Still, in like manner, we
read that the same Spirit is sent by the Son, and was by Him
breathed upon His Apostles. Thus He says Himself, John xv. 26,
" The Comforter, whom I will send unto you from the Father."
John xvi. 7, " If I go not away, the Comforter will not come unto
you ; but if I depart, I will send Him unto you." And in John
xx. 22, after He had risen from the dead, " He breathed on them,
and saith unto them, Receive ye the Holy Ghost."

Now, our principal reasons for concluding that the Spirit of God
proceeds from God the Father are these : namely, that He is called
the Spirit of the Father; that as the Father sends the Son, who is
begotten of Him, so He sends the Spirit; and that He sends Him
especially in that manner which in Scripture is called inspiring
or breathing forth. From all this we conclude that, like as the
Son is begotten, so the Spirit proceedeth of the Father. Yet the
Scriptures set forth the relation of the Spirit to the Son, in all
these respects, in the very same language in which they set forth
the relation of the Spirit to the Father. Hence we conclude, that,
as the Spirit proceedeth from the Father, so He proceeds from the
Son.[2] And though we may question the wisdom of adding the
words *Filioque* to a Creed drawn up by a General Council, without

---

[1] Laud, *Conference with Fisher,* p. 19
(Oxf. 1839), Sect. 9, who quotes Damascene (Lib. i. *Fid. Orth.* c. 11) as saying,
"Non ex Filio, sed Spiritum Filii esse
dicimus."

[2] " Nec possumus dicere quod Spiritus
Sanctus et a Filio non procedat : neque
enim frustra idem Spiritus et Patris et
Filii Spiritus dicitur. Nec video quid
aliud significare voluerit, cum sufflans in
faciem discipulorum ait, *Accipite Spiritum
Sanctum.* Neque enim flatus ille corpo-
reus, cum sensu corporaliter tangendi
procedens ex corpore, substantia Spiritus
Sancti fuit, sed demonstratio per con-
gruam significationem, non tantum a
Patre sed et a Filio procedere Spiritum
Sanctum," &c. — August. *De Trinitat.*
Lib. iv. cap. xx. Tom. viii. p. 829. "De
utroque autem procedere sic docetur,
quia ipse Filius ait, *De Patre procedit.* Et
cum resurrexit a mortuis et apparuisset

discipulis suis, insufflavit et ait, *Accipite
Spiritum Sanctum,* ut Eum etiam de Se
procedere ostenderet. Et ipsa est *Virtus*
quæ *de Illo exibat,* sicut legitur in Evangelio, et sanabat omnes."— Ibid. Lib. xv.
cap. xxvi. p. 998. See also, *De Civitate
Dei,* Lib. xi. c. xxiv. Tom. vii. p. 290 ;
where S. Augustine, showing that the
Holy Spirit is a *Person,* doubts if He can
be called the *goodness* of the Father and
the Son; but observing that the Father
is a Spirit and holy, and the Son is a
Spirit and holy, and yet the Third Person of the Trinity is called the *Holy
Spirit* of the Father and of the Son, he
supposes that that Third Person may be
called the Spirit both of the Father and
of the Son, and the Holiness both of the
Father and of the Son, but yet a substantial Holiness, consubstantial with
both.

the authority of a General Council; we yet do not question the truth of the doctrine conveyed by these words, and which, we believe, was implicitly held by the divines of the Eastern Church, though they shrank from explicit exposition of it in terms.[1]

[1] The great objection which the Eastern Church makes to the *Filioque*, is, that it implies the existence of two ἀρχαί in the Godhead : and, if we believe in δύο ἄναρχοι, we, in effect, believe in two Gods. The unity of the Godhead can only be maintained by acknowledging the Father to be the sole Ἀρχὴ or Πηγὴ θεότητος, who from all eternity has communicated His own Godhead to His co-eternal and consubstantial Son and Spirit. This reasoning is generally true. But, as the doctrine of the Procession of the Spirit from the Father and the Son pre-supposes the eternal Generation of the Son from the Father, it does not follow that that doctrine impugns the Catholic belief in the Μία Ἀρχή.

ARTICLE VI.

Of the Sufficiency of the Holy Scriptures for Salvation.

HOLY Scripture containeth all things necessary to salvation : so that whatsoever is not read therein, nor may be proved thereby, is not to be required of any man, that it should be believed as an article of the Faith, or be thought requisite necessary to salvation.

In the name of the Holy Scripture we do understand those Canonical Books of the old and new Testament of whose authority was never any doubt in the Church.

Of the Names and Number of the Canonical Books.

Genesis.	The Second Book of Chronicles.
Exodus.	
Leviticus.	The First Book of Esdras.
Numbers.	
Deuteronomy.	The Second Book of Esdras.
Joshua.	
Judges.	The Book of Esther.
Ruth.	
The First Book of Samuel.	The Book of Job.
	The Psalms.
The Second Book of Samuel.	The Proverbs.
	Ecclesiastes, or Preacher.
The First Book of Kings.	Cantica, or Songs of Solomon.
The Second Book of Kings.	Four Prophets the greater.
The First Book of Chronicles.	Twelve Prophets the less.

And the other books (as Hierome saith) the Church doth read for example of life and instruction of manners ; but yet doth it not apply them to establish any doctrine.

Such are these following : —

The Third Book of Esdras.	Baruch the Prophet.
The Fourth Book of Esdras.	The Song of the Three Children.
The Book of Tobias.	The Story of Susanna.
The Book of Judith.	Of Bel and the Dragon.
The rest of the Book of Esther.	The Prayer of Manasses.
The Book of Wisdom.	The First Book of Maccabees.
Jesus the Son of Sirach.	The Second Book of Maccabees.

All the books of the new Testament, as they are commonly received, we do receive and account them Canonical.

De Divinis Scripturis, quod sufficiant ad Salutem.

SCRIPTURA sacra continet omnia, quæ ad salutem sunt necessaria, ita, ut quicquid in ea nec legitur, neque inde probari potest, non sit a quoquam exigendum, ut tanquam articulus Fidei credatur, aut ad salutis necessitatem requiri putetur.

Sacræ Scripturæ nomine, eos Canonicos libros veteris, et novi Testamenti intelligimus, de quorum authoritate in Ecclesia nunquam dubitatum est.

De Nominibus et Numero librorum sacræ Canonicæ Scripturæ Veteris Testamenti.

Genesis.	Secundus Liber Paralipomen.
Exodus.	
Leviticus.	Primus Liber Esdræ.
Numeri.	
Deuteron.	Secundus Liber Esdræ.
Josuæ.	
Judicum.	Liber Hester.
Ruth.	Liber Job.
Prior Liber Samuelis.	Psalmi.
	Proverbia.
Secundus Liber Samuelis.	Ecclesiastes vel Concionator.
Prior Liber Regum.	Cantica Salomonis.
Secundus Liber Regum.	IV Prophetæ majores.
Prior Liber Paralipom.	XII Prophetæ minores.

Alios autem libros (ut ait Hieronymus) legit quidem Ecclesia, ad exempla vitæ, et formandos mores : illos tamen ad dogmata confirmanda non adhibet, ut sunt.

Tertius Liber Esdræ.	Baruch Propheta.
	Canticum trium Puerorum.
Quartus Liber Esdræ.	Historia Susannæ.
Liber Tobiæ.	De Bel et Dracone.
Liber Judith.	Oratio Manasses.
Reliquum Libri Hester.	Prior Lib. Machabeorum.
Liber Sapientiæ.	Secundus Liber Machabeorum.
Liber Jesu filii Sirach.	

Novi Testamenti omnes libros (ut vulgo recepti sunt) recipimus, et habemus pro Canonicis.

THIS is the first Article of the Church which can be called controversial. In some respects, it might have seemed natural to have put it as the first Article ; as in the Helvetic Confession the first Article is *De Scriptura Sancta, vero Dei Verbo.* But our reformers wisely put forth, in the beginning of their confession of faith, those doctrines on which the Church universal for fifteen centuries had agreed, and which are the foundations of the Christian faith. Accordingly the first five Articles treat of the Trinity, the Incarnation, the Redemption of the world, the Sanctification of Christians, and the Judgment of all men. Unity on these points was of old times considered to constitute Catholic Christianity ; and by declaring her orthodoxy on these Catholic doctrines, the Church of England, in the very front of her confessions, declares herself orthodox and Catholic.

This done in the first five Articles, she, in the next three, treats of the Rule of Faith, the Scriptures, and the Creeds deduced from them.

The present Article, as it stood in the forty-two Articles of 1552, lacked all the concluding part concerning the Canon of Scripture and the Apocrypha, and treated only of the Sufficiency of Scripture for Salvation. The latter part was added in 1562. The original Article also contained a clause which was omitted in 1562. After the words, " whatsoever is neither read therein, nor may be proved thereby," the words were added, " *although it be sometime received of the godly, and profitable for an order and comeliness,* yet no man ought to be constrained to believe it as an article of faith," &c.

As the Article now stands, it treats of several distinct points, namely, Scripture and Tradition, the Canon of Scripture, the Apocrypha. On all these points demonstration and history are intimately connected ; history in this case being a material part of demonstration. It will therefore be better not to separate them. In the following sections then I propose to consider, —

First. The Sufficiency of Scripture for Salvation ; Secondly. The Canon of Scripture ; Thirdly. The true value of Tradition, and the reading of the Apocrypha.

17

Section I. — THE SUFFICIENCY OF SCRIPTURE FOR
SALVATION.

THAT we may see the force of the words of the Article on this important subject, it will be necessary to consider what opinions were opposed by it. Those opinions were the doctrines of the Church of Rome concerning Scripture and Tradition. It will be well therefore to begin by setting the statements of the Church of Rome and those of the Church of England one against the other; and when we see wherein we differ, we may then proceed to show which is in the right.

Now the decrees of the Council of Trent sufficiently express the doctrines of the Church of Rome. In that Council certain Articles, professedly taken from the writings of the Lutheran divines on the subject of Scripture, were discussed in the third session. And first, the fathers of the Council agreed to condemn the opinion " that all articles of the Christian faith, necessary to be believed, are contained in the Holy Scriptures, and that it is sacrilege to hold the oral Tradition of the Church to be of equal authority with the old and new Testaments." [1] The formal decree of the Council was drawn up in the fourth session, in the year 1546, shortly after the death of Luther, and six years before the putting forth of the forty-two Articles of our own Church in 1552. This decree declares that " the truth is contained *in the written books*, and in the *unwritten traditions*, which, having been received by the Apostles, either from the mouth of Christ Himself, or from the dictates of the Holy Spirit, were handed down even to us; " and that the Council " receives and venerates with *equal feeling of piety and reverence* all the books of the old and new Testament, since one God was the Author of them both, *and also the traditions*, relating as well to *faith* as to *morals*, as having, either from the mouth of Christ Himself, or from the dictation of the Holy Ghost, been preserved by continuous succession in the Catholic Church." [2]

Exactly corresponding with this decree of the Council are the

---

[1] Sarpi, *Hist. of the Council of Trent*, translated by Brent. London, 1676, p. 141.

[2] " Sacrosancta œcumenica et generalis Tridentina Synodus, in Spiritu Sancto legitime congregata, præsidentibus in ea eisdem tribus Apostolicæ sedis legatis, hoc sibi perpetuo ante oculos proponens, ut sublatis erroribus, puritas ipsa Evan- gelii in Ecclesia conservetur : quod promissum ante per prophetas in Scrip- turis sanctis Dominus noster, Jesus Christus, Dei Filius, proprio ore primum promulgavit, deinde per suos Apostolos tanquam fontem omnis salutaris veritatis et morum disciplinæ, omni creaturæ præ- dicari jussit; perspiciens hanc veritatem et disciplinam contineri *in libris scriptis et*

statements of the great Roman Catholic divines. For example, Bellarmine says, " The controversy between us and the heretics consists in two things. The first is, that *we* assert that in Scripture is not expressly contained all necessary doctrine, whether concerning faith or morals, and therefore that, besides the written word of God, there is moreover needed the unwritten word, *i. e.* Divine and Apostolical Tradition. But *they* teach, that all things necessary for faith and morals are contained in the Scriptures, and that therefore there is no need of the unwritten word." [1]

Now these statements are not easily misunderstood. The Church of Rome, both in her Council, and by the mouth of her most eminent divines, asserts that Scripture does not contain all that is necessary for faith and morals; but that there is need of a traditional doctrine, an unwritten word, which is handed down by unbroken tradition in the Church, and which she, the Church of Rome, esteems with the same feelings of piety and reverence with which she receives the Holy Scriptures. It is not merely an Hermeneutical Tradition, *i. e.* certain doctrines handed down from early times, which are useful for clearing up and explaining obscurities in Holy Writ; nor is it an Ecclesiastical Tradition, *i. e.* Tradition concerning Church discipline, rites and ceremonies; but it is a traditional revelation concerning doctrine, in matters of faith and morals, which is not to be found in Scripture, and which is equally certain, equally Divine, and equally to be embraced and reverenced with Scripture itself. Scripture and tradition are parallel, equal, and equally venerable sources of doctrine; and one without the other is not sufficient for salvation.

Such being the statement of the Church of Rome, we may the better understand the statement of the Church of England. Her statement is, as expressed in the Article of 1552, that, however traditions may be " sometimes received by the faithful as godly, and profitable for order and comeliness," yet " Scripture

---

sine scripto traditionibus, quæ ab ipsius Christi ore et Apostolis acceptæ, Spiritu Sancto dictante, quasi per manus traditæ ad nos usque pervenerunt; Orthodoxorum patrum exempla secuta, omnes libros tam veteris quam novi Testamenti, cum utriusque unus Deus sit auctor, *nec-non traditiones* ipsas, tum ad fidem, tum ad mores pertinentes, tamquam vel ore tenus a Christo vel a Spiritu Sancto dictatas, *et continua successione in Ecclesia Catholica conservatas, pari pietatis affectu ac reverentia suscipit ac veneratur.*" — Sess. IV. Can. I. Conc. XIV. 746.

[1] Bellarmin. *De Verbo Dei non Scripto,* Lib. IV. cap. III. " Controversia igitur inter nos et hereticos in duobus consistit. Primum est, quod nos asserimus, in Scripturis non contineri expresse totam doctrinam necessariam sive de fide sive de moribus ; et proinde præter Verbum Dei scriptum, requiri etiam Verbum Dei non scriptum, id est, divinas et Apostolicas traditiones. At ipsi docent, in Scripturis omnia contineri ad fide met mores necessaria, et proinde non esse opus ullo Verbo non scripto."

containeth all things necessary to salvation;" and no man ought
" to be constrained to believe as an article of faith, or repute requisite to the necessity of salvation, whatever is neither read therein,
nor may be proved thereby."

The degree of value which the Church of England has assigned
to Tradition, which, she said, in the forty-two Articles, was " sometimes received by the faithful as godly, and profitable for order,"
we shall see in the third section.   Here we have to show, that, as
regards articles of faith, and as to necessity of salvation, nothing
ought to be required of any man " which is not read in Scripture, nor may be proved thereby."

Scripture, according to the Church of England, rightly interpreted, contains all that is necessary to save the soul.   From it,
by fair and logical inference, may be deduced everything which
ought to be imposed as an article of faith.   It will be seen, hereafter, that she does not despise nor underrate the light of learning,
nor the light of antiquity, but that, as the ground of appeal, she
maintains the supremacy, and the sole supremacy, of the written
word of God.[1]

Now in proving the soundness of . the Anglican, in opposition
to the Romish position, we may proceed in the following order.

We may prove — I. That Scripture is in favour of it ; — II.
That Reason is in favour of it ; — III. That the Primitive
Fathers are in favour of it.

I.   Scripture is in favour of the doctrine of the Anglican Church,
namely, that the written word of God is sufficient for salvation,
containing all necessary articles of faith, and rules of life.

On most questions this argument is the most conclusive that
can be brought; but on the Sufficiency of Scripture we are not
so likely to find Scripture speaking plainly, as on many other
points.   It does indeed bear witness to itself, and yet its witness is
true.   But though both parties have appealed to it, yet neither
party have been satisfied, that, on this particular point, its high
authority will exhaust the subject.

1. To take, first of all, the arguments which have been alleged
from Scripture, as *against* its own sufficiency: we read, that our

---

[1] " Unto a Christian man there can be
nothing either more necessary or profitable than the knowledge of Holy Scripture, forasmuch as in it is contained
God's true Word, setting forth His glory
and also man's duty, and there is no
truth nor doctrine necessary for our jus
tification and everlasting salvation, but
that is, or may be, drawn out of that fountain and well of truth." — Beginning of
the *Homily on Holy Scripture.*

Lord said to His disciples (John xvi. 12) : "I have yet many things to say unto you, but ye cannot bear them now." Therefore it is inferred that there was need of further instruction, orally delivered to the Church, and handed down by tradition, beyond what our Lord revealed, whilst on earth. But the true meaning of the passage is explained by the next verse, which promises that, " when the Spirit of truth was come, He should guide them into all truth." It was to the teaching of the Spirit, by whom the Apostles were afterwards inspired, that our Lord bade them look forward, for the filling up of what His own personal teaching had left deficient. The substance of that teaching of the Spirit, we believe, is preserved to us in the Acts of the Apostles, the Epistles. and the Apocalypse ; not in unwritten tradition.

Again, it is said, " There are also many other things which Jesus did, the which, if they should be written every one, even the world could not contain the books that should be written " (John xxi. 25). Therefore Jesus taught many things not set down in Scripture : we cannot believe that He taught anything super- fluous : therefore there must be something necessary, besides what we read in Scripture. Where are we to seek for this ? Of course, in unwritten tradition.

To this we reply, that doubtless every word spoken by our blessed Lord was most valuable. Many of those words indeed are not in Scripture ; no ! nor yet in tradition : for it never yet was pretended that oral tradition had preserved every word our Saviour uttered. So that, if this argument proves anything, it proves too much ; for it proves, not only the insufficiency of Scripture, but the insufficiency of Scripture and tradition together. What we say is simply, that so much of Christ's divine teaching, and of the teaching of the Spirit to the Apostles, is set down in Scrip- ture, as is necessary for salvation, and for the proving of all neces- sary articles of faith. It is no argument against this, to say that many things, which our Saviour said, are not in Scripture.

The same answer may be given to the argument drawn from the fact, that, during the forty days between His resurrection and His ascension, our Lord " spake of the things pertaining to the kingdom of God " (Acts i. 3). We know, indeed, that His speeches then are not set down in Scripture. But we equally know that they are not to be found in any other tradition. And we do not know that there was anything spoken by Him then, which it is necessary to our salvation that we should know, over and above what we have recorded in Scripture.

It is further urged, that St. Paul cuts short a controversy, not by reference to Scripture, but by appeal to the customs of the Church (1 Cor. xi. 16) : " If any man seem to be contentious, we have no such custom, neither the Churches of God." 'It was a matter of ceremony, namely, that a woman's head should be covered in the house of God ; and assuredly the Church of England fully admits that " the Church hath power to decree rites and ceremonies " (Art. xx.), and that " whosoever, through his private judgment, breaks the traditions and ceremonies of the Church, which be not repugnant to the word of God, ought to be rebuked openly " (Art. xxxiv.)   But this is no proof that doctrines of the faith rest on an authority not written.   It should be sufficient to satisfy any caviller concerning *forms*, that the Churches of God have, or have not, a custom or a form.   But it is not likely that the Apostle would *for doctrine* refer to the Church's customs, when he himself was infallibly guided by the Spirit of God.

But St. Paul, it is said, actually does refer to ordinances and traditions, and forms of words, and a *depositum* to be guarded ; all which are evidently oral traditions of the Church.   " Now I praise you, brethren, that ye remember me in all things, and keep the ordinances, as I delivered them to you," 1 Cor. xi. 2.   " O Timothy, keep that which is committed to thy trust," 1 Tim. vi. 20. " Hold fast the form of sound words which thou hast heard of me, in faith and love which is in Christ Jesus.   That good thing, which was committed unto thee, ($\tau\grave{\eta}\nu$ $\kappa\alpha\lambda\grave{\eta}\nu$ $\pi\alpha\rho\alpha\kappa\alpha\tau\alpha\theta\acute{\eta}\kappa\eta\nu$) keep by the Holy Ghost which dwelleth in us," 2 Tim. i. 13, 14.   " The things that thou hast heard of me among many witnesses, the same commit thou to faithful men, who shall be able to teach others also," 2 Tim. ii. 2.   From all this it is urged, that the Church and the bishops had ordinances intrusted to them, and doctrines committed to them, which they were to watch and guard, and hand down carefully to others.   But all this we readily admit. Timothy was taught by St. Paul : and the doctrine which he had so learned was a sacred deposit which he had carefully to guard, and to teach to those committed to his care ; especially to the clergy under him, and the bishops who were to succeed him.   Before the Scriptures of the new Testament had been written, or at least collected, this must have been a most important principle ; for so only could the torch of truth be kept alight.   And even after the new Testament had been written, and was in the hands of all men, it was doubtless most important that bishops and Churches should be rightly and soundly instructed in the truth

and right meaning of the Scriptures, and should guard themselves
and their flocks against perverting the truth and falling into error.
But there is not therefore any reason to apprehend, that Timothy
or the Church had learned any other doctrines besides those contained in the holy Scriptures, or that the sacred deposit committed
to their charge was any other than the aggregate of Christian doctrine, which they had been taught catechetically, and which they
were to keep from defilement and error by the Holy Ghost which
dwelleth in us.   We well know that the possession of the Scriptures, as a source of truth and as a final appeal, does not supersede
the necessity of Christian education, and sound oral instruction in
the faith : and to every person, nowadays, instructed by Creeds
and Catechisms in the true doctrine of Christ, it might be said,
" Keep that good thing which was committed unto you ; " " Hold
fast the form of sound words." Yet all this instruction and this
sacred deposit may be deducible from Scripture, and virtually
contained in it.

But further, it is said that the Thessalonians are actually bidden to " stand fast and hold the *traditions* which ye have been
taught whether by word or our epistle," 2 Thess. ii. 15.   Therefore the Apostle bids them attend, not only to Scripture, but to
tradition also.   But the word *tradition* means properly nothing
more than *something delivered, the doctrine of our faith delivered to
us.*   And there being two ways of delivering doctrines to us,
either by writing or by word of mouth, it signifies either of them
indifferently.   " ' παράδοσις, *tradition*, is the same with δόγμα, doctrine, and παραδιδόναι is the same with διδάσκειν,' say the gramma-
rians ; and the παραδοθεῖσα πίστις in St. Jude, ' the faith once delivered,' is the same which St. Paul explicates by saying, παραδόσεις
ἃς ἐδιδάχθητε, ' the traditions,' that is, ' the doctrines ye were taught.'
And St. Irenæus (Lib. III. ch. iv.) calls it a tradition apostolical,
that ' Christ took the cup,' and said, ' it was His Blood,' and to
believe in one God, and in Christ ' who was born of a Virgin,'
was the old tradition ; that is the thing which was delivered, and
not at first written, ' which was kept by the barbarians.' " [1]   It
may be added, that the very words of St. Paul, in the passage now
alluded to, prove in themselves that tradition, according to him,
was not necessarily oral tradition, or traditions floating in the
Church ; for he calls his own Epistles, or the doctrine contained in
them, *tradition*, — " *traditions*, which you have been taught either
by word or by our *Epistle*." What therefore the Apostle here

[1] Jer. Taylor, *Dissuasive from Popery*, Part II. Bk. I. Sect. 3.

enjoins on the Thessalonians is simply, that, as he had taught them by preaching, and as he had enjoined them by letter, so they should believe and live. This instruction, thus received, was the tradition to which he alludes. But it by no means follows, because, before Scripture was completed, the Apostles gave oral and epistolary instruction, to which their hearers were to attend, that therefore, after the Scriptures were completed and collected, there must be left, floating about, a stream of traditional truth, which is not to be found in those Scriptures, thus completed and collected. Before the Scriptures of the new Testament were written, there must of course have been need of tradition, or instruction by word of mouth ; and such instruction coming from inspired Apostles was, no doubt, of as much value as what they committed to writing. But the question is, whether they delivered anything essential to our salvation, which they, or some of them, did not subsequently put down in writing, so that it should be carefully preserved, and be a constant witness in the Church. Certainly neither this, nor any of the before-cited passages of Scripture, prove that they did.[1]

Once more, it is said that Christ promised to His Church, "The gates of Hell shall not prevail against it," Matt. xvi. 18 ; "I am with you alway, even unto the end of the world," Matt. xxviii. 20 ; "Whatsoever ye shall bind on earth shall be bound in Heaven," Matt. xviii. 18, &c. ; and that these promises prove that a certain infallibility should reside in the Church, which both makes it a sure keeper of the truth, and renders all its traditions and decrees of sacred authority. But we may reply, that, even if we concede that the whole Church, fully represented, might so claim the promise of Christ to be present with it, and to guide it, that it should not fall into errors in matters of faith ; yet it follows not, that it would be authorized to preserve or to decree any truth which cannot be proved from Scripture. Ancient councils settled many points of faith, and drew up creeds and confessions ; but they professed them to be accordant with, and capable of proof from, Scripture. And though the Church is a keeper and a witness of Holy Writ, and may expound Scripture for the instruction of her children, and in such expositions may look for the promise

---

[1] The passages from Scripture which have been quoted in the text are all alleged by Bellarmine, *De Verbo Dei non Scripto*, Lib. IV.

On the proper meaning of the word *Tradition*, see Jer. Taylor as above ,

Usher, *Answer to a Jesuit*, ch. II. ; Bp. Patrick's *Discourse about Tradition*, in the first volume of Gibson, *Preservative against Popery*, p. 190 ; Van Mildert *Bampton Lectures*, Sermon III.

of Christ and the guidance of His Spirit; it by no means follows, that she has authority to add to " the faith once delivered to the saints," or to set up any standard of doctrine besides that written word of God which is intrusted to her, and to which she is to look as the source of all heavenly wisdom and truth.

2. And here we may dismiss the arguments from Scripture, which have been brought to prove that Scripture does not contain all doctrine necessary for salvation and godliness. We proceed to consider those passages which appear to prove the direct contrary, namely, that all things, of necessity to be believed, are contained in, or may be deduced from, the written word.

The following are amongst the texts commonly alleged :—

" Ye shall not add unto the word which I command you, neither shall ye diminish aught from it." Deut. iv. 2.

" The law of the Lord is perfect, converting the soul." Ps. xix. 7.

" Search the Scriptures; for in them ye think ye have eternal life : and they are they which testify of Me." John v. 39.

" From a child thou hast known the holy Scriptures, which are able to make thee wise unto salvation. . . . . All Scripture is given by inspiration of God, and is profitable for doctrine, for reproof, for correction, for instruction in righteousness, that the man of God may be perfect, throughly furnished unto all good works." 2 Tim. iii. 15–17.

These passages *appear* to prove the perfection and sufficiency of the Scriptures. But it is argued against this inference, that, with regard to the first two passages, they speak of God's commandments and God's law, whether written or unwritten.[1] The third passage may be, and very likely ought to be, translated, not " search," but " ye search the Scriptures." And all the passages relate to the old Testament, not to the new ; for neither could the Jews search the new Testament Scriptures, nor could Timothy have learned the new Testament from his childhood ; since none of the books of the new Testament were then written. If, therefore, these passages prove the sufficiency of Scripture, they prove that the old Testament was sufficient without the new, and therefore prove too much. The passages indeed prove, that all which comes from God is perfect, and very necessary for instruction ; but do not fully prove that nothing but Scripture is necessary.

---

[1] Bellarmine indeed argues that the passage from Deut. iv. 2 applies only to the *unwritten word :* " the word which I *speak* unto you." The word however is not " *speak*," as he renders it, but מְצַוֶּה " *command*," as our translators give it. — Bellarmin. *De Verbo Dei non Scripto,* Lib. IV.

Another argument is drawn from the following passages: —

"Forasmuch as many have taken in hand to set forth in order a declaration of those things which are most surely believed amongst us . . . . it seemed good to me also . . . . to write unto thee in order, most excellent Theophilus, that thou mightest know the certainty of those things wherein thou hast been instructed." Luke i. 1–4.

"These are written that ye might believe that Jesus is the Christ, the Son of God; and that believing ye might have life through His Name." John xx. 31.

These texts do certainly seem to show that the object of writing the Gospels was expressly that men might not be left to the uncertainty of tradition. Many had taken in hand to set forth an account of the Gospel history: St. Luke therefore was moved to commit it carefully to writing, that no vague accounts might mislead Theophilus, but that by the written word he might "know the *certainty* of those things wherein he had before been catechetically instructed." Very similar to this is the language of St. Peter: "I will endeavour that ye may be able after my decease to have these things always in remembrance," 2 Pet. i. 15. It is true that these three passages only apply to the Gospels of St. Luke and St. John, and the Epistles of St. Peter, and perhaps with them to the Gospel of St. Mark; but they nevertheless give the reasons for writing Scripture, and are, as far as they go, a strong presumption against the vagueness and uncertainty of oral, and in favour of the certainty of written, tradition.

Again, ignorance and error in religion are traced to ignorance of Scripture: "Ye do err, not knowing the Scriptures, nor the power of God," Matt. xxii. 29. The peculiar privilege of the Jews is said to be that "to them were committed the oracles of God," Rom. iii. 1, 2. In matters of doubt, all appeals are made to Scripture. The Beroeans are praised, because they "searched the Scriptures daily, whether those things were so," Acts xvii. 11. So under the old Testament it was "to the law and to the testimony: if they speak not according to this word, it is because there is no light in them," Isai. viii. 20; where the law and the testimony must mean the Law of Moses, and the testimony of God given by the Prophets.

Lastly, there is special reprobation of all traditions which add to Scripture or take from it. The passage in the end of the Apocalypse ("If any man shall add unto these things, God shall add unto him the plagues that are written in this book," &c., Rev.

xxii. 18, 19) may indeed apply only to that book itself, and to the uncorrupted preservation of its text. But we cannot have read the Gospels, without seeing how much those who used Jewish traditions are censured and condemned: " Why do ye transgress the commandment of God by your tradition?" " In vain they do worship Me, teaching for doctrines the commandments of men." Matt. xv. 3, 9, comp. Mark vii. 7–13. It is true, the traditions spoken of were Jewish, not Christian traditions. But the principle was much the same. The Pharisees claimed such traditions as divine. They professed, that they were the unwritten word of God, handed down from the time of Ezra, through the doctors of the Law, and the members of the Great Synagogue. They did not deny the value of the written word, but added the unwritten traditions to it. These they considered, not as corrupting, but as completing the truth. Yet our Lord declared that they " made the word of God of none effect by their tradition " (Mark vii. 13). And thus we may fairly infer that our Lord condemns the general principle of making any addition to the written word, by doctrines professedly handed down from father to son. We see, at least, no difference in principle between the oral traditions of the Jewish, and the oral traditions of the Christian Church.

II. We come next to show, that reason is in favour of the Anglican, in opposition to the Roman rule on this subject.

1. The English Church does not hold that unwritten truth is less true than written truth; and if we could be certain that any unwritten doctrine came from Christ and His Apostles, we should receive it with the same reverence that we pay to the written word. But the reason why we rest our faith upon the written word is this: We know that *it* came from God; but we have no certain knowledge that any unwritten tradition did. The former we *know* to be the mid-day light, the other *may be* but an *ignis fatuus*, and lead us into error.

And let it once more be clearly understood, that the question is not, what value there may be in the testimony of the Early Church to certain doctrines of the faith; not, how far early traditions may be useful for the interpreting of Scripture; not, how far we may be right to adhere to the primitive example, in matters of *discipline* and *ceremony*, even those for which we have no Scriptural authority; but it is, whether besides, parallel with, and independent of the Scripture, there is in the Church a *doctrina tradita*, a doctrine handed down from Christ or His Apostles, of equal authority with Scripture, and demanding equal respect.

As has just now been said, when we search for authority in favour of any doctrine, we can tell at once where to go, if Scripture be our rule. But if we have to depend on something besides, where must we look? The former rule is contained in a small compass, is easily accessible, and with proper assistance may be understood. The latter is to be searched for through many folio volumes; is, at last, not certainly to be found; and is at least as difficult as Scripture itself to be understood and explained. Or, if it be said, that it is not in the writings of the fathers, but in the stream of Church tradition, a deposit which was intrusted to the Church and has never been lost by her; we can only reply, that this is even less certain than traditions which may be searched out from ancient writings, and from them proved to have anciently existed. Tradition by word of mouth is a thing proverbially uncertain. In peculiar conditions of society, or for a short time, it may be sufficient for the preservation of truth. But it is evidently unfitted for a body like the Catholic Church; which was to pervade all nations, extend throughout all ages, weather the storm of ignorance and barbarism at one time, and bear up against the scorching and withering glare of learned infidelity at another.

The very fact that the Scriptures were written, and the history of their writing, seem to prove their sufficiency and perfection. When first revelation was given to man, men's lives were so long that there was little danger lest the light of truth should be lost. Adam, Seth, Enoch, Methuselah, Noah, were in fact all but contemporaries. Seth the son of Adam lived to within fifteen years of the birth of Noah. Tradition therefore may have sufficed for them; and yet we have reason to believe, that, even then, the faith was much corrupted. Again, the sons of Noah must have been contemporary with Abraham, to whom another revelation was given; yet Abraham's fathers had become idolaters. And in the few generations from Abraham to Moses the faith again appears to have been corrupted, if not lost; although from the death of Joseph to the birth of Moses not seventy years had passed. Thus, when the world and the Church were under the most favourable circumstances for preserving tradition of the truth unimpaired, it pleased God to leave the world, with occasional revelations indeed, but mostly with only traditional knowledge of the truth. Yet, even so, such knowledge was soon corrupted, and easily lost. After that, God gave a fuller revelation to Moses, and enjoined that it should be committed to writing; and the book of the Law was deposited in the most sacred place of the Sanctuary, and most carefully guarded and watched, as of inestimable value. Thenceforward, when any great prophet was sent to Israel, though, during his lifetime, he orally taught the people, yet his words were ever committed to writing, that they might be preserved after his death. Nor do we know anything now concerning the teaching of any of the prophets, save only what is handed down to us, not by oral, but by written, tradition, namely, the Scriptures of the old Testament.

Most similar was the case with the Christian Church. At first, whilst our Lord and His Apostles were on earth, their personal teaching, and that of those taught by them, might have sufficed. Yet, even then, errors and perversions were creeping in; and if they had not committed the substance of their teaching to writing, the false traditions of the Judaizers, the Cerinthians, or the Gnostics, might have come down through the Church, instead of the true traditions of the disciples of Christ. But we learn from ancient writers, that what the Apostles preached by word of mouth they committed, or caused to be committed to writing, lest the substance of their preaching should be lost.[1] If tradition committed to the Church had been sufficient to preserve the truth, then the writing of the four Gospels, and of the other parts of the new Testament, would have been superfluous. But from the known and well-proved insufficiency of the former, the Apostles, under the guidance of the Spirit, had recourse to the latter mode of insuring a source and a rule of faith.

"The Apostles at first owned these writings; the Churches received them; they transmitted them to their posterity; they grounded their faith upon them; they proved their propositions by them; by them they confuted heretics; and they made them the measure of right and wrong: all that collective body of doctrine,

---

[1] E. g. Μετὰ δὲ τὴν τούτων (i. e. τοῦ Πέτρου καὶ τοῦ Παύλου) ἔξοδον Μάρκος, ὁ μαθητὴς καὶ ἑρμηνευτὴς Πέτρου, καὶ αὐτὸς τὰ ὑπὸ Πέτρου κηρυσσόμενα ἐγγράφως ἡμῖν παραδέδωκε. — Iren. Hær. III. 1.

So again: "Hanc fidem annuntians Joannes Domini discipulus, volens per Evangelii annuntiationem auferre eum qui inseminatus erat hominibus errorem, et multo prius ab his qui dicuntur Nicolaitæ . . . omnia igitur talia circumscribere volens discipulus Domini, et regulam veritatis constituere in ecclesia . . . sic inchoavit in ea quæ erat secundum Evangelium doctrina: In principio erat Verbum. . . ."— Hæres. III. 11.

Τοσοῦτον ἐπέλαμψεν ταῖς τῶν ἀκροατῶν τοῦ Πέτρου διανοίαις εὐσεβείας φέγγος, ὡς μὴ τῇ εἰσάπαξ ἱκανῶς ἔχειν ἀρκεῖσθαι ἀκοῇ. μηδὲ τῇ ἀγράφῳ τοῦ θείου κηρύγματος διδασκαλίᾳ· παρακλήσεσι δὲ παντοίαις Μάρκον, οὗ τὸ εὐαγγέλιον φέρεται, ἀκόλουθον ὄντα Πέτρου λιπαρῆσαι, ὡς ἂν καὶ διὰ γραφῆς ὑπόμνημα τῆς διὰ λόγου παραδοθείσης αὐτοῖς καταλείψοι διδασκαλίας· μὴ πρότερόν τε ἀνεῖναι ἢ κατεργάσασθαι τὸν ἄνδρα, καὶ ταύτῃ αἰτίους γενέσθαι τῆς τοῦ λεγομένου κατὰ Μάρκον εὐαγγελίου γραφῆς.— Euseb. H. E. II. 15. He gives this account on the authority of Papias and Clemens Alexand.

of which all Christians collectively made public confessions, and on which all their hopes of salvation did rely, were all contained in them, and they agreed in no point of faith which is not plainly set down in Scripture." [1]

Now Scripture having been thus evidently designed to correct the uncertainty and supply the deficiency of tradition, it is unreasonable to suppose that God would have suffered Scripture itself, the more certain guide, to be imperfect, and to need the less certain guide, tradition, to supply its defects. Yet, if Scripture itself does not contain the sum and substance of our religion, and all necessary articles of faith, this would be the case.

But as a matter of fact, Scripture has ever been adduced, by divines of all schools and all communions, as capable of proving all the great doctrines of the faith, and all the important rules of duty. We can either prove by it, or deduce from it, the great doctrines concerning the Trinity, the Incarnation, the Atonement, the Sanctification of the Spirit, Original Sin, Justification, the grace of the Sacraments, the privileges of the Church, the Communion of Saints, the Judgment of the great day, and other weighty and cardinal points of faith. And though different schools have differed as to how Scripture should be interpreted on some of these points, yet all have agreed that the true doctrine concerning them may be gathered from Scripture, if interpreted aright. Whatever value, therefore, we may attribute to a *Traditio Hermeneutica*, to traditional interpretations of Scripture ; we ought to be satisfied that all things " to be required of any man as an article of faith, or be thought requisite or necessary to salvation," are so contained in Scripture that they may be either " read therein, or may be proved thereby."

Several things, indeed, all men allow, are contained in Scripture, which are not absolutely necessary to salvation, although they may tend to edification ; and if the lesser matters were inserted there, how can we suppose that the greater would be omitted? Nay, although the Church of Rome often appeals to tradition, as a necessary part of Divine Revelation, yet it may well be questioned, whether even she pretends that any very important truth is to be derived from tradition alone. And assuredly we may safely assert, that there is a total absence of all evidence to prove that there is even professedly any tradition extant to which we are indebted for the knowledge of any great doctrine of the faith, independently of the written word.

[1] Jer. Taylor, *Dissuasive from Popery*, Pt. II. Bk. I. Sect. 3.

2. The principal arguments from reason in favour of the Romanist, and against the Anglican view of this subject, are as follow : —

(1) Tradition was the first rule.   From Adam to Moses all
was traditional ; and from the coming of Christ to the completion
of the Canon of the new Testament, tradition must have been the
principal guide of the Church.   Scripture, therefore, which came
in afterwards, cannot supersede that which was before it, and
which, at first, was sufficient without it.

This argument has already been virtually answered by anticipation.   The duration of men's lives before the time of Moses, and
the presence and personal teaching of inspired Apostles before the
writing of the new Testament, were great safeguards against error.
The fact, that, as these safeguards were withdrawn, God's Providence ordered that the Scriptures should be written and preserved, shows of itself that tradition, which might have been
sufficient then, would not be sufficient now.   We do not say that
Scripture supersedes tradition, but that it is itself the surest tradition, and the only one on which we can safely rely.   It is in fact
the Patriarchal, Levitical, and Apostolical tradition, preserved in
its safest and only certain form.

(2) It is said that Scripture was not written systematically,
but casually, as circumstances occurred, in casual memoirs and
occasional letters ; and therefore cannot be looked on as a systematic collection of doctrine and morality.

This, however, is no proof that the whole sum of necessary
truth may not be extracted from it.   *How* holy men of old were
moved to speak, or to write, seems of little consequence.   God's
wisdom saw fit that it should be in the way in which we have the
Scriptures now.   It is certainly in a more interesting, it is probably in a more profitable way, than if a systematic arrangement
had been adopted.   It is not probable that the Apostles' teaching,
nor even that of our Lord, was always systematic ; and yet in that
all men admit that all necessary truth was contained.   It cannot,
therefore, be necessary to our position to show that the Scriptures
are formally or systematically designed.

(3) The genuineness and canonicity of Scripture itself rest on
tradition, and on tradition alone ; and if tradition is necessary to
prove this, it may equally prove other doctrines.

It is true that historical testimony, and the universal consent
of all the early Christians, are the chief grounds on which we rely
for proof that the various books of the new Testament were the
works of those whose names they bear.   This indeed is, in a great

measure, the way in which we prove the genuineness of every ancient book. We do not know that a book was written by Cæsar
or Tacitus, but by testimony and historical evidence. In like
manner, testimony and historical evidence are essential to prove
that the works ascribed to St. Peter or St. Paul were really theirs.
In this latter case, indeed, we have the most convincing and satisfactory proofs ; for we have the testimony of early Christians,
of early heretics, of ancient heathens, of friends, and of enemies ;
and besides this, the testimony of the Church catholic in general
councils. These are things which we should never lightly value,
under any circumstances ; and when we have to deal with the
question concerning the genuineness of certain books, such a kind
of evidence is the most obvious, the most necessary, and the most
satisfactory possible. But it does not follow that we should give
the same deference to the same testimony, even if such could be
found, on points of doctrine. For the opinions of Cæsar or Tacitus,
we prefer the words of their own books to any testimony external to those books. And so for the doctrines of the Apostles, we
look first and chiefly to what they have written. Besides, we
have concerning the Canon of Scripture an universality of consent which it would be utterly in vain to search for concerning
any doctrine of the faith which is not also to be found in Scripture.
When the Roman Church can bring a like amount of consentient
testimony to prove any doctrine on which Scripture is silent, we
may then, and not till then, entertain the question of a *doctrina
tradita*, parallel to, and of equal authority with, Scripture.

(4) It is farther said, that many necessary things are not set
down in Scripture.

Bellarmine mentions the following : [1] —

a. How women under the old Law might be delivered from
Original Sin, circumcision being only for males; and how
males under eight days old might be saved from it.

b. The Perpetual Virginity of the blessed Virgin Mary, which
has always been believed by the Church, and yet is not in
Scripture.

c. That Easter should be kept on a Sunday, which is necessary
to be believed against the Quarto-decimans.

d. Infant Baptism, which is necessary to be believed; but neither
Romanists nor Protestants can prove it from Scripture.

e. That there is a Purgatory, which Luther himself believed,
and yet admitted that it could not be found in Scripture.

[1] *De Verbo Dei non Scripto*, Lib. IV

If these are all the points that Scripture is silent upon; we need not be very solicitous about its deficiencies. None of them surely can be essential to our salvation. None, except the last two, materially concern our personal faith or practice. The last we not only admit is not in Scripture, but we positively deny that it is true. The last but one, Infant Baptism, we think may be fairly inferred from Scripture, when fully consulted on the subject; and we are very thankful to have the additional testimony of the primitive Church concerning it, which we never reject, as a help and guide to the truth and right understanding of the Scriptures, but only as a distinct and independent authority. The question concerning Easter is one of ceremony, not of faith, and we gladly follow the primitive Church in matters of this nature; although we do not hold, that ceremonies must be one and the same everywhere. The doctrine concerning the Perpetual Virginity is rather a pious opinion, than a necessary article of faith. Our own greatest divines have mostly adhered to the primitive opinion on this subject.[1] But we cannot think that any man's salvation is the surer for believing, or the less sure for disbelieving it.

The question concerning Original Sin, and how women under the Law were delivered from it, and still more, the question concerning infants under eight days old, is as much left in obscurity by tradition, as by Scripture. It is one of those things concerning which we have no revelation.

(5) But it is said, that some of the chief articles of faith, though deduced from Scripture, yet could not be proved from Scripture alone, without the help of tradition and the testimony of the Church. Among the rest are enumerated, the equality of the Divine Persons in the Trinity, the Procession of the Spirit from both the Father and the Son, the Descent into Hell, Original Sin, the change of the Sabbath to the Lord's Day.

The proof of most of these doctrines from Scripture has already been given under the preceding Articles. We maintain, that the equality of the Persons in the Godhead, and the other great doctrines concerning the Trinity, also the Descent into Hell, and Original Sin, are clearly deducible from Scripture alone. We do not indeed reject the testimony of antiquity, but view it, as a valuable guide to the true meaning of Holy Writ; but we maintain that these doctrines might be proved, even without its aid. As to

---

[1] Andrewes's *Devotions*: see Prayers for Monday. Jer. Taylor, *Life of Christ*, § 2. Pearson, *On the Creed*, Art. "Born of the Virgin Mary." Bp. Bull, *Works*, I. p. 96

the Procession of the Holy Ghost, if Scripture will not prove it, certainly tradition will not. In considering the last Article, we saw that the tradition of the Western was different, in some respects, from that of the Eastern Church. The Nicene Creed for some centuries lacked the *Filioque*. And from the evidence in favour of the doctrine, which we deduced from Scripture, it should appear that Scripture speaks more plainly upon it than tradition, or the Church. The change of the Sabbath to the Lord's Day is not an article of faith; but it is doubtless a matter of some moment. It is true, that without the aid of history we might find some difficulty in discovering, whether the early Christians did give up observing the Jewish Sabbath, and kept festival on the first day of the week. But even so, we think, Scripture alone would give us proof that the Lord's Day was to be observed, and that the Jewish Sabbath was not to be observed. Certainly, we read of the first day of the week, as the day on which Christians held their assemblies, administered the Lord's Supper (Acts xx. 7), and collected alms for the poor (1 Cor. xvi. 2). So the Apostle St. John " was in the Spirit on the Lord's Day "(Rev. i. 10). But " Sabbath-days " are enumerated as one of the " shadows of things to come," which belonged to the old dispensation, and so were not binding on Christians (Col. ii. 16, 17). Hence, the new Testament gives us good reason to believe that the obligation to keep the seventh day of the week had passed away, and that the weekly festival of the Christian Church was not Saturday, but Sunday. If it be not conceded that such Scriptural authority be sufficient to satisfy us, we may reply, that the keeping of the Lord's Day is not a question essential to our salvation, like the great doctrines of our faith; and that, therefore, even if we require historical or traditional evidence concerning it, in addition to Scripture, that will not be a case to interfere with this Article of our Church which speaks only of articles of faith, and things necessary to salvation.

(6) Lastly, it is said, Scripture is in many things so obscure, that tradition is necessary to explain its meaning.

To this we reply, that there is, at times, no doubt, some difficulty. The Church of England does not reject the use of all proper aids for the explanation of Scripture. She encourages recourse to human learning, in order to elucidate the language of Holy Writ. She does by no means reject any light, which may be derived from primitive antiquity, and she is anxious to cherish a learned clergy for the instruction of her poorer and more ignorant members. Her rule too concerning Scripture is not, that every uneducated person ought to take the Scriptures in hand, and search out for himself a system of theology. She teaches her children by catechisms and other simple steps to knowledge of the truth. All that she maintains is, that, as a final court of appeal, Scripture is perfect and sufficient. Her children may, by intelligent and humble study of the Scriptures, find in them full authority for all she teaches, and do not require a second, independent authority.

The fathers acknowledge the Scripture to be sufficiently plain, if expounded by comparing Scripture with Scripture. Irenæus tells us to solve the more difficult parts of Scripture by having recourse to those which are easy.[1] And Chrysostom says, " Look for no other teacher ; thou hast the oracles of God ; none teaches thee like these."[2]

" There is no question, but there are many places in the Divine Scriptures, mysterious, intricate, and secret : but these are for the learned, not for the ignorant : for the curious and inquisitive, not for the busied and employed and simple : they are not repositories of salvation, but instances of labour, and occasions of humility, and arguments of forbearance and mutual toleration, and an endearment of reverence and adoration. But all that by which God brings us to Himself is easy and plain."[3]

III. We have, lastly, to prove, that the testimony of the primitive fathers is in favour of the Anglican rule, and not of the Roman.

1. Irenæus says : " We know that the Scriptures are perfect, as being spoken by the Word of God and His Spirit."[4] Again : " We have received the disposition of our salvation by no others but those by whom the Gospel came to us ; which they then preached, and afterwards by God's will delivered to us in the Scriptures, to be the pillar and ground of our faith."[5]

---

[1] Omnis autem quæstio non per aliud quod quæritur habebit resolutionem, nec ambiguitas per aliam ambiguitatem solvetur apud eos qui sensum habent, aut ænigmata per aliud majus ænigma, sed ea quæ sunt talia ex manifestis et consonantibus et claris accipiunt solutionem.— Lib. II. 10. See Beaven's *Account of Irenæus*, p. 138.

[2] *Homil.* IX. *in Ep. Coloss.*

[3] Jer. Taylor's *Dissuasive from Popery,* **Part** II. Bk. I. § 2.

[4] Cedere hæc talia debemus Deo qui et nos fecit, rectissime scientes quia **Scrip**turæ quidem perfectæ sunt, quippe **a** Verbo Dei et Spiritu ejus dictæ. — Lib. II. c. 47.

[5] Non enim per alios dispositionem salutis nostræ cognovimus, quam per eos per quos Evangelium pervenit ad nos : quod quidem tunc præconiaverunt, postea vero per Dei voluntatem in Scripturis nobis tradiderunt, fundamentum **et** columnam fidei nostræ futurum. — **Lib.** III. c. 1.

Tertullian says : "I adore the perfection of Scripture, which
declares to me the Creator and His Works. . . . . Whether all
things were made of preëxistent matter, I have as yet nowhere
read. Let the school of Hermogenes show that it is written. If
it is not written, let them fear the woe which is destined for them
who add to or take away."[1]

Origen says : "The two Testaments . . . . in which every word
that appertains to God may be sought out and discussed, and from
them all knowledge of things may be understood. If anything
remain, which Holy Scripture doth not determine, no third Scripture ought to be had recourse to . . . . but that which remaineth
we must commit to the fire, *i. e.*, reserve it unto God. For God
would not have us know all things in this world."[2]

Hippolytus writes : "There is one God, whom we do not otherwise acknowledge, brethren, but out of the Sacred Scriptures.
For as he who would profess the wisdom of this world cannot
otherwise attain it, unless he read the doctrines of the philosophers,
so whosoever will exercise piety towards God can learn it nowhere
but from the Holy Scriptures."[3]

Athanasius : "The holy and divinely-inspired Scriptures are
of themselves sufficient to the enunciation of truth."[4] Again :
"These are the fountains of salvation, that he who thirsts may be
satisfied with the oracles contained in them. In these alone the
doctrine of salvation is contained. Let no man add to, or take
from them."[5]

Cyril of Jerusalem says, that, "Concerning the divine and holy

---

[1] Adoro Scripturæ plenitudinem qua
mihi et Factorem manifestat et facta.
In Evangelio vero amplius et ministrum
et arbitrum Rectoris invenio, Sermonem.
An autem de aliqua subjacenti materia
facta sint omnia, nusquam adhuc legi.
Scriptum esse doceat Hermogenis offi-
cina. Si non est scriptum, timeat væ
illud *adjicientibus aut detrahentibus* destinatum. — *Adv. Hermogenem*, c. 22. See
also *Apolog.* c. 47. *De Præscript.* c. 6,
&c.

[2] In hoc biduo puto duo Testamenta
posse intelligi, in quibus liceat omne
verbum quod ad Deum pertinet (hoc
enim est sacrificium) requiri et discuti,
atque ex ipsis omnem rerum scientiam
capi. Si quid autem superfuerit, quod
non divina Scriptura decernat, nullam
aliam tertiam Scripturam debere ad auctoritatem scientiæ suscipi. . . . . Sed igni
tradamus quod superest, id est, Deo
reservemus. Neque enim in præsenti

vita Deus scire nos omnia voluit. — Origen. *Homil.* v. *in Levit.*

[3] Εἷς Θεὸς, ὃν οὐκ ἄλλοθεν ἐπιγινώσκομεν,
ἀδελφοὶ, ἢ ἐκ τῶν ἁγίων γραφῶν. Ὃν γὰρ
τρόπον ἐάν τις βουληθῇ τὴν σοφίαν τοῦ αἰῶνος τούτου ἀσκεῖν, οὐκ ἄλλως δυνήσεται τούτου τυχεῖν ἐὰν μὴ δόγμασι φιλοσόφων ἐντύχῃ,
τὸν αὐτὸν δὴ τρόπον ὅσοι Θεοσέβειαν ἀσκεῖν
βουλόμεθα, οὐκ ἄλλοθεν ἀσκήσομεν ἢ ἐκ τῶν
λογίων τοῦ Θεοῦ. — Hippolyt. *Contra Hæresim Noeti,* c. 9.

[4] Αὐτάρκεῖς μὲν γάρ εἰσιν αἱ ἁγίαι καὶ
θεόπνευστοι γραφαὶ πρὸς τὴν τῆς ἀληθείας
ἀπαγγελίαν. — Athanas. *Contra Gentes,*
Tom. I. p. 1.

[5] Ταῦτα πηγαὶ τοῦ σωτηρίου, ὥστε τὴν
διψῶντα ἐμφορεῖσθαι τῶν ἐν τούτοις λιγίων ·
ἐν τούτοις μόνον τὸ τῆς εὐσεβείας διδασκα-
λεῖον εὐαγγελίζεται · μηδεὶς τούτοις ἐπιβαλ-
λέτω, μὴ δὲ τούτων ἀφαιρείσθω. — *Ex Festali Epistola* xxxix. Tom II. p. 39. Edit.
Colon.

mysteries of the faith, even the most casual remark ought not to be delivered without the sacred Scriptures."[1]

Basil : "Believe those things which are written, the things which are nòt written seek not."[2] "It is a manifest defection from the faith, and a proof of arrogance, either to reject anything of what is written, or to introduce anything that is not."[3]

Ambrose : "How can we use those things, which we find not in the Scriptures !"[4]

Jerome : "We deny not those things which are written, so we refuse those which are not written. That God was born of a Virgin we believe, because we read ; that Mary married after she gave birth to Him, we believe not, because we read not."[5]

Augustine : "In those things which are plainly laid down in Scripture, all things are found which embrace faith and morals."[6]

Vincentius Lirinensis begins with the admission, that, "The Canon of Scripture is perfect, and most abundantly sufficient for all things."[7]

Theodoret : "Bring not human reasonings and syllogisms ; I rely on Scripture."[8]

John Damascene : "All things that are delivered to us by the Law, the Prophets, the Apostles, and the Evangelists, we receive, acknowledge, and reverence, seeking for nothing beyond these."[9]

It can scarcely be necessary to bring more or stronger proofs that the fathers with one voice affirm the perfection and sufficiency

---

[1] Δεῖ γὰρ περὶ τῶν θείων καὶ ἀγίων τῆς πίστεως μυστηρίων μηδὲ τὸ τύχον ἄνευ τῶν θείων παραδίδοσθαι γραφῶν.— Cyril. Hierosol. Catech. IV. 12.

[2] Τοῖς γεγραμμένοις πίστευε, τὰ μὴ γεγραμμένα μὴ ζήτει. — Basil. Hom. XXIX. adv. Calumniantes S. Trin.

[3] Φανερὰ ἔκπτωσις πίστεως καὶ ὑπερηφανίας κατηγορία ἢ ἀθετεῖν τι τῶν γεγραμμένων ἢ ἐπεισάγειν τῶν μὴ γεγραμμένων.— Basil. De Fide, c. 1.

[4] Quæ in Scripturis sanctis non reperimus, ea quemadmodum usurpare possumus.— Ambros. Offic. Lib. I. c. 23.

[5] Ut hæc quæ scripta sunt non negamus, ita ea quæ non scripta sunt renuimus. Natum Deum de Virgine credimus, quia legimus. Mariam nupsisse post partum non credimus, quia non legimus.— Hieron. Adv. Helvidium juxta finem, Tom. IV. part II. p. 141, edit. Benedict.

[6] In iis quæ aperte in Scriptura posita sunt, inveniuntur illa omnia quæ continent fidem moresque vivendi. — August.

De Doctrina Christ. Lib. II. c. 9, Tom. III. p. 24.

In like manner : — Proinde sive de Christo, sive de ejus Ecclesia, sive de quacumque alia re quæ pertinet ad fidem vitamque vestram, non dicam nos, nequaquam comparandi ei qui dixit, Licet si nos : sed omnino quod secutus adjecit, Si angelus de cœlo vobis annuntiaverit præterquam quod in Scripturis legalibus et evangelicis accepistis anathema sit.— Aug. Cont. Petilium, Lib. III. c. 6, Tom. IX. p. 301.

[7] Cum sit perfectus Scripturarum Canon, sibique ad omnia satis superque sufficiat. — Vincent. Lirin. Commonitor. c. 2.

[8] Μή μοι λογισμοὺς καὶ συλλογισμοὺς ἀνθρωπίνους προσενέγκῃς · ἐγὼ γὰρ μόνῃ πείθομαι τῇ θείᾳ γραφῇ. — Theodoret. Dial. I. 'Ατρεπτ.

[9] Πάντα τὰ παραδιδόμενα ἡμῖν διά τε νόμου, καὶ προφητῶν καὶ ἀποστόλων καὶ εὐαγγελιστῶν δεχόμεθα καὶ γινώσκομεν καὶ σέβομεν, οὐδὲν περαιτέρω τούτων ἐπιζητοῦντες. — Damascen. Lib. I. De Orthodox. Fide, c. 1.

of the written word, for the end for which it was written, *i. e.*, for a rule of faith, and for a rule of life.[1]

2. (1) But an objection will be urged to these arguments from the fathers, that some of them, and those of no mean importance, clearly speak of a rule of faith which is distinct from the Scriptures; it is therefore evident that they do not appeal to Scripture alone as supreme, perfect, and sufficient. Thus, without question, Irenæus spoke of a κανὼν τῆς ἀληθείας, "a rule of truth," according to which he considered that the Scriptures ought to be interpreted.[2] In the same manner Tertullian appeals to a *Regula Fidei*, "a rule of faith," by which he was guided in interpreting Scripture.[3] Here are two of the earliest fathers appealing to an authority which is certainly not Scripture; and therefore they must have held that something besides Scripture was necessary, and that all things needful for faith and practice were not contained in Scripture.

If, however, we consult the contexts, we shall find that the rule spoken of in both these fathers is the baptismal Creed. Irenæus expressly says that the Canon of Truth, which each one was to keep, was that which was received by him at his baptism;[4] and in the next chapter recites a form or profession of faith, which is very nearly the same as the Apostles' Creed, and which he speaks of as that "faith which the Church scattered throughout the world diligently keeps."[5]

In the very same manner Tertullian writes, "Now we have a rule of faith, which teaches us what we are to defend and maintain, and by that very rule we believe, that there is One God," &c.; he goes on reciting the various articles of the Creed.[6] Here then we see, that the rules of faith of Irenæus and Tertullian were not some independent tradition, teaching doctrines not to be found in Scripture, but the Creeds taught to the Christians, and confessed by them at their baptism, which were in fact epitomes of important Scriptural doctrine, founded on Scripture, and fully according with

---

[1] Divines of the English Church have collected many other passages to the same purpose. See *Laud against Fisher,* § 16; Usher's *Answer to a Jesuit,* ch. 2; Jer. Taylor, *Dissuasive from Popery,* Part II. Bk. I. ch. 2; *Rule of Conscience,* Book II. ch. II. Rule xiv. From some of which works I have taken the above passages, (with one or two exceptions,) merely verifying the quotations.

[2] Οὕτω δὲ καὶ ὁ τὸν κάνονα τῆς ἀληθείας ἀκλινῆ ἐν ἑαυτῷ κατέχων, ὃν διὰ βαπτίσματος εἴληφε, τὰ μὲν ἐκ τῶν γραφῶν ὀνόματα καὶ τὰς λέξεις καὶ τὰς παραβολὰς ἐπιγνώσεται. — Irenæ. I. 9.

[3] Hæc Regula a Christo, ut probabitur, instituta, nullas habet quæstiones, nisi quas hæreses inferunt, et quæ hæreticos faciunt. — Tertull. *De Præscript. Hæret.* c. 14.

Adversus Regulam nihil scire omnia scire. — *Ibid.*

[4] See the last note but one.

[5] Lib. I. 10.

[6] *De Præscript. Hæret.* c. 13.

it. This is a widely different thing from the *Doctrina tradita* of the Church of Rome. Reliance on the latter is opposed to the sufficiency of Scripture; but the rule of Irenæus and Tertullian was based upon Scripture, and in all respects accordant with it.

Clement of Alexandria also, who is almost as early a witness as Tertullian, speaks, like Irenæus, of a κανὼν τῆς ἀληθείας, "a rule of truth," which he also calls κανὼν ἐκκλησιαστικός. But this rule, so far from being something apart from, and of parallel authority with Scripture, is, according to Clement, founded on a harmony of the old Testament with the new. " The ecclesiastical rule," says he, " is the harmony of the Law and the Prophets with the Covenant delivered by the Lord during His presence on earth." [1]

A like sense we must attach to the language of the later fathers, when we find them speaking of a *Regula Fidei*. They considered the fundamental doctrines of the faith, those, that is, contained in the Creeds, to be the great guide for Christians in interpreting Scriptures. Whosoever erred from these erred from the truth; and, in explaining obscure passages, they held that it was very needful to keep in view the necessity of not deviating from the great lines of truth marked out in the baptismal Creeds. This was not to add to Scripture, but to guard it against being wrested to destruction.[2]

(2) But, it may be said, Irenæus, Tertullian, and others, not only appealed to tradition, but even preferred arguing from tradition to arguing from Scripture.

Tertullian especially says: " No appeal must be made to the Scriptures, no contest must be founded on them, in which victory is uncertain. . . . . The grand question is, to whom the Faith itself belongs; in whose hands were the Scriptures deposited . . . . to whom that doctrine was first committed, whereby we are made Christians? For wherever this true doctrine and discipline shall appear to be, there the truth of the Scripture and of the interpretation of it will be, and of Christian tradition." [3]

The meaning, however, of this appeal to tradition in preference to Scripture, both by Irenæus and Tertullian, is this: both were reasoning against heretics. Those heretics mutilated Scripture,

---

[1] Κανὼν δὲ ἐκκλησιαστικὸς ἡ συνῳδία καὶ ἡ συμφωνία νόμου τε καὶ προφητῶν τῇ κατὰ τὴν τοῦ Κυρίου παρουσίαν παραδιδομένῃ διαθήκῃ. — *Strom*. Lib. VI. c. 15, ed. Potter, p. 803.

[2] See Bp. Marsh, *On the Interpretation*

of the *Bible*, Lect. XI.; Bp. Kaye's *Tertullian*, p. 290, &c. ; Bp. Kaye's *Clement of Alexandria*, p. 366 ; Beaven's *Irenæus*, ch. VIII.

[3] *De Præscript. Hæret.* c. 19.

and perverted it. When, therefore, the fathers found their appeal
to Scripture of no effect, partly because the heretics were ready to
deny that what they quoted was Scripture, and partly because they
were ready to evade its force by false glosses and perverted interpretations; then the fathers saw that to reason from Scripture was
not convincing to their opponents, and therefore they had recourse
to the doctrine preserved by the Apostolical Churches, which, they
maintained, were not likely to have lost or to have corrupted the
truth first intrusted to them. It was not, that they themselves
doubted the sufficiency of Scripture, but that they found other
weapons useful against the gainsayers, and therefore brought tradition, not to add to, but to confirm Scripture.[1]

The same may be said concerning the famous work of Vincentius Lirinensis. He begins by admitting that "Scripture is perfect
and abundantly of itself sufficient for all things." But because
various heretics have misinterpreted it, Novatian expounding it one
way, Photinus in another, Sabellius in another, and so on: "therefore," he says, "very necessary it is for the avoiding of such turn-
ings and twinings of error, that the line of interpreting the Prophets and Apostles be directed according to the rule of Ecclesiastical
and Catholic sense."[2]   This is not to introduce a new rule independent of Scripture. It is at most a *Traditio Hermeneutica*, a
rule for the interpreting of Scripture. It still leaves Scripture, as
the fountain of truth; though it guards against using its streams
for other than legitimate purposes.

Finally, we have seen the concurrent testimony of the fathers
to be in favour of the sufficiency of Scripture. If, here and there,
a single passage be apparently unfavourable to this testimony, we
must hold it to be a private opinion of an individual father, and
therefore not worthy of being esteemed in comparison with their
general consent. For it is a rule of Vincentius himself, that
"Whatsoever any, although a learned man, a bishop, a martyr, or
a confessor holds, otherwise than all, or against all, this must be
put aside from the authority of the general judgment, and be
reputed merely his own private opinion."[3]

---

[1] See Beaven's *Irenæus*, p. 136; Bp.
Kaye's *Tertullian*, p. 297, note.
[2] *Commonitor.* c. 2.

[3] *Commonitor.* c. 28. On the true sense
of the perfection of Scripture, see Hooker,
E. P. I. xiii. xiv. II. viii. 5.

Section II. — ON THE CANON OF SCRIPTURE.[1]

AS Scripture is determined by our Church to be the final appeal and only infallible authority concerning matters of faith and practice, it becomes next a subject of the deepest importance to determine, what is Scripture, and what is not. And, as this subject is so important, we naturally look for an authority of the highest kind to settle and determine it. We value, indeed, the decisions of antiquity, we respect the judgment of the primitive Church. But on the question, What is the Word of God? we would, if possible, have an authority as infallible as the word of God; and, if we can have such authority, we can be satisfied with nothing less.

Now such an authority we believe that we possess; and that we possess it in this way: Christ Himself gave His own Divine sanction to the Jewish Canon of the old Testament; and He gave His own authority to His Apostles to write the new. If this statement be once admitted, we have only to investigate historically, what was the Jewish Canon, and what were the books written by the Apostles. We need search no farther; we shall greatly confirm our faith by the witness of fathers and councils; but, if Christ has spoken, we need no other, as we can have no higher warrant.

I. Now, first, we have to consider the question of the *old Testament;* and our inquiry is, Has our Lord Himself stamped with His authority certain books, and left others unauthorized? The answer is, He has. We must not, indeed, argue from the fact of His quoting a certain number of books and leaving a certain number unquoted; for there are six books which can be proved to be Canonical, which the writers of the new Testament never quote; namely, Judges, Ezra, Nehemiah, Esther, Ecclesiastes, Solomon's Song. The fact that these books are not quoted will not destroy their authority; for we have no reason to say that our Lord or His Apostles quoted systematically from all the Ca-

---

[1] The word κάνων signifies a line, or rule, — a standard, therefore, by which other things are to be judged of. It is applied to the *tongue of a balance,* or that small part of the scales which by its perpendicular situation determines the even poise or weight, or by its inclination either way the uneven poise of the things that are weighed. It is applied to the Scriptures, because they have ever been esteemed in the Church " the infallible rule of our faith, and the perfect square of our actions, in all things that are in any way needful for our eternal salvation." — Cosin's *Scholastical Hist. of the Canon,* ch. i.; Jones, *On the Canon,* ch. i.

nonical books, in order to establish their canonicity. But the way
in which our Lord has given His own sanction to a certain definite
number of books, is this: in speaking to the Jews, both He and
His Apostles constantly address them as having the Scriptures, —
Scriptures of Divine authority, and able to make them wise unto
salvation. They never hint that the Jewish Canon is imperfect or
excessive; and hence they plainly show that the Scriptures which
the Jews possessed and acknowledged, were the truly Canonical
Scriptures of the old Testament. Our Lord bids them " Search
the Scriptures," and adds, " they are they which testify of Me "
(John v. 39). St. Paul says, that the greatest privilege of the
Jews was that " unto them were committed the Oracles of God "
(Rom. iii. 2); and tells Timothy, that " from a child he had
known the Scriptures, which were able to make him wise unto
salvation " (2 Tim. iii. 16). Accordingly, our Lord constantly
appeals to those Scriptures as well-known and universally received
books among the Jews, to whom He spoke, quoting them as, " It
is written," or asking concerning them, " How readest thou ? "
Though the Jews are charged with many errors, with corrupting
the truth by tradition, and adding to it the commandments of
men; yet nowhere are they charged with corrupting Scripture,
with having rejected some, or added other books to the Canon.
But it is ever plainly implied that the Canon which they then
possessed, was the true Canon of the old Testament. Thus, then,
by quoting, referring to, or arguing from the old Testament, as it
was then received by the Jews, our Lord stamps with His own
supreme authority the Jewish Canon of the old Testament Scriptures. We have only further to determine from history what the
Jewish Canon, at the time of our Saviour's-teaching, was, and
we have all that we can need. If history will satisfy us of this,
we have no more to ask.

Now the only difficulty lies here. There appear to be two
different books claiming to be the Jewish Scriptures; namely, the
Hebrew Bible, now in the hands both of Jews and Christians,
and the Septuagint. The latter contains all the books contained
in the former, with the addition of the books commonly called the
Apocrypha.

Let us first observe, that the modern Jews universally acknowledge no other Canon but the Hebrew; which corresponds accurately with the Canon of the English Church. Those who know
the fidelity with which for centuries the Jews have guarded their
text, will consider this alone to be a strong argument that the

Hebrew Canon is the same as that cited by our Lord. Every
verse, every word, every letter, of Scripture is numbered by them.
Every large and every small letter, every letter irregularly written,
above the line or below the line, is taken notice of and scrupulously preserved.

But we can go back to more ancient times, and show that the
Canon of the Jews has always been the same. The Babylonian
Talmud recounts the same books that we have now ; namely, in
the Law, the five books of Moses ; among the Prophets, Joshua
and Judges, Samuel and Kings, Jeremiah and Ezekiel, Isaiah and
the twelve minor prophets ; in the Chethubim, Ruth, Psalms, Job,
Proverbs, Ecclesiastes, the Song of Songs, Lamentations, Daniel,
Esther, Chronicles. This was the Canon of the Jewish Church
about A. D. 550.[1]

But one hundred and fifty years earlier than this, Jerome undertook the task of translating the Hebrew Scriptures into Latin.
Theretofore all the Latin translations had been from the Septuagint, and therefore contained all the Apocryphal books. Jerome,
the first of the Latin fathers who could read Hebrew, when under-
taking this important labour, was naturally led to examine into the
Canon of the Hebrew Scriptures. He informs us, that the Jews
had two-and-twenty books in their Bible, corresponding with the
two-and-twenty Hebrew letters. This number they made by
classing two books together as one ; thus, the two books of Samuel
were one, the two books of Kings, Ezra and Nehemiah, Jeremiah
and Lamentations, Judges and Ruth, respectively, were considered
as one each. The books were divided into three classes, the Law,
the Prophets, and the Hagiographa. The first contained the five
books of Moses ; the second contained Joshua, Judges and Ruth,
Samuel, Kings, Isaiah, Jeremiah and Lamentations, Ezekiel, and
the twelve minor prophets ; the third contained Psalms, Proverbs,
Ecclesiastes, the Song of Songs, Job, Daniel, Ezra and Nehemiah,
Esther, Chronicles. The Law, therefore, contained five books, the
Prophets eight, the Hagiographa nine.[2]

To go still farther back, Origen, who was born A. D. 184 and
who died A. D. 255, and who, like Jerome, was learned in Hebrew
and gave great attention to the Hebrew text, (as is well known
from his famous work, the *Hexapla*,) enumerates the same books

[1] Baba Bathra, fol. 14, col. 2. The
books of Moses are called תּוֹרָה The
Law ; the prophetical books נְבִיאִים
The Prophets ; the other books כְּתוּבִים

The Chethubim, *i. e.* The Scriptures or Writings.
[2] Hieron. *Prologus Galeatus*, Op. Tom.
I. p. 318. Ed. Bened.

that Jerome does, except that he adds after all the rest, that there was the book Maccabees apart or distinct from the others.[1]

Still earlier, Melito, bishop of Sardis, made a journey into the East, for the sake of inquiring what were the books held canonical there, and, in a letter to Onesimus, gives a catalogue of these books, precisely corresponding with the present Canon of the Hebrew Scriptures, except that he classes Ezra, Nehemiah, and Esther, under the common name of Esdras.[2] This father lived about the year 160.

We next come to Josephus. He flourished at the time of the siege of Jerusalem, and was therefore contemporary with the Apostles. In the first place, we find in his writings the same threefold division which occurs in Jerome, and has ever since been common with the Jews; namely, the Law, the Prophets, and other books, which he characterizes as "Hymns and Instructions for Men's Lives." A similar division exists in Philo.[3] But Josephus, moreover, divides the Scriptures, as Jerome testifies that the Jews did in his time, into twenty-two books.[4] The only difference between the divisions of Josephus and Jerome is, that, whereas Jerome says there were eight in the Prophets and nine in the Hagiographa, Josephus assigns thirteen to the Prophets, and four to the Hagiographa. We know, however, that the Jews have gradually been augmenting the number of the books in the Hagiographa and diminishing the number in the Prophets, so that there is no great wonder, if between the first and the fourth century there was such a change in their mode of reckoning, that in the first they reckoned thirteen, in the fourth but eight among prophetical books.

Thus then, since we find that Josephus gives the same threefold division which we find afterwards given by Jerome, and also that he gives the same total number of books, namely, twenty-two, though somewhat differently distributed, we might at once naturally conclude that the Jewish Canon in the time of Josephus was the same with the Jewish Canon in the time of Jerome. That is to say, we might conclude that it embraced the books now in the Hebrew Bibles and in the Canon of the English Church, and that it excluded the Apocryphal books, which the English

---

[1] Ap. Euseb. *H. E.* vi. 25 : Ἔξω δὲ τούτων ἐστὶ τὰ Μακκαβαϊκὰ, ἅπερ ἐπιγέγραπται Σαρβὴθ Σαρβανιὲλ. Bishop Cosin interprets this, as meaning that the Books of Maccabees were "out of the Canon." — *History of the Canon,* ch. v

[2] Euseb. *H. E.* iv. 26. See Bp. Cosin as above, ch. iv.

[3] *De Vita Contemplativa,* Tom. ii. p. 475; Marsh, *On the Authority of the old Testament,* Lect. xxxii.

[4] *Contra Apion* i. § 8; Euseb. *H. E.* iii. 10.

Church excludes. But, if we could doubt that this was the case, his own words might set us at rest, for he tells us that the books belonging to the second class (*i. e.* to the Prophets) were written previously to the reign (or to the death) of Artaxerxes Longimanus, and that, though books were written after that time, "they were not esteemed worthy of the same credit with those before them, because there was no longer the exact succession of the Prophets."[1] It was during the reign of Artaxerxes Longimanus that the book of Esther was written, Artaxerxes being, according to Josephus, the Ahasuerus of that book.[2] This would therefore be the last book of his Canon. All the Apocryphal books must have been written long after that reign, and therefore cannot be included in his twenty-two books, compared with which they were not thought worthy of equal credit. It is plain, therefore, that the Canon of Josephus must be the same with that of Jerome.

Now, in the short time which elapsed between our Saviour's earthly ministry and Josephus, no alteration can have taken place in the Canon. Josephus himself tells us, that a copy of the Hebrew Scriptures was preserved in the Temple.[3] And therefore, until the destruction of the Temple, when Josephus was thirty-three years old, that Temple copy existed, and was a protection against all change. He would have had easy access to that Temple copy, and hence is a fully competent witness to its contents. Nay, even without the existence of that copy, which was an invaluable security, we learn from Philo, that in his time the Jews had the same intense veneration for the words of Scripture which we know them to have had afterwards; so that nothing could induce them "to alter one word, and that they would rather die ten thousand deaths than suffer any alteration in their laws and statutes."[4]

We now are arrived at the period when the books of the new Testament were written. Philo and Josephus were in fact contemporaries of Christ and His Apostles. We have already seen,

[1] Ἀπὸ δὲ Ἀρταξέρξου μέχρι τοῦ καθ' ἡμᾶς χρόνου, γέγραπται μὲν ἕκαστα · πίστεως δὲ οὐχ ὁμοίας ἠξίωται τοῖς πρὸ αὐτῶν, διὰ τὸ μὴ γενέσθαι τὴν τῶν προφητῶν ἀκριβῆ διαδοχήν.— *Contra Apionem,* I. § 8; Euseb. *H. E.* III. 10.
[2] *Antiq.* Lib. XI. cap. 6.
[3] Δηλοῦται διὰ τῶν ἀνακειμένων ἐν τῷ ἱερῷ γραμμάτων.—*Antiq.* Lib. V. cap. 17.
[4] Philo-Judæus *Ap. Euseb. Præpar. Evangel.* Lib. VIII. § 6: Μὴ ῥῆμα γ' αὐτοὺς

μόνον τῶν ὑπ' αὐτοῦ γεγραμμένων κινῆσαι, ἀλλὰ κἂν μυριάκις αὐτοὺς ἀποθανεῖν ὑπιμεῖναι θᾶττον τοῖς ἐκείνου νόμοις καὶ ἔθεσιν ἐναντία πεισθῆναι.—See Cosin, *On the Canon,* ch. II.
So Josephus: Δῆλον δ' ἐστιν ἔργῳ πῶς ἡμεῖς τοῖς ἰδίοις γράμμασι πεπιστεύκαμεν · τοσούτου γὰρ αἰῶνος ἤδη παρῳχηκότος οὔτε προσθεῖναί τις οὐδὲν, οὔτε ἀφελεῖν αὐτῶν, οὔτε μεταθεῖναι τετόλμηκεν.— *Contra Apionem,* I. § 8; Euseb. *H. E.* III. 10.

that our Lord and the Apostles quote the Scriptures as well known and universally received, and never hint at their corruption. Our Lord indeed divides them (as we see they were divided by Jerome and the Jews ever since) into three distinct classes, which our Lord calls the Law, the Prophets, and the Psalms,[1] in which "the Psalms" is put for the whole Hagiographa, either because the Psalms stood first among the books of the Hagiographa, or because the Hagiographa may be said to consist chiefly of hymns and poems, which might well be called Psalms.[2] We have to add to this, that in the new Testament every book of the Jewish Canon is distinctly quoted with the exception of six, and those perhaps the six least likely to have furnished passages for quotation; but not one quotation occurs from any one of those books which form a part of what is now called the Apocrypha.[3]

If we could carry the evidence no farther, we might rest satisfied here, that our Lord gave His sanction to the Hebrew, not to the Septuagint Canon. But we can go one step farther, and it is this: one hundred and thirty years before our Lord's birth, the Prologue of the Book of Ecclesiasticus was written, which classes the Hebrew Scriptures into the same three classes, "the Law, the Prophets, and the other books of the fathers." This is a ground for believing that the Jewish Scriptures were the same in number then that they were found to be afterwards. Again, what is not a little important, Targums,[4] some of which are as old as, or older than the Christian era, were made from all the books of the old Testament, but none are to be found of the Apocryphal books. We have Targums of the Law, Targums of the Prophets, Targums of the Chethubim, but no Targums of the Apocrypha.

Our evidence is now pretty nearly complete; we may recapitulate it thus.

We have the threefold division of the Scriptures mentioned — in the Prologue to Ecclesiasticus, by Philo, by our blessed Lord, by Josephus; and the same we find in the time of Jerome, and among all the Jews from that time to this.

---

[1] "That all things must be fulfilled, which were written in the Law of Moses, and in the Prophets, and in the Psalms." — Luke xxiv. 44.

[2] According to the division which existed in our Saviour's time, which probably was the same as that in the time of Josephus, there would have been but four books in the Chethubim or Hagiographa, namely, Psalms, Proverbs, Ecclesiastes, Solomon's Song.

[3] See this proved, — Cosin, *Hist. of Canon*, ch. iii.

[4] The Targums were translations or paraphrases of the Scriptures, made from the original Hebrew into Chaldee, when Hebrew had become a dead language, which was the case soon after the return from captivity. They were read in the synagogues, and formed the ordinary instruments for instruction of the Jews of Palestine in the Scriptures.

We know, that the number of books contained in these three classes was, in the time of Josephus, twenty-two. The same number we find recounted by Origen and Jerome, as belonging to the Jewish Canon, and Origen and Jerome give us their names, which are the names of the books in the present Jewish Canon.

The Canon in the time of Josephus, who was born A. D. 37, must have been the same as that in the time of Christ: as its security was guaranteed by the existence of the Temple copy, to say nothing of the scrupulous fidelity of the Jews, who, as Philo tells us, would have died ten thousand times rather than alter one word.

The Targums, which are paraphrases of the books in the present Hebrew Canon, confirm the same inference ; and some of them are as old as the time of our Lord.

Now we know exactly how the threefold division embraced the books of the Hebrew Canon. We know how, in Origen's time and in Jerome's time, the twenty-two books (which was also the number in Josephus's time) embraced the books of the Hebrew Canon. We know, too, that Melito, less than one hundred years after Josephus, gave, as the books received in the East, a catalogue corresponding exactly with the same Hebrew Canon. But no imaginable ingenuity can ever make the books of the Apocrypha fit into any of these divisions, or agree with any of these lists.

When we add to this, that our Lord and His Apostles, when they gave the sanction of Divine authority to the Jewish Scriptures, quote perpetually nearly all the books of the Hebrew Canon, and quote none besides, no link in the chain seems wanting to prove, that the Jewish Canon is that to which Christ appealed, and which He has commended to us, as the Word of God.

The history of the Septuagint explains the only difficulty in the question. It is briefly as follows : —

In the reign of Ptolemy Philadelphus this version was made at Alexandria. It is impossible, that it could have then contained the books of the Apocrypha, inasmuch as these books were not written till after the date when the Septuagint version was made.; none of them probably having been in existence till about two centuries before the Christian era. At what exact time the Apocryphal books were written respectively, it is not easy to determine. None of them could have been written in Hebrew, which had then become a dead language ; though some may have been composed in Chaldee or Syriac, languages which in the new Testament and in other writings are frequently called Hebrew.[1] However, when these Apocryphal books were written, if in Greek, the originals, if in Chaldee, the Greek translations, were, in all probability, inserted into the Septuagint, along with the still more sacred books of Scripture, by the Alexandrian Jews, who, in their state of dispersion, were naturally zealous about all that concerned their religion and the history of their race. The places which they assigned to the various books, were dependent either on the subject or on the supposed author. Thus the Song of the three Children, the Story of Susanna, and the History of Bel and the Dragon, seemed connected with, and were therefore added to, the book of Daniel. The Greek Esdras seemed naturally to be connected with the Greek translation of the book of Ezra. The Book of Wisdom, being called the Wisdom of Solomon, was added to the Song of Solomon; and the book of Ecclesiasticus, called the Wisdom of Jesus the Son of Sirach, was placed after the Wisdom of Solomon.

No doubt, the Alexandrian Jews ascribed great importance to the books which they thus inserted in the Septuagint version; but Philo, who was an Alexandrian Jew, and who was a contemporary of our Lord's, never quotes them for the purpose of establishing any doctrine; and it is certain that none of them ever got into the Hebrew Canon; nor were they ever received by the Jews of Palestine, amongst whom our blessed Saviour taught, and to whose Canon, therefore, He gave the sanction of His Divine authority.

Now the fathers of the Christian Church for the first three centuries were, with the exception of Origen, profoundly ignorant of Hebrew. It was natural, therefore, that they should have adopted the Greek version as their old Testament; and, accordingly, it formed the original of their Latin version. Hence the books of the old Testament current in the Church were, in Greek the Septuagint, in Latin a translation from the Greek Septuagint;

---

[1] The Book of Ecclesiasticus appears from ch L. 27 to have been written by "Jesus the Son of Sirach of *Jerusalem*;" and in the Prologue of his grandson the words of the book are said to have been Έβραϊστὶ λεγόμενα, written in Hebrew. However, Hebrew was then a dead language, and the Jews spoke Syro-Chaldee, which was what St. Paul spoke when he addressed his countrymen "in the Hebrew dialect," ἐν Ἑβραΐδι διαλέκτῳ, Acts xxii. 1. It is also said that the first book of Maccabees was written in Hebrew; but as some of the events recorded in it happened within one hundred and fifty years from the birth of Christ, it must have been the same Chaldee. Tobit also and Judith are said by Jerome, in his Prefaces to these books, to have been written *Chaldæo sermone*, though it has been thought the Chaldee was only a translation.

both therefore containing the Apocryphal books. It was not till the time of Jerome, that a translation was made from the Hebrew; and hence, in the eyes of many, the whole collection of books contained in the Septuagint and the old Latin translation was naturally viewed with the respect due to Scripture. Many indeed of the fathers, as we shall soon see, knew the difference between the books of the Hebrew Canon and those of the Apocrypha, and knew that the former were Divine, the latter of inferior authority. But still many quoted almost indiscriminately from both; and especially St. Augustine is appealed to, as having given a Catalogue of the old Testament Scriptures, which contained the books of Tobit, Judith, Wisdom, Ecclesiasticus, and the two books of Maccabees.[1] In the Latin Church the name of Augustine stood deservedly high. Though Jerome's labours showed the fallacy of Augustine's opinion, though the Greek fathers never received the Apocryphal books so carelessly as the Latin fathers had done, and though even Augustine himself was aware of the difference between them and the books of the Hebrew Canon; yet the Apocryphal books still kept their place in the Latin Vulgate, and were ultimately adopted by the Council of Trent, as part of the Canon of Scripture. Yet as we can thus easily trace the origin of the mistake, and thereby see that it was a mistake, we need not be led away with it.

This, necessarily very brief, sketch of the grounds on which we believe the present Hebrew Canon to be that to which our Lord gave His sanction, may be sufficient to show on what we rest our belief concerning the sacred books of the old Testament. From such historical evidence we know, that the Scriptures which the Lord Jesus appealed to, authorized, and confirmed, were the books contained in our Hebrew Bibles.[2] We ask no more, and we can receive no more. On such a matter the appeal to such an authority must be final. Fathers and Councils, nay, "the holy Church throughout all the world," would be as nothing, if their voice could be against their Lord's.

We are not, however, in this or in any other question, insensible to the value of the opinions of the fathers, still less of the consent of the early Church. And though we can plainly see what, in this case, may have led some of the fathers into error, we rejoice in being able to show, that, in the main, their testimony

[1] Augustin. *De Doctrina Christiana*, Lib. II. c. 8; *Opera*, Tom. III. pt. I. p. 23.
[2] Passages of the new Testament, where such authority is given to the old, are such as Matt. v. 18. Luke xvi. 29; xxiv. 27, 44. John v. 39. Rom. iii. 1, 2; ix. 4. 2 Tim. iii. 15, 16.

is decisive for what we have already, on other grounds, shown to be the truth.

Now in the second century, A. D. 147, Justin Martyr, himself a native of Palestine, in his Dialogue with Trypho the Jew, though he reproves him for many other things, never reproaches him for rejecting any of the Canonical Scriptures.[1] Melito, A. D. 160, we have already seen, went to Palestine to be satisfied concerning the Canon of the old Testament, and reports that it contained, according to the Christians of that country, the books of our Hebrew Bible.[2] Origen, A. D. 220, the most learned of the early fathers, the famous compiler of the Hexapla, himself a native of and resident at Alexandria, where the Septuagint version was made and received, gives us the same account as Melito.[3]

Athanasius, Bishop of Alexandria, A. D. 340, gives a perfect catalogue of the books of Scripture, enumerating the books of the old Testament just as the English Church receives them now, and mentioning as *not canonical* [4] the Wisdom of Solomon, the Wisdom of Sirach, Esther (*i. e.* the Apocryphal book of Esther), Judith, and Tobit.[5]

Hilary, Bishop of Poitiers, in France, A. D. 350, numbers the books of the old Testament as twenty-two, and gives the names of the very books of the Hebrew Bible used in the English Church, saying that some persons had added to this number Tobit and Judith, to make up twenty-four, the number of the Greek letters, instead of twenty-two, the number of the Hebrew.[6]

Cyril of Jerusalem, A. D. 360, in his Catechetical Lectures, exhorts the catechumens to abstain from the Apocryphal, and to read only the Canonical books of Scripture, giving as the reason, "Why shouldest thou, who knowest not those which are acknowledged by all, take needless trouble about those which are questioned?" He makes the number of the books twenty-two, and

[1] Cosin, *On the Canon*, ch. IV.
[2] Euseb. *H. E.* IV. 26.
[3] Euseb. *H. E.* VI. 25.
[4] Ἕτερα βίβλια τούτων ἔξωθεν · οὐ κανονιζόμενα μὲν, τετυπωμένα δὲ παρὰ τῶν πατέρων.
[5] *Festal. Epist.* XXXIX. *Op.* Tom. II. p. 961, edit. Bened. Tom. II. p. 38. Colon. 1686.
  The only thing to be observed in the catalogue of Athanasius is, that he joins Baruch and the Epistle with Jeremiah; into which mistake many of the fathers fell, from the connection which was made between those books in the LXX. and Latin; though some think, that nothing

more is meant than what is inserted in the book of Jeremiah concerning Baruch, and the Epistle contained in the twenty-ninth chapter of the prophecy of Jeremiah, — not the apocryphal books of these names. See Cosin, ch. VI.

[6] Hilar. *Proleg. in Librum Psalmorum*, § 15, edit. Benedict. p. 9. His Catalogue is Five books of Moses, 5. Joshua, 1. Judges and Ruth, 1. Samuel, 1. Kings, 1. Chronicles, 1. Ezra (including Nehemiah), 1. Psalms, 1. Proverbs, 1. Ecclesiastes, 1. Song of Songs, 1. Minor Prophets, 1. Isaiah, 1. Jeremiah (with Lamentations and Epistle), 1. Daniel, 1. Ezekiel, 1. Job, 1. Esther, 1. In all, 22

gives the same list as Athanasius, *i. e.* the same as the English Canon, with the addition of Baruch and the Epistle to the book of Jeremiah.[1]

The Council of Laodicea, held about A. D. 364, in its fifty-ninth Canon, gives exactly the same list as Athanasius and Cyril. The Canons of this Council were approved by name in the Council of Constantinople in Trullo.[2]

Epiphanius, Bishop of Constance, in Cyprus, A. D. 375, three times numbers the books of the old Testament as we do, and mentions the books of Wisdom and Ecclesiasticus as "doubtful writings," and not counted as among the sacred books "because they were never laid up in the Ark of the covenant." [3]

Gregory Nazianzen, A. D. 376, gives a catalogue, which is the same as the Canon of the English Church, except that he does not mention Esther, which he probably includes in Ezra.[4]

Rufinus, presbyter of Aquileia, A. D. 398, numbers the books of the old Testament as the English Church does at present.[5]

Jerome, the contemporary and friend of Rufinus, gives us, as we have seen, the same catalogue as the Church of England now receives, and enumerates Wisdom, Ecclesiasticus, Judith, Tobit, and the Maccabees, as Apocryphal books.[6]

We have now arrived at the close of the fourth century, and have found that the whole chain of evidence up to that period is in favour, and most decidedly in favour, of the Canon of the English Church. It will be no argument against such testimony, that many of the fathers quote the Apocryphal books, or even quote them as of authority. We have already seen what circumstances led the early Christians, and especially those of the Latin Church, into a somewhat excessive respect for the Apocryphal writings contained in the Septuagint and the ancient Latin Versions.

At the end of the fourth century, and contemporary with Jerome, lived Augustine, Bishop of Hippo. In his book *De Doctrina Christiana*,[7] he enumerates the books of the "whole Canon of Scripture." He reckons in this Canon the books of Tobit, Judith, two books of Maccabees, Wisdom, and Ecclesiasticus. The authority of Augustine is very great. Yet is it not for a moment to be weighed against the testimony of the four preceding centuries, even if his testimony was undoubted and uniform. Yet

---

[1] Cyril. Hieros. *Catech.* IV. § 35.
[2] Concil. Laodicen. Can. LIX. Concil. Quinisext. Can. II.
[3] *Adv. Hæres.* v. LXXVI. *De Mensuris et Ponderibus*, Tom. II. pp. 162, 180.
[4] Greg. Nazianz. *Carm.* XXXIII.

[5] *Expositio in Symbolum Apostolorum,* § 36, *ad calcem Oper. Cyprian.*
[6] *In Prologo Galeato*, Tom. I. p. 322. Ed. Bened.
[7] Lib. II c. 8, edit. Benedict Tom III. p. 23.

this is by no means the case. In the very passage above referred to, he speaks of a diversity of opinion concerning the sacred books, and advises, that those should be preferred which were received by all the Churches; that, of those not always received, those which the greater number and more important Churches received should be preferred before those which were sanctioned by fewer and less authoritative Churches.[1]   But moreover, passages from his other writings tell strongly against the canonicity of the books commonly called the Apocrypha.   Thus he speaks of the Jews being without prophets from the captivity, and after the death of Malachi, Haggai, Zechariah, and Ezra, until Christ.[2]   He tells us, that " the Jews did not receive the book of Maccabees as they did the Law, the Prophets, and the Psalms, to which the Lord gives testimony, as to His own witnesses." [3]   He tells us, that the book of Judith was never in the Canon of the Jews.[4]   He distinguishes between the books which are certainly Solomon's, and the books of Wisdom and Ecclesiasticus, to which custom has given the sanction of his name, but which learned men agreed were not his.[5] And many other proofs have been brought from his works, to show that he was at least doubtful concerning the authority of these books, notwithstanding his catalogue, which included them.[6]

We now come to the Council of Carthage at which it is said that Augustine was present.   The date of this Council is disputed. It is usually considered as the third Council of Carthage, held A. D. 397.   It enumerates the books of Scripture as we have them now, together with Wisdom, Ecclesiasticus, Tobit, Judith, and the two books of Maccabees.[7]   If Augustine was present, it is probable that we ought to interpret the decree of the Council with the same restrictions with which we plainly ought to interpret the words of St. Augustine, who, if he be not altogether inconsistent with him-

---

[1] In canonicis autem Scripturis, Ecclesiarum Catholicarum quam plurium auctoritatem sequatur; inter quas sane illæ sint quæ Apostolicas sedes habere et epistolas accipere meruerunt.   Tenebit igitur hunc modum in Scripturis canonicis, ut eas, quæ ab omnibus accipiuntur Ecclesiis Catholicis, præponat eis quas quædam non accipiunt: in eis vero quæ non accipiuntur ab omnibus, præponat eas quas plures gravioresque accipiunt, eis quas pauciores minorisque auctoritatis Ecclesiæ tenent. — Lib. II. c. 8, edit. Benedict.   Tom. III. p. 23.

[2] De Civitat. Dei, Lib. XVII. cap. 24. Tom. VII. p. 487.   Toto illo tempore ex quo redierunt de Babylonia, post Malachiam, Aggæum, et Zachariam, qui tunc prophetaverunt, et Esdram, non habuerunt prophetas usque ad Salvatoris adventum, &c.

[3] Contra Gaud. Lib. I. c. 31, § 38. Tom. IX. p. 655.

[4] De Civitate Dei, Lib. XVIII. c. 26. Tom. VII. p. 508. In libro Judith : quem sane in Canone Scripturarum Judæi non recepisse dicuntur.

[5] De Civit. Dei, Lib. XVII. c. 20. Tom. VII. p. 483.   Propter eloquii nonnullam similitudinem, ut Salomonis dicantur, obtinuit consuetudo : non autem esse ipsius, non dubitant doctiores.

[6] The whole question is fully sifted by Bp. Cosin, Scholastical History of the Canon, ch. VII.

[7] Conc. Carthag. III. Can. XLVII.

self, must assign a lower degree of authority to the doubtful books than to those which all received. But if it be not so, we must still remember that the Council of Carthage was a provincial, not a general Synod; that it was liable to err; and that in matter of history, if not in matter of doctrine, it actually did err; for by numbering five books of Solomon, it assigned to his authorship Wisdom and Ecclesiasticus, which could not have been written for centuries after his death. We cannot therefore bow to the authority of the Council of Carthage, even if that of St. Augustine be joined to it, against the testimony of all preceding ages, and, above all, against what has been shown to be the witness of our Lord Himself.

The Council of Trent, however, in its fourth session, stamped with its authority all the books which had been enumerated by the Council of Carthage, with the addition of the book of Baruch; and added an anathema against every one who should not receive the whole Canon so put forth, and all the traditions of the Church besides.[1] Thus did the Churches of the Roman communion set themselves against the Churches of God in the times of old, and against all the rest of Christendom in this present time. They, by implication, condemned those ancient fathers, who, as we have seen, almost with one voice preferred the Jewish Scriptures to the Apocryphal writings of the Septuagint. They anathematized, not only the Anglican, and all other reformed Churches, but as well the ancient Churches of the East, who with us reject the Apocrypha, and adhere to the Scriptures which were sanctioned by the Lord.[2] We might speak more strongly of the danger of "cursing whom God hath not cursed;" but we may rest satisfied with the assurance that "the curse causeless shall not come."[3]

---

[1] Concil. Trid. Sess. IV. Decret. I. Sacrorum vero librorum indicem huic decreto adscribendum censuit, ne cui dubitatio suboriri possit, quinam sint, qui ab ipso Synodo suscipiuntur. Sunt vero infra scripti:
Test. V. Quinque Mosis, Jos., Judic., Ruth, 4 Reg., 2 Paralip., Esdræ 1 et 2 (qui dicitur Nehem.), Tobias, Judith, Esther, Job, Psalterium David, cl. Psal., Parab., Ecclesiastes, Cantic. Canticorum, Sapientia, Ecclesiasticus, Esaias, Hieremias cum Baruch, Ezech., Daniel., 12 Proph. Minores, Duo Machabæorum 1 et 2.
Test. N. Quattuor Evangelia, &c. &c. Si quis autem libros ipsos integros cum omnibus suis partibus, prout in Ecclesia Catholica legi convenerunt et in veteri vulgata Latina editione habentur, pro sacris et canonicis non susceperit, et traditiones prædictas sciens et prudens contempserit, anathema sit.

[2] See Suicer, s. v. γραφή. See also Dr. Wordsworth's *Lectures on the Canon*, Appendix B. No. IV., where documents are given, showing the agreement of the Eastern with the Anglican Church on the Canon of Scripture.

[3] On the Canon of the old Testament, see Suicer's *Thesaurus*, s. v. γραφή; Bp Cosin's *Scholastic History of the Canon*; Bp. Marsh, *Lectures*, Part VI. *On the Authority of the old Testament*; Bp. Marsh's *Comparative View*, chap. V. Dr. Wordsworth, in his *Hulsean Lectures on the Canon of Scripture*, has thrown into the Appendix the most important passages

II. The Canon of the new Testament rests on the same authority as the Canon of the old.

As regards the number of books which are to be admitted as Canonical in the New Testament, there is no difference between the Anglican and any other branch of the Church of Christ. Yet on the mode of settling the Canon there is some difference. The Roman Church holds, that we receive the Scriptures, both of the old and new Testament, simply on the *authority* of the Church. It is said, that the Canon was not fixed till the end of the fourth century; and it is inferred, that the Church then, by its plenary authority, determined which books were Scripture, and which were not. Thus virtually the Church has been made to hold a position superior to the Scriptures, as not only " a witness and keeper," but also a judge " of Holy Writ." And though, in the first instance, such authority is conceded to the Church of the fourth century; yet, by implication and consequence, the same authority is claimed for the Church of this day; that is, not for the Church Universal, but for that portion of it which has claimed, as its exclusive title, the name of Catholic, *i. e.* the Church of Rome.

On the other hand, some Protestants have been satisfied to rest the authority of the books of the new Testament on internal evidence, especially on the witness which the Spirit bears with our own spirits that they are the Word of God. The framers of the Belgic Confession, for instance, distinctly assert, that they receive the Scriptures " not so much because the Church receives and sanctions them as Canonical, as because the Spirit witnesses with our consciences that they proceeded from God; and especially because they, of themselves, attest their own authority and sanctity." [1]

Now the Church of England rejects altogether neither the authority of the Church, nor the internal testimony of the Scriptures. Yet she is not satisfied to rest her faith solely on the authoritative decree of any council in the fourth or fifth, still less in any later century; neither can she consent to forego all external testimony, and trust to an internal witness alone, knowing that, as Satan can transform himself into an angel of light, so it

on the subject from the Jewish and early Christian writers, in a form more convenient than they may be seen in Bp. Cosin's most valuable work, as in the latter they are scattered through the notes, whilst in Dr. Wordsworth's book they are given in a compact form at the end.

[1] Idque non tam quod Ecclesia illos pro canonicis recipiat et comprobet: quam quod Spiritus Sanctus nostris conscientiis testetur illos a Deo emanasse: et eo maxime quod ipsi etiam per se sacram hanc suam authoritatem et sanctitatem testentur atque comprobent. — *Confess. Belgica*, Art. v.; *Sylloge Confessionum*, p. 328; Jones, *On the Canon*, Part I. ch. VI.

is possible, that what seems the guidance of God's Spirit may, if not proved, be really the suggestion of evil spirits. Hence we think that there is need of the external word, and of the Church, to teach; lest what seems a light within be but darkness counter-feiting light: and we know, that the fertile source of almost every fanatical error, recorded in history, has been a reliance on inward illumination, to the neglect of outward testimony.[1]

The principle, then, which we assert, is this, that Christ gave authority to His Apostles to teach and to write, that He promised them infallible guidance, and that therefore all Apostolical writings are divinely inspired. We have only to inquire what writings were Apostolical; and for this purpose we have recourse to testimony, or, if the word be preferred, to tradition. The testimony or tradition of the primitive Church is the ground on which the fathers themselves received the books of the new Testament as Apostolical; and, on the same ground, we receive them. We gladly add to this every weight which can be derived from internal evidence, or from the authority of early councils; for we know, that no argument should be neglected, which may fairly confirm our faith. But the first ground on which we receive the new Testament is, that it can be proved to have come from the pens or the dictation of the Apostles of Christ, and that to those Apostles Christ promised infallibility in matters of faith.

1. The promise of inspiration and infallibility appears in such passages as the following: —

" The Comforter, which is the Holy Ghost, whom the Father will send in My Name, He shall teach you all things, and bring all things to your remembrance, whatsoever I have said unto you." John xiv. 25, 26.

" When He, the Spirit of truth is come, He will guide you into all truth, and He will show you things to come." John xvi. 13.

" It is not ye that speak, but the Holy Ghost." Mark xiii. 11.

And what Christ promised, His Apostles claimed. They speak of having the deep things of God revealed to them by His Spirit, 1 Cor. ii. 10. They declare their own Gospel to be the truth, and

---

[1] There is a passage much to the purpose, quoted by Jones (*On the Canon,* Part I. ch. VI.) from the Preface to Baxter's *Saints' Rest.* " For my part, I confess, I could never boast of any such testimony or light of the Spirit nor reason neither, which, without human testimony, would have made me believe that the book of Canticles is canonical and written by Solomon, and the book of Wisdom apocryphal, and written by Philo, &c. Nor could I have known all or any historical books, such as Joshua, Judges. Ruth, Samuel, Kings, Chronicles, Ezra, Nehemiah, &c., to be written by divine inspiration, but by tradition, &c."

anathematize all who preach any other Gospel, Gal. i. 8. They speak of " the mystery of Christ, which in other ages was not made known to the sons of men," as being now revealed to the " Apostles and prophets by the Spirit," Ephes. iii. 4, 5; and treat the Gospel as a faith " once delivered to the saints," Jude 3.

If therefore we believe the new Testament at all, we believe that Jesus Christ gave a promise of inspiration to the Apostles ; and that the Apostles claimed the promise, professed to have received the inspiration, and accordingly assumed to be the only infallible depositaries of the doctrines of the Gospel.

2. We have therefore, in the next place, simply to determine the genuineness of the writings which profess to be Apostolical, and our labour will be finished. If we know that any book was written by an Apostle, we know that, as regards doctrine and faith, it is inspired and infallible, and therefore we receive it into the Canon of Scripture. The primitive Church acted on this principle ; and we act upon the same.

More or less, all ancient writings must be subjected to a test like this. If we wish to know whether certain books were written by Cicero, or Cæsar, or Tacitus, we examine the evidence, and decide according to it. The simple fact that they have ever been received as theirs, is a strong presumption that they proceeded from them. But still we mostly require farther proof.

Now, it is infinitely more important to be assured that a book was written by St. John or St. Paul, than to know that one was written by Cæsar or Cicero. And accordingly God, in His Providence, has afforded us far more abundant evidence concerning the genuineness of the different books of the new Testament, than can be found concerning any other writings of antiquity. That evidence is principally dependent on *testimony*, but is not resolvable into mere *authority*. It is the *witness* of the Church, not merely its *sanction*, to which we appeal.

Now the position of the Church in its earliest ages was such, that its witness on this subject is singularly unexceptionable. During the very lifetimes of the Apostles, it had spread through the civilized world. Europe, Asia, Africa, had all heard the voice of the Apostles, and all had flourishing Churches long before the death of the last of that sacred body. The books which the Apostles had written were therefore not merely to be found in one or two obscure corners of the world, but they were treasured up, and read and reverenced in Rome and Alexandria, in Antioch and Ephesus, in Corinth and Thessalonica, very probably in Spain and Gaul and

Arabia, perhaps even in the remote region of Britain itself. There were therefore witnesses in every corner of the globe. Even where the arms of Rome had not carried conquest, the feet of Apostles had carried good tidings of peace. In many of these Churches, the writers of the sacred books were well known and constant visitors; so that Epistles as from them, or Gospels with their names, could not have been palmed off upon their converts, who could continually have rectified errors of this kind by direct appeal to the living sources of Divine instruction. The writers of the new Testament themselves took care that what they wrote should be widely circulated, and extensively known, when first they wrote it. St. Paul bids the Colossians send his epistle to them to be read as well in the Church of Laodicea (Col. iv. 16). He charges the Thessalonians that they should suffer his epistle to be " read to all the holy brethren " (1 Thess. v. 27). We are informed concerning the Gospels, that they were written, the first by an Apostle, for the use of the Church of Judea;[1] the second, by St. Mark, under the dictation of St. Peter,[2] for the use of those Christians amongst whom St. Peter had been preaching, and who wished to have the substance of it preserved in writing;[3] that St. Luke, the companion of St. Paul, wrote his Gospel at St. Paul's dictation;[4] and that St. John wrote his in his last days at Ephesus, having first seen and approved the other Gospels, writing his own as supplementary to them.[5]

These and similar considerations show that the writings of the new Testament must have had a great degree of publicity, and therefore great protection against forgery and fraud, from their earliest publication. Every separate Church, and every separate city, to which they spread, was a guard against corruption, and a check upon its neighbours. But at the same time, wide as the empire of Christ had spread, it was not then, as now, a collection of disunited communities, but one living, intercommunicating whole. The early records with one voice proclaim that all Christendom was as one man. There was a circulation of life-blood through the whole. A Christian could not go from Rome to Alexandria, or from Alexandria to Ephesus, but he bore a talisman with him, which made him welcomed as a brother. And the degree of intercourse which took place in the very earliest times between far distant Churches, is apparent by the letter of

[1] Euseb. *H. E.* iii. 24; Iren. iii. 1.
[2] Iren. iii. 1 ; iii. 11.
[3] Euseb. i. 15; vi. 14, on the authority of Clemens Alexandrinus.
[4] Iren. iii. 1.
[5] Euseb. iii. 24; Hieron. *De Viris Il-lustribus*, s. v. Joannes.

Clement of Rome to the Church of Corinth, by the solicitude of Ignatius for the different cities, to which he wrote on the eve of his martyrdom, by the journey of Polycarp from Smyrna to Rome to discuss the Paschal controversy, by the appointment of Irenæus, a native of Asia, to the chief bishopric in Gaul, and by numerous similar facts.

We have therefore the following securities that the Churches from the first would preserve the writings of the Apostles safe and in their integrity.

(1) The presence of the Apostles with them, and frequent intercourse among them, whilst the sacred books were in writing.

(2) The publicity given to these books from the first.

(3) The wide diffusion of the Church throughout the world, so that copies would be multiplied everywhere, and one part of the Church would be a check against forgeries in another.

(4) The intimate communion of every part of Christendom with the rest, so that every facility was afforded to every portion of the Church, of knowing what were the Apostles' writings, and of guarding against mistake.

(5) To these we may add, that there were divisions in many Churches even from the Apostles' days, (see 1 Cor. iii. 3, 4; Gal. ii. 4, &c.) which necessarily created independent witnesses, even in individual Churches, each party being a check on the other.

(6) And lastly, that in God's Providence the Apostle St. John lived at the great city of Ephesus for thirty years after the works of the other Apostles had been written; and was thus living in the midst of the civilized world, as a final and authoritative court of appeal, if there could be any doubt as to which were Apostolical, and which Apocryphal writings.

Can we doubt then, that the primitive Church was a body so remarkably constituted that its testimony united, on this particular subject, the singularly opposite merits of unanimity and yet of mutual independence; that it enjoyed the most extraordinary powers for knowing the truth, with no interest in corrupting it, and without the power to corrupt it, even if it had the will?

We conclude therefore, that the Scriptures which the primitive Church held as Apostolical, must have been so. And we may add, that, owing to the wide diffusion of the Church throughout the world, it would have been impossible for a forger in after-times to pass off his forgery on the Church; for, if it was received in one place, it would speedily be rejected in another, and convicted of falsehood, on the sure ground of novelty. The primitive

Church, therefore, was singularly fitted by Providence to be a witness and keeper of Holy Writ ; even a witness and a keeper of it against future as well as present corruptions.

It is impossible to give more than a very brief sketch of the evidence which we derive from the early Church, thus qualified to bear testimony. We may classify it in the following order : —

　(1) Manuscripts of the original.

　(2) Versions in numerous languages.

　(3) Catalogues.

　(4) Quotations and references, and commentaries.

(1) We have manuscripts of the new Testament Scriptures in very great numbers, preserved to us in different quarters of the globe. The testimony which these MSS. bear, all tends to the same point ; namely, the general integrity of the text of the new Testament, as we have it now. These MSS. indeed are so far different from each other as to be independent witnesses ; for, though they agree in preserving the same general text, they differ in verbal minutiæ, and have various readings, like MSS. of all ancient authors ; and it is found that these MSS. can be classed into different families ; so that each family bears a line of testimony distinct from the others. Thus Griesbach distinguished the Greek MSS. into three distinct texts : the Alexandrine, which he found to correspond with the reading of the famous Codex Alexandrinus and with the quotations of Origen, the great Alexandrian critic ; the Byzantine, including those MSS. which in their peculiarities agree with the MSS. which have been brought to us direct from Constantinople ; the Western, to which belong the MSS. which have been chiefly found in Europe, and which in their peculiarities resemble the Latin version. Other critics (as Matthäi, Scholz, &c.) have made different arrangements and classifications ; but all agree in the observation, that we have distinct streams of MSS. coming down to us from the most remote antiquity, and preserving in the main the same text of the new Testament, though differing in minute particulars, sufficient to constitute them in some degree independent witnesses, and existing in the different quarters of the globe. It is true, the most ancient of these MSS. is probably not older than the fourth century ; but it is well known to all scholars, how very ancient a MS. of the fourth century is considered, and how very few MSS. in the world have anything approaching to such antiquity ; and it must be borne in mind, that a MS. of the fourth century represents a text of much earlier date, from which it must have been copied ; and when we

have many independent MSS., and some of them of nearly the same great antiquity, we know that they respectively and independently bear witness to the existence of an older text or texts, to which they owe their original.

Now here is one evidence of the genuineness of our new Testament writings. They are preserved to us in innumerable MSS. in all parts of the world ; MSS. whose authority is of the highest possible character. The books which are thus preserved are not the Apocryphal, but the generally received Canonical books of the new Testament.

(2) We have a great number of ancient versions of the new Testament Scriptures, in the various languages which were vernacular in the early ages of the Church. Thus we have versions in Latin, Syriac, Coptic, Sahidic, Arabic, Ethiopic, Armenian, and other languages. The Versions which are supposed to have the greatest claim to antiquity, are the Latin and the Syriac. That there was a very ancient Latin version, there can be no manner of doubt ; for the rapid diffusion of the Gospel in Europe and Africa made it a matter of great consequence that the new Testament Scriptures should speedily be translated into the Latin tongue. The ancient Italic may, therefore, very probably have been made in the days of the Apostles. The only difficulty of importance is the many alterations which the Latin Versions subsequently underwent, which make it hard to ascertain what MS. fairly represents the most ancient text. Yet all the Latin Versions of any authority, at present in existence, give their testimony, in the main, to the integrity of the text of the new Testament as we have it now. The Peschito Syriac is by most scholars considered to be the oldest of all the versions ; and it has the advantage of being a Version from the Greek into the vernacular tongue of our Lord and His Apostles. It is by many thought to be a work of the first century, and may have been seen by the Apostle St. John. The Syrians themselves held the tradition that it was made by St. Mark. The testimony which it bears concerning the Canon of the new Testament is most satisfactory, so far as it goes. It contains, in literal translation, the four Gospels, the Acts, thirteen Epistles of St. Paul, and the Epistle to the Hebrews, the Epistle of St. James, the first Epistle of St. Peter, and the first of St. John, — that is to say, all our present Canon, except the Apocalypse, the Epistle of St. Jude, the second of St. Peter, and the second and third of St. John. There are many reasons why so ancient a Version should not have contained these last-named

books. If it were made so early as has been supposed, some of the excluded books may not have been written. At all events, it is highly probable that they were not all at once collected into one volume, and some shorter and later pieces are especially likely to have been at first omitted.[1]

(3) We have among very early fathers, regular catalogues of the books of the new Testament, as received and read in the Church.

Origen, the most learned of the Greek fathers, who was born A. D. 185, *i. e.* less than ninety years from the death of St. John, gives a catalogue exactly corresponding with our present Canon.[2]

Eusebius, another most learned and accurate inquirer, born at Cæsarea, in Palestine, A. D. 270, gives a catalogue exactly corresponding with our own, except that he speaks of the Epistles of St. James, St. Jude, 2 Peter, 2 and 3 John, as generally received, yet doubted of by some; and says of the Apocalypse, that, though some doubted, yet others received it; and he himself received it, and considered it as canonical.[3]

Athanasius, Bishop of Alexandria, A. D. 326, and who therefore must have been born in the third century, gives a catalogue exactly corresponding with ours.[4]

Cyril, Bishop of Jerusalem, A. D. 349, gives the same list, with the exception of the Apocalypse.[5]

The Council of Laodicea, A. D. 364, gives the same list as St. Cyril.[6]

Epiphanius, A. D. 370, gives the same list as ours.[7]

Gregory Nazianzen, A. D. 375, who was born about the time of the Council of Nice, gives the same list as ours, omitting the Apocalypse.[8]

Jerome, who was born A. D. 329, was educated at Rome, and was ordained presbyter at Antioch, A. D. 378, gives the same list as ours; except that he observes that most persons in the Latin

---

[1] On the importance of the Syriac version, see Jones, *On the Canon*, Pt. I. ch. XIV.–XIX.

[2] Comment. in Matt. ap. Euseb. *H. E.* VI. 25. In this catalogue he omits St. James and St. Jude. But in his thirteenth Homily on Genesis he speaks of Matthew, Mark, Luke, John, Paul, Peter, James, and Jude, as the authors of the books of the new Testament. In his seventh Homily on the book of Joshua, if we may trust the Latin translation of Rufinus, in which alone it exists, he enumerates all the books which we now have. See Jones, *On the Canon*, Pt. I.

ch. VIII.; Bp. Marsh's *Lectures*, Pt. V. *On Authority of the New Testament*, Lect. XXIV.; Lardner, II. ch. XXXVIII.

[3] *H. E.* III. 25.

[4] *Ex Festali Epist.* XXXIX. Tom. II. p. 961; Edit. Benedict. Tom. II. p. 38, Colon. 1686.

[5] *Cateches.* IV. § 36. He makes mention of certain forged Gospels, ψευδεπίγραφα, and ascribes to the Manicheans a Gospel according to St. Thomas.

[6] Concil. Laodicen. Can. IX.

[7] *Hæres.* 76, c. 5.

[8] Gregor. Nazianz. *Carm.* XXXIII.

Church did not consider the Epistle to the Hebrews as St. Paul's, though he himself held that it was so.[1]

Rufinus, presbyter of Aquileia, contemporary and friend of Jerome, gives the same catalogue as we now possess.[2]

Augustine, Bishop of Hippo, A. D. 394, (born A. D. 355,) gives the same catalogue as ours.[3]

The Council of Carthage (A. D. 397?) gives the same catalogue.[4]

(4) But, besides these formal catalogues, we have from the very first ages a series of quotations, references, and allusions to our sacred books, and in some cases regular harmonies and commentaries upon them.

This is a wide subject. It occupies the first five volumes in the octavo edition of Lardner's most valuable work on *The Credibility of the Gospel History*. An account of it here must necessarily be brief.

The writings of the Apostolical fathers are few in number, and there are many reasons why they should not quote so frequently and fully from the books of the new Testament, as those who succeeded them. Yet there are, nevertheless, a considerable number of references and quotations from the books which we possess as the new Testament Scriptures, even in them.

Clement, who probably died before St. John, especially ascribes the first Epistle to the Corinthians to St. Paul. Words of our blessed Lord, found in the Gospels of St. Matthew, St. Mark, and St. Luke, are recommended with a high degree of respect, but without the names of the Evangelists; and there is reason to think that he alludes to the Acts, the Epistle to the Romans, the two Epistles to the Corinthians, and divers other of the Epistles of the new Testament.[5]

Ignatius, who suffered martyrdom very soon after the death of St. John, in writing to the Ephesians, ascribes the Epistle to that Church to St. Paul, and cites several passages from it. He alludes to St. Matthew's, St. Luke's, and probably to St. John's Gospel; also, probably, to the Acts, Romans, 1 and 2 Corinthians, Galatians, Philippians, 1 Thessalonians, 2 Timothy, 1 Peter, 1 and 3 John. He appears also to have expressions denoting collections of the Gospels and Epistles of the Apostles.[6]

---

[1] *Epist.* L. *ad Paulinum. Opp.* Tom. IV. p. 574; Ed. Bened. On the Epistle to the Hebrews, see *De Viris Illustribus*, s. v. Paulus.
[2] *Exposit. in Symb. Apostol.* § 36, ad calc. Oper. Cyprian.
[3] *De Doctrina Christiana*, Lib. II. c. 8. Tom. III. p. 23.
[4] Concil. Carthag. III. Can. XLVII.
[5] Lardner, II. ch. II.
[6] Ibid. II. ch. V.

Polycarp, Bishop of Smyrna, a disciple of St. John, quotes
Philippians, and speaks of St. Paul as having written to that
Church. He quotes also expressions from St. Matthew and St.
Luke, 1 Corinthians, Ephesians, 1 and 2 Thessalonians; and there
are manifest references to Romans, 1 and 2 Corinthians, Galatians,
Ephesians, 1 and 2 Timothy, 1 Peter, 1 John, and probably to the
Hebrews.[1]

If Barnabas and Hermas are to be reckoned Apostolical, although
there are manifest references to the new Testament in their works,
yet the nature of their writings makes it most improbable that
they should have quoted much from it, and accounts for their comparative silence.[2]

Papias, who was well acquainted with Polycarp, and, as some
think, even with St. John, and was an anxious inquirer about all
that had come from the Apostles and followers of Christ, bears
testimony to the Gospels of St. Matthew and St. Mark, quotes the
first Epistle of St. Peter and the first of St. John, appears to have
a reference to the book of Acts, and there is every reason to suppose he received the Apocalypse. There are no works of his remaining, except a fragment preserved by Eusebius.[3]

Justin Martyr, the first of the fathers of whom we have any
considerable remains, was converted to Christianity about A. D. 133,
flourished chiefly about A. D. 140, i. e. 40 years after the death of
St. John, and died a martyr about A. D. 164 or 167. He has
many quotations from the four Gospels, which he refers to under
the name of the *Memoirs of the Apostles*.[4] He has, moreover,
referred to the Acts, many of the Epistles, and expressly assigns
the Book of Revelation to St. John. In his first Apology, he tells
us that the memoirs of the Apostles and the writings of the
Prophets were read in the assemblies for public worship, and dis
courses made upon them by the presiding presbyter.[5]

---

[1] Lardner. II. ch. VI.

[2] Ibid. II. ch. I. IV.

[3] Euseb. *H. E.* Lib. III. cap. 39; Lardner, ii. ch. IX.

[4] Ἀπομνημονεύματα τῶν Ἀποστόλων,
which he explains by ἃ καλεῖται εὐαγγέλια.
— Apol. I. p. 98, B.
Bishop Marsh in his dissertation *On
the Origin of the Four Gospels*, ch. XV.,
supposes that Justin does not allude to
our present Gospels, but to a certain original document, which the Bishop supposes to have existed, which was early
composed by the Apostles, and from
which the Evangelists compiled their
several Gospels. The words ἃ καλεῖται

εὐαγγέλια he considers an interpolation.
He argues, that *Memoirs of the Apostles*
more probably mean a single work than
a collection of works, and that Justin's
quotations are not exact from our pres
ent Gospels. His arguments are considered by Bishop Kaye, *Writings of Justin
Martyr*, ch. VIII. The last-named prelate seems to have clearly proved that
there is no reason for doubting that our
present Gospels are those cited by Justin,
though, at times, he rather quotes the
purport than the very words of a passage.

[5] *Apol.* I. p. 98; Lardner, II. ch. X.

Tatian, the disciple of Justin Martyr, composed a harmony of the Gospels, called *Diatessaron*.[1]

The circular Epistle of the Churches of Vienne and Lyons, concerning the sufferings of their martyrs in the reign of Marcus Antoninus, uses language from the Gospels of St. Luke and St. John, Acts, Romans, Philippians, 1 Peter, 1 John, and the Revelation.[2]

Irenæus, who was a hearer of Polycarp, the disciple of St John,[3] and became Bishop of Lyons, A. D. 177, assures us that there were four Gospels, and no more,[4] all of which he has largely quoted, with the names of their writers, and has given an account of their composition.[5] He refers the Acts to St. Luke. He quotes all St. Paul's Epistles, except Philemon and the Hebrews, also 1 Peter, 1 and 2 John, and the Apocalypse, which he expressly assigns to St. John the Apostle,[6] and *probably* the Epistle of St. James. "His quotations from the Gospels are so numerous that they occupy more than twelve folio columns in the index of Scripture passages annexed to the Benedictine edition." [7]

Theophilus of Antioch (circ. A. D. 170) quotes St. Matthew, St. Luke, several of St. Paul's Epistles, and we are assured by Eusebius that in his work against Hermogenes he quoted the Apocalypse.[8]

Clement of Alexandria, who lived at the end of the second century, about 100 years after the completion of the Canon of Scripture, quotes all the four Gospels, and especially tells us the origin of St. Mark's.[9] He ascribes the Acts to St. Luke; quotes all St. Paul's Epistles, except the short Epistle to Philemon, and ascribes the Epistle to the Hebrews to St. Paul, though he thinks it was written in Hebrew by St. Paul, and translated into Greek by St. Luke.[9] He quotes three of the Catholic Epistles, namely, 1 John, 1 Peter, Jude; for it is doubtful whether he refers expressly to St. James, or the second Epistle of St. Peter, and the second and third of St. John. The Apocalypse he expressly ascribes to St. John.[10]

Tertullian, presbyter of Carthage, of the same date with Clement, quotes all the books of the new Testament, except perhaps

[1] Lardner, ii. ch. xiii.
[2] Ibid. ch. xvi.
[3] Hieronym. *De V. I. s. v.* Irenæus.
[4] *Adv. Hæres.* iii. 11.
[5] Ibid. iii. 1.
[6] *Adv. Hæres.* iv. 20 ; v. 26.. The time of seeing the Apocalypse is mentioned v. 30; namely, towards the end of the reign of Domitian, if the word ἑωράθη is used of the seeing of the Apocalypse, not, as some think, of the duration of St. John's own life.
[7] Bp. Marsh's *Lectures*, Pt. v. Lect. xxiv.; Lardner, ii. ch. xvii.
[8] Lardner. ii. ch. xx.
[9] Euseb. *H. E.* vi. 14.
[10] Lardner, ii. ch. xxii. ; Bp. Kaye's *Clement of Alex.* ch. viii.

St. James's Epistle, the second of St. Peter, and the third of St. John. The Epistle to the Hebrews he assigns to Barnabas.[1] Dr. Lardner has observed, that "There are perhaps more and larger quotations of the new Testament in this one Christian author than of all the works of Cicero, though of so uncommon excellence for thought and style, in the writers of all characters for several ages.[2]

We are now arrived at Origen, who, as we have seen, gives a complete catalogue of the new Testament, as we have it now.[3]

Dionysius of Alexandria, A.D. 247, quotes the Gospels, Acts, St. Paul's Epistles, especially ascribing the Hebrews to St. Paul, the three Epistles of St. John. On the Apocalypse he has a long dissertation, from which it appears that it was very generally received by Christians as written by St. John, though he himself inclines to attribute it to another John, whom he considered a holy and divinely inspired man.[4]

Cyprian, A.D. 250, quotes all the new Testament except the Epistles to Philemon and the Hebrews, the third of St. John, the second of St. Peter, and St. James. The Apocalypse he often quotes as St. John's.[5]

Methodius, Bishop of Olympus in Lycia, circ. A.D. 260, constantly quotes or refers to the Gospels and Acts, most of St. Paul's Epistles, especially the Hebrews, also 1 Peter, 1 John, and the Apocalypse.[6]

Eusebius has already been adduced as a witness, having given a catalogue of the new Testament Scriptures, as we have them now.

It is unnecessary to continue the list farther. We have already seen that from this time we may find in the works of the fathers full catalogues of the books of the new Testament; and the number of quotations from them in their writings grows fuller and more abundant.

We must add, that heretics quoted and admitted the same Scriptures, with the exception of those outrageous heretics, such as the Gnostics and the Manichees, who were rather heathen philosophers, with a tinge of Christianity, than Christians with a defilement of philosophy. Thus the Montanists, the Donatists,[7] Arius,[8] Photinus,[9] Lucifer,[10] and other schismatics and heretics of the first

---

[1] *De Pudicitia*, c. 20.
[2] Lardner, II. ch. XXVIII. See also Bp. Kaye's *Tertullian*, ch. V. p. 307.
[3] Lardner, ch. XXXVIII.
[4] Ibid. III. ch. XLIII.
[5] Ibid. III. ch. XLIV.
[6] Ibid. III. ch. LVII.
[7] Ibid. ch. LXVII.
[8] Ibid. ch. LXIX.
[9] Ibid. ch. LXXXIX.
[10] Ibid. ch. XCI.

four centuries, received the same sacred books with the Catholic Christians.

Not only heretics, moreover, but heathens and persecutors knew the sacred books and sought to destroy them. Thus in the persecution of Diocletian, there was an edict A. D. 303, that the Christian Churches should be destroyed, and their Scriptures burned. Accordingly, great search was made for the books of the new Testament, and those Christians who, to save themselves, gave up their books to the persecutors, acquired the opprobrious name of Traditores.[1]

When Constantine the Great embraced Christianity, finding that the persecution under Diocletian had diminished the number of copies of the new Testament, he authorized Eusebius Bishop of Cæsarea to get fifty copies of the new Testament written out for him, desiring that they should be skilfully and carefully written on fine parchment.[2]

We have seen then, that numerous MSS., the most ancient Versions, the catalogues given us by the fathers, quotations and references from the time of the earliest Apostolical father, gradually increasing in number, yet numerous from the beginning, the consent of heretics, the enmity of persecutors, — all witness to the existence, from the earliest times, of the new Testament Scriptures; and all this testimony is uniform in favour of the very books which we now possess.

It may be added, that, although it is quite clear that there were certain early writers, such as Clement, Barnabas, and Hermas, highly esteemed, and whose writings were read in some Churches; and though there were some Apocryphal books professing to be the works of the Apostles and Evangelists : yet there is good reason to assert that these books are not quoted by the fathers as authority, and were not received by the Church as Canonical Scripture.[3]

To the external evidence, the internal proofs of genuineness might be added, if time and space would allow. Books which are forgeries generally show, when carefully scrutinized, plain proofs that they are not his whose name they bear. The language, the ideas, the statements of facts, some little circumstance of date or place, some circumstance connected with the character, knowledge, or condition of the author, are found inconsistent and

---

[1] Lardner, ch. LXVI.
[2] Euseb. Lib. IV. c. 36; Lardner, ch. LXX.

[3] See Jones, On the Canon, Part II. ch. I. Observ. III.; Lardner, ch. X. XIV XVII. XXII. XXXVIII. LVII. &c.

incapable of being explained.   Or if this be not the case, there is
a markedly studied effort to avoid all this, and to make the forgery
appear a genuine work.   But the different books of the new
Testament, though written by eight different hands, under vastly
different conditions, have yet defied the efforts of critics to disprove their genuineness.   They only come out the brighter from
every fiery trial.   Their style and language is just what we should
expect from the writers to whom they are ascribed.   They abound
in minute particulars, most naturally and simply introduced, which
correspond accurately with the state of things existing at the time
and in the place in which the authors wrote.   Coincidences have
been pointed out, which the cleverest forger could never have
designed, and which only patient searching could have detected;
whereas, if such coincidences had been designed, they would have
been put prominently forward to meet the view.[1]   In this, and
in similar manners, we may confirm by internal examination the
results deduced from external testimony.

But before we conclude this sketch we must observe, that, in
the accounts of the catalogues and quotations given by the different early fathers, we could not but remark that some books were
less universally quoted, and classed in the catalogues, than others.
We learn, as early as Origen, and more clearly afterwards from
Eusebius, that, though the Church generally received the Canon
of the new Testament as we receive it now, yet some few books
were by some persons considered as doubtful.

Eusebius makes three distinct classes of books,[2] namely : —

ὁμολογούμενοι, those universally received ;

ἀντιλεγόμενοι, those generally received, but doubted of **by**
some ;

νόθοι, *i. e.* Apocryphal books rejected by all but heretics.

In like manner, Cyril of Jerusalem distinguishes between those
παρὰ πᾶσιν ὁμολογούμενα, owned by all, and ἀμφιβαλλόμενα, doubted
of by some.[3]

Now the undoubted books according to Eusebius, which all
received, were the four Gospels, the Acts, thirteen Epistles of St.
Paul, one of St. Peter, one of St. John.   He adds, that Christians
generally received the Hebrews, James, 2 Peter, 2 and 3 John,
Jude, Revelation.   These he esteemed canonical, but tells us that
some doubted concerning their genuineness.   He also mentions
the Epistles of Clement and Barnabas, and the Pastor of Hermas,

---

[1] See Paley's *Horæ Paulinæ*, passim;   [2] *H. E.* III. 3, 25.
Marsh's *Lect.* Pt. v. Lect. xxvi.   [3] Cyril. *Cateches.* iv. 36

as esteemed useful by many, but not to be considered a part of
Canonical Scripture.[1]   Now the principal reasons for doubting the
genuineness and Canonicity of the books which Eusebius speaks
of as ἀντιλεγόμενα, were of this nature.   The Hebrews has not
St. Paul's name, and is thought to be different in style from his
other writings.[2]   St. James might not have been an Apostle, and
therefore his Epistle might have no claim to be in the Canon.
The Apocalypse introduces the name of St. John, contrary to that
Apostle's custom elsewhere ; and some supposed it was written
by John the elder, a person whom Papias mentions, and not by
St. John the Apostle.[3]

To take first the Epistle of St. James ; there is strong reason to
believe, that, whether the writer was James the son of Zebedee,
or James the Lord's brother, he was in any case an Apostle ; for
James the Lord's brother is in Scripture called an Apostle,[4] and
was in all probability the same as James the son of Alphæus, or
Cleopas, (the two names being very probably identical,) his mother
being Mary the sister of the Virgin Mary.[5]   So that there is no
reason to exclude his Epistle from the Canon, because he was not
an Apostle.   But farther, his Epistle is in the Syriac version, and
the authority of the Syrian Church is very important on this head ;
for the Church of Syria bordered on Palestine, where St. James,
the Lord's brother, was bishop, and spoke the same language as
the natives of Palestine itself.   We must remember, too, that
Eusebius tells us that this Epistle was received by the great
majority of Christians ; and that it is by no means wonderful that
an Epistle, written by the Bishop of Jerusalem to the Jews, should
not have become known to the Grecian Churches so soon as
others ; and hence more doubt might arise about it than about
other Epistles.[6]

Of the Epistle to the Hebrews, and the Apocalypse, we learn
that the former was not fully admitted by the Latin, nor the latter
by the Greek Church among Canonical Scriptures.[7]

Of the Epistle to the Hebrews, we may observe that the
absence of the Apostle's name may be fully accounted for by the
fact that he was the Apostle of the Gentiles, not of the circumcision ; and therefore, when he writes to the Jews, he does not
put his name and claim his Apostleship, as not wishing to put for-

---

[1] Euseb. *H. E.* as above ; Lardner,
LXXII.
[2] Hieronym. *De V. I. in Paul.*
[3] Euseb. *H. E.* III. 39.
[4] Gal. i. 19.

[5] See Lardner, VI. ch. XVI.
[6] See Marsh's *Lect.* Pt. v. Lect. XXV.
[7] Hieronym. *Dardan.* Epist. CXXIX
De V. I. s. v. Paul.   1602.

ward the same claim to authority over the Jews which he asserts over the Gentile Churches.[1] But the Epistle is probably referred to by Clement of Rome,[2] and perhaps by Polycarp.[3] We have in its favour the testimony of Origen, Clement of Alexandria, Dionysius of Jerusalem, the Council of Laodicea, Epiphanius, Gregory Nazianzen, Jerome.[4] It is in the Syriac Canon. And, as regards the supposed difference of style from the general writings of St. Paul, the opinion of Clement of Alexandria, that St. Paul wrote the Epistle in Hebrew or Syriac, and that it was translated by St. Luke into Greek, would explain all the difficulty.[5] Yet Mr. Forster appears to have proved, by most careful and accurate comparison, that the style of the Epistle to the Hebrews, notwithstanding the apparent dissimilarity, has all the peculiarity of the writings of St. Paul, a peculiarity so great that the genuineness of the Epistle can hardly be questioned.[6]

The Apocalypse, which is the only other book of any considerable length which is doubted, is ascribed by Papias to John, probably the Apostle. It is the only book which Justin Martyr mentions by name, and he expressly assigns it to St. John. Irenæus constantly quotes it and refers it to St. John. Tertullian and Theophilus of Antioch quote it. Clement of Alexandria assigns it to St. John. So do Origen, Dionysius of Alexandria, Cyprian, Eusebius, Athanasius, Epiphanius, Jerome, the Council of Carthage.[7] All these are witnesses of great importance, and a large number of them living within a century of the date when the book in question was composed. Especially Papias, Justin Martyr, and Irenæus, the very earliest fathers after those called Apostolical, speak much concerning it, and quote frequently from it. Melito, a contemporary of Justin Martyr and Irenæus, is also, according to Eusebius, a witness to the Apocalypse of St. John.[8]

We may now close our brief view of the evidence concerning the Canon of the new Testament; and whilst we rejoice that councils in the fourth century, weighing the evidence, decided on the Canon, and settled it as we have it now, we cannot admit that the present Church receives the Scriptures, whether of the old

---

[1] Clem. Alex. ap. Euseb. *H. E.* vi. 14; Hieron. *In Galat.* cap. i.

[2] Eusebius observes that Clement uses the very language of the Epistle. — *H. E.* iii. 38. It may be added, that the writer of St. Clement's Epistle seems to have been thoroughly imbued with the spirit of the Epistle to the Hebrews.

[3] Lardner, ch. vi.

[4] See the lists above given.

[5] Ap. Euseb. *H. E.* vi. 14.

[6] Forster, *On the Apostolical Authority of the Epistle to the Hebrews.*

[7] See the lists and authorities referred to above.

[8] Καὶ λόγος αὐτοῦ (Μελίτωνος) περὶ προφητείας, καὶ ὁ περὶ φιλονεξίας· καὶ ἡ κλείς· καὶ τὰ περὶ τοῦ διαβόλου καὶ τῆς Ἀποκαλύψεως Ἰωάννου. — Euseb. *H. E.* iv. 26.

Testament or the new, merely on the authority of the Church of the fourth century; inasmuch as the Church of the fourth century itself received them on the testimony of earlier ages, and the present Church receives it on the same. That testimony, even if Councils had been silent, would be of itself amply sufficient to prove that the new Testament Scriptures which we now possess are the genuine works of the Apostles and Evangelists.

Section III. — ON THE REAL VALUE OF TRADITION, AND THE READING OF THE APOCRYPHA.

I. THE Church of England then holds, in conformity with the Church of old, that Scripture is absolutely perfect in relation to the end to which it tends, namely, the teaching us all things necessary to salvation. She denies the existence and rejects the authority of any parallel and equal tradition, of any doctrines necessary to salvation, handed down from generation to generation. But it is not true that the Church of England rejects the proper use of tradition, though she will not suffer it to be unduly exalted. She does not neglect the testimony of antiquity, and cut herself off from the Communion of the Saints of old.

It has been already remarked, that, besides the tradition which the Church of Rome holds necessary to be received, which is a tradition equal and parallel with the Scriptures, there are also traditions which are subservient to Scripture, and calculated to throw light upon it. Such tradition, when kept in its right place, the Church of England has ever used and respected.

Now this tradition is of two kinds, Hermeneutical Tradition, and Ecclesiastical Tradition. The former tends to explain and interpret the Scripture; the latter relates to discipline and ceremonial. With regard to the latter we find that the new Testament has nowhere given express rules for rites, ordinances, and discipline; although we evidently discover that rites, ordinances, and discipline did exist, even when the new Testament was written. For our guidance therefore in these matters, which are useful for edification, but not essential for salvation, we gladly follow the example of the Churches nearest to the Apostles' times, which we conceive to have been ordered by the Apostles themselves, and to be the best witnesses of Apostolic order and Apostolic usages.

Scripture is, at least, not full on these matters; yet they are essential for the regulating and governing of a Church. We appeal therefore, to the purest and earliest models of antiquity. We cannot err in doing this, for in asserting the sufficiency of Scripture, we assert it for the end to which it was designed. As we do not assert it as fit to teach us arts and sciences, so neither do we assert it as designed entirely to regulate Church discipline and ceremony. And where it does not profess to be a perfect guide, we derogate not from its authority in seeking other help. On matters of faith it is complete and full; but not in all things besides.

With regard to Hermeneutical Tradition, we view matters thus. Those early Christians who had the personal instruction of the Apostles and their immediate companions, are more likely to have known the truth of Christian doctrine than those of after-ages, when heresies had become prevalent, when men had learned to wrest Scripture to destruction, and sects and parties had warped and biassed men's minds, so that they could not see clearly the true sense of Holy Writ. Truth is one, but error is multiform; and we know that in process of time new doctrines constantly sprang up in the Church, and by degrees gained footing and took root. We believe therefore, that if we can learn what was the constant teaching of the primitive Christians, we shall be most likely to find the true sense of Scripture preserved in that teaching: and wherever we can trace the first rise of a doctrine, and so stamp it with novelty, the proof of its novelty will be the proof of its falsehood; for what could find no place among the earliest Churches of Christ can scarcely have come from the Apostles of Christ, or from a right interpretation of the Scriptures which they wrote. We do not, in thus judging, appeal to the authority of any individual father, not even if he be one of those who had seen the Apostles, and had received the miraculous gifts of the Holy Ghost. We know that they were fallible men, though we believe them to have been pious and wise men. But we look to their writings for evidence as to what were the doctrines prevalent in the Church during the earliest ages; and we believe that, if we can discover what the doctrines of those earliest ages were, we have a most important clue to guide us in our course through the Scriptures themselves, because we judge that the Church thus early must almost certainly have, in the main, preserved the integrity of the faith, and could not, whilst the voice of Apostolic men was in their ears, have fallen away into error and heresy. We know, that, in those days, men had many advantages over ourselves for the interpreting of the new Testament. A knowledge of the language, the customs, the history of events, which illustrate the Scriptures, was of itself most important. Some of them must have had in their memories the personal teaching of the Apostles, for they were their immediate hearers and followers. Many of them lived within a comparatively short time from their departure. They took the utmost pains to preserve the purity of the Apostolic faith in the Church. The Church of their days had still the *charismata*, or miraculous gifts of the Spirit, visibly poured out upon it; and we may say that in every, or almost every manner, it was qualified, beyond any subsequent Church or age, to understand the Scriptures, and to exhibit the purity and integrity of the Christian faith.

The least, then, that can be said, is that the doctrine of the ancient Church is an useful check on any new interpretation of Scripture. Antiquity is a mark of truth, and novelty a mark of error in religion ; and this rule has ever been found valuable in important controversies. The Socinians have striven to show that Justin Martyr invented the doctrine of the Trinity, deriving it from the writings of Plato. Catholic Christians, on the contrary, have proved, that from the earliest times that doctrine was held in the Church, that therefore it is traceable to the Apostles, and not to Plato, that it springs from a true, not from an erroneous interpretation of Scripture. A like form has the controversy with the Church of Rome assumed. Many of her peculiar doctrines have been proved to owe their origin to comparatively recent times ; and so they have been shown to be unfit to stand the well-known test of Tertullian, that " what is first is true, what is later is adulterate." [1]

Thus then tradition may be useful in the interpretation of Scripture, though not as adding to its authority. We well know that Scripture is perfect in itself, for the end for which it was designed. But we know also, that no aid for its interpretation should be neglected.

That the Church of England takes this view of the right use of tradition, and of the value of the testimony of the primitive Church, will appear from the following documents.

The Convocation of 1571, which passed the XXXIX. Articles in

---

[1] Hæc enim ratio valet adversus omnes hæreses, id esse verum, quodcunque primum, id esse adulterum, quodcunque posterius. — Tertull. *Adv. Prax.* 2.

the form in which we have them now, passed also a code of Canons, in one of which is the following clause : " In the first place let preachers take heed that they deliver nothing from the pulpit, to be religiously held and believed by the people, but that which is agreeable to the old and new Testament, and such as the *Catholic fathers and ancient bishops have collected therefrom.*" [1]

In like manner, in the Preface to the Ordination Service we read, " It is evident to all men reading Holy Scripture, *and ancient authors*, that from the Apostles' time there have been three orders of Ministers in Christ's Church, Bishops, Priests, and Deacons."

So Archbishop Cranmer, the great reformer of our Liturgy and compiler of our Articles, writes, " I also grant that every *exposition* of the Scripture, whereinsoever the old, holy, and true Church did agree, is necessary to be believed. But our controversy here " (that is with the Romanists) " is, whether anything ought to be believed of necessity without the Scripture." [2]

So his great coadjutor Bishop Ridley : " In that the Church of Christ is in doubt, I use herein the wise counsel of Vincentius Lirinensis, whom I am sure you will allow ; who, giving precepts how the Catholic Church may be in all schisms and heresies known, writeth in this manner : ' When,' saith he, ' one part is corrupted with heresies, then prefer the whole world before that one part ; but if the greatest part be affected, then prefer antiquity.' " [3]

Dr. Guest, who was appointed at the accession of Elizabeth, to restore the reformed prayer-book, after it had been disused in the reign of Mary, and who reduced it to nearly its present form, writes thus : " So that I may here well say with Tertullian, That is truth which is first ; that is false which is after. That is truly first which is from the beginning. That is from the beginning which is from the Apostles. Tertullian, *Cont. Prax. Cont. Marc.*" [4]

Bishop Jewel, in his Apology, which is all but an authoritative document, says : " We are come as near as we possibly could to the Church of the Apostles, and of the old Catholic bishops and fathers ; and have directed according to their customs and ordinances, not

---

[1] Imprimis vero videbunt, ne quid unquam doceant pro concione, quod a populo religiose teneri et credi velint, nisi quod consentaneum sit doctrinæ Veteris aut Novi Testamenti, quodque ex illa ipsa doctrina Catholici patres, et veteres episcopi collegerint. — Cardwell's *Synodalia*, I. p. 126.

[2] Cranmer, *On Unwritten Verities;* Jen-

kyn's *Cranmer's Remains*, IV. p. 229. See also p. 126, and III. p. 22.

[3] Gloster Ridley's *Life of Ridley*, p. 613.

[4] Guest to Sir W. Cecil, concerning the *Service Book*, &c. ; Strype's *Annals*, I. Appendix, No. XIV. ; also Cardwell's *Hist. of Conferences*, p. 52.

only our doctrine, but also the Sacraments, and the form of common prayer." [1]

These passages sufficiently prove that our reformers admitted and made use of the appeal to antiquity, in the interpretation of Scripture, and in the establishing of order and discipline. Their wisdom has been followed therein by all the great divines who have succeeded them. Joseph Mede, Hooker, Andrews, Hammond, Overal, Usher, Jeremy Taylor, Bull, Beveridge, Patrick, Waterland, Jebb, Van Mildert, Kaye, G. S. Faber, have been respectively cited as upholding the same principle, and acting upon it.[2]

In the words of Bishop Kaye, " On the subject of religion, there appears to be a peculiar propriety in appealing to the opinions of past ages. In human science we find a regular advance from less to greater degrees of knowledge. Truth is elicited by the labours of successive inquirers; each adds something to the stock of facts which have been previously accumulated; and as new discoveries are continually made, the crude notions of those who first engaged in the pursuit are discarded for more matured and more enlarged views. The most recent opinions are those which are most likely to be correct. But in the case of a Divine revelation, this tentative process can have no place. They to whom is committed the trust of communicating it to others, are thoroughly instructed in its nature and its objects, and possess a knowledge which no inquiries of subsequent ages can improve. What they deliver is the truth itself; which cannot be rendered more pure, though it may, and probably will, be adulterated in its transmission to succeeding generations. The greater the distance from the fountain-head, the greater the chance that the stream will be polluted. On these considerations is founded the persuasion which has generally prevailed, that in order to ascertain what was the doctrine taught by the Apostles, and what is the true interpretation of their writings, we ought to have recourse to the authority of those who lived nearest to their times." [3]

---

[1] *Apolog. Enchiridion Theolog.* p. 184; where see the original more at length.

[2] The student may especially be referred to Bp. Beveridge, Preface to his *Codex Canonum;* Patrick's *Discourse about Tradition,* in the first volume of Gibson's *Preservative against Popery;* Dr. Waterland, *On the Importance of the Doctrine of the Trinity,* ch. vii.; Bp. Jebb's *Pastoral Instructions* — Chapter, *On the Peculiar Character of the Church of England;* Bp. Kaye's *Tertullian,* p. 229. See also Rev. G. S. Faber's *Primitive Doctrine of Justi-*

fication; and also *Primitive Doctrine of Election.* On Ecclesiastical Tradition, or tradition concerning rites and discipline, see Hooker, *E. P.* Bks. ii. and iii.; Bp. Marsh's *Comparative View,* ch. vii.

[3] Bp. Kaye's *Justin Martyr,* ch. i. p. 2. The bishop has satisfactorily shown, that the tradition appealed to by Tertullian in the second century was no other than the kind of tradition admitted by the English Church. See Bp. Kaye's *Tertullian,* p. 297, note.

" We allow," says Bishop Patrick, " that tradition gives us a considerable assistance in such points as are not in so many letters and syllables contained in the Scriptures, but may be gathered from thence by good and manifest reasoning. Or, in plainer words, perhaps, whatsoever tradition justifies any doctrine that may be proved by the Scriptures, though not found in express terms there, we acknowledge to be of great use, and readily receive and follow it, as serving very much to establish us more firmly in that truth, when we see all Christians have adhered to it. This may be called a *confirming tradition:* of which we have an instance in Infant Baptism, which some ancient fathers call an Apostolical tradition." Again: " We look on this tradition as nothing else but the *Scripture unfolded:* not a new thing, but the Scripture explained and made more evident. And thus some part of the Nicene Creed may be called a tradition ; as it hath expressly delivered unto us the sense of the Church of God concerning that great article of our faith, that Jesus Christ is the Son of God, *begotten of His Father before all worlds,* and *of the same substance with the Father.* But this tradition supposes the Scripture for its ground, and delivers nothing but what the fathers, assembled at Nice, believed to be contained there and fetched from thence." [1]

So Dr. Waterland : " We allow no doctrine as necessary which stands only on fathers, or on tradition, oral or written. We admit none for such but what is contained in Scripture, and proved by Scripture, rightly interpreted. And we know of no way more safe in necessaries, to preserve the right interpretation, than to take the ancients along with us. We think it a good method to secure our rule of faith against impostures of all kinds, whether of enthusiasm, or false criticism, or conceited reason, or oral tradition, or the assuming dictates of an infallible chair. If we thus preserve the true sense of Scripture, and upon that sense build our faith, we then build upon Scripture only ; for the sense of Scripture is Scripture." [2]

---

[1] Patrick, *On Tradition,* as above.

[2] Waterland, *On the Importance of the Doctrine of the Trinity,* ch. VII. The note to this passage is as follows : —

" So the great Casaubon, speaking both of himself and for the Church of England, and, at the same time, for Melanchthon and Calvin also : Opto cum Melanchthone et Ecclesia Anglicana, per canalem antiquitatis deduci ad nos dogmata fidei, e fonte sacræ Scripturæ derivata. — Alioquin quis futurus est innovandi finis ? — Etsi omnis mea voluptas est et sola versari in lectione sacræ Scripturæ, nullam tamen inde me hausisse propriam sententiam, nullam habere, neque unquam σὺν Θεῷ εἰπεῖν, esse habiturum. Magni Calvini hæc olim fuit mens, cum scriberet præfationem suam in commentarium Epistolæ ad Romanos ; non debere nos ἐν τοῖς Κυριωτάτοις, a consensu Ecclesiæ recedere," A. D. 1611. Casaub. *Epist.* 744. *Dan. Heinsio,* p. 434. Edit. tertia Rotterdami.

It is indeed most necessary that we do not suffer our respect for antiquity to trench upon our supreme regard for the authority of Scripture. To Scripture we look, as the only source of all Divine knowledge. But when we have fully established this principle, we need not fear to make use of every light with which God has furnished us, for the right understanding of Scripture ; whether it be a critical knowledge of ancient languages, or history, or antiquities, or the belief of the primitive Christians, and the doctrines which holy men of old deduced from those sacred writings, which were to them, as to us, the only fountain of light and truth.

II.   The Article, having declared the sufficiency of Scripture, and set forth the Canon of Scripture, then speaks of those other books which had been always held in high respect, but were not canonical, in the following terms : —

" The other books (as Hierome saith) the Church doth read for example of life and instruction of manners ; but yet doth not apply them to establish any doctrine." [1]

The meaning of these words is, that the Church of God, in all ages, has been used to read the Apocrypha, for example and instruction, but not for doctrine.   This is a simple statement of fact, and if nothing more were said elsewhere, it would need no further explanation.   But, if we look to the Calendar of the Prayer-Book, which was drawn up by the compilers of the Articles, and receives, like the Articles, the assent of all the clergy of the Church, we find that, during a certain portion of the year, in the week-day services, the first lesson is appointed to be read from the Apocrypha.   This is acting on the principle laid down in the Article ; and this is one of those customs of the Church of England which has been most exposed to censure, from those who dissent from her, and from some even of her own children.

There may certainly appear some danger in ordering that to be read, as a lesson of the Church, which is not Canonical Scripture,

---

[1] Ἀπόκρυφα βίβλια or ἀπόκρυφοι βίβλοι, so called either because their authors were unknown ; or because not laid up, like the Canonical books, in the ark ; or because read in private only, not in public also ; though it appears from the XLVIIth Canon of the Council of Carthage, that some apocryphal books were read publicly. Suicer, s. v. ἀπόκρυφοι. Tom. I. p. 458.

The passage of Hierome alluded to is probably : " Sicut ergo Judith et Tobit et Maccabæorum libros legit quidem Ecclesia, sed inter canonicas Scripturas non recipit, sit et hæc duo volumina (h. e. libros Sapientiæ et Ecclesiastici) legat ad ædificationem plebis, non ad auctoritatem Ecclesiasticorum dogmatum confirmandam." — Hieronym. In Libros Salomonis, Chromatio et Heliodoro. Tom. I. p 938. Ed. Ben.

lest it should be mistaken for Scripture; and it is moreover urged against the custom, that the Apocrypha not only is not inspired, but also contains some idle legends, and some erroneous doctrines, and therefore ought not to be admitted to be read in the Church. It is even added, that the Church of Rome has derived some of her errors from, and supports some of her false teaching by, the authority of the Apocrypha.

It may be well, therefore, to state the grounds on which it is probable that our reformers thought fit to retain the Apocryphal lessons, that we may see what is the weight of the objections urged against our Church on the ground of their use.

First, it has been replied to the principal objections, that, if we would exclude all human compositions from the Church, we must exclude homilies, sermons, metrical psalms and hymns, — nay, prayers, whether written or extempore, except such as are taken out of Scripture itself, — that there is no danger that the Apocrypha should be mistaken for Scripture when it is expressly assigned a far lower place, both in the formularies and in the ordinary teaching of the Church, — that, if it be not free from faults, no more is any human composition, and that on this principle we must still rather exclude sermons, psalms, hymns, and even liturgies, — that it is not true that the Church of Rome has derived her errors from the Apocrypha, which does not support them, and by which she could not prove them; for she has derived them from misinterpreting Scripture, from oral tradition, and from her own assumed infallibility.[1]

So much is said in answer to the objections. Farther, in favour of reading the Apocryphal books, their nature and history are alleged. The origin of them has been already alluded to. They were written in the period of time which elapsed between the return from captivity and the birth of Christ. The historical

[1] The following is the answer of the Bishops to the exception of the Puritans at the Savoy Conference against the reading of the Apocrypha: " As they would have no Saints' days observed by the Church, so no Apocryphal chapter read in the Church; but upon such a reason as would exclude all sermons as well as Apocrypha; namely, because the Holy Scriptures contain in them all things necessary either in doctrine to be believed, or in duty to be practised. If so, why so many unnecessary sermons? Why any more but reading of Scriptures? If, notwithstanding their sufficiency, sermons be necessary, there is no reason why the Apocryphal chapters should not be as useful, — most of them containing excellent discourses and rules of morality. It is heartily to be wished that all sermons were as good. If their fear be, that, by this means, those books may come to be of equal esteem with the Canon, they may be secured against that by the title which the Church hath put upon them, calling them Apocryphal; and it is the Church's testimony which teacheth us this difference, and to leave them out were to cross the practice of the Church in former ages." — Cardwell, *Hist. of Conferences*, ch. VII. p. 342.

books of the Apocrypha, therefore, supply a most important link in the history of the Jewish people. Without them we should be ignorant of the fulfilment of many of the old Testament prophecies, especially those in the book of Daniel; and should know nothing of several customs and circumstances alluded to in the new Testament, and essential to its understanding. The other books are mostly pious reflections, written by devout men, who were waiting for the consolation of Israel.

The Alexandrian Jews received them with the most profound respect. The fathers often appealed to them, and cited them; though it has been shown they mostly knew the difference between them and the writings of Moses and the Prophets. It appears that from very early times they were read in most Churches, at least in the West; as in very many were also read the Epistles of Clement and Barnabas, and the Shepherd of Hermas,[1] — not that they were esteemed Canonical, but as of high antiquity and value, and useful for instruction to the people.

In Rufinus we find a distinction between books Apocryphal and books Ecclesiastical.[2] Among the former he classed those which were wholly rejected; among the latter those which were read in Churches. His division therefore is threefold: Canonical, which embraces all those which we now receive into the Canon; Apocryphal, i. e. those which were altogether rejected; and Ecclesiastical, among which he reckons Wisdom, Ecclesiasticus, Tobit, Judith, Maccabees, the Shepherd of Hermas, and the like. This distinction occurs elsewhere, though some of the fathers make only a twofold division, into Canonical and Apocryphal.[3] Now the Ecclesiastical books are what we at this time call the Apocrypha; and forming part both of the Latin and Greek versions of the old

---

[1] Dionysius, a bishop of Corinth in the second century, in a letter to the Church of Rome (ap. Euseb. *H. E.* iii. 16) says, "they read on the Lord's day Clement's Epistle to them in their assemblies;" and Eusebius (*Id.* iv. 23) declares it to have been "universally received, and read in most churches," both in his and former times. The same he says of the Shepherd of Hermas (*Id.* iii. 3), that "it was read in many churches;" which is confirmed by Athanasius (*Epist. Paschal.* xxxix.), and Rufinus (*Exposit. in Symb. Apost.* § 36), both concerning this and other books. — Jones, *On the Canon,* Part i. ch. x.

[2] "Sciendum tamen est,. quod et alii libri sunt qui non Canonici, sed Ecclesiastici a majoribus appellati sunt; ut est

Sapientia Salomonis, et alia Sapientia quæ dicitur filii Sirach, qui liber apud Latinos hoc ipso generali vocabulo Ecclesiasticus appellatur, quo vocabulo non auctor libelli sed Scripturæ qualitas cognominata est. Ejusdem ordinis est libellus Tobiæ et Judith et Maccabæorum libri. In novo vero Testamento libellus, qui dicitur Pastoris sive Hermatis, qui appellatur duæ viæ, vel judicium Petri; quæ omnia legi quidem in Ecclesiis voluerunt, non tamen proferri ad auctoritatem ex his fidei confirmandam. Ceteras vero Scripturas Apocryphas nominarunt, quas in Ecclesiis legi noluerunt." — Rufin. *In Symb. Apost.* § 38.

[3] *E. g.* Cyril. *Cateches.* iv. § 35, where he calls all Apocryphal which are not Canonical.

Testament, they continued to be read in most Churches, from the earliest ages to the time of the Reformation.

It was not peculiar to the English reformers to speak with respect of these books. The foreign reformers use similar language, citing them as a kind of secondary authority; and especially the Swiss and Belgic Confessions, which represent the opinions of the extreme Calvinist section of the Reformation, speak in terms of honour concerning them, the latter allowing them to be read in Churches.[1] It may be added, that the Eastern Churches, which agree with us in the Canon, yet retain the Apocryphal books in their Bibles, and use them as we do.

One more argument ought not to be wholly omitted. The new Testament writers, even our Lord himself, appear often to cite from the Septuagint. We must not consider this as giving full authority to all the books of the Septuagint. Such authority we have already shown to belong only to the books of the Hebrew Canon. But it should appear, that such citations from the Septuagint would naturally commend to the Church the use of that volume as the Greek version of the Scriptures. Now that Greek version contains all the Apocryphal books. If, then, they were so mischievous, or so to be rejected, as some argue, it is scarcely to be accounted for, that neither our Lord nor any of His Apostles give any warning against them, whilst they quote, as of sacred authority, other portions of the volume which contains them.

These views, in the general, appear to have influenced our reformers to retain the Apocryphal books. They have removed them from the Sunday services, and forbidden them to be quoted as authority in matters of faith; but esteeming them as next in value to the sacred Scriptures, from the important information they contain, and from the respect which they have received from the earliest ages, they were unwilling to remove them from the place which they had so long occupied. The reformers were evidently not insensible to the evil of putting anything else on the same footing as the Canonical writings. But this danger, they justly esteemed, would be very small in the reformed Church. And experience has shown, that in this they were right in their

---

[1] *Sylloge Confessionum. Confess. Helvet.* Art. I. p. 17. *Confess. Belgic.* Art. VI. p. 328. The latter runs thus: Differentiam porro constituimus inter libros istos sacros et eos quos Apocryphos vocant: utpote quod Apocryphi legi quidem in Ecclesia possint, et ias sit ex illis eatenus etiam sumere documenta, quatenus cum libris Canonicis consonant; at nequaquam ea est ipsorum auctoritas et firmitas, ut ex illorum testimonio aliquod dogma de fide et religione Christiana certo constitui possit, &c.

judgment, for extreme respect for the Apocrypha has been a feeling in this country almost unknown. In this question, therefore, they appear to have adhered to the maxim which often guided them in matters of doubt, a maxim quoted with so much approbation by the famous Apologist of the English Church, and which originated in the fathers of the Council of Nice : ἔθη ἀρχαῖα κρατείτω — *Let ancient customs prevail.*[1]

---

[1] " Cur id a nobis hodie audiri non potest, quod olim in Concilio Niceno, a tot Episcopis et Catholicis Patribus, nullo refragante, pronunciatum est, ἔθη ἀρχαῖα κρατείτω." — Juelli *Apolog. Enchiridion Theologicum*, p. 158.

On the question of the reading of the Apocrypha in churches, see Hooker, *E. P.* v. 20. Concerning the ancient custom of reading Apocryphal books, see also Bingham, *Eccles. Ant.* Bk. xiv. ch. iii. §§ 14, 15, 16.

The following are the words of a pious and judicious writer, closely attached to a school in the English Church not particularly inclined to pay respect to the Apocrypha : " Man is a creature of extremes. The middle path is generally the wise path ; but there are few wise enough to find it. Because Papists have made too much of some things, Protestants have made too little of them. . . . The Papist puts the Apocrypha into his Canon ; the Protestant will scarcely regard it as an ancient record," &c. — Cecil's *Remains*, p. 364. London, 1830.

[The *commission* to write the Scriptures is contained in the promises quoted on page 167, and the divine *authority* of the New Testament rests on the same promises. But these do not seem to have been made exclusively to the original Apostles, nor to have been fulfilled, as far as writing Holy Scripture is concerned, in all of them. For not all of them contributed to the New Testament, and much of what it contains was written neither by them nor under their guidance, as the Epistles of St. Paul. We are therefore obliged to add that the *testimony* upon which we receive certain books as inspired, is that of the early Church, which by a divinely-guided discrimination accepted what was, and rejected what was not, written by virtue and in fulfillment of those promises ; and that discrimination was based upon evidence part of which is still accessible and can be appreciated by us. — *H. A. Y.* — *J. W.*]

ARTICLE VII.

Of the Old Testament.

THE old Testament is not contrary to the new; for both in the old and new Testament everlasting life is offered to mankind by Christ, who is the only Mediator between God and man, being both God and man. Wherefore they are not to be heard, which feign that the old fathers did look only for transitory promises. Although the Law given from God by Moses, as touching ceremonies and rites, do not bind Christian men, nor the Civil precepts thereof ought of necessity to be received in any commonwealth; yet notwithstanding, no Christian man whatsoever is free from the obedience of the Commandments which are called moral.

De Veteri Testamento.

TESTAMENTUM vetus novo contrarium non est, quandoquidem tam in veteri quam in novo, per Christum, qui unicus est Mediator Dei et hominum, Deus et homo, æterna vita humano generi est proposita. Quare male sentiunt, qui veteres tantum in promissiones temporarias sperasse confingunt. Quanquam Lex a Deo data per Mosen (quoad ceremonias et ritus) Christianos non astringat, neque Civilia ejus præcepta in aliqua republica necessario recipi debeant, nihilominus tamen ab obedientia mandatorum (quæ Moralia vocantur) nullus quantumvis Christianus est solutus.

SECTION I. — HISTORY.

THE Article, as it now stands, is compounded of two of the Articles of 1552, namely, the sixth and the nineteenth. The sixth ran thus: —

"The old Testament is not to be put away, as though it were contrary to the new, but to be kept still; for both in the old and new Testaments everlasting life is offered to mankind only by Christ, who is the only Mediator between God and man. Wherefore they are not to be heard, which feign that the old fathers did look only for transitory promises."

The nineteenth was as follows: —

"The Law, which was given of God by Moses, although it bind not Christian men, as concerning the ceremonies and rites of the same, neither is it required that the civil precepts and orders of it should be received in any commonweal: yet no man (be he never so perfect a Christian) is exempt and loose from the obedience of those commandments which are called moral; wherefore they are not to be hearkened unto, who affirm that Holy Scripture is given only to the weak, and do boast themselves continually of the Spirit, of whom (they say) they have learned such things as they teach, although the same be most evidently repugnant to the Holy Scripture."

I.   We may first consider, what persons have denied the doctrine contained in the original sixth Article, which forms the *first* part of our present Article; and then, who have been opposed to the statements of the original nineteenth Article, of which the substance is contained in the latter part of our present seventh Article.

First then, some early heretics held, that the old Testament was altogether contrary to the new.

The Gnostic sects, who believed in the malignity of matter, would not allow that the Creator of the world could be the Supreme God.   Marcion especially appears to have distinctly taught, that the old Testament was contrary to the new, the former being the work of the Demiurge or Creator, the latter of the Supreme and invisible God.   He is said to have composed a work called *Antitheses*, because in it he set, as it were, in opposition to each other, passages from the old and new Testaments, intending his readers to infer from the apparent disagreement between them, that the Law and the Gospel did not proceed from the same author.   Tertullian wrote a work against Marcion, in the fourth book of which he exposes the inconsistency of this attempt.[1]   Similar opinions prevailed, more or less, among the Valentinians and other Gnostic sects; all of whom attributed the creation to inferior beings, and consequently rejected the old Testament.

The Manichees in like manner, who believed in two principles eternally opposed to each other, as they had views similar to the Gnostics concerning the evil of matter, so they resembled them in their disrespect to the old Testament Scriptures.[2]   And in this they were very probably followed by those mediæval sects of heretics, the Bulgarians, Cathari, and others, who appear to have been infected with Manichean heresy.[3]

It is most probable, however, that the framers of this Article, both in the earlier and in the latter part of it, had in view some of the fanatical sects of the period of the Reformation, especially the Antinomians, who denied the necessity of obedience to the Law

[1] Tertull. *Adv. Marcion*, Lib. iv. Bp. Kaye's *Tertullian*, p. 499, &c.

[2] Deum, qui Legem per Moysen dedit, et in Hebræis prophetis locutus est, non esse verum Deum, sed unum ex principibus tenebrarum. — August. *De Hæres.*

46, Tom. viii. p. 16. See also Socrat. *H. E.* c. 22; Epiphan. *Hæres.* 66, c. 43; Lardner, *Hist. of Manichees*, iii. ch. lxiii.

[3] See Mosheim, *Ecc. Hist.* Cent. xi. pt. ii. ch. v. §§ 2, 3; Cent. xii. pt. ii ch. v. § 4.

of God, and the Anabaptists, who referred all things to an internal illumination; and both of whom were likely to have denied the value and authority of the old Testament.

The opinion that the fathers looked only for transitory promises, has been held, not only by heretics and fanatics, but, more or less, by some, in the main, orthodox Christians. Bishop Warburton, in his famous work, *The Divine Legation of Moses*, has endeavoured to prove that Moses studiously concealed from the Hebrews all knowledge of a future state; and this forms one of the arguments by which he strives to prove the inspiration and Divine authority of the Books of Moses. Though he allows that the later Jews, during and after the Captivity, had a gradually increasing knowledge of the immortality of the soul, yet as regards the earlier times of the Jewish commonwealth, he appears to have denied any such knowledge, even to the patriarchs and prophets.[1]

II. By looking at the wording of the original nineteenth Article, it will appear plainly that the latter part of our present Article is chiefly directed against fanatics, who affirm " that Holy Scripture is given only to the weak, and do boast themselves continually of the Spirit, of whom, they say, that they have learned such things as they teach."

This claim to inward illumination, and consequent neglect of the teaching of Scripture, has constantly characterized fanatical sects in all ages. Those against whom the words of the Article were directed are generally supposed to be the Antinomians and the Anabaptists, who sprang up soon after the rise of the Reformation in Germany. The Antinomians were the followers of Agricola, who carried the doctrine of Justification by faith to the length of rejecting the necessity of moral obedience altogether.[2] The Anabaptists were a constant source of annoyance to the Lutheran reformers. As their name implies, they rejected Infant Baptism, and rebaptized adults. But with this they combined a variety of noxious and fanatic doctrines, which rendered them dangerous both to Church and State. Claiming a high degree of internal illumination, they appear to have sanctioned and committed a number of excesses and crimes, under pretence of special direction and command of God.[3]

[1] See Warburton's *Divine Legation*, Book v. §§ 5, 6.

[2] Mosheim, Cent. XVI. Sect. III. pt. II. ch. I. § 25.

[3] See a history of them, Mosheim, Cent. XVI. Sect. III. pt. II. ch. III. Mosheim also, in the preceding chapter, gives an account of a sect of Libertines

It seems that this Article also incidentally alludes to some persons, who would have retained, not only the moral, but the ceremonial part of the Mosaic Law. This of course must have been true of all the early Judaizing Christian teachers. In the history given of the doctrine of the first Article, we have seen that some part of the Eastern Church was materially corrupted with these Judaizing tendencies. The observance of the Jewish Sabbath, or Saturday, the quartodeciman mode of calculating Easter, and similar observances, have been already mentioned as examples of this kind.

As regards the belief that Christian commonwealths ought to be regulated after the model of the Jewish polity and according to the civil precepts of the old Testament, it seems likely that the Anabaptists of Munster, who seized on that city and set up a religious commonwealth among themselves, endeavoured to conform their regulations in great measure to the laws of the Jewish economy.[1]

In later times, in Great Britain, the Puritans, at the period of the Great Rebellion, were constantly using the language of the old Testament, as authority for their conduct in civil affairs, and as a guide for the administration of the Commonwealth.

It is highly probable that, at the period of the Reformation, the whole question concerning the agreement of the old with the new Testament was a good deal debated. The prominent manner in which the subject of Justification was then brought forward naturally suggested topics of this kind. When men were told, in the strongest terms, that there was not, and could not be, any hope of salvation to them but by faith in Christ; and that this was altogether independent of any merits of their own, and could not be obtained by works of the Law; it obviously and naturally occurred to them to inquire, How then were the fathers under the old Testament saved? *They* had never heard of Christ, and could not be saved by faith in Him. They had only a law of works for their guidance. Can then the old Testament be contrary to the new?

calling themselves Spiritual Brothers and Sisters, who sprang up among the Calvinists in Flanders, and against whom Calvin wrote. They held, that religion consisted in the union of the soul with God, and that such as had attained to such a union were free from the restraints of morality. All ages have been more or less infected by such fanatics. They naturally flourished in a time of such religious excitement as the Reformation.

[1] See Mosheim, as above.

SECTION II. — SCRIPTURAL PROOF.

IN endeavouring to show the correspondence of this Article of our Church with the truth of Scripture, it will be desirable to consider the subjects of it in the order already adopted in speaking of their history.

I.　First, we may consider the statement, that eternal life is offered to mankind, in the old as well as in the new Testament, through Jesus Christ; and that the fathers looked for more than transitory promises.

II.　Secondly, we may treat of the questions concerning the abrogation of the civil and ceremonial, and concerning the permanency of the moral Law.

I.　Now we shall find it more convenient to treat the first division of our subject in the following order: —

1.　To consider the nature of the Law of Moses, and the reason why eternal life is not more clearly set forth as one of its promises.

2.　To speak of the promises, in the old Testament, of a Mediator and Redeemer.

3.　To show, that under the old Covenant there was a hope among the pious of a future state and life eternal.

1.　The character of the Law of Moses was peculiar to itself. God chose the people of Israel to be His own kingdom on earth. There were reasons, some known only to God, others revealed to us, why for two thousand years it pleased Him to preserve His truth amid surrounding idolatry, by committing it entirely to one chosen race.　That people He constituted His own subjects, and ruled over them, as their Sovereign and Lawgiver.　The Jewish commonwealth, therefore, was neither a Monarchy under the Kings, nor an Aristocracy under the Judges, but it was always a Theocracy.　The people had properly no king but God.　Moses was His vicegerent; so was Joshua; and after them the Judges exercised, from time to time, more or less of the same delegated authority.　In the time of Samuel, the people, in a spirit of unbelief, asked for the presence of a visible king, and thereby greatly sinned against God, as dissatisfied with His invisible empire, and rebelling against the government which He had established over them.　He however consented to grant them a temporal ruler, an earthly king. Yet the king so appointed did not rule in his own name, but as the viceroy and lieutenant of the LORD of Hosts, the God of the armies, the King of the kingdom of Israel.

All the laws then were ministered in His name. All the sanction of those laws had reference to Him, as Ruler and Lawgiver. The Tabernacle, and afterwards the Temple, were not simply places of worship; they were rather the Royal Palace, as Jerusalem was the city of the Great King. In the Temple His throne was the mercy-seat, and between the attendant Cherubim He was present in the cloud of glory, to be approached with the homage of incense and prayer, and to be consulted as to His pleasure by His chief minister, the High Priest, with the Urim and Thummim.

Accordingly, the Law given by Moses was the constitution and statute-book of the Theocratic commonwealth. It was indeed a guide for the life and manners of the people; but it was their guide, especially as they were subjects of the temporal government of the Lord. The Almighty is, in His own nature and His own will, unchangeable; and therefore the laws which regulate morality must ever be the same. Hence, when for a time He assumed the government of a temporal kingdom, murder, theft, adultery, and other crimes against justice, mercy, truth, and purity, were forbidden and punished, as a thing of course. But, over and above this, when God became the King of the nation, certain sins against Him became, not only moral, but civil offences. Idolatry was high treason, and direct rebellion. It was not, therefore, as in general, left to the judgment of the hereafter, but was proceeded against at once, as a state crime of the highest magnitude, and punished immediately with temporal death.

The like may be said concerning the destruction of God's enemies, the Amorites, the Amalekites, the Philistines, and others. They were the foes of the King of Israel, and were to be exterminated accordingly.

So again, much of the ceremonial of the Law constituted the state ceremonial of the Invisible King. The earthly sovereign, the priests and the Levites, were His court and His ministers. Custom and tribute were paid to Him, as they would have been naturally paid to the rulers in all the kingdoms of the world.

Now such being the case, we may understand at once why all the sanctions of the Law are temporal, and not eternal. In many instances, indeed, the punishments denounced were to be executed by the civil magistrate. There were rules laid down as to the administration of justice by the inferior officers in the commonwealth of Israel. But in other cases the vengeance denounced is to be executed, not by the inferior magistrate, but by the supreme Head, the King of Israel Himself. Yet still the principle is the same. Whether the King Himself is to be the judge, or the priest, or the magistrate, the reason for the judgment is the same. And accordingly God, who was their King, interfered, not as in other nations by an ordinary Providence, but signally and manifestly, by direct, obvious, miraculous interposition. The obedient subject was rewarded by his bountiful Sovereign with long life and peace and prosperity ; the disobedient was smitten with sickness, afflicted with poverty, or struck down by death.

If at any time the nation became generally disobedient, Prophets were sent to it, who were messengers from the King, to exhort His subjects to preserve their allegiance and return to their duty. Even they, like the Law itself, spoke to the people, for the most part, as subjects of the temporal kingdom of the LORD, and admonished them of the danger of not submitting themselves to their lawful Sovereign.

Whether then we look to the Law or to the Prophets, we can see good reason, why neither eternal life nor eternal death should be the sanction set forth, and the motives pressed upon the people. The Jewish dispensation was in every way extraordinary. We often mistake its nature, by viewing it as if it were the first full declaration of God's will to man ; whereas the patriarchal religion had already existed for full two thousand years before it, and the Law was "added" ($\pi\rho\sigma\epsilon\tau\epsilon\theta\eta$, Gal. iii. 19) to serve only for a time, and for a peculiar purpose. Its object, at least its direct and apparent object, was, not to set forth the way of eternal life, but to be the statute-law of the Theocracy, and to subserve the pur · poses of a carnal and preparatory dispensation, wherein the knowledge of God, and the hopes of a Messiah, were preserved amid the darkness of surrounding heathenism, till the day dawned, and the day-star arose.

The Jews, indeed, who were contemporary with Christ and His Apostles, vainly supposed that the Law of Moses had in it a life-giving power. They stumbled at that stumbling-stone, for they sought eternal salvation, " not by faith in Christ, but as it were by the works of the Law " (Rom. ix. 32). Whereas, the Law was not given for that purpose, but with an object remarkably different from that. " If, indeed, a law had been given, which was capable

of giving life, then would righteousness (or justification) have
been by the Law."[1] But law, though essential for the regulation
of manners, is, of its own nature, incapable of giving eternal salvation; for he who obeys its ordinances can, at most, but deserve to
escape from its penalties. And this is still more emphatically true
of men polluted by sin and compassed by infirmity. For law
provides no propitiation, and offers no spiritual aid. There must
therefore have been something more than law to save men from
eternal ruin; and the Jew, by imagining that the Law could do
this, failed altogether of the righteousness of faith.

Even the sacrifices under the Law had but a temporal efficacy.
They served "for a carnal purifying" (πρὸς τὴν τῆς σαρκὸς καθαρό-
τητα, Heb. ix. 13). They satisfied for offences against the temporal Majesty of the Great King, and screened from the temporal
punishment due to all transgressions of the Law, which He had
enacted. But there was no profession, no promise whatever, that
they should satisfy for the sin of the soul. Indeed, for the heavier
offences there was no propitiation set forth at all; whether these
offences were against the King, or against his subjects. For murder and adultery, for idolatry and blasphemy, there was nothing
left " but a certain fearful looking for of judgment." " The blood
of bulls and of goats could never take away sin;" "could never
make the worshipper perfect as pertaining to the conscience."

2. But beyond all this, there was still another purpose for
which the Mosaic economy was designed. "The Law was a
school-master to bring us to Christ." It was a dispensation professedly preparatory, and imperfect. It was, therefore, so constructed by Infinite Wisdom that there should be an inward spirit
vastly dissimilar from the outward letter of the Law. Accordingly, the whole dispensation, as it was preparatory, so it was
typical. The kingdom of Christ was the great antitype of the old
Theocracy. The Church is a theocracy now, as much as Israel
was then. And so all the ordinances of the temporal kingdom
were types and images of the blessings of the spiritual kingdom.
To this end, as well as to their *immediate* object, served the priests
and the temple, the altar and the sacrifices, the tribute and the
incense, and all the service of the sanctuary. The *letter* then of
the Law could never offer salvation: but the *spirit* did. Nay, the
letter of the Law was necessarily condemnatory, as it gave more
light and brought more obligations; but neither satisfied for trans-

---

[1] Gal. iii. 21. Εἰ γὰρ ἐδόθη νόμος ὁ δυνάμενος ζωοποιῆσαι, ὄντως ἂν ἐκ νόμου ἦν
ἡ δικαιοσύνη.

gressions, nor gave inward sanctification. And so it is written, " The letter killeth, but the spirit giveth life" (2 Cor. iii. 6). The letter brought no promise of immortality, but left men under condemnation; but the spiritual meaning of the Law led men to Christ, and so gave them life.

It will not be necessary to go through the promises of the old Testament and the types of the Law, to show that there was a promise of a mediator, and of redemption from the curse which Adam had brought upon us. The promise to Adam of the seed of the woman, — the promise to Abraham that in his seed all the nations of the earth should be blessed, — the promise to David concerning his son, who should sit upon his throne, — the types of the passover, the scape-goat, the sacrifices on the day of atonement, the consecration of the high priest, the prophecies of David, of Isaiah, of Daniel, of Zechariah, of Malachi, — all readily occur to us as containing predictions, or exhibiting figures, which set forth to the enlightened understanding the hope of future deliverance, and of a Redeemer, who should turn away iniquity.

It is said most truly, that all this was involved in much obscurity; and it can never be denied, that the Jew had a much less clear understanding, a much more partial revelation of " the truth as it is in Jesus," than the least instructed member of the Christian Church. Nay, " the least in the kingdom of Heaven," i. e. in the Gospel dispensation, " is greater " in knowledge " than he who was greatest" before the coming of Christ. But it should not be forgotten that during the patriarchal ages God had revealed Himself to Adam and Enoch, to Noah and Abraham, and perhaps to many besides. We are not to suppose that the light of such primeval revelation, which guided men for more than twenty centuries, was of a sudden quenched in utter darkness. The traditionary knowledge concerning a promised Mediator was no doubt carefully cherished, and served to enlighten much which in the Law, and even in the Prophets, might have been otherwise unintelligible. And hence, the Mediator, though but faintly shadowed out, was yet firmly believed in. We have our Lord's assurance, that " Abraham rejoiced to see His day; he saw it and was glad " (John viii. 56). We have St. Paul's assurance, that the same Abraham, having received the promise of the Redeemer, believed in it, and was justified by faith.[1] And we may well suppose that the faith which guided Abraham guided others, both before and after him.

[1] Rom. iv. 1–20.   Gal. iii. 6–9, 14–19.

At first indeed, and whilst patriarchal tradition yet survived, the intimations of a Mediator in the ancient Scriptures are ₊less distinct and less intelligible. But among the later prophets, when that early tradition may have had less weight, and when the day of Christ was more nearly approaching, the promises may be read more plainly, and the Gospel-history be almost deciphered in the sacred emblems of prophecy.

3. Are we then to suppose, notwithstanding this, that the fathers looked only for transitory promises ?

It is a truth, which, I think, cannot be denied, that Moses does not bring prominently forward the doctrine of a future state. That was a subject which did not fall in with his purpose. His mission was to organize the Jewish Commonwealth, and embody in writing the statute-law of the Theocracy. That Theocracy, as has been said, was a temporal kingdom, though God was its King. Hence naturally he does not bring forward the doctrine of a future life.[1] In addition to the writing of the laws of Israel, Moses gives also a brief, a very brief, sketch of the history of the nation, and of its more illustrious ancestors. It is probable enough that no very frequent allusion to a future existence might occur in this history ; and it is only in the historical, not at all in the legislative writings, that we can expect to meet with it. It has been already explained, that even the prophets, who succeeded Moses, acted much as messengers from the Sovereign of Israel to His rebellious subjects, and hence naturally spoke much concerning obedience to His Law and the sanctions of that Law, which we know were temporal. Yet in many of the prophets, clear notices, not only of a Mediator and a hereafter, but perhaps also of a Resurrection, are to be met with. Even Bishop Warburton, though strongly maintaining that the earlier Jews had no knowledge of a life to come, yet admits that in later times they became fully acquainted with the truth of it.

The principal passages in the books of Moses which seem to prove that the patriarchs believed in an eternity, and that a knowledge of it was general in the days of Moses himself, are as follows : —

(1) The account of the translation of Enoch, Gen. v. 24. This account, indeed, is brief and obscure. We know, however, from other sources what it means, and its obscurity rather seems to

[1] Bp. Warburton asserts that he studiously conceals it. This requires more proof than the Bishop has given. Eternal life was not a sanction of the Law and therefore does not appear in it. It does not follow that it was purposely concealed.

argue that it was, as is most likely, a fact generally known and well understood, and so not needing to be longer dwelt upon. But its obscurity is a little magnified; for we clearly enough learn from the passage, that, whereas in general long life was a promised blessing, yet in the case of Enoch a still greater blessing was conferred. For, whereas all other persons in the same chapter are spoken of as living long and then dying; Enoch's is said to have been comparatively a short life; and then it is said, that, because of his piety, "God took him." "Enoch walked with God; and he was not, for God took him." It is hard to know what other sense could be attached to the passage, except that given it by St. Paul: "Enoch was translated that he should not see death" (Heb. xi. 5). Now people who knew of the translation of Enoch, must have known something of that state of bliss to which he was removed.

(2) Accordingly, Jacob on his death-bed utters an ejaculation utterly unconnected with the immediate context: "I have waited for thy salvation, O Lord" (Gen. xlix. 18). What salvation Jacob could have waited for, who in this very chapter looks forward to far future fortunes for his children, before "the Shiloh should come, and to Him should be the gathering of the people," except it were the salvation of his own soul, which he was just about to breathe forth, has never been clearly explained.

(3) Balaam was so well acquainted with the truth (though so little obedient to it) as "to wish to die the death of the righteous, and that his last end should be like his" (Num. xxiii. 10). Now, the promise of the Law was to the *life* of the righteous; the promises of temporal blessing must all affect life, rather than death. It is natural for a believer in a blessed immortality to wish for such a death, and such a last end as awaits the just. But from a person who believes all God's promises to be made to this life, and looks forward to no life beyond, such an exclamation seems hardly intelligible.

(4) There is a saying of Moses himself which seems probably to imply the same thing. Just before his death he says of Israel, "Oh that they were wise, that they understood this, that they would consider their latter end." It is undoubtedly not certain that אַחֲרִית, "latter end," here, means *death*. Perhaps it should be said, it *probably* does *not* mean *death:* but it means either *futurity*, or *final condition*. And, though we may allow that the force of the passage is not unquestionable, its most natural interpretation would be, that it was a wish that the people of Israe.

were thoughtful of that time when worldly objects of interest should pass away, and their end draw nigh, when wisdom and piety only should profit them.

We come next to the famous passage in the Book of Job.[1] As the words stand in our Authorized Version, they prove Job's belief, not only in a future life, but in a resurrection of the body: " Oh that my words were now written! Oh that they were printed in a book! That they were graven with an iron pen and lead in the rock for ever! For I know that my Redeemer liveth; and that He shall stand at the latter day upon the earth; and though after my skin worms destroy this body, yet in my flesh shall I see God: whom I shall see for myself, and mine eyes shall behold, and not another; though my reins be consumed within me." (Job xix, 23–27.)

There are, without doubt, difficulties in this translation. The passage is in many points obscure, though not more so than the book of Job in general. The more literal rendering of the last three verses is, perhaps, as follows: —

" For I, even I, know that my Redeemer liveth, and hereafter shall stand above the dust. And though, after my skin, this (body) be destroyed, yet from my flesh shall I see God: whom I shall see for myself, and mine eyes shall behold, and no stranger; my reins are consumed within me."

On the whole, whatever rendering is given to it, it is hardly possible that the passage should not *appear* to prove a belief in a future existence. The words " from my flesh " indeed may be interpreted differently, according to the different senses attached to the preposition; and whereas our translators have rendered it " *in* my flesh," some eminent scholars have maintained that we should

---

[1] The date and authorship of the Book of Job is a question in some degree affecting the question in the text. Most scholars consider the book as one of the earliest in the Bible; and many have believed that it was written by Moses. Bp. Warburton argues, that it was not written till the captivity, or the return from captivity; and that it is a dramatic composition rather than a real history (*Divine Legation*, Bk. VI. Sect. II.) The question is not to be settled with a few words. I can only say that it appears to me to bear the marks of great antiquity. It is true that it is not such pure Hebrew as some parts of the old Testament; or rather that it contains a great many Hebrew words and phrases which are not common in the other books of the Bible, and for the explanation of which we must look to the Syriac and Arabic languages. But the style is very little like the style of the later books, which contain a certain number of Chaldaisms and even some Chaldee; such as Daniel, Ezra, Haggai, Zechariah, Malachi, and some of the Psalms. The Aramaisms of Job are very unlike these; and so is the whole style and character of the Hebrew. It is indeed exactly what might be expected from a very ancient writer, who wrote in Hebrew an account of dialogues originally held in an ancient dialect of Arabic. Whether or not Moses was that writer is another question. It seems very doubtful, if not highly improbable.

render it " *without* my flesh." [1] Yet the only difference, which such a different interpretation might cause, would be, that, according to the first, Job hoped to see his Redeemer at the *Resurrection ;* according to the latter, that he expected the same glorious vision as a disembodied spirit.

It is, however, argued that it is very remarkable that no indication save this of a belief in an immortality occurs in the book of Job. It would be natural, it is said, when Job's friends charge him with wickedness, and attribute his sorrows to his sins, that he should at once answer, that, though miserable in this life, he yet had full hope of happiness in a better. As therefore no such reasoning is to be found, we must necessarily conclude that Job was ignorant of a future state ; and that this particular passage, instead of being an anticipation of a future Resurrection, is a prophetic declaration of his belief in what actually afterwards took place ; namely, that, though for a time the disease which afflicted him was permitted to destroy his body, yet, in the end, God should be manifested to defend his cause, and that he should be permitted to see Him with his own eyes.

I am inclined to attribute but little weight to the previous silencé of Job concerning the life to come. Men at that time generally believed that a special Providence brought good upon the righteous, and evil on the wicked in this life ; and in the earlier days of the Jewish commonwealth it doubtless was so. Job shares this belief with his friends ; yet he is conscious of his integrity, and defends himself earnestly against their accusations. It is hardly likely that he should have tried to disprove the justice of a creed which he held himself. Therefore he does not say that they were wrong in believing in a retributive Providence, or urge them to look forward from this life to a better. This would have been

---

[1] So Rosenmüller. Præfixum מ ante בִּשָׂרִי significat defectum, ut Isai. xlix. 15, *An obliviscetur mulier filioli sui* מֵרַחֵם *resecta miseratione,* i. e. ut non misereatur ejus. 1 Sam. xv. 26, *Rejecit te Deus* מִהְיוֹת מֶלֶךְ *ut non sis rex.* Ita מִבְּשָׂרִי accurate respondet priori hemistichio, ut utroque corpus suum dissolvi significet (Schol. in Job xix. 26). Whether the use of מ in the passages thus adduced from Isaiah and Samuel is at all similar to the use of the same preposition in this passage of Job, others must decide. To me it appears that there is little or no analogy. To reject a person, " *from* being king," — to " forget a child *so as not* to love it," — are vastly different notions of the preposition מ from that sought to be attached to it here, namely, " *without* my flesh." Rosenmüller, having given this sense to the preposition, is obliged to say, that it is only by a strong poetical figure that Job is said to see his Redeemer, " without his flesh," signifying merely, that, though much wasted with disease, he yet hoped to live to see his cause defended, and his uprightness vindicated. Should we venture to apply such criticism to any profane author ?

in Job an improbable and unnatural course. But from the singular solemnity with which he ushers in the passage in question, the hope that he expresses that it may "be printed in a book," nay, graven "in the rock for ever," we may well believe that he is about to give utterance to something different from what he has hitherto been speaking of, and to something so important that he wishes it to be preserved, not only for his own time, as a solemn assertion of his innocence, but that it should be handed down to all future generations, as a vital and an eternal truth.

Now nothing could be more appropriate than such an introduction, if Job were about to speak of the general Resurrection, and his hope that he should be comforted and vindicated then. That was an argument unlike any he had urged before, and it was a truth of universal and constant interest, so that he might well wish to have the words which spake of it "printed in a book, yea, graven with an iron pen and lead in the rock for ever."

It is true, there are expressions in the Book of Job which may be interpreted into a denial of the doctrine of a future existence. For instance, "As the cloud is consumed and vanisheth away, so he that goeth down to the grave shall come up no more" (Job vii. 9). "So man lieth down, and riseth not: till the heavens be no more, they shall not awake, nor be raised out of their sleep" (Job xiv. 12). And again (ver. 14) "If a man die, shall he live again?" Bishop Warburton lays great stress on these passages, as proving that Job was ignorant of a Resurrection, and even of a future state. But, in all fairness, do they mean any more than this, that if a man die, he shall live no more in this life; if he goes down to the grave, he shall come up no more, while this world is remaining? This interpretation fully satisfies the force of all the expressions, even of that strongest of all, "man lieth down, and riseth not: till the heavens be no more, they shall not awake." Nay, we may almost venture to say that this last expression has a more than commonly Christian sound; for the new Testament teaches us that the general Resurrection at the last day shall not be, till "the heavens shall pass away with a great noise, and the elements shall melt with fervent heat." (2 Pet. iii. 10, comp. Rev. xx. 11.) It may be added, that the very verse which follows this passage in Job (a passage which is thought so decisive against his belief in a hereafter) appears to carry with it a refutation of such a theory; for in that verse (Job xiv. 13) the patriarch prays that God "would hide him in the grave (בִּשְׁאוֹל *in Hades*), and keep him secret till His wrath was past; that He would appoint him a set time, and then remember him." What could be the meaning of God's hiding him in Hades, or in the grave, till His wrath was past, and then after a set time remembering him, if such language was used by one who knew nothing of life and immortality? For the word *Sheol*, be it observed, whatever diversity of opinion there may be concerning it, has never been supposed by any one to mean anything which is unconnected with the state of the dead. It must be either the grave, or the state of departed souls. Choose which we will; Job wishes for a temporary concealment in the grave, or in the state of the departed, and then to be remembered, and, we can scarce fail to infer, to be raised up again.

With such a hope and such an expectation will well correspond such expressions as, "Though He slay me, yet will I trust Him" (Job xiii. 15). But how shall we interpret them, if they be the language of one whose hopes were all bounded by this life?

In the book of Psalms, David, in a passage which we know to be prophetic of Messiah, speaks as follows: "I have set the Lord always before me; because He is at my right hand I shall not be moved. Therefore my heart is glad, and my glory[1] rejoiceth; yea my flesh also shall rest in confidence.[2] For Thou wilt not leave my soul in Hades, neither wilt Thou suffer Thine Holy One to see corruption. Thou wilt show me the path of life: in Thy presence is the fulness of joy: at Thy right hand there are pleasures for evermore." (Ps. xvi. 8–11.)

In the ears of a Christian such language is so plainly expressive of the hope of resurrection, that it is difficult to attach any other meaning to it. Nay, we know that St. Peter quotes it as a prophecy that Christ should be raised from the dead, His soul not resting in Hades, His body not turning to corruption (Acts ii. 25–31). The passage then, according to the Apostle's comment on it, actually did mean a resurrection. The only question is, Did the Psalmist, when he wrote it, so understand it; or did he write of common things, unconsciously to himself and through the guidance of the Spirit, speaking deep mysteries? It is possible that the latter may have been the case. And yet the words chosen seem to make it improbable. Why does he say, after speaking of the gladness of his heart, and the rejoicing of his spirit, that "even his *flesh* should rest in confidence"? This looks much like an

---

[1] כְּבוֹדִי "My glory," probably a poetical expression for the *heart* or the *soul*. See Gesenius, s. v.   [2] לָבֶטַח in confidence, securely.

assurance that not only the heart might rejoice in God, but even that the body had hope of immortality. And then, " Thou wilt not *leave* my soul in hell." Had he meant that he should not be permitted to die, it would have been natural to say, " Thou wilt not *bring me down* to hell." But he who hopes not to be *left* in Hades, must surely have expectation of first going thither. The words therefore of themselves so plainly imply a resurrection, and are so apparently chosen for the purpose of expressing the hope of a resurrection, that, though we may admit that profound igno- rance on the subject may have kept the prophet from understanding them, and have blinded his eyes that he should not see their sense, yet nothing short of this would have hindered him, who uttered the language, from feeling inspired with a hope full of immortality.[1]

Again, the view which David takes elsewhere of the difference between the end of the righteous and of the wicked is consonant with the hope of a future retribution, and otherwise is unintelli- gible. (Ps. xxxvii. 37, 38.) " Mark the perfect man, and behold the upright: for the end of that man is peace. But the trans- gressors shall be destroyed together: the end of the wicked shall be cut off."

In like manner his confidence in trial and troubles, when the wicked prosper and the just are oppressed, has at least a striking resemblance to the language of one who looks for a time when the just shall be delivered, and the wicked consumed in judgment.

Thus, in Psalm xxiii. 4, David says, " Though I walk through the valley of the shadow of death, I will fear no evil; for Thou art with me ; Thy rod and Thy staff they comfort me." To " walk through the valley of the shadow of death " is probably but a poetical phrase for " to die " ; and to those who looked only for temporal blessings, death would be wellnigh the greatest " *evil*." Hence he who could die and yet " fear no evil," must have had a hope after death. So in Psalm lxxiii., if this were David's, then David, but if not, then Asaph, who is not likely to have known more than David, having spoken of his having envied the wicked, when he saw them in prosperity, and when he found himself chast- ened and afflicted, concludes in this manner: " Thus my heart was

---

[1] It must be remembered that those persons who think Job and David and others ignorant of a future state, yet ad- mit, nay contend, that all their neigh- bours round about were fully cognizant of such a doctrine. (See Warburton, Bk. v. § v.) How then came it to pass that Job, who was an Arab, and David, who was a conqueror, and had dwelt among the Philistines, and become ac- quainted with many peoples, should use language concerning a tenet which they almost must have heard from neighbour- ing nations, and yet not understand it themselves?

grieved, and I was pricked in my reins. So foolish was I, and ignorant; I was as a beast before Thee. Nevertheless I am always
with Thee; Thou hast holden me by my right hand. Thou shalt
guide me with thy counsel, and afterwards receive me to glory"
(Ps. lxxiii. 21–24). The "glory" is not of necessity glory everlasting, but it is hardly necessary to observe that such a sense of
the word suits the context better than any lower interpretation
of it.[1]

As David thus seems to have had hopes of something after
death, so his son Solomon knew, that "when a wicked man dieth,
his expectation shall perish" (Prov. xi. 7); that "The wicked is
driven away in his wickedness, but the righteous hath hope in his
death ' (Prov. xiv. 32). But what hope has the righteous more
than the wicked, or how does the expectation of the wicked, more
than that of the just, perish when he dieth; unless there be a
something after death, which gives hope to the one, but takes it
away from the other? Again, Solomon tells us (Eccles. xii. 7),
that at death " shall the dust return to the earth as it was, and the
spirit shall return to God who gave it;" signifying, as it plainly
seems, that, when the body returns to that from which it was
taken, the spirit shall return into the hand of Him who gave it, not
perishing with the body, but awaiting the judgment of its God.[2]

---

[1] There are, no doubt, some expressions in the Psalms, which seem to imply an ignorance of a future life, e. g. : —
" In death there is no remembrance of
Thee; in the grave who shall give Thee
thanks? (Ps. vi. 5.) " Shall the dust
praise Thee? shall it declare Thy truth?"
(Ps. xxx. 9.) " Wilt Thou show wonders to the dead? shall the dead arise
and praise Thee? shall thy loving-kindness be declared in the grave, or thy
faithfulness in destruction? Shall thy
wonders be known in the dark, and thy
righteousness in the land of forgetfulness?" (Ps. lxxxviii. 10–12.)
These are certainly remarkable expressions, but they do not appear unaccountable in a person who had been
taught by the dispensation under which
he lived to look for temporal blessings
as a reward for obedience, even though
he was a believer in a future state. It is
doubtful whether such language might
not be used even by a Christian. Death
is certainly a part of the curse; and
hence there is no wonder if the pious
Jew dreaded it. And speaking concerning the silence of death does not necessarily imply a total disbelief in a resurrection. The silence and forgetfulness
may mean only forgetfulness as regards
this world.

[2] On this passage see Bishop Bull,
Works, Oxf. 1827, i. p. 29. Bishop Warburton's strongest passage is from Ecclesiastes : —
" The living know that they shall die;
but the dead know not anything, neither
have they any more a reward: for the
memory of them is forgotten." Eccles.
ix. 5. The book of Ecclesiastes is one
the language of which is singularly obscure. The passage in question, if taken
in its context, may, however, be interpreted with no great difficulty. The
royal Preacher observes, that there is one
event to all men, from which no one shall
escape; and whatever good things he
may enjoy in this life, yet death will
surely soon deprive him of them all.
This may naturally embitter earthly enjoyments, for the living know that they
shall die, and they may be assured that
in death they will lose their consciousness of all things that have given them
pleasure here, and receive no more reward or emolument (שָׂכָר) from them.
" Their love and hatred and envy perish; and they have no longer a portion
in anything that is done under the sun."

27

When we come to the prophets, it is scarcely denied by any that we meet with a mention of immortality. , Bishop Warburton, who is probably the ablest writer, at least in the English language, in favour of the opinion that the early Jews knew nothing of a future state, yet admits that in the prophetic writings we begin to see some clear intimations of that doctrine which was to be fully brought to light in the Gospel.

Two remarkable passages are the following: (Isai. xxvi. 19) " Thy dead men shall live; together with my dead body shall they arise. Awake and sing, ye that dwell in the dust; for thy dew is as the dew of herbs, and the earth shall cast out the dead." It is not necessary to determine whether there be here a distinct prophecy of the Resurrection. It is enough to show that Isaiah, and those he wrote for, believed in a Resurrection, if, to express even something else, he uses words to illustrate it, which in their most natural sense imply a Resurrection. When we use a figurative expression, we borrow the figures which we use from things familiar and understood among us.

In the book of Daniel a description is given, which so exactly corresponds with the Christian description of the last Judgment and the general Resurrection, that it must require the greatest ingenuity to give any other sense to it: " At that time thy people shall be delivered, every one that shall be found written in the book. And many of them that sleep in the dust of the earth shall awake, some to everlasting life, and some to shame and everlasting contempt. And they that be wise shall shine as the brightness of the firmament; and they that turn many to righteousness as the stars forever and ever" (Dan. xii. 1–3).

We have already seen (under Art. III.) that the Jews, who lived at the time of our Saviour, with the exception of the sect of the Sadducees, not only believed in the immortality of the soul, but in a Resurrection, and in an intermediate state between death and Judgment. Thus St. Paul's appeal, when he was brought before the Sanhedrim, was agreeable to all, except the sect of the Sadducees: " Men and brethren, I am a Pharisee, the son of a Pharisee; of the hope and resurrection of the dead I am called in question." And the reason of this was, that, though the small and heretical sect of the Sadducees " said there was no resurrection,

---

Now this seems the obvious meaning of the passage beginning ver. 2 and ending ver. 6. Does this prove that Solomon did not believe in a future life? It is plain that he is speaking only of men's losing by death their good things and consciousness of enjoyment *in this life.*

neither angel nor spirit," yet the more orthodox, and more extensive sect of the "Pharisees confessed both" (Acts xxiii. 6, 8).

There may have been sufficient obscurity in the old Testament
Scriptures to admit of the possibility of the existence of two different sects, the one holding, the other denying, a future immortality;
yet there is abundant evidence from the new Testament that the
true interpretation was that adopted by the Pharisees, and that the
Sadducees erred from ignorance and pride. Our Lord indeed,
when the Sadducees came to Him and propounded to Him a difficulty concerning the Resurrection, tells them at once, that they
"erred, not knowing the Scriptures" (Matt. xxii. 29). And
though the passage which our Lord adduces from the books of
Moses (Exod. iii. 6), "I am the God of Abraham, the God of
Isaac, and the God of Jacob," requires some explanation to show
that it proved the doctrine in question, yet it is quite plain that
our Lord reproves the Sadducees for dulness in not having learned
from the old Testament that "all men live to God."

But the passage in the new Testament, which most fully assures us that the ancient fathers looked for heavenly promises, is
the eleventh chapter of the Epistle to the Hebrews. In the first
twelve verses the Apostle had been speaking of the faith of Abel,
Enoch, Noah, Abraham, Sarah, and perhaps of Isaac and Jacob:
and he then adds (vv. 13–16), "These all died in faith, not having received the promises, but having seen them afar off, and were
persuaded of them, and embraced them, and confessed that they
were strangers and pilgrims upon earth. For they that say such
things, declare plainly that they seek a country. And truly, if
they had been mindful of that country from whence they came
out, they might have had opportunity to have returned. But
now they desire a better country, that is, an heavenly: wherefore
God is not ashamed to be called their God, for He hath prepared
for them a city." In like manner (vv. 25, 26) he tells us, that
Moses chose "rather to suffer affliction with the people of God
than to enjoy the pleasures of sin for a season; esteeming the reproach of Christ greater riches than the treasures of Egypt, *for he
had respect unto the recompense of the reward*." And other saints
of the old Testament, he says, "were tortured, not accepting deliverance, that they might obtain *a better resurrection*." Now
those "who seek a better country, that is, a heavenly," those who
despise the pleasures of sin and choose to suffer through life persecution with the people of God, "having respect to the recompense of reward," those who endure torture, "not accepting de-

liverance," that "they may obtain a better resurrection," must certainly have looked for more than transitory promises, even for those very promises of life and immortality which they indeed saw but afar off, but which at length the Lord Jesus by the Gospel fully brought to light.

It may seem unnecessary to add anything further to show that the old Testament is not contrary to the new. Yet it is worth while to remark that the constant quotation of the old Testament by the writers of the new, and their mode of quoting it to confirm and ratify their own teaching, is abundant proof that the one closely corresponds with the other. Our Lord expressly asserts that the old Testament Scriptures are "they which testify of Him" (John v. 39). The people of Berea are spoken of with high commendation, because they searched the old Testament to see whether the preaching of the Apostles was the truth ; and we read that they were so convinced by this daily searching of the Scriptures, that many of them were led to believe (Acts xvii. 11, 12). Nay, St. Paul tells Timothy, that those Scriptures of the old Testament, which he had known from a child, "were able to make him wise unto salvation through faith which is in Christ Jesus." 2 Tim. iii. 15, 16.

It is certain, therefore, that they who wrote, and He in whose name they wrote the Scriptures of the new Testament, so far from holding that the old Testament was different from the new, ever held and taught their entire agreement, and appealed to the old Testament as the strongest confirmation of their doctrine, and as bearing abundant testimony to their sacred mission and their heavenly inspiration.

II. But though the old Testament is not contrary to the new, yet, 1. the ceremonial of the Jewish Law is abolished ; but, 2. the commandments called moral still continue in force.

1. The very end and object of the Jewish ceremonial were such that of necessity it must have passed away. It has already been seen that the Law of Moses was, first, the code of statute-law for the Theocratic commonwealth ; and, secondly, a system of types and emblems preparatory to the coming of the Messiah, who was to fulfil them all. These two purposes it served so long as these purposes existed. But now the Jewish Theocracy has given place to the Christian Church ; and the great Antitype has come, to whom all the typical ceremonies looked forward. There is now therefore no longer any reason for the continuance of the Mosaic

Law. Moses and Elias, the Law and the Prophets, have passed away, and we see no one but Jesus only, to whom we are to listen, as God's beloved Son.

There cannot be at present any kingdom circumstanced as the kingdom of Israel was. God is no longer an earthly Sovereign, reigning exclusively over the Jewish nation as their temporal King. He is indeed the great King in all the earth, but not the particular Ruler of a single commonwealth. The Lord Jesus sits on His Mediatorial Throne. But His is a spiritual dominion. It is indeed that great fifth empire, which Daniel saw imaged by a stone hewn without hands, which in course of time filled the earth. But it is nevertheless a kingdom not of this world; and therefore His servants are not to fight, nor to call down fire from Heaven on their enemies, nor to take the sword, lest they perish by the sword. The weapons of their warfare are not carnal; their citizenship is in Heaven; their fellow-citizens are the saints; their fellow-subjects the household of God.

It is therefore unfit that any kingdom should be governed by the laws, or regulated by the ceremonial of the Jewish polity. The court of an earthly sovereign must be differently ordered from the court of the King of Heaven; the laws, which relate to all the governments of this world, different from those which had reference to the supremacy of the LORD. We have seen that blasphemy, idolatry, and similar offences were under the Jewish economy not merely crimes against religion, they were also distinctly crimes, and that of the highest character, against the State. They tended to nothing less than the dethroning of the King, and putting an usurper in His room. It is therefore clear, that, on principles of civil justice, they were crimes which deserved to be punished with death. But in modern nations they are religious, not civil offences; and though the magistrate may justly restrain such acts or words as tend to the offence of society, or the endangering of morality, yet he would not be justified in proceeding against the blasphemer or the idolater on the principle on which the magistrate was bound to proceed against them in Israel, where their crimes were both civil and religious, derogatory to the honour of God, and at the same time rebellion against the authority of the State. Religious wars and religious persecutions are both utterly alien from the spirit of Christianity. James and John, who would have called down fire, Peter who smote off the ear of Malchus, both thought and acted in the spirit of the Jewish, not of the Christian economy; and were herein types of the Dominicans,

who would convert or destroy by the rack and the flame, and of
the zealots of later times, who in fighting for religious liberty,
shouted as their war - cry, " The sword of the Lord and of
Gideon ! "

We know well how strongly St. Paul condemns those who adhered to the Jewish ceremonial. Our Lord, indeed, had declared
that " one jot or tittle should not pass away till all was fulfilled." [1]
But all was fulfilled when the sceptre departed from Judah, and
so the Jewish commonwealth was dissolved; and when the types
of the Law had their full accomplishment in their great Antitype,
our Prophet, Priest, and King. The argument of the whole Epistle to the Galatians is directed against the observance of Jewish
ceremonies. The Epistle to the Hebrews equally shows that the
Law had " waxed old, and was ready to vanish away," and that,
its accomplishment being perfected in Christ, there was no longer
benefit to be gained by adhering to it. Indeed, in the Epistle to
the Galatians the Apostle declares, that if a man is circumcised,
and strives to keep the Law (*i. e.* the ceremonial Law of Moses),
Christ has become of no effect to him, he has fallen from grace.[2]

But, thus clear though it be, that the ceremonial Law is no
longer binding on a Christian or on a commonwealth, we ought
yet to bear in mind that the organization of the Jewish State
proceeded from above. It was, in some degree, a model republic.
It was, no doubt, in a particular age of the world, under peculiar
circumstances, and with a special object, that the Jewish nation
was set apart to be God's peculiar people, His own kingdom upon
earth. But taking all these into account, we ought still to be
able to derive lessons of political wisdom from the ordinances appointed by the Allwise for the government of His own chosen race.
We can never again see a constitution and a statute-law devised by
infinite Wisdom. We know from our Lord's own words, that in
some respects the enactments of the Mosaic economy, though coming from God, were yet not perfect, because of the hardness of
heart of those for whom they were designed; [3] and therefore, of
course, we must take into account, not only the particular circumstances, but also the particular character of the people; but when
we have made such allowances, we may rest assured that the commonwealth of Israel would be the fittest pattern and type which
legislators could adopt for the government of empires.[4]

---

[1] Matt. v. 18.
[2] Gal. v. 4.
[3] Matt. xix. 8.
[4] The spiritual nature of Christ's king-

dom does indeed preclude the notion of
its being a religion of ceremony. We
must not, however, run into the extreme of supposing that, because the

2. As regards that portion of the Law of Moses which is called moral, we must plainly perceive that it is founded in the eternal principles of justice and truth. It is not a code of enactments, given for the temporary guidance of a temporary government; it is rather a system of moral precepts, for the direction and instruction of rational and accountable beings. Indeed, as God was the King of Israel, moral obedience was in itself a portion of civil obedience. Yet the principle, from which its obligation resulted, was not the relation of a subject to his king, but the relation of a creature to his God. The former was a temporary relation, existing only whilst the Jewish commonwealth should last; the other is an eternal relation, which must endure forever and ever. The moral Law, then, which is God's will, was holy and perfect, even as He is perfect. And St. Paul, when he speaks of it as incapable of justifying, yet carefully guards against any misapprehension of his words, as though he should be supposed to speak disparagingly of the Law itself. He declares that "the Law is holy, and the commandment holy, and just, and good" (Rom. vii. 12). He says that "the Law is spiritual," and the reason why it could not sanctify man was not its own deficiency, for in itself, and for its own end, it was perfect, but because of the weakness and sinfulness of man; because the natural man is "carnal, sold under sin," and so unable to fulfil the law; and the more perfect the Law, the more unable man is to live up to it (Rom. vii. 14). But that it is still binding upon Christians, appears sufficiently from the same Apostle's reasoning, who, when he has shown that by nature man cannot obey the Law, goes on just after to assert, that what could not be done by man's natural weakness, could be, and was done, by the power of God; even "that the righteousness of the Law should be fulfilled in them, who walked not after the flesh, but after the Spirit" (Rom. viii. 4).

Our Lord, in the Sermon on the Mount, not only shows that the moral law is binding on Christians, but shows, moreover, that it is binding in a much stricter and more spiritual sense than was generally understood by the Jews. It had been taught in the Law that we should not commit adultery. But Christ enjoined

temporal or carnal ceremonies of the Mosaic Law were done away in Christ, therefore all outward ordinances are inconsistent with Christian worship. We must remember that man is a creature compounded of soul and body, and therefore needing outward as well as inward agency. Accordingly, our Lord ordained Sacraments, and a ministry; and the Apostles enjoined ordinances of public worship, and exercised ecclesiastical discipline; all which are essential to the existence of a Church in this world, though they may be unnecessary in that city "where there shall be no temple; for the Lord God Almighty and the Lamb shall be the temple of it."

that we should not suffer an impure look, or an unholy thought (Matt. v. 27, 28). It had been taught in the Law, that we should do no murder. But Christ taught that the angry feeling and the angry word, which are the first steps to violence, and might in some cases lead to murder, were breaches of that commandment, and therefore unfit to be permitted in Christian men (Matt. v. 21, 22). The ordinances of the Law were expressed in terms of simple command and prohibition, and were looked on in a light suited to the carnal nature of the dispensation, in which they were given. The Pharisees, who were jealous for the Law, yet mostly looked no farther than the letter, satisfied if they abstained from absolute violation of its negative, and fulfilled the literal injunctions of its positive precepts. But our Lord told His disciples, that, except their righteousness exceeded such righteousness of the Scribes and Pharisees, they should in no case enter into the kingdom of Heaven (Matt. v. 20). His was a spiritual kingdom, and He required spiritual obedience. Mere formal compliance with the ordinances of the Law was insufficient for a Christian, whose heart must be brought into captivity to the will of God. Yet because the obedience must be spiritual, it did not follow that it should not be real. On the contrary, it was to be more real, yea, more strict. For subjection to the spirit of the Law necessarily involves subjection to the letter, though obedience to the letter does not of necessity produce obedience to the spirit. A man may cherish lust and anger without their breaking forth into murder and adultery; but if he checks every rising of evil, he cannot be guilty of the more deliberate wickedness. The first step cannot be arrested, and yet the last plunge be taken.

But if there could be any question as to our Saviour's teaching, one sentence alone should set it at rest: " Whosoever therefore shall break one of these least commandments, and shall teach men so, he shall be called the least in the kingdom of Heaven; but whosoever shall do and teach them, the same shall be called great in the kingdom of Heaven " (Matt. v. 19).

It is most true that some of the moral commandments are accompanied by sanctions which have respect to the state of things under the Jewish Theocracy. For example, the fifth commandment enjoins obedience to parents, with the promise, " that thy days may be long in the land which the Lord thy God giveth thee." But this by no means proves that the injunction is not binding upon all. All we can learn from it is, that, beyond the sanctions by which the eternal will of God is upheld in all religion, natural or revealed, the Jew, as a subject of the Theocracy, had also temporal promises to be expected as the reward of obedience; which, from the peculiar nature of the Mosaic economy, were constantly put prominently forward.   And, in the case of this particular commandment, St. Paul expressly enjoins all Christian children to observe it, on the very ground that it was a commandment of the Law of God.   And he adds, as a special motive for attending to this commandment, that it must plainly have been an important commandment, inasmuch as in the Law it was the first to which a promise was specially attached.   " Children, obey your parents in the Lord, for this is right.   Honour thy father and mother, which is the first commandment with promise;   that it may be well with thee, and that thou mayest live long on the earth " (Eph. vi. 1, 2, 3).   The Apostle first enjoins the duty, quotes in confirmation of his injunction the words of the commandment, and then shows the peculiar importance of that commandment, by pointing out that, under the Mosaic economy, a special promise of blessing was annexed to it.   This by no means shows that we are to fulfil this commandment in hope of that peculiar promise; but it shows that the commandment is binding on Christians as well as upon Jews; and that it is binding, because it is a part of the moral Law given by God to man, which is in itself unchangeable — as unchangeable as He who gave it.

28

ARTICLE VIII.

Of the Three Creeds.

THE Three Creeds, Nicene Creed, Athanasius' Creed, and that which is commonly called the Apostles' Creed, ought thoroughly to be received and believed: for they may be proved by most certain warrants of Holy Scripture.

De Tribus Symbolis.

SYMBOLA tria, Nicenum, Athanasii, et quod vulgo Apostolorum appellatur, omnino recipienda sunt, et credenda, nam firmissimis Scripturarum testimoniis probari possunt.

[The American Article reads, "The Nicene Creed, and that which is commonly called the Apostles' Creed," &c. There is no mention, therefore, of "the Creed of Athanasius," and, correspondently, it does not appear in our Service.

That our Church accepts the Athanasian definition is placed beyond doubt, by the declaration in the Preface to the Prayer Book, that we do not intend to depart "from the Church of England in any *essential* point of doctrine ; " by the retention of the Preface for Trinity Sunday in the office for Holy Communion, and by the adoption of the first five Articles.

That she is not singular in omitting the Athanasian Symbol from her public worship, is proved by the fact that it does not occur in the authorized formularies of the Orthodox Greek Church. And these two facts must, it would seem, place her beyond any well-grounded charge of unsoundness, or even carelessness, on such a vital point.

Bishop White's " Memoirs " show, that all these considerations were present to the minds of the Bishops — White and Seabury — who composed the House of Bishops in 1789. Whether they were equally present to the minds of the other House is, to say the least, uncertain. That body was very strenuous in its opposition, refusing to allow the insertion of the Creed — or, as it should rather be called, Hymn — at all, even with the provision that it might be used or omitted at discretion. This refusal the New England clergy, not without reason, considered intolerant. The difficulty probably arose from those clauses which even Dr. Waterland thought might be separated from the symbol itself. — J. W.|

SECTION I. — OF CREEDS IN GENERAL.

THE Church, after having defined the authority to which she appeals for the truth of her doctrines, proceeds to require belief in those formularies of faith which from very early times had been in constant use in the Church universal, and that upon the principle already laid down, namely, that they are in strict accordance with holy Scripture.

It seems generally admitted that the probable origin of Creeds is to be traced to the form or confession of faith, which was propounded to the Catechumens previously to their baptism. In the Scriptures such forms appear to have been brief. Our Lord commanded that men should be baptized "in the Name of the Father, and of the Son, and of the Holy Ghost:" and perhaps a confession in some such simple form as, "I believe in the Father, and in the Son, and in the Holy Ghost," was all that was at first required. Indeed, Philip required of the Eunuch no more than a profession of a belief that "Jesus Christ was the Son of God."[1] It is probable that the Apostles and their immediate disciples used several Creeds, differing in form, though not in substance. Hence, no certain form existing, all Churches were at liberty to make their own Creed, as they did their own liturgies, not being tied to a particular form of words, so long as they kept to the analogy of faith and doctrine delivered by the Apostles. Then, as heretics arose who denied the fundamental doctrines of the faith, the Creeds became gradually enlarged, to guard the truth from their insidious designs and false expositions.

Dr. Grabe, who examined the question as to what forms were used even in the Apostles' days, came to a conclusion that all the Articles in the Creed commonly called the Apostles' Creed, were in use in the Apostolic Confessions of faith, with the exception of these three, "The Communion of Saints," "the Holy Catholic Church," and "the descent into Hell."[2]

Many confessions of faith are to be found, nearly corresponding with the Creeds which we now possess, in the writings of the earliest fathers. For example, in Justin Martyr, Irenæus, Tertullian, Origen, Cyprian, the Apostolic Constitutions.[3] We have also Creeds of several different Churches preserved to us, agreeing in substance, but slightly varying in form; as the Creed of Jerusalem, Cæsarea, Alexandria, Antioch, Aquileia,[4] &c. But until the time of the Council of Nice, there does not appear to have been any one particular Creed, which prevailed universally, in exactly the same words, and commended by the same universal authority.

[1] See King, *On the Creed*, p. 33 ; Wall, *On Infant Baptism*, II. pt. II. ch. IX. § x. p. 439.

[2] Bingham's *Eccles. Antiq.* Bk. x. ch. III. §§ 6, 7. It is not to be supposed, because these Articles do not occur in the most ancient copies of the Creed, that they were therefore of comparatively modern invention. There is abundant testimony to the doctrines expressed by them in the earliest ecclesiastical writings. Evidence of this may be seen as regards one of them, "The descent into Hell," under Art. III.

[3] These are given at length in Wall, as above ; and in Bingham, Bk. x. ch. IV.

[4] See them at length in Bingham, as above.

The prevalence, however, of some authoritative standard in the Church, although varied by diversity of expression, is apparent from the language of many of the earliest Christian writers. Thus, Irenæus, Tertullian, Clement of Alexandria, and others, speak of a "Canon, or rule of faith, according to which we believe in one God Almighty, and in Jesus Christ, His Son, &c." And it is quite clear that this Κανὼν ἀληθείας, or *Regula fidei*, was no other than the Creed of the Church, expressed in a regular formulary.[1]

The commonest name by which the Creed was designated, was that of Σύμβολον, or Symbolum. The meaning of the term is confessedly obscure. (1) It has been said to have arisen from the fact that the twelve Apostles met together, and each contributed (συνέβαλον) one article to the Creed ; hence called Symbolum, or collation. (2) It has been said to mean a Collation, or Epitome of Christian doctrine. (3) It has been supposed to be, like the Tessera Militaris among the Roman soldiers, a symbol, or sign, by which the soldiers of the Cross were distinguished from heathens or heretics. (4) It has been thought again that it was borrowed from the Military oath (*sacramentum*), by which the Roman soldiers bound themselves to serve their general.[2] (5) And lastly, Lord King has suggested that it may have been borrowed from the religious services of the ancient heathens, who gave to those who were initiated into their mysteries certain signs or marks (*symbola*), whereby they knew one another, and were distinguished from the rest of the world.[3]

It is not very easy to decide which of these five senses may with most propriety be attached to the word. The first is the least probable, inasmuch as the tradition on which it rests appears not to have existed before the fourth century.[4]

The word " Creed," by which these ancient formularies of faith are designated in English, is derived from the word *Credo*, with which the Nicene and Apostles' Creeds commence.

---

[1] See Bingham, Bk. x. ch. iii. § 2; Bp. Marsh, *Lectures*, Camb. 1828, p. 470. See also the meaning of the term, " Rule of faith," discussed under Art. vi.

[2] Symbolum cordis signaculum, et nostræ militiæ sacramentum. — Ambros. Lib. iii. *De velandis Virginibus*, apud Suicer.

[3] Suicer, voc. Σύμβολον. — Bingham, Bk. x. ch. iii. King, *On the Creed*, pp. 6, 11, &c. Wheatley, Dr. Hey, and others have adopted King's derivation. Bingham totally rejects it.

[4] St. Augustine says, the name was given, " quia symbolum inter se faciunt mercatores, quo eorum societas pacto fidei teneatur. Et vestra societas est commercium spiritualium, ut similes sitis negotiatoribus bonam margaritam quærentibus."— Serm. ccxii. *Oper.* Tom. v. p. 985. Paris, 1683.

Section II. — THE APOSTLES' CREED.

RUFINUS mentions a tradition, handed down from ancient times, that, after our Lord's ascension, the Apostles, having received the gift of tongues, and a command to go and preach to all nations, when about to depart from one another, determined to appoint one rule of preaching, that they should not set forth diverse things to their converts. Accordingly, being met together, and inspired by the Holy Ghost, they drew up the Apostles' Creed, contributing to the common stock what each one thought good.[1] The author of the Sermons *de Tempore*, improperly ascribed to Augustine,[2] tells us that "Peter said, I believe in God the Father Almighty; John said, Maker of Heaven and earth; James said, And in Jesus Christ, His only Son, our Lord; Andrew said, Who was conceived by the Holy Ghost, born of the Virgin Mary; Philip said, Suffered under Pontius Pilate, was crucified, dead, and buried; Thomas said, He descended into Hell, the third day He rose again from the dead; Bartholomew said, He ascended into Heaven, and sitteth on the right hand of God the Father Almighty; Matthew said, From thence He shall come to judge the quick and the dead; James the son of Alphæus said, I believe in the Holy Ghost, the Holy Catholic Church; Simon Zelotes said, The Communion of Saints, the Forgiveness of Sins; Jude the brother of James said, The Resurrection of the Flesh; Matthias concluded with, The Life Everlasting."

The principal objections to the truth of these traditions, which are fatal to the last, and nearly fatal to the other, are these: —

First, that Rufinus himself tells us, that the article of the descent into hell was not in the Roman (*i. e.* the Apostles'), nor in the Eastern Creeds. It has been proved by Archbishop Usher and Bishop Pearson, that this statement is true; and also, that two other articles, "the Communion of Saints" and "the Life Everlasting," were wanting in the more ancient Creeds.

Secondly, the formation and existence of the Creed is not mentioned in the Acts of the Apostles, nor in any of the more ancient fathers or Councils; which is most extraordinary, if any such formulary was known to have existed, a formulary which would have

---

[1] Rufinus, *Expositio in Symb. Apost. ad calcem Cypriani*, p. 17, Oxf. 1682; King, p. 24; Bingham, Bk. x. ch. iii. § 5. Bingham translates, "each one contributing his sentence." But Rufinus's words are "conferendo in unum quod sentiebat unusquisque."

[2] Serm. *De Tempore*, 115; *Augustini Opera*, Paris, 1683, Tom. v. Append. p. 395, Serm. ccxli.

had the full authority of Scripture itself, and would therefore, probably, have been continually appealed to, especially in Councils, where new confessions of faith were composed.

Thirdly, it is plain that the ancient Creeds, though alike in substance, were not alike in words; which could never have been the case, if one authoritative form had been handed down from the Apostles.[1]

Fourthly, we may add to this, that the ancients scrupulously avoided committing the Creed to writing; and it is hardly probable, if there was in the Church a deposit so precious as a Creed drawn up by the Apostles, that it would have been left to the uncertainty of oral tradition, or that, if it were so left, it would have been preserved in its perfect integrity.[2]

But though this Creed was not drawn up by the Apostles themselves, it may well be called Apostolic, both as containing the doctrines taught by the Apostles, and as being in substance the same as was used in the Church from the times of the Apostles themselves. This will appear to any one who will compare it with the various ancient forms preserved in the works of the most ancient fathers, and which may be seen in Bingham, Wall, and other well-known writers already referred to.[3]

It was, no doubt, "the work neither of one man nor of one day;" yet it is probable that the Apostles themselves used a form in the main agreeing with the Creed as we now have it, except that the articles concerning the descent into hell, the communion of saints, and the life everlasting, were most likely of later origin. The form indeed was never committed to writing, but, being very short, was easily retained in the memory, and taught to the catechumens, to be repeated by them at their baptism. It differed in different Churches in some verbal particulars, and was reduced to more regular form, owing to the necessity of guarding against particular errors. The form most nearly corresponding to that now called the Apostles' Creed, was the Creed of the Church of Rome; though even that Creed lacked the three clauses mentioned above.[4] And it is an opinion, not without great probability, that the reason why it was called Apostles' Creed was, that the Church of Rome being the only Church in the West which could undeniably claim an Apostle for its founder, its see was called the Apostolic See, and hence its Creed was called the Apostolic Creed.[5]

---

[1] See Suicer, s. v. Σύμβολον; King, p. 26; Bingham, Bk. x. ch. iii. § 5.

[2] See Aug. *Opera*, Tom. v. p. 938. See also King, p. 31.

[3] Suicer, Bingham, and Wall, as above;

Pearson, at the head of every Article in his *Exposition of the Creed*.

[4] Bingham, Bk. x. ch. iii. § 12.

[5] Wall, *On Infant Baptism*, Part ii. ch. ix. p. 472. Oxford, 1835.

It is hardly necessary here to enter into any exposition, or proof from Scripture of the different clauses of the Apostles' Creed. Most of them occur in the Articles of the Church of England. The few which are not expressed in them may be more profitably considered in regular treatises on the Creed, than in a necessarily brief exposition of the Articles.

Section III. — THE NICENE CREED.

WHEN the Council of Nice met, A. D. 325, summoned by the authority of the Emperor Constantine, Eusebius, Bishop of Cæsarea in Palestine, recited to the assembled fathers the Creed, which he professed to have received from the bishops which were before him, into which he had been baptized, even as he had learned from the Scriptures, and such as in his episcopate he had believed and taught. The form of it was as follows: —

" We believe in One God, the Father Almighty, Maker of all things visible and invisible. And in one Lord Jesus Christ, the Word of God, God of God, Light of Light, Life of Life, the only-begotten Son, begotten before every creature ($\Pi\rho\omega\tau\acute{o}\tau\sigma\kappa\sigma\nu$ $\pi\acute{a}\sigma\eta\varsigma$ $\kappa\tau\acute{\iota}\sigma\epsilon\omega\varsigma$, Col. i. 15); begotten of the Father before all worlds, by whom all things were made; who for our salvation was made flesh, and conversed among men, and suffered and rose again the third day, and ascended to the Father, and shall come again with glory to judge the quick and the dead. And we believe in the Holy Ghost."

This confession of faith both Constantine and the assembled bishops unanimously received; and it should seem that this would have been all that was required. But Arius himself, soon after the Council, A. D. 328, delivered a Creed to the Emperor, which was unobjectionable, if viewed by itself, but which studiously omitted anything which might have led him either to express or to abjure his most heretical opinions;[1] namely, that there was a time when

[1] Arius's Creed runs thus: —

" We believe in one God, the Father Almighty, and in Jesus Christ His Son our Lord, begotten of Him before all ages, God the Word, by whom all things were made that are in Heaven and that are in earth; who descended, and was incarnate, and suffered, and rose again, and ascended into Heaven, and shall come again to judge the quick and the dead: and in the Holy Ghost; and in the resurrection of the flesh, and in the life of the world to come, and in the kingdom of Heaven; And in one Cath·

the Son of God was not, that He was made out of nothing, and that
He was not of one substance with the Father. This shows that
there was an absolute necessity that the Council should word its
Confession of faith, not only so as to express the belief of sound
Christians, but also so as to guard against the errors of the Arians.
Accordingly, the symbol set forth by the Council was in these
words : —

"We believe in one God, the Father Almighty, Maker of all
things visible and invisible. And in one Lord Jesus Christ, the
Son of God, begotten of the Father, only-begotten, that is, of the
substance of the Father ; God of God, Light of Light, very God
of very God, Begotten, not made ; being of one substance with
the Father : by whom all things were made, both things in Heaven
and things in earth ; who, for us men and for our salvation, came
down, and was incarnate, and was made man : He suffered, and
rose again the third day : and ascended into Heaven : and shall
come again to judge the quick and the dead. And in the Holy
Ghost.

"And those who say that there was a time when he was not ;
or that before He was begotten, He was not ; or that He was made
out of nothing ; or who say that the Son of God is of any other
substance, or that He is changeable or unstable, these the Catholic
and Apostolic Church anathematizes." [1]

The Nicene Creed thus set forth, and the decrees of the Council
against Arius, were received by the whole Church throughout the
world, and thus marked by the stamp of Catholicity. Athanasius,
in A. D. 363, informs us, that all the Churches in the world, whether
in Europe, Asia, or Africa, approved of the Nicene faith, except a
few persons who followed Arius.[2]

It appears to many that this Creed of the Council of Nice
was but an abridgment of the Creed commonly used in many
parts of the Church, and that the reason why it extended no
further than to the Article, "I believe in the Holy Ghost," was,
because it was intended to lay a stress on those Articles concerning
our Lord, to which the heresy of Arius was opposed. Epiphanius,
who wrote his *Anchorate* some time before the Council of Con-

---

olic Church of God, from one end of the
earth to the other."— Socr. *H. E.* Lib.
I. c. 26 ; Suicer, voc. Σύμβολον ; Bingham, Bk. x. ch. iv. § 10 ; Wall, Part iv.
ch. ix. p. 453.

[1] The Greek may be seen in Routh's
Scriptorum Ecclesiasticorum Opuscula, Tom.
I. p. 351 ; and in Suicer, voc. Σύμβολον ;

also *Athanasii Opera*, Tom. i. p. 247,
Epist. ad Jovian. Colon. 1686.

[2] Καὶ ταύτης σύμψηφοι τυγχάνουσι πᾶσαι
αἱ πανταχοῦ κατὰ τόπον Ἐκκλῆσιαι . . . .
πάρεξ ὀλίγων τὰ 'Αρείου φρονούντων. —
Epist. ad Jovian. Tom. i. p. 246. **See**
Palmer, *On the Church*, Pt. iv. ch. ix.

stantinople, says, that every catechumen repeated at his baptism, from the time of the Council of Nice to the tenth year of Valentinian and Valens, A. D. 373, a Creed in the following words : —

"We believe in One God, the Father Almighty, Maker of Heaven and earth, and of all things visible and invisible : and in the Lord Jesus Christ, the only-begotten Son of God, begotten of the Father before all worlds, that is of the substance of His Father, Light of Light, very God of very God, begotten not made, of one substance with the Father, by whom all things were made, both things in Heaven and things on earth ; who for us men and for our salvation came down from Heaven, and was incarnate of the Holy Ghost and the Virgin Mary, and was made man, and was crucified for us under Pontius Pilate ; He suffered and was buried ; and rose again the third day according to the Scriptures, and ascended into Heaven ; and sitteth on the right hand of the Father ; and He shall come again with glory to judge the quick and the dead ; whose kingdom shall have no end.

"And in the Holy Ghost, the Lord, and Giver of life, who proceedeth from the Father, who with the Father and the Son together is worshipped and glorified, who spake by the prophets. And in one Catholic and Apostolic Church. We acknowledge one Baptism for the remission of sins, We look for the Resurrection of the dead, and the Life of the world to come. Amen.

"And those who say there was a time when He was not, or that He was made out of nothing, or from some other substance or essence, or say that the Son of God is liable to flux or change, those the Catholic and Apostolic Church anathematizes."

This Creed Epiphanius speaks of as handed down from the Apostles, and received in the Church, having been set forth by more than 310 Bishops (the number at Nice being 318).[1]

It has also been observed that Cyril of Jerusalem, who died A. D. 386, and delivered his Catechetical Lectures early in his life, in the eighteenth lecture repeats the following Articles, as part of the Creed : — "In one Baptism of repentance for the remission of sins, and in one Holy Catholic Church ; and in the Resurrection of the flesh ; and in eternal Life." [2]

We must infer then, either that a larger, as well as a shorter Creed was put forth at Nice, such as Epiphanius has recorded, or that such a longer form had existed of old time, and that the

[1] Epiphanius, *In Anchorato,* juxta finem ;
Suicer, s. v. σύμβολον ; Bingham, Bk. x.
ch. iv. § 15.

[2] Cyril, *Catech.* xviii.

Council only specified those parts which bore particularly on the controversy of the day; or, lastly, that shortly after the Council of Nice the Nicene fathers, or some of them, or others who had high authority, enlarged and amplified the Nicene symbol, and that this enlarged form obtained extensively in the Church.[1]

The Council of Constantinople met A. D. 381, consisting of 150 fathers. Their principal object was to condemn the Macedonian heresy, which denied the Deity of the Spirit of God. They accordingly put forth an enlarged edition of the Creed of the Council of Nice. It agreed almost word for word with the Creed of Epiphanius, the only omission being of the following clauses, "that is of the substance of His Father," and "both things in Heaven and things in earth;" which were already fully expressed in other words.

The chief clauses contained in this Creed, which do not occur in the Creed as put forth by the Council of Nice, are as follows: —

"Begotten of the Father before all worlds," "By the Holy Ghost of the Virgin Mary," "Was crucified also for us under Pontius Pilate, and was buried," "Sitteth on the right hand of the Father," "Whose kingdom shall have no end;" and all those clauses which follow the words "We believe in the Holy Ghost."

The most important of these expressions is "the Lord, and Giver of life" (τὸ Κύριον καὶ τὸ ζωοποιὸν). The Arians spoke of Him as a creature. The Macedonians called Him a ministering spirit. In opposition to these, in the Creed of Constantinople, after an expression of belief in the Holy Spirit τὸ Πνεῦμα τὸ ἅγιον is added τὸ Κύριον, "the Lord." This was in allusion to 2 Cor. iii. 17, 18, where the Spirit is spoken of as the Lord (i. e. JEHOVAH); and is called "The Lord the Spirit;"[2] and therefore in this Creed He is called τὸ Πνεῦμα τὸ Κύριον, "the Spirit, which is the LORD."[3]

It is unnecessary to repeat here what was said in the History of the fifth Article, concerning the famous addition of the *Filioque;* which was the chief cause of the schism of the Eastern and Western Churches.

The Creed of Constantinople was solemnly confirmed by the third general Council, the Council of Ephesus, A. D. 431; whose seventh Canon decrees that "No one shall be permitted to introduce, write, or compose any other faith, besides that which was

---

[1] See Suicer and Bingham, as above.
[2] ὁ δὲ Κύριος τὸ Πνεῦμα ἐστιν, and ἀπὸ Κυρίου Πνεύματος.
[3] See Wall, *On Infant Baptism,* II. p. 465.

defined by the holy fathers assembled in the city of Nice with the Holy Ghost."[1]

It is said that the first to introduce the Constantinopolitan Creed into the Liturgy was Peter Fullo, Patriarch of Antioch, about the year 471; and that he ordered it to be repeated in every assembly of the Church.[2]   It is further said, that Timotheus, Bishop of Constantinople, first brought the same custom into the Church of Constantinople, about A. D. 511.[3]   From the East the custom passed into the Western Churches, and was first adopted in Spain by the Council of Toledo, about A. D. 589, when that Church was newly recovered from an inundation of Arianism. The Roman Church appears to have been the last to receive it, as some say, not before A. D. 1014; though others have assigned, with probability, an earlier date.[4]

Section IV. — THE CREED OF ST. ATHANASIUS.

I. THE original of this, as of the Apostles' Creed, is obscure. In former times, many learned men believed it to have been composed by Athanasius, when he was at Rome, and offered by him to Pope Julius, as a confession of his faith.   This was the opinion of Baronius, and in it he was followed by Cardinal Bona, Petavius, Bellarmine, Rivet, and many others of both the Roman and the reformed communions.[5]   The first who entered critically into an examination of the question of its authorship, was Gerard Vossius, in his work *De Tribus Symbolis*, A. D. 1642; who threw strong doubts on the received opinion, having given good reason to believe that this Creed was the work, not of Athanasius, but of some Latin writer, probably much posterior to Athanasius.   Indeed he did not set it higher than A. D. 600.   He was followed by Archbishop Usher, who in his tract *De Symbolis* (A. D. 1647) produced new evidence, of which Vossius was ignorant, agreed with him in denying it to Athanasius, but scrupled not to assign it a date prior to the year 447.

---

[1] Beveridge, *Synodicon,* I. p. 103; Routh's *Opuscula,* II. p. 392.

[2] Πέτρον φησὶ τὸν κναφέα ἐπινοῆσαι . . . . καὶ ἐν πάσῃ συνάξει τὸ σύμβολον λέγεσθαι — Theodor. Lector. *Hist. Eccles.* Lib. II. p. 556, Paris, 1673; Bingham, Bk. x. ch.

IV. § 7; Palmer's *Origines Liturgicæ,* II. ch. IV. § 6.

[3] Theodor. Lector. p. 563; Bingham and Palmer, as above.

[4] Bingham and Palmer, as above.

[5] Bingham Bk. x. ch. IV. § 18.

In the year 1675, Paschasius Quesnel, a learned French divine, published the works of Pope Leo, with some dissertations of his own. In the fourteenth of these, he discusses the authorship of this Creed, and assigns it to Vigilius Tapsensis, an African Bishop, who lived in the latter end of the fifth century, in the time of the Arian persecution by the Vandals. His arguments have so prevailed as to carry a majority of learned writers with him ; amongst whom may be mentioned, Cave, Dupin, Pagi, Natalis Alexander, Bingham.

The principal arguments against the authorship of Athanasius, and in favour of Vigilius, are thus summed up by the last mentioned writer, Bingham.[1] First, because this Creed is wanting in almost all the MSS. of Athanasius' works. Secondly, because the style and contexture of it does not bespeak a Greek, but a Latin author.   Thirdly, because neither Cyril of Alexandria, nor the Council of Ephesus, nor Pope Leo, nor the Council of Chalcedon, have even so much as mentioned it in all they say against the Nestorian or Eutychian heresies. Fourthly, because this Vigilius is known to have published several others of his writings under the borrowed name of Athanasius, with which this Creed is commonly joined." [2]

In 1693, Joseph Antelmi, a learned divine of Paris, in his *Dissertatio de Symbolo Athanasiano*, attacked with great success the opinion of Quesnel, and ascribed the Creed to Vincentius Lirinensis, who flourished in Gaul, A. D. 434.

His arguments appear to have produced considerable effect on the learned world. The famous Tillemont (1697) commends the performance of Antelmi, though still inclining to Quesnel's opinion.   Montfaucon (1698) is convinced that the Creed is not the work of Athanasius nor Vigilius, nor is he convinced that it is due to Vincentius ; but thinks there is great reason to conclude, that it was the work of a Gallican writer or writers, about the time of Vincentius.   In like manner, Muratori, a famous Italian writer (1698), commends the opinion of Antelmi, as nearest to the truth.[3]

Lastly, our learned Dr. Waterland, in his valuable *History of the Athanasian Creed*, having given an account of the opinions of his predecessors, brings many strong arguments to prove that the writer was Hilary, who became Bishop of Arles, A. D. 429, and that he, in all probability, put forth this creed, when he first entered his diocese.

---

[1] Bingham, as above ; Waterland, *Hist.*
of Athanasian Creed, ch. I.

[2] Ibid.

[3] Waterland, as above.

The arguments, by which the time and place in which this Creed was written have been pretty certainly arrived at, may be classed under two heads: 1 External; 2 Internal Proofs.

1. External Proofs are as follows: —

A. D. 670.　　(1) We have ancient testimonies as early as the Council of Autun, A. D. 670, where this Creed is enjoined to be recited by the clergy. After this, Regino, Abbot of Prom in Germany, A. D. 760. The Council of Frankfort, A. D. 794. Theodulph, Bishop of Orleans, A. D. 809. Hincmar, Archbishop of Rheims, A. D. 852, &c.

A. D. 570.　　(2) There is an *ancient commentary*, as early as A. D. 570, by Venantius Fortunatus, an Italian, who became Bishop of Poictiers. Afterwards commentaries by Hincmar, Bishop of Rheims, A. D. 852; Bruno, Bishop of Warzburgh in Germany, A. D. 1033; the famous Abelard, 1120, &c.

A. D. 600.　　(3) There are MSS. as early as the seventh century, and one was found in the Cotton Library by Archbishop Usher, as early as A. D. 600; though this has since disappeared. This is a very early date, considering how few MSS., even of the most ancient writers, are much earlier.

A. D. 850.　　(4) There are *French versions* of the year 850; German, 870; Anglo-Saxon, 930; Greek, 1200, &c.

A. D. 550.　　(5) The reception of this Creed may be shown to have been in Gaul, as early as A. D. 550; Spain, 630; Germany, 787; England, 800; Italy, 880; Rome, 930.

From these considerations we trace the Creed to the middle of the sixth century, when it appears to have been well known, commented on, and treated with great respect; and that more especially in the churches of Gaul.

2. The Internal Evidences are these: —

Not before A. D. 370.　　(1) It was clearly written after the rise of the Apollinarian heresy; for the Creed is full, clear, and minute in obviating all the cavils of that heresy concerning the incarnation of Christ.[1]　This heresy arose about A. D. 360, and grew

A. D. 370.　　to a head about A. D. 370. Epiphanius marks the time when Creeds began to be enlarged in opposition to Apollinarianism, namely, A. D. 373,[2] about which year Athanasius died.

Not before A. D. 416.　　(2) The Creed appears to have adopted several of St. Augustine's expressions and modes of reasoning. Now

---

[1] It will be remembered that the Apollinarians denied a human soul to Christ, and said that the Godhead supplied the place of the rational soul. See August. *Hæres.* 49. Tom. VIII. p. 19.

[2] Epiphanius *Anchorat.* c. 121, ap. Waterland.

he wrote his books on the Trinity about A. D. 416. Especially this Creed contains the famous *Filioque;* and Augustine was the first who brought the doctrine of the Procession from the Son prominently forward; whence he has been charged by the Greeks with being the father of that doctrine. This would make it probable that the Creed was not written much before A. D. 420.

Before A. D. 451.   (3) It appears, however, to have been written before the rise of the Eutychians; for there is not a word plainly expressing the *two natures* of Christ, and excluding *one nature;* which critical terms are rarely or never omitted in the Creeds after the Eutychian times. Nay, though this Creed does in effect oppose this, as well as other heresies, there are expressions in it, which, it has been thought, might have been laid hold of by Eutyches in his favour, and therefore would not have been written after his heresy had arisen; *e. g.* "One, not by conversion of the Godhead into flesh, but by taking of the manhood into God." This might have been perverted to prove the Eutychian dogma, that Christ's manhood was converted into and absorbed in His Godhead. Again, "As the reasonable soul and flesh is one man, so God and man is one Christ." The Eutychians might have argued from this clause, that, as body and soul make up the *one nature* of man, so God and man in Christ made *one nature* also.

Hence it is concluded that this Creed was written before the Council of Chalcedon, where Eutyches was condemned, A. D. 451.

Before A. D. 431.   (4) It was probably before the spread of the Nestorian heresy. It is certain that this Creed does not condemn Nestorianism in the full, direct, and critical terms which Catholics made use of against that heresy. There is nothing about the *Deipara* in it, or about *one Son* only in opposition to two Sons, or about *God* being *born,* or *suffering* and *dying.* But such terms ever occur in Creeds drawn up, or writings directed against Nestorianism. And though terms occur in it which may be held to condemn both Eutychianism and Nestorianism, yet they are not stronger than were used by those who, before the rise of both these heresies, wrote against the Apollinarians, whose doctrine bore considerable resemblance in some points to that of Eutyches, and the maintainers of which often charged the Catholics with something very like the doctrine afterwards held by Nestorius. Hence, in the Apollinarian controversy, the fathers were often led to condemn, by anticipation, both Nestorius and Eutyches. If this reasoning be correct, the Athanasian Creed must have been written before the Council of Ephesus, where Nestorianism was condemned, A. D. 431.

Thus the internal evidence leads us to conclude, that the Athanasian Creed was, in all probability, composed between A. D. 420 and A. D. 431.

As to the *place* where it was made, evidence tends to show that it was *Gaul*.

(1) It seems to have been received first in Gaul. (2) It was held in great esteem by Gallican councils and bishops. (3) It was first admitted into the Gallican Psalter. (4) The oldest versions of it, commentaries on it, citations from it, and testimonies to it, are Gallican, or connected with Gaul. (5) The greatest number of the manuscripts of it, and those of greatest antiquity, are found in Gaul.

From such arguments as these, it has been concluded, with the greatest probability, that this Creed was written in France, and at some time in the interval between A. D. 420 and 431.[1]

The authorship of it then must be assigned to some person or persons, who flourished at this period in the church of Gaul.

Now Vincentius Lirinensis and Hilary of Arles both were Gallican divines, and both flourished at the required time.

Vincentius was a writer of great celebrity and judgment, and his works contained thoughts and expressions which bear a great similarity to the expressions in the Athanasian Creed. It is true his famous work, the *Commonitorium*, is assigned to the date 434, *i. e.* a few years later than the probable date of the Athanasian Creed; but there seems no reason why he should not have written the Creed before the *Commonitorium*.

On the other hand, it is argued by Dr. Waterland, that Hilary was a bishop, which Vincentius was not; and such a work appears much fitter for a bishop than for a private presbyter. He was made a bishop A. D. 429, which falls exactly within the limits assigned for the date of the Creed; and what more likely than that he should have set it forth when he entered on his diocese? He is spoken of as a man of great powers. His writings are said to have been small tracts, but extremely fine; and Honoratus of Marseilles, who wrote his Life, says that he wrote an excellent *Exposition of the Creed*; which is the proper title for the work in question, a work which was rarely called a *Creed* (*Symbolum*) by the ancients. Again, he was a great admirer of St. Augustine (in all but his views of predestination), whence we may account for the similarity of the expressions in this Creed to the language of that father. The resemblance, which is traced to the language of Vincentius,

[1] See Waterland, as above

may have resulted from the fact that Hilary and Vincentius were not only contemporaries, but had been inmates, about the same time, of the same monastery at Lerins; that so Vincentius might borrow expressions from Hilary, to whom he would be likely to look up with respect. Lastly, the style of' this Creed answers well to what is told us of the style and character of Hilary.

To conclude: whether we assign the Athanasian Creed to Hilary or Vincentius, or to both or neither of them, it was pretty certainly the work of some Gallican writer in the beginning of the fifth century. It was very probably called *Athanasian* because it clearly expressed the doctrines which Athanasius so ably defended; and because, when Arianism was rife in Gaul, as it was soon after the publication of this Creed, the Arians very probably called the Catholics Athanasians, and the Creed, which especially and most fully expressed their doctrines, the Athanasian Creed.[1]

II. The particular value of this Creed consists in this, that it guards the doctrine of the Trinity and of the Incarnation against the various heretical subtilties by which it has been explained away: and although it may be argued that most of these heresies are ancient, and therefore out of date, it is far from being true that they may never recur. Arianism, Sabellianism, Apollinarianism, against which it seems chiefly to have been directed, have all been revived in late times; even Nestorian and Eutychian doctrines, which the Creed, as it were, anticipates and condemns, have been more or less approved in our days. And although none of these errors were openly professed, yet the loose way in which many modern writers on Theology often express themselves requires to be restrained by something like the Creed in question, which, by its accurate language, is calculated to produce accuracy of thought.

Even then, if some people may think the damnatory clauses, as they are called, unduly strong, yet the occurrence of one or two strong expressions should not so far weigh with us as to induce us to wish the removal of this confession of our faith from the formularies of the Church. It is, in the main, unquestionably true, that he who, having the means of learning the truth of Christ, shall yet reject and disbelieve it, shall on that account be condemned. It is probable that the damnatory clauses in the Creed of Athanasius mean no more than the words of our Lord, " He that believeth not shall be damned " (Mark xvi. 16). What allowance is to be made for involuntary ignorance, prejudice, or other infirmities, is

---

[1] See Waterland's *History of the Athanasian Creed; Works*, IV.

one of those secret things which belong only to the Lord our God; concerning which we may hope, but cannot pronounce. The Gospel declares that unbelief in the truth shall be a cause of condemnation; and the Church is therefore justified in saying the same. The extreme earnestness and, as to some it seems, harshness, with which the Creed expresses it, resulted from the imminent danger, at the time it was composed, from the most noxious heresy, and the need there was to hedge round the faith of the Church, as it were, with thorns and briers. If we think such language unnecessarily severe, still we must remember that nothing human is free from some mark of human infirmity, and should be slow to doubt the value of a Catholic exposition of the Faith, because one or two expressions seem unsuited to modern phraseology.

The meaning and importance of the different clauses will be best appreciated by observing what errors they respectively opposed. Thus, let us begin with ver. 4: " Neither confounding the Persons, nor dividing the Substance." The Patripassians and Sabellians confounded the Persons; the Arians divided the Substance of the Godhead. After this, the next 14 verses, down to " yet not three Lords, but one Lord," seem principally designed to oppose the Arian heresy, which denied the homo-ousion. Accordingly they declare that in the Holy Trinity there are *Three*, with a distinction of Person, but with an Unity of Substance or Essence; so that, though it is lawful to say that the Father, Son, and Spirit, are distinct Persons, and that each Person is Lord, God, Almighty, uncreated, and incomprehensible, yet it is not lawful to say that there are three Gods, three Lords, three Almighties, three Uncreated, or three Incomprehensibles.[1]

The 19th verse concludes this portion of the Creed, in the words, " For like as we are compelled by the Christian verity to acknowledge every Person by Himself to be God and Lord, so are we forbidden by the Catholic Religion to say, There be three Gods or three Lords." Now the former part of this clause has been supposed by some to speak, so that we might infer from it, that any one Person in the Trinity, by Himself, would constitute the whole Godhead. This, however, is far from being the real or natural sense of the passage. The meaning is this: Each Person in the Trinity is essentially God. And we must not view God as we would a material being, as though the Godhead could be *divided* into three

[1] The original of the word "incomprehensible" is "immensus," *i. e.* ἄπειρος, boundless, immeasurable, or omnipresent. See Waterland, *Hist. of Ath. Cr.* **Ch.** x.; *Works,* IV. p. 385.

different parts, which three united together made up one whole, and
so imagine that the Father alone was not God, but required to have
the Son and the Spirit *added* to Him in order to make up the Godhead.   No! The spiritual unity of the three Blessed Persons in
the Trinity is far closer, more intimate, and more real, than that
unity by which parts make up a whole.   Each by Himself, or considered alone, must be confessed to be God; and yet all make not
up three Gods, but are One in Essence, and therefore but one
God.

The next four verses are opposed to those who confounded the
Persons of the Godhead, making the Father, Son, and Holy Ghost
not only one God, but one Person.   And they state the relations
of the Son to the Father, and of the Holy Ghost to both of
them.

The 23d verse runs thus : " So there is one Father, not three
Fathers: One Son, not three Sons ; One Holy Ghost, not three
Holy Ghosts."   It may be asked here, of what use is this clause ?
Did any heretics ever teach that there were three Fathers, or
three Sons, or three Holy Ghosts?   The answer is, Those who asserted that there were three unoriginated principles (τρεῖς ἄναρχοι),
were considered to teach virtually that there were three Fathers,
or three Sons, or three Holy Ghosts, or a Trinity of Trinities.
Thus one of the Apostolical Canons is directed against presbyters,
who should baptize " in three unoriginated principles, or in three
Sons, or in three Paracletes, or in three Holy Ghosts."   The Council of Bracara denounces those who shall say, " as the Gnostics and
Priscillianists, that there is a Trinity of Trinities."   And Pope
Vigilius decrees, that, if any " baptize in one Person of the Trinity,
or in two, or in three Fathers, or in three Sons, or in three Com-
forters," he should be cast out of the Church.[1]

The Creed from verse 27 treats of the Incarnation, and excludes
the various heretical opinions on this subject.

Some denied that Christ was God, as the Ebionites, Arians, &c.
Others denied that He was Man ; as the Gnostics, the Apollinarians,
and afterwards the Eutychians.   Especially the Apollinarians denied that He was perfect man, having both a reasonable soul and
human flesh besides His Godhead, ver. 30.

Again, the Apollinarians charged the Catholics with saying that
Christ was two, since they assigned Him a human soul as well as
a Divine Spirit.   Therefore the Creed adds, that, " though He be
God and Man, yet He is not two, but one Christ," — a clause which

---

[1] Bingham, *E. A.* Bk. xi. ch. iii. § 4.

afterwards was suitable to oppose the Nestorians, who held that there were two *Persons* united in Christ, ver. 32.

Once more, the Apollinarians made the Godhead of Christ act the part of a soul to His Manhood; which was virtually converting the Godhead into flesh.[1] The true doctrine is, not that God was changed into man, but that the Word of God took human nature into union with His Godhead. Therefore the Creed says, " One, not by conversion of the Godhead into flesh, but by taking of the Manhood into God," ver. 33.

Again, the Apollinarians made a " confusion of substance " in Christ, for they confounded His Godhead and His Manhood; as the Eutychians did afterwards, inasmuch as they made His Godhead act the part of His human soul. Therefore says the Creed " One altogether, not by confusion of substance, but by unity of Person," *i. e.* by uniting both natures in one Person, ver. 34. And this is further explained, that, as in the ordinary man there are two different substances, body and soul, united in one, so in Christ two different natures, God and Man, are intimately united, yet not confounded together, ver. 35: " As the reasonable soul and flesh is one man, so God and Man is one Christ."

Thus the principal clauses of the Creed are drawn up, to obviate the principal errors on the two chief doctrines of the Christian faith. If such errors had never arisen, the accurate language of the Creed would have been useless. But when dangers have been shown to exist, opposition to them seems inevitably forced upon the Church. Peace is infinitely to be desired, but it is better to contend for the faith than to lose it.

The three Creeds in their Original Languages.

1. *Symbolum Apostolorum.*

Πιστεύω εἰς τὸν Θεὸν· Πατέρα παντοκράτορα ποιητὴν οὐρανοῦ καὶ γῆς, καὶ Ἰησοῦν Χριστὸν Υἱὸν αὐτοῦ τὸν μονογενῆ τὸν κύριον ἡμῶν. τὸν συλληφθέντα ἐκ Πνεύματος Ἁγίου, γεννηθέντα ἐκ Μαρίας τῆς παρθένου, παθόντα ἐπὶ Ποντίου Πιλάτου, σταυρωθέντα, θανόντα, καὶ ταφέντα, κατελθόντα εἰς ᾅδου, τῇ τρίτῃ ἡμέρᾳ ἀναστάντα ἀπὸ τῶν νεκρῶν, ἀνελθόντα εἰς τοὺς οὐρανούς, καθεζόμενον ἐν δεξιᾷ Θεοῦ Πατρὸς παντοδυνάμου, ἐκεῖθεν ἐρχόμενον κρῖναι ζῶντας καὶ νεκρούς. Πιστεύω εἰς τὸ Πνεῦμα τὸ ἅγιον, ἁγίαν καθολικὴν ἐκκλησίαν, ἁγίων κοινωνίαν, ἄφεσιν ἁμαρτιῶν, σαρκὸς ἀνάστασιν, ζωὴν αἰώνιον. Ἀμήν.

---

[1] Contentiosissime affirmantes, Verbum carnem factum, hoc est, Verbi aliquid in carnem fuisse conversum atque mutatum. — Augustin. *Hæres.* 55.

2. *Symbolum Constantinopol.*

Πιστεύομεν εἰς ἕνα Θεὸν, Πατέρα παντοκράτορα, ποιητὴν οὐρανοῦ καὶ γῆς, ὁρατῶν τε πάντων καὶ ἀοράτων. Καὶ εἰς ἕνα Κύριον Ἰησοῦν Χριστὸν, τὸν Υἱὸν τοῦ Θεοῦ μονογενῆ, τὸν ἐκ τοῦ Πατρὸς γεννηθέντα πρὸ πάντων τῶν αἰώνων· φῶς ἐκ φωτός, Θεὸν ἀληθινὸν ἐκ Θεοῦ ἀληθινοῦ. γεννηθέντα, οὐ ποιηθέντα, ὁμοούσιον τῷ Πατρί· δι' οὗ τὰ πάντα ἐγένετο, τὸν δι' ἡμᾶς τοὺς ἀνθρώπους, καὶ διὰ τὴν ἡμετέραν σωτηρίαν, κατελθόντα ἐκ τῶν οὐρανῶν, καὶ σαρκωθέντα ἐκ Πνεύματος ἁγίου, καὶ Μαρίας τῆς παρθένου, καὶ ἐνανθρωπήσαντα· σταυρωθέντα τε ὑπὲρ ἡμῶν ἐπὶ Ποντίου Πιλάτου, καὶ παθόντα, καὶ ταφέντα, καὶ ἀναστάντα τῇ τρίτῃ ἡμέρᾳ κατὰ τὰς γραφάς· καὶ ἀνελθόντα εἰς τοὺς οὐρανοὺς, καὶ καθεζόμενον ἐκ δεξιῶν τοῦ Πατρὸς, καὶ πάλιν ἐρχόμενον μετὰ δόξης κρῖναι ζῶντας καὶ νεκρούς· οὗ τῆς βασιλείας οὐκ ἔσται τέλος. Καὶ εἰς τὸ Πνεῦμα τὸ ἅγιον, τὸ Κύριον, καὶ τὸ ζωοποιὸν, τὸ ἐκ τοῦ Πατρὸς ἐκπορευόμενον, τὸ σὺν Πατρὶ καὶ Υἱῷ συμπροσκυνούμενον, καὶ συνδοξαζόμενον, τὸ λαλῆσαν διὰ τῶν προφητῶν. Εἰς μίαν ἁγίαν καθολικὴν καὶ ἀποστολικὴν ἐκκλησίαν· ὁμολογοῦμεν ἓν βάπτισμα εἰς ἄφεσιν ἁμαρτιῶν, προσδοκῶμεν ἀνάστασιν νεκρῶν, καὶ ζωὴν τοῦ μέλλοντος αἰῶνος. Ἀμήν.

3. *Fides Sancti Athanasii.*

1. Quicunque vult salvus esse, ante omnia opus est ut teneat Catholicam Fidem.

2. Quam nisi quisque integram inviolatamque servaverit, absque dubio in æternum peribit.

3. Fides autem Catholica hæc est, ut unum Deum in Trinitate, et Trinitatem in Unitate veneremur:

4. Neque confundentes Personas, neque Substantiam separantes.

5. Alia est enim Persona Patris, alia Filii, alia Spiritus Sancti.

6. Sed Patris, et Filii et Spiritus Sancti, una est Divinitas, æqualis Gloria, coæterna Majestas.

7. Qualis Pater, talis Filius, talis et Spiritus Sanctus.

8. Increatus Pater, increatus Filius, increatus et Spiritus Sanctus.

9. Immensus Pater, immensus Filius, immensus et Spiritus Sanctus.

10. Æternus Pater, æternus Filius, æternus et Spiritus Sanctus.

11. Et tamen non tres æterni, sed unus æternus.

12. Sicut non tres increati, nec tres immensi, sed unus increatus, et unus immensus.

13. Similiter, Omnipotens Pater, Omnipotens Filius, Omnipotens et Spiritus Sanctus.

14. Et tamen non tres Omnipotentes, sed unus Omnipotens.

15. Ita Deus Pater, Deus Filius, Deus et Spiritus Sanctus.

16. Et tamen non tres Dii, sed unus est Deus.

17. Ita Dominus Pater, Dominus Filius, Dominus et Spiritus Sanctus.

18. Et tamen non tres Domini, sed unus est Dominus.

19. Quia sicut singillatim unamquamque Personam et Deum et Dominum confiteri Christiana veritate compellimur; ita tres Deos aut Dominos dicere Catholica religione prohibemur.

20. Pater a nullo est factus, nec creatus, nec genitus.

21. Filius a Patre solo est, non factus, nec creatus, sed genitus.

22. Spiritus Sanctus a Patre et Filio, non factus, nec creatus, nec genitus est, sed procedens.

23. Unus ergo Pater, non tres Patres; unus Filius, non tres Filii; unus Spiritus Sanctus, non tres Spiritus Sancti.

24. Et in hac Trinitate nihil prius aut posterius, nihil majus aut minus, sed totæ tres Personæ coæternæ sibi sunt, et coæquales.

25. Ita ut per omnia, sicut jam supra dictum est, et Unitas in Trinitate, et Trinitas in Unitate veneranda sit.

26. Qui vult ergo salvus esse, ita de Trinitate sentiat.

27. Sed necessarium est ad æternam Salutem, ut Incarnationem quoque Domini nostri Jesu Christi fideliter credat.

28. Est ergo Fides recta, ut credamus et confiteamur, quia Dominus noster Jesus Christus, Dei Filius, Deus pariter et Homo est.

29. Deus est ex substantia Patris ante sæcula genitus: Homo, ex substantia Matris in sæculo natus.

30. Perfectus Deus, perfectus Homo ex anima rationali et hu-:nana carne subsistens.

31. Æqualis Patri secundum Divinitatem: minor Patre secundum Humanitatem.

32. Qui licet Deus sit et Homo, non duo tamen, sed unus est Christus.

33. Unus autem, non conversione Divinitatis in carnem, sed assumptione Humanitatis in Deum.

34. Unus omnino, non confusione Substantiæ, sed unitate Personæ.

35. Nam sicut anima rationalis et caro unus est Homo; ita Deus et Homo unus est Christus.

36. Qui passus est pro salute nostra, descendit ad inferos, tertia die resurrexit a mortuis.

37. Adscendit ad cœlos, sedet ad dexteram Patris; inde venturus judicare vivos et mortuos.

38. Ad cujus adventum omnes homines resurgere habent cum corporibus suis, et reddituri sunt de factis propriis rationem.

39. Et qui bona egerunt ibunt in vitam æternam, qui vero mala, in ignem æternum.

40. Hæc est Fides Catholica, quam nisi quisque fideliter, firmiterque crediderit, salvus esse non poterit.

ARTICLE IX.

ORIGINAL Sin standeth not in the following of Adam (as the Pelagians do vainly talk), but it is the fault and corruption of the nature of every man, that naturally is engendered of the offspring of Adam, whereby man is very far gone from original righteousness, and is of his own nature inclined to evil, so that the flesh lusteth always contrary to the spirit, and therefore, in every person born into this world, it deserveth God's wrath and damnation. And this infection of nature doth remain, yea, in them that are regenerated; whereby the lust of the flesh, called in Greek φρόνημα σαρκὸς, which some do expound the wisdom, some sensuality, some the affection, some the desire of the flesh, is not subject to the law of God. And although there is no condemnation for them that believe and are baptized, yet the Apostle doth confess that concupiscence and lust hath of itself the nature of sin.

PECCATUM originale non est (ut fabulantur Pelagiani) in imitatione Adami situm, sed est vitium, et depravatio naturæ, cujuslibet hominis, ex Adamo naturaliter propagati : qua fit, ut ab originali justitia quam longissime distet, ad malum sua natura propendeat, et caro semper adversus spiritum concupiscat, unde in unoquoque nascentium, iram Dei, atque damnationem meretur. Manet etiam in renatis hæc naturæ depravatio. Qua fit, ut affectus carnis, Græce φρόνημα σαρκὸς (quod alii sapientiam, alii sensum, alii affectum, alii studium carnis interpretantur) legi Dei non subjiciatur et quanquam renatis et credentibus, nulla propter Christum est condemnatio, peccati tamen in sese rationem habere concupiscentiam, fatetur Apostolus.

SECTION I. — HISTORY.

THE origin of evil in the world has, from very early times, been a subject of speculation among philosophers and divines. What the Jewish opinions on the question may have been, is not easy to decide. The rite of circumcision, as administered to infants, may have been understood as showing that infants were born in sin, and had need of the circumcision of the Spirit, to make them partakers of the promises of God. The custom among the Jews to baptize (as well as to circumcise) all proselytes, whether men, women, or children, may seem to indicate that they looked on all, even from their birth, as naturally unclean, and needing a laver or cleansing, before admission to the privileges of their Church.[1]

[1] See the account of this custom at length in Wall's *History of Infant Baptism,* Introd.

That the early fathers of the Christian Church held the universality of human corruption, there can be but little question. A history of infant baptism is also a history of the doctrine of original sin, baptism being for the remission of sin.[1] If there were no original sin, infants could have no need to be baptized. Hence Wall, in his History of Baptism, has brought together, with great labour and fidelity, passages from the earliest writers, showing their belief in the original infection of our nature from Adam. It is not to be expected that the fathers would speak as clearly on this point before, as after the rise of Pelagianism. But a fair inspection of the passages thus cited will convince us that the doctrine was held, almost as clearly as is expressed in our own Article, from the very earliest times of the Church.[2]

For examples of the language of the fathers we may take the following passages: "Besides the evil," says Tertullian,[3] "which the soul contracts from the intervention of the wicked spirit, there is an antecedent, and, in a certain sense, natural evil arising from its corrupt origin. For, as we have already observed, the corruption of our nature is another nature, having its proper god and father, namely, the author of that corruption."

Cyprian, and the council of sixty-six bishops with him (A. D. 253), in their Epistle to Fidus, use the following words: "If then the greatest offenders, and they that have grievously sinned against God before, have, when they afterwards come to believe, forgiveness of sins, and no person is kept off from baptism and this grace, how much less reason is there to refuse an infant, who, being newly born, has no sin save that, being descended from Adam according to the flesh, he has from his very birth contracted the contagion of the death anciently threatened; who comes for this reason more easily to receive forgiveness of sins, because they are not his own but other's sins that are forgiven him?"[4]

---

[1] Mark i. 4. Acts xxii. 16.

[2] See especially the quotations from Clem. Rom. i. pp. 47, 48; Justin Martyr, pp. 64, 68; Tertullian, p. 95; Origen, p. 121; Cyprian, p. 182. Compare Bishop Kaye's *Justin Martyr*, p. 75; *Tertullian*, p. 325.

[3] Malum igitur animæ, præter quod ex obventu spiritus nequam superstruitur, ex originis vitio antecedit, naturale quodammodo. Nam, ut diximus, naturæ corruptio alia natura est, habens suum Deum et patrem, ipsum scilicet corruptionis auctorem. — *De Anima*, c. 41; Bp. Kaye, p. 326. See also cap. 40: Ita omnis anima eousque in Adam censetur, donec in Christo recenseatur; tamdiu immunda, quamdiu recenseatur.

[4] Porro autem si etiam gravissimis delictoribus, et in Deum multum ante peccantibus, cum postea crediderint, remissa peccatorum datur, et a baptismo atque a gratia nemo prohibetur; quanto magis prohiberi non debet infans, qui recens natus nihil peccavit, nisi quod, secundum Adam carnaliter natus, contagium mortis antiquæ prima nativitate contraxit? qui ad remissam peccatorum accipiendam hoc ipso facilius accedit. quod illi remittuntur non propria, sed aliena peccata. — Cyprian. *Epist.* 64 *ad Fidum.* Wall, i. p. 128.

On this, however, as on other articles of faith, there arose here-sies from very early times.   In the second century, about A. D. 180, Florinus, a presbyter of the Church of Rome, taught that God was the author of evil.   This man had been a friend of Irenæus, and a disciple of Polycarp's.   A fragment of a letter from Irenæus ad-dressed to him, in which Irenæus combats his peculiar error, is pre-served by Eusebius.[1]   The Marcionites had, before this, taught the doctrine of two principles, the one of good and the other of evil; and it has been thought probable that it was in opposition to this that Florinus fell into the opposite heresy, and that, in maintaining the sole sovereignty of God, he was led to make Him the author of sin.[2]

The Gnostic heretics in general attributed the origin of sin to matter, which they considered as essentially evil.   Colorbasus, we are told,[3] and Priscillian held, that men's actions were influenced by the stars.[4]   The Manichees, like the Marcionites before them, but more systematically, taught the eternal existence of two opposite and antagonistic principles, to the one of which they attributed the origin of evil.[5]

The great Origen, though using freely those passages of Scrip-ture, which speak of man's natural corruption, and of his being born in sin,[6] yet, from his peculiar theory of the preëxistence of human souls, could scarcely hold that man's sinfulness was derived from the first sin of Adam.   His theory was, that all souls of men have existed in a former state and are confined in bodies, and placed in circumstances according to their conduct in that former state ; and that the bodies, which they now have, are more or less gross according to the qualities of their former crimes.[7]

---

[1] Eusebius, *H. E.* v. 20. See Heylyn, *Historia Quinquarticularis*, ch. I.; Bea-ven's *Irenæus*, p. 24; also Augustin. *Hæres.* 66, Tom. VIII. p. 21.

[2] Lardner's *Hist. of Heretics*, ch. x. § x. Bp. Kaye's *Tertullian*, ch. VII.

[3] Augustin. *De Hæres.* 15.

[4] Augustin. *De Hæres.* 70 ; Adstruunt etiam fatalibus stellis homines colligatos.

[5] See Mosheim, Cent. III. Pt. II. ch. v. The Manichees are said to have taught that "sin was a substance." And Sa-turninus and the Manichees are said to have taught that sin was in man "a na-tura, non a culpa," which accounts for the language of the fathers against them, *e. g.* Theodoret, *Dial.* I.: ἡ ἁμαρτία οὐκ ἔστι τῆς φύσεως ἀλλὰ τῆς κακῆς προαιρέσεως. See Suicer, I. p. 208. The Manichees did not consider sin to lie in a deprava-tion of the whole natural actions and

thoughts of man, but in an evil constitu-tion of a portion of his nature, which they traced to that principle whom they con-sidered as the creator of all the evil in the universe.

[6] See, for example, the passage quoted by Wall, I. p. 121.

[7] See Dupin, *Eccles. Hist.* Cent. III. Art. *Origen.* See also a good, though popular, account of Origen's opinions in the *Biography of the Early Church*, by the Rev. R. W. Evans.

Origen has very generally been charged with semi-Pelagianism, and with being the forerunner of the Pelagian heretics. It is very difficult to judge clearly and impartially about his opinions. A variety of causes tend to obscure them. It is, however, certain that at times he speaks most clearly of all men being born in sin, and needing purification. For example,

In the beginning of the fifth century, a very important heresy sprang up, which called forth more decidedly the sentiments of the Church on this doctrine. Pelagius was a monk residing at Rome, but of British extraction, his name, in his own country, being probably Morgan. Cœlestius, another monk, a native of Ireland, and Julianus, a bishop, were his chief allies. His heresy was spread abroad about A. D. 410, the year that Rome was taken by the Goths. Cœlestius, having endeavored to take priest's orders at Carthage, was accused by Paulinus, a deacon of that Church, of holding several false opinions. About the same time, St. Augustine wrote his first treatise against the same errors. Pelagius had retired into Palestine, whither Augustine sent Orosius, a Spanish presbyter, to accuse him before a synod of bishops at Jerusalem. Here, and at Diospolis, he was acquitted without censure. But in the year 416, two Councils, one at Carthage and another at Milevis, condemned the Pelagian opinions. Innocent, bishop of Rome, was written to by the Councils, and agreed in their decision. But in the year 417 he was succeeded by Zosimus, who, gained over by the ambiguous confession of the Pelagians, and being himself a great admirer of Origen, pronounced in their favour. Augustine, however, with the African bishops, persevered in their opposition; and Zosimus, yielding to their representations, changed his mind and condemned with great severity Pelagius and Cœlestius. They were again finally condemned at the third general council at Ephesus, which met to consider the tenets of Nestorius.[1]

The doctrines charged against Cœlestius at the Council of Carthage (A. D. 412) were —

" That Adam was created mortal, and would have died, whether he had sinned or not. That the sin of Adam hurt only himself, and not all mankind. That infants new born are in the same state that Adam was before his fall. That a man may be without sin, and keep God's commandments, if he will." [2]

Augustine could not speak more plainly than the following : —

Quod si placet audire quid etiam alii sancti de ista nativitate senserint, audi David dicentem : *In iniquitatibus*, inquit, *conceptus sum et in peccatis peperit me mater mea :* ostendens quod quæcumque anima in carne nascitur, iniquitatis et peccati sorde polluitur: et propterea dictum esse illud quod jam superius memoravimus, quia *nemo mundus a sorde, nec si unius diei sit vita ejus.* Addi his etiam potest, ut requiratur quid causæ sit, cum baptisma Ecclesiæ pro remissione peccatorum detur, secundum Ecclesiæ observantiam etiam parvulis baptismum dari ; cum utique si nihil esset in parvulis quod ad remissionem deberet et indulgentiam pertinere, gratia baptismi superflua videretur. — Origen. *Homil. in Levitic.* VIII. num. 3.

[1] See the history of•Pelagius and Pelagianism given by Wall, *Hist. of Infant Baptism*, I. ch. XIX. ; Mosheim, Cent. V. Pt. II. ch. V. ; Neander, IV. pp. 299–362. Also the History of Pelagianism given in the Preface to the tenth volume of the Benedictine edition of St. Augustine's works.

[2] Wall, I. p. 357.

Pelagius himself sent a creed to Innocent, in which he avoids a clear statement concerning original sin, but distinctly asserts, that, though we all need the help of God, we can all keep God's laws, if we will. The principal apponents of Pelagius were Augustine, Jerome, and Fulgentius.[1]

The controversies thus called forth were not soon allayed. A new sect soon arose from the former one, called Semi-Pelagians, whose opinions concerning original sin were not so objectionable as those of Pelagius, but who ascribed far too much to the unassisted strength of the human will.[2]

The sentiments of Pelagius found considerable favour in his native island of Britain, and caused many and grievous troubles to the Church there. Germanus, bishop of Auxerre, and Lupus, bishop of Troyes, were sent over to Britain by the Gallican Church, to confute the growing heresy, and had great success, if we may credit ancient accounts, in opposing both the temporal and spiritual enemies of the Church.[3] The famous Dewi, or St. David, was afterwards greatly distinguished for the zeal and ability with which he opposed the prevailing error and aided in its overthrow. Especially at the Council of Llanddewi Brefi in Cardiganshire, his eloquence and arguments are said to have availed to the silencing of his adversaries, and the establishing of his own celebrity. He was hereupon unanimously erected primate, the aged Dyvrig (Dubritius) resigning in his favour; and he afterwards called another synod at Caerleon, where his exertions were rewarded by the extermination of the heresy.[4]

The schoolmen, in the Middle Ages, as might have been expected, debated much concerning the subject of original sin. *Original Righteousness* they seem to have considered something superadded to the original nature of man, not a part of that nature. According to Luther's statement of their opinions, it was " an ornament added to man, as a wreath upon a maiden's hair is an ornament bestowed on her, and not a part of herself." [5] Original sin, therefore, was the loss or privation of original righteousness, and man

---

[1] The Pelagians endeavoured to prove that some of the ancient fathers, especially of the Greek Church, used their language, and denied the existence of sin in infants. Augustine, in his treatise *contra Julianum*, shows, in opposition to that heretic, that St. Chrysostom (whom Julian had cited in favour of Pelagianism) had in reality plainly expressed the doctrine of original sin. — Aug. *Contra Julianum*, Lib. I. cap. VI. Vol. x. p. 509. Wall, I. p. 416.

[2] See below, under Article X.
[3] Bede, *Hist.* Lib. I. cap. XVII.–XXII. Stillingfleet's *Orig. Britan.* ch. IV. Collier's *Eccl. Hist.* Book I.
[4] Gildas Cambrensis. Rees's *Welsh Saints*, p. 193. Usher, *Brit. Eccl. Antiq.* c. V. xiii. Williams's *Antiq. of the Cymry*, pp. 134, 287.
[5] Luther, *Op.* vi. p. 38, ap. **Laurence** *Bampton Lectures*, p. 56.

was an object of God's displeasure, not as possessing what was offensive to God, but as wanting in that which was pleasing to Him. The body was infected by the fall, whether from the poison of the forbidden fruit, or from whatever cause; but the soul suffered only as deprived of that which Adam possessed, the presence of God and supernatural righteousness, and as having the *imputation of sin* derived from Adam.[1] The infection of the body was indeed *fomes peccati*, a fuel which might be kindled into sin; but the soul contracted *guilt* from imputation of Adam's guilt, not sin from the inheritance of Adam's sin, though deprived of primitive righteousness, a quality dependent on the presence and indwelling of God. St. Augustine had doubted whether the soul as well as the body was derived from the parents, and so contracted sin from them. But the schoolmen, deciding that the soul came direct from God, of necessity were led to deny a direct derivation of sin to the soul, confining its pollution to the body, which then infects the soul; and so they made the defect of the soul to consist in an absence of good, rather than in presence and dominion of evil.[2]

In the Council of Trent there was much discussion of the doctrine of the fathers and schoolmen on this article; after which the following decrees were finally determined on: (1) That Adam by transgressing lost holiness and justice, incurred the wrath of God, death, thraldom to the devil, and was infected both in soul and body. (2) That Adam derived to his posterity death of body, and sin of soul. (3) That sin, transmitted by generation, not by imitation, can be abolished by no remedy but the death of Christ, and that the merit of Christ is applied to children in baptism, as well as to adults. (4) That newly-born children ought to be baptized, as having contracted sin from Adam. (5) That by the grace of baptism the guilt of original sin is remitted, and that all is removed which hath the true and proper nature of sin. And though the concupiscence remaining is called by the Apostle sin,

---

[1] See Laurence, Serm. III. pp. 56–59, and note 2, p. 252.

The fathers appear, almost with one consent, to have held that original righteousness consisted both of natural innocence and of the grace of God vouchsafed to Adam. The one was lost simultaneously with the other. Indeed, the one could not exist without the other. Original righteousness, therefore, according to the primitive teaching, was not only defect of sin, but also the presence of God's Spirit. At the fall, God's Spirit was forfeited, and primeval innocence lost at the same time. See this proved, with his usual learning and clearness of reasoning, by Bp. Bull, *Works*, II. Disc. v. Oxf. 1827. Bp. Bull gives strong reasons for believing this to be both the universal belief of the primitive Church and the doctrine of the sacred Scriptures themselves.

[2] Sarpi, Council of Trent, p. 163. Neander, VIII. pp. 184–198, gives a very interesting account of the scholastic discussions on Original Sin.

the Synod declared that it was not true and proper sin, but was so termed because it ariseth from sin and inclineth to it.[1]

The point on which these decrees differed from the Ninth Article of our Church, is in the entire cancelling of original sin in baptism. According to the Scholastic definition, that original sin consisted in the deprivation of original righteousness, the Council of Trent determined, that in baptism the soul was restored pure into the state of innocency, though the punishments which follow sin be not removed. This all the fathers expounded by saying that the perfection of Adam consisted in an infused quality, which adorned the soul, made it perfect and acceptable to God, and exempted the body from mortality. And God, for the merit of Christ, giveth unto those that are regenerated by baptism another quality called justifying grace, which, wiping out every blemish in the soul, maketh it pure, as was that of Adam ; yea, in some it worketh greater effects than original righteousness, but only it worketh no effect on the body, whereby mortality and other natural defects are not removed.[2]

The Lutherans in this respect differed materially from the fathers of the Council ; especially in maintaining that concupiscence had the nature of sin, and that the infection, though not the imputation of sin, remained in the baptized and regenerate.[3]

The second article of the Augsburg Confession, which is the principal confession of faith of the Lutheran divines, is evidently the source from which our own ninth Article was derived. Without defining the nature of original righteousness,[4] or the mode in which Adam lost it, it declares the doctrine, that every man born naturally from Adam is born in sin, without the faith and fear of God, and with concupiscence, which disease is truly sin and

---

[1] Concupiscentiam Ecclesiam nunquam intellexisse peccatum appellari, quod vere et proprie in renatis peccatum sit, sed quia ex peccato est, et ad peccatum inclinat. — Concil. Trident. Sess. v. Sec. 5. See Anathemas in the fifth Session, Sarpi, p. 173.

A great dispute arose between the Dominicans and Franciscans, the latter insisting that the Virgin Mary should be declared free from the taint of original sin, — the Dominicans maintaining the contrary opinion. (Sarpi, p. 168.) The Council in the end declared, that it did not mean to comprehend the B. Virgin in the decree (p. 173). Augustine had before professed himself unwilling to discuss the question of the Virgin's sinful-

ness, or how far grace might have overcome sin in her, out of reverence to our Lord. (See Wall, *Infant Baptism*, I. p. 404.)

[2] Sarpi, p. 166.

[3] Ideo sic respondemus ; in baptismo tolli peccatum quod ad reatum seu imputationem attinet, sed manere morbum ipsum, &c. — Melancthon. *Loc. Theolog.* p. 122, ap. Laurence, p. 258.

[4] The Saxon confession, however, clearly speaks of original righteousness as something beyond mere innocency, calling it — in ipsa natura hominum lux, conversio voluntatis ad deum. . . . . . ac fuisset homo templum **Dei**, &c. — *Sylloge Confessionum*, p. 246.

deserving of damnation, in all who are not born again by baptism and the Spirit.[1]

Calvin, speaking of original sin, says that " As the spiritual life of Adam consisted in union with his Maker, so alienation from Him was the death of his soul. When the heavenly image was obliterated in him, he did not alone sustain the punishment, but involved all his posterity in it. The impurity of the parents is so transmitted to the children that none are excepted ; and that, not by imitation, but by propagation.". . . " Original sin appears to be an hereditary depravity and corruption of our nature, diffused through all parts of the soul, which first makes men subject to God's wrath, and then brings forth works in us which Scripture calls the works of the flesh.". . . " His destruction is to be ascribed only to man, as he obtained uprightness from God's mercy, and by his own folly fell into vanity.". . . " His sin did not spring from nature, but was an adventitious quality which happened to man, rather than a substantial propriety which from the first was created in him." [2]

Among Calvinistic divines in general there has been a difference concerning the first introduction of sin, chiefly as to whether Adam fell freely or by predestination of God : the sublapsarian Calvinists holding that Adam sinned of his own free will ; the supralapsarians holding that God decreed that he should fall.

The chief point of difference between the two great parties which so long divided the Protestant Churches, the Calvinists and Arminians, was on the *extent* of the vitiation of our nature by the fall. The Calvinists taught that the corruption of man was so great that no spark of moral goodness was left in him ; that he was utterly and totally bad and depraved ; that, however amiable he might be in regard to his fellow-men, yet as regards God and godliness there was no relic of what he once was, any more than in lost spirits and damned souls. The Arminians rejected this strong view of the subject, and, admitting the great corruption of man's heart and intellect, still maintained that some remains of

---

[1] II. *De Peccato Originis.*
Item docent, quod post lapsum Adæ omnes homines, secundum naturam propagati, nascantur cum peccato, hoc est sine metu Dei, sine fiducia erga Deum, et cum concupiscentia, quodque hic morbus, seu vitium originis vere sit peccatum, damnans et afferens nunc quoque æternam mortem his qui non renascuntur per baptismum et Spiritum Sanctum.

Damnant Pelagianos, et alios, qui vitium originis negant esse peccatum, et ut extenuent gloriam meriti et beneficiorum Christi, disputant hominem propriis viribus rationis coram Deo justificari posse. —*Confession of Augsburg.* Compare the Saxon Confession, Art. *De Peccato Originis.*
[2] Calvin, *Inst.* Lib. II. cap. 1, 5, 6, 8, — II.

his original condition might be traced in him; that his mind and will were indeed depraved and incapable of making any independent effort towards true godliness; but that he still differed materially from evil spirits or the spirits of the damned, having a natural conscience, and an appreciation of what is good and of good report.

The Calvinists have generally insisted much on the imputation of Adam's sin to all his posterity, as the true meaning of original sin; though admitting that such imputation was accompanied with actual depravity in the heart of each individual.[1] Calvin himself seems rather to have held that all men were liable to condemnation, because of their own sinfulness derived from Adam, not because of the imputation of Adam's sin.[2]

At the time of the Reformation, the Anabaptists appear to have adopted Pelagian opinions. The article on Original Sin, in the first draught of it as set forth in 1552, begins thus: " Original sin standeth not in the following of Adam, as the Pelagians do vainly talk, which also the Anabaptists do now-a-days renew." Their rejection of infant baptism was of a piece, and naturally connected, with their denial of original sin.

In later times, the Socinians held on this subject thoroughly Pelagian language, and generally denied the corruption of human nature and the need of grace to turn men to godliness.

As regards the Church of England, there have been many attempts, on the one hand, to show that she used the language of the later Calvinists, on the other, to prove that she symbolized with the Arminians. The Articles were drawn up before the great Calvinistic controversy had arisen, and therefore do not use the terms of that controversy. It is pretty certain that, in this, and some of the following Articles, the English reformers symbolized with Melancthon and the Lutheran divines, whose very words in the Confession of Augsburg, or the Wirtemberg Confession, are frequently adopted in the wording of the Articles.[3]

There is nothing said in the Ninth Article on the imputation of Adam's guilt, though that was a favourite subject of scholastic discussion, nor of the question, whether original righteousness meant merely primitive innocence, or consisted moreover in a preternatural gift, and in the indwelling and presence of God. The

---

[1] See, for example, Edwards, *On Original Sin*, Part IV. ch. III. — an able and judicious exposition of the Calvinistic view of this doctrine.

[2] Atque ideo infantes quoque ipsi, dum suam secum damnationem afferunt, *non* alieno, sed suo ipsorum vitio sunt obstricti — Calv. *Inst.* Lib. II. cap. 1, Sect. 8; Laurence, *B. L.* Serm. III. note 8, p. 261.

[3] See Laurence, *B. L.* notes to Serm II., especially notes 8 and 11.

statements are quite general; yet sufficiently guarding the truth that every man naturally engendered of Adam brings into the world a nature inclined to evil, and very far removed from the original righteousness of our first parents; that this sinfulness of his nature deserves the wrath of God; and that, although the condemnation due to it is remitted to all who believe and are baptized, still even in the regenerate the infection, showing itself in the way of concupiscence, remains, and has of itself the nature of sin.

The homily " On the Misery of Man," composed, or at least approved by Cranmer, breathes the same spirit. The homily on the Nativity, in the second book of homilies, drawn up some time later, in the reign of Queen Elizabeth, may be referred to as expressing the doctrine of original sin in somewhat stronger language; the divines of Elizabeth's reign having been brought into more intimate connection with the Calvinistic reformers, and sympathizing more with them, than was the case with the divines of the reign of Edward VI.

SECTION II. — SCRIPTURAL PROOF.

IN considering the Scriptural proof of the doctrine of original sin here, it will be better to confine ourselves strictly to the statements of the Article, avoiding as much as possible those discussions which the Article itself avoids; neither entering into the distinctions of the schoolmen, nor the disputes of the Calvinists, but resting satisfied with the plain practical ground, which our own reformers thought broad and deep enough.

The Article then may be said to embrace the five following propositions : —

I. Original sin is the fault and corruption of our nature, which infects all men.

II. It is not derived by imitation, but inherited by birth.

III. Its extent is such that by it man is very far (*quam longissime*) gone from original righteousness.

IV. It deserves God's wrath and condemnation.

V. Its infection is not entirely removed by baptism, but that infection remains even in the *renati ;* and though there is no condemnation to them that believe and are baptized, yet still lust or concupiscence has the nature of sin.

I. That " original sin is the fault and corruption of our nature, which infects all men," might be inferred from our general knowledge of mankind, and of the evil tempers even of childhood, if we had no express revelation of it.

In the earliest part of the Scripture history the Almighty declared, that " the imagination of man's heart was evil from his youth " (Gen. viii. 21). Job attributed man's weakness and sorrows to the fact that what was clean could not be brought from what was unclean (Job xiv. 4). David, acknowledging his own sin from his youth, confessed that he was " shapen in iniquity, and that in sin did his mother conceive him " (Ps. li. 5). Solomon declared that " there was not a just man on earth, that did good and sinned not " (Eccles. vii. 20). And Isaiah, in foretelling the sacrifice of Christ, gives as the reason for it, that " All we like sheep have gone astray ; we have turned every one to his own way " (liii. 6. See also Gen. vi. 5–12. Job xv. 16. Psalm xiv. 2, 3 ; lviii. 3 ; cvi. 6, &c. Prov. xxii. 15. Jer. xvii. 5, 9.)

These and similar passages, even before the coming of the Gospel, sufficiently showed that there was an evil coextensive with our race and coeval with our birth, from which none were exempt, and which went with us from the cradle to the grave.

There are many passages in the Gospels which show that the same doctrine pervades them ; as our Lord's declaration that " there is none good but One, that is God " (Matt. xix. 17) ; His committing Himself to no man, " for He knew what was in man " (John ii. 24, 25) ; His declaration that no one could enter into the Kingdom of God, " except he were born again of water and of the Spirit " (John iii. 3, 5, 6) ; nay, His institution of baptism, which all who would be saved must receive, showing that there was an uncleanness of nature, which needed to be washed away by grace.

But, of course, the writings of the Apostles, as being the more doctrinal portions of Scripture, treat most systematically on the subject. The whole of the earlier part of the Epistle to the Romans more especially treats of the sinfulness of man, which needs the sacrifice of Christ. The Apostle shows in the first chapter, that the *Gentiles*, notwithstanding the light of nature — the natural conscience which God had given them ; and in the second chapter, that the *Jews*, although to them had been committed the oracles of God, had yet all been condemned by their own acts and

by their own Law.   In the third chapter, he concludes that *all* are
under sin (Rom. iii. 9), that " all have sinned and come short of the
glory of God " (Rom. iii. 23).   In the fifth chapter, he shows that,
from the time of Adam, " death had passed upon all men, for that
all have sinned " (ver. 12).   In the seventh chapter throughout,
he describes the natural man moved by the dictates of conscience
to approve what is good, and yet constrained by a law in his members — the law of sin and death working in him — to follow what is
evil.   He then considers the same natural man instructed by the
revealed Law of God, consenting to the Law that it was good, and
yet unable to fulfil it, because of the sin that dwelleth in him, and
that binds him down to do what is base : so that he even represents
the Law as bringing death rather than life, as showing the good
and the beautiful, as kindling some feelings of desire for better
things, but still as giving no power to reach after them.   And all
this, which he so strikingly describes to us, he tells us results from
this cause, namely, that in man, that is in his natural condition, there
dwelleth no good.   " I know that in me, that is in my flesh, dwelleth no good thing." [1]   In the eighth chapter, he shows how this
defect of our nature is remedied ; that, whereas man by himself
could not please God, whereas the Law was too weak, owing to the
infirmity of man's sinful nature, yet God sent His Son to save, and
His Spirit to sanctify ; and so those who are in the Spirit and no
longer in the flesh, can fulfil the righteousness of the Law.   But
" the *carnal* mind is not subject to the law of God," and " they who
are in the flesh " (*i. e.* in a state of nature, and not under grace)
" cannot please God," Rom. viii. 8.[2]   Just similar is St. Paul's
language in his other Epistles ; see, for example, Eph. iv. 22,

---

[1] Rom. vii. 18: "In my flesh," of
course means in my natural and carnal
state, according to the common Pauline
antithesis of the flesh and the spirit.
No doubt, many persons have thought
that the Apostle in this chapter is speaking of his own struggles against sin still
dwelling in him, when under the dominion of grace.   But it has always appeared
to me that the whole thread of the apostle's argument is broken, and the whole
force of his reasoning destroyed by this
hypothesis.   The fact that he uses the
first person singular need not puzzle us
for a moment.   It is his common habit to
speak in the first person, when he means
to represent himself as the type of others,
of the world at large, or of others situ-
ated like himself.   One sentence in the
chapter, if it stood alone, would be

enough to prove that the Apostle is not
describing the state and conflict of a
regenerate Christian.   It is in v. 14 :
" I am carnal, sold under sin."   The redeemed Christian, " bought with a price,"
and delivered " from the bondage of corruption, into the glorious liberty of the
children of God," can never truly be represented as still " sold under sin."   Christ
has made him free, " and he is free indeed."

[2] We must take care that by the expression, " the flesh," in Rom. vii. viii.
we do not suppose the Apostle to mean
the body, the material part of our being.
This would be the Manichean error.   It
is not the body only, but the whole man,
that the Scriptures speak of as infected
with sin.   Compare John iii. 6.   Gal. v.
19, 20.   1 Cor. iii. 3, 4.

where he speaks of " the old man, which is corrupt according to deceitful lusts ; " Eph. ii. 1, and Col. ii. 13, where he speaks of men, before their conversion and baptism, as having been " dead in trespasses and sin ; " Eph. ii. 3, where he speaks of both Jews and Gentiles as " by nature children of wrath ; " Gal. iii. 22, where he says that " the Scripture hath concluded all under sin."

We can scarcely need fuller proof that the Scriptures describe all men naturally born into the world as subject to the disease of sin.

II. We have next to prove, that " Original sin is not derived from imitation, but inherited by birth."

In the third chapter of Genesis we have an account of the fall of Adam, and the consequent curse upon him, and the ground which he was to till.

Now the old Testament speaks of the impossibility of " bringing a clean thing out of an unclean " (Job xiv. 4), and asks, " What is man, that he should be clean ? Or he which is born of a woman, that he should be righteous ? " (Job xv. 14). The Psalmist, as we have seen, traces his own corruption to the fact that he was " shapen in iniquity, and conceived in sin " (Ps. li. 5). Such expressions imply that the sinfulness of parents passed to their children ; and the universal taint which we have already seen to be existing, is traced to an inheritance derived from father to son.

Such, we cannot doubt, is the meaning of our Lord, " That which is born of the flesh is flesh " (John iii. 6). He was teaching Nicodemus the need which every one had to be born again, before he could see the kingdom of God. Nicodemus marvelled that a man should be born again. Our Lord explains that a spiritual birth was needed. And why ? Because " that which was born of the flesh is flesh." The flesh signifies the natural, carnal, unholy state of man, as contrasted with the holy, spiritual state of the redeemed and regenerate. Now our Lord declared that every man had need of a new birth, because " that which was born of the flesh was flesh." Man inherited by birth the flesh, — a fleshly, an unspiritual, an unholy nature ; therefore he needed a new birth, a birth of the Spirit, which should make him spiritual, even as his former birth of the flesh had made him carnal. This surely sufficiently demonstrates that every man by nature was in a state of defect, and *that*, because he *inherited* defect *by birth*. He was born of parents who were carnal, and therefore he was carnal himself.

Accordingly, St. Paul treats it as a well-known truth, that " in

Adam all die " (1 Cor. xv. 22). And in the Epistle to the Romans
(v. 12) he tells us, that " by one man sin entered into the world,
and death by sin; and so death passed upon all men, for that all
have sinned ; " that " through the offence of one many are dead "
(ver. 15) ; that " by one man's offence death reigned " (ver. 17) ;
that " by the offence of one judgment came upon all men to condemnation " (ver. 18) ; that " by one man's disobedience many
were made sinners " (ver. 19).

It is true that the words thus cited might, if they stood alone,
bear the Pelagian interpretation, that Adam brought in sin by
bringing in the first example of sin, and that his children sinned
after him by imitation of him, not because they derived a sinful
nature from him ; and so judgment passed upon all men, " because
all had sinned," their own personal sins having caused their condemnation.   But St. Paul expressly guards against such an interpretation, by saying (ver. 14) that " death reigned from Adam to
Moses, even over them that had not sinned after the *similitude* of
Adam's transgression." Death was the penalty, which all had paid,
even before the Law of Moses came to give more fully the knowledge of sin; and it had reigned not only in those whose presumptuous wickedness resembled the sin of Adam, but even in
those who had not sinned after that similitude, in infants and idiots,
and such as only inherited the nature, without following the example of Adam.   This doctrine corresponds with the doctrine of our
Lord, " That which is born of the flesh is flesh."

Accordingly, the Apostle, when speaking of human nature in
general, calls it " sinful flesh " (Rom. viii. 3).   Our Lord took our
nature, such as it was derived from Adam, only He was " without
sin ; " but because He took that nature, which was then universally
corrupted, therefore St. Paul says, " He was sent in the likeness
of sinful flesh."   And with this doctrine entirely corresponds all
that the Apostles write of the corruption of men by nature, and of
the change or new birth necessary for every man who is in Christ;
e. g. " The natural man receiveth not the things of the Spirit of
God " (1 Cor. ii. 15).   " I know that in me, that is in my flesh,
dwelleth no good thing " (Rom. vii. 18).   " They that are after the
flesh do mind the things of the flesh " (Rom. viii. 5).   " The carnal
mind is enmity against God; for it is not subject to the law of
God, neither indeed can be.   So then they that are in the flesh
cannot please God " (Rom. viii. 7, 8).   " The flesh lusteth against
the Spirit, and the Spirit against the flesh " (Gal. v. 17).   Again,
" If any man be in Christ he is a new creature " (2 Cor. v. 17).

And the sinfulness of our natural state is called "the old man ; " and Christians are said to have "put off the old man, which is corrupt according to the deceitful lusts, and to have put on the new man, which after God is created in righteousness and true holiness" (Eph. iv. 22–24).

Now all this language appears to prove that sin is a corruption and disease, affecting not only individuals, but the whole of human nature, so that whosoever inherits human nature inherits it so diseased. It is "the flesh," a nature debased and defiled , and whatever is born of the flesh is flesh also. Adam, we find from the second chapter of Genesis, received from God a nature free from sin, and so not subject to shame. But he defiled it with sin, and it became at once subject to shame, and then subject to death. Accordingly, when he handed down that nature to his posterity, he could not hand it down pure as he had received it ; he of necessity gave it to them as he had himself made it, stained with sin, liable to shame, having the seeds of mortality, and subject to condemnation. This view of the subject explains and satisfies the language of Scripture ; and no other view will. There have been popular illustrations of it, such as the comparison of the hereditary taints of disease and insanity, and other ways in which, in God's providence, the sins of the fathers are visited on the children. There have been philosophical discussions concerning the oneness of human nature, interesting in themselves, but unsuited to our limits here.[1] We have already seen that there have been discussions as to whether the body only, or soul and body both, are derived from the parent, and so corrupted by his sins. Even this I have not fully entered into ; though it is plain that Scripture speaks of *man*, not man's body only, as corrupted and condemned. "In Adam all die." From Adam "all have sinned" (Rom. v. 12). Sin is a fault of the soul, and therefore plainly both body and soul are tainted with corruption.

III. We have next to consider the degree or extent of corruption, thus naturally inherited by all men. Does original sin *totally* corrupt all men, so that there is no spark of natural goodness left ? Or are there still relics of what man once was ? still, though in wreck and ruin, some faint outline of his original state of purity ?

---

[1] See for example Hooker, Bk. **v.** ; Wilberforce, *On the Incarnation*, ch. iii. This was the view of St. Augustine, more fully expanded by the realists among the schoolmen.

It has been contended that the words of our Article mean both of these sides of the alternative. Calvinists appeal to the words "quam longissime," in the Latin Article, as proving that man's defection from original righteousness was to the greatest extent possible, that is to say, total and entire.[1] Their opponents argued that the convocation had translated these words by "very far," showing that it was intended only to express a great and serious defection of our race from godliness, not a total destruction of moral sense and feeling.

The Scriptures evidently represent natural sinfulness as very great. The Almighty, speaking of the race before the flood, said that "every imagination of his heart was only evil continually" (Gen. vi. 5). Yet this might apply only to that generation, which had become so wicked as to call for signal judgment and destruction. But then, after the flood, once more God declares that "He will not again curse the ground for man's sake ; *though*[2] the imagination of his heart be only evil from his youth" (Gen. viii. 21). This seems to be a more general proposition, indicating at least that man's heart might prove as evil after the flood as it had done before.

In the book of Job, Eliphaz the Temanite says that God "putteth no trust in His saints, and the heavens are not clean in His sight. How much more abominable and filthy is man which drinketh iniquity like water" (Job xv. 16). We must not always consider the words of Job's friends as of authority in matters of faith, since their judgment is afterwards condemned by God; and we must make allowance for the strong antithesis between *God* and *man ;* yet still the passage shows that to a pious man like Job it was an argument likely to be admitted, that man was so filthy as to "drink iniquity like water."

In Jer. xvii. 9, we read, that "the heart is deceitful above all things and desperately wicked ; who can know it?" It is truly argued that "desperately wicked" is an epithet stronger than the

---

[1] "The Assembly of Divines," in the year 1643, revised the first fifteen Articles with the view of making them speak more clearly the language of Calvinism. The Ninth, according to their revision, was to have stood thus : —

"Original sin standeth not in the following of Adam, as the Pelagians do vainly talk, but, *together with his first sin imputed*, it is the fault and corruption of the nature of every man that naturally is propagated from Adam ; whereby man is *wholly deprived* of original righteousness," &c. And ending with "the Apostle doth confess that concupiscence and lust *is truly and properly* sin." — Neale's *Hist. of Puritans*, v. Appendix, No. vii. London, Baynes, 1822. See also Laurence, *B. L.* p. 196.

[2] "*Though*," the translation of the margin of the English version, probably expresses the כִּי of this passage better than

"*for.*" The conjunction assigns the reason why God had cursed the earth, **not** why He would not curse it again.

original warrants. The Hebrew word אָנֻשׁ signifies rather *danger-ously sick*, and therefore *feeble*, and in a moral sense, *corrupted and depraved.* Yet still the passage shows that the heart of man, taken in the general, is so corrupted and depraved as to be eminently deceitful and hard to know.

To these passages from the old Testament are added the words of St. Paul, " I know that in me, that is in my flesh, dwelleth no good thing," Rom. vii. 18 ; and then again, " The carnal mind is enmity against God ; for it is not subject to the law of God, neither indeed can be," Rom. viii. 7.

Such language undoubtedly proves the very great corruption of the human heart, so that we cannot hesitate to say with our Church, that by nature " man is very far gone from original right-eousness." He is described as " dead in trespasses and sins," and therefore we ought undoubtedly to maintain that his corruption is such as to prevent him from making any efforts to recover himself and turn by his own strength to calling upon God. This is the practical part of the doctrine, and our Church goes no farther.

Those who would push the matter to its greatest length, con-tend that the passages above quoted show that the image of God, in which man was created, was utterly taken from him at the fall ; that he thenceforth had no trace of resemblance to what he once was ; and, though they may not use language so strong, the nat-ural conclusion from that which they do use is, that in a moral point of view there is no distinction between fallen humanity and evil spirits.

Those who differ with them argue that God's image was in-deed defaced by sin, and so the effect and blessing of it lost. But that that image was quite gone they consider disproved by the declaration that " whoso sheddeth man's blood, by man shall his blood be shed ; for in the image of God made He man " (Gen. ix. 6), — by St. Paul's statement, that the man " is the image and glory of God " (1 Cor. xi. 7), — by St. James's reasoning, that it is inconsistent with the same mouth to bless God, and to " curse men, which are made after the similitude of God " (James iii. 9). All these passages, they say, refer to men since the fall, and therefore prove that, whatever effect the fall may have had, it cannot have wholly obliterated the image of the Almighty.

They say farther, that when St. Paul says that " in him, that is in his flesh, dwelleth no good thing," he yet adds, " that to will is present with him, but how to perform that which is good he finds not " (Rom. vii. 18) ; and that he all along represents man as ap-proving of what is right, but unable to accomplish it, — as honoring the law, but not fulfilling it, — as even "delighting in the law of God after the inward man," but finding another law ruling in his members, "which brings him into captivity to the law of sin" (Rom. vii. 22, 23). Hence, though man is captivated and subdued by sin, there must be some relic of his former state to make him see and admire what is good, though unable to follow it ; and so the Apostle speaks of all men as subject to the dictates of natural conscience (Rom. ii. 14, 15), and does not hesitate to reason with unregenerate heathens, of "righteousness, temperance, and judgment to come" (Acts xxiv. 25).

These and like expressions in Scripture, it is thought, are inconsistent with the stronger language which some have used concerning human depravity ; although there is fully enough to show the universal and fearful corruption of our nature, and our utter inability of ourselves to become righteous, or to move upwards towards God and goodness.

IV.   We come next to consider the statement which is made in the Article, that original sin "in every person born into the world deserveth God's wrath and damnation." Dr. Hey thinks that the word "damnation" is not necessarily to be understood of condemnation to eternal death, but may be construed, according to the proper signification of the term, to mean merely condemnation of some kind or other. The language of the Article is undoubtedly guarded, and studiously avoids expressing anything which cannot be clearly proved from Scripture. It is possible, therefore, that this may have been its meaning. But in either sense of the word, we shall probably find fully sufficient support for the doctrine expressed.

The language of St. Paul already quoted, "in Adam all die" (1 Cor. xv. 22), "By one man sin entered into the world, and death by sin ; and so death passed upon all men ; for that all have sinned" (Rom. v. 12), shows that the woe denounced upon Adam, as the effect of his own sin, passed from him to his posterity, as the effect of that sinfulness which they inherited from him. Accordingly, the same Apostle calls all men "children of wrath" (Ephes. ii. 3) ; and that we may be sure that this is true, not only of adults who have sinned wilfully, but even of infants, who have only inherited a sinful nature, we find our Lord, when speaking of the importance of the souls of little children, and of the guardianship of angels over them, attributing the blessings of their condition to

His having delivered them from their original state, which was that of those that are *lost*. " For," said He, " the Son of Man came to seek and to save that which was lost " (Matt. xviii. 11). With this corresponds the before-cited passage of St. Paul : " Death reigned from Adam unto Moses, even over them that had not sinned after the similitude of Adam's transgression."

We find therefore all men, even children, represented as " lost," as " children of wrath," as subject to, and under the reign of " death." And this is said to have been brought in by the sin of one man, even Adam, and to have " passed upon all men ; for that all have sinned."

We cannot fail to infer, that, as Adam by sin became subject to wrath and death, so all men are subject to the same wrath and death, because, by having a nature in itself sinful, they are, even without the commission of actual sin, yet sinners before God, and esteemed as " having sinned."

The death which Adam brought in is clearly (in Rom. v. and 1 Cor. xv.) opposed to the life which Christ bestows. That life is spiritual ; and we therefore reason that the death, which is antithetic to it, is spiritual too. The conclusion is, that every person born into the world has a sinful nature and a sinful heart, which, though it have not broken out in acts of sin, yet constitutes him a sinner, so that he may be said to " have sinned ; " and that, on this account, he is liable to death, whether by death be meant death of the body, or death of the soul.

It appears to me that our Church takes this view of the subject, and so follows closely on the teaching of St. Paul. She has said nothing concerning that hypothesis which was current among the schoolmen, and in general has prevailed amongst the followers of St. Augustine, that Adam's sin was *imputed* to his posterity, and that, as Levi was esteemed to have paid tithes in Abraham, being " yet in the loins of his father " (Heb. vii. 9, 10), so all men are esteemed to have sinned in Adam, and thus have his act of disobedience imputed to them.[1] The hypothesis is ingenious as explaining the language of the Apostle, but seems scarcely to correspond with his assertion that " death passed upon all men for that all

---

[1] See Edwards, *On Original Sin*, Part iv. ch. iii. Bp. Burnet, in stating the objections to this doctrine, gives this among the rest : " It is no small prejudice against this opinion that it was so long before it first appeared in the Latin Church ; that it was never received in the Greek ; and that even the Western Church, though perhaps for some ignorant ages it received it, as it did everything else very implicitly, yet has been very much divided both about this, and many other opinions related to it, or arising out of it." — Burnet **on Art.** ix.

have sinned." [1] It may be said indeed that they are *esteemed* to
have sinned. But the statement is simply that they " *have sinned.*"
And it is much easier to understand that a being of sinful disposition should be considered as having done that to which his disposition inevitably leads him, and which he has only left undone for
lack of opportunity, than it is to suppose that he should be *esteemed*
to have committed an act which was really committed by another,
five thousand years before his birth. At all events, where our
Church leaves it, let it rest.

V. It remains only to show that the infection of original sin is
not (as the Council of Trent ruled it) wholly removed by baptism,
but that it remains even in the *renati ;* and, though there is no
condemnation to them that believe and are baptized, yet the lust
or concupiscence, which remains in all men, has the nature of sin.

1. Let us first remark, that " There is no condemnation to them
that believe and are baptized." This is plain from our Lord's
words in His commission to His Apostles : " He that believeth and
is baptized shall be saved " (Mark xvi. 16). It is not less plain
from the language of St. Peter, who, when asked by his hearers
what they should do for salvation, replied, " Repent, and be baptized " [2] (Acts ii. 38).

The questions which may arise concerning the baptism of young
children, may properly be reserved for the Article which treats
expressly of baptism. Here it is sufficient to observe that our
Church, though not admitting that all *taint* of original sin is done
away in baptism, yet holds that its *condemnation* is remitted. " It
is certain," she says, " by God's word, that children which are
baptized, dying before they commit actual sin, are undoubtedly
saved." [3]

2. But, though we thus believe that the condemnation which

---

[1] The marginal translation of ἐφ' ᾧ "in
whom," would much favour this hypothesis. But it needs proof that ἐφ' ᾧ will
bear such a rendering. Although Augustine, taking the Latin mistranslation
in quo, built on it something of the imputation theory, he explains it very
moderately, namely, that infants sinned
in Adam, because the whole human race
was then contained in Adam, and would
inherit his sinful nature. Quoting Rom.
v. 12, he continues : —

Unde nec illud liquidè dici potest, quod
peccatum Adæ etiam non peccantibus
nocuit, cum Scriptura dicat, *in quo omnes
peccaverunt.* Nec sic dicuntur ista aliena

peccata, tamquam omnino ad parvulos
non pertineant : si quidem in Adam tunc
peccaverunt, quando, in ejus naturâ illâ
insitâ vi quâ eos gignere poterat, adhuc
omnes illi unus fuerunt ; sed dicuntur
aliena, quia nondum ipsi agebant vitas
proprias, sed quicquid erat in futura pro-
pagine, vita unius hominis continebat. —
De Peccatorum Meritis et Remissione. Lib.
III. c. 7, Tom. x. p. 78.

[2] The same appears in express terms
from Rom. viii. 1 : " There is no condemnation to them that are in Christ Jesus."
Compare Gal. iii. 27.

[3] Rubric at the end of the Baptismal
Service.

original sin deserves, is, for Christ's sake, remitted to all that believe and are baptized, and, in the case of infants dying before the commission of actual sin, is remitted on baptism alone ; still we hold that the infection of that sin remains even in the *renati.* The word *renati* occurs twice in the Latin Article, and in the English Article it is translated first " regenerated," and secondly " baptized." It will be seen hereafter on what principles the Church identifies " baptized " and " regenerated ; " it is sufficient for our purpose now to observe that both ideas are embraced in the word used here.

Now that the baptized and regenerate Christian is not free from the infection of original corruption, but has to fight against it, as an enemy still striving to keep him down, and, if possible, to destroy him, appears from the following considerations.

St. James urges Christians not to be in a hurry to be teachers, and gives as a reason that in many things all Christians offend: " In many things we offend all " (James iii. 2). St. Paul, speaking of his own exertions in the service of the Church, says that it will not do for him, when working for others, to neglect himself, but on the contrary, says he, " I keep under my body, and bring it into subjection, lest that by any means, when I have preached to others, I myself should be a castaway " (1 Cor. ix. 27). He bids the Galatians, " If a man be overtaken in a fault, ye which are spiritual restore such an one in the spirit of meekness ; considering thyself, lest thou also be tempted " (Gal. vi. 1). To those who " are risen with Christ," and whom he bids to " seek those things which are above," he yet adds the warning to mortify their earthly members (that is, the members or characteristics of their old man), which he describes as " fornication, uncleanness, inordinate affection, evil concupiscence, and covetousness ; " and further bids them put off " anger, wrath, malice, blasphemy, filthy communication, lying," as being suitable only to the old man which they had put off, and unfitted for the new man which they had put on (Col. i. 1, 5, 8, 9). St. Peter, addressing the Church as " new-born babes " in Christ (1 Pet. ii. 2), yet exhorts them (ver. 11), " as pilgrims and strangers to abstain from fleshly lusts, which war against the soul."

Now all these passages, which clearly concern baptized and regenerate Christians, prove this : that there is still left in them a liability to sin ; that without much care and anxiety all will fall into sin ; and that even under all circumstances, all do " offend in many things." Accordingly, St. John says of those whose " fellowship is with the Father and with His Son Jesus Christ," that " if they say that they have no sin, they deceive themselves, and the truth is not in them" (1 John i. 8). Can anything account for this universally applicable language, except the fact, as stated by our Church, that the infection of original sin remains even in the regenerate or baptized ?

3. Lastly, the Article asserts that " concupiscence and lust hath the nature of sin."

The Council of Trent admitted the existence of lust and concupiscence in the regenerate, and admitted that such concupiscence arose from original sin, and tended to actual sin, but denied that it was sin in itself. The English Church is here at issue with the fathers of the Council.

Her opinion on this point is defended by such passages as these : " Let not sin reign in your mortal bodies, that ye should obey it in the lusts thereof" (Rom. vi. 12), where the lusts of sin seem clearly to be spoken of as sinful. Again, Rom. vii. 7: " I had not known sin but by the Law ; for I had not known lust, except the Law had said, Thou shalt not covet." Here lust and sin seem to be identified. Again, in Matt. v. (especially vv. 28, 29) our Lord speaks of the desire of sin as being itself sin. And in the passage quoted in the Article (Gal. v. 17), St. Paul says that " the flesh lusteth against the Spirit." Now we can hardly understand how the lusts of the natural man should be opposed to the Spirit of God, and yet be sinless. We conclude, therefore, that "lust and concupiscence hath of itself the nature of sin." [1]

---

[1] The connection between *lust* and *sin* is very apparent in the Hebrew language, which derives many of its usages from its theology. Thus הַוָּה signifies both *desire* and *wickedness.* In Arabic هَوًى is *Vasta cupiditas, Amor intensissimus*, from هَوًى to *desire*. So in Hebrew, הַוָּה is (1) *desire*, as in Prov. x. 3, יֶהְדֹּף הַוַּת רְשָׁעִים " He withholdeth the *desire of* the wicked." (2) *wickedness*, as Ps. v. 10, הַוּוֹת קִרְבָּם, " Their inward part is *very wickedness.*" Where the plural form gives intensity.

ARTICLE X.

——◆——

Of Free Will.

THE condition of man, after the fall of Adam, is such, that he cannot turn and prepare himself by his own natural strength and good works to faith, and calling upon God; wherefore we have no power to do good works, pleasant and acceptable to God, without the grace of God by Christ preventing us, that we may have a good will, and working with us,[1] when we have that good will.[2]

De Libero Arbitrio.

EA est hominis post lapsum Adæ conditio, ut sese naturalibus suis viribus et bonis operibus, ad fidem et invocationem Dei convertere ac præparare non possit. Quare absque gratia Dei (quæ per Christum est) nos præveniente, ut velimus, et cooperante dum volumus, ad pietatis opera facienda, quæ Deo grata sunt et accepta, nihil valemus.

Section I.—HISTORY.

THE Article on Free Will naturally follows that concerning Original Sin; and much which was said on the latter subject may be applicable to the explication of the former.

The sentiments of the Apostolical Fathers on Free Will are probably nowhere very distinctly expressed. Their writings are rather practical than controversial; and hence these topics are not very likely to be discussed in them. That they fully and plainly teach the weakness of man, and the necessity of Divine grace, cannot be questioned.

The opinions of Justin Martyr are more clearly and definitely put forth in his extant works than are those of the Apostolical Fathers. In answer to objections which the Jews urged against

---

[1] This is the reading of the copy of the Articles as set forth in 1571. In 1562 the words run "working in us," and such was the reading in 1552.

[2] The Article, as it stood in 1552, began with the words, "We have no power." The former part was prefixed in 1562 by Abp. Parker, having been taken from the Wirtemburg Confession, the words of which are:—

Quod autem nonnulli affirmant homini post lapsum tantam animi integritatem relictam, ut possit sese, naturalibus suis viribus et bonis operibus, ad fidem et invocationem Dei convertere ac præparare, haud obscure pugnat cum Apostolica doctrina et cum vero Ecclesiæ Catholicæ consensu.

The latter part, which constituted the whole of the original Article, has adopted the language of St. Augustine:—

Sine illo vel operante ut velimus, vel cooperante cum volumus, ad bonæ pietatis opera nihil valemus.—De Gratia et Libero Arbitrio, cap. 17. See Abp Laurence, B. L. pp. 101, 235.

the scheme of Christian doctrine, namely, that according to it there
was an inevitable necessity that Christ should suffer, and therefore
a necessity and constraint laid upon the Jews to crucify Him,
Justin denies that God's foreknowledge of wicked actions made
Him the author of those actions. He puts no restraint upon men's
wills, but foretells certain evil actions, not because He causes, but
simply because He foresees them.[1] In like manner, in the first
Apology, which was addressed to heathens, he explains that our
belief in the predictions of the Prophets does not oblige us to
believe that things take place according to fate ; for, if men acted
under a fatal necessity, one could not be praised nor another
blamed.[2] " And in the second Apology he maintains, in opposition
to the Stoics, who believed in an inevitable fate (καθ' εἱμαρμένην
ἀνάγκην πάντα γίνεσθαι), that it is the nature of all men to have
a capacity for virtue and vice ; for unless there were a power of
turning to either, there could be nothing praiseworthy.[3] Yet,
with such a belief in the freedom of human choice, Justin fully
maintained the necessity of Divine grace, and the impossibility of
attaining salvation without the light and aid of God's Spirit.[4]

In the earliest ages the Gnostic and other heretics held, to a
great extent, the doctrines of material fatalism. We have already
seen that some of the Gnostics considered actions as influenced by
the stars. We have seen also, that Florinus taught that God was
the Author of evil, and that Irenæus, who had formerly been his
friend, wrote against him.[5] Against such statements Irenæus constantly maintained human freedom, and denied that the will was a
mere machine acted on by good or evil principles, and itself passive
under them. But the necessity of the grace of God's Holy Spirit
he as strongly expressed, when occasion required.[6]

The Marcionites maintained that the universe was governed by
two independent principles, one of good, and the other of evil.
This naturally led to the belief in a physical restraint on the will
of the creature. Accordingly, Tertullian, in disputing against

---

[1] Dial. cum Tryphone, Opera, p. 290.
[2] Apol. i. Opera, p. 80.
[3] Apol. ii. Opera, p. 45.
[4] E. g. 'Επὶ Θεὸν τὸν πάντα ποιήσαντα
ἐλπίζειν δεῖ πάντας, καὶ παρ' ἐκείνου μόνου
σωτηρίαν καὶ βοηθείαν ζητεῖν· ἀλλὰ μὴ, ὡς
λοιποὺς τῶν ἀνθρώπων, διὰ γένος ἢ πλοῦτον
ἢ ἰσχὺν ἢ σοφίαν νομίζειν δύνασθαι σώζεσθαι.
— Dial. c. Tryph. Opp. p. 329.
Concerning Justin Martyr's opinions on
free will, consult Bp. Kaye's Justin Martyr, p. 75, ch. iii. ; Faber's Primitive
Doctrine of Election, Bk. i. ch. xi

[5] See History of the Ninth Article.
[6] E. g. Sicut arida terra, si non per-
cipiat humorem, non fructificat : sic et
nos, aridum lignum existentes primum,
nunquam fructificaremus vitam, sine suprema voluntaria pluvia. — Adv. Hær.
iii. 19.
Concerning the opinions of Irenæus
on free will, see Faber as above, and
Beaven's Account of Irenæus, ch. xi. p.
112.

them, strenuously contends that freedom of the will was given to Adam.[1] From the same father we learn that Valentinus taught that man was created of three different kinds, — spiritual, animal, and terrestrial ; the first sort as Seth, the second as Abel, the third as Cain ; and that, as the distinction was from birth, it was consequently immutable. The first kind were destined to certain salvation, the last to certain perdition, the lot of the second was uncertain, depending on their greater inclination on the one hand to the spiritual, on the other to the carnal.[2]

The fathers, who were contemporary with these heretics, were naturally led, in disputing against them, to use strong language on the freedom of the will; so that it is no wonder if, after the rise of Pelagius, his followers were ready to quote some of the ancients in defence of their errors.

Origen was one of those who opposed the Marcionite and Valentinian heresies ; and his peculiar system of theology specially led him to more than ordinarily strong assertions of the freedom of the will. He took up the Platonic notion of the preëxistence of souls. The state of all created beings he believed to be regulated by their former actions. All souls were created free. Every rational creature was made capable of good or of evil. Angels and devils were alike created capable of holiness or of wickedness. The devil and his ministers fell by abuse of freedom ; the holy angels stood by a right use of it.[3] Every reasoning being is capable of degenerating or of improvement, according as he follows or resists reason. Men have been placed in different positions in this world ; but it is because of their conduct in a former existence. Jacob was beloved of God more than Esau, because in the former life he had lived more holily.[4] And, as good or evil are *substantially* in none but the Holy Trinity, but all holiness is in creatures only as an *accident*, it follows that it is in us and in our own wills to be holy, or through sloth and negligence to decline from holiness to wickedness and perdition.[5] Holiness is attained or lost, much as music or mathematics. No man becomes a mathematician or a musician but by labour and study, and if he becomes idle and negligent, he will forget what he has learnt, and cease to be skilful in his science

---

[1] Tertull. *Adv. Marcion,* Lib. II. 8, 9, &c.

[2] Tertullian, *De Anima,* c. 21–30. See Bishop Kaye's *Tertullian,* pp. 330, 522.

[3] *De Princip.* Lib. I. cap. 5.

[4] Lib. II. cap. 9, num. 7.

[5] Et per hoc consequens est in nobis esse, atque in nostris motibus, ut vel beati vel sancti simus, vel per desidiam et negligentiam a beatitudine in malitiam et perditionem vergamus, in tantum ut nimius profectus (ut ita dixerim) malitiæ, si quis in tantum sui neglexerit, usque ad eum statum deveniat, ut ea quæ dicitur contraria virtus efficiatur. -- Lib. I. cap. 5, num. 5.

or his art; and so no man will be good who does not practise goodness, and, if he neglects self-discipline and is idle, he will soon lapse
into sin and corruption.[1] Such language assigns so much strength
to man, and keeps out of sight so much the necessity of Divine
grace, that it has been truly said not to have been " without reason
that St. Hierome accuses him of having furnished the Pelagians
with principles ; " though yet in some places he speaks very favourably of grace and of the assistance of God.[2]

In later times, as we have seen already, Manes and his followers
held that good or evil actions were produced by the good or the evil
principle. They appear to have believed that men are acted on by
these powers as an inanimate stock, which must passively submit to
the impulses which move it.[3]

St. Augustine was himself originally a Manichee. In his earlier
treatises he constantly directs his arguments against the Manichean
doctrines, as being those errors with which he was best acquainted,
and which he dreaded most.[4]

After the rise of Pelagianism, and when his efforts were chiefly
directed to the overthrow of that heresy, he speaks less frequently
and clearly in favour of the original freedom of the will, and brings
more prominently out those predestinarian opinions which are so
well known in connection with his name. It would not, however,
be true to say that he materially changed his opinions on that subject ; for in some of his most decidedly Anti-Pelagian writings,
and whilst most strongly maintaining the sovereignty of Divine
grace, he unequivocally asserts the freedom of the human will, as
a gift of God to be used and accounted for.[5]

The tenets of the Pelagians on this subject are expressed in one
of the charges urged against Cœlestius in the Council of Carthage,
" That a man may be without sin, and keep the commandments of

---

[1] Lib. i. cap. 4.

[2] Dupin, *Ecclesiastical Hist.* Cent. iii.
Origen.

It seems as if Clement of Alexandria
pressed the doctrine of free will to a
very undue extent, though not so far nor
so systematically as his great pupil Origen. See Bp. Kaye's *Clement of Alexandria*, ch. x. p. 429.

[3] Beausobre, and apparently Lardner
who quotes him, doubt whether the Manichees did believe the will to be so thoroughly enslaved. See Lardner, *Hist. of
Manichees*, Sec. iv. 13. Vol. iii. p. 474.

[4] For instance, see the treatise *De
Libero Arbitrio, Opp.* Tom. i.

[5] For example, *De Spiritu et Litera,*
§ 52, Tom. x. p. 114.

Liberum ergo arbitrium evacuamus
per gratiam ? Absit, sed magis liberum
arbitrium statuimus. Sicut enim lex per
fidem, sic liberum arbitrium per gratiam
non evacuatur sed statuitur. Neque
enim lex impletur nisi libero arbitrio :
sed per legem cognitio peccati, per fidem
impetratio gratiæ contra peccatum, per
gratiam sanatio animæ a vitio peccati,
per animæ sanitatem libertas arbitrii, per
liberum arbitrium justitiæ dilectio, per
justitiæ dilectionem legis operatio. Ac
per hoc, sicut lex non evacuatur, sed
statuitur per fidem, quia fides impetrat
gratiam, qua lex impleatur : ita liberum
arbitrium non evacuatur per gratiam, sed
statuitur, quia gratia sanat voluntatem,
qua justitia libere diligatur.

God if he will; " [1] or in the passage which Augustine cites from his work, " Our victory proceeds not from the help of God, but from the freedom of will." [2] The Semi-Pelagians, though they did not deny the necessity of grace, yet taught that preventing grace was not necessary to produce the beginnings of true repentance, that every one could by natural strength turn towards God, but that no one could advance and persevere without the assistance of the Spirit of God.[3]

In the ninth century, Goteschalc, a Saxon divine, broached strong predestinarian doctrines, which, of course, more or less embraced the subject of the present Article; for, as he is said to have held that God eternally decreed some men to salvation and others to perdition, he must have held that the will was in a great degree subject to an inevitable necessity.[4] The history of this controversy, however, more properly belongs to the seventeenth Article. The disputes on the doctrines of Goteschalc divided the writers of his day. He was defended by Ratramn, monk of Corby, famous on more accounts than one, and condemned by Rabanus Maurus and Johannes Scotus Erigena.

In the twelfth century flourished Peter, surnamed Lombardus or Lombard, Archbishop of Paris, who wrote a book called *Libri Sententiarum*, in which he compiled extracts from the fathers on different points of faith and doctrine, from which he was afterwards known as the *Magister Sententiarum*, or *Master of the Sentences*. His work became the text-book for future disputants, the storehouse for scholastic polemics, esteemed wellnigh upon a par with Scripture itself.

The schoolmen, who followed him, and flourished chiefly in the thirteenth and fourteenth centuries, discussed to a great extent the questions concerning predestination and the freedom of the will. The most famous of these, as being heads of powerful and opposing parties, were Thomas Aquinas and John Duns Scotus. Thomas Aquinas was a Dominican Friar, of a philosophical spirit and great learning, and was known by the name of *Doctor Universalis*, or *Angelicus*. He was born in Italy, A. D. 1224, and died in 1274.

---

[1] Wall, *Infant Baptism*, I. p. 357; Collier, *Eccl. Hist.* Book I., and the account of Pelagianism given under Article IX.

[2] Victoriam nostram non ex Dei esse adjutorio, sed ex libero arbitrio. — August. *De Gestis Pelagii*, Tom. x. p. 215.

[3] Mosheim, *Eccl. Hist.* Cent. v. pt. II. ch. v. § 26.

Vitalis held that " God did work in us to will, by the Scriptures either read or heard by us ; but that to consent to them or not consent is so in our own power that if we will it may be done." — August. *Epist.* cvii. *ad Vitalem.*

[4] See Mosheim, Cent. ix. pt. II. ch. III.

34

His most famous work is his *Summa Theologiœ.* In philosophy he was a Realist; in Theology, a disciple of St. Augustine; and there-fore opposed to that belief too prevalent among the schoolmen, that the gift of grace was dependent on the manner in which men exercised their merely natural endowmer.ts (*pura naturalia*). Duns Scotus, born at Dunston in Northumberland, about the period of the death of Aquinas, was a Franciscan. He attacked the system of Thomas Aquinas, and acquired the name of *Doctor Subtilis.* He so strongly maintained the doctrine of the freedom of the will as to approximate suspiciously to the error of Pelagius. Duns Scotus was the founder of the School called the *Scotists*, to which the Franciscan friars belonged. The followers of Thomas Aquinas were called *Thomists*, and to these belonged the Domini-cans, who with the Franciscans divided between them the learning of the Christian world in the ages preceding the Reformation.

In reasoning on the subject of the human will, and the need of grace to produce holiness, the school-authors invented a mode of speaking, alluded to in our thirteenth article, by which they endeavoured to reconcile some of the apparent difficulties of the question. They observed that Cornelius, before his baptism and a knowledge of the Gospel, had put up prayers and given alms, which are spoken of in Scripture as acceptable to God.[1] They thought, therefore, that some degree of goodness was attributable to unassisted efforts on the part of man towards the attainment of holiness; and, though they did not hold that such efforts did, of their own merit, deserve grace, yet they taught that in some de-gree they were such as to call down the grace of God upon them, it being not indeed obligatory on the justice of God to reward such efforts by giving His grace, but it being agreeable to His nature and goodness to bestow grace on those who make such efforts. Endeavors, then, on the part of man to attain to godliness were by the schoolmen said to deserve grace *de congruo, of congruity.* But, when once grace was given, then it enabled the recipient to deserve at the hands of God, not only farther grace, but even in the end everlasting life. All this of course was to be considered as depending on the Atonement of Christ; but whatever was pre-supposed, it remarkably tended to the exalting the power of the will, and the strength of unassisted man.[2]

---

[1] Acts x. 4: "Thy prayers and thine alms are come up for a memorial before God."

[2] Laurence, *B. L.* Serm. iv. and the notes to that Sermon *passim.* Neander, vol. viii. pp. 230, 231. Neander points out the marked distinction between the doctrine of grace *de congruo*, as held by Aquinas, and the same doctrine, as held by Alexander of Hales and the Francis-cans.

We now come to the period of the Reformation. The doctrine of grace *de congruo* gave the greatest possible offence to Luther, and called forth much of his strongest language. For example, in his treatise on the *Bondage of the Will* he asserted, that " in his actings towards God, in things pertaining to salvation or damnation, man has no free will, but is the captive, the subject, and the servant, either of the will of God, or of the will of Satan." [1] Again, " If we believe that God foreknows and predestinates everything . . . . it follows that there can be no such thing as free will in man or angel, or any creature." [2] These expressions are characteristic of the vehemence of Luther's temper, when opposing what he considered a dangerous error, and are much stronger than the opinions subsequently expressed by him, and very different from the language of Melancthon and the confessions of the Lutheran Churches.

In the Council of Trent the Lutheran opinions on this doctrine were set forth to be discussed. Much was said on both sides of the question. The Franciscans, as being followers of Scotus, spoke much for the absolute freedom of the will, and in favour of the doctrine of grace *de congruo*. The Dominicans, after St. Thomas Aquinas, repudiated the idea of congruous merit, and maintained the inability of man to turn to good of his own will, since the fall of Adam. The decrees were drawn up, so as to displease either party as little as possible, but with a leaning to the Franciscan doctrines. Those were condemned who said " that since the sin of Adam free will is lost," and that " bad as well as good works are done by the working of God." Yet, at the same time, those were anathematized who said that " a man could be justified without grace," " that grace is given to live well with greater facility, and to merit eternal life, as if free will could do it though with more difficulty ; " and who said that " a man may believe, love, hope, or repent, without the prevention or assistance of the Holy Spirit." [3]

In the earlier days of the Reformation, the Lutherans generally held extreme language on the slavery of the will, and Melancthon himself used expressions which he afterwards withdrew. The more

---

[1] Cæterum erga Deum, vel in rebus quæ pertinent ad salutem vel damnationem, non habet liberum arbitrium, sed captivus, subjectus et servus est vel voluntatis Dei, vel voluntatis Satanæ. — *De Servo Arbitrio, Opp.* Tom. i. p. 432.

[2] Si enim credimus verum esse, quod Deus præscit et præordinat omnia, tum neque falli neque impediri potest sua præscientia et prædestinatione, deinde nihil fieri nisi ipso volente, id quod ipsa ratio cogitur concedere, simul ipsa ratione teste, nullum potest esse liberum arbitrium in homine vel angelo, aut ulla creatura. — *Id.* p. 481.

[3] Sarpi, pp. 134, 210 ; Heylyn, *Historia Quinquarticularis*, pt. i. ch. IV.

matured convictions of this great writer were sober and wise ; and
the confession of Augsburg, whilst affirming that the will of man
" hath not the power to effect the righteousness of God without the
Spirit of God," [1] yet declares that " the cause of sin is the will of
wicked beings, namely, the devil and ungodly men, which, when not
aided by God, turns itself from God, as it is written, When he
speaketh a lie, he speaketh of himself." [2]

The Calvinistic reformers do not hesitate to use the most extreme expressions on the inability of man to do anything but evil.
" The mind of man," says Calvin, " is so wholly alienated from
God, that it can conceive, desire, and effect nothing but what is
impious, perverted, foul, impure, and flagitious ; the heart of sin is
so steeped in venom, that it can breathe forth nothing but fetid
corruption." [3]

The followers of Calvin have, for the most part, used language
similar to their leader. Whether Calvin allowed to Adam free will
in Paradise, or believed that even his fall was predestinated, has
been matter of dispute. Of the Calvinistic divines, those called
Supralapsarians held, as has been mentioned before, that God fore-
ordained that Adam should sin, and therefore denied to him free
will even in a state of innocence. The Sublapsarians held that he
fell of his own will, and not by constraint or through the ordination of God.

Among the bodies of Christians who embraced the Calvinistic
doctrines and discipline, some of the most considerable were the
Churches of Holland and Belgium. The Belgic Confession, put
forth in the year 1567, contains explicit declarations that all things
in the world must happen according to the absolute decree and
ordination of God, though God was not to be called the author of
sin, nor to be blamed for its existence.[4] Several divines of the
Belgic Church had demurred at these doctrines ; and at the end of
the sixteenth and the beginning of the seventeenth century, Jacob
Van Harmin, or Arminius, a pastor of Amsterdam, broached the

---

[1] Non habet vim sine Spiritu Sancto
efficiendæ justitiæ Dei, seu justitiæ spiritualis, quia animalis homo non percipit ea,
quæ sunt Spiritus Dei. — Art. xvii. ;
Sylloge, p. 129.

[2] Art. xix. De causa peccati docent,
quod tametsi Deus creat et conservat naturam, tamen causa peccati est voluntas
malorum, videlicet diaboli et impiorum,
quæ non adjuvante Deo avertit se a Deo,
sicut Christus ait Joh. viii., Cum loquitur mendacium, ex seipso loquitur. —
Syll. p. 130.

[3] Stet ergo nobis indubia ista veritas,
quæ nullis machinamentis quatefieri potest, mentem hominis sic alienatam prorsus a Dei justitia, ut nihil non impium,
contortum, fœdum, impurum, flagitiosum
concipiat, concupiscat, moliatur : cor peccati veneno ita penitus delibutum, ut
nihil quam corruptum fœtorem efflare
queat. — Calv. Institut. Lib. ii. cap. v
19.

[4] Confess. Belgica, Sylloge, p. 234

sentiments generally known by the name of Arminianism. He dying in 1609, and his followers being persecuted by the dominant party, they addressed, in 1610, a *Remonstrance* to the states of Holland, whence they were called *Remonstrants*. Their sentiments on the subject of free will may be gathered from the third and fourth of the five articles, to which, the Arminian doctrines were reduced.

The third article says that " man cannot attain to saving faith of his own free will, in regard that, living in an estate of sin and defection from God, he is not able of himself to think, will, or do anything which is really good." The fourth article runs thus, " The grace of God is the beginning, promotion, and accomplishment of everything that is good in us ; insomuch that the regenerate man can neither think, will, nor do anything that is good, nor resist any sinful temptations without this grace preventing, coöperating, and assisting ; and consequently, all good works which any man can attain to, are to be attributed to the grace of God in Christ. But, as for the manner of the coöperation of this grace, it is not irresistible ; for it is said of many in Scripture, that they did resist the Holy Ghost, as in Acts vii. and many other places." [1]

The disputes between the Remonstrants and their opponents led to the calling of a Synod at Dort, or Dordrecht, at which deputies were present from most of the Protestant Churches of Europe. At this the Arminians were excommunicated, and the doctrines of the Swiss and Belgic reformed Churches declared to be decidedly Calvinistic, and intolerant of the opposite opinions.[2] Both *election* and *reprobation* are declared to be of God alone ; [3] but at the same time, it is affirmed that God is not to be considered as the author of sin ; [4] nor is it to be said that He works on men as logs or stocks, but rather by giving life and energy to their wills.[5] The decrees of the Synod are indeed generally esteemed decidedly supralapsarian, and were unsatisfactory to the English divines who were present during some of their discussions ; [6] but their language seems less exaggerated than some who were opposed to them have been inclined to represent it.[7]

The Church of Rome, after the Council of Trent, was not

---

[1] Heylyn's *Hist. Quinq.* pt. I. ch. V. ; Mosheim, *Eccl. Hist.* Cent. XVII. Sect. II. pt. II.

[2] Heylyn and Mosheim as above.

[3] *Sylloge*, p. 406, Art. VI.

[4] Ibid. p. 409, Art. XV.

[5] Ibid. p. 431, Art. XVI.

[6] See Bp. Hall's *Observations on some Specialities in his Life.*

[7] See, for example, Heylyn, *H. Q.* pt. I. ch. VI.

exempt from the same controversies which divided the Protestants on grace and free will. Molina, a Jesuit, professor at Ebora, in Portugal, in 1588, published a book entitled *Liberi arbitrii concordia cum Gratiæ donis, Divina Præscientia, Prædestinatione, et Reprobatione.* His theory was somewhat similar to that of the Arminians, who taught that grace was given, according as God foresees that man would embrace and make good use of it. The Dominicans were much offended at this work, and accused the Jesuits of reviving Pelagianism. This led to a long and violent contention between the two orders, which caused Clement VIII. to appoint a sort of Council called the Congregation de Auxiliis.[1] The death of Clement VIII., before a settlement of these disputes, did not prevent their continuance under his successor, Paul V. And though Paul did not publicly declare for either side of the question, it is probable that he urged both parties to moderation, being deterred from pronouncing against the Jesuits by the patronage extended to them by the court of France, and from deciding against the Dominicans by the protection of the court of Spain.[2] The controversy, hushed for a time, broke out again in the year 1640, in consequence of the writings of Jansenius, Bishop of Ypres, who revived the doctrines of Augustine, in his book entitled *Augustinus.* His followers were called Jansenists, and were strongly opposed by the Jesuits; the former maintaining the sentiments held by Augustine, Thomas Aquinas, and the Dominicans, the latter holding those of Duns Scotus and the Franciscans. The book of Jansenius was first condemned as a breach of the concord which had been enjoined in the Church, but was afterwards more distinctly prohibited by a solemn bull of Pope Urban VIII., A. D. 1642. The Jansenists however continued to prosper, numbering many able and pious men in their ranks, and appealing to miracles in support of their opinions. But ultimately they were condemned and persecuted by the Bishops of Rome, and the dominant faction of the Church.[3]

Before concluding this sketch of the different controversies in other countries, we must mention the Socinian opinions on free will; which, of course, correspond with their views of original sin : as they appear to consider that man's will is so far free and strong as to need only external, and not internal help towards his sanctification.[4]

After the Reformation, or during the establishment of it *in*

---

[1] Mosheim, Cent. XVI. Sect. III. pt. I.
[2] Ibid. Cent. XVII. Sect. II. pt. I. § 35.
[3] Ibid. Cent. XVII. Sect. II. pt. I. § 40
[4] Ibid. Cent. XVI. Sect. III. pt. II. 17.

England, the first thing which particularly claims our attention is the Article of Free Will in the *Necessary Doctrine*, set forth by King Henry VIII. and signed by Convocation, A. D. 1543. In this it is said that " man has free will now after the fall of Adam ; " and free will is defined, as " a power of reason and will by which good is chosen by the assistance of grace, or evil is chosen without the assistance of the same." [1]

The reformers in the reign of Edward VI. appear to have followed closely upon the steps of the Lutherans (Melancthon and the Confession of Augsburg), in the Articles which concern grace and free will.[2] The Article on free will, in the forty-two Articles of 1552, was immediately succeeded by an Article on grace, which was worded as follows : —

" OF GRACE.

" The grace of Christ, or the Holy Ghost by Him given, doth take away the stony heart and giveth an heart of flesh. And although those who have no will to good things, He maketh them will, and those that would evil things, He maketh them not to will ; yet nevertheless he enforceth not the will. And therefore no man, when he sinneth, can excuse himself as not worthy to be blamed or condemned, by alleging that he sinned unwillingly or by compulsion."

During the Marian persecution, the English Divines who fled to Frankfort and other places on the Continent, by being thrown into contact with foreign reformers, were drawn into the controversies which agitated them. Many came back with strong prejudices in favour of the Calvinists, while others were strongly disposed to maintain Lutheran views. There were therefore three distinct parties in the Church in the early part of the reign of Elizabeth. Some were for the restoration of popery; others inclined to Lutheran views of grace and of the Sacraments; and a third party had imbibed Calvinistic sentiments of predestination and church discipline, and Zuinglian sentiments on sacramental grace. The last were the forerunners of the Puritans, who soon became non-conformists, and finally dissenters. They acquired the name of Gospellers, and called their opponents Freewillers. Archbishop Parker and the leading men of the day wisely strove to heal the divisions, and softened down the language of our formularies so as to include as many as possible within the pale of the

---

[1] *Formularies of Faith in the Reign of Henry VIII.* p. 359, where see the Article of Free Will at length.

[2] See Laurence, *B. L. passim*, especially Sermon v.

National Church; and among other measures of conciliation the *Article on Grace* was omitted, to satisfy the Calvinistic section of the Church.[1]

The controversies, however, between the high Church and the Puritan divines, both on points of doctrine and of discipline, continued to divide the Church. Whitgift, Archbishop of Canterbury, in doctrine agreed with Calvin, but in discipline was a high Episcopalian. During his primacy were drawn up the famous Lambeth Articles, which he would gladly have imposed on the Church, but which never received the authority of the queen, the parliament, or the convocation. The first of these Articles says, that " God hath from eternity predestinated some men to life, others He has reprobated to death; " and the ninth asserts, that " it is not in the will or power of every one to be saved." [2]

In the conference held at Hampton Court in the reign of King James I. A. D. 1603, an effort was made on the part of the Puritan divines to obtain an alteration in some of the XXXIX Articles, and to have them made more conformable to Calvinistic language ; but no alteration was effected, owing to the opposition of the King and of the Bishops to the arguments of the Puritans.[3]

The Articles remain therefore as they were put forth in 1562, and afterwards in 1571. And those on the subject of grace, free will, and other similar subjects, are the same as those drawn up in 1552, by Cranmer and his fellows, with the exception of the omission of the Article on Grace which was then the tenth Article, and the prefixing of the first part of the present tenth (originally the ninth Article) down to the word " wherefore."

There have been, ever since the reign of Elizabeth, two parties in the English Church, one holding the doctrines of Calvin, and the other opposing those doctrines, and each party has considered the Articles to speak their own language. It is however an undoubted truth that the Articles were drawn up before Calvin's works had become extensively known, or had become in any degree popular in this country. It is probable that they speak the language neither of Calvin, nor of Arminius ; and between the extreme opinions, which had prevailed among the Schoolmen and others, they held a middle course, carefully avoiding the dogma of congruous merit, maintaining jealously the absolute necessity of preventing grace to enable us to will or to do according to the

---

[1] Heylyn's *H. Q.* pt. iii. ch. xvii. On the state of parties, &c. in Elizabeth's reign, see Soames's *Elizabethan Religious History.*

[2] Heylyn's *H. Q.* pt. iii. ch. xx.

[3] Heylyn, pt. iii. ch. xxii., Cardwell's *History of Conferences*, p. 178, &c.

commandments of God, but not minutely entering into the questions concerning the freedom of man before the fall, or the degree of free agency left to him since the fall.

Section II. — SCRIPTURAL PROOF.

THE ninth Article having asserted that man by the fall is " very far gone from original righteousness," there arises at once a probability that he is weak and helpless towards good. In reasoning therefore on that Article, it was natural in some degree to anticipate some of the conclusions of this.

Yet still, unless it be clearly conceded that by the fall man became *totally* corrupt, with no shadow of the image of God in which he was created, and with a mind nearly approaching, if not actually similar, to the mind of devils; it would be possible that such a degree of strength might remain to him that he might make some independent efforts towards holiness, and in some degree prepare himself for the reception of grace. As therefore the ninth Article does not define the exact amount of man's defection from original righteousness, it was quite necessary to state the doctrine of his utter helplessness in this.

The subject, as it is stated in the Article, seems to divide itself into the two following heads.

I. Since the fall, man has no power by his own natural strength to turn himself to faith and godliness, or to do good works acceptable to God. But the grace of God is absolutely necessary to enable him to do this.

II. The grace of God acts in two ways.

1. First, it is preventing grace, giving a good will.

2. Afterwards, it is coöperating grace, working in and with us, when we have that good will.

I. First, then, since the fall, man has no power by his own natural strength to turn himself to faith and holiness, or to do good works acceptable to God. But the grace of God is absolutely necessary to enable him to do this.

Here the point to be proved is simply this. Whatever degree

35

of defection is implied in the fall, whatever natural amiability any individuals of the human race may possess, no one, by mere natural strength, and without internal help from God, can believe or do what is, in a religious point of view, pleasing or acceptable to God.

1. In the sixth chapter of St. John our Lord says, "No man can come unto Me, except the Father which hath sent Me draw him" (ver. 44); and again, "Therefore said I unto you, no man can come unto Me, except it were given him of My Father" (ver. 65).

Now here the proposition is quite general. All mankind are included in the sentence, "No man can come" to Christ, except it be given him of God, except God the Father draw him. This is a plain statement of natural weakness, and of the need of preventing grace. It shows that by nature man is apart from Christ, and that only the gift of God and the drawing of God can bring him to Christ.

To this argument the Pelagians answer, that no doubt it is necessary that God should draw us, if we are to come to Him; but the way in which He draws us is not by internal assistance and the motions of His Spirit in our hearts, but externally, by the calls of His word, the warnings of His Providence, the ordinances of His Church. Thus, therefore, say they, He may be said to draw us, and thus it is given us of Him to come to Christ. But we may reply to this objection, that such an interpretation is inconsistent with the whole drift of our Lord's discourse. The Capharnaite Jews, who heard Him, were staggered at His sayings, and disbelieved them. Externally the word of God was drawing them then, but they murmured against it, and refused to listen to it. Accordingly our Lord tells them that it was from an absence of *inward* sanctification that they rejected the *outward* calls of His word. If they came to Him, it must be by the drawing of the Father, through the grace of His Spirit; for, says He, "No man can come unto Me, except the Father, which hath sent Me, draw him; and I will raise him up at the last day. As it is written in the Prophets, And they shall be all taught of God. Every man therefore that hath heard, and that hath learned of the Father, cometh unto me" (vv. 44, 45). If by these words is meant only the outward drawing by external means, it is plain that all who heard Him had such drawing in its most efficient form; yet most of them rejected Him. It is evident that they lacked something more than this. That being taught of God, that learning of the Father,

which would bring them to Christ, must therefore have been something within them, not the calls of His word without ;· and hence
we may conclude that our Lord's words show it to be an invari-
able rule, a truth coextensive with the nature of fallen man, that
no one can come to Christ, or, what is the same thing, turn and
prepare himself to faith and calling upon God, without the internal
operations of the Spirit of God.

2. To confirm this view of the subject, let us recur to what
we saw, in considering the ninth Article, was the doctrine of Scripture concerning our original corruption.

Our Lord states (John viii. 34) that "whosoever committeth sin
is the servant (δοῦλος *the slave*) of sin." Now all men by nature
commit sin, and therefore are slaves of sin. This is what St. Paul
calls "the bondage of corruption" (Rom. viii. 21). This natural
state of man is, both by our Lord and by the Apostle, contrasted
with the liberty of the soul under a state of grace. "If the Son
shall make you free, ye shall be free indeed" (John viii. 36), says
Christ ; and St. Paul calls it "the glorious liberty of the children
of God" (Rom. viii. 21). In like manner our Lord distinguishes
between the state of a servant and the state of a son (John viii. 35).
Nay, so complete is this servitude of sin by nature, that St. Paul,
more than once, calls it *death*. He speaks of people as by nature
"*dead* in trespasses and sins" (Ephes. ii. 1 ; Col. ii. 13). He says of
those who had been delivered from this state by grace, that "God
had *quickened* them together with Christ" (Ephes. ii. 5) ; that those
who were baptized into the death of Christ, having been *dead* in
trespasses and sins, God had "*quickened* together with Him" (Col.
ii. 12, 13). Now slavery and death are the strongest terms to express utter helplessness that language admits of. So, freeing from
slavery and quickening or raising to life, as plainly as possible, indicate a free gift, independent of the will or power of the recipient,
and show that the recipient must previously have been in a condition, as unable to free himself as the bondsman, as unable to
quicken himself as a dead man.

In accordance with all this, St. Paul (in Rom. vii. viii., a passage considered in the last Article) argues at length, that man,
being by nature "carnal, sold under sin," even if able to admire
what is good, was utterly unable to perform it (Rom. vii. 14–21),
there being a law, ruling in his members, which makes him captive
to the law of sin (v. 23). And then he tells us, that the way in
which this bondage must be broken is by the Spirit of God taking
possession of and ruling in that heart, in which before sin had

ruled, and so delivering it from the law of sin. " For the law of
the Spirit of life in Christ Jesus hath made me free from the law
of sin and death " (viii. 2).

Not only is such helplessness of the unregenerate man plainly
taught by our Lord and His Apostles, but we farther find, that
the very mind and understanding are represented as darkened by
the natural state of corruption, and so incapable of comprehending
and appreciating spiritual truth, until enlightened by the Spirit of
God. Thus " the natural man receiveth not the things of the Spirit
of God ; . . . . neither can he know them, because they are spiritually discerned " (1 Cor. ii. 14, comp. Rom. viii. 5 ,6, 7 ; Jude 19).
Man by nature has no discernment of those things which belong
to the Spirit of God ; and if so, it is quite clear, that, if he ever
attains to spiritual discernment, it must be given him preternat-
urally.

To this belong all the passages concerning the new birth ; for
if a new birth be necessary, there must, before it, be an absence
of that life which is the product of such a birth. Accordingly,
God is represented as begetting us of His own will (James i. 18).
To enter into the kingdom, a man must be born again, of water,
and of the *Spirit* (John iii. 3, 5). In Christ Jesus a new creation
availeth (Gal. vi. 15). It is not by works of righteousness which
we have done, but according to His own mercy that God saveth
us, by the washing of regeneration, and renewing of the Holy Ghost
(Tit. iii. 5).

In like manner, the Scriptures, when speaking of the good works
of Christians, represent them as due, not to any independent effort
of the human will, but altogether to the grace of God working in
them. Thus our Lord, in a parable, fully declares the whole
source and spring of Christian holiness to be the life and virtue
derived from Him. He likens Himself to a Vine, and all His
disciples to branches. We know, that branches of a tree derive
life and strength from the sap, which is sent into them from the
root and stem. In like manner our Lord tells us, that, by being
branches of Him, we may bring forth good fruit, but that, apart
from Him, we can do nothing. " Abide in Me, and I in you. As
the branch cannot bear fruit of itself, except it abide in the vine ;
no more can ye, except ye abide in Me. I am the Vine, ye are
the branches. He that abideth in me, and I in him, the same
bringeth forth much fruit ; for without Me (χωρὶς ἐμοῦ, apart from
Me) ye can do nothing (John xv. 4, 5).

So constantly is this dependence of the Christian upon Divine grace urged by the sacred writers, that they frequently call to our remembrance, not only that we owe our first turning from evil to the quickening of God's Spirit, but that even the regenerate and the faithful believer is at every step dependent upon the illumination, guidance, strength, and support of the same Divine Comforter and Guide. So St. Paul, writing of himself and other regenerate Christians, says, " Not that we are sufficient of ourselves to think anything as of ourselves : but our sufficiency is of God " (2 Cor. iii. 5). When urging his faithful converts to " work out their own salvation with fear and trembling," he adds as an encouragement to them, " For it is God that worketh in you both to will and to do of His good pleasure " (Phil. ii. 13). And when speaking with thankfulness of the labours which he himself had been enabled to undergo for the sake of the Gospel, he adds, " Yet not I, but the grace of God which was with me " (1 Cor. xv. 10).

Now all this language of Scripture seems plainly to prove that by nature man has no free will to do good, no power to make independent efforts towards holiness. There is an iron tyranny, a law of sin and death, which keeps him in bondage and deprives him of the power to escape, and even of the discernment of spiritual things, which would make him desire deliverance. From this law of sin and death the Spirit of life can set him free ; from this bondage the Son can make him free indeed ; but none besides. Nay! he is sleeping the sleep of spiritual death, and therefore needs internal as well as external aid to rouse him ; aye! a new creation, a new birth, a new life. And even when set free, quickened, regenerate, he continues still able to act and think uprightly only so long as he derives strength from Christ ; just as the branch can bear no fruit, except it derive sap and strength from the stem on which it grows.

II. It being thus proved that by nature man, corrupted by the fall, is not in possession of free will, or more properly, that his will, though unrestrained by God, is yet warped and led captive by evil spirits and his own bad propensities, it remains that we consider the effects of God's grace upon the will, when setting it free from this captivity. The Article describes these effects, as follows : —

1. God's grace prevents us, that we may have a good will.

2. It works in us, or with us, when we have that good will.

The passages of Scripture which have been already brought to bear in the former division of the subject, may appear to have sufficiently demonstrated these two propositions.

1. The necessity of preventing grace follows, of course, from the

doctrine that man, of himself, cannot turn to God. For, if he cannot turn of himself, he must either remain forever alienated, or must need some power to turn him. In the language of the prophet, " Turn Thou me, and I shall be turned " (Jer. xxxi. 18). Accordingly, we read continually of the first turning of the heart as coming from God. God is said to be "found of them that sought Him not, and made manifest to them that asked not after Him " (Isai. lxv. 1 ; Rom. x. 20). We read of His opening people's "hearts so that they attend to the things spoken " (Acts xvi. 14) ; and we are taught that He " worketh in us both to *will* and to do " (Phil. ii. 13) ; so that the regenerate and sanctified Christian is declared to be God's " *workmanship* created in Christ Jesus unto good works " (Eph. ii. 10). God is said to have " wrought " believers for immortality and glory (2 Cor. v. 5). The " new man " is said to be " *created* in righteousness and true holiness " (Eph. iv. 24).

Such passages, and all others which speak of new birth and new creation, show plainly that God's grace prevents us, waits not, that is, for us to make advances to Him, but graciously comes forward to help us, whilst yet we are without strength. They show too, that whereas by nature the will was corrupt and not tending to God, bound down and taken captive to the law of sin, so when the grace of God renews it, it is no longer in slavery, but free, choosing life and holiness, not by compulsion, but by free choice and love. " The Son makes us free indeed " (John viii. 36). " The law of the Spirit of life makes us free from the law of sin and death " (Rom. viii. 2). There is a " glorious liberty for the children of God " (Rom. viii. 21). It is, " to liberty " that we " have been called " (Gal. v. 13) ; for, " where the Spirit of the Lord is, there is liberty " (2 Cor. iii. 17).

We see then the contrast which exists between the will in its natural corrupt state, and the will in its regenerate and purified state. In the former it is enslaved ; in the latter it is free. Satan keeps it a bond-slave in the first ; God sets it free in the last. Then it could only choose evil ; now it is free to choose good. Then under the law of sin and death ; now under " the perfect law of liberty " (James i. 25).

2. But the will, thus set free, needs farther support, guidance, and strength. The new-born Christian has still a conflict to undergo, for which he requires the whole armour of God. This is expressed in the Article, by the words " working with us when we have that good will."

The Latin Article has the word *cooperante*, which in the first English translation was rendered " working *in* us ; " but in 1572 it was expressed somewhat more closely after the Latin., " working *with* us."

Such expressions of course imply that when the will is renewed there is need of farther grace to support it, but, at the same time, that the renewed man is to exert himself in the strength of that grace, and to work under its influence.

The doctrine of coöperation has been opposed by many as assigning too much strength to man. Man, say they, is altogether too weak either to begin the work of grace, or even, after that work is begun, to contribute anything towards its completion. It is patching the pure robe of Christ's righteousness to add any of the filthy rags of man's works to it. Accordingly, St. Paul attributes all his own labours, not to himself, but to " the grace of God which was with him " (1 Cor. xv. 10) ; and says, " I no longer live myself (ζῶ δὲ οὐκέτι ἐγώ), but Christ liveth in me " (Gal. ii. 20). And it is written that God " worketh *in* us," not *with* us, " both to will and to do " (Phil. ii. 13).

Whether coöperation be a good expression or not, and whether it be altogether reverent to speak as if the Holy Spirit of God and man's renewed will act in concert together, is of course fairly open to question. In general, no doubt the Scriptures speak of God's working *in* us, rather than *with* us. Yet the doctrine of our Article, rightly understood, rests on a sound foundation.

In the first instance indeed man's will is represented as being under bondage. Spiritually we are described as slaves, blind, dead. But as we have seen, the Son is said to " make us free ; " the " law of the Spirit of life frees us from the law of sin and death ; " and so we are brought into " the glorious liberty of the children of God." Thus it appears that Christ's service is indeed perfect freedom. The will, no longer enslaved and bowed down, is set at liberty and enabled to act ; and though, whenever and howsoever it acts in a good direction, it is always acting under the guidance and governance of the Spirit of God, yet it does not follow that that guidance is a yoke of bondage, or of irresistible necessity. Accordingly, when the Apostle has explained how the Spirit frees us from the law of sin, and brings us into the glorious liberty of God's children (Rom. viii. 2–21), he tells us a little farther on, that whereas we still continue weak and ignorant, " the Spirit *helpeth* our infirmities " (ver. 26). In the very same breath in which he tells us that " it is God that worketh in us both to will and to do," he bids us "work out our own salvation with fear and trembling" (Phil. ii. 12, 13). And so he speaks of himself as using all kinds of self-discipline (1 Cor. ix. 27), and as "pressing forward to the mark for the prize of the high calling" (Phil. iii. 14).

To this purpose are all the exhortations of Scripture addressed to those who are under grace, not to miss the blessings which God has prepared for them. For example, we have warnings not to "defile the temple of God," *i. e.* not to pollute with sin our bodies, in which God's Spirit dwells (1 Cor. iii. 17) ; not to grieve, not to quench the Spirit (Eph. iv. 30 ; 1 Thess. v. 19) ; not to neglect the gift which is in us, but to stir it up (1 Tim. iv. 14 ; 2 Tim. i. 6) ; not to "receive the grace of God in vain" (2 Cor. vi. 1), " to stand fast," and not "fall from grace" (Gal. v. 1–4) ; "to take heed lest there be an evil heart of unbelief in departing from the living God" (Heb. iii. 12); to "look diligently, lest any man fail of the grace of God" (Heb. xii. 15); when we think we are standing, "to take heed lest we fall." (1 Cor. x. 12).

Now all such passages do indeed plainly presuppose that all the good we can do comes from the Spirit of God working in us. Yet they seem as plainly to prove that that blessed Spirit does not move the will as a mere machine, so that it is impossible for it to resist or neglect His blessed influences. It seems plain from them, that under those influences, and guided by them, the renewed heart moves willingly ; and that, whenever those influences do not produce their full effect, it is because the remains of corruption in that heart resist and counteract them. And this is all that is meant in the Article by the term *cooperante*, " working with us."

If, indeed, according to the sentiment of Luther, quoted in the former section, man's will was first a mere bond-slave of sin, and after grace equally a slave, or machine, moved passively and irresistibly by the Spirit, we can hardly understand how it should be that men are not all equally abandoned before grace, and all equally moving onward to perfection under grace. Since by that theory the will is entirely passive under the motions of the Spirit, opposing no obstacle to them, and therefore, as we should suppose, likely in all persons to be fully and perfectly sanctified.

The doctrine of Scripture, however, is evidently expressed in the words of our Article. God must give the will, must set the will free from its natural slavery, before it can turn to good ; but then it moves in the freedom which He has bestowed upon it, and never so truly uses that freedom, as when it follows the motions of the Spirit. Yet clearly there remains some power to resist and to do evil. For, though "those that have no will to good things God maketh them to will; . . . Yet, nevertheless, He enforceth not the will."[1] And so, although He must work in us, yet we, under His influences, must strive and press forward, not resisting Him, not neglecting, but stirring up His gifts in our hearts.

[1] **Art. of 1552.**

ARTICLE XI.

———•———

Of the Justification of Man.

WE are accounted righteous before God, only for the merit of our Lord and Saviour Jesus Christ, by faith, and not for our own works or deservings: Wherefore, that we are justified by faith only is a most wholesome doctrine, and very full of comfort, as more largely is expressed in the Homily of Justification.

De Hominis Justificatione.

TANTUM propter meritum Domini et Servatoris nostri Jesu Christi, per fidem, non propter opera et merita nostra, justi coram Deo reputamur. Quare sola fide nos justificari, doctrina est saluberrima, ac consolationis plenissima, ut in homilia de justificatione hominis fusius explicatur.

SECTION I. — HISTORY.

IT is probable that natural religion inclines all men, uninstructed by Revelation, to seek for pardon and acceptance with God, either by attempting to live up to His law, or by making some personal sacrifices as an atonement for offences against it. The robe laid before the statue of Athena, or the hecatomb offered to Phœbus, were to compensate for sins against their divinity.

If we look to Jewish history, we shall find the prophets remonstrating with the Israelites for thinking that ceremonial observances would satisfy for the breach of God's commandments, and their sincerest penitents acknowledging that sacrifices would not profit them, but that they needed to be purged as with hyssop, and new created in heart (Psalm li.). Hence we may readily see, that the temptation of the Jews was to seek God's favour, when they had fallen from it, by ceremonial rites, without sufficient reference to the spirit of the ritual; as with many it was to seek the same favor by a rigid observance of a mere formal obedience, such as our Lord reproves in the Pharisees, and as St. Paul declares to have been the cause of the fall of his countrymen (Rom. ix. 31, 32). The Rabbins appear to have taught that a man's good deeds would be weighed against his bad; and that if the former preponderated, he would be accepted and rewarded.[1] And forgetting or neglecting the spiritual significance of their prophecies and sacrifices, they expected a Messiah indeed, but a triumphant conqueror,

---

[1] See Bull, *Harmon. Apost.* II. xvi. 8.

not one who by His death would expiate their sins; and so the Cross of Christ was a stumbling-block and offence to them. They were profoundly ignorant that Christ should be to them "the end of the Law for righteousness," that by Him alone all who believed in Him should receive justification and life.[1]

It has been thought also, that some among the Jews held that a man would be saved, even without holiness, who simply embraced the creed of Abraham, acknowledging the unity of the Godhead and the Resurrection of the dead; a view which seems to have been adopted by Mohammed in the Koran. Accordingly, it has been said, that, as St. Paul in his Epistles condemned the former error of his fellow-countrymen, so St. James directed his Epistle against the latter: the one showing, that neither ceremonial observances nor legal obedience could satisfy the demands of God's justice, but that an atonement and true faith were necessary; the other, that a mere creed was not calculated to please God, when the life was not consistent with it.[2]

The sentiments of the fathers on the subject of justification have afforded matter for much discussion. According to some, they taught nearly the doctrine of the Council of Trent; according to others, they nearly spoke the language of Luther. The truth appears to lie in neither of these statements. Justification had not been in early times the cause of much debate. No fierce contests had arisen upon it. Hence, no need was felt for accurate definitions concerning it. The statements of the fathers are therefore generally rather practical than formal. They dwell much on the Atonement, and the meritorious cause of pardon; so much so, that they could see the Blood of Christ in the scarlet thread which Rahab tied in her window, and His Cross in the stretched out hands of Moses, when Israel prevailed over Midian.[3] But they do not appear ever to have entered thoroughly into the question of justification, as it was afterwards debated in the time of the schoolmen, and, still more, of the reformers.

It is remarkable, that probably the most express statement on the subject which occurs in all the writings of the fathers, is to be found in the very earliest of all, Clement of Rome. Speaking of faithful men of old, he writes, "They were all therefore greatly glorified, not for their own sake, or for their own works, or for the

---

[1] See Bull, *Harmon. Apost.* II. xvii. 3.
[2] See Michaelis, *Introduction to the New Testament*, IV. ch. XXVI. § 6, who considers this to have been the cause of St. James's argument on justification, and that his Epistle was written before St. Paul's, or at least before he had seen St. Paul's writings.
[3] Clem. Rom. *Epist.* 1 *ad Corinth.* 12. Barnab. *Epist.* 12.

righteousness that they themselves wrought ; but through His will.
And we also, being called by the same will in Christ Jesus, are
not justified by ourselves, neither by our own wisdom, or knowledge, or piety, or any works which we did in holiness of heart, but
by that faith by which God Almighty has justified all men from
the beginning: to whom be glory for ever and ever.   Amen." [1]

The passage is important, not only because of its antiquity, but
because of its distinctness. The word "justify" appears to be
used, as our Article uses it, for "to account righteous;" not, as
the Council of Trent, for "to make righteous" by infusion of holiness ; and the instrument of such justification is declared to be and
ever to have been, not "wisdom, knowledge, piety, or works done
in holiness of heart, but" "faith." [2]

With regard to the statements of the later fathers, we must
carefully bear in mind, that, without question, they attributed the
salvation of man solely and perfectly to the Blood of Christ ; that
they did not look to be saved because they had deserved salvation,
but because Christ had satisfied for their sins ; but though this is
thus far plain, it will not enable us to come to any certain conclusion as to their views concerning the doctrine of justification
scholastically considered.

Such passages as the following show the spirit of the fathers, as
regards their reliance on the Atonement of Christ. "Let us
without ceasing hold steadfastly to Him, who is our hope, and the
earnest of our righteousness, even Jesus Christ, who His own self
bare our sins in His own body on the tree ; who did no sin, neither

[1] Clem. Rom. *Epist.* I. cap. 32.
[2] Πάντες οὖν ἐδοξάσθησαν, οὐ δι' αὐτῶν, ἢ
τῶν ἔργων αὐτῶν, ἢ διὰ τῆς δικαιοπραγίας ἧς
κατειργάσαντο, ἀλλὰ διὰ τοῦ θελήματος αὐτοῦ.
Καὶ ἡμεῖς οὖν διὰ θελήματος αὐτοῦ ἐν Χριστῷ
Ἰησοῦ κληθέντες, οὐ δι' ἑαυτῶν δικαιούμεθα,
οὐδὲ διὰ τῆς ἡμετέρας σοφίας, ἢ συνέσεως, ἢ
εὐσεβείας, ἢ ἔργων ὧν κατειργασάμεθα ἐν
ὁσιότητι καρδίας · ἀλλὰ διὰ τῆς πίστεως, δι' ἧς
πάντας τοὺς ἀπ' αἰῶνος ὁ παντοκράτωρ Θεὸς
ἐδικαίωσεν · ᾧ ἔστω δόξα εἰς τοὺς αἰῶνας τῶν
αἰώνων. Ἀμήν.
Almost the only question which may
be raised on the passage is, Does St.
Clement contrast faith with works done
before the grace of God, or works after
the grace of God, i. e. evangelical works ?
Dr. Waterland says, "It is of great
weight with him, that so early and so
considerable a writer as Clement of
Rome, an apostolical man, should so interpret the doctrine of *justifying faith* as
to oppose it plainly even to evangelical
works, however exalted." — *Works,* IX.

p. 452. Mr. Faber thinks that, "Indisputably, *by the very force and tenor of their
definition* (i. e. as being works done in
holiness of heart), they are works performed after the infusion of holiness into
the heart by the gracious spirit of God."
— *Primitive Doctrine of Justification,* p. 83.
Mr. Newman, on the other hand, contends that "in holiness of heart" means
no more than "piously," "holily ;" and
that "works which we did in holiness of
heart" (as the article is omitted before
ἔργων though not the former substantives
σοφίας, εὐσεβείας, &c., and the verb κατειργασάμεθα is in the aorist) would more
naturally, though perhaps not necessarily, signify an hypothetical, not a real
case, as in those words of St. Jerome
afterwards quoted by Mr. Faber, p. 122,
"Convertentem impium per solam fidem
justificat Deus, non per opera quæ non
habuit." — Newman, *On Justification,* p
436.

was guile found in His mouth ; but suffered all for us that we might live through Him." [1]

" For this cause did our Lord vouchsafe to give up His Body to destruction, that through the forgiveness of our sins we might be sanctified; that is, by the sprinkling of His Blood." [2]

" By His stripes healing is conferred on all who come to the Father by Him." [3]

" All men fall short of the glory of God, and are justified not by themselves, but by the coming of the Lord." [4]

" I will not glory because I am righteous, but because I am redeemed. I will glory, not because I am free from sins, but because my sins are forgiven me ; not because I have profited, nor because any one hath profited me, but because Christ is my Advocate with the Father, and because Christ's Blood hath been shed for me." [5]

" Our righteousness . . . . is such in this life that it consists rather in remission of sins than in perfection of virtue." [6]

"Not to commit sin, is the righteousness of God ; but man's righteousness consists in the mercy of God." [7]

Thus far it is plain that the fathers believed what the Scriptures taught and what the Article of our Church maintains, that " we are accounted righteous before God only for the merit of our Lord and Saviour Jesus Christ, and not for our own works or deservings." And if anywhere they seem to speak a language not strictly in accordance with this doctrine, we ought in fairness to conclude that they do not mean really to contradict themselves, though they speak broadly and as the Scriptures speak, concerning the necessity of that " holiness, without which no man shall see the Lord." But when we come to technical terms, and express definitions, we shall find considerable difficulty in ascertaining the sense attached to them in the patristic writings. We have already seen something like a distinct statement in Clement of Rome, and something nearly approaching it may be found in those who followed him. A few examples I have thrown into the note.[8]   Yet

[1] Polycarp, *Epist.* viii.
[2] Barnab. *Ep.* v.
[3] Just. M. *Dial.* p. 366. See also Bp. Kaye's *Justin Martyr*, p. 77.
[4] Iren. iv. xxxvii. See also Beaven's *Irenæus*, p. 194.
[5] Ambros. *De Jacobo et Vita Beat.* i. 6. See Newman, *On Justification*, p. 401.
[6] August. *De Civit.* xix. 27. See Calvin, *Institut.* iii. 12.
[7] Non peccare Dei est justitia ; hominis autem justitia, Dei indulgentia. — Bernard, *Sermon.* 21 et 23 in Cantic. See Calvin, *Institut.* iii. 12. See also Neander, viii. p. 218.

[8] Οὐ γὰρ δή γε εἰς βαλανεῖον ὑμᾶς ἔπεμπεν Ἡσαΐας ἀπολουσομένους ἐκεῖ τὸν φόνον καὶ τὰς ἄλλας ἁμαρτίας, οὓς οὐδὲ τὸ τῆς θαλάσσης ἱκανὸν πᾶν ὕδωρ καθαρίσαι, ἀλλὰ ὡς εἰκὸς πάλαι τοῦτο ἐκεῖνο τὸ σωτήριον λουτρὸν ἦν, ὃ εἵπετο τοῖς μεταγινώσκουσι, καὶ μηκέτι αἵματι τράγων καὶ προβάτων ἢ

it seems, on a general examination of the most remarkable passages from the ancient writings on this subject, that it is extremely difficult to say whether the fathers always understood the word "justification" in a forensic sense, as signifying acquittal from guilt and imputation of righteousness, or rather, as, in addition to that, containing in it the notion of infusion of righteousness. It has already been observed that we must not expect in their words the precision of controversy, where no controversy had been raised. In order of time, acquittal from guilt and infusion of righteousness (or what in modern Theology have been called justification and sanctification) go together, and are never separated. Therefore, though at times the fathers seem to use the term "justification" merely in its forensic sense, yet sometimes they speak too as if it included the idea of making just, as well as of esteeming just.

For example, in one place St. Chrysostom (on Rom. viii. 33: " It is God that justifieth; who is he that condemneth?") writes: " He does not say, it is God that forgave our sins, but, what is much greater, *It is God that justifieth.* For when the Judge's sentence declares us just (δικαίους ἀποφαίνει), and such a Judge too, what signifieth the accuser?"[1] Here he seems to speak as if he considered justification as no more than " declaring or pronouncing just." Yet, in other parts of the same work, he clearly shows that in justification he considered something more to be included than remission and acquittal. Thus, in the Eighth Homily on Rom. iv. 7, (" Blessed are they whose iniquities are forgiven,") we read: " He seems to be bringing a testimony beside his purpose. For it does not say, Blessed are they whose faith is reckoned for righteousness. But he does so purposely, not inadvertently, to show the greater excellence. For if he be blessed that by grace

σποδῷ δαμάλεως, ἢ σεμιδάλεως προσφοραῖς καθαριζομένους, ἀλλὰ πίστει διὰ τοῦ αἵματος τοῦ Χριστοῦ, καὶ τοῦ θανάτου αὐτοῦ, ὃς διὰ τοῦτο ἀπέθανεν. κ. τ. λ. — Just. M. *Dial.* p. 229, d.

Non incognitus igitur erat Dominus Abrahæ, cujus diem concupivit videre : sed neque Pater Domini; didicerat enim a Verbo Domini, et credidit ei; quapropter et deputatum est ei ad justitiam a Domino. Fides enim quæ est ad Deum altissimum justificat hominem. — Irenæ. IV. 13. See also IV. 27.

His igitur consideratis pertractatisque pro viribus quas Dominus donare dignatur, colligimus non justificari hominem præceptis bonæ vitæ nisi per fidem Jesu Christi, hoc est non lege operum sed **fi**dei; non litera sed spiritu, non facto-

rum meritis sed gratuita gratia. — Augustus. *De Spiritu et Litera,* cap. 22.

Convertentem impium per solam fidem justificat Deus, non opera bona quæ non habuit: alioquin per impietatis opera fuerat puniendus. Simul attende, quia non peccatorem dicit justificari per fidem sed impium, hoc est, nuper credentem asseruit.

Secundum propositum gratiæ Dei.] Qui proposuit gratis per solam fidem peccata dimittere. — Hieron. *In Epist. ad Rom.* cap. iv. Tom. v. pp. 937, 938. The Benedictine editors consider this commentary as not Jerome's. See also *In Epist. ad Galat.* cap. iii.

[1] *Homil. in Ep. ad Rom.* xv. See **also** Hom. VII. on ch. iii. 27.

received forgiveness, much more he that is made just and that manifests faith." Again, Homil. x. on Rom. v. 16, (" the free gift is of many offences unto justification,") he argues that " it was not only that sins were done away, but that righteousness was given." It is true that to be esteemed righteous is more than to be esteemed sinless ; as the one would only deliver from punishment, the other give a right to reward; and so St. Chrysostom may only mean that justification is more than pardon, because to be accounted righteous is more than to be acquitted of guilt. But it appears to have been common to many of the fathers to leave in some uncertainty the question, whether justification did or did not contain in it the making that of which it involved the imputation.

This is especially observable in the works of St. Augustine. For example, in the 45th chapter of the *De Spiritu et Litera*, where he is reasoning on the words of St. Paul, " The doers of the Law shall be justified." He asks " What is to be justified but to be made just by Him who justifies the ungodly, so that from ungodly, he becomes just ? " and so he concludes, that by this phrase St. Paul means that " they shall be made just who before were not so, not who before were just ; that so the Jews, who were hearers of the Law, might understand that they need the grace of a justifier that they might become doers of the Law." Or else, he proposes to interpret it in the other way, " *shall be justified,* as though it were said, shall be held and accounted righteous ; just as it is said of a certain one, *He willing to justify himself,* that is, to be held and esteemed just." So then Augustine appears to leave it an open question, whether to *justify* is to *make,* or to *esteem* and *hold* as righteous.

Yet, though there be such ambiguity, we need be but little solicitous on the subject; but rather conclude, that " the point having never been discussed, and those fathers never having thoroughly considered the sense of St. Paul, might unawares take the word (justify) as it sounded in the Latin, especially the sense they affixed to it signifying a matter very true and certain in Christianity." [1]

Dr. Waterland, in his treatise on *Justification,* [2] has collected a great number of passages from the fathers, to show that they considered every person at his baptism to receive the gift of justification. Our limits will not allow us to follow him at length. But if we take justification to mean remission of sin and admission into

---

[1] Barrow, ii. Sermon v. *On Justification by Faith.*
[2] Waterland's *Works,* ix. p. 442.

God's favour, it needs but very slight acquaintance with the writings of the early Christians to know, that as they confessed their faith " in one baptism for the remission of sins," so they universally taught that all persons duly receiving baptism, and not hindering the grace of God by unbelief and impenitence, obtained in baptism pardon for sin, admission into the Christian Church and covenant, and the assistance of the Holy Spirit of God; and that so they were thenceforth " children of God, members of Christ, and inheritors of the kingdom of heaven."

To sum up what has been said. In the essence of this Article the fathers' language is clear. They held, that all hope of salvation must spring from the mercy of God through the merits of Christ. They taught, that every person baptized (not forfeiting the grace by sin and impenitence) was looked on as a member of the body of the faithful, and so in favour with God. They spoke too of faith as that state of salvation in which we receive justification and life. But (if at least we make some exceptions) they do not speak in the clear and controversial language of later days; nor is it always certain, whether by the word *justified* they understand that a man's faith is accounted to him for righteousness, or that, being the great sanctifying principle, it is the instrument whereby God works in him holiness.

It would be beside our purpose and exceed our limits to investigate at length the definitions of the schoolmen. Learned discussions are liable to much misunderstanding. But the impressions popularly conveyed by the teaching of the scholastic divines, and especially the view which was taken of them by Luther and their opponents, are very important to our right apprehension of the controversy at the time of the Reformation.

In the first place it appears that the schoolmen generally understood justification to mean not infusion of righteousness, but forgiveness of sins. It is true, they looked on it as the immediate result of, and as inseparably connected with grace infused; but their definitions made justification to mean, not the making righteous, but the declaring righteous.[1]

It is not to be supposed that they denied or doubted that such

---

[1] Primo quæritur, an justificatio impii sit remissio peccatorum? Et videtur quod non . . . . Sed *contra* est quod dicitur in Glossa Rom. viii. Super illud " Quos vocavit, hos et justificavit." Glo. remissione peccatorum: ergo remissio peccatorum est justificatio. — Aquinas, *Quæstion. Disput.* quæst. 28, Art. i. quoted by Laurence, *Bampt. Lect.* p. 119.

Neander, viii. p. 222, gives an interesting account of the scholastic discussions on justification. His statements appear different from those in the text, but it is only so at first sight.

justification sprang primarily from the grace of God, and meritoriously from the death of Christ.   The faults charged upon their
system are, that they looked for merit *de congruo*, and *de condigno*,
that they attached *efficacy* to *attrition*, that they inculcated the doctrine of *satisfaction*, and that they assigned grace to the Sacraments
ex opere operato.

Luther especially insists that these scholastic opinions were
directly subversive of the doctrine of St. Paul, and of the grace of
God.   " They say," he writes, " that a good work before grace is
able to obtain grace of *congruity* (which they call *meritum de congruo*), because it is meet that God should reward such a work.
But when grace is obtained, the work following deserveth eternal
life of debt and worthiness, which they call *meritum de condigno*.
. . . . For the first God is no debtor, but because He is just and
good, He must approve such good work, though it be done in
mortal sin, and so give grace for such service.   But when grace is
obtained, God is become a debtor, and is constrained of right and
duty to give eternal life.   For now it is not only a work of free-
will, done according to the substance, but also done in grace, which
makes a man acceptable to God, that is to say, in charity."   " This
is the divinity of the kingdom of antichrist ; which here I recite,
that St. Paul's argument may be the better understood, for two
things contrary to one another being put together may be the
better understood." [1]

Again, the compunction for sin which might be felt before the
grace of God was given, was called *attrition ;* compunction arising
from the motions of God's Spirit being called *contrition*.   Now
attrition was considered as a means whereby God predisposed to
grace.   So that it had in it some merit *de congruo*, and so of its
own nature led to contrition and to justification.[2]

There being some difficulty in knowing whether a man's repentance was *contrition* or merely *attrition*, the Church was supposed to
come to his aid with the power of the keys.   The sacrament of
penance added to attrition, and works of satisfaction being enjoined,
the conscience was to be stilled, though it might yet be uncertain
whether true repentance and lively faith had really been attained.[3]

---

[1] Luther, on Galatians, ii. 16.
[2] See Laurence, *B. L.* Lect. IV. and VI.
Also notes on Lect. VI.   The following is
one sentence from a long passage quoted
by him, p. 321, from Scotus, Lib. IV.
dist. IV. quæst. 2.
" Potest ergo dici quod Deus disponit
per attritionem, in alique instanti dare

gratiam : et pro illa attritione, ut pro merito, justificat, sicut est meritum justifi-
cationis.   Et licet non continuaretur idem
actus circa peccatum in genere naturæ et
moris, qui prius, adhuc in illo instanti in-
funderetur gratia, qui jam præcepit meritum de congruo."

[3] Laurence, as above, and p. 320.

Once more, the doctrine that the Sacraments worked grace and so effected justification independently of the faith of the receiver, and merely *ex opere operato*, was by the reformers charged upon the schoolmen, as overthrowing the doctrine of justification, through faith, by the merits of Christ.[1] And at last when by attrition perfected by penance, satisfaction, and absolution, and through the grace of God passing into contrition, the sinner was believed to be pardoned, and his soul justified before God, it still remained a question whether there was not a certain amount of temporal punishment to be endured, in this life perhaps, but more probably in purgatory, before the soul be received into full favour with God, and be pronounced " not guilty " in His presence.

The abuses which prevailed at the time of the Reformation connected with the above doctrines are popularly known. Hence, especially, the merit attached to pilgrimages, and other works of satisfaction, which were thought capable of averting the temporal punishments yet due to sin; although of course eternal punishment could be averted only by the merits of Christ. Hence, too, the famous sale of indulgences, which first prompted Luther to take the steps which led rapidly to his breach with the see of Rome.

It is possible that much of the teaching of the schoolmen, and of the more learned and pious of the divines of the Middle Ages, may, when fairly interpreted, admit of a sense far more innocent han we are apt to attribute to it, and might, if confined to the schools, have produced comparatively little mischief. But the effect produced upon the popular mind was evidently noxious. Nothing can be more plain than the fact, that reformers, in all countries, felt that the great evil against which they had to fight was the general belief that man could merit God's favour by good deeds of his own, and that works of mercy, charity, and self-denial, procured (through the intercession of Christ, or perhaps of the Virgin Mary) pardon for sin and acceptance with God.

It was in opposition to all this, that Luther so strongly propounded his doctrine of " justification by faith only." He saw the extreme importance of teaching men to acknowledge their own weakness, and to rely on the Atonement "as a full, perfect, and sufficient sacrifice for the sins of the whole world." Salvation was to be ascribed to grace, not to be claimed as a right; and with the view of effectually destroying all hope from *claims*, he adopted the language of St. Paul, and put forth in its strongest possible form, as the *articulus stantis aut cadentis ecclesiæ*, the statement,

[1] Laurence, p. 324.

that "justification is by faith only," without works, love, or holiness. That is to say, he asserted that man is justified through, or because of the merits of Christ, and that the sole *instrument* of his justification is *faith*. This faith indeed will produce charity, and so good works ; but, when considered as justifying, it must be considered as apart from holiness, and charity, and good works.

The vehemence of his temper, and the great importance which he attached to his doctrine, led him to state it in language which we may not approve. Such language, if used now, when very different errors prevail from those most common in Luther's time, might, in all probability, lead to Antinomianism and fanaticism of all kinds. But it is necessary to put ourselves into Luther's position, and to take a fair view of the man, whose energy brought about the greatest revolution in history, in order to judge fairly of his language and opinions.

For example, Luther stated that faith alone, not faith informed or perfected by charity, was that which justified. This seems opposed to the language of St. James (ch. ii. 14, &c.), and even to the language of St. Paul, who tells us that it is "faith, which worketh by love," which "availeth in Christ Jesus " (Gal. v. 6). Accordingly, the schoolmen had distinguished between *fides informis*, a faith which was merely speculative, and had in it neither love nor holiness, and *fides formata*, or faith which is perfected by the charity and good works which spring from it ; to which faith they attributed the office of justifying.[1] Now this statement, that it is *fides formata* which justifies, Luther denied. By so doing it will be thought by many that he contradicted Scripture, the fathers, the homilies of our own Church, and the sentiments of many contemporary reformers. But the ground on which he did so he himself clearly explains to us. The schoolmen and Romanist divines, according to him, taught that faith, furnished with charity, justified the sinner, in order that they might assign the office of justification, not to the faith, but to the charity : that so it might be said, Faith justifies indeed ; but it is because of the merit of that charity, and of those good works which it contains, and which give it all its efficacy. " Faith," he says, is, according to them, " the body and the shell ; charity the life, the kernel, the form, and furniture." " But we," he continues, " in the stead of this charity, put

[1] On this scholastic distinction see Calvin, *Instit.* Lib. iii. ch. ii. § 8. Also Neander, viii. 220, 221. Calvin himself denies the justice of the distinction on this ground : Fides in Christi notitia sita est. Christus nisi cum Spiritus sui sanctificatione cognosci nequit. Consequitur fidem a pio affectu nullo modo esse distrahendam. A very different argument from Luther's.

faith, and we say that faith apprehends Jesus Christ, who is the form which adorns and furnishes faith . . . . As the schoolmen say that charity adorns and furnishes faith, so do we say that it is Christ which furnishes or adorns faith, or rather, that He is the very form and perfection of faith. Wherefore Christ apprehended by faith and dwelling in the heart is the true Christian righteousness, for which God counteth us righteous, and giveth us eternal life." [1]

Faith then, he taught, will justify, not because it is full of love, but because it is full of Christ. Therefore, too, he thought it necessary to state that faith justified, before it had charity or good works with it; though, of necessity, it must produce charity and good works, as soon as it has justified. Faith he compares to the bride, Christ to the bridegroom. The bride will be alone with the Bridegroom, but as soon as she cometh forth from the bridechamber, she will be attended by her bridesmaids and followers, good works and holiness.

The earnestness with which he pursued his object, and the infinite importance which he attached to it, led him into vehemence of expressions, and perhaps inaccuracy of statements, which only the circumstances of the case can extenuate. At times he seems to speak as if faith itself was the cause, not merely the instrument, of salvation. At other times he writes as if good works were rather to be avoided than desired. But it is fair to consider these expressions as the result of inadvertence and the impetuosity with which he pleaded a favourite cause, when we find statements of the evil of Antinomianism, and the excellency of those works which spring from faith, in other portions of the very same writings.[2]

It should be added, that Luther plainly put forth the statement that the sins of the believer are imputed to Christ, and so that Christ's righteousness is imputed to the believer.[3] He speaks often of the desirableness of attaining to personal assurance of salvation, and at times appears to identify this assurance with justifying faith.[4]

[1] Luther on Galat. ii. 16. See also on Gal. ii. 17; v. 16.

[2] For example, on Gal. iii. 22: "When we are out of the matter of justification, we cannot enough praise and extol those works which God has commanded. For who can enough commend the profit and fruit of only one work, which a Christian does in and through faith? Indeed, it is more precious than heaven and earth." See also on Gal. iii. 19, 23, 27, &c.

[3] See on Gal. ii. 16; iii. 13.

[4] See on Gal. iii. 13. *Opera*, 1554. Tom. v. p. 350. Concerning Luther's view of the connection of justification with baptism, we may refer to his commentary on Gal. iii. 27, Tom. v. p. 369. There he says, "We have by nature the leathern coat of Adam, but we put on Christ by baptism." In Baptismo non datur vestitus legalis justitiæ aut nostrorum operum, sed Christus fit indumentum nostrum . . . . Evangelice Christum induere, non est legem et opera, sed inæstimabile donum induere, scilicet re

The council of Trent was much occupied in discussing Luther's doctrine of justification.   Indeed, the Tridentine fathers appear to have gone to the consideration of it, with the conviction that all his errors might be resolved into this one.[1]

It was universally agreed among these divines, that faith justifies.   But what justifying faith was, or how it justified, was much debated.   " All agreed, that justifying faith is an assent to whatsoever is revealed by God, or determined by the Church to be believed ; which, sometimes being joined with charity, sometimes remaining without it, they distinguished into two sorts : one, which is found in sinners, which the schools call unformed, solitary, idle, or dead ; the other, which is only in the good, working by charity, and therefore called formed, efficacious, and lively. "   But it was not universally agreed that justifying faith was to be called faith formed by charity ; Marinarus, a Carmelite, objecting that St. Paul did not say that faith was formed by charity, but that it worketh by charity.[2]

There was much discussion concerning works before grace, and merit *de congruo ;* in which the Franciscans maintained, whilst the Dominicans denied, that good works could be done without the Spirit of God, and so merit grace of congruity.[3]   But concerning works after grace, all agreed to condemn Luther, who denied intrinsic goodness to works done in and after grace, and asserted even that they were sins.   These, they all asserted, having been wrought by the Spirit of God, were essentially good and perfect.[4]   They all agreed too, that only faith could not be said to justify, since God and the Sacraments do justify, as causes in their several kinds.[5]

But the principal points of the difficulty were : first, Is a man justified, and then acts justly ? or, Does he act justly, and then is justified ? and, secondly, Is the word " justify " to be used in the forensic sense of imputing righteousness ; or does it mean infusion of habitual righteousness into the heart ?   On the latter point there was much difference of opinion ; the Franciscans strongly opposing the forensic sense, which was as strongly upheld by Marinarus. None doubted that Christ had merited for us, but some blamed the word to *impute*, because it was not found in the fathers ; whilst others said that, agreeing on the thing, it was needless to dispute about the word ; a word which it appears the Dominicans especially

missionem peccatorum, justitiam, pacem, consolationem, lætitiam in Spiritu Sancto, salutem, vitam, et Christum ipsum. See also *De Sacr. Baptism.* Tom. I. p. 72.
 [1] Sarpi, *Hist.* Lib. II. p. 178.

[2] Ibid. p. 183.
[3] Ibid. p. 185.
[4] Ibid. p. 186.
[5] Ibid. p. 183.

would have accepted, as showing that all was from Christ, but that they suspected any word which was popular with the Lutherans.[1]

After many such discussions as these, the Council finally drew up sixteen heads and thirty canons or anathemas on the subject of justification, yet so guarded and obscure that each party wrote treatises to prove that the decisions were in their favour.[2] The most important of the decrees were the following: (2) That God sent His Son to redeem both Jews and Gentiles. (3) But that, though He died for all, yet those only enjoy the benefit to whom His merit is communicated. (4) That the justification of the wicked is a translation from the state of a son of Adam to that of a son of God, which, since the Gospel, is not done without baptism or the vow thereof. (5) That the beginning of justification in adults proceeds from preventing grace. (7) That justification is *not only remission of sins, but sanctification* also ; and has five causes : the final, God's glory and eternal life ; the efficient, God ; the meritorious, Christ ; the instrumental, the sacraments ; and the formal, righteousness, given by God, received according to the good pleasure of the Holy Ghost, and according to the disposition of the receiver, receiving together with remission of sins, faith, hope, and charity. (8) That, when St. Paul saith that man is justified by faith and *gratis*, it ought to be understood, because faith is the beginning, and the things which precede justification are not meritorious of grace.[3]

Among the *anathemas*, some of the most important are : (1) That a man may be justified without grace. (11) That man is justified only by the imputation of the justice of Christ, or only by remission of sins without inherent grace, or charity ; or that the grace of justification is only the favour of God. (12) That justifying faith is nothing but confidence in the mercy of God, who remitteth sins for Christ. (14) That man is absolved and justified, because he doth firmly believe that he is justified.[4]

These articles and canons show the difference between Luther and the Council of Trent, so far as we can be certain of the design of the latter. Yet the most eminent divines present in the Council, after its decrees, debated on their sense ;[5] so that at last it was necessary to make a decree against all notes, glosses, and commentaries ; the Pope reserving to himself the right of solving difficulties, and settling controversies on the subject.[6]

[1] Sarpi, *Hist.* Bk. II. p. 187.
[2] Ibid. p. 202.
[3] Concil. Trident. Sess VI. capp. 2, 3, 4, 5, 7, 8.
[4] Concil. Trident. Can. 1, 11, 12, 14.
[5] Sarpi, Bk. II. p. 215.
[6] Ibid. Bk. VIII. p. 762.

Roman Catholic writers since the Reformation have generally gone against the forensic sense of the word "justify ; " have held, that God by grace implants inherent righteousness in the heart, makes the sinner righteous by union with Christ and the indwelling of His Spirit, and that then He esteems him, what in fact He has made him, a holy and righteous man. Their view has been thus stated by one who may be supposed to have carefully studied it. "It appears that they hold two things : — that the presence of grace implies the absence of mortal sin ; next, that it is a divine gift bringing with it the property of a continual acceptableness, and so recommending the soul to God's favour so as to anticipate the necessity of any superadded pardon." [1]

To return to the Lutheran divines : Melancthon, the Confession of Augsburg, and generally the more moderate Lutherans, softened and explained the strong language of Luther. With them Faith was trust (*fiducia*), or fiduciary apprehension. It was made clear, that faith in itself had no virtue, but that the meritorious cause of justification was the death and satisfaction of Jesus Christ. So that justification by faith was even said to be a *correlative* term for justification or salvation by the merits and death of Christ. Nay, justification by faith was even called a *Paulina figura*, by which was meant that we are saved by grace, and not by claims or merits of our own.[2]

---

[1] Newman, *On Justification*, p. 396. See also Bellarmine, *De Justific.* ; and Barrow, II. Sect. v. p. 79.

Bellarmine states the causes of justification thus : 1. *The final cause*, God's glory and our salvation. 2. *The efficient cause*, God's goodness and Christ's merits. 3. *The material cause*, the mind or will of man, in which righteousness abides, and in which are formed the dispositions predisposing to the formal cause. 4. *The formal cause*, internally, the habit of grace ; externally, the righteousness of Christ. *De Justific.* Lib. I. cap. 2. Justification he denies to consist in remission of sins or imputation of righteousness only, but asserts it to have for its formal cause the infusion of habitual righteousness. Lib. II. cap. 3, 6, 15. Good works he asserts to be meritorious of eternal life, but that, because they are wrought in us by the grace of God. Lib. v. cap. 12, *et passim*.

[2] Fide sumus justi, id est, per misericordiam propter Christum sumus justi ; non quia fides sit virtus, quæ mereatur remissionem sua dignitate. — Melancth. *Loci Theolog. de Argum. Advers.* p. 286. Laurence, *B. L.* p. 333.

Cum dicitur, Fide justificamur, non aliud dicitur, quam quod propter Filium Dei accipiamus remissionem peccatorum et reputemur justi . . . . Intelligatur ergo propositio *correlative*, Fide justi sumus, id est, per misericordiam propter Filium Dei sumus justi seu accepti. —Mel. *Loc. Theol. de Voc Fidei*, f. 199, 2. Newman, *On Justif.* p. 278.

Cum igitur dicimus *Fide justificamur*, non hoc intelligimus, quod justi sumus propter ipsius virtutis dignitatem, sed hæc est sententia, consequi nos remissionem peccatorum, et imputationem justitiæ per misericordiam propter Christum . . . . Jam bonas mentes nihil offendet *novitas hujus Paulinæ figuræ*, Fide justificamur, si intelligant proprie de misericordia dici, eamque veris et necessariis laudibus ornari. Quid potest enim esse gratius conscientiæ afflictæ et pavidæ in veris doloribus quam audire, hoc esse mandatum Dei, hanc esse vocem sponsi Christi, ut statuant certe donari remissionem peccatorum seu reconciliationem, non propter nostram dignitatem, sed gratis, per misericordiam, propter Christum, ut beneficium sit certum. — Confessio August. 1540. *De Fide, Sylloge Confessionum*, Oxf. 1827, p. 182.

Thus then it was ruled, that the peculiar significance of St. Paul's language, and of the Lutheran use of it, implied, not an opposition of faith to charity, or of faith to holiness, but an opposition of the merits of Christ to the merits of man, of the mercy of God to the claims which a sinner might suppose himself to have for acceptance in God's presence.

Still it was clear that, in some sense, *faith* was made the *instrument* or *formal* cause of justification. And the question still remained, Had such faith love in it, or was it to be considered as apart from love? We have seen that Luther declared that justifying faith had not love in it till it had justified; and to his definitions some of the Lutherans adhered, though he may himself afterwards have in some degree modified them.

Melancthon and the moderate Lutherans appear to have spoken rather differently. Melancthon says, that " no doubt there are love and other graces in faith; but that, when St. Paul says, ' we are justified by faith,' he means, not by the virtue of that grace, but by the mercy of God, for the sake of the Mediator." [1] The Confession of Augsburg declares, that "faith cannot exist except in those who repent; " that " among good works, the chief is faith, which produces many other virtues, which cannot exist till faith has been conceived in the heart." [2] Again, it reconciles St. James and St. Paul, by explaining that St. James speaks of a mere historical faith, whilst St. Paul speaks of reliance on God's mercy in Christ.[3] It distinctly asserts, that faith brings forth good works, and quotes with approbation the words of St. Ambrose, *Fides bonæ voluntatis et justæ actionis genitrix est.*[4] All then, but a few of the more rigid Lutherans, agreed that it was a living, not a dead faith, a faith full of good works, not a bare and historical assent to truth, which justified the soul. Still, the question remained, Was it *fides, quæ viva est,* or, *fides qua viva est,* (*i. e.* faith, which is living, *or* faith, because it is living,) which justifies? Some thought, that if it were considered as justifying because it was living, then there would be some merit attached to that which quickened it, or which

---

[1] Concedo in fiducia inesse dilectionem, et hanc virtutem et plerasque alias adesse oportere; sed cum dicimus, Fiducia sumus justi, non intelligatur nos propter virtutis istius dignitatem, sed per misericordiam recipi propter Mediatorem, quem tamen oportet fide apprehendi. Ergo hoc dicimus correlative.—Melancth. *Loci Theolog. de Argum. Advers.* p. 284. Laurence, *B. L.* p. 332. Newman, *Justific.* p. 10.

[2] Nec existere fides potest nisi in his qui pœnitentiam agunt, quia fides consolatur corda in contritione et terroribus peccati .... Inter bona opera, præcipuum est et summus cultus Dei fides ipsa, et parit multas alias virtutes, quæ existere non possunt, nisi prius corda fidem conceperint. — *Confess. August. Syll. Conf* p. 83.

[3] *Sylloge Conf.* pp. 181, 182.

[4] Ibid. p. 183.

showed it to be alive, *i. e.* to charity. " Modes were invented of explaining the difficulty, which savoured more of metaphysical subtlety than of practical wisdom, such as that mentioned by Bishop Bull : " Faith justifies, pregnant with good works, but not as yet having given birth to them." [1]

Bucer, a divine, who had some concern in our own Reformation, and whose opinions are therefore particularly interesting to us, seems to have been very moderate on this subject. He expresses his regret that language should be used concerning faith alone, to the exclusion of holiness, such as to offend well-meaning men. He considers that no one should object to the additions of *viva* or *formata* as applied to justifying faith ; since it is plain that St. Paul spoke of a living faith as justifying, and only meant to exclude self-righteousness.[2]

Several controversies concerning justification arose among the Lutherans, even in the lifetime of Luther. Osiander, A. D. 1550, broached some opinions, the exact nature of which it may be difficult to define. They appear to have been chiefly, " that faith does not justify by applying and embracing the righteousness of the Man Christ, but by uniting to Christ, who then by His Divine nature dwells in the heart, and that this union both justifies before God, and sanctifies the sinner." There was probably, however, something more than this, or it would hardly have excited the vehement opposition of so mild a man as Melancthon.[3]

Of a very different kind were the errors of Agricola, (A. D. 1538,) who is accused of having carried the doctrine of *faith alone* to its most noxious extreme. He is esteemed the founder of the Antinomians ; and is said to have held that all licentiousness and sin were allowable, if only Christ was received and embraced by a lively faith. He was vigorously opposed by Luther.[4]

To proceed from the Lutheran to the Calvinistic reformers : they appear for the most part to have symbolized with Luther in his general statement concerning justification. They declared that *to justify* was a forensic term signifying to *remit sins*, and pronounce *righteous*.[5] They said, that we receive this justification not by

---

[1] Bull, *Harm. Apostol.* Diss. Prior. VI. 2.

[2] See especially on Psalm xi. quoted by Bull, *Harm. Apostol.* Diss. Post. II. 8.

[3] Mosh. *Ch. Hist.* Art. XVI. § III. part II. See also Calv. *Instit.* III. cap. xi. 5–11, who accuses him of opinions bordering on Manicheism.

[4] Mosh. as above.

[5] Justificatio significat Apostolo in disputatione de Justificatione, *peccata remittere, a culpa et pœna absolvere, in gratiam recipere, et justum pronunciare.* — *Confess. Helvet. Sylloge*, p. 51.

Nos justificationem simpliciter interpretamur acceptionem, qua nos Deus in gratiam receptos pro justis habet — Calvin, *Inst.* III. xi. 2.

works, but by faith in God's mercy ; and because faith receives
Christ, our righteousness, and ascribes all to God's grace in Christ,
therefore justification is attributed to faith, and that chiefly because of Christ, not because it is any work of ours.[1]   They considered it to consist especially in the imputation of our sins to
Christ, and of Christ's righteousness to us ; and strenuously denied
that justification was in consequence of any internal sanctification
wrought in us by the indwelling of the Holy Ghost, and the faith
which He inspires.[2]   They denied that justification was of faith
and works conjoined.[3]   But when the question arose, Is the faith
which justifies to be considered as alone, and *informis*, or lively, and
full of good works, (*formata*) ? they seem to have decided that it
was the latter and not the former.   Although Calvin complained
that the distinction was nugatory, inasmuch as faith never could
exist apart from the holiness which it produces.[4]

Our own reformers soon embraced the doctrine of Luther, with
such modifications as their own wisdom suggested.   In the Articles set forth in 1536, justification is defined to signify remission
of sins and acceptance into the favour of God.   We are said to
attain this justification for the only mercy and grace of the Father,
freely for Jesus Christ's sake, through contrition and faith joined
with charity ;[5] language which is repeated in the *Institution of a
Christian Man.*[6]

As on other subjects, the English reformers' views grew more
fixed and definite after the death of Henry VIII.   The Homily
of Salvation, and the 11th Article of 1552, expressed definitively
the judgment of Cranmer and his companions on justification.
The 11th Article, as drawn by them, ran thus : " Justification by

---

[1] *Sylloge*, p. 52.

[2] Deus nos justificat non imputans nobis peccata, sed imputans Christi nobis
justitiam.   *Sylloge*, p. 52.

Hinc et illud conficitur, sola interces-
sione justitiæ Christi nos obtinere ut coram Deo justificemur.   Quod perinde
valet ac si diceretur hominem non in
seipso justum esse, sed quia Christi justitia imputatione cum illo communicatur :
quod accurata animadversione dignum
est. Siquidem evanescit nugamentum
illud, ideo justificari hominem fide, quoniam illa Spiritum Dei participat quo justus redditur : quod magis est contrarium
superiori doctrinæ quam ut conciliari unquam queat.   Neque enim dubium, quin
sit inops propriæ justitiæ, qui justitiam
extra seipsum quærere docetur. — Calv.
Inst. iii. xi. 23.

[3] Calv. *Inst.* iii. xi. 13, 14.

[4] Quapropter loquimur in hac causa,
non de ficta fide, de inani et otiosa et
mortua, sed de viva, vivificanteque, quæ
propter Christum, qui vita est et vivificat,
quem comprehendit, viva est et dicitur,
ac se vivam esse vivis declarat operibus.
Nihil itaque contra hanc nostram doctrinam pugnat Jacobus ille, qui de fide
loquitur inani et mortua, quam quidam
jactabant, Christum autem intra se viven-
tem per fidem non habebant. — *Confess.
Helvet. Sylloge*, p. 53. See also Calvin,
Inst. iii. ii. 8, quoted above.

[5] *Formularies of Faith in the Reign of
Henry VIII.* Oxford, p. 12.

[6] Ibid. p. 209.

only faith in Jesus Christ, in that sense as it is declared in the
Homily of Justification, is a most certain and wholesome doctrine
for Christian men." The Article as it stands now is somewhat
differently worded, but probably conveys the same sense. Both
send us to the " Homily of Justification " as the interpreter of the
sense in which the Church of England understands " Justification
by faith ; " and therefore the definitions of this homily, if we can
discover them, are the definitions of the Anglican Church concerning this debated point. There is no homily entitled the Homily
of Justification, but the Homily of Salvation treats expressly of
justification ; and it has therefore always been understood, either
that this homily alone, or this conjoined with that which precedes
and that which follows it, is the homily referred to in the Article.

The Article itself, as it now stands, appears to speak very much
the language of Melancthon and the Confession of Augsburg ; for
its statement of the doctrine of justification by faith is, that " We
are accounted righteous before God only for the merits of our Lord
and Saviour Jesus Christ, by faith, and not for our own works or
deservings." This is language very similar to that of Melancthon,
quoted above, who considered justification by faith, and salvation
by grace, to be correlative terms ; and to that of the Confession of
Augsburg, which calls justification by faith a *Paulina figura* for
remission of sins by mercy, for the sake of Christ. For further
explanation the Article sends us to the homily, which teaches as
follows.

It begins by defining justification to be " the forgiveness of sins
and trespasses." " This justification or righteousness, which we so
receive of God's mercy and Christ's merits, embraced by faith, is
taken, allowed, and accepted for our perfect and full justification.
. . . . God sent His Son into the world to fulfil the Law for us,
and by shedding of His most precious Blood, to make a sacrifice
and satisfaction, or (as it may be called) amends to His Father for
our sins, to assuage His wrath and indignation conceived against
us for the same. Insomuch that infants, being baptized and dying
in their infancy, are by this sacrifice washed from their sins, brought
to God's favour, and made His children, and inheritors of His
Kingdom of Heaven. And they which in act or deed do sin after
baptism, when they turn again to God unfeignedly, they are likewise washed by this sacrifice from their sins, in such sort that there
remaineth not any spot of sin that shall be imputed to their damnation. This is that justification of righteousness which St. Paul
speaketh of when he saith, *No man is justified by the works of the*

law, but freely, by faith in Jesus Christ. Gal. ii. . . . . The Apostle toucheth specially three things, which must go together in our justification. Upon God's part, His great mercy and grace : upon Christ's part, justice, that is, the satisfaction of God's justice . . . upon our part, true and lively faith in the merits of Jesus Christ, which yet is not ours, but God's working in us . . . . Therefore St. Paul declareth here nothing upon the behalf of man concerning his justification, but only a true and lively faith, which nevertheless is the gift of God, and not man's only work without God.   And yet

How it is to be understood that faith justifieth without works.

that faith doth not shut out repentance, hope, love, dread and the fear of God, to be joined with faith, in every man that is justified, but it shutteth them out from the office of justifying.   So that, although they be all present together in him that is justified, yet they justify not altogether ; nor the faith also doth not shut out the justice of our good works, necessarily to be done afterwards of duty towards God : (for we are most bounden to serve God in doing good deeds, commanded by Him, in His holy Scripture, all the days of our life :) but it excludeth them, so that we may not do them to this intent, to be made just by doing of them." [1]

Again — " The true understanding of the doctrine, we be justified freely by faith without works, or that we be justified by faith in Christ only, is not that this our own act to believe in Christ, or this our faith in Christ, which is within us, doth justify us, and deserve our justification unto us (for that were to count ourselves to be justified by some act or virtue which is within ourselves) ; but the true understanding and meaning thereof is, that although we hear God's word and believe it ; although we have faith, hope, charity, repentance, dread and fear of God within us, and do never so many good works thereunto ; yet we must renounce the merit of all said virtues, of faith, hope, charity, and all other virtues and good deeds which we either have done, shall do, or can do, as things that be far too weak and insufficient and imperfect to deserve remission of our sins and our justification ; and therefore we must trust only in God's mercy, and that sacrifice which our High Priest and Saviour Jesus Christ, the Son of God, once offered for us upon the cross, to obtain thereby God's grace and remission, as well of our original sin in baptism, as of all actual sin committed by us after our baptism, if we truly repent and turn unfeignedly to Him again.   So that as St. John the Baptist, although he was never so virtuous and godly a man, yet in this matter of forgiveness of sin, he did put the peo-

[1] First Part of the *Homily of Salvation.*

ple from him, and appointed them to Christ, saying thus unto them : *Behold the Lamb of God, which taketh away the sins of the world,* John i. ; even so, as great and godly a virtue as the lively faith is, yet it putteth us from itself, and remitteth or appointeth us unto Christ, for to have only by Him remission of our sins, or justification. So that our faith in Christ (as it were) saith unto us thus : It is not I that take away your sins, but it is Christ only ; and to Him only I send you for that purpose, forsaking therein all your good virtues, words, thoughts, and works, and only putting your trust in Christ." [1]

It is plain that the doctrine contained in these extracts (from a homily which has unusual authority, as being virtually assented to by every one who signs the Articles) is briefly as follows. That, which the English reformers meant by justification by faith, is, that we can never deserve anything at God's hands by our own works, — that therefore we must owe our salvation only to the free mercy of God, who, for the sake of His Son Jesus Christ, pardons and accepts all infants who are baptized in His name, and all persons who sin after baptism, when by His grace they are brought to repentance and conversion, — that justification is especially assigned to faith, not because of any peculiar excellence in faith itself, but rather because faith sends us from itself to Christ, and because by it we apprehend Christ and rest upon Him only for acceptance with God, — that, though therefore we ascribe justification to faith only, it is not meant that justifying faith either is or can be without its fruits, but that it is ever pregnant and adorned with love, and hope, and holiness.

Language in strict conformity with this was uniformly held by those who had the chief hand in drawing up the Articles and compiling the Liturgy, and is to be found in those semi-authoritative documents which were from time to time set forth by them.[2]

---

[1] Second Part of *Homily of Salvation.* Also concerning the difference between a dead and living faith, and the reconciliation of St. Paul and St. James, see Part 3. See also the conclusion of the 3d part of the *Homily on Prayer ;* the 2d part of the *Homily on Almsdeeds,* near the middle ; the conclusion of the second *Homily of the Passion,* and particularly the whole of the *Homilies of Faith and Good Works.*

[2] We may refer particularly to the following : Cranmer's *Catechism,* Oxf. pp. 98, 114, 115, 143, 205; Cranmer's *Works;* ed. Jenkyns, Oxf. ii. p. 121, iii. 553.

Justification is thus briefly explained in Edw. VI.'s Catechism : " As oft as we use to say that we are made righteous and saved by faith only, it is meant thereby, that faith or rather trust alone, doth lay hand upon, understand, and perceive our righteous making to be given us of God freely : that is to say, by no deserts of our own, but by the free grace of the Almighty Father. Moreover, faith doth engender in us the love of our neighbour, and such works as God is pleased withal. For if it be a true and lively faith, quickened by the Holy Ghost, she is the mother of all good saying and doing . . . . And although good works

Owing to the unhappy divisions of later times in the Church of England, there has been no small difference among her divines on this head of justification; a difference, however, which there is good reason to hope is rather apparent in scholastic and logical definitions, than in its bearing on vital truth or practical godliness.

The great Hooker wrote a treatise on Justification, in which he strongly impugns the doctrine of the Church of Rome concerning justification by infusion of righteousness, and maintains the principle of imputation, distinguishing the righteousness of justification as external to us, the righteousness of sanctification as internal.[1]

Bishop Bull in his *Harmonia Apostolica* admits that sense of justification by faith, which, he says, all the sounder Protestants have attached to it, namely, Salvation by grace only. He takes justification in the forensic sense, the meritorious cause of which is Christ, the instrument or formal cause being *fides formata*, or faith accompanied by good works.[2]

Dr. Barrow, in the first five of his Sermons on the Creed, discusses the nature of faith and justification with great learning and moderation. Justification he shows to be a forensic term, to be given for the sake of Christ, to be the result of God's mere mercy, apart from our deserts; yet he considers baptism and faith to be the conditions of justification, and faith to include its effects. Faith is a hearty reception of the Gospel, first exerting itself by open avowal in baptism, to which time therefore the act of justification especially pertains. Yet too every dispensation of pardon granted upon repentance may be also termed justification. Hence every

cannot deserve to make us righteous before God, yet do they so cleave unto faith, that neither can faith be found without them, nor good works be anywhere without faith." — (*Enchiridion Theolog.* i. p. 25.)

So Noel's Catechism : Ad Dei misericordiam confugiendum est qua gratis nos in Christo nullo nostro merito nec operum respectu, amore et benevolentia complectitur; tum peccata nobis nostra condonans, tum justitia Christi per Fidem in ipsum ita nos donans ut ob eam, perinde ac si nostra esset, ipsi accepti simus . . . . *M.* Non ergo inter hujus justitiæ causas Fidem principem locum tenere dicis, ut ejus merito nos ex nobis justi coram Deo habeamur ? *A.* Nequaquam : id enim esset Fidem in Christi locum substituere . . *M.* Verum an a bonis operibus ita separari hæc justitia potest, ut qui hanc habet, illis careat ? *A.* Nequaquam . . . . *M.* Justitiam ergo, Fidem, ac bona opera, natura coherentia esse dicis, quæ proinde non

magis distrahi debeant quam Christus illorum in nobis author a seipso divelli possit. — *Enchirid. Theolog.* i. p. 282.

Jewel's *Apology :* Itaque unicum receptum nostrum et perfugium esse ad misericordiam Patris nostri per Jesum Christum, ut certo animis nostris persuadeamus illum esse propitiationem pro peccatis nostris; ejus sanguine omnes labes nostras deletas esse . . . . Quamvis autem dicamus nihil nobis esse præsidii in operibus et factis nostris, et omnis salutis nostræ rationem constituamus in solo Christo, non tamen ea causa dicimus laxe et solute vivendum esse, quasi tingi tantum et credere, satis sit homini Christiano, et nihil ab eo aliud expectetur. Vera Fides viva est, nec potest esse otiosa. — *Enchirid. Theolog.* pp. 131, 132.

[1] *Discourse on Justification,* &c. *Works,* iii. pt. ii. p. 601. Oxf. 1836.

[2] Bull's *Harm. Apost.* and *Examen Censuræ.* *Works,* Oxf. iii. iv.

person is justified freely for Christ's sake at his baptism, continues justified whilst he is in a state of lively faith, and returns to a state of justification, if he have fallen from it, by repentance.[1]

Dr. Waterland, in a very able tract on the same subject, argues, that the causes of justification are (1) the moving cause, God's grace and goodness ; (2) the meritorious cause, Christ; (3) the efficient cause, the Holy Spirit — that its instruments are (1) baptism ; (2) faith — that its conditions are, (1) faith ; (2) obedience.[2]

Mr. Alexander Knox, a writer of great originality and piety, expressed himself unable to believe the protestant doctrine of justification. The forensic sense of the word seemed to him too like a legal fiction : and he could not believe that God could pronounce any one just, or account any one righteous, who had really no such inherent quality as justice or righteousness. Accordingly, he solved the difficulty by asserting that God pronounces those righteous by justification, whom He has already made so by sanctification.[3]

In still later days, Mr. Faber has written an able work to prove that in the earliest Christian writers, from Clement of Rome downwards, the word justification is used strictly in its forensic sense, and that justification is ascribed to faith alone.[4]

Lastly, not very long before his secession to the Church of Rome, Mr. Newman published a most logical treatise, in which he professes to steer a middle course between the Roman and the Lutheran doctrines. He takes the forensic sense of the term justification — and asserts, that it is conferred in baptism, is maintained by faith, and consists in the indwelling of the Spirit of God, and the being made members of the Body of Christ.[5]

Whatever speculative differences may have existed of late or in times gone by, it is no small comfort to know, that it has been allowed by all that fallen man cannot of himself become worthy of eternal salvation, that he stands in need both of pardoning mercy and sanctifying grace, that this mercy and this grace have been procured for him by the all-prevailing merits of the Redeemer, and that these blessings, offered to all, may be appropriated to the individual believer by that faith which the Holy Spirit will implant, and which must produce love and holiness and all good fruits. The

---

[1] *Works*, fol. Vol. ii. especially Sermons iv. v.

[2] Waterland, *On Justification, Works.* Van Mildert, ix. p. 427

[3] Knox's *Remains.*

[4] Faber's *Primitive Doctrine of Justification.*

[5] Newman, *On Justification ;* see especially Lect. iii. vi. ix.

divines of Trent and their most extreme antagonists have denied none of these propositions.

Section II. — SCRIPTURAL PROOF.

1. SENSE of the word *Justification.*

The word which we render *just* or *righteous* (namely, δίκαιος, or in the Hebrew צַדִּיק) has two principal significations: the one popular, the other accurate. In its popular signification, it is nearly equivalent to *good, holy, pious,* (ἀγαθός, εὐσεβής, חָסִיד) ; and is used commonly of men, who are living a pious and upright life, not according to the perfect standard of the law of God, but subject to such imperfection and impurity as is common to man. Examples of this usage may be found in the following, among many other passages: Gen. vi. 9. Ps. xxxvii. 12. Prov. iv. 18; xxiv. 16. Matt. i. 19; x. 41; xxiii. 29. Mark vi. 20. Luke ii. 25. Acts x. 22. James v. 16. In its more accurate sense, δίκαιος signifies absolutely, strictly, and perfectly righteous or just, without defect or impurity, like the holy Angels, or like God Himself. As for instance, in Job ix. 2. Matt. xxvii. 19. Luke xxiii. 47. Rom. ii. 13; iii. 10. 1 Tim. i. 9. In which, as in most similar passages, the word particularly seems to express *innocent, not guilty,* with reference to a tribunal of justice, or question of crime. The same distinction is equally observable in the substantive *righteousness* (צֶדֶק δικαιοσύνη) ; which at one time stands for strict and perfect justice, (as in Acts xvii. 31. Rom. iii. 5. Rev. xix. 11, &c.) ; at other times for such goodness, holiness, or good deeds, as men under the grace of God are capable of (as in Ps. xv. 2. Isai. xxxii. 17. Matt. v. 10, 20; vi. 33. Acts xiii. 10. Rom. vi. 18, 19, 20; viii. 10; xiv. 17. Eph. v. 9; vi. 14. Heb. xii. 11).

The verb δικαιόω, which strictly corresponds with the Hebrew causative verb הִצְדִּיק, and is translated in English " *to justify,*" in some degree partakes of the ambiguity of the adjective, from which it is formed ; yet, not so as, fairly considered, to introduce much difficulty into the doctrine of which we have to treat.

1. The literal signification of the verb, whether in Hebrew or in Greek, is "to make righteous." It may therefore, of course, be used for something like an infusion of righteousness into the mind

or character of a man ; and the passive may signify the possession
of that righteousness so infused ; and such a sense appears probably to belong to it in Rev. xxii. 11, " He that is righteous, let him
be righteous still " (ὁ δίκαιος δικαιωθήτω, in some MSS. from a gloss
δικαιοσύνην ποιησάτω.") [1]

2. But a very slight examination of the question can scarcely
fail to convince us, that the commoner use of this verb in the
Scriptures is in the sense of a judicial sentence ; and

(1) It signifies to execute a judicial act, in the general,
towards a person, and to do him right, whether in acquitting or
in condemning him. Thus in 2 Sam. xv. 4 : " Oh! that I were
made a judge in the land, that every man which hath any suit or
cause might come unto me, (וְהִצְדַּקְתִּיו καὶ δικαιώσω αὐτὸν) and I
would *justify* him," that is, do him right.

So Ps. lxxxii. 3 : " Defend the poor and the fatherless, *justify*
(הַצְדִּיקוּ δικαιώσατε) the poor and needy," *i. e.* do them right.

(2) Especially it signifies to pronounce sentence in a man's
favour, acquit him, free him from punishment. Deut. xxv. 1 :
" The judges .... shall justify the righteous, and condemn the
wicked."

1 Kings viii. 32. 2 Chron. vi. 23 : " Then hear Thou in Heaven,
and do, and judge Thy servants, condemning the wicked, to bring
his way upon his head ; and justifying the righteous, to give him
according to his righteousness."

Prov. xvii. 15 : " He that justifieth the wicked, and he that
condemneth the just, even they both are abomination unto the
Lord." So Exod. xxiii. 7. Psalm li. 4.

And so in the new Testament, Matt. xii. 37 : " By thy words
thou shalt be justified, and by thy words thou shalt be condemned "
(*i. e.* in the day of Judgment: see ver. 36).

(3) In consequence of this sense of the word *to justify*, it is
sometimes used in general for to *approve* or *esteem* a person *just*.
So Matt. xi. 19, " Wisdom is justified of her children." In Luke x.
29 ; xvi. 15, we read of people who "justified themselves." Luke
xviii. 14, " The publican went home *justified*," (*i. e.* approved
either by God or his own conscience,) " rather than the Pharisee."
Luke vii. 29, " All the people justified God," (*i. e.* declared their
approbation of God's dealings in the mission of John,) " being baptized with John's baptism."

---

[1] The following passages have also been   Job xxxv. 7, 8.   Ezek. xvi. 52.   Ecclus
thought to have the word in this sense,   xviii. 22 ; xxxi. 5.
but perhaps without sufficient ground:

39

(4) So again, *to justify* is used for *to free from burdens* or *obligations*, such as the obligations which a particular law imposes on us, as Rom. vi. 7, " He that is dead is freed from sin " (literally is "justified," δεδικαίωται).

It appears, then, that in passages where the word " to justify " occurs with no particular reference to the doctrine of this Article, it is almost always used in a sense more or less connected with the ideas of acquittal, pardon, acceptance, or approbation : *i. e.* in a forensic or judicial sense. It remains to see, whether this is the sense in which St. Paul uses it, when directly and especially treating on justification by faith. Now this will appear, if we consider and compare the following passages. In Rom. v. 9, we read, " Being *justified by His Blood*, we shall be saved from wrath through Him." With this compare Eph. i. 7, " in whom we have redemption through His Blood, *the forgiveness of sins.*" Again, if we compare Rom. iii. 24, 25, 26, we cannot fail to conclude that *justification* is a synonym for *remission of sins.* " Being justified freely by His grace, through the redemption which is in Christ Jesus ; whom God hath set forth to be a propitiation through faith in His blood, to declare His righteousness *for the remission of sins* that are past, through the forbearance of God ; to declare, I say, His righteousness, that He might be just, and the justifier of him that believeth in Jesus."

Then the word *justify* is used as equivalent to *count or impute righteousness* and to *cover sin.* This appears plainly from Rom. iv. 5, 6, 7.

Again, by comparing Rom. v. 9 with Rom. v. 10, it seems that to *justify* is synonymous with to *reconcile with God ;* for πολλῷ μᾶλλον δικαιωθέντες, " much more being justified," in the one verse, answers to πολλῷ μᾶλλον καταλλαγέντες, " much more being reconciled," in the other.

Once more, *justification* is directly opposed to *condemnation*, as in Rom. v. 18, " By the offence of one (judgment came) upon all men to *condemnation*, even so by the righteousness of One (the free gift came) upon all men unto *justification* of life." [1] Again, in

---

[1] It has been argued, (Bellarm. *De Justif.* l. 2, c. 3.) that as Adam's sin was *infused* into his posterity, so this passage must mean that in justification Christ's righteousness is *infused* into His disciples. To which it has been replied, (Barrow, II. Sermon v. p. 80.) that justification and condemnation being " both acts of God, and it being plain that God condemning doth not infuse any inherent unrighteousness into man, neither doth He justifying (formally) (if the antithesis must be pat) put any inherent righteousness into him : inherent unrighteousness in the former case may be a consequent of that condemnation, and inherent righteousness may be connected with this justification ; but neither *that* nor *this*

Rom. viii. 33, 34, " Who shall lay anything to the charge of God's elect ?   It is God that *justifieth*.   Who is he that *condemneth* ? " [1]

But which is more important than the comparison of particular passages, if we consider the whole course of St. Paul's reasoning in the earlier chapters of the Romans, we must be led to conclude that by justification he means acquittal from guilt and acceptance with God.   He begins by proving that all men, Jews and Gentiles, are *condemned* by the law (whether of Moses or of nature) under which they lived (Rom. i. ii.)   He shows from the Law itself that the Jews as well as the Gentiles were guilty before God (Rom. iii. 9–19) ; and that therefore all the world (if the Gospel be not taken into account) are lying under God's wrath and subject to His condemnation.   And this course of reasoning leads him to the conclusion, that if we would have *justification* at all it must be not by the works of law, but by the faith of Christ (Rom. iii. 20).   Now in such a connection, what must justification mean ?   Man subject to the law (whether revealed or natural) had so much sinned as to be subject to *condemnation*.   The thing to be desired was his *justification ;* which justification could be only by the free grace of God through Christ.   Surely then that *justification* must mean pardon for the sins which he had committed, and deliverance from the condemnation into which his sins had thrown him.

This is further shown immediately afterwards by the case and the language of saints of the old Testament.   Abraham was justified (or as it is explained, " accounted righteous ") by faith, not by his own good works and deservings.   And David looks on a state of blessedness as one in which a man has " his iniquities forgiven, and his sins covered " (Rom. iv. 1–8).   The thing then which all the world needed, and which could be obtained only through God's mercy in Christ, was covering of sin, and forgiveness of iniquity. This therefore must be what St. Paul means by the term *Justification.*

II. Sense of the word *Faith.*

Having arrived at a conclusion as to the sense of the words *jus-*

---

may formally signify those qualities respectively : as the inherent unrighteousness consequent upon Adam's sin is not included in God's condemning, so neither is the inherent righteousness proceeding from our Saviour's obedience contained in God's justifying men."

[1] The antithesis is not in the least degree altered, if the punctuation and trans-lation of this passage, which is more probably correct, be adopted.   Τίς ἐγκα-λέσει κατὰ ἐκλεκτῶν Θεοῦ ; Θεὸς ὁ δικαιῶν ; τίς ὁ κατακρίνων ; Χριστὸς ὁ ἀποθανὼν, κ. τ. λ. : " Who shall lay anything to the charge of God's elect ?   Shall God who justifieth ?   Who is he that condemneth ? Is it Christ, who died, &c. ? "

tify and *justification*, it becomes necessary, in order to appreciate
the meaning of the words *Justification by faith*, and the doctrine
expressed by those words, to examine the usages of the term *faith*
in Scripture, and especially in the writings of St. Paul.

According to its derivation the word should mean persuasion of
the truth of anything. But this does not decide its force as a theological virtue, still less its signification in the peculiar language of
St. Paul. There can be little doubt that it is used in very different senses in different parts of Scripture.

For example : —

1. It is used to signify truth or good faith (like אֱמֶת, *fides*) in
Matt. xxiii. 23, " the weightier matters of the Law, judgment,
mercy, and *faith ;* " and in Rom. iii. 3 : " Shall their unbelief make
the *faith* (or faithfulness) of God without effect ? "

2. It is used of the assurance given by one person to another,
Acts xvii. 31, " whereof He hath given *assurance* unto all men "
(πίστιν παράσχων πᾶσι).

3. It is used as a term to designate the Christian Religion, " the
faith " or " the faith of Christ." So Acts vi. 7, " were obedient to
the faith." Acts xiii. 8, " seeking to turn away the deputy from
the faith." Rom. i. 5, " for obedience to the faith among all nations," εἰς ὑπακοὴν πίστεως ἐν πᾶσι τοῖς ἔθνεσι (*i. e.* to convert all nations to the Christian Religion). So xvi. 26. Comp. Eph. iii. 17;
iv. 5. Phil. i. 25. 1 Tim. iv. 1. Tit. i. 1, 4. James ii. 1.
Jude, 3, 20. Rev. ii. 13 ; xiv. 12. In this sense St. Paul appears
especially to use it in his Epistle to the Galatians ; where perhaps
we may consider, that in his constant antithesis of Law and Faith,
he is contrasting the Law of Moses, or the Religion of the Jews,
with the Faith of Christ, or the Religion of the Gospel. Some of
the more obvious usages of the word in this sense in the Epistle to
the Galatians are in the following: Gal. i. 23, " now preacheth the
faith which once he destroyed," iii. 23, " Before faith came (πρὸ τοῦ
δὲ ἐλθεῖν τὴν πίστιν), we were kept under the Law, shut up unto the
faith which should afterwards be revealed " (εἰς τὴν μέλλουσαν ἀποκα-
λυφθῆναι πίστιν). The same sense is apparent in the whole context
(vv. 24, 25, 26) ; where it is taught us, that both Jews and Gentiles become children of God by the faith (*i. e.* by embracing the
religion or Gospel) of Jesus Christ, having put on Christ by being
baptized into Him.

Accordingly, Gal. vi. 10, we read of Christians as being οἰκεῖοι
τῆς πίστεως, servants of the Gospel, domestics of the Christian faith.[1]

---

[1] So אֱמֶר, is used for "true religion," Ps. lxxxvi. 11.

4. There are passages in the Epistles in which it seems plain that faith is spoken of as separable from its results, as an assent to Christian truth without the heart being duly moved by it, and so the life corresponding with it. That is to say, faith is used in that sense which the schoolmen called *fides informis*.

Thus St. Peter (2 Pet. i. 5) bids men " *add* to their faith virtue" and all other Christian graces, as though faith might be considered as apart from other graces. St. Paul (1 Cor. xiii. 2) speaks of a faith strong enough to move mountains, and yet capable of being conceived of as without charity, and so of no value ; and in the same chapter (ver. 13) speaks of faith, hope, charity, as three distinct graces, two of which shall pass away, and one, namely, charity, shall abide ; and declares this charity to be the greatest of the three. Especially St. James (ii. 14–26) considers the case of faith without works, and declares such a faith unable to justify.

5. Yet, on the other hand, since it is the nature of faith to open the eye of the mind to things spiritual, and to bring home to it the view of Heaven, and hell, of God's justice and mercy, of man's liability to judgment, and Christ's Atonement and Mediation ; therefore it is most commonly spoken of as an operative and active principle, " purifying the heart" (Acts xv. 9), and " working by love " (Gal. v. 6). Accordingly, in Heb. xi. St. Paul attributes to the energy of faith all the holiness and heroism of the saints and martyrs in times of old.

6. Especially, as the principal subjects of God's revelations are His promises, therefore faith came to mean πεποίθησις, *fiducia*, reliance on the truth of God's promises, or trust in His mercy and grace.

Of such a nature was that faith which gave men strength to benefit by the miraculous powers of Christ and His Apostles, Matt. ix. 2, 22 : " Thy faith hath made thee whole." Acts xiv. 9, St. Paul perceived that the cripple at Lystra " had faith to be healed." See also, Matt. viii. 16 ; ix. 29; xvii. 20 ; xxi. 21. Mark ii. 5; iv. 40 ; v. 34 ; x. 52 ; xi. 22. Luke v. 20 ; vii. 9 ; viii. 25, 48 ; xvii. 5, 6 ; xviii. 42. Acts iii. 16. Jam. v. 15.

So St. James speaks of " praying in faith, nothing wavering " (James i. 6), that is, praying in a spirit of trust in God and reliance on His promises. St. Peter (1 Pet. v. 9) tells us to resist the devil " stedfast in the faith," *i. e.* steadily relying on the help of God. Of such a nature seems to be " the shield of faith " (Eph. vi. 16), which can " quench the fiery darts of the wicked one." So we read of " faith and patience," of " the patience and faith of the saints,"

(Rev. ii. 19; xiii. 10), evidently signifying their resignation and *trust* in God under trials and afflictions. So perhaps we may say that in the above-cited eleventh of Hebrews, faith is represented as a full conviction that what God had promised He was able and willing to perform; hence a trust or reliance on God's truth and promises, by which men overcame earthly temptations and difficulties, despised the world, and fought a good fight. See especially vv. 10, 11, 13, 14, 16, 19, 26, 27.

Thus much of *faith* generally. The question next arises, In what sense does St. Paul use the word when he speaks of faith as justifying? Is justifying faith a bare historical assent? Is it but a synonym for the religion of Christ? Is it trust and confidence in God? Is it to be considered, as full of its fruits and lively in its operation, or apart from all such, or at least prior to them?

Let us examine those passages of Scripture, whether St. Paul's or not, in which it is certain or probable that faith and justification are considered together, and see what attributes are assigned to the faith so spoken of.

Justifying faith then is: —

1. The work and gift of God.

Matt. xvi. 17. John vi. 29, 44, 45. Phil. i. 29.

2. The character of the regenerate.

Compare Gal. v. 6, with Gal. vi. 15; whence it will appear that regeneration and justifying faith are used convertibly.

3. The sign of regeneration.

1 John v. 1: " Whosoever believeth that Jesus is the Christ is born of God," his faith being the proof of his regeneration.

4. It is seated in the heart, not merely in the understanding.

Rom. x. 10: " With the heart man believeth unto righteousness."

5. Is not dead.

See James ii. 14–26; which proves clearly that, if faith is dead and so without works, it does not profit.

6. But, on the contrary, is a full conviction of the truth of God's promises and reliance on them.

See Heb. xi. 19, where Abraham's faith, when he offered up Isaac, is described as an "accounting that God was able to raise him up even from the dead;" which is the very example adduced by St. Paul, when he is specially treating on the subject of justifying faith (Rom. iv. 18–20), and by St. James, when he is rectifying errors on the same important subject (James ii. 23, &c.)

7. It worketh by love.

Gal. v. 6; where we read that that which " *availeth* " (*i. e.* justifieth) " in Christ Jesus," is " faith which worketh by love."

8. Accordingly it sanctifies.

Acts xxvi. 18 : " That they may receive forgiveness of sins, and
inheritance among them which are *sanctified by faith that is in Me.*"

9. It purifies the heart.

Acts xv. 9: " Purifying their hearts by faith."

10. It overcomes the world.

1 John v. 4 : " This is the victory that overcometh the world,
even our faith."

Compare Hebrews xi., throughout the whole of which we have
a description of faith as that which overcomes the world.   And
with this again compare (as before) Rom. iv. ; where the same
kind of reasoning is used, and the same example adduced concerning *justifying* faith, as in Heb. xi. concerning faith *in the general.*

11. It is evidently connected with its results, and by a kind of
synecdoche considered as containing them,[1] or pregnant with them.

This will plainly appear, if we examine the three passages in
which Abraham's faith is said to have been imputed to him for
righteousness, *i. e.* to have been justifying.

Those three passages are Gen. xv. 6. Rom. iv. James ii. 21–23,
to which may be added Heb. xi. 8–10.

In Gen. xv. we read of God's promise to Abraham, that he
should have a son in his old age, whose seed should be as the stars
of heaven for multitude.   And unlikely as this was, and against
all natural probability, Abraham " believed in the Lord ; and He
counted it to him for righteousness," ver. 6.

In Rom. iv. St. Paul quotes this instance of Abraham's faith, and
illustrates it thus (ver. 18–22) : " Who against hope believed in
hope, that he might become the father of many nations ; according
to that which was spoken, So shall thy seed be.   And being not
weak in faith, he considered not his own body now dead, when he
was about an hundred years old, neither yet the deadness of
Sarah's womb ; he staggered not at the promise of God through
unbelief; but was strong in faith, giving glory to God, and being
fully persuaded that what He had promised He was able also to
perform.   And therefore it was imputed to him for righteousness."

Now St. James (ii. 21–23) reasons on the subject thus : " Was
not Abiaham our father justified by works when he had offered
Isaac his son upon the altar ?   Seest thou how faith wrought with
his works, and by works was faith made perfect ?   And the Scrip-

---

[1] See Barrow.

ture was fulfilled which saith, Abraham believed God, and it was
imputed unto him for righteousness; and he was called the friend
of God."

And similar effects of his faith St. Paul himself speaks of, Heb.
xi. 8 : " By faith, Abraham, when he was called to go out into a
place which he should after receive for an inheritance, *obeyed;* and
he went out, not knowing whither he went."

See also verses 9–12.

From all which passages it is sufficiently apparent, that when
the Scriptures speak of the *faith* of Abraham, which *justified* him,
they understand by it a faith of such nature that a man is persuaded by it to disregard all earthly considerations, and to resign
himself, contrary to all his worldly interests, to obedient conformity
with the will of God.

12. As it was seen of faith in general, that it had special reference to the promises and mercies of God, so it will be found that
justifying faith has special reference to the Person, sufferings, and
mediation of the Lord Jesus Christ, and to God's promises in Him.
For example, John iii. 14, 15 : " As Moses lifted up the serpent in
the wilderness, even so must the Son of Man be lifted up ; that
whosoever believeth in Him should not perish, but have eternal
life." John vi. 40: " This is the will of Him that sent Me,
that every one which seeth the Son, and believeth on Him, may
have everlasting life." Ver. 47 : " Verily, verily, I say unto you,
he that believeth on Me hath everlasting life." Acts x. 43 :
" Through His Name whosoever believeth in Him shall receive
remission of sins." xvi. 31 : " Believe on the Lord Jesus Christ,
and thou shalt be saved, and thy house." Rom. iii. 25, 26 : " Whom
God hath set forth to be a propitiation through faith in His blood,
to declare His righteousness for the remission of sins that are past,
through the forbearance of God ; to declare, I say, at this time, His
righteousness, that He might be just, and the justifier of Him which
believeth in Jesus." x. 9 : " If thou shalt confess with thy mouth
the Lord Jesus, and shalt believe in thine heart that God hath
raised Him from the dead, thou shalt be saved." See also John i.
12; iii. 16, 18, 36 ; v. 24 ; vi. 29, 35 ; xi. 25, 26 ; xvi. 27 ; xvii.
25. Acts xiii. 38, 39; xx. 21. Rom. iii. 22 ; iv. 5, 24 ; x. 4.
Philem. 5. 1 John iii. 23 ; v. 1.

So much indeed is this the character of faith, (at least of that
active faith which, as we have seen, is the faith which justifies,)
that by it Christ is said to dwell in the heart. Ephes. iii. 17 :
" That Christ may dwell in your hearts by faith." And so it not

only has reference to the work of Christ for us, but it is both the proof of Christ's dwelling in us, and the instrument whereby He dwells in us.

III. General View of *Justification* in Scripture.

Having premised thus much concerning the meaning attached to the term Justification, and to the grace of justifying faith, by the inspired writers in the new Testament, we may now perhaps proceed to state more fully and formally the doctrine of Scripture concerning justification, or pardon and acceptance with God.

In the general, then, we may state concerning the justification of man, that

1. The moving cause is God's mercy.

2. The *meritorious* cause is Christ's Atonement.

But we know, that, notwithstanding the infinite mercy of God, and the fulness and all-sufficiency of the sacrifice of Christ, yet all men do not benefit by this grace. Therefore we learn that there is need of something internal to connect with the external work of our salvation; Christ in the heart connecting with Christ on the cross; the work of the Spirit to be united to the work of the Redeemer. Hence

3. The immediate efficient cause is the Holy Spirit, who moves the heart by His influences, leads to Christ, regenerates and renews.

4. The first instrument by which God conveys pardon, under ordinary circumstances, is Baptism. Hence this is the first instrument of justification. This will appear from the following.

Even John's baptism (*a fortiori* Christ's) was a "baptism of repentance for the remission of sins," *i. e.* for justification. Mark i. 4. Luke iii. 3. When our Lord instituted His baptism, it was with the promise that all who so far believed the preaching of the Apostles as to embrace the faith of Christ and be baptized into it, " should be saved," Mark xvi. 16. When the Apostles were asked by their converts what they should do, they replied, " Repent, and be baptized every one of you in the name of Jesus Christ for the *remission of sins*," Acts ii. 37, 38. After St. Paul's conversion to the faith, Ananias called on him to " arise and be baptized, and wash away his sins," Acts xxii. 16.

The Apostle couples being "*washed*" with " sanctified and justified," 1 Cor. vi. 11 ; speaks of the Church as " cleansed with the washing of water," Eph. v. 26 ; and places the " washing of regeneration " as a synonym or parallel with the " being justified,"

40

Tit. iii. 5, 7.   See likewise Rom. vi. 4, 7.   Col. ii. 12, 14.   1 Pet. iii. 21, &c.

Baptism is that which places us in a state of covenant with God, and hence, in St. Paul's words, is that in which " we put on Christ," and are esteemed " the children of God by the faith in Christ," Gal. iii. 26, 27.   Hence a person receiving baptism is put in a position to receive from God the gifts which He has covenanted to give to us in His Son ; and the first of those gifts is acceptance into His favour and remission of our sins, that is, justification.

5. The state of heart in which a man must be, who is accepted or justified, is a state of faith, Rom. x. 10.   Eph. iii. 17.   Accordingly, when justification is considered subjectively, or as connected with the state of the Christian's heart, the instrument is said to be faith.   Faith, therefore, may be considered either as the *instrument*, or as the *state* of justification.

6. When a man is said by St. James to be justified *by works ;* it is not because his works procure him acceptance meritoriously, but because they are the sign, and fruit, and necessary results of that sanctification by the Spirit which unites him to the Atonement of Christ, and are the necessary and inseparable concomitants — or, in fact, parts — of his faith, as much as light is part of the sun, or fruit is part of the tree which bears it.

Such may be fairly considered as a general view of the doctrine of justification as commonly taught in Scripture.   But in order to a full investigation of this question, it is necessary to understand the peculiar signification attached by St. Paul to what may be considered his favorite formula, namely : —

IV. Justification by faith.

Now it is quite clear that St. Paul's great object in the Epistle to the Romans was to put down all *claims* on the part of man to reward, for services done by him to God.   Accordingly, in the first three chapters he shows all men, whether Jews or Gentiles, to be *sinners*, and so *deserving*, not justification or acquittal, but condemnation.   His conclusion is, that if we are saved, it must be by the merits of Christ or by free grace only ; without any *claims* on our part on the score of desert.   This truth he expresses under the formula of " Justification by faith."

Hence we conclude, that, in the language of St. Paul, " justification by faith," and " free salvation by grace," are (as it has been seen that Melancthon, the Confession of Augsburg, and our own Article and Homilies, teach) correlative or convertible expressions. The former means the latter.

That this is the case will appear more plainly, if we read connectedly but a very few of the passages in which St. Paul especially propounds his doctrine of justification, *e. g.* Rom. iii. 23, 24, 28 : " All have sinned and come short of the glory of God ; being *justified freely by His grace,* through the redemption that is in Christ Jesus, whom, &c. . . . therefore we conclude, that a man is *justified by faith* without the deeds of the law."

Eph. ii. 8 : " By grace are ye saved through faith," &c.

Tit. iii. 4, 5, 7 : " After that the kindness and love of God our Saviour toward man appeared, not by works of righteousness which we have done, but according to His mercy He saved us . . . that being justified by His grace, we should be made heirs according to the hope of eternal life."

So Rom. iv. 25; v. 1, 9, 16, 20, 21, compared together, clearly show the same thing. " Who was delivered for our offences, and was raised again for our justification. Therefore, being justified by faith, we have peace with God," Rom. iv. 25 ; v. 1. " Much more then, being now justified by His Blood, we shall be saved from wrath through Him," v. 9. " The judgment was by one to condemnation ; but the free gift is of many offences unto justification," ver. 16. " Where sin abounded, grace did much more abound : that as sin hath reigned unto death, even so might grace reign through righteousness unto eternal life by Jesus Christ," vv. 20, 21.

But although we may readily come to the conclusion that justification by faith is little more than a synonymous expression for justification or salvation by free grace ; yet we can scarcely doubt, that there is something in the nature of faith which especially qualifies it to be put in a formula to denote *grace* in opposition to *claims.*

Now this would be the case, if *faith* in the argument of the Epistle to the Romans meant nothing more than " the Christian Religion ; " which it sometimes appears to mean, especially in the Epistle to the Galatians. For, as the religion of Christ is that by embracing which we embrace God's offers and promises of pardon, it might naturally be put to represent those promises and that grace by which pardon is given. But we can hardly conclude that this is the signification of justifying faith in the Epistle to the Romans ; because St. Paul especially adduces the case of Abraham, as a subject of justifying faith (Rom. iv. 1, &c.). But Abraham could no more have been considered as justified by the Gospel or the religion of Christ, than any other person under the old dispensation; and could not have been spoken of, as living under the Gospel, in opposition to such as lived under the Law.

It should appear, therefore, that it is not Christ's religion, considered as a whole, which is meant by the Apostle when he speaks of *justifying faith;* but that it is that special religious grace which is called faith, and the qualities of which we have lately investigated. Accordingly we must search for something in the nature of faith itself, or of its objects, which renders it fit to be put in the formula of St. Paul, as the representative of grace, and as opposed to self-justifying claims.

1. First then, faith is a state of heart in which a man is, and is not an enumeration of so many works or good deeds, which a man has done, and for which he may be supposed to claim reward. It therefore fitly and naturally represents a state of grace, in contradistinction to a state of claim, or self-justification. It is that state in which a man is who is regenerate, and so in union with Christ. Yet at the same time, as in the case of the penitent thief upon the cross, it may exist even before it can have brought forth external good works, and therefore obviously cannot recommend us to God on the score of meritorious services, which we have rendered to Him. It is therefore the symbol of acceptance by free mercy, apart from human claims.

2. Next, its character is to rely on the power and promises of God, and not on the strength or works of man. For the eye of faith, seeing Him who is invisible, contrasts His power with its own weakness. Hence it becomes nearly identified with trust (*fiducia*). Such emphatically was the character of Abraham's faith, so specially referred to by the Apostle, which led him to leave his country and sacrifice his son, because " he counted Him faithful who had promised." Hence faith becomes a fit symbol for renunciation of claims and deserts, and trust in God's mercy and pardoning grace.

3. Faith is, perhaps even more than other graces, clearly and obviously the gift of God. We know that we cannot force or contro. our own belief, and therefore feel that we require the eyes of our understanding to be enlightened by inspiration from above. Therefore again faith is less likely than other graces to be made a ground for boasting.

4. Lastly, although this may not be its exclusive object, yet its peculiar and principal object is Christ, and His Atonement and Mediation. Hence, according to Luther, faith is " full of Christ." Hence, according to a greater than Luther, " Christ dwells in our

hearts by faith." Hence faith, leading to Christ and looking to Christ, is, by a natural transition, spoken of in Scripture as if it were invested with attributes which are really above it, and as though it effected that of which it is but the instrument, and whose cause and Author is God in Christ.

To the belief indeed, that justifying faith, as spoken of by St. Paul, means merely a reliance on the Atonement, the often-adduced instance of Abraham seems at first sight opposed. For Abraham, whom St. Paul brings forward as the type of justifying faith, is not spoken of as having full confidence in the pardoning grace of Christ; but his faith, in the instance alluded to (Gen. xv. 5, 6), had reference to God's promise, that his seed should be as numerous as the stars of Heaven. It was *this* faith that was counted to him for righteousness; and, though it may be argued that there was in this promise of God concerning his offspring virtually contained a promise of the Messiah ; yet it can hardly be said, that Abraham's belief that God would multiply his seed, meant a belief that he should himself be saved by the merits of Christ, and that, on this account, it was justifying faith.

We must then probably infer that some of the general charac-ters of faith above referred to, rendered Abraham acceptable to God ; and that so his faith was counted for righteousness. And this consideration certainly causes some little difficulty in our appre-ciation of the doctrine laid down by St. Paul. Still, if we examine the whole of his reasoning in the first five chapters of the Epistle to the Romans, we shall find that the great object on which he speaks of the Christian's faith as fixed is the work of Christ, and God's acceptance of us in Him. Even where he adduces the example of Abraham, and insists that Abraham was justified, not by his own merits, but by his faith ; he concludes, that, in like manner, faith shall be imputed to us for righteousness, " if we believe in Him that raised up Jesus our Lord from the dead, who was delivered for our offences, and raised again for our justification " (Rom. iv. 24, 25). And the following chapter is all devoted to considering the reparation which the righteousness of ,Christ has made for the ruin which Adam's sin had produced.

It appears, therefore, that the faith of Abraham must have been alleged, rather as illustrative of, than as identical with, the faith of the Christian. It was of the same kind with the Christian's faith, .n so far as all faith has the same general characters, and has therefore a similar acceptableness with God. But the peculiar faith of the Christian is that by which he apprehends Christ. As the High-priest laid his hand upon the head of the scapegoat, and by confessing, conveyed the sins of the congregation to the scapegoat, that they might be taken away, so the believer lays his hand on the Head of the Great Sacrifice. He believes in the Redeemer of the world, and in God's love through Him. His soul rests upon his Saviour. His faith therefore is a bond of union with the incarnate Godhead; and so becomes the instrumental cause of justification in us; the meritorious cause of which is all in Christ.

And on this ground most especially it seems, that the Apostle, when labouring to show that human merit and human efforts must fail to bring us to God, and to render us acceptable to Him, produces, and insists so strongly on his peculiar statement of "Justification by faith." [1]

V. Certain questions on the Doctrine of Justification.

1. Is justification an act or a state?

Some persons have decided that it is an act, taking place at a particular moment, never to be repeated. Others, that it is a state, which continues or is lost, as the case may be.

If it be the former, it must be limited either (1) to baptism, when, as has been shown, there is promise of remission of sins; or (2) to the moment which may be considered as the turning-point from a life of sin to a life of repentance, faith, and holiness, — a moment known only to God; or (3) to the day of Judgment, when the wicked shall be condemned, and the pious shall be absolved or justified. Either or all of these may be considered as the moment of transition from condemnation to justification, or pardon and acceptance.

But Scripture seems rather to represent justification, as a *state* of acceptance before God. It is quite certain, that some persons are represented as in favour, grace, or acceptance with God, that is justified; others as under His wrath, and liable to condemnation. The prophet Ezekiel (xxxiii. vv. 12–19) contrasts the condition

---

[1] This is excellently expressed in the following passage from Cardinal Toletus (in cap. iii. ad Roman. annot. 17) quoted by Bp. Forbes, *Considerationes Modestæ de Justificatione*, Lib. I. c. III. § 17 : —

Quia nempe in fide magis manifestatur, hominem non propria virtute, sed Christi merito justificari : sicut enim in aspectu in serpentem Deus posuit sanitatem in deserto, quia aspectus magis indicabat, sanari virtute serpentis, non operis alicujus proprii aut medicinæ alicujus ; ita fides ostendit, justificari peccatores vir-tute et merito Christi, in quam credentes salvi fiunt, non propria ipsorum virtute et merito. Ea causa est cur fidei tribuitur (justificatio) maxime a S. Paulo qui a justificatione legis opera et humanum meritum aut efficaciam excludere, et in sola Christi virtute et merito collocare nitebatur : idcirco meminit fidei in Christum. Hoc nec pœnitentia nec dilectio nec spes habent. Fides enim immediatius ac distinctius in Eum fertur, cujus virtute justificamur.

of the righteous and the wicked, showing the one to be a condition of acceptance, the other of condemnation : the former continuing so long as the character continues the same, and lost as soon as that character is lost ; the latter in like manner continuing, until the wickedness is forsaken and the life renewed, and then giving place to the former, the condition of favour or pardon.   In like manner our Lord (John xv. 1–10) speaks of His disciples as clean through His word, and continuing so whilst they abide in Him ; but if they abide not in Him, then to be cast forth as a branch, withered, and even burned (see especially vv. 3–6).   Language just similar to this is used by St. Paul (see Rom. vi. 1, 2, 19 ; xi. 20, 21. Gal. v. 4. Col. i. 22, 23. Heb. x. 38, 39).   From all which we can hardly fail to conclude that justification before God is a *state* in which a person continues so long as he continues united to Christ, abiding in Him, having Christ dwelling in his heart, being the subject of His grace, and of the sanctification of the Spirit.

If therefore the premises are correct, we may define justification to be a state of pardon and acceptance in the presence of God, bestowed upon us freely for Christ's sake, by the mercy of God, which is first given in baptism to all who receive that sacrament aright, which continues so long as the subject continues in a state of faith, which fails when he falls from the state of faith, and which is restored again when by grace and repentance he is restored to a state of faith.   So that we may say, whilst in a state of faith, so long in a state of justification : whilst a believer, so long a justified person.   Hence too, concerning the distinction drawn by Luther, that faith is *alone* when it justifies, and that after justification is effected, then come in charity, and good works, and holiness, we may infer that such a distinction can be true only when considered in the abstract, but not as a matter of practical experience.   For practically and really, where there is acceptance, there is faith and sanctification, and, springing from them and reigning with them, are all the graces of a Christian's life.

2. It having been laid down, that faith (*fœta operibus*) may be considered, either as the *state* or the *instrument* of justification, it may be a question, whether we ought to say that faith, or faith and good works, or faith and holiness, are the *condition* or *conditions* of justification.

The answer to this question, as given by many divines of high authority in the Church, has been in the affirmative.   But the question is, whether or not we can deduce an affirmative answer from the Scripture.   No doubt, faith and holiness are, as regards

justification, graces *sine quibus non.* There is no justification nor
salvation where there is not faith, love, holiness, obedience. But
when we state that faith and good works are *conditions*, we in effect
suppose the Almighty to offer us what have been called the *Terms
of the Gospel;* terms that is of the following kind : " Now that
by Christ's mediation God's wrath has been appeased, if you will
repent, believe, and obey, you shall be saved." Conditions imply
a bargain of this kind. Now there may be no objection to looking
on the matter in some such light as this ; but it does not appear to
be the form in which the Scriptures represent God's dealings with
us. The new Testament seems to speak of us as pensioners on
the bounty of God's grace. Especially when justification by faith
is spoken of, " it is *of faith*, that it might be *by grace*," Rom. iv. 16.
And though it is true that it would be an act of immeasurable
grace for God to pardon our past sins, on condition that, by His
help, we avoided sin and lived holily for the future, yet this does
not appear to be the statement anywhere made by the Apostles ;
nor does such an act of grace come up to the standard of that
infinite mercy of God in Christ Jesus, which is revealed to us in
the Gospel. It has already been shown that one peculiar reason
why justification by faith represents free salvation by grace is,
that faith is itself most clearly " the gift of God." Therefore it is
spoken of as the instrument of our justification, not because it is
a *condition*, which we can make with Him, but because it is itself
a gift which He bestows on us.

Besides, if we could make conditions with God, even after He
had accepted an atonement for the past, it might be hard to say
that " boasting " was altogether " excluded " (Rom. iii. 27). Excluded indeed it might be in strict justice, because the forgiving of
past sins, and the accepting of imperfect obedience for the future,
would be, of itself, an act of boundless grace, when we deserve nothing but condemnation. But still, comparing ourselves with ourselves,
we might easily be inclined to feel proud of even imperfect obedience, if it were made the condition of our salvation. Therefore,
we may perhaps fairly conclude, that salvation is not of works, not
merely not as the cause, but not even as the terms or conditions of
our justification. Nor is faith itself the condition on which God
accepts us, although it is the instrument by which He justifies us,
and the state in which we are when justified.

3. Whereas it is taught by St. Paul that a man is justified by
faith, and yet it is taught both by St. Paul and throughout
the new Testament that we shall be judged according to **our**

works, [1] are we driven to conclude that there is an inconsistency in the statements of Scripture ?

The answer to this is, that as all persons who are justified are regenerate and in a state of faith, their faith and regeneration will necessarily be to them the source of holiness and good works. Now the clearest tokens both to men and angels of their internal condition of faith and sanctification must be their good works; nay, the clearest proof even to themselves. Hence, that they should be judged by their works, and rewarded according to their works, is thoroughly consistent with God's dispensations. The meritorious cause indeed of their salvation is Christ's Atonement; the instrument by which they are brought into covenant with God is baptism; the means whereby their state of acceptance is maintained is faith; but the criterion by which their final state will be determined shall be works. And all these are so knit up together in the redeemed, regenerate, believing, sanctified Christian, that it is nowise derogating from the excellence of the one to ascribe its proper office, in the economy of salvation, to the other.

4. The ordinary instruments of justification being baptism and faith, can a person be justified where either of these is wanting ?

That persons can be justified without faith where faith is impossible, may appear from the case of infants. Though they are too young for active faith, yet clearly are they not so for salvation, nor therefore for justification. Our Lord bids us bring little children to Him, and says that " of such is the Kingdom of Heaven " (Mark x. 14). And St. Paul says, the children of believing parents are holy (1 Cor. vii. 14). And if infant baptism be a custom for which we have sufficient authority, then, as baptism is for the remission of sins, it follows that infants in baptism may receive remission of sins or justification, though not yet capable of faith. Similar reasoning is applicable to the case of idiots, or persons otherwise irresponsible, who, like infants, are incapable of active faith, but of whom we may reasonably hope that they are not incapable of salvation. As regards baptism, that, as a general rule, it is the ordinance of God, without which we cannot look for the promises of God, is quite apparent from passages already referred to, such as Mark xvi. 16. Acts xxii. 16. Gal. iii. 26, 27, &c. In these and similar passages remission of sins is promised to such as believe the Gospel, and submit to baptism. Yet, as we have seen

---

[1] See, for instance, Matt. xvi. 27; Rom. ii. 6; 1 Cor. iii. 8; 2 Cor. v. 10; 1 Peter i. 17; Rev. ii. 23, xx. 13, xxii. 12.

concerning faith, that though generally necessary, yet cases may and do exist where it is impossible, and so not required, in like manner we may reasonably conclude that cases may exist in which baptism may be dispensed with. Though Christ has appointed baptism, and we have no right to look for His blessing if we neglect it, yet we cannot presume to limit His mercy even by His own ordinances. Indeed, we find in the Acts of the Apostles (x. 4, 44) a case, the case of Cornelius, in which God accepted and poured His Holy Spirit on a person who had not been baptized; and though St. Peter thought it necessary that baptism should be at once administered to him, and thereby taught us the deep value of that Sacrament, still this case sufficiently shows that God does at times work without the intervention of means appointed by Himself, and therefore teaches us that we must not exclude from salvation those who, from ignorance or inability, have not received the blessing of baptism.

5. Is the language of St. James opposed to the doctrine of St. Paul?

It has been already seen that St. Paul means by Justification by faith, free salvation by God's grace; and that, where he speaks of faith as the instrument of justification, he means a lively faith, productive of good works. (See especially Rom. vi.) St. James probably wrote against such as abused the doctrine of St. Paul, and taught that a speculative barren faith, or mere orthodoxy, was sufficient for salvation without the fruits of faith. Accordingly, he asks, " Can this faith save him?" He says, " Faith, if it have not works, is dead, being alone." [1] But it must be observed that St. Paul never speaks of a dead faith as profiting. On the contrary, he declares that faith without charity would be nothing (1 Cor. xiii. 2). It is plain, therefore, that St. Paul considers faith as pregnant with its results, though not as justifying because of its results, and does not design to put in opposition to one another faith and the

---

[1] James ii. 14, 17.

Many people have endeavoured to reconcile St. Paul and St. James, by supposing that the former speaks of justification before God, the latter of justification in the sight of men. But it is quite clear that St. James speaks of the same kind of justification as St. Paul, from James ii. 14, 23. In the former verse he speaks of faith without works as not capable of *saving* a man; *i. e.* of course, of justifying him before God, for justification before man can never *save.* And in the latter verse, he adduces the case of Abra-

ham, as of one who had a faith which brought forth works, and says, it was this kind of faith which was imputed to him for righteousness, *i. e.* clearly before God. Evidently the two apostles differ in their use of the word "faith," not in their use of the word "justify." Both speak of justification before God: but one says that we are justified by faith, *i. e.* by a *living* faith; the other denies that we are justified by mere faith, *i. e.* (according to his own explanation) by a *dead* faith.

good works which naturally spring out of a lively faith, but rather faith and legal works, — " the works of the Law," — works done in a self-justifying spirit, and looked on as meriting reward.   Faith, therefore, he declares, justifies without such works, — the works of the Law ; but he does not say that a faith which does not bring forth the works of faith, will justify.   On the other hand, St. James asserts that faith will not justify, if it do not bring forth good works ; but by good works he means evangelical works, the works of faith, not legal works, the works of the Law.   Hence, there is no necessary contradiction in the language of the two Apostles. St. James simply considers justifying faith as *including* the works of *faith*.   St. Paul considers justifying faith as *excluding* the works of the *Law*.[1]

[1] Sine operibus fidei, non legis, mortua est fides. — Hieron. in Gal. iii.   Ille dicit de operibus quæ fidem præcedunt, iste de iis quæ fidem sequuntur. — Augustin. *Liber de Diversis Quæstionibus.*   Quæst. 76, Tom. vi. p. 68.

[On the dispute with regard to *fides informis* and *fides formata* (see p. 291), the following remark deserves attention :   " There is probably some truth on each side.   We are justified by a faith which is at least potentially a *fides formata ;* although the *office* of justifying belongs not to the works of faith but to faith itself."   *England* vs. *Rome* (H. B. Swete), p. 35, note. — *J. W.*]

ARTICLE XII.

——◆——

Of Good Works.

ALBEIT that good works, which are the fruits of faith, and follow after justification, cannot put away our sins, and endure the severity of God's judgment; yet are they pleasing and acceptable to God in Christ, and do spring out necessarily of a true and lively faith; insomuch that by them a lively faith may be as evidently known, as a tree discerned by the fruit.

De Bonis Operibus.

BONA opera, quæ sunt fructus fidei, et justificatos sequuntur, quanquam peccata expiare, et divini judicii severitatem ferre non possunt : Deo tamen grata sunt, et accepta in Christo, atque ex vera et viva fide necessario profluunt, ut planè ex illis, æque fides viva cognosci possit, atque arbor ex fructu judicari.

SECTION I.— HISTORY.

THE great length at which the last Article was considered renders it less necessary to say much upon this. Our present twelfth Article did not exist in the forty-two Articles of King Edward's reign, but was added in the year 1562, after the accession of Queen Elizabeth. It .is evidently intended as a kind of supplement to the eleventh, lest that should be supposed to teach Solifidianism. Archbishop Laurence traces the wording of it to a passage in the Wirtemburg Confession, to which it certainly bears great resemblance.[1]

The general object of the Article was, no doubt, to oppose the Antinomian errors, which had originated with Agricola, and which there was some danger might spring from Lutheranism.[2] With such the whole Reformation was charged by the divines of the Roman communion, and therefore it was the more needful that the reformers should protest against them.

There are certain particular expressions also in the Article which require to be explained historically. We have seen that the schoolmen talked of good works, done without the grace of God,

---

[1] The passage is :—
De Bonis Operibus.
Non est autem sentiendum, quod in bonis operibus, quæ per nos facimus, in judicio Dei, ubi agitur de expiatione peccatorum, et placatione divinæ iræ, ac merito æternæ salutis, confidendum sit.

Omnia enim bona opera, quæ nos facimus, sunt imperfecta, nec possunt severitatem divini judicii ferre. — Laurence, *B. L.* Notes on Serm. II. p. 235.

[2] Mosh. *Ch. Hist.* Cent. XVI. § III. pt. II. as quoted in the last Article.

meriting grace *de congruo.* " To this Luther and the reformers opposed the statement that works done without the grace of God might be apparently, but were not really good. And to this purpose is the thirteenth Article of our Church, which we have soon to consider. Luther asserted that good works, which are pleasing to God, are not wrought but in faith ; for " whatever is not of faith is sin ; " and where there is faith, there is justification ; therefore good works follow, not precede justification. Our Article uses this language without in this place discussing the merits of it. In the thirteenth Article the question is more fully entered on. It may be mentioned that language very similar had before been used by Augustine, and from him very probably was it borrowed by Luther. " Good works," says that father, " follow a man's justification, do not precede it in order that he may be justified." [1]

Another expression in the Articles is, that " good works cannot put away our sins and endure the severity of God's judgment." In the historical account of the last Article we saw that the Council of Trent condemned Luther for denying intrinsic goodness to works done after grace, and asserted that, as they were wrought by the Spirit of God, they were essentially good and perfect. The Council also taught that to the justified God's commandments are possible, that justification is preserved and increased by good works, that the good works of the just, which are the gifts of God, are withal the merits of the justified.[2]

We have seen also that Bellarmine and the Romanist divines assert, that good works which are wrought in us by the grace of God are, by virtue of that grace, meritorious of eternal life ; [3] *i. e.* according to the schoolmen, they merit reward *de condigno.* The words of our Article are evidently opposed to these opinions. For, though they speak plainly of the necessity and value of works wrought by grace, they declare that " they cannot put away our sins, and endure the severity of God's judgment."

SECTION II. — SCRIPTURAL PROOF.

WE may perceive, from what has been said, that the Article opposes three doctrines.

---

[1] Sequuntur opera bona justificatum, non præcedunt justificandum. — *De Fide et Operibus,* c. 14.
[2] Session vi. Canons 18, 24, 32.

[3] Bellarmine, *De Justificatione,* Lib. **v.** cap. 12, quoted in the History of Art.

XI

I. Merit *de congruo;* — II. Merit *de condigno;* — III. Antinomianism.

Or otherwise the Article teaches : —

I. That good works follow after justification ;

II. That though they spring from the grace of God and a lively faith, still they cannot put away sin and endure the severity of God's judgment.

III. Yet (1) that in Christ they are pleasing to God : and (2) That they spring out necessarily of a true and lively, *i. e.* a justifying faith, insomuch that by them a lively faith may be as evidently known as a tree is discerned by its fruit.

I. The question of merit *de congruo* and works before justification being the special subject of the next Article, we may defer its consideration till we consider that Article.

II. That the good works of justified men are not perfect enough to put away sin, and endure the severity of God's judgment, may be proved as follows.

Our Lord tells us, that after we have done all that is commanded us " we are still unprofitable servants, having done only that which was our duty to do " (Luke xvii. 10). But, if this be the case, how can we ever do anything to put away our former sins ? Our best deeds leave us still unprofitable ; and if we had never sinned, we should still have only done our duty, and could claim no reward. But when we have sinned, it is clear that no degree of subsequent obedience (which would have been due even if we had not sinned) can cancel the sins which are past. And to this we must add that, even under grace, obedience is never perfect. " In many things we offend all," says St. James (iii. 2) ; and St. John tells us that " if we say that we have no sin, we deceive ourselves" (1 John i. 8). And both the Apostles are evidently speaking to and of regenerate Christians. The Psalmist prays God not to " enter into judgment with him, because in His sight *no man living* could be justified " (Psalm cxliii. 2). Accordingly, St. Paul argues that the person who is blessed in God's sight is not the man who lives blameless in the Law, but " he whose iniquities are forgiven and whose sins are covered," even " the man to whom the Lord will not impute sin " (Rom. iv. 7, 8). " All have sinned and come short of the glory of God ; " and therefore must be "justified freely by His grace, through the redemption which is in Christ Jesus " (Rom. iii. 23, 24). Such passages fully prove that, in whatever strength or power

good works are wrought, they are not perfect enough to put away
sin, and to endure the judgment of God.

Still, though the Church denies the *merit* of good works, and
their sufficiency to screen us from the wrath and endure the judgment of God, she yet teaches,

III. 1. That in Christ, they are pleasing and acceptable to God;
and 2, that they do necessarily spring out of a true and lively faith.

1. In Christ they are pleasing and acceptable to God.

(1). The words *in Christ* are introduced to remind us that whatever is good in us must spring from the grace of Christ, and whatever in us is acceptable to God is acceptable for Christ's sake.   In
all the servants of Christ, God sees the image of His Son.   In all
the members of Christ, God sees the Spirit of His Son descending
from the Head to the Members, like the holy oil on Aaron's head,
which flowed down to the skirts of his clothing.   In all the branches
of the heavenly Vine, God sees the fruit thereof, as put forth by
virtue of the life and nourishment derived from the Vine itself;
and that Vine is Christ.   In every wedding-guest who has on the
wedding-garment, the King sees the wearer clothed in the robe of
His own Son, and acknowledges them all as His children : " for we
are all the children of God by faith in Christ Jesus : for as many
as have been baptized into Christ have put on Christ " (Gal. iii. 26,
27).   Accordingly, the Scriptures constantly, when they speak of
Christians and the works of Christians as pleasing to God, teach us
that it is " in Christ."   So we read, " There is now no condemnation to them that are in Christ Jesus " (Rom. viii. 1).   " In Christ
Jesus neither circumcision availeth anything, nor uncircumcision ;
but faith which worketh by love " (Gal. v. 6).   " We are His
workmanship, created in Christ Jesus unto good works " (Ephes.
ii. 10).   We are to " do all in the name of the Lord Jesus " (Col.
iii. 17).   We are to " offer spiritual sacrifices, acceptable to God
by Jesus Christ " (1 Pet. ii. 5).   We are to " give thanks always
for all things unto God and the Father in the name of our Lord
Jesus Christ " (Eph. v. 20).   " By Him we are to offer the sacrifices of praise to God " (Heb. xiii. 15).

(2) But then the good deeds which Christians perform in Christ
are *pleasing and acceptable to God*.

Our Lord tells us, that " not every one that saith unto Him,
Lord, Lord, shall enter into the kingdom of Heaven ; but he that
doeth the will of His Father which is in Heaven " (Matt. vii. 21).
He assures us of the reward of those who have left all for His sake,

that they shall receive a hundredfold, and eternal life (Mark x. 29, 30). He tells us, that, " if we forgive, we shall be forgiven; that if we give, it shall be given to us" (Mark xi. 26 ; Luke vi. 37, 38). He shows us by parables, that those who of two talents make five, shall receive five cities; those who make of five talents ten, shall receive ten cities (Matt. xxv. 14–30. Compare Luke xix. 12–26). He tells us that at the judgment-day they who have fed the hungry, clothed the naked, and visited the afflicted, shall be placed on the right hand, and go into life eternal (Matt. xxv. 31–46). He tells us of " a prophet's reward," and " a right-eous man's reward " (Matt. x. 41, 42). And, in short, assures us that He will " reward every man according to his works" (Matt. xvi. 27).

So, from His Apostles we learn, that " in every nation he that feareth Him and worketh righteousness, is accepted with Him " (Acts x. 35): that the sacrifice of our bodies is " acceptable to God " (Rom. xii. 1): that the labour of Christ's servants " shall not be in vain in the Lord" (1 Cor. xv. 58): that " God loveth a cheerful giver" (2 Cor. ix. 7): that, if we are not " weary in well-doing, in due season we shall reap, if we faint not " (Gal. vi. 9): that our new creation in Christ Jesus is " unto good works, which God hath beforehand ordained that we should walk in them " (Eph. ii. 10): that the new man " after God is created in right-eousness and true holiness" (Eph. iv. 24): that our call is " not to uncleanness, but to holiness" (1 Thess. iv. 7): that " every one who nameth the name of Christ must depart from iniquity" (2 Tim. ii. 19); must " be careful to maintain good works" (Tit. iii. 8): that " without holiness no man shall see the Lord" (Heb. xii. 14): that with " such sacrifices " for His service " God is well pleased ". (Heb. xiii. 16): that " pure religion and undefiled before God and the Father is this, to visit the fatherless and widows in their affliction, and to keep himself unspotted from the world" (Jas. i. 27): that faith with-out works will not profit (Jas. ii. 14): that " to do well and suffer for it, and take it patiently, is acceptable to God " (1 Pet. ii. 20): that whatsoever we ask of God we receive, if " we keep His commandments, and do those things which are pleasing in His sight: " and that " he that keepeth His commandments dwelleth in Him, and He in him" (1 John iii. 22, 24. Compare Rom. vi. *passim*, Rom. viii. 1–14, and the concluding chapters of all St. Paul's Epistles).

Thus we plainly see that good works wrought in Christ are not

only useful and desirable, but are absolutely necessary for every
Christian, and are pleasing and acceptable to God. " We do not
take away the *reward*, because we deny the *merit* of good works.
We know that in the keeping of God's commandments there is
great reward (Ps. xix. 11) ; and that unto him that soweth righteousness there shall be a *sure reward* (Prov. xi. 18). But the
question is, whence he that soweth in this manner must expect to
reap so great and so sure a harvest ; whether from God's justice,
which he must do, if he stand upon merit, or from His mercy, as a
recompense freely bestowed out of God's gracious bounty, and not
in justice due for the worth of the work performed. Which question, we think the prophet Hosea hath sufficiently resolved, when
he biddeth us *sow to ourselves in righteousness, and reap in* MERCY
(Hos. x. 12). Neither do we hereby any whit detract from the
truth of that axiom, that *God will give every man according to his
works ;* for still the question remaineth the very same, whether
God may not judge a man according to his works, when He sitteth
upon the throne of grace, as well as when He sitteth upon the
throne of justice ? And we think here, that the Prophet David
hath fully cleared the case in that one sentence, Psalm lxii. 12,
' *With thee, O Lord, is* MERCY ; for thou rewardest every one according to his work.'

" Originally therefore, and in itself, we hold that this reward
proceedeth merely from God's free bounty and mercy ; but accidentally, in regard that God hath tied Himself by His word and
promise to confer such a reward, we grant that it now proveth in
a sort to be an act of justice ; even as in *forgiving of our sins*, which
in itself all men know to be an act of mercy, He is said to be *faithful and just* (1 John i. 9), namely, in regard of the faithful performance of His promise." [1]

To conclude, then, the Scriptures prove, and the Church teaches,
that, not upon the ground of merit, but yet according to God's will
and appointment, good works, wrought in Christ, are necessary for
every Christian, are pleasing and acceptable to God, and will in
the end receive " great recompense of reward," even that " crown
of righteousness, which the Lord, the righteous Judge, will give in
that day" (2 Tim. iv. 8).

2. That good works " do spring out necessarily of a true and
living faith," is a proposition which may be considered to have
been incidentally but fully proved in treating on the eleventh
Article. It may therefore here be sufficient to refer but briefly

---

[1] Usher, *Answer to a Jesuit*, ch. XII.

to a few of the passages of Scripture in which this is most plainly set forth.

The sixth chapter of Romans throughout is an explanation entered into by the Apostle, to show that this doctrine of justification does not supersede the necessity of good works; inasmuch as justified persons walk in newness of life, are made free from sin, and become servants of righteousness. The eleventh chapter of Hebrews is an enumeration of signal works of holiness, which were produced through the energizing power of the faith by which the saints of old lived and acted. St. James, in his famous chapter (ii. vv. 14–26), explains at length, that if faith be living, it will necessarily bring forth works, and that if there be no works, the faith is dead. We read of being "sanctified by faith" in Christ (Acts xxvi. 18). God is said to "purify the heart by faith" (Acts xv. 9). Faith is said to be "the victory which overcometh the world" (1 John v. 4). The faith which "availeth in Christ Jesus," is called "faith which worketh by love" (Gal. v. 6).

Perhaps the strongest proof of this proposition is, that in all those writings of St. Paul (especially his Epistles to the Romans and the Galatians) where he peculiarly treats of faith, he passes directly from faith to speak of holiness, counselling Christians, as the consequence of his doctrine concerning faith, to bring forth good works. This we may observe in the latter chapters of both these Epistles, and indeed of all his Epistles. The eleventh chapter of Hebrews indeed, which professes to explain to us what faith is, does so almost entirely by giving a list of the works which have sprung from it; just as one who wished to describe the excellence of a fruit-tree would dwell chiefly on the beauty and goodness of its fruit.

We may be assured, therefore, that we cannot assign too high a place to good works, so long as we do not assign to them the power of *meriting* salvation. They spring from faith, and they feed faith; for the more faith is called into action, the brighter and the stronger it grows. And as in the bodily economy of man, good health gives birth to good spirits, and yet again, good spirits support and invigorate health; so it is in his spiritual life. Faith gives rise to holiness, and holiness gives energy to faith.

ARTICLE XIII.

| *Of Works before Justification.* | *De Operibus ante Justificationem.* |

WORKS done before the Grace of Christ, and the inspiration of His Spirit, are not pleasant to God, forasmuch as they spring not of faith in Jesus Christ; neither do they make men meet to receive grace, or (as the school-authors say) deserve grace of congruity; yea, rather, for that they are not done as God hath willed and commanded them to be done, we doubt not but they have the nature of sin.

OPERA quæ fiunt ante gratiam Christi et Spiritus ejus afflatum, cum ex fide Jesu Christi non prodeant, minime Deo grata sunt; neque gratiam, ut multi vocant, de congruo merentur; immo cum non sint facta, ut Deus illa fieri voluit et præcepit, peccati rationem habere non dubitamus.

SECTION I. — HISTORY.

THIS Article is intimately connected with the four preceding Articles, and is intended, probably, to prevent any mistakes, and more fully to explain some points in them.

In the former Articles an account has been given of most of the errors against which this Article is directed; and the very wording of it shows that the scholastic doctrine of congruous merit is especially aimed at. Here, however, it may be proper to remark that the question has arisen concerning the nature of heathen virtue, a question of great difficulty, on which the fathers touched, both before and after the Pelagian controversy. Clement of Alexandria particularly speculated much upon the mode in which God's grace and the teaching of Christ visited men before the coming of the Gospel. " His notion was, that philosophy was given to the Gentiles by God, for the same purpose for which the Law was given to the Jews: in order to prepare them for justification under the Gospel by faith in Christ." " It is certain, however, that Clement did not believe that heathen virtue possessed of itself any efficacy towards justification. For he says, that every action of the heathen is sinful, since it is not sufficient that an action is right; its object or aim must also be right." [1]

---

[1] Bishop Kaye, on the Writings of Clement of Alexandria, p. 426. See also pp. 122, *seq.*

Indeed, these opinions of Clement do not seem to interfere at
all with the doctrine of this Article ; for Clement evidently considered that God mysteriously worked in the Gentiles by His grace,
using, as an external means, the imperfect instrument of their own
philosophy.   So that whatever good, he thought, might have
existed in heathens, he still ascribed to God's grace, and therefore
did not consider their goodness " as works done before the grace
of Christ." [1]

We have already seen, how the Pelagians and Semi-pelagians [2]
denied the necessity of preventing grace ; and held that, in the first
instance, God only called men by His word and ordinances, and
that by their own strength such as were called might turn to God,
and seek His assistance.

In controversy, they appear to have referred to the case of
virtuous heathens, many of whom might put to shame the lives of
Christians.   To Julianus, who advances this argument, Augustine
replies at great length.   Augustine's position was, that " what was
not of faith was sin."   Julianus supposes the case of a heathen,
who covers the naked and does works of mercy ; and asks, " If a
Gentile have clothed the naked, is this act of his therefore sin,
because it is not of faith ? " [3]   Augustine replies that it is ; " not
because the simple act of covering the naked is sin, but because
none but the impious would deny, that not to glory in the Lord, on
account of such a work, was sin." [4]   He then goes on to argue,
that a bad tree cannot bring forth really good fruit, that an unbelieving tree is a bad tree, and that apparently good works are not
always really so, as the clemency of Saul in sparing Agag was sin.
So he, who does unbelievingly, whatever he does, does ill ; and he
who does ill, sins.[5]   The good works which an unbeliever does are
the works of Him, who turns evil to good.   But without faith we
cannot please God.[6]   If the eye be evil, the whole body is dark ;
whence we may learn, that he who does not do good works with
the good intention of a good faith (that is, of a faith which worketh
by love), his whole body is full of darkness.   And since the good
works, or apparent good works, of unbelievers cannot bring them
to Heaven, we ought to hold, that true goodness can never be

---

[1] See Bishop Kaye, as above, p. 122,
&c.

[2] See History of Art. IX. and X.

[3] Si gentilis, inquis, nudum operuerit,
numquid quia non est ex fide, peccatum
est ?

[4] Prorsus in quantum non est ex fide,
peccatum est.   Non quia per se ipsum

factum est, quod est nudum operire, peccatum est ; sed de tali opere non in Domino gloriari, solus impius negat esse
peccatum. — *Cont. Julianum*, Lib. IV. c.
30.

[5] Cap. 31.

[6] Cap. 32.

given but by the grace of God through Christ, so as to bring a man to the kingdom of God.[1]

This was the kind of reasoning, which the fathers of that day used against the Pelagian arguments, that truly good deeds might be done without the grace of God.[2]

The doctrine of the schoolmen concerning grace of congruity bore a suspicious resemblance to that of Semi-pelagians. In the history of the ninth, tenth, and eleventh Articles enough has been said on this subject ; and of the zeal with which Luther maintained the absolute necessity of preventing grace, in order that man should make any efforts, or take any steps towards godliness.[3]

The case of Cornelius (Acts x.) was an argument often made use of in favour of grace of congruity. He, it was said, was a Gentile, and therefore not under the influence of God's grace ; and yet it was told him, " Thy prayers and thine alms are come up for a memorial before God " (ver. 4). Hence it was argued, that he did what was acceptable to God, though without the grace of God.

Luther treats Cornelius as a man who had faith in a promised Mediator, although he did not yet know that that Mediator was come ; and so, he argues, that his good deeds were of faith, and therefore acceptable.[4]

At the Council of Trent the general opinion was strongly against Luther on these points. Catarinus indeed maintained, with great learning, that " man, without the special help of God, can do no work which may be truly good, though morally, but sinneth still." In confirmation of which, he quoted Augustine, Ambrose, Prosper, Anselm, and others. He was violently opposed by the Franciscans, but supported by the Dominicans.[5]

In the end, the seventh canon of the sixth session of the council condemned those who said, " That works done before justification are sins, and that a man sinneth the more, by how much the more he laboureth to dispose himself to grace." [6] Which canon does not

---

[1] Aut certe quoniam saltem concedis opera infidelium, quæ tibi eorum videntur bona, non tamen eos ad salutem sempiternam regnumque perducere : scito nos illud bonum hominum dicere, illam voluntatem bonam, illud opus bonum, sine Dei gratia quæ datur per unum Mediatorem Dei et hominum nemini posse conferri ; per quod solum homo potest ad æternum Dei donum regnumque perduci. Cap. 33. See also Augustine, De Fide et Operibus, where, in opposition to the Pelagian opinion that good works must be *added* to faith, he contends that good works *spring* from faith.

[2] The reader may see many passages from Jerome, Prosper, and others, to the same effect, in Usher's *Answer to a Jesuit*, ch. xi.

[3] See especially Luther on Gal. ii. 16.

[4] Luther on Gal. iii. 2.

[5] Sarpi, pp. 183–185.

[6] Session vi. Can. 7, and Sarpi, p. 210.

exactly contradict the words of our Article, except it be in the last sentence of it.

The Lutheran Confessions of faith speak very reasonably on this subject. The twentieth article of the Confession of Augsburg states a principal reason for maintaining justification by faith to be, that we might not think to deserve grace by our own good works antecedent to grace.[1]

Our own reformers seem to have been influenced by a very similar view. The Homilies say, that " without faith can no good work be done, accepted and pleasant to God." " Without faith all that is done of us is but dead before God; although the work seem never so gay and glorious before man."[2]

Again, " As the good fruit is not the cause that the tree is good, but the tree must first be good before it can bring forth good fruit; so the good deeds of man are not the cause which maketh man good, but he is first made good by the Spirit and grace of God, that effectually worketh in him, and afterwards he bringeth forth good fruits."[3]

" They are greatly deceived that preach repentance without Christ, and teach the simple and ignorant that it consisteth only in the works of men. They may indeed speak many things of good works, and of amendment of life and manners : but without Christ they be all vain and unprofitable. They that think that they have done much of themselves towards repentance, are so much the farther from God, because they do seek those things in their own works and merits, which ought only to be sought in our Saviour Jesus Christ, and in the merits of His death and passion and bloodshedding."[4]

Section II. — SCRIPTURAL PROOF.

THE subjects embraced by the Article are, —

I. That works before grace and the inspiration of the Spirit are not pleasing to God, forasmuch as they are not of faith.

II. They do not make men meet to receive grace de congruo.

[1] Sylloge, pp, 130, 131.
[2] First part of Homily on Good Works.
[3] Second part of the Homily on Alms-deeds.
[4] First part of the Homily of Repent-ance.

III. Rather, as not being done as God hath willed, it is believed that they have the nature of sin.

Of these three positions, the second must follow from the proof of the first. For if good works without grace are not pleasing to God, they cannot predispose to grace. As regards the *title* of the Article, " Of Works before Justification," we may observe, that it was probably adopted because the question discussed in the Article itself went, at the time of the Reformation and the Council of Trent, under that name.[1] All questions concerning merit *de congruo*, and works done before grace, were considered as embraced in the general term, " the question concerning works before justification." The Article itself says nothing about *justification*. All that it determines is, that, in order for works to be acceptable to God, they must be done by the grace of God, and must spring from a principle of faith.

Against the whole tenor of the Article, and in favour of all which it condemns, the principal arguments from Scripture are such as these. Certain passages of Scripture seem to speak highly of particular individuals, who were not Christians or true believers, e. g. Naaman the Syrian, and Cornelius the centurion. They had not the faith of Christ, and yet their good deeds are approved. It may, however, be replied, that both of them evidently acted from a principle of faith. Naaman went to the prophet and sought relief, because he believed that, as a prophet, he had power to heal him. Again, Cornelius, though not a Jew, was evidently a believer in the One true God, a *proselyte of the gate*, if not a *proselyte of righteousness ;* and therefore we cannot say that he had no faith, nor that he was without the grace of God.

The same may be said of the Ninevites. Their repentance, it is argued, was accepted by God ; and yet they were heathens, and therefore not true believers. But it is certain that their repentance sprang from their faith in Jonah's preaching, and may very probably have been produced by that Holy Spirit who at all times has striven with men : and hence it was not of the nature of simple, naked, unassisted efforts to do good.

[1] Luther had used this language, that a man was justified first, and then did good works : and so " works before justification," became a common expression. Our Church in the xiith Article speaks of good works as " following after justification." We are not, of course, bound to consider that every act of a man, who is not in a state of full sanctification, is therefore devoid of goodness and of the nature of sin. This article sufficiently explains both its own meaning and the meaning of the phrase, " follow after justification," in the xiith Article, namely, that no works are good which do not come of grace.

A stronger argument against the doctrine of this Article seems derivable from the language of St. Paul, Rom. ii. 14, 26, 27. There he speaks of the Gentiles or heathens, " which have not a law," and yet " do by nature the things contained in the Law," and so " are a law unto themselves." And he says, that " if the uncircumcision keep the righteousness of the Law, shall not his uncircumcision be counted for circumcision ? And shall not uncircumcision which is by nature, if it fulfil the Law, judge thee, who by the letter and circumcision dost transgress the Law ? " Here the apostle seems to speak as if the heathen, who had not the revealed knowledge of God's will, yet might so do His will as to be acceptable with Him.

In like manner, many learned men, of the Reformed Communions, as well as of the Roman, understand St. Paul's reasoning in Gal. iv. to be like what was shown in the last Section to have been the opinion of Clement of Alexandria; namely, that before the Gospel both Jews and Gentiles were kept by God in a state of bondage or tutelage, waiting for the liberty of the children of God ; that to the heathen their condition was one of elementary servitude, preparatory to the Gospel, as was that of the Jews. If the first seven verses of this chapter be compared carefully with the eighth and ninth, there will appear some ground for such an interpretation. From these passages it is argued, that heathens, who could not have faith, and were not subjects of grace, were yet capable in their degree of pleasing God.

To this reasoning we may reply, that nothing can be more obscure than the question as to God's dealings with, and purposes concerning the heathen world. Revelation is addressed to those whom it concerns, and tells us very little of the state of those to whom it is not addressed. Our business is to follow Christ, and not to ask " Lord, and what shall this man do ? " There is a marked purpose in Scripture not to satisfy man's idle curiosity. The question therefore, at times so much debated, whether it be possible or impossible that the benefits of Christ's redemption should reach to those millions of human beings who never have heard and never could hear of Him, is left in deep obscurity ; and when people have reasoned on the subject, their arguments have mostly been inferences deduced from other doctrines, and not express statements of Scripture.

This much, however, we may fairly conclude, that if the passages just referred to prove that the heathen can do what is pleasing to God, and be accepted by Him, it is because His Holy Spirit can plead with them, even through the imperfect means of natural religion. St. Paul says, it was God's will that men " should seek the Lord, if haply they might feel after Him " (Acts xvii. 27). And he is there speaking of the world in its times of heathen darkness. It is possible that there may have been an imperfect faith, even " in times of ignorance which God winked at." We know not, but that they who touched but the hem of Christ's garment, may have found virtue go out of it.

But with regard to the teaching of our Article, we may fairly conclude that it rather refers to the case of persons within, not without the sound of the Gospel. This is the practical question. It does not concern us practically to know how it may be with the heathen ; although, of course, their case affects the general question. And the case of the heathen is so obscure, that we can hardly be justified in bringing it to throw light on a case which concerns ourselves and our own state before God.

But it may be farther said that God approves of justice, and temperance, and charity, in themselves, and of themselves ; and therefore if a man who has neither faith nor grace, acts justly, and does mercy, and lives soberly, God must approve and be pleased with such acts, just as he would disapprove and hate the contrary. But, in reply, it is urged, that God sees the heart, and loves what is good in us, only when it springs from a good source. Indeed, there are some sinners much greater sinners than others, whom He will visit with " greater damnation." But though in themselves He loves justice and mercy, He does not love and accept the man who does them, unless that man does them from right motives ; and as " every good and perfect gift is from above," we infer that good motives cannot come but from Him, " who worketh in us to will as well as to do according to His good pleasure." The man " dead in trespasses and sins," must have life given him from above, before he can walk in newness of life, and do what is well pleasing in God's sight.

Having thus considered the principal objections, we may now proceed to prove our propositions.

I. And first : " Works done before the grace of Christ, and the inspiration of His Spirit, are not pleasing to God, forasmuch as they spring not of faith."

The language concerning the new birth may come in here. John iii. 3 : " Except a man be born again, he cannot see the kingdom of God : " the language of our Lord to His disciples, John xv.

43

5, " Without Me ye can do nothing : " and the language of St. Paul
concerning the state of the unregenerate and carnal mind, " In me,
that is in my flesh, dwelleth no good thing," Rom. vii. 18. " The
carnal mind is not subject to the law of God, neither indeed can be.
So then they that are in the flesh cannot please God," Rom. viii. 7,
8. All these and many similar passages were considered at length
under Article IX.; and they surely prove that the natural man,
without the aid of God, cannot bring forth fruits which are pleasing
to God. As our Lord says expressly, " Abide in Me, and I in
you. As the branch cannot bear fruit of itself except it abide in
the vine ; no more can ye, except ye abide in Me," John xv. 4.[1]

But, moreover, as it is taught us that the source of all true holiness is faith, so if our good works do not spring from faith, they cannot be pleasing to God. Thus, " without faith it is impossible to
please God," Heb. xi. 6. " The just shall live by faith," Rom. i. 17.
Nay ! we are even told that " whatsoever is not of faith is sin,"
Rom. xiv. 23 : and that evidently, because apparently good works, if
not springing from a good source, are not really good.

Hence the statement of our Article seems fully borne out, that
" works done before the grace of Christ and the inspiration of His
Spirit, are not pleasant to God, forasmuch as they spring not of
faith."

II. The second proposition follows from the first: namely, that
works done without grace do not make men meet to receive grace
de congruo.

If they are not acceptable to God, it is manifest that they cannot
procure grace from Him. It is true, that " the Law of the Lord is
an undefiled law, converting the soul;" and that he who strives
earnestly to fulfil God's commandments may always expect to have
his exertions assisted by fuller supplies of the grace of God.[2] But
this is because God loves to reward His grace in us by farther gifts
of that grace — because all those earnest strivings are in themselves
proofs of the Spirit of God working in us. Good works are in no
degree to be underrated ; and the more a man does of them, the
more he is likely to gain strength to do more.

This is the regular course of growth in grace. Even naturally,
good habits are acquired by performing good actions: and spiritually, those that use the grace of God find it increasing in them.

---

[1] The reader may refer to what was
said under Art. x. on Free Will.
[2] On this principle it is that " If any
man will (θέλῃ) do the will of God, he

shall know of the doctrine, whether it be
of God," John vii. 17. " God resisteth
the proud but giveth grace to the humble," 1 Pet. v. 5.

But this is quite a distinct view of the case from that taken by the maintainers of congruous merit.   Their doctrine is that a man, without any help from God, and by a strong effort of his own will, can so fulfil the commandments, as, though not of actual right, yet, on a certain principle of congruity, to draw down the grace of God upon him.   Scripture, on the contrary, seems to teach that every attempt of this kind is displeasing, as being the result of arrogance and self-sufficiency.   The Pharisees, who thought themselves not blind, are told that that was the very cause of their condemnation, whereas, if they were aware of their own weakness, they should receive their sight.   " If ye were blind, ye should have no sin ; but now ye say, We see ; therefore your sin remaineth " (John ix. 41). The Jews are spoken of as cast off and blinded, because they sought to find their way to God, and to attain to righteousness, through the works of the Law, and through their own righteousness, instead of by the faith of Christ (see Rom. ix. 30, 31) ; for they " were ignorant of God's righteousness, and going about to establish their own righteousness, they did not submit themselves to the righteousness of God " (Rom. x. 3).

III.   The Article concludes by saying, that forasmuch as such works " are not done as God hath willed and commanded them to be done, we doubt not but that they have the nature of sin."

Works done in self-righteousness, done with a view to justify ourselves by our own merits, are not done as God hath willed, but in a wrong spirit and temper ; and therefore, proceeding from a bad principle, must be bad.   There may be in such works a mixture, as there often is, of good with the bad motive.   This God alone can see, and will approve the good, whilst He disapproves the bad.   Many a person tries to do right, acting in ignorance, and on the principle that such a mode of action is what God has appointed, and what He will reward.   Such a person may have very imperfect knowledge of the truth, and may not be sufficiently aware of his own weakness, and his own need of Divine strength. But mixed with such errors, there may be pure principles of faith and desire to serve God ; and God, who sees the heart, may give more blessing to such a person than to many a better instructed Christian.   The Article, however, may be quite right, notwithstanding, in saying that works, not springing from grace, and not done in faith, have the nature of sin.   As a general proposition, it is true that " whatever is not of faith is sin."   And the spirit which leads a man, instead of relying on God's mercy in Christ, and seeking the aid of His Spirit, to rely on his own unassisted efforts, is also sin.   It is a virtual denial of human infirmity, of the Atonement of Christ, and of the need of the Spirit.

Again, the only thing, which makes good works to be good, is the fact that God has commanded them.   Hence, if we find them not done in the way and for the end to which God has ordained them, we are justified in saying that they are not good works, but bad works.   The passages quoted from the Homilies in the former section show sufficiently that this was what the reformers meant by the words of the Article.

ARTICLE XIV.

Of Works of Supererogation.

VOLUNTARY works, besides, over and above God's commandments, which they call Works of Supererogation, cannot be taught without arrogancy and impiety: for by them men do declare, that they do not only render unto God as much as they are bound to do, but that they do more for His sake than of bounden duty is required: whereas Christ saith plainly, When ye have done all that are commanded to you, say, We are unprofitable servants.

De Operibus Supererogationis.

OPERA, quæ supererogationis appellant, non possunt sine arrogantia, et impietate prædicari. Nam illis declarant homines, non tantum se Deo reddere, quæ tenentur, sed plus in ejus gratiam facere, quàm deberent, cum apertè Christus dicat: Cum feceritis omnia quæcunque præcepta sunt vobis dicite, servi inutiles sumus.

SECTION I.—HISTORY.

THERE is nothing in the earliest fathers which bears much on the subject of this Article, unless it be that they appear to have attached more than due importance to martyrdom. Thus the baptism of blood was considered equivalent to baptism by water; and some perhaps, appear to have ascribed merit to it, such as to cancel sins. Hermas for instance speaks of the martyrs as having " all their offences blotted out, because they have suffered death for the name of the Son of God." [1] And again says of them, when compared with the rest of the redeemed, that they have " some glory above the others." [2] And so Tertullian says, that " all sins are forgiven to martyrdom." [3] But with reference to the last-named writer, it has been clearly shown, that with all his high esteem for martyrdom, he expressly maintained that it was impossible for martyrs to have an excess of holiness above what was required, as not being in themselves sinless. It was the custom in his days for persons who had lapsed in persecution to be restored to the communion of the Church, at the intercession of martyrs and confessors ; a custom which was often much abused. Writing

---

[1] *Simil.* IX. 29. [2] *Vis.* III. 28.
[3] Omnia huic operi delicta donantur. *Apol.* sub. fin.

on this subject, Tertullian says, " Who but the Son of God can by
His own death relieve others from death?   He, indeed, delivered
the thief at the very moment of His passion ; for He had come for
this very end, that, being Himself free from sin and perfectly holy,
He might die for sinners.   You then, who imitate Christ in pardoning sins, if you are yourselves sinless, suffer death for me.   But
if you are yourself a sinner, how can the oil out of your cruise
suffice both for you and me ? " [1]

In this admiration, however, of the early Church for martyrdom,
and in the admission of the intercession of the martyrs for the deliverance of others from church-censures, we may perhaps trace the
germ of the doctrine of works of supererogation.[2]

In the respect which they paid to virginity we may find
another source for the same error ; for it is well known, that they
gave the fullest latitude to those words of our Lord and of St.
Paul, in which they speak of celibacy as a favourable state of life
for the development of Christian graces, and for devotion to the
service of the Cross.

On this subject especially St. Paul writes, " Concerning virgins,
I have no commandment of the Lord; yet I give my advice "
(1 Cor. vii. 25) ; *De virginibus autem præceptum Domini non habeo,
sed consilium do.*   From this expression it was very early inferred
that the Scriptures made a distinction between *precepts*, which are
binding on all men, and *counsels*, which it is desirable to follow,
but which are not obligatory on the conscience.   Thus St. Cyprian,
speaking of celibacy, says, " The Lord does not command this, but
exhorts to it.   He lays not on a yoke of necessity, when the free
choice of the will remains.   But whereas he says, that in His Father's house are many mansions, He points out the way to the
better mansions." [3]   St. Augustine writes, " It is not said, Thou
shalt not marry, as it is said, Thou shalt not commit adultery,
Thou shalt not kill.   The latter are exacted, the former is offered.
If the one is observed, there is praise.   If the other is neglected,

---

[1] *De Pudicitia,* Cap. 22. See Bishop
Kaye, *Tertullian,* p. 336.
    Like this is the language of Augustine,
quoted by Bp. Beveridge on this Article :
Etsi fratres pro fratribus moriantur, tamen in peccatorum remissionem nullius
sanguis martyris funditur, quod fecit Ille
(*i. e.* Dominus Christus) pro nobis.   August. *In Joh.* tract 84.

[2] *Rogare legem,* to propose a law.   *Ero-
gare,* to make a law for paying a sum of
money out of a public treasury.   So the
word is used for lending or paying out.

Hence *supererogare,* to pay over and
above.   In Luke x. 35, προσδαπανάω is
in the Vulgate *supererogo,* to spend more.
— Hey, iii. p. 403.

[3] Nec hoc jubet Dominus sed hortatur :
nec jugum necessitatis imponit, quando
maneat voluntatis arbitrium liberum.
Sed cum habitationes multas apud Patrem suum dicat, melioris habitaculi hos-
pitia demonstrat : habitacula ista meliora
vos petitis, carnis desideria castrantes,
majoris præmium in cœlestibus obtine-
tis. — Cypr. *De Habitu Virginum,* p. 102.

there will be condemnation." [1]　And St. Jerome distinguishes between a precept and a counsel, as that the one involves necessity of obedience, the other leaves a liberty of accepting or refusing.[2]

The distinction thus early made may have had a legitimate foundation in Holy Writ. But, in process of time, there grew out of it the doctrine of works of supererogation, as connected with a belief in the merits of martyrdom, and of voluntary celibacy. The increase of monasticism, and the increasing respect paid to every kind of ascetic observance, cherished this belief. In the language of the confession of Augsburg, " The monks taught that their mode of life was a state of perfection, because they observed not precepts only, but counsels also. This error is greatly at variance with Gospel truth ; for thus they pretended so to satisfy the commands of God as even to exceed them. And hence arose the grievous error, that they claimed merits of supererogation. These they applied to others, that they might be satisfactions for other men's sins." [3]

The full-grown form of the doctrine was, that a man may not only keep the law of God, so as to do all that is actually enjoined on him, but may be so full of the grace of God as even to do more than God's law enjoins, and thereby deserve even more than his own salvation. This excess of merit, which was supposed to be attained by some of the greater saints, formed a deposit, which was intrusted to the Church, and which the Roman pontiff, the vicar of Christ, could for reasonable causes, by the power of the keys, unlock, and grant to the faithful, in the way of indulgences, and for the remission of temporal punishment.

In the Council of Trent, the last decrees read and approved were concerning the granting of indulgences. The council anathematized those who said they were unprofitable, and, though forbid-

---

[1] Non enim sicut *Non mœchaberis, non occides*, ita dici potest, non nubes. Illa exiguntur, ista offeruntur. Si fiunt ista, laudantur : nisi fiunt illa, damnantur. In illis Dominus debitum imperat vobis ; in his autem si quid amplius supererogaveritis, in redeundo reddit vobis. — August. *De Sancta Virginitate*, cap. 30. *Opera*, Tom. VI. p. 355.

[2] Ubi consilium, ibi offerentis arbitrium, ubi præceptum datum, ibi necessitas est servientis. Hieron. ad Eustochium, *De Servanda Virginitate*. So in the Sermons *De Tempore*, ascribed to Augustine, Sermon LXI. De Virginitate dicitur, Qui potest capere, capiat. De justitia non dicitur, Qui potest facere,

sed Omnis arbor, quæ non facit fructum bonum exscindetur, et in ignem mittetur. See these and some other passages quoted by Bellarmine, *De Monachis*, Lib. II. cap. 7, 11. Tom. II. pp. 363, 380.

The words of S. Chrysostom are much to this purpose on Rom. viii. : οἱ πνευματικοὶ πάντα πράττουσιν ἐπιθυμίᾳ καὶ πόθῳ, καὶ τοῦτο δηλοῦσι τῷ καὶ ὑπερβαίνειν τὰ ὑποτάγματα. Thus rendered by Bp. Jer. Taylor, " Spiritual men do their actions with much passion and holy zeal, and give testimony of it by expressing it in the uncommanded instances." — *Rule of Conscience*, II. 3, 12 ; which see.

[3] *Sylloge*, p. 223.

ding their sale and other abuses, yet commanded that they should be retained as profitable for Christian people.[1] There is no express mention of works of supererogation.

It is scarcely necessary to add, that all the reformed Churches and sects, of whatever class or denomination, have rejected the doctrine of the Romanists concerning works of supererogation.

Section II. — SCRIPTURAL PROOF.

THE principal arguments in favour of the doctrine of the Roman Church on this subject may be found in the writings of Cardinal Bellarmine, in the second book of his treatise *De Monachis.* He assumes the principle, a principle which rightly understood need not be controverted, that in some passages of Scripture advice is given, where there is not a positive command: and then he infers that, " as our Lord distinguishes counsels from precepts, He plainly shows that men justified by the grace of God can not only fulfil the law, but even do some works most pleasing to God, which have not been commanded." [2]

Now this inference may fairly be considered a *petitio principii ;* for advice, when coming from our Lord or His Apostles, may be a counsel tending indeed to spiritual good, but yet, if followed, not enabling to do more than is commanded, but only putting in the road to obtain more grace and strength from above.

Bellarmine, besides referring to several passages of the fathers, some of which have been already quoted, brings forward very many texts of Scripture to prove his position. The greater number of these appear so little relevant, that I shall make no apology for considering those only which appear to have some weight.

1. The first which we may mention is the counsel given by our Lord to the man who came to Him, and asked, " Good Master, what good thing shall I do that I may have eternal life ? " Our Lord first replies, " Keep the commandments." The young man then says that he has kept all these from his youth, and adds,

---

[1] Sarpi, p. 757.

[2] *Controvers. General.* Lib. iv. *De Indulgentiis,* Tom. iii. p. 1124. Dominus consilia a præceptis distinguens, ostendit posse homines justificatos per gratiam Dei non solum implere legem, sed etiam aliqua alia opera Deo gratissima facere, quæ imperata non sint. He quotes especially the case of the young man, Matt xix. 16, &c.

" What lack I yet? " Jesus said unto him, " If thou wilt be perfect,
go and sell that thou hast, and give to the poor, and thou shalt
have treasure in Heaven : and come and follow Me." [1] Bellarmine
argues that this last sentence of our Lord's could not have been a
command, but was a counsel of perfection, which, if obeyed, would
have been more than was the young man's duty, *i. e.* a work of
supererogation. This he proves as follows : It was not a precept ;
for to the question, " What shall I do that I may have eternal
life ? " the answer is " If thou wilt enter into life keep the commandments." Therefore the keeping the commandments would be
sufficient for salvation. And the advice afterwards given tended to
perfection, not to salvation.[2]

But if we attentively consider the whole conversation, we shall
see that this interpretation will not satisfy the case. In the first
place, the young man asks, " What good thing he should do to have
eternal life ; " to which our Lord gives the general reply, that, " if
he would be saved, he must keep the commandments." The young
man, evidently not ill disposed (see Mark x. 21), but with an undue notion of his own strength and goodness, then says, that he has
kept all the commandments from his youth, and, as though he could
see no deficiency in his own conduct, asks again, " What lack I
yet ? " Now it was to this question, " What lack I ? " that our Lord
gave the reply now under consideration. That reply, therefore,
was intended to show the young man what he *lacked :* and if he
lacked something, it is quite clear that the supplying of that lack,

---

[1] Matt. xix. 16–21.
[2] Lib. ii. *De Monachis,* cap. 9, Tom.
ii. p. 368, &c.
The cardinal replies to many arguments which have been brought against
his interpretation of this history : *e. g.*
St. Jerome and Bede considered the
young man's question as a tempting of
our Lord, but Chrysostom refutes this
opinion, by showing that none of the
Evangelists blame him, and Bellarmine
adds, that St. Mark (x. 21), says that
" Jesus beholding him loved him." Calvin (*Inst.* Lib. iv. cap. 13) had argued
that our Lord could not have placed perfection in selling all things, since in 1
Cor. xiii. 3, we read " though I give all
my goods to feed the poor . . . . and
have not charity, it profiteth me nothing." Calvin also observes, that the
young man could not really have kept
all the commandments, for one is, " Thou
shalt love the Lord thy God with all thy
heart," &c. ; and he who does this will
give up everything, and therefore, of

course, all his wealth, for Him. Peter
Martyr too had said, that it could not be
a counsel, but a precept, when our Lord
said, " If thou wilt be perfect, sell all
that thou hast ; " for in Matt. **v.** 48,
" Be ye perfect " is a precept ; and therefore whatever teaches us to be perfect
must be of the nature of a precept also.
To this Bellarmine tries to reply, that
there are different kinds of perfection,
some necessary for salvation, but a higher
degree for a higher grade of glory. P.
Martyr also says, that this command
was given to the young man alone, and
that therefore it was necessary for his
perfection, but not for every one's, for he
is perfect who obeys God's laws. Bellarmine answers, No ! The command was,
" If thou wilt enter into life, keep the
commandments ; " this was addressed to
all. So we ought to infer that the saying,
" If thou wilt be perfect, sell all that thou
hast," was equally addressed to all. **He**
quotes Ambrose, Jerome, and Augustine,
as agreeing with him in this view.

or deficiency, could not be a work of supererogation, but a work of duty or obligation. This is further proved by the conduct of the young man, who, when he had heard our Lord's reply, "went away sorrowful." That is to say, he felt not able and willing to do what our Lord had said was needful for him to do. He had asked what was necessary for his salvation. The first answer gave him satisfaction; for it did not fully convince him of his weakness. The second probed him to the quick, and showed him that the strength of purpose which he supposed himself to possess, was not such as to lead him to renounce all for the kingdom of God. And so, when he had gone away sorrowful, our Lord does not say, A rich man shall hardly become perfect, or do works of supererogation; but He says, "Verily I say unto you, that a rich man shall hardly *enter into the kingdom of Heaven.* And again I say unto you, It is easier for a camel to go through the eye of a needle, than for a rich man to *enter into the kingdom of God.*" It was unfitness for the kingdom of Heaven, not unfitness for a supereminent degree of glory, which the rich man showed, when, at our Lord's bidding, he could not sell all that he had.

Whence it appears, that this saying of our Lord's was a precept, and not a counsel. It was like the command given to Abraham to kill his son. It was a trial of his faith and of his readiness to obey. The faithful servant of God will give up all, even that he loves the best, for Him whom he serves. Abraham's dearest treasure was his son, and he was ready to sacrifice him. The young man's treasure was his wealth, and he went away sorrowful. The one was shown to be true and firm in the faith. The other's faith was proved to be doubtful and wavering.

Bellarmine, however, farther contends that, whereas it follows in the 27th verse, "Peter answered and said unto Him, Behold we have forsaken all, and followed Thee; what shall we have therefore?" if the command was only given to the young man, and not to all men, then our Lord would have said to Peter, "I will give nothing to you, I spoke only to this young man;" (*Nihil vobis dabo, nam soli illi juveni loquutus sum*); whereas the answer ac'ually given is (*Amen dico vobis, &c.*) "Verily I say unto you, that ye who have followed Me . . . . shall sit on twelve thrones . . . . and *every one* who hath forsaken houses, or brethren, or sisters, or father, or mother, or wife, or children, or lands, for my sake, shall receive an hundred-fold, and shall inherit everlasting life." The cardinal's conclusion is therefore, that to *all* men it is a *precept*, "keep the commandments," and to *all* men it is a *coun-*

scl, " sell that thou hast, and give to the poor." The Apostles obeyed the precept and the counsel both, and so did more than their duty; the young man kept only the precepts, and so won Heaven, but not more than Heaven.

There is evidently a fallacy here. No doubt, it is not commanded to all men to sell all that they have ; for St. Paul bade Timothy " charge those who are rich in this world " (not to sell their possessions, but) " not to trust in uncertain riches," " to do good, to be rich in good works, ready to distribute, willing to communicate " (1 Tim. vi. 17, 18). But though all men are not expressly called to sell all that they have, yet at the time of our Lord's presence upon earth, He did call all His immediate followers to give up everything for His sake ; and the most obvious and decided way of giving proof of zeal for His service and love to Him, was to forsake parents and brethren, house and lands, and to follow Him who had no place to lay His head.[1] Thus, as Abraham evidenced his faith by being ready to slay his son, so the Apostles evidenced theirs by forsaking their homes ; and the rich young man could not find it in his heart to sacrifice so much, because his faith was not so true. Here is no room for works of supererogation, nor even for counsels of perfection.

2. Another of Bellarmine's proofs[2] is drawn from 1 Cor. ix. ; in which St. Paul asserts, that he might have received payment for his ministry, that he might have led about a wife at the expense of the Church ; but that he would not do anything of this kind, lest his glorying should be made void. Taking the Latin version as his guide, Bellarmine reasons, that, though St. Paul might have fulfilled all his duty, if he had taken payment of the Church, yet he would not take reward, that he might obtain greater glory. And he argues against Peter Martyr (who interprets the *gloriam* of ver. 15 to " mean glorying before men ") that St. Augustine had written, *Bonum est magis mihi mori, quam ut gloriam meam quis evacuet. Quam gloriam ? nisi quam habere voluit apud Deum in Christo ?*[3] But *pace tanti viri,* be it said, that the Greek word is καύχημα, which means *boasting ;* and that a greater than St. Augustine has written that " no flesh should glory (or boast) in God's presence."[4] The passage in St. Paul can hardly mean anything

---

[1] We must remember that there was a perfectly general precept to this effect: " He that loveth father or mother more than me is not worthy of me," Matt. x. 37. And again : " If any man come to me, and hate not his father and mother, and wife and children, and brethren and sisters, yea, and his own life also, he can not be my disciple," Luke xiv. 26.

[2] Tom. II. p. 378.

[3] *Lib. de Opere Monachorum,* c. 10.

[4] 1 Cor. i. 29. Comp. Rom. iii. 27 ; iv 2. Eph. ii. 9.

but this: that, whereas he, as an Apostle, had a right to be charge-
able to the Church, he had yet refused to be so, that he might have
the more influence for good over those among whom he ministered.
As he says in the nineteenth verse of the same chapter, " Though
he was free from all men, yet he made himself the servant of all,
that he might gain the more." Thus he was able to boast, that he
had cost them nothing; and they therefore could not charge him
with avarice or private views. To make his glorying in this respect void would have been to deprive him of his influence over
them, and therefore of that power to do good which lay so near
his heart.

3. But the most cogent argument from Scripture, in favour of
works of supererogation, is drawn from the passages in which our
Lord and St. Paul, whilst highly honouring marriage, yet give the
preference to a life of celibacy. The passages in question are
Matt. xix. 10, 11, 12, and 1 Cor. vii. *passim*, especially 7, 8, 25–
28, 32–40.

On the first passage, Bellarmine observes, that to live a life of
celibacy cannot be a precept, because of the high commendation
which our Lord had just bestowed upon matrimony, and yet, he
says, it is evident that it has a reward in Heaven, because our Lord
declares that " some have made themselves eunuchs " (*i. e.* have
lived a life of celibacy) " for the kingdom of Heaven's sake," and
then adds, " He that is able to receive it, let him receive it " (Matt.
xix. 12). In like manner, on 1 Cor. vii. he observes, that the
advice to abstain from marriage is evidently a *counsel;* and that it
is a counsel of not merely human wisdom, but proceeding from the
Spirit of God; which he fully proves from ver. 25, 40; where the
Apostle declares that, though there had been " no commandment
of the Lord," yet he gave his judgment as one who had " obtained
mercy of the Lord to be faithful," ver. 25; and that in thus giving
his judgment, he felt assured that he had the Spirit of God,
ver. 40.[1]

Luther, he says, only admitted a temporal advantage to be attached to celibacy, and such has been the exposition of many Protestants; namely, that so a man may escape cares, and anxieties,
and *that* especially in time of persecution. Against such Bellarmine quotes the words of St. Augustine;[2] who truly maintained,

---

[1] Δοκῶ δὲ κἀγὼ Πνεῦμα Θεοῦ ἔχειν,
where, according to the well-known
usage of St. Paul and others, δοκεῖν is
far from implying doubt.

[2] *De Sancta Virginitate*, c. 13. Unde
mirabiliter desipiunt, qui putant hujus

continentiæ bonum non esse necessarium
propter regnum cœlorum, sed propter
præsens sæculum, quod scilicet conjugia
terrenis curis pluribus atque arctioribus
distenduntur, qua molestia virgines et
continentes carent, &c.

that the Apostle spoke of spiritual as well as temporal benefits to be derived from celibacy.

From Luther, Bellarmine passes to Melancthon, who went farther than Luther, and admitted that some spiritual good might be derived from an unmarried state, such as more freedom and time for prayer and preaching.[1] But to the temporal benefits admitted by Luther, and to the spiritual benefits allowed by Melancthon, Bellarmine adds a third, namely, to please God and obtain greater reward. He observes that the words *propter instantem necessitatem*, "because of the present distress" (ver. 26), do not mean that we may escape present troubles, but that they rather mean, *propter brevitatem temporis*, "because of the shortness of the time;" as it is said (ver. 29), "But this I say, brethren, the time is short." Against Melancthon he says, that in ver. 34 the Apostle commends the state of an unmarried female, saying, that "she careth for the things of the Lord, that she may be holy both in body and in spirit;" and that this shows that virginity has of itself a sanctity both of body and spirit, according to the words of Jerome (lib. I. *Contra Jovinian*): *Illa virginitas hostia Christi est, cujus nec mentem cogitatio, nec carnem libido maculant.* From ver. 35, where St. Paul says he speaks thus "for that which is comely," *ad id quod honestum est*, Bellarmine argues that the apostle calls continence a thing *per se honestam et decoram et proinde Deo charam*, "a thing in its own nature comely and honourable, and therefore dear to God." And again, in ver. 40, the words "She is happier if she so abide," he says, plainly mean, she will be happier in the world to come.[2]

Now in this reasoning of the distinguished Romanist divine there appears a considerable mixture of truth and error. Let us admit, as we cannot doubt, that the Apostle wrote under the guidance of the Spirit; let us admit that he gave a *counsel*, not a *precept;* for plainly it is no commandment of God that men should not marry, but only that they should "abstain from fornication." Let us admit that both our blessed Lord and St. Paul spoke of abstaining from marriage, for the sake of some advantages which an unmarried life has, as regards spiritual employments and spiritual meditations. The divines of our own communion have admitted this as freely as those of the Roman Church.[3] There seems no reason to

---

[1] In Locis, cap. *De Castitate.*

[2] Beatior autem erit, si sic permanserit, id est, ut exponit, in futuro sæculo. Bellarmine treats of Matt. xix. *Controv. Gener.* Tom. ii. p. 367. Cf. 1 Cor. vii.

[3] For example, see Bp. Burnet on this Article, and Milner, *Hist. of the Church*, Cent. i. ch. xi. ; Cent. ii. ch. viii.; divines of a school peculiarly disinclined from any concessions to the Romanists. On the proper distinction between precepts and counsels, the student may read with great advantage Bp. Jer. Taylor,

doubt, that both our Lord and St. Paul speak of some to whom a
peculiar gift has been given, and who can, by living unmarried, devote themselves more unreservedly to the work of the Gospel, and
the service of the Lord.   Marriage brings with it the anxieties of
family and worldly business, and many of those " cares of this life,"
which may, if not checked, choke the good seed.   From all such
celibacy is free.   Therefore, though marriage be a state ordained of
God, yet some, thinking to give their whole lives to religious employments, have abstained from marriage, " have made themselves
eunuchs for the kingdom of Heaven's sake ; " and such a determination, in such as are " able to receive it," our Lord has honoured
with His sanction, " Let him receive it."   And so it is with the counsel of St. Paul.   He tells us, that " the time is short, it remaineth
that they that have wives be as though they had none . . . that they
who use this world, be as though they used it not ; [1] for the fashion
of this world passeth away."   Accordingly, to such as have the gift
of continence he gives his advice, that it may help them on more in
their course of godliness, if they continue to live a life less burdened
with the cares of this world than is the life of those who are
united in marriage.   Such a life is not indeed to be commended to
all men, and the Apostle carefully guards himself against forcing the
conscience, or " casting a snare upon " them.   But it is a life which
has many advantages.   The unmarried have nothing to do but care
for the things of the Lord ; whilst the married cannot but be anxious
to please not only God, but the partner of their earthly pilgrimage.
Much therefore as there is of blessing in the married state, honourable as it is in all men, and a κοίτη ἀμίαντος, a state undefiled ; still
those who have contracted it are, like Martha, necessarily " cumbered
about much serving," whilst the unmarried, like Mary, have more
leisure to " sit at the feet of Jesus," able to " attend upon the Lord
without distraction." [2]   Therefore it is that the Apostle counsels an
unmarried life, because of " the present distress ; " because, it may
be, of the distress and anxieties of this present life, which are much
unfavourable to the attainment of holiness, and which especially be-
set those who are tied in the bond of matrimony. [3]

This exposition will fairly satisfy the language both of Christ and

---

Rule of Conscience, Book ii. ch. iii. Rule
12.
   [1] 1 Cor. vii. 31 : " As though they used
it not," ὡς μὴ καταχρώμενοι.   Καταχρᾶσθαι
here probably signifies to *use.*   Comp. 1
Cor. vii. 31 ; ix. 18.
   [2] 1 Cor. vii. 35.   In the words πρὸς τὸ
εὐπρόσεδρον τῷ Κυρίῳ ἀπερισπάστως,

it has been thought that St. Paul especially alludes to Mary's " sitting at Jesus'
feet."   Luke x. 39.
   [3] Propter instantem necessitatem.]   Id
est, præsentis vitæ solicitudinem, quæ
multum potest obesse justitiæ, et qua
præcipue juncti matrimoniis implicantur.
— Hieron. in 1 Cor. vii.

of His Apostle. But we deny that St. Paul, when instituting a comparison between marriage and celibacy, speaks of the latter as having more merit than the former; or that the one shall ensure a higher place in Heaven than the other. It may be to some persons a state more favourable for growth in grace, though, for obvious reasons, it may be a snare to others. But, as marriage is a thing holy in itself, so we do not learn that celibacy is holier. " One is not a better chastity than the other. Marriage is a κοίτη ἀμίαντος, an undefiled state, and nothing can be cleaner than that which is not at all unclean." [1] And therefore, though we fully admit the honour due to a holy celibacy, we yet deny that it has any merit at all, as nothing in man can merit from God; and still more do we deny that it can have merit of supererogation.[2]

The above are the only arguments from Scripture, adduced by Bellarmine, which can be considered as of weight or importance; and we may therefore fairly consider that, in answering them, we have shown that Scripture does not countenance the doctrine which our fourteenth Article condemns. It remains to show, that there are passages and statements in the Scriptures directly at variance with that doctrine, and utterly inconsistent with it.

1. In the first place Scripture shows that all men, even those under the dominion of grace, are still imperfect and full of infirmity. David says, that " there is none that doeth good, no not one " (Ps. xiv. 3); St. James says, that " in many things we offend, all " (Jas. iii. 2); and St. John says, that " if we say that we have no sin we deceive ourselves " (1 John i. 8). But if it be true that all men have sinned and " in many things offend," then it is quite clear that no man can be so perfectly holy as not only to fulfil all God's law, but even to exceed it. And as the Psalmist spoke, in the four-

---

[1] Jer. Taylor, as above.

[2] A passage, not noticed by Bellarmine, may seem to countenance the doctrine that the sufferings of the saints were beneficial, not only to themselves, but to the Church; and that therefore their merits were more than enough for their own salvation. The passage is Col. i. 24, " Who now rejoice in my sufferings for you, and fill up that which is behind of the afflictions of Christ in my flesh for His body's sake, which is the Church." But if we carefully consider the passage, we cannot suppose that the Apostle means that there was anything deficient in the sufferings of Christ, or that His infinite merits needed addition from the sufferings of His servant. The true meaning of the passage is this: Every servant of Christ has need to be conformed to the likeness of the sufferings of his Lord. St. Paul considered, that there was somewhat lacking in him, that there was somewhat yet behind of " the affliction of Christ," before he could be thoroughly conformed to His likeness; and earnestly desiring to be made like his Lord, he gladly took every additional trial as only bringing him nearer to His image; and all these trials he endured for the sake of the Church, which he served, and to which he preached the Gospel of Christ. There is no mention of vicarious suffering on the part of St. Paul, of supererogatory merit, or of addition to the full, perfect, and sufficient sacrifice of Christ upon the Cross.

teenth Psalm, " to those that were under the Law " (see Rom. iii. 10, 19), so St. James and St. John evidently spoke to those who were under grace ; as the whole context evinces.   Hence we must conclude that even under grace no man lives actually spotless in God's commandments.

2. But even if we could live wholly without spot, and never offend in thought, word, or deed, even so our Lord teaches us that such a spotless obedience would still leave us undeserving of reward. " When ye shall have done all those things which are commanded you, say We are unprofitable servants : we have done that which was our duty to do " (Luke xvii. 10).   What room is there then for the doctrine which teaches, that a man may do enough for his salvation and attain to glory by keeping the precepts ; and then by observing counsels may merit still more ?   Even if we could keep all the precepts, we should be unprofitable, having no right to reward, but merely to exemption from punishment.[1]   Something more than obedience to precepts is required, even for salvation ; and where, then, is the foundation on which to build still higher merit ?

3. Again, in the parable of the ten virgins, when the five foolish virgins found their oil fail, they are represented as going to the wise virgins, and asking to borrow oil from them.   But the wise answered that they had not enough for themselves and others too, showing that no one can have holiness or grace enough to supply another's deficiencies, but that each one must seek pardon and grace for himself (Matt. xxv. 9).

4. Then the precepts of the Gospel are so full and comprehensive that everything, even the highest degree of perfection, is contained in them.   Under the Law, indeed, if the letter only was observed, the statutes contained but a certain express catalogue of duties : but the spiritual sense of the Law, as enforced by our Saviour, enjoins such an entire surrender of all the faculties of the body, soul, and spirit to the service of Christ, that nothing conceivable can exceed or overpass it.   This will be quite apparent, if we read our Lord's exposition of the Law, in the Sermon on the Mount (Matt. v. 27, *seq*), where a thought or a look of evil is deadly sin ; or His declaration that no one can be His disciple who hates not his

---

[1] Quod sub præcepto est, si non impleatur, punit. Impletum morte tantum caret ; quia nihil ex se dat, sed quod debet, exsolvit. — Hieron. in 1 Cor. vii.

It is true, that the divines of the Roman communion always presuppose that it is the atonement of Christ which gives efficacy and merit to the works of the saints. But we must remember that our Lord, in the passage from Luke xvii. 10, spoke to His own disciples, — those very saints who are supposed not only to have merited life, but to have laid up a store of good works, more than was needed for their salvation.

nearest friends and his own life, if need be, for Christ's service; or His summary of the commandments — unbounded love to God, and perfect love to man (Matt. xxii. 37, 38, 39) ; " Thou shalt love the Lord thy God with all thy heart, and with all thy soul, and with all thy mind; and thou shalt love thy neighbour as thyself." We cannot conceive either saint or angel more perfect than this: and yet all this is *commanded* — is of the nature of a *precept*, not of counsels only. The language of St. Paul's exhortation is equally strong ; that we present ourselves " as living sacrifices to God " (Rom. xii. 1), that we " cleanse ourselves from all filthiness of flesh and spirit, *perfecting* holiness in the fear of God " (2 Cor. vii. 1). " Finally, whatsoever things are true, whatsoever things are honest, whatsoever things are just, whatsoever things are lovely, whatsoever things are of good report ; if there be any virtue, and if there be any praise, think on these things " (Phil. iv. 8). Can anything go beyond these things which it is our duty to do? But if any man seem to be contentious, St. Peter tells us, as a plain command, to aim " to be holy as Christ is holy " (1 Pet. i. 15, 16) : and Christ Himself concludes His teaching concerning the strict and spiritual nature of the Law with the words, " Be ye therefore perfect, as your Father which is in heaven is perfect " (Matt. v. 48). Till then we can learn that God's grace has ever made man as perfect as God, we can never believe that man has ever fully lived up to the *precepts* of the Gospel. Where is the room for higher graces still ?

5. Lastly, we may observe that the whole of the doctrine of works of supererogation arises from a false view of the principles of Christian obedience. If we look for merit, it must be to Christ. Christian obedience is not a task of so much work to be done, and so much reward to be expected. When it is sound and perfect, it springs from a true faith and a holy love. And as no degree of perfection can excel the obedience which would be yielded by perfect love, so nothing can excel that holiness at which every Christian is bound to aim. The obedience of the Gospel is not the task-work of a slave, but the perfect freedom of a son.

45

ARTICLE XV.

Of Christ alone without Sin.

CHRIST in the truth of our nature was made like unto us in all things, sin only except; from which He was clearly void, both in His flesh and in His Spirit. He came to be the lamb without spot, who, by sacrifice of himself once made, should take away the sins of the world; and sin (as St. John saith) was not in Him. But all we the rest, although baptized and born again in Christ, yet offend in many things; and if we say we have no sin, we deceive ourselves, and the truth is not in us.

De Christo, qui solus est sine peccato.

CHRISTUS, in nostræ naturæ veritate, per omnia similis factus est nobis, excepto peccato, a quo prorsus erat immunis, tum in carne, tum in Spiritu. Venit ut Agnus, absque macula, qui mundi peccata per immolationem sui semel factam tolleret, et peccatum (ut inquit Johannes) in eo non erat: sed nos reliqui etiam baptizati, et in Christo regenerati, in multis tamen offendimus omnes. Et si dixerimus, quia peccatum non habemus, nos ipsos seducimus, et veritas in nobis non est.

SECTION I. — HISTORY.

THE history of the greater part of the doctrine contained in this Article may be considered as involved in the history of some of the preceding Articles, especially of the ninth. We spoke there of the Pelagian heresy, and observed that Pelagius held that it was possible for a man, even without the grace of God, to keep God's law, and live a life of perfect holiness. St. Augustine, we saw in his arguments against Pelagianism, still expressed unwillingness to discuss the question of the sinfulness of the blessed Virgin Mary, out of reverence to her Son and Lord. Pelagius had held that it was necessary for our religion that we should confess the Virgin to be sinless (*i. e.* that we might not hold our Saviour to be born in sin). St. Augustine answers, " Concerning the Virgin Mary, I am not willing, for the honour of our Lord, to hold any dispute, when we are talking about sin. For how do we know what more grace was bestowed on her to overcome all sin, who had the honour to conceive and bring forth Him who certainly had no sin ? " [1]

---

[1] August. *De Natura et Gratia.* Wall, *Inf. Bapt.* i. p. 404. The passage from Augustine is from c. 42. Tom. x. p. 144: —

Excepta itaque sancta virgine Maria, de qua propter honorem Domini nullam prorsus cum de peccatis agitur, haberi volo quæstionem. Unde enim scimus, quid ei plus gratiæ collatum fuerit ad vincendum omni ex parte peccatum ? &c.

This scruple, which early prevailed about the Virgin, in the course of years grew into a doctrine. But for a length of time the doctrine was privately held, not publicly expressed. In the year 1136 the Canons of Lyons brought the doctrine of the Immaculate Conception of the Virgin into the ecclesiastical offices; for which act of rashness they were severely censured by St. Bernard. But about the year 1300, the celebrated Schoolman, John Duns Scotus, a Franciscan Friar, strenuously maintained the total exemption from sin of the Blessed Virgin, and grounded it upon the omnipotency of God, who could free her from sin, if He chose. Thenceforward the Scotists and Franciscans ever advocated the dogma of the Immaculate Conception.[1]

At the Council of Trent this question was hotly debated; the Franciscans excepting the Virgin from all taint of sin, the Dominicans labouring to comprehend her name under the common law. The pope commanded that the contention on the subject should be omitted, for fear of causing a schism. Both parties acquiesced in silence, on the condition that when the decrees were made it should merely be added that there was no intention to include the Blessed Virgin in the decrees concerning original sin.[2] It was therefore left an open question, although the Franciscans had the better reason of the two parties to be satisfied.[3]

[1] Sarpi, *Council of Trent*, p. 178.

[2] Sarpi, pp. 164, 169, 171.

[3] [Some further historical details may properly be added, relating to the action of the papacy.

In 1476, Sixtus IV. issued the Bull *Cum Præcelsa*. In it he encouraged the celebration of the Festival of the Immaculate Conception. In 1488, by the Bull *Grave nimis*, he forbade that either those who hold the opinion of the immaculate conception, or those who hold its contrary, should be charged with heresy or mortal sin. These two Bulls were formally accepted by the Council of Trent. *Sess. V. Decree concerning Original Sin.*

In 1570, Pius V. issued the Bull *Super Speculam*. This Bull allowed either opinion, and forbade all controversy in public, though it allowed discussion in the schools.

In 1617, Paul IV. issued the Bull *Beati pacifici*, in which, under heavy penalties, he renewed the constitutions of Sixtus IV. and Pius V.

In 1622, Gregory XV. took a step in advance, by forbidding any one, till it should be otherwise ordered, to assert *in public* that the Virgin was conceived in original sin, though he declared that he did not deny or controvert the opinion that she was. At the same time he allowed any one to assert the immaculate conception, only not attacking the other opinions, while, *without permission from the Holy See*, no one was permitted to assert the conception in original sin at all. In the same year another Bull, *Eximii atque Singularis*, allowed the Dominicans, in their own schools, to discuss the opinion.

Alexander VII., in 1671, issued the Bull *Solicitudo omnium Ecclesiarum*, which, while it favoured the opinion of the immaculate conception, yet forbade those who held the opposite opinion to be charged with heresy.

Finally, on the 8th of December, 1854, Pius IX. by the Bull *Ineffabilis*, created this opinion into an Article of the Faith, without even the pretence of consulting a General Council, consolidating and concentrating in himself a power, *in spiritualibus*, which neither Hildebrand nor Innocent had ever attempted to exercise, and accepting, or rather demanding, assent to the most *ultramontane* theory of the papal authority. There the matter rests at present, but *the end is not yet.*

Already the claim is advanced, that the Blessed Virgin *merited* this grace of

It was also decreed in the Council of Trent that all the taint of original sin is washed away in baptism.[1]   And the Lutherans were condemned for saying that God's commands were not possible to the just.[2]   From these canons of the council it might naturally follow, that a person baptized and justified may fully keep God's commands, and live a life of spotless holiness.   But what is even more to the purpose still, is the Romish doctrine of works of supererogation.   For, if such works are possible, it must first be possible that he who does them should be perfectly sinless.   Otherwise he could not do, not only his duty, but more than his duty.   Accordingly this Article of our Church, " Of Christ alone without sin," follows immediately on that concerning Works of Supererogation.   The one is very probably intended as a supplement and strengthener to the other ; so that, whereas in the last Article it was said that no man can do more than God's law requires, so in this it is added, that no man in this life can fully live up to its requirements, but *all* offend many times ; and none, even of the baptized and regenerate, is quite free from sin.

That part of the Article which alleges that Christ was free from sin need not be considered historically, for none but those who deny His Divinity can deny His sinlessness.   And the greatest heretics, even mere Humanitarians, have respected the Saviour as a pure and holy Being.

Section II. — SCRIPTURAL PROOF.

THE subjects treated on in the Article are, —

  I. That Christ was without sin, although in all other things made like unto us.

  II. That all other men (even though baptized and born again in Christ) yet offend in many things.

  I. That Christ, though perfect man, was yet free from sin, prop-

---

the immaculate conception, because of her holiness in a *preëxistent state*. How long will it take to extend that preëxistence to *eternity,* and then to argue from eternal existence, *participation in the Divine Nature ?*
  The Abbè Laborde, *On the Impossibility*

of the Immaculate Conception, may well be consulted ; while, to see the weakness of the arguments in defence of this fearful novelty, one need only read the *Treatise* of the Cardinal Lambruschini. — J. W.]
  [1] Sess. v. Can. 5.
  [2] Sess. vi. Can. 18.

erly forms a part of the doctrine of the Incarnation, and is therefore intimately connected with Article II.

The eternal Son of God, the second Person in the Godhead, took into that Person the perfect nature of man. That nature of man had become defiled and debased. And it was that He might purify and restore it that He took it into Himself. But the question is, whether, when He took the nature, He was obliged to take its corruption with it. If so, we may well believe that the Incarnation would have been impossible. God is of purer eyes than to behold iniquity. Much less can we suppose that God would take iniquity and corruption to Himself, into union with His own spotless purity and holiness.

But though human nature, in all naturally engendered of Adam, is stained with the sin of Adam, yet sin is not a *part* of human nature, but a *fault* of it.[1] The Manicheans held that matter was essentially evil, and so human nature was evil, because matter was a part of it. But matter as well as spirit comes from God, and so is of itself, like all His creatures, " very good." Sin, therefore, which we all inherit, is a corruption and evil addition to our nature, not an essential and integral part of it. Whether it consists in a withdrawal of the indwelling and presence of God, and a consequent rebellion of the lower principles of man's nature,[2] or whether there be moreover a kind of taint or poison, which, working in him, produces sin, and renders him liable to death ; in either case original sin is not human nature, but an accident of that nature ; a quality as distinct from humanity as is any particular bodily disease, such as madness, or consumption, or neuralgia.

When therefore Christ took our nature, it was not essential to its perfection that He should take our sinfulness. Sin not being a part, but a fault of nature, He might be " made in all things like unto us," even though sin were excepted. Our *liability* to sin indeed He must have taken ; for else He could not have been " in all things tempted like as we are." Adam had a liability to sin, and therefore was susceptible of temptation, before he was

---

[1] The Manichees held that sin was a natura non a culpa: *i. e.* because they thought one portion of our nature (*i. e.* the body) essentially evil. But the fathers taught that it was not τῆς φύσεως, ἀλλὰ τῆς κακῆς προαιρέσεως : " not of nature, but of an evil determination of the will : " (see History of Art. ix. note). And our ninth Article teaches, not that it is part of our nature, but " the fault and corruption of our nature."

[2] " Man's corruption consists, first, in the deprivation of the Divine guidance, which he has rejected, for " the light shined in darkness, and the darkness comprehended it not ; " and secondly, in the correspondent rebellion of the lower principles of his body and his soul." — Wilberforce on *The Incarnation*, p 74.

actually guilty of sin, and so defiled and corrupted by it. And Christ, who was the second Adam, who came on purpose that He might conquer where Adam had fallen, and so restore that nature which Adam had debased, was, by the constitution of that nature which He adopted, liable to be assailed by the same dangers that Adam had been assailed by. But His own essential holiness and the supporting power of his Godhead enabled Him to endure temptation, and so made it impossible that He should fall under it. Thus He became a fit representative of our race, as much as Adam was. He had all our nature, with all its natural weaknesses ; and all that He lacked was that which was no proper part of, but only a vicious addition to our nature, namely, our sin. Nay, He even condescended to take our sicknesses. He was liable to hunger and weariness, and death. Many indeed of our sicknesses are the natural results of sin, of gluttony or intemperance, anger or passion. These He, who had no sin, could not have. Yet He took, not only human nature, but mortal nature ; and though He was too holy to defile Himself with our sin, yet He was not too glorious to submit to our death.

The passages of Scripture which prove this part of the doctrine of the Article, are sufficiently numerous and familiar. Thus it is announced to Mary, " That *Holy Thing* which shall be born of thee shall be called the Son of God " (Luke i. 35). " The prince of this world," said our Lord, " hath nothing in Me " (John xiv. 30). He was " the Holy One, and the just " (Acts iii. 14). God " made Him to be sin for us who knew no sin " (2 Cor. v. 21). " He was in all things tempted like as we are, yet without sin " (Heb. iv. 15). " An High Priest, holy, harmless, undefiled, separate from sinners, and made higher than the heavens ; " not like those " high priests who have infirmity," and needing to " offer up sacrifices, first for their own sins, and then for the people's " (Heb. vii. 26, 27, 28). He " did no sin, neither was guile found in His mouth " (1 Pet. ii. 22). He " was manifested to take away our sins, and in Him is no sin " (1 John iii. 5).

The words of the Article, that " He came to be the Lamb without spot " are from the following : —

" He was led as a Lamb to the slaughter, and as a sheep before her shearers is dumb, so He openeth not His mouth " (Isai. liii. 7). " The next day John seeth Jesus coming unto him, and saith, Behold the Lamb of God which taketh away the sin of the world " (John i. 29). " Christ, who through the Eternal Spirit offered Himself without spot to God " (Heb. ix. 14). Redeemed " with the precious Blood of Christ, as of a Lamb without blemish and without spot" (1 Pet. i. 19. Comp. Exod. xii. 5; Lev. xxii. 19, 20, 21).

II. The second part of the Article, that "all other men offend in many things, even though baptized and born again," has been already considered at some length under the ninth Article. It was there shown that the taint of sin pervaded the whole human race, and that every one naturally born of Adam was subject to it; that even the regenerate had still the remains of such corruption; and that that concupiscence, which still remains in them, has the nature of sin.[1]

It may be sufficient here to recite a few of the passages of Scripture on which more especially the proof of this assertion depends.

" If they sin against thee," says Solomon, " for there is no man that sinneth not" (1 Kings viii. 46). " In Thy sight," says David, " shall no man living be justified " (Ps. cxliii. 2). " Who can say," asks the wise man, " I have made my heart clean, I am pure from my sin? " (Prov. xx. 9). " We have proved both Jews and Gentiles, that they are all under sin " (Rom. iii. 9). " Death passed upon all men, for that all have sinned" (Rom. v. 12). " The Scripture hath concluded all under sin " (Gal. iii. 22). " In many things we offend, all " (James iii. 2). " If we say that we have no sin, we deceive ourselves, and the truth is not in us " (1 John i. 8). " Let not sin reign in your mortal body, that ye should obey it in the lusts thereof" (Rom. vi. 12). " I had not known sin but by the Law: for I had not known lust except the Law had said, Thou shalt not covet " (Rom. vii. 7). So " the flesh lusteth against the Spirit " (Gal. v. 17).

The last two passages show that lust or concupiscence hath the nature of sin.

2. The principal objections which may be urged against this part of the doctrine of the Article, are such as the following.

In some passages of Scripture people are called blameless: as (Luke i. 6), Zacharias and Elizabeth are spoken of as " both righteous before God, walking in all the commandments and ordinances of the Lord, blameless." In a like manner St. Paul speaks of himself as having " lived in all good conscience before God to this day " (Acts xxiii. 1); as exercising himself " to have a con-

---

[1] Ανθρώπων οὐδεὶς ἀναμάρτητος, ἑνὶ γὰρ μαρτυρεῖται, ὅτι ἁμαρτίαν οὐκ ἐποίησε. Basil. **M.** *Orat. de Pænitentia.* Suicer. I. 207.

science void of offence toward God and toward man" (Acts xxiv. 16); as having been before his conversion, "touching the righteousness which is in the Law, blameless" (Phil. iii. 6).

Such passages seem to argue *blameless* perfection. But we may answer that Zacharias could not have been perfect, or he would not have disbelieved the Angel when he promised him a son, and so have been smitten with dumbness for his want of faith (Luke i. 20). St. Paul, when he speaks of himself as blameless touching the righteousness of the Law, was a persecutor of the Church, and though he did it ignorantly in unbelief, and so obtained mercy, yet we can hardly consider it as consistent with perfection; and though he speaks of himself as exercising himself to have a conscience void of offence, yet we know that he did "not count himself to have apprehended," that he was sensible of "infirmities" (see 2 Cor. xi. 30; xii. 10, &c.); that he felt it necessary to "keep under his body, and bring it into subjection" (1 Cor. ix. 27). Nay, we know that he was liable to infirmity, for so sharp a contention rose between him and Barnabas, that they could not continue together in the work of the Gospel, but were obliged to separate one from another. We must therefore understand the word *blameless* in a more popular sense, not as if those of whom it is predicated were free from all stain of sin, but as meaning that they lived an upright, godly life, ever striving to keep a conscience free from offence, and never yielding to those wilful sins which offend society, or destroy the work of God's grace in the soul, or even give cause of deep and bitter regret to him who yields to them.

Again, it is said of the Christian under grace, that "the law of the Spirit of life makes him free from the law of sin and death" (Rom. viii. 2). This is true of all good Christians, but it does not mean that they are made perfect and wholly free from sin, but that the Spirit of God sets them free from the *bondage* and *slavery* of sin, and gives them freedom and strength to "fulfil the righteousness of the Law."

The same reasoning nearly applies to the words of St. John, "Whosoever is born of God doth not commit sin" (1 John iii. 9). This is true of every regenerate man as regards his new nature, the new man created in him. That new man is pure and holy, hating sin and avoiding it. Still however there are the remains of the old man, causing in him those infirmities which more or less are common to all. A regenerate man does not live in admitted sin. If he does, his new life has failed and is stifled. But, he still "in many things offends," and, "if he says he has no sin, he deceives himself;" because, in this world, the old nature may be kept in subjection and bondage, but is never thoroughly extinguished, until the last enemy has been destroyed, and all things are put in subjection under the feet of Christ.

It is true, we are bid to be holy, as Christ is holy (1 Pet. i. 15); to "be perfect, as our Father which is in Heaven is perfect" (Matt. v. 48). But we can infer from these exhortations no more than this. It is our part to set before us the highest possible standard at which to aim. Christ took our nature, that He might make us partakers of His nature; and we are never to be satisfied, unless we grow daily more and more like to Him. But it does not follow, that we shall ever attain to such perfect conformity to His Image, until we become "like Him, by seeing Him as He is."

We come, lastly, to consider the case of the Blessed Virgin. That she was a person of most singular holiness, most highly honoured of God, and most affectionately beloved by her Divine Son, no candid reader of Scripture can doubt. The Angel salutes her, "Hail, thou that art highly favoured: [1] the Lord is with thee; Blessed art thou among women" (Luke i. 28). Her cousin Elizabeth saluted her, by the Holy Ghost, saying, "Blessed art thou among women;" and though she was her near kinswoman, yet wondered at the honour done to herself in that "the Mother of her Lord should come unto her" (Luke i. 42, 43). Mary herself said of herself, that "all generations should call her blessed" (Luke i. 48). The Lord in His youth was subject to her (Luke ii. 51). At His death, and with His dying accents, He commended her to the care and guardianship of His most devoted and best loved disciple (John xix. 26, 27). We learn of her, that she was the first who, hearing the blessed teaching of her Son, "kept all His sayings in her heart" (Luke ii. 51). We find her following Him, with unwearied and dauntless affection, to the foot of His Cross (John xix. 25); and, when all but His most faithful followers were dispersed, continuing with the Apostles "with one accord in prayer and supplication" (Acts i. 14).

All this is but what we should expect. Doubtless among women there never lived a holier than she who was chosen to the highest honour that ever befel created being. That honour, indeed, to be the tabernacle of Incarnate Godhead, to cherish the infant years, minister to the wants, and soothe, if such there were, the early sufferings of the Redeemer of mankind, to be the only earthly

[1] Κεχαριτωμένη. The margin has " *Or*, graciously accepted, *or*, much graced."

46

instrument by which God wrought the mystery of the Incarnation, is an honour so high that we can hardly wonder if ages of ignorance gave undue reverence to her who had such favour of God.[1]

Yet it has been remarked that on three separate occasions our Lord and her Lord used of, and to her, language at least bordering on censure. At the marriage in Cana, the words, " Woman, what have I to do with thee?" (John ii. 4) (though not sounding so strong in the Greek as in the English language) have been esteemed in all ages as words of rebuke.[2] Before this, when He was but twelve years old (Luke ii. 49), as His mother and Joseph sought for Him, He reproves them for not knowing the high mission on which He came : " How is it that ye sought Me? Wist ye not that I must be about My Father's business?" Lastly, when His mother and His brethren sought to speak with Him, the answer to those who told Him of it was, " Who are My mother and My brethren? And He stretched forth His hand towards His disciples and said, Behold My mother and My brethren! For, whosoever shall do the will of My Father which is in Heaven, the same is My brother, and sister, and mother" (Matt. xii. 48, 49, 50).

Very similar to this was that saying, when a certain woman " lifted up her voice and said unto Him, Blessed is the womb that bare Thee, and the paps which Thou hast sucked. But He said, Yea rather, blessed are they that hear the word of God and keep it " (Luke xi. 27, 28). There was indeed no denial of the blessedness of being His mother ; still less was there any denial that His mother was blessed. But the privilege of being the mother of Jesus was not in itself so great as the blessing of doing the will of God. Now those who argue that the Virgin was perfectly free from sin, argue so from the very fact of her being the mother of the Immaculate Saviour. But surely, if the fact of being His

---

[1] " Man is a creature of extremes . . . . Because Papists have made too much of things, Protestants have made too little of them . . . . Because one party has exalted the Virgin Mary to a divinity, the other can scarcely think of that *most highly favoured among women* with common respect." — *Remains of the Rev. Richard Cecil*, p. 364. Ninth Edition. Lond. 1830.

[2] τί ἐμοὶ καὶ σοὶ γύναι; the word γύναι may easily be used as a term of respect, and might as well have been rendered "lady" as "woman." Every one knows that ladies of the highest rank would have been so addressed in Greek. But the fathers all acknowledged rebuke in the sentence. ἐπέπληττε τῇ μητρί, says Athanasius (*Contra Arian.* Orat. 4) ; ἐπετίμησεν ἀκαίρως αἰτούσῃ, says Chrysostom (*In Matt.* hom. 45) ; 'Ο δὲ ἐπιτιμᾷ αὐτῇ οὐκ ἀλόγως, says Theophylact. See Beveridge on this Article. Epiphanius says that these words were used that no one might esteem the Blessed Virgin of a higher nature than woman, with special view to the heresies which would one day arise (*Hæres.* 79, Collyridiani).

mother proved that she was sinless, it would have brought with it, or have been the proof of, a blessing so great that there could have been no room for the " Yea! rather blessed."

We may conclude, therefore, that the Virgin Mary, though " highly favoured," " blessed among women," and, doubtless, unusually sanctified, was yet no exception to the rule that all mankind, Christ only excepted, are stained with sin, and liable to offend in many things.[1]

[1] The subject of the Perpetual Virginity of the Virgin Mary, which has some affinity to the question discussed in the text, may be seen treated at length by Pearson *On the Creed*, Article, " Born of the Virgin Mary." See especially the notes. See also Jer. Taylor's *Life of Christ*, § 2. Bp. Bull's *Works*, i. Serm. iv. ; and Professor Mill's *Accounts of our Lord's Brethren*.

ARTICLE XVI.

Of Sin after Baptism.	*De Peccato Post Baptismum.*

NOT every deadly sin willingly committed after baptism is sin against the Holy Ghost, and unpardonable. Wherefore the grant of repentance is not to be denied to such as fall into sin after baptism. After we have received the Holy Ghost we may depart from grace given and fall into sin, and by the grace of God we may arise again and amend our lives. And therefore they are to be condemned which say they can no more sin as long as they live here, or deny the place of forgiveness to such as truly repent.

NON omne peccatum mortale post baptismum voluntarie perpetratum, est peccatum in Spiritum Sanctum, et irremissibile. Proinde lapsis a baptismo in peccata, locus pœnitentiæ non est negandus. Post acceptum Spiritum Sanctum possumus a gratia data recedere, atque peccare, denuoque per gratiam Dei resurgere, ac resipiscere; ideoque illi damnandi sunt, qui se, quamdiu hic vivant, amplius non posse peccare affirmant, aut vere resipiscentibus veniæ locum denegant.

SECTION I. — HISTORY.

THE Article as it now stands is very nearly the same as the fifteenth Article of A. D. 1552. But in the Articles of 1552, the sixteenth Article followed out the subject of the fifteenth, and treated expressly of Blasphemy against the Holy Ghost.

The Article which we now have, treats of, or alludes to

I. Deadly sin after baptism, and the possibility of repentance for such sin.

II. The sin against the Holy Ghost.

III. The possibility of falling from grace.

The first of these three divisions is that which forms the main subject of the Article; the other two being incidentally alluded to. The third, however, is spoken of in somewhat decided terms, and being a point on which there has been no little controversy, requires to be considered.

I. As regards the possibility of repentance and forgiveness for sins committed after baptism and the grace of God, there was some stir even in early ages of the Church.

Some of the Gnostics, who affected great asceticism, appear to have held also very rigid notions of the divine justice and the irremissibility of sins.   Clement of Alexandria says that Basilides taught that "not all sins, but only sins which were committed involuntarily or through ignorance, were forgiven."[1]

The Church itself in early times was very severe in its censures against heinous crimes, and very slow in admitting offenders to Church-communion.   It appears that in the second and third centuries, persons who committed small sins might be admitted frequently to repentance, but that great and flagrant offenders were put to penance and reconciled to the Church but once.   In the case indeed of some very grievous, deadly, and often-repeated sins, the Church seems to have refused communion even at the last hour. The meaning of which severity doubtless was, that offenders might not mock God and the Church with feigned repentance, turning again to sin like the swine to their wallowing in the mire.[2]

The Montanists carried this rigour much farther than the Catholics; for they not only refused repeated penances and reconciliation, but did not allow to the Church the power of forgiving great sins after baptism, even once.   Tertullian, in those writings which he composed before he became a Montanist, speaks of grievous sins as once, and but once, remitted by the Church.   After he had joined the sect of the Montanists, he distinguishes between venial sins, (such as causeless anger, evil speaking, rash swearing, falsehood,) and sins of a heinous and deadly character, such as murder, idolatry, fraud, denying Christ, blasphemy, adultery, fornication. Of these latter he says there is no remission, and that even Christ will not intercede for them.[3]

St. Clement of Alexandria in one place seems to say that there is no repentance but once after baptism.[4]   It is probable that he refers to a passage in the *Pastor* of Hermas, where we read that there is but one penitence, namely, when we descend into the water, and so receive remission of sins.[5]   But whereas it is pretty certain that Hermas speaks of the repentance and remission of sins in baptism to be once given and never repeated, but does not thereby

---

[1] Clem. Alex. *Strom.* iv. p. 634, Potter; Mosheim, *De Rebus ante Constant.* sæc. 2, c. 48; King, *On the Creed*, p. 358; Bp. Kaye's *Clem. Alex.* p. 269.

[2] See this subject fully considered by Bingham, *Eccles. Antiq.* Bk. xvi. c. x.; Bk. xviii. c. iv.   He quotes Hermas, Clem. Alex., Tertull., Origen, the Council of Eliberis, Ambros., Augustine, &c.; see especially Bk. xviii. c. iv. § 1.

[3] Bp. Kaye's *Tertullian*, pp. 20, 254, 339; Tertullian, *De Pudicitia*, c. 19; see also Lardner, *Hist. of Heretics*, Bk. ii.

ch. xix. sect. 8; Mosheim, *Eccl. Hist.* Cent. ii. pt. ii. ch. v.

[4] Ὁ μὲν οὖν ἐξ ἐθνῶν καὶ τῆς προβιότητος ἐκείνης ἐπὶ τὴν πίστιν ὁρμήσας, ἅπαξ ἔτυχεν ἀφέσεως ἁμαρτιῶν. ὁ δὲ καὶ μετὰ ταῦτα ἁμαρτήσας, εἶτα μετανοῶν, κἂν συγγνώμης τυγχάνῃ, αἰδεῖσθαι ὀφείλει, μηκέτι λουόμενος εἰς ἄφεσιν ἁμαρτιῶν . . . . δόκησις τοίνυν μετανοίας, οὐ μετάνοια, τὸ πολλάκις αἰτεῖσθαι συγγνώμην, ἐφ' οἷς πλημμελοῦμεν πολλάκις. — *Stromat.* ii. § 13, p. 460.

[5] Herm. *Past. Mandat.* iv. 3; Cotel. p. 96.

mean to exclude from repentance after baptism ; [1] so it appears that
Clement of Alexandria speaks either of one *public* penance, which
might be conceded by the Church,[2] or that he simply means that
to repent and return again continually to former sins proves the
repentance not to have been real, but feigned and hypocritical.
Yet some have thought that the language both of Hermas and
Clement prepared the way for the severity of Origen and the errors
of the Novatians.

Origen appears to have thrown out the opinion, that persons who
had once embraced the Gospel and been baptized, and then denied
the faith, could not be readmitted to repentance nor obtain pardon
of sin.[3]

The sect of the Novatians arose about the middle of the third
century. Novatian, their founder, a presbyter of Rome, had on a
former occasion been chosen by the Church of that city to write to
Cyprian on the subject of restoring the lapsed to communion.[4] In
the year 251, Cornelius was elected Bishop of Rome, a post to
which Novatian aspired. Novatian had himself secured three
bishops, ignorant and inexperienced men, to consecrate him to the
bishopric. But not succeeding in his hopes of holding possession
of the see, he set up a schismatical communion. He does not
appear to have held any heretical doctrine ; but he denied to the
Church the power of restoring to communion those who had lapsed
in persecution. Eusebius indeed says, that he denied to them the
hope of salvation ; [5] but it seems more probable, from the language
of Cyprian and others, that he exhorted them to repent, and to seek
for pardon, but refused to offer them any consolation, or to admit
them again to any church-privilege in this life.[6]

---

[1] Consult Cotelerius's note on this passage of Hermas.

[2] So his words are explained by Lumper, *Hist. Theolog. Crit.* Tom. iv. p. 388.
Bp. Jeremy Taylor writes, " Whereas
some of them " (*i. e.* of the fathers) " use
to say that after baptism, or after the
first relapse, they are ' unpardonable,'
we must know that in the style of the
Church, ' unpardonable ' signifies such
to which, by the discipline and customs
of the Church, pardon may not be ministered. They were called ' unpardonable,' not because God would not pardon
them, but because He alone could." —
On Repentance, ch. ix. § 3. All that is
said in this section about the fathers' doctrine of repentance is well worth reading.

[3] Origen. *Tract.* 35 *in Matthæum ;* see
Abp. Potter's note on the before-cited
passage of Clem. Alex.

[4] The letter is in the collection of the
letters of Cyprian, Epis. xxx.

[5] *H. E.* vi. 43; ὡς μηκέτ' οὔσης αὐτοῖς
σωτηρίας ἐλπίδος. So Epiphan. *Adv. Hær.*
Hær. xxxix. λέγων μὴ εἶναι σωτηρίαν, ἀλλὰ
μίαν μετάνοιαν.

[6] *Epist.* 55, *juxta finem.* There he
describes the Novatians as urging repentance, but excluding from peace :
" hortari ad satisfactionis pœnitentiam, et
subtrahere de satisfactione medicinam ;
dicere fratribus nostris, plange et lacry-
mas funde, et diebus ac noctibus inge-
misce, et pro abluendo et purgando delicto tuo largiter et frequenter operare,
sed extra ecclesiam post omnia ista mo-
rieris : quæcumque ad pacem pertinent,
facies, sed nullam pacem, quam quæris,
accipies."

Whether he extended this severity to heinous sins in general is not apparent ; but it seems that the sect of the Novatians, who owed their origin to him, refused communion to the penitent after other heavy offences besides lapsing in persecution.[1] The Novatians arrogated to themselves the title of *Cathari,* or *pure ;* and refused to acknowledge the baptism of those Churches which admitted the lapsed to penance and communion.

The Church Catholic, however, rejected at once the severity of Novatian's sentiments. Eusebius, on the authority of Cornelius, mentions a council of bishops, who met at Rome and condemned the folly of Novatian.[2] Still the sect of the Cathari continued, and appears to have flourished throughout the fourth and part of the fifth century. But the fathers of the Church uniformly esteemed them heretics, and expressed their belief in the remissibility of sin, on repentance, after baptism.[3]

St. Cyprian says, that to a lapsed Christian, who repents, prays, and exerts himself, God gives pardon and restores his arms, so that he may fight again, strengthened for the conflict by the very sorrow for his sins. And he, thus strengthened by the Lord, may make glad the Church, which he had saddened, and obtain not only pardon, but a crown.[4] St. Gregory Nazianzen calls penitence another baptism, but rougher and more troublesome ; and says that owning the infirmity and fickleness of man, he gratefully accepts for himself, and willingly imparts to others, this grace of repentance ; aware that he himself is compassed with infirmities, and that with that measure he metes it shall be measured to him again. The Novatian he calls the modern Pharisee, and asks if he would not have allowed the repentance of David, or the return of Peter after he had denied his Lord, or the contrition of the incestuous Corinthian, to whom St. Paul confirmed his love.[5]

---

[1] " Igitur, hoc nullum habet dubium, adultam ecclesiam Novatianam non modo perfidos Christianos, verum etiam omnium capitalium criminum reos alienos a se voluisse." — Mosheim, *De Rebus ante Constant. Magnum,* sæc. tertium, § XVI.

[2] *H. E.* VI. 43, *juxta finem.*

[3] See Cyprian, Eusebius, and Epiphanius, as above ; Mosheim, *De Rebus ante Constant. Magnum,* sæc. III. §§ XV. XVI.; Lardner, III. pt. II. ch. 47; Cave, *Histor. Liter.* Tom. I. p. 91.

[4] " Pœnitenti, operanti, roganti, potest (Deus) clementer ignoscere .... dat Ille et arma rursus quibus victus armetur, reparat et corroborat vires, quibus fides instaurata vegetetur. Repetet certamen suum miles, iterabit aciem, provocabit hostem, et quidem factus ad prœlium fortior per dolorem. Qui sic Deo satisfecerit, qui pœnitentia facti sui, qui pudore delicti, plus et virtutis et fidei de ipso lapsus sui dolore conceperit, exauditus et adjutus a Domino, quam contristaverat nuper, lætam faciet Ecclesiam : nec jam solam Dei veniam merebitur, sed coronam." Cypr. *De Lapsis, fin.* p. 188.

[5] Οἶδα καὶ πέμπτον (βάπτισμα) ἔτι τῶν δακρύων, ἀλλ' ἐπιπονώτερον. ὡς ὁ λούων καθ' ἑκάστην νύκτα τὴν κλίνην αὐτοῦ, καὶ τὴν στρωμνὴν τοῖς δάκρυσιν .... ἐγὼ μὲν οὖν (ἄνθρωπος εἶναι γὰρ ὁμολογῶ ζῶον τρεπτὸν καὶ ῥευστῆς φύσεως) καὶ ἔχομαι τοῦτο προθύμως, καὶ προσκυνῶ τὸν δεδωκότα, καὶ τοῖς

St. Ambrose says, that, as our blessed Lord calls all that are
weary and heavy laden to come unto Him, those cannot be reckoned
as His disciples, who, whilst they have need of mercy themselves,
yet deny it to others.[1]   The Novatians granted pardon to smaller,
not to greater crimes ; but God, says St. Ambrose, makes no such
distinction, who has promised His mercy to all, and gives to all
His priests the power of loosing without any exception.   Only, if
the crime be great, so must be the repentance.[2]

Other early heretics are mentioned, as agreeing with the
Novatians in their severity against the lapsed.   The Apostolici are
reckoned by Epiphanius as an offset from the Encratites or Cathari.
Their opinions concerning marriage and all worldly indulgences
were highly ascetic, and they refused to receive those who once
fell.[3]   The Meletians were an Egyptian sect.   They arose about
the time of Diocletian's persecution.   Meletius, their founder, was
Bishop of Lycopolis in the Thebaid.   He was deposed by Peter,
Bishop of Alexandria, and set up a schismatical communion under
Alexander, the successor of Peter.   They ultimately joined the
Arians, as being the great enemies of Alexander.   Epiphanius and
Augustine ascribe to them the same severity to the lapsed which
characterized the Novatians.[4]   The Luciferians, who followed
Lucifer, Bishop of Cagliari in Sardinia, avoided communion with
those who had lapsed to Arianism, and with those bishops who
restored the lapsed.   It should seem from Jerome that the Luciferians did not altogether exclude laymen who had lapsed from
returning to communion, but would on no account receive repentant bishops and presbyters ; arguing from our Lord's words, " Ye
are the salt of the earth : but if the salt have lost its savour, wherewith shall it be salted." [5]

ἄλλοις μεταδίδωμι καὶ προεισφέρω τοῦ ἐλέου
τὸν ἔλεον. Οἶδα γὰρ καὶ αὐτὸς ἀσθένειαν
περικείμενος, καὶ ὡς ἂν μετρήσω, μετρηθησό-
μενος. Σὺ δὲ τί λέγεις ; τί νομοθετεῖς, ὦ
νέε φαρισαῖε, καὶ καθαρὲ τὴν προσηγορίαν,
οὐ τὴν προαίρεσιν, καὶ φυσῶν ἡμῖν Ναυατοῦ
τὰ μετὰ τῆς αὐτῆς ἀσθενείας ; οὐ δέχῃ μετάνοιαν ; οὐ δίδως ὀδυρμοῖς χώραν ; οὐ δακρύεις
δάκρυον; Μὴ σύ γε τοιούτου κριτοῦ τύχοις
. . . . οὐδὲ τὸν Δαβὶδ δέχῃ μετανοοῦντα, ᾧ
καὶ τὸ προφητικὸν χάρισμα ἡ μετάνοια συνε-
τήρησεν ; οὐδὲ Πέτρον τὸν μέγαν παθόντά
τι ἀνθρώπινον περὶ τὸ σωτήριον πάθος ;
. . . . οὐδὲ τὸν ἐν Κορίνθῳ παρανομήσαντα ;
Παῦλος δὲ καὶ ἀγάπην ἐκύρωσεν, ἐπειδὴ τὴν
διόρθωσιν εἶδε, καὶ τὸ αἴτιον, ἵνα μὴ τῇ πε-
ρισσοτέρᾳ λύπῃ καταποθῇ ὁ τοιοῦτος. — Greg.
Naz. *Orat.* 39, Tom. I. p. 634, Col. 1690.

[1] "Unde liquet eos inter Christi dis-
cipulos non esse habendos, qui dura pro
mitibus, superba pro humilibus sequenda
opinantur : et cum ipsi quærant Domini
misericordiam, aliis eam denegant; ut
sunt doctores Novatianorum, qui mun-
dos se appellant." — *De Pœnitentia,* Lib.
I. c. I.

[2] " Sed Deus distinctionem non facit,
qui misericordiam suam promisit omnibus, et relaxandi licentiam omnibus sacerdotibus suis sine ulla exceptione con-
cessit.   Sed qui culpam exaggeravit,
exaggeret etiam pœnitentiam." — Ibid.
c. 2.

[3] Epiphan. *Hæres.* 61.

[4] Epiphan. *Hæres.* 63 ; August. *Hæres*
48.

[5] Hieron. *Adv. Luciferianos,* Tom. IV
pt. II. p. 290, *seq.*

At the period of the Reformation, it appears that some of the sects which then arose, most probably the Anabaptists in particular, revived in some degree the Novatian errors. The XIth Article of the Confession of Augsburg, which is the source of the XVIth Article of the Church of England, condemns the Novatians by name, for refusing repentance to the lapsed, and afterwards condemns the Anabaptists, though for another error, namely, the denial that persons once justified ever lose the grace of God.[1] Dr. Hey thinks that both the German and English reformers had chiefly in view the Anabaptists, in their condemnation of this extreme rigour against the lapsed.[2]

In the fourteenth session of the Council of Trent, several decrees and canons were drawn up upon penance, whereby it was defined that, for sins after baptism, the sacrament of penance was essential and sufficient; the form of the sacrament being contrition, confession, and satisfaction. It was determined that it was necessary to pardon that every mortal sin should be confessed, but not every venial sin.[3]

The continental reformers were very express in asserting the efficacy of repentance for remission of sin after baptism. Thus, the Confession of Augsburg says, that " Remission of sins may be granted to those who lapse after baptism, at any time when they turn to God. And the Church ought to grant absolution to such."[4] The Helvetic Confession declares, that " there is access to God and pardon for all who believe, with the exception of those guilty of the sin against the Holy Ghost; therefore the old and new Novatians are to be condemned."[5]

The sentiments of the English Reformers appear plainly, both in the wording of this Article, and in several of the Homilies. For example, in the First Book of Homilies we read, " They, which in act or deed do sin after baptism, when they turn again to God unfeignedly, they are likewise washed by this sacrifice from their sins, in such sort that there remaineth not any spot of sin that shall be imputed to their damnation."[6]   " We must trust only in

---

[1] *Confess. Augs.* Art. xi.; *Sylloge*, p. 172.
[2] *Lectures*, iii. p. 436.
[3] *Conc. Trid.* Sess. xiv. Can. i. iv. &c.; Sarpi, p. 326.
[4] " De pœnitentia docent, quod lapsis post baptismum contingere possit remissio peccatorum, quocunque tempore cum convertuntur. Et quod ecclesia talibus redeuntibus ad pœnitentiam impertire absolutionem debeat." — Conf. August. Art. xi.; *Syll.* p. 172.

[5] " Docemus interim semper et omnibus peccatoribus aditum patere ad Deum, et hunc omnino omnibus fidelibus condonare peccata, excepto uno illo peccato in Spiritum Sanctum. Ideoque damnamus et veteres et novos Novatianos atque Catharos." — *Confess. Helvet.* Art. xiv.; *Syllog.* p. 50.
[6] *Homily of Salvation*, pt. i.

47

God's mercy, and that sacrifice which our High Priest and Saviour, Christ Jesus the Son of God, once offered upon the Cross, to obtain thereby God's grace and remission, as well of our original sin in baptism as of all actual sin committed by us after our baptism, if we truly repent and turn to Him unfeignedly again." [1] And in the Second Book of Homilies we are told, " Repentance is never too late, so that it be true and just." [2] " Although we do, after we be once come to God, and grafted in his Son Jesus Christ, fall into great sins . . . . yet if we rise again by repentance, and with a full purpose of amendment of life do flee unto the mercy of God, taking sure hold thereon, through faith in his Son Jesus Christ, there is an assured and infallible hope of pardon and remission of the same, and that we shall be received again into the favour of our heavenly Father." [3]

II. Concerning the sin against the Holy Ghost, the language of our Article is directed against an opinion, which was first broached by Origen.

Origen and Theognostus taught, that the blasphemy against the Holy Ghost was, when those who in baptism had received the gift of the Spirit, returned again to sin ; and that such had never forgiveness.   Origen, we are told, assigned as a reason for this, that, whereas God the Father pervades and embraces all things, animate and inanimate, and the power of God the Son extends more immediately to the rational creatures of God, among whom are heathen men who have never yet believed ; the Spirit of God, on the contrary, is in those only who have received the grace of baptism. Hence, when Gentiles and unbelievers sin by blasphemy, they sin against the Son, who is in them, yet they can be forgiven.   But when baptized Christians sin, their iniquity proceeds to the Spirit of God, who dwells in their hearts, and therefore they have never forgiveness.

St. Athanasius wrote a treatise expressly on the subject, in which he first states, and then examines and confutes, this notion of Origen's. He observes, that the occasion of our Lord's speaking of the sin against the Holy Ghost was the blasphemy of the Pharisees, who disbelieved the miracles of Christ, and ascribed them to Beelzebub.   They, he remarks, had never been baptized, and yet they had either committed, or were in imminent danger of committing, the sin against the Holy Ghost.

Athanasius himself appears to maintain, that the blasphemy

---

[1] *Homily of Salvation*, pt. II.   [2] *Homily of Repentance* pt. I.   [3] Ibid.

against the Son of Man was the disbelieving and blaspheming
against our blessed Lord, when as yet only His human nature
was manifested; but that blasphemy against the Holy Spirit was
continuing to deride and speak evil of Him, when He had given
plain and irrefragable proofs of His Godhead and Divine nature.[1]
The author, under his name, of the Questions to Antiochus, says,
that they blasphemed the Holy Spirit, that is, the Divine nature of
the Son who said that He cast out devils by Beelzebub. To them,
he says, there is no remission in this world, nor in the next. But,
he adds, we must understand this, not that he who blasphemes
and repents, but that he who blasphemes and does not repent,
shall never be forgiven; for no sin is unpardonable in the presence
of God to those who holily and worthily repent; and then he
adds, that there are three baptisms which purge away sin: the
baptism of water, the baptism of blood, i. e. martyrdom, and the
baptism of tears, i. e. repentance; and that many, who had defiled
by backsliding their holy baptism, have yet been cleansed and
accepted by the baptism of tears.[2]

Many, both ancient and modern, have followed in the steps of
Athanasius, and given a like interpretation of the blasphemy against
the Spirit. St. Chrysostom appears to take the same view; namely,
that blasphemy was irremissible, which was uttered after the discovery and experimental proof of the Spirit's working. But then
he appears to deny remission of such sin, not only to the impenitent, but even to those who repent.[3]

St. Augustine has some very excellent observations on the subject. He shows that neither Jews nor Gentiles were kept from
pardon, because they had blasphemed Christ and the Holy Spirit
in their unconverted state; nor yet that persons who had been
baptized in infancy, and had grown up in ignorance, were refused
forgiveness, because in their state of ignorance they resisted the
Spirit and spoke against Him. He shows too, that even baptized
persons lapsing, or becoming heretics, were yet admitted to the
peace of the Church on their conversion and repentance; and
enumerates among such heretics, Sabellians, Arians, Manichæans,
Cataphrygians, Donatists. And then concludes, that the sin
against the Spirit of God, which hath never forgiveness, is a final
and obdurate continuance in wickedness, despite of all the calls

---

[1] Athanas. In Illud Evangelii, Quicunque
dixerit.
[2] Athan. Quæstiones ad Antiochum,
Quæst. LXXI. LXXII.

[3] οὐκ ἀφεθήσεται οὐδὲ μετανοοῦσι. —
Chrysost. Homil. XLI. in Matt. ap. Suic.
Tom. I. p. 700.

of God to repentance, joined with a desperation of the mercy
of God.[1]

That the Church at large rejected the theory of Origen, though
the Novatians appear to have adopted it, is plain from their admitting offenders after baptism, even the most heinous, to penance and
absolution.   They did not indeed restore them readily and lightly,
as we do at present, but after a long term of penitence and exclusion from church-privileges ; yet still, after sufficient satisfaction had
been given to the Church, all offenders were ecclesiastically pardoned, and the sinner restored to peace and communion.   For example,
for fornication, the offender was expelled three years from the
public service of the Church, three years more he was in the station
of hearers, three years more in the station of the prostrate, and
then was received to full communion.   The term was double for
adultery, and three times as long for murder.   There was, however,
some discretion allowed to the bishop, who might contract the term
of discipline upon just ground of reason ; and especially if there
was imminent danger of death, the clemency of the fathers determined that the sinner should not be permitted to enter on his long
last journey without provision for it, and without participation in
the holy sacraments.[2]   These rules were not the same in all dioceses and all parts of the Church.   Thus the council of Ancyra enjoins seven years' penance for adultery ; [3] for such as had sacrificed,
three years of prostration, and two years more as communicants
without oblation ; [4] and for those who had sacrificed two or three
times, it enjoins a penance of six years.[5]   But the diversity in the
measure of penance only proves identity of principle.

III. The question of the possibility of falling from grace may be

---

[1] Augustin. *Epist. ad Romanos Expositio inchoata*, 14–23.   Tom. iii. par.
ii. p. 933–940.   See especially, c. 22, p.
939 : " Si ergo nec Paganis, nec Hebræis,
nec hæreticis, nec schismaticis nondum
baptizatis ad baptismum Christi aditus
clauditur, ubi condemnata vita priore in
melius commutentur ; quamvis Chris-
tianitati et Ecclesiæ Dei adversantes antequam Christianis sacramentis ablueren-
tur, etiam Spiritui Sancto quanta potu-
erunt infestatione restiterint ; si etiam
hominibus, qui usque ad sacramentorum
perceptionem veritatis scientiam percep-
erint, et post hæc lapsi Spiritui Sancto
restiterunt, ad sanitatem redeuntibus et
pacem Dei pœnitendo quærentibus, aux-
ilium misericordiæ non negatur ; si denique de illis ipsis, quibus blasphemiam in
Spiritum Sanctum ab eis prolatam Dominus objecit, si qui resipiscentes ad Dei
gratiam confugerunt, sine ulla dubita-
tione sanati sunt : quid aliud restat nisi,
ut peccatum in Spiritum Sanctum, quod
neque in hoc sæculo neque in futuro
dimitti Dominus dicit, nullum intelligatur nisi perseverantia in nequitia et in
malignitate, cum desperatione indulgen-
tiæ Dei ? "

[2] See Marshall's *Penitential Discipline*,
especially ch. ii. pt. ii. § 1, and Appendix, Num. i. ; Gregory Nyssen's *Canonical Epistle to Letoius*.

[3] Concil. Ancyrani, Can. xx. ; Beveridge, *Pandect*. Tom. i. p. 397.

[4] Can. vi. ; Beveridge, i. p. 380.

[5] Can. viii. ; Beveridge, i. 382.

considered as intimately connected with the doctrine of God's predestination, and therefore might properly come under the XVIIth
Article. Yet, as it is certainly in some degree treated of in this
Article, and may be separated from the question of predestination,
we may not refuse to consider it here.

The earliest fathers, Clement, Ignatius, Justin Martyr, Irenæus,
and others, speak of God's election and of predestination to grace
and life. But, as we shall see in the next Article, it is not immediately certain in what sense they use this language of holy Scripture.
The controversies which afterwards arose concerning the Pelagian
heresy, and the predestinarian doctrines of St. Augustine, induced
persons to use more accurate terms : and Augustine himself argues
that the fathers did not teach his doctrines, because no heresy had
arisen which made it necessary to expound them.[1]   It seems, however, tolerably certain that the fathers of the second century spoke
of the possibility of falling away from grace, and held that those who
had received the gift of the Holy Spirit might afterwards reject it
and be lost.   Justin Martyr says, that " God will accept the penitent, as if he had never sinned, and will treat him who turns from
godliness to impiety, as a sinner and unjust.   Wherefore our Lord
Jesus Christ says, " In whatsoever I find you, I will judge you." [2]
Irenæus says, that whereas God gives grace, those who profit by it
will receive glory, but those who reject it will be punished.[3]   He
compares children of God, who disobey Him, to sons of men who
are disinherited by their fathers ; and says that if we disobey God,
we shall be cast off by Him.[4]   Clement of Alexandria speaks of
his Gnostic or perfect Christian, as praying for the permanence
and continuance of that good which he already possesses.[5]   Tertullian indeed, in his later treatises, especially after he had become a
Montanist, seems to say that a person who fell away from grace

---

[1] *De Prædestinatione,* § 27, Tom. x. p.
808 ; *De Dono Perseverantiæ,* § 53, Tom.
x. p. 851.

[2] *Dialog.* p. 267.

[3] " Dedit ergo Deus bonum, quemadmodum et Apostolus testificatur in eadem
epistola, et qui operantur quidem illud,
gloriam et honorem percipient, quoniam
operati sunt bonum, cum possint non
operari illud ; hi autem qui illud non
operantur, judicium justum recipient
Dei, quoniam non sunt operati bonum,
cum possint operari illud." — *Adv. Hær.*
iv. 71.

[4] " Quemadmodum enim in hominibus
indicto audientes patribus filii abdicati,
natura quidem filii eorum sunt, lege vero

alienati sunt, non enim hæredes fiunt na-
turalium parentum : eodem modo apud
Deum, qui non obediunt Ei, abdicati ab
Eo, desierunt filii Ejus esse . . . Verum
quando credunt et subjecti esse Deo perseverant et doctrinam Ejus custodiunt,
filii sunt Dei ; cum autem abscesserint,
et transgressi fuerint, Diabolo adscribun-
tur principi, ei qui primo sibi, tunc et
reliquis causa abscessionis factus est." —
Ibid. iv. 80. See also Beaven's *Irenæus,*
p. 166.

[5] 'Ο γνωστικὸς δὲ ὢν μὲν κέκτηται παρα-
μονήν, ἐπιτηδειότητα δὲ εἰς ἃ μέλλει ἀποβαί-
νειν, καὶ ἀϊδιότητα ὢν λήψεται, αἰτήσεται. —
Strom. Lib. vii. 7, p. 857.

had never been a Christian. In his tract *De Præscriptione* even, which was probably written before his Montanism, he speaks of no one as a Christian, but such as endured to the end.[1] . But in his tract *De Pudicitia*, which was written when he had become a Montanist, in commenting on those words of St. John, " He who is born of God sinneth not," he argues that venial sins, such as causeless anger, rash swearing, &c., all Christians are liable to ; but that deadly sin, such as murder, idolatry, blasphemy, impiety, no good Christian, no child of God, will commit.[2] Bishop Kaye even thinks that the language of Tertullian in his *later* writings is directly opposed to the doctrine of our XVIth Article. But he observes that as there was no controversy on the subject of perseverance in his days, we must not construe his expressions too strictly.[3] The time when this question really came to be discussed was after the rise of Pelagianism, and when St. Augustine had stated his predestinarian opinions. Perseverance was a natural part of his doctrine of predestination ; for, whereas he taught that some men were predestinated to eternal salvation, whilst others were permitted to fall by their own sins into condemnation, it followed of necessity that he should believe some to be predestinated to final perseverance, and others not. In his work *De Correptione et Gratia*, he calls those elect who were predestinated to eternal life ;[4] and observes that those who did not persevere were not properly to be called elect, for they were not separated from the mass of perdition by the foreknowledge and predestination of God ; and though, when they believed and were baptized and lived according to God, they might be called elect, yet it was by those who knew not the future, not by God, who saw that they would not persevere.[5]

The clergy of Marseilles and other parts of Gaul, being offended at the predestinarianism expressed in this and other treatises of Augustine, Prosper and Hilary wrote to him a statement of their objections. These letters of Hilary and Prosper called forth a reply from St. Augustine, in two books ; the former on the Predestination of the Saints, the other on the Gift of Perseverance. In the latter, he asserts perseverance to be the gift of God, not given equally to all, but only to the predestinated. Whether a person has received this gift must in this life ever be uncertain ; for, however long he may have persevered in holiness, yet if he does not persevere to the end, he cannot have received the grace of perse-

---

[1] " Nemo autem Christianus, *nisi qui ad finem usque perseveraverit.*" — *De Præscript. Hæretic.* c. 3.
[2] *De Pudicitia*, c. 19.
[3] Bp. Kaye's *Tertullian*, p. 340.
[4] *De Corrept. et Grat.* § 14.
[5] Ibid. § 16.

verance.[1] He says, that of two infants equally born in sin, by
God's will one is taken, one left; that, of two grown persons, one
follows God's call, another refuses to follow it; and all this is
from the inscrutable judgments of God. And so, of two pious
persons, why to one is granted final perseverance, to another it is
not granted, is to be resolved into the still more inscrutable judgments of God.[2]

It appears plainly that St. Augustine held two distinct predesti-
nations : one predestination to regeneration and a state of grace,
the other predestination to perseverance and to final reward. We
find him continually speaking of persons predestinated to be brought
into the Church, and so by God's grace brought to baptism, and
therein regenerate, but not necessarily on that account persevering
to the end. Nay, he speaks of persons continuing in a state of
grace for many years, but yet finally falling away.[3] Such were
predestinated to regeneration, and to receive grace and sanctification, but for some unknown though doubtless just cause, they were
not predestinated to final perseverance. God is pleased to mix
those who will not persevere with those who will, for good and
wise reasons, on purpose that he who thinketh he standeth should
take heed lest he fall.[4] In this life it was utterly impossible for
any one to know whether he would persevere or not.[5] He might
live ten years and persevere for five, and yet for the last five fall
away.[6] We may see examples of God's hidden counsels in the
case of some infants who die unregenerate, others who die regenerate ; the former lost, the latter saved. And of those who are regenerate and grow up, some persevering to the end, others permitted to live on till they lapsed and fell away, and so are lost, who if
they had died just before they lapsed, would have been saved; and
again others, who had lapsed, preserved in life till they repented
again, who, if they had been taken away before repentance, would
have been damned.[7]

---

[1] *De Dono Persererantiæ, Opp.* Tom.
x. p. 822. See especially §§ 1, 6, 7, 10,
15, 19.

[2] " Ex duobus autem piis, cur huic
donetur perseverantia usque ad finem,
illi non donetur, inscrutabiliora sunt judicia Dei . . . Nonne postremo utrique
vocati fuerant, et vocantem secuti, utrique ex impiis justificati, et per lavacrum
regenerationis utrique renovati ? Sed si
hæc audiret ille, qui sciebat, procul dubio
quod dicebat, respondere posset et dicere :
Vera sunt hæc, secundum hæc omnia
ex nobis erant; verumtamen secundum

aliam quandam discretionem non erant
ex nobis, nam si fuissent ex nobis, man-
sissent utique nobiscum." — Ibid. § 21.

[3] See especially *De Corrept. et Grat.*
20, 22 ; *De Dono Perseverantiæ,* 1, 21, 32,
33, &c.

[4] *De Don. Persev.* 19.

[5] " Utrum quisque hoc munus accep-
erit, quam diu hanc vitam ducit, incer-
tum est. Si enim prius quam moriatur
cadat, non perseverasse utique dicitur, et
verissime dicitur." — Ibid. § 1.

[6] Ibid.

[7] Ibid § 32

It is of considerable importance to observe the nature of St. Augustine's doctrine of perseverance, as it materially differs from the doctrine most generally held by later predestinarians. St. Augustine did not hold that persons who had once received the gift of God's Spirit could never lose it, or at least, could never be finally lost. On the contrary, he plainly taught that persons might receive the gift of regeneration, and might persevere in holiness for a time, and yet, if they had not the gift of perseverance, might fall away at the last. In short, he held that predestination to grace did not necessarily imply predestination to glory. A person might receive the grace of God and act upon it, and yet not persevere to the end; and hence it was that he held that, even if a person had all the signs and tokens of a child of God, it was quite impossible in this life to say whether he was predestinated to persevere to the end.[1]

The question of final perseverance, and of the falling from grace, thenceforth became a natural part of discussions concerning predestination.

At the time of the Reformation all these subjects were hotly discussed. The Council of Trent found nothing to condemn in the writings of Luther, or of the Lutheran divines, on the subject of predestination, or of final perseverance;[2] but from the writings of the Zuinglians several articles were drawn out which were considered deserving of condemnation. Among these there were, (5) That the justified cannot fall from grace. (6) That those who are called, and are not in the number of the predestinated, do never receive grace. (8) That the justified is bound to believe for certain that in case he fall from grace he shall receive it again.[3]

The divines of Trent, though not entirely at one concerning some questions of predestination, agreed to censure these concerning final perseverance, with admirable concord. They said that it had always been an opinion in the Church, that many receive grace and keep it for a time, who afterwards lose it, and are damned at the last. They alleged the examples of Saul, Solomon, and Judas, of whom our Lord said, "Of those whom thou hast given me have I lost none save the son of perdition." To these they added Nicholas, one of the deacons, and for a conclusion of all, the fall of Luther.[4]

The language of Luther, on all the subjects connected with predestination, varies a good deal. Earlier in his life he was a

---

[1] See *ante*, note 5, p. 375, and *De Dono Perseverantiæ, passim*.
[2] Sarpi, p. 197.   [3] Ibid.   [4] Ibid. p. 200.

high predestinarian; but later he seems to have materially changed his views. In his commentary on the 17th chapter of St. John, he speaks of all disputes on predestination as having sprung from their author the devil.[1] In his commentary on the Galatians (ch. v. 4), he speaks plainly of falling from grace, and says that " he who falls away from grace, loses expiation, remission of sins, righteousness, liberty, life, &c., which Christ by His death and resurrection deserved for us; and, in their room, acquires wrath and God's judgment, sin, death, slavery to the devil, and eternal damnation." [2]

The XIth Article of the Confession of Augsburg, which is clearly the source of our own XVIth Article, condemns the Anabaptists, who say that persons once justified cannot again lose the Holy Spirit.[3] From which we may conclude, first, that such was the teaching of the Anabaptists; and secondly, that the Lutherans viewed it altogether as an Anabaptist error.

The Calvinist divines, on the contrary, have generally believed that grace once given was indefectible; and this is in fact their doctrine of perseverance. Calvin himself held, that our Lord and St. Paul taught us to confide that we should always be safe, if we were once made Christ's; and that those who fall away may have had the outward signs, but had not the inward truth of election.[4]

The English reformers, as we have already seen, adopted in this Article the language, not of the Zuinglians and Calvinists, but of the Confession of Augsburg and the Lutherans. This is apparent from the wording of the Article itself, which evidently follows the wording of the Confession of Augsburg; and also from the Homilies, and other documents, both before and after the drawing up of the Articles. " The Necessary Doctrine " has been appropriately cited, which says, " It is no doubt, but although we be once justified, yet we may fall therefrom . . . . And although we be illuminated, and have tasted the heavenly gift, and be made partakers of the Holy Ghost, yet we may fall and displease God." [5] The whole of the Homily " Of Falling from God " holds language of the same character. It should be read throughout, being a practical discourse, from which extracts would fail to give a right impression. It is impossible to doubt, that the doctrine contained in it is, that

---

[1] *Opp.* Tom. v. p. 197.

[2] *Opp.* Tom. v. p. 405.

[3] " Damnant et Anabaptistas, qui negant semel justificatos iterum posse amittere Spiritum Sanctum." — *Sylloge,* p. 173.

[4] " Quid hinc nos discere voluit Christus, nisi ut confidamus perpetuo nos fore salvos, quia illius semel facti sumus ? " &c. — *Instit.* Lib. III. c. xxiv. 6, 7.

[5] *Formularies of Faith in the Reign of Henry the Eighth,* p. 367.

we may once receive the grace of God, and yet finally fall away from Him. These were documents drawn up at the period of the Reformation, shortly before the putting forth of the Articles. The second book of Homilies, written early in the reign of Queen Elizabeth, and of nearly the same date with the final revision of the Articles, breathes the same spirit throughout. The language of the Homily called " The First Part of the Information of certain parts of Scripture " may be referred to as a specimen. After reciting examples from Scripture of the sins of good men, it continues, " We ought then to learn by them this profitable lesson, that if so godly men as they were, which otherwise felt inwardly of God's Holy Spirit influencing their hearts with the fear and love of God, could not by their own strength keep themselves from commiting horrible sin, but did so grievously fall that without God's mercy they had perished everlastingly ; how much more ought we then, miserable wretches, which have no feeling of God within us at all, continually to fear, not only that we may fall as they did, but also be overcome and drowned in sin, as they were not."

The Homily on the Resurrection has the following : " Ye must consider that ye be therefore cleansed and renewed that ye should henceforth serve God in holiness and righteousness all the days of your life, that ye may reign with Him in everlasting life (Luke i.) If ye refuse so great grace whereto ye be called, what other thing do ye than heap to you damnation more and more, and so provoke God to cast His displeasure upon you, and to revenge this mockage of His holy sacraments in so great abusing of them ? Apply yourselves, good friends, to live in Christ, that Christ may still live in you," &c.

Similar is the tone breathed by the Liturgy itself. In the Baptismal Service we are taught to pray, that the baptized child " may ever remain in the number of God's faithful and elect children." In the Catechism the child, after speaking of himself as in a state of salvation, adds, " I pray unto God to give me His grace that I may continue in the same unto my life's end." And in the Burial Service we pray that God will " suffer us not at our last hour for any pains of death to fall from " Him.

In the reign of Queen Elizabeth the sympathy which had sprung up with the Calvinistic reformers of the continent made the teaching of our English divines approximate more nearly to the teaching of the Calvinists. Near the end of that reign a dispute arose at Cambridge, originating in the teaching of Barret, a fellow of Caius College, who preached *ad clerum* against Calvin's doctrines about predestination and falling from grace. Barret was complained of to Archbishop Whitgift, who at first took his part ; but at last, at the earnest request of the heads of Colleges, sent for him to Lambeth, where he was directed not to teach like doctrines again. The dispute so originating was continued between Dr. Whitaker, the Regius Professor, and Dr. Baro, the Margaret Professor, of Divinity. Whitaker, who took the high Calvinistic side, was sent by his party to Lambeth, where he proposed to the Archbishop to send down to Cambridge a series of Articles, nine in number, stamped with the authority of the archbishops and bishops, in order to check the progress of what he called Pelagianism. Archbishop Whitgift was thus induced to call a meeting of bishops and other clergy. The theses of Whitaker were submitted to them, and with some few alterations, which however were of considerable importance, they were passed by the meeting and sent down to Cambridge. The Queen censured Whitgift for the whole proceeding ; and he promised to write to Cambridge, that the Articles might be suppressed. These were the famous *Lambeth Articles*. The fifth and sixth concerned falling from grace and certainty of salvation. The fifth as proposed by Whitaker ran thus, " True, living, and justifying faith, and the influence of the Spirit of God, is not extinguished, nor fails, nor goes off, in those who have once been partakers of it, either totally or finally." The divines at Lambeth erased the words " in those who have once been partakers of it," and substituted for them " in the elect ; " thus making the doctrine more nearly correspond with Augustine's, rather than, as it did in Whitaker's draught of it, with Calvin's. The sixth Article, in Whitaker's draught, said that " A man who truly believes, that is, who has justifying faith, is sure, from the certainty of faith, concerning the remission of his sins and his eternal salvation through Christ." For " certainty of faith " the Lambeth divines substituted " full assurance of faith," using that word as signifying, not a full and absolute certainty, such as is the certainty of matters of science or of the principles of the faith, but rather a lesser degree of certainty, such as is obtained in matters of judicial evidence and legal trials.[1]

---

[1] The Vth and VIth Articles as drawn by Whitaker were, —

" V. Vera, viva, et justificans fides et Spiritus Dei Sanctificans non extinguitur, non excidit, non evanescit *in iis qui semel ejus participes fuerunt*, aut totaliter aut finaliter.

" VI. Homo vere fidelis, id est fide justificante præditus, certus est *certitudine* fidei, de remissione peccatorum suorum et salute sempiterna sua per Christum."

In the Vth the Lambeth Divines for *in iis qui semel ejus participes fuerunt*, substituted *in electis*.

In the VIth for *certitudine* they substi-

Soon after the accession of James I., A. D. 1604, the conference was held at Hampton Court. Dr. Reynolds, the speaker for the Puritans, moved, among other things, that the Articles be explained and enlarged. For example, whereas in Art. XVI. the words are these: "After we have received the Holy Ghost, we may depart from grace," he wished that there should be added, "yet neither totally nor finally;" and also that "the nine assertions orthodoxal concluded at Lambeth might be inserted into that book of Articles." On this point he was answered by the Bishop of London; no alteration of the kind was conceded, the Articles remaining as they were before, and the Lambeth Articles never having received any sanction of the Church or the Crown.[1]

Section II. — SCRIPTURAL PROOF.

THE first thing we have to show from holy Scripture is, that "every deadly sin committed after baptism is not unpardonable," and that "the place of forgiveness is not to be denied to such as truly repent."

To prove this proposition, it will be desirable (1) to show that sins after baptism are not generally unpardonable. (2) To consider those texts of Scripture, which are thought to prove the great heinousness and unpardonable nature of some sins, especially if committed after baptism.

I. First, then, sins after baptism are not generally incapable of being pardoned.

Baptism is the first step in the Christian life, by which we are admitted into the covenant, and to a share of the pardoning love of God in Christ. Under the Jewish dispensation there was no such thing as baptism ordained by God; but circumcision admitted into God's covenant with Abraham, and to a participation in the blessings of the congregation or Church of the Jews. Now it is a truth universally admitted, that the blessings we receive under the Gospel are greater than those which the Jews received under the Law. Especially, under the Gospel and in the Church of Christ, there is

---

tuted *plerophoria.* — See Strype's Whitgift, L. IV. c. 17.

[1] Cardwell, *Hist. of Conferences,* p. 178.

a fuller fountain of mercy and grace opened to all. " There is a fountain open for sin and for uncleanness," such as .ne Jews had only in figure. " The Law was given by Moses, but *grace* and truth came by Jesus Christ " (Joh. i. 17). Yet under the Law it is quite certain that there was a continual sacrifice offered for the sins both of priests and people, and a continual promise of pardon to the returning and penitent sinner. The prophet Ezekiel (ch. xxxiii. 12–20) by God's commandment clearly expounds to the Israelites, that, of those within the covenant, if the righteous man turn from his righteousness, he shall surely die ; but if the wicked " turn from his sin, and do that which is lawful and right," " none of his sins that he hath committed shall be mentioned unto him ; he hath done that which is lawful and right; he shall surely live." So the prophet David, after deliberate murder and adultery, was yet at once restored on his repentance. If then under the Law those who sinned were admitted to pardon, but under the Gospel, that is to say after baptism, those who sin are not admitted to pardon, then is the Gospel a state of less, instead of greater, grace than the Law ; then those who have been made partakers of Christ, have been admitted to a sterner law and a less merciful covenant than those who were baptized into Moses, and admitted to that carnal commandment, which made nothing perfect.

It is true, indeed, that the greater God's mercies are, the heavier will be the punishment of those who slight them. " If they who despised Moses' law died without mercy, of how much sorer punishment shall he be thought worthy, who hath trodden under foot the Son of God ? " (Heb. x. 28, 29). Yet, that the slighting of God's mercies should be of so great guilt, results from the fact that those mercies are so great: and, if the grant of repentance be withheld from the Christian, which was conceded to the Jew, then we may say, that God's mercies under the Law were greater than are His mercies under the Gospel.

Thus then we may naturally infer that pardon of sin would be given to Christians, and that sin committed after baptism would not in general exclude the sinner from all hope of repentance. Such reasoning is fully confirmed by the language of the new Testament. The Lord's Prayer was ordained for the use of those who might call Almighty God their Father. We therefore may clearly see that it was to be used only by children of God. Now in baptism we are made children of God. In the Lord's Prayer, then, God's baptized children are taught to pray that their sins should be forgiven them. And our blessed Lord comforts us with the assurance, that, " if we forgive men their trespasses, our heavenly Father will also forgive our trespasses " (Matt. vi. 14). So in the parable of the Prodigal Son (Luke xv.), it is a *son* that leaves his *father*, and who on his repentance is welcomed home and pardoned. The parable plainly sets before us, that, if we, as sons of God, leave our Father's home and revel in all iniquity, still on true and earnest repentance we shall be received, pardoned, comforted.

To the chief ministers of His Church our Lord gave the power of binding and loosing; binding by censure upon sin, but loosing again by absolution and reconciliation (Matt. xviii. 18) ; and to confirm this power to them the more strongly He declared : " Whose soever sins ye remit, they are remitted unto them ; and whose soever sins ye retain, they are retained " (John xx. 23). If the reconciliation of offenders to the Church be so sanctioned in Heaven, can there be a doubt that there is also pardon in Heaven for such as, having so offended, have repented and been reconciled ?

We have instances in the new Testament of the Apostles giving hope of pardon, and restoring communion to those who had sinned most heavily after baptism. · Thus Simon Magus, just after he was baptized, showed himself to be " in the gall of bitterness and the bond of iniquity ; " yet St. Peter urged him to repent of his wickedness, and to pray God, if perhaps the thought of his heart might be forgiven him [1] (Acts viii. 22, 23). Even of the man who after baptism had committed incest, and whom St. Paul (1 Cor. v. 1–5) bids the Corinthians to excommunicate, he yet gives hope that " his spirit may be saved in the day of the Lord Jesus " (ver. 5). And when the incestuous man had given signs of true sorrow for his sin, but a very short time after his excommunication, the Apostle ordered him to be restored to communion, declares that he ministerially pardoned his offences in the name and as the minister of Christ (2 Cor. ii. 10) ; recommends the Corinthians to comfort him, that he should not be swallowed up with overmuch sorrow (ver. 7); and assures them, with reference to the same subject, that " godly sorrow worketh repentance to salvation not to be repented of " (2 Cor. vii. 10). Nay ! he expressly says that the object of excommun·cating the guilty man was that his " spirit might be saved " (1 Cor. v. 5).

Again, St. Paul exhorts the Galatian Church. " Brethren, if a man be overtaken in a fault (ἐν τινὶ παραπτώματι) you, which are spiritual, restore such an one in the spirit of meekness, considering thyself, lest thou also be tempted." The words made use of are

---

[1] καὶ δεήθητι Θεοῦ, εἰ ἄρα ἀφεθήσεταί σοι ἡ ἐπίνι ια τῆς καρδίας σου.

perfectly general, and we may infer from them, as a general rule, that a man entrapped or overtaken by any kind of transgression or backsliding is, on his repentance, to be restored to communion. In the latter part of the second Epistle to the Corinthians (xii. 20, 21), the Apostle speaks of his apprehension that he shall be grieved at the state of the Corinthian Church, for he feared that many of the Corinthian Christians had committed all those sins which most grievously defile the temple of God (ἀκαθάρσια, πόρνεια, ἀσέλγεια), even every kind of uncleanness; but then the way in which he adds καὶ μὴ μετανοησάντων, " and have not repented," seems clearly to indicate that the poignancy of his grief was derived from their impenitence; and that for those who repented there was still room for pardon and hope.

St. Peter tells us, that God " is long-suffering to usward " (meaning, as we may suppose, to Christians), " not willing that any should perish, but that all should come to repentance " (2 Pet. iii. 9). St. John says that, as all men are sinners, so " if we confess our sins, He is faithful and just to forgive us our sins." And when he writes to Christians, calling them his " little children," and exhorting them that they sin not, he yet adds, " If any man sin, we have an advocate with the Father, Jesus Christ the righteous; and He is the propitiation for our sins." Here we have an evident address to those who were members of Christ's Church by baptism, an earnest exhortation to them not to sin, yet an encouragement to those who fall into sin, not to despair, as there is yet an Advocate, yet propitiation, through Jesus Christ (1 John i. 9; ii. 1, 2). St. James (James v. 13–15) enjoins, that if any member of the Church be sick, he should send for the clergy, the elders of the Church, to pray over him, and, among other blessings, promises that " if he have committed sins they shall be forgiven him." Lastly, in the Apocalypse, referring to men who had been seduced from their faith to all the abominations of the worst kind of heresy, our blessed Lord speaks of " giving time to repent; " and threatens heavy punishment, " unless they repent of their deeds " (Rev. ii. 20–22).

The general promises to repenting sinners do not, of course, belong to our present inquiry. Such promises may have been made to such as had not been baptized, and may be performed only in baptism. But those now adduced all evidently concern Christians, who had been brought to Christ by baptism, and who had afterwards fallen into sin. And they seem clearly to prove, that not even the deadliest sin committed by a baptized person makes it utterly impossible that, on hearty repentance and true faith, he should be forgiven.

There are indeed some passages of Scripture, and some very serious considerations, which have led to the belief that deadly sin after baptism has never forgiveness; and these we must take into account.

The fact that St. Paul speaks of the whole Church and every individual Christian as temples of the Holy Ghost (1 Cor. iii. 16; vi. 19; 2 Cor. vi. 16; Eph. ii. 22), joined with many similar considerations, shows that at our baptism we are set apart and consecrated to be temples of God. And then St. Paul declares that "if any man defile the temple of God, him shall God destroy; for the temple of God is holy, which temple ye are" (1 Cor. iii. 17). In like manner, we know that in baptism we are made members of Christ (see Gal. iii. 27; Ephes. iv. 15, 16, &c.). And St. Paul, reminding the Corinthians of this, says: "What, know ye not that your bodies are the members of Christ? Shall I then take the members of Christ, and make them the members of an harlot? God forbid" (1 Cor. vi. 15). Such sayings prove, with exceeding force, the great wickedness of sin, and especially of sins of uncleanness, when committed by a baptized Christian; who thereby "sinneth against his own body" (1 Cor. vi. 18), and against the Holy Ghost, whose temple his body has been made. So our blessed Saviour, speaking of Christians as branches of the Vine, whose root and stem is Christ, says that, "If a man abide not in Me, he is cast forth as a branch, and is withered" (John xv. 6).

These passages, however, though they show the great guilt of sinning against grace, do not prove such sins to be unpardonable, though probably they suggested the opinion that sin after baptism was the sin against the Holy Ghost, which hath never forgiveness.

There are strong and very fearful passages in the first Epistle of St. John, which have still more led to some of the opinions disclaimed by the Article we are now considering. In 1 John iii. 6, 8, 9, we read that, "Whosoever abideth in Him, sinneth nct. . . . He that committeth sin is of the devil. . . . Whosoever is born of God doth not commit sin; for his seed remaineth in him; and he cannot sin, because he is born of God." This passage led Jovinian to teach that a baptized Christian could never sin; and has been one argument from which it has been inferred, that, if by any means this high estate of purity should be lost, it would be lost irrevocably. Jerome, in his answer to Jovinian,[1] well explains the

---

[1] *Adv. Jovinian.* Lib. ii. *circ. init.* Tom. iv. pt. ii. p. 193.

general tenour of St. John's reasoning. He remarks that St. John exhorts those whom he addresses as little children, to keep themselves from idols (1 John v. 21) ; showing that they were liable to be tempted like others, and to fall ; that he writes to them not to sin ; and assures them still that, if they sin, they have an Advocate in the Lord Jesus Christ (1 John ii. 1, 2) ; that their best way of knowing that they know Christ is to keep His commandments (ver. 4) ; that he, who says he abides in Him, ought to walk as He walked (ver. 6). " Therefore," he continues, " St. John says, ' I write unto you, little children,' since ' every one who is born of God sinneth not,' that ye sin not, and that ye may know that ye abide in the generation of God, so long as ye do not sin ; yea, those who continue in God's generation cannot sin. For what communion hath Christ with Belial ? If we have received Christ as a guest into our hearts, we put to flight the devil. But if we sin again, the devil enters through the door of sin, and then Christ departs." This seems a correct account of St. John's reasoning, and shows that what he means is, that the regenerate man, so long as he continues in the regenerate state, overcomes sin and casts it out ; but if he falls from the regenerate state and sins, then he becomes again the servant of the devil. But it neither proves, that the regenerate man cannot sin, nor that, if he does, his fall is irrecoverable.

But St. John (1 John v. 16, 17) speaks of the distinction between " sin unto death," and " sin not unto death ; " and encourages us to pray for the latter, but not for the former. Bp. Jeremy Taylor has some good remarks on this verse. " Every Christian," he says, " is in some degree in the state of grace, so long as he is invited to repentance, and so long as he is capable of the prayers of the Church. This we learn from those words of St. John, ' All unrighteousness is sin, and there is a sin not unto death ; ' that is, some sorts of sin are so incident to the condition of men, and their state of imperfection, that the man who hath committed them is still within the methods of pardon, and hath not forfeited his title to the promises and covenant of repentance ; but ' there is a sin unto death ; ' that is, some men proceed beyond the measures and economy of the Gospel, and the usual methods and probabilities of repentance, by obstinacy, and preserving a sin, by a wilful, spiteful resisting, or despising the offers of grace and the means of pardon ; for such a man St. John does not encourage us to pray ; if he be such a person as St. John described, our prayers will do him no good ; but because no man can tell the last minute or period of

49

pardon, nor just when a man is gone beyond the limit ; and because the limit itself can be enlarged, and God's mercies stay for
some longer than for others, therefore St. John left us under the
indefinite restraint and caution; which was decretory enough to
represent that sad state of things in which the refractory and impenitent have immerged themselves, and yet so indefinite and cau-
tious, that we may not be too forward in applying it to particulars,
nor in prescribing measures to the Divine mercy, nor in passing
final sentences upon our brother, before we have heard our Judge
Himself speak. 'Sinning a sin not unto death' is an expression
fully signifying that there are some sins which though they be
committed and displeased God, and must be repented of, and need
many and mighty prayers for their pardon, yet the man is in the
state of grace and pardon, that is, he is within the covenant of
mercy ; he may be admitted, if he will return to his duty : so that
being in a state of grace is having a title to God's loving-kindness,
a not being rejected of God, but a being beloved of Him to certain
purposes of mercy, and that hath these measures and degrees."

Again, " Every act of sin takes away something from the contrary grace, but if the root abides in the ground, the plant is still
alive, and may bring forth fruit again. 'But he only is dead who
hath thrown off God for ever, or entirely with his very heart.' So
St. Ambrose. To be 'dead in trespasses and sins,' which is the
phrase of St. Paul (Eph. ii. 1), is the same with that expression
of St. John, of 'sinning a sin unto death,' that is, habitual, refractory, pertinacious, and incorrigible sinners, in whom there is
scarcely any hope or sign of life. These are they upon whom, as
St. Paul's expression is, (1 Thess. ii. 16,) 'the wrath of God is
come upon them to the uttermost, εἰς τὸ τέλος, unto death.' So was
their sin, it was a sin unto death ; so is their punishment." [1]

But by far the most terrible passages in Scripture, on the danger of backsliding and the difficulty or impossibility of renewal, are
to be found in the Epistle to the Hebrews. We learn indeed from
Tertullian (*De Pudicitia*), that the difficulty of the 6th chapter
of that Epistle was the main reason why the Roman Church was
so long in admitting it into the Canon.

In the 10th chapter we read that, "if we sin wilfully after we
have received the knowledge of the truth, there remaineth no more
sacrifice for sins; but a certain fearful looking for of judgment and
fiery indignation, which shall devour the adversaries. He that de
spised Moses' law, perished without mercy under two or three wit

[1] *Of Repentance,* ch IV § 2

nesses ; of how much sorer punishment, think ye, shall he be thought worthy, who hath trodden under foot the Son of God, and hath counted the Blood of the Covenant an unholy thing, and hath done despite to the Spirit of Grace ? " (Heb. x. 26–29). The peculiar strength of this passage is in the words, " If we sin wilfully after we have received the knowledge of the truth, there remaineth no more sacrifice for sins." The word " *sin* " in the first clause, is here supposed by many to mean " apostatize." So in IIos. xiii. 2, we read וְעַתָּה יוֹסִפוּ לַחֲטֹא " Now they add moreover to sin ; " where the sin spoken of is a revolting from God, and apostatizing to Baal. And, as regards the " remaining no more sacrifice for sin," the Apostle had been showing, throughout the early verses of the chapter, that the priests under the Law kept constantly offering sacrifices, year by year and day by day (vv. 1–11). But Christ offered but *one* sacrifice for sin, and by that one sacrifice hath perfected all that are sanctified (vv. 12–14). So then, if we reject the sacrifice of Christ, and after a knowledge of its saving efficacy, apostatize willingly [1] from the faith, there are not now fresh sacrifices, " offered year by year continually ; " and by rejecting the one sacrifice of Christ, we cut ourselves off from the benefit of His death ; and since we have chosen sin instead of God, there is no new sacrifice to bring us to God.

Another of the hard sentences, which has led to a belief in the irremissibility of post-baptismal sin, is Heb. xii. 17. The Apostle, warning against the danger of falling from grace, bids us take heed, lest there be " any fornicator or profane person like Esau, who for one morsel of meat sold his birthright. For ye know how that afterward, when he would have inherited a blessing, he was rejected ; for he found no place of repentance, though he sought it carefully with tears." There can be no doubt, that Esau is here propounded to us as a type of those who, having been made sons of God by baptism, and so, having a birthright and promised inheritance, by thoughtlessness and sensuality, " for one morsel of meat," throw themselves out of God's favour, and, leaving God's family, return to the condition of mere sons of Adam. St. Paul reminding us that, when Esau had sold his birthright, he found no place for repentance, even when he sought it with tears, puts us on our guard against the like folly, by fear of the like fate. Yet it does not follow of course, that every person who lives unworthily of his baptismal privileges, shall be denied access to repentance. We can

---

[1] ἑκουσίως בְּיָד רָמָה with a high hand, and Rosenmüller thereon ; Kuinoel on presumptuously. See Numb. xv. 29, 30 ; Heb. x. 26.

never, when we yield to sin, know that God will give us repentance; and we may die in our sin.   And even if we repent, our
repentance, like Esau's, may be too late ; after the door is shut, and
when it will not do to knock.   We are told elsewhere of those who
came and cried, " Lord, Lord, open unto us," and who received no
answer but, " I know you not" (Matt. xxv. 11, 12).   Such a late
repentance is that of those who would repent in the grave, perhaps of some who seek only on the bed of death.   But if we follow
out the history of Esau, we may gain at least this comfort from it,
that, even late as he had put off his seeking repentance, so late that
he could never be fully restored, yet, though not to the same position as before, he was still restored to favour and to blessing (Gen.
xxvii. 38, 39).   So that we may hope from this history, as set
forth to us for a type, that, though such as cast away their privileges as Christians find it hard to be reinstated in the position
from which they fell, and may, perhaps, never in this world attain
to like blessedness and assurance as if they had never fallen, still
the door of repentance is not shut against them.   Their place in
their Father's house may be lower ; but still it is not hopeless that
there may, and shall, be a place for them.

The strongest passage, and that on which the Novatians most
rested their doctrines, remains yet to be considered.   It is Heb.
vi. 4, 5, 6 : " It is impossible for those, who were once enlightened,
and have tasted of the heavenly gift, and were made partakers of
the Holy Ghost, and have tasted the good word of God, and the
powers of the world to come, if they shall fall away, to renew them
again to repentance ; seeing they crucify to themselves the Son of
God afresh, and put Him to an open shame."

The Syriac Version, Theodoret, Theophylact, and others of the
ancients, who are followed by Ernesti, Michaelis, and many learned
men of our own times, understand by the word " enlightened "
(ἅπαξ φωτισθέντας) here, and in Heb. x. 32, "baptized."   Clement
of Rome, Justin Martyr, and others of the very earliest Christians,
used the word in this sense.[1]   But whether we admit this to be
the right interpretation or not, we must allow the passage to teach
that a person, after baptism and Christian blessing and enlightenment, may so fall away that it may be impossible to renew him to
repentance.   The words made use of seem to say that persons
once baptized, endued with God's Holy Spirit, made partakers of
the Christian Church,[2] if they despise all these blessings, rejecting,

---

[1] See Suicer, s. v. φωτίζω, φωτισμὸς.   [2] δυνάμεις μέλλοντος αἰῶνος, the very
Also Bingham, E. A. i. iv. 1, xi. i. 4   phrase used in the LXX. (cf. Isai. ix. 6)

and, as it were, afresh crucifying the Son of God, cannot be again restored to repentance. The difficulty of the passage lies almost wholly in two words, παραπεσόντας, "having fallen away," and ἀνακαινίζειν, "to renew." Most commentators consider the word "fall away," which occurs here only in the New Testament, to signify total apostasy from the faith.[1] If indeed the other two participles (ἀνασταυροῦντας and παραδειγματίζοντας) be to be coupled with it, as in apposition to, and explanation of it, then we may well conclude that it can mean no less. It is the case of those "who sin wilfully after they have received the knowledge of the truth," of him from whom one devil had been cast out, but to whom it had returned with seven worse devils. Rejecting their faith and their baptism, they fall away from Christ, reproach and crucify Him afresh, as much reject Him for their Saviour as they who actually nailed Him to the Cross. Bishop Taylor describes them as persons, who, "without cause or excuse, without error or infirmity, choosingly, willingly, knowingly, called Christ an impostor, and would have crucified Him again if He were alive ; that is, they consented to His death by believing that He suffered justly. This is the case here described, and cannot be drawn to anything else but its parallel; that is, a malicious renouncing charity, or holy life, as these men did the faith, to both which they have made their solemn vows in baptism ; but this can no way be drawn to the condemnation and final excision of such persons who fall into any great sin, of which they are willing to repent."[2]

And for the other word of difficulty, ἀνακαινίζειν, "to renew," some think we must understand *to rebaptize*. The Church has no power to rebaptize those who fall away ; and so, as first they were washed in the waters of baptism from original sin, to wash them again from their guilt of apostasy.[3] Others understand to *admit by absolution to the fellowship of the Church*, and so restore them to repentance and penance, when they have once thoroughly apostatized.[4] Others understand, that, whereas they have rejected the

of the Christian Church. See Hammond, *in loc.* Rosenmüller and Kuinoel both understand these words of the Kingdom of Christ, the Reign of Messiah. Hence "the powers of the world to come" would be the blessed effects of Christ's kingdom and gospel.

[1] παραπίπτειν is the translation of the LXX. for אֵים Ezek. xxii. 4, and מָעַל Ezek. xiv. 13. Schleusner compares 2 Chron. xxix. 19, where the LXX. translate בְּמַעֲלוֹ, ἐν ἀποστασίᾳ αὐτοῦ.

[2] *On Repentance*, ch. IX. sect. 4.

[3] Dr. Hammond, *in loc.* observes that, as ἐγκαινίζειν is to dedicate, consecrate, so, ἀνακαινίζειν is to reconsecrate. Persons utterly apostate could not be reconsecrate. There was no power to repeat their baptism, nor, if utterly apostate, could the Church readmit them by penance to Church-communion.

[4] Many understand ἀνακαινίζειν as applied to the ministers of the Church. It is "impossible for the ministers of Christ to renew them again ; " that is, there is

Gospel and all its means of grace, their case has become hopeless, because no other covenant can be provided for them: "There remaineth no more sacrifice for sins." No new method of salvation will be devised for them; and as they have utterly given up the one already provided, rejected Christ, and despised His Spirit, so it is impossible that any other should renew them. "Other foundation can no man lay, save that which is laid, which is Jesus Christ;" "for there is no means of salvation but this one; and this one they hate, and will not have; they will not return to the old, and there is none left by which they can be *renewed*, and therefore their condition is desperate." [1]

On the whole, there can be no doubt of the awful severity of the language of this passage, and of the warning it gives us against falling from grace; but, when we compare it with other passages somewhat like it, and contrast with it those which assure us of God's readiness to receive the penitent sinner, and to give repentance even to those who sin after grace given; we can hardly fail to conclude that it concerns particularly extreme cases, and not those of ordinary occurrence; and that, though it proves the heinousness of sinning against light and grace, and shows that we may so fall after grace as never to recover ourselves, yet it does not prove that there is no pardon for such baptized Christians as sin grievously, and then seek earnestly for repentance.

The fact that our Lord left to His Church the power of the keys, allowing its chief pastors to excommunicate for sin and restore on repentance, and that the Apostles and first bishops ever exercised that power, shows that even great sins (for none other led to excommunication) do not exclude from pardon. Nay, "Baptism is εἰς μετάνοια , the admission of us to the covenant of faith and repentance; or as Mark the anchorite called it, πρόφασίς ἐστι τῆς μετανοίας, the introduction of repentance, or that state of life that is full of labour and care, and amendment of our faults; for that is the best life that any man can live; and therefore repentance hath its progress after baptism, as it hath its beginning before; for first, 'repentance is unto baptism,' and then 'baptism unto repentance.' . . . . Besides, our admission to the holy Sacrament of the Lord's Supper is a perpetual entertainment of our hopes, because then and there is really exhibited to us the Body that was broken and the Blood that was 'shed for the remission

no other sacrament by which we can restore offenders to the same position in which they were before their fall, and in which they were once placed by the sacrament of baptism.

[1] Bishop Jeremy Taylor, as above

of sins.' Still it is applied, and that application could not be necessary to be done anew, if there were not new necessities; and still we are invited to do actions of repentance, 'to examine ourselves, and so to eat.' All which, as things are ordered, would be infinitely useless to mankind, if it did not mean pardon to Christians falling into foul sins even after baptism."[1]

We may therefore conclude that, severe as some passages of Scripture are against those who sin wilfully against light and grace, and strict as the discipline of the early Church was against all such offenders, there is yet nothing to prove that heinous sin committed after baptism cannot be pardoned on repentance. The strongest and severest texts of Scripture seem to apply, not to persons who have sinned and seek repentance, but to apostates from the faith, who are stout in their apostasy, and hardened in sin.

II. Our next consideration is the "Sin against the Holy Ghost."

The statements of Scripture already considered have, as we have seen, been supposed by some to show that the sin against the Holy Ghost must be falling grievously after baptism. For, as it has been supposed that these statements make deadly sin after baptism the unpardonable sin, and our Lord makes blasphemy against the Holy Ghost to be unpardonable, and both our Lord and St. John (1 John v. 16) seem to speak as if there were but one unpardonable sin, therefore deadly sin after baptism and the blasphemy against the Holy Ghost must be identical. The foregoing arguments seem sufficiently to have shown that this hypothesis is untrue.

If we examine the circumstances under which our Lord uttered His solemn warnings concerning blasphemy against the Holy Ghost, we may probably the better understand the nature of that sin. He had been casting out a devil, thereby giving signal proof of His Godhead. But the Pharisees, instead of believing and acknowledging His heavenly mission, ascribed His power to Satan and Beelzebub (Matt. xii. 24). Those who thus resisted such evidence were plainly obstinate and hardened unbelievers, such as, we may well believe, were given over to a reprobate mind, and such as no evidence of the truth could move to faith and penitence. Accordingly, many believe that by thus rejecting the faith, and ascribing the works of our Lord's Divinity to the power of evil spirits, they had committed the sin against the Holy Ghost.

[1] Jeremy Taylor, *On Repentance*, ch. ix. sect. 2.

That they were *very near* committing that sin there can be little
doubt. They had stepped upon the confines, they had uttered dar-
ing and desperate blasphemy. They had reviled the holy Son of
God. They had called His works of love and goodness the works
of the devil, thereby confounding light with darkness. But still
our Lord consents to reason with them. He still puts forth parables, by which to convince them that they were in error (Matt.
xii. 23–30). And He would scarce do this, if there were no hope
that they might repent, no possibility that they might be forgiven.
And then He warns them. Warning and reasoning are for those
who may yet take warning and conviction, not for those to whom
they would·be useless.

And of what nature is His warning? They had just blasphemed
Him, disbelieved His mission, disregarded His miracles. Yet
He tells them in gracious goodness, that all manner of sin and
blasphemy which men commit shall be forgiven them, that even
blasphemy against Himself, the Son of Man, shall be forgiven;
but then He adds, that, if they went farther still, and committed
the same sin moreover against the Spirit of God, it should never
be forgiven, neither in this world, nor in the world to come (vv.
31, 32).

Now Christ was then present with them as the Son of Man.
The glory of His Godhead was veiled under the likeness of sinful
flesh. Those were " the days of the Son of Man ; " and " the
Spirit was not yet given, because that Jesus was not yet glorified."
There is no doubt, that it must have been deadly wickedness which
led men to doubt the truth of His doctrine when taught with such
power from His sacred lips, and proved so mightily by the works
which He wrought. But the full power of the Gospel had not
been put forth; especially the Spirit had not been poured on the
Church, — a blessing so great, that it made it expedient for His
disciples that even Jesus should go away from them in order that
He might give it to them (John xvi. 7). But when the Spirit was
poured forth, then all the means of grace were used; Jesus working without, and the Spirit pleading within. And in those who
received the word and were baptized, the Spirit took up His dwelling, and moved and ruled in their hearts. This then was a state
of greater grace, and a more convincing state of evidence to the
world and to the Church, than even the bodily presence of the
Saviour as the Son of Man. Accordingly, resistance to the means
of grace, after the gift of the Spirit, was worse than resistance
during the bodily presence of Christ. Resisting the former, re-

fusing to be converted by it, rejecting its evidence, and obstinate impenitence under its influence, was blasphemy against the Son of Man. Still even this could be forgiven ; for farther and yet greater means of grace were to be tried, even on those who had rejected Christ. " The Gospel was to be preached unto them, with the Holy Ghost sent down from heaven " (1 Pet. i. 12). But this mission of the Comforter was the last and highest means ever to be tried, the last and greatest dispensation of the grace of God. Those, therefore, who after this still remained obstinate, still rejected Christ in His kingdom, as they had rejected Him in His humility, still refused to be converted, ascribed the gifts of His Apostles and the graces of His Church, not to the Spirit of God, but to the spirit of evil, such men blasphemed not only the Son of Man — the Word of God when veiled in human flesh — but they rejected and blasphemed the Spirit of God, and so had never forgiveness.

This seems the true explanation of the sin against the Holy Ghost, namely, obstinate, resolute, and wilful impenitence, after all the means of grace and with all the strivings of the Spirit, under the Christian dispensation as distinguished from the Jewish, and amid all the blessings and privileges of the Church of Christ.

And this view of the subject does not materially differ from the statement of St. Athanasius, namely, that blasphemy against Christ, when His manhood only was visible, was blasphemy against the Son of Man ; but that, when His Godhead was manifested, it became blasphemy against the Holy Ghost : nor from that of St. Augustine, that the sin against the Spirit of God is a final and obdurate continuance in wickedness, despite of the calls of God to repentance, joined with a desperation of the mercy of God.[1]

III. The last subject to which we come is the question of Final Perseverance, or the Indefectibility of Grace.

The Article says, " After we have received the Holy Ghost, we may depart from grace given and fall into sin, and by the grace of God we may arise again and amend our lives." The arguments which have been already gone into, concerning the grant of repentance and pardon to those who sin after baptism and the grace of God, sufficiently prove, the latter clause of the above statement. Indeed the former clause may be considered as proved also ; for if there is a large provision in the Gospel and the Church for forgiveness of sins and reconciliation of those who, having received the Spirit, have fallen away, then must it be possible, that, " after

---

[1] See the statement of their opinions in Sect. I.

we have received the Holy Ghost, we may yet depart from grace
and fall into sin." Jovinian indeed held that every truly baptized
person could sin no more. But such an error has been very uncommon in the Church, so uncommon that it is scarcely needful
to prove that a person may have received grace and yet be
tempted and fall into sin ; as David so grievously fell in the matter
of Uriah, or as St. Peter, when he denied his Lord. But the
question, whether a person who. has once received grace can ever
fall finally and irrecoverably, has been much agitated since the
days of Zuingle and Calvin ; and though possibly not expressly
determined by the wording of this Article, it yet properly comes
to be considered here.

The doctrine of the Zuinglians and high Calvinists has been,
that if a man has once been regenerate and endued with the Holy
Ghost, he may fall into sin for a time, but will surely be restored
again, and can never finally be lost. We have seen, on the contrary, that St. Augustine and the more ancient predestinarians
held that grace might have been given, but yet, if a person was
not *predestinated to perseverance*, he might fall away. We have
seen that the Lutherans held that grace given might yet be lost
utterly. We have seen that the reformers of the Church of
England, whether following St. Augustine in his views of predestination or not, appear clearly to have agreed with him, and with
Luther and the Lutherans, in holding that grace might be lost,
not only for the time, but finally.

1. The passages of Scripture most in favour of the doctrine
that those who have once been regenerate can never finally fall
from grace, are such as follow.

Matt. xxiv. 24, which must be set aside, if rightly translated.[1]
Luke xxii. 32, which shows that our Lord prays for His servants.
John vi. 39; John x. 27, 28; but these last must be compared
with John xvii. 12, which shows, that though the true sheep of
Christ never perish, yet some may, like Judas, be given Him for
a time, and yet finally be sons of perdition. Rom. viii. 38, 39,
xi. 29, show that God is faithful, and will never repent of His
mercy to us, and that, if we do not wilfully leave Him, no created
power shall be able to pluck us out of His hand. They *prove* no
more than this.

Stronger by far are such passages as 1 Cor. i. 8, 9 ; Phil. i. 6 ;

---

[1] The English version translates εἰ
δυνατὸν " if *it were* possible." The whole
strength of the passage as favouring the
Calvinistic theory is in the words *it were*,
which are not in the Greek. Render it
" if possible," and the argument is gone.

2 Thess. iii. 3. Yet they are addressed to whole Churches, all the members of which are not certainly preserved blameless to the end. The confidence expressed concerning the Philippians (Phil. i. 6) cannot have meant that it was impossible for any of them to be lost ; for St. Paul afterwards exhorts them to " work out their salvation with fear and trembling " (ii. 12), and to "stand fast in the Lord " (iv. 1). So that we must necessarily understand the Apostle's confident hope to result from a consideration of the known goodness and grace of God, and also of the Philippians' own past progress in holiness. " He conjectured," as Theophylact says, " from what was past, what they would be for the future." [1]

The passages which speak of Christians as *sealed*, and having the " earnest of the Spirit," (see 2 Cor. i. 21, 22 ; Ephes. i. 13 ; iv. 30,) are thought to teach the indefectibility of grace ; because what is sealed is kept and preserved. But sealing probably only signifies the ratifying of a covenant, which is done in baptism. And though the giving of the Spirit is indeed the *earnest* of a future inheritance, it does not follow that no unfaithfulness in the Christian may deprive him of the blessing, of which God has given him the earnest and pledge, because a covenant always implies two parties, and if either breaks it, the other is free.

So again Jas. i. 17 tells us of the unchangeableness of God, and 2 Tim. ii. 19 shows that He " knoweth them that are His." But neither proves that *we* may not change, nor that all who are now God's people will continue so to the end, though he knoweth who will and who will not.

The expression " full assurance of hope " (Heb. vi. 11) has been thought to prove that we may be always certain of continuance, if we have once known the grace of God. But the Apostle does not ground the " assurance of hope " on such a doctrine. His words are : " We desire that every one of you do show the same diligence to the full assurance of hope to the end ; that ye be not slothful, but followers of them who through faith and patience inherit the promises." This shows, that our assured hope will spring from a close walk with God, and that slothfulness, or a lack of diligence, is likely to impair our hope and disturb our assurance. The more diligent we are, the more hope we shall have ; our hope not being grounded on the indefectibility of grace, but on the evidences of our faith given by a consistent growth in grace.

---

[1] ἀπὸ τῶν παρελθόντων καὶ περὶ τῶν μελλόντων στοχαζόμενος. — Theophyl. *in loc.* quoted by Whitby, whom see.

Again, 1 Pet. i. 4, 5, speaks of an inheritance " reserved in heaven for those who are *kept* by the power of God, through faith unto salvation." The word "*kept*" is in the Greek φρουρουμένους, *i. e.* " guarded as in a garrison." The figure represents believers as attacked by evil spirits and wicked men, but defended by the power of God, through the influence of their faith. It does not show that all believers are kept from falling away ; but that they are guarded by God through the instrumentality of their faith. "If" then " they continue in the faith " (Col. i. 23), " if they hold the beginning of their confidence steadfast unto the end " (Heb. iii. 14), then will " their faith be able to quench all the fiery darts of the wicked one " (Eph. vi. 16), and will " overcome the world " (1 John v. 4). But, as it is expressly said that it is " through faith " that they are " kept" or " guarded," we cannot infer that their faith itself is so guarded that it can by no possibility fail.[1]

But the strongest passage on this side of the question is 1 John iii. 9 : " Whosoever is born of God doth not commit sin ; for his seed remaineth in him : and he cannot sin, because he is born of God." From this Jovinian inferred that a regenerate man could never sin again ; but the Zuinglian and Calvinist infer, that the regenerate man having the seed of life in him, may indeed fall into sin, but is sure to recover himself again, and to be saved at the last. If the text proves anything about indefectibility of grace, it plainly proves Jovinian's rather than Calvin's position ; namely, that the regenerate man never falls into sin at all, not merely that he does not fall finally.

The truth is, the Apostle is simply contrasting the state of the regenerate with that of the unregenerate, and tells us, that sin is the mark of the latter, holiness of the former. " He that doeth righteousness is righteous . . . he that committeth sin is of the devil " (vv. 7, 8). Here is the antithesis. It is like the statement, " A good tree cannot bring forth evil fruit, neither can a corrupt tree bring forth good fruit " (Matt. vii. 18). This does not mean, that a good tree can never cease to be good, and so cease to bear good fruit.[2] So it is with that of St. Paul, " The carnal mind cannot be subject to the law of God " (Rom. viii. 7). But it is not meant, that a man of carnal mind may not be converted, and then love holiness and God's law. So Ignatius writes, " Spiritual men can-

---

[1] See Whitby and Macknight on 1 Pet. i. 4, 5.

[2] " Bona arbor non fert malos fructus, quamdiu in bonitatis studio perseverat."

— Hieron. *In Matt.* vii. 18, Tom. iv. pt. ii. p. 25, cited by Dr. Hammond on 1 John iii. 9.

not do the things of the flesh ; " [1] that is, obviously, so long as they continue spiritual.

Just so St. John. He points out the difference between the righteous and the wicked; namely, that the former do righteousness, the latter commit sin. Then he says, " Every one that is born of God [2] cannot sin, because of the seed of God which is in him." He is righteous, and therefore doeth righteousness; he is a good tree, and therefore cannot bring forth bad fruit ; he is spiritual, and therefore cannot do carnal things. But this does not prove that he may not fall from grace, and so lose his title to be a son of God, and also that seed of God in his heart which keeps him from sin. " The regenerate man," says Jerome, " cannot sin so long as he continues in the generation of God . . . . but, if we admit sin, and the devil enters into the door of our hearts, Christ goes away." [3]

2. So much of the arguments from Scripture by which the doctrine that grace in the regenerate can never fail has been maintained. Against this doctrine many passages of Scripture are alleged.

(1) There are frequent statements of the condemnation and rejection of such as, having been in a state of grace, fall away from it, and which it is hard to believe are only meant to frighten us away from an impossible danger. Such are

Ezek. xviii. 24 ; xxxiii. 18. Matt. v. 13. Matt. xxiv. 46–51, comp. Luke xxi. 34–36. Heb. x. 26–29, 38. 2 Pet. ii. 20–22.

(2) There are declarations, that those only " who endure to the end " shall be saved, those " who keep their garments " shall be blessed; that " if we continue in the faith grounded and settled, and be not moved away," we shall be presented holy in the sight of God.

Matt. x. 22. Col. i. 22, 23. Heb. iii. 6. Rev. xvi. 15.

Thus final salvation is promised not merely to present, but to continuing and persevering faith.

---

[1] Ignat. Ad Eph. c. viii.

[2] πᾶς ὁ γεγεννημένος. Rosenmüller says that it is the same as γεννητός יְלוּד, Job xiv. 1, or τεκνὸν, as in ver. 10. And Dr. Hammond observes, that the perfect participle indicates that we must not refer the words "born of God" to the moment or instant of regeneration, but to the continuing state of regeneration. It indicates not a transient, but a permanent condition.

[3] He thus explains the passage in St. John : " Propterea, inquit, scribo vobis, filioli mei ; omnis, qui natus est ex Deo, non peccat, ut non peccetis ; et tamdiu sciatis vos in generatione Domini permanere quamdiu non peccaveritis. Immo, qui in generatione Domini perseverant peccare non possunt. Quæ enim communicatio luci et tenebris ? Christo et Belial ? . . . . Si susceperimus Christum in hospitio nostri pectoris, illico fugamus Diabolum. Si peccaverimus, et per peccati januam ingressus fuerit Diabolus, protinus Christus recedit."—Hieron. Adv. Jovin. Lib. ii. init. Tom. iv. Par. ii. p. 193.

(3) Accordingly, there are numerous warnings against falling away, exhortations to stand fast, and prayers for perseverance and against falling.

Rom. xi. 20, 21.   1 Cor. x. 1–10, 12.   1 Cor. xvi. 13.   Col. ii. 6, 7, 8,   1 Thess. v. 19.   Heb. iii. 12; xii. 15, 16.   2 Pet. iii. 17.   Jude 20, 21, 24.   Rev. xvi. 15.

All these passages speak of the danger of falling away, and of the final condemnation of such as fall, and warn and pray against falling. The advocates for the doctrine of final perseverance say, that although all grace comes only from God, yet He ordains means to be used for obtaining grace ; so, although perseverance is the gift of God, and never withholden from such as receive grace at all ; yet warnings against backsliding, and declarations concerning the punishment of backsliders, are useful and necessary means to keep believers in a state of watchfulness, and therefore are instruments in God's hands to work in them the grace of perseverance, which however could as easily be given without them, and will assuredly be given to all who have once been regenerate. Their opponents reply, that such reasoning is an evident attempt to explain away the obvious sense of Scripture ; God's threatenings could never be denounced against a sin which was impossible. If utter falling away in the regenerate is, in God's counsels, a thing which cannot occur, then can we believe that God would give the most solemn warnings to be found in the whole of Scripture against it ? Would the Apostle put up the most earnest prayers against it ? Would the condemnation pronounced upon it be so severe and so terrible ? But it is argued farther, that,

(4) There are express and positive statements, that men may, nay, do, fall away from grace given and accepted, and so do finally perish.

The parable of the sower (Matt. xiii. Mark iv. Luke viii.) contains a statement of this kind. Four different kinds of hearers are there described. Of these, one, the way-side hearer, disregards it altogether; one, compared to good ground, receives and profits by it, and brings forth fruit to life eternal. But two kinds, those like the stony ground, and those like the thorny ground, embrace it and profit by it for a time, and *then fall away*. The seed in the stony ground springs up (Matt. xiii. 5). Such hearers received the seed with joy (ver. 20), but they last only for a while (ver. 21) ; they " for a while believe, but in time of temptation fall away " (Luke viii. 13). So the seed which falls among thorns springs up ; but the thorns spring up with it, and choke it. " The cares of this world and the deceitfulness of riches choke the word ' (Matt. xiii. 22).

Again, the parable of the Vine and the Branches (John xv. 1-10) teaches the same thing. Christ's disciples are compared to branches of a Vine, the Lord Himself being that Vine. "Every branch," He says, "*in Me* that beareth not fruit, He " (*i. e.* God the Father) "*taketh away*" (ver. 2). "I am the Vine, ye are the branches; he that abideth in Me, and I in him, the same bringeth forth much fruit; for without Me ye can do nothing. *If a man abide not in Me, he is cast forth as a branch, and is withered,* and men gather them, and cast them into the fire, and they are burned " (vv. 5, 6).

Heb. vi. 4-8, seems to contain a positive statement that men do sometimes so fall away from grace already received as to fall not only finally but hopelessly : " It is impossible for those who were once enlightened, and have tasted of the heavenly gift, and were made partakers of the Holy Ghost, and have tasted the good word of God, and the powers of the world to come, if they shall fall away, to renew them again unto repentance ; seeing they crucify to themselves the Son of God afresh, and put Him to an open shame," &c.

So 2 Pet. ii. 21, 22. The Apostle is evidently speaking of persons who *had* fallen away from grace, apostates from the faith of Christ. For though, in ver. 20, he speaks only hypothetically, " If after they have escaped the pollutions of the world," &c., yet in vv. 21, 22, he speaks of their apostasy as having actually occurred : " It had been better for them not to have known the way of righteousness, than, after they have known it, to turn from the holy commandment delivered unto them. But *it is happened* (συμβέβηκε) unto them according to the true proverb, The dog is turned to his own vomit again ; and the sow that was washed to her wallowing in the mire."

(5) Finally, it is contended that, with all these proofs from Scripture that grace given may be lost, the doctrine of the indefectibility of grace would never have been thought of, but that it fell naturally into a system. Accordingly, the more ancient predestinarians, like Augustine, though they believed in the irrespective and immutable decrees of God, yet did not teach the doctrine of absolutely indefectible grace. But Calvin's great characteristic was his logical acuteness, which led him to form all his doctrines into harmonious systems. He could never leave mysterious doctrines in their mystery, on the principle that our finite intellects

are permitted to grasp only part of the great plans of infinite Wisdom. The doctrine of final perseverance seemed necessary to the harmony and completeness of the predestinarian scheme ; and on that account, not because Scripture taught it, it was adopted and received.

ARTICLE XVII.

———◆———

Of Predestination and Election.

PREDESTINATION to life is the everlasting purpose of God, whereby (before the foundations of the world were laid) He hath constantly decreed by His counsel, secret to us, to deliver from curse and damnation those whom He hath chosen in Christ out of mankind, and to bring them by Christ to everlasting salvation, as vessels made to honour. Wherefore they which be endued with so excellent a benefit of God be called according to God's purpose by His Spirit working in due season: they through grace obey the calling : they be justified freely : they be made sons of God by adoption ; they be made like the image of His only-begotten Son Jesus Christ ; they walk religiously in good works, and at length, by God's mercy, they attain to everlasting felicity.

As the godly consideration of predestination and our election in Christ, is full of sweet, pleasant, and unspeakable comfort to godly persons, and such as feel in themselves the working of the Spirit of Christ, mortifying the works of the flesh, and their earthly members, and drawing up their mind to high and heavenly things, as well because it doth greatly establish and confirm their faith of eternal salvation to be enjoyed through Christ, as because it doth fervently kindle their love towards God : so, for curious and carnal persons, lacking the Spirit of Christ, to have continually before their eyes the sentence of God's predestination is a most dangerous downfall, whereby the Devil doth thrust them either into desperation, or into wretchlessness of most unclean living, no less perilous than desperation.

Furthermore, we must receive God's promises in such wise, as they be generally set forth to us in Holy Scripture : and, in our doings that will of God is to be followed, which we have expressly declared unto us in the Word of God.

De Prædestinatione et Electione.

PRÆDESTINATIO ad vitam, est æternum Dei propositum, quo ante jacta mundi fundamenta, suo consilio, nobis quidem occulto, constanter decrevit, eos quos in Christo elegit ex hominum genere, a maledicto et exitio liberare, atque (ut vasa in honorem efficta) per Christum, ad æternam salutem adducere. Unde qui tam præclaro Dei beneficio sunt donati, illi Spiritu ejus, opportuno tempore operante, secundum propositum ejus, vocantur, vocationi per gratiam parent, justificantur gratis, adoptantur in filios Dei, Unigeniti ejus Jesu Christi imagini efficiuntur conformes, in bonis operibus sancte ambulant, et demum ex Dei misericordia pertingunt ad sempiternam felicitatem.

Quemadmodum prædestinationis, et electionis nostræ in Christo pia consideratio, dulcis, suavis, et ineffabilis consolationis plena est, vere piis, et iis qui sentiunt in se vim Spiritus Christi, facta carnis, et membra, quæ adhuc sunt super terram, mortificantem, animumque ad cœlestia et superna rapientem : tum quia fidem nostram de æterna salute consequenda per Christum plurimum stabilit, atque confirmat, tum quia amorem nostrum in Deum vehementer accendit : ita hominibus curiosis, carnalibus, et Spiritu Christi destitutis, ob oculos perpetuo versari prædestinationis Dei sententiam, pernitiosissimum est præcipitium, unde illos diabolus protrudit, vel in desperationem, vel in æque pernitiosam impurissimæ vitæ securitatem. Deinde promissiones divinas sic amplecti oportet, ut nobis in sacris literis generaliter propositæ sunt, et Dei voluntas in nostris actionibus ea sequenda est, quam in verbo Dei habemus, diserte revelatam.

———

SECTION I. — HISTORY.

THE XVIIth Article is almost, word for word, the same as the original Article of 1552.

The questions concerning God's eternal predestination are by no means peculiar to the Christian religion. The Essenes among the Jews, Zeno and the Stoics, and the followers of Mohammed, were all rigid predestinarians; believing that all the affairs of the world and the actions of the human race were ordered by an eternal and inexorable decree.

In the Christian Church there has never been any doubt or question, but that the Scriptures teach us concerning the election and predestination of God. All Christians believe in the doctrine of election. The question is, therefore, not whether the doctrine of election is true, but what the meaning of election is. Now on this point there is a vast variety of sentiment.

1. *Calvinism.* The doctrine of Calvin and the Calvinists is, that from all eternity God predestinated a certain fixed number of individuals, irrespective of anything in them, to final salvation and glory; and that all others are either predestined to damnation, or, at least, so left out of God's decree to glory that they must inevitably perish.

2. *Arminianism.* The doctrine of Arminius and the Arminians is, that, from all eternity, God predestinated a certain fixed number of individuals to glory; but that this decree was not arbitrary, but in consequence of God's foreknowledge, that those so predestinated would make a good use of the grace given; and that, as God necessarily foresees all things, so foreseeing the faith of individuals, He hath, in strict justice, ordered His decrees accordingly.

According to both these schemes, *election is to life eternal:* and the *elect* are identical with *the finally saved.*

3. *Nationalism.* The opinion of Locke and some others is, that the election, spoken of by God in Scripture, does not concern *individuals* at all, but applies only to *nations;* that, as God chose the Jews at one time to be His people, so He has since ordained certain nations to be brought into the pale of the Christian Church. Here the *elect* are all *Christian nations.*

4. *Ecclesiastical Election.* Others have held, that, as the Jews of old were God's chosen people, so now is the Christian Church; that every baptized member of the Church is one of God's elect, and that this election is from God's irrespective and unsearchable decree. Here therefore *election* is to *baptismal privileges*, not to final glory; and the elect are identical with the *baptized;* and the election constitutes *the Church.*

5. Some have held, that there is an election to baptism of some individuals, and again an election out of the elect: so that some

are elected by God's inscrutable decree to grace, and from among these some by a like inscrutable decree to perseverance and to glory. Here the *elect* are, in one sense of the word, identical with the *baptized ;* in another sense of the word, with the *finally saved.*

6. Lastly, some have taught, that, whereas to all Christians grace enough is given to insure salvation, if they will use it, yet to some amongst them is given, by God's eternal decree, a yet greater degree of grace, such that by it they must certainly be saved. This is the theory which has sometimes been called *Baxterian,* from Richard Baxter, the distinguished nonconformist divine.

The subject of predestination naturally embraces other cognate subjects, such as original sin, free-will, final perseverance, particular redemption, and reprobation. The three former have been considered under the IXth, Xth, and XVIth Articles respectively, and much of the history of the predestinarian controversy will be found under the history of those Articles.[1]

From the classification above given it will be evident, that the mere use of the terms election or predestination by a writer will not at all determine in what sense that writer uses them, nor to which of the six classes above enumerated his doctrines may be assigned.

Among the earlier fathers, especially those of the apostolic age, the language used is mostly general, and therefore difficult to fix to a particular meaning.

Clement of Rome speaks of a sedition in the Church, " as alien and foreign from the elect of God." [2] " Ye contended," he writes, " day and night for the whole brotherhood, that, with compassion and a good conscience, the number of His elect might be saved." [3] To the same Church of Corinth he speaks of God as having " made us unto Himself a part of the election. For thus it is written, When the Most High divided the nations, when He separated the sons of Adam, He set the bounds of the nations according to the number of the angels ; His people Jacob became the

---

[1] The five points of Calvinism, as they are called, are, —

1. Predestination, including Predestination, or election to life eternal, and Reprobation, or Predestination to damnation.

2. Particular Redemption, *i. e.* That Christ died only for a chosen few.

3. Original Sin.

4. Irresistible Grace, or effectual calling, the opposite to which is Free will.

5. Final Perseverance.

[3] τῆς ἀλλοτρίας καὶ ξένης τοῖς ἐκλεκτοῖς τοῦ Θεοῦ μιαρᾶς καὶ ἀνοσίου στάσεως.— 1 *Ep. ad Corinth.* 1.

[4] εἰς τὸ σώζεσθαι μετ' ἐλέους καὶ συνειδήσεως τὸν ἀριθμὸν τῶν ἐκλεκτῶν αὐτοῦ. —: 1 *Ep. ad Corinth.* 2.

portion of the Lord, and Israel the lot of His inheritance. And in another place he saith, Behold the Lord taketh to Himself a nation from the midst of the nations, as a man taketh the first-fruits of his threshing-floor, and from that nation shall come the Holy of Holies." [1] " In love have been perfected all the elect of God." [2] " Now God, who seeth all things, the Father of spirits and the Lord of all flesh, who hath elected our Lord Jesus Christ, and us by Him to be His peculiar people, grant to every soul," [3] &c.

Ignatius addresses the *Church* of Ephesus as " blessed through the greatness and fulness of God the Father, predestinated before the worlds continually to glory, — glory enduring, unchangeable, united, and elected in true suffering according to the will of God the Father, and of Jesus Christ our God. " [4]   In the same manner he addresses " the holy Church which is in Tralles " as " beloved by God the Father of Jesus Christ, *elect* and worthy of God." [5]

Hermas, in the book of his Visions, constantly speaks of God's *elect :* " God, who hath founded His holy Church, will remove the heavens and the mountains, the hills and the seas, ... all things shall be made plain to His elect," . . . . or, " shall be filled with His elect." [6] " Canst thou report these things to the elect ? " [7] " Go ye and declare to the elect of God His mighty acts." [8]   The Apostles, bishops, and ministers are said to have ministered to the elect of God.[9]

---

[1] Πατέρα ἡμῶν, ὃς ἐκλογῆς μέρος ἐποίησεν ἑαυτῷ. Οὕτω γὰρ γέγραπται· Ὅτε διεμέρισεν ὁ Ὕψιστος ἔθνη, ὡς δὲ ἔσπειρεν υἱοὺς Ἀδὰμ, ἔστησεν ὅρια ἐθνῶν κατὰ ἀριθμὸν ἀγγέλων· ἐγενήθη μερὶς Κυρίου λαὸς αὐτοῦ Ἰακὼβ, σχοίνισμα κληρονομίας αὐτοῦ Ἰσραὴλ· καὶ ἐν ἑτέρῳ τόπῳ λέγει· Ἰδοὺ Κύριος λαμβάνει ἑαυτῷ ἔθνος ἐκ μέσου ἐθνῶν, ὥσπερ λαμβάνει ἄνθρωπος τὴν ἀπαρχὴν αὐτοῦ τῆς ἅλω· καὶ ἐξελεύσεται ἐκ τοῦ ἔθνους ἐκείνου ἅγια ἁγίων. — 1 *Ep. ad Corinth.* 29.

[2] ἐν ἀγάπῃ ἐτελειώθησαν πάντες οἱ ἐκλεκτοὶ τοῦ Θεοῦ. — Ibid. 49.

[3] Ὁ παντεπόπτης Θεὸς καὶ Δεσπότης τῶν πνευμάτων καὶ Κύριος πάσης σαρκὸς, ὁ ἐκλεξάμενος τὸν Κύριον Ἰησοῦν Χριστόν, καὶ ἡμᾶς δι᾽ αὐτοῦ εἰς λαὸν περιούσιον, δώῃ, κ. τ. λ. — Ibid. 58.

[4] Ἰγνάτιος, ὁ καὶ Θεοφόρος, τῇ εὐλογημένῃ ἐν μεγέθει Θεοῦ Πατρὸς πληρώματι, τῇ προωρισμένῃ πρὸ αἰώνων διὰ παντὸς εἰς δόξαν, παράμονον, ἄτρεπτον, ἡνωμένην καὶ ἐκλελεγμένην, ἐν πάθει ἀληθινῷ, ἐν θελήματι τοῦ Πατρὸς καὶ Ἰησοῦ Χριστοῦ τοῦ Θεοῦ ἡμῶν, τῇ ἐκκλησίᾳ τῇ ἀξιομακαρίστῳ τῇ οὔσῃ ἐν Ἐφέσῳ τῆς Ἀσίας, κ. τ. λ. — Ignat. *Ad Ephes.* 1.

[5] Ἰγνάτιος, ὁ καὶ Θεοφόρος, ἠγαπημένῃ Θεῷ Πατρὶ Ἰησοῦ Χριστοῦ ἐκκλησίᾳ ἁγίᾳ, τῇ οὔσῃ ἐν Τράλλεσιν τῆς Ἀσίας, ἐκλεκτῇ καὶ ἀξιοθέῳ. — Ignat. *Ad Trall.* 1.

[6] " Ecce Deus virtutum qui . . . . virtute sua potenti condidit ecclesiam suam quam benedixit : ecce transferet cœlos ac montes, colles ac maria, et omnia plana (al. plena), fient electis ejus ; ut reddat illis repromissionem quam repromisit," &c. — Lib. i. *Vis.* i. 3.

[7] " Potes hæc electis Dei renunciare ? " — Lib. i.

[8] " Vade ergo et enarra electis Dei magnalia ipsius. Et dices illis quod bestia hæc figura est pressuræ superventuræ. Si ergo præparaveritis vos, poteritis effugere illam, si cor venturum fuerit purum et sine macula. . . . . Væ dubiis iis, qui audierint verba hæc et contemperint ; melius erat illis non nasci." — Lib. i. *Vis.* iv. 2.

[9] " Apostoli et episcopi et doctores et ministri, qui ingressi sunt in clementia Dei, et episcopatum gesserunt, et docuerunt, et ministraverunt sancte et modeste electis Dei qui dormiverunt quique adhuc sunt." — Lib. i. *Vis.* iii. 5.

Here we have the elect spoken of as identical with the Church. We even find language which seems to prove that Hermas considered the elect as in a state of probation in this world which might end either in their salvation or in their condemnation. "Then shall their sins be forgiven which they have committed, and the sins of all the saints, who have sinned even to this day, if they shall repent with all their hearts, and put away all doubts out of their hearts. For the Lord hath sworn by His glory concerning His elect, having determined this very time, even now, if any one shall sin, he shall not have salvation."[1] On the other hand, in one passage he seems to speak of a mansion of glory for the elect in the world to come : " The white colour represents the age to come, in which shall dwell God's elect; since the elect shall be pure and spotless unto eternal life."[2]

These are the principal passages in the Apostolical Fathers concerning election and predestination. It would be a great point gained, if we could clearly ascertain their sentiments on this subject. They lived before philosophy had produced an effect on the language of theology. Now there is no question on which philosophy is likely to have produced greater effect than on the question concerning God's eternal decrees. When, therefore, we come to the writings of such men as Justin, Clement of Alexandria, and Origen, we naturally doubt, whether they speak the language of the Church in their days, or the language of their own thoughts and speculations.

In the passages above cited, there is no marked trace of any of the three schemes which have been designated respectively as Calvinism, Arminianism, or Nationalism. One passage from Clement may seem to speak the language of Nationalism ; but it is only in appearance. That ancient father applies the term " nation " to the Christian Church ; but it is plain that he merely means, that, as the Israelites of old were chosen to be God's peculiar people, so now His Church is, as it were, a nation chosen out of the nations. He speaks indeed of " the number of God's elect being saved," as though there were a definite number of God's elect, who should be saved in the end ; language which, we shall see, is used also by

---

[1] " Tunc remittentur illis peccata, quæ jampridem peccaverunt, et omnibus sanctis qui peccaverunt usque in hodiernum diem, et si toto corde suo egerint pœnitentiam, et abstulerint a cordibus suis dubitationes. Juravit enim Dominator ille, per gloriam suam, super electos suos, præfinita ista die, etiam nunc si peccaverit aliquis, non habiturum illum salutem." — Lib. i. *Vis.* ii. 2. Compare with this the passage cited in note 8 of last page.

[2] " Alba autem pars superventuri est sæculi in quo habitabunt electi Dei, quoniam immaculati et puri erunt electi Dei in vitam æternam." — Lib. i. *Vis.* iv. 3.

Justin and Irenæus. Whether this was intended in the sense which would be affixed to it by Augustine or Calvin, must be a question. We may almost certainly say, it was not so used by Justin Martyr. There is also one passage, the last quoted from Hermas, in which the term *elect* seems used of those who are chosen to life eternal. All the other passages from the apostolical fathers identify the whole Church of God with the election, and therefore the elect with the baptized. It is most undesirable to put any force on language of such importance as the language of writers in the apostolic age. But on a fair review of the whole, it can hardly appear that these fathers speak of election in any sense but one of the two following: either (1) as an election of individuals to the Church and to baptism, or (2) possibly as an election first to baptism, and then a further election out of the baptized to glory. On the first sense, the passages seem clear and decided; on the second, it seems but reasonable to admit that there is great doubt.

In the history of the doctrine of free will,[1] we saw that Justin Martyr ascribed free agency to all human beings, and argued that God does not cause actions, because He foresees them.[2] On the contrary, he defends Christians against the charge that they believed in a fatal necessity. Our belief in the predictions of the prophet does not oblige us to believe that things take place according to fate. "This only," he says, "we hold to be fated, that they who choose what is good shall obtain a reward; that they who choose what is evil shall be punished."[3] So again soon after, he says that "we assert future events to have been foretold by the prophets, not because we say that they should so happen by fatal necessity, but because God foreknew the future actions of all men."[4] And presently again he speaks of God deferring the punishment of the wicked, till the "foreknown number of the good and virtuous should be fulfilled."[5] Accordingly Bishop Kaye has concluded that, if Justin Martyr speaks anywhere of predestination *to life eternal*, it is in the Arminian sense, or, as it has been called, *ex prævisis meritis.*[6] But when Justin Martyr especially speaks of God's election, he appears clearly to intend by it an election of individuals out of the world, and the bringing them by His calling to be

---

[1] Art. x. Sect. 1. p. 261.
[2] *Dial.* p. 290.
[3] ἀλλ' εἱμαρμένην φαμὲν ἀπαράβατον ταύτην εἶναι, τοῖς τὰ καλὰ ἐκλεγομένοις, τὰ ἄξια ἐπιτίμια· καὶ τοῖς ὁμοίως τὰ ἐναντία, τὰ ἄξια ἐπίχειρα. — *Apol.* 1. p. 81.

[4] *Apol.* 1. p. 82 a.
[5] καὶ συντελεσθῇ ὁ ἀριθμὸς τῶν προεγνωσμένων αὐτῷ ἀγαθῶν γιγνομένων καὶ ἐναρέτων, κ. τ. λ. — *Apol.* 1. p. 82 d.
[6] Bp. Kaye's *Justin Martyr,* p. 82.

of His peculiar people the Church. Thus, he is speaking of the Christian Church in antithesis to the Jewish, and he says, " We are by no means a despicable people, nor a barbarous nation, like the Phrygians and the Carians ; but God hath elected us, and has manifested Himself to those who asked not for Him. Behold I am God, saith He, to a nation that called not on my Name." Then, speaking of the calling of Abraham by the grace of Christ, he continues, " By the same voice He hath called us all, and we have come out of the polity in which we lived, living evilly, after the manner of the other inhabitants of the world," [1] &c.

It is probable therefore that, to whatever cause Justin Martyr may have assigned the final salvation of Christians, their *election* he considered to be a calling in from the people of the world to be members of the Church of Christ ; as Abraham was called from among the Gentiles to be the founder of the chosen race.

Irenæus, like Clement of Rome and Justin Martyr, speaks of a definite number of persons who shall be saved, and holds the opinion that the world shall last till this number is perfected. Yet he does not hint that any particular individuals were predestinated, of which that number should consist.[2] As regards predestination to eternal death, he clearly speaks of that as the result of God's foreknowledge of the wickedness of those whom He condemns, and says that the reason why God gave Pharaoh up to his unbelief was that He knew he never would believe.[3] He asserts too, that God puts no constraint on any one to believe ; but that, foreknowing all things, He has prepared for all fitting habitations.[4] Thus he was evidently no believer in the doctrine since called reprobation, nor in irresistible grace, or effectual calling.

But it is probable that the meaning which he attached to the

---

[1] Οὐκοῦν οὐκ εὐκαταφρόνητος δῆμος ἐσμὲν, οὐδὲ βάρβαρον φῦλον, οὐδὲ ὁποῖα Καρῶν ἢ Φρυγῶν ἔθνη, ἀλλὰ καὶ ἡμᾶς ἐξελέξατο ὁ Θεὸς, καὶ ἐμφανὴς ἐγενήθη τοῖς μὴ ἐπερωτῶσιν αὐτὸν. Ἰδοὺ Θεός εἰμι, φησὶ τῷ ἔθνει οἳ οὐκ ἐπεκαλέσαντο τὸ ὄνομά μου . . . . καὶ ἡμᾶς δὲ ἅπαντας δι' ἐκείνης τῆς φωνῆς ἐκάλεσε, καὶ ἐξήλθομεν ἤδη ἀπὸ τῆς πολιτείας ἐν ᾗ ἐζῶμεν, κ. τ. λ. — *Dial.* p. 347.

[2] καὶ διὰ τοῦτο πληρωθέντος τοῦ ἀριθμοῦ οὗ αὐτὸς παρ' αὐτῷ προώρισε, πάντες οἱ ἐγγραφέντες εἰς ζωὴν ἀναστήσονται . . . . ἵνα τὸ σύμμετρον φῦλον τῆς προορίσεως ἀπὸ Θεοῦ ἀνθρωπότητος ἀποτελεσθὲν τὴν ἁρμονίαν τηρήσῃ τοῦ Πατρὸς. — *Adv. Hær.* ii. 72.

[3] " Deus his quidem qui non credunt, sed nullificant eum, infert cæcitatem. . . . Si igitur et nunc, quotquot scit non credituros Deus, cum sit omnium præcognitor tradidit eos infidelitati eorum, et avertit faciem ab hujusmodi, relinquens eos in tenebris, quas ipsi sibi elegerunt; quid mirum, si et tunc nunquam crediturum Pharaonem, cum his qui cum eo erant, tradidit eos suæ infidelitati," &c — Lib. iv. 48.

[4] " Nec enim lumen deficit propter eos qui semetipsos excæcaverunt, sed illo perseverante quale et est excæcati per suam culpam in caligine constituuntur. Neque lumen cum magna necessitate subjiciet sibi quemquam : neque Deus coget eum, qui nolit continere ejus artem. Qui igitur abstiterunt a paterno lumine et transgressi sunt legem libertatis, per suam abstiterunt culpam, liberi arbitrii et suæ potestatis facti. Deus autem omnia præsciens, utrisque aptas præparavit habitationes," &c. — Lib. iv. 76 ; *Conf.* Lib. v. 27, 28.

Scriptural term election was, that God chose and elected certain
persons to baptism and to be members of His Church. In speaking of Esau and Jacob, as types of the Jewish and the Christian
Church, he explains St. Paul's language, in the ninth of Romans,
as meaning that God, who knoweth all things, was foretelling the
rejection of the Jews, and the election of the Gentile Church.[1]
Explaining the parable of the vineyard let out to husbandmen, he
says that God first planted the vineyard of the human race by the
creation of Adam and the election of the fathers ; then let it out
to husbandmen, the Jews, surrounding it with a hedge, built a
tower, and elected Jerusalem. But when they did not believe, He
sent His Son, whom they slew. Then the tower of election being
exalted and beautified, the vineyard, no longer walled round, but
laid open to the world, is let to other husbandmen, who will bring
forth the fruits. For the Church is everywhere illustrious ; everywhere the wine-press is dug round, because those who receive the
Spirit are everywhere. And soon after, he says that the same
Word of God who formerly elected the patriarchs has now elected
us.[2] Thus it appears that Irenæus looked on the Jews as formerly,
and on the Christian Church as now, the elect people of God ; and
so he calls " the Church the synagogue or congregation of God,
which He hath collected by Himself." [3]

Tertullian says little or nothing to guide us to his view of the
doctrine of election, except that, in arguing against certain heretics,
he maintains that it is unlawful so to ascribe all things to the will of
God as to take away our own responsibility and freedom of action.[4]

[1] " In ea enim epistola quæ est ad
Romanos, ait Apostolus : *Sed et Rebecca ex
uno concubitu habens Isaac patris nostri ; a
Verbo responsum accepit, ut secundum electionem propositum Dei permaneat, non ex
operibus, sed ex vocante, dictum est ei : Duo
populi in utero tuo, et duæ gentes in ventre
tuo, et populus populum superabit, et major
serviet minori.* Ex quibus manifestum est
non solum prophetationes patriarcharum,
sed et partum Rebeccæ prophetiam fuisse
duorum populorum : et unum quidem
esse majorem, alterum vero minorem ;
et alterum quidem sub servitio, alterum
autem liberum ; unius autem et ejusdem
patris. Unus et idem Deus noster et
illorum ; qui est absconsorum cognitor,
qui scit omnia antequam fiant ; et propter hoc dixit ; *Jacob dilexi,* Esau autem
odio habui." — Lib. iv. 38.
[2] " Plantavit enim Deus vineam humani generis, primo quidem per plas-
mationem Adæ, et electionem patrum :
tradidit autem eam colonis per eam legis

dationem quæ est per Moysem ; sepem
autem circumdedit, id est, circumtermi-
navit eorum culturam ; et turrim ædifi-
cavit, Hierusalem elegit . . . . Non credentibus autem illis, &c. . . . . tradidit
eam Dominus Deus non jam circumval-
latam, sed expansam in universum mundum aliis colonis, reddentibus fructus
temporibus suis, turre electionis exaltata
ubique et speciosa. Ubique enim præ-
clara est ecclesia, et ubique circumfossum
torcular : ubique enim sunt qui suscipi-
unt Spiritum . . . . Sed quoniam et patriarchas qui elegit et nos. idem est Verbum Dei," &c. — Lib. iv. 70.
[3] " *Deus stetit in synagoga,* &c. De Patre et Filio et de his qui adoptionem
perceperunt, dicit : hi autem sunt ecclesia. Hæc enim est synagoga Dei, quam
Deus, hoc est, Filius ipse, per semetipsum collegit." — Lib. iii. 6.
[4] " Non est bonæ et solidæ fidei, sic
omnia ad voluntatem Dei referre : et ita
adulari unumquemque, dicendo nihil fieri

Clement of Alexandria appears to have used the same language as his predecessors, concerning the Church as the election, and all Christians as the elect of God. He especially defines the Church as the general assembly of the elect.[1] So he quotes Hermas as saying, that the Church is held together by that faith by which God's elect are saved.[2] The Church, according to Clement, is the body of Christ, a holy and spiritual company; but they who belong to it, but live not uprightly, are, as it were, but the flesh of the body.[3] He holds the Church to be one, into which are collected all those who are righteous according to the purpose (κατὰ πρόθεσιν); and continues, that the Church is one, which collects together by the will of God those already ordained, whom God hath predestinated.[4]

But then when we come to the ground or cause of God's election, we find that Clement seems to speak of it as being God's foreknowledge. Thus, in the last passage referred to, he says, the Church embraces " all whom God hath predestinated, having foreknown that they would be righteous before the foundation of the world." [5] So he speaks of each person as partaker of the benefit, according to his own will; for the choice and exercise of the soul constitutes the difference of the election.[6] Accordingly, Bishop Kaye thinks, " it is evident that Clement must have held the doctrine of predestination in the Arminian sense; " [7] and Mr. Faber says, that " this prescientific solution is for the first time enounced by the speculative Clement of Alexandria." [8]

Whether Justin and Irenæus had in any degree enounced the same before, may be a fair question. The causation of sin they clearly refused to attribute to God, declaring that, where He is said to have hardened, it was because He foresaw the sinner was irreclaimable. And though Clement of Alexandria speaks more clearly than either of them, concerning God's foreknowledge as the

sine jussione Ejus: ut non intelligamus aliquid esse in nobis ipsis. Cæterum excusabitur omne delictum, si continuerimus nihil fieri a nobis sine Dei voluntate." — *De Exhortatione Castitatis*, c. 2. See Bishop Kaye's view of Tertullian's opinion on this subject in his account of Tertullian, p. 341.

[1] τὸ ἄθροισμα τῶν ἐκλεκτῶν ἐκκλησίαν καλῶ. — *Stromat.* VII. p 846, Potter.

[2] Ἡ τοίνυν συνέχουσα τὴν ἐκκλησίαν, ὡς φησὶν ὁ ποιμὴν, ἀρετὴ ἡ πίστις ἐστὶ, δι' ἧς σώζονται οἱ ἐκλεκτοὶ τοῦ Θεοῦ. — *Stromat.* Lib. II. p. 458, Potter.

[3] See Stromat. Lib. VII. p. 885.

[4] μίαν εἶναι τὴν ἀληθῆ ἐκκλησίαν, εἰς ἣν

οἱ κατὰ πρόθεσιν δίκαιοι ἐγκαταλέγονται . . . μόνην εἶναι φάμεν τὴν ἀρχαίαν καὶ καθολικὴν ἐκκλησίαν . . . . δι' ἑνὸς τοῦ Κυρίου συνάγουσαν τοὺς ἤδη κατατεταγμένους, οὓς προώρισεν ὁ Θεὸς. — *Strom.* VII. p. 899.

[5] οὓς προώρισεν ὁ Θεὸς, δικαίους ἐσομένους πρὸ καταβολῆς κόσμου ἐγνωκώς. — Ibid.

[6] μεταλαμβάνει δὲ τῆς εὐποιίας ἕκαστος ἡμῶν πρὸς ὃ βούλεται· ἐπεὶ τὴν διαφορὰν τῆς ἐκλογῆς ἀξία γενομένη ψυχῆς αἵρεσίς τε καὶ συνάσκησις πεποίηκεν. — *Strom.* γ. sub fine, p. 734.

[7] Bp. Kaye, *Clement. Alex.* p. 434.

[8] Faber, *Primitive Doctrine of Election*, p. 269.

ground of His predestination, yet he does not differ from them in the view that the Church of God is composed of the elect people of God.

Some divines of the Roman Communion[1] have endeavoured to discover the doctrines of St. Augustine in the writings of Clement; but it is only because he ascribes the beginning, the continuance, and the perfection of religion in the soul, to the grace of God, that they have thence inferred that, as it is all of grace, so it must all be of absolute predestination. Yet every one, but slightly acquainted with the predestinarian controversy, must know, that the chief disputants on every side of this troublesome argument have all alike agreed in ascribing the whole work of religion in the soul to God's grace and the operations of His Spirit; the question having only been, Is that grace irresistible or not? Is the freedom of the will utterly extinguished by it, or not? The passage especially referred to by Bossuet, in proof of the Austinism (so to speak) of Clement, is the prayer with which he concludes his *Pædagogue*, and which is simply, — that God would grant us, that following His commandments we may become fully like Him, and that He would grant, that all passing their lives in peace, and being translated into His kingdom or polity, having sailed over the waves of sin, may be borne through still waters by His Holy Spirit, and may praise God, Father, Son, and Holy Ghost; day and night unto the perfect day. And to this prayer he adds, that "Since the *Pædagogue* (*i. e.* the Word of God) has brought us into His Church, and joined us to Himself, it will be well for us being there to offer up thanksgiving to the Lord, in return for His gracious guidance and instruction.[2] This passage, however, rather corresponds with what we have seen to be the general doctrine of Clement, as probably of his predecessors, namely, that God's election brought men to baptism and to His Church, and that His grace, given to them there, enabled them, if not determined to quench the Spirit, to go on shining more and more unto the perfect day.

From this time forth, although the belief in God's election of individuals into His Church, and a frequent identification of the Church with the elect, is observable in all the patristic writers of eminence; yet when the question concerning the final salvation of

[1] Bossuet, *Défense de la Tradition et des Saints Pères*, Tom. II. Liv. XII. chap. 26; Lumper, *Historia Theologico-Critica*, Tom. IV. p. 285.

[2] *Pædagog.* Lib. III. *sub fine*, p. 311. The concluding words are, ἐπεὶ δὲ εἰς τὴν ἐκκλησίαν ἡμᾶς καταστήσας ὁ Παιδαγωγὸς αὐτὸς ἑαυτῷ παρακατέθετο τῷ διδασκαλικῷ καὶ πανεπισκόπῳ Λόγῳ, καλῶς ἂν ἔχοι ἡμᾶς ἐνταῦθα γενομένους, μισθὸν εὐχαριστίας δικαίας, κατάλληλον ἀστείου παιδαγωγίας αἰνῃ ἀναπέμψαι Κυρίῳ.

individuals was brought into contact with the question of the Divine decrees, that solution of the difficulty, since called Arminian, was generally adopted.

Origen, the pupil of Clement of Alexandria, himself the greatest speculator of early times, and the great maintainer of the freedom of the will, adopted it in its fullest and most definite form. He expressly says, that God, who foresees all things, no more causes man's sins, nor forces his obedience, than one who looks at a person walking in a slippery place is the cause that he should stumble.[1] Such was the progress of opinion among the early Christians, and so general was the spread of the foreknowledge theory in the third and fourth centuries, that our great Bishop Andrewes considered almost all the fathers to have believed in a foreseen faith, " which," he adds, " even Beza confesses ; "[2] and Hooker, himself an illustrious disciple of St. Augustine, says that " all the ancient fathers of the Church of Christ have evermore with uniform consent agreed that reprobation presupposeth foreseen sin as a most just cause, whereupon it groundeth itself." [3]

So much was this the case, that even St. Augustine himself, when first entering upon the question of predestination, taught that it was contingent on God's foreknowledge of the faith or unbelief of individuals.[4] But his farther progress in the Pelagian controversy, where he had to contend against those who grievously abused the doctrine of man's free will, led him to reconsider the questions concerning the grace of God and His predestination and purpose. Indeed he asserts, and that truly, that, before the Pelagian controversy, he had written concerning free will almost as if he had been disputing against Pelagians.[5] But his statements concerning God's foreknowledge, as antecedent to his predestination, he absolutely retracts.[6] Thenceforth his belief appears to have been,

<hr />

[1] Ὥσπερ εἴ τις ὁρῶν τινα διὰ μὲν ἀμαθίαν προπετῆ διὰ δὲ τὴν προπέτειαν ἀναλογίστως ἐπιβαίνοντα ὁδοῦ ὀλισθῆρας, καὶ καταλάβοι πεπεῖσθαι ὀλισθήσαντα, οὐχὶ αἴτιος τοῦ ὀλίσθου ἐκείνῳ γίνεται· οὕτω νοητέον τὸν Θεὸν προεωρακότα ὁποῖος ἔσται ἕκαστος, καὶ τὰς αἰτίας τοῦ τοιοῦτον αὐτὸν ἔσεσθαι καθορᾶν καὶ ὅτι ἁμαρτήσεται τάδε γινώσκει, καὶ κατορθώσει τάδε· καὶ εἰ χρὴ λέγειν οὐ τὴν πρόγνωσιν αἰτίαν τῶν γινομένων · οὐ γὰρ ἐφάπτεται τοῦ προεγνωσμένου ἁμαρτησομένου ὁ Θεὸς, ὅταν ἁμαρτάνῃ · ἀλλὰ παραδοξότερον μὲν, ἀληθὲς δὲ ἐροῦμεν, τὸ ἐσόμενον αἴτιον τοῦ τοιάνδε εἶναι τὴν περὶ αὐτοῦ πρόγνωσιν· οὐ γὰρ. ἐπεὶ ἔγνωσται, γίνεται, ἀλλ' ἐπεὶ γίνεσθαι ἔμελλεν, ἔγνωσται.— Origen. Philocal. c. XXIII.

[2] Andrewes, *Judgment of the Lambeth Articles.*

[3] *Answer to a letter of certain English Protestants.*

[4] " Respondemus. præscientia Dei factum esse, qua novit etiam de nondum natis, qualis quisque futurus sit . . . Non ergo elegit Deus opera cujusquam in præscientia, quæ ipse daturus, sed fidem elegit in præscientia : ut quem sibi crediturum esse præscivit, ipsum elegerit cui Spiritum Sanctum daret, ut bona operando etiam vitam æternam consequeretur." — *Proposit. Ex. Epist. ad Romanos Expositio.* Tom. III. pars 2, 916.

[5] *Retractationum,* Lib. I. cap. IX. Tom. I. p. 15.

[6] " Item disputans quid elegerit Deus in nondum nato . . . . ad hoc perduxi ratiocinationem, ut dicerem, *Non ergo elegit Deus opera cujusquam in præscientia,*

that Adam fell freely,[1] that, all mankind being born in sin, God's inscrutable wisdom and mercy, for good reasons, but reasons unknown to us, determined to rescue some from sin and damnation.[2] Accordingly, He prepared His Church, and predestinated some to be brought into the Church by baptism, who thereby became partakers of regenerating grace. These, and these only, could be saved.[3] Yet there was a further decree, even concerning the regenerate, namely, that some of them should die before committing actual sin, and therefore be saved; but that, of those who grew up to maturity, some should be led on by the grace of God to final perseverance, and therefore to glory: whereas others, not being gifted according to God's eternal purpose with the grace of perseverance, would not persevere at all; or if they persevered for a time, would in the end fall away and be lost.[4] It would have been just that all should be damned; it is therefore of free mercy that some should be saved.[5] God therefore graciously frees some, but leaves others by just judgment to perdition.[6] "Of two infants, both born in sin, why one is taken and the other left; of two grown persons, why one is called so as to follow the calling, the other, either not called, or not called so as to follow the calling; these are in the inscrutable decrees of God. And of two godly men, why to one is given the grace of perseverance, but to another it is not given, this is still more in the inscrutable will of God. Of this, however, all the faithful ought to be certain, that one was predestinated, and the other not," &c.[7] The baptized and regenerate may be called of the elect, when they believe and are baptized, and live according to God; but they are not properly and fully elect, unless it is also ordained that they shall persevere and live holily to the end.[8]

These statements of St. Augustine gave considerable uneasiness to many who agreed with him in his general views of doctrine.

quæ ipse daturus est; sed fidem elegit in præscientia, ut quem sibi crediturum esse præscivit, ipsum elegerit cui Spiritum Sanctum daret, ut bona operando etiam vitam æternam consequeretur: nondum diligentius quæsiveram, nec adhuc inveneram qualis sit electio gratiæ." — Retract. Lib. I. cap. XXIII. Tom. I. p. 35.

[1] De Corrept. et Grat. 28, Tom. x. p. 763.

[2] De Dono Perseverantiæ, 31, p. 837; De Corrept. et Gratia, § 16, Tom. x. p. 758.

[3] De Dono Perseverantiæ, 23, Tom. x. p. 832.

[4] Ibid. § 1, Tom. x. pp. 821, 822; § 2, p. 823; § 21, p. 831; §§ 32, 33, p. 838.

[5] De Natura et Gratia, cap. v. Tom. x. p. 129.

[6] De Dono Perseverantiæ, § 35; Tom. x. p. 839.

[7] De Dono Perseverantiæ, § 21, Tom. x. p. 831: "De duobus autem parvulis originali peccato pariter obstrictis, cur iste assumatur, ille relinquatur; et ex duobus ætate jam grandibus, cur iste ita vocetur, ut vocantem sequatur; ille autem aut non vocetur, aut non ita vocetur inscrutabilia sunt judicia Dei. Ex duobus autem piis, cur huic donetur perseverantia usque in finem, illi non donetur inscrutabiliora sunt judicia Dei. Illud tamen fidelibus debet esse certissimum, hunc esse ex prædestinatis, illum non esse."

[8] De Correptione et Gratia, § 16, Tom. x. p. 758.

The members of the monastery of Adrumetum were especially troubled by these discussions.[1] In consequence, St. Augustine wrote his treatises *De Gratia et Libero Arbitrio*, and *De Correptione et Gratia*. In a short time, the clergy of Marseilles doubting the soundness of St. Augustine's view, Prosper and Hilary [2] wrote letters to him, stating the scruples of the Gallican clergy, thanking him in general for his defence of the truth, but saying that hitherto the Catholic faith had been defended, without recourse to such a theory of predestination.[3] The Gallican clergy state, that their own belief had hitherto been that God's predestination was founded on prevision of faith.[4]

Of these Massilians there appear to have been two parties, one infected with Semi-Pelagian errors, the other sound and catholic.[5] Both, however, agreed in being startled and displeased with the doctrines of St. Augustine, and in esteeming them new and unheard of. Among those who were thus dissatisfied, Prosper mentions Hilary of Arles,[6] a bishop of the first learning and piety of that age.

In answer to these letters Augustine wrote his two treatises, *De Prædestinatione Sanctorum* and *De Dono Perseverantiæ*. He acknowledges, as in his book of Retractations, that he now saw more clearly than formerly; [7] yet he says that he had implicitly taught the same doctrines before, but heresies bring out more clearly the truth.[8] He also says, the earlier fathers did not write much on these doctrines, because they had no Pelagius to write against.[9] Still he thinks that he can find support from passages in St. Cyprian, St. Gregory Nazianzen, and St. Ambrose. From St. Cyprian he quotes, " We must glory in nothing, as we have nothing of our own." [10] And again he refers to St. Cyprian's interpretation of the petition in the Lord's prayer, " Hallowed be thy Name," as meaning, that we pray that His name may be

---

[1] See the correspondence of Augustine with Valentinus. — August. *Opp.* Tom. II. pp. 791–799.

[2] Generally supposed to be the Bishop of Arles, though the Benedictine editor gives good reasons for thinking it may have been another person of the same name.

[3] " Quid opus fuit hujuscemodi disputationis incerto tot minus intelligentium corda turbari ? Neque enim minus utiliter sine hac definitione, aiunt, tot annis, a tot tractatoribus, tot præcedentibus libris et tuis et aliorum, cum contra alios, tum maxime contra Pelagianos, Catholicam fidem fuisse defensam." — *Epist.*

Hilar. § 8 ; Aug. *Opp.* Tom. x. p. 787. See also *De Dono Persev.* § 52, Tom. x. p. 850.

[4] Ibid. § 4.

[5] *Epist. Prosper.* § 3 ; Aug. *Op.* Tom. x. p. 779 ; *De Prædestinat.* § 2, p. 791.

[6] *Epist. Prosper.* § 9, p. 873.

[7] *De Prædestin.* § 7, Tom. x. p. 793.

[8] *De Dono Persever.* § 53, Tom. x. p. 851.

[9] *De Prædestin.* § 27, p. 808.

[10] " In nullo gloriandum, quando nostrum nihil sit." — Cypr. *Ad Quirinum,* Lib. III. Cap. 4 ; August. *De Prædest.* § 7, Tom. x. p. 753 ; *De Dono Persever.* § 36, p. 841 ; § 48, p. 848.

sanctified in us.   And this he further explains to signify that we
pray that we, who have been sanctified in baptism, may persevere
in that which we have begun.[1]   Hence St. Augustine concludes
that Cyprian held the doctrine of perseverance in the Augustinian
sense of that doctrine.

From Gregory Nazianzen he cites an exhortation to confess the
doctrine of the Trinity, which concludes with an expression of
confident hope, that God, who first gave them to believe, would
also give them to confess the faith.[2]

From Ambrose he alleges two passages.   In one, St. Ambrose
simply argues, that, if a man says he followed Christ because it
seemed good to himself to do so, he does not deny the will of God,
for man's will is prepared by God.[3]   The other passage is as follows : " Learn also, that He would not be received by those not
converted in simplicity of mind.   For if He would, He could from
indevout have made them devout.   Why they received Him not,
the evangelist has himself related, saying, *Because His face was as
of one going to Jerusalem.*   For the disciples were desiring to be
received into Samaria, but those whom God thinks good He calls,
and whom He wills He makes religious." [4]

These are the passages alleged by St. Augustine, in proof that
more ancient fathers than himself held his view of predestination.
With the exception of the last from St. Ambrose, it will appear to
most people, that, if St. Augustine had not brought weightier arguments from Scripture than he did from the fathers, he would
hardly have succeeded in settling his system so firmly in the minds
of his followers.   The language of the last passage indeed appears,
at first sight, strongly to resemble the language of St. Austin.
But it is by no means clear that even this passage does not accord
with the views of those fathers who held the election of individuals
to the Church and to baptismal grace, but believed that any farther
predestination was from foreseen faith ; and it is capable of proof,

[1] Cyprian, *In Dominic. Orat.* ; August.
De Dono Persever. § 4, p. 824.
[2] δώσει γάρ εὖ οἶδα ὁ τὸ πρῶτον δοὺς, καὶ
τὸ δεύτερον, καὶ μάλιστα. — Greg. Nazianz.
Oratio 44 *in Pentecosten.*
"Gregorium addamus ét tertium qui
et credere in Deum, et quod credimus,
confiteri, Dei donum esse testatur . . . .
*Dabit enim, certus sum : qui dedit quod pri-
mum est, dabit et quod secundum est :* qui
dedit credere, dabit et confiteri." — Aug.
De Dono Persever. 49, p. 849.
[3] " Quod cum dicit, non negat Deo visum : a Deo enim præparatur voluntas

hominum. Ut enim Deus honorificetur
a sancto, Dei gratia est." — Ambros.
Comment. in Lucam apud August. Ibid.
[4] "Simul disce, inquit, quid recipi nol-
uit a non simplici mente conversis. Nam
si voluisset, ex indevotis devotos fecisset.
Cur autem non receperint eum, evangelista ipse commemoravit, dicens, Quia
facies ejus erat euntis in Jerusalem. Dis-
cipuli autem recipi intra Samariam
gestiebant. Sed Deus quos dignatur vocat, et quem vult religiosum faciet." —
Ambros. *Comment. in Lucam,* Lib. VII
apud Augustin. Ibid.

that such were in fact the views generally held by St. Ambrose.[1] This passage, if fairly interpreted, contains probably no contradic‧tion of his other statements.

It is, of course, a question of no small interest, whether St. Augustine's elders in the faith held the same doctrine with himself on the predestination of God, or whether he was the first to dis‧cover it in Scripture. That so learned a divine could find no stronger passages in any of their writings than those just mentioned, is much like a confession of the difficulty of the proof. His own opinions must have great and deserved weight; but if they were novel, we can hardly accept them as true. The passages already quoted from the earliest fathers are all we have to guide us in this question; for it seems now an admitted fact, that from Ori‧gen to St. Augustine *irrespective individual election to glory* was unheard of.

Soon after the correspondence with the Massilian Christians, A. D. 430, St. Augustine died, " without any equal," says Hooker, " in the Church of Christ, from that day to this." Prosper fol‧lowed in the steps of his great master with constancy and success; but he exceeded him in the strength of his predestinarian senti‧ments: for, whereas Augustine held that the wicked perish from their natural sins, being passed over in God's decree, but not act‧ually predestinated to damnation, Prosper seems plainly to have taught the reprobation of the non-elect.[2] He drew up a book of sentences from the writings of St. Augustine;[3] and with the aid of Celestine and Leo, Bishops of Rome, was successful in oppos‧ing the Pelagian heresy.

Not long after, we read of a priest named Lucidus, who, taking up Augustine's predestinarianism, carried it into lengths to which Augustine had never gone. Faustus, Bishop of Riez, who him‧self was inclined to Semi-Pelagianism, succeeded in inducing him to recant. A synod was assembled at Arles, A. D. 475, where the errors of Lucidus were condemned, and his recantation was re-

---

[1] See this very successfully shown by Faber, *Primitive Doctrine of Election*, Bk. I. ch. VIII. p. 168, &c. The following passage shows clearly, that he held the views of Clement and Origen concerning God's prevision of faith as the ground of His predestination to glory. In dis‧cussing Matt. xx. 23, he writes: " Deni‧que ad Patrem referens addidit: Quibus paratum est, ut ostenderet Patrem quo‧que non petitionibus deferre solere, sed meritis, quia Deus personarum acceptor non est. Unde et Apostolus ait, Quos

præscivit, et prædestinavit. Non enim ante prædestinavit quam præsciret, sed quorum merita præscivit, eorum præmia prædestinavit." — *De Fide ad Gratianum*, Lib. v. cap. 2, *sub fine.*

Mr. Faber has clearly shown that else‧where St. Ambrose maintains the doc‧trine of ecclesiastical election.

[2] *Epist. ad Ruffinum*, Cap. XIV.; Ap‧pend. ad *Op. Augustin.* Tom. x. p. 168.

[3] See Appendix to Vol. x. of St. Au‧gustine's Works, p. 223, *seq.*

ceived. Some of these errors were, that " God's foreknowledge depresses men to hell, — that those who perished could not have been saved, — that a vessel of dishonour could n?ver become a vessel of honour, — that Christ did not die for all meri, nor wills all men to be saved." [1]

In the year 529 was held the second Council of Orange, at which Cæsarius of Arles presided. Its canons and decrees bear the signatures of fourteen bishops, and were approved by Boniface II., Bishop of Rome. They are chiefly directed against the errors of the Semi-Pelagians. But to the twenty-five canons on this subject there are appended three declarations of doctrine. 1. That by the grace of baptism all baptized persons can, if they will, be saved. 2. That if any hold that God has predestinated any to damnation, they are to be anathematized. 3. That God begins in us all good by His grace, thereby leading men to faith and baptism, and that, after baptism, by the aid of His grace, we can do His will. [2] These propositions of the Council of Orange, coming immediately after canons against Semi-Pelagianism and exaggerated notions of free will, express as nearly as possible a belief in Ecclesiastical Election, (*i. e.* election to the church and to baptismal privileges,) but reject the peculiar doctrines of St. Austin.

Some mention was made of Goteschalc in the history of the Xth Article. [3] He was a Benedictine monk of the convent of Orbais in the diocese of Soissons, about A. D. 840. He was a great admirer of St. Augustine, and revived his views of predestination ; though, like Lucidus, he appears to have gone much beyond his master. If we may believe the account of his doctrines given by Hincmar, he taught that there was a double predestination, of the elect to glory, and of the reprobate to death. God, of His free grace, has unchangeably predestinated the elect to life eternal ; but the reprobate, who will be condemned by their own demerits, He has equally predestinated to eternal death. [4] He taught also, that Christ did not die for those who were predestinated to damnation, but only for those who were predestinated to life. [5] Rabanus Maurus, Archbishop of Mentz, opposed him with great zeal, and summoned a council at Mentz, A. D. 848, which condemned Got-

---

[1] Conc. Tom. IV. p. 1041. See also Hooker's Works, edit. Keble, Oxford, 1836 ; Vol. II. Appendix, p. 736, notes.
[2] Concil. IV. 1666 ; Appendix to Vol. X. of St. Augustine's Works, p. 157.
[3] See above, p. 265.

[4] Hincmar, *De Prædestin.* Cap. 5 ; Cave, *Hist. Lit.* Tom. I. p. 528.
[5] Hincmar, Ibid. c. 27 ; Cave, Ibid. Archbishop Usher wrote a history of the controversy concerning Goteschalc.

eschalc's opinions, and then sent him to Hincmar, Archbishop of Rheims, who assembled a synod at Quiercy, which degraded him from the priesthood, obliged him to burn the tract which he had delivered to Rabanus Maurus in justification of his doctrines, and committed him to prison, where he lay for twenty-one years, and then died.[1]

The discussions between Thomists and Scotists, among the schoolmen, have also been referred to under Art. X.[2] The former were followers of Thomas Aquinas, who himself followed St. Augustine. They appear to have held irrespective predestination to life; but to have admitted neither reprobation, partial redemption, nor final perseverance, in the sense in which the two former were held by Lucidus and Goteschalc.[3]

We saw, under Article X., how strongly Luther, in his earlier writings, spoke of the slavery of the human will, and the necessity under which it was constrained.[4] In the first edition of the *Loci Theologici*, Melancthon held language of the same kind. But in the second edition these expressions were all withdrawn; and, as we saw in the last Article, Luther, later in life, condemned what are called Calvinistic views of election. Archbishop Laurence has shown, by abundant and incontrovertible evidence, that after the diet of Augsburg, A. D. 1530, when the famous Lutheran Confession was presented to the Emperor, Luther and Melancthon entirely abandoned the high views of absolute predestination which they had at first adopted. Luther continually exhorted his followers to abstain from all such speculations, and to believe that because they were baptized Christians, they were God's elect, and to rest in the general promises of God.[5] Luther expressly approved [6] of the later edition of Melancthon's *Loci Theologici*, put forth A. D. 1535, in which his former views of predestination were retracted.[7]

---

[1] See Cave, as above; and Mosheim, Cent. IX. pt. II. ch. III.

[2] See above, p. 266. See also Neander, *C. H.* VIII. p. 171.

[3] Archbishop Laurence, in the learned notes to his *Bampton Lectures*, seems to contend that none of the schoolmen believed in predestination, in the absolute and irrespective sense in which St. Augustine held it. But it seems to me that the very passages which he quotes from Aquinas prove that he did hold Augustine's view of predestination to life, though he clearly denied reprobation, and the certainty of individual perseverance: *e. g.* "Deus habet præscientiam etiam de peccatis; sed prædestinatio est

de bonis salutaribus." — Aquin. *Exposit. in Rom.* cap. 8; Laurence, p. 353. See also the passages immediately following, and the quotations from Aquinas *ap.* Laurence, p. 152; where his view of perseverance seems exactly the same as that which we have seen above to have been St. Augustine's.

[4] Above, p. 267.

[5] See Laurence, *Bampton Lectures*, note 6, to Serm. VII. pp. 355, *seq.* See especially Lutheri *Opera*, VI. p. 355; Laurence, pp. 356, 357.

[6] Preface to Vol. I. of his Works. Wittenb. 1545; Laurence, p. 250.

[7] See Laurence, p. 249; Serm. II. note 16. Serm. VII. note 7.

53

He himself speaks of the predestinarian controversies set on foot
in his own time, as the work of the devil.[1] Melancthon too, in the
strongest terms, condemned what he called the Stoical and Manichean rage, and urged all people to fly from such monstrous
opinions.[2]

The doctrine both of Luther and Melancthon, after their first
change of opinion, appears to have been very nearly that which,
we have reason to conclude, was the doctrine of the earliest fathers.
They clearly taught that Christ died for all men, and that God
willed all to be saved. They held, that all persons brought to
baptism and to the Church were to be esteemed the elect people of
God, having been led to baptism by the gracious purpose of God.
They taught too, that God's purposes were to be *generally* considered, and His promises *generally* interpreted, *i. e.* as implying
His *general* designs concerning Christians and the human race,
and as concerning classes of persons, according to their respective
characters.[3]

Zuinglius was an absolute predestinarian, ascribing all things
to the purpose and decrees of God; but he materially differed
from the Calvinist divines who followed him, in holding that God's
mercies in Christ, though given irrespectively, and from absolute
predestination, were bestowed not only on Christians, but on infants
who die without actual sin, and on heathens, who " had · grace to
live a virtuous life, though ignorant of the Redeemer." [4]

In the Council of Trent, when the question of predestination
was discussed, no fault was found with the Lutheran statements on
this head; but several points were found for discussion in the
writings of the Zuinglians. Many of the Tridentine divines took
views of predestination similar to those of St. Augustine, though

---

[1] *Opp.* Tom. v. p. 197. See under
History of Article xvi.

[2] See his language largely quoted,
Laurence, pp. 159, 162, 163, 241, 359,
366, 367, 370. Some of the same passages may be seen in Faber, *Primitive
Doctrine of Election*, pp. 350, 351, 352.

[3] Luther's sentiments on universal
grace are shown by Archbishop Laurence,
pp. 160, 359. On his and Melancthon's
belief in baptismal election see p. 157;
e. g. " Quicquid hic factum est, id omne
propter nos factum, qui in illum credimus,
et in nomen ejus baptizati, et ad salutem
destinati, atque electi sumus." — Luth.
Opp. Tom. vii. p. 355; Laurence, p.
157.

" De effectu electionis teneamus hanc
consolationem; Deum, volentem non

perire totum genus humanum, semper
propter Filium per misericordiam vo-
care, trahere et colligere *Ecclesiam*, et recipere assentientes, atque ita velle semper aliquam esse ecclesiam, quam adju-
vat et salvat." — Melancth. *Loc. Theolog.
De Prædest.*; Laurence, p. 357. See
other passages there to the same effect.
See also Faber, *Prim. Doct. of Election,*
p. 374, note; who brings numerous passages from Melancthon to prove that he
held election to baptismal grace.

[4] " Nihil restat, quo minus inter gentes
quoque Deus sibi deligat, qui observent
et post fata illi jungantur; libera est
enim electio ejus." — Zuing. *Oper.* Tom.
ii. p. 371; Faber, *Prim. Doct. of Election,*
p. 373; Laurence, *Serm.* v. notes 1, 2, pp.
295–302.

these were strongly opposed by the Franciscans. Catarinus propounded an opinion much like that afterwards held by Baxter, that of Christians, some were immutably elected to glory, others were so left that they might or might not be saved. All agreed to condemn the doctrine commonly called Final Perseverance.[1]

Calvin, with the love of system and logical precision which was so characteristic of him, rejected every appearance of compromise, and every attempt to soften down the severity of the high predestinarian scheme. Advancing, therefore, far beyond the principles of his great master, St. Augustine, he not only taught that all the elect are saved by immutable decree, but that the reprobate are damned by a like irreversible sentence, a sentence determined concerning them before the foundation of the world, and utterly irrespective of the foreknowledge of God.[2] Nay ! God's foreknowledge of their reprobation and damnation is the result of His having predestinated it; not His predestination the result of His foreknowledge.[3] The very fall of Adam was ordained, because God saw good that it should be so ; though, why he saw good, it is not for us to say. But no doubt He so determined, partly because thereby the glory of His Name would be justly set forth.[4] Those who are thus elect to glory, and those only, are *called effectually*, *i. e.* irresistibly ; whereas the non-elect, or reprobate, have only the external calls of the word and the Church.[5] Those thus effectually called, are endued with the grace of final perseverance, so that they can never wholly fall away from grace.[6]

These views, with little variation, were adopted by the different bodies of Christians which were reformed on the Calvinistic model. Sufficient account has been given under Article X. of the principal proceedings of the Synod of Dort. The Remonstrants, who agreed with Arminius, and against whom that synod directed its decrees, had adopted that theory concerning God's predestination which had been current among the fathers from Origen to

---

[1] Sarpi, p. 197.

[2] " Aliis vita æterna, aliis damnatio æterna præordinata." — *Institut.* III. xxi. 5. " Quod ergo Scriptura clare ostendit dicimus, æterno et immutabili consilio Deum semel constituisse quos olim semel assumere vellet in salutem, quos rursum exitio devovere. Hoc consilium quoad electos in gratuita ejus misericordia fundatum esse asserimus, nullo humanæ dignitatis respectu : quos vero damnationi addicit, his justo quidem et irreprehensibili, sed incomprehensibili ipsius judicio, vitæ aditum præcludi." — Ibid. III. xxi. 7.

[3] *Institut.* III. xxi. 6.

[4] " Lapsus enim primus homo, quia Dominus ita expedire censuerat : cur censuerit, nos latet. Certum tamen est non aliter censuisse, nisi quia videbat nominis sui gloriam inde merito illustrari." — Lib. III. xxiii. 8.

[5] Lib. III. xxiv. 1, *seq.*

[6] Lib. III. xxiv. 6, 7.

Augustine.[1] They taught that God's predestination resulted from
His foreknowledge. They ascribed all good in man to the grace
of the Spirit of God; but they held, that God determined to save
eternally those who, He foresaw, would persevere in His grace to
the end, and that He destined to damnation those who, He knew,
would persevere in their unbelief. These views were rejected and
condemned by the synod, which distinctly enunciated the five
points of Calvinism.[2]

The disputes on the same subject, which have prevailed in the
Church of Rome since the Council of Trent, were all sufficently
alluded to under Article X.[3]

The doctrine of our own Reformers on this deep question, and
the meaning of the XVIIth Article, have been much debated.
The Calvinistic divines of our own communion have unhesitatingly
claimed the Article as their own; although the earnest desire
which they showed in the reign of Queen Elizabeth, to introduce
the far more express language of the Lambeth Articles, shows
that they were not fully satisfied with the wording of it. On the
other hand, the Arminians assert that the seventeenth Article exactly expresses their own views. The Arminians agree with the
Calvinists in holding that God, by his secret counsel, hath predestinated some to life eternal, others to eternal death. They differ
from them in that, whereas the Calvinists attribute this predestination to God's sovereign, irrespective, and though doubtless just, yet
apparently arbitrary will, the Arminians attribute it to His eternal
foreknowledge. Now the Article says nothing concerning the *moving cause* of predestination; and therefore speaks as much the language of Arminius as of Calvin. The latter clauses of the Article
appear specially designed to guard against the dangers of the Calvinistic theory, and therefore the former cannot have been intended
to propound it. Moreover the sentiments concerning election most
prevalent in the Church before the Reformation were that God
predestinated to life and death, not according to His absolute will,
but according as He foresaw future faith or unbelief; and there
being no ground for supposing that the English reformers had been
mixed up with any of the predestinarian controversies of Calvin
and the Swiss reformers, there is every ground, it is said, for sup-

---

[1] Calvin himself owns that Ambrose,
Origen, and Jerome, held the Arminian
view of election. — *Institut.* III. xxii. 8.
[2] See Mosheim, Cent. XVII. Sect. II.
ch II. § 11; Heylyn, *Histor. Quinquartic.*

Part II. ch. IV. And for the decrees of
Dordrecht on Predestination, see *Syllog∝
Confess.* p. 406.
[3] Above, pp. 269, 270.

posing that the Article ought to be taken in the Arminian, not in the Calvinistic sense.

In what sense the English reformers really did accept the doctrine of God's election, and in what sense the XVIIth Article is to be interpreted, is truly a question of considerable difficulty. The language of Cranmer and Ridley, and of our own Liturgy, Articles and Homilies, is remarkably unlike Calvin's concerning effectual calling and final perseverance.[1] It is also clear, that the English Reformers held, and expressed in our formularies, with great clearness and certainty, the universality of redemption through Christ.[2] So that, in three out of five points of Calvinism, Particular Redemption, Effectual Calling, and Final Perseverance, the English reformers were at variance with Calvin.

Still, no doubt, it is possible that they may have been un-Calvinistic in all these points, and yet have agreed with St. Augustine on the general notion and causation of God's predestination; for we have seen that Augustine's views were materially different from Calvin's.

It is pretty certain that Calvin's system had not produced much influence, at the time the XVIIth Article was drawn up. It is true, the first edition of his *Institutes* was written early in his career; and that contains strong predestinarian statements. But the great discussion on this head at Geneva, and the publication of his book *De Prædestinatione*, did not take place till A. D. 1552, the very year in which the Articles were put forth.

It has moreover been clearly shown, that the earlier Articles of the Church of England were drawn up from Lutheran models, agreeing remarkably with the language of Melancthon and the Confession of Augsburg.[3] Archbishop Laurence has plainly proved that the greatest intimacy and confidence existed between Cranmer and Melancthon; that for a series of years during the reign of Henry VIII. and Edward VI. both the king and the leading reformers were most desirous of bringing Melancthon to England, and that nothing but the death of Edward VI. prevented the establishment of Melancthon in the chair of divinity at Cambridge, formerly filled by Erasmus and Bucer.[4] All this must have been

---

[1] Concerning *effectual calling* see particularly the original xth Article, quoted p. 271; and the whole History of Article x. On Final Perseverance, see History of Art. xvi.

[2] " The offering of Christ once made is that perfect redemption, propitiation, and satisfaction for *all the sins of the whole world.*" — Art. xxxi. " God the Son, who hath redeemed me and *all mankind.*" — Catechism. " A full, perfect, and sufficient sacrifice, oblation, and satisfaction for the sins of the whole world."— Prayer of Consecration at the Holy Communion.

[3] See Laurence's *Bampton Lectures, passim,* and the historical sections to several of the foregoing Articles.

[4] See Laurence, *Sermon* I. note 3, p. 198.

pending at the very time the XVIIth Article was composed.
Nay! there is even some reason to think that Cranmer was induced to draw up this Article by suggestion of Melancthon, who,
when consulted by Cranmer (A. D. 1548) on the compilation of a
public confession on this particular question, wrote recommending
great caution and moderation, adding that at first the stoical disputations about fate were too horrible among the reformers, and in-
jurious to good discipline ; and urging that Cranmer " should think
well concerning any such formula of doctrine." [1]

From such facts it is inferred that the Lutheran, not the Calvinist reformers, had weight, and were consulted on the drawing up
of this Article ; and that, as Lutheran models were adopted for the
former Articles, so, although there is no Article in the Confession
of Augsburg on predestination, yet the views of that doctrine current among the Lutheran divines were more likely to prevail than
those among the Calvinists, who had as yet had no influence in
Great Britain.

The published writings of Cranmer and Ridley have remarkably
little which can lead to an understanding of their own views of
God's predestination.   We hear that Ridley wrote a " godly and
comfortable treatise " on " the matter of God's election ; " but it
has never yet come to light.   In the letter wherein he speaks of
having prepared some notes on the subject, he says, " In these
matters I am so fearful that I dare not speak further, yea, almost
none otherwise than the very text doth, as it were, lead me by the
hand. " [2]

Cranmer's writings are, even more than Ridley's, free from statements on God's predestination.   But Archbishop Laurence has
brought several passages from Latimer, Hooper, and other contemporaneous divines of the Church of England, which show that they
held decidedly anti-Calvinistic sentiments, and which prove that
even the Calvinism of Bradford was of the most moderate kind.[3]

If from the writings of the reformers we pass to the formularies
of the Church, the Liturgy, the Catechism, and the Homilies, we
shall find that they appear to view the election of God as the choosing of persons to baptism, the elect as identical with the baptized,
or, what is the same thing, with the Church of Christ throughout

---

[1] " Nimis horridæ fuerunt initio Stoicæ
disputationes apud rostros de fato, et
disciplinæ nocueru·nt.   Quare te rogo, ut
de tali aliqua formula doctrinæ cogites."
— Melancth. *Epist.* Lib. iii. Epist. 44 ;
Laurence, p. 226.

[2] Letter to Bradford in the Library
of Emmanuel College, Cambridge, Ridley's *Remains,* Parker Society's edition, p.
367.

[3] See Laurence, *Sermon* viii. note 8,
p. 389–394.

the world. Thus, in the Catechism, every baptized child is taught
to say, " God the Holy Ghost, who sanctifieth *me* and all the *elect*
people of God." In the Baptismal Service we pray that the child
" now to be baptized, may receive the fulness of God's grace, and
ever remain in the number of His faithful and *elect* children." In
the daily service we pray, " Endue thy ministers with righteousness,
and make thy *chosen* people joyful. O Lord, save thy people, and
bless thine inheritance." Where God's inheritance, the Church,
is evidently the same as His " chosen " or elect " people," whom
we pray that He will bless, save, and make joyful. In the Burial
Service, we pray God to " accomplish the number of His *elect,* and
hasten His kingdom, that *we,* with all those departed," &c. Where
the *we* appears to be connected with God's *elect.* In the Homily
of falling from God all Christians are plainly spoken of as the
" chosen " (*i. e.* elect) " vineyard of God," which yet by falling
away may be lost. " If we, which are the chosen vineyard of
God, bring not forth good fruits, that is to say, good works . . . .
He will pluck away all defence, and suffer grievous plagues . . . .
to light upon us. Finally, if these serve not, He will let us lie
waste, He will give us over . . . ." &c.

From all these considerations, it is more probable that an Article
drawn up by Cranmer should have expounded the doctrine of ecclesiastical or baptismal election, than that it should have contained
the doctrine of Calvin or Arminius. For both the other documents
drawn up by himself, and the writings of his great counsellor, Melancthon, exhibit the clearest evidence of their belief in such ecclesiastical election. Add to which, the early fathers, whose writings
Cranmer most diligently searched, are very full of the same mode
of explaining the truth.

The question still remains, after all this historical probability,
Will the wording of the Article bear this meaning ? or are we absolutely constrained to give another interpretation to it ? Persons
but little acquainted with scholastic disputations and with the language of controversy are apt at first sight to think the XVIIth Article obviously Calvinistic, though others, somewhat better read, are
aware that it will equally suit the doctrine of Arminius: but both
might be inclined to suppose that it could not express the opinions
of Melancthon and of the majority of the primitive fathers, and
what, we have seen reason to conclude, were Cranmer's own opinions. Let us see whether this is the case.

In the first place then, the words of the concluding paragraph in
the Article have been shown to bear so remarkable a resemblance

to the language of Melancthon (language particularly objected to by Calvin [1]), that it could hardly have been accidental. " Furthermore," it runs, " we must receive God's promises in such wise as they be *generally* set forth in holy Scripture ; and in our doings that will of God is to be followed, which we have expressly declared to us in the word of God." The word *generally* is in the Latin *generaliter*, which means not *for the most part*, but *universally* or *generically*, i. e. as concerning classes of persons. Now Melancthon writes, " And if other things may be nicely disputed concerning election, yet it is well for godly men to hold that *the promise is general or universal. Nor ought we to judge otherwise concerning the will of God than according to the revealed word*, and we ought to know what God hath commanded that we may believe," [2] &c.

But in the beginning of the Article we read of " predestination to life," and of God's purpose " to deliver from curse and damnation : " expressions which may seem tied to the notion of election embraced by Augustine, Calvin, and Arminius, namely, predestination to life eternal. It is, however, to be noted, that it would quite suit the way of thinking common to those who held ecclesiastical election, to speak of election to baptism as *election to life*, and as *deliverance from curse and damnation*. For the Church of Christ is that body, which, having been purchased by the Blood of Christ, is destined to life eternal, and placed in a position of deliverance from the curse of original sin. Baptism is for the remission of sin. All baptized infants have been elected therefore to life, and delivered from curse and damnation. The election to life eternal indeed is mediate, through election to the Church, not immediate and direct. Every baptized Christian has been chosen out of the world to be placed in the Church, in order that he may be brought by Christ to everlasting salvation, as a vessel made to honour. He may forfeit the blessing afterwards, but it has been freely bestowed on him. All persons endued with such an excellent benefit of God are called according to His purpose by His Spirit. They are freely justified and made Sons of God by adoption (language specially used in the Catechism of baptized children) ; they be made like the image of the only-begotten, Jesus Christ, for the baptized Christian is said to be regenerate after the likeness of Christ. The next step in his course is to walk in good works ; the last to attain, by God's mercy, to everlasting felicity.

---

[1] See Laurence, p. 180.

[2] " Et si alia subtiliter de electione disputari fortasse possunt, tamen prodest piis tenere quod *promissio sit universalis.* Nec debemus *de voluntate Dei aliter judi-* care quam juxta *Verbum revelatum,* et scire debemus, quod Deus præceperat, ut credamus." — *Opera,* IV. p. 498; Laurence, pp. 172, 362, 363.

Such language then, which is the language of the Article, suits the baptismal theory as well as the Calvinistic theory ; and it has been contended with great force by Archbishop Laurence and Mr. Faber, that no other sense can be properly attached to it.

On the whole, however, it seems worthy of consideration, whether the Article was not designedly drawn up in guarded and general terms, on purpose to comprehend all persons of tolerably sober views. It is hardly likely that Cranmer and his associates would have been willing to exclude from subscription those who symbolized with the truly admirable St. Augustine, or those who held the theory of prevision, so common among those fathers whose writings Cranmer had so diligently studied. Nor, again, can we imagine that anything would have been put forth markedly offensive to Melancthon, whose very thoughts and words seem embodied in one portion of this Article, as well as in so many of the preceding. Therefore, though Cranmer was strong in condemning those who made God the author of sin, by saying that He enforced the will ; though he firmly maintained that Christ died to save all men, and would have all men to be saved ; though he and his fellows rejected the Calvinistic tenet of final perseverance ; they were yet willing to leave the field fairly open to different views of the Divine predestination, and accordingly worded the Article in strictly Scriptural language, only guarding carefully and piously against the dangers which might befal " carnal and curious persons." After long and serious consideration, I am inclined to think this the true state of the case. I am strongly disposed to believe that Cranmer's own opinions were certainly neither Arminian nor Calvinistic, nor probably even Augustinian ; yet I can hardly think that he would have so worded this Article, had he intended to declare very decidedly against either explanation of the doctrine of election.

It seems unnecessary to do more than briefly allude to the painful controversies to which this fruitful subject gave rise in the Church of England, since the Reformation. A sufficient account was given, under Article XVI., of the disputes which led to the drawing up of the Lambeth Articles, which, though accepted by Archbishop Whitgift and a majority of the divines at Lambeth, never had any ecclesiastical authority. The first four of these were designed to express distinctly the *Calvinistic* doctrines of election and reprobation ; though the bishops softened down a few of the expressions in Whitaker's original draught, so as to make

them a little less exclusive.[1] The Puritan party at Hampton Court
wished that these "nine assertions orthodoxal" should be added
to the XXXIX. Articles, and also that some of the expressions in
the XXXIX. Articles which sounded most against Calvinism
should be altered or modified; but their wish was not obtained.[2]
There have ever since continued different views of the doctrine
of predestination amongst us, and different interpretations of this
XVIIth Article. It were indeed much to be wished that such
differences might cease ; but from the days of St. Augustine to
this day, they have existed in the universal Church ; and we can
scarcely hope to see them utterly subside in our own portion of it.

Section II. — SCRIPTURAL PROOF.

IN investigating the Scriptural doctrine of Election, it is of the
utmost consequence to keep close to Scripture itself, and to
keep clear of philosophy. The subject of God's foreknowledge
and predestination must be full of difficulty, and our question can
only be, what is revealed to us, not what may be abstract truth.

[1] The Lambeth Articles, after revision
by the bishops, were as follows : —

1. Deus, ab æterno, prædestinavit
quosdam ad vitam, quosdam reprobavit
ad mortem.

2. Causa movens prædestinationis ad
vitam, non est prævisio fidei aut perseverantiæ, aut bonorum operum aut ullius
rei quæ insit in personis prædestinatis,
sed sola voluntas beneplaciti Dei.

3. Prædestinatorum definitus et certus
est numerus, qui nec augeri nec minui
potest.

4. Qui non sunt prædestinati ad salutem necessario propter peccata sua
damnabuntur.

5. Vera, viva et justificans Fides, et
Spiritus Dei justificantis non extinguitur,
non excidit, non evanescit, in electis, aut
finaliter aut totaliter.

6. Homo vere fidelis, i. e. fide justificante præditus, certus est, Plerophoria
Fidei, de remissione peccatorum suorum,
et salute sempiterna sua per Christum.

7. Gratia salutaris non tribuitur, non
communicatur, non conceditur universis
hominibus, qua servari possint, si volu-
erint.

8. Nemo potest venire ad Christum,
nisi datum ei fuerit, et nisi Pater eum
traxerit. Et omnes homines non trahun-
tur a Patre, ut veniant ad Filium.

9. Non est positum in arbitrio aut
potestate uniuscujusque hominis salvari.

We saw under Article xvi. the alterations introduced by the Lambeth Divines
into Propositions 5 and 6, thereby materially modifying the sense. The first
proposition expresses a general truth, to
which all assent. In the second Whitaker
had " Causa efficiens," which the bishops
altered to "movens;" for the moving
cause of man's salvation is not in himself, but in God's mercy through Christ.
So, instead of the last words in Whitaker's second Proposition, "sed sola, et ab-
soluta, et simplex voluntas Dei," they put
" sed sola voluntas beneplaciti Dei," because our salvation springs from God's
good pleasure and goodness. Yet even
so modified (and with such modifications
all their original force was lost) the Articles did not approve themselves to the
Queen or the best of our then living
divines.

[2] Cardwell's Conferences, pp. 178, seq.

The disputes between the Calvinists and Arminians took, unhappily, a metaphysical, almost more than a Scriptural turn. The Calvinists were unable to believe in the contingency of events certainly foreknown, and in the absolute sovereignty of God, if limited by His knowledge of the actions of subordinate beings. The Arminians, truly contending that an action was not made compulsory because it was foreseen, held it inconsistent with the justice of God to destine some to be saved and others to be lost. Both argued from natural religion ; and both gave weighty reasons for their inferences. But both should have seen that there was a limit to all such investigations, which no human intelligence could pass ; and that those very arguments which reduced their adversaries to the greatest difficulties, might often, if pursued further, have told against themselves.

It is quite certain that, if we carry out our investigations on such subjects to their fullest extent, we must at length reach a point which is impassable, but where we are at least as much in difficulty and darkness as at any previous step in our course. Thus, why God, who is all holy and merciful, ever permitted sin to exist, seeing He could have prevented it ; why, when sin came, not only into the creation, but into this world, He did not wholly, instead of partially, remove its curse and power ; why the child derived it from its parent ; why the unsinning brute creation is involved in pain and death, the wages of sin ; why, whereas one half of the infants who are born die before the age of reason and responsibility, yet God does not cause all to die in infancy who, He foresees, will, if they live, live wickedly : — these and like questions, which puzzle us as to the omnipotence, the justice, or the goodness of God, and which neither Scripture nor philosophy will answer, ought to teach us that it is not designed that we should be satisfied on these deep subjects of speculation, concerning which Milton has described even angelic beings as lost in inextricable difficulty.

There is another line of reasoning, which has been taken in this controversy, somewhat more bearing on practical questions, and yet leading us beyond the reach of human intelligence. The Calvinist feels deeply that all must be ascribed to the grace of God, and nothing to the goodness of man. Therefore, he reasons, all holiness must come from an absolute decree ; for, if not, why does one accept grace, another refuse it ? If the grace be not irresistible, there must be something meritorious in him who receives, compared with him who resists. Both indeed may resist God's grace ; but he indeed who resists the least, so as not to quench the Spirit, must be considered as relatively, if not positively, meritorious. The Arminian, on the contrary, admitting that merit is not possible for man, yet contends that the belief in an irreversible decree takes away all human responsibility, makes the mind of man a mere machine, and deprives us of all motives for exertion and watchfulness. Even these arguments lead us to difficulties which perhaps we cannot solve. We are clearly taught to believe, that sinful man can deserve no good from God, and derives all he has from Him. We are also taught to feel our own responsibility in the use of the grace given us, and the necessity of exerting ourselves in the strength of that grace. There may be some difficulty in harmonizing the two truths; but we have no right to construct a system based upon one of them, and to the exclusion of the other. If we cannot see, as many think they can, that they form parts of one harmonious whole, we must be content to accept them both, without trying to reconcile them.

Now the doctrine of Calvin rests on two premises: 1. That election infallibly implies salvation. 2. That election is arbitrary. The Arminians admit the first premiss, which is probably false, and reject the second, which is probably true. If we would fairly investigate the question, we must begin by a determination not to be biassed by the use of words, nor to suffer ourselves to be led by a train of inductive reasoning. The former is a mistake which prevails extensively on almost all religious questions, and is utterly subversive of candour and truth; the latter is altogether inadmissible on a subject so deep as that under consideration.

To begin with the old Testament, a portion of Scripture too much neglected in this controversy, we read much there of God's election: and it is perhaps to be regretted, that our authorized translation has used the words *choose, chosen, choice,* in the old Testament, and the words *elect* and *election* in the new Testament, whereas the original must be the same in both, and the ideas, contained under both phrases, identical.

Now who are the persons spoken of in the old Testament as God's elect or chosen people? Plainly the seed of Abraham, the children of Israel. Let us then observe, first, the ground of their election; secondly, to what they were elect?

It is quite apparent, from innumerable statements of Moses and the prophets, that the cause or ground of God's election of the people of Israel was not, as on the Arminian hypothesis, foreseen faith, but God's good pleasure, springing from motives unknown to us. It was not for "their righteousness, for the uprightness of their heart, that they went in to possess the land." The Lord did " not give them the good land to possess for their righteousness: for they were a stiff-necked people" (Deut. ix. 5, 6). " Only the Lord had a delight in their fathers to love them, and He chose their seed after them above all people" (Deut. x. 15). " The Lord will not forsake His people for His great name's sake; because it hath pleased the Lord to make you His people" (1 Sam. xii. 22). " I will be the God of all the families of Israel, and they shall be my people . . . I have loved thee with an everlasting love; therefore with loving-kindness have I drawn thee" (Jer. xxxi. 1, 3). " I have loved you, saith the Lord, yet ye say, Wherein hast thou loved us? Was not Esau Jacob's brother? saith the Lord; yet I loved Jacob, and I hated Esau" (Mal. i. 2, 3): a passage, which, as explained by St. Paul (Rom. ix. 13), clearly expresses God's purpose to choose the seed of Jacob in preference to that of Esau, irrespectively of the goodness of the one or the other.

The Arminian hypothesis, therefore, of foreseen faith is clearly inapplicable to the election spoken of in the books of the old Testament. The cause and ground of it was plainly God's absolute irrespective decree. But then *to what* was the election so often mentioned there? We have discovered its ground; can we discover the correct idea to be attached to the action itself?

It is evident that the whole Jewish nation, and none but they, were the objects of God's election. " O children of Israel . . . . you only have I known of all the families of the earth " (Amos iii. 1, 2). " Thou art an holy people unto the LORD thy God; the LORD thy God hath chosen thee to be a special people unto Himself, above all people that are upon the face of the earth " (Deut. vii. 6). " The LORD had a delight in thy fathers to love them, and He chose their seed after them, even you among all people, as it is this day " (Deut. x. 15). " The Lord hath avouched thee this day to be His peculiar people, as He hath promised thee, and that thou shouldest keep all his commandments: and to make thee high above all nations which He hath made, in praise, and in name, and in honour; and that thou mayest be an holy people unto the LORD thy God " (Deut. xxvi. 18, 19). And, " What one nation in the earth is like thy people, like Israel, whom God went to redeem for a people to Himself? . . . For Thou hast confirmed to Thyself Thy people Israel, to be a people unto Thee for ever: and Thou, LORD, art become their God " (2 Sam. vii. 23, 24). " Blessed is the nation whose God is the LORD, and the people whom He hath chosen for His own inheritance " (Psal. xxxiii. 12). " The LORD hath

chosen Jacob unto Himself, and Israel for His peculiar treasure "
(Psal. cxxxv. 4). "Thou, Israel, art My servant, Jacob whom I
have chosen, the seed of Abraham My friend . . . I have chosen
thee and not cast thee away" (Isai. xli. 8, 9). "Yet now hear,
O Jacob, my servant, and Israel whom I have chosen" (Isai. xliv.
1). "For Jacob, My servant's sake and Israel Mine elect" (Isai.
xlv. 4). "Considerest thou not what this people have spoken,
saying, The two families which the Lord hath chosen, He hath
even cast them off?" (Jer. xxxiii. 24.)

All these passages tell exactly the same tale, and explain to us the
nature and object of God's election, as propounded under the old
Testament. Were the Jewish people, who are thus constantly
called God's elect, elected to an unfailing and infallible salvation of
their souls? Most assuredly not. Nay, they were not elected to
infallible possession even of all the *temporal* blessings of God's people. Victory over their enemies, entrance into, in the first place,
and then quiet possession of, the promised land were made contingent on their obedience to God's will (see Deut. vii., viii. *passim*).
But that to which they were chosen, was to be God's "peculiar
people," — to be "a holy people," consecrated to the service of
God,— to have the covenant and the promises, and to be the
Church of God. Yet still, there was "set before them life and
death, cursing and blessing:" and they were exhorted to "choose
life:" "that they might dwell in the land which the LORD sware
to their fathers" (Deut. xxx. 19, 20).

We see therefore, first, that the cause of God's election was ar-
bitary; secondly, that the election itself was to blessing indeed, but
it was the blessing of privilege, not of absolute possession. And
even of those chosen to be brought out of Egypt, and to become
God's people in the wilderness, by abusing their privileges, all but
two perished before they reached the promised land; and those
chosen to live in Canaan, as God's Church and people then on
earth, were continually provoking God's indignation, and bringing
down a curse instead of a blessing upon them.

The seed of Abraham then, the children of Israel, were the only
elect people of God at that time upon earth; but their election
was to the privilege of being God's Church, the subjects of His
Theocratic kingdom, the recipients of His grace, and the depositaries of His truth. This is the whole nature of election, as propounded to us in the Law and the Prophets. If there were any further election, and of what nature it may have been, as far as the
old Testament went, was one of the "secret things, which belong
to the LORD our God."

Some people indeed argue, that, if one person or body of persons is predestined to light and privilege, and another is debarred from them, it is one and the same thing as if one was predestined to salvation and another to damnation; for, if the one is not certainly saved, the other is certainly lost: and so, if election to glory be not taught, reprobation to damnation is. But this is, first of all, an ex·ample of that mode of induction which is so objectionable in ques·tions of this sort. And next, it remains to be proved, either that privilege leads of necessity to salvation, or that absence of privilege leads inevitably to damnation. However, it will, no doubt, be gen·erally conceded that the Jew was placed in a more favourable state for attaining salvation than the Gentile, and *that*, as we have seen, from an arbitrary decree of God. This, it will be said, is as inconsistent with our ideas of justice, as anything in the system of Calvin or Augustine. Admit this, and you may as well admit all. The question, however, still remains the same; not what men are willing to admit, but what the Bible reveals. This election to light and privilege is evidently analogous to those cases which we see in God's ordinary Providence: some born rich, others poor; some nursed in ignorance, others in full light; some with pious, others with ungodly parents; and now too, some in a Christian, others in a heathen land; some with five talents, others with but one. Why all this is, we cannot tell; why God is pleased to put some in a position where vice seems all but inevitable, others where goodness seems almost natural, we know not; nor again, as has been said before, why He does not ordain that all who He foresees will be wicked, should die in infancy. We know and see, that such is His pleasure. The secret motives of His will we are not told, and we cannot fathom. We are left to believe that, though hidden from us, they must be right. What we are taught is, how to avail ourselves of the privileges, whatever they may be, which we have; to escape the dangers, and profit by the advantages of our position. This is practical, and this is revealed truth.

To return to the old Testament. As we have seen, we there read much of election; and it is always election of a certain body of persons, by an arbitrary decree, to the blessings and privileges of being of the Church of God. And we observe another thing, namely, that, whereas none but the Israelites were elected to such privileges then, there were yet many prophecies of a time when other persons, individuals of other nations, should be chosen by God, and made partakers of the same privileges with the Jews, — the same privileges enhanced and exalted. Nay, the Jews **are** threatened, as a body, with rejection from privilege for their sins ; a remnant only of them being to be retained in the possession of blessing; and with that remnant, a host from other nations to be brought in and associated.

When we come to the *new Testament*, we must bear in mind that the Apostles were all Jews, but their mission was to proclaim that the Jewish Church had passed away, and to bring in converts to the Christian Church. Especially St. Paul had to found a Church among the Gentiles, and to bring the Gentiles into the fold of Christ. Nothing therefore could be more natural, or more in accordance with the plan of the Apostles, than, as it were, to apologize to the Jews, and to explain to the Gentiles the new condition which the Almighty had designed for His Church in the world. It would be most natural that they should enlarge upon the truth that in God's eternal counsels there were general purposes of mercy for mankind, to be effected by means of bringing persons into Christ's Church, and therein by the graces of His Spirit conforming them to the likeness of His Son ; that though hitherto His mercy in this respect had been confined to the Jews His further plans having been hid for ages and generations, yet now it was revealed that the Gentiles should with the Jews be fellow-heirs (see Col. i. 25, 26, Eph. iii. 5, 6) ; that, therefore, whereas heretofore the seed of Abraham had been the only chosen people of God, yet now the whole Catholic Church, composed of both converted Jews and Gentiles, were His chosen people ; and God, who, of His good pleasure, for a time elected only the Jews, had, by the same good pleasure, now chosen individuals both of Jews and Gentiles, to be members of His Church and heirs of the grace of life. In thus reasoning, it is most natural that the Apostles should constantly compare the state of Christians with the state of the Jews, and so continually use old Testament language, adopting the very expressions of Moses and the prophets, and simply applying them to the altered condition of the world, and to the enlarged condition of the Church. Thus, were the Jews constantly spoken of as a holy people, as called and chosen of God ? In like manner, St. Paul begins scarce any Epistle without calling the Church addressed in it either holy, called, or elect (see Rom. i. 6, 7 ; [1] 1 Cor. i. 9, 24 ; 2 Cor. i. 1; Eph. i. 1; Phil. i. 1; Col. i. 2; 1 Thess. i. 4 ; 2 Thess. ii. 13 ; 2 Tim. i. 8–10 ; Heb. iii. 1, &c.). Were the Jews spoken of as " a peculiar people, a kingdom of priests, a holy nation " (Exod. xix. 5, 6) ? St. Peter addresses the Christian Church as

---

[1] κλητοῖς, ἁγίοις, not as in our version, " called to be saints," but, " called, holy,' as the Syriac.

"a chosen generation, a royal priesthood, a peculiar people, that they should show forth the praises of Him who hath called them cut of darkness into His marvellous light; which in times past were not a people, but now are the people of God." [1] So too, in his very first. salutation of the Church, composed as it was of Jewish and Gentile converts, he calls them " strangers or sojourners, scattered abroad, elect according to the foreknowledge of God the Father " (1 Pet. i. 2) ; where, like St. Paul, he no doubt uses this expression with special reference to the objection which the Jews made to the calling of the Gentiles. They thought that God's plan was only to call the children of Israel. But no ! the Apostle speaks of the *Church* (a Gentile as well as a Jewish Church) as chosen and preordained, by a foreknown and predestinated counsel of God, kept secret hitherto, but now made manifest.[2]

This mode of treating the question is nowhere more apparent than in the opening of the Epistle to the Ephesians. There St. Paul is addressing a Gentile Church. Having first saluted its members, as " the holy persons in Ephesus, and the faithful in Christ Jesus," he at once proceeds to give God thanks for having blessed the Christian Church with all spiritual blessings in Christ Jesus, according as He had chosen that Church in Him before the foundation of the world ; the object of such election being, that it might be made holy and without blame before him in love ; God having predestinated its members to the adoption of children (as the Jews had of old been children of God), through Jesus Christ to Himself, according to the good pleasure of His will, to the praise of the glory of His grace (Eph. i. 3–6). He then proceeds to speak of the Church's blessing in having redemption through the Blood of Christ, and says, that now God has made known His hitherto hidden will, that in the dispensation of the fulness of time all things were to be collected together under one Head in Christ, both things in heaven and things on earth (vv. 9. 10). And he continues, that in Him " *we* (that is, those who have believed from among the Jews) have obtained an inheritance, being predestinated according to His purpose," &c. " In whom ye also (ye Gentile Christians) trusted, after that ye heard of the word of truth " (vv. 11–13).[3]

---

[1] 1 Pet. ii. 9, 10. St. Peter has here adopted the very words addressed to the Jewish people in Exod. xix. 5, 6, xxiii. 22, as rendered by the LXX. Ἔσεσϑέ μοι λαὸς περιούσιος ἀπὸ πάντων τῶν ἐϑνῶν . . . ὑμεῖς· ϳὲ ἔσεσϑέ μοι βασίλειον ἱεράτευμα καὶ ἔϑνος ἅγιον.

[2] Comp. 1 Pet. v. 13 ; where he speaks of the *whole Church* at Babylon as " elect together with " those churches to whom he writes.

[3] The force of the 14th verse is almost lost in our translation ; its peculiarity consisting in its use and adaptation of the

The Apostle next proceeds to give thanks for their conversion and faith, and to pray for their further grace and enlightenment (Eph. i. 15, 16; ii. 10). He reminds them of their former Gentile state, when they were without Christ, and aliens from the commonwealth of Israel (ii. 11, 12); and tells them, that now they are brought nigh by Christ, who hath broken down the partition wall between Jews and Gentiles, and reconciled both Jews and Gentiles to God in one body, preaching peace to the Gentiles, who were far off, and to the Jews, who were nigh (vv. 13–17). He says, that they are therefore now no longer far off from God, but are made fellow-citizens of the same city, the Church, with the saints, and of the same household of God, and are built on the same foundation, and all grow together to one holy temple in the Lord (vv. 18–22). All this was a mystery, in other ages not made known, but now revealed to apostles and prophets by the Spirit, namely, that it had been part of God's eternal purpose of mercy that Gentiles should be fellow-heirs with Jews, both members of the same body, the Church, and partakers of the same promise in Christ by the Gospel (iii. 3–6).

The Churches, which the Apostles thus addressed as elect, and on which they impress the blessings and privileges of their election, are still treated by them as in a state of probation, and their election is represented, not merely as a source of comfort, but also as full of responsibility. Thus, to the Ephesians, of whose election we find St. Paul spoke so strongly in the first chapter, he says, " I . . . beseech you that ye walk worthy of the vocation wherewith ye are called " (Ephes. iv. 1). And he thenceforth continues through the whole of the remainder of the Epistle, teaching them how to live, so as not to forfeit their blessings — not to be " like children tossed to and fro " (iv. 14) — not to " walk henceforth as other Gentiles " (17) — not to grieve the Spirit (30) — not to be partakers with fornicators and unclean livers, who have no inheritance in God's kingdom (v. 1–7) — to " have no fellowship with the unfruitful works of darkness " (11) — to " walk circumspectly, not

old Testament language to the Christian Church. The words rendered in our version, " until the redemption of the purchased possession," mean more likely " with reference to the ransom of God's peculiar people, or, of the people whom God hath made His own; " εἰς ἀπολύτρωσιν τῆς περιποιήσεως. See Exod. xix. 5, 6; xxiii. 22. So the LXX. read Malachi iii. 17, where it appears prophetic of the Gentile Church. Compare the language of St. Peter, quoted in the last note but one, who calls the Church λαὸς εἰς περιποίησιν. St. Paul, (Acts xx. 28,) speaking to the Ephesians, calls them the Church of God, ἣν περιεποιήσατο διὰ τοῦ ἰδίου αἵματος. The expression appears to mean " the people whom God made His own," so first applied to the Jewish, afterwards to the Christian Church. See Schleusner on this word, Hammond, Rosenmüller and Macknight on Ephes. i. 14, and on 1 Pet. ii. 9.

as fools, but as wise " (15) — not to be " drunk with wine, but to be filled with the Spirit " (18) — to " put on the whole armour of God, that they might be able to stand against the wiles of the devil," knowing that they had a contest against wicked spirits; that so they might " be able to withstand in the evil day, and having done all, to stand " (vi. 11, 12, 13).

Just similar is his language to other Churches. Thus, the Philippians, whom he calls " saints," he bids to " work out their own salvation with fear and trembling " (Phil. ii. 12 ; compare iii. 12–16). The Colossians, whom he speaks of as having been " translated into the kingdom of God's dear Son," he bids " to put on, as the elect of God, holy and beloved," all Christian graces (iii. 12–17) ; and to avoid all heathen vices (iii. 5–9) ; and *that* on the very principle that they were to consider themselves as brought into a new state in Christ (iii. 9, 10). The Thessalonians, whom he tells that he " knows their election of God " (1 Thess. i. 4), he warns against sloth and sleep (1 Thess. v. 6), urges them to put on Christian armour (v. 8, 9), exhorts them not to " *quench* the Spirit " (v. 19). And to Timothy he says of himself, that he " endures all things for the elect's sake ; " and *that, not* because the elect are *sure* of salvation, but in *order that* " they may *also obtain* the salvation which is in Christ Jesus with eternal glory " (2 Tim. ii. 10).

In exactly the same manner, St. Peter, as we have seen, addresses those to whom he writes as " elect," and whom he calls " an elect generation," (1 Pet. i. 2; ii. 9) : but he still urges them to " abstain from fleshly lusts," (ii. 11) ; to " pass the time of their sojourning here in fear," (i. 17) ; to be " sober and watch unto prayer " (iv. 7) ; to " give diligence to make their calling and election sure " (2 Pet. i. 10) ; to " beware lest, being led away with the error of the wicked, they fall from their own steadfastness " (2 Pet. iii. 17).

All this is in the same spirit and tone. It is, allowing for the change of circumstances, just as the prophets addressed the Jews. The prophets addressed the Jews, and the apostles addressed Christians, as God's chosen people, as elect, predestinated to the Church, to grace, to blessing. But then, they urge their blessings and election as motives, not for confidence, but for watchfulness. They speak to them as having a conflict to maintain, a race to run ; and they exhort them not to quench the Spirit, who is aiding them, to beware lest they fall from the steadfastness of their faith, to be sober and watch to the end.

Let us turn next to the Epistle to the Romans. In the ninth chapter more especially, St. Paul considers the question of God's rejecting the unbelieving Jews, and calling into His Church a body of persons elected from among Jews and Gentiles. The rejection of his fellow-countrymen he himself deeply deplores; but there was a difficulty and objection arising, which he sets himself directly to solve. God has chosen Israel for His people. He had given them " an everlasting covenant, even the sure mercies of David." Could then the rejection of the Jews be explained consistently with God's justice, His promises, and His past dealing with His people ? Objections of this kind the Apostle replies to. And he does so by showing that God's dealings now were just as they had always been of old. Of old He gave the promise to Abraham, but afterwards limited it to his seed in Isaac. Then again, though Esau and Jacob were both Isaac's children, He gave the privileges of His Church to the descendants of Jacob, not to those of Esau ; and that with no reference to Jacob's goodness ; for the restriction of the promise was made before either Jacob or Esau were born ; exactly according to those words by Malachi, where God, speaking of His calling of the Israelites, says, " Jacob have I loved, but Esau have I hated." (Rom. ix. 6–13.) This restriction therefore of God's promises, first to Isaac, and then to Jacob, corresponded exactly with His purposes now revealed in the Gospel, namely, to bring to Christian and Church privileges that *portion* of the Jews who embraced the Gospel, and to cast off the rest who were hardened in unbelief. From verse 14 to verse 19, St. Paul states an objection to this doctrine of God's election, which he replies to in verse 20. The objection he states thus, " Shall we say then that there is injustice with God ? " For the language of Scripture seems to imply that there is, God being represented as saying, " I will have mercy on whom I will have mercy," which shows that it is of God's mercy, and not of man's will. Again, it is said to Pharaoh, " For this cause have I raised thee up, that I might shew My power in thee." So that it seems to be taught us, that God shows mercy on whom He will, and hardens whom He will. It may therefore be reasonably said, why does He yet find fault with the sinner ; " for who hath resisted His will ? " (vv. 14–19). This objection to God's justice the Apostle states thus strongly, that he may answer it the more fully. His reply is, that such complaints against God for electing the Jewish people, and placing Pharaoh in an exalted station, and bearing long with his wickedness, are presumptuous and arrogant. " Nay, but O man, who art thou that repliest against

God? Shall the thing formed say to him that formed it, Why hast thou made me thus? Hath not the potter power over the clay to make one vessel unto honour and another unto dishonour?" (vv. 20, 21).[1] Shall man complain because God ordained the Jews for a place of eminence in His Church, or raised Pharaoh as king of Egypt to a position of honour, and yet a position in which he would only the more surely exhibit his wickedness? We know not the secret motives of God's will. What if the real reason of all this were, that " God, willing to manifest His wrath, and to make His power known," as He did with Pharaoh, so now also has endured with much long-suffering the unbelieving Israelites, who are " vessels of wrath " already " fitted to destruction," in order " that He might make known the riches of His glory on the vessels of mercy, which He had afore prepared for a position of honour, even on us, who are that Church of Christ, which He hath now called, not of the Jews only, but also of the Gentiles?" (vv. 20–24).

If we will cast aside preconceived doctrines and conventional phraseology, it will surely appear that such is the plain meaning of this memorable chapter. The Apostle is explaining the justice of God's dealings, in having long borne with the Jewish race, and now casting them off and establishing a Church composed partly of the remnant of the Jews, partly of Gentile converts. Herein He only acted as He had ever done, calling first the seed of Abraham His chosen, then the seed of Isaac, elected from the elect, and again (elected once more out of them) the seed of Jacob; and as He had borne long with Pharaoh's wickedness, that He might make him the more signal monument of His vengeance, so perhaps it was with the Jews. He had borne long with them, partly in

---

[1] See Jer. xviii. 2-10. "The scriptural similitude of the potter and the clay is often triumphantly appealed to as a proof that God has from eternity decreed, and what is more, has *revealed to us* that He has so decreed the salvation or perdition of each individual, without any other reason assigned than that such is His will and pleasure: 'we are in His hands,' say these predestinarians, 'as clay is in the potter's, who hath power of the same lump to make one vessel to honour and another to dishonour,' not observing, in their hasty eagerness to seize on every apparent confirmation of their system, that this similitude, as far as it goes, rather makes against them; since the potter never makes any vessel for *the express purpose* of being broken and destroyed. This comparison accordingly agrees much better with the view here taken; the potter, according to his own arbitrary choice, makes 'of the same lump one vessel to honour, and another to dishonour,' *i. e.*, some to nobler and some to meaner uses; but all for *some* use; none with the design that it should be cast away and dashed to pieces: even so the Almighty, of His own arbitrary choice, causes some to be born to wealth or rank, others to poverty and obscurity; some in a heathen and others in a Christian country; the advantages and privileges bestowed on each are various, and, as far as we can see, arbitrarily dispensed; the final rewards or punishments depend, as we are plainly taught, on the use or abuse of these advantages." — Archbp. Whately, *Essays on the Writings of St. Paul.* Essay III. on Election, an essay full of clear and thoughtful statements and elucidations.

mercy, and partly that He might magnify His power, and show the severity of His justice.

The same subject is kept in view, more or less, throughout the two following chapters.   In the 11th he again distinctly recurs to the bringing of a portion of the Jewish race into the Church of Christ, not indeed the whole nation — but restricted again, as it once was in Isaac, and afterwards in Jacob.   He instances the case in which all Israel seemed involved in one common apostasy, and yet God told Elias that there were seven thousand men who had not bowed the knee to Baal.   Even so it was at the time of the Gospel.   All Israel seemed cast off, but it was not so; a remnant remained, a remnant was called into the Church, chosen or elected into it by the grace of God.   " Even so at this present time also there is a remnant according to the election of grace." Rom. xi. 5.

We may now proceed to the passage which, even more than any of the preceding, may be considered as the stronghold either of the Calvinist or the Arminian.   Each claims it as unquestionably his own.   The passage is Rom. viii. 29, 30 : " For whom He did foreknow, He also did predestinate to be conformed to the image of His Son, that He might be the first-born among many brethren.   Moreover, whom He did predestinate, them He also called : and whom He called, them He also justified : and whom He justified, them He also glorified."

The Calvinist contends that the passage plainly speaks of predestination to eternal glory ; the various clauses showing the progress, from the first purpose of God, through calling and justifying, to the final salvation of the elect soul.   The Arminian replies, that, though it is true that the passage speaks of predestination to eternal glory, yet it is evidently on the ground of foreseen faith ; for it begins with the words "whom He did foreknow ;" showing that His foreknowledge of their acceptance of His grace was the motive of His predestination of their glory.   That the Arminian has scarcely ground for this argument seems clear from the use of this word " foreknew " in Rom. xi. 2 ; where " God hath not cast away His people whom He foreknew," can scarcely mean otherwise than " whom He had predestinated to be His Church of old."   But then, though it seems that the passage speaks of an *arbitrary purpose*, yet it cannot be proved to have any *direct* reference to *future* glory.   The verbs are all in the *past* tense, and none in the *future*, and therefore cannot certainly be translated as *future*.   Either " whom He hath justified, them He hath glorified,"[1] or " whom

---

[1] οὓς δὲ ἐδικαίωσε, τούτους καὶ ἐδόξασε.

He *justifies*, them He also *glorifies*," would correctly render it; since the aorist expresses either a *past* or a *present*. Hence the passage was uniformly understood by the ancients as referring not to *future* glory of Christians in the world to come, but to that *present* glorification of the elect, which consists in their participation in the high honour and privilege bestowed by God upon His Church.[1] And, as they viewed it, so grammatical accuracy will oblige us to understand it. And if so, then we must interpret the passage in correspondence with the language in the Epistle to the Ephesians, and in the chapter already considered in the Epistle to the Romans. " Those whom God in His eternal counsels chose before the foundation of the world, His elect people, the Church, He designed to bring to great blessings and privileges; namely, conformity to the likeness of His Son, calling into His Church, justification, and the high honor and glory of being sons of God and heirs of the kingdom of heaven." [2]

It would exceed our limits, if we were to consider all the passages bearing on this doctrine in the Gospels and Acts of the Apostles. The parable of the vineyard (Matt. xx. 1–16), and of the wedding feast (Matt. xxii. 1–14), evidently speak the language of ecclesiastical election, the calling of the Jews, and then the election of the halt and maimed heathen from the highways and hedges into the Christian Church.[3]

In the Acts, we read of God's " adding to the Church such as should be saved," (τοὺς σωζομένους, those who were being saved,) where the words plainly mean that God brought into His Church those whom He chose to the privileges of a state of salvation [4] (Acts ii. 47).

---

[1] See Faber, *Prim. Doct. of Election*, who quotes, from Whitby, Origen, Chrysostom, Œcumenius, Theodoret, Theophylact, pseudo-Ambrosius, and Jerome, as concurring in this interpretation of " glorified."

[2] I have myself little doubt that this is the meaning of the passage, divested of conventional phraseology, which cramps our whole mind in these inquiries. But I should wish to guard against dogmatizing too decidedly on such passages. I think this passage and one other (John vi. 37–39) to be the strongest passages in favour of the theory of St. Augustine; and their full weight ought to be given them. Some sound and learned divines have thought, that the new Testament evidently speaks of election to grace, and that most of the passages on the subject

relate to this, but that there are also passages which relate to a further election out of the elect, to glory.

[3] The words with which these two parables end, seem, at first sight, an exception to the use of the word *elect* in the Scriptures; namely, " Many are called, but few chosen : " πολλοὶ μὲν κλητοὶ, ὀλίγοι δὲ ἐκλεκτοί. It is, however, merely a different application of the same term. Many are called to Christian privileges, but only those who make a good use of them are chosen to salvation. Notwithstanding, then, a different application of the word *chosen*, the principle laid down appears to be precisely the same.

[4] τοὺς σωζομένους. Dr. Hammond (on Luke xiii. 23, and 1 Pet. ii. 6, in which he is followed by Lowth on Isaiah i. 9, Ezek. vii. 6) considers this expression

In Acts xiii. 48, we hear of persons "believing, as many as were ordained to eternal life," which sounds at first much like the doctrine of Calvin. But in the first place, the word here rendered *ordained*, is nowhere else employed in the sense of *predestinated;* and if it is to be so interpreted here, we must perforce understand it as meaning, that they were predestinated to the reception of that Gospel which is itself the way to eternal life, and which, if not abused, will surely lead to it. Otherwise the passage would prove, that all those who heard the Apostles and embraced the Gospel and the Church, must have been finally saved; a thing in the highest degree improbable, and wholly inconsistent with experience.[1]

In the Gospel of St. John we have two or three passages, supposed to speak markedly the language of Calvinism.

1. "All that the Father giveth Me shall come to Me; and him that cometh to me I will in no wise cast out" (John vi. 37).

2. "And this is the Father's will which hath sent Me, that of all which He hath given Me I should lose nothing, but should raise it up again at the last day" (John vi. 39).

3. "Have not I *chosen* you twelve, and one of you is a devil?" (John vi. 70).

4. "My sheep hear my voice, and I know them, and they follow me: and I give unto them eternal life; and they shall never perish, neither shall any pluck them out of My hand. My Father, which gave them Me, is greater than all; and no (man) is able to pluck them out of My Father's hand" (John x. 27–29).

5. "Because ye are not of the world, but I have *chosen* you out of the world, therefore the world hateth you" (John xv. 19).

6. "Holy Father, keep through Thine own Name those whom thou hast given Me, that they may be one, as We are. While I was with them in the world, I kept them in Thy Name: those that Thou gavest Me I have kept, and none of them is lost, but the son of perdition; that the Scripture might be fulfilled" (John xvii. 11, 12).

Some of these passages, taken by themselves, undoubtedly bear a very Calvinistic aspect, especially the second and the fourth. But if we take them altogether, they explain each other. The whole then seems a connected scheme. The Father gives a Church of disciples to His Son; who also Himself chooses them

---

as synonymous with the "remnant" or "escaped," שָׁרִיד, so often spoken of in the old Testament. The Syriac renders the words by ܫܰܘܦ ܗܳܕܶ ܕܰܚܒ̣ܺ ‖ qui salvi fiebant in cœtu vel ecclesia.

[3] See Hammond on this verse, and

from the world. Those that the Father thus gives to the Son, assuredly come to Him, and are joined unto his fellowship.[1] It is not the will of God that any of these should perish. "He willeth not the death of a sinner." "It is not the will of the Father that one of these little ones should perish." Whilst our blessed Lord was on earth with His Church, He preserved and guarded it by His presence; and when He left it, He prayed the Father that He would guard and support His disciples, "not taking them from the world, but keeping them from the evil" (John xvii. 15). The faithfulness of God is pledged to support His tempted servants, and His greatness secures them against all dangers, and assures them, that none shall be able to take them out of Christ's hands. Yet that their final perseverance and salvation are not so certainly secured, as that, because they have been given to Christ they can never at last be condemned, is evidenced by the case of Judas Iscariot, who, in the third and sixth of the above passages, is numbered with Christ's elect,[2] and with those whom the Father had given Him; yet still is mentioned, as one who, notwithstanding Christ's own presence and guidance, had fallen away and perished. He, like the rest, had been of Christ's sheep, elect to discipleship and grace; but, having quenched the Spirit, and been unfaithful, he was not chosen to salvation.[3]

Whatever then be philosophically true concerning man's freedom and God's sovereignty and foreknowledge; the question which is practical to us is, How far has God revealed in His word the grounds of His dealings with us? If the foregoing investigation has been fairly conducted, we must conclude, that the revelation which has been given us concerns His will and purpose to gather together in Christ a Church chosen out of the world, and that to this Church and to every individual member of it He gives the means of salvation. That salvation, if attained, will be wholly due to the grace of God, which first chooses the elect soul to the blessings of the baptismal covenant, and afterwards endues it with

also his notes on Luke xiii. 23; 1 Pet. ii. 6.

[1] Compare John x. 16: "Other sheep I have, that are not of this fold" (Gentiles, not Jews): "them also I must bring, and they shall hear My voice: and there shall be one fold, and one shepherd."

[2] Compare, "I speak not of you all; I know whom I have chosen," (meaning Judas). John xiii. 18.

[3] I cannot see that any force is put upon the passages from St. John by the explanation and paraphrase in the text.

It seems to me that, when all are compared together, no other sense can be attached to them. Yet, as above noted, the passages marked 2 and 4, and Romans viii. 29, 30, are the passages most favourable to the theory of St. Augustine. And it is so fearful a thing to put a strained interpretation on the words of Christ, in order to adapt them to a system, that I would not willingly err, by pressing on others those interpretations which seem to me to be undoubtedly true.

power to live the life of faith. If, on the other hand, the proffered
salvation be forfeited, it will be in consequence of the fault and
wickedness of him that rejects it. Much is said of God's will,
that all should be saved, and of Christ's death as sufficient for all
men; and we hear of none shut out from salvation, but for their
own faults and demerits. More than this cannot with certainty
be inferred from Scripture; for it appears most probable that what
we learn there concerns only predestination to grace, there being
no revelation concerning predestination to glory.

The old Testament, our blessed Lord, St. Paul, St. Peter, and
St. John, and after them the earliest Christian Fathers, seem thus
in perfect harmony to speak of God's election of individuals to His
Church. Of any further election we cannot say that they did
speak. New and more subtle questions were brought in by philosophers, like Clement and Origen, which were more fully worked
out by the powerful intellect of St. Augustine, whose contact with
philosophic heretics tempted him to philosophic speculations. In
later times the disputations of the schoolmen still mingled meta·
physics with theology; till the acute but over-bold mind of Calvin
moulded into full proportion a system, which has proved the fertile
source of discord to all succeeding generations. In the hands of
the great Genevan divine it was not allowed to be quiet and otiose,
but became the basis and groundwork of his whole scheme of
theology. Much of that scheme was sound and admirable; but
it was so made to bend and square itself to its author's strong
view of predestination, that it lost the fair proportions of Catholic
truth.

Deep learning and fervent piety have characterized many who
have widely differed in these points of doctrine. It is well for us,
disregarding mere human authority and philosophical discussions,
to strive to attain the simple sense of the Scriptures of God. But
it is not well, when we have satisfied ourselves, to condemn those
who may disagree with us; nor, because we see practical dangers
in certain doctrines, to believe that all who embrace those doctrines
must of necessity fall into evil, through the dangers which attach
to them. Discussions on subjects such as this do not, perhaps, so
much need acuteness and subtilty, as humility and charity.

ARTICLE XVIII.

Of obtaining Eternal Salvation only by the Name of Christ.

De speranda æterna salute tantum in nomine Christi.

THEY also are to be had accursed that presume to say, that every man shall be saved by the law or sect which he professeth, so that he be diligent to frame his life according to that law, and the light of nature. For Holy Scripture doth set out unto us only the name of Jesus Christ, whereby men must be saved.

SUNT et illi anathematizandi, qui dicere audent unumquemque in lege aut secta quam profitetur esse servandum, modo juxta illam et lumen naturæ accurate vixerit, cum sacræ literæ tantum Jesu Christi nomen prædicent, in quo salvos fieri homines oportet.

SECTION I. — HISTORY.

THE early fathers with great unanimity assert, that salvation is only to be had through Christ, and in the Church of Christ. So Ignatius says, " Let no one be deceived. Even heavenly beings and the glory of angels and principalities, visible and invisible, unless they believe in the Blood of Christ, even for them is condemnation." [1] " If any one be not within the altar, he is deprived of the bread of God." [2]

Irenæus says, " The Church is the entrance to life, all who teach otherwise are thieves and robbers." [3] " They are not partakers of the Spirit who do not come into the Church, but they defraud themselves of life." [4]

Origen says, " Let no one deceive himself; out of this house, *i. e.* the Church, no one is saved." [5]

Cyprian, in speaking of the unity of the Church, says, that " Whoever is separated from the Church is separated from the

---

[1] Μηδεὶς πλανάσθω· καὶ τὰ ἐπουράνια, καὶ ἡ δόξα τῶν ἀγγέλων, καὶ οἱ ἄρχοντες ὁρατοί τε καὶ ἀόρατοι, ἐὰν μὴ πιστεύσωσιν εἰς τὸ αἷμα Χριστοῦ, κᾀκείνοις κρίσις ἐστίν. — *Ad. Smyrn.* VI.

[2] Ἐὰν μή τις ᾖ ἐντὸς τοῦ θυσιαστηρίου, ὑστερεῖται τοῦ ἄρτου τοῦ Θεοῦ. — *Ad. Ephes.* V.

[3] " Hæc (h. e. ecclesia) est enim vitæ introitus ; omnes autem reliqui fures sunt et latrones." — *Adv. Hær.* III. 4.

[4] " Spiritus ; cujus non sunt participes omnes qui non concurrunt ad ecclesiam, sed semetipsos fraudant a vita . . . . ubi enim ecclesia ibi et Spiritus Dei." — Ibid. III. 40. See the whole chapter.

[5] " Nemo ergo sibi persuadeat, nemo seipsum decipiat ; extra hanc domum, id est, extra ecclesiam, nemo salvatur." — *Homil. in Jesum Nave,* III. num. 5

promise of the Church ; that if a man have not the Church for his mother, he hath not God for his father ; and that, as to be saved from the deluge it was needful to be in the ark, so to escape now, we must be in the Church." [1]

Lactantius writes that, " if a person have not entered into, or have gone out of the Church, he is apart from salvation." [2]

Statements in great number to the same purport might be quoted. The necessity of cleaving to Christ, of being baptized, and of belonging to the Church, is much and constantly dwelt upon ; and so the rejection of baptism is often spoken of as excluding from life.

In the Recognitions of Clement, a spurious but still a very early work, we find it argued from St. Matthew, that " if a person is not baptized, not only will he be deprived of Heaven, but will not be without danger in the resurrection, however good his life may have been." [3]

St. Cyril of Jerusalem says, " No one can be saved without baptism except the martyrs." [4]

St. Gregory Nazianzen held, that infants who die without baptism " will neither be glorified, nor yet be punished." [5]

And so the pseudo-Athanasius says, "it is clear that baptized children of believers go spotless and as believers into the kingdom. But the unbaptized and heathen children neither go to the kingdom nor yet to punishment, seeing they have not committed actual sin." [6]

When the Pelagian controversy had arisen, the question was considerably agitated, as to how far it was possible for the unbaptized to be saved. And as the Pelagians underrated baptism, their opponents naturally insisted on it more strongly.

St. Augustine, the great anti-Pelagian champion, denounces, as

[1] " Quisquis ab ecclesia segregatus adulteræ jungitur, a promissis ecclesiæ separatur. Nec pervenit ad Christi præmia, qui relinquit ecclesiam Christi. Alienus est, profanus est, hostis est. Habere jam non potest Deum Patrem, qui Ecclesiam non habet matrem. Si potuit evadere quisquam qui extra arcam Noe fuit, et qui extra ecclesiam foris fuerit, evadet." — De Unitate Ecclesiæ. Oxf. 1682, p. 109.

[2] " Sola Catholica ecclesia est quæ verum cultum retinet. Hic est fons veritatis, hoc est domicilium fidei, hoc templum Dei : quo si quis non intraverit, vel a quo si quis exierit, a spe vitæ ac salutis æternæ alienus est." — Lactant. Lib. IV. c. 30 ; see Pearson, On the Creed, p. 350.

[3] " Si quis Jesu Baptisma non fuerit

consecutus, is non solum cœlorum regno fraudabitur, verum et in resurrectione mortuorum non absque periculo erit etiamsi bonæ vitæ et rectæ mentis prærogativa muniatur." — Coteler. I. p. 501, c. 55 ; see also p. 551, c. 10.

[4] εἰ τις μὴ λάβῃ τὸ βάπτισμα, σωτηρίαν οὐκ ἔχει πλὴν μόνον μαρτύρων, οἳ καὶ χωρὶς τοῦ ὕδατος λαμβάνουσι τὴν βασιλείαν. — Cateches. III. 7.

[5] τοὺς δὲ μήτε δοξασθήσεσθαι, μήτε κολασθήσεσθαι περὶ τοῦ δικαίου Κριτοῦ, ὡς ἀσφραγίστους μὲν, ἀπονήρους δὲ, ἀλλὰ παθόντας μᾶλλον τὴν ζημίαν ἢ δρασάντας. — Oratio XL. Tom. I. p. 653. Colon.

[6] τὰ δὲ ἀβάπτιστα καὶ τὰ ἐθνικὰ, οὔτε εἰς βασιλείαν εἰσέρχονται · ἀλλ' οὔτε πάλιν εἰς κόλασιν. ἁμαρτίαν οὐκ ἔπραξαν. — Quæstiones ad Antiochum, Quæst. CXIV.

a Pelagian error, the opinion that unbaptized infants could be saved.[1] He denies that any can be saved without Baptism and the Eucharist.[2] The Pelagians seem to have promised to infants unbaptized a kind of mean between Heaven and Hell. This Augustine utterly condemns;[3] and he himself positively asserts that no one apart from the society of Christ can be saved.[4] Baptized infants, he says, at death passed into eternal life, unbaptized into death.[5]

In the work of the pseudo-Ambrosius, which is generally attributed to a writer of the name of Prosper, who is evidently a follower of St. Augustine, we read of some infants as regenerate to eternal life, others, unregenerate passing to perpetual misery.[6]

The earlier fathers, however, though, as we have seen, strongly stating that baptism, faith in Christ, union with the Church, are the only appointed means of safety, held language far less severe than St. Augustine's on the possibility of salvation to the heathen and the unbaptized. Justin Martyr, for instance, appears to have had the notion that ancient philosophers received some revelation from the Son of God, and so were led to oppose Polytheism.[7] Similar views must have occurred to Tertullian, who looked on Socrates as having some insight into Divine truth;[8] and thought that a kind of inspiration had reached the ancient philosophers.[9] Yet he seems to have believed the heathen generally under the dominion of the powers of darkness; and Bishop Kaye thinks his opinion of the necessity of baptism must, if he had entertained the question at all, have led him to decide against the salvability of the heathen.[10] There may, however, exist a strong persuasion of the necessity of baptism, without a decided dogmatizing on the condition of those to whom it has not been offered; and, in any case, on subjects so profound as this, we cannot always insist that any author shall be consistent with himself. Clement of Alexandria,

---

[1] See *De Gestis Pelagii*, c xi. Tom. x. p. 204.

[2] *De Peccatorum Meritis et Remissione*, Tom. x. p. 15.

[3] *De Anima et ejus origine*, c. 9, Tom. x. p. 343.

[4] *De Peccatorum Meritis et Remissione*, c. 11, Tom. x. p. 80.

[5] *De Dono Perseverantiæ*, c. 30, 31, Tom. x. p. 837.

[6] *De Vocatione Gentium*, Lib. i. cap. 7; Lib. ii. cap. 8. Vossius attributes it to Prosper, bishop of Orleans in the sixth century, not to Prosper of Aquitaine, the disciple of St. Augustine.

[7] Οὐ γὰρ μόνον Ἕλλησι διὰ Σωκράτους ὑπὸ λόγου (*i. e.* ratione) ἠλέγχθη ταῦτα, ἀλλὰ καὶ ἐν βαρβάροις ὑπ' αὐτοῦ τοῦ Λόγου μορφωθέντος καὶ ἀνθρώπου γενομένου καὶ Ἰησοῦ Χριστοῦ κληθέντος. — *Apol.* i. p. 56. Comp. *Dial.* pp. 218, 220.

[8] "Idem (Socrates) et quum aliquid de veritate sapiebat, deos negans," &c.— *Apolog.* c. 46.

[9] "Taceo de philosophis, quos superbia severitatis et duritia disciplinæ ab omni timore securos, nonnullos etiam afflatus Veritatis adversus Deos erigit." — *Ad Nationes*, Lib. i. c. 10. See Bishop Kaye's *Tertullian*, pp. 174, 345.

[10] See as above, p. 345.

whose sympathies were strong with the ancient philosophers, speaks
of the Law as given to the Jews, and philosophy to the Greeks,
before the coming of Christ. He considers philosophy as having
borrowed much from Revelation, and thinks it was capable by
God's appointment of justifying those who had no opportunity of
knowing better.[1]

This charitable hope concerning the salvability of the heathen,
though naturally less entertained by divines who, like Augustine,
were engaged in opposing Pelagianism, is not confined to the earliest fathers. St. Chrysostom, in commenting on St. Paul's argument in the second chapter of Romans, verse 29, evidently implies,
that the religious and virtuous Gentile might have been saved,
whilst the ungodly Jew would be condemned.[2] On the contrary,
St. Augustine, with reference to the same passage, understood by
the Gentile which does *by nature* the things of the Law, not the
uninstructed heathen, but the Gentile Christian, who does *by grace*
the things of the Law.[3]

We have seen that Gregory Nazianzen and the pseudo-Athanasius
believed in an intermediate state between Heaven and hell for
heathens and infants unbaptized. In this they are followed by
Pope Innocent III., and some of the schoolmen : and, no doubt,
out of this arose the belief in a *limbus* for those children who die
before baptism and before the commission of actual sin.

To proceed to the period of the Reformation : the Council of
Trent anathematizes all who deny that baptism is necessary to salvation ;[4] which however is not the same thing as deciding on the
state of the unbaptized.

Among the foreign reformers, Zuinglius believed that all infants
and heathens might partake of God's mercies in Christ.[5] Luther
denies in plain terms remission of sins to any without the Church.[6]
But the Lutheran Confessions do not appear to say much on this
head. Calvin, though appearing to think baptism the only means
whereby elect infants could be regenerate and so saved, if they
died,[7] yet argues forcibly against such as consign all unbaptized infants to damnation.[8] Still he says of the visible Church, that we

---

[1] Ἠν μὲν οὖν πρὸ τῆς τοῦ Κυρίου παρουσίας εἰς δικαιοσύνην Ἕλλησιν ἀναγκαία φιλοσοφία. — Strom. I. p. 331.   φιλοσοφία δὲ ἡ
Ἑλληνική, οἷον προκαθαίρει καὶ προεθίζει τὴν
ψυχὴν εἰς παραδοχὴν πίστεως. — Strom. VII.
p. 839.   εἰκότως οὖν Ἰουδαίοις μὲν νόμος,
Ἕλλησι δὲ φιλοσοφία μέχρι τῆς παρουσίας,
ἐντεῦθεν δὲ ἡ κλῆσις ἡ καθολικὴ εἰς περιούσιον δικαιοσύνης λαόν. — Strom. VI. p. 823.

[2] Chrysost. Hom. VI. in Epist. ad Rom.

[3] De Spiritu et Litera, § 43, Tom. X. p.
108. Comp. Contra Julianum, Lib. IV. 23,
24, 25, Tom. X. p. 597.

[4] Sess. VII. Can. V. De Baptismo.

[5] See on this subject under Art. XVII.

[6] Catechismus Major. Op. Tom. V. p.
629.

[7] Institut. IV. xvi. 17.

[8] Ibid. IV. xvi. 26.

have no entrance into life, unless she, our Mother, conceives us in her womb; and without her bosom is no remission of sins or salvation to be hoped for.[1]

Cranmer's Catechism was published by him A. D. 1548. It was translated from the Latin of Justus Jonas, a Lutheran divine. Sometimes in the translation alterations were introduced by Archbishop Cranmer, or under his direction, which are peculiarly calculated to show his own opinions. One strong passage on the subject of this Article is translated literally and with all the force of the original: "If we should have heathen parents and die without baptism, we should be damned everlastingly."[2] But another passage, which cannot be considered stronger, if so strong, is left out in the translation, apparently because Cranmer was unwilling so decidedly to dogmatize on this question.[3]

In the first Book of Homilies we read, "If a heathen man clothe the naked, feed the hungry, and do such other like works; yet because he doth them not in faith for the honour and love of God, they be but dead, vain, and fruitless works to him. Faith it is that doth commend the work to God; for, as St. Augustine saith, whether thou wilt or no, that work which cometh not of faith is nought; where the faith of Christ is not the foundation, there is no good work, what building soever we make."[4]

Noel's Catechism is a work drawn up long after the putting forth of the Articles, and therefore not, like the writings of Cranmer and Ridley or the first Book of Homilies, historically calculated to elucidate the Articles; yet from the approbation it received in the reign of Elizabeth, it has been looked on as of high authority in the Church of England. Its words on this subject are: —

"*M.* Is there then no hope of salvation out of the Church?

[1] "Non alius est in vitam ingressus nisi nos ipsa (h. e. visibilis ecclesia) concipiat in utero, nisi nos pariat, &c. Extra ejus gremium nulla est speranda peccatorum remissio, nec ulla salus." — IV. i. 4.

[2] Cranmer's *Catechism*, Oxford, 1829, p. 39 of the Latin, p. 51 of the English. See Preface, p. xvi.

[3] The passage is in the Latin, p. 106. "Et ut firmiter credamus has immensas, ineffabiles, infinitas opes et thesauros veros, primitias regni cœlorum et vitæ æternæ, tantum in ecclesia esse, nusquam alibi, neque apud sapientes et philosophos gentium, neque apud Turcicam illam tot millium hominum colluviem, neque apud papisticam illam et titulo tenus ecclesiam inveniri." These words are omitted in page 125 of the English; yet the following words occur in the same page: "Without the Church is no remission of sin." In the Confutation of Unwritten Verities (*Works*, IV. p. 510) Cranmer says, "To that eternal salvation cometh no man but he that hath the Head Christ. Yea, and no man can have the Head Christ which is not in His Body the Church."

[4] First Part of *Homily on Good Works.* Compare the language of St. Augustine, *Contra Julianum*, Lib. IV. quoted under Art. XIII. p. 332.

"*A*. Without it there can be nothing but damnation and death."[1]

The above - cited passages show, that the English reformers strongly held the doctrine that without Christ, without baptism, apart from the Church, no salvation is offered to man, and that if we reject them, we have no right to look for it. It might even seem that they took the strong views of St. Augustine against the salvability of the heathen or of infants unbaptized, under any circumstances. Yet there are some indications of reluctance to assume so decided a position. It has already been observed, that it is very possible to assert strongly that no other means of salvation are *offered*, that no other hope is *held out*, without determining positively that all who are cut off from the means of grace, inevitably perish. Many of the fathers appear to have thought this a consistent view of the case. Calvin, as we have seen, denied salvation out of the visible Church, and yet would not allow that all unbaptized infants perish. And so Cranmer, though translating one strong passage from Justus Jonas, has left another out of his Catechism, probably because he would not pronounce definitely on the state of heathens and persons in ignorance.

As to the wording of the Article itself, it comes naturally and properly between the Article on God's election of persons into His Church, and the Article which defines the Church itself. It condemns that latitudinarianism which makes all creeds and all communions alike, saying that all men may be saved by their own sect, so they shape their lives according to it, and to the law of nature. The ground on which it protests against this view of matters is, that the Scriptures set forth no other name but Christ's whereby we may be saved. . The opinion here condemned therefore is, not a charitable hope that persons who have never heard of Christ, or who have been bred in ignorance or error, may not be inevitably excluded from the benefit of His atonement ; but that cold indifference to faith and truth which would rest satisfied and leave them in their errors, instead of striving to bring them to faith in Christ and to His Body the Church, to which alone the promises of the Gospel are made, and to which by actual revelation God's mercies are annexed.

---

[1] *M*. Nullane ergo salutis spes extra damnatio exitium atque interitus esse Ecclesiam? *A*. Extra eam nihil nisi potest."

Section II. — SCRIPTURAL PROOF.

THE teaching of the Article will be sufficiently established, if we show : —

I. That Holy Scripture sets out to us only the name of Jesus Christ, whereby men may be saved.

II. That salvation is therefore offered only in the Church.

III. That accordingly, we have no right to say that men shall be saved by their own law or sect, if they be diligent to frame their life according to that law and the light of nature.

I. The first proposition appears from such passages as these, " He that believeth on the Son hath everlasting life : and he that believeth not the Son shall not see life ; but the wrath of God abideth on him " (John iii. 36).   " No man cometh unto the Father, but by Me " (John xiv. 6).   " Other foundation can no man lay than that is laid, which is Jesus Christ " (1 Cor. iii. 11).   " There is one God, and one Mediator between God and men, the man Christ Jesus, who gave Himself a ransom for all " (1 Tim. ii. 5, 6). " He is the propitiation for our sins : and not for ours only, but also for the sins of the whole world " (1 John ii. 2).   " This is the record, that God hath given to us eternal life, and this life is in His Son.   He that hath the Son hath life ; and he that hath not the Son of God hath not life " (1 John v. 12).   Compare Mark xvi. 15, 16 ; John i. 29 ; iii. 14, 15, 17 ; v. 40 ; x. 9 ; xx. 31 ; Acts xiii. 38 ; Rom. vii. 24, 25 ; 2 Cor. v. 18, 19 ; 2 Tim. i. 10 ; Heb. v. 9 ; xi. 6 ; xii. 2.   " Neither is there salvation in any other ; for there is none other name under Heaven given among men, whereby we must be saved " (Acts iv. 12).   " To Him give all the prophets witness, that through His name whosoever believeth in Him shall receive remission of sins " (Acts x. 43). " Sirs, what must I do to be saved ?   And they said, Believe on the Lord Jesus Christ, and thou shalt be saved, and thy house " (Acts xvi. 30, 31).

II. The second proposition appears from this : —
When our Lord had offered the propitiation, by which **He**

57

became the Saviour of mankind, He commissioned His Apostles
to preach the Gospel and to found the Church ; and " He said unto
them, Go ye into all the world, and preach the Gospel to every
creature : He that believeth and is baptized shall be saved ; but
he that believeth not shall be damned" (Mark xvi. 15, 16).

Accordingly, when St. Peter's sermon at the feast of Pentecost had produced a wonderful effect on those that heard it, so
that they cried, " Men and brethren, what shall we do ? then Peter said unto them, Repent, and be baptized every one of you in the
name of Jesus Christ for the remission of sins " (Acts ii. 37, 38).
And so, in like manner, whensoever persons were converted to
the faith, they were at once baptized into the Church. Compare
Acts viii. 12, 13, 36, 38; ix. 18; x. 47, 48; xvi. 33 ; xix. 5,
xxii. 16, &c.

Hence, St. Peter (1 Pet. iii. 21) speaks of baptism as saving
us, like the ark of Noah ; for baptism places us within the Church,
which, like Noah's ark, is the place of refuge for Christ's disciples
in the flood of ungodliness around it.   And St. Paul tells us, that,
" As many as are baptized into Christ have put on Christ" (Gal.
iii. 27).   And as thus baptism, by placing us within the Church,
puts us in a place of safety, a state of salvation, so it is the
Church only which is said to be saved.   Christ is called " the
Head of the body the Church " (Col. i. 18), and so is said to be
" the Saviour of the body " (Ephes. v. 23), of which He is the
Head.   He represents Himself as the Vine, and all members of
His Church as branches of that Vine ; and then says, " I am the
Vine, ye are the branches : he that abideth in Me, and I in him,
the same bringeth forth much fruit : for without Me ye can do
nothing.   If a man abide not in Me, he is cast forth as a branch,
and is withered " (John xv. 5, 6).

Again we read, that " Christ loved the *Church*, and gave Himself for it ; that he might sanctify and cleanse it with the washing
of water by the word, that He might present it to Himself a
glorious Church : " &c. (Ephes. v. 25, 26, 27).   And accordingly,
when first God's grace by the preaching of the Apostles was
bringing men to Christ, and to the Christian faith, we are told
that " the Lord added unto the Church daily such as were being
saved "($\tau o \grave{v} \varsigma \ \sigma \omega \zeta o \mu \acute{e} v o v \varsigma$) (Acts ii. 47).

III. As to believe in Christ, to be baptized into His Name,
and incorporated into His Church, are the appointed means to

salvation ; so to reject Him and continue in unbelief is the way to be lost. When the Gospel was to be preached, our Lord promised that those who believed so as to be baptized should be saved, or placed in a state of salvation; but He added, " He that believeth not shall be damned " (Mark xvi. 16). So He said of those that rejected Him, " He that believeth not is condemned already, because he hath not believed in the Name of the only-begotten Son of God; and this is the condemnation, that light is come into the world, and men loved darkness rather than light, because their deeds were evil " (John iii. 18, 19). " He that rejecteth Me, and receiveth not My words, hath one that judgeth him ; the word that I have spoken, the same shall judge him at the last day " (John xii. 48). And to St. John He declared that " the unbelieving . . . . shall have their part in the lake which burneth with fire and brimstone " (Rev. xxi. 8).

It is unnecessary to multiply proofs, that, as there is no salvation offered but by Christ and to those who believe and are baptized in His Name, so those who reject Him shall be rejected ; and that therefore we cannot hold out the hope of salvation to those who adhere to another sect or law, as though they might be saved by that, if only they lived up to its requirements. If it were necessary to add more, we might refer to those passages in which it is declared that, after the Gospel was come, the Law of Moses, being done away, could never give salvation to those who lived under it, (see Rom. iii. 9, 23 ; ix. 31, 32; Gal. ii. 16, 21; iii. 21, 22 ; v. 2, 4, &c.) If the Law of Moses could not justify, a law which did come from God ; much less can we believe that any other creed, of man's device, could be safe for any to abide in.

The question concerning the salvability of the heathen need hardly be discussed. It is quite certain that Scripture says very little about them. Its words concern and are addressed to those who can hear and read them, not to those who hear them not. The fact appears to be, that no religion but Christ's, no society but His Church, is set forth as the means of our salvation. Those who have these means proposed to them, and wilfully reject them, must expect to be rejected by Christ. Whether there be any mercy in store for those who, nursed in ignorance, have not had the offer of this salvation, has been a question ; and it is not answered in this Article. If we have some hope that they may be saved, still we must certainly conclude, *not that their own law or sect will save them*, but that Christ, who tasted death for every man, and is the propitiation for the sins of the whole world, may have mercy on them, even though they knew Him not.[1]

[1] Passages, such as Psalm ix. 17, "The wicked shall be turned into hell, and all the nations that forget God," are brought forward as proving that all heathen nations shall be damned. Yet *hell* in this case is *Hades*, not *Gehenna;* and on the other hand, Rom. ii. 11–16, Acts xvii. 26, 27, 30, appear to prove that it is not impossible heathens may be capable of salvation. No doubt the reason why so little is said about them is, that it is impossible that what is said can reach them.

"I hold it to be a most certain rule of interpreting Scripture that it never speaks *of* persons, when there is a physical impossibility of its speaking *to* them. .... So the heathen, who died before the word was spoken, and in whose land it was never preached, are dead to the word; it concerns them not at all; but, the moment it can reach them, it is theirs, and for them." — Dr. Arnold's *Life and Correspondence,* Letter LXV.

ARTICLE XIX.

———

Of the Church.	*De Ecclesia.*
The visible Church of Christ is a congregation of faithful men, in the which the pure word of God is preached, and the Sacraments be duly ministered, according to Christ's ordinance in all those things that of necessity are requisite to the same.	Ecclesia Christi visibilis est cœtus fidelium, in quo verbum Dei purum prædicatur, et Sacramenta quoad ea quæ necessario exiguntur juxta Christi institutum recte administrantur. Sicut erravit Ecclesia Hierosolymitana, Alexandrina, et Antiochena ; ita et erravit Ecclesia Romana, non solum quoad agenda, et cæremoniarum ritus, verum in his etiam quæ credenda sunt.
As the Church of Jerusalem, Alexandria, and Antioch, have erred, so also, the Church of Rome hath erred, not only in their living and manner of ceremonies, but also in matters of faith.	

———

Section I.— HISTORY.

AFTER speaking of God's election, probably meaning thereby election to the blessings of His Church ; after declaring that the promise of salvation is not to be held out to all persons of all sects and religions ; the Articles proceed to define the Church itself, into which God predestinates individuals to be brought, and which is appointed as the earthly home of those who embrace the Gospel and would be saved.

A distinct definition was naturally called for at the Reformation, when great schisms were likely to arise, and when the Church of Rome claimed to be the only true Church of God, and made communion with the Pope a necessary note of the Church. Such distinct definitions we may not always meet with in earlier times.

Ignatius calls the Church, " the multitude or congregation that is in God ; " [1] says of the three orders of clergy, that " without these there is no Church ; " [2] and, " wheresoever the bishop shall appear, there let the multitude also be ; as where Jesus Christ is, there is the Catholic Church." [3]

Justin Martyr identifies the Church with those called Chris-

---

[1] τὸ ἐν Θεῷ πλῆθος. — *Trall.* 8.
[2] χωρὶς τούτων ἐκκλησία οὐ καλεῖται. — *Ibid.* 3.

[3] ὅπου ἂν φανῇ ὁ ἐπίσκοπος, ἐκεῖ τὸ πλῆθος ἔστω · ὥσπερ ὅπου ἂν ἡ Χριστὸς Ἰησοῦς ἐκεῖ ἡ καθολικὴ ἐκκλησία. — *Smyrn.* 8.

tians, partakers of the name of Christ; speaks of it as one synagogue and one assembly; and says, it is as the daughter of God.[1]

Irenæus speaks of the Church as consisting of " those who have received the adoption; for this is the synagogue of God, which God the Son has assembled by Himself." [2]   It is the Paradise of God planted in the world; and the fruits of the garden are the Holy Scriptures.[3]   It is spread throughout the world, sown by Apostles and their followers, holding, from them, the one faith in the Trinity, Incarnation, Redemption, and General Judgment.[4]   It is one, though universal.[5]   Its Head is Christ.[6]   It is a visible body, animated by one Spirit, everywhere preaching one and the same faith, one and the same way of salvation.[7]   The tradition, or doctrine of the Apostles is carefully preserved in the Church, and the succession of pastors and bishops from the Apostles.[8]   He says, the successors of the first bishops might be enumerated in many Churches; and singles out more particularly the Churches of Rome and Smyrna, giving a catalogue of the bishops of Rome from St. Peter and St. Paul.[9]

Tertullian speaks of the Church as composed of all the Churches founded by Apostles, or offsprings of Apostolic Churches, and living in the unity of the same faith and discipline.[10]

The Church, according to Clement of Alexandria, is the assembly of the elect,[11] the congregation of Christian worshippers; [12] the devout Christians being, as it were, the spiritual life of the body of Christ, the unworthy members being like the carnal part.[13]

Origen says, the Church is the body of Christ, animated by the Son of God, the members being all who believe in Him.[14]   The

---

[1] Ὅτι τοῖς εἰς αὐτὸν πιστεύουσιν, ὡς οὖσι μιᾷ ψυχῇ καὶ μιᾷ συναγωγῇ, καὶ μιᾷ ἐκκλησίᾳ ὁ λόγος τοῦ Θεοῦ, ὡς θυγατρὶ τῇ ἐκκλησίᾳ τῇ ἐξ ὀνόματος αὐτοῦ γενομένῃ, καὶ μετασχούσῃ τοῦ ὀνόματος αὐτοῦ (Χριστιανοὶ γὰρ πάντες καλούμεθα), κ. τ. λ. — Dial. p. 287.

[2] Hær. iii. 6.

[3] v. 20.

[4] i. 2 (where the faith of the Church is given nearly in the words of the Creed); v. 20.

[5] i. 3; iii. 11; v. 20.

[6] iii. 18; v. 18.

[7] τοῦτο τὸ κήρυγμα παρειληφυῖα, καὶ ταύτην τὴν πίστιν, ὡς προέφαμεν, ἡ ἐκκλησία καίπερ ἐν ὅλῳ τῷ κόσμῳ διεσπαρμένη, ἐπιμελῶς φυλάσσει, ὡς ἕνα οἶκον οἰκοῦσα, καὶ ὁμοίως πιστεύει τούτοις ὡς μίαν ψυχὴν καὶ τὴν αὐτὴν ἔχουσα καρδίαν, καὶ συμφώνως ταῦτα κηρύσσει, καὶ διδάσκει, καὶ παραδίδωσιν, ὡς ἓν στόμα κεκτημένη. — Lib. i. cap. 3; also Lib. v. cap. 20.

[8] Lib. iii. cap. 3.

[9] Ibid.

[10] De Præscript. Hæretic. 20, 21.

[11] Οὐ νῦν τὸν τόπον ἀλλὰ τὸ ἄθροισμα τῶν ἐκλεκτῶν, ἐκκλησίαν καλῶ. — Strom. vii. p. 846.

[12] τὸ ἄθροισμα τῶν ταῖς εὐχαῖς ἀνακειμένων.   " The congregation of those who dedicate themselves to prayer." — Strom. vii. p. 848.

[13] Σῶμα δὲ ἀλληγορεῖται ἡ ἐκκλησία Κυρίου, ὁ πνευματικὸς καὶ ἅγιος χορός· ἐξ ὧν οἱ τὸ ὄνομα ἐπικεκλημένοι μόνον, βιοῦντες δὲ οὐ κατὰ λόγον, σάρκες εἰσί. — Strom. vii. p. 885.

[14] Λέγομεν ὅτι Σῶμα Χριστοῦ φασὶν εἶναι οἱ θεῖοι λόγοι, ὑπὸ τοῦ Υἱοῦ τοῦ Θεοῦ ψυχούμενον, τὴν πᾶσαν τοῦ Θεοῦ ἐκκλησίαν, μέλη δὲ τούτου τοῦ Σώματος εἶναι ὡς ὅλου τοὺς δὲ τίνας τοὺς πιστεύοντας. — Contra Celsum, vi. 48.

visibility of the Church he expresses by saying that we should give no heed to those who say, " ' There is Christ,' but show Him not in the Church, which is full of brightness from the East to the West, and is the pillar and ground of the truth." [1]

Cyprian calls the Church the Mother of all the children of God; compares it to the ark of Noah, in which all, who would be saved, should take refuge; and says that, whilst it puts forth its rays through all the world, yet it is but one light.[2]

Athanasius we find speaking of Christ as the foundation of the Church;[3] and of unfaithful Christians as the tares among the good seed.[4]

Cyril of Jerusalem says, The Church is called *Ecclesia* (assembly), because it calls out and assembles together all; just as the Lord says, " Assemble all the congregation to the door of the tabernacle of witness " (Lev. viii. 3). The Church is called Catholic, because it is throughout all the world; because it teaches universally all truth; because it brings all classes of men into subjection to godliness; because it cures all spiritual diseases, and has all sorts of spiritual graces. It is distinguished from sects of heretics, as the Holy Catholic Church, in which we ought to abide, as having been therein baptized.[5]

Gregory Nazianzen calls it a Vineyard, into which all are summoned as to their place of work, as soon as they are brought to the faith; into which, however, they actually enter by baptism.[6]

St. Ambrose says, The faith is the foundation of the Church; not St. Peter, but St. Peter's faith; for the Church is like a good ship beat against by many waves; but the true faith, on which the Church is founded, should prevail against all heresies.[7]

As the remains of the great fathers, who flourished late in the fourth and early in the fifth century, are far more voluminous than those of their predecessors; so also the increase of heresies, and

[1] "Non debemus attendere eis qui dicunt, *Ecce hic Christus*, non autem ostendunt Eum in Ecclesia, quæ plena est fulgore ab oriente usque ad occidentem, quæ plena est lumine vero, quæ est columna et firmamentum veritatis." — *Comm. in Matthæ.* c. xxiv. See Palmer *On the Church.* i. pt. i. ch. iii.

[2] " Ecclesia Domini luce perfusa per orbem totum radios suos porrigit, unum tamen lumen est . . . . Habere jam non potest Deum Patrem, qui ecclesiam non habet matrem. Si potuit evadere quisquam qui extra arcam Noe fuit; et qui extra ecclesiam foris fuerit, evadet," &c. — *De Unitate Ecclesiæ,* pp. 108, 109, Fell.

[3] *Contra Arian.* iii. p. 444, Colon.
[4] *De Semente,* p. 1064.
[5] *Cateches.* xviii. 11, which see at length.
[6] *Oratio Quadragesima,* p. 650, Colon.
[7] " Fides ergo est Ecclesiæ fundamentum. Non enim de carne Petri, sed de fide dictum est, quia portæ mortis ei non prævalebunt: sed confessio vincit infernum. Nam cum Ecclesia multis tanquam bona navis fluctibus sæpe tundatur, adversus omnes hæreses debet valere Ecclesiæ fundamentum." — *De Incarnationis Sacramento,* cap. v.

especially the schism of the Donatists, led to their speaking oftener and more fully of the Church and its blessings; and this is observable more in the Latin than in the Greek writers.

With Chrysostom, the Church is Christ's Body, and the thought of this ought to keep us from sin. And though the Head is above all principality and power, yet the body is trampled on by devils — so unworthy are members of Christ.[1] This body consists of all believers, some honourable, some dishonourable members.[2] It is both one and yet many ; and the regenerating Spirit is given to all in baptism.[3]

With Rufinus, the true Church is that in which there is one faith, one baptism, and a belief in one God, Father, Son, and Spirit; and the Church, thus pure in the faith, is spotless.[4]

With Jerome and Augustine, the Church is the ark of Noah, which St. Peter said was a type of our salvation by baptism. But, as there were evil beasts in the ark, so bad Christians in the Church.[5] The meaning of *Church* (Ecclesia) is, according to Jerome, *congregation*.[6] It is not held together by walls, but by the truth of its doctrines. And where the true faith is, there is the Church.[7] Its head is in Heaven, but its members upon earth.[8] It is built on prophets and apostles ;[9] and there is no Church without a priesthood.[10]

Augustine says, "The Church (*Ecclesia*) is so named from vocation or calling."[11] It is the New Jerusalem ;[12] the Robe of Christ ;[13] the City of the Great King ;[14] the City of God.[15] It is the field of God ;[16] in which, however, spring both tares and wheat.[17] It is not only visible, but bright and conspicuous. It is a city set on a hill, which cannot be hid.[18] It may be as clearly known, and as certainly recognized, as was the risen Body of

---

[1] Hom. iii. *In Epist. ad Ephes.*

[2] Hom. x. *In Ephes.*

[3] Hom. xxx. *In* 1 *Corinth.*

[4] *Expositio in Symbolum Apostol.* Art Sanctam Ecclesiam Catholicam.

[5] Hieronym. *Adv. Lucifer.* Tom. iv. p. 302; August. *Enarr. in Psalm.* xxiv. Tom. iv. p. 131.

[6] *Comment.* Lib. iii. *in Proverb.* c. xxx.; Ecclesia enim congregatio vocatur. Tom. v. p. 590.

[7] " Ecclesia non parietibus consistit, sed in dogmatum veritate ; Ecclesia ibi est, ubi fides vera est." — *Comm. in Psalm.* cxxxiii. Tom. ii. Append. p. 472.

[8] " Caput in cœlo, membra in terra." — *Ps.* xc. Tom. ii. App. p. 361.

[9] *Comment. in Ps.* xvii. Tom. ii. Appendix, p. 393.

[10] "Ecclesia non autem, quæ non habet sacerdotes." — *Adv. Lucifer.* Tom. iv. p. 302.

[11] " Ecclesia ex vocatione appellata." *In Epist. ad Roman. Inchoata Expositio,* Tom. iii. pt. ii. p. 925.

[12] *De Civitate Dei,* Tom. vii. p. 594.

[13] Ibid. p. 452.

[14] Ibid. p. 479.

[15] Ibid. pp. 335, 510.

[16] *Enarr. in Ps.* cxxxiv. Tom. iv. p. 1497.

[17] *Serm.* xv. *de* 8 v. *Psalm* xxv. Tom. v. p. 89 ; *Serm.* cxxiii. *In Vigiliis Paschæ,* Tom. v. p. 967.

[18] *Enarr. in Psalm.* lvii. Tom. iv. p. 547 ; *Serm.* xxxvii. *De Proverb.* cap. xxxi. Tom. v. p. 181.

Christ by St. Thomas.[1] The Church below consists of all believers; the Church above, of the angels of heaven.[2] The
Church is not all pure and free from stain; the just are mingled
with the unjust.[3] The Church indeed now is washed with water
by the word (Eph. v. 26); yet not to be " without spot or wrinkle "
(Eph. v. 27), till the Resurrection.[4] After the Resurrection, the
bad members shall be taken away, and there shall be none but the
good.[5] No doubt, baptism cleanses those who receive it from all
sin; but after baptism fresh sins may be committed; and therefore, from that to the Judgment, there is constant need of remission.[6] So essential are the Sacraments to the existence of the
Church, that Augustine says the Church is formed by the two
Sacraments, which flowed from the side of Christ, just as Eve was
formed out of the side of Adam, who was a type of Christ.[7]

It naturally strikes us, that the above and similar statements of
the fathers concerning the Church are not, for the most part, of
the nature of logical definitions. They are essentially practical,
and even devotional in their character. Yet by comparing them
together, we may find that the very definitions of our own Article
are implicitly given by them. Thus we have heard their teaching,
— that the Church is a visible body, capable of being known and
recognized, — that the very word Church means congregation, —
that it is a congregation of believers, or of the faithful, — that its
great support and characteristic is the true faith preserved by it, —
that baptism admits to it, — that it is essential to its existence to
have a rightly ordained ministry, who are able to minister the Sacraments, which Sacraments are even spoken of as forming the
Church.[8]

The Creeds do not exactly define, but give titles to distinguish
the Church. The Apostles' Creed calls it the Holy Catholic
Church; and the Constantinopolitan Creed calls it One, Holy,
Catholic, and Apostolic. Its *unity* depends on unity of foundatior,

---

[1] *Enarr. in Ps.* cxlvii. Tom. iv. p. 1664.

[2] " Ecclesia deorsum in omnibus fidelibus, Ecclesia sursum in angelis." —
Enarr. in Psalm. cxxxvii. Tom. iv. p.
1527.

[3] *De Civitate Dei,* i. 35; xviii. 48, 49;
Tom. vii. pp. 30, 531.

[4] *De Perfectione Justitiæ,* Tom. x. p.
183

[5] Serm. cclii. *In Diebus Pasch.* Tom.
v. p. 1041.

[6] *De Gestis Pelagii,* Tom. x. p. 206.

[7] " Quod latus lancea percussum in
terra sanguinem et aquam manat; procul

dubio sacramenta sunt quibus formatur
Ecclesia, tanquam Eva facta de latere
dormientis Adam, qui erat forma futuri."
— Serm. ccxix. cap. 14, *In Vigiliis Pas-
chæ,* Tom. v. p. 962. The same idea is
expressed by St. Chrysostom, *Homil. in
Johan.* 85, Tom. ii. p. 915. See under
Art. xxv.

[8] When St. Augustine says that the
Church is formed by the Sacraments, he
means that we are first joined to the
Church by baptism, and preserved in
spiritual life and church-communion by
the Eucharist.

unity of faith, unity of baptism, unity of discipline, unity of communion.   Its *holiness* springs from the presence of Christ, the
sanctification of the Holy Spirit, the graces conferred upon its
members by partaking of its Sacraments and living in its communion.   Its *apostolicity* results from its being built on the foundation
of Apostles and Prophets, continuing in the doctrine and fellowship
of the Apostles, holding the faith of the Apostles, governed and
ministered to by a clergy deriving their succession from the
Apostles.

The designation *Catholic*, used in all the Creeds and throughout
the writings of the fathers, originated probably in the universality
of the Christian Church, as distinguished from the local nationality
of the Jewish synagogue.   The same Christian Church, one in its
foundation, in its faith, and in its Sacraments, was spread universally
through all nations.   But, as sects and heresies separated by degrees
from the one universal Church, forming small and distinct communions among themselves ; the term Catholic, which at first applied to
all who embraced the religion of Jesus, was afterwards used to express that one holy Church which existed through all the world,
undivided, and intercommunicating in all its branches, as contra-
distinguished from heretics and schismatics.   Hence Catholic, in
one view of the term, became nearly identified with orthodox.
And so, whilst the one Catholic Church meant the true Church
throughout the world, yet the true and sound Church in a single
city would be called the Catholic Church of that city,[1] its members
would be called Catholic Christians, and the faith which they held
in common with the universal Church, was the Catholic faith.
Accordingly, St. Cyril admonishes his people, that, if ever they
sojourned in any city, it was not sufficient to inquire for the Church,
or the Lord's house ; for Marcionists and Manichees, and all sorts
of heretics, professed to be of the Church, and called their places
of assembly the House of the Lord ; but they ought to ask, Where
is the Catholic Church ?   For this is the peculiar name of the Holy
Body, the Mother of us all, the Spouse of the Lord Jesus Christ.[2]

The unity and catholicity of the Church were imminently perilled by the schism of the East and West, when the entire Latin
Church ceased to communicate with the entire Eastern Church.
From that time to this there has been no communion between
them ; though possibly neither branch has utterly rejected the

---

[1] Thus Constantine writes to the
Church of Alexandria : "Constantine
the Great, Augustus, to the people of
the Catholic Church of Alexandria." —
See Athanasii *Opera*, i. 772, 773, 779 ;
Colon. Suicer, ii. 14.
[2] *Cateches.* xviii. 12.

other from a share in the unity of the Church and of the faith.[1]

The gradual corruption in the Western Church perilled still further unity and catholicity. The unity of communion was preserved through the West of Europe; but important points of faith and practice were corrupted and impaired. Hence the many protests and divisions in Germany, England, and other parts of Europe, ending in that great disruption known as the general Reformation.

At that period, some even of those who were sensible of the corruptions, felt that to adhere to the communion of Rome was essential, if they would abide in the fellowship of the Apostles and the unity of the Catholic Church. Others, as Luther, Melancthon, Zuinglius, held that sound faith and purity of doctrine were more essential to catholicity than undivided communion even with the bishops and existing Church of their own land; arguing that a Church could not be Catholic which did not soundly hold the Catholic faith, and duly administer the holy Sacraments. Luther indeed never wished to separate from the Church, but ever appealed to a true general council; and the Confession of Augsburg declared that the Lutherans differed in no Article of faith from the Catholic Church,[2] holding that the Churches ought *jure divino* to obey their bishops. Bishops, it is said, might easily retain their authority, if they would not command things contrary to good conscience. All that was sought was that unjust burdens should not be imposed, which were novel, and contrary to the custom of the Catholic Church.[3]

Our own reformers had a less difficult part to play, for though, in order to return to primitive purity of faith, they were obliged to separate from most of the continental Churches, they were themselves, for the most part, the bishops and clergy of the national Church; and there was therefore no internal secession from the jurisdiction of the Episcopate, though there was necessary alienation from the great body of the Church.

In this unhappy state of things, the Church, which remained in communion with Rome, arrogated to itself the name (too often since conceded to it) of the Catholic Church; maintaining, that she was the one true Church, from which all others had separated off, — that communion with the see of St. Peter was essential to

---

[1] On this subject consult Palmer, *On the Church*, i. pt. i. ch. ix. sect. 2.
[2] *Confess. August.* A. D. 1531, Art. xxi. *Sylloge*, p. 133.
[3] *Syll.* p. 157. See also Palmer, i. pt. i. ch. xii. § 1, p 361.

the unity, catholicity, and to the very existence of the Church, and
that all who were separated from that communion were heretics
and schismatics.

This led naturally to definitions of the Church on the part of the
reforming clergy and the reformed Churches.   The VIIth Article
of the Confession of Augsburg is evidently the origin of the XIXth
Article of our own Church.   There we find it said, that " There
is one Holy Church to abide forever.   And the Church is a congregation of saints, in which the Gospel is rightly taught, and the
Sacraments rightly administered." [1]

Luther, in commenting on the Article in the Creed concerning
the Holy Catholic Church, says, " Church, or *Ecclesia*, means properly the congregation or communion of Christians ; " and expounds
that Article of the Creed thus, " I believe that there is a certain
congregation and communion of saints on earth, gathered together
of holy men under one Head, Christ; collected by the Holy Spirit,
in one faith and one sentiment, adorned with various gifts, but
united in love, and accordant in all things, without sects or schism.
. . . . Moreover, in this Christianity we believe that remission of
sins is offered, which takes place by means of the Sacraments and
absolution of the Church." [2]

Calvin defines the Visible Church as " the multitude of men
diffused through the world, who profess to worship one God in
Christ; are initiated into this faith by baptism; testify their unity
in true doctrine and charity by participating in the Supper; have
consent in the Word of God, and for the preaching of that Word
maintain the ministry ordained of Christ." [3]

The English reformers have given, in works of authority, some
definitions of the Visible Church, besides that contained in this
Article.   The second part of the Homily for Whitsunday (set forth
early in Elizabeth's reign, therefore, after the Articles of 1552, but
before the final sanction of the XXXIX. Articles by the Convocation of 1562 and 1571) gives the following, as the notes of the
Church : " The true Church is an universal congregation or fellowship of God's faithful and elect people, built upon the foundation of
the Apostles and Prophets, Jesus Christ Himself being the head
corner-stone, Ephes. ii.   And it hath always these notes or marks

---

[1] *Conf. August.* Art. VII. *Sylloge,* p.
125, also p. 171.

[2] *Catechismus Major.* Opera, Tom. v.
p. 628.

[3] " Universalem hominum multitudi-
nem in orbe diffusam quæ unum se Deum
et Christum colere profitetur ; Baptismo
initiatur in Ejus fidem : cœnæ participatione unitatem in vera doctrina et cari-
tate testatur : consensionem habet in
verbo Domini, atque ad ejus prædicatio-
nem ministerium conservat a Christo institutum." — *Institut.* Lib I. s. 7.

whereby it is known: pure and sound doctrine, the Sacraments ministered according to Christ's holy institution, and the right use of ecclesiastical discipline."

Very similar are the statements of the Catechism of Edward VI. A. D. 1553, the year after the first draught of the Articles. " The marks of the Church are, first, pure preaching of the Gospel : then brotherly love : thirdly, upright and uncorrupted use of the Lord's Sacraments, according to the ordinance of the Gospel: last of all, brotherly correction and excommunication, or banishing those out of the Church that will not amend themselves. This mark the holy fathers termed discipline." [1]

Noel's Catechism also enumerates, first, sound doctrine and right use of the Sacraments, and then the use of just discipline.[2]

Bishop Ridley gave a definition exactly conformable to the above : " The holy Catholic or universal Church, which is the communion of saints, the house of God, the city of God, the spouse of God, the body of Christ, the pillar and stay of the truth ; this Church I believe, according to the Creed: this Church I do reverence and honour in the Lord.   The marks whereby this Church is known unto me in this dark world, and in the midst of this crooked and froward generation, are these, — the sincere preaching of God's Word ; the due administration of the Sacraments ; charity ; and faithful observances of ecclesiastical discipline, according to the Word of God." [3]

The difference which strikes us between these definitions and that of the Article is, that in them there is added to the notes in the Article, " the observance of ecclesiastical discipline," or, as the Homily terms it, of " the ecclesiastical keys."   Now it is probable that the compilers of the Articles, who elsewhere made this use of the keys one note of the Church, omitted it in the Article itself, as considering that it was implied in the due administration of the Sacraments.   For what is the power of the keys and the observance of discipline, but the admission of some to, and the rejection of others from, the Sacraments and blessings of the Church ?   Where, therefore, the Sacraments are duly ministered, there too discipline must exist.[4]

---

[1] *Enchirid. Thoeologicum*, I. p. 26.
[2] Ibid. I. p. 276.
[3] Conferences between Nicholas Ridley and Hugh Latimer, Ridley's *Works*, Parker Society edition. p. 123.
[4] The definition of the Church by the Roman Catholic divines does not materially differ from those of the Reformers, except in one important point. Bellarmine gives it as follows : " Nostra sententia est ecclesiam unam tantum esse, non duas, et illam unam et veram esse cœtum hominum ejusdem Christianæ fidei professione et eorundem sacra mentorum communione colligatum, sub regimine legitimorum pastorum, *ac præcipue unius Christi in terris Vicarii Romani pontificis*." — *Controvers. General.* Tom. II. p. 108, Lib. III. *De Ecclesia, c.* 2.

It may be right to say something of the *invisible* Church. The Article says nothing of the *invisible* Church ; but as it uses the term " *visible* Church," it implies a contradistinction to something invisible. Now " *invisible Church* " is not a Scriptural term, but a term of comparatively late origin ; and there are two different views of its meaning. Some persons by it understand the saints departed, who, in Paradise or the unseen place (Hades), are no longer militant and visible, but form part of the true Church of God, — the Church in fact in its purified and beatified condition, freed from its unsound members, and " without spot or wrinkle, or any such thing."

Others, however, (and the Reformers were mostly of this opinion,) believed that within the visible Church we might conceive to exist a body of true saints, persons not only communicating with the outward Church, but, moreover, really sanctified in heart, who not only now partook of Church-privileges, but would forever reign with Christ. These formed the invisible Church, whom none knew but God ; whereas the visible Church was composed of faithful and unfaithful, of tares and wheat.[1]

It is however certain, that the Article confines itself to the consideration of the visible Church, and gives us no authoritative statement concerning the invisible Church. And, indeed, the reformers themselves vary considerably in their statements on the subject, though the sad corruptions in the visible Church in their days led them naturally to apply some of the promises in Scripture to a secret body, and not to the universal Church. There does not appear anything in the Liturgy or formularies of the Church which specially alludes to this distinction of the visible and invisible Church. The Church spoken of there is the Body of Christ, the ark of Christ's Church, and still the congregation of all who profess and call themselves Christians, the congregation of Christian people dispersed through the world, built on the foundation of Apostles and Prophets, the blessed company of all faithful people, into which a child is incorporated by baptism, of fellowship with which the

---

[1] Calvin expounds this doctrine at length, *Inst.* Lib. IV. cap. i. It may be seen in the writings of the English Reformers, *e. g. The Institution of a Christian Man.* See *Formularies of Faith in the Reign of Henry VIII.* p. 52; Edward VI. *Catechism, Enchir. Theol.* p. 24; Noel's *Catechism*, Ibid. p. 272; Cranmer's *Works*, III. p. 19; Ridley's *Works*, p. 126.

The fathers do not appear to have recognized this distinction, although in St. Augustine and some others there are frequent and evident allusions to the difference of the body of the really faithful and the mere outward communion of the Church. St. Augustine mentions it as an error of the Pelagians, that they looked on the Church as composed of perfectly holy persons, *Hæres.* 88. And afterwards, Calvin attributes the same opinion to the Anabaptists, *Inst.* IV. i. 13.

adult is assured by communion, and for all members of which we pray that they may be led into the way of truth, and so walk in the light of truth, that at last they may attain to the light of everlasting life. And so we pray "for all estates of men in God's Holy Church, that every member of the same, in his vocation and ministry, may truly and godly serve Him," [1] that is, may be faithful, not unworthy members of the Body.

II. The latter part of the Article concerns the errors of one portion of the Church, the Church of Rome.

The Church of Rome claimed to be the whole Catholic Church. Here we declare our belief that she is but one branch or portion of the Catholic Church, and that an erring branch, erring not only in practice and discipline, but in matters of faith. This is illustrated by reference to the Churches of Jerusalem, Antioch, and Alexandria, all of which are said to have erred in doctrine as well as discipline ; and, like them, the Church of Rome is said to have erred. In what points Jerusalem, Alexandria, and Antioch may be considered as having erred in matters of faith is a question which has been mooted by expositors of this Article. Dr. Hey thinks it was in favouring Arianism and condemning Origen. The great point on which the Western Church separated from the

---

[1] Collect for Good Friday.

The following are the other principal expressions in the Liturgy and Prayers concerning the Church : —

"That it may please Thee to rule and govern Thy holy Church universal in the right way," &c. (Litany). "More especially we pray for the good estate of the Catholic Church, that it may be so guided and governed by Thy good Spirit, that all who profess and call themselves Christians may be led into the way of truth," &c. (Prayer for all Conditions of Men). "Who hast purchased to Thyself an universal Church by the precious Blood of Thy dear Son. . . . Who of Thy Divine Providence hast appointed divers orders in Thy Church" (Prayers for Ember Weeks). "Merciful Lord, we beseech thee to cast Thy bright beams of light upon Thy Church, that it being enlightened by the doctrine of thy blessed Apostle and Evangelist St. John, may so walk in the light of Thy truth that it may at length attain to the light of everlasting life" (Collect for St. John's day). "O Almighty God, who hast knit together thine elect in one communion and fellowship in the mystical Body of Thy Son Christ our Lord" (Collect for All Saints). "O Almighty God, who hast built Thy Church upon the foundation of Apostles and Prophets, Jesus Christ Himself being the head corner-stone" (Collect for St. Simon and St. Jude). The Prayer "for the whole state of Christ's Church militant here in earth" is a prayer for all states of men, kings and councils, bishops and curates, all the people in health or sickness. The first prayer for the child to be baptized asks, "that he, being delivered from Thy wrath, may be received into the ark of Christ's Church." And after the baptism we thank God that He hath "incorporated him into His holy Church." So in the Post-Communion we thank God for feeding us in the Sacrament, thereby assuring us that we are very members "incorporate in the mystical Body of His Son, which is the blessed company of all faithful people." In the bidding prayer ministers are enjoined to move the people to join them in prayer in this form : "Ye shall pray for Christ's holy Catholic Church, that is, for the whole congregation of Christian people dispersed throughout the whole world, and especially for the Churches of England, Scotland and Ireland," &c. (Canon 55).

Eastern was the doctrine of the procession of the Third Person
of the Trinity.　It was an acknowledged fact in the West, that on
this point the Eastern Churches had erred.　When therefore the
Article, writing in condemnation of errors in the Church of Rome,
speaks first of the errors of the Eastern Churches, perhaps it
specially alludes to that point in which the Church of Rome would
hold, in common with the Church of England, that these Churches
had erred.　So the statement would be a kind of *argumentum ad
hominem*, a premise sure to be granted.　But this part of the Article is directed against Romanist, not against Eastern or Alexandrian errors, which are only introduced *obiter*.　Some might expect
the Article to have denounced the Church of Rome, not as a
Church in error, but as the synagogue of Antichrist, an antichristian assembly, not an erring Church.　No doubt, at times, such is
the language of the reformers, who, in their strong opposition to
Romanist errors, often use the most severe terms in denouncing
them.　But in their most sober and guarded language, not only
our own, but Luther, Calvin, and other continental reformers,
speak of the Church of Rome as a Church, though a fallen and
corrupt Church.

Thus Luther says, "We call the Church of Rome holy, and
the bishops' sees holy, though they be perverted and their bishops
impious.　In Rome, though worse than Sodom and Gomorrha,
there are still Baptism and the Sacrament, the Gospel, the Scripture, the ministry, the name of Christ and God.　Therefore the
Church of Rome is holy."　"Wherever," he adds, "the Word
and Sacraments substantially remain, there is the holy Church,
notwithstanding Antichrist reigns there, who, as Scripture witnesseth, sits not in a stable of demons or a pigsty, or an assembly
of infidels, but in the most noble and holy place, even the temple
of God." [1]

Calvin, writing to Lælius Socinus, maintains the validity of
Popish baptism, and says that he does not deny some remains of
a Church to the Papists.[2]　In another epistle to the same he
writes, "When I allow some remains of a Church to the Papists,
I do not confine it to the elect who are dispersed among them;
but mean, that some ruins of a scattered Church exist there; which
is confirmed by St. Paul's declaration, that Antichrist shall sit in
the temple of God." [3]

---

[1] *Comment. in Galat.* i. 2; Opp. Tom.
v. pp. 278, 279.
[2] Calv. *Zozino Epistolæ*, p. 51, Amste-
lod. 1667.

[3] "Quod ecclesiæ reliquias manere in
papatu dico. non restringo ad electos qui
illic dispersi sunt: sed ruinas dissipatæ
ecclesiæ illic extare intelligo.　Ac ne

As to the writings of our reformers, to begin with the reign of Henry VIII., the *Institution of a Christian Man* has, " I do believe that the Church of Rome is not, nor cannot worthily be called the true Catholic Church, but only a particular member thereof " . . . . " and I believe that the said Church of Rome, with all the other particular Churches in the world, compacted and united together, do make and constitute but one Catholic Church or body." [1] So the *Necessary Doctrine*, " The Church of Rome, being but a several Church, challenging that name of *Catholic* above all other, doeth great wrong to all other Churches, and doeth only by force and maintenance support an unjust usurpation." [2]

In Cranmer's Catechism, after a denunciation of the great sin of worshipping images of the saints, it is said : " Thus, good children, I have declared how we were wont to abuse images; not that I herein condemn your fathers, who were men of great devotion, and had an earnest love towards God, although their zeal in all points was not ruled and governed by true knowledge; but they were seduced and blinded partly by the common ignorance that reigned in their time, partly by the covetousness of their teachers," [3] &c. Here the members of the Church before the Reformation are spoken of as pious, though ignorant and misled. So Cranmer frequently charges popery, not on the people, but on the Pope and the friars who deluded them.[4] In his appeal at his degradation, he says, " Originally the Church of Rome, as it were the lady of the world, both was and also was conceited worthily, the mother of other Churches." He then proceeds to speak of corruptions introduced into the Roman and afterwards into other Churches, " growing out of kind into the manners of the Church their mother ; " he says, there is no hope of Reformation from the Pope, and therefore from him appeals to a " free general council " of the whole Church ; and adds, that he is " ready in all things to follow the judgment of the most sacred word of God, and of the holy Catholic Church." [5]

So then, although the English, like the foreign reformers, frequently called the papal power Antichrist, the Man of sin, the Beast, &c., deplore and condemn the idolatrous state of the Church

---

mihi longis rationibus disputandum sit, nos Pauli auctoritate contentos esse decet, qui Antichristum in templo Dei sessurum pronunciat."—*Epist.* p. 57. See also *Institut.* IV. ii. 12.

[1] *Formularies of Faith*, p. 56.

[2] p. 247.

[3] *Catechism*, pp. 26, 27.

[4] *Works*, III. p. 365. " I charge none with the name of papists but that be well worthy thereof. For I charge not the hearers, but the teachers, not the learners, but the inventors of the untrue doctrine."

[5] *Works*, IV. pp. 125, 126, 127.

before the Reformation, and of the Church which continued in union with Rome after the Reformation, and in consequence often use language which appears to imply that the Church of Rome was no true Church at all; still they often speak, as this Article does, of the Church of Rome as yet a Church, though a corrupt, degenerate, and erring Church. Accordingly, the XXXth Canon declares : " So far was it from the purpose of the Church of England to forsake and reject the Churches of Italy, France, Spain, Germany, or any such like Churches, in all things that they held or practised, that, as the *Apology of the Church of England* confesseth, it doth with reverence retain those ceremonies which do neither endamage the Church of God, nor offend the minds of sober men ; and only departed from them in those particular points wherein they were fallen both from themselves in their ancient integrity, and from the Apostolical Churches, which were their first founders."

The tone and temper of the Church of England appears therefore to be that of a body earnestly and steadfastly protesting against Romanism, against all the errors, abuses, and idolatries of the Church of Rome, and the usurpation of the See of Rome ; but yet acknowledging that, with a fearful amount of error, the Churches of the Roman communion are still branches, though corrupt branches of the universal Church of Christ.

The divine who has been commonly considered as the most accredited exponent of the principles of the Church of England, thus speaks in her behalf: " In the Church of Christ we were (*i. e.* before the Reformation), and we are so still. Other difference between our estate before and now we know none, but only such as we see in Judah ; which, having some time been idolatrous, became afterwards more soundly religious by renouncing idolatry and superstition. . . . The indisposition of the Church of Rome to reform herself must be no stay unto us from performing our duty to God; even as desire of retaining conformity with them could be no excuse if we did not perform our duty. Notwithstanding, so far as lawfully we may, we have held and do hold fellowship with them. For even as the Apostle doth say of Israel, that they are in one respect enemies, but in another beloved of God (Rom. xi. 28) ; in like sort with Rome we dare not communicate touching her grievous abominations, yet, touching those main parts of Christian truth wherein they constantly still persist, we gladly acknowledge them to be of the family of Jesus Christ." [1]

[1] Hooker, *Eccl. Pol.* iii. i. 10.

This is not the language of one great man; but most consistent with it have been the sentiments of almost all those eminent writers of our Church, who are known and reverenced as the great types of Anglican piety, learning, and charity.[1] It is infinitely to be desired that there should be no relaxation of our protest against error and corruption; but the force of a protest can never be increased by uncharitableness or exaggeration. Let Rome throw off her false additions to the Creed, and we will gladly communicate with her; but, so long as she retains her errors, we cannot but stand aloof, lest we should be partakers of her sins.

Section II. — SCRIPTURAL PROOF.

THE word ἐκκλησία, rendered *Church*, should, according to its derivation, signify persons called out from among others for some purpose. At Athens, the *Ecclesia* was the general assembly of the people, convened by the crier for legislation. In the old Testament, the word is often used by the LXX. to translate the Hebrew קָהָל, which commonly expresses the assembly or congregation of the people of Israel.[2] Accordingly, when adopted in the new Testament, it is used to signify the whole assembly or congregation of the people of God under the Gospel, as it had been before to signify the congregation of the people of God under the Law. And as συναγωγή, *Synagogue*, was the more frequent word for the congregation of the Jews; so perhaps our Lord and his Apostles adopted, by preference and for distinction's sake, the word ἐκκλησία, *Church*, for the congregation of Christians.

1. Now it is well known and obvious, that the word *Congregation*, as read in the old Testament, not only meant an assembly of the people gathered together at a special time for worship, but was constantly used to express the whole body of worshippers, the whole people of Israel, the congregation which the Lord had purchased (*e. g.* Ex. xii. 19. Lev. iv. 15. Num. xvi. 3, 9; xxvii. 17. Josh. xxii. 18, 20. Judg. xxi. 13, 16. Ps. lxxiv. 2).

---

[1] The student may consult Palmer, *On the Church*, ch. xi. where he will find quotations from Bp. Hall, Archbp. Usher, Hammond, Chillingworth, Field, &c.

[2] קָהָל is often rendered ἐκκλησία, as Deut. ix. 10; xviii. 16; Judges xxi. 8; 1 Kings viii. 65; 2 Chron. vii. 8, 12; often it is rendered συναγωγή, as Exod. xvi. 1–3; Lev. iv. 13, 14, 21; Num. xvi. 3; xx. 6. In Psalm xxii. 22, " In the midst of the *Congregation* will I praise Thee," is rendered by the Apostle, " In the midst of the *Church* will I praise Thee" (Heb. ii. 12). So St. Stephen speaks of "the Church in the wilderness" (Acts vii. 38), meaning the congregation of the Israelites.

This too, *mutatis mutandis*, is the ordinary acceptation of the word *Church*, in the new Testament. It applies to the society of Christians, to those who believe in Christ, to those who live in Christian fellowship, and partake of Gospel privileges. For example: " Give none offence, neither to the Jews nor to the Gentiles, nor to the Church of God " (1 Cor. x. 32).[1] " On this rock I will build My Church " (Matt. xvi. 18). " Saul made havoc of the Church " (Acts viii. 3). " Persecuted the Church of God " (1 Cor. xv. 9). " The Lord added to the Church such as should be saved " (Acts ii. 47). " Fear came on all the Church " (Acts v. 11). " The Church is subject unto Christ " (Eph. v. 24). " God hath set some in the Church, first Apostles, secondarily prophets," &c. (1 Cor. xii. 28).

2. But it also signifies the Church, or body of Christians in a particular town or country. Thus we read of " the Church which was at Jerusalem " (Acts viii. 1); " the Church which was at Antioch " (Acts xiii. 1); " the elders of the Church at Ephesus " (Acts xx. 17); " the Church of God which is at Corinth " (1 Cor. i. 2. Compare Rom. xvi. 1, 4; 1 Cor. xvi. 1; Col. iv. 16; Rev. ii. ; iii. &c. &c.)

3. It is used even for a single family of Christians, or a single congregation meeting for worship, as the first Christians did, in a private house, *e. g.* " Priscilla and Aquila, and the Church that is in their house " (Rom. xvi. 5. 1 Cor. xvi. 19); " Nymphas and the Church which is in his house " (Col. iv. 15); " The Church in thy house " (Philem. 2). And accordingly, at times we find the word used in the plural, as signifying the various congregations of Christians, whether in one single city, or throughout the world; as Acts ix. 31; xv. 41. Rom. xvi. 4. 1 Cor. vii. 17; xi. 16; xiv. 33; xvi. 1, 19. Rev. i. 4, 11; ii. 23, &c.

We may say therefore, that as the *Congregation* among the Jews signified either a body of worshippers, or more often the great body of worshippers assembled at the temple or tabernacle, or the great body of the Jewish people considered as the people of God; so the *Church* amongst Christians signifies, in the new Testament, either a single congregation of Christians, or the whole body of Christians in a particular place, or the whole body of Christians dispersed throughout the world.

In our Article the word *Church* is interpreted *Congregation*, probably on the ground of the above considerations; namely,

---

[1] In this passage the "Church" is used to distinguish Christians from Jews and heathens.

because such is the original meaning of the word, and such its application many times in Scripture. The Church is called "a Congregation of *faithful men*," *cœtus fidelium*, because those of whom the Church is composed are the professed believers in Jesus Christ, that body of people "first called Christians in Antioch" (Acts xi. 26).

The name which our Lord Himself most frequently uses for the Church is, "the kingdom of God," or "the kingdom of Heaven." The prophets constantly spoke of the Messiah as the King who should reign in righteousness (Isai. xxxii. 1), the King who should reign and prosper (Jer. xxiii. 5), the King of Israel, who should come to Zion, "just, and having salvation"(Zech. ix. 9). Daniel foretold that, when the Assyrian, Medo-Persian, and Grecian empires had passed away, and after the fourth great empire of Rome had been established, "the God of Heaven should set up a kingdom, which should never be destroyed" (Dan. ii. 44); that the Son of Man should have given Him "dominion, and glory, and a kingdom, that all people, nations, and languages, should serve Him" (Dan. vii. 14). These prophecies led the Jews to expect that Messiah should set up a temporal kingdom, with all the glory and splendour of the kingdoms of this world. Our Lord Himself, therefore, uses the language of the Prophets, and the language current among the Jews, continually calling the Church, which He was to establish, by the name of kingdom: "My kingdom," "kingdom of God," "kingdom of Heaven," though often correcting the mistaken views entertained of it, and explaining that His kingdom was not of this world. (See Matt. iii. 2; iv. 17; xii. 28; xiii. 38. Mark i. 14; iv. 11, 26, 30; x. 15. Luke iv. 43; vii. 28; viii. 1; ix. 2, 62; xvi. 16. John iii. 3. Acts i. 3; &c.)

Having premised thus much concerning the names or titles of that body of which the Article treats, we may next proceed to consider how the Scriptures prove the various statements of the Article.

1. That the Church is a visible body of believers.

2. That the pure word of God is held and preached in it.

3. That the Sacraments are duly ministered in it, according to Christ's ordinance.

1. First, then, the Church is a visible body of believers.

This, we have already observed, does not interfere with the belief that there is a body of persons within the Church, known only to God, who differ from the rest, in being not only in outward privilege, but also in inward spirit, servants of Christ; whom some have called the invisible Church, and who being faithful unto death, will enter into the Church triumphant. Nor does it interfere with a belief that the saints who are in Paradise, and perhaps also the holy angels of heaven, are members of the Church invisible, the company of God's elect and redeemed people. What we have to deal with here, is the Church of God, considered as Christ's ordinance in the world, for the gathering together in one body of all believers in Him, and making them partakers of the various means of grace.

It is argued indeed *in limine*, that the Church and kingdom of Christ cannot be visible, because our Lord said, " The kingdom of God cometh not with observation. Neither shall they say, Lo, here! or, lo there! for, behold the kingdom of God is within you " (Luke xvii. 20, 21). This, however, proves no more than this. The Pharisees, who had asked " when the kingdom of God should come?" expected a kingdom of earthly glory, pomp, and splendour. Our Lord answered, that this was not the way in which His kingdom should come, not with observation, nor so that men should point out, Lo here! as to a splendid spectacle. On the contrary, God's reign in the Church should not be like an earthly king's, but in the hearts of His people.[1]

But it is plain, both from prophecy and the new Testament, that the Church was to be, and is, a visible company. " The mountain of the Lord's house was to be established on the top of the mountains, and all nations were to flow unto it " (Isai. ii. 2). Among the earthly kingdoms, Christ's kingdom was to grow up gradually, like a stone hewn without hands, till it became a mountain and filled the earth, breaking in pieces and consuming the worldly empires (Dan. ii. 35, 44). The kingdom of heaven in the Gospels is compared to a field sown with good and bad seed growing together till the harvest; to a marriage supper, where some have no wedding-garments; to a net taking good and bad fish, not separated till the net be drawn to the shore; by which we cannot fail to understand the outward communion of Christians in this world, in which the faithful and unfaithful live together, not fully separated till the Judgment (Matt. xiii. 24–30, 47–50; xxii. 11,

---

[1] Many consider that the passage ought to be rendered not " within you," but " *amongst* you," ἐντὸς ὑμῶν, i. e. Though you expect to see some *sign* of a kingdom, yet in truth the kingdom of God is already come among you, and you have not recognized it. But it is to be noted that in the new Testament the words *Kingdom of God* signify three things : — 1. The reign of Christ in His Church on earth. 2. The reign of Christ in the hearts of His people. 3. The reign of Christ in the eternal kingdom of glory.

12). Such parables would be inapplicable to an invisible company, and can only be interpreted of a visible body.

Our Lord distinctly commanded, that, if a Christian offended against his brother, the offence should be told to the Church (Matt. xviii. 17). But if the Church were not a visible and ascertainable body, such a thing could not be. Accordingly our Lord addresses His Church, as "the light of the world, a city set on a hill, that cannot be hid" (Matt. v. 14). St. Paul gives Timothy directions how to act as a bishop, that he might "know how to behave himself in the house of God, which is the Church of the living God, the pillar and ground of the truth" (Tim. iii. 15). This would be unintelligible, if the Church were only an invisible spiritual society of faithful Christians, and not an outward organized body. So, when first persons were brought in large numbers to believe the Gospel, we are taught that all those who were placed in a state of salvation were "added to the Church" (Acts ii. 47); evidently, from the context, by the rite of baptism. This again plainly intimates that the Church was a definite visible body of men. The same appears from such expressions as the following: "Fear came on all the Church" (Acts v. 11); "a great persecution against the Church" (Acts viii. 1); "assembled themselves with the Church" (Acts xi. 26); "God hath set some in the Church, first Apostles, secondarily prophets" (1 Cor. xii. 28). The clergy are called "the elders of the Church"(Acts xx. 17. James v. 14) who are "to feed the Church of God" (Acts xx. 28), to "take care of the Church of God" (1 Tim. iii. 5). People are spoken of as cast out of the Church (3 John 10). The same thing appears again from what is said of local or national Churches, which, being branches of the one universal Church, are evidently and constantly spoken of as the visible society of Christians in their respective cities or countries. (See Acts xi. 22; xiii. 1; xiv. 23; xv. 3, 22. Rom. xvi. 1, 16, 23. 1 Cor. vi. 4; vii. 17; xi. 16; xiv. 33; xvi. 1, 19. Gal. i. 22. 1 Thess. ii. 14. Rev. i. 4, &c.)

Accordingly, St. Paul, when he speaks of the unity of the Church, speaks not only of spiritual, but of external unity also; for he says, "There is one *body*, and one spirit" (Eph. iv. 4). And our blessed Lord, when praying for the unity of His disciples, evidently desired a visible unity, which might be a witness for God to the world; "that they also may be one in Us, that the world may believe," &c. (John xvii. 21).

We conclude therefore that, as the primitive Church always

held, so Scripture also teaches, that the Church is not merely a spiritual and mystical communion of faithful Christians, known only to God, but is a visible body of those who are outward followers of Christ, consisting partly of faithful, partly of unfaithful, but all professed believers in the Gospel.

2. The first characteristic given us of this body is, that the pure Word of God, or, in other language, the true faith, is kept and preached in it.

The Church is called by St. Paul "the pillar and ground of the truth" (1 Tim. iii. 15); whence it is manifest that a main province of the Church is to maintain and support the truth. Our blessed Lord prayed for His disciples, that the Father would "sanctify them through His truth" (John xvii. 17). He promised to the Apostles that "the Spirit of truth should guide them into all truth" (John xvi. 13). He bade them "go and teach all nations" (Matt. xxviii. 19). And we learn of the first converted Christians, that they continued in the Apostles' doctrine and fellowship" (Acts ii. 42). Accordingly, the Apostles speak of the faith as ONE (Ephes. iv. 5); of the faith once delivered to the saints (Jude 3); urge Christians "earnestly to contend for" it (Jude 3); and desire their bishops " to rebuke them sharply, that they may be sound in the faith" (Tit. i. 13).

Hence to introduce false doctrine or heresy into the Church is described as damning sin. St. Peter speaks of those " who privily shall bring in damnable heresies" (2 Pet. ii. 1). St. Paul classes heresies among the works of the flesh (Gal. v. 20). He says, " If any man preach any other Gospel unto you than that ye have received, let him be anathema" (Gal. i. 9). He bids Timothy withdraw himself from those "who teach otherwise, and consent not to wholesome words, even the words of our Lord Jesus Christ, and to the doctrine which is according to godliness" (1 Tim. vi. 3, 5). And to Titus he says, " A man that is an heretic, after the first and second admonition, reject" (Tit. iii. 10). St. John bids, " If there come any unto you, and bring not this doctrine, receive him not into your house, neither bid him God speed " (2 John 10). He says, " Whosoever abideth not in the doctrine of Christ, hath not God " (2 John 9). And calls all who " deny the Father and the Son," or " deny that Jesus Christ has come in the flesh," not Christians, but Antichrists (1 John ii. 22. 2 John 7).

Thus Scripture represents the Church as a body holding the truth, nay, " the pillar and ground of the truth ; " and heretics, or persons holding vital error, are spoken of as apart from God, to be rejected, and not received as fellow-Christians or members of Christ's Church.

The wording of our Article, " the pure word of God," may be somewhat difficult.   Some would confine the meaning of it within very narrow limits, others would extend it to an indefinite latitude. We must notice, that the expression is not, " the word of God is purely preached," but, " the pure word of God is preached."   If the former words had been used, we might have doubted in what body of Christians God's Word was always purely preached, with no mixture of falsehood or error.   But " the pure word of God " is preached, wherever the main doctrines of the Gospel are preserved and taught.   The question, however, of " fundamentals " has always been considered difficult ; and different persons have chosen to make different doctrines fundamental, according to their own peculiar views of truth.   Hence, some have excluded almost all Christians except themselves from holding the pure word of God ; others have scarcely shut out Arians, Socinians, or even Deists.   We may be sure the Church intended to maintain the purity of Christian truth, yet without the narrowness of sectarian bigotry.   The way in which her own formularies are drawn up, — the first five Articles being almost a repetition and enforcement of the chief Articles of the Creed, and the eighth containing the Creeds themselves, — the question addressed to all members of the Church before admission to baptism, in the Catechism and in sickness, as to whether they believed the Creed, — the repetition on every Sunday and holyday of two of the Creeds, and once every month of the third, in the public service by the congregation, — the expressed adherence by the reformers to the decrees of the first four General Councils, — the general agreement to the same effect by the primitive Church, with which the reformers declared themselves to be in perfect accordance and unison : — these, and the like considerations, make it nearly certain that the compilers of the Article would have, and must have intended, that all who truly believed the Creeds of the Church were so far in possession and belief of " the pure word of God " as not to have forfeited the character of Christians, or the fellowship of the Christian Church.

3. The next mark of the Church is, that " the Sacraments be duly ministered, according to Christ's ordinance."   We know, that, among the Jews, circumcision and the passover were essential to the existence of the people as the congregation of the Lord, and that he who rejected or neglected either was to be cut off from His people (Gen. xvii. 14.   Exod. xii. 15).   When the Lord Jesus

60

founded His Church, He appointed the two Sacraments to supersede the two great ordinances of the Synagogue, namely, baptism,
to initiate the convert or the child, the Eucharist, to maintain communion with Himself and with His people.

The command which He gave to His Apostles was to " make
disciples of all nations by baptizing them " (Matt. xxviii. 19) : that
is to say, persons from all nations, who believed the Gospel, were
to be admitted into the number of the disciples, the Church of
Christ, by the Sacrament of baptism. We know that the Apostles
acted on this command, ever receiving by the rite of baptism all
who had been converted to the truth. (See Acts ii. 38, 41 ; viii.
12, 13, 36–38 ; ix. 18 ; x. 47, 48 ; xvi. 14, 15, 33 ; xix. 3, 5.
Rom. vi. 3, 4.   Gal. iii. 27.   Col. ii. 11, 12. 1 Pet. iii. 20, 21, &c.)
Nay ! our Lord Himself declared, " Except a man be born of *water*
and of the Spirit, he cannot enter into the kingdom of God " (John
iii. 5).   Whence it is quite clear, that a Christian Church must
administer baptism according to our Lord's command and the example of the Apostles, for otherwise its members could not be
" born of water."

But our blessed Lord, moreover, commanded His Apostles to
break the bread and bless the wine in remembrance of Him ; and
declared the bread broken and the cup poured out to be His Body
and Blood (Matt. xxvi. 26–30).   Moreover, He declared that except a Christian received the grace of His Body and Blood, he had
no life in him (John vi. 53).   Accordingly, we ever find that the
Apostles and the Apostolic Churches "continued stedfastly in the
breaking of bread " (Acts ii. 42; xx. 7, 11. 1 Cor. x. 16, 17 ; xi.
17, &c.) ; believing and declaring, that the " cup which they blessed
was the communion of the Blood of Christ, and the bread which
they brake was the communion of the Body of Christ " (1 Cor.
x. 16).

These two Sacraments, therefore, Baptism and the Holy Communion, were the ordinance of Christ, essential to the existence
of His Church, steadily administered by His first ministers, and
received by His early disciples, as completely as Circumcision and
the Passover in the old dispensation of the Jews.   The Article
therefore justly asserts, that it is a necessary note of the Church,
that the Sacraments should be duly ministered, according to the
ordinance of Christ.

4. There is still one more point to be noticed.   The Article says
the " pure word of God " is not only to be held, but to be
"*preached;* " and that the Sacraments are to be " DULY *ministered*

according to Christ's ordinance." The first expression at once suggests the question, " How shall they hear without a preacher? and how shall they preach except they be sent?" The second expression suggests the inquiry, How can sacraments be DULY *ministered?* and, whom has Christ authorized to minister them? The definition evidently implies the consideration of a ministry: even as we saw both fathers and reformers mentioning a duly or-dained ministry as essential to the character of a Church. The present Article may possibly have less distinctly enunciated this, because in two future Articles the subject is specially treated.

It is a truth hardly questioned, that our Lord did ordain a minis-try for the preaching of the word, and that those so ordained did exercise that ministry, and considered themselves as sent by Christ to fulfil it. (See Matt. x.; xxviii. 19, 20. Luke x. 1, 16. John xx. 21, 23. Acts xx. 20; xxvi. 17. 1 Cor. iv. 1; ix. 16, 17; xii. 28. 2 Cor. i. 1. Gal. i. 1. Eph. iv. 11, 14. Phil. i. 1. Col. iv. 17. 1 Tim. iii. 1. Tit. i. 5. 1 Pet. v. 1, &c. &c.) It is also quite certain that those to whom He gave authority to bap-tize, and those whom He commanded to bless the cup and break the bread in the Communion, were His commissioned and ordained Apostles (see the institution of the Eucharist in Matt. xxvi, and of Baptism in Matt. xxviii). Moreover, we never hear of any one in the new Testament, except a minister of God, attempting to baptize or to administer the Holy Communion. We know equally well, that the practice and belief of the Primitive Church was that none but bishops and presbyters should minister the Communion, and, ordinarily *at least,* none but bishops, priests, or deacons, should preach or baptize.

Thus then we conclude, that to the right preaching of the Word, and to the due administration of the Sacraments according to Christ's ordinance, a ministry, such as Christ ordained, is necessary, and therefore is included in the definition of this Article.

Moreover, as Baptism was to be with water, and the Eucharist with bread and wine, these elements must be used in order that they be duly administered; and, with the elements, that form of words which Christ has prescribed, at least in the case of Baptism, where a distinct form has been given. And so, the Sacraments, to be duly administered, need first the right elements, then the right form of words, and lastly, a ministry according to the ordinance of Christ.

5. It has been already noticed, that the definitions of the Arti-cle may be fairly considered as including the statement given in

the Homily and in other partly authoritative documents, that one note of the Church is discipline, or the power of the Keys. For, if the Sacraments be duly ministered, unfit persons must be shut out from them; and if there be a duly constituted ministry, that ministry must have the power of the Keys committed by Christ to His Church. But, as this subject falls more naturally under Article XXXIII., we may defer its fuller consideration for the present.

The formularies of our Church have expressed no judgment as to how far the very being of a Church may be imperilled by a defect in this particular note of the Church; as by mutilation of the Sacraments, imperfect ordination, or defective exercise of the power of the Keys. At the present time, these questions force themselves on us. But the English Church has been content to give her decision as to the right mode of ordaining, ministering Sacraments, and exercising discipline, without expressing an opinion on the degree of defectiveness in such matters which would cause other communions to cease from being Churches of Christ.

II. "The Church of Rome hath erred, not only in living and manner of ceremonies, but also in matters of faith."

So many of the Articles specially enter upon the errors of the Church of Rome that the subject may require very brief notice here. By "matters of faith" probably it is not intended to express articles of the Creed. Had the Church of Rome rejected the Creeds, and those fundamental articles of the faith contained in them, the Church of England would probably have considered her distinctly as a heresy, and not as a corrupt and erring Church. But there are many errors which concern the faith of Christ, besides those which strike at the very foundation, and would overthrow even the Creeds themselves.

Amongst these we may reckon all those novelties and heterodoxies contained in the Creed of Pope Pius IV., or of the Council of Trent. They are thus reckoned up by Dr. Barrow: 1. Seven Sacraments. 2. Trent doctrine of Justification and Original Sin. 3. Propitiatory sacrifice of the Mass. 4. Transubstantiation. 5. Communicating under one kind. 6. Purgatory. 7. Invocation of Saints. 8. Veneration of Relics. 9. Worship of Images. 10. The Roman Church to be the Mother and Mistress of all Churches. 11. Swearing Obedience to the Pope. 12. Receiving the decrees of all synods and of Trent.[1]

It is true that these do not involve a denial of the Creeds, but

[1] Barrow, *On the Pope's Supremacy*, p. 290, conclusion.

they are additions to the Creeds, and error may be shown in excess, as well as in defect of belief. They are to be received by all members of the Church of Rome, as articles of faith. They are not with them mere matters of opinion. Every priest is required to swear that they form parts of the Catholic faith, without which no one can be saved.[1] Now the Church of England holds all of them to be false : several of her Articles are directed against these very doctrines as fabulous and dangerous ; and therefore she must conclude, that " the Church of Rome hath erred, not only in living and manner of ceremonies, but also in " those very points which she herself has declared to be " matters of faith."

[1] The Creed of Pope Pius IV. begins with a declaration of firm faith in the various Articles in the Nicene, or Constantinopolitan Creed ; and then continues with a like declaration of firm faith in the twelve novelties enumerated in the text. It finally rejects and anathematizes all things rejected and anathematized by the Council of Trent. And concludes with a solemn vow and profession of all this as "the true Catholic faith, out of which no one can be saved." " Hanc veram Catholicam fidem extra quam nemo salvus esse potest . . . . sponte profiteor ac veraciter teneo, spondeo, voveo ac juro. Sic me Deus adjuvet et hæc sancta Dei evangelia." *Concil. Trident. Canones et Decreta*, pp. 370-373, Monast. Guestphalorum, 1845.

ARTICLE XX.

◆

Of the Authority of the Church.

THE Church hath power to decree rites or ceremonies, and authority in controversies of faith. ; and yet it is not lawful for the Church to ordain anything that is contrary to God's word written, neither may it so expound one place of Scripture that it be repugnant to another. Wherefore, although the Church be a witness and a keeper of Holy Writ; yet, as it ought not to decree anything against the same, so besides the same ought it not to enforce anything to be believed for necessity of salvation.

De Ecclesiæ Authoritate.

HABET Ecclesia ritus sive cæremoniat authoritatem; quamvis Ecclesiæ non licet quicquam instituere, quod verbo Dei scripto adversetur, nec unum scripturæ locum sic exponere potest, ut alteri contradicat. Quare licet Ecclesia sit divinorum librorum testis et conservatrix, attamen ut adversus eos nihil decernere, ita præter illos nihil credendum de necessitate salutis debet obtrudere.

SECTION I.— HISTORY.

THE history of this Article is famous, owing to the dispute concerning the first clause of it: " The Church hath power to decree rites or ceremonies, and authority in controversies of faith." The Article of 1552 (then the XXIst Article) had not the clause. Moreover, the first draught of the Articles in Elizabeth's reign (A. D. 1562) had it not. In this form the Articles were signed by both houses of convocation; and the original document so signed, is now in the library of Corpus Christi College, Cambridge. Yet this document had never synodical authority, for it never received the ratification of the crown. Before the royal assent was given, some alterations were made : namely, the addition of this clause, and the omission of Article XXIX. The clause itself was taken from the Lutheran Confession of Wurtemberg, from which source Archbishop Parker derived most of the additions which were made in Queen Elizabeth's reign to the Articles drawn up by Crammer in the reign of Edward VI.[1] It is supposed that the Queen's wish induced the council to make this alteration. And when it had been made, the Latin edition of R. Wolfe was published in 1563, printed by the Queen's command, and with a declaration of her

---

[1] In the Wurtemberg confession are the words : " Credimus et confitemur quod . . . . hæc ecclesia habeat jus judicandi de omnibus doctrinis . . . . quod hæc ecclesia habeat jus interpretandæ Scripturæ." — Laurence, *Bamp. Lect.* p. 236

royal approval. This copy, therefore, is considered as possessed of full synodical authority. The fine *English* edition, printed by Jugge and Cawood in 1563, has not the clause,[1] and this is very probably the copy of the Articles submitted to Parliament, which passed an Act (13 Eliz. Cap. 12) giving the authority of statute law to what had already received the authority of the Queen and convocation.

After this, the printed copies varied, some omitting, but most retaining the clause. It does not appear that any English copy received the authority of convocation till 1571; and then, no doubt, the copy corresponded with one of those printed by Jugge and Cawood, with the date 1571. Dr. Cardwell gives an accurate reprint of one of these, containing the disputed clause.[2] Yet there were other editions, put forth by the same printers, with the same date 1571, some retaining, others omitting the clause. From that time the greater number of editions have the clause. Dr. Cardwell enumerates editions of 1563, 1571, as omitting it; and as retaining it, editions of 1563, 1571, 1581, 1586, 1593, 1612, 1624, 1628, and all subsequent editions.[3] All subscriptions, therefore, and acts of Parliament, after this period, had reference to the Article with the first clause as forming part of it; and not to the form in which it was first passed by convocation, before the Queen's sanction was obtained.

Important as the question concerning this clause has been thought, it is truly observed that that portion of it concerning rites and ceremonies is fully expressed in Article XXXIV.; and that that portion which concerns controversies of faith is virtually contained in the latter part of this Article itself.

It is not necessary to spend much time in proving that the primitive Church claimed a certain authority, both in matters of ceremony and in controversies of faith. This is self-apparent from the fact, that, when any disputes arose, whether of doctrine or of discipline, synods and councils continually met to decide upon them, and declare the judgment of the Church. Where a judgment is pronounced, authority must be claimed. The first general council of Nice was assembled for the express purpose of giving the judg‧ ment of the Church, represented by the fathers of that council, on a most important point of doctrine, namely, the Deity of the Son

---

[1] Though it had not this clause, inserted at the Queen's desire, yet it omitted Art. xxix., expunged by the Queen's desire. The Articles were therefore, as so passed by Parliament, only thirty-eight in number. They are given by Dr. Cardwell, *Synodalia*, i. p. 53.

[2] *Synodal.* i. p. 98.

[3] See Cardwell's *Synodalia*, i. pp. 34, 53, 73, 90, &c.; and the authorities referred to by him.

of God, and on a matter of ceremony, namely, the time of keeping Easter. The Epistle of Constantine to the Churches, written as it were from the council, urges all Christians to receive the decrees of the bishops so assembled as the will of God.[1]

The fathers certainly taught that the authority of the Church was to be obeyed and received with deep respect. Irenæus says, " Where the Church is, there is the Spirit of God . . . . but the Spirit is truth." [2]   Tertullian, " Every doctrine is to be judged as false which is opposed to the truth taught by the Churches, the Apostles, Christ, and God." [3]   St. Cyril says, " The Church is called Catholic, because it teaches universally, and without omission, all doctrines needful to be known." [4]   Passages to the same purport might be abundantly multiplied, if evidences of so well-known a fact could be required.

When controversies arose, whether about doctrine, or about rules and ceremonies and Church-ordinances, such as the keeping of Easter, the rebaptizing of heretics, or the enforcing of discipline on the lapsed, it could hardly be but that the Church should exercise some discretion, and pronounce some judgment. Most of the canons of the early councils will be found to be on matters of discipline ; and as Scripture generally left them undecided, it was necessary for the representatives of the Church to use the best judgment they could upon them. To this end they strove, looking for the guidance of the Spirit, following Scripture where it gave them light, and on those points on which Scripture was silent, following that rule unanimously adopted at Nice, " Let the ancient customs prevail," τὰ ἀρχαῖα ἔθη κρατείτω.[5]

Yet, that the fathers held the authority of Scripture to be primary and paramount, and considered that the Church had no power to enact new articles of faith, nor to decree anything which was contrary to the Scriptures, has already been shown sufficiently, and the proof needs not to be repeated here.[6]   The power of the Church they held, not as an authority superior or equal to the Scriptures, but as declaratory of them when doubtful, and decretory on matters of discipline.

---

[1] Euseb. *De Vita Constantin.* III. 20.

[2] " Ubi enim ecclesia, ibi et Spiritus Dei ; et ubi Spiritus Dei, illic ecclesia et omnis gratia. Spiritus autem veritas." — Lib. III. cap. 40.

[3] Omnem vero doctrinam de mendacio præjudicandam quæ sapiat contra veritatem Ecclesiarum et Apostolorum et Christi et Dei." — *De Præscript. Hæret.* c. 21.

[4] διὰ τὸ διδάσκειν καθολικῶς καὶ ἀνελλει-πῶς ἅπαντα τὰ εἰς γνῶσιν ἀνθρώπων ἐλθεῖν ὀφείλοντα δόγματα. — *Cateches.* XVIII. 11. See Palmer, *On the Church,* II. pt. IV. ch. IV.

[5] The principle of observing traditionary ceremonies, where Scripture is silent, is laid down by Tertullian, *De Corona,* c. 3, 4, 5. See Palmer, II. pt. IV. ch. IV.

[6] See above, p. 147, *seq.*   Article VI. Sect. I. III.

The reformers in general did not deny such authority to the Church, to interpret Scripture in case of disputes upon doctrine, nor to adopt or retain ceremonies of ancient custom or human institution, not contrary to the teaching of Scripture. Thus the Confession of Augsburg says, " We do not despise the consent of the Catholic Church . . . . nor are we willing to patronize impious opinions, which the Church Catholic has condemned." [1] It declares that there are indifferent ceremonies, which ought to be observed for the good order of the Church.[2] But on the other hand, it pronounces that " the bishops have no power to decree anything contrary to the Gospel." [3]

Calvin, denying that the Church has any power to introduce new doctrines, yet gladly admits, that when a discussion concerning doctrine arises, no more fit mode of settling it can be devised than a meeting of bishops to discuss it. And he mentions with approbation the Councils of Nice, Constantinople, and Ephesus.[4]

The language of the English reformers is still plainer. The Preface to the Book of Common Prayer gives reasons why the Church abolished some and retained other ceremonies ; and though it speaks of ceremonies as but small things in themselves, it yet declares that the wilful transgression " and breaking of a common rule and discipline is no small offence before God."

Cranmer appealed to a general council, protesting, " I intend to speak nothing against one holy Catholic and Apostolic Church, or the authority thereof; the which authority I have in great reverence, and to whom my mind is in all things to obey :" [5] and declaring, " I may err, but heretic I cannot be ; forasmuch as I am ready in all things to follow the judgment of the most sacred word of God, and of the holy Catholic Church." [6] He declares his agreement with Vincentius Lirinensis, who taught that " the Bible is perfect and sufficient of itself for the truth of the Catholic faith, and that the whole Church cannot make one article of faith ; although it may be taken as a necessary witness of the same, with these three conditions, that the thing which we would establish thereby hath been believed in all places, ever, and of all men." [7] In short, his judgment appears to have been clearly, that " every

---

[1] " Non enim aspernamur consensum catholicæ Ecclesiæ . . . . nec patrocinari impiis aut seditiosis opinionibus volumus, quas ecclesia Catholica damnavit." — Confess. August. 1540. Art. 21 ; Sylloge, p. 189.
[2] Pars I. Art. xv. 1531 ; Sylloge, p. 127 ; 1540, p. 174.

[3] Sylloge, p. 154.
[4] Instit. IV. ix. 13.
[5] Appeal at his Degradation, Works, IV. p. 121.
[6] Ibid. p. 127.
[7] Answer to Smythe's Preface, III. p. 23.

exposition of Scripture in which the whole Church agreed," was to be received ; but that the Church had no power to decree *Articles of faith* without the Scripture, though rites indifferent she might decree.[1]

The origin of the dispute about the first clause in this Article was the repugnance of the Puritan divines to the use of the surplice and other Church ordinances. This feeling arose in the reign of Edward VI., and the controversies gendered by it continued to rage fiercely in Elizabeth's. The Puritans contended, not only that the Church could not enact new articles of faith, but that no rites nor ceremonies were admissible but those for which there was plain warrant in the new Testament. It is probable that Elizabeth and her councillors wished to have a definite assertion of the power of the Church to legislate on such points ; and therefore insisted on the distinct enunciation of the principle by the clause in question, notwithstanding that it was virtually included in other statements or formularies. The controversy reached its height in the reign of Charles I. ; and one of the charges against Archbishop Laud was, that he had introduced this clause into the Articles, it not having been previously to be found there.[2] On the subject itself the great work of Hooker was composed ; one main and principal object of that work being to prove the right which the Church Catholic and particular national Churches have to legislate on matters indifferent, and to enact such rites and ceremonies as are not repugnant to the teaching of Holy Writ.

Section II. — SCRIPTURAL PROOF.

THERE are contained in this Article three positive or affirmative, and two negative or restraining assertions.

    I. The affirmative are : —
        1. The Church is a witness and keeper of Holy Writ.
        2. The Church hath power to decree rites and ceremonies.
        3. The Church hath authority in controversies of faith.

[1] See especially IV. p. 229, quoted above, in p. 185, under Article VI. See also *Works*, III. pp. 509, 517 ; IV pp. 77, 126, 173, 223, 225, &c.

[2] That this charge is unfounded has already appeared.

II. The restraining assertions are : —
 1. It is not lawful for the Church to ordain anything contrary to God's word written.
 2. Besides the written word, she ought not to enforce anything to be believed for necessity of salvation.

I. 1. The Church is a witness and keeper of Holy Writ, forasmuch as that unto it, as unto the Jews of old, " are committed the oracles of God " (Rom. iii. 2).   As the Jews had the Old Testament Scriptures " read in the synagogues every Sabbath-day " (Acts xv. 21) ; so the Christian Church has the Scriptures of both Testaments read continually in her assemblies. In no way can she more truly fulfil her office of " pillar and ground of the truth " than by preserving and maintaining those Scriptures in which the truth is to be found. The Scriptures are a sacred deposit left to the Church, to guard and to teach. The manner in which the ancient Churches collected and preserved the sacred writings, and handed them down to us, and the abundant evidence which we have that they have been received by us in their integrity, were considered at length under Art. VI.[1]

We, the children of the Church, must, in the first instance at least, receive the word of God from her. She, by our parents and her ministers, puts the Bible into our hands, even before we could seek it for ourselves. To her care her Lord has intrusted it. She keeps it, and testifies to us that it is the word of God, and teaches us the truths contained in it. Her ministers are enjoined " to hold fast the form of sound words " (2 Tim. i. 13) ; " to preach the word instant in season and out of season " (2 Tim. iv. 2). And so she leads us, by preaching and catechizing, and other modes of instruction, to take the Bible in our hands, and read it for ourselves.

In these and many similar modes, the Church is a witness, as well as a keeper of Holy Writ. We can hardly conceive a state of things in which it could be otherwise. If the Church had not carefully guarded the Scriptures at first, they would have been scattered and lost, and spurious writings would have partially taken the place of the true. If she did not, by her teaching and her ministry, witness to us that the Scriptures were from above, and so lead us to read and reverence them, we should be obliged to wait till the full maturity of reason and manhood before we could learn what was the word of truth, and should then have patiently to go through for ourselves all the evidence which might

[1] See Art. VI. Sect. II.

be necessary to convince us that the Bible, and not the Koran or the Veda, was that which contained " the lively oracles of God."

2. The Church has power to decree rites and ceremonies.

In the term " rites and ceremonies " of course we do not include things of the same nature as Sacraments, or other ordinances of the Gospel. Two Sacraments were ordained of Christ, and the Church cannot make others like them. Ordination is from Christ's authority, and we learn from Scripture that it is to be performed by imposition of hands. The Church cannot alter this, either by dispensing with it, or putting something different in its room. By " rites and ceremonies," therefore, are meant things comparatively indifferent in themselves, — the adjuncts and accidents, not the essence and substance of holy things.

Certain rules are specially prescribed to us in Holy Scripture for regulating public worship, and for ministering the ordinances of God. But these rules are mostly general, and the carrying out of them must be regulated by some authority or other. The rules given are such as the following: " Let all things be done decently and in order " (1 Cor. xiv. 26, 40). Yet how to arrange all things so that they should be done decently and in order, we are not always told. Occasionlly, indeed, the Apostles gave something like specific directions; as, for instance, St. James's command not to allow the poor to sit in a low place, and the rich in a good place (James ii. 1, 10) ; St. Paul's directions about the seemly administration of the Lord's Supper (1 Cor. xi. 17–33) ; and again, St. Paul's command that men should be uncovered and women veiled (1 Cor. xi. 4–16), and that women should keep silence in the churches (1 Cor, xiv. 34). Yet, though in these few points there may be something like fixed rules laid down, the Church is generally left to arrange so that in her public worship all things should be done " decently, in order, and to edifying," without specific directions for every particular. Nay! St. Paul, when so strongly insisting on men being uncovered and women covered, concludes by arguing that, if any people are disposed to be contentious on this head, they ought to yield their own judgment to the customs of the Church. " If any man seem to be contentious, we have no such custom, neither the Churches of God " (1 Cor. xi. 16). Thus, therefore, the very principle laid down in Scripture seems to be that the Church should order and arrange the details of public worship, so as may be most calculated to honour God and edify the people ; just as St. Paul left Titus at Crete " that he might set in order the things which were wanting " in the Church of that land

(Tit. i. 5). Indeed, unless by authority some rules for public worship were made, decency and order could never exist. Thus, whether prayer should be of set form or extempore — whether the minister should wear a peculiar dress — whether baptism should be by immersion or by pouring — whether at the Eucharist we should kneel or sit, and numerous other like questions, have all reference to rites and ceremonies. If the public authority of the Church could not enjoin anything concerning them, what utter confusion might exist in our assemblies! At one time prayer might be extempore, and at another from a prayer–book. One minister might wear a surplice, another an academic gown, a third his common walking-dress, and a fourth a cope, or some fantastic device of his own. One person might kneel, another stand, and another sit at receiving the Communion. Would any one coming in to such an assembly " report that God was in us of a truth ? " And with the variety of opinion and feeling among Christians, much worse than this might easily occur, if the Church had no power to decree its rites and ceremonies. Yet we are taught concerning this very matter of decent solemnity, that " God is not the author of confusion, but of peace, as in all the churches of the saints" (1 Cor. xiv. 33).

Thus then the injunctions of the Apostles, and the absolute necessity of the case, lead to the conclusion that the Church must have " power to decree rites and ceremonies." . And we may add, that all bodies of Christians, however opposed to ceremonial, have yet exercised the power of decreeing rites for their own bodies. However bare and free from ornament their public worship may be, yet in some way or other it is ordered and regulated, if it be public worship at all. Baptism and the Lord's Supper are ministered with some degree of regularity ; preaching and praying are arranged after some kind of order ; and how simple soever that order may be, it is an order derived from the authority of their own body, and not expressly prescribed in Scripture. Scripture teaches all things essential for salvation ; but all minutiæ of ceremonial it neither teaches nor professes to teach. Such therefore must be left, in some degree, to the authority and wisdom of the Church.[1]

3. The Church has, moreover, authority in controversies of faith.

This statement of the Article as necessarily follows from the nature of the case as the two already considered. It is only ne-

---

[1] See on this subject more especially Hooker, *Eccl. Pol.* Bk. iii.

cessary to keep in mind the qualifications which the latter part of the Article suggests.

Our Lord gave authority to His Church to bind and to loose, and to excommunicate those who would not hear the church. The Apostles enjoined that heretics, persons that teach false doctrine or deny the truth, should be shunned, excommunicated, and put out of the Church.[1] Now, if the Church has no power to determine what is true and what is false, such authority would be a dead letter, and the Apostles' injunctions would be vain. All heretics claim Scripture as on their side. If the Church is not allowed to exercise authority in controversies of faith, she could never reject heretics, unless indeed they went so far as to deny the truth of Scripture altogether. In order therefore to exercise that discipline and power of the Keys which Christ committed to her, the Church must have authority to decide on what is truth, and what is falsehood.

The Church is a society founded by God, for the very purpose of preserving, maintaining, and propagating the truth. If she had no power to discern truth from error, how would this be possible? Her ministers are enjoined to teach and to preach the truth of the Gospel; not simply to put the Bible into the hands of the people, and leave them to read it. Their commission is, " Go and teach all nations . . . . teaching them to observe all things whatsoever I have commanded you " (Matt. xxviii. 19, 20). They are " by sound doctrine to convince the gainsayers " (Tit. i. 9). They are " to feed the Church of God " (Acts xx. 28) : to give " the household of God their portion of meat in due season " (Luke xii. 42). The chief pastors of the Church are to " commit to faithful men, who shall be able to teach others also," that truth which they have themselves received (2 Tim. ii. 2). And they are enjoined to " rebuke men sharply, that they may be sound in the faith " (Tit. i. 13).

All this implies authority, — authority to declare truth, to maintain truth, to discern truth from error, to judge when controversies arise, whether one party is heretical or not, and to reject from communion such as are in grievous falsehood and error.

There are promises to the Church, and titles of the Church, which confirm these arguments. The Church is called " an holy temple in the Lord . . . . a habitation of God through the Spirit " (Eph. ii. 21, 22). Individual Christians believe that they shall

---

[1] Matt. xviii. 17, 18. Acts xx. 30. 2 Thess. iii. 6. 1 Tim. i. 3; vi. 3. Tit. i 11 ; iii. 10. See Art xix, Sect. ii. 5.

be guided into truth by the indwelling Spirit of God; how much more therefore that Church which is not only composed of the various individual Christians, who are partakers of the Spirit, but is also itself built up for God's Spirit to dwell in it? Our blessed Lord promises to His Church, that " the gates of hell shall never prevail against it " (Matt. xvi. 18); and that He will be with its pastors "always, even unto the end of the world " (Matt. xxviii. 20). Such a promise implies the constant presence, assistance, and guidance of Him who is the Church's Head, and His assurance that the power of evil shall never be able to destroy the faith of the Church, or take away God's truth from it; for, if once the faith of the Church should fail, the Church itself must fail with it. Hence the Church, having always the presence and guidance of Christ, the indwelling of His Spirit, and the assurance that the gates of hell shall never prevail against her; we must conclude that the Church will be guarded against anything like universal or fundamental error. And so we may say, that she not only is authorized to give judgments in matters of faith, but also has a promise of direction in judging.

This further appears from the Church being called " the pillar and ground of the truth " (1 Tim. iii. 15). Bishop Burnet contends that this is a metaphor, and that we must not argue too much on metaphor. But, if we never try to understand the figures of Scripture, we must neglect a very large and most important portion of Scripture. Indeed, almost all that is taught us about God and the world of spirits is taught us in figurative language, because it is above our common comprehension, and therefore conveyed to us by parables and metaphors. And the figure here is a very obvious one. It may mean a little more, or a little less, but its general meaning is plain enough. And that meaning surely is, that God has appointed His Church in the world, that it may hold fast, support, and maintain the truth: and not only is it *ordained* for this end, but as all God's ordinances are surely fitted for their purpose, so the Church is *qualified* also to uphold the truth which is committed to it.

Therefore we conclude, that by God's appointment, and according to plain language of Scripture, " the Church hath authority in controversies of faith."

II. But the authority of the Church is not a supreme and independent authority. In matters of faith, it is the authority of a judge, not the authority of a legislator. Truth comes from God

not from the Church. The written word of God is the record of
God's truth; and no other record exists. He alone is the Legislator, and the Scriptures contain the code of laws which He has
ordained. To maintain those laws and the truth connected with
them, and, so far as possible, to enforce them, is the duty of the
Church. But she has no authority either to alter or to add to
them.

She may judge therefore, but it must be according to the laws
which have been made for her. She has authority, but it is an
authority limited by the Scriptures of truth.

Such is the nature of all judicial power. We say the judges
of the land have authority to pronounce judgments; but they must
pronounce their judgments according to the law. They have no
power to alter it, no power to go beyond it. The only power
which they have, is to enforce and administer; and, where it is
obscure or doubtful, to do their best to interpret it.[1]

This is exactly the limitation which we find that the Article
truly assigns to the authority of the Church. She has power to
decree rites and ceremonies, and authority in controversies of
faith; but in thus doing: —

1. She must not ordain anything contrary to God's word written, nor explain one place of Scripture so as to contradict another.

2. Besides the written word, she ought not to enforce anything
to be believed for necessity of salvation.

The first limitation is self-apparent, if we admit the word of
God to be the word of God. For whatever authority be assigned
to the Church, it would be fearful impiety to give it authority
superior to God Himself. It is probable, that this limitation is
more particularly intended to apply to the power of ordaining
ceremonies, as the second applies to articles of faith. If so, it
means that the Church may ordain ceremonies in themselves indifferent, but she may not ordain any which would be repugnant
to the written word. Thus for example, it would mean that forms
of prayer, clerical vestments, and the like, are within the province
of the Church to decide upon; but image-worship, or the adoration
of the host, being contrary to the commandments of God, are beyond her power to sanction or permit.

The second limitation applies to doctrine, and is almost a repetition of a portion of Article VI. already considered.[2] It denies to

---

[1] In the early councils, it was customary to place the Gospels on a throne
or raised platform in the midst of the
assembly, to indicate that in them were
contained the rules by which the decisions of the council must be framed.

[2] "Holy Scripture containeth all things
necessary to salvation, so that whatso

the Church the power to initiate in matters of faith. She may not enforce upon her children new articles for which there is no authority in the Bible ; but may interpret Scripture, and enforce the articles of faith to be deduced from thence.

Hence we may see that the Article determines that there is but one supreme primary authority, that is to say, the written tradition of the will of God, the holy Scriptures, His lively oracles. The authority of the Church is ministerial and declaratory, not absolute and supreme. And the decisions of the Church must always be guided by, and dependent on, the statements and injunctions of the written word of God.[1]

ever is not read therein, nor may be proved thereby is not to be required of any man, or be thought required of any man, that it should be believed as an article of faith, or be thought requisite or necessary to salvation." — Art. vi.

[1] Neither the right nor the duty of *Private Judgment*, if properly understood, is interfered with by the statements of this Article. It is the duty of every Christian to search the Scriptures in order to learn God's will from them. Yet this neither supersedes the propriety of individuals paying deference to the judgment of the whole Church, nor does it preclude the Church from forming a judgment. It is the right and the wisdom of every citizen to acquaint himself with the laws of his country, and to endeavour to render them an intelligent obedience. Yet this does not take away from a competent authority or tribunal the right of pronouncing according to them. The following words of an eminent English divine seem to put the whole question in its true light, and in the light in which our Church has constantly viewed it : " Far am I, by what I have now said, from endeavouring to weaken or undermine the rights of ecclesiastical authority. We do readily acknowledge that every Christian Church in the world has a right and authority to decide controversies in religion that do arise among its members, and consequently to declare the sense of Scripture concerning those controversies. And though we say that every private Christian hath a liberty left him of examining and judging for himself, and which cannot, which ought not to be taken from him ; yet every member of a Church ought to submit to the Church's decisions and declarations so as not to oppose them, not to break the communion or the peace of the Church upon account of them, unless in such cases where obedience and compliance is apparently sinful and against God's laws." — Archbishop Sharp, *Works*, v. p. 63. Oxf. 1829.

[One great difficulty concerning the authority of the Church in matters of faith arises from the fact that many people seem to expect to hear the Church speaking with definite precise statements in answer to every doubt that may arise, or every question we may choose to put to her ; or else they imagine that to be what is or ought to be claimed by the believers in an authoritative Church. But observe : —

1. The only Church that claims to possess that kind of authority has contradicted herself, repeatedly. (See Janus, " The Pope and the Council, cap. iii. sect. 3.)

2. That kind of power was never promised to the Church. (St. Matt. xvi. 18, xxviii. 20.)

3. The promises referred to justify us in expecting a general indefectibility, not a special and particular infallibility.

4. This is all that is possible without a second Incarnation ; for which, accordingly, Dr. Manning (*The Temporal Mission of the Holy Ghost*) against all facts, contends.

5. This authority, is not a vague thing of no practical consequence, but covers all the essentials of Doctrine and Discipline.

6. The voice of the Church is not gathered from a single utterance, but from general consent or from a single utterance ratified by general consent according to the rule of S. Vincent of Lerins. *Common.* caps. ii. iii. — *J. W.*]

ARTICLE XXI.

Of the Authority of General Councils.

GENERAL Councils may not be gather-ed together without the commandment and will of Princes. And when they be gathered together (forasmuch as they be an assembly of men, whereof all be not governed with the Spirit and Word of God), they may err, and sometimes have erred, even in things pertaining unto God. Wherefore things ordained by them as necessary to Salvation have nei-ther strength nor authority, unless it may be declared that they be taken out of Holy Scriptures.

De Authoritate Conciliorum generalium.

GENERALIA concilia sine jussu et volun tate Principum congregari non possunt; et ubi convenerint, quia ex hominibus constant, qui non omnes Spiritu et Ver-bo Dei reguntur, et errare possunt, et interdum errarunt etiam in his quæ ad Deum pertinent; ideoque quæ ab illis constituuntur, ut ad salutem necessaria, neque robur habent, neque authoritatem, nisi ostendi possint e sacris literis esse desumpta.

[This Article is omitted in the American Revision, "because it is partly of a local and civil nature, and is provided for, as to the remaining parts of it, in other Articles." Not a very sufficient reason for an unfortunate omission.

As some persons have argued from the omission, in 1562 and 1571, of Articles XLI. and XLII. of 1552, that the Church of England intended to allow Millenari-anism and Universalism, so others have urged, that, by omitting this Article, the American Church, if it did not assert, at least allowed the infallibility of a General Council. The one line of argument is worth as much as the other, both being worthless. — *J. W.*]

WE saw, in considering the last Article, that our Lord Jesus Christ had given a certain promise of guidance and inde-fectibility to His Church, by which we may conclude, that the whole Church shall never utterly fail or be absorbed in one gulf of error. We saw too, that the Church had a right to judge in controversies of faith, so as to expel from her communion those whom she determined to be fundamentally wrong.

If these premises be true, the voice and judgment of the Church universal must be of great value and importance, not as superseding but as interpreting Scripture. And this voice of the Church has been considered to be audible, in the general consent of Christians of all, and more especially of early times. Those doctrines which the Church of Christ at all times, everywhere, and universally, has received, have been esteemed the judgment of the Catholic Church. This is the universality, antiquity, and agreement, the "semper, ubique et ab omnibus" of Vincentius Lirinensis.[1] It is true, no doctrine of the faith has been received so universally that it never has been spoken or written against. But a large number of doctrines (all, in fact, clearly enunciated in the Creeds) have been upheld by the vast majority of Christians from the beginning to the present day. There never was a time, not even the short-lived but fearful reign of Arianism, in which the Church in general did not hold all these doctrines; and those who dissented from them formed a comparatively small, if not always an insignificant, minority. And as regards these fundamental truths, there would never be any difficulty in following the rule which Vincentius gives in explanation of his own canon, namely, "If a small part of the Church holds a private error, we should adhere to the whole. If the whole be for the time infected by some novel opinion, we should cleave to antiquity. If in antiquity itself there be found partial error, we should then prefer universal decisions before private judgments." [2] This rule will embrace all the Articles of the Creeds of the Church. But new errors may arise, and men's minds may be sadly perplexed by them, and difficulties of various kinds may spring up, in which the voice of the Christian Church may never have plainly spoken; and the question may almost of necessity occur, Shall the abettors of such or such an opinion be esteemed heretics or not, be continued in, or rejected from, the communion of Christians? In such cases, which may be cases of great emergency, the only way in which the Church can speak is by a council of representatives.

Among the Jews, questions of importance and difficulty were referred to the Sanhedrim, a council of seventy-one elders, which sat at Jerusalem. In the Christian Church, the first example of such an assembly is what has by some been called the first general council, held by the Apostles and elders and brethren at Jerusalem, concerning the question of circumcising the Gentile converts (Acts xv.).

Afterwards we hear of no council for some considerable period. But during the third century several provincial synods sat, for the

---

[1] Vincentius Lirinens. *Commonit.* c. 2.

[2] " Quid igitur faciet Christianus Catholicus, si se aliqua ecclesiæ particula ab universalis fidei communione præciderit ? Quid utique nisi ut pestifero corruptoque membro sanitatem universi corporis anteponat ? Quid si novella aliqua contagio non jam portiunculam tantum, sed totam pariter ecclesiam commaculare conetur ? Tunc etiam providebit, ut antiquitati inhæreat, quæ prorsus jam non potest ab ulla novitatis fraude seduci. Quid si in ipsa vetustate, duorum aut trium hominum, vel certe civitatis unius aut etiam provinciæ alicujus error deprehendatur ? Tunc omnino curabit ut paucorum temeritati vel inscitiæ si qua sunt universaliter antiquitus universalis Concilii decreta præponat," &c. — *Commonit.* c. 3.

determining of matters either of doctrine or discipline. Thus Victor held a council at Rome, A. D. 196, concerning the keeping of Easter; in which year other councils were held, in other places, on the same subject. St. Cyprian held several councils at Carthage, on the subject of the lapsed, and the rebaptizing of heretics (A. D. 253, 254, 255.) Councils were held at Antioch, A. D. 264, 265, to condemn and excommunicate Paul of Samosata. And many others for similar purposes were convened, in their respective provinces, during the third and early part of the fourth century. Yet hitherto they were but partial and provincial, not general councils of the whole Church. At last, during the disturbances which were created by the propagation of the Arian heresy, Constantine the Great, having been converted to Christianity, and giving the countenance of the imperial government to the hitherto persecuted Church of Christ, summoned a general council of all the bishops of Christendom, to pronounce the judgment of the Church Catholic concerning the Divinity of the Son of God. The council met A. D. 325. The number of bishops that assembled at this great synod is generally stated to have been 318, besides priests and deacons. The council decided by an immense majority for the doctrine of the ὁμοούσιον, drew up the Nicene Creed, and published twenty canons on matters of discipline.

1. This was the first general or œcumenical council. Following this were five others, also generally received as œcumenical. 2. The council of Constantinople, summoned by the Emperor Theodosius, A. D. 381, which condemned Macedonius, and added the latter part to the creed of Nice. 3. The council of Ephesus, called by the younger Theodosius, A. D. 431, which condemned Nestorius. 4. The council of Chalcedon, called by Marcianus, A. D. 451, which condemned Eutyches. 5. The second of Constantinople, summoned by the Emperor Justinian, A. D. 553, confirmatory of the councils of Ephesus and Chalcedon. 6. The third of Constantinople, convened by the Emperor Constantine Pogonatus, A. D. 680, which condemned the Monothelites.

These six are the only councils which have been acknowledged by the Universal Church. There are two or three others, called œcumenical by the Greek Church, and many called œcumenical by the Latin Church, which, however, have never received universal approval.[1] Even the fifth and sixth have not been quite so univer-

---

[1] The Greeks number eight general councils, adding to the above six the second council of Nice under Irene and her son Constantine, A. D. 787, and the fourth of Constantinople, A. D. 869, under the Emperor Basil.

sally esteemed as the first four. The fifth, though generally acknowledged in the East, was for a time doubted by several of the
Western bishops. Gregory the Great said he reverenced the first
four synods as he did the four Evangelists ; evidently considering
those four as far more important than those which followed them.[1]
And the reformers, both foreign and Anglican, and probably the
divines of the English Church in general, have more unhesitatingly
received the first four, than the fifth and sixth councils ; though it
has been thought that the reason for this may be, that the fifth and
sixth were considered as merely supplementary to the preceding
two, and therefore as virtually included in them.

1. These few well-known and unquestioned facts are, of themselves sufficient to give us an insight into the nature, constitution,
and authority of general councils. In the first three centuries no
general council was ever held. The reason of this may be mani-
fold. In the first century Apostles were yet alive, whose inspired
authority could have been subject to no appeal. Indeed the meeting of Apostles and elders at Jerusalem may be called a council ;
but its force is derived, not merely from Christ's promise of guidance to His Church, but also from His assurance of inspiration to
His apostles. Then, too, the Church was small ; Jerusalem was the
visible centre of unity ; the Apostles gathered together there could
readily, by common consent, meet and unite in expression of their
decisions. But a century later, and the Church was spread from
India in the east, to Gaul and Lusitania in the west; from Ethiopia
southward, to the remotest northern Isles of Britain. There was
singular difficulty in all its bishops meeting in one spot. A general
gathering of all the spiritual heads of Christendom would have been,
like enough, a signal for general persecution. There was no one
power which could summon all together, and which all would be
bound to obey.[2] And therefore it would have been morally, and
perhaps physically impossible to gather a council from all portions
of the Church. But when not only was the Roman empire subject
to one man, but that one man became the patron and protector of
the Church, his power enabled him to enjoin all bishops who were
his subjects to meet him, or to send deputies to a general synod ;
and his safe-conduct assured against the violence, at least of heathen
persecutors. Hence, by the very nature of the case, general coun-

---

[1] Gregor. *Epist. ad. Joann. Constan-
tinop. Episc. Epistol.* Lib. i. c. 24.
[2] I must assume that the Bishop of
Rome had not that supremacy which
the Pope has since claimed and exercised ; though this is not the place to
prove the assumption.

cils were at first never summoned, and when summoned, it was by
" the commandment and will of princes."

Formidable heresies had risen before, but at first they were sufficiently met by the zeal and energy of catholic bishops; then local
synods condemned and suppressed them.   But the rise of Arianism
required a more stringent remedy, and a more distinct declaration
of the voice of the Church.   The evils of Arianism were not confined to Arius and his followers.   Macedonians, Nestorians, Eutychians, Monothelites, all sprang out of the same grievous controversies ; and the six general synods were successively summoned for
the end of pruning off these various offshoots of the one noxious
plant.

So then general synods were the result of peculiar exigencies,
and were summoned by the only power which could constrain general obedience, — obedience that is of meeting to deliberate, not, it
is to be hoped, of deciding according to the imperial standard of
truth.   This constituted them, so far as they were so, general and
œcumenical.   When the Bishop of Rome had attained to the full
height of his sacerdotal and imperial authority, claiming an universal
dominion over the Church of Christ, by virtue of succession to the
primacy of St. Peter, he began to exercise the power, for many
centuries enjoyed only by the emperors, of calling together general
councils of the Church, himself presiding in them.   The question
of presidency we may lay aside, as we have to deal only with the
right to summon.   Now, it is quite true that there was no inherent
and inalienable right in the Roman emperor, nor in any other secular prince, to summon ecclesiastical synods.   Therefore the bare
fact of their being summoned by the emperor, gave them no special authority.   But the imperial was the only power which could
command general obedience.   Hence, when the emperor summoned, all portions of Christendom obeyed ; and so a council, as
nearly as possible œcumenical, was gathered together.   But when
the Pope claimed the same authority, the result was not the same.
The bishops of the Roman obedience felt bound to attend, when
the chief pontiff summoned them ; but the eastern prelates felt no
such obligation, and the bishops belonging to the ancient patriarchates of Constantinople, Antioch, and Alexandria refused to attend
to a command issuing from the Patriarch of Rome.   The ground,
therefore, on which this Article asserts that princes only have a
right to summon general councils is that such only have power to
compel attendance at them.   Neither the Greek nor the reformed
Churches admit the authority claimed by the Pope, and therefor℈

their bishops would not assemble at his command. There is no single individual governor, nor any ten or twelve ecclesiastical governors, who, if they agree together, could with authority summon a council. All bishops are *de jure* equal and independent, and might refuse to obey citations from other bishops; and their refusals would invalidate the authority of the council called.

At the time of the Reformation there was a great effort to call a free general council. Luther appealed to such. So did our own Cranmer. But it was to a real and free council. The pope summoned the Council of Trent; but the reformers refused to acknowledge his authority to call it, or to admit that, so called, it was a real council of the whole Church. Soon after the Church of England had thrown off the supremacy of the Bishop of Rome, declarations to the above effect were made by English bishops and by convocation. The words of the latter are, " We think that neither the Bishop of Rome, nor any one prince of what estate, degree, or preëminence soever he be, may, by his own authority, call, indict, or summon any general council, without the express consent, assent, and agreement of the residue of Christian princes." [1] Their argument is, that when the Roman emperor had absolute and universal control, his commandment alone was sufficient to insure the attendance of bishops from all quarters of the world. But now there is no such supreme authority. The pope claims it; but it is an usurpation. The only conceivable mode of insuring universality now would be, that all Christian princes in all parts of Christendom should agree together to send bishops to represent their respective Churches; and such an agreement would correspond with the ancient mode of convoking councils, as nearly as in the present state of things is possible.[2] A supreme spiritual authority, such as is claimed by the pope, we do not acknowledge; but as all bishops are subject to their respective sovereigns, the joint will of all Christian princes might produce an œcumenical synod; but no other plan of proceeding seems likely to do so.

2. But when councils are gathered together, from whence do they derive their authority? There is no distinct promise of infal-

---

[1] " The judgment of Convocation concerning general Councils." It is signed by " Thomas Cromwell, Thomas Cantuariensis, Johannes London, with thirteen bishops; and of abbots, priors, archdeacons, deans, proctors, clerks, and other ministers, forty-nine." See Appendix to Cranmer's *Works*, iv. p. 258; also Burnet, *Reform.* i. App. B. iii. No. 5; Collier, *Eccl. Hist.* ii. App. 2037.

[2] See also " The Opinion of certain of the Bishops and clergy of this realm, subscribed with their hands touching the general Council," probably A. D. 1537. It is signed by Cranmer as archbishop, eight other bishops, the Abbot of Westminster, and three others.— Jenkyns's *Cranmer*, iv. p. 266.

libility to councils in Scripture. Nay ! there is probably no distinct allusion to councils at all. To the bishops and rulers of the Church indeed there is a promise of Christ's guidance and presence, and Christians are enjoined to " obey " and " follow the faith " " of those who have the rule over them." [1] Hence the judgment of our own spiritual guides is much to be attended to ; and when our spiritual rulers meet together and agree on matters either of doctrine or discipline, there is no question but that their decisions are worthy of all consideration and respect. Yet infallibility is certainly not promised to any one bishop or pastor, and though they are assured of Christ's presence and guidance, yet promises of this kind are all more or less conditional ; and it is only to the universal Church that the assurance belongs, " the gates of hell shall not prevail against it." Individual bishops, we know, may err. Hence assemblies of individual bishops may err ; because, though they have the grace of ordination, yet all may not be pious men, " governed with the Spirit and word of God." [2]

If indeed all the chief pastors of the Church could meet together and all agree, we might perhaps be justified in considering their decision as the voice of the universal Church ; and the promises of Christ to His Church are such as might lead us to believe that that Church could not universally be heretical, and therefore that its universal judgment must be sound. But no synod ever had, nor perhaps ever can have, such conditions as these. Those hitherto held have consisted of a minority of the bishops of the whole Church ; and most important portions of the Church have been but very slenderly represented. Though, therefore, one bishop may be supposed to represent many others ; yet even in political matters we often feel an assembly of deputies to speak but imperfectly the voice of a people, and in ecclesiastical and spiritual things this must be much more probable. We cannot say then, that the whole Church speaks by the voices of a minority of her bishops, even when they are quite agreed.

Again, it is not quite certain that our Lord's promises to His Church render it impossible that the major part of that Church should for a time be corrupted by error. God gave many and great promises to Israel ; and yet at one time there were but seven thousand knees that had not bowed to Baal. The promises indeed assure us that the Church shall not become totally corrupt, nor

---

[1] Heb. xiii. 7, 17. Compare Acts xx. 28–31 ; Tit. i. 13 ; iii. 10, &c.
[2] See the sentiments of Bishop Ridley to this effect, corresponding to the word-

ing of the Article. — Ridley's *Works*, p. 130, Parker Society edition, Cambridge 1841.

continue so finally. But we have seen, that Vincentius himself supposes the possibility of the Church for a time being largely, and indeed in the greater part of it, led astray by some novelty of doctrine. Now a council composed of a minority of bishops of the Church might, in a corrupt age, consist of those very bishops who had embraced the novelties, from which the great body of the Church was not then exempt. What would then be the value of the decisions of such a council? We may perhaps reasonably hope, that the gracious and superintending Providence of Christ would never allow the Church, which is His Body, and of which He is the present and animating Head, to be so represented, or misrepresented. But there is nothing in the nature of councils to assure us against such an evil. Councils have hitherto always consisted of a minority. Even that minority has not always been unanimous; and it might be, that the same minority might represent the worse, instead of the sounder part of the Church, in a corrupt and ignorant age.

We hear enough of councils, even in the best ages, to know that the proceedings at them have not always been the wisest, or the most charitable; that some of those who attended them were not the most highly to be respected; and that other motives, besides zeal for the truth, have had too much influence in them. The words of Gregory Nazianzen are famous: " If I must write the truth," he says, " I am disposed to avoid every assembly of bishops; for of no synod have I seen a profitable end; rather an addition to, than a diminution of, evils; for the love of strife and the thirst for superiority are beyond the power of words to express." [1] Every reader of Church history must feel that there is too much truthfulness in this picture.

The question then arises, of what use are universal synods? and what authority are we to assign them? The answer is, that so far as they speak the language of the universal Church, and are accredited by the Church, so far they have the authority, which we saw under the last Article to be inherent in the Church, of deciding in controversies of faith. Now we can only know that they speak the language of the Church when their decrees meet with universal acceptance, and are admitted by the whole body of Christians to be certainly true. Every general council which has received this stamp to its decisions may be esteemed to speak the

---

[1] ἐχω μὲν οὕτως. εἰ δεῖ τἀληθὲς γράφειν, ὥστε πάντα σύλλογον φεύγειν ἐπίσκοπων, ὅτι μηδεμιᾶς συνόδου τέλος εἶδον χρηστόν· μηδὲ λύσιν κακῶν μᾶλλον ἐσχηκυίας, ἢ προσθήκην. Αἱ γὰρ φιλονεικίαι καὶ φιλαρχίαι· ἀλλ' ὅπως μηδὲ φορτικὸν ὑπολάβῃς οὕτω γράφοντα· καὶ λόγου κρείττονες, κ. τ. λ. — Epist. 55, Procopio. Tom. I. p. 814, Colon. 1690.

language of the universal Church; and as in some cases the judgment of the universal Church could not otherwise have been elicited, therefore we must admit their importance and necessity. Now the first six, or at least the first four, general councils have received this sanction of universal consent to their decisions. Their decrees were sent round throughout the Christian world; they were received and approved of by all the different national Churches of Europe, Asia, and Africa; the errors condemned by them were then, and ever have been, counted heresies; and the creeds set forth by them have been acknowledged, reverenced, and constantly repeated in the Liturgy, by every orthodox Church from that time to this.[1]

Thus then the true general synods have received an authority which they had not in themselves. "It is," as the Lutheran Confession expresses it, "the legitimate way of healing dissension in the Church to refer ecclesiastical controversies to synods."[2] But those synods have universal authority only when they receive catholic consent. When the Church at large has universally received their decrees, then are they truly general councils, and their authority equal to the authority of the Church itself.

Supposing then a synod to assemble, and to draw up articles of doctrine, or rules of discipline, even though it have been legally assembled by an authority qualified to convene it, and to insure attendance at it, still we hold it possible that it should err, not only in its mode of reasoning, or in matters indifferent, but "even in things pertaining to God." Hence, when its decrees came forth, especially if they concerned things " necessary to salvation," we should not esteem them to have strength nor authority " until they were compared with Holy Scripture, and could be declared to be taken out " of it. The council itself would be bound to decide on the grounds of Scripture, no power having the right to prescribe anything as " requisite or necessary to salvation, which is not read therein, nor may be proved thereby." The Church would be bound to examine the decisions of the council itself, on the grounds of Scripture, and would not be justified in receiving those decisions unless it found that they were " taken out of Holy Scripture." But when the Church had fully received, and stamped

---

[1] Not only episcopal churches have so admitted the decrees of the general councils, but that the reformers and reformed bodies of Christians in Germany, Switzerland, &c. have admitted them, may appear both from their confessions and the writings of their divines — e. g.

see *Corfess. August.* **Art. xxi.**; *Sylloge*, p. 189; Calvin, *Institut.* iv. ix. 8, 13.

[2] " Hæc est usitata et legitima via in ecclesia dirimendi dissensiones, videlicet ad synodos referre controversias ecclesiasticas." — *Conf. August.* ubi supra.

with its approval the acts of the council, then would they assume the form of judgments of the Church concerning the doctrines of Scripture.[1] This was the case with the great Councils of Nice Constantinople, Ephesus, and Chalcedon. They put forth their decisions as their interpretations of the word of God. They enjoined nothing " as necessary to salvation," but what they " declared to have been taken out of Holy Scripture." All Christendom received their interpretations as sound and true : and, from that day to this, they have been admitted by the Catholic Church as true articles of faith. This has stamped them with an authority of Scriptural truth, and Catholic consent, of which the constitution of the Councils themselves could not give us full certainty and assurance.[2]

3. Concerning the assertion of the Article, that " some general councils have erred," Bishop Burnet justly observes that it " must be understood of councils that pass for such." The later councils summoned by the Pope, and acknowledged only by the Western Churches and those in obedience to Rome, were commonly called General Councils at the time of the Reformation, as they still are in the Roman Church, though never acknowledged by the Churches of the East.[3]

Of these, the fourth Council of Lateran, under Innocent III. A. D. 1215, asserted the doctrine of Transubstantiation.[4] The Council of Constance, A. D. 1414, forbade the cup to the laity.[5] The Council of Florence, A. D. 1439, decreed the doctrine of Purgatory.[6] The Council of Trent added to the Nicene Creed a confession of belief in seven sacraments, Transubstantiation, Purgatory, Invocation of Saints, Image-worship, &c. &c.

The decrees of these councils, though called general, have never received the assent of the Eastern Churches, and cannot therefore be of universal authority. None of the above-mentioned doctrines,

---

[1] Calvin, as above referred to, says : " Sic priscas illas synodos, ut Nicænam, Constantinopolitanam, Ephesinam primam, Chalcedonensem, ac similes, quæ confutandis erroribus habitæ sunt, libenter amplectimur, reveremurque ut sacrosanctas, quantum attinet ad fidei dogmata : nihil enim continent quam puram et nativam Scripturæ interpretationem quam sancti patres, spirituali prudentia, ad frangendos religionis hostes, qui tunc emerserant, accommodarunt."—*Institut.* IV. ix. 8. Compare *Confess. Helvet.* Art. XI.; *Sylloge*, pp. 41, 42.
[2] On the subject of the authority of general synods, see Palmer, *On the Church,*

Part IV. ch. 8 ; whose view is the same as that taken in the text.
[3] According to the Roman Church the First Council of Lateran summoned by Pope Calixtus II. A. D. 1123, was the 9th general Council. The other general councils allowed by the Latin Church are, Second Lateran, A. D. 1139. Third Lateran, 1179. Fourth Lateran, 1215. Lyons, 1245. Lyons, 1274. Vienne, 1311. Constance, 1414. Basle, 1431. Florence, 1439. Fifth Lateran, 1512. Trent, 1546.
[4] Conc. Lateran, IV Can. I.
[5] Sess. XIII.
[6] Concil. Florent. *De Purgat.*

which they sanctioned, can be found in Scripture, but may all be proved to be contrary to Scripture. They are all denied in those Articles of our own Church which we have next to consider, and which we shall have to justify from Holy Writ. Hence, we can have no difficulty in concluding, that some (so-called) General Councils have erred, even in things pertaining to God.

[NOTE. The statement that General Councils may not be gathered "without the commandment and will of Princes," probably caused the omission of this Article in the American revision.

It should be remembered, however, that it is aimed against the Papal usurpation, and interference with the Civil power. The Pope — as in the famous dispute of Boniface VIII. and Philip le Bel — claimed the right of calling the clergy out of the several countries in which they lived, without the consent of the civil power, and the words above quoted were intended to meet this claim. So Bishop Burnet, Dr. Hey, Mr. Hardwicke, and even Mr. Newman in Tract XC. explain them.

The student should specially bear in mind (a) the proper work of a General Council, and (b) its proper authentication.

The first is, not to invent new Articles of faith, but to testify to, to set forth more carefully, and to guard antecedent truth. So that, while it is not an *infal lible judge*, it may be a *faithful witness*. The second is found, not in the confirmation of the Pope or any other person, but in the acceptance of the Council by the entire Church. As to the rules laid down by some Romish writers, that a General Council must be called by the Pope, that he must preside, &c. they are all confuted by a simple reference to the four great General Councils. If those rules are sound, they were not General Councils; if they were General Councils, those rules are un founded. — *J. W.*]

ARTICLE XXII.

Of Purgatory.	*De Purgatorio.*
THE Romish doctrine concerning purgatory, pardons, worshipping and adoration, as well of images, as of reliques, and also invocation of saints, is a fond thing, vainly invented, and grounded upon no warranty of Scripture, but rather repugnant to the Word of God.	DOCTRINA Romanensium de purgatorio, de indulgentiis, de veneratione, tum imaginum, tum reliquiarum, necnon de invocatione sanctorum, res est futilis, inaniter conficta, et nullis Scripturarum testimoniis innititur; immo verbo Dei contradicit.

SECTION I. — HISTORY.

THE three preceding Articles concerned the Church visible. This treats of the Church invisible.

The only difference between the wording of this Article and the XXIIId of Edward VI. is, that whereas this has "The Romish doctrine," that had "The doctrine of the school-authors."

The Article is so comprehensive that many volumes might be written upon it. It will be necessary therefore to study brevity. It evidently treats of two principal points. I. Purgatory, and the pardons or indulgences connected with the doctrine concerning it. II. The Worship of images and relics, and the Invocation of Saints.

I. 1. Purgatory.

Under the IIId Article we saw that the Jews and the early Christians uniformly believed in an intermediate state between death and judgment. But their language and expectations, at least those of the earliest fathers, are inconsistent with a belief that any of the pious were in a state of suffering, or that the sufferings of the wicked were but for a time only.

Clemens Romanus says, that "Those who have finished their course in charity, according to the grace of Christ, possess the region of the godly, who shall be manifested in the visitation of the Kingdom of Christ." [1]   Justin Martyr says, "The souls of the godly remain in a certain better place, the unjust and wicked in a worse,

---

[1] ἔχουσιν χώραν εὐσεβῶν. — Clem. *Ad Cor.* i. 50.

awaiting the day of judgment."[1]   Irenæus argues from the parable
of Dives and Lazarus, that "each sort of men receive, even before
the judgment, their due place of abode."[2]   Tertullian speaks of
Paradise "as a place of divine pleasantness, destined to receive the
spirits of the just."[3]   So Cyprian, "it is for him to fear death who
is unwilling to go to Christ."[4]   "Do not suppose death the same
thing to the just and the unjust.   The just are called to a refresh-
ing, the unjust are hurried away to torment; speedily safety is
given to the faithful, to the unfaithful punishment."[5]   This, he
shows, is not peculiar to martyrs or eminent saints.   "Abraham,
Isaac, and Jacob, did not suffer martyrdom, yet were honoured
first among the patriarchs ; and to their company every one is
gathered, who is believing and righteous and praiseworthy."[6]

We may, however, early trace a belief that, as death itself was a
part of the curse, so every one was to look forward, not for the rest
of the intermediate state, but for the joys of the resurrection ; a
delay of the resurrection, and a continuance of the death of the
body, being esteemed in itself penal, and the result of sin.   Indeed,
St. Paul (2 Cor. v. 2, 4, 6) taught, that to be unclothed was an
evil; though it would be better to be "absent from the body," since
thereby we might be "present with the Lord."   Hence, Irenæus
speaks of the time between death and judgment as "a period of
condemnation, resulting from man's disobedience."[7]   And Tertullian says, that "sin, though small in amount, may be to be punished
by delay of the resurrection : "[8] of which passage more hereafter.

This leads to the consideration of *Prayer for the Dead*.   There
can be no question that this custom very early prevailed among
Christians.   It is first mentioned by Tertullian, who speaks of the
common practice of the Church to make oblations for the dead on

[1] τὰς μὲν τῶν εὐσεβῶν ψυχὰς ἐν κρείττονί
ποι χώρῳ μένειν, κ. τ. λ. — *Dial.* p. 223 ;
*Conf. Quæst. et Respons. ad Orthodox. Jus-
tino Imputat.* qu. 5.
[2] "Dignam habitationem unamquamque gentem percipere etiam ante judicium." — Lib. ii. 63.   Compare Lib. v.
31, quoted above, p. 97.
[3] "Locum divinæ amœnitatis recipiendis sanctorum spiritibus destinatum."
— *Apol.* i. 47.
[4] "Ejus est mortem timere qui ad Christum nolit ire."— Cyp. *De Mortalitate*, p.
157, Oxon. 1682.
[5] "Non est quod putetis bonis et malis
interitum esse communem.   Ad refrigerium justi vocantur, ad supplicium rapi-
untur injusti : datur velocius tutela fiden-
tibus, perfidis pœna." — Ibid. p. 161.

[6] "Ad quorum convivium congregatur
quisquis fidelis et justus et laudabilis invenitur." — Ibid. p. 163.
The reasoning of the whole treatise *De
Mortalitate* is of the same kind, and quite
inconsistent with a belief that good men
going out of this life have a penal state
to undergo before attaining to rest and
happiness.
[7] "Ut quemadmodum caput resurrexit
a mortuis, sic et reliquum corpus omnis
hominis qui invenitur in vita, impleto
tempore condemnationis ejus, quæ erat
propter inobedientiam, resurgat."— Iren.
iii. 21.
[8] "Modicum quoque de ictum mora resurrectionis illic luendum " — *De Anima*,
c. 58.

the anniversary of the day of their death, which they called their birthday ; who says also, that widows prayed for the souls of their husbands that they might have refreshment and a part in the first resurrection.[1] The like is mentioned by Origen,[2] Cyprian,[3] Cyril of Jerusalem,[4] Gregory Nazianzen,[5] Ambrose,[6] Chrysostom,[7] and others of the earliest fathers ; and prayers and thanksgivings for the dead occur in all the ancient Liturgies, as in that to be found in the Apostolical Constitutions, in the Liturgies of St. James, St. Mark, St. Basil, St. Chrysostom, &c.

On this early practice, dating unquestionably from the second century, the school-authors and the Romanist divines ground one of their strongest arguments to prove that a belief in Purgatory was primitive and apostolic. For why, say they, were prayers offered for the dead, unless they could profit them ? and how could they profit them, except by delivering from the pains of Purgatory, or shortening their duration ?

Yet it is to be observed, that many of the very prayers alleged by the Roman Catholic controversialists do of themselves prove that those who composed them could not have believed the persons prayed for to be in purgatory. The prayers for the dead in the ancient Liturgies are offered for all the greatest saints, for the Virgin Mary, the Apostles and martyrs, whom even the Roman Church has never supposed to be in purgatory. Thus the Clementine Liturgy, found in the Apostolical Constitutions,[8] has the words, " We offer to Thee (i. e. we pray) for all the saints who have pleased Thee from the beginning of the world ; the patriarchs, prophets, righteous men, apostles, martyrs," &c. The Liturgy called St. Chrysostom's prays for all departed in the faith, patriarchs, prophets, apostles, &c. : and " especially for the holy, immaculate, blessed Theotokos, and ever-virgin Mary." [9] This alone is sufficient to prove that prayer for the dead did not presuppose Purgatory, and was in no degree necessarily connected with it. Indeed, many of the ancients who speak of praying for the dead positively declare their firm belief that those for whom they prayed were in peace, rest, and blessedness, and therefore certainly not in fire and tor-

---

[1] " Oblationes pro defunctis, pro natalitiis annua die facimus." — De Corona Milit. c. 3. " Pro anima ejus orat, et refrigerium interim adpostulat ei, et in prima resurrectione consortium, et offert annuis diebus dormitionis ejus." — De Monogamia, c. 10.

[2] Lib. ix. In Rom. xii.

[3] Epist. 34, Edit. Fell, 39, p. 77.

[4] Catech. Myst. v. 6, 7.

[5] Orat. in Cæsar. juxta fin.

[6] Epist. ii. 8, Ad Faustinum.

[7] Hom. 41, in 1 ad Corinth.

[8] Constitut. Apostol. Lib. viii. cap. 12.

[9] ἐξαιρέτως τῆς παναγίας, ἀχράντου, ὑπερευλογημένης δεσποίνης ἡμῶν Θεοτόκου καὶ ἀειπαρθένου Μαρίας. — Chrysost. Liturq. Græc.

ment; [1] and it is not too much to affirm, that none of the ancient prayers had anything like an allusion to a Purgatory. Nay, even in the ancient Roman missals were the words, "Remember, O Lord, Thy servants which have gone before us with the sign of faith, and *sleep in the sleep of peace;* To them, O Lord, and to all *that are in rest in Christ*, we beseech Thee to grant a place of refreshment, of light and peace." [2]

It has been so common to admit the false premiss of the Romanist divines, (namely, that prayer for the dead presupposes a Purgatory,) that it is to many minds difficult to understand on what principles the early Christians used such prayers. One of those principles was, doubtless, that all things to us unknown are to us future. Present and future are but relative ideas. To God nothing is future; all things are present. But to man, that is future of which he is ignorant. As then we know not with absolute certainty the present condition or final doom of those who are departed; their present condition is relatively, and their final doom, absolutely, future to our minds. Hence, it was thought, we are justified in praying that it may be good, even though the events of their past life may have already decided it. Again, the Resurrection is yet to come, and therefore the full bliss of the departed is yet future. Hence the ancients prayed for a hastening of the Resurrection, much in the spirit of our own Burial Service, and of the petition in the Lord's Prayer, "Thy kingdom come." [3] Thus St. Ambrose prayed for the Emperors Gratian and Valentinian, that God would "raise them up with a speedy resurrection." [4] And the Liturgies constantly ask a speedy and a happy resurrection to those who have died in the Lord. [5]

Another portion of these prayers was Eucharistic or thanksgiving; whereby they gave God thanks both for the martyrs and for all that had died in the faith and fear of God; [6] and these com-

---

[1] See this shown in very numerous instances by Archbishop Usher, *Answer to a Jesuit*, ch. vii., and by Bingham, *E. A.* Bk. xv. ch. iii. § 16.

[2] "Memento etiam, Domine, famulorum famularumque tuarum, qui nos præcesserunt cum signo fidei, et dormiunt in somno pacis. Ipsis, Domine, et omnibus in Christo quiescentibus, locum refrigerii lucis et pacis ut indulgeas deprecamur."— *Bibl. Patr.* Gr. Lat. Tom. ii. p. 129, quoted by Usher and Bingham, as above.

[3] See Bp. Bull, Sermon iii. *Works,* i. p. 71, Oxf. 1827.

[4] "Te quæso, summe Deus, ut charis-simos juvenes matura resurrectione suscites et resuscites."— Ambros. *De Obit. Valentini, in ipso fine;* Usher, as above.

[5] See numerous examples, quoted by Usher as above.

[6] "The term of εὐχαριστήριος εὐχή, 'a thanksgiving prayer,' I borrow from the writer of the Ecclesiastical Hierarchy, (Dionys. *Eccles. Hierarch.* cap. vii.) who, in the description of the funeral observances used of old in the Church, informeth us, first, that the friends of the dead accounted him to be, as he was, blessed, because that, according to his wish, he had obtained a victorious end, and thereupon sent forth hymns of thanksgiving to

memorations of the departed were thought most important, as tes-
tifying a belief in the doctrine of "the Communion of Saints,"
and that the souls of those who are gone hence are still living, still
fellow-heirs of the same glory, and fellow-citizens of the same kingdom with ourselves.[1]

These were the chief reasons for prayers for the dead in public
Liturgies. In the more private devotions, the solicitude which
had existed for beloved objects whilst on earth was still expressed
for their souls, when they had gone hence and were in the middle
state of the dead. For, though they held that "what shall be to
every one at the day of judgment is determined at the day of his
death,"[2] yet they thought it not unreasonable to pray that even
those who they hoped were safe might not lose that portion of
blessedness which they supposed to be in store for them.[3] There
were also some private opinions,—as that the "more abundant
damnation" of the damned might be lessened,[4]—that there was
a first resurrection, at which some eminent saints rose before the
rest, and to this they prayed that their friends might attain,[5]—that
all men, even the best and holiest, had at the day of judgment a
baptism of fire to go through, which should try their works, even
though they should be saved in it: of which baptism more presently. Such private and particular opinions influenced the prayers
of those who adopted them; but they were all unconnected with
the doctrine of purgatory.[6]

The prayers for the dead, thus early prevalent, were in process
of time, in the Roman Church, converted into prayers for souls
in purgatory. At the beginning of the Reformation, it was first
proposed to eradicate all traces of this doctrine from the Liturgies,
but to retain such prayers for the dead as were accordant with
primitive practice and belief. Accordingly, the first Liturgy of
Edward VI. contained thanksgiving for all those saints " who now
do rest in the sleep of peace," prayer for their " everlasting peace,"

the Author of that victory, desiring that
they themselves might come unto the
like end." — Usher, as above.

[1] Epiphan. *Hæres.* LXXV. n. VII.

[2] "Quod enim in die judicii futurum
est omnibus, hoc in singulis die mortis
impletur."— Hieronym. *In Joel,* cap. 2;
Usher, Ibid.

[3] See this exemplified in the prayer of
St. Augustine for his mother Monica. —
Confess. Lib. IX. cap. 13, quoted by Bing-
ham, Lib. XV. ch. III. § 16.

[4] " Ut tolerabilior sit damnatio."—
Aug. *Enchirid. ad Laurent.* cap. CX. Bingham, Ibid.

[5] This was a Millenarian opinion, and
was held by Tertullian. — *De Monogam.*
cap. 10; *Cont. Marcion.* Lib. III. cap. 25;
Bingham, Ibid.

[6] The student should by all means read
Usher's *Answer to a Jesuit,* ch. VII. *On
Prayer for the Dead;* and Bingham, Bk.
XV. ch. III. §§ 15, 16. See also Field, *Of
the Church,* Bk. III. c. 9, 17; Jer. Taylor, *Dissuasive from Popery,* pt. I. ch. I.
§ IV.; Bramhall, *Answer to M. De la Mille-
liere,* I. p. 59, of the Anglo-Catholic Library; Bull's *Works,* I. Serm. III. &c.

and that "at the day of the general resurrection all they which be of the mystical body of the Son, might be set on His right hand." But the reformers afterwards, fearing from what had already occurred that such prayers might be abused or misconstrued, removed them from the Communion and Burial services. Yet still we retain a thanksgiving for saints departed, a prayer that we, with them, may be partakers of everlasting glory, and a request that God would "complete the number of His elect, and hasten His kingdom, that we, with all those who are departed out of this life in His faith and fear, may have our perfect consummation and bliss in His eternal and everlasting glory." Such commemorations of the dead sufficiently accord with the spirit of the primitive prayers, without in any degree laying us open to the danger that ill-taught or ill-thinking men might found upon them doctrines of deceit or dangerous delusions.

We have seen then, that the doctrine of the ancients concerning the intermediate state was inconsistent with a belief in purgatory, and that their custom of praying for the dead had no connection with it. Yet we may trace the rise of the doctrine itself by successive steps from early times.

In the first two centuries there is a deep silence on the subject. At the end of the second, Tertullian considered that Paradise was a place of divine pleasantness appointed to receive the souls of the just.[1] But early in the third century, Tertullian had left the Church, and joined the Montanists; and there is a passage in one of his treatises, written after he became a Montanist, which deserves attention. In that treatise (*De Anima*) he indeed clearly speaks of all the righteous as detained *in inferis*, waiting in Abraham's bosom the comfort of the resurrection;[2] and says, that doubtless in the intermediate state (*penes inferos*) are punishments and rewards, as we may learn from the parable of Dives and Lazarus.[3] This appears inconsistent with any purgatorial notion; yet some consider that he had an idea of the kind, because he explains twice in this treatise the words, "Thou shalt not come out thence till thou hast paid the very last farthing," to mean, that even "small offences are expiated by delay of resurrection."[4] He

---

[1] *Apol.* i. 45, quoted above.
[2] Tertull. *De Anima*, 55.
[3] Ibid. 58.
[4] "Ne .... judex te tradat angelo executionis, et ille te in carcerem mandet inferum, unde non dimittaris, nisi modico quoque delicto mora resurrectionis expenso." — Ibid. 35.

"In summa carcerem illum quem evangelium demonstrat inferos intelligimus, et novissimum quadrantem, modicum quoque delictum mora resurrectionis illic luendum interpretamur; nemo dubitabit animam aliquid pensare penes inferos salva resurrectionis plenitudine per carnem quoque." — Ibid. 58.

seems, however, to consider that they will be more fully punished at the judgment.[1] And even this interpretation of Scripture, which is evidently very different from the doctrine of purgatory, he says that he derived, not from the teaching of the Church, but from Montanus.[2]

Contemporary with Tertullian, though somewhat his junior, was Origen. If Tertullian derived a notion somewhat resembling purgatory from a heretic, Origen derived a notion also bearing some resemblance to it from a heathen. His views of the nature of the human soul were borrowed from Plato. He believed it to be immortal and preëxistent, always in a state of progress or decline, and ever receiving the place due to its attainments in holiness, or defection to wickedness. Hence, he did not believe the purest souls of the redeemed, or the holy angels themselves, incapable of sinning, nor the very devils out of all hope of recovery.[3] In accordance with this theory, he was obliged to consider that all the pains of the damned were merely purgatorial, and that their sins would be expiated by fire.[4] To this he applied those passages of Scripture which speak of "a fiery trial," and of the fire as to "try every man's work of what sort it is" (1 Cor. iii. 13–15). He held that at the day of judgment all men must pass through the fire, even the saints and prophets. As the Hebrews went through the Red Sea, so all must pass through the fire of the judgment. As the Egyptians sank in the sea, so wicked men shall sink in the lake of fire: but good men, washed in the blood of the Lamb, even they, like Israel, must pass through the flood of flame ; but they shall go through it safe and uninjured.[5] All must go to the fire. The Lord sits and purifies the sons of Judah. He who brings

[1] See the concluding words in the last-cited passage.

[2] " Hoc enim Paracletus (h. e. Montanus) frequentissime commendavit, si quis sermones ejus ex agnitione promissorum charismatum admiscuit."— Ibid.
There is a passage in Cyprian (Epist. 55 ad Antonian. p. 109, Oxf. 1682) from which it is supposed that he adopted this view of Tertullian, whom he called " his Master." Rigaltius has shown that the language thus used by Cyprian applies to the penitential discipline of the Church, not to a purgatorial fire after death. It is true, the wording of this passage looks like Tertullian's reasoning. But Cyprian's language is so constantly opposed to the notion of purgatory, that it is scarcely possible that he should have consistently held that doctrine. See the pas-

sages above quoted from his treatise De Mortalitate. So the following : " Quod interim morimur, ad immortalitatem morte transgredimur ; nec potest vita æterna succedere, nisi hinc contigerit exire. Non est exitus iste, sed transitus : et temporali itinere decurso, ad æterna transgressus."— De Mortalitate, 12, p. 164. "Amplectamur diem, qui assignat singulos domicilio suo, qui nos istinc ereptos, et laqueis sæcularibus exsolutos Paradiso restituit et regno." — Ibid. 14, p. 166.

[3] De Principiis, Lib. .. cap. 6, n. 3, Hieronym. In Jonæ Proph. c. iii.; Augustin. De Civit. Dei, Lib. xxi. c. 17, Tom. vii. 637. See Laud against Fisher, § 38.

[4] Origen, De Principiis, Lib. ii. cap. 10, n. 5 ; Homil. in Levitic. vii. n. 4.

[5] Homil. iii. in Ps. xxxvi. num. 1

much gold with little lead, shall have the lead purged away, and
the gold shall remain uncorrupted. The more lead there is, the
more burning there will be. But if a man be all leaden, he shall
sink down into the abyss, as lead sinks in the water.[1]

This theory of Origen is so far from being the same with the
Romanist's purgatory, that, first of all, he places it instead of hell;
and secondly, so far from looking for it between death and the resurrection, he taught that it would take place after the resurrection,
at the day of judgment. Yet to this speculation, the offspring of
human reason and Platonic philosophy, we may trace the rise of
the doctrine on which the Church of Rome has erected so much
of her power, and which has been so fatally pregnant with superstition. The theories of Origen were interesting, his character
and learning were captivating; and so his name and opinions had
much weight with those who followed him. Accordingly, we find
eminent writers both in the East and West embracing his speculations. Lactantius held all judgment to be deferred till the resurrection; then eternal fire should consume the wicked, but it should
try even the just. Those who had many sins would be scorched
by it, but the pure would come off scathless.[2] Gregory Nazianzen, with the same idea, speaking of various kinds of baptism,
Moses's baptism, Christ's baptism, the martyr's baptism, the baptism of penitence, adds, "and perhaps in the next world men will
be baptized with fire, which last baptism will be more grievous
and of longer duration, which will devour the material part like
hay, and consume the light substance of every kind of sin."[3] Ambrose again, using almost the words of Origen, says, "that all must
pass through the flames, even St. John and St. Peter."[4] And
elsewhere he adopts Origen's illustration of the Israelites and
Egyptians passing through the Red Sea, comparing it with the
passage of all men through the fire of judgment.[5] Hilary too
speaks of all, even the Virgin Mary, as to undergo the trial of fire
at the day of judgment, in which souls must expiate their offences.[6]
Gregory Nyssen in like manner speaks of "a purgatorial fire after
our departure hence," and of "the purging fire, which takes
away the filth commingled with the soul."[7]

---

[1] *Homil. in Exod.* vi. num. 4.

[2] Lactant. vii. 21.

[3] τυχόν ἐκεῖ τῷ πυρὶ βαπτισθήσονται τῷ
τελευταίῳ βαπτίσματι τῷ ἐπιπονωτέρῳ καὶ
μακροτέρῳ, ὁ ἐσθίει τὸν χόρτον, τὴν ὕλην, καὶ
δαπανᾷ πάσης κακίας κουφότητα. — Greg.
Nazianz. *Oratio* xxxix. *juxta finem.*

[4] *Serm. XX. in Psal.* 118.

[5] *In Psal.* 36.

[6] " Cum ex omni otioso verbo rationem
simus præstituri, diem judicii concupis-
cemus, in quo subeunda sunt gravia illa
expiandæ a peccatis animæ supplicia,"
&c. — Hilar. *In Ps.* 118, lit. *Gimel.*

[7] μετὰ τὴν ἐνθένδε μετανάστασιν, διὰ τῆς
τοῦ καθαρσίου πυρὸς χωνείας. — *Orat. De*

All these views spring from the same source, and tend to the same conclusion. They arise from Origen's interpretation of 1 Cor. iii. 13–15; and they imply a belief, not in a purgatory between death and resurrection, but in a fiery ordeal through which all must pass at the day of judgment, which will consume the wicked, but purify the just.

We come now to St. Augustine. His name is deservedly had in honour, and his opinions have borne peculiar weight. He too, like Origen and Ambrose, speaks of the fire of judgment, which is to try men's works.[1] But he goes further still. In commenting on the passage of St. Paul, so often referred to, (1 Cor. iii. 11–15,) he says, that if men have the true foundation, even Jesus Christ, though they may not be pure from all carnal affections and infirmities, these shall be purged away from them by the fire of tribulation, by the loss of things we love, by persecution, and in the end of the world by the afflictions which antichrist should bring; in short, by the troubles of this life. But then he adds, that some have supposed that after death some further purging by fire was awaiting them who were not fully purified here, and he says, " I will not argue against it ; for perhaps it is true." [2] He does not set it forth as an article of faith. He does not speak of it as a doctrine of the Church. He does not propound it as an acknowledged truth. He does not lay it down as a settled opinion. He merely alleges it as a probable conjecture. He holds it to be uncertain, whether all tribulation is to be borne here, or some hereafter; or whether some hereafter instead of some here. But he thinks perhaps some such opinion is true. He says at least, it is not incredible.[3] The very mode in which he sets forth his doubts and queries shows that no certain ground could be taken upon the subject, as deduced from undoubted language of Scripture, or primitive teaching of the Church. In fact, he acknowledges the

Mortuis, Tom. iii. p. 634, Paris, 1638. τοῦ καθαρσίου πυρὸς τὸν ἐμμυχθέντα τῇ ψυχῇ ῥύπον ἀποκαθηράντος. — *Ibid.* p. 635. See *Laud against Fisher,* § 38.

[1] *De Civitate Dei,* xvi. 24, xx. 25, Tom. vii. pp. 437, 609.

[2] "Post istius sane corporis mortem, donec ad illum veniatur, qui post resurrectionem corporum futurus est damnationis ultimus dies, si hoc temporis intervallo spiritus defunctorum ejusmodi ignem dicuntur perpeti, quem non sentiant illi qui non habuerunt tales mores et amores in hujus corporis vita, ut eorum ligna, fœnum, stipula consumatur ; alii vero sentiant qui ejusmodi secum ædificia portaverunt, sive ibi tantum, sive ideo hic ut non ibi, sæcularia, quamvis a damnatione venialia concremantem ignem transitoriæ tribulationis inveniant, *non redarguo, quia forsitan verum est.*" — *De Civit. Dei,* xxi. 26, Tom. vii. p.649.

[3] " Tale aliquid etiam post hanc vitam fieri, *incredibile non est, et utrum ita sit quæri potest, et aut inveniri aut latere,* nonnullos fideles per ignem quendam purgatorium quanto magis minusve bona pereuntia dilexerunt, tanto tardius citiusque salvari."— *Enchiridion ad. Laurent.* cap. 69, Tom. vi. p. 222. See also *De Fide et Operibus,* cap. 16, Tom. vi. p. 180.

great difficulty of the passage in St. Paul, simply speaks of the purgatorial view as having been suggested, and thinks it not impossible or improbable. In this form of it, it was in fact an evident novelty in the days of St. Augustine.[1]

A century and a half later, Pope Gregory I. laid it down distinctly, that " there is a purgatorial fire before the judgment for lighter faults." [2] From this time a belief in purgatory rapidly gained ground in the Western Church. Visions and apparitions of the dead were appealed to, as witnesses for the existence of a state of purgation for those souls who were detained in prison waiting for the judgment.[3] Thomas Aquinas and other schoolmen discussed the subject with their usual ingenuity, and more fully explained the situation of purgatory, its pains, and their intensity. But the Greek Church, divided from the Latin on other points, was never agreed with it on this.

In the year 1431 met the synod of Basle, which promised much reformation, and effected none. Thither a deputation had come from the Emperor of Constantinople ; and by it a hope was excited that the breach between the two long-divided branches of the Church might now be healed. Eugenius IV. Bishop of Rome, who at first endeavoured in 1437 to translate the Council of Basle to Ferrara, now strove to remove it to Florence (A. D. 1439). Only four of the Bishops left Basle at his command, the rest continuing their sitting there till 1443, forming a council acknowledged as œcumenical by great part of Europe, though opposed to the pope. However, several Italian bishops met at Florence, and were joined by the Greek emperor and some bishops from the East. In this synod the Greek deputies were induced to acknowledge, that the Bishop of Rome was the primate and head of the Church, that the Holy Spirit proceedeth from the Father and the Son, and *that there is a purgatory.* These decrees were signed by about sixty-two Latin bishops, by John Palæologus the emperor, and by eighteen Eastern bishops. On their return to Constantinople the Greek prelates were received with the greatest indignation by those

---

[1] We must by no means imagine that the fathers uniformly interpreted this passage of the Corinthians either of a purgatorial fire at judgment, or before the judgment. For example, St. Chrysostom distinctly expounds it of a probatory, not a purgatory fire ; and understands that those who suffer loss are those who are damned eternally, and that their " being saved yet so as by fire " means that they shall be preserved from annihila-

tion, not from suffering by the fire. — See *Hom.* IX. *in* 1 *Corinth.*

[2] " De quibusdam levibus culpis esse ante judicium purgatorius ignis credendus est." — Gregor. *Dial.* Lib. IV. cap. 39. Also *In Psalm.* iii. *Pœnitent. in princip:* . Usher, *Answer to a Jesuit,* ch. VI. ; *Laud against Fisher,* § 38.

[3] See Jer. Taylor, *Dissuasive from Popery,* pt. I. ch. I. § 4, Vol. X. p. 150, *Works.* London, 1822.

whom they might be supposed to represent. The decrees of Florence were utterly and most summarily rejected in the East, the synod was altogether repudiated, and has never since been recognized. The patriarchs of Antioch, Alexandria, and Jerusalem, who were represented by deputies in the council, joined in the protest against it. To this day the Eastern Church has never acknowledged it, nor does it accept any of its decrees, whether concerning the Procession, the Pope, or Purgatory.[1]

The Council of Trent, A. D. 1563, professing to be " taught by the Holy Spirit, the Scriptures, and tradition of the fathers," decreed, that there is a purgatory, and that souls there detained are aided by the sacrifice of the altar. It, however, forbade the people to be troubled with any of the more subtle questions on the subject.[2]

The divines of the Church of Rome have not been so careful as the council to avoid entering into minute discussion. Bellarmine has a whole book on the circumstances of purgatory. In this, he first discusses for whom purgatory is reserved. Then he argues that souls there detained can neither merit nor sin ; then, that they are sure of salvation. Then he resolves the question, Where is purgatory ? Next he discusses, whether souls pass straight from purgatory to Heaven, or whether there be a Paradise besides. He discusses how long purgatory lasts, of what nature is its punishment, whether its fire is corporeal, (which he solves in the affirmative,) whether demons torment the souls there, (which he leaves in doubt). And lastly, he teaches how prayers aid the souls in purgatory, and what kind of prayers they should be.[3]

2. Pardons or Indulgences.

These, in the sense intended by this Article and taught by the Church of Rome, sprang out of the doctrine of Purgatory.

In the Primitive Church, when Christians had lapsed in persecution, or otherwise incurred the censure of the Church, it was not uncommon for the bishops to relax the penances which had been enjoined on them, either when there was danger of death, or at the intercession of the martyrs or confessors in prison, or from some other worthy cause.[4] Very early, the custom of martyrs interceding appears to have been abused ; and the high esteem in which martyrdom was held, led to the precipitate reception of their prayers

---

[1] *Concil.* Tom. XIII.; Fleury, LIV.; Gibbon, ch. LXVI. LXVII.; Usher, as above; Palmer, *On the Church* pt. IV. ch. XI. § 5.

[2] Sess. XXV. *Decretum de Purgatorio.*
[3] Bellarmin. *De Purgatorio*, Lib. II.
[4] Tertullian *Ad Martyres*, c. I.; Cypr *Ep.* 15 *ad Martyres*; Euseb. *H. E.* v. 2.

for offenders, to the interruption of the right discipline of the Church.[1]

The Council of Ancyra, and, soon after, the Council of Nice, gave bishops express authority to restore offenders to communion, and to shorten the term of their penitential probation, on consideration of past good conduct or present tokens of true repentance.[2] This was reasonable enough. But all good is liable to abuse. In process of time, liberal almsgiving was accepted in lieu, or at least in mitigation of penance : the beginning of which custom is charged, though probably without justice, on our own Archbishop Theodore.[3] Here was a loop-hole for all evil to creep in. The subsequent sale of indulgences easily rose out of the permission to substitute charity to the poor or to the Church for mortification and humiliation before God.

But the obtaining of such exemptions is a wholly different thing from the modern doctrine of the Roman Church concerning indulgences. Indulgences indeed now are said to be exemptions from the *temporal punishment of sins*. But in the term *temporal punishment* are included not only Church-censures, but the pains of purgatory ; and it is held, that the Bishop of Rome has a store or treasure of the merits of Christ and of the saints, which, for sufficient reasons, he can dispense, either by himself or his agents, to mitigate or shorten the sufferings of penitents, whether in this world or the world to come ; [4] this power not, of course, extending to the torments of hell, which are not among the *temporal* punishments of sin. Some of the Roman Catholic divines acknowledge that no mention of such indulgences is to be found in Scripture or in the fathers. Many of the schoolmen confess that their use began in the time of Pope Alexander III., at the end of the twelfth century. Indeed, before this time, it is hardly possible to discover any traces of them. The first jubilee, or year of general indulgence, is said to have been kept in the pontificate of Boniface VIII., 1300 years after Christ. And the famous bull, *Unigenitus*, was issued by Pope Clement VI. fifty years after the first jubilee,

---

[1] See Tertullian, *De Pudicit.* c. 22.

[2] Concil. Ancyran. Can. v. ; Concil. Nicæn. I. Can. XII.; Marshall's *Penitential Discipline*, ch. III. § 2.

[3] Theodore became Archbishop of Canterbury, A. D. 670. The custom of purchasing exemption of penance by almsgiving can be proved to be of greater antiquity than this. See Marshall, as above.

[4] "Recte Clemens VI. Pont. in Constitutione, Extravagantis, quæ incipit

Unigenitus . . . . declaravit, extare in Eccl. thesaurum spiritualem ex passionibus Christi et sanctorum conflatum." — Bellarmin. *De Indulgentiis*, Lib. I. cap. 2.

"Restat igitur ut passiones sanctorum, si ullo modo dispensari debeant, extra sacramentum solum, idque per solutionem solius reatus pœnæ temporalis dispensari debeant." — Ibid. cap. 3.

See also cap. 10, where Indulgences are shown to apply either to penance in this life or purgatorial pains in the next.

A. D. 1350.[1] It was not without discussion and opposition that this custom grew and prevailed.[2] It reached its greatest height of corruption in the Pontificate of Leo X., when Tetzel, the agent of that pope, openly selling indulgences in Germany, roused the spirit of Luther, and so hastened the Reformation. This led to more formal discussion and consideration of the grounds of it. The Council of Trent decreed, that " the treasures of the Church should not be made use of for gain, but for godliness." [3] It declared, that " the power of granting indulgences was given by Christ to His Church," that, according to ancient usage, " it is to be retained in the Church ; " and it anathematizes those " who assert that indulgences are useless, or that the Church cannot grant them." Yet it enjoins moderation in their use, lest " by too great facility in granting them ecclesiastical discipline be enervated ; " and forbids all abuses, whereby profit has been sought by them, and through which scandal has arisen from heretics.[4]

II. 1. " Worshipping and adoration as well of images as of relics."

We have strong testimony from the earliest times against anything like image-worship, or the use of images or pictures, for the exciting of devotion. Irenæus speaks of it as one of the errors of some of the Gnostics, that they had images and pictures, which they crowned and honoured, as the Gentiles do, professing that the form of Christ, as He was in the flesh, was made by Pilate.[5] Clement of Alexandria repeatedly speaks of the impropriety of making an image of God, the best image of whom is man created after His likeness.[6] Origen quotes Celsus as saying that Christians could not " bear temples, altars, and images ; " and proceeds to justify the forbidding of statues and images, showing that Christians rejected them on a higher principle than the Scythians and nomad tribes of Libya.[7] He contends, that it is folly to make images of God, whose best image are those virtues and graces which the Word forms within us, and by which we imitate Him,

---

[1] Jer. Taylor, *Dissuasive from Popery*, ch. I. § 3, Vol. x. p. 138 ; Bellarmin. *De Indulgentiis*, Lib. I. cap. 2.
[2] See Bp. Taylor, as above. who refers to Franciscus de Mayronis and Durandus as having disputed against it. See also Bellarmine, as above.
[3] Sess. XXI. cap. IX.
[4] Sess. XXV. *Decretum de Indulgentiis.*
[5] Iren. *Adv. Hær.* I. 24, *ad finem.* Comp. Epiphan. *Hæres.* XXVII. n. 6, who charges

the Carpocratians with worshipping images of Christ, together with those of the philosophers, as the Gentiles do. So Augustine (*Hæres.* VII.) accuses them of worshipping images of our Lord, of St. Paul, Homer, and Plato.
[6] *Strom.* Lib. v. 5, Tom. II. p. 662, **Lib.** VI. 18, Tom. II. p. 825, Lib. VII. 5, **Tom.** II. p. 845, &c.
[7] *Cont. Cels.* Lib. VII. 62, *seq.*

the " First-born of every creature," in whom, of all things, is the
highest and noblest image of the Father.[1]   So Minucius Felix asks
" What should I form as an image of God, when, if you think
rightly, man is himself God's image ? " [2]   Exactly in like manner
argues Lactantius : " That is not God's image which is made
with man's fingers, with stone or brass : but man himself, who
thinks and moves and acts ; " and he says, " it is superfluous to
make images of gods, as if they were absent, when we believe
them to be present." [3]   Athanasius as plainly condemns the adoration of images, whether in their use the Supreme Being be to be
worshipped, or only angels and inferior intelligences.[4]

The Romanist divines lay great stress on the early mention of
the use of the sign of the cross and of emblematical figures.   But,
how far either of these are from resemblance to the later use of
images, it is impossible that any one can be unmindful.   Symbols
of the faith were unquestionably very early adopted, perhaps from
the very first ; and have been retained, not only in the Anglican,
but in the Lutheran and other reformed communions.

Tertullian speaks of the symbol, on a chalice, of the Good
Shepherd carrying the lost sheep on his shoulders.[5]   This was not
even a figure of our Saviour, but merely an emblem of Him ; and
this is the only instance ever mentioned by writers of the first
three centuries.   The sign of the cross, we learn from the same
father, was constantly made by the first Christians on their fore-
heads, at their going out and coming in, at meals, at bathing, at
lying down and rising up ; and all this, he says, had been handed
down by ancient custom and tradition.[6]   But though they thus
used the sign of the Cross, to remind them of Him who was crucified, it was not to worship it.   " We neither worship crosses, nor
wish for them," says Minucius Felix ; [7] for the heathens had charged
upon Christians that they paid respect to that instrument of punishment which they deserved.[8]   But the cross was esteemed emblematical of the doctrine of the Cross, and a badge to distinguish
Christian from heathen men.   If ever the early Christians were
likely to have worshipped the cross, it was when the Empress
Helena, mother to Constantine the Great, found, or thought she
found the true cross on which our Lord was crucified.   But how
little was this the case, we learn from the words of St. Ambrose.

---

[1] *Cont. Cels.* Lib. VII. 18.
[2] Minuc. Felic. *Octavius*, p. 313. Lugd.
Batav. 1672.
[3] *Instit.* II. 2.
[4] *Orat. cont. Gentes.* Tom. I. p. 22, Col.
1686.

[5] *De Pudicit.* c. 7.
[6] *De Corona M.* c. 3.
[7] *Octav.* p. 284.
[8] Ibid. p. 86 ; Tertull. *Apol.* c. 16.

He tells us that Helena found the nails with which our Lord was crucified, and placed one in the crown worn by Constantine. " Wise Helena," he says, " who exalted the cross on the head of kings, that Christ's cross might be adored in kings." [1]　But then he remarks that Helena worshipped that great King who was crucified, " not the wood on which He was crucified; that would be a heathenish error, a vanity of impious men; but she worshipped Him who hung upon the cross." [2]　In vain therefore is the ancient use of the cross, or even the respect paid to the figure of it, alleged as a proof of the antiquity of image-worship.　Indeed, it has not been the cross, but the Crucifix, the figure of the crucified Saviour, which has tempted to an idolatrous worship of it.

We have seen that it was charged against the Gnostics as an error, that they had an image of our Saviour, and paid it honour as the heathen do.　Eusebius tells us that the people of Paneas had a statue, said to have been erected by the woman who was healed of an issue of blood, and supposed to be a likeness of our blessed Saviour.　Eusebius remarks on it, that it is no great wonder if the heathen who were healed by our Saviour should have done such things as this, when pictures of St. Peter, and St. Paul, and of Christ Himself, were said to be preserved; all this being after the heathen manner of honouring deliverers.[3]　It is true, Sozomen tells us, that, when Julian had removed this statue, and the heathen had insulted it and broken it in pieces out of hatred to Christ, the Christians gathered up the fragments and laid them up in the Church.[4]　But it follows not, because the Christians of his day did not wish to see a statue which was esteemed a likeness of our Saviour treated with contempt, that they therefore intended to adore it.　They did not set it up in the Church to worship, but simply brought in the fragments there, that they might not be insulted.

It is not improbable that, about the beginning of the fourth century, there was some inclination to bring pictures into churches; for at the Council of Eliberis in Spain, A. D. 305, one of the canons ordered, that " no picture should be in the church, lest that, which is worshipped or adored, be painted on the walls." [5]　At the latter

<hr>

[1] " Sapiens Helena, quæ crucem in capite regum levavit, ut crux Christi in regibus adoretur." — Ambros. *De Obitu Theodosii, juxta finem.*

[2] " Habeat Helena quæ legat (h. e. *titulum in crucem a Pilato inscriptum*) unde crucem Domini recognoscat. Invenit ergo titulum, Regem adoravit, non lignum utique, quia hic gentilis est error,

et vanitas impiorum, sed adoravit **Illum** qui pependit in ligno," &c. — Ibid.

[3] ὡς εἰκὸς τῶν παλαιῶν ἀπαραφυλάκτως οἷα σωτῆρας ἐθνικῇ συνηθείᾳ παρ' ἑαυτοῖς τοῦτον τιμᾶν εἰωθότων τὸν τρόπον. — *H. E.* VII. 18.

[4] Sozomen. v. 21.

[5] Concil. Eliber. can. 36 : " Placuit picturas in ecclesia esse non debere, ne

end of the fourth century, we are told that Paulinus, Bishop of Nola, to keep the country-people quiet, when they met to celebrate the festival of the dedication of the church of St. Felix, ordered the church to be painted with portraits of martyrs and Scripture history, such as Esther, Job, Tobit, &c.[1]

Nearly at the same time, or a little earlier, Epiphanius, going through Anablatha, a village in Palestine, " found there a veil hanging before the door of a church, whereon was painted an image of Christ, or some saint — he did not remember which. When he saw in the church of Christ an image of a man, contrary to the authority of Scripture, he rent it, and advised that it should be made a winding-sheet for some poor man." [2] Here we have the strong testimony of a bishop and eminent father of the Church, not only against image-worship, but even against the use of pictures in the house of God.

At the end of the fourth century again, St. Augustine says that he knew of many who were worshippers of tombs and pictures, and who practised other superstitious rites. But he says, the Church condemns all such, and strives to correct them as evil children.[3] He himself declares, that it is impiety to erect a statue to God in the Church.[4] He contends against the argument of the heathens, that they only used the image to remind them of the being they worshipped, saying that the visible image naturally arrested the attention more than the invisible deity ; and hence the use of such an outward symbol of devotion is calculated to lead to a real worship of the idol itself, even of the gold and silver, the work of men's hands. And then he answers the objection, that Christians in the administration of the Sacraments had vessels made of gold and silver, the work of men's hands. " But," he asks, " have they a mouth, and speak not ? have they eyes, and see not ? or do we worship them, because in their use we worship God ? That is the chief cause of the mad impiety, that a form like life has so much power on the feelings of the wretched beings as to make it-

---

quod colitur aut adoratur, in parietibus depingatur." — See Jer. Taylor, *Dissuasire*, pt. i. ch. i. § 8; Bingham, *E. A.* Bk. viii. ch. viii. § 6.

[1] Paulin. *Natal.* 9, *Felicis*; Bingham, Bk. viii. ch. viii. § 7.

[2] Epiphan. *Epist. ad Johan. Hierosol.* translated by St. Jerome. *Ep.* 60 : Bellarmine (*De Imagin.* Lib. ii. c. 9) argues that the passage is an interpolation. But it is in all the MSS., and its genuineness is admitted by Petavius (*De Incarnation.*

Lib. xv. c. 14, 4, 8). See Bingham, as above.

[3] " Novi multos esse sepulcrorum et picturarum adoratores, &c. . . . . quos et ipsa (Ecclesia) condemnat, et quotidie tanquam malos filios corrigere studet." — *De Moribus Ecclesiæ,* i. c. 34, §§ 74, 75, Tom. i. p. 713.

[4] *De Fide et Symbolo*, c. vii. Tom. vi. p 157 ; Comp. *De Consensu Evangelist,* i. 16, Tom. iii. pt. ii. p. 11.

self to be worshipped, instead of its being manifest that it is not living, and so ought to be contemned," [1] &c.

From all this it is manifest, that in the fourth century, among ignorant Christians, a tendency to pay reverence to pictures or images was beginning to appear in some parts of the Church ; the Church herself and her bishops and divines strongly opposing and earnestly protesting against it.   Towards the close of this century, and afterwards, we hear of pictures (not statues) introduced into churches.   Yet these pictures were not pictures of our Lord and His saints, but rather historical pictures of Scripture subjects, such as the sacrifice of Isaac, or of martyrdoms, or, as we saw from Paulinus, of Job and Esther, and other famous characters of old. About the same time, pictures of living kings and bishops were admitted into the church, and set up with those of martyrs and Scripture histories.   But as with the dead, so neither with the living, was worship either probable or designed.[2]   However, danger of this kind soon arose.   By degrees not pictures only, but statues were brought in.   And in the sixth century, we find that Serenus, Bishop of Marseilles, ordered all the images in the churches of his diocese to be defaced and broken ; whereupon Gregory the Great writes to him, to say that he approved of his forbidding images to be worshipped, but that he blamed him for breaking them, as they were innocent of themselves, and useful for the instruction of the vulgar.[3]

In the eighth century arose the famous Iconoclastic controversy of Constantinople.   Philippicus Bardanes, the emperor, with the consent of John, patriarch of Constantinople, began by pulling down pictures from the churches, and forbade them at Rome 'as well as in Greece.   Constantius, Bishop of Rome, opposed him, and ordered pictures of the first six councils to be placed in the porch of St. Peter's.   The controversy, thus kindled, raged during the reigns of several subsequent emperors, especially of Leo the Isaurian, and his son Constantine Copronymus, who were zealous Iconoclasts, and the Empress Irene, as zealous for the opposite party, who were called Iconoduli.   In the reign of Constantine Copronymus, a council was summoned at Constantinople, A. D. 754, called by the Greeks the Seventh General Council, but rejected by the Latins, which condemned the worship and all use of images.   In

---

[1] *In Psalm.* cxiii. ; Serm. II. §§ 4, 5, 6.
[2] See Bingham, *E. A.* Bk. VIII. ch. VIII. §§ 9, 11.
[3] " Quia sanctorum imagines adorari vetuisses, omnino laudavimus : fregisse vero reprehendimus," &c. — Gregor. Lib. IX. Ep. 9 ; Bingham, as above ; Jer. Taylor, as above.

the reign of Irene, A. D. 784, the second Council of Nice was summoned by that empress, which reversed the decrees of the Council
of Constantinople, and ordained that images should be set up, that
salutation and respectful honour should be paid them, and incense
should be offered; but not the worship of *Latria*, which is due to
God alone.[1] The decrees of this synod were sent by Pope Adrian
into France, to Charlemagne, to be confirmed by the bishops of his
kingdom; Charlemagne having also received them direct from
Greece. The Gallican bishops, having thus a copy of the decrees,
composed a reply to them, not objecting to images, if used for historical remembrance and ornament to walls, but absolutely condemning any worship or adoration of them.[2] This work (the *Libri
Carolini*) was published by the authority of Charlemagne and the
consent of his bishops, A. D. 790.[3] Charlemagne also consulted the
British bishops, A. D. 792, who, abhorring the worship of images,
authorized Albinus to convey to Charlemagne, in their name, a
refutation of the decrees of the second Council of Nice. In 794,
Charlemagne assembled a synod at Frankfort, composed of 300
bishops from France, Germany, and Italy, who formally rejected
the Synod of Nice, and declared that it was not to be esteemed
the seventh general council.[4] It has been shown, indeed, that the
Synod of Nice was not received in the Western Church for five centuries and a half; and it was very long before there was any real
recognition of image-worship in the West, except in those Churches
immediately influenced by Rome.[5]

In 869, the Emperor Basil assembled another council at Constantinople, attended by about one hundred Eastern bishops and
the legates of Pope Adrian. This confirmed the worship of images,
and is esteemed by Romanists as the eighth general council. Yet
it is wholly rejected by the Eastern Church, and was evidently for
a long time not acknowledged in the West.[6] It was rejected by

---

[1] In the VIIth Session a profession of
faith was read and signed by the legates
and bishops, deciding that images of
Christ, the Virgin, and the saints, should
be exposed to view and honoured, but not
vorshipped with *Latria*; but that lights
should be burned before them and incense
offered to them, as the honour so bestowed upon the image is transferred to the
original.

[2] " Dum nos nihil in imaginibus sper-
namus nisi adorationem . . . non ad ado-
randum, sed ad memoriam rerum gesta-
rum et venustatem parietum habere per-
mittimus. — *Lib. Carol.* Lib. III. c. 16.

[3] The Caroline books are still extant.
The Preface may be seen in Mr. Har-
vey's learned and useful work, *Ecclesiæ
Anglicanæ Vindex Catholicus*.

[4] See Dupin, *Eccl. Hist.* Cent. VIII.;
Mosheim, *Eccl. Hist.* Cent. VIII. pt. 2,
ch. 3; Usher, *Answer to a Jesuit*, ch. X.;
Bp. Bull, *Corruption of Church of Rome,
Works*, II. p. 275, &c.; Palmer, *On the
Church*, part IV. ch. X. § 4.

[5] Palmer, as above.

[6] Palmer, *On the Church*, pt. IV. ch. X
§ 5.

the next Council of Constantinople, held A. D. 879, which itself also is rejected by the Western Church.

The Council of Trent, which is supposed to fix the doctrines of the Roman Church, enjoins that " Images of Christ, the Virgo Deipara, and the saints, shall be retained in churches, and due honour and veneration given to them, not because any divinity or virtue is believed to be in them, for which they are to be worshipped, nor because anything is to be sought from them, or faith reposed in them, as by the Gentiles, who placed their hope in images; but because the honour which is paid to them is referred to their prototypes; so that by means of the images, which we kiss and bow down before, we adore Christ and reverence the saints, whose likeness they bear." [1]

2. The worshipping of relics is so much connected with the adoration of images and invocation of saints, that we may pass it over the more briefly.

No doubt, there was an early inclination to pay much respect to the remains of martyrs. We know from all antiquity, that the custom prevailed of meeting at their tombs and celebrating the days of their martyrdom. We find that the Smyrnæan Christians were disappointed at not being allowed the body of Polycarp, as many desired to be able to take it away. Yet they indignantly repudiated the notion that they could worship it.[2] The importance attached to the finding of the true cross by St. Helena is an example of a similar feeling. As the bones of Elisha restored a dead man to life, so the ancients early believed that miraculous powers were often conferred on the dead bodies of the martyrs. Such Gregory Nazianzen attributes to the ashes of St. Cyprian, and speaks of his body as a benefit to the community.[3] A little later, Vigilantius, a Gaul by birth, but a presbyter of the church of Spain, declaimed against the veneration which men had in his time learned to pay to the tombs and relics of the martyrs. It is probable, that he charged his fellow Christians with practices of which they were not guilty; yet it is not unlikely, that in the more rude and ignorant neighbourhoods, that, which was at first but natural respect, was even then approaching to mischievous superstition. St. Jerome wrote fiercely against him, most distinctly and vehemently repelling the charge that Christians worshipped the relics of the saints. " Not only," he says, " do we not worship relics, but not the sun, the moon, angels nor archangels, cherubim nor seraphim, nor any

---

[1] **Sess. xxv.** *De Invocatione, &c. Sanctorum et Sacris Imaginibus.*

[2] *Martyr. Polycarpi*, c. 17.

[3] *Orat.* XVIII. Tom. I. pp. 284, 285.

name that is named in this world or in the world to come ; lest we
should serve the creature rather than the Creator, who is blessed
forever. We honour the relics of the martyrs, that we may worship Him whose martyrs they are. We honour the servants, that
their honour may redound to their Lord's." [1] His contemporary,
St. Augustine, seems to have been more alive than St. Jerome to
the growing evil. He graphically describes and complains of the
custom, then beginning, of people wandering about and selling relics, or what they said to be relics, of those who had suffered martyrdom.[2]

Still it has been proved, that, in the early ages, the Church
never permitted anything like religious worship to be offered to the
relics of the saints.[3] The respect paid to them sprang from that
natural instinct of humanity, which prompts us to cherish the mortal remains, and all else that is left to us, of those we have loved
and honoured whilst in life ; and the belief of the sacredness and
future resurrection of the bodies of Christians, joined with the wish
to protect them from the insults of their heathen persecutors, added
intensity to this feeling. With the progress of image-worship and
of the invocation of the saints, grew (and perhaps still more rapidly)
the undue esteem of relics, to which sanctity seemed to belong :
until at length the relics of saints were formally installed amongst
the objects of worship, and set up with images for the veneration
of the faithful.[4]

3. The Invocation of Saints.

For this practice no early authority can be pleaded, but against
it the strongest testimony of the primitive Christians exists. They
assert continually, that we should worship none but God. Thus
Justin Martyr : " It becomes Christians to worship God only." [5]
Tertullian : " For the safety of the Emperor we invoke God, eternal, true, and living God . . . . Nor can I pray to any other than
to Him, from whom I am sure that I may obtain, because He alone
can give it." [6] Origen : " To worship any one besides the Father,
the Son, and the Holy Ghost, is the sin of impiety." [7] Lactantius

---

[1] Hieronym. *Epist.* 37, *ad Riparium.*
Tom. iv. part ii. p. 279.

[2] " Alii membra martyrum, si tamen
martyrum, venditant."— *De Op. Monach.*
c. 28, Tom. vi. p. 498.

[3] See on this subject Bingham, *E. A.*
Bk. xxiii. cap. iv. §§ 8, 9 : also (referred
to by him) Dallæus *De Objecto cultus Relig-*
iosi, Lib. iv.

[4] See *Concil. Trident.* Sess. xxv. ;
Bellarmin. *De Reliquiis Sanctorum*, Lib.
iv. &c.

[5] τὸν Θεὸν μόνον δεῖ προσκυνεῖν. — *Apol.*
i. p. 63.

[6] " Nos pro salute imperatorum Deum invocamus æternum, Deum verum,
Deum vivum . . . Hæc ab alio orare non
possum, quam a quo me scio consecutu-
rum, quoniam et ipse qui solus præstat."
— *Apol.* c. 30.

[7] " Adorare quem, iam præter Patrem
et Filium et Spiritum Sanctum impietatis est crimen." — *Comment. in Epist. ad*
Roman. Lib. i. n. 16. Comp. *In Jesum*

complains of the extreme blindness of men (*i. e.* heathens), who could worship dead men.[1] And Athanasius argues from St. Paul's language (1 Thess. iii. 11), that the Son must be God, and not an angel or any other creature, since He is invoked in conjunction with His Father.[2]

In the circular Epistle of the Church of Smyrna, narrating the martyrdom of St. Polycarp, which took place about A. D. 147, it is said, that the Jews prevented the giving of the body to the Christians for burial, " lest forsaking Him who was crucified, they should begin to worship this Polycarp ; " " not considering," writes the Church of Smyrna, " that neither is it possible for us to forsake Christ, who suffered for the salvation of all who are saved in the whole world, the spotless One for sinners, nor to worship any other." [3]

No doubt, the early Christians, believing in " the communion of saints," had a lively conviction that saints departed were still fellow-worshippers with the Church militant, and thought that those in Paradise still prayed for those on earth.[4] But it does not therefore follow, that they considered that those who joined with us in prayer, ought to be themselves addressed in prayer. On the contrary, we have express evidence that those who believed the saints at rest to pray for the saints in trial, believed that they did so without being invoked. So Origen, " When men, purposing to themselves things which are excellent, pray to God, thousands of the sacred powers join with them in prayer, though not themselves called on or invoked." [5] Nay! he is here specially arguing against Celsus, who would have had men invoke others of inferior power, after the God who is over all ; and he contends that, as the shadow follows the body, so if we can move God by our prayers, we shall be sure to have all the angels and souls of the righteous on our side, and that therefore we must endeavour to please God alone.[6] In the same book he repeatedly denies that it is permitted us to worship

---

Nave, Hom. **vi.** 3 : " Non enim adorasset, nisi agnovisset Deum."

[1] " Homines autem ipsos ad tantam cæcitatem esse deductos, ut vero ac vivo Deo mortuos præferant." —*Instit.* ii. c. i.

[2] νῦν δὲ ἡ τοιαύτη δόσις δείκνυσι τὴν ἑνότητα τοῦ Πατρὸς καὶ τοῦ Υἱοῦ οὐκ ἂν γοῦν εὔξαιτο τις λαβεῖν παρὰ τοῦ Πατρὸς καὶ τῶν Ἀγγέλων· ἢ παρά τινος τῶν ἄλλων κτισμάτων, οὐδ' ἂν εἴποι τις, δῴη σοι ὁ Θεὸς καὶ Ἀγγελος. — *Contra Arian.* Orat. iv.

[3] οὐδὲ ἕτερόν τινα σέβεσθαι. — S. *Polycarpi Martyrium,* c. 17 ; Coteler. Tom. ii. p. 200.

[4] *e. g.* Origen writes : " Ego sic arbitror, quod omnes illi, qui dormierunt ante nos, patres pugnent nobiscum, et adjuvent nos orationibus suis. Ita namque etiam quendam de senioribus magistris audivi dicentem," &c. — *In Jesum Nave,* Hom. xvi. 5.

[5] ὥστε τολμᾶν ἡμᾶς λέγειν, ὅτι ἀνθρώποις μετὰ προαιρέσεως προτιθεμένοις τὰ κρείττονα, εὐχομένοις τῷ Θεῷ, μυρίαι ὅσαι ἄκλητοι συνεύχονται δυνάμεις ἱεραί.— *Cont. Celsum,* Lib. viii. c. 64.

[6] *Cont. Cels.* Lib. viii. c. 64.

angels, who are ministering spirits, our duty being to worship God
alone.[1]   And whereas Celsus had said, that angels (δαίμονες) belonged to God, and should be reverenced, Origen says, " Far from
us be the counsels of Celsus, that we should worship them.   We
must pray to God alone who is over all, and to the only-begotten
Son, the first-born of every creature, and from Him must ask, that,
when our prayers have reached Him, He, as High Priest, would
offer them to His God and our God, to His Father, and the Father
of all who live according to His word." [2]

St. Athanasius observes, that St. Peter forbade Cornelius to worship him (Acts x. 26), and the angel forbade St. John, when he
would have worshipped him (Rev. xxii. 9).   " Wherefore," he adds,
" it belongs to God only to be worshipped, and of this the angels
are not ignorant, who, though they excel in glory, are yet all of
them creatures, and are not in the number of those to be adored,
but of those who adore the Lord." [3]

In like manner the Council of Laodicea, held probably about
A. D. 364,[4] forbids Christians to attend conventicles where angels
were invoked, and pronounces anathema on all such as were guilty
of this secret idolatry, inasmuch as they might be esteemed to have
left the Lord Jesus, and given themselves to idolatry.[5]   Theodoret
tells us, that the reason why this canon was passed at Laodicea
was because in Phrygia and Pisidia men had learned to pray to
angels; and even to his own day, he says, there were oratories of
St. Michael among them.[6]

We hear of another early example of an heretical tendency to
creature-worship, which seems almost providentially to have been
permitted, in order that there might be an early testimony borne
against it.   Epiphanius tells us that, whereas some had treated the
Virgin Mary with contempt, others were led to the other extreme
of error, so that women offered cakes before her, and exalted her to
the dignity of one to be worshipped.[7]   This, he says, was a doctrine invented by demons.   " No doubt the body of Mary was
holy; but she was not a God."   Again, " The Virgin was a vir-

---

[1] *Cont. Cels.* VIII. num. 35, 57.
[2] Ibid. num. 26.   See the like argument, *Cont. Cels.* v. num. 4.
[3] Athanas. *Cont. Arian.* Orat. III. Tom.
I. p. 394.
[4] The date is uncertain, some placing
it as early as A. D. 314, others as late as
A. D. 372.
[5] *Concil. Laodic.* Can. XXXV.
Ὅτι οὐ δεῖ χριστιανοὺς ἐγκαταλείπειν τὴν
ἐκκλησίαν τοῦ Θεοῦ καὶ ἀπιέναι καὶ ἀγγέλους

ὀνομάζειν καὶ συνάξεις ποιεῖν· ἅπερ ἀπηγόρευ-
ται.   εἴ τις οὖν εὑρεθῇ ταύτῃ τῇ κεκρυμμένῃ
εἰδωλολατρείᾳ σχολάζων, ἔστω ἀνάθεμα, ὅτι
ἐγκατέλιπε τὸν Κύριον ἡμῶν Ἰησοῦν Χριστὸν,
τὸν Υἱὸν τοῦ Θεοῦ, καὶ εἰδωλολατρείᾳ προ-
σῆλθεν.
[6] Theodoret, *In Coloss.* ii. and iii. ;
Usher, *Answer to a Jesuit,* ch. IX.; Suicer,
s. v. ἄγγελος.
[7] *Hæres.* 79.

gin, and to be honoured; yet not given us to be worshipped, but herself worshipper of Him who was born of her after the flesh, and who came down from Heaven and from the bosom of His Father." He then continues, that " the words ' Woman, what have I to do with thee?' were spoken on purpose that we might know her to be a woman, and not esteem her as something of a more excellent nature, and because our Lord foresaw the heresies likely to arise." Again he says, " Neither Elias, though he never died, nor Thecla, nor any of the saints, is to be worshipped." [1] If the Apostles " will not allow the angels to be worshipped, how much less the daughter of Anna," *i. e.* the blessed Virgin. " Let Mary be honoured, but let the Father, the Son, and the Holy Spirit be worshipped. Let no man worship Mary." [2] " Therefore though Mary be most excellent, holy, and honoured, yet is it not that she should be adored." [3]

Thus early did the worship of the Virgin show itself, and thus earnestly did the Christian fathers protest against it. [4]

Gregory Nazianzen flourished nearly at the same time with Epiphanius, towards the end of the fourth century. Archbishop Usher says, that his writings are the first in which we meet with anything like an address to the spirits of the dead. [5] It is worth while to see how this is. First, then, let us premise, that he expressly declares all worship of a creature to be idolatry. He positively charges the Arians with idolatry, because they, not believing the Son of God to be fully equal and of one substance with the Father, yet offered prayers to Him. [6] It is plain, therefore, that any address made by him to the departed could not be intended to be of the nature of that inferior worship, which the Arians offered to the Son, believing Him only the chief of the creatures of God. Yet it is clear that he believed, though not with certainty, that departed saints took an interest in all that passed among their friends and brethren on earth. [7] He had even a pious persuasion that they still continued as much as ever to aid with their prayers those for whom they had been wont to pray on earth. [8] And he ventures to think, if it be not too bold to say so, (εἰ μὴ τολμηρὸν τοῦτο εἰπεῖν,)

---

[1] οὔτε τις τῶν ἁγίων προσκυνεῖται.

[2] ἐν τιμῇ ἔστω Μαρία, ὁ δὲ Πατὴρ, καὶ Υἱὸς καὶ ἅγιον Πνεῦμα προσκυνείσθω, τὴν Μαρίαν μηδεὶς προσκυνείτω.

[3] καὶ εἰ καλλίστη ἡ Μαρία καὶ ἁγία καὶ τετιμημένη, ἀλλ' οὐκ εἰς τὸ προσκυνεῖσθαι.

[4] Bellarmine quotes a passage from Athanasius (*De Deipara Virgine, ad finem*) which would, if genuine, prove that St. Athanasius sanctions the worship of the Virgin; but the tract is known to be spurious, and was evidently written after the rise of the Monothelite heresy.

[5] Usher, *Answer to a Jesuit*, ch. IX.

[6] Greg. Nazianz. *Orat.* XL. Tom. I. p. 669.

[7] καὶ γὰρ πείθομαι τὰς τῶν ἁγίων ψυχὰς τῶν ἡμετέρων αἰσθάνεσθαι. — *Epist.* 201, p. 898.

[8] *Orat.* XXIV. p. 425.

that the saints, being then nearer to God, and having put off the
fetters of the flesh, have more avail with Him than when on earth.[1]
In all this he does not appear to have gone further than some who
preceded him; nor is there anything in such speculations beyond
what might be consistent which the most Protestant abhorrence of
saint-worship and Mariolatry. Let us then see how it influenced
him in the addresses which he is supposed to have made to the
departed. In his first oration against Julian, speaking rhetorically,
he addresses the departed emperor Constantius, " Hear, O soul of
the great Constantius, if thou hast any sense or perception of these
things, thou and the Christian souls of emperors before thee."[2]
So, in his funeral oration on his sister Gorgonia, he winds up
thus: " If thou hast a care for the things done by us, and pious
souls have this honour of God, that they perceive such things, receive this our oration, in the place of many funeral rites."[3] Yet
these addresses, so far from resembling the prayer in after-times
offered to the saints, do in themselves effectually bear witness that
no such prayers were ever at that time sent up to them. In
oratorical language, in regular oratorical harangues, Gregory addresses himself to the souls of the departed. In one case he, as
it were, calls on the soul of Constantius to witness; in the other
he addresses his sister, and trusts that she may be satisfied with
the funeral honours done to her. But in both instances he expresses doubt whether they can hear him, and in neither does he
make anything like prayers to them.

All good things are liable to abuse; and the affectionate interest
which the first Christians felt in the repose of the souls who had
gone before them to Paradise, their belief that they still prayed
with them and for them, no doubt, in course of time engendered
an inclination to ask the departed to offer prayers for them, and so
by degrees led to the Mariolatry and saint-worship of the Church
of Rome. We have seen, however, the clearest proofs that nothing of the sort was permitted or endured in the first four centuries.
Later than that, we have distinct evidence in the same direction
from those great lights of the Church, St. Chrysostom and St.
Augustine. The former protests against angel-worship as the most
fearful abomination, and attributes its origin to the inventions of
the devil.[4] St. Augustine replies to a charge brought by the Man-

---

[1] *Orat.* xix. p. 288.

[2] 'Ακουε καὶ ἡ τοῦ μεγάλου Κωνσταντίου
ψυχὴ, εἴ τις αἴσθησις, ὅσαι τε πρὸ αὐτοῦ
βασιλέων φιλόχριστοι. — *Orat.* iii. p. 50.

[3] εἰ δέ τις σοὶ καὶ τῶν ἡμετέρων ἐστι

λόγος, καὶ τοῦτο ταῖς ὁσίαις ψυχαῖς ἐκ Θεοῦ
γέρας, τῶν τοιούτων ἐπαισθάνεσθαι, δέχοιο
καὶ τὸν ἡμέτερον λόγον, ἀντὶ πολλῶν καὶ
πρὸ πολλῶν ἐνταφίων. — *Orat.* xi. p. 189.

[4] ὁ διάβολος τὰ τῶν ἀγγέλων ἐπεισήγαγε,

ichees, that the Catholics worshipped the martyrs, saying that Christians celebrated the memories of martyrs to excite themselves to imitation, to associate themselves in their good deeds, to have the benefit of their prayers; but never so as to offer up sacrifice (the sacrifice of worship) to martyrs, but to the God of martyrs. " The honour," he continues, " which we bestow on martyrs, is the honour of love and society, just as holy men of God are honoured in this life; but with that honour which the Greeks call *Latria*, and for which there is no one word in Latin, a service proper to God alone, we neither worship nor teach any one to worship any but God." [1]

Unhappily, some even of this early time, whose names are deservedly had in honour, were not so wise. St. Jerome, the contemporary of St. Chrysostom and St. Augustine, gave too much encouragement to the superstitions which were taking root in his day. Vigilantius, whatever his errors may have been, seems wisely to have protested against the growing tendency to venerate the relics and bones of the martyrs, and even called those who did so, idolaters. St. Jerome repudiates indeed all idolatrous worship. " Not only do we not worship and adore the relics of martyrs, but neither sun nor moon, nor angels, nor archangels, cherubim nor seraphim, nor any name that is named, in this world or in the world to come, lest we should serve the creature more than the Creator, who is blessed forever." But he earnestly defends the sanctity of the martyrs' relics. Vigilantius had argued, that the souls of Apostles and martyrs were either in the bosom of Abraham, or in a place of rest and refreshment, or beneath the altar of God (Rev. vi. 9). But Jerome contends, that " they follow the Lamb whithersoever He goeth (Rev. xiv. 4); and as the Lamb is everywhere present, so we may believe them to be; and as demons wander through the earth, can we argue that the souls of martyrs must be confined to one place?" On the contrary, he thinks that they may frequent the shrines where their relics are preserved, and where their memorials are celebrated. He expresses belief in miracles wrought at the tombs of martyrs, and that they pray for us after their decease. He defends the custom of lighting torches

βασκαίνων ἡμῖν τῆς τιμῆς. — *Homil.* IX. in *Coloss.* See also *Homil.* V. VII. *in Coloss.;* Bingham, *E. A.* XIII. iii. 3.

[1] " Colimus ergo martyres eo cultu dilectionis et societatis, quo et in hac vita coluntur sancti homines Dei, quorum cor ad talem pro evangelica veritate passionem paratum esse sentimus. At vero illo cultu, quæ Græce *Latria* dicitur, Latine uno verbo dici non potest, cum sit quædam proprie Divinitati debita servitus, nec colimus, nec colendum docemus nisi unum Deum." — *Contr. Faustum,* Lib. XXI. c. 20, Tom. VIII. p. 347; Bingham, XIII. iii. 2.

before the martyrs' shrines, denying that it is idolatrous to do so.[1]
Here, though such language is far different from what we read in
after-ages, we yet clearly trace the rise and gradual progress of
dangerous error.

The temptation to turn the mind from God to His creatures is
nowhere more likely to assail us than in our devotions. The multitude, converted from heathenism, who had all along worshipped
deified mortals, readily lapsed into the worship of martyrs. The
noxious plant early took root, and though for a time the wise and
pious pastors of the Church kept down its growth, still it gained
strength and sprang up afresh; until in ages of darkness and ignorance it reached a height so great, that, at least among the rude
and untaught masses, it overshadowed with its dark branches the
green pastures of the Church of Christ.

It is unnecessary to trace its progress. It grew steadily on,
though still checked occasionally. During the Iconoclastic controversy, one of the canons of the Council of Frankfort forbade not
only image-worship, but the invocation of saints (A. D. 794);
which, however, had been upheld by the opposite party at the second Council of Nice (A. D. 787).

Our Article especially condemns the "*Romish* doctrine" of invocation of saints, for which, of course, we must consult the decrees of the Council of Trent. That council simply enjoins, that
the people be taught "that the saints reigning with Christ offer
their prayers for men to God, and that it is good and useful to invoke them as suppliants; and for the sake of the obtaining of
benefits from God through Jesus Christ our Lord, who is our only
Redeemer and Saviour, to have recourse to their prayers." The
calling this idolatry it declares to be impious.[2] The creed of the
council has one article, "As also that the saints reigning with
Christ are to be venerated and invoked, and that they offer up
prayers for us to God, and that their relics are to be venerated."[3]

This is the mildest statement of the doctrine. Unhappily the
practice has far exceeded it; and that too in the public and authorized prayers of the Romish Church. It would be an irksome task

---

[1] *Epist.* 37, *ad Riparium*, Tom. IV. pt.
II. p. 279.

[2] "Docentes eos, sanctos una cum
Christo regnantes orationes suas pro hominibus offerre, bonum atque utile esse
suppliciter eos invocare, et ob beneficia
impetranda a Deo per Filium ejus Jesum
Christum, Dominum Nostrum, qui solus
noster Redemptor et Salvator est, ad

eorum orationes, opem auxiliumque con-
fugere," &c.— Sess. XXV. *De Invocatione
Sanctorum, &c.*

[3] "Similiter et sanctos una cum Christo
regnantes venerandos et invocandos esse,
eosque orationes Deo pro nobis offerre,
eorumque reliquias esse venerandas." —
Bulla Pii IV. *Super Forma Juramenti
Professionis Fidei.*

to collect the many expressions of idolatrous worship with which the Blessed Virgin is approached; and they are too well known to make it necessary.

It is desirable to observe the distinctions which Romanist divines make between the worship due to God, and that paid to the Blessed Virgin and the saints. They lay it down, that there are three kinds of worship or adoration : first, *latria*, which belongs only to God ; secondly, that honour and respect shown to good men ; thirdly, an intermediate worship, called by them *dulia*, which belongs to glorified saints in general, and *hyperdulia*, which belongs to the human nature of Christ, and to the Blessed Virgin.[1]

They determine, that the saints are to be invoked, not as primarily able to grant our prayers, but only to aid us with their intercessions ; although they admit, that the forms of the prayers are as though we prayed directly to them ; as for instance in the hymn : —

> Maria mater gratiæ,
> Mater misericordiæ,
> Tu nos ab hoste protege,
> Et hora mortis suscipe.

They say, moreover, that the saints pray for us through Christ, Christ prays immediately to the Father.[2]

It has seemed unnecessary to say anything of the views concerning the various subjects of this Article, as entertained by the different Protestant communions. All the reformed bodies of Europe have agreed in condemning the belief in purgatory, image-worship, and saint-worship. The Calvinistic bodies are more rigid than the Church of England and the Lutherans, in their rejection of all outward symbolism and emblems in their worship and places of worship. The Lutherans retain, not only the cross, but pictures and the Crucifix in their churches ; but, of course, they exhibit nothing like adoration to them. The Church of England has retained the cross as the symbol of redemption, and has encouraged the architectural adornment of her churches, but she has generally rejected the Crucifix, and whatever may appear to involve the least danger of idolatrous worship.

---

[1] See Bellarmine, *De Sanct. Beatit.* Lib. i. cap. 12. [2] Ibid. c. 17.

Section II. — SCRIPTURAL PROOF.

I. 1. Purgatory.

On this subject, and indeed on all the subjects of this Article, the burden of proof evidently lies with those who maintain the affirmative side of the question. If there be a purgatory, and if saints and images be objects of adoration, there should be some evidence to convince us that it is so.

The proofs from Scripture alleged in favour of purgatory are of two kinds: —

(1) Passages which speak of prayer for the dead.

(2) Passages which directly bear upon purgatory.

(1) The passages alleged in favour of prayer for the dead are:

2 Macc. xii. 42–45: where Judas is said to have "made a reconciliation for the dead, that they might be delivered from sin."

Tobit iv. 17: "Pour out thy bread," *i. e.* give alms to obtain prayers from the poor, "at the burial of the just, but give nothing to the wicked."

1 Sam. xxxi. 13: "They took their bones and buried them under a tree at Jabesh, and fasted seven days." This fasting is supposed to have been for the souls of Saul and his son.

1 Cor. xv. 29: "Else what shall they do which are baptized for the dead?" that is, who fast and weep, being baptized in tears for the dead.

2 Tim. i. 16, 18: "The Lord give mercy to the house of Onesiphorus . . . . The Lord grant unto him that he may find mercy of the Lord in that day." Where it is contended that Onesiphorus must have been dead, for St. Paul, who prays for present and future blessings to other people, here evidently prays for the bereaved family of Onesiphorus, and for Onesiphorus himself, that he may be blessed at the day of judgment.

In answer to all this we may say, that the only clear passage in favour of prayer for the dead is from the apocryphal book of Maccabees, which, not having the authority of Scripture, is merely of the force of Jewish tradition. But how little Jewish traditions are to be regarded in proof of doctrine, our Lord's condemnation of them is evidence enough. It certainly may be argued from this that the Jews sometimes used prayers for the dead, which no doubt was the case. But it would be very difficult to show that any sect among them believed in a purgatory. Of all the passages from the canonical Scriptures, the last cited (from 2 Tim. i. 18) is the only one that has any appearance of really favouring prayer for the dead. No doubt, some Protestant commentators (e. g. Grotius) have believed that Onesiphorus was dead. But if it be so, St. Paul's words merely imply a pious hope that, when he shall stand before the judgment-seat "in that day," he may "obtain mercy of the Lord," and receive the reward of the righteous, and not the doom of the wicked. There is certainly nothing in such an aspiration which implies the notion that he was, at the time it was uttered, in purgatory, and that St. Paul's prayers might help to deliver him from it. On the contrary, if the words be used concerning one already dead, they will furnish a proof from Scripture, in addition to the many which have been brought from antiquity,[1] that prayer for the dead does not of necessity presuppose a belief in purgatory. The early Christians undoubtedly did often pray for saints, of whose rest and blessedness they had no manner of doubt. Hence it would be no proof of the doctrine of purgatory, even if fifty clear passages, instead of a single doubtful one, could be brought to show that the Apostles permitted prayer for the dead.

(2) The passages which are brought as directly bearing on purgatory, are Ps. xxxviii. 1: "O Lord, rebuke me not in thy wrath; neither chasten me in Thy hot displeasure." "Wrath" is said to mean eternal damnation; "hot displeasure," to mean purgatory.

Ps. lxvi. 12: "We went through fire" (i. e. purgatory) "and through water" (i. e. baptism); "but Thou broughtest us out into a wealthy place."

Isai. iv. 4: "When the Lord shall have washed away the filth of the daughters of Zion, and shall have *purged* the blood of Jerusalem from the midst thereof by the spirit of judgment, and by the spirit of *burning.*"[2]

Isai. ix. 18. Mic. vii. 8, 9.

Zech. ix. 11: "As for thee also, by the blood of thy covenant I have sent forth thy prisoners out of the pit wherein is no water." This is interpreted of Christ's descent into hell, to deliver those who were detained in the *limbus patrum.*

Mal. iii. 3: "He shall sit as a refiner and purifier of silver; and He shall purify the sons of Levi, and purge them," &c.

---

[1] See Section I. i. 1.

[2] Bellarmine cites Augustine (*De Civit. Dei,* Lib. xx. c. 25) as interpreting this of purgatory. Augustine, however, does not interpret it of purgatory, but of that trial by fire which Origen, and others after him, supposed was to take place at the judgment-day.

Matt. xii. 32 : " It shall not be forgiven him neither in this world, *neither in the world to come ;* " i. e. evidently in purgatory, for in hell there is no forgiveness.

Matt. v. 22 : Our Lord speaks of three kinds of punishments, the judgment, the council, and hell. The latter belongs to the world to come ; therefore the two former must. Hence there must be some punishments in the next world besides hell.

Matt. v. 25, 26 : " Agree with thine adversary quickly, whiles thou art in the way with him ; lest at any time the adversary deliver thee to the judge, and the judge deliver thee to the officer, and thou be cast into prison. Verily I say unto thee, thou shalt by no means come out thence, till thou hast paid the uttermost farthing." The last words show that the *prison* must be purgatory, a temporal, not an eternal punishment. Otherwise, how would anything be said about coming out of it ?

1 Cor. iii. 12–15 : " Now if any man build upon this foundation, gold, silver, precious stones, wood, hay, stubble ; every man's work shall be made manifest : for the day shall declare it, because it shall be revealed by fire ; and the fire shall try every man's work of what sort it is. If any man's work abide which he hath built thereupon, he shall receive a reward. If any man's work shall be burned, he shall suffer loss : but he himself shall be saved ; yet so as by fire."

Luke xvi. 9, xxiii. 42, are also quoted ; but it is difficult to see how they can be made to bear on the question. Also Acts ii. 24, where our Lord is said to have " loosed the pains of death," *i. e.* to have delivered the souls from *limbus.* And Phil. ii. 10, Rev. v. 3, which speak of beings " in Heaven and earth and *under the earth.*" Where, " under the earth," it is contended, must mean purgatory.

These are all that are alleged by Bellarmine as proofs from Scripture that there is a purgatory between death and judgment. He adds, however, arguments from the fathers, whose sentiments have been already considered, and many from visions of the saints, which it will be unnecessary to consider.[1] His principal argument from reason is, that, although sins are forgiven to all true penitents for the merits of Christ, yet it is as regards their eternal, not their temporal punishment ; for we know that many devout penitents have to suffer the temporal punishments of their sins, though the eternal be remitted. Thus natural death, which is the result of sin, the temporal wages of sin, befals all men, those who are saved

[1] Bellarmine, *De Purgatorio,* Lib. i. c. 3–8, &c.

from, as well as those who fall into, death eternal. So David had his sin forgiven him, but still his child died. Eternally he was saved, but temporally punished. Now it often happens that persons have not suffered all the temporal punishment due to their sins in this life ; and therefore we must needs suppose, there is some state of punishment awaiting them in the next.[1]

It appears at first sight, to a person unused to believe in purgatory, almost impossible that such a doctrine could be grounded on such arguments. If indeed the doctrine were proved and established on separate grounds, then perhaps some of the passages quoted above might be fairly alleged in illustration of it, or as bearing a second and mystical interpretation, which might have reference to it. But what is fair in illustration may be utterly insufficient for demonstration.

It is not too much to assert, that only one of the texts from Scripture cited by Bellarmine can be alleged in direct proof. If he rightly interpret 1 Cor. iii. 12–15, that may be considered as a direct and cogent argument ; and then some of the other passages might be brought to illustrate and confirm it. But if that were put out of the question, we may venture to say even Roman Catholic controversialists would find the Scriptural ground untenable. The passages in St. Matthew (v. 26, xii. 32, " Thou shalt by no means come out thence till thou hast paid the uttermost farthing," and, " It shall not be forgiven him, neither in this world, neither in the world to come ") may indeed be supposed to speak of temporal punishments in the next world. But if they prove anything, they prove more than the Roman Catholic Church would wish, namely, that the pains of *hell* are not eternal ; for it is evidently hell which is the punishment of unrepented and unpardoned sin. Those who go to purgatory, are, on the showing of its own advocates, those who have received forgiveness of their sins, but need the purgation of suffering, either here or hereafter, to fit them for Heaven. The truth is, that the words of our Lord indicate merely, first, that as a great debtor is imprisoned till he has paid the last farthing, so a man who is not delivered here from the burden of his sins must remain in punishmemt for ever, as his debt is too heavy ever to be paid off; and next, that he who sins against the Holy Ghost has *never* forgiveness ; and it is added, " neither in this world, neither in the world to come," to impress more forcibly both the fearfulness and the eternity of his condemnation.

To recur, then, to 1 Cor. iii. 12–15 ; Bellarmine himself quotes

---

[1] Bellarmine, *De Purgatorio*, Lib. i. cap. 11.

St. Augustine [1] as saying that it is one of those hard passages of St. Paul, which St. Peter speaks of as wrested by unstable men to their destruction, and which St. Augustine wishes to be interpreted by wiser men than himself. If so, it is hardly prudent or modest to build such a doctrine as purgatory upon it. Bellarmine himself recounts many different interpretations of the different figures in the passage, as given by different fathers and divines. That all the fathers did not interpret it of purgatory is most certain; for St. Chrysostom has already been quoted as interpreting it of eternal damnation. But more than that, those fathers whose interpretation seems most suitable to the Romanist belief, do not understand the passage of purgatory, but of a purgatorial or probatory fire, not between death and judgment, but at the very day of judgment itself, when all works shall be brought up and be had in remembrance before the Lord. This has already been shown in the preceding section. And indeed it is not possible justly to give an interpretation of the passage nearer to the Romish interpretation than this. The expression " the day " is understood by all who interpret it of the next life to mean " the day of judgment." " The day " cannot certainly be well understood of the hidden and unrevealed state of the dead in the intermediate and disembodied state. If, therefore, the passage refers to the next world at all, it must mean that at the day of judgment all works shall be revealed, and tried, as it were, in the fire. Those who have built on the right foundation shall be saved; though, if their superstructure be of an inferior quality (whatever be meant by the superstructure), it shall be lost. This might indeed be made to suit the doctrine of Origen, but is utterly inapplicable to the doctrine of purgatory.

But even Origen's doctrine it will not well suit, if the context be fully considered. St. Paul had been speaking of himself and Apollos, as labourers together in the work of evangelizing the world and building the Church (vv. 5–9). The Church he declares to be God's building (ver. 9), even a temple for the indwelling of the Spirit (ver. 16). Now he says, the only possible foundation which can be laid is that which has been laid already, even Jesus Christ, (ver. 11). But the builders (*i. e.* ministers of Christ), in building the Church on this foundation, may make the superstructure of various materials, some building of safe and precious materials, gold, silver, and precious stones; others of less valuable or less durable, wood, hay, and stubble What then must be the meaning of this? Clearly, either that in building up the

[1] *De Fide et Operibus,* c. 15.

Church, they may upon the foundation, Christ, build sounder or less sound doctrines, — or, (which seems a still more correct interpretation of the figures,) that they may build up soundly instructed and confirmed believers, or, by negligence and ignorance, may train less orthodox and steadfast Christians. There is evidently nothing about the good or bad works of Christian men built on the foundation of a sound faith. It is the good or bad workmanship of Christian pastors in building up the Church of Christ. To proceed then: when the Christian minister and master-builder has thus finished his work, the day will prove whether it be good or bad. If his building be stable, it will endure, and he will be blessed in his labours and " receive a reward " (comp. 1 Cor. ix. 17). But if his superstructure be destroyed; if those, whom he has built up in the faith prove ill instructed and unstable, he will himself suffer loss, he will lose those disciples, who would have been " his crown of rejoicing in the presence of the Lord Jesus Christ at His coming " (1 Thess. ii. 19) ; and even he himself will escape, as it were, out of the fire.[1] It may be that the fiery trial means " the day " of judgment: for then all men's works shall be manifested; and the building of the Christian pastor or Apostle shall be then proved good or evil, by the characters and works of those whom he has converted and taught. But, as whatever doth make manifest is called " the day," therefore many think, and that with much ground of reason, that " the day " here spoken of was that day of trial and persecution which was awaiting the Church. That day was indeed likely to prove the faithfulness of the converts, and therefore the soundness of the pastor's building. St. Paul often speaks of unsound teachers; and if they had built up unstably, the day of persecution was likely to reveal it, to show the hollowness of their disciples, and to cause them loss. And such a trial would be " so as by fire." Elsewhere the term " fiery trial " is applied to persecution and affliction. St. Peter speaks specially of the trial of faith by affliction, as being like that of gold in the furnace, the very same metaphor with that used here by St. Paul (1 Pet. i. 7) ; and, again with the same meaning, tells the Christians that they should not " think it strange concerning the fiery trial which was to try them," but to rejoice, as it would the more fit them to partake of Christ's glory.

But whether we interpret *the day* and the *fiery trial* of persecution here or of judgment hereafter, there is no room in either for

---

[1] ὡς διὰ πυρός. The expression is " so as by fire ; " a proverbial expression for an escape from great danger. See Grotius and Rosenmüller, *in loc.*

purgatory. Purgatory is not a time of trial on earth, nor is it at the time of standing before the Judgment-seat of Heaven. Therefore it is not the fiery trial of St. Paul, nor is it *the day*, which shall try of what nature is the superstructure erected by the master-builders on the one foundation of the Christian Church.

If then the texts alleged in favour of purgatory fail to establish it, we may go on to say that there are many which are directly opposed to it. It was promised to the penitent thief, " To-day thou shalt be with Me in Paradise " (Luke xxiii. 43). St. Paul felt assured, that it was better " to depart, and to be with Christ " (Phil. i. 23), " to be absent from the body, and present with the Lord" (2 Cor. v. 8) ; having no apprehension of a purgatorial fire, in the middle state ; apparently laying it down as a principle concerning pious men, that whilst " at home in the body they are absent from the Lord ; " and that they may be confidently willing to leave the body, that they may be with the Lord (see 2 Cor. v. 6–9). Not one word about purgatory is ever urged upon Christians, to quicken them to a closer walk with God. All the other " terrors of the Lord" are put forth in their strongest light " to persuade men ; " but this, which would be naturally so powerful, and which has been made so much of in after-times, is never brought forward by the Apostles. Nay ! St. John declares that he had an express revelation concerning the present happiness of those that sleep in Jesus, namely, that they were blessed and at rest. " I heard a voice from Heaven saying unto me, Write, Blessed are the dead which die in the Lord from henceforth ; yea, saith the Spirit, that they may rest from their labours " (Rev. xiv. 13). When we couple such express declarations as these with the exhortations not to grieve for the dead in Christ, the general assurances concerning the blessedness of the death of the righteous, and concerning the cleansing from all sin by the blood of Christ, and then contrast them with the very slender Scriptural ground on which purgatory rests, it will be scarcely possible to doubt, that that doctrine was the growth of after-years, and sprang from the root of worldly philosophy, not of heavenly wisdom. Compare Luke xxi. 28 ; John v. 24 ; Eph. iv. 30 ; 1 Thess. iv. 13, &c. ; 2 Thess. i. 7 ; 2 Tim. iv. 8 ; 1 John i. 7 ; iii. 14.

2. Pardons or Indulgences.

The doctrine of pardons, and the custom of granting indulgences, rest on two grounds, namely, 1, purgatory, 2, works of supererogation. Indulgences, as granted by the Church of Rome, signify a remission of the temporal punishment of sins in purgatory ; and the power to grant them is supposed to be derived from the supe.abundant merits of Christ, the Virgin Mary, and the saints. It is argued by Romanist divines that (1) A double value exists in men's good deeds, first of merit, secondly of satisfaction : '(2) A good deed, as it is meritorious, cannot be applied to another ; but, as it is satisfactory or expiatory, it can : (3) There exists in the Church an infinite store of the merits of Christ, which never can be exhausted : (4.) And, in addition to this, the sufferings of the Virgin Mary (herself immaculate) and of the other saints, having been more than enough for their own sins, avail for the sins of others. Now, in the Church is deposited all this treasure of satisfactions, and it can be applied to deliver the souls of others from the temporal punishment of sins, the pains of purgatory.[1] That such a power exists in the pope is argued from the command to St. Peter, " to feed the sheep of Christ," and the promise to him of the keys of the kingdom, of authority to bind and to loose. That the good deeds of one man are transferable to another, is thought to be proved by the article of the Creed, " I believe in the communion of saints," and by the words of St. Paul, " I will very gladly spend and be spent for you " (2 Cor. xii. 15) ; " I endure all things for the elect's sake " (2 Tim. ii. 10) ; " I rejoice in my sufferings for you, and fill up that which is behind of the afflictions of Christ in my flesh for His body's sake, which is the Church " [2] (Col. i. 24).

Both the doctrine of purgatory and that concerning works of supererogation have already been considered ; and we have seen that they have no foundation in Scripture. Hence the practice of granting indulgences, which rests on them, must necessarily be condemned. The Romanist divines admit that indulgences free not from natural pains, or from civil punishments.[3] They never profess that they can deliver from eternal death. Hence, if there be no purgatory, there can be no room for indulgences.

If there be, as they state, an infinite store of Christ's merits committed to the Church, one would think it needless to add the sufferings of the Virgin Mary and of the saints. As to the claim, to dispense the benefits of these sufferings, founded on the promise of the keys to St. Peter, I hope to consider more at length the whole question of binding and loosing, of retaining ,and remitting sins, and of the pope's succession to St. Peter, under future Articles. Suffice it here that we remember, 1, that there is no

---

[1] Bellarmine, *De Indulgentiis*, Lib. i. cap. ii. 2, 3, 7.

[2] Ibid. Lib. i. c. 3. The last-cited passage, Col. i. 24, was considered under Art. xiv. p. 351, note.

[3] Bellarmin. Ibid. Lib. i. c. 7.

foundation for the figment of purgatory in Scripture, and that its gradual rise is clearly traceable ; 2, that none of the saints, not even the Blessed Virgin, were free from sin, nor able to atone for their own sins ; 3, that works of supererogation are impossible ; 4, that therefore indulgences, partly derived from superabundant works of satisfaction performed by the saints, and having for their object the freeing of souls from purgatory, must be unwarranted and useless.

II.   1. The Worshipping and Adoration of Images.

We can readily believe that the champions of image - worship would find a difficulty in discovering Scriptural authority for their practice.   But it rather surprises us to learn that their whole stock of argument is derived from the *old Testament;* in which no sin is so much condemned as the worship, nay, even the making of idols. The distinction between idols and images, it seems hard to understand.   That images may lawfully be placed in temples, is argued from the fact that Moses was commanded to make the Cherubim of gold, and place them on each side of the mercy-seat, (Ex. xxv. 18) ; and that Solomon carved all the walls of the temple " round about with carved figures of Cherubim " (2 Kings vi. 29), and " he made a molten sea — and it stood upon twelve oxen — and on the borders were lions, oxen, and Cherubim " (1 Kings vii. 23, 25, 29).[1]   That the second commandment[2] does not forbid making images, but only making them with the object of worshipping them, is also contended ; and thus far we have no reason to complain.   There may be a superstitious dread, as well as a superstitious use, of outward emblems.   No doubt, much as the Jew was bidden to hold idolatry in abhorrence, he was not only permitted, but commanded to place emblematical figures in the house of the Lord.   It is further said, that the brazen serpent which Moses set up by God's ordinance in the wilderness (Num. xxi. 8, 9) was an example of the use of images for religious purposes.   This was a

[1] See Bellarmine, *De Ecclesia Triumphante,* Lib. ii. cap. ix. ; *Controvers.* Tom. ii. p. 771.

[2] The second commandment is joined with the first, according to the reckoning of the Church of Rome.   This is not to be esteemed a Romish novelty.   It will be found so united in the Masoretic Bibles; the Masoretic Jews dividing the tenth commandment (according to our reckoning) into two.   What the Roman Church deals unfairly in is, that she teaches the commandments popularly only in epitome ; and that so, having joined the first and second together, she virtually omits the second, recounting them in her catechisms, &c. thus, 1 Thou shalt have none other gods but me. 2 Thou shalt not take the Name of the Lord thy God in vain.   3 Remember that thou keep holy the Sabbath day, &c.   By this method her children, and other less instructed members, are often ignorant of the existence in the Decalogue of a prohibition against idolatry.

figure of the Lord Jesus, the expected Messiah; and the wounded Israelites were taught to look up to it for healing and deliverance. But beyond this it is said, that the Jews actually did adore the Ark of the Covenant, and that in so doing they must have adored the Cherubim which were upon it. And this most strangely is inferred from the words, " Exalt ye the LORD your God, and worship at His footstool; for He is holy " (Ps. xcix. 5) ; where the Vulgate reads, *Adorate scabellum ejus, quoniam sanctus est;* or, as some quote it, *quoniam sanctum est.*[1]

With every desire to feel candid towards those who are opposed to us, it is difficult to know how to treat such arguments as these. We willingly concede, that the iconoclastic spirit of the Puritans was fuller of zeal than of judgment ; for if the figures of Cherubim were commanded in the temple, figures of angels and saints and storied windows in our cathedrals could scarcely be impious and idolatrous. But when we are told that the existence of such symbols near the mercy-seat involved a necessity that the Jew should worship them, we scarcely know whither such reasoning may carry us. If the Cherubim in the temple were worshipped, why were the golden calves of Jeroboam so foully idolatrous? It is mostly considered, that Jeroboam borrowed these very figures from the carvings of the sanctuary. How could that be holy in Jerusalem, which was vile in Dan and Bethel? Nay! the sin of Jeroboam was specially, that he made the calves to be *worshipped;* whereas in the temple they were not for worship, but for symbolism. As for the brazen serpent, it was no doubt, like the Cherubim, a proof that such symbols are allowable ; and was also the instrument (like the rod of Moses) by which God worked wonderful miracles. But when it tempted the people to worship it, Hezekiah broke it in pieces (2 Kings xviii. 4), as thinking it better to destroy so venerable a memorial of God's mercies, than to leave it as an incentive to sin.

The argument from Ps. xcix. 5, is the only one which Bellarmine (in many learned chapters on the subject) alleges in direct proof from Scripture that images are not only lawful, but adorable. Even if the Vulgate rendering (*adorate scabellum*) were correct, it would be a forlorn hope, with which to attack such a fortress as the second commandment. But the Hebrew (הִשְׁתַּחֲווּ לַהֲדֹם) is far more correctly rendered by the English version, " Bow down before His footstool." Though to *fall down before* God may be to worship Him, yet *to fall down before his footstool* is not necessarily

---

[1] See Bellarmine, *De Ecclesia Triumph.* Lib. I. c. XIII. Lib. II. c. XII. Tom. II. pp 708, 781.

to worship His footstool. Hence the word may at times be properly translated, " *to worship ;* " but here such a translation is altogether out of place.

In short, if the Roman Church had never approached nearer to idolatry than the Jews when they worshipped in the courts of the temple, within which were symbolical figures of oxen and cherubim, than the high priest, when once a year he approached the very ark of the covenant and sprinkled the blood before the mercy-seat, or than the people in the wilderness, when they looked upon the brazen serpent and recovered, there would have been no controversy and no councils on the subject of image-worship. But when we know, that the common people are taught to bow down before statues and pictures of our blessed Saviour, of His Virgin Mother, and of His saints and angels ; though we are told that they make prayers, not to the images, but to those of which they are images, yet we ask, wherein does such worship differ from idolatry ? No heathen people believed the image to be their God. They prayed not to the image, but to the god whom the image was meant to represent.[1] Nay ! the golden calves of Jeroboam were doubtless meant merely as symbols of the power of Jehovah ; and the people, in bowing down before them, thought they worshipped the gods " which brought them up out of the land of Egypt " (1 Kings xii. 28). But it is the very essence of idolatry, not to worship God in spirit and in truth, but to worship Him through the medium of an image or representation. It is against this that the second commandment is directed : " Thou shalt not make to thyself any graven image, nor the likeness of anything that is in heaven or earth, or under the earth — Thou shalt not bow down to it, nor worship it." And it is not uncharitable to assert, that the ignorant people in ignorant ages have as much worshipped the figure of the Virgin and the image of our Lord upon the cross, as ever ignorant heathens worshipped the statues of Baal or Jupiter, or as the Israelites worshipped the golden calf in the wilderness. It must even be added, painful as it is to dwell on such a subject, that divines of eminence in the Church of Rome have taught unchecked, that to the very images of Christ was due the same supreme worship which is due to Christ Himself, — even that *latria*, with which none but the Holy Trinity and the Incarnate Word must be approached.[2]

---

[1] See this exactly stated, *Arnob. adv. Gentes,* Lib. vi.

[2] See this proved by numerous passages from distinguished Romanists by Archbishop Usher, *Answer to a Jesuit,* chap. x. Dublin, 1624, p. 449. " Constans est theologorum sententia " (says Azorius the Jesuit) " imaginem eodem honore et cultu honorari et coli, quo colitur id cujus est imago." — Jo. Azor. *Institut Moral.* Tom. i. Lib. ix. cap. 9.

Bellarmine himself, who takes a middle course, states the above as one out of three current opinions in the Church, and as held by Thomas Aquinas, Caietan, Bonaventura, and many others of high name ; [1] and though he himself considers the worship of *latria* only improperly and *per accidens* due to an image, yet he says that " *the images of Christ and the saints are to be venerated, not only by accident or improperly, but also by themselves properly, so that themselves terminate the veneration, as in themselves considered, and not only as they take the place of their Exemplar.*" [2] If this be not to break one, and that not the least of God's commandments, and to teach men so, it must indeed be hard to know how God's commandments can be broken, and how kept. Even enlightened heathenism seldom went so far as to believe the worship to be due *properly* to the idol itself, and not merely to its original and prototype.

It is unnecessary to recite the Scriptures which speak against idolatry and image-worship ; they are so patent and obvious. See for example, Exod. xx. 2–5 ; xxxii. 1–20. Levit. xix. 4 ; xxvi. 1. Deut. iv. 15–18, 23, 25 ; xvi. 21, 22 ; xxvii. 15 ; xxix. 17. 2 Kings xviii. 4 ; xxiii. 4. Ps. cxv. 4. Isai. ii. 8, 9 ; xl. 18, 19, 25 ; xlii. ; xliv. ; xlvi. 5–7. Acts xvii. 25, 29. Rom. i. 21, 23, 25. 1 Cor. viii. 4 ; x. 7 ; xii. 2. 1 John v. 21. Rev. ix. 20.

2. Worshipping and Adoration of Relics.

The arguments brought from Scripture to defend relic worship are — that miracles were wrought by the bones of Elisha (2 Kings xiii. 21), by the hem of Christ's garment (Matt. ix. 20–22), by " the shadow of Peter passing by " (Acts v. 15), by handkerchiefs and aprons brought from the body of St. Paul (Acts xix. 12), — that the rod of Aaron and the pot of manna were preserved in the temple, — that it is said (in Isai. xi. 10), " In Him (Christ) shall the Gentiles trust, and His sepulchre shall be glorious ; " *In Eum gentes sperabunt, et erit sepulchrum Ejus gloriosum.* [3]

---

[1] *De Eccles. Triumph. Lib.* II. c. XX. ; *Controvers.* Tom. II. p. 801. Thomas Aquinas says : " Sic sequitur quod eadem reverentia exhibeatur imagini Christi et ipsi Christo. Cum ergo Christus adoretur adoratione latriæ consequens est quod ejus imago sit adoratione latriæ adoranda." — *Summa*, pt. III. quæst. 25, Artic. 3. See Usher, as above.

[2] " Imagines Christi et sanctorum venerandæ sunt, non solum per accidens, vel improprie, sed etiam per se proprie, ita ut ipsæ terminent venerationem ut in se considerantur, et non solum ut vicem gerunt exemplaris." — Ibid. c. 21, p.

802. He goes on to show, that it should neither be said nor denied (especially in public discourses), that images should be worshipped with *latria* (c. XXII.). The images of Christ *improperly and by accident* receive *latria* (c. XXXIII.). He concludes by saying : " Cultus, qui per se, proprie debetur imaginibus, est cultus quidem imperfectus, qui analogice et reductive pertinet ad speciem ejus cultus, qui debetur exemplari." — c. XXV. p. 809.

[3] Bellarmin. *De Eccl. Triumph. Lib.* II. cap. III. ; *Cont. Gen* Tom. II. p. 746.

The last argument is derived solely from the Latin translation. The Hebrew, the Greek, the Chaldee, and other versions, have "His rest," or "His place of habitation shall be glorious." (מְנֻחָתוֹ *ἀνάπαυσις*). Even if it meant the sepulchre, which it does not, it would not follow that because it was glorious or honourable, therefore it should be adored. There can be no question, that God has been pleased to give such honour to His saints, that in one instance the dead body of a prophet was the means of restoring life to the departed, that in another, handkerchiefs brought from an Apostle were made instruments of miraculous cure. But we have no instance in Scripture of the garments or the bones of the saints being preserved for such purposes. All evidence from Holy Writ goes in the opposite direction. The Almighty buried the body of Moses, so that no man should know where it lay, Deut. xxxiv. 6; which seems purposely to have been done, that no superstitious reverence should be paid to it. The bones of Elisha, by which so wonderful a miracle was wrought, were not preserved for any purpose of worship or superstition. The body of the holy martyr St. Stephen was by devout men " carried to his burial, and great lamentation was made over him ; " but no relics of him are spoken of, nor of St. James, who followed him in martyrdom. Their bones were evidently, like those of their predecessors the prophets, left alone, and no man moved them (2 Kings xxiii. 18). The pot of manna and the rod of Aaron were preserved as memorials of God's mercy ; but no one can imagine any worship paid to them. And the only relic to which we learn that worship was paid, namely, the brazen serpent, was on that very account broken in pieces by Hezekiah ; and he is commended for breaking it (2 Kings xviii. 4), though of all relics it must have been the noblest and most glorious, reminding the people of their deliverance from Egypt, and giving them assurance of a still more glorious deliverance, to which all their hopes should point. But the very first principle of Scripture truth is, " Thou shalt worship the Lord thy God, and Him only shalt thou serve " (Matt. iv. 10). And though by degrees a superstitious esteem for the relics of martyrs crept into the Church, yet we have clear evidence that for some time no undue honour was paid to them, and that when it was, the pious and learned, instead of fostering, strove to check the course of the error. The contemporaries of St. Polycarp indignantly denied that they wished for his body for any superstitious purposes, or that they could worship any but Christ.[1] And St. Augustine reproved the

---

[1] See especially *Martyr. Polycarp.* c. 17, referred to above.

superstitious sale of relics, which, by his day, had grown into an abuse.[1] Yet the Roman Church has authoritatively condemned such as deny that the bodies of martyrs or the relics of the saints are to be venerated.[2] And some of her divines have even sanctioned the paying of the supreme worship of *latria* to the relics of the cross, the nails, the lance, and the garments of the crucified Redeemer.[3]

3. Invocation of Saints.

The divines of the Church of Rome defend this practice as follows : —

(1) Saints, not going to purgatory, go straight to Heaven, where they enjoy the presence of God.

(2) Being then in the presence of God, they behold, in the face of God, the concerns of the Church on earth.

(3) It is good to ask our friends on earth to pray for us ; how much rather those who, being nearer God, have more avail with Him.

(4) The Scripture contains examples of saint-worship.

(1) The first position is sought to be established from Scripture, thus, —

The thief on the cross went straight to Paradise, *i. e.* to Heaven ! (Luke xxiii. 43). " We know that if our earthly house of this tabernacle be dissolved, we have a house not made with hands, eternal in the heavens " (2 Cor. v. 1, comp. ver. 4). " When He ascended up on high, He led captivity captive " (Eph. iv. 8). " Having a desire to depart, and to be with Christ " (Phil. i. 23). " The way into the holiest of all was not yet made manifest, while as the first tabernacle was yet standing " (Heb. ix. 8). " Ye are come unto mount Zion, and unto the city of the living God, the heavenly Jerusalem, to the general assembly of the first-born who are written in heaven . . . and to the spirits of just men made perfect " (Heb. xii. 22, 23). " Lord Jesus, receive my spirit " (Acts vii. 59). White robes are given to the martyrs who cry from under the altar, *i. e.* the glory of the body after the resurrection (Rev. vi. 11). " These are they which came out of great tribulation, and have washed their robes and made them white in the blood of the Lamb. Therefore are they before the throne of God, and serve Him day and night in His temple " (Rev. vii. 14, 15).

<hr/>

[1] Augustin. Tom. vi. p. 498.
[2] Concil. Trident. Sess. xxv. *De Invocatione, Veneratione, et Reliquiis Sanctorum.*
[3] " Reliquiæ crucis, clavorum, lanceæ, vestium Christi, et imago crucifixi sunt latria veneranda." — Joh. de Turrec. *In Festo Invent. Crucis,* q. 3 ; Beveridge, on Artic. xxii.

It is admitted that in the old Testament the saints, being as yet
in the *limbus patrum*, and therefore not in Heaven, could not be
prayed to;[1] but since Christ's descent into Hell and resurrection
from the dead, all who die in Him, if not needing to go to purgatory, go straight to glory, and therefore, reigning with Christ, may
be invocated.

It must be remembered, that these arguments for the immediate
glorification of the saints run side by side with arguments for a purgatory. The latter is an absolutely necessary supplement to the
former: without it, the Roman Catholic divines could not get rid
of the force of the arguments in favour of an intermediate state.
The two must therefore succeed or fail together. Now, it is
unnecessary to repeat the arguments already brought forward
against purgatory, or those (under Article III.) in proof that souls
go, not straight to Heaven after death, but to an intermediate state
of bliss or woe, awaiting the resurrection of the dead. All we
need consider now is this. Do the above texts of Scripture con-
travene that position? The first proves, that the thief went with
our Saviour where He went from the Cross; that is, not to
Heaven, but to Hades, to the place of souls departed, which, in the
case of the redeemed, is called Paradise. Our Lord went not to
Heaven till he He rose from the grave.[2] The second proves that,
when this body is dissolved, we may yet hope, at the general Resurrection, for a glorified body. But the context proves clearly,
that, between death and judgment, the souls of the saints remain
without the body, in bliss, but yet longing for the resurrection.
(See 2 Cor, v. 2, 3, 4, 6, 8, 10). The passage from Ephes. iv.
only proves that Christ conquered death. That from Phil. i. shows
that the disembodied spirit in Paradise is admitted to some presence
with its Saviour; as does that from Acts vii. Heb. ix. 8, merely
teaches that Christ is the way to Heaven, a way not *manifested*
under the old Law. Heb. xii. speaks of the Church as composed
of the first-born, whose names are in God's book, and as having
fellowship with the angels, and with departed saints, who have finished their course. The first passage from the Apocalypse (vi. 11),
if taken in its context (see Rev. vi. 9), is a strong proof that even
martyrs are in a state of expectant, not of perfect bliss; and if the
white robes really mean the glorified body at the resurrection, then

---

[1] "Notandum est ante Christi adventum qui moriebantur non intrabant in
cœlum, nec Deum videbant, nec cognos-
cere poterant ordinarie preces supplican-
tium. Ideo non fuit consuetum in V.
Testamento ut diceretur, Sancte Abraham, ora pro me: sed solum orabant
homines ejus temporis Deum." — Bellarmine, *De Eccles. Triumph.* i. 19

[2] See above, pp. 88, 95, &c.

must we believe yet more clearly than ever, that the very martyrs remain " under the altar " until the time of the resurrection of the just. The second passage (from Rev. vii. 14, 15) is probably a prophetic vision of the bliss of the saints, *after the general judgment*, and therefore plainly *nihil ad rem*.

It is said by the Romanists that a few *heretics* have denied the immediate beatification of the saints, *Tertullian*, Vigilantius, the Greeks at Florence, Luther, Calvin ;[1] and it is inferred that all the orthodox fathers have maintained it.[2] Tertullian is here a heretic, though, when he seems to favour purgatory, he is a Catholic divine. But the truth is, even their own divines have allowed, that a very large number of the greatest names of antiquity believed that the saints did not enjoy the vision of God till after the general judgment. Franciscus Pegna mentions, as of that persuasion, Irenæus, Justin M., Tertullian, Clemens Romanus, Origen, Ambrose, Chrysostom, Augustine, Lactantius, Victorinus, Prudentius, Theodoret, Aretas, Œcumenius, Theophylact, and Euthymius.[3] And our own great Bishop Bull pronounces it to have been the doctrine of the whole Catholic Church for many ages, " that the souls of the faithful, in the state of separation, though they are in a happy condition in Paradise, yet are not in the third Heaven, nor do enjoy the beatific vision till the Resurrection . . . . Nay, this was a doctrine so generally received in the time of Justin Martyr, that is, in the first succession of the Apostles, that we learn from the same Justin that there were none but some profligate heretics that believed the souls of the faithful, before the Resurrection, to be received into Heaven. (*Dialog. cum Tryphone*, pp. 306, 307. Paris, 1636)."[4]

Yet this immediate beatification of the saints is the very foundation of saint-worship. That can be but a slender foundation for so vast a superstructure, which the first fathers and the greatest writers of antiquity (even our enemies being the judges) could not find in the word of God, and did not believe to be true. Conceding the utmost that we can, we must yet maintain that the evidence from Scripture is far more against, than in favour of, this foundation, and that the first and greatest of the fathers utterly rejected it.

(2) If the first position cannot be established, of course the sec-

---

[1] See Bellarmine, *De Ecclesia Triumphante*, I. 1 ; *Controv. Gener.* Tom. II. p. 674.

[2] The testimonies in favour of it from the fathers are cited, Bellarmine, *ubi supra*, Lib. I. c. 4, 5.

[3] Fr. Pegna, in part. II. *Directorii Inquisitor.* comment. 21, apud Usher *Answer to a Jesuit*, chap. IX. ; who quotes also Thomas Stapleton to the same purport.

[4] Bull, *Vindication of the Church of England*, § XII.

ond must fall; though even if the first were granted, it does by no
means seem to follow that the second would stand. For even if
saints departed always behold the face of God, it does not certainly
follow that thereby they have the omniscience of God. That they
continue to take an interest in their fellow-worshippers, children of
the same Father, members of the same body with themselves, we
may reasonably believe; but that they know all the prayers which
each one on earth utters, even the secret silent prayer of the heart,
we cannot at least be certain — or rather we should think most
improbable.

(3) It is said that saints on earth pray for each other, and exhort one another to pray for them, (Heb. xiii. 18, James v. 16);
why not then ask the saints in light to pray for us, who, nearer the
throne of God, have more interest with Him?

Yet, who does not see the difference between joining our prayers
with our brethren on earth, so through the one Mediator drawing
nigh to God in common supplication for mercies and mutual intercession for each other, and the invocating saints above, with all
the circumstances of religious worship, to go to God for us, and so
to save us from going to Him for ourselves? If, indeed, we could
be quite certain, that our departed friends could hear us, when we
spoke to them, there might possibly be no more evil in asking them
to continue their prayers for us, than there could be in asking those
prayers from them whilst on earth, — no evil, that is, except the
danger that this custom might go further and so grow worse. This,
no doubt, was all that the interpellation of the martyrs was in the
early ages; and if it had stopped here, it would have never been
censured. But who will say that Romish saint-worship is no
more?

In the Church of Rome, when it is determined who are to be
saints, they are publicly canonized, *i. e.* they are enrolled in the
Catalogue of Saints; it is decreed, that they shall be formally held
to be saints, and called so; they are invoked in the public prayers
of the Church: churches and altars to their memory are dedicated
to God; the sacrifices of the Eucharist and of public prayers are
publicly offered before God to their honour; their festivals are celebrated: their images are painted with a glory round their heads:
their relics are preserved and venerated.[1] They are completely
invocated as mediators between God and man; so that those who
fear to go to God direct, are encouraged to approach Him through
the saints, as being not so high and holy as to inspire fear and

[1] Bellarmine, *De Ecclesia Triumph.* i. 7.

dread.[1]   Herein the very office of Christ is invaded, "the ONE Mediator between God and man" (1 Tim. ii. 5) ; a High Priest, who can " be touched with the feeling of our infirmities," and through whom we may " come boldly unto the throne of grace, that we may obtain mercy, and find grace to help in time of need " (Heb. iv. 15, 16).   Nay, more than this, direct prayer is made to the saints for protection and deliverance ; and even in prayer to God Himself, He is reminded of the protection and patronage of the saints.[2]   And we know, that, not only among the vulgar, but with the authority of the most learned, and those canonized saints, prayers have been put up to the Blessed Virgin, to use a mother's authority, and command her Son to have mercy upon sinners.[3]   What support can all this derive from the injunctions to us in Scripture to pray for one another, and the assurances that " the effectual fervent prayer of a righteous man availeth much " ?

(4) Next it is alleged, that Scripture contains positive examples of the worship of saints and angels.

Bellarmine cites the following : —

Ps. xcix. 5 : " Exalt ye the Lord our God, and worship at His footstool ; for He is holy," (*Adorate scabellum pedis ejus, quoniam sanctum est*) : a passage which has been already considered.   Gen. xviii. 2, xix. 1, Abraham and Lot bow down to the angels.   Numb. xxii. 31, Balaam, when he saw the angel, "fell flat on his face." 1 Sam. xxviii. 14, " And Saul perceived that it was Samuel, and he stooped with his face to the ground, and bowed himself." 1 Kings xviii. 7, " And as Obadiah was in the way, behold Elijah met him, and he knew him, and fell on his face, and said, Art thou that my Lord Elijah ? "   2 Kings ii. 15, " When the sons of the prophets saw him, they said, The spirit of Elijah doth rest upon Elisha : and they came to meet him, and bowed themselves to the

---

[1] One reason alleged in favour of saint-worship is " Propter Dei reverentiam : ut peccator, qui Deum offendit, quia non audet in propria persona adire, occurrat ad sanctos, eorum patrocinia implorando." — Alexand. de Hales, *Summa*, pt. IV. quæst. 26, memb. 3, artic. 5. Vide Usher, *ubi supra*.

[2] " Grant, we beseech Thee, Almighty God, that Thy faithful, who rejoice under the name and protection of the most blessed Virgin Mary, may, by her pious intercession, be delivered from all evils here on earth, and be brought to the eternal joys of Heaven.   Through." — " Coll. for the Feast of the name of B. V. Mary ; " " Missal for the Laity,"

published by authority of Thomas Bishop of Cambysopolis, and Nicholas Bishop of Melipotamus, Sept. 25, 1845.

[3] " Imperatrix et Domina nostra benignissima, jure matris impera tuo dilectissimo Filio Domino nostro Jesu Christo, ut mentes nostras ab amore terrestrium ad cœlestia desideria erigere dignetur." — Bonaventura, *Corona B. Mariæ Virginis, Oper. Tom.* VI.

" Inclina vultum Dei super nos : coge Illum peccatoribus misereri." — *Id. in Psalterio B. Mariæ Virginis*, Ibid.

See Archbishop Usher, as above, who gives many passages at length from Bernardin de Bustis, Jacob de Valentia, Gabriel Biel, &c., to the like effect.

ground before him." Josh. v. 14, 15 ; when Joshua knew that
he was in the presence of the Captain of the Lord's host, " he fell
on his face to the earth, and did worship." The angel did not
forbid him to worship him, but said, " Loose thy shoe from off thy
foot, for the place whereon thou standest is holy." Dan. ii. 46,
" The king Nebuchadnezzar fell upon his face, and worshipped
Daniel ; and commanded that they should offer an oblation and
sweet odour to him." [1]

Now, in the first place, it is certainly not a little strange, that,
whereas the divines of the Church of Rome tell us that no prayers
were offered to the old Testament saints, because they were in the
limbus patrum, and not in Heaven ; [2] yet, in their Scriptural proof
of saint-worship, they bring all their arguments from the old Testament only. There must be something rotten here. And we
need not go far to see what the ground of their preference for such
a line of argument is. The Eastern form of salutation to princes,
honoured guests, and elders, was, and still is, a profound prostration of the body, which is easily construed into an act of religious
worship. Now Abraham and Lot evidently (from the context and
from Heb. xiii. 2) did not know that the angels who appeared to
them were angels. They thought them strangers on a journey,
and exercised Eastern hospitality to them. They perceived that
they were strangers of distinction, and exhibited Eastern tokens
of respect. Thus, " being not forgetful to entertain strangers, they
entertained angels unawares."

The same may be said of all the above instances, except perhaps the last two. Falling down at the feet was the common mode
of respectful salutation, and that especially when favours were to
be asked. Thus Abigail fell at the feet of David (1 Sam. xxv.
24) ; Esther fell at the feet of Ahasuerus (Esth. viii. 3) ; the servant is represented as falling at the feet of his master (Matt. xviii.
29). This was no sign of religious worship. Even Balaam,
though he fell down before the angel, by no means appears to have
worshipped him. He fell down from fear, and in token of respect.
The case of Joshua, when he met the Captain of the Lord's host,
may be different. It is well known to have been the belief of many
of the fathers, and of many eminent divines after them, that the
Captain of the Lord's host was the second Person of the Holy
Trinity, the eternal Son of God.[3] And it is certainly as fair to

---

[1] Bellarmin. *De Eccles. Triumph.* i. 13 ;　　[3] See Justin M. *Dialogus,* p. 284 ; Euseb.
Cont. Gen. Tom. ii. p. 708.　　　　　　*H E.* i. 2.
[2] See Bellarmin. Ibid. i. 19, as quoted
above.

infer from the worship paid to him, that he was God, as to infer from it, that worship ought to be paid to any beside God.

We are reduced then to one single instance, and that the instance of an idolatrous king, who soon afterwards bade every one worship a golden image. He indeed appears, in a rapture of astonishment, to have fallen down to worship the prophet Daniel — not a glorified saint reigning with Christ — but one of those old fathers, who had to abide after death in the *limbus*, until our Lord's descent to Hades should rescue them.

But is there no instance in the new Testament? The new Testament is ever the best interpreter of the old. Are there no examples of the worship of saints or angels there? The Roman Catholic divines have not adduced any; but their opponents cannot deny that there are some cases of such worship recorded, and those too of a worship which cannot be explained to mean merely bowing down in token of respect to a superior.

One example is that of Cornelius: "as Peter was coming in, Cornelius met him, and fell down at his feet and worshipped him" (προσεκύνησεν). This is very like the case of Nebuchadnezzar and Daniel; but with this advantage over it, that Cornelius was no idolater, and St. Peter was not a prophet of the old Testament, for whom the schoolmen tell us a *limbus* was in store, but the chief of the Apostles, to whom the keys of the kingdom were committed, from whom the Roman Pontiff inherits his right to forgive and retain sins, and who (on their showing) at death was sure of passing straight to the highest kingdom of glory, thenceforth to reign with Christ, and to receive the prayers of the faithful. How then does St. Peter, whose authority none will question, treat the worship of Cornelius? "Peter took him up, saying, Stand up: I myself also am a man" (Acts x. 25, 26).

We may remember another case somewhat similar, though not quite identical, when "the Apostles Barnabas and Paul rent their clothes, and ran in among the people, crying out and saying, Sirs, why do ye these things? we also are men of like passions with you" (Acts xiv. 14, 15). But perhaps we shall be told that it was *latria* not *dulia*, that the men of Lycaonia meant to pay to them.

However, we are not confined to saint-worship in the new Testament; we can discover manifest traces of angel-worship too. Twice, one whose example we may rarely refuse to follow, the blessed Apostle St. John, fell down to worship the angel, who showed him the mysteries of the Apocalypse. The same word (προσκυνῆσαι) is used here as was used of Cornelius and St. Peter,

and as is used (in the .LXX.) of Nebuchadnezzar and Daniel
(προσεκύνησε, Dan. ii. 46). And what does the angel of God say
to the Apostle ? " See thou do it not; I am thy fellow-servant,
and of thy brethren, that have the testimony of Jesus: worship
God" (Rev. xix. 10). And again, "See thou do it not: for I am
thy fellow-servant . . . . worship God " (Rev. xxii. 9).

These are cases as plain as any in the old Testament can be.
It is not very likely that St. John would have offered the supreme
worship of *latria* to the angel. Therefore, no doubt, all kind of
worship was forbidden him. And if only *latria* be forbidden, but
dulia be a pious or necessary custom, it is certainly remarkable
that neither the angel explained to St. John, nor St. Peter to
Cornelius, nor St. Paul to the people of Lycaonia, the very important distinction between *latria* and *dulia*, the great sin of offering
the former, and the great piety of offering the latter, to created but
glorified intelligences; especially as the ambiguous word *worship*
(προσκυνῆσαι) includes them both. Moreover, as God's revelations
became successively clearer, and there is a gradual *development* of
Divine truth, it is truly unaccountable that so large a germ of
saint and angel-worship as the Roman Catholics discover in the
old Testament, should have developed into nothing more manifest
than what we thus find in the new. St. Paul, we know, earnestly
warns his converts against " the worshipping of angels,"— and the
word he uses (θρήσκεια) appears to comprehend all kinds of worship
(Col. ii. 18). St. Paul was not a writer who neglected accurate
distinctions, and we may fairly say, he was as profound a reasoner
and as deep a theologian as any human being, even under Divine
revelation, was ever privileged to become. But there is no question raised by him about *dulia* or *hyperdulia*. It is simply " Let no
man beguile you of your reward, in a voluntary humility, and worshipping of angels " (Col. ii. 18). It is a fearful thing to think, that
this voluntary humility, and unauthorized worship of inferior beings,
may beguile of their reward those who should worship God only.

One more instance is too pregnant to be omitted. Once, and
but once, in the history of the Bible, do we hear that an angel
claimed worship for himself. And he claimed it of Him whose
example in worship, as in everything else, we are bound to follow.
An angel of exceeding power once said to Jesus, " All these things
will I give Thee, if Thou wilt fall down and worship me. Then
said Jesus unto him, Get thee hence, Satan; for it is written, Thou
shalt worship the Lord thy God, and Him only shalt thou serve "
(Matt. iv. 9, 10).

ARTICLE XXIII.

Of Ministering in the Congregation.

De Vocatione Ministrorum.

It is not lawful for any man to take upon him the office of public preaching, or ministering the Sacraments in the Congregation, before he be lawfully called, and sent to execute the same. And those we ought to judge lawfully called and sent, which be chosen and called to this work by men who have public authority given unto them in the Congregation, to call and send ministers into the Lord's vineyard.

Non licet cuiquam sumere sibi munus publice prædicandi, aut administrandi sacramenta in Ecclesia, nisi prius fuerit ad hæc obeunda legitime vocatus et missus. Atque illos legitime vocatos et missos existimare debemus, qui per homines, quibus potestas vocandi ministros, atque mittendi in Vineam Domini, publice concessa est in Ecclesia, cooptati fuerint, et asciti in hoc opus.

Section I. — HISTORY.

AFTER the Articles concerning the Church comes naturally this concerning the ministry.

The wording of the Article demands some attention. The first sentence is derived from the fourteenth Article of the Confession of Augsburg, as drawn up in 1531. That article runs: "De ordine Ecclesiastico docent, quod nemo debeat in Ecclesia publice docere, aut Sacramenta administrare, nisi rite vocatus." [1]

In the XIII. Articles, supposed to have been agreed upon between the English and German divines, (A. D. 1538,) the Xth Article is: "De ministris Ecclesiæ docemus, quod nemo debeat publice docere, aut sacramenta ministrare, nisi rite vocatus, et quidem ab his, penes quos in ecclesia, juxta verbum Dei et leges ac consuetudines uniuscujusque regionis, jus est vocandi et admittendi." [2]

The twenty-fourth of the XLII. Articles of 1552, is worded exactly as our present twenty-third, and evidently only slightly changed from the above-cited Article of 1538. [3]

---

[1] *Sylloge*, p. 127. In 1540 we find the following clause added : "Sicut et Paulus præcipit Tito ut in civitatibus presbyteros constituat." — *Syll.* p. 174.

[2] Then follows a declaration, that no bishop should intrude on another diocese, and that the wickedness of ministers hinders not the grace of the Sacraments. — Jenkyns's *Cranmer*, IV. Appendix, p. 286.

[3] The heading of the Articles both in those of 1552 and in those of 1662 is, *Nemo in Ecclesia ministret nisi vocatus.*

As it now stands, it contains two parts : —

I. That no one may assume the office of the ministry without a lawful call and mission.

II. That calling and mission can only be given by certain authorities, who are the ministers of ordination.

The latter portion of the Article is somewhat vaguely worded : the reason for which is easily traced to the probable fact, that the original draught of the Article was agreed on in a conference between the Anglican and Lutheran divines. It would have been painful to the latter, if a strong assertion of the need of episcopal ordination had been inserted, when they were debarred from episcopal regimen. Hence it is but generally asserted, that lawful calling can only be given by those, " who have public authority in the Church to send labourers into the Vineyard." But then we may observe, that the authority of the English Ordinal is expressly made the subject of Article XXXVI.; and to see the force of the latter on our present Article, we must have recourse to the Ordinal, as expressing the mind of the reformers on this subject.

One expression in this Article requires to be especially observed. In the Confession of Augsburg, the XIII. Articles of 1538, and the Latin Articles of 1552, 1562, 1571, the word *Ecclesia* occurs twice. But in the English translations this word is rendered *Congregation*. To a modern reader, used to the language of Congregational dissenters, this translation has a different sound to that, which it must have had at the time of the Reformation. The ancient Church of the Jews is called " the Congregation of the Lord." The XIXth Article defines the Church as a " Congregation of faithful men," &c. Accordingly, the word *Ecclesia*, instead of being rendered *Church*, is rendered *Congregation*, meaning the whole Congregation of Christ's people, *i. e.* the Church or Body of Christ. The more modern idea of a Congregational election of ministers had evidently not suggested itself, or the word would have been avoided.

We may now proceed to our history.

I. No one can question, that very early in the Church there existed a distinction widely marked between the Clergy (κλῆρος, κληρικοὶ, *Clerici*) and the *Laity* (λαὸς, *Laici*). The only doubt which can be raised, is, whether such a distinction was quite primitive, or came in, in the second and third centuries, through the ambition of ecclesiastics.

It is a most happy circumstance, that the very earliest of the

Christian fathers, *Clemens Romanus*, the companion of St. Paul, has left us clear testimony on this head. Giving instructions concerning the duty of Christians towards those who minister to God, he first adduces the examples of the Jewish economy, in which the chief priest, and the Levite, have all their proper ministries, " and the layman is confined within the bounds of what is commanded to laymen." [1] He then goes on to say, " The Apostles have preached to us from our Lord Jesus Christ; Jesus Christ from God. Christ therefore was sent by God, the Apostles by Christ; so both were orderly sent according to the will of God . . . . Having received their commands . . . . and preaching through countries and cities, they appointed the first-fruits of their conversions to be bishops and deacons over such as should afterwards believe, having first proved them by the Spirit." [2] Then again, referring to the election of the seed of Aaron to the priesthood, in order to avoid contention,[3] he continues : " So likewise our Apostles knew by our Lord Jesus Christ, that there should contentions arise upon account of the ministry ; And therefore, having a perfect foreknowledge of this, they appointed persons, as we have said before, and then gave direction, how, when they should die, other chosen and approved men should succeed in their ministry. Wherefore we cannot think that those may justly be thrown out of their ministry who were appointed by them, or afterwards chosen by other eminent men, with the consent of the whole Church . . . . Blessed are those presbyters who, having finished their course before those times, have obtained a faithful and perfect dissolution ; for they have no fear, lest any one should turn them out of the place which is now appointed for them." [4]

Here, in the very earliest of the fathers, we have plainly the distinction of clergy and laity, the clergy spoken of at one time as presbyters, at another as bishops and deacons ; their mode of appointment in succession from the Apostles, and the duty of the people to be submissive and affectionate to them.

Ignatius speaks in language so strong, of the necessity of obedience to bishops, presbyters, and deacons, that the very strength of the expressions has been the chief reason for doubting the genuineness of his epistles. The seven shorter epistles, since Bishop Pearson's able defence of them, have generally been admitted to be genuine. The late discovery of a Syriac translation of three of them has again opened the question ; their learned editor and

---

[1] ὁ λαϊκὸς ἄνθρωπος τοῖς λαϊκοῖς προσταγμασιν δέδεται. —Clem. R. 1 *In Corinth* c. 40.

[2] Ibid. c. 42.

[3] c. 43.

[4] c. 44.

translator contending that the Syriac represents the true text, and
that even the shorter Greek epistles, which are longer than the
Syriac, have suffered from interpolation. This is no place to enter
into a controversy of such extent; it is, however, satisfactory to
find, that the short Syriac epistles, as they contain the most important testimonies to the great doctrine of the Trinity and the
Incarnation,[1] so do they contain most strong and unmistakable language on the ministry and the three orders of the ministry : " Give
heed to the bishop, that God also may give heed to you. My soul
be for those[2] who are subject to the bishop, presbyters, and deacons : may I have my portion with them in God." [3]

Irenæus speaks distinctly of successions of presbyters in the
Church from the time of the Apostles ; [4] says, that he was able to
reckon up those who had been made bishops by the Apostles, and
their successors even to his own time ; [5] and recounts the succession
of bishops at Rome from St. Peter and St. Paul, and at Smyrna
from St. Polycarp ; [6] to which successions he attaches deep importance.

Clement of Alexandria distinguishes the presbyter and deacon
from the layman,[7] and the lay from the priestly.[8] He uses the
term κλῆρος, clergy ; [9] and speaks of the three degrees in the
Church militant, of bishops, presbyters, and deacons,[10] which he
compares to the angelic orders in Heaven.[11]

Tertullian bears testimony to the existence of a distinction between clergy and laity in his day; and charges the heretics with
confounding the offices of layman and cleric.[12] The three orders of
bishops, presbyters, and deacons, are enumerated together ; [13] and
he tells us that the chief priest, i. e. the bishop, had the right to
baptize, as also had presbyters and deacons, but not without the
authority of the bishop.[14]

---

[1] See, for instance, Ignatius *Ad Ephes.*
c. 1, 9, 18 (19 in the Greek), *Ad Polyc.*
c. 8, where the Syriac has all the same
remarkable expressions as the Greek.
See especially in the first passage,
Ephes. c. 1, ἀναζωπυρήσαντες ἐν αἵματι Θεοῦ

[2] Ἀντίψυχον ἐγὼ τῶν ὑποτασσομένων, κ.
τ. λ.
[3] Ignat. *Ad Polyc.* c. 6.
[4] *Adv. Hær.* III. 2.
[5] "Habemus annumerare eos, qui ab
Apostolis instituti sunt Episcopi in ecclesiis, et successores eorum usque ad nos."
— III. 3.
[6] Ibid.
[7] κἂν πρεσβύτερος ᾖ, κἂν διάκονος, κἂν
λαϊκός. — *Stromat.* Lib. III. p. 552.

[8] *Stromata*, Lib. v. pp. 665, 666 ; where
λαϊκῆς ἀπιστίας is opposed to ἱερατικὴ δια-
κονία.
[9] " *Quis dives salvetur*," p. 959.
[10] *Stromat.* Lib. vi. p. 793.
[11] See Bp. Kaye's *Clement of Alexan
dria*, p. 463.
[12] " Alius hodie episcopus, cras alius :
hodie diaconus qui cras lector ; hodie
presbyter, qui cras laicus. Nam et laicis sacerdotalia munera injungunt." — *De
Præscript.* c. 41.
[13] See the last passage; also *De Fugâ*,
c. 11.
[14] "Dandi (baptismum) quidem habet
jus summus sacerdos, qui est episcopus ;
dehinc presbyteri et diaconi, non tamen
sine episcopi auctoritate, propter ec lesiæ
honorem." — *De Baptismo*, c. 17.

He speaks of receiving the Eucharist only from the presbyters.[1]
The office of the bishop was, according to him, of apostolic institution; and in the Catholic Church the successions of the bishops
could be traced to the Apostles, as the succession at Smyrna from
Polycarp, placed there by St. John, that at Rome from Clemens,
placed there by St. Peter.[2]

It is true that Tertullian claims for all Christians, that they are
priests, and contends that, in places where there are no clergy,
laymen may exercise the priestly offices, may baptize, and even
celebrate the Eucharist. But this is only in case of extreme necessity; his strong assertion of this is in a tract, written after he had
seceded from the Church; and, even allowing the utmost possible
weight to the passage, it does not prove the non-existence of a distinct order of the clergy, but only that, in case of absolute necessity, that distinction was not to be observed.[3]

Origen is very express on the office of the clergy,[4] on the power
of the keys as committed to them,[5] on the duty of obedience to
them.[6]

We are now arrived at the Cyprianic age, when no one doubts
that the distinction between lay and cleric was strongly marked
and much insisted on. Some have contended, that the distinction
was not from the first; but none can deny, that by this time it
was universally accepted. Hilary the deacon, whose commentaries
on St. Paul's epistles are appended to the works of St. Ambrose,
is indeed cited as saying that, in the beginning, in order to increase
the Church, the power to preach and baptize was given to all, but
that, when the Church spread abroad, a more regular constitution
was ordained, so that none of the clergy were permitted to intrude
into offices not committed to themselves.[7] But this does not prove
even that Hilary thought the distinction of lay and cleric not to be
Apostolical. It is most probable from the context, that by the
word *all, omnibus,* he means not all the *faithful,* but all the *clergy;*

---

[1] " Eucharistiæ sacramentum non de
aliorum manu quam præsidentium sumimus." — *De Corona,* 3.

[2] *De Præscript.* c. 32.

[3] *De Exhort. Castitat.* c. 7. See also
De Baptismo, c. 17. And consult Bp.
Kaye's *Tertullian,* p. 224; and Bingham,
E. A. Bk. I. ch. v. sect. 4.

[4] See *Homil.* II. *in Numer.; Homil.*
XIII. *in Lucam.*

[5] *In Matt.* Tom. XII. num. 14.

[6] *Homil.* XX. *in Lucam.* "Si Jesus
Filius Dei subjicitur Joseph et Mariæ,
ego non subjicior episcopo, qui mihi a

Deo ordinatus est pater? Non subjiciar
presbytero qui mihi Domini dignatione
præpositus est?"

[7] " Ut cresceret plebs et multiplicare-
tur omnibus inter initia concessum est
et evangelizare et baptizare et Scripturas
in ecclesia explanare. At ubi autem
omnia loca circumplexa est ecclesia, con-
venticula constituta sunt, et rectores et
cætera officia in ecclesiis sunt ordinata,
ut nullus de clero auderet, qui ordinatus
non esset, præsumere officium, quod sci-
ret non sibi creditum." — Hilar. Diac. *In
Epist. Eph.* c. IV. v. 12.

who at first performed all sacred functions indiscriminately, but afterwards were limited according to their distinctions of bishop, presbyter, and deacon. And even if he meant that all the faithful had at first a ministerial commission; yet still he clearly intended to fix the more regular constitution of the Church to the Apostolic age, before the close of which the Church might be said to have spread itself everywhere, and therefore needed regular establishment.[1] So that this passage makes nothing against the Apostolical origin of the order of clergy, and their distinction from the laity.[2]

So necessary did the fathers consider the office of the ministry, that St. Jerome tells us, " There is no Church where there are not priests." [3] And St. Chrysostom says, " Since the Sacraments are necessary to salvation, and all these things are performed by the hands of the priesthood, how, without them, shall any man be able to avoid the fire of hell, or to obtain the promised crown ? " [4]

The opinions of Christians of all ages, and almost all sects, have been in favour of the necessity of a distinct call to the ministry, and of an order regularly set apart for the executing of that office. Luther condemns it as an error invented by the devil, that men should say that they have a talent from the Lord, and therefore must of necessity assume the office of preaching. They should wait, till they are called to the ministry. If their Master wants them, He will call them; " If they teach uncalled, it will not be without injury to themselves and their hearers; for Christ will not be with them." [5] The Confession of Augsburg speaks of the ministry of the word and Sacraments as divinely instituted; condemns the Anabaptists, who teach that men can receive the Spirit, without the external word ; and says, that none may minister the word and Sacraments, not rightly called to it.[6] The Helvetic Confession of the Zuinglians declares the office of minister to be " ancient and ordained of God ; not of recent, or of human ordination." [7] Calvin says, that " no one must be accounted a minister

---

[1] See Bingham, Book i. c. v. § 4, and Mr. Morrison's note to his translation of Neander's *Church History*, i. p. 252.

[2] St. Jerome tells us the reason of the name κλῆρος, *clerici*, " Propterea vocantur *clerici*, vel quia de sorte sunt Domini, vel quia Dominus sors, id est pars, clericorum est." — *Ad Nepotian. De Vita Clericorum*, Tom. iv. Part ii. p. 259.

[3] " Ecclesia non est, quæ non habet sacerdotes."— *Dial. c. Lucifer.* c. 8.

[4] Εἰ γὰρ οὐ δύναταί τις εἰσελθεῖν εἰς τὴν βασιλείαν τῶν οὐρανῶν, ἐὰν μὴ δι' ὕδατος καὶ Πνεύματος ἀναγεννηθῇ, καὶ ὁ μὴ τρώγων τὴν σάρκα τοῦ Κυρίου, καὶ τὸ αἷμα αὐτοῦ πίνων,

ἐκβέβληται τῆς αἰωνίου ζωῆς, πάντα δὲ ταῦτα δι' ἑτέρου μὲν οὐδενὸς, μόνον δὲ διὰ τῶν ἁγίων ἐκείνων ἐπιτελεῖται χειρῶν, τῶν τοῦ ἱερέος λέγω, πῶς ἄν τις τούτων ἐκτὸς, ἢ τὸ τῆς γεεννῆς ἐκφυγεῖν δυνήσεται πῦρ, ἢ τῶν ἀποκειμένων στεφάνων τυχεῖν ; — Chrysost. *De Sacerdot.* Lib. iii.

[5] " Qui non vocatus docet, non sine damno, et suo, et auditorum, docet, quod Christus non sit cum eo." — Luther, *In Galat.* i. 1, Tom. v. p. 215.

[6] *Confess. August.* pars i. Art. v. *Syllog.* p. 24, Art. xiv. p. 127.

[7] *Confess. Helvet.* c. xviii. ; *Syllog.* p. 65.

of Christ, except he be regularly called. . . . If so great a minister as St. Paul dares not arrogate to himself to be heard in the Church, but because he has been ordained to this office by the Lord's command, and faithfully discharges his duty, how great would be his impudence whc should seek this honour destitute of both these qualifications!"[1]

The Church of England especially expresses her opinions in the Ordinal, where, besides the language of the Preface and the words of the Services themselves, it is ordered, that " There shall be a sermon declaring . . . . how *necessary* the order of priests is in the Church of Christ."

Since the Reformation, sects have arisen which underrate the necessity of the ministry and of a call to it. The Anabaptists appear to have done this. The latter Remonstrants, as represented by Episcopius, seem to have thought a fluency of speech and acceptableness to the congregation a sufficient mission.[2] The Quakers, and several fanatical sects, investing all Christians with ministerial authority, have abrogated all distinction of lay and clerical. But these are not much to be considered in a history of religious opinions.

II.   The Article next speaks of those ministers being lawfully called and sent, who derive their calling and mission from certain persons having public authority in the Church to call and to send.

It is necessary then to consider, whether there have always been certain persons invested with such public authority; who such persons were; and who are recognized as such by the English Church.

It is the plain record of all antiquity, that ordination was anciently conferred by the highest order of the ministry. This will probably be questioned by no one. We have seen that St. Clement, the earliest Christian writer except those of the new Testament, speaks of the Apostles as having appointed successors to themselves in the ministry and government of the Church. We have seen that Irenæus speaks of a regular succession from the Apostles in the Churches, and that he counts up the succession in the Churches of Rome and of Smyrna. A like testimony we have brought from Tertullian. The farther we proceed, the clearer the evidence becomes, that no ordinations took place, except by those

---

[1] Calvin, *Institut.* IV. iii. 10. See Palmer, *On the Church*, pt. I. ch. VIII.
[2] See *Episcop. Disp.* 76, Thes. 4, 5;

Remons. Conf. c. 22, § 1; Ford, *On the Articles*, Art. XXIII.

who thus succeeded to the ministry of the Apostles, deriving their orders in direct descent from them.

The only difficulty which seems to occur is this. In the new Testament, it is conceded that *Bishop* (ἐπίσκοπος) and *Presbyter* (πρεσβύτερος) were synonymous and convertible terms. In after-ages we find them distinguished ; the title *Bishop* being tied to the first, the title *Presbyter* to the second order of the ministry. Theodoret[1] and Hilary the deacon[2] tell us, that " the same persons were originally called indiscriminately bishops and presbyters, whilst those who are now called bishops, were called Apostles. But afterwards, the name *Apostle* was appropriated to such only as were Apostles indeed, and then the name *Bishop* was given to those who were before called Apostles." [3] The question is, Was this really the state of the case from the first, or is it the invention of a later age? Were there always three orders of ministers? or originally but two, the aristocratical by degrees changing into a 'monarchical government ? There have been many (such as Blondel, Daillé, Lord King, &c.) who have asserted, that there were but two orders, *presbyters* and *deacons ;* that by degrees, where there were several presbyters, one was elected to preside over the rest; but that he was no more distinct from them, than the dean of a cathedral is from the rest of the chapter, or than the rector or vicar of a large parish is from the assistant curates and ministers of the various chapelries connected with it, — in short a ruling or presiding elder, but not a bishop. By degrees, they say, these ruling elders arrogated to themselves to be a superior order to their brethren, and claimed exclusively that authority to ordain and to execute discipline, which had before been vested in the whole body of the presbytery.

It is quite certain, that in the beginning of the third century, *i. e.* one hundred years after the Apostles, there existed in the Church the three orders of bishops, presbyters, and deacons. Thenceforward, in every part of the world whither Christianity had spread, no Church was to be found where bishops did not preside and ordain. They are well-known rules, that " what has been religiously observed by the Apostolical Churches, must appear to have been handed down from the Apostles themselves." [4] And that, " what is held by the Universal Church, and not ordained by any council, but has always been retained in the Church, is to be

---

[1] *Comm. in* 1 *Tim.* iii. 1.
[2] Hilar. Diac. *In Ephes.* iv.
[3] See Bingham, *E. A.* Book II. ch. II. § 1.

[4] " Constabit id esse ab Apostolis traditum, quod apud ecclesias apostolorum fuerit sacrosanctum." — Tertull. *C. Marcion.* Lib. IV c. 5; cf. *De P'æscript.* c. 17.

believed to have come down from Apostolical authority."[1] So then the burden of proof must lie with those who contend that a custom universally prevailing at a very early period was an innovation, and not a tradition.

Let us, however, see whether the chain of evidence is not complete even from the Apostles.

Clemens Romanus, it is true, mentions only bishops and deacons, and afterwards presbyters; from which it has been inferred that bishops and presbyters were still used indiscriminately for the same office, as in the new Testament. Yet his epistle contains at least inferential proof of the existence of three orders at the time he wrote. In the first place, he himself evidently writes with authority, as representing the whole Church in the great city of Rome. "The Church of God, which is at Rome, to the Church of God which is at Corinth."[2] This exactly corresponds with what we are told by Irenæus and all subsequent testimonies, that Clement was bishop of Rome. Then, in speaking of the ministry as ordained by the Apostles, when they themselves were about to depart, and enjoining the laity to be observant of it, he specially compares the Christian clergy to the three orders of the Levitical priesthood. " The same care must be had of the persons that minister unto Him : for the chief priest has his proper services ; and to the priests their proper place is appointed ; and to the Levites appertain their proper ministries : and the layman is confined within the bounds of what is commanded to laymen."[3] This, be it observed, is exactly the language of later fathers. In allusion to this resemblance the presbyters are constantly called *sacerdotes;* the bishop, *summus sacerdos;* the deacons, *Levitæ.* And it will facilitate our understanding of the whole question, if we bear in mind, that, as the high priest was still a priest, and only distinguished from the other priests by one or two points of official preëminence, so the fathers constantly speak of the bishop as still a presbyter ($\sigma\nu\mu\pi\rho\epsilon\sigma\beta\acute{\nu}\tau\epsilon\rho\text{os}$, 1 Pet. v. 1), but as distinguished from the other presbyters by the power of ordination and jurisdiction.

If we believe the seven shorter epistles of Ignatius to be genuine, they abound in passages concerning the three orders of the ministry, so plain that no language can be stronger or more signif-

---

[1] "Quod universa tenet ecclesia, nec conciliis institutum, sed semper retentum, non nisi auctoritate apostolica traditum rectissime creditur." — Augustin.

Adv. Donatist. Lib. IV. c. 24, Tom. IX. p 139.

[2] Clem. 1 *Ad Cor* c. 1.

[3] c. 40.

icant.[1] If, on the contrary, we incline to receive the epistles of the Syriac version, not as abbreviated, but as the genuine epistles, we have already seen, that they contain a passage in which subjection to the bishops, presbyters, and deacons, and especially to the bishop, is most earnestly and solemnly enjoined.[2]

In the account of the martyrdom of Ignatius, we are told that the cities and Churches of Asia sent their bishops, presbyters, and deacons to meet him.[3]

Hegesippus (ab. A. D. 158) relates of himself, that, as he was travelling to Rome, he communicated with many bishops, and especially speaks of having intercourse with Primus, the Bishop of Corinth. He also relates the succession of certain bishops of Rome. And speaks of Simon, the son of Cleopas, as second Bishop of Jerusalem.[4] Here we find the three great cities, Jerusalem, Rome, and Corinth, in each of which there must have been several presbyters, yet still each presided over by a single bishop.

Irenæus undoubtedly calls the same persons by the name of bishops and presbyters ; but we should be misled by the mere indiscrimate use of names, if we concluded that therefore there was in his day no such thing as a church-officer superior to the general body of presbyters. On the contrary, we have already seen that he lays great stress on the power of tracing up the succession of ministers in the Churches unbroken to the Apostles ; and this succession he traces, not by the whole body of presbyters in each, but by the single individuals at the head. Thus, he says, the Apostles St. Peter and St. Paul gave the bishopric of Rome to Linus, to him succeeded Anacletus, to Anacletus Clemens, to Clemens Evarestus, to him Alexander, then Sixtus, Telesphorus, Hyginus, Pius, Anicetus, Soter, Eleutherius. In the like manner he speaks of a regular descent of the heads of the Church of Smyrna from Polycarp.[5] Here it is evident, that the regular ordination and succession of doctrine in the Church is maintained, not by parity of presbyters, but by successive ordination of chief pastors, who in their turn had power to ordain others.

It has been already mentioned, that Clement of Alexandria considers " the degrees (αἱ προκοπαὶ) in the Church on earth of bishops, presbyters, and deacons, to be imitations of the angelic glory, and of that dispensation which is said to await those who live in right-

---

[1] See Ign. *Ad Ephes.* 3, 4, 5, 6; *Magnes.* 2, 6, 13 ; *Trall.* 2, 7; *Philadelph.* 1, 4, 7, 10 ; *Smyrn.* 8, 12; *Polyc.* 6.
[2] *Epist. ad Polycarp.* c. 6, cited above.
[3] *Martyr. Ignatii*, Coteler. II. p. 174
[4] Ap. Euseb. *H. E.* IV. 22.
[5] Irenæ. Lib. III. c. 3.

eousness according to the Gospel.   These, according to the Apostle, being raised into the clouds, will first minister (διακονεῖν), then, receiving an advancement in glory, be enrolled in the presbytery until they come to the perfect man." [1]   Here it is evident that Clement alludes to the existence of three orders in the ministry, which might successively be passed through, and which he fancifully considers like the progressive degrees of glory hereafter.   Elsewhere also he speaks of presbyters, bishops, and deacons, saying that there are various precepts or suggestions in the Scriptures pertaining to particular persons, " some for presbyters, some for bishops, some for deacons," [2] &c.

The testimony of Tertullian has already been sufficiently adduced, when we were on the subject of the distinction of clergy and laity.   He, more than once, enumerates the three orders.[3]   In one instance he asserts that presbyters and deacons could not baptize without the authority of the bishop ; [4] challenges heretics to trace, as the Catholics could, the succession of their bishops to the Apostles ; [5] and complains that among heretics the offices of bishops, deacons, presbyters, and laics, were all confounded.[6]

Origen continually distinguishes between bishops, priests, and deacons.   Bishop Pearson [7] has quoted ten passages from his writings, in seven of which the distinction is plainly marked, and the three orders are expressly enumerated.

All these writers lived within a hundred years of the Apostles. St. John is said to have died A. D. 100, and Origen to have been born A. D. 186.   From the time of Origen the case admits of no question.   The first fifty of the canons of the apostles use the word *bishop* thirty-six times, in appropriation to him, that is the ruler or president of the church, above the clergy and laity ; twenty-four times the bishop is expressly distinguished from the presbyter ; and fourteen times indicated as having particular care for government, jurisdiction, censures, and ordinations committed to him.[8] The first canon expressly enjoins, that a bishop be consecrated by

---

[1] *Stromat.* VI. p. 793.   See also, Bp. Kaye's *Clem. Alex.* p. 463.

[2] αἱ μὲν πρεσβυτέροις, αἱ δ᾽ ἐπισκόποις · αἱ δὲ διακόνοις, κ. τ. λ. — *Pædag.* III. p. 309.

[3] *De Baptismo,* c. 17, *De Fugâ,* c. 11.

[4] Ibid. c. 17, cited above.

[5] *De Præscrip. Hæretic.* c. 32.

[6] Ibid. c. 41, cited above.

[7] *Vindiciæ Ignat.* ap. Coteler. Tom. II pt. II. p. 320.

[8] See Bp. Taylor's *Episcopacy Asserted.* Sect. XXIV.

All this occurs in the first fifty Canons, which are received as authentic, being quoted by the Council of Nice, Constantinople, Ephesus, Chalcedon, Antioch, and Carthage.   They were undoubtedly not apostolical, but are generally referred to the middle of the third century.   Bp. Beveridge thinks they were collected by Clement of Alexandria. They seem to be appealed to as authority by Tertullian, Cyprian, Constantine the Great, Alexander of Alexandria, and Athanasius.   See *Codex Canonum Eccles. Prim.* illus. a Gul. Beveregio.

two or three bishops. The second, that a presbyter or deacon be
ordained by one bishop. The thirty-fifth forbids bishops to ordain
out of their own dioceses. The thirty-seventh decrees synods of
bishops. The thirty-eighth enjoins bishops to have the superintend-
ence of all ecclesiastical affairs; and the thirty-ninth forbids presbyters and deacons to do anything without the knowledge of their
bishop.[1]

Having now reached the age of Cyprian, when the existence of
a regular diocesan episcopacy is not questioned by the most skepti-
cal; if we look back on the testimonies above cited, it is surely not
too much to assert, that for scarcely any of the undoubted events
of ancient history does there exist anything like the weight of contemporary evidence that we have from the first, that, in the first
century after the Apostolic age, there was a marked distinction between bishops, presbyters, and deacons; or that, if the *names* of
bishops and presbyters were not always distinguished, there was
still clearly a separation between the functions of the ordinary presbyter and those of the president, chief priest, or bishop of the
Church. There is nothing like such evidence for the existence of
the laws of Draco, or the usurpation of Pisistratus, of the kingdom
of Crœsus, or the battle of Marathon, for the wars of Carthage,
or the very being of such persons as Brennus, or Pyrrhus, or Han-
nibal.

In the age of Cyprian (*i. e.* about A. D. 250), we have abundant evidence as to the state of the Church. We know, for instance, that Cornelius, Bishop of Rome, had forty-four presbyters under him;[2] that Cyprian himself, in like manner, presided
over a considerable body of presbyters. The latter never hesitates
to claim supreme authority, under God, over his presbyters and
deacons; and complains bitterly, if any of the presbytery give not
due honour to him as their bishop.[3] The privileges of the presbytery were indeed carefully preserved to them; and we have no
reason to believe that, at this early period, nearly so great an im-
parity prevailed, as we afterwards meet with. The dioceses were
very small compared with their extent in modern times. One
bishop generally had the care of one large town and its immediate
suburbs: whence the original name of a diocese was not διοικήσις

---

[1] Beveregii *Synodicon*, Tom. i. pp. 1,
24–27.
[2] Euseb. vi. 43.
[3] See, for instance, *Epistol.* xvi. " Quod
enim non periculum metuere debemus
de offensa Domini quando aliqui de Pres-
byteris nec Evangelii nec loci sui memo-
res, sed neque futurum Domini judicium,
neque nunc sibi propositum episcopum
cogitantes, quod nunquam omnino sub
antecessoribus factum est, cum contumelia præpositi totum sibi vendicant ? "

(*diocese*), but παροικία (*parochia*), a word not expressing, as of late times, a single congregation or parish, but implying the whole town and its immediate neighborhood; that is, such a precinct or district as a single bishop could govern with the assistance of his presbyters.[1] The power of bishops too over their presbyters was, in early times, limited in many ways. The Council of Carthage (A. D. 348) ordained, that three bishops should judge a deacon, and not less than six should censure a presbyter.[2] Presbyters were always looked on as assessors and counsellors to their bishop.[3] Bishops weighed all things by common advice, and did nothing but after deliberation, and with consent of their clergy.[4] Presbyters were considered as, equally with the bishops, invested with the dignity of the priestly office;[5] and in the African Churches and the Latin, though not in the East, all the presbyters present assisted the bishop in the ordination of a presbyter, by laying their hands on his head.[6]

Yet there is no example of ordination ever being intrusted to presbyters only. On one occasion, a presbyter of Alexandria, named Colluthus, pretended to act as a bishop, but a council of bishops, assembled at Alexandria under Hosius (A. D. 324), declared his ordinations null and void.[7]

Those who advocate the parity of bishops and presbyters, appeal to the language of St Chrysostom and St. Jerome; who undoubtedly maintained with great earnestness the dignity of the office of presbyter, and esteemed it very little inferior to the episcopate. Yet their very words distinctly show, that in one point, and that the point now in question, the bishop had a power not intrusted to the presbyter. St. Chrysostom says, that " bishops excel presbyters *only in the power of ordination*."[8] And St. Jerome asks, " what does a bishop which a presbyter does not, *except*

---

[1] See Suicer, s. v. παροικία; and Bingham, *E. A.* Bk. IX. c. 2.

[2] *Concil. Carthag.* I. Can. 11; see Bingham, Bk. II. ch. III. sect. 9.

[3] Σύμβουλοι τοῦ ἐπισκόπου, συνέδριον καὶ βουλὴ τῆς ἐκκλησίας. — *Constit. Apostol.* Lib. II. c. 28.

[4] " Quando a primordio episcopatus mei statuerim, nihil sine consilio vestro, et sine consensu plebis, mea privata sententia gerere." — Cyprian, *Epist.* XIV.; *Op. Cyp. Epist.* p. 38.
" Omni actu ad me perlato placuit contrahi presbyterium, qui et hodie præsentes fuerunt, ut firmato consilio, quid circa personam eorum observari deberet, consensu omnium statueretur."—Cornelius

Cypriano, *Epist.* XLIX.; *Op.* Cypr. *Epist.* p. 92. See Bingham, Bk. II. ch. XIX. sect. 8.

[5] " Qui cum Episcopo Presbyteri sacerdotali honore conjuncti." — Cyprian. *Ad Lucian. Epist.* LXI. See Bingham, II. xix. 14.

[6] It was so ordained by the fourth Council of Carthage, and there is a rule to the same purpose in the constitutions of the Church of Alexandria. See Bingham, II. xix. 10.

[7] Athanas. *Opp.* I. p. 732, Colon. See Bingham, II. iii. 6; Palmer, *On the Church*, pt. VI. ch. IV.

[8] χειροτονία μόνῃ. — *Hom.* IX. in 1 ad *Tim.*

ordaining?"[1] It is true that St. Jerome, arguing from the language of St. Paul to Timothy, contends that *Episcopus* and *Presbyter* originally designated the same office, and thinks that one was afterwards placed above the rest, to avoid schism in the Church. This, however, is evidently only his own private inference from Scripture. He relates indeed, that at Alexandria, from the time of St. Mark to Heraclas and Dionysius, the presbyters used to elect one from among themselves, and, having placed him aloft (*in excelsiori gradu*), saluted him Episcopus; as if an army should make a general (*imperator*), or a body of deacons an archdeacon.[2] But we cannot infer from this, that St. Jerome means to say that there was no distinct consecration of the bishop so elected; for it is merely of the election, not of the ordination of their bishop, that he speaks; and he simply adduces this as an instance of what he believed to be one of the ancient forms of episcopacy; namely, the appointment by the presbyters of one from among themselves to preside over them.[3]

Hilary the deacon says, that " the ordination of bishop and presbyters is the same, for both are priests; but the bishop is first; for every bishop is a presbyter, not every presbyter a bishop."[4] All this is true, except inasmuch as he says there is no difference between the ordination of a bishop and a presbyter; and this is evidently the private opinion (deduced from the language of St. Paul) of a person not much to be relied on, and who afterwards joined the Luciferian schism.   What he says in another place,[5] that " in Egypt, even to his days, presbyters *sealed* (consignant), in the absence of the bishop," does not mean that they *ordained*, but that they *confirmed;* and, no doubt, in the early ages, presbyters were sometimes permitted to confirm, by delegation of the episcopal power.[6]

The only decided opponent of episcopacy in primitive times was Aerius, a presbyter of the Church of Sebaste, in Armenia, of the fourth century.   He had a quarrel with his bishop, Eustathius, and was thence led, among other errors, to declare that bishops and presbyters were altogether equal, and that a presbyter could ordain, as well as a bishop.   Epiphanius says, he was altogether an

---

[1] "Quid enim facit, *excepta ordinatione,* episcopus, quod presbyter non faciat?" — *Epist. ad Evangelium,* Ep. 101; *Op.* Tom. IV. pars II. p. 802.

[2] Ibid.

[3] See Bishop Hall, *Episcopacy of Divine Right,* Pt. II. Sect. 15; Bp. J. Taylor, *On Episcopacy,* Sect. 32; Bingham,

II. iii. 5; Palmer, *On the Church,* pt. VI. ch. IV.

[4] *In* 1 *Tim.* iii. *in Oper. Ambros.*

[5] *In Ephes.* iv. "Denique apud Ægyptum presbyteri consignant, si præsens non sit episcopus."

[6] See Bingham, Bk. XII. ch. II. sect. 2, 4; Palmer, pt. VI. ch. I. VI.

Arian heretic ('Αρειανὸς μὲν τὸ πᾶν). His sentiments were wholly rejected by the Catholics, and his sect driven from all quarters of the Church;[1] it being a settled doctrine at that day, that the order of bishops excelled the order of presbyters, "inasmuch as the order of bishops can beget fathers to the Church by ordination, but the order of presbyters can but beget sons by baptism."[2]

The review, then, which has been taken of the primitive testimony, proves this: that, in the earliest ages, in every quarter of the world whither the Church had penetrated, whilst all Churches had their regular ministers of the two orders of presbyters and deacons, yet in every city there was one chief presbyter, presiding over the clergy of that city and its suburb (παροικία), and that to him was committed the power of ordination, or, in the language of the Article, he had "public authority given him in the Church, to call and send ministers into the Lord's Vineyard." Whether he was to be esteemed of a different order, or of the same order, differing only in degree;[3] in any case, by universal consent, he was the minister of ordination. Other presbyters, equally with him, received authority to teach, to baptize, to minister the Eucharist; but he only had authority to ordain. Such authority was believed to have been derived to bishops from the Apostles. And the principle on which their ordinations were deemed valid, was, not merely that they themselves had the priestly office, but that they had received authority (authority by regular episcopal descent) to give ordination and mission to others.

Those who maintain the validity of presbyterian orders, do so on the ground that bishops were themselves but presbyters. Those who maintain that episcopal ordination is necessary, reply that even though bishops be themselves presbyters, yet they only, and not all presbyters alike, had the authority to ordain; and therefore that without them ordination could not take place. This was the constant creed of the fathers, and of the schoolmen after them.

---

[1] Epiphanius, *Hæres.* 75; August, *Hæres.* 54.

[2] Epiphanius, Ibjd.

[3] The fathers, the schoolmen, and divines, both of the Roman and reformed episcopal churches, have seemed doubtful whether bishops and presbyters were of different degrees in the same order, or of different orders. The distinction between presbyter and deacon has always been esteemed as greater than that between bishop and presbyter; the eminence of the bishop over the presbyter consisting chiefly in the power of ordina-tion. Mr. Palmer enumerates as advocates for identity of order, but inferiority of degree, Clemens Romanus, Polycarp, Irenæus, Clemens Alexand., Tertullian, Firmilian, Jerome, Hilary the deacon, Chrysostom, Augustine, Theodoret, Sedulius, Primasius, Isidore Hispalensis, Bede, Alcuin, the Synod of Aix, in 819, Amalarius, Hugo S. Victor, Peter Lombard, Alexander Alensis, Bonaventura, Albertus Magnus, Thomas Aquinas, Scotus, Cajetan, Durandus, the Council of Trent, and many reformers of the 16th century. Palmer, pt. IV. ch. I.

The Council of Trent, and the later writers in the Church of
Rome, have not greatly insisted on the three orders, but have generally classed together the first and second, bishops and presbyters,
under the common name of *sacerdotes, priests;* influenced herein
by the high importance which they attached to the priesthood,
and by the disposition to reserve supreme episcopal authority to
the pope.[1] Yet they have never thought of permitting any but
the bishop to administer ordination, which is by them esteemed a
Sacrament of the Church; but have ever held bishops to be successors of the Apostles, superior to presbyters, and qualified, which
the other clergy were not, to confirm and to ordain.[2]

At the time of the Reformation, the Lutherans, meeting with
nothing but opposition from the bishops, were constrained to act
without them. Yet Luther and his followers constantly acted
under appeal to a general council. The Confession of Augsburg
fully conceded to bishops the power of the keys, *i. e.* of preaching
the Gospel, of remitting and retaining sins, and of administering
the Sacraments;[3] and declared, that bishops should retain all their
legitimate authority, if only they would not urge such traditions as
could not be kept with a good conscience.[4] The Lutherans earnestly protested, that they much wished to retain episcopacy, but
that the bishops forced them to reject sound doctrine, and therefore
they were unable to preserve their allegiance to them; and they
" openly testified to the world, that they would willingly continue
the canonical government, if only the bishops would cease to exercise cruelty upon the Churches."[5]

The Calvinists, though in like manner rejecting their bishops,
who would have bound them to Rome, declared themselves ready
to submit to a lawful hierarchy. Calvin said that those who
would not submit themselves to such, were deserving of any ana-

---

[1] The Council of Trent, Sess. XXIII.
cap. 2, reckons seven orders of ministers,
sacerdotes, diaconi, subdiaconi, acolythi,
exorcistæ, lectores, ostiarii. The Council of Nice itself (Can. 3) had given the
name of κλῆρος to others besides bishops,
presbyters, and deacons; and the third
Council of Carthage made a Canon (Can.
23) on purpose to confirm the title to
them. (Bingham, I. v. 7.)

[2] Vid. *Concil. Trident.* Sess. XXIII.
cap. 4.

[3] Confess. August. *De Potestate Eccle-
siastica, Sylloge,* pp. 151, 225.

[4] Ibid. pp. 157, 231.

[5] " Episcopi sacerdotes nostros aut co-
gunt hoc doctrinæ genus, quod confessi
sumus, abjicere et damnare, aut nova et

inaudita crudelitate miseros et innocentes
occidunt. Hæ causæ impediunt quo
minus agnoscant hos episcopos nostri
sacerdotes. Ita sævitia episcoporum in
causa est, quare alicubi dissolvitur illa
canonica politia, quam nos magnopere
cupiebamus conservare. Ipsi viderint
quomodo rationem Deo reddituri sint,
quod dissipant ecclesiam. Porro hic iterum volumus testatum, nos libenter con-
servaturos esse ecclesiasticam et canoni-
cam politiam, si modo episcopi desinant
in nostras ecclesias sævire." — *Apologia
Confessionis,* Art. VII. § 24. See Bp.
Hall's *Episcopacy,* Int. Sect. 3. The
above passage is given at greater length
in Dr. Wordsworth's *Theophilus Anglica-
nus,* ch. XI.

thema.[1] Even Beza thought it insane to reject all episcopacy ; and
wished that the Church of England might continue to enjoy forever that singular bounty of God.[2]

John Knox himself was not a favourer of that parity of ministers
which Andrew Melvill afterwards introduced into the Kirk of Scotland, but may be considered as, more or less, a witness for the distinction of bishops and presbyters.[3]

In the English Church, the primitive rule of episcopal ordination
and apostolical descent has never been infringed. The Article
under consideration is the only authorized formulary, which seems
in the least degree ambiguous. The ambiguity, however, is not
real but apparent only ; as it is clearly stated that not all who are
themselves ministers can ordain ; but only those invested with
public authority in the Church to send others into the Vineyard.
This is a complete description of a bishop, who is a chief presbyter
invested, over and above other presbyters, with the power of sending labourers into the Vineyard.

The first germ of this Article we have already seen, in the Articles agreed on between the Lutheran and Anglican divines, A. D.
1538.[4] About the same year, or soon after, a paper was written
by Cranmer, *De Ordine et Ministerio Sacerdotum et Episcoporum*,
in which the divine authority of priests and bishops, the superiority
of bishops, and their succession from the Apostles, are strongly
maintained.[5] The same kind of language is used in the *Institution
of a Christian Man*, set forth nearly at the same time, or somewhat
earlier.[6] In the year 1540, Henry VIIIth, in regard of a more
exact review of the *Institution of a Christian Man*, appointed several learned men to deliberate about sundry points of religion, and
to give in their sentiments distinctly. Seventeen questions were
proposed to them concerning the Sacraments and ordination.[7] All
agreed, except one, that bishops had the authority to make presbyters ; and almost all agreed, that none besides had this power. Their
general opinion was, that a bishop further required consecration,
though Cox thought institution with imposition of hands sufficient.

[1] "Talem nobis hierarchiam si exhib-
eant in qua sic emineant episcopi, ut
Christo subesse non recusent, ut ab Illo
tanquam ab unico Capite pendeant et ad
Ipsum referantur : . . . tum vero nullo
non anathemate dignos fatear, si qui
erunt, qui non eam reverentur, summa-
que obedientia observant." — Calvin. *De
Necessitate Reform. Eccl-s.* See also *Institut.* IV. c. 10. See Hall, as above.

[2] 'Fruatur sane ista singulari Dei

beneficentia, quæ utinam illi sit perpet-
ua." — *Beza ad Sarav.* apud Hall, *Episcopacy*, Sect. 4.

[3] Harington's *Notes on the Church of
Scotland.* ch. III.

[4] Cranmer's *Works*, by Jenkyns, IV.
p. 286.

[5] Ibid. p. 300.

[6] *Formularies of Faith in the Reign of
Henry VIII.* p. 101.

[7] Strype's *Cranmer*, p. 110.

But at this time Cranmer appears to have been much wavering on the subject of ordination. He had imbibed a very high notion of the Divine prerogative of Christian princes ; and some of his answers indicate a belief, that Christian kings, as well as bishops, had power to ordain ministers. Still he adds, as if doubtful of the soundness of his position, " This is mine opinion and sentence at this present, which nevertheless I do not temerariously define, but refer the judgment thereof wholly to your majesty." [1] Several of the other divines had afterwards a hand in drawing up the Liturgy and the Ordinal ; and all had expressed opinions diametrically opposite to the Archbishop. But the Archbishop's own appears to have been only a theory hastily taken up, and as speedily relinquished, at a period when all opinions were undergoing a great revolution, and when the reformers were generally inclined to overrate the regal, and underrate the episcopal authority ; since kings in most parts of Europe fostered, and bishops checked the progress of the Reformation. It is to be observed that the *Necessary Doctrine*, which was the result of this *review* of the *Institution of a Christian Man*, contains the strongest language concerning " order," as " the gift or grace of ministration in Christ's Church, given of God to Christian men by the consecration and imposition of the bishop's hands," and concerning a continual succession even to the end of the world.[2] This was set forth A. D. 1543. In 1548, Cranmer himself put out what is called Cranmer's Catechism, which, though not written by him, was translated and published by his authority. In this the Apostolical descent, Episcopal ordination, and the power of the Keys, are strongly enforced and greatly enlarged upon.[3] Bishop Burnet remarks on it, that " it is plain that Cranmer had now quite laid aside those singular opinions which he formerly held of the ecclesiastical functions ; for now, in a work which was wholly his own, without the concurrence of any other, he fully sets forth their divine institution." [4] In 1549, Cranmer and twelve other divines drew up the *Ordinal*, where it is declared that, " from the Apostles' times, there hath been three orders of Ministers in Christ's Church : Bishops, Priests, and Deacons ; " it is said that none were admitted to them but " by public prayer, with imposition of hands ; " and it is enjoined that hereafter all persons to be ordained shall be

---

[1] See Jenkyns's *Cranmer*, II. p. 98, where Cranmer's answers are given. All the replies are to be found in the Appendix to Burnet *On the Reformation*, and Collier's *Ecclesiastical History*. See also Jenkyns's preface to his edition of *Cranmer*, I. p. xxxii. &c.

[2] See at length *Formularies of Faith*, p. 277.

[3] See Cranmer's *Catechism*, p. 193, &c. Oxford, 1829.

[4] Burnet, *History of Reformation*, II pt. 2.

admitted according to the form laid down in the Ordinal, which is nearly the same as that still used in the Church of England. In 1552, the *Reformatio Legum* was published, the chief writer of which was the Archbishop. In this again the three orders, of bishop, presbyter, and deacon, are distinctly treated of. For bishops are claimed the powers of jurisdiction and ordination, and all three orders are spoken of as evidently holding their offices on Scriptural authority and by Divine appointment.[1] Cranmer therefore could only have entertained for a short time the peculiar opinions which in 1540 he unhappily expressed.[2] It is only necessary to add, that the Ordinal is expressly sanctioned and authorized, not only as part of the Book of Common Prayer, but by the XXXVIth Article;[3] and we may observe, that, not only is episcopal ordination enjoined by it, but in its present form it forbids that any shall hereafter be " accounted or taken to be a lawful bishop, priest, or deacon in the United Church of England or Ireland, or suffered to execute any of the said functions, except he be called, tried, examined, and admitted thereunto, according to the form hereafter following, or hath had formerly episcopal consecration or ordination."[4]

Section II. — SCRIPTURAL PROOF.

WE may proceed, as in the last section, to show that, —

I. There is a regular order of ministers in the Christian Church set apart for sacred offices, and that no one may assume their functions, except he be lawfully called and sent.

[1] *Reform. Leg.* Tit. *De Ecclesia et Ministris Ejus,* capp. 3, 4, 10–12.

[2] The question concerning Archbishop Cranmer's remarkable expressions in 1540. and subsequent change of opinion, is ably disposed of by Chancellor Harington, *Succession of Bishops in the Church of England.* See also his *Two Ordination Sermons.* Exeter, 1845.

[3] The Church of England has always acted on the principles laid down in the Preface to the Ordinal, although many of her writers have shown consideration for the difficulties of the Continental Protestants. It has been asserted by Mr. Macaulay, *Hist. of England,* I. p. 75, that " in the year 1603 the province of Canterbury " (*i. e.* in Canon 55) " solemnly recognized the Church of Scotland, a Church in which episcopal ordination was unknown, as a branch of the holy Catholic Church of Christ." This state-ment has been clearly disproved by Chancellor Harington, who has demonstrated that at least a titular episcopacy then existed in Scotland, and that there was " a full determination to restore a regularly consecrated episcopacy." See a *Letter on the LVth Canon and the Kirk of Scotland,* by E. C. Harington, M. A. Rivingtons, 1851.

[4] The following writers may be consulted by the student, both as containing the arguments for episcopacy and the succession of ministers, and as showing the judgment of the great Anglican divines on the subject. Hooker, Bk. VII. ; Hall, *Episcopacy of Divine Right ;* Taylor, *On Episcopacy ;* Chillingworth, *Divine Institution of Episcopacy ;* Leslie, *On the Qualifications to administer the Sacraments ;* Potter, *On Church Government ;* Bingham, E. A. Bk. II. ; Palmer, *On the Church,* Part VI.

II. There are regular ministers of ordination, to whom public authority is given to send labourers into the Vineyard.

I. The example of the old Testament priesthood is clearly to the point. One out of the twelve tribes was set apart for sacred offices in general, and of that tribe one whole family for special priestly ministration.

It is said truly, that the priesthood, and especially the high priesthood, was typical of Christ. He is the great High Priest over the House of God. Therefore, it is argued, all other priesthood has ceased. It is however equally true, that the kings and prophets of old were as much types of Christ as were the high priests. Christ is our Prophet, Priest, and King. Yet still it is lawful that there should be kings and prophets under the Gospel, for we read of many prophets in the Church (Acts ii. 17; xi. 27; xiii. 1; xv. 32; xxi. 9, 10. 1 Cor. xii. 28. Eph. iv. 11); and we are specially enjoined to " honour the king " (1 Pet. ii. 17).

In one sense, doubtless, there are no such prophets, kings, or priests now, as there were under the Law. Kings were then rulers of the theocracy, vicegerents of God in governing the Church of God. Prophets were sent to prepare the way of Him who was to come. Priests offered up daily sacrifice of propitiation, in type of the Lamb of God, who taketh away the sins of the world. So, in such a sense, are there now neither prophets, priests, nor kings. But as the coming of *the* King and Prophet has not abolished the kingly or prophetic office, so the coming of the Great High Priest has not of necessity done away with all priestly functions in the Church, but only with such as of their own nature belonged to the typical and ceremonial dispensation. Nay! we may fairly argue, that as sacred things in the old Testament needed the ministry of consecrated officers, so the still more sacred things of the new Testament would be likely to need the attendance of those specially set apart. And, without controversy, the Gospel and the Sacraments are greater and more sacred than the Law and the sacrifices; and hence, " if the ministration of death . . . . was glorious," we could easily imagine, that the " ministration of the Spirit would be rather glorious; " that " if the ministration of condemnation was glory, much more would the ministration of righteousness exceed in glory" (2 Cor. iii. 7, 8, 9). In the old Testament the priests were appointed, first to minister in the sacrifices, and then to teach the people (Lev. x. 11. Deut. xxxiii. 10. Hagg. ii. 11. Mal. ii. 7). We still need the ministration, not of sacrifices, but of Sacraments; and the instruction of the Church is at least as necessary as the instruction of the Jews.

It is said, however, that all Christians are priests, and that a distinct ministry is therefore needless and inconsistent (see 1 Pet. ii. 9; Rev. i. 6; v. 10). But it is to be observed, that wherever Christians are said to be *priests*, they are also said to be *kings*. We know that the kingly character, which Christ bestows on His people, has not abolished monarchy; why should their priestly character have abolished ministry? Besides which, the very passages in the new Testament in which Christians are called a "royal priesthood," "kings and priests," are absolute quotations from the old Testament, where the very same titles are given to all the people of the Jews. "Ye shall be unto me a kingdom of *priests*, a holy nation" (Exod. xix. 6). The Septuagint Version of Exodus and the Greek of St. Peter are almost the same. The one did not forbid a special priesthood in Israel; the other therefore cannot disprove a ministry in the Church. It was indeed argued on one occasion, that the sanctity of the whole congregation made it useless to have priests at all.[1] But how far the argument was safe the sequel showed, when the earth swallowed up Korah and his company, and fourteen thousand of the people died of the plague, because they had listened to his reasoning (Num. xvi. 32, 33, 45–49). It is difficult to see, where the difference lies between this statement of Korah and the modern denial of a Christian ministry, on the ground that all the Christian Church is a holy and spiritual priesthood; and it is difficult to understand what can be, if this be not, the "gainsaying of Core," so strongly rebuked by St. Jude (ver. 11).

Now it was foretold by Isaiah (lxvi. 21) that, when the Gentiles were brought in, that is in the days of the Church of Christ, some among them should be taken "for priests and for Levites." This looks much like a prophecy of a ministry to be established under the Gospel, with some analogy to that under the Law. Accordingly, our blessed Lord, even during His own personal ministry, whilst the Great High Priest was bodily ministering on earth, appointed two distinct orders of ministers under Himself, first, Apostles (Matt. x. 1), secondly, the seventy disciples (Luke x. 1); and this with evident reference to the twelve tribes of Israel, and the seventy elders among the Jews. He gave them power to preach

[1] Numb. xvi. 3: "Ye take too much upon you, seeing all the congregation are holy, every one of them, and the LORD is among them; wherefore then lift ye up yourselves above the congregation of the LORD?"

the Gospel (Matt. x. 7.   Luke x. 9), to bless those that received
them (Matt. x. 12, 13.   Luke x. 5, 6), to denounce God's judgments on those that rejected them (Matt. x. 14.   Luke x. 10, 11).
He assured them, that he that received them received Him, that
he that despised them despised Him (Matt. x. 40.   Luke x. 16).
And He further endued them with miraculous powers, because of
the peculiar exigencies of their ministration.   Moreover, He promised to give them the keys of the kingdom, that they might bind
and loose ; *i. e.* excommunicate offenders and absolve the penitent
(Matt. xvi. 19; xviii. 18).   All this was whilst He Himself went
in and out among them, as the chief minister of His own Church.
When He was about to suffer, He instituted one of the Sacraments
of His Church, and gave especial authority to the Apostles to minister it (Luke xxii. 19; 1 Cor. xi. 24, 25 ; compare 1 Cor. x. 16) ;
it being apparent from the statement of St. John, that they had
before received authority, not only to preach, but to baptize (John
iv. 2).   At last, when He had risen from the dead, He gave fuller
commission to those who were now to be the chief ministers in
his kingdom, to go forth with His authority to preach and to baptize (Matt. xxviii. 19).   He said unto them, " Peace be unto you :
as My Father hath sent Me, even so send I you.   And He breathed on them, and said unto them, Receive ye the Holy Ghost : [1]
whose soever sins ye remit, they are remitted unto them ; and
whose soever sins ye retain, they are retained " (John xx. 21, 22,
23).   He enjoined them to feed His sheep (John xxi. 15, 17).
Lastly, He promised to be " with them alway, even to the end of
the world " (Matt. xxviii. 20).   Then He left the Church, thus
organized with Apostles and elders ; and ten days afterwards
sent down the miraculous, enlightening gifts of the Spirit, the
more fully to qualify His chosen ministers for the work which lay
upon them.   Accordingly, the Apostle says, " When He ascended
up on high, He gave gifts unto men, ... He gave some (as)
Apostles, and some (as) prophets, and some, evangelists, and some,
pastors and teachers, for the perfecting of the saints, for the work
of the ministry, for the edifying of the Body of Christ " (Eph. iv.
8, 11, 12, &c.).

The ministry so constituted continued to work.   The college
of Apostles was perfected by the addition of Matthias (Acts. i.

---

[1] " The Holy Ghost," for the work of
the ministry, the ordaining influences of
the Spirit.   It could not have been the
ordinary operations of the Spirit, for they
had been long living under them ; nor
was it the miraculous baptism of the
Church with the Holy Ghost, which did
not come upon them till the day of Pentecost, Acts ii. 1.

26). The Apostles preached, baptized, broke bread, (*i. e.* ministered the Holy Communion,) and governed the Church: Afterwards, believers multiplying, and the Apostles and elders not having leisure to attend to the secular affairs of the Church, they ordained the third order of deacons, whose ordination was performed by
laying on of hands; and so they also were then empowered to
preach and to baptize (Acts viii. 5, 12, 13, 38,), though not to perform some functions peculiar to the Apostles (Acts viii. 15–17).

Thenceforward we find baptism, breaking of bread, and preaching, ever performed by regular ministers, Apostles, elders, deacons.
The Apostles, as they go on their missionary journeys, " ordain
them elders in every Church " (Acts xiv. 23). The " elders "
meet with the Apostles in solemn council about the affairs of the
Church (Acts xv. 2). When St. Paul takes leave of the Churches,
he sends to the " elders " and addresses them with the exhortation,
" Take heed unto yourselves, and to all the flock, over which the
Holy Ghost hath made you overseers, to feed the Church of God
which He hath purchased with His own Blood " (Acts xx. 17, 28).
We find from the inscriptions of the Epistles, that the settled
Churches had " bishops and deacons " (Phil. i. 1). St. Peter exhorts the " elders " of the Church to " feed the flock of God " (1 Pet.
v. 1, 2). St. James bids the sick to send for the " elders of the
Church to pray over them " (James v. 14). St. Paul speaks of himself and other Christian pastors, as " ministers of Christ, and stewards of the mysteries of God " (1 Cor. iv. 1). He exhorts Archippus
to take heed to the ministry, which he had received of the Lord,
to fulfil it (Col. iv. 17). Especially, we find in his Epistles to
Timothy and Titus, that towards the end of his own Apostleship
he appointed others, who had previously received the gift of God
by the laying on of hands (1 Tim. iv. 14. 2 Tim. i. 6), that they
might, as the Apostles had hitherto done, " ordain elders in every
city " (Tit. i. 5. 1 Tim. i. 3; v. 21, 22, &c.) Directions are given
for proving, examining, and commissioning elders, presbyters or
bishops, and deacons, which was to be done by the laying on of
the hands of those chief ministers, themselves thus apostolically
sent. (See 1 Tim. iii. 1–13; v. 21, 22. Tit. i. 5–7, &c.) The
elders so ordained were esteemed worthy of double honour, especially if they ruled well and laboured in the word and doctrine
(1 Tim. v. 17). And the Church is exhorted to obey those who
had thus " the rule over them, and who watched for their souls,
as they that must give account " (Heb. xiii. 17). Thus we find,
that a regular ministry was established, ordained after a set form,

by laying on of the hands of Apostles or other chief ministers empowered' by them; that they preached and administered the Sacraments; that they were called ministers and stewards of God's mysteries; that they were urged faithfully to fulfil their ministry, and that the people were urged to attend to them and respect them. Those who sent them forth were exhorted to be careful and circumspect how they ordained them.

Now, all this proves, that this public office not only existed, but was not to be undertaken except by persons lawfully called and sent. St. Paul reasons, that the Jewish priesthood could not be undertaken except by him " that is called of God, as was Aaron " (Heb. v. 4). He even adds, that " Christ also glorified not Himself to be made an High Priest " (ver. 5). But the Gospel ministry was more glorious than that of the Law; " for if the ministration of condemnation be glory, much more doth the ministration of righteousness exceed in glory " (2 Cor. iii. 9). Hence we reasonably should conclude, that it too could not be self-assumed. And we find accordingly, that the Apostles ask, " How shall they preach except they be sent? " (Rom. x. 15); that they highly estimate the importance and difficulty of the office, saying, " Who is sufficient for these things? " (2 Cor. ii. 16); that they dissuade people from rashly seeking to intrude into it (James iii. 1); and that, so far from considering all Christians as equally ministers of Christ, they ask, " Are all Apostles, are all prophets, are all teachers? " (1 Cor. xii. 29). On the contrary, they plainly teach us, that the Church is a body, in which God ordains different stations for different members, some to be eyes, others ears, some hands, others feet; all necessary, all to be honoured, but some in more honourable place than the rest.

II. The new Testament contains evidence, that, besides the ordinary ministers, namely, presbyters and deacons, there were always certain chief presbyters who were ministers of ordination, having authority to send labourers into the Vineyard.

Under the Law, besides the ordinary priests and Levites, there was always the high priest, and therefore three orders or degrees of ministry. When our blessed Lord Himself was upon earth, He ordained two orders of ministers under Himself, the Apostles and the seventy disciples. Here again was a threefold cord, Christ answering to the high priest, the Apostles to the priests, the seventy to the Levites. But our Lord was to depart from them; and for the future government of His Church we find a promise, that " in the regeneration " (*i. e.* in the new state of things under the Gospel of Christ, the renovation of the Church) the twelve Apostles should " sit upon twelve thrones, judging the twelve tribes of Israel " (Matt. xix. 28). " What are the twelve tribes of Israel, but the whole Church of God? For whereof did the first Christian Church consist, but of converted Jews? And whither did our Saviour bend all His allusions, but to them? They had their twelve *princes of the tribes of their fathers* (Numb. i. 16). They had their seventy elders, to bear the burden of the people (Numb. xi. 16, 17). The Son of God affects to imitate His former polity, and therefore chooses His twelve and seventy disciples to sway His evangelical Church.[1]

Thus, when the Saviour in body departed from them, He left behind Him twelve Apostles to sit on the thrones or seats of government in the Church, and under them seventy elders to act with them, as their fellow-labourers and assessors. (See Acts xv. 22, &c.) Soon after the ascension, the Apostles were moved to appoint a third order, the order of deacons. And thus once more the number was complete, resembling the number of the Aaronic ministry, and embracing, 1, Apostles ; 2, elders ; 3, deacons. The former two were appointed and ordained by the Lord, the third was from the Apostles.[2]

Whilst the Lord Jesus was present with them, He alone ordained. (See Matt. x. Luke x. John xx. &c.). After His ascension (except in the cases of St. Matthias and St. Paul, who were constituted to the Apostleship by Christ Himself) the Apostles acted as the ministers of ordination. (See Acts vi. 3, 6 ; xiv. 23. 2 Tim. i. 6. Tit. i. 5). Under them, we find continual mention of two orders of ministers, presbyters or elders, (who are also called bishops,) and deacons. (Acts xx. 17. Phil. i. 1, &c.). The Apostles in all things undertook the government of, and authority over the Churches, giving directions to the inferior ministers, and

---

[1] Bishop Hall's *Episcopacy*, Sect. 2.

[2] [The statements of this paragraph must, I think, be taken with some modification. There is no evidence in the New Testament that the *seventy* of the Gospels became, *ipso facto,* the presbyters or elders of the Apostolic Church. That these elders may have been selected from that body, is highly probable. There is patristic authority to prove it. But the same authority asserts that the seven deacons were also selected from the seventy ; a thing which would be inexplicable, had the seventy been made presbyters by our Lord. (See the pas-

sages cited in Archbishop Potter *On Church Government,* p. 48, Am. ed.)

What is certain is, that Paul and Barnabas " ordained them elders in every Church " which they founded in their first missionary journey (Acts xiv. 23) ; following, herein the example of the mother Church of Jerusalem (Acts xi. 30), and furnishing a pattern for all Churches. The institution of the order is not recorded, as that of deacons is. Its existence, however, is certain, and so the main argument remains untouched. — *J. W.*]

superintending them. (See Acts xv.; xix. 1–5; xx. 17–35.
1 Cor. iv. 16–21; v. 3–5. 2 Cor. ii. 9, 10; x. 1–14; xii. 20,
21, &c.) It is very true that the Apostles speak, when addressing the elders, with brotherly kindness, calling themselves *fel-
low-elders* (συμπρεσβύτεροι, 1 Pet. v. 1); but no one can question
their own superiority to them; and when they are mentioned together, they are distinguished as "the Apostles and elders," — a
phrase occurring three times in Acts xv. But the time was to
come, when the Apostles should be taken from the Church, as
their Lord had left it before. Did they then make provision for its
government after their departure, and for a succession to themselves, as ministers of ordination? The Epistles to Timothy and
Titus plainly answer this question. Timothy and Titus had themselves been presbyters, ordained by (2 Tim. i. 6), and companions
of St. Paul. Towards the end of his own ministry, and when his
own apostolical cares had largely increased, he appointed them to
take the oversight of two large districts, the one of Ephesus (where
we know there were several elders or presbyters, Acts xx. 17),
the other of Crete, famous for its hundred cities. In these respective districts, he authorized them to execute full apostolical authority, the same kind of authority which he himself had exercised in
his own larger sphere of labour. They were to regulate the public services of the Church (1 Tim. ii. 1, 2, &c.), — to ordain presbyters and deacons by the laying on their hands (1 Tim. iii. 1–
14; v. 22. Tit. i. 5), — to provide that sound doctrine should be
taught (1 Tim. i. 3; iii. 15; iv. 6, 16. 2 Tim. i. 13; ii. 14. Tit.
i. 13), — committing carefully to faithful men the office of teaching,
which they had themselves received from the Apostles (2 Tim. ii.
2), — to execute discipline, honouring the diligent (1 Tim. v. 17),
— hearing complaints and judging those complained of (1 Tim. v.
19, 20, 21, 24), — admonishing those that erred (Tit. i. 13), but
excommunicating those that were heretical (Tit. iii. 10). All this
power is committed to them, as a solemn charge, to be accounted
for before God, and as a commandment to be kept without spot,
unrebukable, to the coming of our Lord Jesus Christ (1 Tim. i.
18; v. 21; vi. 13. 2 Tim. iv. 1); and grace for this ministry is
specially said to have been given them by the putting on of the
hands of the Apostles (2 Tim. i. 6).

Now, here is the case of two persons placed in a position previously occupied by none but the Apostles, with special power of
jurisdiction and ordination. Before this, we find no such powers in
any but the Apostles. Now we find them committed to Timothy

and Titus. Is it not plain that, as our Lord left the Apostles with chief authority over His Church, having elders and deacons under them, so now the Apostles, themselves about to depart, leave Timothy and Titus, and others like them, with the same authority which they themselves had received from Christ?

It is only necessary, in order to complete the chain of evidence, that we observe what we meet with in the Revelation of St. John. There, seven great Churches are written to; one of which is the Church of Ephesus, of which we know that there were many elders there, and that afterwards Timothy was appointed as chief minister over them all. Each of these Churches is addressed through one presiding minister, who is called *Angel*, a name of the same import as *Apostle*. And these angels are compared to stars, placed to give light to the Churches (Rev. i. 20). Can we doubt then, that there was in each of these Churches one person, whose ministry was superior to the rest, as Timothy's had been to that of the presbyters and deacons under him?

The evidence therefore of the new Testament seems clear and uniform, that there ever existed three orders of ministers: *First*, (1) Our Lord, (2) the Apostles, (3) the seventy. *Secondly*, (1) the Apostles, (2) the elders, (3) the deacons. *Thirdly*, (1) Persons like Timothy and Titus, called *angels* by St. John, (2) the elders, presbyters, or bishops, (3) the deacons. Moreover we find that, in all these cases, ordinations were performed by the first order of these ministers, by the laying on of hands; except where our Lord Himself ordained, when He did not lay on His hands, but breathed on His disciples (John xx. 22).

The only arguments of any weight, which are urged against the above, appear to be the following:

1. *Bishops* and *presbyters* are in Scripture convertible terms, which shows that their subsequent distinction was an invention of the priesthood.

The answer to this has been already given in the words of Theodoret. The second order of ministers, whose general and proper designation was elders or presbyters, are in a few instances called by St. Paul *Episcopi*, bishops, or overlookers. The first order were called Apostles, and, by St. John, Angels. There are obvious reasons why these two latter names should have been afterwards considered too venerable to be given to ordinary ministers; and hence the name *bishop*, originally used to designate the overlookers of a flock, was afterwards appropriated to those who were overlookers of the pastors. But the bishops of after-times " never

thought themselves and their order to succeed the Scripture, Ἐπίσκοποι, but the Scripture Ἀπόστολοι. They were διάδοχοι τῶν Ἀποστόλων, the *successors of the Apostles.*" [1]

2. A second argument is, that, in Acts xiii. 1–3, Barnabas
and Saul are said to have been ordained by some who were not
Apostles.

This was no ordination, but merely a setting apart for a special
labour ; which was done, according to the pious custom of early
days, with fasting, prayer, and imposition of hands. (Comp. Acts
xiv. 23.) That it was no ordination, appears from the fact, that
St. Paul was made an Apostle by our Lord, at the very time of
his conversion. See Acts xxvi. 17, where our Lord constitutes
him an Apostle to the Gentiles. The words are, εἰς οὓς νῦν σε ἀπο-
στέλλω. And St. Paul himself always declares, that he had his
ministry, "not *of* men, neither *by* man, but by Jesus Christ and
God the Father" (Gal. i. 1).

3. It is said again, Timothy was ordained "with the laying on
of the hands of the *presbytery*" (1 Tim. iv. 14).

It is certain, however, that bishops and presbyters are not so different, but that a bishop is still a presbyter, though all presbyters
are not bishops. So Apostles were still presbyters, (1 Pet. v. 1) ;
though all presbyters were not Apostles. Hence, the presbytery
may have in this case consisted only of those of the first order.
At all events, St. Paul took part in Timothy's ordination, for, in 2
Tim. i. 6, he speaks of the grace of ordination as given to Timothy,
"by the putting on of his (St. Paul's) hands." Hence, Timothy
was certainly not ordained by *presbyters only*, without the presence,
and laying on of hands of an Apostle. It may have been thus early
permitted to presbyters to join with Apostles in laying on of their
hands at the ordinations of other presbyters, as it has since been in
the Western Church ; but this at least gives no sanction to mere
presbyterian ordination.

We must conclude then with Hooker, "If anything in the
Church's government, surely the first institution of bishops was from
Heaven, even of God." [2] And with Bp. Hall, " What inevitable necessity may do, we now dispute not," yet " for the main substance," episcopacy " is utterly indispensable, and must so continue
to the world's end." [3]

---

[1] Bentley, *On Freethinking*, p. 136, quoted by Wordsworth, *Theoph. Anglic.*
[2] Hooker, vii. v. 10.

[3] Bp. Hall's *Episcopacy*, Pt. ii. Sect.
22.

ARTICLE XXIV.

———◆———

Of speaking in the Congregation in such a tongue as the people understandeth.

De loquendo in Ecclesia lingua quam populos intelligit.

It is a thing plainly repugnant to the Word of God, and the custom of the Primitive Church to have Publick Prayer in the Church, or to minister the Sacraments in a tongue not understanded of the people.

Lingua populo non intellecta, publicas in Ecclesia preces peragere, aut Sacramenta administrare, Verbo Dei, et primitivæ Ecclesiæ consuetudini plane repugnat.

Section I.— HISTORY.

THE Article itself appeals to the custom of the primitive Church. The testimony of the fathers we must naturally expect to find only incidentally; for, unless the custom of praying in a strange tongue had prevailed in early times, the idea would probably never have occurred to them, and so they would not be likely to say anything against it. There are however several important proofs to be found, that such a custom did not prevail, but that prayers were offered up in the churches in the vernacular tongue.

Greek, Latin, and Syriac were languages spoken by the great bulk of the nations first converted to Christianity; and therefore the earliest liturgies and translations of the Scriptures were sure to be in these tongues. But moreover, the Egyptians, Ethiopians or Abyssinians, Muscovites, Armenians and others, had liturgies in the vernacular.[1]

The sacred Scriptures were early rendered into the tongues of the nations which had been converted to the faith. Even before the coming of Christ, we know that the Scriptures were translated into Greek for the Alexandrian Jews, and into Chaldee for the Jews of Palestine, to whom their original Hebrew had become obsolete. Under the Gospel the Syriac translation of the new Testament is by many ascribed to the age of the Apostles; at all events, it is a very early work. Latin versions were scarcely, if

---

[1] See Usher, *Historia Dogmatica de Scripturis et Sacris Vernaculis,* cap. VIII. sect. v., where he proves this from the confession of eminent Romanist divines

73

at all, posterior to the Syriac. Thus the numerous tribes which spoke Greek, Latin, or Syriac, had from the beginning the Scriptures, as well as the common Prayer of the Church, in languages understood by them. Moreover, there were very early versions into the Coptic, Sahidic, Ethiopic, Arabic, Armenian, Gothic, Sclavonic, and Anglo-Saxon; a fact too well known to require proof.[1]

Again, we have evidence from the writings of the fathers, that the custom of the primitive Christians was, that the whole congregation should join in the responses and in the singing of psalms and hymns; a custom which proves that both the psalms and the liturgies must have been in intelligible dialects.[2] For instance, St. Cyril writes, "When the priest says, "Lift up your hearts," the people answer, "We lift them up unto the Lord;" then the priest says, "Let us give thanks unto the Lord," and the people say, "It is meet and right." [3] St. Chrysostom says, that "Though all utter the response, yet the voice is wafted as from one mouth." [4] And St. Hilary speaks of people standing without the Church, and yet able to hear the voice of the congregation within, offering up prayer and praise.[5] So the emperor Justinian in one of his laws especially enjoins bishops and presbyters, in public prayers and Sacraments, to speak, not secretly, but with such a voice as may be well heard by the people.[6]

But, beyond all this, we have plain testimonies of the fathers, that both the Scriptures were read and the prayers offered in a tongue intelligible to the assembled multitude. Justin Martyr says, that, among the early Christians, "the commentaries of the Apostles and writings of the prophets were first read; and then, when the reader had ceased, the president made an oration exhorting the people to remember and imitate the things which they had heard." [7] Such an exhortation would have been useless, if the language in which the writings of the Prophets and Apostles were read had not been a language familiar to the congregation. There is a well-known passage in Origen,[8] where he asserts, that, "the Greeks used Greek in their prayers, the Romans Latin, and so

---

[1]. See Bingham, *E. A.* Bk. XIII. ch. IV. § 5; Horne, *Introduction to Scriptures*, II. pt. I. ch. II.

[2] See Usher, as above, cap. VIII. sect. IV; Bingham, *E. A.* Bk. XIII. ch. IV. sect. II.

[3] *Catech. Mystagog.* v.

[4] *Homil. in* 1 *Cor.* xiv.; *Homil.* xxxvi. *iuxta fin.*

[5] "Audiat orantis populi, consistens quis extra ecclesiam, vocem; spectet celebres hymnorum sonitus; et inter divinorum quoque sacramentorum officia, responsionem devotæ confessionis accipiat." — Hilar. *In Psalm.* lxv.; Usher, *ubi supra.*

[6] Justinian, *Novell.* 137. See Usher, as above.

[7] *Apolog.* I. p. 98.

[8] Origen *C. Celsum.* VIII. 37.

every one in his own language prays to God, and gives thanks, as he is able : and the God of all languages hears them that pray in all dialects, even as if all spake with but one voice." From Jerome we learn, that sometimes more than one language was used in the same service, because of the presence of men from different nations. He says, that, " at the funeral of Paula, the Psalms were sung in Greek, Latin, and Syriac, because men of each of those languages were there." [1] Indeed, eminent schoolmen and Roman Catholic divines, as Lyra, Thomas Aquinas and Harding, hav fully allowed that in the primitive Church prayers were offered up in the vulgar tongue, that the people might be the better instructed.[2]

The way in which the use of a dead language for public worship came in, is pretty obvious. The Romans, as masters of the western world, strove to impose their own language on their colonial subjects. Thus the common tongue of Europe was Latin. The ecclesiastics were in constant connection with Rome, the centre of civilization, the chief city of Christian Europe. Thus the language most generally understood became too the language of liturgical worship. By degrees, out of the ancient Latin grew the French, the Italian, the Spanish, and other dialects. Still the old Latin liturgies were preserved, and for a long time were, with no great difficulty, understood. By this time the clergy throughout the western Church had become still more closely united to Rome. More too of mystery had grown over men's minds with regard to the Church's sacred ordinances. Hence all things conspired to make the clergy willing to leave in the language of the central city the prayers of the distant provinces. And thus the change, which became needful when men's languages had changed, was never effected. A feeling too that, as the Church was one and yet universal, so there should be but one universal tongue in which her prayers and praises should go up to God, lent a colouring of piety and poetry to the old custom of having Latin liturgies. And so till the Reformation, no efficient attempt was made to reform what many must have deemed an error, and to make the worship of God, to people as well as priests, a reasonable service.

When this question came to be discussed in the Council of Trent, it was forbidden by an anathema to say that the mass should

[1] Hieron. *Ad Eustochium, Epitaphium Paulæ Matris, juxta fin.* Tom. IV. Part II. p. 687.
[2] Lyra, in 1 *Cor.* xiv. 17; Aquinas *In* 1 *Cor.* xiv. Vol. XVI. fol. 84; Harding,

Contra Juellum, Art. 3, sect. 28. See Usher, as above; Jer. Taylor, *Dissuasive,* pt. I. ch. I. sect. 7; Bingham, Bk. XIII. ch. IV.

not be celebrated in any but the vulgar tongue, or the consecration not performed in a low voice.[1] And though in modern times some prayers are offered in the churches of the Roman communion in tongues understood of the people, yet the mass is never celebrated except in Latin, both to avoid profanation, and lest the very words which are supposed to have been used from the beginning should lose any of their force or sacredness by translation.

SECTION II. — SCRIPTURAL PROOF.

IT is not likely that there should be very much said in Scripture on this subject. The Bible seldom suggests, even to condemn, errors into which men had never fallen. Certainly, however, we can find no trace among the Jews of the use of prayers in an unknown tongue, nor yet among the Apostolic Christians.

The only case in point appears to be that of the exercise of the gift of tongues among the Corinthian Christians. The purpose for which that miraculous power was conferred, was evidently, that the Gospel might be preached by unlearned men to all nations, peoples, and languages. Some of the Corinthian converts, having received the gift by the laying on of the hands of the Apostles, used it to ostentation, not to edification, speaking in the congregations in languages not understood by those who were present. St. Paul rebukes this in the xivth chapter of his first Epistle ; and there incidentally shows, that prayer in a tongue not intelligible to the congregation is contrary to the due order of the Church and the will of God. This is especially observable in verses 14–17 : " If I pray in an unknown tongue, my spirit prayeth, but my understanding is unfruitful. What is it then ? I will pray with the spirit, and I will pray with the understanding also ; I will sing with the spirit, and I will sing with the understanding also. Else, when thou shalt bless with the spirit, how shall he that occupieth the room of the unlearned say Amen at thy giving of thanks, seeing that he understandeth not what thou sayest ? " So again ver. 19 : " In the Church I had rather speak five words with my understanding, that by my voice I might teach others, than ten thousand words in an unknown tongue." And ver. 28 : " If there be no interpreter, let him " (*i. e.* the person who can speak only in a tongue unknown

[1] Sess. XXII. Can. 9. See also Sarpi, *Hist. of the Council of Trent*, p. 540.

to the hearers) "keep silence in the Church; and let him speak to himself and to God."

All these arguments seem as clearly against having liturgies in a dead language, as against the custom which had grown up in the Church of Corinth, of using the gift of tongues when there was none to interpret them. Prayer is to be with the understanding, not with the spirit only. Prayer and thanksgiving are not to be offered publicly in words, to which the unlearned cannot say Amen. A man may pray in such words in private to God, but not publicly in the Church. The reason assigned is, " God is not the author of confusion, but of peace, as in all the churches of the saints " (ver. 33). And the general rule laid down is, " Let all things be done to edifying " (ver. 26).

No arguments from expediency seem fit to be set against such decisions of the Apostles. Now the only arguments of any weight for retaining Latin in the Liturgies are arguments from expediency. For instance, it is said, Latin is a general language, and so, well for the whole Church to use. But it is more true to say, that it is generally unknown, than that it is generally known; for it is only the learned in all lands that understand it; the masses of the people (who have souls to be saved as well as the more instructed) do not understand it anywhere. It is said, that the holy services are kept from profanation by being veiled in the mystery of a difficult tongue. But it is surely more profanation, when people mutter sacred things, or listen to them being muttered, without understanding them, than when they reverently and intelligently join with heart and mind in solemnizing them. It is said again, that the use of the dead language fixes and preserves the sacred services; so that words used from Apostolic times are still used by the Church; and the mass is celebrated in the same syllables in which it was said by the primitive bishops. This, if extended to the whole service of the mass, is not strictly true; for the Roman missal does not actually agree with the various primitive liturgies, which primitive liturgies have considerable varieties among themselves. If the statement be confined to the very words of consecration; then surely we ought to use, not Latin, but Greek, in which these words are to be found in the new Testament. If these be any virtue in the very words themselves, we are no nearer the original, if we say, *Hoc est Corpus Meum*, than if we say, *This is My Body*.

In short, the custom of having prayers in an unknown tongue appears to have originated in a kind of accident, but to have been

perpetuated by design. It originated in the Latin becoming
obsolete in Europe, and the prayers not being translated, as the
various European dialects grew up. It was then found to be a
means of keeping up mystery, and so priestly power ; and therefore it was preserved. But it is evidently without authority from
Scripture, or from the primitive Church

ARTICLE XXV.

Of the Sacraments.

SACRAMENTS ordained of Christ be not only badges or tokens of Christian men's profession, but rather they be certain sure witnesses, and effectual signs of grace, and God's good will towards us, by the which He doth work invisibly in us, and doth not only quicken, but also strengthen and confirm our Faith in Him.

There are two Sacraments ordained of Christ our Lord in the Gospel, that is to say, Baptism and the Supper of the Lord.

Those five commonly called Sacraments, that is to say, Confirmation, Penance, Orders, Matrimony, and extreme Unction, are not to be counted for sacraments of the Gospel, being such as have grown partly of the corrupt following of the Apostles, partly are states of life allowed in the Scriptures, but yet have not like nature of Sacraments with Baptism, and the Lord's Supper, for that they have not any visible sign or ceremony ordained of God.

The Sacraments were not ordained of Christ to be gazed upon, or to be carried about, but that we should duly use them. And in such only as worthily receive the same they have a wholesome effect or operation: but they that receive them unworthily, purchase to themselves damnation, as St. Paul saith.

De Sacramentis.

SACRAMENTA a Christo instituta, non tantum sunt notæ professionis Christianorum, sed certa quædam potius testimonia, et efficacia signa gratiæ atque bonæ in nos voluntatis Dei, per quæ invisibiliter Ipse in nos operatur, nostramque fidem in se non solum excitat, verum etiam confirmat.

Duo a Christo Domino nostro in Evangelio instituta sunt sacramenta, scilicet, Baptismus et Cœna Domini.

Quinque illa vulgo nominata Sacramenta; scilicet, Confirmatio, pœnitentia, ordo, matrimonium, et extrema unctio, pro sacramentis evangelicis habenda non sunt, ut quæ partim a prava apostolorum imitatione profluxerunt, partim vitæ status sunt in scripturis quidem probati, sed sacramentorum eandem cum Baptismo et Cœna Domini rationem non habentes, ut quæ signum aliquod visibile, ceu cæremoniam a Deo institutam non habeant.

Sacramenta non in hoc instituta sunt a Christo, ut spectarentur aut circumferrentur; sed ut rite illis uteremur, et in his duntaxat, qui digne percipiunt, salutarem habent effectum: Qui vero indigne percipiunt, damnationem (ut inquit Paulus) sibi ipsis acquirunt.

THE main substance of this Article is taken from the XIIIth Article of the Confession of Augsburg, the very words of which are adopted in the first part of it.[1] The Articles agreed on between the Anglican and Lutheran reformers, in 1538, had one Article (the IXth) to the same purport; though that went on to speak of Infant Baptism.[2] The XXVIth Article of 1552 contained nearly the same statements as the present XXVth; but had

---

[1] "De usu Sacramentorum docent; quod *Sacramenta instituta sint, non modo ut sint notæ professionis inter homines, sed magis ut sint signa et testimonia voluntatis Dei erga nos, ad excitandam et confirmandam fidem* in his qui utuntur . . . . proposita, &c." — *Confess. August.* Art. XIII.

[2] Cranmer's *Works* by Jenkyns, IV.; Appendix, p. 285.

no reference to the seven Sacraments.   It asserted that the wholesome effect of the Sacraments was not *ex opere operato*, " *of work wrought.*"   Moreover, there was the following sentence in it by way of introduction, which is almost in the words of St. Augustine : " Our Lord Jesus Christ hath knit together a company of new people with the Sacraments, most few in number, most easy to be kept, most excellent in signification, as is Baptism and the Lord's Supper." [1]

We may divide the Article, as it now stands, into four heads.

I.   Concerning the number of the Sacraments of the Gospel.

II.   Concerning their efficacy.

III.   Concerning their proper use.

IV.   Concerning their worthy reception.

The whole Article is introductory to the six next in order after it, and is rather concerned with definitions than aught else.   And as such I purpose to consider it.

I.   The word Sacrament (*Sacramentum*) is an ecclesiastical, rather than a Scriptural term.   It is used indeed in the Latin translations for the Greek word μυστήριον, *mystery.*   Yet the technical use of both these terms in the Christian Church is rather patristic than Apostolical.   The original meaning of the word *Sacramentum* was (1) anything sacred, hence (2) a sacred deposit, a pledge, and (3) most commonly, an oath, especially the military oath, which soldiers took to be faithful to their country, and obey the orders of their general.   Whether the first, or the last and ordinary sense of the word was the origin of the ecclesiastical usage of it, may be a question.

The earliest application of the term to anything Christian is to be found in the well-known letter of Pliny the younger to the emperor Trajan; in which he speaks of the Christians as wont to meet together on a certain fixed day, before sunrise, when they chanted hymns to Christ as to God, and *bound themselves by a Sacrament* not to commit any sort of wickedness.[2]   It is possible,

---

[1] The words of St. Augustine are : " Sacramentis numero paucissimis, observatione facillimis, significatione præstantissimis, societatem novi populi colligavit, sicuti est Baptismus Trinitatis nomine consecratus, communicatio Corporis et Sanguinis Ipsius ; et si quid aliud in Scripturis Canonicis commendatur." —Epistol. 54, *Op.* Tom. II. p. 124.   He uses nearly the same words, *De Doct. Christ.* Lib. III. c. 9, Tom. III. pars I. p. 49.

[2] " Adfirmabant autem, hanc fuisse summam vel culpæ suæ. vel erroris, quod essent soliti, stato die, ante lucem convenire, carmenque Christo quasi Deo dicere secum invicem ; seque *Sacramento* non in scelus aliquod obstringere, sed ne furta, ne latrocinia, ne adulteria committerent, ne fidem fallerent, ne depositum appellati abnegarent."—Plin. *Epist* 97.

that the word *Sacrament* here meant simply *an oath*. Yet since
Pliny reported it, as the Christians had told it to him, it is probable enough, that he used the very word which he had heard
from them, and that they used it in the Christian and technical
sense, howsoever Pliny may have understood it. It is generally
supposed that its *application* in this passage was to the Supper of
the Lord.[1]

In Tertullian, the earliest of the Latin fathers, we find the
notion of the military oath applied to the Christian's baptismal
vow, to serve faithfully under the banner of the cross. "We were
called to the warfare of the living God, when we made answer according to the words of the Sacrament (*in Sacramenti verba res-
pondimus*). No soldier goes to war with luxuries," [2] &c.

This, however, is an exception to the rule. The commoner
use of the word is either for a sacred rite in general, an outward
sign of some more hidden reality — or else for certain particular,
more exalted rites of the Gospel and the Church. It has, in short,
a more extended, and a more restricted force. In its more extended sense, it signified little more than a religious ordinance or a
sacred sign. Thus Tertullian, speaking of the charges of infanticide, brought by the heathens against the Christians, says that
Christians were charged with "the Sacrament of infanticide." [3]
He calls our Lord's anointing by the Holy Ghost, *Sacramentum
unctionis*.[4] St. Cyprian speaks of the many Sacraments contained
in the Lord's Prayer.[5] He calls the three hours of prayer, "a Sacrament of the Trinity." [6] He says, the manna was "a Sacrament
of the equality with which Christ diffuses His gifts of light and
grace upon His Church ; and that the Red Sea was a Sacrament
(*i. e.* a divinely ordained figure) of baptism." [7] Accordingly, we
hear some of the ancients speaking of the two great ordinances of
Baptism and the Eucharist, not as each but one Sacrament, but as
each containing two Sacraments. In Baptism, the two Sacraments
were the water, and the chrism which was anciently used after it.[8]

---

[1] See Waterland, *On the Eucharist*, ch.
I.

[2] *Ad Mart.* 3 ; conf. *De Spectaculis*,
24 ; *De Corona*, 13 ; *De Idololatria*, 6, &c.
Cf. Hieronym. *Epist.* I. *ad Heliodorum :*
" Recordare tyrocinii tui diem, quo
Christo in baptismate consepultus, in
sacramenti verba jurasti." — *On the Baptismal Profession*, see Bingham, XI. vii. 6.

[3] " Dicimur sceleratissimi, de sacramento infanticidii."—*Apolog.* 7.

[4] *Adv. Praxeam*, 28 ; see Bp. Kaye,
Tertullian, p. 358.

[5] " Qualia autem sunt, fratres dilectis-
simi, orationis Dominicæ sacramenta,
quam multa, quam magna breviter in
sermone collecta." — Cypr. *De Oratione
Dominica*, T. 142. Oxford, 1682.

[6] " Horam tertiam, sextam, nonam,
sacramento scilicet Trinitatis."—Ibid. E.
154.

[7] Ibid. *Epistol.* 69, al. 76, E. 187.

[8] Immediately after baptism in the
early ages, followed the unction or
chrism, and confirmation, or the laying
on of hands. So Tertullian: "Exinde

In the Eucharist, the two Sacraments were the bread and the wine. Thus St. Cyprian twice speaks of regeneration as to be obtained by the reception of both Sacraments ; where the context shows, that the two Sacraments mean the washing of water and the imposition of hands, considered as parts of the one ordinance of Baptism.[1] And so Isidore speaks of four great Sacraments, namely, Baptism and Chrism, the Body and the Blood of Christ.[2]

The use of the term *Sacrament* then was very different among the fathers from its ordinary use amongst us. Yet there was with them also a more restricted use of the term ; and there is abundant proof that the two great Sacraments of Baptism and the Eucharist were markedly separated from, and preferred before all other sacraments or ordinances. It is observed, that Justin Martyr in his first apology, (see pp. 93, 97,) when giving an account of the Christian religion and of its rites, mentions only Baptism and the Supper of the Lord. Tertullian uses the word *Sacramentum* with the common laxity of the early writers, yet he specially applies it to Baptism, which he calls *Sacramentum Fidei*,[3] *Aquæ*,[4] *Lavacri*,[5] and to the Eucharist, which he calls *Sacramentum Eucharistiæ*.[6] He does not seem to have applied it to any of the five Romish Sacraments, except to marriage, concerning which he specially alludes to the Latin translation of Eph. v. 32, where μέγα μυστή-ριον is rendered *magnum Sacramentum*.[7] The same is the case

---

egressi de lavacro perungimur benedicta unctione." — *De Baptismo*, 7. " Dehinc manus imponitur, per benedictionem invocans, et invitans Spiritum Sanctum." —c. 8. Confirmation was anciently considered part of baptism, and followed on it immediately. See Bingham, xii. 3 ; Suicer, s. v. χρίσμα, ii. 1534 ; ἔλαιον, i. 1077 ; and Hooker, Bk. v. ch. 66

Confirmation was sometimes delayed from the difficulty of obtaining the presence of a bishop at the time of baptism ; but unction seems to have been always administered with baptism. "Ungi quoque necesse est eum, qui baptizatus sit, ut accepto Chrismate, id est, unctione, esse unctus Dei, et habere in se gratiam Christi possit." — Cypr. *Epist.* lxx. E. 190.

The custom of anointing after baptism was retained by our reformers in the first Service Book, though omitted in the second. The following was the form prescribed. " Then the priest shall anoint the infant upon the head, saying, Almighty God, the Father of our Lord Jesus Christ, who hath regenerate thee

by water and the Holy Ghost, and hath given thee remission of all thy sins, He vouchsafe to anoint thee with the unction of His Holy Spirit, and bring thee to the inheritance of everlasting life. Amen." — *Two Liturgies of Edw. VI.* Oxf. 1838, p. 334.

Confirmation was not considered essential to the receiving of the Holy Ghost in baptism, but was " only a sacramental complement." — See Hooker, v. ch. lxvi. § 6, and St. Jerome, as cited there.

[1] " Tunc demum plene sanctificari, et esse Filii Dei possunt, si sacramento utroque nascantur," &c. — *Epist.* lxxii. E. 196, Cf. *Ep.* lxxiii. p. 207. See also Bingham, xii. i. 4.

[2] " Sunt autem sacramenta, baptismus et chrisma ; corpus et sanguis Christi." — Isidor. *Origin.* Lib. v꞉. c. xix. apud Bingham, *ubi supr.*

[3] *De Anima*, i.

[4] *De Baptismo*, 1, 12.

[5] *De Virgin. Veland.* 2.

[6] *De Corona*, 3.

[7] *De Jejuniis*, 3. See Bishop **Kaye's** *Tertullian*, p. 358.

with the later Latin fathers. St. Augustine, when contrasting the
Sacraments of the Law with those of the Gospel, speaks of the
former as many, but the latter as very few, and then enumerates
only Baptism and the Communion : in one passage adding, " and
if there be any other commended to us in the Canonical Scriptures :"
but in another, instancing only Baptism and the Lord's Supper.[1]
In like manner, speaking of Adam and Eve as types of Christ and
the Church, he says that, " As from the side of Adam when sleeping sprang Eve, so from the side of Christ sleeping on the Cross
flowed the Sacraments of the Church " (*Sacramenta Ecclesiæ profluxerunt*), *i. e.* the two Sacraments typified by the water and the
blood.[2] Elsewhere he says, " The water and the blood which
flowed from the side, were the twin Sacraments of the Church
(*Ecclesiæ gemina Sacramenta*), the water in which the bride is
purified, the blood with which she is endowed." [3]

The same thing is observable among the Greeks. Though they
use the word *mystery*, as the Latins do *Sacrament*, for any sacred
sign ; yet baptism and the Eucharist are markedly distinguished
from all other ordinances. Ignatius speaks of them as the two
rites, which may not be celebrated without the bishop's authority.[4]
St. Cyril couples " the holy mysteries of baptism," and the
" spiritual and heavenly mysteries " " of the Holy Altar," as those
things for which the catechumens were trained.[5] St. Chrysostom joins together Baptism and the Lord's Supper, as the two
ordinances necessary to salvation. " If none can enter into the
kingdom of Heaven except he be born again of water and the
Spirit, and if he who eateth not the Flesh of the Lord nor
drinketh His blood is cast out of life eternal, and if these things are
performed by the hands of the priests," [6] &c. So he speaks, almost
in the same terms with St. Augustine, of the blood and water from
our Saviour's side, as typifying the two mysteries or Sacraments

---

[1] In the one passage, *Epist.* 54, given above, he says : " Sicuti est baptismus Trinitatis nomine consecratus, communicatio corporis est sanguinis ipsius, et si quid aliud in Scripturis Canonicis commendatur."

In the other passage, *De Doctrina Christiana*, Lib. III. c. 9, he says simply : " Sicuti est baptismus et celebratio Corporis et Sanguinis Domini."

[2] *In Johann. Evang.* cap. IV. tract. XV. Tom. III. pars 2, p. 409.

[3] " Percussum est enim latus Ejus, ut evangelium loquitur, et statim manavit sanguis et aqua, quæ sunt Ecclesiæ gem-

ina sacramenta ; aqua ex qua est sponsa purificata, sanguis ex quo invenitur esse dotata." — *De Symb. ad Catech.* 15, Tom. VI. p. 562.

This latter book is not certainly Augustine's ; though the Benedictine editors consider this genuine, and the three tracts which follow it spurious. The like sentiments occur often in St. Augustine. See *Serm.* CCXIX. c. 14; *In Vigiliis Paschæ*, quoted under Art. XIX. Sect. I.

[4] *Smyrn.* VIII.

[5] *Cateches.* XVIII. 14.

[6] *De Sacerdot.* III.

by which the Church is constituted.[1]   In which expressions he is followed, nearly word for word, by Theophylact.[2]

With whatever latitude therefore the word *mystery* and *Sacrament* are used in their general acceptation by the fathers, there is still a higher and more special signification, in which they are applied to the two great ordinances of the Gospel, instituted by Christ Himself.[3]

As for the number *seven* insisted on by the Church of Rome, we cannot find it in the writings of the fathers.   Peter Lombard is said to have first devised it in the twelfth century, and from him it was adopted generally by the Schoolmen.[4]   It was laid down with authority in a decree to the Armenians, sent from the Council of Florence 1439, which runs only in the name of Pope Eugenius.[5] It was then confirmed by the provincial Council of Sens, otherwise called the Council of Paris, A. D. 1528 ;[6] after that, by the Council of Trent, A. D. 1547.[7]   It finally stands as part of the Creed of Pope Pius IV.[8]

The confessions of all the reformed Churches speak of but *two* Sacraments of the Gospel.[9]   In England, the *Articles about Religion* and the *Necessary Doctrine*, put forth in Henry VIIIth's reign, in 1536 and 1543 respectively, retain the notion of seven Sacraments. Even the first book of Homilies, A. D. 1547, speaks of " the Sacrament of matrimony," and that, immediately after speaking of the " Sacrament of baptism." [10]   Cranmer's Catechism speaks of three Sacraments as instituted by Christ, baptism, absolution, the Lord's Supper.[11]   But the final judgment of the reformed Church of England appears first in this Article ; secondly, in the language of the Catechism, where Sacraments are defined as outward signs of inward grace, " ordained by Christ Himself," and are said to be

---

[1] ἐξῆλθε δὴ γὰρ ὕδωρ καὶ αἷμα. οὐκ ἁπλῶς, οὐδὲ ὡς ἔτυχεν, αὗται ἐξῆλθον αἱ πηγαί · ἀλλ' ἐπειδὴ ἐξ ἀμφοτέρων τούτων ἡ ἐκκλησία συνέστηκε · καὶ ἴσασιν οἱ μυσταγωγούμενοι δι' ὕδατος μὲν ἀναγεννώμενοι, δι' αἵματος δὲ καὶ σαρκὸς τρεφόμενοι. ἐντεῦθεν ἀρχὴν λαμβάνει τὰ μυστήρια. — *Homil. in Johann.* 85, Tom. II. p. 915.
Elsewhere he speaks of the blood and water being εἰς τύπον τῶν μυστηρίων, for a type of the Sacraments. — Tom. v. *Homil.* cxviii.

[2] Οὐχ ἁπλῶς ταῦτα γίνεται, ἀλλ' ἐπεὶ τῇ ἐκκλησίᾳ ἡ ζωὴ διὰ τούτων τῶν δύο γίνεται καὶ συνίσταται, δι' ὕδατος μὲν γεννώμεθα, δι' αἵματος καὶ σώματος τρεφόμεθα. — Theophyl. *In Johannis,* cap. xix. See Suicer, s. v. μυστη ···

[3] It should be added that both *mys-*

tery and *Sacrament* were κατ' ἐξοχὴν applied to the Eucharist.   See Suicer, as above, and Waterland, *On the Eucharist,* ch. i.

[4] Lombard *Sentent.* Liv. iv. dist. ii. § i.

[5] *Decret. Eugen. Papæ* iv. *ad Armenos ap.* Labb. *Concil.* Tom. xiii. p. 534.

[6] Can. x. ; Labb. *Concil.* Tom. xiv. p. 454.

[7] Sess. vii. Can. i.   See Archbishop Bramhall, *Answer to M. De la Milletière,* Bramhall's *Works,* i. p. 55.   Oxf. 1842.

[8] See *Sylloge Confessionum,* p. 4.

[9] See Luther's *Catechismus Major, Opera,* Tom. v. p. 636 ; *Sylloge Confessionum,* pp. 75, 127, 277, 349, 876.

[10] *First Part of the Sermon of Swearing.*

[11] Cranmer's *Catechism,* p. 183.   On the effect of Absolation, see p. 202.

" *two* only as generally necessary to salvation ; " and thirdly, in the
second book of Homilies, the words of which are so much to the
purpose that we may well refer to them here : " As for the number
of them, if they should be considered according to the exact signification of a Sacrament, namely, for the visible signs, expressly
commanded in the New Testament, whereunto is annexed the
promise of free forgiveness of our sins, and of our holiness and
joining in Christ, there be but two : namely, baptism and the
Supper of the Lord. For, although absolution hath the promise
of forgiveness of sin ; yet by the express word of the new Testament it hath not this promise annexed and tied to the visible sign,
which is imposition of hands. For this visible sign (I mean laying
on of hands) is not expressly commanded in the new Testament to
be used in absolution, as the visible signs in baptism and the Lord's
Supper are : and therefore absolution is no such Sacrament as
baptism and the communion are. And though the ordering of
ministers hath His visible sign and promise, yet it lacks the promise
of remission of sins, as all other Sacraments except the two above-
named do. Therefore neither it, nor any other Sacrament else, be
such Sacraments as Baptism and the Communion are. But in
general acceptation the name of a Sacrament may be attributed to
anything, whereby an holy thing is signified. In which understanding of the word the ancient writers have given this name, not
only to the other five, commonly of late years taken and used for
supplying the number of the seven Sacraments ; but also to divers
and sundry other ceremonies, as to oil, washing of feet, and such
like ; not meaning thereby to repute them as Sacraments in the
same signification that the two fore-named Sacraments are. *Dionysius, Bernard, de Cœna Domini, et Ablut. pedum.* " [1]

In this passage we see clearly our own Church's definition of a
Sacrament, and the points of difference between ourselves and the
Romish divines. The Homily defines a Sacrament of the Gospel
to be " a visible sign expressly commended to us in the new Testament, whereunto is annexed the promise of free forgiveness of
our sins, and of our holiness and joining in Christ." This closely
corresponds with the words of the Catechism : " An outward and
visible sign of an inward and spiritual grace given unto us, ordained
by Christ Himself, as a means whereby we receive the same "
spiritual grace, " and a pledge to assure us thereof." And again,
the definition of this XXVth Article is of similar significance :
" Sacraments *ordained of Christ be* . . . . certain sure witnesses,

---

[1] *Homily on Common Prayer and Sacraments.*

and effectual (*efficacia*) signs of grace, and God's good-will towards us, by the which He doth work invisibly in us."

Now this definition does not exclude matrimony, confirmation, absolution, and orders, from being *in some sense* Sacraments; but it excludes them from being " *such* Sacraments as baptism and the Communion." No other ordinances but baptism and Communion have an express sign ordained by Christ Himself, and annexed thereto the promise of free forgiveness of sins," and " of inward and spiritual grace given to us." Therefore these have clearly a preëminence over all other ordinances, and may therefore κατ' ἐξοχὴν be called Sacraments of the Gospel: being also the only ordinances which are " generally necessary to salvation."

It seems hardly needful to enter on a full consideration of each of the five Romish Sacraments here. Four out of the five the Church of England admits, at least in a modified form. This Article declares them to be " such as have grown partly of the corrupt following of the Apostles, partly to be states of life allowed in the Scriptures." Matrimony is especially to be called a " state of life allowed in the Scriptures." It is possible, that orders and confirmation may be so called also. Yet orders, confirmation, and penance or absolution, as the Roman Church administers them, are mixed with some superstitious ceremonies. Hence perhaps they, as well as extreme unction, may be considered in the Article, to have " grown " (in their Roman Catholic or mediæval form) " of the corrupt following of the Apostles."

1. *Confirmation*, in the primitive Church, followed immediately on baptism, and, as above noted, was made ordinarily a part of baptism. Tertullian and Cyril of Jerusalem both speak of the catechumens as first receiving baptism, and then immediately on their coming out of the water, receiving chrism and imposition of hands.[1] The separation of confirmation from baptism arose, sometimes from the difficulty of obtaining the presence of a bishop, sometimes from the reconciling of heretics, who were confirmed but not rebaptized, and latterly from the deferring the confirmation of infants; it being thought good that, though baptized, they should delay their confirmation till they were trained and seasoned for serving as soldiers in the army of Christ.[2] The result has been that, after the first ages, confirmation became a separate rite from

---

[1] Tertullian, *De Baptismo*, 7, 8, quoted above. Cyril. *Catech. Myst.* III. 1, Ὑμῖν ὁμοίως ἀναβεβηκόσιν ἀπὸ τῆς κολυμβήθρας τῶν ἱερῶν ναμάτων ἐδόθη χρίσμα. — See Bingham, XII. i. 1; Suicer, s. vv. σφρα- γίς, χρίσμα.
[2] See Hooker, Bk. v. lxvi. 7.

baptism, and we still continue it as such, believing that so it is more fit for edifying.

2. *Ordination* we esteem, scarcely less than does the Church of Rome, as an appointment of Christ Himself. We believe that God gives grace for the office of the ministry to those who receive it aright. We observe that, though our Lord commanded no particular sign, yet the Apostles always used the laying on of hands. But with regard to the inward grace, we read not that forgiveness of sins or personal sanctification were promised to its right reception, but rather the Holy Ghost for the work of the ministry. Therefore, although we retain it as essential for the maintenance of a rightly constituted ministry in the Church, yet we place it not on a par with the two Sacraments of baptism and Communion: which are the means of obtaining and increasing spiritual life to our souls, and of binding together the company of God's people in one.[1]

3. *Matrimony* is not so much a Sacrament of the Gospel as " an honourable estate, instituted of God in the time of man's innocency ; " it is neither a badge, "by which Christian men are discerned from others, which be not christened ; " nor is it a means, whereby pardon of sins and inward sanctification are conveyed to us by the Spirit of God. Hence again, though, like other sacred ceremonies, it may be called a Sacrament, and anciently was so called, it comes not under our definition of a Sacrament of the Gospel. In the Epistle to the Ephesians (v. 32), St. Paul does indeed say concerning it, " This is a great mystery ; " or rather (Τὸ μυστήριον τοῦτο μέγα ἐστίν), " This mystery is great." The Latins have translated his words *magnum est Sacramentum ;* and so it has been argued, that matrimony is specially called a Sacrament. It is plain, however, that St. Paul's meaning is merely this. The marriage of Adam and Eve (and indeed marriage in the general) was esteemed by the Jews, and is constantly spoken of in the new Testament, as a figure, type or *mystery* of the union and marriage betwixt Christ and his Church. The fathers all seem to understand it so. Tertullian says, that Adam's calling Eve " bone of his bone and flesh of his flesh," was a great Sacrament concerning Christ and His Church.[2] St. Chrysostom understands it that marriage was an allegory of Christ's union to His Bride, the Church. " That it was something great and wonderful, Moses, or rather

---

[1] " In nullum nomen religionis sive veræ sive falsæ coagulari homines possunt, nisi aliquo signaculorum vel sacramentorum visibilium consortio colligantur."—August. *C. Faustum*, XIX. 11. See Wordsworth, *Theophil. Anglic.* ch. VIII.

[2] " Nam etsi Adam statim prophetavit, magnum illud sacramentum in Christum et Ecclesiam : *Hoc nunc os ex ossibus meis*," &c. — *De Anima*, c. 11. See also *De Exhort. Castitat.* c. 5.

God, intimated. For the present, however, saith he, I speak con-·
cerning Christ, both that He left the Father, and came down, came
to the Bride, and became one Spirit. *For he that is joined unto the
Lord is one Spirit.* And he says well, *It is a great mystery.* And
then as though he were to say, nevertheless the allegory does not
destroy affection, he adds, *Let every one of you in particular so love
his wife even as himself.*" [1] So too Theodoret and Theophylact [2]
explain it, namely, that the Apostle speaks of marriage as a mystery or allegory of Christ and the Church.

4. *Penance* in the Church of Rome consists of three parts: confession, absolution, and satisfaction. The origin of it was in the
early penitential discipline of the Church. In the primitive ages,
when baptized Christians had committed grievous sins, they were
placed for a time in the position of penitents. Their discipline
consisted of three parts: namely, 1, confession; 2, separation from
the Church; 3, absolution.

At first it appears that confession was made publicly by the
offender in the face of the Church, and was probably an humble
acknowledgment of sins which already had given offence to the
company of believers.[3] Yet very early it was commended to penitents to seek out for themselves a wise spiritual adviser, to whom
they should confide their more secret offences, that, if he judged it
expedient, such offences might afterwards be confessed in the face
of the congregation.[4] In process of time the bishops appointed a
regular officer or penitentiary, to hear these private confessions, and
to judge whether they should be made public or not. Socrates
says, this officer was first appointed for the restoration of those
who had lapsed in the Decian persecution;[5] though Sozomen thinks
such a minister must have been necessary, and so in existence from
the first.[6] The duty of this penitentiary was, to inquire into the
nature of the penitents' offences, to prescribe to them certain
modes of humiliation, and if needful a public acknowledgment of
their sins; and then to give them absolution.[7] In course of time,
a scandalous offence having been confessed to a presbyter in the

---

[1] Chrysost. *In Ephes.* v. 32, *Homil.* xx.
[2] Theodoret and Theophylact, *ad hunc
locum.* See Suicer, s. v. μυστήριον. See
also Hammond and Whitby *On Ephes.* v.
33. Macknight has an excellent note on
the passage.
[3] See Tertullian, *De Pœnitentia*, c. 9,
10; Augustin. *Homil.* xlix. 3, Tom. v.
p. 1054.
[4] So Origen: "Tantummodo circum-
spice diligentius cui debeas confiteri pec-

catum tuum . . . . Si intellexerit et
præviderit talem esse languorem tuum
qui in conventu totius Ecclesiæ exponi
debeat et curari, ex quo fortassis et
cæteri ædificari poterunt. et tu ipse facile
sanari," &c. — Origen *In Ps.* xxxvii. *Homil.* 2.
[5] Socr. *H. E.* Lib. v. c. 19.
[6] Sozomen, Lib. vii. c. 16.
[7] Ibid.

Greek Church, which produced a public excitement, Nectarius, Bishop of Constantinople, was induced to abolish the office of penitentiary.[1] St. Chrysostom was the immediate successor of Nectarius. It appears from his writings, that public confession still continued to be a part of discipline;[2] although we have reason to think that the congregation was not always informed of the exact nature of the crimes for which the penitent was suffering penance and confessing guilt, but only that they knew them to be great and deadly offences.[3] This much, however, we learn from the writings both of St. Chrysostom and of his great contemporary, St. Augustine, that the Church in their days did not consider private confession of private sins essential to salvation, but only the public confession of public scandals necessary to the discipline of the Church. " What have I to do with men," says St. Augustine, " that they should hear my confessions ? "[4] " I do not compel you," says St. Chrysostom, " to discover your sins in the presence of men. Unfold your conscience before God, show Him your wounds, and from Him seek healing."[5]

Leo the Great, who was Bishop of Rome, A. D. 440, is said to have been the first innovator on the penitential discipline of the Church ; for he forbade sins which had been confessed to the priest to be published in the Church, deciding that private confession was sufficient for the clearing of the conscience of the offenders.[6] Theodore, Archbishop of Canterbury in the seventh century, is said to have been the first who altogether abolished public penance for private sins.[7] Redemption of penance also by pecuniary fines became, in process of time, a common practice, which some also refer to Theodore as the originator.[8] Along with private confession grew the custom of private absolution.[9] And afterwards the form itself of absolution became more peremptory and authoritative ;[10] till at length auricular confession, followed by absolution and satisfaction, was elevated to the full dignity of a necessary Sacrament.

---

[1] Socr. Sozom. Ibid.

[2] *Epist. ad Innocent.* Tom. III. p. 517 ; *In Epist. ad Ephes. Hom.* III. Tom. XI. p. 23 ; *In Epist. ad Ebræ. Hom.* IV. Tom. XII. pp. 48, 49.

[3] August. *In Symbol. ad Catechumen.* Lib. I. c. 15.

[4] " Quid mihi ergo est cum hominibus, ut audiant confessiones meas, quasi ipsi sanaturi sint omnes languores meos ? " — *Confession.* Lib. x. c. 3, Tom. I. p. 171.

[5] Οὐδὲ γὰρ εἰς θεατρόν σε ἄγω τῶν συνδούλων τῶν σῶν, οὐδὲ ἐκκάλυψαι τοῖς ἀνθρώποις ἀναγκάζω τὰ ἁμαρτήματα· τὸ συνειδὸς ἀνάπτυξον ἔμπροσθεν τοῦ Θεοῦ καὶ αὐτῷ δεῖξον τὰ τραύματα, καὶ παρ' αὐτῷ τὰ φάρμακα αἴτησον: Chrysost. *De Incomprehensibili Dei Natura,* Hom. v. § 7, Tom. I. p. 490.

[6] Leo. *Epist.* 136, *ad Episc. Campan.*

[7] " Theodorus, homo græcus, primus aperte morem sustulit publice de criminibus occultis pœnitendi." — Morinus *De Administ. Pœnitent.* x. 17, 2, quoted by Marshall in *Penitential Discipline,* ch. III. § I.

[8] Marshall, ch. III. § 2.

[9] Ibid. § 3.

[10] Ibid. § 4.

The Council of Trent anathematizes all who deny it to be truly and properly a Sacrament, instituted by Christ Himself,[1] and necessary to salvation *jure divino*, or who say that the method of confessing secretly to the priest alone (which the Church Catholic has observed from the beginning) is alien to Christ's institution and of human invention.[2]

The reformed Churches have generally abolished auricular confession, as obligatory and sacramental. The Lutherans indeed still retain it, as a regular part of Church order and discipline. The Augsburg Confession declares concerning confession, that it is right to retain private absolution in the Church, but that it is not necessary in confession to enumerate every individual sin.[3] Calvin also recommended both private confession to a pastor, and private absolution when needed for the remedy of any special infirmity ; but he says, it should not be made obligatory upon all, but only commended to such as need it.[4] Our own reformers appear to have taken the same wise and moderate view. Ridley, the greatest light of the English Reformation, writes shortly before his death : " Confession unto the minister, which is able to instruct, correct, comfort, and inform the weak, wounded, and ignorant conscience, indeed I ever thought might do much good in Christ's congregation, and so, I assure you, I think even to this day." [5] So the second part of the Homily of Repentance, after condemning the auricular confession of the Church of Rome, says, " I do not say, but that if any do find themselves troubled in conscience, they may repair to their learned curate or pastor," &c. The exhortation to the Communion bids those, who cannot quiet their own consciences, come to the curate, " or some other discreet and learned minister of God's word, and open his grief, that by the ministry of God's holy Word he may receive the benefit of absolution, together with ghostly council and advice, to the quieting of his conscience, and avoiding of all scruple and doubtfulness." In the service for the Visitation of the Sick, it is enjoined on the minister, that he shall move the sick person " to make a special confession of his sins, if he feel his conscience troubled with any weighty matter ; " and a form of absolution is appointed to be used, after such confession, to those who " humbly and heartily desire it." Thus the Church of England provides for all troubled consciences the power of relieving themselves, by making confession of guilt to their pastor.

[1] Sess. xiv. Can. i.
[2] Can. vi.
[3] *Conf. August.* Art. xii. ; *Sylloge*, p. 173.

[4] *Institut.* Lib. iii. c. iv. §§ 12, 14.
[5] Letter to West, dated from Bocardo, in Oxford, April 8, 1554 ; *Letters of the Martyrs*, p. 30. London, 1837.

or " any other discreet and learned minister," and so gives them comfort and counsel ; but does not bind every one of necessity to rehearse all his private sins to man, nor elevate such useful confession into a Sacrament essential to salvation.[1]

The question concerning the power of the keys, as exercised by the ministers of God, may well be reserved to a future Article. It may be sufficient to observe here, that the chief Scripture ground for private confession is to be found in the language of St. James, chap. v. 14–16. There the Apostle counsels the sick to send for the presbyters of the Church who are to pray over them ; and it is promised that such prayers shall be especially effectual for the pardon of sins. It is then added, " Confess your faults one to another, and pray one for another, that ye may be healed. The effectual fervent prayer of a righteous man availeth much" (ver. 16). And this is illustrated by the efficacy of the prayers of the prophet Elijah, at whose intercession rain was first withheld, and then given again. The context, in which all this occurs, compared with the promise given by our Lord to His ministers (Matt. xviii. 18. John xx. 23), and with the custom of the Church from the earliest times, has been ever considered as a ground for the practice continued in the Church of England, that the sick should be especially visited by the clergy, should be moved to confession of sins, and should look to the prayers of the minister as means for obtaining from God pardon, grace, and if it be His will, restoration to health and strength.[2]

There can be no doubt, that a distressed conscience may be soothed and guided by confidence in a spiritual adviser. Most people, much in earnest, and much oppressed with a sense of sin, have yearned for such confidence. Hence the Church should always afford to the sin-stricken soul the power of unburdening itself. But, on the other hand, whatever tends to lead people to substitute confession to man for confession to God, and to make the path of repentance less rugged than the Gospel makes it, must be dangerous. Such is the systematic and compulsory confession of the Church of Rome, followed as it is by absolution and penance, which too often seem to speak peace to the soul, perhaps before its peace is sealed in Heaven. The penitent finds it far easier to unburden his soul to the priest, than to seek, day and night, with broken spirit, for pardon from God : and, when he has once confided his griefs to his spiritual guide, he easily substitutes that guide's

[1] The student is especially referred for a history of this subject to Marshall's *Penitential Discipline*, ch. II. III.

[2] See Dr. Hammond on this passage of St James.

counsels for the dictates of his own conscience: and no counsels from without can speak as fearfully as the whispers of remorse within. Hence the danger of healing the wound lightly, — of substituting false peace for that peace which can come only from a true penitence, and from the sense of God's pardoning love through Christ. Confession has been well called "the luxury of repentance."[1] Access to it is not to be denied to the dying, the perplexed, or the broken-hearted; but it is to be feared for the morbid spirit, and still more to be feared, as a mere routine of ordinary life, as a salving over of the conscience stained by sin, and seeking an easy deliverance from its warnings and reproofs.

5. *Extreme Unction* is an ordinance concerning which we differ from the Church of Rome more than on the other four. We admit the proper use of confirmation, confession, orders, and matrimony; but extreme unction we neither esteem to be a Sacrament, nor an ordinance of the Church at all. As used in the modern Church of Rome, it implies unction with olive oil, blessed by the bishop, and applied by the priest to the five senses of the dying man. It is considered as conveying God's pardon and support in the last hour. It is administered when all hope of recovery is gone, and generally no food is permitted to be taken after it.

The Roman Catholic controversialists can find no primitive authority for this ordinance, except that of Pope Innocent the First, in the fifth century.[2] In a letter to Decentius[3] he answers a question, whether the sick might be anointed with oil, and whether the bishop might anoint? He replies that this might be done, arguing from the language of St. James. But, if extreme unction were then a Sacrament of the Church, it is impossible that one bishop should have asked this question of another; or, if he did, that the other should not at once have reminded him that it was a well-known sacrament of immemorial usage.[4] This is the only authority from patristic ages that the Romanist divines can bring.

They insist, therefore, the rather on the authority from Scripture. That authority, however, is but slender. When our Lord sent out His Apostles and gave them power to "heal the sick," "they anointed with oil many that were sick, and healed them" (Mark vi. 13). Here unction was evidently an outward sign similar to that used by our Saviour, when He made clay and put it to the blind man's eyes. It was connected with the miraculous power

---

[1] Taylor's *Notes from Life.*
[2] See Bellarmine, *De Extrema Unctione,* cap. iv.
[3] *Epist.* i. *ad Decentium,* c. 8.
[4] See Burnet on this Article.

of healing. That power lasted for some time in the Church. Accordingly, St. James desires the sick to send for the elders of the Church, to whom the miraculous gifts were mostly committed, and enjoins that with prayer for the pardon of sins should be joined anointing with oil, in order to the restoration of health ; that as the Apostles used unction upon those whom they healed, so the elders of the Church, who had the gift of healing, should do likewise. " Is any sick among you? let him call for the elders of the Church ; and let them pray over him, anointing him with oil in the name of the Lord : and the prayer of faith shall save the sick, and the Lord shall raise him up " (James v. 14, 15). Here the end of the anointing appears to be that " the Lord should raise him up." Now this exactly corresponds with the miraculous cures of the early ages, but not at all with the extreme unction of late times. Extreme unction is only administered when recovery is hopeless. St. James enjoined unction with the special object of recovery. So long then as miraculous powers remained in the Church, it was reasonable that anointing of the sick should be retained ; but, when those powers ceased, it was reasonable that the unction should cease also.

It was very natural, however, that, when the miraculous powers began to decline, the custom of anointing, which at first had reference to bodily diseases, should still be continued with reference to spiritual maladies. Yet we cannot trace clearly the transition. The use of oil, connected with real or supposed miracles, is frequently alluded to; but it is not till late that there occurs any clear reference to it, as a religious or sacramental rite. Innocent III. at the end of the twelfth century, is quoted by Bellarmine next to Innocent I.[1] His witness is, no doubt, plain enough. A still fuller confirmation of extreme unction is given by Pope Eugenius in the Council of Florence ; at which, it will be remembered, there was an intention of reconciling the Greek with the Latin Church.[2] The Greeks still practise unction, but do not esteem it a Sacrament. At the Council of Trent there were four canons passed, declaring extreme unction to be a Sacrament, instituted by Christ, conferring good, remitting sins, and comforting the infirm.[3]

The English reformers retained a form of anointing the sick in the first Service Book of Edward VI. ; though it does not appear

---

[1] Bellarmine, Ibid. Bellarmine indeed refers to Origen, *Hom.* II. *in Levit.* ; Chrysostom, *De Sacerdot.* III. &c. ; but he acknowledges that he only refers to them as quoting the words of St. James, not as speaking of the Sacrament of extreme unction ; of which they certainly do not speak. To anything farther he can call no witness, after Innocent I., before Alcuin.

[2] *Decretum Eugenii ad Armen. ubi supra*

[3] Sess. XIV.

that they attributed any sacramental efficacy to it, but merely allowed it to be used " if the sick person desired it," with a prayer for pardon of sins and restoration of bodily health.[1] Cranmer had long before, A. D. 1540, expressed his opinion, that there was no ground in Scripture or antiquity for considering the number of the Sacraments to be seven; and especially had pronounced, that " Unction of the sick with oil to remit venial sins, as it is now used, is not spoken of in Scripture, nor in any ancient author." [2] The second Service Book entirely omitted all reference to unction in the service for the Visitation of the Sick.

The merits of the question rest entirely on the two following points of inquiry : 1. Is the passage in St. James to be considered as Apostolical authority for the institution of a Sacrament in the Church ? or has it reference to the cure of bodily disease ? 2. Is the doubtful answer of Pope Innocent I., in the fifth century, sufficient ground for believing that extreme unction had prevailed from the first? or, on the contrary, do the deep silence of his predecessors, and his own hesitating reply, argue plainly, that they " had no such custom, neither the churches of God ? " Roman Catholics answer affirmatively to the former of these alternatives. Reformed Churches undoubtingly adopt the latter.

Having thus considered what the Article says (I.) concerning the *number* of the Sacraments, we have paved the way for the rest of its statements. Limiting the name Sacrament to Baptism and the Eucharist, we have merely to consider (II.) what are the benefits we receive by; (III.) what is the right use of these two ordinances; and (IV.) who are their proper recipients?

II. The efficacy of the Sacraments.

This question must be discussed more particularly in the XXVIIth and XXVIIIth Articles. To speak generally on it now, we may observe, that the doctrine of the fathers on this subject was very clear and strong from the very first. Ignatius speaks of a Christian's baptism as his spiritual armour,[3] and, concerning the Eucharist he writes, " If a man be not within the altar, he is deprived of the bread of God." [4] " I desire the bread of God, which is the Flesh of Christ, and as drink I long for His Blood, which is love incorruptible." [5] The Epistle of Barnabas, which

---

[1] *Two Liturgies of Edward VI.* p. 366.

[2] See " Questions and Answers on the Sacraments," *Works*, II. pp. 100, 103.

[3] τὸ βάπτισμα ὑμῶν μενέτω ὡς ὅπλα.

— *Ad Polyc.* VII. This passage is in the Syriac version.

[4] *Ad Eph.* v.

[5] *Ad Rom.* VII. This passage also is in the Syriac.

though probably not written by the companion of St. Paul, is doubt-less one of the earliest remains of Christian antiquity, speaks of " That baptism, which brings forgiveness of sins," and says, " That we go down into the water full of sins and pollutions, but come up again bringing forth fruit." [1] Justin Martyr, in his account of the Christian Sacraments, speaks of men as " regenerated " and receiving remission of sins in the water of baptism,[2] and as receiv-ing in the Eucharist, not " common bread and common drink," but " the Flesh and Blood of the incarnate Jesus." [3] Irenæus is as clear on both the grace of baptism and the reception of Christ in the Eucharist.[4] Tertullian speaks of the " blessed Sacrament of water, in which, washed from the sins of our former blindness, we are liberated to life eternal ; " in which we " as fish are born, after the pattern of our Ἰχθὺς, Jesus Christ." [5] In the Lord's Sup-per he speaks of feeding on the Body and Blood of Christ, that our soul may be fattened of God.[6] These are all writers of the first century from the Apostles.

It would keep us needlessly long, if we were to go through all the writers of the early ages. It may fairly be said, that with one voice they proclaim their belief that great spiritual blessings are to be obtained, by all faithful recipients, both in baptism and in the Supper of the Lord. The grace of the former they call remis-sion of sins, regeneration, illumination ;[7] the grace of the latter they call the Body and Blood of Christ. In both they looked to receive Christ ; in both they hoped for pardon of sins, and the pres-ence of the Spirit of God. The full meaning of these phrases we shall have to consider in the following articles. Let it suffice here to refer to the pregnant words of St. Augustine, in which he con-trasts the Sacraments or ordinances of the Law with those of the Gospel ; a change having been made, by which the Sacraments have become " easier, fewer, more healthful." " The Sacraments of the new Testament," he says, *give salvation*, whereas those of the old Testament only *promised a Saviour*." [8] Here we have the view of evangelical Sacraments which pervades all Christian antiq-uity, namely, that they differ from the ordinances of the old Law in this ; the ordinances of the old Law were but pledges of future bless-

---

[1] *Epistol. Barnab.* c. 12.
[2] *Apol.* I. p. 93.
[3] Ibid. p. 97.
[4] See Lib. I. c. 18; Lib. III. c. 19; Lib. v. c. 2, &c.
[5] *De Baptismo*, c. 1. " Nos pisciculi, secundum ἰχθὺν nostrum Jesum Chris-tum, in aqua nascimur." Alluding to the word ΙΧΘΥΣ containing the initial

letters of our Lord's Name and titles, Ἰησοῦς Χριστὸς Θεοῦ Υἱὸς Σωτήρ.
[6] *De Resurr. Carnis*, c. 8.
[7] φωτισμὸς. — See Suicer, s. h. v
[8] " Sacramenta N. Testamenti dant salutem ; Sacramenta V. Testamenti promiserunt Salvatorem." — *Enarr. in Ps.* lxxiii. § 2, Tom. IV. p. 769.

ings, not means to convey them, but the Sacraments of the Gospel not only promised Christ, but, to those who receive them in faith, they are means whereby God gives Christ to the soul.

We read, however, of some early heretics who denied the grace or the necessity of the Sacraments. Irenæus ascribes to some of the Gnostics the error of saying, that outward and material sacraments were unnecessary, so the soul were illuminated;[1] an opinion consistent enough with the ultra-spiritualism of that sect, which made all excellence to consist in spiritual enlightenment, and esteemed all matter to be evil and the source of sin. One of the errors for which St. Jerome attacked Jovinian, was, that he altogether separated baptism by the Spirit from baptism by water, saying that a man who had been baptized by the Spirit would never sin after, but that, if he sinned again, it was a proof that he had received only water-baptism, but not spiritual baptism.[2] The Manichees, like the Gnostics, and probably on the same principles, believing baptism to have no efficacy, never administered it to their converts.[3] The Messalians were a sect of mystics, who are described as devoting themselves wholly to prayer, and avoiding even labour for their bodily necessities.[4] It appears that they had a very low esteem of the Sacraments, so that Theodoret accuses them of denying any efficacy whatever to baptism;[5] though there is some reason to think that he has exaggerated their errors.[6] It is probable enough that, wherever mysticism prevailed, such a disregard of external ordinances would prevail also. Those medieval sects which derived their errors from Gnostic or Manichean sources, would naturally underrate Sacraments, as having material elements, which such heretics regarded as essentially evil. Accordingly, we learn that the Paulicians in the ninth century refused to celebrate the Lord's Supper, and probably in like manner rejected outward baptism.[7] The Bulgarians and Albigenses are said to have sprung from the Paulicians; and, though it is difficult to arrive at the truth concerning the tenets of these persecuted sects, we may yet probably infer, that one of their errors was an underrating of the value of baptism and the Eucharist.

The time, however, for these subjects to be most fiercely con-

---

[1] *Hæres.* I. c. 18, p. 91. Edit. Oxon. 1702.
[2] Hieronym. *Adv. Jovinianum*, Lib. II. Tom IV. pt. II. p. 193.
[3] August. *De Hæres.* c. 46; Bingham, *E. A.* Bk. XI. ch. II. sect. 4.
[4] Epiphan. *Hæres.* LXXX.; Augustin. *Hæres.* LVII

[5] Theodoret. *Hæret. Fab.* Lib. IV. c. 10.
[6] See Bingham, *E. A.* Bk. XI. ch. II sect. 5.
[7] See Mosheim, *E. H.* Cent. IX. pt. II. ch. V. Also Bingham, *E. A.* Bk. XI. ch. II. sect. 4.

tested would naturally be the period of the Reformation. We must leave the discussion on Transubstantiation, which agitated the Church in the Middle Ages, for the Articles which treat expressly on the Lord's Supper. Suffice it here to observe, that the school-authors, in their investigations concerning sacramental efficacy, were led, not merely to insist on the value of the Sacraments as means, in the use of which God's Spirit works, but also to lay down the principle, that the Sacraments are so in their own nature vehicles of grace, that, *ex opere operato*, from the mere fact of their administration, they convey Christ to the soul. Such a reception of Christ may not indeed be always to salvation; nay, it may be to condemnation; but still the Sacrament administered always brought with it a spiritual grace. This doctrine was fixed, as the doctrine of the Roman Church, by the decrees of the Council of Trent. They anathematized all, who deny that the Sacraments contain grace,[1] or that this grace is conferred by them *ex opere operato*.[2]

All the reformed, whatever differences may have existed between them on these subjects (and such differences were sufficiently great), appear to have much objected to the statement of the *opus operatum*. To them such a statement seemed to imply, not that Sacraments were means through which God was pleased to work, and which He had promised to bless, but rather, that they were of the nature of magical incantations, which, however carelessly administered, could not be separated from their effects upon the soul. The very elements therefore became the objects of adoration. The water of baptism was in itself holy and the source of holiness; the consecrated wafer was the Body of the Son of God. Extremes generate extremes: and we learn that the anabaptists and other fanatics were led to such extravagance of opposition to the extravagance of Romanism, as impiously to mock the blessed Sacrament of the Eucharist; so that " railing bills against it were fixed upon the doors of St. Paul's Cathedral and other places, terming it *Jack in a box*, *The Sacrament of the halter*, *Round Robin*, and such like irreverent terms." [3]

Among the continental reformers, *Zuinglius*, *Luther*, and *Calvin*, adopted three different views of the Sacraments.

Zuinglius rejected sacramental grace entirely. He held Sacraments to be bare signs, outward tokens of Christian profession, but

---

[1] Sess. VII. Can. VI. " Si quis dixerit, sacramenta novæ legis non continere gratiam, quam significant . . . . anathema sit."

[2] Sess. VII. Can. VIII. " Si quis dix-erit per ipsa novæ legis sacramenta ex opere operato non conferri gratiam . . . . anathema sit."

[3] Ridley's *Life of Ridley*, p. 216, re-ferred to by Dr. Hey on this Article.

in no sense means of grace. He defined a Sacrament to be "an external symbol, by which we testify what we are, and what is our duty, just as one who bears a national costume or badge testifies that he belongs to a particular nation or society." [1] And again, "A Sacrament is the sign of a sacred thing; when therefore I speak of the Sacrament of Christ's Body, I mean no more than that bread which is the figure and type of Christ's Body." [2]

Luther, on the contrary, maintained the great importance and spiritual efficacy of the Sacraments. "We can lay it down as a rule," he writes, "that where are the Eucharist, Baptism, the Word, there is Christ, remission of sins, and life eternal." [3] In the Eucharist, it is well known that he believed that, with the consecrated bread and wine, there are delivered to the recipient the very Body and Blood of Christ; the elements not being transubstantiated, but the Body of Christ being consubstantially united with them. [4] Of the other Sacrament he taught, that, as man is born naturally full of sins, so in baptism he is born spiritually, regenerated, justified. His sins are buried there, and righteousness rises instead of sins. [5] "St. Paul," says he, "teaches that baptism is not a sign, but a clothing in Christ, yea, that Christ Himself is our clothing. Wherefore baptism is a most potent and efficacious rite." [6]

Calvin took a kind of mean between Luther and Zuinglius. Concerning Sacraments in general, he writes, that "though they are figures, yet not naked and empty figures, but having their truth and substance united to them; not only representing, but offering grace. We ought never to separate the substance of the Sacraments from the Sacraments themselves. We ought not indeed to confound them, but to rend them asunder is absurd." [7] The

---

[1] "Sacramentum quid] Sacramentum ergo . . . . symbolum externum, quo quales simus, et quodnam sit officium testamur, significat. Ut enim, qui crucem gestat albam, sese Helvetum esse, et posthac semper fore testatur," &c. — De Baptismo, Zuinglii Opera, 1581, Tom. i. fol. 60.

[2] "Sacramentum quid] Sacramentum est sacræ rei signum. Cum ergo Sacramentum Corporis Christi nomino, non quicquam aliud, quam panem, qui Corporis Christi pro nobis mortui figura et typus est, intelligo." — De Cœna Domini, Opera, Tom. i. folio 274.

[3] In Genesin. c. iv. Opera, Tom. vi. fol. 62.

[4] Of this more under Art. xxviii. Meanwhile, see his treatise De Sacramento Altaris, Tom. i. fol. 78 ; Catechismus Major, Tom. v. p. 640.

[5] "Quemadmodum enim mater illo carnali partu plenum peccatis puerum et iræ filium edit, ita baptismus edit spiritualem partum, et regenerat nos, ut justificati simus filii gratiæ. Sic peccata in baptismo demerguntur, et emergit pro peccatis justitia." — De Sacramento Baptismi, Tom. i. fol. 72.

[6] "Docet ergo Paulus baptismum non signum, sed indumentum Christi, immo ipsum Christum indumentum nostrum esse. Quare baptismus potentissima ac efficacissima res est." — In iii. cap. Ad Galat. Tom. v. fol. 370.

[7] "Figuris igitur et signis, quæ sub oculorum sensum cadunt, ut naturæ nostræ imbecillitas requirit, ostenditur : ita tamen ut non sit figura nuda et simplex, sed veritati suæ et substantiæ conjungitur . . . . Sed hoc adjungemus, Sacramenta Domini nullo modo a substantia

word is joined to the external sign, and hence Sacraments have their efficacy . . . . Christ breathed on His Apostles, and they received, not His breathing only, but the Spirit of God. Wherefore? but because Christ had promised? So in baptism we put on Christ, we are washed in His Blood, our old man is crucified, that the righteousness of God may reign in us. In the sacred Supper we are fed spiritually by the Body and Blood of Christ. Whence so great effects, but from the promise of Christ, who effects and makes good by His Spirit what He testifies by His Word?" [1] In regard to the grace received by *infants* in baptism, it is probable, as we shall see hereafter, that Calvin's predestinarian theory materially influenced his views. But as regards adult recipients both of baptism and the Lord's Supper, he clearly taught, that to the faithful God gives, in the one remission and regeneration, in the other, the *real* but *spiritual* presence of Christ's Body and Blood. On the question of the Eucharist especially he differed from the Romanists, in that he rejected transubstantiation, — from the Lutherans, in that he rejected consubstantiation, — from the Zuinglians, in that he maintained a *real* presence of Christ, though he held that presence to be *spiritual*, not *carnal*.[2]

The Calvinistic communions, including the English Puritans and Non-Conformists, have generally followed Zuinglius rather than Calvin in their Sacramental theory; though by no means agreeing with the former on many other points of theology.

The Anglican reformers have sometimes been charged with Zuinglian sentiments concerning the Eucharist. On this subject, however, it is capable of evident proof, that they symbolized, not with Zuinglius, but with Calvin, though not deriving their views from him. On baptism their language is stronger, not only than

---

et veritate sua separari oportere. Ea quidem ne confundantur, distinguere non tantum convenit, sed etiam omnino necessarium est. Sed ita dividere ut alterum sine altero constituatur, absurdissimum."— *De Cœna Domini*, Calvini *Opuscula*, pp. 133, 134.

[1] " Observent lectores externo et visibili symbolo simul verbum conjungi, nam et hinc sacramenta vim suam mutuantur: non quod in voce, quæ auribus personat, inclusa sit Spiritus efficacia; sed quia a testimonio Verbi pendet eorum omnium effectus, quæ ex sacramentis percipiunt fideles. Flat Christus in Apostolos: hi non flatum modo sed Spiritum quoque recipiunt. Cur? nisi quia illis Christus promittit? Similiter in Baptismo Christum induimus, abluimur Ejus sanguine, crucifigitur vetus homo noster, ut regnet in nobis Dei justitia. In sacra Cœna spiritualiter Christi carne et sanguine pascimur. Unde tanta vis, nisi ex Christi promissione, qui Spiritu Suo efficit ac præstat quod verbo testatur." — Calvinus *In Evangelium Johannis*, c. xx. v. 22.

[2] " Necesse est igitur nos in Cœna *vere* Corpus et sanguinem Christi recipere . . . . quemadmodum panis in manu distribuitur, ita Corpus Christi, ut Ejus participes simus, nobis communicari." — *De Cœna Domini Opuscula*, p. 134.

" Cæterum hoc imprimis tenendum, ut *carnalis* omnis imaginatio excludatur, animum oportere sursum in cœlos erigere, ne existimemus Dominum nostrum Jesum Christum eo dejectum esse ut in elementis corruptibilibus concludatur." — Ibid. p. 147.

Calvin's, but even than Luther's.   But of their views concerning
these two Sacraments separately, we must reserve the consideration for the present.   Meanwhile, let us observe a few of their
statements on Sacraments in general.

We have already noticed their language in this XXVth Article,
that Sacraments are "effectual signs of grace, by the which God
doth work invisibly in us."   We have compared the language of
the Homily, in which Sacraments are defined to be " visible signs
expressly commanded in the new Testament, whereunto is annexed the promise of free forgiveness of sins, and of our holiness
and joining in Christ."   We have seen that the Catechism uses
terms of the same significance, calling Sacraments "outward and
visible signs of inward and spiritual grace," which grace is not
merely promised, but "given unto us;" saying also that they
were "ordained by Christ Himself" to be, not only "a pledge to
assure us " of that grace, but also "a means whereby we receive
the same."

In like manner Nowell's *Catechism*, a semi-authoritative document, has the following: "How many Sacraments hath God ordained in His Church?   *A*. Two: Baptism, and the Holy Supper,
which are commonly used among the faithful.   For by the one we
are born again, and by the other we are nourished to everlasting
life." [1]   Jewel's *Apology*, a similar authority, having denied the
Romish doctrine of Transubstantiation, adds: " But when we say
this, we lower not the nature of the Lord's Supper, nor teach it to
be a mere frigid ceremony, and that in it nothing is done, as some
calumniously say that we teach.   For we assert, that Christ truly
exhibits Himself present with us in His Sacraments; in baptism,
that we may put Him on; in the Supper, that we may feed on
Him by faith and in Spirit, and from His Cross and Blood have
everlasting life: and this we assert to be done, not coldly and perfunctorily, but in very deed and truth." [2]   The *Reformatio Legum*
again condemns those who would take the Sacraments " for naked
signs and external marks, whereby the religion of Christian men
may be discerned from others." [3]   And to refer once more to the
Homilies, " The sermon for repairing and keeping clean the
churches " speaks of the house of God as that " wherein be ministered the Sacraments and mysteries of our redemption.   The fountain of our regeneration is there presented to us; the partaking
of the Body and Blood of Christ is there offered unto us; and

---

[1] See the *Enchiridion Theologicum*, i. pp.
313, 314.
[2] *Enchiridion Theolog.* i. p. 129.

[3] "Pro nudis signis et externis tantum
indiciis." — *Reformatio Legum, De Hær·si-
bus,* c. 17, quoted by Hey

shall we not esteem the place where so heavenly things are handled ? "

It may seem needless to add private testimonies of the individual reformers. Yet the names of Cranmer and Ridley stand justly so much at the head of our Reformation that we may well hear one word from each of them. Cranmer, in his *Answer to Gardiner*, writes " Likewise when he (the minister) ministereth to our sight Christ's holy Sacraments, we must think Christ crucified and pre-sented before our eyes, because the Sacraments so represent Him, and be His Sacraments, not the priest's. As in baptism we must think that, as the priest putteth his hand to the child outwardly and washeth him with water, so must we think that God putteth to His hand inwardly and washeth the infant with His Holy Spirit, and, moreover, that Christ cometh down upon the child and apparelleth him with His own Self. And as at the Lord's holy table, the priest distributeth wine and bread to feed the body, so must we think that inwardly by faith we see Christ feeding both body and soul to eter-nal life." [1]   " In all ages," says Ridley, " the devil hath stirred up some light heads to esteem the Sacraments but lightly, as to be empty and bare signs." [2]   " And as all do agree hitherto in the aforesaid doctrine, so all do detest, abhor, and condemn the wicked heresy of the Messalonians, which otherwise be called Euchites, which said that the holy Sacrament can do neither good nor harm ; and do also condemn those wicked anabaptists, which put no dif-ference between the Lord's table and the Lord's meat and their own." [3]

It is not necessary to pursue the history of this subject to more modern times. The Quakers, and some other sects, have not only undervalued Sacramental grace, but actually have rejected all use of the Sacraments. The foreign Protestants, with the exception of the Lutherans, seem mostly to adopt Zuinglian opinions ; as have the generality of dissenters among ourselves. In the English Church, those who have formed their theological views for the most part on the Puritan model, have taken in general low ground on the Sacraments, especially on the Sacrament of baptism, whilst the opposite school have zealously maintained the reality and im-portance of Sacramental grace. The period of Bishop Hoadley and the Bangorian controversy has been pointed to as an era from which lower sacramental doctrines have been very commonly admitted among churchmen. In the present day it is painfully

[1] Cranmer's *Works*, by Jenkyns, III. pp. 553, 554.
[2] *Works*, Parker Society, p. 114.
[3] *Ridley's Works*, Parker Society, p. 9.

known to every one with what fierceness the flame of discord has burst forth, on the subject of those very ordinances of grace which were instituted by Christ on purpose to bind together in one fold and one flock the blessed company of all true believers.

III.   Concerning the proper use of the Sacraments, the Article says, —

" The Sacraments were not ordained of Christ to be gazed upon or to be carried about, but that we should duly use them."   This sentence alludes to the elevation and procession of the host in the Church of Rome ; and, as a similar statement is made, with more direct reference to those customs, in Article XXVIII. we may reserve the consideration of the question for the present.   Thus much only we may remark, that the Tridentine definition, that " the grace of the Sacraments is contained in the Sacraments," naturally led to the adoration of the elements themselves : whereas the doctrine that Sacraments have no efficacy of their own nature, but are ordinances of God, which He is pleased to honour, and by which He has promised to work, will lead to a reverent esteem and diligent use of them, but not to a superstitious veneration of the mere instruments.   This is the difference between Rome and England.

IV.   The last question treated of is the worthy reception of the Sacraments.

" In such only as worthily receive the same, have they a wholesome effect or operation ; but they that receive them unworthily, purchase to themselves damnation, as St. Paul saith."

This statement also is virtually repeated concerning baptism in Art. XXVII. and still more clearly concerning the Eucharist in Art. XXIX.

Highly as the fathers speak, and often with no expressed reservation or restriction, concerning sacramental grace and the potency of the Sacraments, yet, when occasion offers, we may always observe that they did not so tie the grace to the ordinance as to believe that the impenitent and the unbelieving would benefit by it.   Origen, though plainly speaking of remission of sins and the gift of God's Spirit as the grace of baptism, yet observes that " *all are not Israel that are of Israel ;* nor are all baptized with the Spirit who are baptized with water . . . . Some who have received baptism have been unworthy to receive the Holy Spirit. Simon had received baptism, but as he came with hypocrisy for

grace, he was rejected from the gift of the Spirit." [1] Again, he says
that all persons washed with water were not washed to salvation.
It was so with Simon Magus. And, accordingly, he urges on
catechumens to prepare themselves diligently for baptism, lest they
receive the water only, not the Spirit of God. "He who is baptized to salvation receives water and the Holy Spirit; but Simon,
not being baptized to salvation, received water, but not the Spirit
of God." [2]

Tertullian says, he denies not that the pardon of sins is assured
to those who are baptized, but yet he says, we ought to labour
that we attain that blessing. God suffers not the unworthy to
come to His treasures. "Some," he remarks, "think that God
must make good His promises, even to the unworthy, and would
make His liberality a slavish obligation." But Tertullian himself
plainly indicates his belief, that baptism to such unworthy recipients would not be the fountain of life, but rather *symbolum
mortis*, the mark of death. [3]

Just in the same spirit, St. Cyril in the preface to his Catechetical Lectures; in which, though he speaks very excellent things
of the blessings of baptism and Communion, yet he warns against
unworthy approach to them, and diligently prepares his catechumens for worthy reception of them. He begins by propounding
to them the sad example of Simon Magus. "Simon Magus," says
he, "of old came to the laver. He was baptized, but not illuminated. He washed his body with the water, but enlightened
not his heart with the Spirit. His body descended and rose up
again, but his soul was not buried with Christ, nor raised again
with Him." [4] He then goes on to speak of the man without
the wedding garment, and to bid them beware of such conduct as his. He tells them, they have full time for preparation.
"If," he adds, "thou remainest in evil purpose, he who warns
thee will be blameless, but look not thou to receive grace. The
water will receive thee, but the Spirit will not receive thee." [5]

Just so St. Augustine: "All the Sacraments are common, but
not the grace of the Sacraments to all . . . . The laver of regeneration is common to all baptized in the name of the Trinity; but
the grace of baptism is not common to all. For heretics, and
false brethren in the Catholic Church, have the same baptism." [6]
"The Sacrament is one thing, the grace of the Sacrament another.

---

[1] *In Numeros, Homil.* III. num. 1.
[2] *In Ezekiel, Hom.* VI. num. 5. See
Lumper *De Vita et Scriptis Origenis,* Art.
XIII.
[3] *De Pænitentia,* c. 6.
[4] *Cyril. Hierosol. Præfatio Cateches.* I.
[5] Ibid. III.
[6] *In Ps.* 77, Tom. IV. pp. 816, **817**

How many eat of the altar, and die, aye! and die by eating. Wherefore saith the Apostle, He eateth and drinketh condemnation to himself." [1] " If, therefore, thou wilt know that thou hast received the Spirit, ask thine own heart, lest perchance thou hast the Sacrament, but not the virtue of the Sacrament." [2]

The Scholastic disputes concerning the grace of the Sacraments originated the theory of the *opus operatum*. The Sacraments were thought to be so completely vehicles of grace that they themselves contained and conveyed the grace which was proper to them. Thus the elements in the Eucharist were believed to be changed into the substance of Christ's Body and Blood; and by whomsoever the bread and wine were received, by the same the Body and Blood of Christ were eaten and drunk. To the unworthy indeed the reception was not to salvation, but to condemnation; yet still it was a real receiving, not only of the Sacrament, but also of the grace of the Sacrament. So Simon Magus was believed to have received, not only baptism, but the grace of baptism, yet not to life, but to death. He was said to have been regenerated by baptism, but regenerate to a greater condemnation. The fathers' expressions were made to bear this meaning, when they speak in glowing terms of the blessings to be expected in the reception of the sacraments. [3] But a hundred such strong statements can never be fairly alleged against a single sentence occurring in qualification or explanation of them. How often soever it be said that baptism is regeneration, and the Eucharist a feeding upon Christ's Body and Blood; a single statement, that this is true only of worthy recipients, is sufficient to prove that such a qualification is always to be understood.

The Roman Church, however, has adopted the theory of the *opus operatum*, and stamped it with synodal authority. Yet in the

---

[1] *In Johann.* cap. 6, Tract XXVI. Tom. III. pars. II. p. 498, c.

[2] *In Epist. Johann.* cap. IV. Tract VI. Tom. III. pars II. p. 868, f. Compare p. 840, c. See also *De Civitate Dei*, Lib. XXI. cap. 25. Tom. VII. p. 445, *seq.*

[3] Thus St. Augustine is supposed to have asserted, that Simon Magus received the Holy Ghost in baptism. He is speaking of the many gifts which a man may receive, and yet lack charity; he continues, " Respice ad munera ipsius Ecclesiæ. Munus sacramentorum in baptismo, in eucharistia, in cæteris sanctis sacramentis; quale munus est? Hoc munus adeptus est et Simon Magus. Prophetia quale munus est? Propheta-

vit et Saul malus rex," &c. S. Augustin. *In Ps.* ciii. Serm. I. 9. Tom. IV. p. 1136. It does not appear to me that anything in this passage is inconsistent with a belief that the grace of the Sacrament may be withheld from the impenitent. At all events, such a vague statement can never be pressed against such positive statements as those given above from the same father. In one passage indeed he leaves it as a kind of open question, whether Simon Magus was regenerated to greater condemnation, or whether he was born of water, but not of the Spirit. He seems to incline to the latter alternative. — *De Baptismo c. Donatist.* Lib. VI. c. 12. Tom. IX. p. 169.

very canon which asserts that the Sacraments *contain grace*, it is added, that " they *confer* grace on those *who do not place a bar*." [1]

If it were not added soon after [2] that the " Sacraments confer grace, *ex opere operato*," we might believe that the Tridentine fathers did not materially differ from the statements of our own reformers; *to place a bar* being much the same as *to receive unworthily*.

The reformers all strongly opposed the doctrine of the *opus operatum*.

The Lutherans, who of all the reformed bodies were considered to hold the highest view of the Sacraments, yet plainly rejected the belief that grace was inseparably tied to the reception of them. Luther complains, that the schoolmen and the papists dreamed of virtue infused into the water of baptism ; but he held the gift of the Spirit to the baptized to result from the promise of God to them, but that the water was still but water. [3] So, though by the doctrine of consubstantiation Christ's very Body would be received with the bread, yet, as the bread is not said to be changed into Christ's Body, it is possible that by the unworthy the bread alone might be eaten, but the Body and Blood might not be communicated In this, as in many respects, consubstantiation is much different from transubstantiation ; since, according to the latter, the substance of the bread and wine is utterly annihilated, and nothing remains but the substance of the Body and Blood, so that all who receive the Sacrament, must receive by it the very substance of Christ.

It is unnecessary, for the present, to say more concerning our own reformers' views of this subject ; they are plainly expressed in this and the following Articles ; and we shall hear more of them under Art. XXVII. and XXVIII.

---

[1] *Concil. Trident.* Sess. VII. can. VI. " Si quis dixerit sacramenta novæ legis non continere gratiam, quam significant, aut gratiam ipsam *non ponentibus obicem non conferre*, anathema sit."

[2] Ibid. Canon VIII.

[3] See Laurence's *Bampton Lectures,* Note on Sermon VII. pp. 157, 158.

ARTICLE XXVI.

———◆———

Of the Unworthiness of the Ministers, which hinders not the effect of the Sacrament.

ALTHOUGH in the visible Church the evil be ever mingled with the good, and sometimes the evil have chief authority in the Ministration of the Word and Sacraments, yet forasmuch as they do not the same in their own name, but in Christ's, and do minister by His commission and authority, we may use their ministry, both in hearing the Word of God, and in receiving of the Sacraments. Neither is the effect of Christ's ordinance taken away by their wickedness, nor the grace of God's gifts diminished from such as by faith and rightly do receive the Sacraments ministered unto them ; which be effectual, because of Christ's institution and promise, although they be ministered by evil men.

Nevertheless, it appertaineth to the discipline of the Church, that inquiry be made of evil Ministers, and that they be accused by those that have knowledge of their offences ; and finally being found guilty, by just judgment be deposed.

De vi Institutionum Divinarum, quod eam non tollat malitia Ministrorum.

QUAMVIS in ecclesia visibili, bonis mali semper sunt admixti, atque interdum ministerio verbi et sacramentorum præsint, tamen cum non suo, sed Christi nomine agant, ejusque mandato et auctoritate ministrent, illorum ministerio uti licet, cum in verbo Dei audiendo, tum in sacramentis percipiendis. Neque per illorum malitiam effectus institutorum Christi tollitur, aut gratia donorum Dei minuitur, quoad eos qui fide et rite sibi oblata percipiunt, quæ propter institutionem Christi et promissionem efficacia sunt, licet per malos administrentur.

Ad Ecclesiæ tamen disciplinam pertinet, ut in malos ministros inquiratur, accusenturque ab his, qui eorum flagitia noverint, atque tandem justo convicti judicio deponantur.

———————————

SECTION I. — HISTORY.

IT is natural, in treating of the doctrines contained in this Articie, to begin with the question concerning heretical baptism, which agitated the primitive Church. Tertullian denies that the heretics administered Christian baptism at all, because they did not believe in the same God nor the same Christ with the Christians. Hence the rebaptizing of heretics was not, according to him, a repetition of the one baptism ; for their former baptism was, strictly speaking, not Christian baptism at all, being baptism into a different faith from that of the Gospel.[1] The same rule seems to be laid down by the Apostolical Canons, the 46th canon commanding the deposition of any " bishop, presbyter, or deacon, who admitted

---

[1] Tertull. *De Baptismo*, c. 15.

the baptism or sacrifice of heretics " (comp. canons 47, 68).   In
the famous dispute between Stephen, Bishop of Rome, and Cyprian,
Bishop of Carthage, the latter, and the African bishops who
were with him, denied the validity of baptism by heretics and
schismatics also.   The baptism of heretics, Cyprian, like Tertullian,
held to be baptism into another religion than the Gospel, into the
faith of another God than the Father, Son, and Holy Ghost.
Hence, he concluded that such baptism must be void.[1]   But,
moreover, the baptism of schismatics appears to have been rejected
by the African bishops ; because according to the interrogation in
baptism, (" Dost thou believe in the life eternal, and remission of
sins in the Holy Church ? ") they held that remission of sins could
not be given but in the Church.[2]

Stephen, Bishop of Rome, took the directly opposite view, admitting all baptism, whether by schismatics or heretics, so it was
with water in the name of the Trinity ; and such has been the rule
of the Latin Church ever since.   The Greek Church has taken
a middle course, rejecting heretical, but admitting schismatical baptism.

This was quite a different question from that on which this
Article is treating.   But, in the controversy, the African Church
used language as if they thought that one reason why heretics
could not administer baptism aright, was because they themselves
had not the grace of baptism, and so could not bestow it on others.
" What prayer," they ask, " can a sacrilegious and impious priest
offer ?   As it is written, God heareth not sinners ; but who wor-
ships Him and doth His will, him He heareth.   And who can
give what he hath not ? or how can a person perform spiritual
offices, who hath himself lost the Holy Spirit ? " [3]   Such a statement, which must be considered as *obiter dictum*, was perhaps
naturally put forth as one among other arguments, without having
been maturely weighed or traced out to all its consequences.
When, however, in the fourth century, arose the famous schism of
the Donatists, more was made of it than might at first have been
intended.   The Synodical letter in which that statement is made
was addressed to certain bishops of the Numidians.   Now the
Donatist faction arose among the Numidians.   It originated in an
opposition to the election of Cæcilianus into the see of Carthage.
His opponents, the Numidian bishops, accused his consecrator,

---

[1] Cyprian, *Epist.* 73, *Jubaiano Fratri,*   *de Rebaptizandis Hæreticis in Epistol. Cyp-*
p. 203.   *riani, Epist.* 70, p. 190.
[2] *Epistola Synodica Numidis Episcopis,*   [3] Ibid. p. 191.

Felix, of being a *traditor* (*i. e.* one who in Diocletian's persecution had delivered up the sacred writings to the heathen magistrates to be burned) ; and hence they denied that his consecration was valid ; for a bishop in deadly sin could not confer the grace of ordination.[1] The length to which this controversy went, was very great. The Donatists (as they were called from their chief leader Donatus) became a large and influential sect, having no fewer than 400 bishops of their own. They refused all communion with the African Church, of which Cæcilianus was the chief bishop, and even rebaptized those who came over to their own faction. They naturally referred to the authority of Cyprian and his contemporary bishops, and made the most of their statements concerning the invalidity of heretical baptism.

The controversy which thus arose, hinged much on the question with which we have now to deal. The Donatist writers (Petilianus, Parmenianus, Cresconius) appear to have maintained the invalidity of the acts of those ministers who were in deadly sin ; and seemed almost to deny the position, that a true church can contain " the evil mingled with the good." Augustine and Optatus were their chief opponents ; and some of the most valuable treatises of the former were called forth by this dispute.

Augustine lays it down as a rule, that ministers do not confer remission of sins, or the grace of the Sacraments, but that the Holy Spirit confers them through their ministry.[2] The remission of sins is given by virtue of the Sacraments, not by the merit of him who ministers them.[3] " It matters not to the integrity of baptism, how much the worse he is who ministers it. For there is not so much difference between the bad and the worse, as between the good and the bad. Yet when a bad man baptizes, he gives no other thing than a good man gives." [4] Still he seems to agree in some measure with Cyprian ; for he says that heretical baptism, although it be real baptism, yet tends not to salvation, but to destruction.[5]

St. Chrysostom bears a like testimony in the Greek Church, at the same time. " It is not just," he writes, " that those who approach by faith should receive hurt from the symbols of our sal-

---

[1] See the *History of the Donatists,* Mosheim, Cent. IV. pt. II. ch. V.

[2] " Satis ostenditur non ipsos id agere, sed per eos utique Spiritum Sanctum." — *Contra Epistolam Parmeniani,* Lib. II. c. 11. Tom. IX. p. 41.

[3] *De Baptismo contra Donatistas,* Lib. IV. c. 4, Tom. IX. p. 124, a.

[4] " Nihil interest ad integritatem baptismi, quanto pejor id tradat. Neque enim tantum interest inter malum et pejorem, quantum interest inter bonum et malum : et tamen cum baptizat malus, non aliud dat quam bonus." — Ibid. Lib vI. c. 24, p. 174, f.

[5] Ibid. Lib. v. c. 22, p. 156, b.

vation through the wickedness of another." [1]   So again, " God uses
to work even by unworthy persons, and in no respect is the grace
of baptism injured by the life of the priest." [2]

Isidore of Pelusium is very clear to the same effect: " If a
wicked man approaches the altar and unholily handles sacred things,
he shall bear his punishment, but the altar receives no contamina-
tion." [3]   " He that is baptized receives no damage from the symbols of salvation, if the priest be not a good liver." [4]

There can be no greater obstacle to the progress of religion
than inconsistency in its professors, and especially in its ministers.
The earnest and enthusiastic naturally sigh for a state of things
which shall be free from all such blemishes, and picture to themselves a Church, the members of which shall be all sincere, and its
ministers holy.   They ill endure that the tares shall grow up with
the wheat until the harvest.   The Montanists, the Cathari, and
later, the Anabaptists, were of this spirit.   In the Middle Ages the
ill-living of the lower class of friars appears to have been a great
cause of scandal to the laity, and a principal ground for the cry of
reformation.   We know that Wickliffe and his followers inveighed
loudly against such corruption; and it is probable enough that
much was said at that period concerning the damage that might
occur from the ministrations of ungodly men.   The council of
Constance (Sess. VIII.) condemned the errors of Wickliffe, contained in forty-five propositions; the fourth of which imputes to
him the doctrine that " a bishop or priest in mortal sin cannot
ordain, baptize, or consecrate."   The Council of Trent (Sess. XIV.
De Pœnit. cap. 6) decrees, in like manner, that those are in error
who contend that the power of absolution is lost by wicked priests;
for they exercise this power as Christ's ministers and by virtue of
their ordination.

Whatever may have been the popular feeling on this subject
among the advocates of reformation in general, there is no
doubt that the Anabaptists (in conformity with their general
principle, that the whole Church should be pure and sincere) [5]

---

[1] Οὐ δίκαιον ἦν διὰ τὴν ἑτέρου κακίαν
εἰς τὰ σύμβολα τῆς σωτηρίας ἡμῶν τοὺς
πίστει προσιόντας παραβλάπτεσθαι. — Homil. LXXXVI. in Johannem.   See Suicer,
Tom. II. p. 383.
[2] νυνὶ δὲ καὶ δι' ἀναξίων ἐνεργεῖν ὁ Θεὸς
εἴωθε, καὶ οὐδὲν τοῦ βαπτίσματος ἡ χάρις
παρὰ τοῦ βίου τοῦ ἱέρεως παραβλάπτεται.
— Homil. VIII. in I ad Corinth.   This passage is quoted by Bp. Beveridge on this
Article.

[3] Isidor. Pelus. Epist. 340, Lib. III.;
Suicer, ubi supra.
[4] ὁ τελούμενος οὐδὲν παραβλάπτεται εἰς τὰ
σωτηριώδη σύμβολα, εἰ ὁ ἱερεὺς μὴ εὖ βιοὺς
εἴη, ἀλλ' αὐτὸς μὲν παντώς. — Epist. 37,
Lib. II. Suic. II. 1083.
[5] Mosheim says, they taught that
" the Church of Christ ought to be exempt
from all sin." — Cent. XVI. sect. III. pt.
II. §§ 5, 17.

held the impropriety of receiving Sacraments from ungodly ministers.[1]

The foreign reformers, however, like the English, rejected these notions of the necessity of personal holiness in the minister to the validity of his ministrations. The VIIIth Article of the Confession of Augsburg is the original of this XXVIth Article of our Church. It was a little modified in the Vth of the Articles agreed on between the Anglicans and Lutherans in 1538, which contains a paragraph nearly word for word the same as the former part of our present Article. The Article stands now exactly as it did in 1552.[2]

It has been thought that, besides what we have been considering, the Roman Catholic doctrine of " Intention " may have been aimed at. This, however, does not appear probable. The Lutheran Article especially mentions " The Donatists and others like them ; " and the state of the Church at the time of the Reformation, the disaffection of the laity to the clergy, the scandals said to exist in the lesser monasteries, the irregular lives of the mendicant friars, the ignorance of some among the reformed clergy, the springing up of Anabaptist sentiments,— all these things sufficiently point out a reason and necessity for such an Article as the present. The Roman doctrine of Intention is indeed of most " desperate conse-

---

[1] See *Reformatio Legum de Hæresibus*, c. 15, which is cited by Hey.
[2] *Confession of Augsburg.*

Art. VIII.

A. D. 1531.

Quanquam Ecclesia proprie sit congregatio sanctorum et vere credentium ; tamen cum in hac vita multi hypocritæ et mali admixti sint, licet uti sacramentis quæ per malos administrantur, juxta vocem Christi, "sedent Scribæ et Pharisæi in Cathedra Mosis," &c. Et sacramenta et verbum propter ordinationem et mandatum Christi sunt efficacia, etiamsi per malos exhibeantur.

Damnant Donatistas et similes, qui negabant licere uti ministerio malorum in ecclesia, et sentiebant ministerium malorum inutile et inefficax esse.

A. D. 1540.

Cum autem in hac vita admixti sint Ecclesiæ multi mali et hypocritæ, qui tamen societatem habent externorum signorum cum ecclesia, licet uti sacramentis, quæ per malos administrantur, juxta vocem Christi, &c.

Portion of the Vth Article of 1538.

" Et quamvis in Ecclesia secundum posteriorem acceptionem mali sint bonis admixti, atque etiam ministeriis verbi et sacramentorum nonnunquam præsint ; tamen cum ministrent non suo, sed Christi, nomine, mandato et auctoritate, licet eorum ministerio uti, tam in verbo audiendo quam in recipiendis sacramentis, juxta illud, ' Qui vos audit, me audit.' Nec per eorum malitiam minuitur effectus, aut gratia donorum Christi rite accipientibus ; sunt enim efficacia propter promissionem et ordinationem Christi, etiamsi per malos exhibeantur."

quence." If no Sacrament is valid, unless the priest intends that it should be so ; then we know not whether our children be baptized, our wives married, our communions received, or our bishops consecrated. And this last question has been made much use of by the Church of Rome against the Church of England. It is urged, that a bishop or presbyter, who has a defective view of the grace of the Sacrament, cannot rightly administer it, because he does not intend to convey the full grace of that Sacrament. The bishops, for instance, who consecrated Archbishop Parker and others in the reign of Elizabeth, had a defective view of the effects of ordination and of the power of the clergy ; they therefore did not intend to give, nor the consecrated ministers to receive, the full grace and privileges of the priesthood. Hence those ministers were not rightly consecrated.

This Article was not originally directed against this error ; but it virtually and in effect meets it. Plainly, the relying on the intention of the minister results from a sort of belief that the minister himself is the depositary of grace, and can dispense that grace of his own will. If then, in outwardly ministering a Sacrament, he does not intend to confer the benefits of the Sacrament, they will not be conferred. Such seems the rationale of the doctrine of Intention. This Article, on the contrary, truly sets forth, that the clergy minister the Sacraments, not " in their own name, but in Christ's, and do minister by His commission and authority ; " and that the Sacraments be " effectual because of Christ's institution and promise, though they be ministered by evil men." So then, it is not because ministers will or intend to bestow grace, but because Christ has ordained to give grace through their ministry. If then they rightly administer, and we rightly receive the ordinance, we need not consider what is the mind of the priest, since it is not in the power of man's intention to frustrate the gracious purposes of God. Were it otherwise, no Church could be sure of its orders, no Christian of his baptism. For none can tell, whether in Rome, or Greece, or England, that some careless or some malicious bishop may not have been indifferent, or opposed to the conferring of ordination, and so the whole line of succession have been cut off, and all the orders of the Church invalidated. None can tell that an evil minister may not secretly have cursed his infant, whilst outwardly invoking a blessing on him, and so his baptismal privileges may have been annulled. But if we believe Christ's Sacraments to be blessed, and Christ's ministers to have authority, not as themselves indued with grace, but as instruments, whereby God pours it down upon us, then we need not fear to lose the treasure, though the vessel be but earthen, and itself fit only to be burned.[1]

The concluding paragraph in the Article lays it down, that inquiry ought to b· made of evil ministers, and that if they are found guilty, they should by just judgment be deposed. There is not need of much history here. From the first, such discipline prevailed, and has prevailed in every Church and sect. Thus the twenty-fifth of the Canons of the Apostles enjoins, that "a bishop or priest found guilty of fornication or perjury shall be deposed."[2] The twenty-seventh commands, that a bishop or priest who strikes one of the faithful, be deposed.[3] The ninth canon of the first Council of Nice forbids that any be advanced to the order of presbyter who have been previously guilty of any grievous sin; and, if it be found out afterwards that he had so sinned, he is to be deposed.[4]

But so patent and obvious has been this custom of the Church, to inquire concerning scandalous ministers, to remove them that have erred, and, if possible, to forbid the ordination of the undeserving, that it is needless to enlarge on it. Of course, there have been times of laxer, and times of stricter discipline; but all times and all Churches have admitted the principle.

Section II.—SCRIPTURAL PROOF.

1. THE first statement of the Article is, that "In the Visible Church the evil are ever mingled with the good." We saw something of this under Article XIX. It is clearly proved by our Lord's comparison of His kingdom to a field, in which tares and wheat grow together till the harvest (Matt. xiii. 24–30, 37–43); to a net, containing fish of every kind, that is, both the wicked and the just (Matt. xiii. 47–50); to a marriage-feast, where some have the wedding garment, some have not; all, "both bad and good," having been gathered into it (Matt. xxii. 10, 11). So St. Paul compares the Church to a great house, "in which there

---

[1] The Council of Florence (*Instr. Armenor. Concil.* Tom XIII. p. 535) and the Council of Trent (Sess. VII. can. XI.) require only an *implicit* intention in the minister, *i. e.* to do what the Church doth, or what Christ instituted. But this distinction, which seems to have some justice in it, is easily drawn out so as to save themselves, and yet to enable them to condemn us. The student may refer to Abp. Bramhall, *Protestants' Ordination Defended*, v. p. 210, *Lib. of Anglo-Cath. Theology.*

[2] Beveridge, *Synodicon*, Tom. I. p. 16.
[3] Ibid. p. 17.
[4] Ibid. p. 70.

are not only vessels of gold and silver, but also of wood and earth, and some to honour, and some to dishonour " (2 Tim. ii. 20). These arguments are so conclusive, as, according to St. Augustine, to have converted even the Donatists.[1]

The Article adds, that " sometimes the evil have chief authority (*præsint*) in the ministration of the word and Sacraments." We need go no further than Judas for proof of this. Our Lord Himself gave all the same authority to him that He gave to the rest of the Apostles; and yet He knew, when He chose him, that he was a devil (John vi. 70, 71). And so, later in the new Testament, we read of Diotrephes (3 John 9), and others, who, though ministers of God, were not men of godliness. Our Lord Himself describes especially the character of some. who should be made " rulers over his household, to give them meat in due season," but who should " smite their fellow-servants, and eat and drink with the drunken," and who at last should be " cut asunder, and have their portion with the hypocrites " (Matt. xxiv. 45–51).

2. It should hardly need much argument to prove, that that ministry which Christ permitted in His Church, may lawfully be used by His people. If He ordained Judas, we may use the ministry of such as Judas, and yet not lose blessing. And so He taught us, " The scribes and Pharisees sit in Moses' seat: all therefore whatsoever they bid you observe, that observe and do ; but do not ye after their works: for they say and do not " (Matt. xxiii. 2, 3). And the Apostles plainly teach, that not holiness in the minister, but God's blessing on their ministry, is the cause of good to His Church and growth to our souls. It was not by their " own power and holiness " that they made the lame to walk ; but " His name through faith in His name " (Acts iii. 12, 16). Paul may have " planted, and Apollos watered ; but God gave the increase. So then neither is he that planteth anything, neither he that watereth ; but God that giveth the increase " (1 Cor. iii. 6, 7). Paul and Apollos were but " ministers, by whom men believed, even as the Lord gave to every man " (ver. 5). Great and glorious as the ministration was (2 Cor. iii. 7, 8), yet the treasure was in " earthen vessels, that the excellency might be of God, and not of" them (2 Cor. iv. 7).

3. Still, though we do not believe that God's ordinances lose their effect, because unworthy hands administer them ; yet it is obviously to be much desired, that those who minister in holy

---

[1] See Pearson, *On the Creed*, Art. IX. p. 344, who quotes Augustine, *lib. post collationem,* c. 9, 10.

things should themselves be men of holiness. If ungodly members should be excommunicated, much more should ungodly
ministers be deposed. For, not only do such hinder the free
course of the Gospel, and offend weak brethren; but the torch of
truth and holiness is most surely lit and handed on by those in
whose heart it is burning and bright. The old Testament teaches
that " the priests should be clothed with righteousness " (Ps. cxxxii.
9) ; and that the Lord " will be sanctified in them that come nigh
Him" (Lev. x. 3). In the new Testament, besides general instructions concerning discipline, there are special instructions concerning the discipline of the clergy. These are mostly to be
found in the Epistles to Timothy, who, as bishop, has directions
given him concerning the importance of " laying hands suddenly
on no man " (1 Tim. v. 22), concerning the mode of receiving an
accusation against an elder (ver. 19), and as to how he was to
rebuke those that sinned (ver. 20). This is a matter too plain to
be insisted on; the common instincts of our nature and the
universal practice of Christians consenting render argument unnecessary.

ARTICLE XXVII.

Of Baptism.

BAPTISM is not only a sign of profession, and mark of difference, whereby Christian men are discerned from others that be not christened, but it is also a sign of Regeneration or new Birth, whereby, as by an instrument, they that receive Baptism rightly are grafted into the Church; the promises of forgiveness of sin, and of our adoption to be the sons of God by the Holy Ghost, are visibly signed and sealed; Faith is confirmed, and Grace increased by virtue of prayer unto God. The Baptism of young Children is in any wise to be retained in the Church, as most agreeable with the institution of Christ.

De Baptismo.

BAPTISMUS non est tantum professionis signum, ac discriminis nota, qua Christiani a non Christianis discernantur, sed etiam est signum regenerationis, per quod, tanquam per instrumentum, recte Baptismum suscipientes, ecclesiæ inseruntur, promissiones de remissione peccatorum, atque adoptione nostra in filios Dei per Spiritum sanctum visibiliter obsignantur, fides confirmatur, et vi divinæ invocationis gratia augetur.

Baptismus parvulorum omnino in Ecclesia retinendus est, ut qui cum Christi institutione optime congruat.

Section I. — DEFINITION OF DOCTRINE.

IT is, unhappily, well known to every one, how much discord has arisen on the subject of baptismal grace. On the one side, men, perceiving that in Scripture the new birth of the Spirit is closely coupled with new birth by water, and that the ancient Church ever identified baptism with regeneration, have unhesitatingly taught that regeneration is the grace of baptism, never separated from it, but when the recipient places a bar against it by impenitence. On the other side, it has been observed, that the grace of regeneration is a death unto sin and a new birth unto righteousness; that it extends to an entire renewal of the moral nature of man, restoring him to the image of Him who created him; that no such change as this can be attributed to the washing with water; that such a change can only result from the influences of God's Spirit, subduing the perverse will, and bringing the whole man into captivity to the obedience of Christ; and that, as a matter of fact and experience, the vast majority of the baptized never have undergone, and never do undergo, a change so momentous and unmistakable.

The difference of opinion has often been considered to depend on the different tenets of the opposing parties concerning pre-

destination; the Calvinist denying that baptized infants are regenerate, because grace once given can never be forfeited; the anti-
Calvinist explaining the apparent anomaly, that the baptized are
often practically unregenerate, by saying that the grace has been
given, but lost by unfaithfulness. Something beyond this, however, must be at the root of the disagreement; for St. Augustine,
and a large number of zealous predestinarians, have held high doctrine on baptismal grace; whilst many, who reject the tenet of
absolute predestination, have been as strongly opposed to the doctrine of baptism, which Augustine and many of his followers have
allowed.

It is perhaps too much to say that the diversity is dependent
on mere difference of definition. Yet accurate definition is no
doubt very desirable; and it is probable that, if both parties
understood either their own or their opponents' principles better,
they would find many more points of contact, and many fewer
grounds of disagreement than at present. As it is, both sides see
one important aspect of truth, and both perhaps often overlook its
opposite, and equally necessary phase. On the one hand, the
importance of training up children as heirs of immortality and
recipients of the seed of life, is much and rightly insisted on; on
the other side, too much overlooked. But again, the belief in the
grace of baptism at times has led to some degree of formalism and
neglect of spiritual vitality; whilst those who deny that grace
have exhibited a greater zeal for conversion of souls from sin and
error, because putting no trust on the supposed existence of a
spark of grace derived to all professing Christians in the initiatory
Sacrament.

May there not be a possibility of holding the truth which
there is on both sides, without the error of either?

Baptism is confessedly an embracing the service of God, an
enlisting into the army of Christ, to fight under His banner, the
Cross. Every one, therefore, who is baptized, is thenceforth bound
to be a faithful follower of Him whose soldier he has professed
himself. But it is not God's plan to entail responsibilities on us,
without giving us the power to fulfil them. Hence naturally we
might expect that, when He has called us to His service, He
would furnish us with arms and strength to the contest. It is
better therefore to begin with God's gifts to us: for we can only
give Him of His own: 'Εκ Διὸς ἀρχώμεσθα.

1. We know then, first of all, that God, in Christ, has made
with man a *covenant of grace*. The terms of that covenant are on

God's part, that He, for Christ's sake, not for our merit, freely, fully, graciously pours down upon undeserving sinners, (1) pardon of sin ; (2) the aid of the Spirit ; (3) in the end, everlasting life. All this is given us *in Christ*. No terms are in the first place required from us ; for we have none to give. We have but to accept the offer of free pardon made to rebellious subjects, and, with pardon, of strength for the future to obey.

Now baptism is the formal act by which we are admitted into covenant with God. It is the embracing of God's covenant of grace in Christ: in the case of adults, by their own deliberate choice ; in the case of infants, by God's merciful appointment, and according to the election of grace.

We cannot doubt of the truth of God's promises. Hence we may be assured, that He will make good His covenant to all that are brought within the terms of it : *i. e.* to all who are baptized. Hence again, we infer that the promises to the baptized, and therefore the blessings of baptism, are : —

(1.)　Pardon of sins.

(2.)　The aid of the Spirit of God.

(3.)　If not forfeited, everlasting life.

2. But, moreover, baptism is the engrafting into the *Church*, to which belong the covenant and the promises. The Church is the body of Christ ; and Christ is its covenanted Head. Hence we see another relation consequent on baptism ; namely, that we thereby become members of Christ. And indeed without this we could not receive the blessings of the covenant. For pardon and grace can only flow to us from Christ. It is *in Him* that God gives us both, — that God will give us everlasting life. " In Him is life." " He that hath the Son hath life, and he that hath not the Son of God hath not life."

So too, the Church is the family of God, as well as the body of Christ. Hence by baptism we become, not only members of the mystical body of the Lord, but adopted children of our heavenly Father. God thenceforward looks on us as united, according to covenant, to His Son, and hence as His children by grace ; and if children, then heirs, heirs of God and joint heirs with Christ.

Thus, in the language of the Catechism, we are made in baptism members of Christ, children of God, and therefore inheritors of the kingdom of heaven.[1]

---

[1] Inheritance, be it observed, implies not certainty of possession, but the possibility of being disinherited. Thus St. Paul : " Let us therefore fear, lest, a

All this results from the nature of a covenant and the nature of the Church.

But here a great practical question has arisen, which it is of the utmost importance not to disregard. Does all this merely indicate a new outward federal relation of the baptized to God ? or does it imply a spiritual change in the soul itself, and a moral change of disposition ? A federal relation it undoubtedly points out ; for the soul is by baptism taken into covenant in Christ. But a covenant on God's part implies the faithfulness of the Covenanter. Hence, undoubtedly, baptism guarantees a *spiritual change* in the condition of the recipient. But we must not confound a spiritual change in the condition of the soul, with a moral change of the disposition and tempers. It is a great *spiritual* change to be received into Christ's Church, to be counted as a child of God, to obtain remission of sins, and to have the aid and presence of the Spirit of God. But a *moral* change can only be the result of the soul's profiting by the spiritual change. If the presence of the Sanctifier does not produce sanctification, no moral change has been effected. If the pleadings of the Spirit have been rejected, and the soul has remained unmoved under them, it cannot be said that there is a moral renovation of the character.[1]

We may therefore define the *internal* grace of baptism to consist rather in the assured presence of the Renovator, than in the actual renovation of the heart. The latter is indeed the natural result of the influence of the former ; but it requires also another element, namely, the yielding of the will of the recipient to the previous influences of the Sanctifier.[2]

promise being left us of entering *into His rest,* any of you should seem to come short of it " (Heb. iv. 1). There may be a promise of future blessing, which may be forfeited by sin (Comp. Heb. xii. 15, 16, 28).

[1] [A change *of* the spirit is a different thing from a change *in* the spirit, and yet each is a *spiritual* change. — J. W.]

[2] Hooker (though rather practical and devotional, than formal and logical in his statements) seems to say much the same as I have said in the text. "Baptism is a Sacrament which God hath instituted in His Church, to the end that they which receive the same might be incorporated into Christ, and so through His precious merit obtain as well that saving grace of imputation which taketh away all former guiltiness, as also that infused Divine virtue of the Holy Ghost, *which giveth to the powers of the soul their first disposition towards future newness of life.*"—

Eccl. Pol. v. ix. 2. Waterland more accurately defines the distinction (in the case especially of infant baptism) between the grace given in baptism, called regeneration, and the effects of it when cultivated in the heart and life, called renovation. "Regeneration is a kind of renewal, but then it is of the spiritual state considered at large ; whereas renovation seems to mean a more particular kind of renewal, namely, of the inward frame or disposition of the man. . . . Regeneration may be granted and received (as in infants) where that renovation has yet no place at all for the time being." Again, "Regeneration and renovation differ in respect to the effective cause or agency ; for one is the work of the Spirit in the use of water, that is of the Spirit singly, since water really does nothing, is no agent at all ; *but the other is the work of the Spirit and the man together."* Again, " It may reasonably be presumed that

It is unnecessary to inquire here, whether the presence of God's Spirit is not vouchsafed to others besides the baptized. We have instances of such in Cornelius, whose prayers and alms were accepted, whilst he was yet in ignorance of the Gospel; and upon whom the Holy Ghost fell, before he had received the baptism of water (Acts x. 4, 44, 47). The point to be remembered is this, that to the baptized the aid of the Spirit is *promised by covenant;* and therefore to them it is *assured.* Others *may* receive it, according to the will of God; but cannot *claim* it, according to His promise.

Now this fact, that baptism, from the very nature of the covenant, carries with it an assurance of pardon for sins, of adoption into the Church, and of aid from the Spirit, is sufficient to warrant the term, "Baptismal Regeneration." Birth into the Church and adoption into the family of God, remission of original sins in *infants*, and of all *past* sins in *worthily receiving adults*, and the gift of the Spirit to renew and sanctify, comprise the elements of the new birth, the germ of spiritual life. Hence they are called by the Church "Spiritual Regeneration." Yet, as God's gifts of grace are not compulsory, it follows that the baptized, by his own perverseness, may reject them all. Whether then he received baptism in infancy or in maturity, if he has not profited by its blessings, he has never received such a renovation of heart and nature that he can be called *practically* regenerate. Nay! his *heart* is unregenerate, although his outward state and his covenanted privileges be never so great. He yet needs conversion and renewal of spirit. And hence it comes to pass, that many of our greatest divines (*e. g.* Hammond, J. Taylor, Beveridge), who held distinctly the doctrine of baptismal grace, or baptismal regeneration, yet constantly spoke of some of the baptized as still unregenerate; be-

---

from the time of their new birth by water and the Spirit (which at that very moment is a renewal of their state to Godward) the renewing also of their heart may come gradually in, with their first dawnings of reason, in such measure as they shall be capable of; in a way to us imperceptible, but known to that Divine Spirit who regenerates them, and whose temple thenceforth they are, till they defile themselves with actual and grievous sin. In this case it is to be noticed that regeneration precedes, and renovation commonly follows after." — Waterland, *On Regeneration*.

Bishop Bethell appears to adopt the same view: "Regeneration is a spiritual grace, and, in a certain sense, every spiritual grace may be said to be moral, because it effects a change in a man's moral nature. But the word Moral, to speak more properly, implies choice, and consciousness, and self-action, and faculties or dispositions expanding themselves into habits; and hence moral graces or virtues are, as Waterland expresses himself, 'the joint work of the Spirit and the man.'"—*Doctrine of Regeneration in Baptism.* Fifth Edition, p. 247.

I must venture to say that, agreeing fully in the general statement of all these passages, I should rather speak of the "yielding of the man's will to the Spirit of God," than of "the joint work of the Spirit and the man." The latter sounds to me too much like a claim of independence for weak and sinful humanity.

cause, though God could not be supposed to have failed to make good His promise to them, yet they had not yielded to His Spirit's gracious influences; and so their hearts had never been renewed "after the image of Him that created them;" and they had continued in darkness and in the bondage of corruption, though "called to the glorious liberty of the children of God."

If we take this as the explanation of the great doctrine in question, we may see at once:—

1. That the absence of practical results, and of anything like practical spiritual life in many of the baptized, is not to be accounted for *merely and solely* by the theory that such have early fallen away from grace and from a state of holiness once effected; for from the first they may never have yielded to the gracious workings of the Spirit, and so real practical holiness may never have been produced.

2. Nor, again, must it be accounted for by the hypothesis, that their regeneration is in a state of abeyance, until their own will rises to meet and coöperate with the grace bestowed upon them. For this hypothesis seems to savour of Semi-pelagianism, making the will, as it were, an independent agent, coördinate and equally efficient with the Holy Spirit; and allowing it a spontaneous movement towards good. Whereas, sound evangelical truth will teach us to consider the will utterly incapable of moving towards holiness, till *first* quickened to it by the grace of God.

3. But the real solution of the difficulty will appear to be, that, though God never failed of His promise, and though the aid and presence of His Spirit were ever vouchsafed to the recipients of baptism, yet their wills had never yielded to be renewed by it; and therefore, though subjects of the grace of God, they had never brought forth the fruits of holiness.

Yet all baptized persons, though not personally sanctified, have a relative holiness: For,—

1. They are members of the Church, which is holy; branches therefore of the true Vine, even if they are fruitless branches, and so withering and dying. They have a covenanted relation to, and a spiritual union with Christ, who is the Head of His Body mystical.

2. They are adopted into the family of God; and, though they be from the first rebellious and prodigal sons, yet they have a covenanted title to be regarded as children, and moreover, if they return from their wanderings, to be received and welcomed as children.

3. They have been solemnly set apart and dedicated to God, consecrated to be temples of the Holy Ghost: and as such, have a real, even though it may be a rejected presence of the Spirit assured to them. That presence will, if they cultivate and obey it, truly sanctify them, but, if not cultivated, but resisted, it will leave them in unfruitfulness.[1]

A distinction must be drawn between adult and infant recipients.

1. In the case of adults, faith and repentance are necessary prerequisites ; and without them we must not expect the blessings of the Sacrame.it. But then the reason why these graces are requisite is not because they contribute their share to the production of the grace of baptism. That would be to derogate from the free gift of God, and from the bounty of the Giver. On the contrary, we must ever esteem the grace of God to be free and unmerited, and not attracted to us by any good which is in us. It is not the active quality of our faith which makes us worthy recipients. That would be to make faith a fellow-worker with, and in itself independent of the Spirit of God ; which is closely bordering on Semipelagian heresy. But, though our faith cannot be of that meritorious character, that it should elicit grace from above, yet our impenitence and unbelief are permitted to act as obstacles to the free-working of the grace of God ; and, by our own obstinacy and hardness of heart, we may " quench the Spirit."

Hence, that there may be no impediment to their regeneration, a believing and penitent spirit must be cultivated in those who are to be baptized ; lest, like Simon Magus, they receive the washing of water, but still remain, as regards their hearts and consciences, "in the gall of bitterness and the bond of iniquity."

2. Concerning infants the case is different. Active faith in them is not possible ; nor is it even to be desired. It is not the active character of his faith which seems to qualify the adult. It is rather, that it implies and assures an absence of that repelling obstinacy and hard-heartedness which makes sinners reject the mercy of the Lord.

The very helplessness of infants is, in this case, their protection.

---

[1] Whether the Spirit ever finally leaves in this life the soul which has been consecrated to Him, and utterly ceases to plead with it, is a question too hard to answer. God's covenant is to give His Spirit ; and if we do not drive Him away, he will abide with us forever, and lead us daily onward. Thus our baptism may be called a life-long work. Even when resisted and grieved, we may hope that He does not soon "take His everlasting flight." Yet we cannot say that there may be no period of impenitence, when God shall swear in His wrath, " My Spirit shall no longer plead."

We cannot too much remember, that God's gifts come from Him and not from us ; from His mercy, not our merits, our faith, or our obedience. The only obstacle which infants can offer to grace, is the taint of original corruption. But to say that original sin is a bar to receiving remission of original sin (which is one chief grace of this Sacrament), is a positive contradiction in terms.

Again, the theory that the faith of parents or of sponsors is necessary to give effect to baptism in infants, is not to be maintained for an instant.[1] This were to cross the whole principle of evangelical mercy. It would be to make the child's salvation hinge on its parent's faithfulness. It would make God's grace contingent, not even on the merits of the recipient, but actually on the merits of the recipient's friends. Sponsors, after all, are probably of human institution, and therefore cannot affect a divine ordinance. And this theory does sadly derogate from the grace of God, which acts ever freely and spontaneously ; and grievously magnifies the office of human faith, which is humbly to receive mercy, not arrogantly to deserve it.[2]

Once more, the theory that infants have need of a " prevenient act of grace," to make them meet for remission of sins, is evidently founded on a low appreciation of God's pardoning love. The very thing which makes them meet for pardon, is their helpless sinfulness. This is their very plea for mercy ; and cannot therefore be the bar opposed to it. If they were not sinful, they would need neither pardon nor grace. Active hostility and wilful obstinacy they cannot exhibit. And God's mercy in Christ extends to the pardon of all sinners, who do not wilfully reject it. Hence the Church has ever held, that there is nothing in the character of infants (whose sinfulness is inevitable, and not wilfully contracted) which can offer an insuperable obstacle to receiving the grace of remission of sin, or the aid of the Spirit of God.

But, though it be true that infants can, at the time of their baptism, oppose no obstacle, lest they should receive pardon and grace ; and though therefore, in case of their death before actual sin, we believe in the certainty of their salvation ; yet we must bear in mind, that the pardon of sin and the aid of the Spirit, assured (and therefore surely given) at baptism, will not have produced an entire change of their nature, eradicating the propensity to sin, and

---

[1] That is to say, beyond the fact that, without an act of faith on the part of parents or sponsors, infants would not come to baptism at all.

[2] It is quite another question how far any but the children of Christians and believers are proper subjects of baptism. This may be the case from God's appointment, not because of an imputation to the infant of the parent's fitness for grace.

new creating a sanctified heart. The grace of the Spirit, we may believe, will, as the reason opens and the will developes, plead with their spirits, prompt them to good and warn them from evil; and, if not resisted, will doubtless lead them daily onwards in progressive holiness. But the power too to resist, which they did not possess in infancy, will daily increase with their increasing reason and activity; and their *actual and internal sanctification* will result only from an obedient yielding to the grace of the Sanctifier; and will be utterly abortive, if, through sinful propensities and sinful indulgence of them, that grace be stifled, disregarded, or abused.

Thus, though we may not define the grace of the Spirit, vouchsafed in infant baptism, to be a " mere potential principle," and, until it be stirred up, " dormant and inactive ; " yet we may define it, so as to understand that its active operations are only to be expected when the dawning reason and rising will themselves become active and intelligent; and that anything like a real moral renovation of disposition and character can only be looked for, where the adolescent will does not resist and quench the gracious influences of the Spirit of God, but suffers itself to be moulded and quickened into a state of subjection to the good pleasure of the Lord, and of likeness to the character of Christ.

Yet this need not prevent us from believing that the aid of the Spirit has been vouchsafed, even to those who have never profited by it. It is possible for a branch to be grafted into a vine, and a stream of nourishment to flow from the root to it; and yet, if a knot or obstacle exist in the branch, the life of the vine may never reach the engrafted member ; from no fault in the parent stem, but from the hardening of the bough itself. It is in like manner possible, that the infant grafted into the true Vine, a member of the Body mystical of Christ, may, through its own fault as it grows to maturity, fail of deriving grace from the life of the Spirit, and yet there be no unfaithfulness on the part of the Giver, no want of liberality in the Fountain of goodness. And this seems sufficiently to account for the well-known and familiar fact, that so many millions of baptized Christians grow up to manhood with no profit from their baptism, and when grown up, can be considered, in their spiritual condition, as no better, if not worse, than heathen men : except, at least, that they are in the formal covenant of grace, and are therefore admitted to its outward ordinances ; have probably from time to time the Spirit's warnings and pleadings ; and have the assurance too, that, on their repentance and conversion,

God will ever receive them to His mercy, and welcome them as prodigal *sons* returning to their *Father*, as *sheep* coming back to the *Shepherd* of their souls.

Section II. — SCRIPTURAL PROOF.

HAVING thus defined the doctrine, we may proceed to consider the Scriptural evidence for its truth.[1]

I.   First, let us see what aid we can derive from the old Testament, and from Jewish rites and language.

1.   It is an acknowledged fact, that circumcision among the Jews was the typical and corresponding rite to baptism in the Church. It admitted into the Mosaic covenant; as baptism admits into the Christian. It was given to Abraham for that very end, that it might be the initiatory rite, the seal and token of the covenant between God and the posterity of Abraham. (See Gen. xvii. 9–14; Acts vii. 8.) The person who had received circumcision, was a partaker of God's promises to the Israelites. (See Exod. xii. 48.) The person who neglected it, was to be cut off from the people (Gen. xvii. 14; Exod. iv. 24, &c.) St. Paul himself draws the parallel between this Jewish rite and the Christian rite of baptism; which latter he calls " circumcision made without hands " (Col. ii. 11, 12). And from his language it is plain that the parallel altogether holds good, allowing for this important difference, that circumcision admitted to a legal or carnal covenant, baptism admits to a spiritual covenant.

2.   In addition to circumcision, thus given by God, it is well known that the Jews, in admitting proselytes from heathenism, ever added a form of washing, or baptism. They baptized all, men, women, and children, of any proselyted family; and then they esteemed them as new-born from their Gentile heathenism into the Church or family of Israel. The language which they used con-

---

[1] The principal heads or divisions of the subject considered in this section are : —

I.   The light to be derived from the old Testament.

II.   Baptism considered as admitting us to a *Covenant;* involving a promise, **1,** of pardon; 2, of spiritual aid; 3, of eternal life.

III.   Baptism considered as admitting to the *Church;* which is, 1, the Body of Christ; 2, the Family of God : 3, the Kingdom of Heaven; 4, the Temple of the Holy Ghost.

IV.   Baptism, as related to spiritual regeneration.

V.   Objections considered and answered.

cerning such, was very remarkable. " If any one become a prose-lyte, he is like a child new-born." " The gentile that is made a proselyte, and the servant that is made free, behold, he is like a child new-born; and all those relations which he had while either a gentile or a servant, they now cease from being so." Nay! they even taught that men might *legally* marry those who had been their former relations; though, for edification and propriety, it was forbidden.[1]

This well accounts for the way in which the Jews understood the baptism of John. They knew that baptism implied admission into a new covenant or faith; and when he baptized, they thought he did so because the age of Messias was come, and that he himself must be either the Messiah, or else Elias, who was to prepare the way for Him. (See John i. 19, 25.) Those, too, who were baptized of him, came confessing their sins, because in the baptism of proselytes it had been always the custom to examine into the spirit and motives of the converts, before they were admitted to the rite of initiation.[2]

Our Lord was ever pleased to adapt His teaching and ordinances to the habits and understanding of the people whom He taught. The Lord's Prayer is a collection from familiar Jewish forms.[3] The cup in the Lord's Supper was taken from the wine-cups used, by ordinary custom, at the ancient Passover, one of which was called " the cup of blessing." [4] These were but human institutions; yet our gracious Saviour, stooping to man's infirmities, sanctioned with His approval, and sanctified with His blessing, things which before had but earthly authority. There can be little, or no doubt, that it was so with baptism. Washing was a common mode of typical purification, in use on all occasions with the Jews: especially it was ordained for the ceremonial purification of proselytes. And accordingly, our Lord adopts and authorizes it, as the means for the admission of proselytes or converts from Judaism or heathenism into the Gospel and the Church: for admitting to a participation of the covenant of grace, as circumcision had admitted to the covenant of works.

Circumcision then, and Jewish baptism, were both types and precursors of Christian baptism; and from the signification and use of them we may infer somewhat concerning the signification and use of baptism.

3. Besides these, there were certain great events in old Testa-

---

[1] See Lightfoot, *H. H.* on John iii. 3.
[2] See at length Lightfoot, *H. H.* on Matt. iii. 6. See also Wall, *On Infant Baptism*, Introduction, *passim*.

[3] Lightfoot, on Matt. vi. 9.
[4] Lightfoot, on Matt. xxvi. 27.

ment history to which the Apostles point as typical of baptism, especially the ark of Noah, and the passage of the Red Sea. In the ark of Noah, God's chosen people were saved, so as by water, from the destruction of a perishing world. The ark was, as it were, the body of the Church, in which all who entered it might be safe. To this, St. Peter tells us, baptism is the counterpart (ἀντίτυπον) (1 Pet. iii. 21); because by baptism we have access to the Church, and to that salvation which God has ordained in the Church.

4. The passage of the Red Sea was the first step of the Israelites from the land of their bondage. Before they passed it, they were slaves; after they had passed it, they were free, their enemies were overthrown, and they were delivered. Yet it was a passage, not into Canaan, but into the wilderness; deliverance from inevitable bondage, but not deliverance from fighting and toil. They had yet forty years to wander, before the passage of Jordan should lead them into rest. In these forty years' wanderings they had contests, temptations, and dangers. Though saved from Pharaoh, their disobedience and unbelief overthrew most of them in the wilderness; and but few of those who had passed through the sea, ever reached the home of their inheritance. St. Paul (1 Cor. x. 1–12) sets this before us, as a type of Christian baptism and Christian life. Baptism is to us a rite ordained for our deliverance, — deliverance from sin and the slavery of sin; but it is only our first step in the course of our profession; and if we, like the Israelites, though bathed in the waters and fed from the manna and the rock, yet lust, and murmur, and tempt Christ, and commit idolatry and impurity, we must expect to fall under the power of the serpent, to be destroyed of the destroyer, and never to enter into that promised land, which is nevertheless the inheritance prepared for us of God.

II. Baptism then is admission into the Christian covenant, as circumcision was admission into the Jewish covenant. Now a covenant implies two parties, and certain stipulations. In the case of enemies it requires a mediator. In the old covenant, the parties were God and the Jews: the Mediator was Moses: the stipulations were, " This do : " and then the promise was, " Thou shalt live." The whole dispensation was worldly and legal. It had no promise of *eternal* life, but only of temporal prosperity. It had no sacrifice which could take away sin (Heb. x. 4). It had no assurance of the aid of the Spirit of God.[1]

---

[1] See some reflections on this subject, Art. VII. sect. II. p. 197

But the new covenant is widely different : a covenant of grace, not a covenant of works ; not after the law of a carnal commandment, but after the power of an endless life. Its promises are not earthly, but heavenly. Its Mediator is not Moses, but Jesus Christ. In Him there is forgiveness of sins. From Him flows the Spirit of grace. By Him is an everlasting inheritance. And so God Himself describes the blessings to those within the new covenant to be, that He would be " merciful to their unrighteousness," and no more remember their sins ; and that He would " put His laws into their minds, and write them in their hearts " (Heb. viii. 10, 12).

We may see at once therefore, wherein circumcision and baptism differ ; why neither remission of sins nor spiritual aid were promised to the recipients of the former ; why both are promised to the recipients of the latter. Neither could belong to a covenant of works ; neither could flow from their Mediator Moses. Both are parts of the covenant of grace ; both flow to us from our Mediator Christ. In short, God's part in the new covenant is this : He assures to us pardon, the Spirit, life eternal. This, however, involves a response on our parts. We promise renunciation of sin, faith in the Gospel, obedience to the commands. This is the covenant between God and man, made in Christ. But God's part must come first. We cannot move a step till He gives us life. We are helpless, but in His strength. Hence God must first move to give us grace, before we can move to do Him service. He will not break His part of the covenant. He will not keep back His promise. Therefore, when we are baptized, being received into the covenant, we may be sure that God will give us, 1, pardon in Christ, 2, help through Christ : if we reject both, we shall fail of the final promise, which is, 3, eternal life. But the failure will be from us, not from Him : from our will not responding to His motions ; from our spirit not yielding to the influence of His Spirit ; not from a keeping back on His part of pardon or grace. All this seems to be the necessary result of the striking of a covenant, which is done at the baptismal font, between us and God.

To this view of the subject belong the questions and answers made at Baptism. The Church recounts God's promise, " to receive the person baptized, to release him of his sins, to sanctify him with the Holy Ghost, to give him the kingdom of Heaven, and everlasting life : " and adds, " which promise He, *for His part*, will most surely keep and perform." But then she goes on to

require, that the person to be baptized (or his sureties, if he be an
infant) shall respond to God's promises, by engaging to fulfil his
part of the covenant, namely, to renounce the devil, to believe all
the articles of the Christian faith, and obediently to keep God's commandments.   This custom has existed from the very earliest times.
It is mentioned by Tertullian (who wrote but a hundred years
after the Apostles) as having prevailed in the Church, by immemorial tradition.[1]   The ancients very generally understood St. Peter
to allude to this, in the famous passage concerning the ark of Noah
(1 Pet. iii. 21).[2]   There, having spoken of the deliverance of
Noah and his family from the deluge, which overwhelmed the
wicked, he goes on to say, that baptism is the counterpart of ($\dot{a}\nu\tau\acute{\iota}\tau\upsilon$-
$\pi o\nu$, that which actually corresponds with and resembles) the ark.
For, as the ark saved Noah, so baptism saves us.[3]   But then, lest
it should appear as if he taught baptism to act as a charm or incan-
tation, *ex opere operato*, he adds, " not the putting away the filth
of the flesh, but the answer of a good conscience towards God."[4]
That is to say, the mere washing with water will not save the soul.
It is the appointed ordinance for bringing the soul into the ark of
the Church, into covenant with God, and therefore into a state of
salvation.   God's Spirit and blessing too are assured to its recipients.   But, in order that it may be a truly saving ordinance, the
conscience of the recipient must respond to the mercy of God; just
as the catechumen is required to make answer to the interroga-
tions then proposed to him.   " The answer of a good conscience "
most probably alludes to the pledge given by the baptized in
reply to the questions; but it seems still farther to indicate, that
as the lips then move in answer to the questions of the minister,
so, if the ordinance is to be truly life-giving, the heart of the respon-
dent must move in obedience to the grace received by it, must
spring up in response to the good motions of the Spirit of God.

To return then to what was said above; God's part in the covenant is to give, (1) pardon or remission of sins, (2) the aid of the
Spirit, and (3) (in the end, and our part of the covenant not being

---

[1] *De Coron. Milit.* c. 3.

[2] See Cave, *Primitive Christianity,* pt. I.
ch. x. p. 315; Bingham, *H. E.* Bk. xi.
ch. vii. sect. 3; Neander, *Church History,*
I. sect. III.

[3] 'Ὃ καὶ ἡμᾶς ἀντίτυπον νῦν σῴζει βάπτισμα.

[4] ἐπερώτημα properly signifies *question*
or *questioning.*   So the Vulgate, *conscientiæ bonæ interrogatio in Deum;* which is
too literal to be intelligible.   We must

probably understand a metonymy of *question* for *answer.*   So the Syriac renders it
" Not when you wash the body from filth
but when you confess God in a pure
conscience."   So the fathers evidently
interpret it, as Tertullian: *Anima respon-
sione sancitur.* — *De Resurrect.* c. 48.   So
more modern interpreters, for the most
part, *e. g.* Erasmus : *Quo fit, ut bona conscientia respondeat apud Deum.*   And Beza : *Stipulatio bonæ conscientiæ apud Deum.*

violated) eternal life. Now these are just the blessings which
are not only the obvious promises of the baptismal covenant, but
which moreover Scripture couples immediately with the actual
rite of baptism.

1. Remission of sins is promised to the baptized.

Even John the Baptist preached "the baptism of repentance,
for the remission of sins" (Mark i. 4) ; although he constantly
pointed to " One mightier than himself, who should baptize with the
Holy Ghost" (Mark i. 7, 8). But Christian baptism is far more
distinctly spoken of as bringing this grace with it. St. Peter told
the multitude convinced by his preaching, to " repent and be baptized in the name of Jesus Christ, *for the remission of sins*" (Acts
ii. 38). Ananias bade Saul of Tarsus, " Arise and be baptized, and
wash away thy sins" (Acts xxii. 16). In allusion to this doctrine
of God's pardoning love, assured to those who come for it in baptism, we find St. Paul mentioning, as one of the requisites for drawing near to God through our great High Priest, that we should
have " our bodies washed with pure water" (Heb. x. 22). Again
he tells us, that Christ cleanses the Church " by the washing of
water" (Eph. v. 25, 26). And when he reminds the Corinthians
of their past lives of sin and impurity, he comforts them by adding,
" But ye have been *washed*, but ye have been sanctified," &c. (1
Cor. vi. 11). In which passage, it is true, that " *washed* " may be
to be taken figuratively ; yet at least the figure is borrowed from
baptism, and the more literal and obvious interpretation of it would
apply it directly to baptism. In another place, we find, " the
washing of regeneration " put as the correlative of justification (see
Tit. iii. 5, 7). According to such words of Scripture, the Constantinopolitan Creed contains the clause, " I acknowledge one
Baptism for the remission of sins ;" where, although some lay all
the stress on the word " *one*," as intended to prohibit the iteration
of baptism, yet it cannot be denied, that the words " for the remission of sins " indicate the belief of the council that that grace was
annexed to baptism, a belief which the fathers of that council repeatedly have expressed in those works of theirs which have come
down to us.

2. The aid of the Holy Spirit is promised to the baptized. This
is the express declaration of St. Peter in the passage just quoted.
" Repent, and be *baptized*, every one of you in the name of Jesus
Christ, for the remission of sins ; and *ye shall receive the gift of the
Holy Ghost*." And lest it should be thought that this meant but
the temporary, miraculous gifts of the Spirit, he continues, " for the

promise is to you, and to your children, and to all that are afar off,
even as many as the Lord our God shall call " (Acts ii. 38, 39).

It is scarcely necessary to add proofs to so plain a statement;
yet we find direct evidence in the history of the Acts, that the
presence of the Spirit accompanied the administration of baptism.
Thus, in the case of Cornelius and his household, who had received
the Holy Ghost by direct effusion from above, St. Peter immediately enjoined, that baptism should be administered to them, that
the outward rite should not be wanting to whom the inward grace
was already given (Acts x. 47, 48). Certain Ephesian converts
had not received the Holy Ghost. St. Paul, finding this to be the
case, then asked them, "Unto what they were baptized?" and
they said, "Unto John's baptism." Whereupon, the Apostle enjoined them to be baptized in the name of the Lord Jesus; and
when they had been so baptized, he laid his hands on them, and
they received the Holy Ghost (Acts xix. 2, 6). It is probably
true that, in both these instances, the miraculous gifts of the Spirit
were given; yet the connection between the gift of the Spirit
and the Sacrament of baptism is plainly pointed out by them; confirming the doctrine which the words of St. Peter so distinctly
have laid down.

3. Eternal life is promised to the baptized.

Here indeed we must qualify the promise. Eternal life is not so
much a present gift, as a future contingency. It is a treasure laid
up for us; not a deposit committed to us. Both pardon and grace
may be forfeited; yet they are present possessions. Heaven is not
a present possession, but a promised inheritance. Still it is part of
the promise of the covenant, and therefore one of the blessings of
the baptized. The very commission to admit into the covenant by
baptism expressed this.

The Apostles were to make disciples of ($\mu a \theta \eta \tau \epsilon \acute{v} \sigma a \tau \epsilon$) all nations
(Matt. xxviii. 19). The Gospel was to be preached to every creat-
ure. He that so believed it as to be baptized, was *to be saved;*
he that disbelieved and rejected it, was to be damned (Mark xvi.
15, 16). *Salvation* then was promised us to follow on belief and
baptism; where plainly we must understand, not eternal life, but
the way to life — *a state of salvation.* So it is said that "the Lord
added to the Church daily such as should be saved" ($\tau o \grave{v} s \, \sigma \omega \zeta o \mu \acute{\epsilon}-$
$\nu o v s$): the Lord, that is, brought into His Church by baptism all
those who were being saved, or placed in the way of salvation.
And so St. Peter says, that, like the ark of Noah, "baptism doth
now *save* us" (1 Pet. iii. 21). In all such passages (and many

might be added looking the same way) baptism is declared to be a *saving* ordinance : salvation appears to be attached to it. Yet it is evident, from the whole tenor of Scripture, that the title to such salvation is defeasible ; that the promise of eternal life, though sure on God's part, may be made of none effect by us ; so that, " a promise being left us of entering into His rest, we may come short of it."

Yet thus we see that, as we are admitted to covenant by baptism, so baptism has the promise, 1, of pardon ; 2, of spiritual aid ; 3, of everlasting life.

III. The Ark then, into which we are thus admitted by baptism, is the *Church*. The Church is the great company of baptized Christians, the number of those who are within the covenant.

Here we have another relation to consider ; the baptized not only embraces the covenant, but he is formally grafted into the Church. Now the Church in Scripture is called, 1, the Body of Christ ; 2, the Household or Family of God ; 3, the Kingdom of Heaven.

1. Christians therefore by baptism are made members of the Body of Christ.

St. Paul tells us, that the Church is one Body of which Christ is the Head, and all Christians the different members (1 Cor. vi. 15, xii. 12–27. Eph. iv. 15, 16. Col. ii. 19). " Ye," he says, addressing the whole Church of Corinth, " are the Body of Christ, and members in particular " (1 Cor. xii. 27). And he shows us how we become members of that Body, when he says, " By one Spirit are we all *baptized* into one Body " (1 Cor. xii. 13). By a very similar figure our Lord calls Himself the Vine, and His disciples the branches ; and as St. Paul tells us that the Body of the Church derives strength and vigour from the Head (Eph. iv. 16), so our Lord says that the branches of the Vine derive life and nourishment from the Vine (John xv. 1–8). Yet it is plain enough that, in both the Lord's and His Apostle's teaching, it is not meant that none but the devout believer can be a member of Christ ; for St. Paul reasons with the Corinthians against causing divisions in the one Body, and so losing the blessing of belonging to it (1 Cor. xii.) and against making their bodies, which are members of Christ, to become members of an harlot, and so liable to be destroyed (1 Cor. vi. 13–20). And our blessed Lord explains to His hearers, that those branches of the true Vine which do not bear fruit, or do not abide in Him, shall be cast forth and withered and burned (John xv. 2, 6).

Another expression of Holy Scripture, concerning the union of the Christian to his Saviour, is especially applied by St. Paul **to** baptism : " As many of you as have been baptized into Christ, have put on Christ," (Χριστὸν ἐνεδύσασθε, put on Christ as a garment). And again, referring to his favourite figure of the Head and the Body, he tells the Christian Church that they are complete, " in Him, which is the Head of all principality and power : in whom also ye are circumcised with the circumcision made without hands " . . . . " *buried with Him in baptism, wherein also ye are risen* with Him, through the faith of the operation of God, who hath raised Him from the dead " (Col. ii. 10–12. Comp. Rom. vi. 3, 4).

On such authority it is that the Church has ever taught its children to say, that in baptism they were made " members of Christ ; " that is, members of that mystical Body of which Christ is the Head, and to which He communicates grace and strength, as the head communicates vigour to the body, or the vine sends forth life and strength into its several branches.

The question, which has been raised, whether this union be real and vital, or merely formal and federal, seems altogether inadmissible. It is plainly real and life-giving, except the fault of the individual renders it ineffectual. The branch grafted into the Vine is really united to it ; yet it may fail of deriving life from it. Though it die, it will still be a dead *branch*. Then, indeed, it may be, that its attachment to the Vine cannot be strictly called vital union. Yet all the language of our Lord and of St. Paul shows, that the members of Christ, the branches of the Vine, are really privileged to draw life and strength from Him, and may surely receive that life and strength, unless they reject or disregard it. (See John xv. 4. Eph. iv. 16, 17. Col. ii. 18, 19). If they reject or disregard it, they will then, but by their own fault, lose the benefit of membership, and in the end be cut off (John xv. 6).

2. The Church is also called the Household or Family of God (Gal. vi. 10. Eph. ii. 19 ; iii. 15).

Accordingly, when persons are baptized into the faith of Christ, they are said to be made children of God ; and that, by right of their union with Christ, who is the true only-begotten Son of God. Thus the Apostle tells us, that all who have embraced the faith of the Gospel are made children of God ; because they put on Christ in baptism. " Ye are all the children of God by the faith in Jesus Christ (διὰ τῆς πίστεως ἐν Χριστῷ Ἰησοῦ) : for as many of you as have been baptized into Christ, have put on Christ " (Gal. iii. 26, 27. Compare iv. 5).

Hence the Church says, that in baptism we are 'made, not only

" members of Christ," but also " children of God." Baptism is
the seal of our adoption. We are brought into God's family, God's
household, the Church; and thus " to all, who receive Him, does
Christ give power to become the sons of God " (John i. 12). Yet
here again we must make the same reservation. Though the baptized have a covenanted title to be God's children, and hence are
permitted to approach Him as their Father; there is nothing which
says that they shall not be prodigals, that they shall not even " go
astray from the womb," and so lose all the privileges and blessings
of sonship. As there may be an union to the true Vine, which,
because the branch draws not its own nourishment, ends in cutting
off and casting into the fire; so there may be a sonship, which
leads only to disinheriting.

If the privileges vouchsafed in baptism be profited by, the sonship will be real, living, lasting. If the privileges be neglected or
despised, the sonship will become but nominal, and to be done away.
For, " as many as are led by the Spirit of God, they " only are
the true " sons of God " (Rom. viii. 14). " In this the children
of God are manifest, and the children of the devil; whosoever
doeth not righteousness is not of God, neither he that loveth not his
brother " (1 John iii. 10).

3. The Church is called a kingdom, " the kingdom of heaven "
(Matt. iii. 2; v. 19, &c. &c.) It is the spiritual reign of Christ
upon earth; the Israel, of which He is the King.

Accordingly, all Christians by baptism are admitted into the
earthly kingdom of Christ; and " except a man be born again of
water and of the spirit, he cannot enter into this kingdom " (John
iii. 5). The baptized then are the subjects of Christ here. They
may prove rebellious subjects, and so be cast out of the kingdom,
but still they are enrolled among His subjects; and if they are
faithful, they shall continue His subjects in the eternal kingdom of
His glory.

Nay! this right results to them from another title, namely, that
they are sons. " If children, then heirs, heirs of God, and joint-
heirs with Christ" (Rom. viii. 17). And so the Church, having
taught us that we are " children of God," teaches us also, that we
are " inheritors of the kingdom of heaven." We are " begotten
again to an inheritance incorruptible, and undefiled, and that
fadeth not away, reserved in heaven for us " (1 Pet. i. 3, 4). Yet
heirs may be disinherited. The inheritance is sure; but the heirs
may be prodigal. And, as the branch may wither, and the child
may be an outcast, so the heir may be cut off, and the inheritance
never be attained.

4. There is one more character of the Church to which we may refer, namely, that it is set apart to be a temple of the Spirit of God.

St. Paul describes the whole Church as " fitly framed together, growing into an holy temple in the Lord ; " and speaks of individual Christians, as " builded together " in it, so that the whole should become " an habitation of God through the Spirit " (Eph. ii. 21, 22. Comp. 1 Pet. ii. 5). So again, he calls the whole Corinthian Church " the temple of the living God " (2 Cor. vi. 16). Hence the individual Christian, when brought into the Church, becomes a portion of that sacred building, which is consecrated for the Spirit to dwell in.

But moreover, St. Paul speaks of Christians as in like manner set apart to be individually God's temples ; and urges this upon them, as a motive why they should keep their bodies holy, and not pollute them with sin ; lest they should defile the temple of God, and be destroyed for desecrating so sacred an abode. " Know ye not that ye are the temple of God, and that the Spirit of God dwelleth in you ? If any man defile the temple of God, him shall God destroy : for the temple of God is holy, which temple ye are " (1 Cor. iii. 16, 17). " Flee fornication. . . . . What, know ye not that your body is the temple of the Holy Ghost which is in you ? " &c. (1 Cor. vi. 18, 19).

This seems to teach us, that, as the whole Church is God's temple, so every member of the Church is consecrated to be a temple of the Holy Ghost, — as a member of Christ, so a temple of the Spirit. But, as unholiness will defile the member of Christ, and spoil the blessedness of membership, so sin will pollute the temple of God, and bring destruction, rather than salvation, on such as walk after the flesh, not after the Spirit. The Holy Ghost, if not repelled, will come and dwell with, and sanctify every member of the Church ; but if dishonoured, not only may He take His flight, but the guilt will be aggravated by the holiness of the heavenly Visitor, thus driven from His dwelling-place.

IV. We come, lastly, to speak of what has been most commonly called the special grace of baptism, namely, *Regeneration* or the *new birth*.

We have indeed anticipated the consideration of this already. If by baptism we are all made " members of Christ, children of God, and inheritors of the kingdom of heaven," then are we new-born in baptism ; for therein we are joined to Christ, cut out of the wild olive-tree, and grafted into the good tree, born into the Church, into the family of God, as children of our Father which is in heaven. Moreover, if then the Spirit of God becomes our assured guest and present help, the first germ of spiritual life must be ours : and this is all that is meant by new birth.

The theology of later days, among the Zuinglians and Calvinists, but still more among the Arminians, has attached a different sense to *regeneration ;* identifying it with *conversion* or *renovation*, and denying its existence, except in such persons as attain to a state of true sanctification. Enough has already been said in the way of definition. It is merely needful here to show, that as Scripture assigns certain graces to baptism, so it speaks of those graces under the name of *regeneration*. In John iii. our Lord especially seems to refer to the Jewish language concerning the baptism of proselytes. Of them the Jews were wont to say, that at their baptism they were born anew, and had entered on a new life. So our Lord says of proselytes to the Gospel or Kingdom, that "except a man be born of water and of the Spirit, he cannot enter into the kingdom of God" (ver. 5). And when Nicodemus expresses his astonishment, our Lord says, " Art thou a master in Israel, and knowest not these things ? " (ver. 10) : as though the language of his own nation and of the masters in it might have taught him some understanding of the words of Christ. The Calvinistic divines have followed the Zuinglians, in denying that baptism is here alluded to at all. They think, that, by " water and the Spirit," we must understand only " the Spirit which washes as with water." [1] But it is a strong argument against this interpretation, which is brought by Hooker, and was before him admitted by Zuingle,[2] that " of all the ancients there is not one to be named, that ever did otherwise expound or allege the place than of external baptism." [3] " When the letter of the law hath two things plainly and expressly specified, water and the Spirit ; water, as a duty required on our parts, the Spirit, as a gift which God bestoweth ; there is danger in presuming so to interpret it, as if the clause which concerneth ourselves were more than needeth. We may by such rare expositions attain perhaps to be thought witty, but with ill advice." [4]

Confirmatory of the meaning of these words of our Lord is that expression of St. Paul where he speaks of us as " saved by the washing of regeneration," λοῦτρον παλιγγενεσίας, (Tit. iii. 5) ;

---

[1] Calvin. *Institut.* iv. xvi. 25.
[2] *Opera,* Tom. i. fol. 60, *De Baptismo.*
[3] Hooker, Bk. v. sect. 58.
[4] Ibid. sect. 59.

a passage which, like the last, the whole ancient Church understood of the laver of baptism.

So much has been said already concerning our becoming children of God, clothed in Christ, and members of Christ, — concerning our being buried with Christ and rising again with Him, — concerning our being baptized into the Church by the Spirit of God, (see Gal. iii. 26, 27. Rom. vi. 4. Col. ii. 12. 1 Cor. xii. 13), all bearing on the subject of our new birth, that it is scarcely necessary to do more than again refer to such expressions here, in confirmation of the just cited passages, which distinctly speak of being born again in baptism.[1]

I have purposely delayed this part of the subject to the last; because here we meet with the chief difficulty and the greatest diversity of opinions. Many, who perhaps will concede that baptism admits to covenant with God and to the Church of Christ, and therefore to a participation in the blessings of the covenant, namely, remission of sins, the aid of the Spirit, and the promise of eternal life, will yet refuse to call these blessings by the name of regeneration. To them that name bears a deeper signification. It implies *renovation* of the whole man, or, in the school-language, an *infused habit of grace*. We so naturally identify the thing signified with the name by which we have been used to signify it, that we almost as readily part with a truth, as with the word by which we have known that truth. It is like the name of one dear to us, dear almost as the bearer of that name.

At all events, then, let us understand, that it is the word in which the difference lies, rather than the substance. Let us remember, that regeneration is itself a figure of speech. I do not mean, that the birth of the Spirit is an unreality. God forbid! it is as real as, if not more real than, natural birth. But when we call it a birth, or regeneration, we adopt natural images to express spiritual truths. In figures there is always a *likeness*, but not an *identity*, between the image and that which it represents. Now the term or figure, *regeneration*, has been applied in various languages to many things. We saw that the Jews applied it to the manumission of a slave, to the conversion and reception into

---

[1] We may especially compare St. Paul's teaching, that we are buried with Christ, and raised again with Him in baptism (Rom. vi. 4. Col. ii. 12), with St. Peter's teaching, that " God hath begotten us again to a lively hope by *the resurrection* of Jesus Christ from the dead " (1 Pet. i. 3). St. Paul's exhortation consequent on such doctrine is, " If ye be risen with Christ, seek those things which are above" (Col. iii. 1). St. Peter's is, "Laying aside all malice, &c., as new-born babes desire the sincere milk of the word, that ye may grow thereby " (1 Pet. ii. 1, 2).

their Church of a proselyte. Heathens too have used like terms, to express initiation into their mysteries, and the like. But it is obvious, that a much greater change than any of these takes place in the condition of a person who is grafted into the Christian Church, pardoned of his sins, and with the grace of the Spirit bestowed to quicken him. And hence, with great propriety, such a person may be said to be new-born. However, the fathers often used glowing terms of the blessings thus given to the baptized; so that it might be easy to suppose that with them regeneration signified far more than this, and involved of a certainty newness of life and sanctification of heart. The schoolmen followed to its consequences the language which had been used by their predecessors; making it to include an entire eradication of original corruption, and an infused habit of holiness in the heart. Thus the term "regeneration" came to signify far more than its original force implied; and hence Zuingle, and after him the Calvinists, and still more strongly the Arminians, adopting the scholastic view of regeneration, saw clearly that such an extent of grace was not the grace of baptism, and were so led to deny that regeneration took place in baptism at all, and to assign it to a different, and generally subsequent, period of life.

No little difficulty again may probably have arisen from want of observing that the figure, regeneration, may not unreasonably have a twofold significance. For first, it may be used of the time when the new-creating grace is bestowed upon us, secondly, it may be applied to the hearty reception of that grace by the subject of it, and to the springing up and growth of it in his heart and life. So, the person baptized may be said to be new-born, because the quickening Spirit is given to him; and yet, afterwards, the same person may be called unregenerate, because the life of the Spirit (rejected and uncultivated) has never grown up in him. This we have already seen in the language of St. Paul. In one place he says, we are all made children of God by being baptized into the faith of Christ (Gal. iii. 26, 27). In another, that only they can truly be called sons of God, who are led by the Spirit of God (Rom. viii. 14).

Does not the very same reasoning explain the often objected language of St. John? He it is who records the discourse in which the Lord Jesus tells us that a man must "be born again of water and of the Spirit," — a passage which all antiquity expounded of the new birth of baptism. Yet he too tells us, that "he who is born of God sinneth not" (1 John iii. 9); and that

faith is the evidence of new birth; for that " he that believeth
that Jesus is the Christ is born of God" (1 John v. 1). He too
tells us, that in " this the children of God are manifest, and the
children of the devil; whosoever doeth not righteousness is not
of God, neither he that loveth not his brother" (1 John iii. 10).
The distinction between the one and the other set of passages
seems still the same — the distinction namely between the germ
and the expanded blossom — between the principle calculated to
produce holiness, and the actual renewal and sanctification of the
heart.

We may add, that the different objects in view in the different
passages explain the difference in the use of terms. Our Lord
was instructing Nicodemus how a man must first come to Him
and be admitted into His kingdom; and so He points out to him
baptism by water, to be accompanied by its covenanted grace of
God's Holy Spirit. St. John, on the contrary, was plainly com-
bating the errors of certain heretics, who prided themselves on
their *Gnosis* or illumination, and who claimed to be born of God,
though neglecting holiness and the fruits of the Spirit. The
Apostle therefore tells them, that real new birth showed itself in a
renewal of the heart, that a sound faith and an active obedience
manifested the true sons of God, and that to pretend to know God,
and yet not to keep His commandments, was to act the part of a
liar and dissembler (1 John ii. 3, 4, 6, 22; iii. 7–10, 24; iv. 2;
v. 1, 2, 4).

It is said, probably with justice, that the past tenses, used by
St. John, show that he meant to speak, not only of those who had
once been regenerate, but of those who yet retained their new life
of the Spirit, and had not fallen away from it by sin.[1] Yet it
seems to me, that, apart from all questions of grammatical nicety,
it may be correct enough to admit the doctrine of regeneration in
baptism, in the acceptation already expounded; and yet, to say
that regenerate Christians, true children of God, live a life of faith,
overcome the world, and keep themselves by the Spirit from the
commission of wilful sin. And this will exactly explain the
language of St. John: and will furnish an unfailing key to those
passages which seem to differ with each other, because some speak
of us as born anew in baptism, whilst others deny the grace of
regeneration to any but such as walk after the Spirit, and live the
life of the Spirit.

---

[1] *e. g.* πᾶς ὁ γεγεννημένος ἐκ τοῦ   Jerome, and reflections upon it, may be
Θεοῦ ἁμαρτίαν οὐ ποιεῖ. — 1 John iii. 6.   found under Art. xvi.
The exposition of this passage by St.

V. Some objections considered.

The chief objections which have been made to the statements of the Church concerning baptismal grace, apply to an imaginary view of the subject, rather than to that stated in the foregoing pages.

1. On the hypothesis that " regeneration " always means a real change or renovation of the moral character, a conversion of the heart from sin to godliness, it is urged that such grace cannot be given in baptism. As a matter of fact, we see a large proportion of baptized infants growing up with no sign that their natural corruption has been subdued, and a new heart created within them. If all the change, that is to be looked for in our souls, be such as we see daily exhibited in the life of the baptized, then we must sadly dilute and explain away the language of the Scriptures concerning the new birth, the new creation, the regenerate and converted soul. The belief that this language applies merely to what takes place in baptism, is calculated to lower our standard of Christian holiness and our estimate of the effects of the operations of the Spirit. In our actual experience we know that many mere formalists have taken shelter under the doctrine of baptismal regeneration, satisfied to believe that all the necessary change had passed upon them then, and that they need look for no more.

I am fully prepared to go all lengths with those who would protest against such mere heartless formalism as this. But such protest applies to a totally different view of the doctrine of baptism from that which has been taken above. It is a most important truth that, if we would enter into the kingdom, we must undergo a great moral change of heart and nature ; and it is most true, that many have grown up from baptism, and gone down to the grave, without ever undergoing such a change. Such (as has been already observed) are practically unregenerate. Still they may have had given them all the grace which has been above defined to be the grace of baptism. Yet, though God made good His promise, they may never have embraced it. He may, at baptism, have received them to His Church and favour, and have bestowed on them the grace of His Spirit. Yet they may never have responded to the grace, never have yielded to the influence, and so never have profited by the aid of the Spirit. Though grafted into the Vine, they drew no life from it. They were dead branches, and in the end were to be burned.

Still the grace which they derived from their baptism may be correctly called regeneration ; because, if it had been accepted, instead of being rejected, it would have gone on springing up in them, as a well of life. The new creation, like the natural creation, is progressive. Strong men are first helpless infants. A particular period must be fixed, as the moment of birth. None can be so truly pointed out, as that when first by covenant the Spirit is given, and the soul is counted in Christ, and not in Adam. Now that period is baptism. It is the starting-post of the Christian race; the seed-time of spiritual growth; the moment when the Spirit of God breathes into the nostrils the breath of life. Yet it by no means is meant, that the race always is run, because he who should run it is at the starting-post; nor that the seed grows up, because it is then sown; nor even that the infant quickens into life, because God's Spirit is there to kindle it. And if it be so, still it is but the first beginning of life. The new creation goes on through life. It is first the seed, then the blade, then the ear, then the full corn in the ear (Mark iv. 28). Thus Luther, whilst admirably stating his views of baptismal grace, observes, that the grace of baptism is not a thing transient and confined to the moment, but which, if cultivated, remains and renovates through the whole course of life.[1]

If then a person has been baptized, but still remains with his carnal nature unrenewed; we are not to conclude that God was unfaithful, though the man has been unfruitful. But we are still to look upon that person as practically unregenerate; and we ought to try to bring him to conversion of heart, to a real change of soul and spirit. We may indeed still hope, that God's Spirit, promised in baptism, will be ever ready to aid him, when he does not continue obstinately to resist. But we must look, that "Christ should again be formed in him," — that he should "be converted and become as a little child," before we can pronounce that he is a true son of God. It has been the custom of the Church to call such a change, when wrought after baptism, not *regeneration*, but *conversion* or *renewal;* but the practical effect is the same: namely, that at conversion that change is really and practically wrought upon the soul, which actually was not produced at baptism, but which, except for his own fault, would have been wrought by the Spirit assured to the baptized.[2]

---

[1] *De Sacramento Baptismi, Op.* Tom. i. p. 72. The marginal heading is *Baptismus durat per vitam.*

[2] We must not, however, deny that true renovation or conversion is at times the immediate effect of God's grace given in infancy. John the Baptist was not the only one that ever was "sanctified from his mother's womb." Nor would our Lord have said concerning children, that "of such is the kingdom of heaven," if they were never both the subjects of God's renewing grace, and themselves obedient to that grace. Too generally,

2. Another objection is drawn from the Calvinistic scheme. Baptismal grace is supposed to contradict the doctrine of final perseverance. The Calvinistic scheme teaches, that grace is always irresistible, and that grace once given always abides. The soul, once in a state of grace, is always in a state of grace. If therefore grace was given at baptism, it can never fail.

The most rigid form of Calvinism might make this inevitable. Yet very high predestinarians have thought otherwise. Augustine held that persons might be predestinated to grace, but not to perseverance; nay, that they might be ordained to persevere for a time, yet not to the end.[1] Calvin himself does not seem to have held his doctrine of perseverance so rigidly as to make it impossible that God should give some degree of aid to such as reject it. At all events, many, who have followed him a great way in his predestinarianism, have believed that grace might be given in baptism, yet rejected and forfeited by sin. Of such was our own Hooker, and many other of our most eminent divines. It has been already shown, that the more extreme and exaggerated forms of the doctrine of final perseverance are not sanctioned by our own formularies, nor, it is believed, by the word of God. (See Art. XVI.)

3. A third objection is, that all the promises of God are to faith; that it is by faith we embrace Christ, and through faith receive the Spirit of God; that therefore to make baptism the means of receiving grace, is to put it in the place of faith.

It is undoubtedly true that an adult should not come to baptism without faith; and that, if he comes in an unbelieving spirit, he cannot expect to find grace in the Sacrament. But the objection, to the extent to which it has been urged, would magnify the office of faith beyond all reason, and utterly beside the teaching of Scripture. It cannot be that faith is requisite before any grace can be given; for it is quite certain, that there can be no faith unless grace has first been given to generate faith. Otherwise we are inevitably Pelagians. "The natural man receiveth not the things of the Spirit of God." Therefore, it is quite clear, that there must be some quickening from the Spirit, before there can be any faith. To magnify faith, so as to make it essential to the *first* reception of grace, is to take away "the free gift of God." If

---

alas! the dew of God's Spirit is early wiped from the heart. But there have been many pious men, who have grown up from childhood in the faith and fear of God; many of whom we read in the lives of God's servants; some whom we ourselves have been privileged to know and esteem.

[1] See his statements under Art. XVI.

God cannot give till we believe, His gift is not free, coming down from the bounty of Him "who giveth liberally and upbra'deth not," but is attracted (that we say not merited) by our faith.

Besides, this would go near to damn all infants. They cannot have faith. Yet unless they be regenerated, they are not within the promise of eternal life (John iii. 3, 5).￼ This is Calvin's argu-- ment against impugners of infant baptism. Infants, he contends, must be capable of regeneration, though they are not capable of faith; else they could not receive purgation from innate córruption. "How," ask they, "can infants be regenerate who know neither good nor evil?" We reply, "God's work is not of none effect, though not down to our understanding. It is clear, that infants who are saved, must first be regenerate. For, if they bear a cor- rupt nature from their mother's womb, they must be purged of it before entering God's kingdom, where nothing entereth, polluted, or defiled." [1]

Luther, who of all men spoke most earnestly of the importance of faith and its office in justifying, uses still stronger language in condemnation of this opinion. He complains, that Papists and An- abaptists conspire together against the Church of God, "making God's work to hinge on man's worthiness. For so the Anabaptists teach, that baptism is nothing, unless the person baptized be believ- ing. From such a principle," he says, "it needs must follow that all God's works are nothing, unless the recipient be good. Bap- tism is the work of God; but a bad man maketh that it is not the work of God." We may add, though not subscribe to, his vehe- ment conclusion, "Who sees not in such Anabaptists, not men pos- sessed, but demons possessed by worse demons?" [2]

4. A fourth objection is as follows. In the case of adults it is admitted that baptismal grace will not be bestowed on such recipi-

[1] *Institut.* IV. xvi. 17.
[2] *Præfatio in Epist. ad Galat. Opera,* Tom. v. p. 271.

One school of divines amongst us is supposed to insist very much on this necessity of faith, as though without it God could not act. I am sure the better instructed and more pious among them would shrink from any such extreme statement. Let me instance the justly venerated names of Cecil, Scott, Wilber- force, Simeon. They, and such as they, may have used language unlike the Church's language on holy baptism, but I feel no doubt they would have repudiated the language which Luther, in the text, quotes as the arguments of the Anabap- tists. To speak of one of them; Mr.

Simeon's views of baptism do not appear to have been very distinctly propounded. Perhaps he varied a little in his views at different times. I hardly see any dif- ference between many of his statements and my own. In his *Sermons on the Holy Spirit,* indeed, he asserted that "Bap- tism was a change of state, but not a change of nature;" but this probably meant no more than a denial that bap- tism necessarily involved an *actual moral* change, a real internal renovation; for in his sermons on the Liturgy he has expressed himself in terms almost as clear in favour of properly explained baptismal grace as any of the Fathers or Anglican reformers could have used. —See *Excellency of the Liturgy,* Sermon II

ents as come in an unbelieving and impenitent spirit.   But if there
be already repentance and faith, there must be already regeneration, and therefore regeneration cannot be given in baptism.

Here again the misunderstanding results from difference of definition.   The Church calls the grace of baptism by the name of regeneration, for reasons already specified ; but she does not deny
that God may work in the souls of men previously to their baptism ; nay ! she does not deny that there may be true spiritual life
in them before baptism.   But that spiritual life she does not call
the new birth, till it is manifested in the Sacrament of regeneration.
We must remember that the terms *new birth* and *regeneration* are
images borrowed from natural objects, and applied to spiritual objects.   In nature, we believe life to exist in the infant before it is
born, — life too of the same kind as its life after birth.   Nay ! if
there be no life before it is born, there will be none after it is born.
So, the unbaptized may not be altogether destitute of spiritual life ;
yet the actual birth may be considered as taking place at baptism ;
when there is not only life, but life apparent, life proclaimed to the
world ; when the soul receives the seal of adoption, is counted in
the family of God, and not only partakes of God's grace and mercy,
but has a covenanted assurance and title to it.

5. One more objection we may notice.   It is said that Sacraments and all outward ordinances are but the husk and shell : the
life of God in the soul is the kernel and valuable part of religion.
Let us regard the latter, and then we may throw the former away.

But we may reply, that He who has made the kernel, has made
too the husk and the shell.   In the natural creation, He has ordered that no seed shall grow to maturity if the husk and shell are
untimely stripped off from it.   If we have a treasure in earthen
vessels, we may not rashly break the vessels, lest the treasure be
lost.   In God's kingdom of nature, he has created for man a body
as well as a spirit ; we must not think to insure the life of the spirit
by disregarding and despising the body.   Such conduct seems precisely that of Naaman the Syrian, who refused to bathe in the
waters of Jordan, as seeing no natural virtue in them to heal his
leprosy.   But had he persisted in his refusal, he would have returned to Syria a leper as he came.   It was not the waters of Jordan that healed him : it is not the water of baptism which heals us.
But God appointed both them and it ; and to despise His appointment may be to forfeit His grace.

6. There is indeed one difficulty which 1 cannot solve, which
Scripture has not solved.   How is it, that if God's Spirit is given

to every infant baptized, some profit by the gift, and others profit not? It cannot be that God is faithful to His promise in one case and not in others. Nor again, can we believe that there is some inherent merit and excellence in the one child, but not in the other. This is one of the deep things of God, — of the secret things which belong to the Lord our God. Why one heart responds to the calls of grace, one steadily resists them, we inquire in vain. If we gain a step in the inquiry, we only find a new inquiry beyond it. The Calvinistic theory cuts the knot; but it leaves harder knots uncut. It is safer to admit the difficulty, — to acknowledge the impotence of our own intellects to disentangle it, — and humbly to rest satisfied with adoring, reverent, trusting, patient faith. We may feel assured concerning our God, that, though clouds and darkness are round about Him, yet righteousness and judgment are the habitation of His seat.

Section III. — HISTORY.

IT has generally been considered, that on the doctrine of baptismal grace the testimony of primitive antiquity is more than ordinarily clear, uniform, and consentient. A very high esteem of the Sacraments pervades the writings of all the fathers, and is especially apparent in their respect for baptism. The controversies of later days, of course, had never arisen. Many of the early writers were rather eloquent rhetoricians, than accurate reasoners. We may therefore expect to find extreme and exaggerated statements. Yet such language (allow what you will for it) is the index to something more solid than itself. It would never have been used concerning things of little moment, or low estimation.[1]

---

[1] I have been induced to enter more fully into the question of the patristic doctrine of Baptism than I should otherwise have done, owing to the doubts which have lately been thrown upon it by various writers, and especially by Mr. Faber, in his *Primitive Doctrine of Regeneration*. Whatever comes from Mr. Faber deserves consideration. There is one argument which appears of weight in his treatise, namely, that the fathers ever *identify* baptism with circumcision. Yet the careful reader will observe that every passage from the fathers which Mr. Faber adduces to this purpose, speaks of circumcision as a *type* of baptism, not as *identical* with baptism. We have already seen that the fathers distinguished between the Sacraments of the old Testament and those of the new. "The sacraments of the new Testament *give* salvation; those of the old Testament *promise* a Saviour" (August. *In Ps.* lxxiii. Tom. iv. p. 769, quoted under Art. xxv.) The same distinction is constantly referred to: "The former carnal circumcision is made void; and a second spiritual is assigned" (Cyprian. *Testimon.* i. 8.) "No other advantage attended on circumcision, except that by it the Jews were distinguished from other nations. But our circumcision, I mean the grace

The most obvious example of this is to be found in the fact, that the fathers ordinarily call the Sacraments themselves by the name of the grace of the Sacraments. Thus baptism is perpetually called *regeneration* or *illumination;* not the Sacrament of regeneration, but simply regeneration. So the Eucharist is called the Body and Blood of Christ. And again, *to be regenerated* is used for *to be baptized.* All this is without qualification. And if these expressions stood alone, we should naturally infer that the primitive Christians believed the grace of the Sacraments to be inseparably tied to the Sacraments, and to be wrought by them *ex opere operato.* Happily, however, abundant testimonies exist, to prove that they esteemed unworthy recipients partakers of the Sacrament, but not partakers of its life-giving power. This has already appeared by what was said on the subject under Article XXV. It is very difficult to convey a correct impression of the teaching of four or five centuries on such a subject as this, by the quotation of a few isolated passages. I will endeavour to exhibit it, as well and as honestly as I can, in the small space which must necessarily be allotted to it. And, I believe, we shall see every reason to conclude that the fathers held that conversion of heart did not accompany baptism, when unworthily received, or not duly profited by; but that they did hold that remission of sins and the grace of the Spirit were promised to accompany baptism, and that that grace, if yielded to and cultivated, would regenerate and new create the soul. Hence, they assigned the name of regeneration to the Sacrament to which regenerating grace was promised; and sometimes, no doubt, they spoke as if regeneration were tied to that Sacrament. Yet still we shall see that, when they explained themselves accurately, it always appeared that the Sacrament did not work *ex opere operato;* but that the effect was to be attributed to God's Spirit acting, according to covenant, on the soul, when the soul did not harden itself against His grace.

We may remember then, that Ignatius calls baptism the Christian's arms,[1] meaning probably, that, as the Christian at baptism enlists as Christ's soldier, so then he is furnished with armour from above to fight in His service. We may remember also the strong statement of Barnabas, or the writer under his name: " We de-

---

of baptism, has a healing free from pain, procures us myriads of good things, and fills us with the grace of the Holy Spirit " (Chrysostom, *Homil.* XL. *in Genesin,* quoted by Bishop Beveridge on this Article). It may well be doubted whether one single passage from the fathers can be found, in which circumcision is made of the same force as baptism, or in which any legal ordinance is placed on a level with the Sacraments of the Gospel.

[1] *Ad. Polyc.* c. 6, quoted under **Art.** XXV.

scend into the water full of sins and pollutions, and ascend out of
it full of good fruits." [1] So Hermas speaks of our "life being saved
by water;" [2] and again he says, "Before a man receives the Name
of the Son of God, he is destined to death; but when he receives
that seal, he is freed from death, and delivered to life. That seal
is water, into which men descend bound over to death, but ascend
out of it assigned to life." [3] Justin Martyr, professing to give to
the heathen emperors an account of the Sacraments and ordinances of the Christian Church, thus describes to them the rite of
baptism: "As many as are persuaded and believe that what we
teach is true, and undertake to lead lives agreeable to the same,
are brought by us to a place where there is water, and are regenerated, after the same manner of regeneration in which we ourselves were regenerated; for they are washed in the water, in the
name of the Father and Lord of the Universe, and of our Saviour
Jesus Christ, and of the Holy Ghost." [4] The reason of this, he
says, is that, as in our first birth we, without our own knowledge,
and of necessity, were born in sin, "so we should no longer remain children of necessity and ignorance, but become children of
choice and knowledge, and should receive in the water remission
of all our former sins." [5]

Irenæus, in like manner, puts regeneration as a synonyme of
baptism, — "baptism, which is regeneration to God." [6] So, when
speaking of the commission given by our Lord to baptize, he says,
"Committing to His disciples *the power of regeneration*, He said to
them, Go ye and teach all nations, baptizing them," [7] &c. Accordingly, he speaks of infants as born anew by Christ to God. [8] Yet,
on the other hand, he appears not to have esteemed the mere reception of baptism as a proof that there would be newness of life.
It was the Sacrament of regeneration, but it would be life-giving,
only if its grace was cultivated, and so productive of faith. Therefore he describes the Christian as by nature like a wild olive-branch,
which is grafted into a good olive; not losing the nature of the
flesh, but suffering a transmutation from the carnal to the spiritual
man. But the good olive, neglected, becomes wild; so the negli-

---

[1] *Epist. Barnab.* c. 11; also quoted,
Art. xxv.

[2] Hermas, Lib. i.; *Vision.* iii. c. 3.

[3] Lib. iii. *Similitud.* ix. c. 15.

[4] ἔπειτα ἄγονται ὑφ' ἡμῶν ἔνθα ὕδωρ ἐστὶ,
καὶ τρόπον ἀναγεννήσεως, ὃν καὶ ἡμεῖς αὐτοὶ
ἀνεγεννήθημεν, ἀναγεννῶνται, κ. τ. λ. —
Apolog. i. p. 93.

[5] ἀφέσεώς τε ἁμαρτιῶν ὑπὲρ ὧν προημάρ-
τομεν τύχωμεν ἐν τῷ ὕδατι. — *Apolog.* i. p.
94.

[6] τοῦ βαπτίσματος τῆς εἰς Θεὸν ἀναγεννήσεως. — Lib. i. c. 18. Edit. Grabe, p. 88.

[7] "Et iterum potestatem regenerationis in Deum demandans discipulis, dicebat eis, *Euntes docete gentes, baptizantes
eos*," &c. — Lib. iii c. 19, p. 243.

[8] "Omnes enim venit per semetipsum
salvare; omnes, inquam, qui per eum
renascuntur in Deum, infantes et parvulos, et juvenes, et seniores." -- Lib
ii. c. 39, p. 160.

gent Christian ceases to be fruitful, and returns to his old condition
of a mere natural man. He, who does not by faith obtain and
keep the grafting in of the Spirit, will be but flesh and blood, not
capable of inheriting the kingdom of God.[1]

In the time of Irenæus some Gnostic heretics had rejected
Sacraments on the ground that they were material, and that all
matter was impure.[2] Soon after, we find Tertullian ascribing this
error to the Cainites.[3] Against them he wrote his treatise *De
Baptismo.* He begins it thus: "Happy the Sacrament of our
water, whereby being cleansed from the sins of our former blindness
we are made free unto eternal life! . . . . We, as lesser fish, after
our IXΘΥΣ, Jesus Christ, are born in water, nor are we safe, except
we abide in the water."[4] "Water first brought forth that which
had life; so that there may be no wonder if in baptism the waters
should be life-giving."[5] "Thus the nature of water, sanctified by
the Holy One, itself also received the power of sanctifying."[6]
"Wherefore all waters obtain, after prayer to God, the Sacrament
of sanctification. For the Spirit straightway cometh down from
the Heavens above, and is over the waters, sanctifying them from
Himself; and they so sanctified acquire the power of sanctifying."[7]
He shortly afterwards explains his belief, that the Spirit is not
given' in the water, but that in the water the angel cleanses and
purifies, and prepares for the Holy Spirit, to be given in the imposition of hands, which anciently formed a part of the baptismal
ordinance.[8] So, speaking of water flowing from the Rock, he says,
"*If that Rock was Christ,* without doubt we see baptism blessed
by the water in Christ. How great is the grace of water for the
confirmation of baptism before God and His Christ! Never is
Christ without water, forasmuch as He Himself is washed in
water."[9] Again he calls baptism "the most holy laver of new
birth;"[10] and declares that none can be saved without baptism.[11]

---

[1] See at length, Lib. v. c. 10, p. 413.
[2] Irenæus, Lib. i. c. 18, p. 91.
[3] *De Baptismo,* c. 1, 13.
[4] Ibid. c. 1. See under Art. xxv.
[5] c. 3.
[6] c. 4.
[7] *De Baptismo.*
[8] "Non quod in aquis Spiritum Sanctum consequamur; sed in aqua emundati
per angelum, Spiritui Sancto præpara-
mur." — c. 6, conf. c. 7.
Of the imposition of hands following
immediately on baptism, and considered
as a part of it, see under Art. xxv. Mr.
Faber quotes this passage thus: "Not
that we obtain the Holy Spirit in the
merc water, but, being cleansed under the

angel in the water, we are prepared by
the Holy Spirit." — *Primitive Doctrine of
Regeneration,* p. 138. There is nothing
about *mere* water in Tertullian. What
he means is obvious enough. Alluding
to the stirring of the pool of Bethesda by
the angel, he considered that water-baptism was appointed for remission of sins;
but that the grace of the Holy Spirit did
not come upon the recipient until the
bishop had laid his hands on him.
[9] Ibid. c. 9.
[10] "Sanctissimo lavacro novi natalis."
— c. 20; comp. *De Anima,* c. 41; *Cont.
Marcion.* Lib. i. c. 28; *De Pœnitentia,* c. 6.
[11] "Præscribitur nemini sine baptismo
competere salutem, ex illa, maxime, pro-

Yet, on the other hand, very strong as these expressions appear, we must judge that Tertullian did not teach the *opus operatum;* for we find him exhorting the candidates for baptism to prepare for it with the most earnest and frequent prayers, fastings, and watchings, and with confession of all past sins; evidently, that they might not miss the grace to be expected in it.[1] And to unworthy receivers he believed that the Sacrament would be, not the fountain of life, but the sign of death.[2]

The doctrine of Clement, Tertullian's great contemporary at Alexandria, and of Clement's still more illustrious pupil and successor, Origen, seems to have been just the same. " The Pædagogue," *i. e.* Christ, says St. Clement, " forms man from the dust, *regenerates him with water,* gives him increase by the Spirit, and instructs him by the Word." [3] " Being baptized, we are illuminated; being illuminated, we are adopted as sons; being adopted, we are perfected; being perfect, we are rendered immortal . . . . This work (*i. e.* baptism) is called by many names, grace, illumination, that which is perfect, and the laver. Laver, because by it we are washed from sins; grace, because the punishment due to our sins is remitted; illumination, because by it we see that holy and saving light, *i. e.* by it we are clear-sighted to behold the Divine; that which is perfect, for what is lacking to him who knoweth God?[4] " Our sins are remitted by one sovereign remedy, baptism according to the word (λογικῷ βαπτίσματι). We are washed from all our sins, and at once are no longer evil. This is one grace of illumination,[5] that a man is no longer the same in manners as before he was washed. For knowledge rises along with illumination, shining around the mind; and immediately we, who were unlearned, are called learners (μαθηταὶ); this learning having at some former time been conferred on us; for it is not possible to name the precise time:[6] for catechetical teaching leads to

nunciatione Domini, qui ait, *Nisi natus ex aqua quis erit, non habet vitam "* — *De Baptismo,* c. 10.

[1] c. 20.

[2] " Symbolum mortis."—*De Pœnitentia,* c 6. See above, Art. xxv. Tertullian's inclination to deny remission to deadly sins after baptism (see on Art. xvi. sect. 1.) originated partly from his high esteem for baptism, partly from his own highly ascetic temper.

[3] *Pædagog.* Lib. i. c. 12, p. 156, line 18.

[4] Ibid. Lib. i. c. 6, p. 113, line 27.

[5] φωτίσματος — this is a common name for baptism among all the fathers.

[6] οὐ γὰο ἂν ἔχοις εἰπεῖν τὸν χρόνον.

Mr. Faber (*Prim. Doct. of Regeneration,* pp. 131, 144) puts this clause in capitals, and cites it as proving that Clement did not hold God's grace to be given in baptism, but at any time before, in, or after baptism. The force of his argument, however, entirely depends on his having dissociated the passage from its context; for the context in which it stands exactly disproves his position. Clement is explaining the great blessings of baptism; but he also explains that catechumens were regularly trained for it, and that they had reason to expect that their previous preparation, with which they came to the Sacrament, would be specially blessed,

faith, and faith, at the very time of baptism, is instructed by the Spirit." [1]

It may be remembered that, under Article XXV., Origen was quoted as saying, that some, who receive baptism unworthily, receive not the Spirit of God with it; as Simon Magus, "not being baptized to salvation, received water, but not the Spirit of God." [2] Yet Origen distinctly asserted that baptism was ordained for remission of sins and spiritual regeneration. "Children," says he, "are baptized for the remission of sins . . . . By the sacrament of baptism the uncleanness of our birth is put away; and therefore even infants are baptized . . . . In the regeneration of baptism, the Sacrament is received, that, as Jesus, according to the dispensation of the flesh, was purified after His birth by an oblation, so we should be purified by spiritual regeneration." [3] We have already spoken of the error, into which Origen fell, of believing that deadly sin after baptism was the sin against the Holy Ghost. [4] Such a notion would have been impossible, had not a very high esteem of the blessings of baptism been prevalent when he wrote.

This brings us to the age of Cyprian. Thenceforth it would be far easier to convict the fathers of holding the *opus operatum*, than of doubting that grace was given in baptism. Cyprian himself says, "All who come to the Divine laver, by the sanctification of baptism put off the old man by grace of the saving laver, and being renewed by the Holy Spirit, are purged of the filth of the old contagion by a second birth." [5] "Thence begins the origin of all faith, and a salutary entrance to hope of eternal life." [6] His own experience of the blessings of baptism he sets forth in the enthusiastic language of a young convert. [7] We perhaps need not attribute very much weight to such a glowing picture; for the passage was written soon after his baptism; and Augustine has expressed his opinion, that it was in the taste of a young writer, not of a matured divine. [8] Cyprian appears to have followed Tertullian in con-

---

and their faith instructed, ἅμα τῷ βαπτίσματι, "at the very moment of baptism." Bishop Bethell has some good remarks in reply to this argument of Mr. Faber. Bethell, *On Regeneration*, pp. 254–260. Fifth edition.

[1] *Pædagog.* Lib. I. c. 6, p. 116, line 13.

[2] *In Numeros, Homil.* III. num. I.; *In Ezechiel. Hom.* VI. num. V. cited under Art. XXV.

[3] "Parvuli baptizantur in remissionem peccatorum. . . . . Et quia per baptismi sacramentum nativitatis sordes deponuntur, propterea baptizantur et parvuli. . . . In regeneratione baptismi assumitur sac-

ramentum et quomodo Jesus secundum dispensationem carnis oblatione purgatus est, ita etiam nos spiritali regeneratione purgamur." — *Homil.* XIV. *in Lucam.*

[4] See under Art. XVI. sect. I.

[5] *De Habitu Virginum.* Oxf. 1682, p. 103.

[6] *Epistol.* LXXIII. p. 203.

[7] *Ad Donatum de Gratia Dei, circ. init.* p. 2.

[8] Augustine, *De Doctr. Christ.* IV. 14. The passage from Cyprian is quoted by Bishop Bethell. — Fifth edit. p. 127.

sidering chrism, or the imposition of hands, essential to the completion of the grace of baptism.[1]

From Cyprian we may pass to the great Athanasius. A few
words will express his doctrine. "He who is baptized, puts off
the old man, and is renewed, being born again of the grace of the
Spirit."[2]

It is natural, on this subject, to turn with much interest to the
works of St. Cyril of Jerusalem ; whose Catechetical Lectures
were addressed to catechumens preparing for baptism. His pref-
atory lecture sets forth at once the great blessings of baptismal
grace, and the great need of duly preparing the mind of the adult
recipient, lest by unbelief or hypocrisy he should miss the benefit.
To those who were training for it he says, that already "the savour of blessedness was upon them, and they were gathering spiritual flowers, to wreathe heavenly crowns. The blossoms of the trees
have budded ; may the fruit be brought to perfection." But he
adds, that an honest intention was necessary to blessing ; "for
though the body be present, yet if the mind be absent, it is of no
avail."[3] He then goes on to speak of Simon Magus, as brought
to baptism, but not enlightened ; "dipping his body in the water,
but not permitting the Spirit to illuminate him."[4] He therefore bids
his catechumen to look, "not on the bare water, but to salvation
from the working of the Spirit."[5] The blessings, however, of the
Sacrament, if duly accepted, he rates at the highest value. "Great
is the baptism which is set before you. Liberty to the captives ; remission of sins ; death of sins ; regeneration of the soul ; garment
of light ; holy seal, indissoluble ; chariot to heaven ; delight of
Paradise ; procuring for us the kingdom ; the free gift of the adoption of sons."[6] "Jesus sanctified baptism by being Himself bap-

---

[1] See *Ep.* LXXII. p. 196 ; *Epist.* LXXIII.
p. 207, quoted under Art. XXV.
Mr. Faber quotes, as of great consequence to his own theory, the former of
these passages : "Tum demum plene
sanctificari et esse filii Dei possunt, si
sacramento utroque nascantur, cum scriptum sit, *Nisi quis renatus fuerit ex aqua et
Spiritu*," &c. — *Prim. Doct. of Regener.* p.
68. He strangely infers that Cyprian
held *water* to be one sacrament, and the
Spirit the other ; as though any Divine
could really call God's Holy Spirit a
Sacrament : *i. e.* an *outward sign* of an
inward grace. So common a book as
Bingham's *Antiquities* will tell us that the
two sacraments by which Tertullian and
Cyprian believed regeneration to be bestowed upon us, were water and imposi-

tion of hands, both then considered parts
of baptism. — See Bingham, XII. i. 1,
4.

[2] Ὁ δὲ βαπτιζόμενος τὸν μὲν παλαιὸν
ἀποδιδύσκεται· ἀνακαινίζεται δὲ ἄνωθεν γεννηθεὶς τῇ τοῦ Πνεύματος χάριτι. — *Epist.*
IV. *ad Serapion.* 13. The passage is given
more at length by Bishop Bethell, p. 311.

[3] *Præfat. Catech.* 1.

[4] Ibid.

[5] Μὴ τῷ ψιλῷ τοῦ ὕδατος πρόσεχε, ἀλλὰ
τῇ τοῦ ἁγίου Πνεύματος ἐνεργείᾳ τὴν σωτηρίαν
ἐνδέχου. — *Catech.* III. 2. See Beveridge
on this Article.

[6] Μέγα τὸ προκείμενον βάπτισμα. αἰχ-
μαλώτοις λύτρον· ἁμαρτημάτων ἄφεσις· θάνα-
τος ἁμαρτίας· παλιγγενεσία ψυχῆς· ἔνδυμα
φωτεινόν· σφραγὶς ἁγία ἀκατάλυτος· ὄχημα
πρὸς οὐρανόν· παραδείσου τρυφή· βασιλείας

tized." [1] "By baptism the sting of death is destroyed." [2] "Thou descendest into the waters dead in sins; thou risest again quickened in righteousness." [3]

Gregory Nazianzen sums up the blessings of baptism in words which bear a striking resemblance to those above quoted from Cyril. "Baptism (τὸ φώτισμα) is the splendour of souls, the change of life, the answer of the conscience to God. It is the aid of our infirmity, the putting off of the flesh, the following the Spirit, the participation of the word, the correction of images (πλασμάτων ἐπα- νόρθωσις), the drowning of sin, the participation of light, the destruction of darkness, the chariot of God, the travelling with Christ, the confirmation of faith, the perfecting of the mind, the key of the kingdom, the change of life, the destruction of slavery, the loosing of chains, the conversion of the constitution (συνθέσεως μεταποίησις), the most beautiful and glorious of the gifts of God . . . . It is illumination, more holy than all other illuminations . . . . It is called gift, charisma, baptism, unction, illumination, the clothing of incorruption, the bath of regeneration, the seal," [4] &c. &c. Elsewhere he speaks, like Cyril, of the need of diligent preparation, and counsels: "Let the laver wash, not thy body only, but thine image." [5] And, in one place, he seems to consider, that all the graces of baptism might possibly, though not probably, be given before the reception of the Sacrament, to which the Sacrament itself would then be the seal; for of his sister Gorgonia he says, that "to her almost alone baptism was not the gift of grace, but the seal only." [6]

St. Ambrose in the West, contemporary with St. Gregory in the East, calls the dividing of the waters of Jordan by Elijah (whereby some of the water must have flowed back to its source) "a type of the Sacrament of salutary laver; by which infants, who have been baptized, are reformed from a state of wretchedness, to the primitive state, in which they were created." [7]

One word more from St. Chrysostom. Comparing God's pardon to us with the pardon granted to criminals by earthly rulers, he says, that, if kings were to pardon, and even to invest their offend-

---

πρόξενον · υἱοθεσίας χάρισμα. — *Catech. Præfat.* 10. St. Basil has almost word for word the same sentence. — *Exhortat. ad Baptism.* Tom. I. p. 413.

[1] *Catech.* III. 8.

[2] Ibid.

[3] *Catech.* III. 9: νεκρὸς ἐν ἁμαρτίαις καταβὰς, ἀναβαίνεις ζωοποιηθεὶς ἐν δικαιοσύνῃ. — Comp. *Catech.* xx. 4, 5.

[4] Greg. Naz. *Orat.* xl. *Opp.* Tom. I. p. 638. Colon.

[5] Ibid. p. 661.

[6] καὶ μόνη σχεδὸν, ἵν' εἴπω τόλμησας, σφραγὶς ἀλλ' οὐ χάρισμα ἦν τὸ μυστήριον. — *Orat.* xi. Tom. I. p. 188.

[7] "Significat salutaris lavacri futura mysteria; per quæ in primordia naturæ suæ qui baptizati fuerint parvuli a malitia reformantur." — *Comment. in Evangel. Luc.* Lib. I. § 37. The passage is given more at length by Wall, *Infant Baptism*, pt. I. c. 13.

ing subjects with their own royalty, they still could not free them from their sins. "It is God only who does this; which He will accomplish in the laver of regeneration. For His grace touches the soul, and eradicates its sins " . . . . "As when iron or gold is recast, it is made pure and new again; so the Holy Spirit, recasting the soul in baptism, as in a furnace, consumes its sins, and makes it shine with more purity than the purest gold." [1]

If we stopped here, might we not conclude, that the fathers *uno ore* affirm that baptism, rightly administered and duly received, is an ordinance appointed by God, in which He promises to receive the sinner to Himself, to give Him for Christ's sake pardon of his sins, and to bestow upon him the gift of the Spirit? And, although some rhetorical language may obscure their meaning, is it not yet clear, that this grace is not to be looked for from baptism, as though it worked as a charm, but that baptism is to be diligently prepared for, and its grace made use of; and that the unbelieving and the hypocrite may receive the water without receiving the Spirit of God, enhancing his condemnation, rather than obtaining remission of his sins?

We have yet to consider the views of St. Augustine. No one speaks more fully, no one has a juster claim to be heard. Perhaps the greatest of uninspired divines, he has influenced, more than any, the opinions of all succeeding generations. The reformers especially drank deeply from the fountain of his thoughts. He writes, not with the rhetoric of an orator, but with the logic of a thoughtful reasoner, and yet with the eloquence of an earnest and devoted Christian.

His predestinarian sentiments may, doubtless, have affected his views of baptismal grace. It has been asserted that, in one point only, he materially differed from Calvin. Both believed that God's predestination was irrespective of individuals, and to eternal life. But Calvin held, that once regenerate a person could never finally fall; and so taught that none but those elect to glory could receive regeneration in baptism. Augustine, on the contrary, held that *all* infants are regenerate in baptism; and therefore, that the regenerate may fall away. It has, however, been said that this difference is not real, but apparent only; for that, by *regeneration* Calvin meant *a moral change of disposition*, but Augustine meant only a *beneficial federal change of relative condition*. [2]

If we remember what was said of Augustine's predestinarianism

---

[1] Chrysost. *Homil. in* 1 *Epist. ad Corinth. Homil.* xl.

[2] Faber, *Prin. Doct. of Election*, Bk. i. ch. vii. p. 81, &c.

(under Arts. XVI. XVII.), we shall see that this statement falls short of the truth. We there saw, that St. Augustine distinctly taught, not only that persons regenerate in baptism might finally fail of salvation, but even that persons might believe, and live for some years in a state of piety and godliness, and yet fall away and be lost. He distinguished between predestination to grace, and predestination to perseverance. He said indeed, that persons could not with the strictest propriety be called elect who had not the gift of perseverance ; but yet that persons might be baptized, regenerate, believing, and for a time persevere — " that a man might live for ten years and persevere for five, and yet for the last five fall away and be lost." [1] " We call those elect," he writes, " and Christ's disciples, and children of God, because they are to be so called, whom we see having been regenerated, living piously ; but then only are they truly to be called so, if they *continue* in that for which they so are called." [2] " They were then in a good state, but because they did not continue in it, *i. e.* did not persevere unto the end, therefore the Apostle says, *they were not of us*, even when they were with us, that is, they were not of the number of sons, even when they had the faith of sons." [3] &c. He takes the case of two godly men : to one perseverance is given, to the other not. This is God's inscrutable decree (*inscrutabiliora sunt judicia Dei*). One, no doubt, was of the predestinated ; the other, not. " Yet were not both created by God, born of Adam, made out of the earth, and received souls of like nature ? Nay ! had not both been called, and had followed Him that called them ? Had not both been justi-fied, though before ungodly, and both by the laver of regeneration made new creatures ? " (*utrique ex iniquis justificati, et per lava-crum regenerationis utrique renovati*). " Whence then," he asks, " this distinction ? " and he resolves it into the decree of God.[4]

Now here is the great difference between Augustine and Calvin. Whatever the latter may have held, the former certainly did *not* hold, that *grace inevitably leads to glory.*

With respect to the meaning which Augustine attached to the term *regeneration* as applied to baptism, it is, perhaps, not in-correct to say that he held that it was not conversion of heart or " a moral change of disposition," but rather, " a *beneficial* federal change of relative condition." His own words clearly prove that he did not believe the necessary consequences of baptism to be con-

---

[1] See quotations and references under Art. XVI. sect. I. Art. XVII. sect. I.; es-pecially *De Corrept. et Grat.* §§ 16, 20, 22; *De Dono Persev.* 1, 19, 21, 32, 33.

[2] *De Corrept. et Grat.* § 22, p. 762.
[3] Ibid. § 20, p. 761.
[4] *De Dono Persev.* § 21, Tom. x. p. 831.

version of heart, nay, that in infants conversion of heart could not
be the *immediate* consequence of baptism.[1] Yet we may venture
to say, that he was too profound a thinker and too sound a divine
to have believed that baptism admitted us into a new federal
relation with God, or, in plainer words, that it brought us into
a new covenant of grace, without also believing that it made us
partakers of the *blessings* of that covenant.   He could never have
taught, that, under the dispensation of the Gospel, God would
bring us into a covenanted relationship with Himself, thereby
saddling us with fresh obligations to obey Him, without also be-
stowing upon us the power which would enable us to fulfil those
obligations.

The view which he takes of the difference between baptized
and unbaptized infants, clearly shows his high estimation of baptismal blessing.   We need not herein follow his teaching, but it is
quite certain that he held that all unbaptized infants, if they died
in infancy, would perish everlastingly ; and, on the other hand, he
clearly held that if they died in infancy, having been baptized, they
passed at once into eternal life.[2] The distinction between the state
of the baptized and the unbaptized infant he thus clearly marks :
" In infants, born but not baptized, Adam may be recognized ; in
infants, born and baptized, and hence born again, Christ may be
recognized." [3]   He identifies baptized with believing infants (*fidelibus infantibus, id est, in Christo baptizatis*) ; and says of them,
that, " though infants, they are members of Christ, partakers of His
Sacraments, that they may have in them life." [4]   When they are
baptized, nothing less is done than that they are incorporated into

---

[1] " Quibus rebus omnibus ostenditur
aliud esse sacramentum baptismi, aliud
conversionem cordis, sed salutem hominis
ex utroque compleri ; nec si unum horum
defuerit, ideo putare debemus consequens
esse ut et alterum desit ; quia et illud sine
isto potest esse in infante, et hoc sine illo
potuit esse in latrone, complente Deo sive
in illo, sive in isto, quod non ex voluntate
defuisset ; cum vero ex voluntate alterum horum defuerit, reatu hominem in-
volvi. *Et baptismus quidem potest inesse,
ubi conversio cordis defuerit : conversio autem
cordis potest quidem inesse non percepto baptismo, sed contempto non potest.*" — *De Baptismo contra Donatistas*, Lib. IV. c. XXV. §
32, Tom. IX. p. 141.
[2] " Absit ut causam parvulorum sic
relinquamus, ut esse nobis dicamus in-
certum. utrum in Christo regenerati si
moriantur parvuli, transeant in æternam
salutem, non regenerati autem transeant

in mortem secundam." — *De Dono Persever.* § 30, Tom. x. p. 837.
" Cum videant alios parvulos non regeneratos ad æternam mortem, alios autem regeneratos ad æternam vitam tolli
de hac vita." — Ibid. § 32.
" Cum moriuntur infantes, aut merito regenerationis transeunt ex malis ad
bona, aut merito originis transeunt ex
malis ad mala." — *De Prædestinat.* § 24,
Tom. x. p. 806.
" Quia parvulus non baptizatus non
intrat in regnum cœlorum, et tu dicis
et ego." — *Serm.* 294, c. 7, Tom. v. p.
1186.
[3] " In parvulis natis et nondum baptizatis agnoscatur Adam : in parvulis natis et baptizatis et ob hoc renatis agnoscatur Christus." — *Serm.* 174, c. 8, Tom.
v. p. 834.
[4] " Infantes sunt, sed membra ejus
sunt. Infantes sunt, sed sacramenta ac-

the Church, that is, are joined to the Body and members of Christ; and this, he says, is so important, that without it they would be damned.[1] However holy their parents may have been, they themselves cannot be free from the taint of original sin, but by baptism.[2] But in baptism it is effected by God's grace, that all original sin is made void. Yet it is not so made void, that concupiscence is also destroyed with it, but only so that, if the child dies, it shall not operate to his destruction. If, however, the infant lives, and grows to an age of understanding and responsibility, he will have need to fight against that concupiscence, and, by God's help, he may overcome it, unless he have received God's grace in vain.[3] Those then, who are baptized, receive remission of all their sins.[4] Infants cannot believe, when they are baptized, nor make responses and stipulations for themselves. Therefore the response of others is sufficient for their consecration.[5] In Cornelius, spiritual sanctification preceded the Sacrament of regeneration; but in baptized infants the Sacrament of regeneration precedes; and if they hold fast Christian piety, conversion in heart will follow, the Sacrament of which preceded in body.[6] But how is such conversion of heart to follow? If baptism be a *mere* outward change, nothing in it could give hope of future conversion of heart. Accordingly, St. Augustine teaches that, "in baptized infants, though they know it not, the Spirit of God dwelleth."[7] And again, that "a power is given them, by which, from the sons of this world, they may become the sons of God."[8]

I believe these quotations give a faithful representation of the general teaching of St. Augustine on baptism. They are not garbled extracts; but, on the contrary, if consulted at length, will

cipiunt. Infantes sunt, sed mensæ Ejus participes fiunt, ut habeant in se vitam." — Ibid. c. 6.

[1] *De Peccat. Merit. et Remiss.* Lib. III. c 4, Tom. x. p. 78.

[2] Ibid. c. 12, p. 83.

[3] "In parvulis certe gratia Dei per baptismum . . . id agitur ut evacuetur caro peccati. Evacuatur autem non ut in ipsa vivente carne concupiscentia conspersa et innata repente absumatur et non sit ; sed ne obsit mortuo, quæ inerat nato. Nam si post baptismum vixerit, atque ad ætatem capacem præcepti pervenire potuerit, ibi habet cum qua pugnet, eamque adjuvante Deo superet, si non in vacuum gratiam Ejus susceperit, si reprobatus esse noluerit."— *De Peccat. Meritis et Remiss.* Lib. I. c. 39, Tom. x. p. 39.

[4] *De Civit. Dei,* Lib. I. c. 27, Tom. VII. p. 25.

[5] *De Baptismo c. Donatist.* Lib. IV. c. 24, Tom. IX. p. 141.

[6] "Ita in baptizatis infantibus præcedit regenerationis sacramentum ; et si Christianam tenuerint pietatem, sequetur etiam in corde conversio ; cujus mysterium præcessit in corpore."—Ibid. p. 140.

[7] "Dicimus ergo in baptizatis parvulis, quamvis id nesciunt, habitare Spiritum Sanctum."— *Epist.* 187 *ad Dardan.* c. VIII. Tom. II. p. 586. So also, "Ad templum Dei pertinent parvuli, sanctificati sacramento Christi, regenerati Spiritu Sancto." — Ibid. c. VI. 684.

[8] "Frustrata potestate captivatoris sui, et data potestate qua fiant ex filiis hujus sæculi filii Dei." — *De Nuptiis et Concupiscentia,* Lib. I. c. 22, Tom. x. p. 292.

be found to give only more fully the same impression of the
writer's meaning. Is it not plain then, that his meaning is, as
nearly as possible, coincident with the doctrine laid down in the
two preceding sections?

He teaches, that baptism is not in itself conversion of heart;
and of adults he says, that a person may be baptized with water,
but not born of the Spirit.[1] In infants also, he says, that the
Sacrament of regeneration precedes conversion of heart. He considers that the regeneration of baptism consists in a grafting into
the Church, the body of Christ; a remission of all original sin, so
that baptized infants dying in infancy are sure of salvation; and,
moreover, in an assured presence of the Holy Spirit, which, if not
obeyed, will profit them nothing; but which, if held fast, and not
received in vain, will lead, with the opening reason, to that faith
and conversion in heart, of which, in unconscious infancy, they had
been incapable. Accordingly, he uses the term "child of God" in
a twofold signification. At one time, he speaks of all the baptized
as regenerate in Christ, and made children of God, by virtue of
that Sacrament. At another time, he speaks of baptismal grace
as rather enabling them to become, than as actually constituting
them God's children; and says that, in the higher and stricter
sense, persons are not to be called sons of God unless they have
the grace of perseverance, and walk in the love of God.[2]

It has very justly been observed, concerning this teaching of
St. Augustine, that over and above the great value of his own
judgment and testimony, he appeals to the uniform voice of an
tiquity, and declares that, in his baptismal doctrine, he proceed
upon principles which from the earliest ages have been admitted
in the Church.[3]

---

[1] He asserts that one of two things
must be determined: either that adults
receiving unworthily, like Simon Magus,
are born of water and of the Spirit, but
to their destruction, not to their salvation; or else that the hypocritical, and
those not converted in heart, must be esteemed to have been baptized, but not
born of the Spirit. — *De Baptismo c. Donatist.* Lib. VI. c. 12, Tom. IX. p. 169.

[2] See the passages quoted above. See
also *In Epistol. Johann.* c. 3, Tract. VI. 6,
7, Tom. III. par. II. pp. 859, 860, where
he argues that though a man may have
received the Sacrament of baptism, so
great a thing that it makes a new man
by remission of all his sins ("ut novum
hominem faciat dimissione omnium peccatorum"); yet if he have not charity,

he must not say that he is born of God.
("Habeat caritatem: aliter non se dicat
natum ex Deo.") The sons of God are
distinguished from the children of the
devil only by charity. Those who have
charity are born of God. Those who
have not charity are not born of God.

[3] "Quod universa tenet Ecclesia, nec
conciliis institutum, sed semper retentum
est, non nisi authoritate Apostolica traditum, rectissime creditur." — Lib. IV. c.
24, Tom. IX. p. 140.

On this Mr. Faber remarks: "Thus
by this remarkable attestation he becomes
as it were a host of witnesses in himself." (*Prim. Doct. of Regeneration*, p.
324.) I am much pained at being obliged
to express decided dissent from some of
the positions of Mr. Faber, a writer for

It is needless to trace the chain of fathers beyond St. Augustine. The scholastic discussions too may have had a sufficient interest in themselves, but we have neither need of, nor space for them here, and must at once pass to the period of the Reformation.

The Council of Trent declared that in baptism not only remission of original sin was given, but also all, which properly has the nature of sin, is cut off. In the regenerate there is nothing which God hates. Concupiscence indeed remains ; but has not the nature of sin, and will never hurt those who fight against it.[1] As a general principle, the Council decided (Sess. VII. can. VIII.), that the Sacraments confer grace *ex opere operato*.

Luther and the Lutheran reformers are clear and express in their assertion of baptismal grace. Luther lays great stress on Gal. iii. 27 ; which he says " is much to be observed against fanatical spirits, who lower the dignity of baptism, and speak impiously concerning it. St. Paul, on the contrary, adorns it with glorious titles, calling it the laver of regeneration and of the renewing of the Holy Ghost. And here, he says, all baptized persons have put on Christ ; as though he would say, Ye received not by baptism a sign or watchword (*tesseram*), by which you were enlisted into the number of Christians, as many fanatics of our day think, who make baptism a mere watchword, *i. e.* a short and empty sign. ' But as many,' he says, ' as have been baptized have put on Christ,' that is, Ye have been snatched from the Law into a new nativity, which was effected in baptism. Therefore ye are no longer under the Law, but are clothed with a new garment, *i. e.* Christ's righteousness. St. Paul therefore teaches that baptism is not a sign, but a clothing in Christ, yea, that Christ Himself is

whom I entertain much respect, and in whose writings I have taken great interest. I believe that his view of the subject cannot be so different from that which I have taken above, as might at first appear. His great argument is that the fathers did not believe moral renovation or conversion of heart to be the necessary concomitant of baptism. Of this I think there can be no doubt. Mr. Faber himself fully admits that " all sin is pardoned in baptism " (p. 321). He also holds that God's predestination, as revealed to us in Scripture, is not, as Arminians teach, *ex prævisis meritis* : nor yet, as Calvinists teach, to eternal glory ; but, as the fathers teach, to baptismal blessing ; and that all baptized persons **may**, if they will, become elect to glory.

(See *Prim. Doct. of Election, passim.*) Surely, then, he must consistently hold that all baptized persons are entitled to the aid of God's Holy Spirit. I am therefore quite at a loss to understand him, when I find him stating that infants, from original sin, " cannot be worthy recipients of baptism . . . . without an antecedent operation to make them worthy " (p. 345). Surely original sin is not a bar to God's pardoning mercy in Christ, nor to the grace of His Spirit, to quicken us from such sin. And how to believe that an antecedent operation is necessary to make them worthy, except on Arminian or Calvinistic principles, I cannot imagine.

[1] Sess. v. *De Pecc. Origin.* See also under Art. IX. pp. 244, 245

our clothing. Wherefore baptism is a most potent and efficacious rite."[1] "To be baptized in God's name, is not to be baptized by man, but by God. Wherefore, though it be done by man's hands, we must believe and hold that it is the work of God."[2] "God Himself honours baptism with His Name, and confirms it with His own power (*sua virtute*)."[3] "Separated from the Word, it is but water. Joined with the Word, it is Christ's Sacrament."[4] "The effect of baptism is remission of sins and the gift of the Holy Spirit."[5] Some had urged, that to ascribe such blessings to baptism was to attribute salvation, not to faith, but to works. Luther replies, that one of the objects of faith, and one of those things on which faith rests, is the grace of God in baptism. Besides, baptism is not our work, but God's. On God's work we rely for salvation, not on men's. And baptism is not the work of the bather, but of God.[6]

He denies that, in the case of infants, there is any need of faith. God's work is not rendered ineffectual, because they have no power to believe.[7] The work of God is then begun in the soul; but the effect of baptism is a thing which remains through the whole of life.[8] For the mortification of the body of sin, which is part of the grace proper to baptism, is a work which we are constantly to experience through life, till the sin be altogether abolished, and we rise and reign with Christ.[9] "This life therefore is a perpetual spiritual baptism, till we die."[10] "Baptism is the deluge of grace; as Noah's deluge was the deluge of wrath."[11] Baptism does not take away sin. "But in it God makes a covenant with you." "Immediately from your baptism God begins to renew you. He bestows on you His Spirit, and the Spirit begins immediately to mortify your nature and sins, and so to prepare you for death and resurrection." "God pledges Himself not to impute to you the remains of sin, which still cleave to you, nor to condemn you on their account."[12] A baptized person may therefore humbly say: "I know my works to be impure and defiled; but I am baptized, and I know that God, who cannot lie, has bound Himself to me in baptism, not to impute my sins to me, but rather to mortify them in me and abolish them."[13] All this, however, on God's part,

[1] Luther *In* III. *ad Galat.* Tom. v. p. 370.
[2] *Catechismus Major*, Tom. v. p. 657.
[3] Ibid.
[4] Ibid.
[5] Ibid.
[6] Ibid. p. 638.
[7] Ibid. p. 639.
[8] Ibid.
[9] *Præfat. in Epist. ad Romanos* Tom. v. p. 100.
[10] *De Sacramento Baptism.* Tom. I p. 72.
[11] Ibid. p. 72.
[12] Ibid. p. 74.
[13] Ibid.

Luther considers to involve a corresponding obligation on ours, to
use the grace so assured to us, and to mortify by its help the deeds
of the body.[1]

Zuinglius took a view the exact opposite to Luther's, on this
Sacrament, as on Sacraments in general. He begins by stating,
that almost all, whoever went before him, from the very times of
the Apostles, have erred concerning baptism.[2] He states his own
opinion to be, that a person who is signed by the sign of baptism,
promises that he will be a hearer and disciple of God, and that he
will obey His laws. " If," he says, " the Sacraments were the
things they signified, then could they not be signs. For the sign
and the thing signified cannot be the same. Baptism therefore
is the sign which binds and initiates us to Jesus Christ." [3] " External baptism with water contributes nothing to the washing away
of sin." [4] To get rid of a difficulty which naturally presented itself, he says that " Original sin does not deserve damnation, if a
person have believing parents. . . . Original sin is a disease, which
yet is not blameworthy in itself, nor can bring with it the pain of
damnation . . . . until a person, corrupted by its contagion, trans-
gresses God's law ; which then mostly happens, when he sees and
understands that law." [5] Accordingly, he argues for the undoubted
salvation of infants, baptized or unbaptized.[6]

Calvin, in his general view of Sacraments, was in accord neither
with Luther nor Zuinglius. It is by no means easy to define his
doctrine of baptism. Inconsistency is very little his character ; yet
on baptism he appears to have been somewhat inconsistent with
himself. His peculiar predestinarian system made it difficult for
him to believe that infants received grace ; because, according to

---

[1] De Sacramento Baptism. Tom. i. p.
73. Melancthon speaks exactly like Luther : " Quod Deus approbat baptismum
parvulorum, hoc ostendit, quod Deus dat
Spiritum Sanctum sic baptizatis."— Melancthon. Opp. Tom. i. p. 61.

" Sentimus eos (h. e. parvulos) in baptismo fieri filios Dei, accipere Spiritum
Sanctum, et manere in gratia tamdiu,
quoad non effundant eam peccatis actualibus ea ætate, quæ jam dicitur rationis
compos." — Tom. iv. pp. 664. See Bethell, On Regeneration, p. 155 ; Laurence,
Doctrine of the Church of England on Baptism. Third edit. p. 89.

[2] " Illud mihi ingenue circa libri ini-
tium dicendum est : fere omnes eos, quotquot ab ipsis Apostolorum temporibus
de baptismo scribere instituerunt, non
in paucis (quod pace omnium hominum

dictum esse velim) a scopo aberravisse."
— Zuinglius, De Baptismo Oper. pars 2,
Tigur. 1581, Tom. i. fol. 60.

[3] Ibid.

[4] " Externus baptismus ergo qui aqua
constat, ad peccatorum ablutionem nihil
facit." — Ibid. fol. 71.

[5] " Peccatum ergo originale damnationem non meretur, si modo quis paren-
tes fideles nactus fuerit. . . . Unde colligimus peccatum originale morbum quidem
esse, qui tamen per se culpabilis non est,
nec damnationis pœnam inferre potest
. . . . donec homo contagione hac corrup-
tus legem Domini transgreditur, quod
tum demum fieri consuevit, cum legem
sibi positam videt et intelligit." — Tom.
i. fol. 90.

[6] Compare his De Peccato Originali
Declaratio, Tom. i. fol. 116, seq.

him, grace given was always effectual, not to be resisted, never to
be lost. Yet his sacramental system led him to teach, that Sacraments were effectual means of grace, by which God acted on the
recipient, unless the recipient opposed an impenitent and unbelieving heart. If we took only his famous work, the *Institutes*, (which
was a youthful production, but from the general principles of
which he never departed,) we might think his views of baptism
scarcely higher than Zuingle's. He argues, indeed, against the
Anabaptists, that infants must be proper recipients of baptism,
because they can be saved, and can only be saved by being regenerate; and therefore they must be fit to receive the Sacrament of
regeneration.[1] He objects to the statement, that baptism is a mere
badge or watchword (*tessera*), whereby Christians, like soldiers,
may be distinguished among men.[2] Yet he seems to make baptism
little more than a figure or sign of an inward blessing; not a
means also, whereby that blessing may be conferred. " Baptism
is a sign of our initiation, whereby we are admitted into the society
of the Church; that being grafted into Christ, we may be counted
among the sons of God. Moreover, it was given us, that it might
serve for our faith with Him, and for our confession before men." [3]
We must not suppose that water can wash away our sins. St.
Paul connects the word of life and baptism of water together
(Eph. v. 26), signifying that the promise of our ablution and sanctification is brought by the word, and sealed by baptism.[4] Still,
he says that those who receive baptism with a right faith, perceive
the efficacy of Christ's death in mortifying their flesh, and of His
resurrection in renewal of the spirit; as the branch derives nourishment from the stock into which it is grafted.[5] Original sin,
which of itself would bring certain damnation, is by no means abolished by baptism; but the elect and believers are assured by baptism, that the guilt of original sin will not condemn them.[6] Ananias, when he exhorted Saul to " arise and be baptized, and wash
away his sins " (Acts xxii. 16), did not mean that in baptism, or
by virtue of baptism, sins were remitted; but that by baptism he
might have testimony and assurance, that his sins had already been
remitted.[7] As regards infants: the children of faithful parents,
dying before the age of reason, are certainly saved, whether baptized or not baptized. Therefore the children of faithful parents
are not baptized, that they may then first become sons of God, but

---

[1] *Instit.* IV. xvi. 17.
[2] Ibid. IV. xv. 1.
[3] Ibid.
[4] IV. xv. 2.

[5] IV. xv. 5.
[6] IV. xv. 10.
[7] IV. xv. 15.

rather are by a solemn sign then received into the Church, because by virtue of the promise they already belonged to the body of Christ.[1] He denies that John iii. 5, has any reference to baptism ; [2] and, on the whole, seems to teach, that elect children (among whom are all children of the faithful dying before the age of reason) receive from God the grace of remission and regeneration, and therefore are sealed with the seal of baptism, the effect of which is not to be confined to the period of baptism, but endures throughout life.[3]

Here, then, notwithstanding some difference of expression, and a material difference about the guilt of original sin,[4] there is no considerable disagreement between Calvin and Zuinglius on the grace of baptism. I do not know that Calvin ever retracted any of the opinions which he thus expressed. I will not say, that he ever materially modified them. Perhaps other expressions, which he used afterwards, may be reconciled with all that has just been referred to. Yet certainly, in some of his later works, he speaks much more favourably of the grace of baptism ; as though, when off his favourite system, he were constrained, by the evidence of Scripture, to attach more importance to it. In the Catechism which he composed for the children of the Church of Geneva, (which bears date A. D. 1545,) he teaches it to be " certain that pardon of sins and newness of life are offered to us in baptism." [5] It is possible enough, that this Catechism was itself designed for the use of (presumed) elect children. It must therefore be read with some allowance. Yet, in other of his works, somewhat similar statements may be found. In his commentary on the Acts of the Apostles (in Acts ii. 38), he says, that we cannot indeed receive miraculous gifts, as the Apostles ; yet the promise, " Ye shall

---

[1] " Unde sequitur, non ideo baptizari fidelium liberos, ut filii Dei tunc primum fiant, qui ante alieni fuerunt ab ecclesia ; sed solenni potius signo ideo recipi in ecclesiam, quia promissionis beneficio jam ante ad Christi corpus pertinebant." — *Instit.* IV. xv. 22. Comp. *Epist.* 193.

[2] IV. xvi. 25.

[3] See IV. xv. xvi. *passim ;* especially xvi. 22, xv. 3, &c. Comp. III. iii. 9.

[4] Zuinglius held that original sin would not damn any in whom it had not broken out in actual sin. Hence that all infants, dying in infancy, were saved. Calvin held that it was, of its own nature, fraught with damnation ; but that, in the case of elect infants, the curse was reversed.

[5] " *M.* Verum, annon aliud aquæ tribuis, nisi ut ablutionis tantum sit figura ?

" *P.* Sic figuram esse sentio, ut simul annexa sit veritas. Neque enim, sua nobis dona pollicendo, nos Deus frustratur. Proinde et peccatorum veniam et vitæ novitatem offerri nobis in baptismo et recipi a nobis certum est.

" *M.* Quomodo per baptismum nobis hæc bona conferuntur ?

" *P.* Quia nisi promissiones illic nobis oblatas respuendo infructuosas reddimus, vestimur Christo, Ejusque Spiritu donamur." — *Catechismus Ecclesiæ Genevensis,* J. Calvino Authore. *Calvini Opuscula.* Genevæ. 1552.

receive the Holy Ghost," applies to all ages of the Church, in a
more exalted sense than any promise of mere miraculous gifts.
"To baptism therefore the grace of the Spirit will ever be annexed, unless an impediment from us occurs." [1]   Again he says,
"We must take notice, that no mere figure is proposed to us in
baptism, but that an exhibition of the thing signified is annexed to
it ; for God never fallaciously promises, but really fulfils, what he
signifies by figure.   But then again, we must take heed not to tie
God's grace to the Sacraments ; for the administration of baptism
profits nothing, except where God thinks fit." [2]   In another place,
after bidding us direct our minds in baptism, not to the water, but
to Christ, he adds : "But if any one, relying on this, should make
baptism a mere frigid spectacle, and void of all grace of the Spirit,
he will be much deceived." [3]   And again he tells us, that in Sacraments the sign is joined with the word ; and then there is grace
received by the faithful.   "So Christ breathed on His Apostles.
They received, not only the breathing, but the Spirit too.   Why?
Because of Christ's promise.   So in baptism, we put on Christ,
are washed with His blood ; our old man is crucified, and God's
righteousness reigns in us . . . . Whence so great a power, but
from Christ's promise, who effects and makes good by His Spirit
what He witnesses by His word !" [4]

Notwithstanding these statements, which are certainly very different from those of Zuingle, it is probable that Calvin limited the
reception of sacramental grace to the elect.   There can be little
doubt that he was not always consistent on this head ; yet I think
it cannot be denied that he did believe some grace to be promised
in baptism.   But then God's promises he limited to the elect.
Hence, he probably believed that the elect received an accomplishment of these promises, and therefore remission of sins, and
God's Spirit in baptism ; but that the non-elect received the sign
only, without the grace. [5]

The followers of Calvin have, for the most part, been purely
Zuinglian in their views of baptism : not indeed all predestinarians

---

[1] "Baptismo igitur semper annexa erit
Spiritus gratia, nisi a nobis impedimen-
tum occurrat." — J. Calvin. *Commentar.
in Act. Apostol.* c. ii. v. 38.

[2] Ibid. *in* c. xxii. 16.

[3] Ibid. c. xi. 16.

[4] "Flat Christus in Apostolos : hi non
flatum modo, sed Spiritum quoque recipiunt.   Cur ? nisi quia illis Christus promittit ?   Similiter in baptismo Christum
induimus, abluimur Ejus sanguine, cru-

cifigitur vetus homo noster, ut regret in
nobis Dei justitia.   In sacra Cœna spiritualiter Christi Carne et Sanguine pascimur.   Unde tanta vis, nisi ex Christi
promissione, qui Spiritu suo efficit ac
præstat, quod verbo testatur ?" — J.
Calv. *In Johann.* c. xx. 22.

[5] "Neque enim quicquam prodest ex-
terna baptismi administratio, *nisi ubi vix
Deo visum est.*" — *In Act. A¡os'ol* **xxii.**
16.

since Calvin's time ; but those who have expressly adopted Calvin's predestinarianism. It may be added, that the Arminians, who sprang from the Calvinists, though on one point at least widely separated from them, not only agreed with them in their Zuinglian view of baptism, but far more decidedly repudiated baptismal grace than the Calvinists themselves, calling baptism by the name to which Calvin had specially objected, a mere watchword, or badge of profession (*Tessera*).[1]

Our own English reformers seem to speak very strongly and plainly. It has been said of late, that it is impossible they could hold the doctrine that infants uniformly receive remission of sins and the assured help of God's Spirit in baptism, because they were all Calvinists. It cannot be meant that they were, in all respects, followers of Calvin ; for such an assertion would be obviously and notoriously untrue. The statement probably implies no more than that they were predestinarians, *i. e.* believers in an absolute and irrespective predestination of individuals to eternal glory. There is very slight, if any, foundation, even for this. Yet allowing it to be true, it is by no means a consequence, that Cranmer and Ridley must have followed out to its natural conclusions this doctrine of irrespective decrees. Calvin did, no doubt, though even he appears to have had some misgivings about baptism. But much greater men than Calvin held the same doctrine of irrespective personal election to glory, but did not follow it out to what may seem its inevitable consequences, — for instance, St. Augustine and Luther ; though the latter appears ultimately to have shunned all discussions on predestination. If the English reformers were absolute predestinarians, it is quite certain that they took Augustine's, not Calvin's view. Now Augustine's, as has been shown, did not in any way influence his baptismal doctrines. There can therefore be no propriety in disposing at once of the opinions of the Anglican reformers, by saying that they were predestinarians, and that they therefore could not but have coincided with Calvin on baptism.

Here, as elsewhere, Cranmer and Ridley must be our great authorities, because they were the chief compilers both of the Articles and the Liturgy. It was their genius which directed the Reformation, and their spirit which is infused into its formularies.

---

[1] " Baptismus ritus est, quo fideles tanquam sacra tessera confirmantur de gratiosa Dei erga ipsos voluntate." — Limborch. *Theol.* Lib. IV. c. 67, § 5. " Baptismum non esse lavacrum regenerationis satis . . . . constare potest." — Ibid. § 10. See Bishop Bethell, p. 171, *seq.*

Cranmer, in 1548, published his Catechism, translated and modified from the Latin of a Lutheran divine, Justus Jonas.   In that
Catechism the statements are remarkably like Luther's.   It is
said, that " without the word of God water is water, and not baptism ; but when the word of the living God is joined to the water,
then it is baptism, and water of wonderful wholesomeness, and the
bath of regeneration, as St. Paul writeth." [1]   Again, " We ought
not to have an eye only to the water, but to God rather, which did
ordain the baptism of water, and commanded it to be done in His
name.   For He is Almighty, and able to work in us by baptism,
forgiveness of our sins, and all those wonderful effects and operations for the which He ordained the same, though man's reason is
not able to conceive the same.   Therefore, consider, good children,
the great treasures and benefits whereof God maketh us partakers,
when we are baptized, which be these.   The first is, that in baptism our sins be forgiven us, as St. Peter witnesseth.   Let every
one of you be baptized for the forgiveness of his sins.   The second
is, that the Holy Ghost is given us . . . . according to this saying
of St. Peter, Let every one of you be baptized in the name of
Christ, and then ye shall receive the gift of the Holy Ghost.   The
third is, that by baptism the whole righteousness of Christ is given
us . . . . Fourthly, by baptism we die with Christ." [2]   It is then
said, that before baptism we cannot have peace or quietness of conscience.   " But, after our sins in baptism be forgiven us, and we
believe the promise of God, and so by our faith be justified, then
our consciences be quieted." [3]   A sinner that is not baptized, " although he had the Holy Ghost to this effect to help him to fight
against sin, yet oftentimes he is overcome and falleth into sin.
. . . . But when in baptism the righteousness of Christ is given
and imputed to him, then he is delivered from all those perils.
For he knoweth for a surety that he hath put upon him Christ, and
that his weakness and imperfection is covered and hid with the
perfect righteousness and holiness of Christ." [4]   Once more, " The
second birth is by the water of baptism, which Paul calls the bath
of regeneration, because our sins be forgiven us in baptism, and
the Holy Ghost is poured into us as God's beloved children." [5]
" He that is baptized may assuredly say thus, I am not now in the
wavering opinion that I only suppose myself to be a Christian man,
but I am in a sure belief that I am made a Christian man ; for I

[1] Cranmer's *Catechism*, pp. 191, 192.   [4] Ibid. pp. 188, 189.
[2] Ibid. p. 186.   [5] Ibid. p. 182.
[3] Ibid. p. 187.

know for a surety that I am baptized, and I am sure also that baptism was ordained of God . . . . and the Holy Ghost doth witness that he which is baptized hath put on him Christ." [1]

So completely is this Luther's language, that similar statements, word for word, may be taken from all parts of his writings. But it nevertheless appears exactly to exhibit the sentiments of Cranmer, who adopted it; for the same tone pervades all his subsequent writings; and I know of no single contrary statement, though I have carefully read and noted all his remains, with special reference to this doctrine. He attributes no holiness to the water itself; [2] denies the grace of baptism to those who come feignedly, "who be washed with sacramental water, but be not washed with the Holy Ghost, and clothed with Christ." [3] But as to others (infants or worthily receiving adults) he teaches, that "Through baptism in this world the body is washed and the soul is washed: the body outwardly, the soul inwardly; the work is one;" [4] and that "that doctrine is not to be suffered in the Church which teacheth that we are not joined to Christ by baptism." [5] "As in baptism we must think that, as the priest putteth his hand to the child outwardly, and washeth him with water; so must we think that God putteth to His hand inwardly, and washeth the infant with His Holy Spirit, and moreover, that Christ Himself cometh down upon the child, and apparelleth him with His own self." [6]

His great friend and contemporary, Bishop Ridley, calls baptism by the name of "regeneration;" [7] says that "the water in baptism is sacramentally changed into the fountain of regeneration;" [8] that "the water in baptism hath grace promised, and by that grace the Holy Spirit is given; not that grace is included in water, but that grace cometh by water." [9]

There was little dispute in England at the time of the Reformation about baptism. Most of the passages above cited occur in controversy with Romanist divines; and it is truly remarkable that Cranmer, instead of maintaining lower ground than the Romanists on baptismal grace, maintains rather higher ground; for the Romanist divines were inclined to derogate from the dignity of baptism, in order the more to elevate the importance of the Commu-

---

[1] Cranmer's *Catechism*, p. 184.
[2] *Works*, III. p. 490.
[3] Ibid. II. p. 439. See also III. pp. 322, 323.
[4] IV. p. 39.
[5] Ibid. p. 42.
[6] Ibid. III. p. 553. See also II. pp. 302, 340; III. pp. 65, 118, 171, 276, 490, 534, 553: IV. pp. 39–44, 55, &c.
[7] *Works*, Park. Soc. p. 57.
[8] Ibid. p. 12.
[9] Ibid. p. 240.

ion.[1] The most systematic statements are to be found in Cranmer's Catechism, which, as noticed above, uses the very language
of Luther. Luther appears exactly to have followed, on this head,
his great master, St. Augustine. We may therefore naturally infer, that the sentiments of Cranmer and Ridley were nearly those
of Augustine. Certain it is, they were not those of Zuinglius nor
of Calvin. A few quotations can never bring out the full force of
an author's meaning. The works of Cranmer are readily to be obtained. In the notes I have put a considerable number of references. It is easy to turn to them, and each reader may convince
himself whether the context does not fully bear out the impression
which the extracts convey.

If from the reformers who first drew up our services and Articles, we turn to those of the reign of Elizabeth, who adopted and
slightly modified them, we shall find no different language. Jewel's *Apology* says, that " Baptism is the Sacrament of remission of
sins, and of our washing in the Blood of Christ."[2] " We assert,
that Christ exhibits Himself truly present in His Sacraments : in
baptism, that we may put Him on,"[3] &c. In Nowell's *Catechism*,
a work like Jewel's *Apology*, to be esteemed semi-authoritative, the
child is taught thus : " *M.* what is the hidden and spiritual grace
in baptism ? *A.* It is twofold : namely, remission of sins and regeneration . . . . *M.* You seem to make the water only a certain figure of divine things ? *A.* A figure indeed it is, but by no means
empty and fallacious ; but such, that to it the verity of the things
themselves is joined and tied. For, as God truly offers to us in
baptism pardon of sins and newness of life, so are they certainly received by us. Far be it from us to suppose that God would mock
us with vain images ! *M.* Do we then receive remission of sins by
mere outward washing and sprinkling ? *A.* By no means ! For Christ
alone washes off the stains of our souls with His own Blood. It
were impious to attribute this honour to an outward element,"[4] &c.

If we pass to the formularies themselves, we may begin with the
Articles agreed on between the Anglican and Lutheran divines in

---

[1] See this especially in the " Disputation with Chedsey," Cranmer's *Works*,
iv. pp. 41, 42.
Latimer has been much referred to, as
having in one passage denied the connection between baptism and regeneration. Archbp. Laurence (*Doctrine of the
Church of England on Baptism*, Third
Edition, pp. 43–45) has shown that Latimer's general teaching coincided with
Cranmer's. I have not quoted Bp. Lat-

imer, because there is nothing to connect him with the drawing up either of
the Articles or the Liturgy ; and therefore his testimony is no more important
than that of any other divine of the
period.
[2] *Juelli Apologia, Enchirid. Theolog.* p.
127.
[3] Ibid. p. 129.
[4] *Noelli Catechismus Enchirid. Theolog.*
pp. 314, 315; cf. p. 321.

1538. In them it is said, that " in baptism remission of sins a e
the grace of Christ is offered to infants and adults . . . . that infants
in baptism attain remission of sins and grace, and become children
of God, because the promise of grace and life eternal extends not
only to adults but also to infants . . . . But because infants are
born with original sin, they need remission of that sin, and this is
so remitted that its imputation is taken away. Howbeit the corruption of nature or concupiscence remains in this life, although it
begins to be healed, because the Holy Spirit, even in infants, is efficacious and cleanses them." [1] If we refer to the Articles of 1536,
the Bishops' Book, A. D. 1537, and the King's Book, A. D. 1543,
we shall find them all agreeing to teach, that " infants by the Sacrament of baptism receive remission of sins, the grace and favour
of God, and be made thereby very sons and children of God ; " [2]
that " the effect and virtue of this Sacrament is forgiveness of sins
and grace of the Holy Ghost ; " [3] that infants, " being offered in
the faith of the Church, receive forgiveness of their sins, and such
grace of the Holy Ghost, that, if they die in the state of their infancy, they shall thereby undoubtedly be saved." [4]

The First Book of Homilies is the earliest public document of
the reign of Edw. VI. In the " Homily of Salvation" (Part I.)
it is stated, " that infants, being baptized and dying in their infancy,
are by this sacrifice washed from their sins, brought to God's favour,
and made His children, and inheritors of His kingdom of heaven ; "
and that " we must trust only in God's mercy and the sacrifice . . .
offered on the cross, to obtain thereby God's grace and remission,
as well of our original sin in baptism, as of all actual sin committed
after our baptism, if we truly repent."

The Second Book of Homilies was not published till the reign of
Elizabeth, yet it now is united with the First ; and we may therefore quote them together. In a former Article we saw that baptism and the Supper of the Lord were described as the two Sacraments having " visible signs, whereunto is annexed the promise of
free forgiveness of our sins, and of our holiness and joining in
Christ." [5] The " Homily of repairing of Churches " says of the

---

[1] " Et quod per baptismum offerantur remissio peccatorum et gratia Christi, in-fantibus et adultis . . . . et quod infantes per baptismum consequantur remissi-onem peccatorum et gratiam, et sint filii Dei, quia promissio gratiæ et vitæ æternæ pertinet non solum ad adultos, sed etiam ad infantes . . . . Quia vero infantes nascuntur cum peccato originis, habent opus remissione illius peccati, et illud ita remittitur ut reatus tollatur, licet corruptio naturæ seu concupiscen-tia manet in hac vita, etsi incipit sanari, quia Spiritus Sanctus in ipsis etiam infantibus est efficax et eos mundat." — See Cranmer's *Works*, IV. pp. 279, 280.

[2] *Formularies in the Reign of Henry VIII.* pp. xix. 7, 93.

[3] Ibid. p. 253.

[4] Ibid. p. 254.

[5] *Hom. of Common Prayer and Sacra-ments.*

Church, that " The fountain of our regeneration is there presented
unto us." The " Homily of the Passion," that " We be therefore
washed in our baptism from the filthiness of sin, that we should live
afterward in the pureness of life."

The next authoritative document, after the First Book of Homilies, was the First Service Book of Edw. VI. This was compiled
in the same year (1548) that Cranmer's Catechism was put forth.
The Baptismal Service in that Book differs from our present ser-
ice for infant baptism, in that the latter lacks some of the ceremonies which were retained in the former. The doctrinal statements
(if prayers can be said to contain statements) are the same. It is,
however, desirable to postpone the consideration of these till the
last. Yet one portion of the First Service Book we must not omit.
It is the Catechism. Here we have (drawn up by Cranmer and
set forth in the same year with his larger Catechism already cited)
all the portion of our present Church Catechism, down to the end
of the Lord's Prayer. The latter part, concerning the Sacraments,
was not added till after the Hampton Court Controversy, in the
reign of James I., more than fifty years later. The teaching in
the earliest questions, however, was, as it still continues : " Who
gave you that name ? My godfathers and godmothers in my baptism, wherein I was made a member of Christ, a child of God, and
an inheritor of the kingdom of heaven." The child is taught to
call this " a state of salvation," and to speak of himself as " sanctified by God the Holy Ghost," like " all the elect people of God."

Immediately before the Catechism in the First Service Book
there is a rubric, which now stands in the baptismal service, to the
following purport: " It is certain by God's word, that children
being baptized, if they depart out of this life in their infancy, are
undoubtedly saved." [1] These were the principal public documents
put forth at the period of the Reformation, in which baptism is
treated of, with the exception of the Articles, and the services for
Infant Baptism. Let us then next take the Articles. These were
published A. D. 1552, four years after the First Service Book and
Cranmer's Catechism, and the same year as the Second Service
Book. Those Articles which treat on baptism, were not altered in
the reign of Elizabeth.

Besides the Article on Baptism itself, one or two expressions

[1] Archbishop Laurence (*Doctrine of
Church of England on Baptism*, p. 98)
quotes a passage from the *Reformatio
Legum*, a document drawn up by Cranmer which most satisfactorily shows
that the English reformers by no means
adopted the opinions of the later fathers
and of the schoolmen, that all unbaptized infants must inevitably perish.
" Quod longe secus habere judicamus,"
are the words used. See also Laurence,
B. L. p. 70.

occur in the earlier Articles, Thus, in that on original sin (now the IXth), we read in the English, "although there is no condemnation to them that believe and are baptized." In the Latin the word rendered "baptized" is *renatis*, "born again." And the Article "Of Christ alone without sin" (now the XVth) says: "All we the rest, although baptized and born again in Christ." In both these there appears an identification of baptism and regeneration.

To proceed to our present Article, the XXVIIth. It is difficult to find any exact model on which it is framed. It bears little resemblance to any former Article, in any other confession, either English or foreign. It is evidently penned with considerable caution. It begins with a denial of the Zuinglian notion, that "baptism is a mere sign of profession or mark of difference." It continues, that it is "a sign of regeneration or new birth." So far, however, its statement is not much more than Zuinglius's. But then it adds, "*whereby, as by an instrument*, they, who receive baptism rightly, are grafted into the church; the promises of forgiveness of sin and of our adoption to be the sons of God, by the Holy Ghost are visibly *signed and sealed*." The concluding words of the paragraph contain considerable difficulty. "Faith is confirmed and grace increased by virtue of prayer to God," *vi divinæ invocationis*. The Latin and the English do not correspond, and appear to convey different ideas. The former would indicate that the invocation of God, which accompanies the act of baptism, confirms faith and increases grace. The latter would imply, that the prayers of the congregation might, over and above the ordinance of God, be blessed to the recipient's soul, so that, whereas he might receive grace by God's appointment, whether prayer accompanied baptism or not; yet the addition of prayer was calculated to bring down more grace and to confirm faith. Whence the confusion sprang, if such it were, it may be hard to say. The Latin and English have both authority; but one does not explain the other. Perhaps they rather supply than explain each other.

The Articles then speak the same language as the other formularies of our Church, on the subject of baptismal grace. Yet it has been truly observed, that the Article which expressly treats of baptism speaks less distinctly than any other authorized document, and is more easily explained away. Why this should have been is not apparent. The primate, and his coadjutor Ridley, perpetually, both before and after the publication of the Articles, expressed their own views in strong and unmistakable language. It is cer-

tain that the bishops and clergy in general were not more disposed to Zuinglian doctrines than the primate ; but, on the contrary, were rather more favourable to Romanism and doctrines
verging on Romanism.   The Article could not therefore have been
softened to please them.   It is not impossible, that the king himself, young as he was, may have had some leaning to the Swiss
reformers, and that to please him, and perhaps to satisfy some
foreign divines, a certain degree of ambiguity may have been admitted.

We must remember, that the office for Infant Baptism was put
out nearly at the same time with the Articles, that it was enjoined
by the same authority, that it is of equal obligation on the clergy,
and of still greater interest to the laity of the Church.   Its meaning has been a fertile source of trouble in the present century.
Yet, if fairly considered, its sense can scarcely be ambiguous.

It perhaps would be conceded that, if the sentiments of the reformers were clearly known and fully established, the natural sense
of the service would be no longer doubtful.   We have had copious
extracts from their works ; and their own doctrine has been given
in their own words.   Most of their statements must have concerned *infant* baptism ; for so little was adult baptism known in their
day, that no office for adult baptism was appointed till nearly a
hundred years after them.   We know that they speak of infants
as regenerated in baptism.   The only questions which can occur
are these : Did they believe *all* baptized infants to be regenerated, or only some ?   And, if so, what did they mean by regeneration ?

A considerable number of men, whose piety forbids us to doubt
their honesty, suppose that the reformers believed *some*, but *not
all*, infants to be regenerated in baptism.   Such persons therefore
say, that the well-known strong expressions in the baptismal service must be interpreted with some reservation.   They adopt the
notion of a charitable hypothesis.   The Church charitably hopes
that a particular child may be regenerate, and therefore fearlessly
expresses its conviction that he *is* regenerate.   In special confirmation of this theory, they adduce the office for Adult Baptism,
where nearly the same expressions are used, and where it is impossible to be sure that regeneration is bestowed ; for confessedly
to adults grace is given only when there is sincerity and faith.
To this they add the Burial Service ; where we give God thanks
for taking our departed brother out of this world, evidently on the
charitable supposition that he is fit for a better.

Now it is quite plain that the office for Adult Baptism **cannot** explain the office for Infant Baptism; for this reason. The office for Adult Baptism was not drawn up till a hundred years after that for Infant Baptism, *i. e.* in the reign of Charles II. It was so worded as to be as like as possible to the more ancient office for infants; and as few alterations as could be were adopted. An office drawn up A. D. 1661 cannot interpret one drawn up in 1552. Or if it be supposed that the bishops of 1661 were likely to understand the language of their predecessors in 1552, then we may listen to *their* explanation of the office for Infant Baptism, the strong terms of which were objected to by the puritans. " Seeing," say these very bishops, who compiled the office of Adult Baptism, " that God's Sacraments have their effects, where the receiver doth not *ponere obicem*, put any bar against them (which children cannot do), we may say in faith of *every* child that is baptized, that it is regenerated by God's Holy Spirit; and the denial of it tends to anabaptism," [1] &c.

The Burial Service does not seem a case in point. There is there no positive assertion of the certainty of the individual's bliss, as there is of the certainty of the infant's regeneration in the baptismal service. Concerning the individual, we indeed give thanks that God has " been pleased to deliver him from the miseries of this sinful world." But, as regards his resting in Christ, we only say, " as our *hope* is this our brother doth." The expression, " in sure and certain hope of the resurrection to eternal life," is a *general* proposition, affecting all men, and not specially the individual. The very words then of the Burial Service express plainly a charitable and comfortable *hope.* Those of the baptismal service, on the contrary, contain a positive *assertion*, and a consequent thanksgiving. The one therefore cannot explain the other.

But is it in any manner likely that the reformers should have intended a charitable hope, where they express an undoubting confidence? The belief that some were regenerate in baptism, and others were not, was, to say the most of it, a perfectly new notion in their day. The fathers believed *all* infants to be regenerate; so did the schoolmen; so did the whole mediæval Church; so did Luther and the Lutherans. Zuingle and the Zuinglians, on the contrary, believed that no one was regenerate in baptism; with them baptism was a mere outward sign. With Calvin and his followers originated the idea that the elect might receive grace, but the non-elect be left unblessed, in the Sacrament of baptism.

---

[1] Cardwell's *Hist. of Conferences*, p. 356.

It is quite certain that, early in their career, our reformers could have known nothing of this theory. It was not until late, that they had any connection whatever with the Calvinistic divines. But if, at any period in their lives, they obtained from Geneva a perfectly new light on the subject of infants receiving baptismal grace, is it not most strange that their writings should exhibit no trace of this? From 1536 to 1555 we have their documents and disputations. The same tone and statements, concerning baptism and the grace of baptism, prevail from first to last. In the Articles of 1536, in the Bishops' Book of 1537, in the Articles of 1538, in the King's Book of 1543, in Cranmer's Catechism, the Baptismal Service, the Church Catechism of 1548, in the Second Service Book and the Articles of 1552, in the Answer to Gardiner 1551, and the Disputation with Chedsey 1554, exactly the same general assertions occur. There is nothing said about *all* infants, still less is anything said about excluding any. Unworthy adults are excluded, but infants never. Is it not most probable that the utter silence concerning the inclusion of all, or the exclusion of some, resulted from the fact that Calvin's theory, which is not very apparent even in his own published works, had never been brought to their notice? that they therefore used the ordinary language of those who went before them, speaking in the general of infants as the subjects of the grace of God, and not caring to specify *all*, because not dreaming that *some* could be excluded?[1] In fact, their own sentiments, to any one who will fairly examine their writings, must seem plainly to have been these. All men, infants as well as elders, are subject to original sin, and as such, subject to the wrath of God. But all too are subjects of the redeeming love of God. He would have all to be saved. He freely offers pardon and grace to all. Thus, even of unbaptized infants we may hope that they shall share the blessings of the atonement, and dying in infancy, shall be saved from the curse of sin. But baptism is God's special ordinance for bringing them into covenant with Him. Of those infants therefore who have been baptized, we do not *hope*, but we *know*, that

---

[1] It will be remembered that Calvin's difficulty was this. His theory was, that grace was never given but irresistibly, and once given, never was withdrawn. Hence, if given to an infant, it must, sooner or later, renew his nature, and save his soul. Hence, again, if grace was given in baptism, the child must be saved. The predestinarians before him had not this idea. Augustine, and probably all predestinarians from him to Calvin, held that grace might be bestowed, but not profited by. Hence God's Spirit and aid might be given to an infant, but he never grow up the holier for it, because he resisted and quenched the Spirit; and even if he were renewed at first, if not predestinated to perseverance, he might fall away. Unless it can be proved, that our reformers had adopted Calvin's theory of irresistible grace and final perseverance, it cannot be probable that they should have entertained his difficulties about baptism.

as they are partakers of the covenant of grace, so they are partakers of the assurance of pardon, and moreover have a right to those graces of the Holy Spirit, which, if cultivated, as they grow up, will surely new-create in them a sanctified nature, mortifying and destroying their old and corrupt nature, and making them sons of God indeed. Hence, as they are by baptism entitled to regenerating grace, we do not scruple to use the language of Scripture and antiquity, and to call them, regenerate in baptism. Yet we do not thereby intend that original corruption is quenched in them, or that their whole moral disposition is changed; but only, that they are new-born into the Church, that their sin of nature is not imputed to them, and that they have an assurance of that spiritual aid, which, if not hindered, will renew, convert, and restore them.

It will be no small confirmation to the belief that this was their sentiment concerning baptism, if we learn that the model on which their baptismal services were formed was not Calvinistic, nor Zuinglian, but Lutheran. Archbishop Laurence has shown that, on the subject of our formularies in general, there was much correspondence between the English and the Lutheran divines.[1] But it has been proved, beyond the possibility of doubt, that the sources of our present office for Infant Baptism were, *first*, the Service in common use in the mediæval Church, and still in the Church of Rome; *secondly*, a formulary adopted by Luther for his own followers in Germany; *thirdly*, a Service composed by Melancthon and Bucer for the use of the Archbishop of Cologne, which was itself adapted from the ancient Liturgy of Nuremburg.[2] This fact directly associates our own formularies with those, first of the ancient Church, secondly, of the Lutheran reformers. The parts of the more ancient services which were deemed superstitious, such as chrism and exorcism, were omitted. But the doctrine involved is evidently the same as that held by Luther and Melancthon; who, it has been seen, followed and symbolized with St. Augustine.

Section IV. — INFANT BAPTISM.

SO much space has been occupied on the earlier part of this Article, that the latter part must be very briefly considered;

---

[1] See Laurence's *Bampton Lectures, passim.*

[2] Appendix to Laurence's *Doctrine of the Church of England on Baptism.*

especially as some of what has been already said may bear on the question of infant baptism.

We have already traced the analogy between circumcision and baptism. The latter indeed excels the former, as the new covenant excels the old; but both were alike initiatory rites, the means of entering into covenant with God, and the seal of that covenant. If children could be admitted into the covenant of works, why not, *a fortiori*, into the covenant of grace? If, before they knew good from evil, they were capable of being bound by an obligation to do good and to renounce evil, and that without the assurance of quickening grace, how can they be incapable of admission to the promises of pardon, to the offer of life eternal, to the mercy and love of Him " who came to seek and to save that which was lost?" In that case, the blessings of the old covenant, instead of being more limited, must have been more extended than those of the new; and the Law, which was given by Moses, must have been more merciful than the grace and truth, which came by Jesus Christ. The parallel too is the more exact, if we remember, that to adults circumcision was " the seal of the righteousness of faith " (Rom. iv. 11); and so was not given to Abraham, till he had believed. But this prerequisite in adults was no prerequisite in infants. The infant children of the Israelites, and of the converts to Judaism, were all circumcised, though they could have no faith to qualify them.

We saw, in a former Section, that not only circumcision, but baptism, was practised among the Jews; and that, when they admitted proselytes into their communion, they not only circumcised all the males, but baptized all, male and female, infant and adult.[1] When therefore our Lord sent out His disciples to " make proselytes of all nations by baptizing them " (μαθητεύσατε πάντα τὰ ἔθνη, βαπτίζοντες αὐτοὺς, Matt. xxviii. 19), He addresses persons, who had been ever used to the mode of proselyting, or admitting of proselytes, which He commanded; and, as they had always seen infants, as well as adults, baptized for such proselytism, they could only have understood that they too were to practise *infant* baptism. Unless therefore there were a special bar put upon such a practice, our Lord's words naturally implied that the practice was according to His will. The omission to specify infants is only analogous to the omission of commands to perform other obvious duties which were well understood before, and which the first teachers of Christianity took naturally for granted.

[1] See Lightfoot on Matt. iii.; Wall, *Infant Baptism*, Introduction, quoted in sect. 11

The necessity of baptism has constantly been inferred from our Lord's declaration, " Except a man [1] be born of *water*, and of the Spirit, he cannot enter into the kingdom of God " (John iii. 5). But the same supreme authority declared too concerning infants, that " of such is the kingdom of God " (Mark x. 14). If so, they must be capable of baptism, both by water and the Spirit. Otherwise, one would think, they cannot be capable of entering into that kingdom, which is said specially to appertain to them. The whole of our Lord's teaching, on that occasion, when infants were brought to Him, seems to show, as plainly as possible, the propriety of infant baptism. If young children ought to be brought to Christ, and He has peculiar pleasure in and love for them, then can there be no possible reason why we should keep them from the Sacrament of His love. It may be said that we thereby bind them, without their own consent, to obligations which they might be unwilling to contract. But every human being, created by God, and redeemed by Christ, is, baptized or unbaptized, bound to believe, to love, to obey Him; and hence, whether acknowledged or not, the obligation exists. And, moreover, if in baptism responsibility is undertaken, far greater is the blessing than the responsibility: for let it ever be remembered, that it is admission not to a covenant of works and to a bargain, " This do, and thou shalt live; " but that it is to a covenant of grace, to pardon, and mercy, and spiritual aid, and the promise of eternal life. Great therefore are the blessings of baptism; and, though of course there are consequent obligations, yet they are only such as, more or less, would exist for the unbaptized.

Again, the statement of St. Paul, that the children of Christian parents are holy (1 Cor. vii. 14), is fairly alleged as a proof that Christians' children are fit recipients of the first Christian Sacrament. The other Sacrament, which is a renewal of the covenant made in the first, may be fitter for the adult and intelligent; but there can be nothing to keep the infant from the first. If it be said that he has original sin, this, so far from keeping him from baptism, is his very reason for needing it. For though we may hope that, under the Gospel of the grace of God, sin will not be imputed where it has not been actual and wilful; yet baptism is " for the remission of sin " (Mark i. 4); and there is no way, but baptism, whereby we can place the infant in formal covenant with God, and therefore within the terms of the covenant, and having the *assurance* that his sins shall not be imputed to him, and that, if he go hence, his soul shall be safe.

[1] τὶς, any one.

The words of St. Peter, again, sound much like an encouragement to bring the young to baptism. For when he had exhorted those who asked what they should do, to be " baptized in the name of Jesus Christ for the remission of sins," and assured them that then they should " receive the Holy Ghost ; " he added, " For the promise is to you and to your *children* " (Acts ii. 38, 39).

Lastly, though it is true that we read nothing of infants being baptized by any of the Apostles, it being on every account far more likely that we should hear of the baptism of adults, yet we do find that whole households were baptized by them, in more cases than one (Acts xvi. 15, 33 ; 1 Cor. i. 16) ; and in households it is most likely that there must have been children.

If we consult the records of antiquity, we shall find every reason to believe that the practice of infant baptism prevailed from the very first. Justin Martyr wrote his Second Apology about A. D. 148 (*i. e.* 48 years after the death of the last Apostle). He there speaks of persons 60 and 70 years old, who had been made disciples to Christ in their infancy.[1] How can infants be made disciples, but by baptism ? And if these had been baptized in their infancy, it must have been during the lifetimes of the Apostle St. John, and of other apostolic men. Irenæus, next in succession to Justin, says : " Christ came to save all by Himself ; all, that is, who by Him are regenerated to God, — infants and little ones, and boys and youths and old men. Therefore He went through every age, being made an infant for infants, that He might sanctify infants." [2] &c. If we consider that Irenæus, like other of the fathers, commonly calls baptism by the name of regeneration, this passage will seem conclusive of the custom and doctrine in his day.

Tertullian is an important, though unwilling witness. He shows that in his day (about a century from the Apostles) the custom of baptizing infants prevailed, and that sponsors were wont to answer for them ; but he himself advocated a delay in baptism ; for he thought the innocent age of infants could scarcely need the haste of bringing them to baptism ; he thought also that sponsors might, from death or other causes, be unable to fulfil their duties, and he considered it better to seek remission of sins later in life, when temptations were less likely to make men fall away.[3] This was his own reasoning against the custom of the Church, showing what that custom of the Church, against which he reasoned, was. His

---

[1] πολλοί τινες καὶ πολλαὶ ἑξηκοντοῦται καὶ ἑβδομηκοντοῦται, οἱ ἐκ παίδων ἐμαθητεύθησαν τῷ Χριστῷ, ἄφθοροι διαμένουσι.—Justin. *Apol.* II. p. 62.

[2] " Omnes venit per semetipsum sal-

vare ; omnes, inquam, qui per Eum renascuntur in Deum ; infantes et parvulos, et pueros, et juvenes, et seniores," &c. — Irenæus, Lib. II. c. 39, p. 160.

[3] *De Baptismo*, c. 18.

own view arose from his fear of the heinousness of sin after baptism, which we have already considered.

Origen, a few years later, bears ample testimony to the custom of infant baptism. "Infants," he says, "are baptized for the remission of sins;" and he gives the reason, that "none is free from pollution, though his life be but of one day on the earth." [1] He tells us also, that "the Church received a custom handed down from the Apostles, to give baptism even to infants." [2] Origen, it is observed by Wall, was born about 85 years after the Apostles, and his family had long been Christian.

The next father of note is Cyprian. In his day (circ. A. D. 250) there arose a question as to what day a child should be baptized. Fidus, an African bishop, wrote to him to inquire whether baptism, like circumcision, should be always deferred till the eighth day; or whether, if need required, it might be administered at once. An answer was returned by Cyprian and a council of sixty-six bishops. The unanimous judgment of the council was, that there was no need of such delay, for "the mercy and grace of God is to be denied to none that is born." [3] If anything could be an obstacle to persons obtaining the grace of baptism, they argue, adults would be rather hindered by their grievous sins. But if no one is so kept from baptism, how much less infants, who have no sins but such as they derived by inheritance from Adam. [4]

The foregoing testimonies all occur in the first century and a half from the Apostles. It would be easy, but in this brief sketch it is unnecessary, to carry the chain further down. For a moment we may notice the view taken by Gregory Nazianzen, as it seems remarkable and indeed unaccountable. He gives his judgment, that, in case of danger, baptism ought to be administered without delay; but if there be no danger, he advises that it be deferred for about three years. [5] Why deferred at all, if to be deferred but three years, he does not explain.

That, among the later fathers, baptism was not so universally administered in infancy as amongst ourselves, there does indeed seem reason to conjecture. The great potency which many attached to it, and the fear of the contraction of heinous sin after it, appear to have induced some to delay its administration. Thus

---

[1] Origen. *In Luc. Homil.* xiv.

[2] "Pro hoc (*i. e.* propter peccatum originis) Ecclesia ab Apostolis traditionem suscepit etiam parvulis baptismum dare."—Origen. *In Epist. ad Roman.* Lib. v. 9.

[3] "Universi potius judicavimus nulli homini nato misericordiam Dei et gratiam denegandam." — Cyprian. *Epist.* 64 *ad Fidum.*

[4] Ibid. See this part of the passage quoted under Art. ix. p. 240, note 4.

[5] Greg. Naz. *Orat.* xl. Tom. i. p. 658, A.

Constantine was not baptized till he was dying.[1]   St. Augustine,
though his mother was a Christian, did not receive baptism in his
infancy.   He himself deplores the delay, but says it was owing to
his mother's fear of the great temptations which seemed impending
over his boyhood, to which she thought it better " to expose the
clay, whence her son might afterwards be moulded, than the cast
when made." [2]

Such instances, resulting from peculiar scruples, are no proofs
that the custom of baptizing in infancy did not prevail from the
first.   Augustine himself clearly asserts, that the Church both
held the custom, and believed the efficacy of infant baptism, from
all times, and so universally, that it could only have received it
from the Apostles.[3]

---

[1] Euseb. *Vita Constantin.* Lib. iv. c.
62.

[2] August. *Confess.* Lib. i. c. 11.

[3] *De Baptismo, c. Donatistas*, Lib. iv.
c. 24, Tom. ix. p. 140, cited in the last
section.

ARTICLE XXVIII.

Of the Lord's Supper.

THE Supper of the Lord is not only a sign of the love that Christians ought to have among themselves one to another; but rather is a Sacrament of our Redemption by Christ's death: insomuch that to such as rightly, worthily, and with faith, receive the same, the Bread which we break is a partaking of the Body of Christ; and likewise the Cup of Blessing is a partaking of the Blood of Christ.

Transubstantiation (or the change of the substance of Bread and Wine) in the Supper of the Lord, cannot be proved by Holy Writ; but is repugnant to the plain words of Scripture, overthroweth the nature of a Sacrament, and hath given occasion to many superstitions.

The Body of Christ is given, taken, and eaten, in the Supper, only after an heavenly and spiritual manner. And the mean, whereby the Body of Christ is received and eaten in the Supper, is Faith.

The Sacrament of the Lord's Supper was not by Christ's ordinance reserved, carried about, lifted up, or worshipped.

De Cœna Domini.

CŒNA Domini non est tantum signum mutuæ benevolentiæ Christianorum inter sese, verum pctius est sacramentum nostræ per mortem Christi redemptionis. Atque adeo, rite, digne et cum fide sumentibus, panis quem frangimus est communicatio corporis Christi; similiter poculum benedictionis est communicatio sanguinis Christi.

Panis et vini transubstantiatio in Eucharistia ex sacris literis probari non potest; sed apertis Scripturæ verbis adversatur, sacramenti naturam evertit, et multarum superstitionum dedit occasionem.

Corpus Christi datur, accipitur et manducatur in Cœna tantum cœlesti et spirituali ratione. Medium autem, quo Corpus Christi accipitur et manducatur in Cœna, fides est.

Sacramentum Eucharistiæ ex institutione Christi non servabatur, circumferebatur, elevabatur, nec adorabatur.

Section I.— HISTORY.

THIS Article treats generally of the Lord's Supper, but more especially of the presence of Christ in that Sacrament, and of the mode in which He is received there. On this mysterious doctrine there have been four principal opinions: 1, Transubstantiation; 2, Consubstantiation; 3, The real spiritual presence; 4, The denial of any special presence altogether.

1. Transubstantiation is the doctrine of the Church of Rome. As stated by school-authors, and other more subtle reasoners among them, it means that in the Eucharist, after the words of consecration, the whole *substance* of the bread is converted into the *substance* of the Body of Christ, and the *substance* of the wine into the *substance* of His Blood; so that the bread and wine no

longer remain, but the Body and Blood of Christ are substituted in their places. This, however, is said to be true only of the *substance*, not of the *accidents*. The accidents (such as colour, shape, taste, smell, consistence, &c.) all remain unchanged. The substance, which is interior to, and not necessarily dependent on these external accidents, is that which is converted. Yet we are not to call it a mere spiritual change, (though some of their writers have allowed even this,) but the change is a real and miraculous conversion of the substance of the bread and wine into the very Body of Christ, which was born of the blessed Virgin and crucified on Calvary.

2. Consubstantiation is considered to be the doctrine of Luther and the Lutherans. It differs from transubstantiation, in that it does not imply a change in the substance of the elements. Those who hold this doctrine teach, that the bread remains bread, and the wine remains wine ; but that with, and by means of the consecrated elements, the true, natural Body and Blood of Christ are communicated to the recipients.

3. The doctrine of a real, spiritual presence is the doctrine of the English Church, and was the doctrine of Calvin, and of many foreign reformers. It teaches that Christ is really received by faithful communicants in the Lord's Supper; but that there is no gross or carnal, but only a spiritual and heavenly presence there ; not the less real, however, for being spiritual. It teaches, therefore, that the bread and wine are received naturally ; but the Body and Blood of Christ are received spiritually. " The result of which doctrine is this : it is bread, and it is Christ's Body. It is bread in substance, Christ in the Sacrament; and Christ is as really given to all that are truly disposed, as the symbols are : each as they can ; Christ as Christ can be given ; the bread and the wine as they can ; and to the same real purposes to which they were designed ; and Christ does as really nourish and sanctify the soul as the elements the body." [1]

4. The fourth opinion is that of Zuinglius, who taught that the Eucharist is a bare commemoration of the death of Christ, and that the bread and wine are mere symbols and tokens to remind us of his Body and Blood.

The subject on which we are entering is one which has produced folios of controversy; alas! what should have been for our peace becoming to us an occasion of falling. But a brief view is all that is here possible.

---

[1] Jer. Taylor, *On the Real Presence*, sect. 1. 4.

When we consider the language of the fathers, one or two cautions are necessary. Of course their words were not measured
and guarded, as ours have been in our times of trouble. Their
writings are often rhetorical, that we say not sometimes turgid.
They treat such questions as these practically, not argumentatively.
Now in such writings, it may be very difficult to tell the exact
intention of the writer, when subsequent ages have drawn subtle
distinctions.

Thus much we must premise as unquestionable. The whole primitive Church evidently believed in *a presence* of Christ in the Eucharist. All spoke of feeding there on Christ; eating His Body
and drinking His Blood. But then was it a spiritual presence or
a carnal presence? Did they teach a carnal eating and drinking of
Christ's natural Flesh and Blood? or did they intend a spiritual
manducation, — an eating spiritually and a drinking in by the soul
of the life-giving efficacy of the Body broken and the Blood shed?
Did they believe the bread and wine to be actually and literally
transmuted into Flesh and Blood? or did they think the bread and
wine still to remain bread and wine, though constituted Sacraments
of Christ, means in God's hand of conveying to us Christ's Body and
Blood, and so, after Christ's own example, to be called by the *name*
of His Body and Blood?

Here is the question; and it must be carefully noted. If there
were no other alternative, but that the fathers must have been either
Papists or Zuinglians, — must have held either a carnal presence, or
none at all; then we must perforce acknowledge that they believed
in a carnal presence, and were transubstantialists. For some presence they undoubtedly taught; some mode of feeding on Christ they
undeniably believed in. But another alternative is possible, and
has been acknowledged as possible, even by eminent scholastic and
Romanist divines. They may have believed a spiritual presence.
They may have thought, that the Eucharist conveyed Christ
really, and yet spiritually, to the recipient; and they may have
taught, that the soul was truly nourished by spiritually feeding on
His Flesh and Blood, as truly as the body is nourished by carnally
feeding upon bread and wine.

Whichever they held, a carnal or a spiritual presence, they
may easily have used language which would sound like the carnal
presence. There can be little doubt that their faith and feelings
inclined them to the mysterious, and there was no controversy,
no apparent need of caution. But then we may observe, that
one clear statement that the presence was spiritual, or that the

substance of the bread and wine remained, must outweigh statements innumerable, which merely sound like a belief in transubstantiation or in a carnal presence.   For the latter would naturally
occur where people believed in a *real* presence, and had never
learned the necessity of guarding their words, lest they should be
thought to teach a carnal and natural presence; but the former
could never come from the lips or pens of those who acknowledged
a literal change of the elements, and that the natural Body of the
Lord was actually eaten by all who communicate.

For instance, Roman Catholics will never say, that the bread
and wine remain unchanged, and that the feeding is *only* spiritual.
But Protestants, of many different communions, have freely declared
that Christ's " Body and Blood are verily and indeed taken." Nay !
it is acknowledged by them, that the Body of Christ then received
is the very Body that was born of the Virgin Mary, that was
crucified, dead, and buried.   For there is no other Body, no other
Blood of Christ.   Christ's Body is now glorified, but still it is the
same Body, though in its glorified condition.   It is not even
denied that we receive that Body really, substantially, corporally :
for although the word " *corporally* " seem opposed to " spiritually,"
yet it is not so of necessity.   And, as we acknowledge that it is a
Body which we receive, so we cannot deny its presence corporally,
i. e. after the manner of a Body.   Only, when we come to explain
ourselves, we say, that, though it be Christ's very Body we receive
in the Eucharist, and though we cannot deny even the word
corporal concerning it; yet as Christ's Body is now a spiritual
Body, so we expect a spiritual presence of that Body ; and we do
not believe, that we *naturally* and *carnally* eat that which is now
no longer carnal and natural ; but that we spiritually receive
Christ's Spiritual Body into our souls, and spiritually drink His
life-giving Blood with the lips of our spirit.[1]   Moreover, it has
been abundantly acknowledged, not only by our English divines, but
by Protestants of all sorts, that the elements, after consecration,
may be called by the name of those things which they represent.
But then we call them so, not because we believe them to have
lost their original nature, and to have ceased to be what they were,
but because, being hallowed to a new and higher purpose, they may
be called that which they are the means of communicating.

It was necessary to say thus much, that we might not be
startled by strong terms ; and so conclude at once that we had
found a doctrine, before it had yet entered even into men's dreams.

---

[1] See this excellently laid down by Bp. Taylor, *On the Real Presence*, sect. i. 9–11.

With this precaution, we shall readily see in the fathers abundant evidence that the carnal doctrine of transubstantiation had not risen in their days. Let us take one or two of the strongest expressions, and which, if not explained and qualified by other statements, would seem conclusive for transubstantiation and a natural presence.

St. Jerome and others speak of the clergy as making the Body of Christ.[1] Yet, as the words of consecration make the bread the Sacrament of Christ's Body, and so the means of conveying His Body to the communicant, and as it was an acknowledged mode of speech, and fully sanctioned by the language of our Lord, to call the consecrated bread by the name of that of which it was the type and Sacrament; it was not unnatural that the priest, by his consecration, should be said to make Christ's Body and Blood, even by those who believed no more than a spiritual and sacramental communication of them to the faithful.

St. Chrysostom writes, "When you behold the Lord sacrificed and lying, and the priest standing by the sacrifice and praying, and the congregation sprinkled with that precious Blood (καὶ πάντας ἐκείνῳ τῷ τιμίῳ φοινισσομένους αἵματι) . . . . are you not immediately transported to Heaven, and dismissing from your soul every fleshly thought, do you not with naked spirit and pure mind see the things which are in Heaven? Oh wonderful! Oh! the love of God! who, seated with the Father above, is held at that moment by the hands of all; and who gives Himself to those who desire to receive Him. And all see this by the eyes of faith."[2] "Behold thou seest Him, thou touchest Him, thou eatest Him. He gives Himself to thee, not only to see, but to touch, to eat, and to receive within . . . . How pure should he be who partakes of that sacrifice! the hand that divides His Flesh, the mouth filled with Spiritual fire, the tongue empurpled with His awful Blood!"[3] Now these expressions are so strong that even believers in transubstantiation could hardly use them without a figure. The Roman Catholics allow that the *accidents* of the bread and wine remain unchanged; and would hardly therefore in literal language

---

[1] "Absit ut de his quidquam sinistrum loquar, qui Apostolico gradui succedentes Christi Corpus sacro ore conficiunt, per quos et nos Christiani sumus; qui claves regni cœlorum habentes," &c. — Hieron. *Ad Heliodorum, Epist.* v. Tom. iv. part ii. p. 10.

[2] *De Sacerdot.* iii. § 4.

[3] Ἰδοὺ αὐτὸν ὁρᾷς, αὐτοῦ ἅπτῃ, αὐτὸν ἐσθίεις . . . αὐτὸς δὲ ἑαυτόν σοι δίδωσιν,

οὐκ ἰδεῖν μόνον, ἀλλὰ καὶ ἅψασθαι καὶ φαγεῖν καὶ λαβεῖν ἔνδον . . . τίνος οὖν οὐκ ἔδει καθαρώτερον εἶναι τὸν ταύτης ἀπολαύοντα τῆς θυσίας; ποίας ἡλιακῆς ἀκτῖνος τὴν χεῖρα τὴν ταύτην διατέμνουσαν τὴν σάρκα, τὸ στόμα τὸ πληρούμενον πυρὸς πνευματικοῦ, τὴν γλῶσσαν τὴν φοινισσομένην αἵματι φρικωδεστάτῳ. — Chrys. *Hom.* 83 *in Matt.* c. 26.

speak of the tongue as assuming the purple colour of Christ's
Blood. But hyperbolic expressions are common with St. Chrysostom and his contemporaries; and they use such language, that
they may exalt the dignity of the blessed Sacrament; that they
may induce communicants to approach it with devotion and reverence; that they may turn their minds from the visible objects
before them to those invisible objects which they represent, and
which as St. Chrysostom says, they may " see by the eye of faith."

Still more remarkable perhaps are the expressions used by
others of the Greek, especially the later Greek fathers, concerning the change (μεταβολὴ, μεταστοιχείωσις) in the Sacraments. So
Gregory Nyssen says, " These things He gives by virtue of the
benediction upon it, transmuting the nature of the things which
appear."[1] And Theophylact (the last of the Greek fathers, A. D.
1077), " Therefore the merciful God, condescending to us, preserves the form of bread and wine, but transforms them into the
virtue of His Flesh and Blood."[2] Those who translate μεταστοι-
χειοῦν by *transelementare*, think that we have here the very word
made use of, which exactly answers to the Roman Catholic doctrine of transubstantiation, namely, a change of the elements into
something different from their original substance. Yet first of all
transelementare is not certainly, nor probably, a right translation.[3]
Secondly, Gregory Nyssen is speaking not only of a change in the
Eucharist, but in the Sacraments generally; and whatever sanctifying efficacy may have been attributed to the water in baptism,
no change of its substance was ever believed to take place.
Thirdly, Theophylact only says that the elements are changed into
the *virtue* or *efficacy*, not into the *substance* of Christ's Flesh and
Blood, — a very notable distinction. Fourthly, he uses the same
word (μεταστοιχείωσις) of changes very unlike transubstantiation, *e. g.*
the change of our bodies to the state of incorruption, and the change
that is made in the faithful, when they are united to Christ.[4]
Lastly, we shall find abundant proof from Greek fathers, centuries
before Theophylact, to show that a conversion of substance was

---

[1] ταῦτα δὲ δίδωσι τῇ τῆς εὐλογίας δυνάμει
πρὸς ἐκεῖνο μεταστοιχειώσας τῶν φαινομένων
τὴν φύσιν. — Gregor. Nyssen. *In Orat.
Catechet.*

[2] Διὰ τοῦτο συγκαταβαίνων ἡμῖν ὁ φιλάν-
θρωπος· τὸ μὲν εἶδος ἄρτου καὶ οἴνου φυλάτ-
τει· εἰς δύναμιν δὲ σαρκὸς καὶ αἵματος με-
ταστοιχεῖοι.—Theophyl. *In Evangel. Marc.*
cap. cxiv.

[3] Suidas has μεταστοιχείουσα, μετασχημα-
τίζουσα, μεταπλάττουσα. Suicer argues

at length that *transelementare* will not
properly express its sense. (See Suicer, ii. pp. 363, 364.) Jer. Taylor (*On
the Real Presence*, sect. xii. num. 5) adduces the words of Suarez, the learned
Jesuit, in acknowledgment that μεταστοιχείωσις does not properly convey the
meaning of *transubstantiation.*

[4] Theophyl. *In Luc.* xxiv. *et in Joh.* vi
apud Jer. Taylor, *ubi supra.*

not believed by the early Greek Church; and therefore, that Theophylact's transelementation must have meant something else, or that he himself must have adopted comparatively modern views.

The same observations apply to the passages cited from St. Cyril of Jerusalem, where he speaks of Christ's changing the water into wine, and then adds, " Let us therefore with full assurance receive Christ's Body and Blood ; for His Body is given to thee in the figure of bread, and His Blood in the figure of wine." [1] But here St. Cyril happily explains himself; for soon after he speaks of the Capharnaite Jews as offended at our Lord's sayings in John vi. 53. And this, he says, was from their carnal interpretation of His words: " They, not receiving His saying spiritually, being offended went backward, thinking that He invited them to the eating of flesh." [2] He then compares the Eucharist to the shew-bread, and says that, " as the bread is fitted for the body, so the Word for the soul. Look not therefore as on bare bread and wine, for they are, according to the Lord's saying, His Flesh and Blood." [3] The context plainly shows the conversion to be spirit-ual, not as the Jews had understood our Lord, as indicating a lit-eral σαρκοφαγία, or banquet upon flesh.

There is a famous passage, which the Roman Catholic contro-versialists coupled with the last from St. Cyril, and much insisted on, as plainly in their favour. It comes from the tract *De Cœna Domini*, in former times attributed to St. Cyprian, but which the Benedictine editors assign to Arnoldus, of Bona Vallis, a contem-porary of St. Bernard. It speaks of the bread as " changed, not in form, but in nature." [4] The words of our own reformer shall explain that, even if the language were (as it is not) St. Cyprian's, it would not prove him a supporter of transubstantiation. " The bread is changed, not in shape nor substance, but in nature, as Cyprian truly saith ; not meaning that the natural substance of bread is clean gone, but that by God's word there is added

---

[1] ἐν τύπῳ γὰρ ἄρτου δίδοταί σοι σῶμα, καὶ ἐν τύπῳ οἴνου δίδοταί σοι τὸ αἷμα. — Cyril. Hieros. *Catec. Mystagog.* IV. 1.

[2] ἐκεῖνοι μὴ ἀκηκοότες πνευματικῶς τῶν λεγομένων, σκανδαλισθέντες, ἀπῆλθον εἰς τὰ ὀπίσω, νομίζοντες ὅτι ἐπὶ σαρκοφαγίαν αὐτοὺς προτρέπεται. — Ibid.

[3] Μὴ πρόσεχε οὖν ὡς ψιλοῖς τῷ ἄρτῳ καὶ τῷ οἴνῳ· σῶμα γὰρ καὶ αἷμα Χριστοῦ κατὰ τὴν δεσποτικὴν τυγχάνει ἀπόφασιν. — *Cat. Myst.* IV. 2.

[4] " Panis iste, quem Dominus discipu-lis porrigebat, non effigie, sed natura, mutatus, omnipotentia Verbi factus est caro." — *De Cœna Domini.* The tract is

usually printed in the Appendix of the works of Cyprian. In the Oxford edi-tion it is in Appendix, p. 39, and the above passage, p. 40. In the edition of Venice, 1729, it is App. p. xcix. There is also a famous passage from St. Am-brose, *De Myst* IX. § 52, where he speaks of Christ's words as changing the prop-erties of the elements: " valebit Chrisii Sermo ut species mutet elementorum ; " and again, mutare naturas. The answer in the text to the passage from the Pseudo-Cyprian equally applies to this from St. Ambrose. See also Bp. Cosin, *Hist. of Transubstant.* ch. VI. 14.

thereto another higher property, nature and condition, far passing the nature and condition of common bread, that is to say, that the bread doth show unto us, as the same Cyprian saith, that we be partakers of the Spirit of God, and most purely joined unto Christ, and spiritually fed with His Flesh and Blood: so that now the said mystical bread is both a corporal food for the body, and a spiritual food for the soul." [1]

We must not omit one passage from St. Hilary, which contains certainly some startling expressions. He is arguing against heretics, who held that the Unity of the Father and the Son was unity of *will*, not unity of nature. He quotes against them John xvii. 21, 23: " That they may be one, even as We are one: I in them, and Thou in Me, that they may be made perfect in one." And he contends, that the unity of the Father and the Son must be an unity of nature, not merely of will; inasmuch as the indwelling of Christ in His people is not by concord of will, but by verity of nature; for He took the nature of our flesh, on purpose that He might dwell in us according to that human nature; and by His human nature He dwelleth in us and we in Him. Hence our union with Him is by unity of nature, *i. e.* human nature. So in like manner, His union with the Father is by unity of nature, *i. e.* Divine nature. In the course of this argument he says, " If Christ therefore really took flesh of our body, and He is truly that Man who was born of Mary, and we truly under the mystery receive His Flesh, by means of which we shall be one; for the Father is in Him and He in us; what room is there for mere unity of will, when the natural property effected by the Sacrament, is the Sacrament of perfect unity ? Christ Himself says concerning the truth of His nature in us, *My flesh is meat indeed, and my blood is drink indeed. Whoso eateth my flesh, and drinketh my blood dwelleth in me, and I in him.* Concerning the truth of His Body and Blood there is no room for doubt ; for now by our Lord's witness and our own faith, it is truly Flesh, and truly Blood. And these received, and taken in by us, make that we be in Christ and Christ in us." [2]

[1] Cranmer, *Remains*, II. p. 340; *Defence of the Catholic Doctrine*, Bk. II. ch. XI.

[2] " Quisquis ergo naturaliter Patrem in Christo negabit neget prius non naturaliter vel se in Christo, vel Christum sibi inesse; quia in Christo Pater, et Christus in nobis, unum in his esse nos faciunt. Si vere igitur carnem corporis nostri Christus assumpsit, et vere homo ille, qui ex Maria natus fuit, Christus est, nosque vere sub mysterio carnem corporis sui sumimus; (et per hoc unum erimus, quia Pater in eo est, et Ille in nobis ;) quomodo voluntatis unitas aperitur, cum naturalis per sacramentum proprietas, perfectæ sit sacramentum unitatis: De naturali in nobis Christi veritate ipse ait : *Caro mea vere est esca, et sanguis meus vere est potus. Qui edit carnem meam,*

The passage, strong as it is, does not stagger those who admit a true but spiritual presence of Christ's Body in the receiving of the Eucharist, and a true but spiritual union of Christians to the human nature of their Lord. " For as concerning the word *truly*," they say, " it setteth not lively forth a real and substantial presence ; for Christ is truly in all His faithful people, and they truly eat His Flesh and drink His Blood, and yet not by a real and corporal, but by a spiritual and effectual presence." [1] " And although he saith that Christ is naturally in us, yet he saith also that we be naturally in Him. And nevertheless in so saying, he meant not of the natural and corporal presence of the substance of Christ's Body and of ours ; for as our bodies be not after that sort within His Body, so is not His Body after that sort within our bodies . . . And as the union between Christ and us in baptism is spiritual . . . so likewise our union with Christ in His holy Supper is spiritual . . . and therefore Hilarius, speaking there of both the Sacraments, maketh no difference between our union with Christ in baptism and our union with Him in His holy Supper." [2]

Now, although such passages admit of an explanation, whether we adopt the transubstantialist theory or the doctrine of a true but spiritual presence in the Eucharist ; yet it must be conceded that, if all the language of the fathers was similar to the above-quoted sentences, there would be just reason to suspect that, from the first, transubstantiation, or something near akin to it, was the doctrine of the Church. But it is easy to bring a chain of testimonies, from the very earliest ages through many centuries, which cannot be interpreted to mean transubstantiation, or a carnal presence, but which declare, though plainly for a real, yet as plainly for a spiritual feeding upon Christ.

The apostolical fathers, for the most part, speak in terms so general, that it is often almost doubtful, whether they speak of the Eucharist, or of that spiritual feeding upon Christ as the bread of life, which all allow to be possible, even without the Eucharist. Thus

---

et bibit sanguinem meum, in me manet, et ejo in eo. De veritate carnis et sanguinis non relictus est ambigendi locus : nunc enim et ipsius Domini professione et fide nostra, vere caro, et vere sanguis est. Et hæc accepta et hausta efficiunt ut nos in Christo et Christus in nobis sit." — Hilar. *De Trinitate*, Lib. viii. § 13, p. 222. Edit. Benedict.

[1] Cranmer's *Answer to Gardiner*, Works, iii. p. 254.

[2] Cranmer's *Defence of the Catholic Doctrine, &c.* Works, ii. pp. 406, 407. N. B. Just before the passage above quoted, Hilary had spoken of the union of Christians to Christ in baptism, as he speaks afterwards of their union in the Eucharist : "Docet Apostolus ex natura sacramentorum esse hanc fidelium unitatem, ad Galatas scribens, *Quotquot enim in Christo baptizati estis, Christum induistis*," &c. — *De Trin.* Lib. viii. p. 218. Ed. Ben.

Ignatius, " I delight not in the food of corruption, nor in the pleasures of this life ; I desire the bread of God, which is the Flesh of Christ, and His Blood I desire as drink, which is love incorruptible." [1] Again, " Let no one be deceived ; if any one be not within the altar, he is deprived of the bread of God." [2] His high esteem for the grace of this Sacrament he shows in general expressions, e. g. " breaking one and the same bread, which is the medicine of immortality, our antidote that we die not, but live forever in Christ Jesus." [3] One passage in this early father alludes to certain sects of the Gnostics or Docetæ, who not believing that the Saviour had ever taken real human flesh, refused to receive the Eucharist, because they would not acknowledge it to be the Body of Christ. " They abstain from the Eucharist and public prayer, because they confess not the Eucharist to be the Flesh of our Saviour Jesus Christ, which suffered for our sins, and which the Father of His goodness raised from the dead." [4] From which we may fairly conclude, that the fathers called the consecrated bread the Body of Christ, and that some early heretics did not admit the language, or perhaps even the Sacrament, because they disbelieved in the existence of Christ's Body. But even Bellarmine allows, that the question between Ignatius and the heretics was not the doctrine of the Eucharist, but the doctrine of the Incarnation.[5] Whatever may have been the belief of the Church as to the *mode* of receiving Christ's Body in the Eucharist, the heretics would have been equally likely to reject the Eucharist, as not acknowledging that Christ had a body at all. For the Eucharist, which symbolizes, and is the means of receiving His Body, presupposes its reality. Another passage from Ignatius is as follows : " Hasten therefore to partake of the one Eucharist ; for there is but one Flesh of our Lord Jesus Christ, and one cup for the unity of His Blood ; one altar, as also one bishop," [6] &c. Here the exhortation is to avoid schism, partaking of the one Eucharist, where is exhibited to us the oneness of the Saviour we receive, and so the unity of the Church.

[1] Ignat. *Ad Roman.* VII. The passage is in the Syriac.
[2] Ignat. *Ad. Ephes.* V.
[3] *Ad Ephes.* XX.
[4] *Ad Smyrn.* VII. The passage is not in the longer epistles, but it is in the shorter (esteemed the genuine) epistles of Ignatius, and it is cited by Theodoret (*Dial.* 3) and is maintained to be genuine by Cotelerius, Tom. II. p. 37, note *in loc*. The Greek is εὐχαριστίας καὶ προσευχῆς ἀπέχονται, διὰ τὸ μὴ ὁμολογεῖν τὴν εὐχα-

ριστίαν σάρκα εἶναι τοῦ Σωτῆρος ἡμῶν Ἰησοῦ Χριστοῦ, τὴν ὑπὲρ ἁμαρτιῶν ἡμῶν παθοῦσαν, ἣν χρηστότητι ὁ Πατὴρ ἐγειρεν.
[5] *De Eucharistia,* I. 1, cited by Bp. Cosin, *Hist. of Transubstantiation,* ch. VI. 11.
[6] Σπουδάσατε οὖν μιᾷ εὐχαριστίᾳ χρῆσθαι · μία γὰρ σὰρξ τοῦ Κυρίου ἡμῶν Ἰησοῦ Χριστοῦ, καὶ ἓν ποτήριον εἰς ἕνωσ.ν τοῦ αἵματος αὐτοῦ, ἓν θυσιαστήριον ὡς ε'ς ἐπίσκοπος κ. τ. λ. — *Ad Philadelph.* IV.

Justin Martyr describes the Eucharistic feast to the heathen emperor.   He speaks first of the bread and wine as blessed by the presiding presbyter; and then says, " This food is called by us Eucharist, which no one is allowed to take, but he who believes our
doctrines to be true, and has been baptized in the laver of regeneration, for the remission of sins, and lives as Christ has enjoined.
For we take not these as common bread and common drink.   For
like as our Saviour Jesus Christ, having been made flesh by the
Word of God, had flesh and blood for our salvation, so we are
taught that this food, which is blessed by the prayer of the Word
that cometh from Him, by conversion of which our flesh and blood
are nourished, is the Flesh and Blood of Him, the Incarnate Jesus." [1]
There is manifestly in this passage what may be called High Eucharistic doctrine.   Justin was plainly no Zuinglian.   The Christians
of his day took not the consecrated elements " for common bread
and common wine."   But, if Justin was no Sacramentarian,
neither was he a transubstantialist.   Whereas he says it is not
common bread, he evidently believes it to be yet *bread;* otherwise
he would naturally have left out the epithet *common*, and have
said, that they esteemed it no longer bread *at all*.   Moreover, he
speaks of the elements as changed into the nourishment of our
flesh and blood.   But he would never have said this had he believed them to have literally become the unchangeable and incorruptible Body of the Lord.   It is evident, therefore, that he held
no change in the elements, but a Sacramental change; although
he undoubtedly declares, that in the Eucharist the Christians were
taught that there was a reception of the Body and Blood of Christ.
Dr. Waterland argues, that consubstantiation is as much excluded
by this passage as transubstantiation,[2] though Bishop Kaye appears
to admit that it sounds not unlike the former.[3]   Still he has justly
added, that in the Dialogue with Trypho Justin states the bread
to be in commemoration of Christ's Body, and the cup of His

---

[1] οὐ γὰρ ὡς κοινὸν ἄρτον, οὐδὲ κοινὸν
πόμα ταῦτα λαμβάνομεν, ἀλλ᾽ ὃν τρόπον
διὰ λόγου Θεοῦ σαρκοποιηθεὶς Ἰησοῦς
Χριστὸς ὁ Σωτὴρ ἡμῶν, καὶ σάρκα· καὶ
αἷμα ὑπὲρ σωτηρίας ἡμῶν ἔσχεν, οὕτως
καὶ τὴν δι᾽ εὐχῆς λόγου τοῦ παρ᾽ αὐτοῦ
εὐχαρισθεῖσαν τροφὴν ἐξ ἧς αἷμα καὶ σάρκες
κατὰ μεταβολὴν τρέφονται ἡμῶν, ἐκείνου τοῦ
σαρκοποιηθέντος Ἰησοῦ καὶ σάρκα καὶ αἷμα
ἐδιδάχθημεν εἶναι. — Justin. *Apol.* I. p.
98.

  " As it appears to me, Justin in this
passage does not intend to compare the
manner, in which Jesus Christ being

made flesh by the Word of God hath
flesh and blood for our sake, with that
in which the bread and wine . . . . became the Flesh and Blood of Christ;
but only to say that, as Christians were
taught that Christ had flesh and blood,
so were they also taught that the bread
and wine in the Eucharist are the Body
and Blood of Christ; ὃν τρόπον is merely
equivalent to *as*." — Bishop Kaye, *Justin Martyr,* pp. 87, 88, note.

[2] Waterland, *On the Eucharist,* ch. **VII**

[3] Bp. Kaye's *Justin Martyr,* p. 74.

Blood ;[1] and in another place applies to them the expression " dry
and liquid food ; "[2] and such language would scarcely have been
used by a believer in the natural, though the language of the former passage might be readily adopted by a believer in the spiritual
presence.

Our next witness is Irenæus. " As the bread from the earth,
receiving the invocation of God, is no longer *common bread*, but the
Eucharist, consisting of *two* things, *earthly* and *heavenly ;* so also
our bodies, receiving the Eucharist, are no longer corruptible,
but have hope of eternal resurrection."[3]   Here we have evidently
the substance of the bread remaining, still an *earthly* element.
Yet it is no longer *common* bread, for by consecration there is a
heavenly or spiritual grace united to it, which makes it not mere
bread, but the Eucharist.

Irenæus had to contend against the Gnostics, who denied the
reality of the Body of Christ.   In more than one place he argues,
from the real substantial character of the Eucharistic elements,
that the Flesh and Blood of Christ, of which they were the representatives, must be substantial and real.   This will make his language sometimes sound as though he believed in a natural presence of that Flesh and Blood ; yet, if we remember his object and
attentively observe his words, we shall think otherwise.   " That
cup," he says, " which is a creature, He recognized to be His
Blood which is shed, with which He imbues (δεύει) our blood ;
and the bread which is a creature, He affirmed to be His own
Body, by which our bodies grow.   When, therefore, both the mingled cup and the created bread receive the word of God, and become the Eucharist of Christ's Blood and Body, and by them the
substance of our flesh grows and consists, how can they say, that
the flesh is not capable of the gift of God, namely of life eternal,
when it is fed by Christ's Body and Blood, and is a member of
Him ? "[4]

In a fragment edited by Pfaff, we have a clear explanation of
Irenæus's view, that, by the Holy Spirit descending on the Eucharist, the Elements become so the Body and Blood of Christ, that,
though they yet remain *figures* or *emblems*, still the partakers of

---

[1] περὶ τοῦ ἄρτου ὃν παρέδωκεν ἡμῖν ὁ
ἡμέτερος Χριστὸς ποιεῖν εἰς ἀνάμνησιν τοῦ τε
σωματοποιήσασθαι, κ. τ. λ. — *Dialog.* p. 296.

[2] τῆς τροφῆς αὐτῶν ξηρᾶς καὶ ὑγρᾶς, ἐν
ᾗ καὶ τοῦ πάθους ὃ πέπονθε δι᾿ αὐτοῦ ὁ
Θεὸς τοῦ Θεοῦ μέμνηται. — *Dial.* p. 345.

[3] Ὡς γὰρ ἀπὸ γῆς ἄρτος προσλαμβα-
νόμενος τὴν ἔκκλησιν τοῦ Θεοῦ, οὐκέτι

κοινὸς ἄρτος ἐστὶν, ἀλλ᾿ εὐχαριστία, ἐκ δύο
πραγμάτων συνεστηκυῖα · οὕτως καὶ τὰ
σώματα ἡμῶν μεταλαμβάνοντα τῆς εὐχαριστίας μηκέτι εἶναι φθαρτά, τὴν ἐλπίδα
τῆς εἰς αἰῶνας ἀναστάσεως ἔχοντα. — Irenæ.
Lib. iv. 32 (Lib. iv. 18, Bened.)

[4] *Adv. Hær.* v. 2.   Of this passage we
may observe, that if Irenæus had meant

those emblems obtain pardon and eternal life.[1]   In another fragment quoted from him by Œcumenius, we read, that during persecution some slaves had informed against their masters, having misinterpreted the language used concerning the Eucharist, and so supposing that their masters fed on human flesh. This, Irenæus says, arose from their having heard the divine Communion called the Blood and Body of Christ; "and they, *thinking it was in reality flesh and blood*, gave information accordingly."[2]   The inference obviously is, that Irenæus did not think the bread and wine to have become really Flesh and Blood. So he, like Justin Martyr, is a witness against the Roman doctrine, and yet perhaps, as Waterland observes, still more against the mere figurists or memorialists. For it is certain, that he believed the Body and Blood of Christ to be verily and indeed taken in the Eucharist; but still he gives no indication of a belief in a change of the elements, acknowledging them to be *emblems* (ἀντίτυπα), and not thinking that those who partook of them, were indeed feeding upon flesh and blood.[3]

Tertullian says, " The petition, *Give us this day our daily bread*, may be spiritually interpreted. For Christ is our bread. I, said He, *am the bread of Life:* and just before, *The Bread is the Word of the Living God, who came down from Heaven:* and also because His Body is understood in Bread, *This is My Body.* (*Tum quod et Corpus Ejus in pane censetur, Hoc est Corpus Meum.*) Therefore, by asking our daily bread, we seek perpetuity in Christ and to be undivided from His Body."[4]   Again he writes, " Our body is fed with the Body and Blood of Christ, that our soul may be fattened of God."[5]   He speaks of Christ, as *calling* bread His Body.[6] " Bread," again we read, "by which He represents His very Body."[7]   So also, " Having taken bread and distributed it to

that the elements were changed in substance into Christ's Body and Blood, he would never have spoken of them as nourishing our bodies, which implies the idea of digestion, acknowledged to be blasphemy.

[1] καὶ ἐνταῦθα τὴν πρόσφοραν τελέσαντες ἐκκαλοῦμεν τὸ Πνεῦμα τὸ ἅγιον, ὅπως ἀποφήνῃ τὴν θυσίαν ταύτην καὶ τὸν ἄρτον σῶμα τοῦ Χριστοῦ· ἵνα οἱ μεταλάβοντες τούτων τῶν ἀντιτύπων τῆς ἀφέσεως τῶν ἁμαρτιῶν καὶ τῆς ζωῆς αἰωνίου τύχωσιν. — Irenæi *Scripta Anecdota*, fragm. 2, p. 29.

[2] οἱ δοῦλοι οὗτοι, μὴ ἔχοντες πῶς τὸ τοῖς ἀναγκάζουσι καθ᾽ ἡδονὴν ἐρεῖν, παρ᾽ ὅσον ἤκουον τῶν δεσποτῶν, τὴν θείαν μετάληψιν αἷμα καὶ σῶμα εἶναι Χριστοῦ, αὐτοὶ νομίσαντες τῷ ὄντι αἷμα καὶ σάρκα εἶναι, τοῦτο

ἐξεῖπον τοῖς ἐκζητοῦσι. — *Fragmentum ab Œcumenio in Comment. ad* 1 *Petri Epist.* cap. 3, p. 498, *allegatum ;* Irenæi *Op.* Grabe, p. 469.

[3] There is an excellent chapter in Beaven's *Irenæus* on the subject of Irenæus's statements concerning the Eucharist.

[4] *De Oratione*, c. 6.

[5] " Caro Corpore et Sanguine Christi vescitur, ut et anima de Deo saginetur." — *De Resur. Carn.* c. 8.

[6] " Christus . . . panem corpus suum appellans." — *Adv. Judæ.* c. 10.

[7] " Panem quo ipsum Corpus suum repræsentat." — *Adv. Marcion.* Lib. I. c. 14.

" Repræsento — to exhibit as present;

His disciples, He made it His body by saying, This is my Body,
i. e. the figure of My Body. But there would be no figure, if
there were no true Body. A mere phantom, without substance,
would admit no figure." [1] In the last passage, he is arguing, like
Ignatius and Irenæus, against those who denied a Body to our Lord.
Now surely this testimony is plain. The bread is not really
Christ's Body, but a figure of His Body, with which however He
is pleased to recall (*repræsentare*) His Body to His followers. In
this bread His Body is understood (*censetur*) or accounted ; and so
our bodies are fed with His Body, that our souls may be nourished
of God. Though the bread then is a figure ; yet the feeding on
Christ is not merely figurative, but real, and spiritual. He is the
Bread of life ; and by feeding on Him we receive perpetual and
indivisible union to His Body.

Clement of Alexandria, of the same date with Tertullian, says,
" The Blood of the Lord is twofold: the one natural or carnal,
whereby we are redeemed from corruption ; the other spiritual,
whereby we are anointed ; and this is to drink the Blood of Jesus,
to be partakers of the Lord's incorruptibility. Also the Spirit is
the 'power of the Word, as the Blood is of the flesh." [2] He then
goes on to speak of the wine mingled with water ; and says, that
the mixture of the drink and of the Logos is called the Eucharist
— " Blessed and glorious grace, by which those, who partake in
faith, are sanctified both body and soul." " Christ," he says a little
farther on, " partook of wine ; for He was a man. He blessed it
too, saying, *Take, drink, this is My Blood*, the blood of the vine.
He thus calls allegorically the Word, who was poured forth for
many for the remission of sins, the sacred stream of gladness . . . .
He showed that what He blessed was wine, by saying to His disciples, *I will not drink of the fruit of this vine till I drink it with you
in My Father's Kingdom.*" [3] Clement was a very mystical writer ;

ὑποτυπόω, præsentem esse facio, ob oculos pono, refero. Repræsentare dicuntur
pictores. Item oratores graphice quip-
piam describentes." — Facciolati.
[1] " Acceptum panem et distributum
discipulis, corpus illum suum fecit, Hoc
est Corpus Meum, dicendo, id est, figura
Corporis Mei. Figura autem non fuisset. nisi veritatis esset Corpus. Cæterum
vacua res, quod est phantasma, figuram
capere non posset." — *Adv. Marcion.* Lib.
iv. c. 40.
[2] Διττὸν δὲ τὸ αἷμα τοῦ Κυρίου · τὸ μὲν
γάρ ἐστιν αὐτοῦ σαρκικὸν, ᾧ τῆς φθορᾶς
λελυτρώμεθα · τὸ δὲ πνευματικὸν, τουτέστιν
ᾧ κεχρίσμεθα · καὶ τοῦτ' ἐστι πιεῖν το αἷμα

τοῦ Ἰησοῦ, τῆς Κυριακῆς μεταλαμβάνειν
ἀφθαρσίας · ἰσχὺς δὲ τοῦ Λόγου τὸ πνεῦμα, ὡς
αἷμα σαρκός. — *Pædag.* Lib. ii. c. 2, p.
177.
[3] Εὖ γὰρ ἴστε, μετέλαβεν οἴνου καὶ αὐτὸς ·
καὶ γὰρ ἄνθρωπος καὶ αὐτός. Καὶ εὐλόγησέν
γε τὸν οἶνον, εἰπὼν, λάβετε, πίετε · τοῦτό
μου ἐστὶ τὸ αἷμα, αἷμα τῆς ἀμπέλου · τὸν
Λόγον, τὸν περὶ πολλῶν ἐκχυννόμενον εἰς
ἄφεσιν ἁμαρτιῶν, εὐφροσύνης ἅγιον ἀλλη-
γορεῖ νᾶμα . . . ὅτι δὲ οἶνος ἦν τὸ εὐλογη-
θὲν, ἀπέδειξε πάλιν, πρὸς τοὺς μαθητὰς
λέγων. Οὐ μὴ πίω ἐκ τοῦ γεννήματος τῆς
ἀμπέλου ταύτης, μέχρις ἂν πίω αὐτὸ μεθ'
ὑμῶν ἐν τῇ βασιλείᾳ τοῦ Πατρὸς ἡμῶν. —
Pædag. Lib. ii. c. 2, p. 186.

but we can discern this much at least from the foregoing passages : that, whilst he attached great spiritual blessings to the Eucharist, he yet believed the substance of the wine to remain in it, and the Blood received therein to be spiritual, not natural Blood.

In Origen, as in his predecessors, we perceive at the same time deep reverence for the Body of Christ received in the Eucharist, and yet a belief that the reception of that Body was spiritual and heavenly, not carnal and natural.   " When ye receive the Body of the Lord, with all caution and reverence ye preserve it ; lest any, the least thereof, be lost, or any portion of the consecrated gift pass away." [1]   " Acknowledge that they are figures, which are written in the sacred volumes ; therefore as spiritual, not carnal, examine and understand what is said.   For, if as carnal you receive them, they hurt, not nourish you.   Not only in the old Testament is there a letter which killeth ; but also in the new there is a letter which killeth him who does not spiritually consider it. For, if according to the letter you receive this saying, *Except ye eat My Flesh and drink My Blood,* that letter killeth." [2]

St. Cyprian, in his 63d Epistle, is very full on the subject of the cup in the sacrament.   He is writing there against the Aquarii, who rejected wine as evil, and so used water at the communion. He argues that the tradition of the Lord should be preserved ; and that nothing should be done but what Christ did before : that therefore " the Cup, which is offered in commemoration cf Him, be offered mixed with wine.   For whereas Christ says, *I am the true Vine,* the Blood of Christ is surely wine, not water.   Nor can it appear that in the cup is His Blood, with which we are redeemed, if wine be absent, by which Christ's Blood is represented." [3]   There is much there to the same purpose.   But these words alone prove, that Cyprian, whilst calling the consecrated wine the Blood of Christ, and believing (as is abundantly evident through his writings everywhere) that there was in the Sacrament a real partaking

---

[1] " Cum suscipitis Corpus Domini, cum omni cautela et veneratione servatis, ne ex eo parum quid decidat, ne consecrati muneris aliquid dilabatur." — *In Exod. Hom.* xiii.

[2] " Agnoscite quia figuræ sunt quæ in divinis voluminibus scripta sunt, et ideo tanquam spiritales et non tanquam carnales examinate et intelligite quæ dicuntur. Si enim quasi carnales ista suscipitis, lædunt vos et non alunt. Est enim et in evangeliis litera quæ occidit. Non solum in veteri Testamento occidens litera deprehenditur ; est et in novo Testamento litera quæ occidat eum qui non

spiritaliter quæ dicuntur adverterit. Si enim secundum literam sequaris hoc ipsum quod dictum est : *Nisi manducaveritis carnem meam, et biberitis sanguinem meum,* occidit litera." — *In Levit. Hom.* vii. n. 5.

[3] " Ut calix, qui in commemoratione Ejus offertur, mixtus vino offeratur. Nam cum dicat Christus ; *Ego sum vitis vera ;* sanguis Christi, non aqua est utique, sed vinum. Nec potest videri sanguis Ejus, quo redemti et vivificati sumus, esse in calice, quando vinum desit calici quo Christi sanguis ostenditur." — Cyprian. *Epist.* lxiii. ; *Cœcilio Fratri,* p. 148. Oxf.

of Christ, yet considered that there was still remaining the substance of the wine; for, says he, "The Blood of Christ is wine," *i. e.* that cup which we drink, acknowledging it to be the Blood of Christ, is wine. Moreover, he considered the wine to be a representation or means of showing Christ's Blood, and the cup to be offered in commemoration of Him.

St. Athanasius, quoting John vi. 16–63, observes, "Christ distinguished between the flesh and the spirit, that believing not only what was apparent, but also what was invisible, they might know that what He spake was not carnal but spiritual. For to how many could His Body have sufficed for food that this might be for nourishment to all the world? But therefore He made mention of His ascension into heaven, that He might draw them from understanding it corporally; and that they might understand that the Flesh He spoke of was heavenly food from above, and spiritual nourishment given them by Him. *For*, says He, *the things that I speak unto you they are spirit and they are life.* Which is as though He had said, My Body, which is shown and given for the world, shall be given in food, that it may be spiritually distributed to every one, and become to each a preservative unto the resurrection of eternal life." [1]

We have already heard St. Cyril of Jerusalem, the contemporary of Athanasius, declare his belief, that the Body and Blood of Christ are given us under the figure of bread and wine, and that the Capharnaites were misled by interpreting our Lord carnally, as though He meant a banquet upon flesh, not, as He ought to be interpreted, spiritually. [2] So, in a former lecture, speaking of the unction, which was given with baptism, figuring the anointing of the Holy Ghost, he writes, "Beware of supposing this bare unction. For as the bread of the Eucharist, after the invocation of the Holy Ghost, is no longer mere bread (οὐκ ἔτι ἄρτος λιτὸς), but the Body of Christ; so also this holy ointment is no longer simple ointment, nor common, after the invocation, but the gift of Christ. . . . While thy body is anointed with the visible ointment, thy soul is

---

[1] τὸ πνεῦμα πρὸς τὰ κατὰ σάρκα διέστειλεν, ἵνα μὴ μόνον τὸ φαινόμενον, ἀλλὰ καὶ τὸ ἀόρατον αὐτοῦ πιστεύσαντες μάθωσιν, ὅτι καὶ ἃ λέγει οὐκ ἐστι σαρκικὰ ἀλλὰ πνευματικά· πόσοις γὰρ ἤρκει τὸ σῶμα πρὸς βρῶσιν, ἵνα καὶ τοῦ κόσμου παντὸς τοῦτο τροφὴ γένηται; ἀλλὰ διὰ τοῦτο τῆς εἰς οὐρανοὺς διαβάσεως ἐμνημόνευσε τοῦ υἱοῦ τοῦ ἀνθρώπου, ἵνα τῆς σωματικῆς ἐννοίας αὐτοὺς ἀφελκύσῃ καὶ λοιπὸν τὴν εἰρημένην σάρκα βρῶσιν ἄνωθεν οὐράνιον, καὶ πνευματικὴν τροφὴν παρ' αὐτοῦ διδομένην μάθωσιν. ἃ γὰρ λελάληκα, φησὶν, ὑμῖν πνεῦμα ἐστι καὶ ζωή. ἴσον τῷ εἰπεῖν, τὸ μὲν δεικνύμενον καὶ διδόμενον ὑπὲρ τοῦ κόσμου δοθήσεται τροφὴ, ὡς πνευματικῶς ἐν ἑκάστῳ ταύτην ἀναδίδοσθαι, καὶ γίνεσθαι πᾶσι φυλακτήριον εἰς ἀνάστασιν ζωῆς αἰωνίου. — Athanas. *In illud Evangelii*, "Quicumque dixerit," *Op.* Tom. i. p. 979.

[2] Cyril. *Cateches. Mystag.* iv. 1, cited above.

sanctified by the Holy, life-giving Spirit." [1] Here is a denial that
the bread is *mere* bread, not that it still continues really bread; and
a statement that it is the Body of Christ, but so the Body of Christ,
as the unction was believed to be the Holy Ghost; *i. e.* not in a
natural change of the substance, but in spirit, and power, and life.

St. Jerome clearly distinguishes between the natural Body and
Blood of Christ, which were crucified and shed, and the spiritual
Body and Blood of Christ, which are eaten and drunken by the
faithful.[2] And so we must explain that language of his, which,
as we saw above, appeared to savour of the later doctrine of the
Latin Church. St. Chrysostom too, who used such glowing terms
of the real presence of Christ, elsewhere explains himself, that we
should look on all Sacraments, not outwardly and carnally, but
spiritually and with the eyes of our souls.[3] And in the Epistle to
Cæsarius, which is mostly esteemed to be his, and if not his, was
certainly by a contemporary of his, we read that, " before the bread
is consecrated, we call it bread ; but, when it is consecrated, it is
no longer called bread, but is held worthy to be called the Body
of the Lord, yet still the substance of the bread remains." [4]

We must now proceed to St. Augustine, whom all agree to honour. He has so much to the purpose, that how to choose is difficult. " Prepare not thy teeth, but thy heart." [5] " Why make
ready thy teeth and thy belly? Believe, and thou hast eaten." [6]
" Our Lord hesitated not to say, *This is my Body*, when He gave
the sign of His Body." [7] " Spiritually understand what I have
spoken to you. You are not to eat that Body, which you see, and

---

[1] *Cat. Myst.* III. 3.

[2] " Dupliciter vero sanguis Christi et
caro intelligitur : vel spiritualis illa et
divina, de quo Ipse dixit: *Caro mea vere
est cibus, et sanguis meus vere est potus:* et,
*Nisi manducaveritis carnem meam, et san-
guinem meum biberitis, non habebitis vitam
æternam:* vel caro et sanguis quæ cru-
cifixa est et qui militis effusus est lancea.
Juxta hanc divisionem et in sanctis
ejus diversitas sanguinis et carnis accipitur, ut alia sit caro quæ visura est salu-
tare Dei, alia caro et sanguis quæ regnum
Dei non queant possidere." — Hieronym.
In Ephes. cap. i. v. 7. Tom. IV. pt. I. p.
328.

[3] τί δέ ἐστι τὸ σαρκικῶς νοῆσαι; τὸ ἁπλῶς
εἰς τὰ προκείμενα ὁρᾶν, καὶ μὴ πλέον τι φαν-
τάζεσθαι. τοῦτο γάρ ἐστι σαρκικῶς. χρὴ δὲ
μὴ οὕτω κρίνειν τοῖς ὁρωμένοις, ἀλλὰ πάντα
τὰ μυστήρια τοῖς ἔνδον ὀφθαλμοῖς κατοπτε-
΄ειν. τοῦτο γάρ ἐστι πνευματικῶς. — Chrysost. *In Joann.* c. vi. ; *Homil.* XLVII. Tom.
VIII. p. 278.

[4] " Sicut enim antequam sanctificetur
panis, panem nominamus : divina autem
illum sanctificante gratia, mediante sacerdote, liberatus est quidem ab appellatione
panis ; dignus autem habitus Dominici
Corporis appellatione, *etiamsi natura panis
in ipso permansit,* et non duo corpora, sed
unum Corpus Filii prædicamus," &c. —
Chrysost. *Ad Cæsarium Monach.* Tom. III.
p. 743. On the history and genuineness
of this Epistle see Cave, *Histor. Literar.*
Tom. I. p. 315; Routh's *Scriptor. Eccles.
Opuscula,* p. 479; Jenkyns's *Cranmer,* II.
p. 325, note.

[5] " Noli parare fauces, sed cor." —
De Verbis Domini, Serm. 33, Tom. V. p.
566.

[6] " Quid paras dentes et ventrem ?
Crede et manducasti." — *In Joann. Tract.*
25, Tom. III. pars. II. p. 489.

[7] "Non enim Dominus dubitavit dicere
Hoc est Corpus Meum, cum signum daret
Corporis sui." — *Contra Adimantum,* Tom.
VIII. p. 124.

drink that Blood, which they will shed, who will crucify me. I
have commended to you a Sacrament. Spiritually understood, it
will quicken you. Though it must be visibly celebrated, yet it
must invisibly be understood." [1] " What you see is bread and the
cup. But as your faith requires, the bread is Christ's Body, the
cup His Blood. How is the bread His Body? and the wine His
Blood? These things, brethren, are therefore called Sacraments,
because in them one thing is seen, another understood. What appears has a bodily form : what is understood has a spiritual fruit." [2]
" The Body and Blood of Christ will then be life to each, if what
is visibly received in the Sacrament be in actual verity spiritually
eaten, spiritually drunk." [3]

Theodoret may be our last witness, a witness against transubstantiation, but not against the truth of Christ's presence, nor the
real participation in His Body and Blood. " Our Saviour," he
tells us, " changed the names of things ; giving to His Body the
name of bread, and to the bread the name of His Body. His object was, that those who partake of the mysteries, should not have
regard to the nature of the visible elements, but by the change
of names, might believe that change which is wrought by grace.
For He, who called His own Body food and bread, and again
called Himself a vine, He honoured the visible symbols with the
name of His Body and Blood, *not changing the nature, but adding
to the nature grace.*" [4] And afterwards he says, " The mystic symbols depart not after consecration from their own nature, for they
remain in the former substance ; yet we understand what they have

---

[1] " Spiritaliter intelligite quod locutus
sum : non hoc Corpus quod videtis man-
dicaturi estis, et bibituri illum sanguinem
quem fusuri sunt qui me crucifigent.
Sacramentum aliquod vobis commen-
davi. Spiritaliter intellectum, vivifica-
bit vos. Etsi necesse est illud visibiliter celebrari, oportet tamen invisibiliter
intelligi." — *In Psalm.* xcviii. Tom. iv.
p. 1066.

[2] " Quod videtis, panis est et calix,
quod vobis etiam oculi vestri renunciant:
quod autem fides vestra postulat instru-
enda, panis est Corpus Christi, calix sanguis Christi . . . . Quomodo est panis
corpus Ejus? et calix, vel quod habet
calix, quomodo est sanguis Ejus? Ista,
fratres, ideo dicuntur sacramenta, quia
in eis aliud videtur, aliud intelligitur.
Quod videtur, speciem habet corpora-
lem, quod intelligitur fructum habet spir-
italem." — *Serm.* 272 *ad Infantes*, Tom. v.
pars i. p. 1103.

[3] " Vita unicuique erit Corpus et Sanguis Christi, si quod in sacramento visibiliter sumitur, in ipsa veritate spiritaliter manducetur, spiritaliter bibatur." —
Serm. 2, *De Verbis Apostoli*, Tom. v. pars
i. p. 64.

[4] Ὁ δέ γε Σωτὴρ ὁ ἡμέτερος ἐνήλλαξε τὰ
ὀνόματα· καὶ τῷ μὲν σώματι τὸ τοῦ συμβό-
λου τέθεικεν ὄνομα, τῷ δὲ συμβόλῳ τὸ τοῦ
σώματος. οὕτως ἄμπελον ἑαυτὸν ὀνόμασας,
αἷμα τὸ σύμβολον προσηγόρευσεν.
Δῆλος ὁ σκοπὸς τοῖς τὰ θεῖα μεμυημένοις.
ἐβουλήθη γὰρ τοὺς τῶν θείων μυστηρίων
μεταλαγχάνοντας, μὴ τῇ φύσει τῶν βλεπομέ-
νων προσέχειν, ἀλλὰ διὰ τῆς τῶν ὀνομάτων
ἐναλλαγῆς πιστεύειν τῇ ἐκ τῆς χάριτος γεγεν-
νημένῃ μεταβολῇ. ὁ γὰρ δὲ τὸ σῶμα σῖτον
καὶ ἄρτον προσαγορεύσας, καὶ αὖ πάλιν ἑαυτὸν ἄμπελον ὀνομάσας, οὗτος τὰ ὁρώμενα
σύμβολα τῇ τοῦ σώματος καὶ αἵματος προση-
γορίᾳ τετίμηκεν, οὐ τὴν φύσιν μεταβαλῶν,
ἀλλὰ τὴν χάριν τῇ φύσει προστεθηκώς. —
Dial. 1. ed. Sirmond. Tom. iv. p. 17.

become, and believe and adore, as though they were what they are believed to be." [1]

Space and time will not allow us a longer list of authorit:es. Those already adduced have been fairly chosen, and should be fairly weighed. The Christian student must not argue for victory, but search for truth. That search is seldom unattended by difficulties. Yet may it not in this case be safely concluded, that, weighing all considerations, and notwithstanding some remarkable phrases, the doctrine of the early ages was not in favour of a miraculous change in the consecrated elements, not in favour of a carnal presence of the natural Body of the Lord, but in favour of a real, effectual, life-giving presence of Christ's spiritual Body communicated to the faith, and feeding the souls, of His disciples ?

There is, perhaps, another possible alternative. The early Church held firmly Christ's presence in His Sacraments. The tendency was, for the most part, not to explain, but to veil such subjects in a reverential mystery. It may therefore have been that, whereas a spiritual presence was originally and generally recognized, yet some may have suffered their reverence to degenerate into superstition, and have spoken, and perhaps thought, as though there were a carnal presence. There was probably a vagueness of apprehension on the subject among some. Their very religion tended to foster this. But one thing is certain, namely, that the doctrine of a carnal presence was never the ruled doctrine of the primitive ages, was not received, or rather was emphatically denied, by many of the greatest of the fathers, and that it does not come down to us with the sanction and authority of that which was always, everywhere, and by all men, anciently acknowledged (*quod semper, quod ubique, quod ab omnibus traditum est*). And another thing is most certain, namely, that, if any of the fathers did contemplate any beside a spiritual presence, it was not in the way of transubstantiation, but rather of consubstantiation. For, let us take the example of St. Hilary, who, if any one, used language most like the language of later ages. Still the very object of his reasoning was to prove, that in Christ's Person there are two natures : one not extinguished, because the other is added. He illustrates this by the bread of the Eucharist, which still retains the nature of the bread unchanged, although the nature of

---

[1] Οὐδὲ γὰρ μετὰ τὸν ἁγιασμὸν τὰ μυστικὰ σύμβολα τῆς οἰκείας ἐξίσταται φύσεως· μένει γὰρ ἐπὶ τῆς προτέρας οὐσίας καὶ τοῦ σχήματος καὶ τοῦ εἴδους, καὶ ὁρατά ἐστι καὶ ἁπτά, οἷα καὶ πρότερον ἦν, νοεῖται δὲ ἅπερ ἐγένετο καὶ πιστεύεται, καὶ προσκυνεῖται ὡς ἐκεῖνα ὄντα ἅπερ πιστεύεται. — *Dial.* 2, ed. Sirmond. Tom. IV. p. 85.

Christ's Body is added to it. Now, interpret this how we may, it is a plain witness against transubstantiation. It may mean consubstantiation; it may mean a spiritual presence; but transubstantiation it cannot mean: for it was an error of Eutyches, not of the orthodox St. Hilary, that the human nature of the Saviour was absorbed and transubstantiated into the Divine.[1]

We must now pass on to the controversies of the Middle Ages. About A. D. 831, Paschasius Radbert, a monk, and afterwards abbot of Corbie, maintained the corporal presence.[2] Whether even he taught the full-grown doctrine of transubstantiation, or only consubstantiation, our divines have questioned. Certainly he speaks some things very unlike the former, and even more resembling the doctrine of spiritual feeding.[3] Yet he says, that " after the consecration nothing but the Body and Blood of Christ are to be believed;" an expression nearly approaching, if not fully expressing, the Roman doctrine.[4]

Rabanus Maurus, Archbishop of Mentz, a divine of the highest credit in the Church, wrote against the statements of Paschasius. The work is lost indeed; but the evidence of its former existence is strong and clear.[5]

Johannes Scotus Erigena, who at this period lived at the court of Charles the Bald, and sometimes with our own king Alfred, and who at his death was esteemed a martyr, and placed in the Roman Calendar, wrote a book by the command of the Emperor Charles, against the substantial change in the Sacraments; a book, which, two hundred years afterwards, was condemned at the council of Verceil, upon the ground that it made the bread and wine to be mere empty signs.[6]

Bertram too, or Ratramnus, a monk of Corbie, wrote, also at the desire of Charles the Bald, concerning this doctrine, which now began to agitate the Church. The book is still extant, and is well worthy to be read. Its genuineness has been attacked by the

---

[1] See above, p. 69.

[2] Cave places him A. D. 841.

[3] " Christus ergo cibus est angelorum, et sacramentum hoc vere caro ipsius et sanguis, quam spiritualiter manducat et bibit homo." — De Corpore et Sanguine Domini, c. 5.

[4] " Quia voluit (Dominus), licet in figura panis et vini, hæc sic esse, omnino nihil aliud quam caro Christi et sanguis post consecrationem credenda sunt." — Ibid. cap. 1.

Bishop Cosin gives several specimens of his language (Hist. of Transubstantiation, ch. xxv. s. 29), and argues, that there is nothing in his whole book " that favours the transubstantiation of the bread, or its destruction or removal." However, he quotes Bellarmine and Sirmondus as esteeming him so highly, that they were not ashamed to say that he was the first that had written to the purpose concerning the Eucharist; but there are some spurious additions to his book, which speak a stronger language than the book itself. See also Cave, H. L. Tom. ı. p. 535.

[5] See Cave, H. L. p. 542.

[6] Ibid. Tom. i. p. 549.

Roman Catholic writers, but with little success. Others have charged him with heresy ; whilst others again have allowed him to be Catholic, but yet, like other Catholics, not free from some errors.[1] The book was finally prohibited by the Council of Trent. Bertram's statements are clear for the spiritual, and against the carnal presence in the Eucharist. " The change," he says, " is not wrought corporally, but spiritually and figuratively. Under the veil of the material bread and wine the spiritual Body and Blood of Christ exist . . . . Both (the bread and wine), as they are corporally handled, are in their nature corporal creatures ; but, according to their virtue, and what they become spiritually, they are the mysteries of Christ's Body and Blood." [2] " By all that hath been hitherto said, it appears, that the Body and Blood of Christ, which are received by the mouths of the faithful in the Church, are figures in respect of their visible nature ; but in respect of the invisible substance, that is the power of the Word of God, they are truly Christ's Body and Blood. Wherefore, as they are visible creatures, they feed the body ; but as they have the virtue of a more powerful substance, they do both feed and sanctify the souls of the faithful." [3]

The Middle Ages, if favourable to a reverent, were not less favourable to a superstitious spirit. Hence the principles of Paschasius were more likely to gain ground than those of Bertram ; yet there are not wanting testimonies, for some time later, in favour of the spiritual and against the carnal presence. Especially it has been observed that the doctrine of the Anglo-Saxon Church was more than others in accordance with the primitive truth. The famous Ælfric was born probably about A. D. 956, and died about 1051. He was abbot, some say of St. Albans, others of Malmesbury or Peterborough ; and afterwards Archbishop of York.[4] Some valu-

---

[1] *Index Expurgator.* Belgic. jussu et auctoritate Philip. II., cited by Aubertin. *De Eucharist.* p. 930 ; Cosin's *Hist. of Transubst.* ch. v. § 35 ; Bishop Taylor, *On the Real Presence,* § XII. 32.

[2] " At quia confitentur et Corpus et Sanguinem Christi esse, nec hoc esse potuisse nisi facta in melius commutatione, neque ista commutatio corporaliter sed spiritualiter facta sit, necesse est ut jam figurata facta esse dicatur : quoniam sub velamento corporei panis, corporeique vini, spirituale corpus Christi, spiritualisque sanguis existit . . . . Secundum namque quod utrumque corporaliter contingitur, species sunt creaturæ corporeæ ; secundum potentiam vero, quod spiritual-

iter factæ sunt, mysteria sunt Corporis et Sanguinis Christi." — Ratramnus, *De Corpore et Sanguine Domini.* London, 1686, p. 24.

[3] " Ex his omnibus, quæ sunt hactenus dicta, monstratum est quod corpus et sanguis Christi, quæ fidelium ore in ecclesia percipiuntur figuræ sunt secundum speciem visibilem : At vero secundum invisibilem substantiam, i. e. divini potentiam Verbi, Corpus et Sanguis vere Christi existunt. Unde secundum visibilem creaturam corpus pascunt, juxta vero potentioris virtutem substantiæ, mentes fidelium et pascunt et sanctificant." — Ibid. p. 64.

[4] See Cave, *H. L.* Tom I. p. **588 ;**

able fragments of his writings remain in Latin and Anglo-Saxon, full of clear statements on the doctrine in question. "This is not," he says, "that Body in which He suffered for us, but spiritually it is made His Body and Blood."[1] "That housel" (*i. e.* the Eucharist) "is Christ's Body, not bodily but ghostly: not the Body which He suffered in, but the Body of which He spake, when He blessed bread and wine to housel, a night before His suffering,"[2] &c.

Not much later than Ælfric was Berengarius, Archdeacon of Angers, who appears to have been a man of great piety. He strenuously maintained the doctrine, which had been taught by Bertram, Scotus, and Ælfric, teaching that the bread and wine remained in their natural substance, yet not denying the invisible grace of the Sacrament. It is probable that many of the Gallican Church sided with him. He was condemned, however, and with him the writings of Johannes Erigena, by a Council at Verceil under Leo IX., A. D. 1050, on the ground that they taught the bread and wine in the Eucharist to be only bare signs. Under Victor the Second, another Council was held at Tours, A. D. 1055, at which Hildebrand presided as legate, where Berengarius freely declared that he did not believe the bread and wine to be mere empty shadows. Under Nicholas II., a new council was called at Rome (A. D. 1059); where Berengarius was forced to recant, and to declare that the "bread and wine after consecration became the very Body and Blood of Christ, and that they are touched and broken by the hands of the priests, and ground by the teeth of the faithful, not sacramentally only, but in truth and sensibly." After a time, however, he again maintained the doctrine of the spiritual presence; and Lanfranc, afterwards Archbishop of Canterbury, entered the lists of controversy against him, in whose work are fragments preserved to us of the writings of Berengarius. At length Hildebrand came to the papal chair, as Gregory VII. He summoned another council at Rome, A. D. 1078; and another A. D. 1079. At the former Berengarius acknowledged, that the real

Soames's *Anglo-Saxon Church*, ch. IV. pp. 218–229. There appear to have been two Ælfrics, one Archbishop of Canterbury, and the other of York. The latter, a friend and disciple of the former, is generally supposed to have been the author of the Homilies. See Hardwick, *Ch. Hist. of the Middle Ages*, p. 187.

[1] "Non sit tamen hoc sacrificium Corpus Ejus in quo passus est pro nobis, neque Sanguis Ejus, quem pro nobis effudit: sed spiritualiter Corpus Ejus efficitur et sanguis." — *Ælfrici Epistola ad Wulfstanum;* Routh. *Opuscula*, p. 520.

[2] From Ælfric's *Epistle to Wulfsine, Bishop of Sherburn,* Routh. p. 528. The passage quoted is from the Old English translation of the reign of Queen Elizabeth. The Anglo-Saxon is given by Dr. Routh (*loc. cit.*) with the English and Latin versions.

Body and Blood of Christ were present at the Eucharist, without saying anything of transubstantiation ; and it is supposed that the Pope was satisfied with this, and unwilling to proceed further. But at the latter, the enemies of Berengarius prevailed, and he was forced to declare that the bread and wine are substantially converted into the Body and Blood of Christ, which Body after consecration is present, not only sacramentally, but in verity of substance.[1]

It is very doubtful when the term *transubstantiation* was first used. It is said to have been invented by Stephen, Bishop of Augustodunum, about the year 1100, in his book *De Sacramento Altaris*.[2]

Under Innocent III., A. D. 1216, sat the famous Council of Lateran, by which that term, and the full form of the doctrine, were sanctioned and made authoritative. Seventy chapters were drawn up by Innocent himself. When proposed to the Council, they were received without debate, and silence was supposed to imply consent. The first chapter is directed against the Manichæan heresy, and among other things, declares that, in the sacrifice of the Mass, " Christ's Body and Blood are really contained under the species of bread and wine, the bread being transubstantiated into His Body, and the wine into His Blood." [3] It has been acknowledged by the Schoolmen and Romanists, that before this Council the doctrine of transubstantiation was not an article of the faith.[4] From this time, however, it became established as part of the Creed of the Roman Church. The Council of Constance, A. D. 1415, in the eighth session, condemned Wicliffe for denying the doctrine of transubstantiation, and of the corporal presence. The Council of Florence, A. D. 1439, at which Greek bishops and deputies were present, left the doctrine untouched. But the instruction to the Armenians, which runs only in the name of Pope Eugenius, and was not submitted to the Council, but which Roman Catholic authors often cite as a synodical decree, says, that " by virtue of the

---

[1] " Corde credo et ore profiteor panem et vinum quæ ponuntur in altari, per mysterium sacræ orationis et verba nostri Redemptoris substantialiter converti in veram ac propriam et vivificatricem carnem et sanguinem Domini nostri Jesu Christi, et post consecrationem esse verum Christi Corpus, quod natum est de Virgine, et quod pro salute mundi oblatum in cruce pependit — non tantum per signum et virtutem sacramenti, sed et in proprietate naturæ et veritate substantiæ." — *Concil.* Tom. x. p. 378. See Cosin's *Hist. of Transubst.* ; also Mosheim, *E. H.* cent. xi. part ii. ch. iii.

[2] In *B. Patrum*, Tom. x. p. 412. See Jer. Taylor *On the Real Presence*, sect. xii. 32.

[3] *Concil.* Tom. xi. p. 117.

[4] See Bramhall's *Answer to M. de la Milletière*, pt. i. disc. i. ; *Works, Anglo-Cath. Lib.* i. p. 14; Jer. Taylor, *On the Real Presence*, § i. 2.

89

words of Christ, the substance of the bread and wine is turned into the substance of His Body and Blood."[1]   At length the Council of Trent, A. D. 1551, decreed, that by "consecration there is a conversion of the whole substance of the bread and wine into the substance of Christ's Body and Blood."[2]   An anathema is pronounced against all who deny such change of the substance (the forms yet remaining), a change which the Church Catholic aptly calls transubstantiation.[3]   Finally in the Creed of Pope Pius IV., (A. D. 1563,) there is a profession of faith, that the Body and Blood of Christ, together "with His Soul and Divinity, are truly and really and substantially in the Eucharist, and that there is a conversion of the whole substance of the bread into His Body, and of the whole substance of the wine into His Blood; which conversion the Church Catholic calls transubstantiation."[4]

The doctrine then of transubstantiation, and (as it is improperly called) *the real presence*, is the established doctrine of the Roman Church.   There is still, however, a room for difference of statement and difference of thought upon the subject.   It appears to be ruled, that the substance only, not the accidents, undergo a change. Now it is almost questionable, whether the accidents do not comprise all the properties of matter.   If so, the change may still be spiritual rather than material.   And here we get a phenomenon by no means without parallel in other Roman Catholic articles of faith. For, as in saint worship some only ask departed friends to pray for them, whilst others bow down to the stock of a tree; so in the Eucharist, the learned and enlightened appear to acknowledge a far more spiritual change than is taught to the equally devout but more credulous multitude.   For the latter all kinds of miracles have been devised, and visions, wherein the Host has seemed to disappear, and the infant Saviour has been seen in its room; or where Blood has flowed in streams from the consecrated wafer, impiously preserved by unbelieving communicants.   But on the other hand, by the more learned and liberal, statements have been made perpetually in acknowledgment of a spiritual rather than a carnal presence; and such as no enlightened Protestant would cavil at or refuse.

---

[1] See Cosin, *On Transubstantiation*, Bk. VII. § 30.

[2] Sess. XIII. cap. iv.

[3] Sess. XIII. *De Eucharist.* can. IV.

[4] "Profiteor pariter in missa offerri Deo, verum, proprium et propitiatorium sacrificium pro vivis et defunctis, atque in sanctissimo Eucharistiæ sacramento esse vere, realiter et substantialiter corpus et sanguinem, una cum anima et divinitate Domini nostri Jesu Christi, fierique conversionem totius substantiæ panis in corpus, et totius substantiæ vini in sanguinem, quam conversionem Catholica Ecclesia transubstantiationem appellat."

St. Bernard of Clairvaux, the immediate forerunner of the schoolmen (A. D. 1115), acknowledged no feeding but a spiritual feeding.[1] Peter Lombard, the famous Master of the Sentences (A. D. 1141), though speaking of the conversion of the bread and wine, declines to determine whether that conversion be formal or substantial, or of some other kind.[2] Aquinas (A. D. 1255) spoke of Christ's Body as present, not bodily but substantially;[3] a distinction not easy to explain. Durandus (A. D. 1320) said that, though we believe the presence, we know not the manner of the presence.[4] Cuthbert Tonstal, Bishop of Durham, said that, "Before the Lateran Council it was free to every one to hold as they would concerning the manner; and that it would have been better to leave curious persons to their own conjectures."[5] Cardinal Cajetan writes, that "The real Body of Christ is eaten in the Sacrament, yet not corporally but spiritually. Spiritual manducation, which is made by the soul, reaches to the flesh of Christ, which is in the Sacrament."[6] And Gardiner, in his controversy with Cranmer says, "The Catholic teaching is, that the manner of Christ's presence in the Sacrament is spiritual and supernatural, not corporal nor carnal, not natural, not sensible, nor perceptible, but only spiritual, the how and manner whereof God knoweth."[7]

Let us now pass to the doctrines of the Reformation, merely observing by the way, that the dogma of transubstantiation, though formally decreed by the Roman Church, has never been adopted by the Greek. Luther, if not the inventor, has been esteemed the great patron of the doctrine of consubstantiation. Whilst rejecting the idea of a change in the substance of the elements, he believed in a presence *with* the elements, of the material substance of Christ's Body and Blood. He appears to have had recourse to the same illustration which had been used to explain the union of the Divine and human natures in Christ; namely, that, as in red-hot iron there is the nature both of iron and fire, so in the Eucharist

---

[1] "Eadem Caro nobis, sed spiritualiter utique, non carnaliter exhibeatur." — *Sermo. De S. Martino.* See Jer. Taylor, *Real Presence*, § 1. 8; Cosin, *On Transubstantiation*, ch. VII. § 13, who gives several quotations from St. Bernard to this effect.

[2] "Si autem quæritur qualis sit illa conversio, an formaliter an substantialiter, vel alterius generis, diffinire non sufficio." — *Sent.* IV. *Dist.* 10. See Cosin, as above, § 15.

[3] See Jer. Taylor, as above, § XI. 20.

[4] "Verbum audimus, motum senti-

mus, modum nescimus, præsentiam credimus." — Neand. *Synops. Chron.* p. 203, quoted by Jer. Taylor, as above, § 1. 2.

[5] Tonstal, *De Eucharist.* Lib. I. p. 46; Jer. Taylor, as above.

[6] "Manducatur verum Corpus Christi in sacramento, sed non corporaliter, sed spiritualiter. Spiritualis manducatio, quæ per animam fit, ad Christi carnem in sacramento existentem pertingit." — *Opusc.* Tom. II. Tract. 2, *De Euch.* c. v.; Jer. Taylor, as above, § VII. 8.

[7] Cranmer's *Works*, III. p. 241, *Answer to Gardiner.*

there is both the bread and the Body of the Lord. Strong as are
his expressions in the arguments which he used with the Sacramentarians, still from his less controversial statements, we may
almost be led to think that Luther did not much go beyond a faith
in the spiritual presence. Controversy often produces extreme
statements : and it may have been so with him.[1] He does indeed
say in a comparatively uncontroversial tract, that there are "the
real Body and Blood of Christ *in* and *under* the bread and wine." [2]
But then he speaks of faith as the means whereby we obtain the
benefits of the Sacrament, as that to which they are exhibited.[3]

As to the public documents of the Lutherans, the Confession of
Augsburg simply declares, that the Body and Blood of Christ are
really given with the bread and wine.[4] But the Saxon Confession
says, that " In this communion Christ is truly and substantially
present, and His Body and Blood are truly exhibited to those who
receive." [5]

The great leader among the reformers, of those who took an
opposite view to Luther, was Zuingle. He was not satisfied to
reject a material presence ; but he even denied a presence of any
sort. With him the bread and wine were empty signs. Feeding
on Christ was a figure for believing in Him. The Communion
was but a ceremony to remind us of Him. Spiritual manducation
was resting upon the mercy of God.[6] He probably may have modified these statements afterwards ; yet they thoroughly belonged to
his system.

Calvin took a middle course between Luther and Zuingle. With
the former he acknowledged a real presence of Christ in His Supper ; with the latter he denied a corporal or material presence.
Having stated the view of the Sacramentarians, that to eat the
Flesh and drink the Blood of Christ is merely to believe on Him,
he says, " But to me Christ appears to have intended something

[1] See, for instance, *De Sacramento Altaris, Opp.* Tom. i. p. 82.

[2] "Esse verum corpus et sanguinem
Domini Nostri Jesu Christi, in et sub
pane et vino per verbum Christi."—*Catechismus Major,* Tom. v. p. 641.

[3] Ibid.

[4] " De Cœna Domini docent quod cum
pane et vino vere exhibeantur corpus et
sanguis Christi, vescentibus in Cœna
Domini."—*Confess. August.* Art. x. ; *Sylloge,* p. 172.

[5] " Vere adesse Christum, et vere exhiberi sumentibus corpus et sanguinem
Christi." — *Sylloge,* p. 282.

[6] " Sacramentaliter edere esse aliud

non potest quam signum aut symbolum
edere."— *De Vera et Falsa Religione, Opera
Zuinglii,* pars 2, Tom. i. fol. 215. He
denies that there can be any spiritual
Body of Christ, except His Church, fol.
216. Again : " Sacramentum est sacræ rei
signum. Cum ergo Sacramentum Corporis Christi nomino, non quicquam
aliud, quam panem, qui Corporis Christi
pro nobis mortui figura et typus est, intelligo."— *De Cœna Domini,* Ibid. fol. 274.
" Spiritualiter edere Corpus Christi nihil
est aliud, quam spiritu ac mente niti misericordia et bonitate Dei, propter Christum." — *Fidei Christianæ Expositio,* Ibid
fol. 555.

more express and sublime in that famous discourse of His, where He commends to us the eating of His flesh; namely, that by a real participation of Him we be quickened; which He therefore designated under the words eating and drinking, lest any should think that the life we derive from Him is received by simple cognition. For as, not the sight, but the eating of the bread gives nourishment to the body, so it is needful that, for the soul to be wholly partaker of Christ, it should be quickened by His virtue to life eternal." [1]

The elements, according to him, receive the name of Christ's Body and Blood, " because they are, as it were, instruments whereby Christ distributes them to us." [2] And, " if we believe the truth of God, we must believe that there is an inward substance of the Sacrament in the Lord's Supper joined to the outward signs; and so, that, as the bread is given by the hands, the Body of Christ is also communicated, that we be partakers of Him." [3] " That Body, which you see not, is to you a spiritual aliment. Does it seem incredible, that we are fed by the Flesh of Christ, which is so far from us? We must remember, that the work of the Spirit is secret and wonder-working, which it would be profane to measure by our intelligence." [4] Thus then to receive Christ in the Eucharist is not merely to believe in Him; yet it is by faith we are enabled to receive Him. By believing we eat Christ's Flesh, because by faith our feeding on Him is effected; and that feeding is the fruit of faith. " With them," (*i. e.* the Zuinglians,) he writes,

---

[1] *Institut.* IV. xvii. 5.

[2] " Corporis vero et sanguinis nomen eis attributum, quod sint velut instrumenta, quibus Dominus Jesus Christus nobis ea distribuit." — Calvinus, *De Cœna Domini, Opuscula.* Genevæ, 1552, p. 133.

[3] " Ita in communione, quam in Christi corpore et sanguine habemus, dicendum est, mysterium spirituale esse, quod nec oculis conspici, nec ingenio humano comprehendi potest. Figuris igitur et signis, quæ sub oculorum sensum cadunt, ut naturæ nostræ imbecillitas requirit ostenditur; ita tamen ut non sit figura nuda et simplex, sed veritati suæ et substantiæ conjuncta. . . . .

" Necesse est igitur nos in Cœna vere corpus et sanguinem Christi recipere, cum utriusque communionem Dominus repræsentet. Quid enim sibi vellet, nos panem comedere ac vinum bibere, ut significent carnem ipsius cibum esse nostrum, et sanguinem potum, si veritate spirituali prætermissa, vinum et panem solummodo præberet. . . . .

" Itaque fatendum est si vera sit repræsentatio quam adhibet Deus, in cœna substantiam interiorem sacramenti visibilibus signis conjunctam esse, et quemadmodum panis in manu distribuitur, ita Corpus Christi, ut Ejus participes simus, nobis communicari. Hoc certe etiam, si nihil aliud esset, nobis abunde satisfacere deberet, cum intelligimus Christum nobis in Cœna veram propriamque corporis et sanguinis sui substantiam nobis donare — ut pleno jure ipsum possideamus, et possidendo in omnem bonorum suorum societatem vocemur." — Ibid. pp. 133, 134.

[4] " Corpus, quod nequaquam cernis, spirituale est tibi alimentum. Incredibile hoc tibi videtur, pasci nos Christi carne, quæ tam procul a nobis distat? Meminerimus, arcanum et mirificum esse Spiritus Sancti opus, quod intelligentiæ tuæ modulo metiri sit nefas." — Calvin. *In* 1 *Cor.* xi. 24, cited by Waterland, *On the Eucharist*, c. VII.

"the feeding is faith: with me the power of feeding comes as a consequence of faith."[1]

Melancthon, the disciple, friend, and successor of Luther, is supposed to have hesitated between a material and a spiritual presence. In the Confession of Augsburg, which is due to him, we have already seen strong words, which sound like consubstantiation. He is said to have used in earlier days the word *corporaliter*, to express the mode in which Christ communicates His Flesh and Blood in the Eucharist, but to have avoided such expressions, after much intercourse on the question with Œcolampadius.[2] After Luther's death, he had the chief voice and influence among the Lutherans; and through his peaceful counsels in Germany, and Calvin's sound views in Switzerland, much greater concord prevailed on this question among the continental Protestants, than had existed during the lifetime of the great reformer of Wittemberg; the Lutherans and Zuinglians both consenting to modify their views and statements.[3] Insomuch that Hooker observed concerning them: " By opening the several opinions which have been held, they are grown for aught I can see on all sides, at the length to a general agreement concerning that which alone is material, namely, the real participation of Christ, and of life in His Body and Blood by means of this Sacrament."[4]

From the continental Protestants, we must turn to England. Cranmer and Ridley appear to have retained the doctrines of the corporal presence and of transubstantiation throughout the reign of Henry VIII. The formularies of that reign all seem to teach it. Ridley is said to have been converted to a belief in the spiritual (instead of the natural) presence, by reading the treatise of Bertram or Ratramn, probably about the year 1545.[5] At this time Cranmer was zealous for transubstantiation. But Ridley communicated to the Archbishop what he had discovered in the writings of Ratramn; and they then set themselves to examine the matter with more than ordinary care.[6] Ridley indeed refused to take the credit of converting Cranmer;[7] but Cranmer himself always acknowledged his obligations to Ridley.[8] It has been thought that Cranmer went through two changes: to consubstantiation first, and then to the spiritual feeding; and most probably

---

1 " Illis manducatio est fides, mihi ex fide potius consequi videtur." — *Institut.* IV. xvii. 5.

2 See Jer. Taylor, *On Real Presence*, § I. 9.

3 See Mosh. *E. H.* Cent. XVI. sect. III. pt. II. ch. I. 27, and ch. II. 12.

4 Hooker, *E. P.* Bk. v. ch. LXVII. 2.

5 Ridley's *Life of Ridley*, p. 166.

6 Burnet, *Hist. of Reformation*, pt. II. Bk. I. p. 107.

7 *Ridley's Life*, p. 169.

8 *Cranmer's Remains*, (Jenkyns,) IV. p. 97.

there may have been some gradual progress in his convictions.[1] Yet it was constantly affirmed by him that, before he put forth the translation of the Catechism of Justus Jonas, commonly called Cranmer's Catechism, he had fully embraced the spiritual doctrine, and that the strong phrases there used concerning the real presence and the real feeding on Christ, were intended of a spiritual presence and a spiritual feeding, not of consubstantiation.[2]

After this both Cranmer and Ridley, to whom we are chiefly indebted for our formularies, maintained a doctrine nearly identical with that maintained by Calvin, and before him by Bertram. With the latter Ridley expresses his entire accordance.[3] He constantly declares that, whilst he rejects all presence of the natural Body and Blood, in the way of transubstantiation, he yet acknowledges a real presence of Christ, spiritually and by grace, to be received by the faithful in the Communion of the Eucharist.[4] Cranmer has by some been thought to incline nearer to Zuinglianism; yet, if fair allowance be made for hasty expressions in the irritation of controversy, it will probably appear that he, like Ridley, followed the doctrine of the ancient Church, and held a real reception of Christ in the Spirit. Certainly we find him writing as follows: "I say (as all the holy fathers and martyrs used to say) that we receive Christ spiritually, by faith with our minds eating His Flesh and drinking His Blood : so that we receive Christ's own very natural Body, but not naturally nor corporally."[5] "It is my constant faith and belief, that we receive Christ in the Sacrament, verily and truly . . . But . . . you think a man cannot receive the Body of Christ verily, unless he take Him corporally in his corporal mouth . . . My doctrine is that . . . He is by faith spiritually present with us, and is our spiritual food and nourishment, and sitteth

---

[1] The subject is discussed by Dr. Jenkyns, note to *Cranmer's Works*, IV. p. 95.

[2] Cranmer's *Works*, II. p. 440, III. pp. 13, 297, 344.

[3] See *Enchiridion Theologicum*, I. p. 56.

[4] "I say that the Body of Christ is present in the Sacrament, but yet sacramentally and spiritually (according to His grace) giving life, and in that respect really, that is, according to His benediction, giving life. . . . The true Church of Christ doth acknowledge a presence of Christ's Body in the Lord's Supper to be communicated to the godly by grace and spiritually, as I have often showed, and by a sacramental signification, but not by the corporal presence of the Body of His Flesh." — *Works*, Parker Society, p. 236.

"That heavenly Lamb is (as I confess) on the table : but by a spiritual pres ence, and not after any corporeal presence of the Flesh taken of the Virgin Mary." — Ibid. p. 249.

"Both you and I agree in this, that in the Sacrament is the very true and natural Body and Blood of Christ, even that which is born of the Virgin Mary . . . . We confess all one thing to be in the Sacrament, and dissent in the manner of being there. I confess Christ's natural Body to be in the Sacrament by Spirit and grace . . . . You make a proper kind of being, inclosing a natural Body under the shape and form of bread and wine."—Fox, *Martyrs*, II. p. 1598. Lond. 1597, cited by *Laud against Fisher*, § 35.

[5] *Remains*, III. p. 5.

in the midst of all them that be gathered together in His Name ; and this feeding is spiritual feeding and an heavenly feeding, far passing all corporal and carnal feeding, in deed and not in figure only, or not at all, as you most untruly report my saying to be." [1] " I say that the same visible and palpable Flesh that was for us crucified, &c. &c., is eaten of Christian people at His Holy supper . . . The diversity is not in the Body, but in the eating thereof ; no man eating it carnally, but the good eating it both sacramentally and spiritually, and the evil only sacramentally, that is, figuratively." [2]

These sentiments of our reformers are undoubtedly embodied in our Liturgy and Articles. One thing indeed has been thought to savour of a tendency to Zuinglianism. The first Service Book of Edward VI., drawn up undoubtedly after Cranmer had embraced the doctrine of the spiritual presence, contained, as did all the ancient Liturgies, an invocation of the Holy Ghost to bless the bread and wine ; " that they might be unto us the Body and Blood of Christ." This was omitted in the second Service Book ; probably lest the grace of the Sacrament should thus seem to be tied to the consecrated elements. But a still more remarkable departure from the ancient forms was this. Whereas, in the first Service Book, the words of administration were, " The Body of our Lord Jesus Christ, which was given for thee, preserve thy body and soul unto eternal life ; " in the second Service Book they were merely, " Take and eat this, in remembrance that Christ died for thee, and feed on Him in thy heart by faith with thanksgiving." [3] This seemed to imply that the reformers believed in no real spiritual reception of Christ's Body in the Eucharist, but only in a remembrance of His death and passion. Accordingly, in the reign of Elizabeth the two forms were combined together, and have ever since continued in use in the Church. But though this change looked like an inclination on the part of the earlier reformers to the doctrine of the mere figurists, yet it is by no means certain that some of the alterations in the Service Book were agreeable to our leading divines ; [4] and notwithstanding this alteration, there remained numerous statements in our formularies to prove that a real but spiritual presence of Christ was, and is the doctrine of the reformed Church of England.

Thus we are told in the exhortation to communion, that God

---

[1] *Remains*, iii. pp. 288, 289.
[2] Ibid. p. 340.   See also ii. p. 441, iv.
p. 16.

[3] *Two Liturgies of Edward VI.* p. 297. Oxf. 1838.
[4] See above, p. 12, note 1.

" hath given His Son our Saviour Jesus Christ, not only to die for us, but also to be our spiritual food and sustenance in that holy Sacrament." It is said that, " if with a true penitent heart and lively faith we receive that holy Sacrament . . . . we spiritually eat the Flesh of Christ, and drink His Blood." In what is called the " prayer of humble access," we ask that God would " give us grace so to eat the Flesh of His dear Son Jesus Christ, and to drink His Blood, that our sinful bodies may be made clean by His Body, and our souls washed through His most precious Blood." In the prayer of consecration, we speak of being " partakers of His most blessed Body and Blood ; " and in the post-communion we thank God that He doth " vouchsafe to feed us with the spiritual food of the most precious Body and Blood of His Son our Saviour Jesus Christ." So likewise in this Article it is professed, that " to them who worthily receive, ... the bread which we break is a partaking of the Body of Christ, and likewise the cup of blessing is a partaking of the Blood of Christ." All these are expressions in the second Service Book of Edward VI., and in the Articles drawn up in that reign. The latter part of the Catechism is of later date, but in strict accordance with the earlier documents. Its words are, that " the Body and Blood of Christ are verily and indeed taken and received by the faithful in the Lord's Supper."

In this XXVIIIth Article, as first drawn up A. D. 1552, there was a clause stating, that Christ in bodily presence is in Heaven, and therefore that we ought not to confess " the real and bodily presence (as they term it) of Christ's Flesh and Blood in the Sacrament of the Lord's Supper." This nearly corresponds with the statement of the rubric at the end of our present communion Service.[1] Both the clause in the Article and the rubric were omitted in Elizabeth's reign, lest persons inclined to the Lutheran belief might be too much offended by it ; and many such were in the Church, whom it was wished to conciliate. The rubric was again restored in the reign of Charles II. The meaning of it clearly is, not to deny a spiritual, but only a " corporal presence of Christ's natural Flesh and Blood," " and a consequent adoration of the

---

[1] Concerning that rubric see above, p. 106, note 1, p. 113, note 2.

Luther much insisted on the ubiquity of the human nature of our blessed Lord, derived to it from the union with the Divine nature. But we must not believe the human nature transubstantiated into the Divine, as Eutyches taught.

St. Augustine observes that Christ, according to His human nature, is now on God's right hand, and thence shall come to judgment; and according to that nature He is not everywhere. " Cavendum est enim, ne ita divinitatem adstruamus hominis, ut veritatem Corporis auferamus." — *Epist.* 187, Tom. II. p. 681, quoted above, p. 113, note 2. See this subject most admirably handled by Hooker, *E. P.* v. 55.

elements, as though they did not remain still in their very natural substances."

The Homilies are very express. " Thus much we must be sure to hold, that in the Supper of the Lord there is no vain ceremony, no bare sign, no *untrue figure of a thing absent* (Matt. xxvi.); but as the Scripture saith, The table of the Lord, the bread and cup of the Lord, the memory of Christ, the annunciation of His death, yea, the communion of the Body and Blood of the Lord, in a marvellous incorporation, which by the operation of the Holy Ghost (the very bond of our conjunction with Christ) is through faith wrought in the souls of the faithful, whereby not only their souls live to eternal life, but they surely trust to win to their bodies a resurrection to immortality "[1] (1 Cor. x.)

Bishop Jewel, who perhaps was the chief writer of this Second Book of Homilies, says in his Apology: " We plainly pronounce in the Supper the Body and Blood of the Lord, the Flesh of the Son of God, to be truly exhibited to those who believe."[2]   And again, after protesting against transubstantiation, he says, " yet when we say this, we do not lower the Lord's Supper, nor make it a mere frigid ceremony.   We assert, that Christ exhibits Himself really present in the Sacraments ; in baptism, that we may put Him on, in His Supper, that we may feed on Him by faith and in spirit . . . . and this we say is not done perfunctorily, nor frigidly, but in very deed and truly."[3]

It appears, then, that our reformers symbolized herein with Calvin ; though it is not likely that they learned their doctrine from him.   Points of difference may be discovered between them ; but in the main, Calvin, Melancthon in his later views, and the Anglican divines, were at one.   There have, no doubt, been different ways of explaining the spiritual presence, among those who have agreed to acknowledge such a presence.   But perhaps the safest plan is to say, that because it is spiritual, therefore it needs must be mystical.   And so Bishop Taylor concludes, that our doctrine differs not from that of ancient writers, who acknowledged Christ's presence, but would not define the manner of His presence.   For

---

[1] *Second Book of Homilies,* "First part of the Sermon Concerning the Sacrament."

[2] "Diserteque pronunciamus in cœna credentibus vere exhiberi Corpus et Sanguinem Domini, carnem Filii Dei." — Juelli *Apologia. Ench. Theolog.* p. 126.

[3] "Non tamen cum ista dicimus, extenuamus Cœnam Domini aut eam frigidam tantum cæremoniam esse docemus. . . . . Christum enim asserimus, vere sese præsentem exhibere in sacramentis suis ; in baptismo, ut Eum induamus, in cœna, ut Eum fide et spiritu comedamus, et de Ejus cruce et sanguine habeamus vitam æternam ; idque dicimus non perfunctorie et frigide, sed re ipsa et vere fieri." — Ibid. p. 129.   Compare Noel's *Catechism, Ench. Theol.* p. 320, where the same doctrine is propounded.

he observes that we say, " the presence of Christ is real, and it is spiritual ; and this account still leaves the Article in its deepest mystery ; because spiritual perfections are indiscernible, and the word ' spiritual ' is a very general term, particular in nothing but that it excludes the corporal and natural." [1]

It would be endless, and it is unnecessary, to say much concerning our divines since the Reformation. Some perhaps, who have followed Calvin in his predestinarian theory, have followed, not him, but Zuingle, upon the Sacraments. And this too may have been the bent of those who afterwards more especially followed Arminius, both here and on the Continent.[2] But from the time of the Reformation to the present, all the great luminaries of our Church have maintained the doctrine which appears in the face of our formularies ; agreeing to deny a corporal, and to acknowledge a spiritual feeding in the Supper of the Lord. It is scarcely necessary to recount the names of Mede, Andrewes, Hooker, Taylor, Hammond, Cosin, Bramhall, Usher, Pearson, Patrick, Bull, Beveridge, Wake, Waterland. All these have left us writings on the subject, and all have coincided, with but very slight diversity, in the substance of their belief. They have agreed, as Hooker says, that " Christ is *personally* present ; albeit a part of Christ be *corporally* absent ; " [3] that " the fruit of the Eucharist is the participation of the Body and Blood of Christ " — but that " the real presence of Christ's most blessed Body and Blood is not to be sought for in the Sacrament (*i. e.* in the elements) ; but in the worthy receiver of the Sacrament." [4]

SECTION II. — SCRIPTURAL PROOF.

I. *The Words of Institution.*

WE know that almost all the sacrifices, among both Jews and Gentiles, were succeeded by a feast upon the body of the sacrificed victim ; the persons, who thus fed upon the sacrifice, declaring their interest in the sacred rite, and through it entering

---

[1] Jer. Taylor, § 1. 2.
[2] There is a very pious work by one of the Arminian writers in the English Church (Horneck's *Crucified Jesus*). It has much to edify and spiritualize, but

if I understand it, its doctrine is purely Zuinglian.
[3] Book v. lxvii. 11.
[4] Book v. xvii. 6.

into covenant with the God.[1] Now the Passover was the most solemn and significant of all the sacrifices of the Law, the most remarkable of all the types of our redemption.   In its first institution, it was ordained that the lamb should be slain, evidently in the way of a propitiatory offering,[2] in order that the destroying angel, which smote the Egyptians, might not destroy those for whom this offering was made.   Yet no one had a claim to exemption from the destruction, except those on whose lintels and doorposts the blood of the lamb was sprinkled, and who had partaken of the feast upon the lamb slain, — they and all their households.[2] The feast was, as it were, the consummation of the sacrifice ; the efficacy of the latter being assured only to those who partook of the former.

It is not a little observable then, that our blessed Saviour, the night before He suffered, or (if we take the Jewish reckoning from evening to evening) the very day on which He suffered, superseded the typical feast of the Passover by the commemorative feast of the Eucharist.   He first, according to the Law, ate the Passover with His disciples.   Then, supper being ended,[4] and probably after He had washed the feet of His disciples,[5] He instituted a new rite appropriate to the New Covenant, but with peculiar reference to the rite under the Old Covenant.   With the Passover, by Divine ordinance, there had been always eaten unleavened bread ; and, by immemorial custom, there had been four cups of wine poured out ; over each of which thanks were offered up, "and of which the third cup was specially called the cup of blessing." [6] Now the bread and the wine, thus eaten and drunk solemnly at the Passover, our Lord adopts, as the signs or elements for the institution of His new Sacrament.   The bread at the Passover was blessed and broken, the wine was blessed and poured out.[7]   These same ceremonies our Lord now uses.   He breaks the bread and blesses it ; He pours out the wine and blesses it.   In the feast of the Passover the bread and wine had been but subordinate ; the latter not even of Divine authority.   Our Lord makes them now the. chief.   Before, the chief place had been occupied by the Paschal Lamb.   It was slain and eaten in commemoration of the first Passover, in type and

[1] See Cudworth, *True Notion of the Lord's Supper*, ch. I.
[2] See the true sacrificial nature of the Passover proved, Cudworth, as above. ch. II.
[3] Exod. xii. 2-13.

[4] μετὰ τὸ δειπνῆσαι, Luke xxii. 20.
[5] John xiii. 2, *seq.*
[6] Buxtorf, *De Cœna Dom.* § 22; Lightfoot, *H. H.* on Matt. xxvi. 26, 27.
Lightfoot, Ibid.

anticipation of the Saviour Himself. But now that the type was succeeded by the antitype, and that the feast must therefore be commemorative, not anticipatory, our Lord puts the bread and wine in place of the flesh of the Lamb; that, as the latter had been eaten as a type of Him, so the former should be eaten and drunk in remembrance of Him.

It has been observed, that the lamb, when set on the table to be eaten at the Passover, was commonly called by the Jews "the body of the Paschal Lamb;" and it seems not unnatural to suppose that our Lord, as adopting otherwise on this occasion their customs and language, should here also have alluded to their common phrase. They had spoken of eating "the body of the lamb" (גּוּפוֹ שֶׁל כֶּבֶשׂ שֶׁל הַפֶּסַח), and when He blessed the Bread, He said of it, "This is My Body;" as though He would say, "Heretofore you ate the body of the Lamb, a type of Me to be delivered to death for you. Now I abrogate this forever; and instead, I give you My Body to be crucified and broken for you; and so hereafter, when you eat this bread, think not of the Paschal Lamb, which, like all types, is now done away in Me; but believe that you feed on My Body broken, to deliver you, not from Egyptian bondage, but from the far worse bondage of death and hell." [1]

Again, when our Lord had broken and blessed the bread, and giving it to His disciples, had called it His Body, He then took the cup, poured it out, blessed it, and called it His Blood. And it is observable that, as when Moses sprinkled the people with the blood of the sacrifice, he said of it, "Behold the blood of the Covenant;" [2] so our Lord and Saviour, in giving His disciples this cup to drink, said of it, "This is My Blood of the New Covenant" (Matt. xxvi. 27; Mark xiv. 24).

In almost all respects then, the institution of the Eucharist was likened to the sacrificial feasts of the Jews; most especially to the feast of the Passover.[3] It had only this point of difference:

---

[1] Buxtorf, *De Cœna Dom.* § 25; Lightfoot, *H. H.* on Luke xxii. 19.

[2] Exod. xxiv. 8; Heb. ix. 20.

[3] A question has been raised whether our Saviour and His disciples had been eating the Paschal lamb or not, before He instituted the Eucharist; the ground for the question being that other well-known doubt, namely, Was the Thursday or the Friday the day on which the Passover ought to be eaten? However this latter may be solved, there seems no possibility of evading the force of Luke xxii. 15:

"With desire have I desired to eat *this Passover* with you before I suffer." (Comp. Matt. xxvi. 17-19; Mark xiv. 12-16). The true solution of the difficulty has always appeared to me to be this. The commandment was that the Passover should be slain on the 14th day of the month, "between the two evenings," בֵּין הָעַרְבַּיִם (Exod. xii. 6); that is to say, from the evening of the 14th to the evening of the 15th day of the month, according to the common

that, whereas in all the ancient feasts the victim was actually killed, and then its natural body was eaten ; here the feast was instituted (though on the day of His death, yet) before our blessed Lord was crucified, and bread and wine were substituted in the room of His natural Flesh and Blood. Yet the bread and wine He called His Body and Blood; even as the flesh of the lamb was called the body of the Paschal lamb. And we can scarcely fail to infer that, as the flesh of the old sacrifice was never called the Body of Christ, but (what it really was) the body of the lamb, and as on the contrary the elements in the newly founded feast *were* called the Body and Blood of Christ, so the new festival must have had a closer connection with the great and true sacrifice than had the slaughtered victim, which represented Him in the old festival. The bread and wine were His Body and Blood, in a sense beyond that in which the Paschal lamb was Christ; that is to say, not merely in a figure, but in more than a figure.

Now this the very nature of the case would lead us to expect. Under the Law were mere lifeless ceremonies; but under the Gospel there is substance, instead of shadow. Under the Law there were sacrifices of slain beasts ; and the feast was therefore on the flesh of slain beasts. But under the Gospel there is no sacrifice, but of the Lamb of God ; and a feast upon the sacrifice must therefore be a feeding upon Him ; and we may add, that though the Law were true as coming from God, yet emphatically and peculiarly the Gospel is *the truth*. Hence, if in the legal ceremony there was a true feeding upon the victim, we cannot doubt that in the Gospel Sacrament there is a true feeding on the Saviour. And yet once more, the Law was carnal, but the Gospel is spiritual. And so, whereas the Paschal festival involved a carnal eating of the typical sacrifice, we infer that the Eucharistic festival would involve a spiritual eating of the true Sacrifice. And hence, as in all respects the Passover squared well with the place it occupied in its own dispensation, the Eucharist would fall into its place in the higher dispensation. The one a feast on a sacrifice ; the other a feast on a Sacrifice. The one on the lamb ; the other on the Lamb of God. The one true ; the other true.

Jewish mode of counting time. Thus our Lord ate the Passover on the right day, *i. e.* on the evening of the 14th ; yet He was crucified on the same day ; for from evening to evening was but a single day. And this will solve all the difficulty in John xviii. 28 ; for many of the Jews may not have eaten the Passover on the morning of the Friday, though our Lord had eaten it on the evening of the Thursday. See *Duty of Observing the Christian Sabbath*, by Samuel Lee, D. D., &c. note 15; where he quotes the Gemara on the Jerusalem Talmud in confirmation of this interpretation of Exod xii. 6.

But the one carnally true; the other spiritually, and therefore even *more* true.

There are three things especially to be observed in the form of institution: 1, the blessing; 2, the declaration; 3, the command.

1. The blessing. " Jesus took bread and blessed it:" so say St. Matthew (xxvi. 26) and St. Mark (xiv. 22). This was the custom with the Jews. The master of the house pronounced over the bread a form of benediction, placing both his hands upon it. And this blessing, we are told, was by them called קִדּוּשׁ *i. e.* sanctification.[1] Whether or not our Lord adopted the common form of words, we cannot tell. At all events, He gave utterance to some words of blessing, whereby He set apart the bread from its common use, to a new, sacramental and sacred purpose.

For *blessed* (εὐλογήσας) St. Luke (xxii. 17) and St. Paul (1 Cor. xi. 24) have *gave thanks* (εὐχαριστήσας). The words seem nearly synonymous. They are so used concerning the blessing of the bread, when our Lord fed the four thousand with the seven loaves (Mark viii. 6, 7): the Vulgate translates (εὐχαριστια) by *benedictio* (1 Cor. xiv. 16): and the Hebrew word בֵּרֵךְ *to bless,* is rendered indifferently by words which signify either *blessing* or *thanksgiving.* And so, no doubt, our Lord and Saviour, when consecrating this bread to a sacred ordinance, gave thanks to God His Father, and with the thanksgiving joined a blessing; which changed the bread, not in substance, not in quantity, not in quality — but in use, in purpose, in sanctity; so that what before was common, now became sacramental bread; even the sacrament and mystery of the Body of Christ.[2]

2. From the blessing we pass to the declaration: —

" Take, eat; this is My Body." So St. Matthew, St. Mark, St. Luke, St. Paul. St. Luke adds, " which is given for you" (xxii. 19). St. Paul, " which is broken for you" (1 Cor. xi. 24).

There is a little more difference in their account of the cup. St. Matthew and St. Mark say, " This cup is My Blood of the new Testament which is shed for many." St. Luke and St. Paul say, " This cup is the new testament in My Blood."

We have already compared these phrases with the Jewish form of speech, and have seen how the one throws light upon the other. We have seen also reason to infer, that the ordinance thus instituted was for the purpose of a spiritual feast upon the one true Sacrifice, a feeding on the Body and the Blood of Christ. But

---

[1] Buxtorf, as above, § 46.
[2] Ibid. § 48. Compare Waterland, *On the Eucharist,* ch. **v. 3.**

we have now come to a point, where those who believe in the verity of the feeding upon Christ, branch off from each other into two opposed and unhappily hostile divisions. The Protestant admits that the words of institution assure us of the blessing of feeding upon Christ, and give us ground to call the consecrated elements Christ's Body and Blood. But the Romanist maintains, that they moreover assure us that the bread, when blessed, no longer remains bread, but has become the very natural Flesh of Christ, and in a like manner the wine His natural Blood. The Romanist reasons from the plain meaning of the words, and the duty reverently to believe what Christ has spoken. "This *is* My Body;" therefore it is no longer bread. And to make it clearer, they say that, whereas the substantive "*bread*" ($ἄρτος$) is masculine, the relative "*this*" ($τοῦτο$) is neuter; and that therefore the word *this* means not, "This Bread is My Body;" but on the contrary means, "This, which is no longer bread, is My Body."[1] The grammatical argument is too futile to keep us long. Bread, being a thing without life, though in Greek and Latin it is expressed by a masculine substantive, in wellnigh all languages might be referred to by a neuter pronoun; and though we could not say *Hoc est frater meus;* yet we may say *Hoc est aqua,* or *Hoc est panis.* Nay! would it not have been a more singular mode of speech, if our Lord, when He took the bread in His hand, instead of saying concerning it, $τοῦτο$, *hoc, this thing,* had said, $οὗτος$, *hic, he?*

But more weight lies in the verb $ἐστὶ$, *is;* and yet, if no better argument than its use could be adduced, we must admit that the mere figurists have almost as strong ground as the transubstantialists. If the simple use of the substantive verb proves an absolute change of substance, how are we to interpret "The seed is the word; the field is the world; the reapers are the angels; the harvest is the end of the world; I am the door; I am the vine?"[2] We cannot here understand a substantial change, but must admit a figure of speech. And so, in truth, we must admit in the Eucharist; for though we acknowledge Christ's presence, and not only acknowledge but rejoice in it; yet we hold not that presence to be in the material bread; nor can these words prove that it is there. The passage which perhaps most nearly corresponds to this, is that wherein St. Paul says that "That Rock was Christ" (1 Cor. x. 4). It is indeed generally contended that the Rock was Christ by a mere figure of speech; and hence the illustration is urged to support the doctrine of the figurists. But this is scarcely true.

[1] Bellarmine, Lib. I. *De Eucharistia,* ch. x.   [2] See Taylor, *Real Presence,* sect. VI.

If the illustration be correctly interpreted, it will prove the *real* but the spiritual presence of the Body of Christ. The Apostle's argument is strictly this : The Israelites, in their pilgrimage in the wilderness, were like Christians, subjects of grace. Christ followed, and Christ fed them. They had bread from Heaven, and drank out of the rock ; and as the literal manna fed their bodies, so there was a heavenly manna prepared for their souls. And as from the rock of stone Moses called forth the stream of water ; so there was with them also a spiritual Rock, by which their souls were watered ; and that spiritual " Rock was Christ." It was not then, we may observe, that the *spiritual Rock* was a figure of Christ. *The rock of stone* was a *figure* of Christ ; but *the spiritual Rock* — " *that* Rock *was* Christ." So it is in the Eucharist. The bread in the Eucharist is an emblem of the Bread of life : but *that* Bread is Christ. As with the natural rock in the wilderness there was present the Spiritual Rock, which is Christ : so with the natural bread in the Sacrament there is present the Spiritual Bread, which is Christ's Body.

And next for the cup. Our Lord calls it, " My Blood of the new Covenant ; " or, according to St. Luke, " The new Covenant in My Blood [1] which is shed for you." The reference here to the language of the old Testament, and to the rites of sacrifice, has been already noticed.[2] If we take the words as recorded by St. Matthew and St. Mark, " This is My Blood of the new Covenant," they will mean, " As in the old dispensation God made covenant with Israel with the blood of beasts, so now He makes covenant with Christians through the Blood of Christ ; and this wine is the emblem of that Blood, and the means of partaking of its benefits." If we take St. Luke's version (which is also St. Paul's), then we must understand, " The blood of old was the sign and pledge of the Covenant, the medium of its ratification. This cup is the sign and pledge of the new Covenant, which is now to be ratified in My Blood."

In either case we see obviously in the Eucharist a federal rite.

---

[1] I unhesitatingly translate *Covenant*, not Testament, believing that διαθήκη should always in the Bible be rendered Covenant. The only apparent exception is in Heb. ix. 15–20. Even here, however, Covenant will probably make the more pertinent sense. See Professor Scholefield's *Hints for a New Translation, ad h. l.*

[2] τοῦτο τὸ ποτήριον ἡ καινὴ διαθήκη ἐν τῷ αἵματί μου, τὸ ὑπὲρ ὑμῶν ἐκχυνόμενον (Luke xxii. 20). The participle prop-

erly agrees with ποτήριον, though it may by a solecism refer to αἷμα. Lightfoot *H. H. in loc.* says, " This seems to have reference to that cup of wine which was every day poured out in the drink-offerings in the daily sacrifice, for that also was poured out for the remission of sins. So that the bread may have reference to the body of the daily sacrifice, and the cup to the wine of the drink-offering "

As sacrifices, and especially feasts on sacrifices, were the means of ratifying covenants between man and man, or between man and God; so the Eucharistic feast upon the Sacrifice is the means of ratifying the covenant between the Lord and His people. The Blood of the covenant was shed upon the cross. So peace has been made. But the peace is accepted, and the covenant assured by this sacred banquet; where we are God's guests, and where the spiritual food spread for us is the Lamb slain for our sins, and where our souls may be washed by His most precious Blood.[1]

3. The third thing to be observed in the institution of the Eucharist is the command, " This do in remembrance of Me " (Luke xxii. 19; 1 Cor. xi. 24, 25).

This do, τοῦτο ποιεῖτε. *Hoc facite.* Do what? Make My Body? Sacrifice Me? If our Lord had commanded them to make His Body, why did He say "in remembrance of Me ?" Remembrance and actual bodily presence are scarcely compatible ideas. Besides, did our Lord then sacrifice Himself? Surely not. It was the next morning that He offered up Himself a Sacrifice; not then, when He sat with them at meat. But, just as, when the first Passover was instituted, the Israelites were commanded " to keep this feast by an ordinance for ever " (Exod. xii. 14; xiii. 10),— to sacrifice the lamb and eat it, as they had been instructed by Moses: so the disciples are commanded to observe this new feast, even as they were instructed by their Master and Lord. " Do this," *i. e.* " Do what you now see Me do." Break the bread, bless it, and consecrate it; then distribute among yourselves, and eat it; and likewise with the wine. And this all is to be done " in remembrance of Me." The Passover was in remembrance of the deliverance from Egypt and from the destruction of the first-born; and when it was kept, the Israelites were to tell their children what the ordinance meant (Exod. xiii. 8). But this Sacrament is a remembrance of greater deliverance, and of that gracious Master who wrought the deliverance; and " as often as we eat this bread and drink this cup, we do shew the Lord's death till He come " (1 Cor. xi. 26). In all ways therefore it may be a remembrance of Christ: but specially it is a remembrance of His death. It is a memorial, a showing forth of that sacrifice which He offered on the cross, and which we feed upon in our souls. As it is a commemoration of the sacrifice, so may it be called a commemorative sacrifice. But, as Christ was Himself present alive when He instituted the ordinance, and as He did not *then* offer up Himself a sacrifice on the

---

[1] See Cudworth, as above, ch. VI.

cross, nor hold in His own sacred hands His own crucified Body; so we believe not, that we are commanded to offer Him up afresh, or that we are to expect to feed upon His natural Flesh and Blood. His Body has been offered up once for all, a full, perfect, and sufficient sacrifice. We may present the remembrance of that sacrifice to God, may tell it out to the world, may believe that, whilst we eat the symbols with our mouths, we feed upon the Saviour in our spirits; but we have no warrant to believe, and we could find no greater comfort in believing, that Christ was to be newly sacrificed every day, and His very Flesh and Blood to be eaten and drunk by our bodily mouths.

II. *Our Lord's Discourse at Capernaum.* John vi.

A great many, both of the Roman Catholic divines and of the mere figurists, have denied that the discourse in the sixth chapter of St. John has any reference to the grace of the Eucharist. The motive of such denial is obvious; for it is next to impossible to admit that the Eucharist is there referred to, without also admitting that no material presence is tenable, and at the same time, that some real spiritual feeding of the soul is promised. It is said indeed that the discourse was delivered before the Eucharist was instituted, and therefore could not have applied to it: an argument, which must surely seem very strange, if we consider how very much our Lord's discourses are anticipatory and prophetic. Indeed almost all His teaching seems suitable to instruct His followers in "the things pertaining to the Kingdom of God," the things that were to be in His Church and reign upon earth, rather than suitable to the time of His bodily presence. So His discourse with Nicodemus was as much anticipatory of the institution of baptism, as this discourse at Capernaum was of the institution of the Holy Communion. And, to bring but one more example, if our Lord be never supposed to speak and to teach but concerning things already revealed and manifested, what could have been His meaning in His many declarations that Christians "must *take up their Cross*, and follow Him;" [1] when as yet all those who heard Him knew not for certain that He would die at all, and most assuredly understood not "what death He should die?"

It is quite clear then, that the mystery of the discourse in St. John vi. required something to make it intelligible. Many even of our Lord's disciples were so offended at it, that they at once "went back, and walked no more with Him" (ver. 66). What

[1] See Matt. x. 38, xvi. 24; Mark viii. 34, x. 21; Luke ix. 23, xiv. 27.

so sorely puzzled them must doubtless have sunk deep into their memories; and when next our blessed Saviour used the same lan guage as He had used on this memorable occasion, is it not cer- tain, that His first words would recur with all their force, and that the teaching of the first discourse would be coupled with that of the second? Now the only occasions on which we read that Jesus said anything about eating His Flesh and drinking His Blood, were, first in this instance at Capernaum, secondly at the last Pass- over, when He instituted the Eucharist. How the disciples who heard both discourses could fail to couple them together, it is hard to conceive. In the former, inestimable blessings were said to accom- pany the eating and drinking of Christ's Body and Blood: in the latter, a special mode appeared to be pointed out, by which His Body and Blood might be eaten and drunken. Both, no doubt, sounded strange and wonderful. Those who wondered at them both, would naturally compare the one with the other, to see if the one would not explain the other.

And surely the one does explain the other. In the sixth chap- ter of St. John we read that our Lord had just fed five thousand men with five loaves and two fishes. They who had seen the miracle, on the next day followed Jesus; but as He well knew, not for spiritual blessing, but that they might again be fed and be filled (v. 26). To this carnal and unbelieving multitude He en- joins, "that they should labour not for earthly, but for spiritual food, which endureth unto everlasting life" (v. 27); and taking occasion of their own reference to the manna in the wilderness (v. 31), He tells them, that, as God gave their fathers manna, so now He would give them "true bread from Heaven" (v. 32). He then declares Himself to be " the Bread of life: " and adds, " he that cometh to Me shall never hunger, and he that believeth on Me shall never thirst" (v. 35), *i. e.* neither hunger nor thirst, be- cause, thus coming and believing, he shall be fed upon the Bread of life. The Jews, who were present, now begin to murmur. They disbelieve the Saviour's saying, that He had come down from Heaven, supposing that they knew both His father and His mother. He then goes on, not to explain His statements, but to enforce, and rather put them with more mystery and difficulty. He tells them that, not only had He come down from Heaven, that not only was He the Bread of life, but that, whereas the fathers ate manna and died, yet those who should eat that Bread, should never die. And then most startling words of all, He says that the bread which He should give was His Flesh, which he would give for the life of the world (v. 51). And when this saying caused fresh striving amongst them, He adds, " Verily, verily, I say unto you, Except ye eat the Flesh of the Son of Man, and drink His Blood, ye have no life in you. . . . My Flesh is meat indeed, and My Blood is drink indeed. . . . As the living Father hath sent Me, and I live by the Father; so he that eateth Me, even he shall live by Me " (vv. 53–57).

Now those who tell us that this had no reference to the Eucharist, say that nothing is here meant but that faith in the death of Christ is the great means of union to Christ, and that which raises us to life and immortality. But surely Calvin's belief, that something more express and sublime is intended by such striking language, must commend itself to our reason. It is not the way of Scripture to expound to us simple doctrines by such mysterious language; but rather by simple figures and analogies to bring down deep doctrines in some degree to the level of our capacities. Yet, if all this discourse be merely to teach us that we must believe in the death of Christ, we have an example of most difficult language, and, we may add, language most likely to give offence, in order to express what requires no figures to make it intelligible, when simply and plainly stated. But if it be true, that to those who believe in Christ, to those who come to Him believing, He, in some manner far above our comprehension, so communicates His blessed Self, so joins them to Him by an ineffable union, that they may be said to be one with Him, and He with them, that He dwelleth in them and they in Him, that as He liveth by the Father so they live by Him; — if this and the like of this be true, then can we understand, that some deep language, some strong metaphors, may be needful to express the doctrine, and that the greater and more mysterious the blessing, the stranger and more hard to understand may be the language.

Now, certainly it is true that the faithful Christian lives by union to the glorified, divine humanity of His Lord. Christ, who is one with the Father by His Godhead, becomes one with His disciples by His manhood: and by an union with us, which is ineffable, and to be comprehended only by a devout and reverent believing, He supports, sustains, and feeds that spiritual life which He creates in us. That this is one chief fruit of His incarnation, all Scripture bears witness. That this, and perhaps much more than this, is taught in the chapter we are considering, there can be no reasonable question. And, although faith is an essential instrument for enabling us to receive such blessing (see v. 35); yet something much deeper and sublimer than the mere act of believing is plainly intended by it, — even that in spirit we are truly joined to the Man Christ Jesus, our great Head and Lord; that our whole spiritual man is sustained and nourished by Him; that by His life we live; by His might and power our weakness is upheld and strengthened. We do not presume to say that this is all the mystery conveyed to us by the language of our Lord. But this we may boldly affirm is the character, though it be not the sum of the mystery. And when we come to find the like language used by Him concerning the holy ordinance which He established at His passion, can we fail to infer, that with that ordinance, rightly and faithfully partaken of, are communicated those very blessings which in the discourse at Capernaum are so marvellously expressed?

Such thoughts must free us from the frigid notions of the disciples of Zuinglius; but will they lead us to the carnal notions of the transubstantialists? Most surely, No! There are two statements, in the chapter we are considering, quite fatal to the doctrine of the material presence. One is, where our Lord tells us that whosoever eats of the bread of life shall " not die " (ver. 51), " shall live for ever " (ver. 58): that " he who eateth His Flesh and drinketh His Blood, hath eternal life " (ver. 54). Now, if the bread and wine in the communion are changed into the substance of the Body and Blood, then every unworthy partaker, notwithstanding his unworthiness, partakes of Christ's Body and Blood; and hence, according to this chapter, eating the bread of life shall " not die " — " shall live for ever " — " hath eternal life." He cannot, as St. Paul says, eat to condemnation, but must eat to salvation. The other statement is stronger still. When those who heard murmured at our Lord's promise to feed them with His Flesh and Blood, Jesus said unto them, " Doth this offend you? What and if ye shall see ($\dot{\epsilon}\grave{\alpha}\nu$ $o\hat{\upsilon}\nu$ $\theta\epsilon\omega\rho\hat{\eta}\tau\epsilon$) the Son of Man ascend where He was before? It is the spirit that quickeneth, the flesh profiteth nothing; the words that I speak unto you, they are spirit, and they are life " (vv. 61–63). Do my words offend you? If ye see Me ascend where I was before, how then will ye judge? Will ye then be still more offended, thinking my words still more impossible? Or will ye then begin to understand the truth, and to know that they must be spiritually interpreted? The mistake ye have made, is that ye have interpreted them carnally. But it is the spirit which profiteth; the flesh profiteth nothing. The words that I speak unto you, they are spirit, and they are life. Such was the obvious meaning of our Lord's reply; and it penetrates to the very depths of the difficulty. The meaning of the discourse was all spiritual. The feeding on Christ's Body and Blood is a spiritual feeding. No other feeding profits. It would do no good. To eat the material substance of His Flesh, and drink the material substance of His Blood, would be useless. It is the spirit only which gives life; and the words which He had spoken, were spirit and life. And be it noted, whether the discourse did, by anticipation, concern the Eucharist, or whether it did not, yet this much is clear: we have it revealed in the unfailing and unerring words of our Redeemer, that carnally to eat His Flesh and drink His Blood would profit us nothing; and therefore we may be assured infallibly, that such a carnal feeding, being profitless, would never have been ordained by Him in a Sacrament for His Church.

III. *The statements of St. Paul.*

These occur in 1 Cor. x. and 1 Cor. xi.

The argument from the former chapter (1 Cor. x.) is of this nature. The Christians of Corinth, living among idolaters, were tempted to join in idol-feasts, at which meats that had been offered in sacrifice were solemnly and religiously eaten. However innocent it may be to eat meat of any kind, St. Paul points out that it is no longer innocent when the eating it implies a participating in an idolatrous ceremony, especially an idolatrous sacrifice. He that partakes of a sacrificial feast declares thereby his respect for the sacrifice, and his interest in it. He claims to be a partaker of the sacrifice. The Apostle illustrates this in three ways: first, by our participation of the sacrifice of Christ in the Eucharist (vv. 16, 17); secondly, by the Jews' participation in the sacrifices of which they eat; thirdly, by the heathen's participation of the sacrifices of demon-gods. To take the last two illustrations first. He observes with regard to " Israel after the flesh," that " they which eat of the sacrifices are partakers (κοινωνοὶ) of the altar." That is to say, by eating of the meat of the sacrifice they have a share, a participation in the benefit of that which is offered on the altar (v. 18). As for the Gentiles, he says, that they offer sacrifice, not to God, but to demon-gods (δαιμονίοις); and it is unbecoming in Christians to be partakers or communicants (κοινωνοὶ) of demon-gods. Nay! it is altogether inconsistent to drink of the cup of the Lord, and of the cup of demon-gods; to partake of the Lord's table, and the table of demon-gods (vv. 20, 21); the " table of demon-gods " here meaning the feast upon the

heathen sacrifices, " the table of the Lord " meaning the banquet
of the Holy Communion, and probably alluding to Malachi i.
7, 12 ; where the expression " table of the Lord " is used in immediate connection with the word " altar," and refers to the sacrificial
feasting connected with the Jewish sacrifices. In juxtaposition
then, and immediate comparison with these feasts on Jewish and
heathen offerings, St. Paul places the Christian festival of the
Eucharist ; and as he tells the Corinthians, that the Israelites in
their feasts were partakers of the altar, and the heathen partook
of the table of devils, so he says, Christians partake of the Lord's
table.   But more than this, he asks, " The cup of blessing which
we bless, is it not a joint-partaking (κοινωνία) of the Blood of
Christ ?   The bread which we break, is it not a joint-partaking
of the Body of Christ ?   For we being many are one bread, and
one body ; for we are all partakers of that one bread " (vv. 16, 17).
The natural signification of the word κοινωνία, and the sense deducible from the context, require that it should be rendered, as
above, *joint-partaking* or *joint-participation*.[1]   The parallel is between partaking of idol sacrifices, partaking of Jewish sacrifices,
and partaking of the Christian Sacrifice, *i. e.* Christ.   And the
17th verse is added to show, that by such participation there is a
joint fellowship, not only with Christ, the Head, but with His
whole Body the Church.

Now, what must we infer from this teaching ?   Does it not
plainly tell us, that the feeding at the Lord's table corresponds with
the feeding at the Jewish altar and the heathen idol-feasts.   That,
as the latter gave them participation in their sacrifices and their
demon-gods, so the former gives us participation of Christ's Body
and Blood !   This much we cannot, and we would not deny.   The
bread and wine are to us means or instruments, whereby, through
God's grace, we become partakers of the sacrifice of the Body and
Blood of Christ.   But, on the other hand, must we therefore infer,
that we partake of Christ's Body, naturally and materially ?   The
very words appear to teach us otherwise.   If there were a real
change of the elements into Christ's natural Flesh and Blood, it
seems altogether unaccountable, that the force of the argument
should have been weakened by the introduction of the word
κοινωνία *participation*.   If the bread be literally and substantially

---

[1] κοίνος common, κοινόω to make common, impart, κοινωνὸς a partaker, κοινωνία
participation.   This is the natural meaning.   κοινωνία means also close communion or joint partnership.   St. Paul ordinarily uses κοινωνία for *partaking*.   See 2
Cor. viii. 4, ix. 3.   Comp. κοινωνοὶ ix. 18.
In Rom. xv. 26, Heb. xiii. 16, κοινωνία is
communication.

the Body, it would have been more natural to say, " Is not the bread which we break, Christ's Body?" And the inference would be immediate; Can we eat Christ's Body and demon-sacrifices together? The word κοινωνία, on which the peculiar strength of the passage depends, whilst it clearly points to the Eucharistic elements as ordained means to enable us to partake of the Body and Blood of Christ, yet shows too that they are *means of partaking*, not themselves changed into the substance of that which they represent. They are ordained, that we may partake of Christ; but they are not Christ themselves.

The other passage of St. Paul (1 Cor. xi. 19–30) has the same object as that which we have just considered; namely, to increase our reverence for " the dignity of this holy mystery." The early Christians appear to have joined with the reception of the communion an *agape* or love-feast. In such a feast it was seemly, that the rich should provide for the poor, and that all things should be in common. But in Corinth, a city long famous for luxury, the richer Christians appear to have overlooked the Christian principle, and to have made their feasts of charity minister to their own indulgence, rather than to their poor neighbours' wants. This was in itself wrong; it was not, as the Apostle says, to eat the Lord's supper;[1] and it was despising the church of God, — shaming those who had no houses to feast in. And what made it worst of all was this, that with these feasts of charity was joined a reception of the Holy Communion; and to receive that at a time when some were feasting gluttonously, and others suffering from hunger, was to treat contemptuously the most sacred and blessed ordinance of the Lord. It was receiving that Sacrament unworthily. It was not only treating the agape as a private feast, and one in which self-indulgence was permissible, but it was making the Eucharist itself a common thing.

To enforce his lesson on this subject, the Apostle reminds the Corinthians of the mode and the words in which our Lord had instituted the Eucharist. This part of his teaching we have already considered. But he goes on to reason that, as our Lord had instituted bread and wine as Sacraments of His Body and Blood, " therefore whosoever shall eat this bread, and drink this cup of the Lord unworthily, shall be guilty of the Body and Blood

---

[1] κυριακὸν δεῖπνον φαγεῖν, v. 20. This probably does not refer to the Eucharist, but to the *Agape*, the feast of charity, which was joined with it. See Hammond and Whitby, *in loc.;* Waterland, *On the Eucharist*, ch. i. 8; Suicer, s. v. 'Αγαπαὶ; Cave, *Primitive Christianity*, pt. i. ch. ii.; Bingham, *E. A.* Bk. xv. ch. vii. §§ 6, 7, 9.

of the Lord," ver. 27.   He then exhorts to self-examination, ver.
28, and adds, ver. 29 : " For he that eateth and drinketh unworthily, eateth and drinketh to himself condemnation, not setting
apart as holy the Body of the Lord " (κρίμα ἑαυτῷ ἐσθίει καὶ πίνει,
μὴ διακρίνων τὸ Σῶμα τοῦ Κυρίου).[1] The Lord's own words of
institution pointed to this Sacrament as the means of participating
in His Body and Blood ; he therefore who received that Sacrament, not as a thing most sacred and venerable, but as part or
adjunct of a common feast, was guilty of great and heinous impiety,
because he did not set apart as a holy thing the Body of the
Lord.   This is the plain meaning of the passage, according to the
obvious rendering of the original ; and it certainly teaches a lesson
of deep reverence, and speaks home plainly to our faith.   It seems
an unanswerable argument against those who esteem the Eucharist
as " a bare sign of a thing absent."   We, of the Church of England,
who believe Christ really present in His Sacraments, and spiritually
there feeding our souls, as much as those who look for a natural
reception of Him, can feel the truth and awfulness of such apostolic
warnings.   We do not differ with the believers in transubstantiation, so far as their statement goes, that in the Eucharist there is
a real presence of the Lord.   And therefore we feel, as they do,
that to receive unworthily is to do dishonour to the Body of Christ.
Our difference with them is not concerning the truth of Christ's
presence, which the Apostle's words seem forcibly to teach us ; but
we differ with them only concerning the mode.   That they define
carnally, whilst we believe it mystically.   And herein we can
scarcely use words more apposite than the words used long ago
by Calvin : " If any ask me concerning the mode, I am not
ashamed to confess the mystery to be more sublime than my intellect can grasp, or than words can tell ; and, that I may speak more
openly, I essay rather than understand.   Therefore here I embrace
without controversy the truth of God, in which I may safely
acquiesce.   He pronounces His Flesh the food of my soul, His
Blood the drink.   I offer my soul to be fed with such aliments.
In His sacred Feast He bids me, under symbols of bread and wine,

---

[1] διακρίνων, discernens, separating,
setting apart as holy. So the Syriac,
ܦܪܘܫ.   To discern, as we in modern
English use that word, is only a secondary and improper sense of διακρίνειν, as
it is also of discernere. The natural
meaning is to separate, to make a distinction
of one thing from another. It is used in
classical as well as in Hellenistic Greek,
with the sense of to set apart for holy purposes. So Pindar, Olymp. x. 54–56 : Περὶ
δὲ πάξαις ἄλτιν μὲν ὅγ' ἐν καθαρῷ διακρίνει.
The plain meaning therefore of St. Paul
is, that people who mixed up the Eucharist with a profane feast, treated the
Lord's Body, which is given us there, as
no better than a common thing, not as
sacred and holy.

to take His Body and Blood, to eat and to drink. I doubt not but that He really offers, and that I receive. All I reject is what is in itself absurd, unworthy of the heavenly majesty of Christ, or alien from the verity of His nature as man." [1] So Calvin; and so our own Hooker: "What these elements are in themselves it skilleth not. It is enough that *unto me that take them* they are the Body and Blood of Christ. His promise in witness hereof sufficeth. His word He knoweth which way to accomplish. Why should any cogitation possess the mind of a faithful communicant; but, O my God, Thou art true: O my soul, thou art happy?" [2] It is in this way that the Scriptures have left it: so the devout soul has ever embraced it: and so we may safely and thankfully receive it, — not speculate curiously, nor expound carnally; but believe and live.

[1] *Institut.* IV. xvii. 32.   [2] *E. P.* Bk. v. ch. LXVI. 12.

NOTE.

I HAVE confined myself in this Article almost wholly to the presence in the Eucharist, and the mode of receiving Christ's Body and Blood. The latter part of the Article has thereby been deprived of its due attention. It is, however, but a simple corollary. Elevating the host resulted from a belief in transubstantiation. If that doctrine be rejected, we shall not believe the wafer to have been really transformed into Christ's Body, and so shall not worship it, nor elevate it for worship. There is evidently no Scriptural authority for the elevation of the Host, the command being, " Take, *eat.*" The Roman ritualists themselves admit, that there is no trace of its existence before the 11th or 12th centuries; and no certain documents refer to it till about A. D. 1200. See Palmer, *On the Church,* Vol. I. part I. ch. XI p. 311.

[Two particulars of the Tridentine doctrine of Transubstantiation are especially to be noted for their contrast to the Anglican doctrine of the real Spiritual Presence in the Eucharist.

(1.) The annihilation of the elements. With regard to which, remember: —

(*a.*) The absence of Scriptural proof.

(*b.*) The patristic teaching that the elements remain in their original substance; especially the use by Gelasius and others of the accepted Eucharistic doctrine as an argument against the Eutychians. See Pearson *On the Creed,* p. 247, and note.

(*c.*) That if this view is correct, it is a solitary instance of a miracle which contradicts the senses, instead of appealing to them.

(2.) The identification of the consecrated elements not with the Body and Blood of. Christ, but with His entire Personality by affirming the presence in them of His Human Soul. With regard to which, remember: —

(*a.*) The absence of Scriptural proof. The language is, "this is my Body," "this is my Blood," not "this is I myself;" the sole exception being St. John vi. 57: "He hat eateth me, even he shall live by me," where the manner of feeding upon Christ had been explained in the preceding verse to be the eating of His flesh and drinking of His Blood.

(*b.*) The language of the Fathers is similar.

(*c.*) So also is the statement of the Orthodox Eastern Church, Guettée, *Exp. de la Doctrine,* p. 135.

On the subject of the Eucharistic Presence, see the invaluable Introduction to Part II. of the *Principles of Divine Service* by Archdeacon Freeman. — *H. A. Y. — J. W.*]

ARTICLE XXIX.

Of the Wicked which eat not the Body of Christ in the use of the Lord's Supper.

De manducatione Corporis Christi, et impios illud non manducare.

THE Wicked, and such as be void of a lively faith, although they do carnally and visibly press with their teeth (as *St. Augustine* saith) the Sacrament of the Body and Blood of Christ, yet in no wise are they partakers of Christ : but rather, to their condemnation, do eat and drink the sign or Sacrament of so great a thing.

IMPII, et fide viva destituti, licet carnaliter et visibiliter (ut Augustinus loquitur) corporis et sanguinis Christi Sacramentum dentibus premant, nullo tamen modo Christi participes efficiuntur.

Sed potius tantæ rei Sacramentum, seu symbolum, ad judicium sibi manducant et bibunt.

SECTION I. — HISTORY.

IF the last Article be true, this most probably follows on it. There are but two possible views of the question. Either the wicked and unbelieving do not eat Christ's Body and Blood, but only their sacred symbols ; or they eat the Body and Blood, but to condemnation, not to salvation. The former alternative has generally been held, in latter times, by the advocates of a spiritual feeding; the latter, by the believers in transubstantiation, and, I suppose, by most believers in consubstantiation. The fathers' teaching is naturally obscure on this point. They so constantly called the symbols by the name of that they symbolized, that they would commonly speak of eating the Body of Christ, when they meant only the consecrated bread, the Sacrament of His Body. Yet plain passages occur, which are strongly in favour of the view taken by our reformers in this Article.

Origen speaks concerning " the Word who was made flesh, the true food, which no wicked man can eat. For, if it were possible that one continuing in wickedness should eat Him who was made flesh, the Word, the living bread ; in vain would it have been written, *whoso eateth this bread shall live forever.*" [1] Cyprian tells

---

[1] Πολλὰ δ' ἂν περὶ αὐτοῦ λέγοιτο τοῦ Λόγου, ὃς γέγονε σὰρξ καὶ ἀληθινὴ βρῶσις, ἣν τινα ὁ φάγων πάντως ζήσεται εἰς τὸν αἰῶνα, οὐδενὸς δυναμένου φαύλου ἐσθίειν αὐτήν· εἰ γὰρ οἶόν τε ἦν ἔτι φαῦλον μένοντα ἐσθίειν τὸν γενόμενον σάρκα Λόγον ὄντα, καὶ ἄρτον ζῶντα, οὐκ ἂν ἐγέγραπτο, ὅτι πᾶς ὁ φάγων τὸν ἄρτον τοῦτον ζήσεται εἰς τὴν αἰῶνα. Origen. *In Matt.* xv. Comment.

a story of the Eucharistic bread becoming a cinder in the hands of one who had lapsed, as a proof that Christ could not be received by the unworthy communicant.[1]   So St. Hilary, " The bread that came down from Heaven, is not taken but by him who hath the Lord, and is a member of Christ." [2]   St. Augustine is quoted in the very words of the Article.   Some part of the passage is thought by the Benedictine editors to have been interpolated; which I will put between brackets.   What remains, however, is fully sufficient to serve the purpose for which it is adduced.   " By this, he who abides not in Christ, nor Christ in him, without doubt eats not [spiritually] His Flesh, nor drinks His Blood; [though he carnally and visibly press with his teeth the Sacrament of His Body and Blood] ; but rather he eats and drinks, to his condemnation, the Sacrament of so great a thing." [3]   So elsewhere, he clearly distinguishes between sacramental eating and real eating: " *Whoso eateth My flesh and drinketh My blood, dwelleth in Me, and I in him.* Here our Lord shows what it is, not only sacramentally, but really, to eat Christ's Body and drink His Blood ; even to dwell in Christ and Christ in him.   And He said this, as much as to say, Whosoever does not abide in Me and I in him, let him not say, nor think that he eats My Body or drinks My Blood." [4]   So Jerome also says, that " lovers of pleasure rather than lovers of God eat not the Flesh, nor drink the Blood of Jesus." [5]

It has been argued indeed, that the prayer in the ancient Liturgies, for the descent of the Holy Ghost upon the elements, implied of necessity a belief that after that descent the elements of themselves become so truly the Body and Blood of Christ, that the com-

[1] " Et quidem alius, quia et ipse maculatus sacrificio a sacerdote celebrato partem cum cæteris ausus est latenter accipere, sanctum Domini corpus edere et contrectare non potuit : cinerem ferre se, apertis manibus invenit. Documento unius ostenditur, Dominum recedere cum negatur, nec immerentibus ad salutem prodesse quod sumitur, quando gratia salutaris in cinerem, sanctitate fugiente, mutatur." — Cyprian. *De Lapsis*, p. 133, Fell.

[2] " Panis qui descendit de cœlo, non nisi ab eo accipitur qui Dominum habet, et Christi membrum est." — Hilar. *De Trinit.* Lib. VIII.

[3] " Ac per hoc qui non manet in Christo, et in quo non manet Christus, procul dubio nec manducat [spiritualiter] carnem Ejus, nec bibit Ejus sanguinem [licet carnaliter et visibiliter premat dentibus sacramentum corporis et sanguinis Christi :] sed magis tantæ rei sacramentum ad judicium sibi manducat et bibit." — *In Joan. Tract.* 26, Tom. III. pars II. p. 500.

[4] " Denique Ipse dicens *Qui manducat Carnem meam, et bibit Sanguinem meum, in Me manet, et Ego in eo ;* ostendit quid sit non sacramento tenus, sed re vera Corpus Christi manducare, et Ejus sanguinem bibere : hoc est enim in Christo manere, ut in illo maneat et Christus. Sic enim hoc dixit, tanquam diceret, Qui non in me manet, et in quo Ego non maneo, non se dicat aut existimet manducare Corpus meum aut bibere sanguinem meum." — *De Civitate Dei*, Lib. XXI. c. 25, Tom. VII. p. 646.

[5] " Omnes voluptatis magis amatores, quam amatores Dei . . . . nec comedunt carnem Jesu, neque bibunt sanguinem Ejus; de quo Ipse loquitur : *Qui comedit carnem meam, et bibit sanguinem meum, habet vitam æternam.*" — Hieronym. *In Isai.* c. 66, ver. 17. Tom. III. p. 506.

municants, whether worthily or unworthily receiving, must necessarily partake of the Body and Blood.   This, if it means anything
of the kind, means the full doctrine of transubstantiation.   But no
such conclusion can be deduced from the fact of the invocation.
For first, the like invocation of the Spirit was made in baptism ;
and of this we hear much earlier than of the invocation in the Eucharist.[1]   Now, though the fathers believed, as the English reformers did, that the Holy Ghost " would sanctify the water to the
mystical washing away of sin ; "[2] yet they neither believed in a
change of the substance of the water, nor in an admixture of the
Holy Spirit with the water ;[3] nor that an unworthy recipient obtained the blessing of the Spirit's sanctification.   We must suppose
the same principle to apply to the sanctification of the symbols in
the Eucharist.   As the minister was to consecrate, so the fathers
looked for the Spirit to bless the elements to a sacred use.   " We
beseech the merciful God," says St. Cyril, " to send the Holy
Ghost upon the elements ; that He may make the bread Christ's
Body and the wine His Blood.   For, undoubtedly, whatever the
Holy Ghost touches, that is sanctified and changed." [4]

But, though the Holy Spirit sanctifies and changes, it follows not
that the change is a change of substance.   The sanctification of the
elements is to a sacred use and office, — to a new relation, not to
a new nature.   Accordingly, St. Cyril speaks afterwards of the
illapse of the Holy Spirit, as making the elements holy, and at the
same time making the communicant holy.   " Holy also are ye,
being now endowed with the Spirit." [5]   So, some of the ancient
Liturgies have a prayer for the descent on the communicants first,
and then on the elements.[6]   And so, in several Liturgies, and
especially in the Gregorian Sacramentary,[7] from thence derived
to the canon of the mass, the words " to us," are inserted ;
thereby restricting the blessing upon the elements to their effects
on the recipient.   Nay ! that transubstantiation could not have
been intended, has been admitted by many Romanist divines ; inas-

---

[1] Tertull. De Baptismo, c. 4.
[2] Office of Public Baptism.
[3] μιγνύντων τὰ ἄμικτα, says Basil, of
those who spoke of the mixture of the
Spirit and water. Basil, De Sp. S. Tom.
III. p. 30. See Waterland, On the Eucharist, ch. x.
[4] Cyril Hierosol. Catech. Mystag. v.
c. 7. This is the oldest certain mention
of the custom ; i. e. in the middle of the
fourth century. The next oldest form is
in the Apostolical Constitutions, Lib. VIII.
c. 12 : " We beseech Thee, O God, to send
Thy Holy Spirit on this Sacrifice . . .

that He may make this bread to become
the Body of Thy Christ, and this cup to
become the Blood of Thy Christ." — See
Waterland, as above.
[5] Ibid. c. 19.
[6] " Super nos et super hæc dona."
(See the Liturgies in Fabricius and
Renaudotius, cited by Waterland, as
above.)
[7] " Quam oblationem Tu, Deus, in omnibus quæsumus benedictam facere dig-
neris, ut nobis corpus et sanguis fiat," &c.
— Cited by Waterland.

much as, in the Greek Liturgies, the invocation of the Spirit followed the words of institution. Now, the Latin divines fix the consecration to the words of institution. Hence, if there be any truth in transubstantiation, the change must, according to them, have taken place before the invocation, and could not therefore be the effect of the invocation.[1] In short, " all circumstances show, that the true and ancient intent of that part of the service was not to implore any physical change in the elements, no, nor so much as a physical connection of the Spirit with the elements, but a moral change only in the elements, as to relation and uses, and a gracious presence of the Holy Spirit upon the communicants." [2]

But, when a belief arose in the *opus operatum*, and in the absolute change of substance in the elements, then, naturally, it was held, that not only the faithful, but even the unbelieving, must receive the very Body and Blood of Christ, though of course the latter, only to condemn them. And then too, the fathers (who spoke freely of the elements under the name of that they signified, and, no doubt, believed in a sanctification of them to holy purposes) were cited as holding the same language, and as witnesses to the same doctrine.

It seems by no means necessary that the like result should follow from the doctrine of *consubstantiation*. Indeed Luther greatly abhorred the *opus operatum*. Still, I suppose, the Lutherans rather inclined to the belief that the wicked eat the Body of Christ, yet impiously, and to their ruin. And so this Article was, for a time, expunged by Queen Elizabeth and her Council; [3] probably as not agreeable to those members of the Church who were of Lutheran sentiments. All other branches of the Reformation seem to have agreed that, as the presence of Christ was not in the elements, but only vouchsafed with the elements " to the faithful," so His presence would be withheld from those who were unfaithful and impenitent.

Section II. — SCRIPTURAL PROOF.

IN one sense of the words, then, we may admit that every communicant eats Christ's Body and drinks His Blood ; because he eats the symbol which is called His Body (*corpus, h. e. figura*

---

[1] Waterland, as above, p. 407. (Cambridge, 1737.) The subject is very fully discussed in this place by Dr. Waterland.

[2] Ibid.

[3] See above, Introduction, p. 15

corporis), and drinks the symbol which is called His Blood. But all that has been said in former Articles to disprove the doctrine of the *opus operatum*, applies here. The actual reception of Christ's Body and Blood is the reception, not of the outward sign, but of the inward grace. Now, the inward grace of the Sacraments be- longs only to the faithful, not to the impenitent and unbelieving. Of course, if we admit a physical change in the elements, we must believe Christ's Body to be eaten, not only by the wicked, but, as has been often argued, by mice or dogs, or any other animal, that may accidentally devour a portion of the consecrated bread. Hence the contrary position to the statement of this Article follows, of necessity, on the doctrine of transubstantiation. But then, the op- posite doctrine of an efficacious, spiritual presence, and that rather in the recipient than in the element, seems inevitably to issue in the doctrine here propounded.

As for the direct statements of the new Testament, we must lay aside the words of institution ; which will not aid us, until we have determined whether they imply a spiritual or a carnal presence ; and confine our attention to the eleventh chapter of 1 Cor. and to the sixth chapter of St. John. In the former we are told, that " whosoever shall eat this bread and drink this cup of the Lord, unworthily, is guilty of the Body and Blood of the Lord " (ver. 27) ; and that " he that eateth and drinketh unworthily, eateth and drinketh condemnation to himself, not setting apart as holy the Lord's Body " (ver. 29). Perhaps the first view of this pas- sage rather appears to favour the doctrine of the *opus operatum*. The unworthy communicant is " guilty of the Body and Blood of the Lord," which he pollutes ; and he eats and drinks condemna- tion because he does not set apart and treat with reverence the Lord's Body. At least, candour may oblige us to admit that there is nothing in St. Paul's words thus cited, which will not square with the hypothesis that every recipient equally eats the Flesh and drinks the Blood of Christ. But, on the other hand, we are justi- fied in contending that there is nothing inconsistent with our own belief, that the wicked do not eat Christ. In the former case, we can see how great the profanation would be ; but in the latter, it is still very fearful. The feast provided for the faithful is doubtless a spiritual feast on the Lord's Body and Blood ; hence, the profane receiver is unquestionably " guilty concerning Christ's Body and Blood " (ἔνοχος τοῦ σώματος, κ. τ. λ.). And again, as the bread and wine are the means of communicating to us the Body and Blood of Christ ; so he, who treats the Eucharist as part of a mere common feast, (which the Corinthians did,) does clearly refuse to treat with reverence, and to set apart as holy the Body of the Lord.

But if there be any ambiguity in the words of St. Paul, there can be none in the words of our Lord. He plainly tells us, "He that eateth My Flesh and drinketh My Blood, dwelleth in Me, and I in him" (John vi. 56). "He that eateth Me, even he shall live by Me" (ver. 57). "He that eateth of this bread shall live forever" (ver. 58). "Whoso eateth my Flesh and drinketh My Blood hath eternal life; and I will raise him up at the last day" (ver. 54). Now all this is plain, that the real feeding on Christ is to salvation, not to condemnation. All are agreed, that the wicked do not profit, but rather suffer loss by eating in the Eucharist. But then, if they do not profit, we inevitably infer from the words of our Lord, that they have not eaten His Flesh nor drunk His Blood; for those who do so, "live by Him," — "live forever," — "have eternal life," — have Him dwelling in them, — "have eternal life, and are raised up at the last day."

The only escape from the inference seems to be in an assertion, that John vi. does not refer to Eucharistic feeding, but to spiritual feeding apart from the Eucharist. But whatever conclusion we may come to on that head, the statement seems clear and general, "He that eateth Me shall live by Me" (ver. 57). Now, granting that this eating of Christ may be apart from the Eucharist, yet is it not quite clear that, *howsoever it be*, it is life-giving? The proposition is perfectly universal. Though, therefore, we may admit that it may be applicable to a mere spiritual feeding by faith, yet we must contend that, if in the Eucharist it be *real*, then it must bring life with it. "He that eateth shall live." The only question is therefore — who eateth? Whosoever eateth, if the eating be real eating, eateth life. If, therefore, in the Eucharist a man really feeds on Christ, he lives by Him. Hence, those who eat and drink unworthily, cannot really feed on the Lord's Body; though, "to their condemnation, they do eat and drink the Sacrament of so great a thing." And this seems, at the same time, to prove the proposition of our Article, and to disprove the whole theory of transubstantiation, and of the natural presence.

83

ARTICLE XXX.

Of both Kinds.

De utraque Specie.

THE Cup of the Lord is not to be denied to the Lay-people : for both the parts of the Lord's Sacrament, by Christ's ordinance and commandment, ought to be ministered to all Christian men alike.

CALIX Domini laicis non est denegandus, utraque enim pars Dominici Sacramenti ex Christi institutione et præcepto, omnibus Christianis ex æquo administrari debet.

SECTION I.—HISTORY.

IT is not so much as pretended by the more candid Roman Catholics, that there is patristic authority for withdrawing the cup from the laity.

In the earliest account we have of the ministration of the Eucharist, that of Justin Martyr, we read that " the deacons gave *to every one* that was present to partake of the bread, over which thanks had been offered, and *of wine* mixed with water, and that they carried them also to those not present."[1] This is fully confirmed by St. Cyprian, who speaks of the deacons as " offering the cup to those who were present."[2] St. Chrysostom especially notices, that there was no distinction between priests and laymen in this respect : " Whereas under the old Covenant the priests ate some things, and the laymen others ; and it was not lawful for the people to partake of those things, of which the priest partook ; it is not so now, but one Body is placed before all, *and one cup.*"[3]

These and similar expressions of the fathers are fully borne out by the language of the ancient liturgies ; from which we infer, not only that both elements were administered alike to clergy and laity, but that they were ministered separately. The fear of spilling the

---

[1] Εὐχαριστήσαντος δὲ τοῦ προεστῶτος καὶ ἐπευφημήσαντος πάντος τοῦ λαοῦ, οἱ καλούμενοι παρ᾽ ἡμῖν διάκονοι διδόασιν ἑκάστῳ τῶν παρόντων μεταλαβεῖν τοῦ εὐχαριστηθέντος ἄρτου καὶ οἴνου καὶ ὕδατος, καὶ τοῖς οὐ παροῦσιν ἀποφέρουσι.— Justin. *Apol.* I. p. 97.

[2] " Ubi solennibus adimpletis calicem

diaconus offerre præsentibus cœpit."— Cyp. *De Lapsis*, p. 94, Fell.

[3] Οὐ καθάπερ ἐπὶ τῆς παλαίας τὰ μὲν ὁ ἱερεὺς ἤσθιε, τὰ δὲ ὁ ἀρχόμενος · καὶ θέμις οὐκ ἦν τῷ λαῷ μετέχειν ὧν μετεῖχεν ὁ ἱερεὺς, ἀλλ᾽ οὐ νῦν, ἀλλὰ πᾶσιν ἓν σῶμα πρόκειται καὶ ἓν ποτήριον.— Chrysost. *Homil.* XIV. *in* 1 *Cor.*

consecrated wine (of right to be regarded reverently, but in the course of time regarded superstitiously) led to the administering the two elements together, by dipping the consecrated bread into the cup; which custom still continues in the Eastern Churches. But the doctrine of transubstantiation naturally led to the belief that, inasmuch as the elements were wholly changed into the substance of Christ, therefore whole Christ, Body and Blood, was contained in either element; and hence that, if only one element was received, yet Christ was fully received under that one element.

It was not at first without opposition, both from councils and from eminent divines, that the custom which this belief gave rise to, gradually gained ground. Thus the xxviiith canon of the Council of Clermont (A. D. 1095) decrees, that all, who shall communicate at the altar, shall receive the Body and Blood of Jesus Christ under both kinds, if there be no provision to the contrary.[1] And in the next century, Geoffrey, Abbot of Vendome, censures the custom of a certain monastery, where both species were not administered separately, but the bread was steeped in the wine.[2]

In the time of the schoolmen, however, the question was pretty much discussed, whether it was lawful to receive in one kind only. They were by no means agreed that either element could be dispensed with. But the temptation to withhold the cup was great. Thereby the danger was avoided of spilling on the ground the sacred Blood of Christ. Thereby too, it was left in the power of the priesthood to dispense only so much as they chose, even of the ordinance of Christ.[3]

There was scarcely any corruption of Popery so much complained of by Wickliffe, Huss, and other early reformers, as this withholding from the faithful what they cherished, as a portion of their birthright. It was one of the abuses which, it was fondly

---

[1] See Dupin, Cent. xi. Vol ix. p. 74.

[2] Dupin, Cent. xii. Vol. x. p. 133.

[3] It is a remarkable acknowledgment of Cardinal Bona, that "always, everywhere, from the very first foundation of the Church to the 12th century, the faithful always communicated under the species both of bread and wine."

"Certum est omnes passim clericos et laicos, viros et mulieres sub utraque specie sacra mysteria antiquitus sumpsisse, cum solemni eorum celebrationi aderant, et offerebant et de oblatis participabant. Extra sacrificium vero, et extra ecclesiam semper et ubique sub una specie in usu fuit. Primæ parti assertionis consentiunt omnes, tam Catholici quam sectarii; nec eam negare potest, qui vel levissima rerum Ecclesiasticarum imbutus sit. Semper enim et ubique, ab ecclesiæ primordiis usque ad sæculum duodecimum, sub specie panis et vini communicarunt fideles: cœpitque paulatim ejus sæculi initio usus calicis obsolescere, plerisque episcopis eum populo interdicentibus ob periculum irreverentiæ et effusionis." — Bona, Rev. Liturg. Lib. ii. c. 18, n. 1, quoted by Bingham, E. A. xv. v. 1.

hoped, the Council of Constance (A. D. 1415) would reform and eradicate. But so far from reforming it, that famous Council decreed that, as the reception of one element was sufficient for the receiving wholly both the Body and Blood of Christ, so the Eucharist should be received by the laity in one kind only.[1]

This decree led to serious results in Germany. The sects of the Calixtines and Taborites sprang up in opposition to it; the former protesting against the depriving them of an inalienable right and privilege, the latter not satisfied with protesting, but having recourse even to arms and violence.[2]

It is only further necessary to add, that, whilst every reformed Church in Christendom restored to the laity the cup in the Eucharist, the Council of Trent, following the Council of Constance, decreed anathemas against all who held, that both kinds were necessary to all the faithful — against all who denied that the Catholic Church had been led by just causes to order the laity and the non-ministering clergy to communicate under the species of bread alone — and against all who denied that whole Christ was received according to His own institution under one kind.[3]

SECTION II. — SCRIPTURAL PROOF.

THE only passages in Scripture which can be appealed to, are those which relate to the institution of the Eucharist. In all of these there appears no difference between the bread and the cup, save only this: that in St. Matthew (xxvi. 27) our Lord is specially related to have used, concerning the latter, the words "Drink ye *all* of it," and in St. Mark (xiv. 23) it is specially recorded, that "they *all* drank of it;" whereas, concerning the bread, it is only said, "Take, eat." If therefore we can at all infer that one should be of more universal extent and applicability than the other, our inference should surely be rather in favour of the cup, than in favour of the other element.

But I believe it is never argued that Scripture gives authority for the withdrawing of the cup. The mode of argument is this. It is true, all the Apostles received both elements. But

---

[1] Concil. Constant. Sess. XIII. See also Mosheim, Cent. XV. ch. II. § 8.　　[2] Mosheim, Cent. XV. pt. II. ch. III. §§ 5, 6.　　[3] Sess. XXI. Cap. I II. III

then all were priests. This therefore is not sufficient ground for assuming that the laity are of necessity to receive both elements. It is granted, that it is not a matter *de fide* and of absolute obligation to withdraw the cup from laymen, but merely a Church-ordinance, for greater decency and edification. It is indeed necessary to consecrate both bread and wine, in order to follow our Lord's example; and, for the same reason, necessary that some one should receive them both. Hence the officiating priest always communicates in both kinds. But it is no injury to the rest, that they receive but in one kind, for whole Christ (Body and Blood and Spirit and Godhead) is received perfectly under either species; and therefore he who receives but one, has no need to receive more. It is a similar case to that when our Lord said to St. Peter, " He that is washed needeth not save to wash his feet, but is clean every whit " (John xiii. 10).

Now this is surely very unsafe reasoning. It is true, the Apostles were all ministers of Christ. But if this be ground for withdrawing the cup, it might be as well pleaded for withdrawing the Sacrament altogether from the laity. There were at that memorable Passover none present but our Lord and His Apostles. But surely the example was intended for all the Church. Besides which, the Church of Rome withholds the cup, not only from the laity, but even from all the clergy, except the consecrating priest; which clearly is inconsistent with the original institution, wherein our Lord did not drink of it Himself alone, but said, " Drink ye *all* of it," and " they *all* drank."

If we take St. Paul's statements and reasonings in 1 Cor. x. xi., we shall find much ground to conclude that not only presbyters, but the people too, partook of the two elements. His addresses, warnings, exhortations in those two chapters are evidently general. We should almost infer, that they were rather to the laity, than to the clergy. It is more likely that laymen, than that clergymen, should have been guilty of partaking of idol feasts, and of neglecting to hallow the feast of the Eucharist. Now one argument by which he tries to persuade the Corinthian Christians not to eat what had been offered to idols is, " Ye cannot drink *the cup of the Lord* and the cup of devils " (1 Cor. x. 21). This would be no great argument to laymen, unless they were permitted to drink " the cup of the Lord." And in the following chapter he presses on them the duty of self-examination before communion, and of reverently partaking of that holy Sacrament, in terms which show clearly that all those whom he addresses, *i. e.* both clergy and

laity, were wont to receive both the bread and the cup: " As often
as ye eat this bread *and drink this cup*, ye do show the Lord's
death till he come ; wherefore *whosoever* shall eat this bread and
drink this cup of the Lord unworthily, shall be guilty of the Body
and Blood of the Lord.   But let a man (*i. e.* any man, whosoever
receives the Sacrament) examine himself, and so let him eat of
that bread *and drink of that cup* " (1 Cor. xi. 27–29).

With such strong evidence, that the cup was not only instituted by our blessed Lord, but also received by all His people, it
is surely very hazardous to conclude from certain inductions of
reason, that one half of His ordinance may be withheld from the
great body of His Church.   On what do we rest, as an assurance
that we shall receive blessing in the use of Sacraments, but on our
knowledge that we are acting in obedience to our Lord's commands, doing as He has ordained that we should do, and therefore
have a right to expect that He will give that grace which He has
promised to give in the due administering of his ordinances ?
But if we, resting on our own fallible judgments, curtail His
ordinances, and administer but half of what He has enjoined,
what right have we to expect a blessing to rest upon us ?   A
Sacrament is no Sacrament without these three requisites : the
minister, the ordained elements, and the words of consecration.   We
should not think baptism valid, if we substituted sand for water;
nor the Eucharist valid, if we substituted water for wine, or meat
for bread ; although the rite which of old answered to the Eucharist, was celebrated with the flesh of lamb.   It leaves therefore a
very serious question, whether the Sacrament is a valid Sacrament
when there is only ministered one half of what Christ ordained,
of what the Apostolic Christians received, and of what the
Catholic Church administered for very many centuries after the
Apostles.

It is quite clear that only one thing can give even a colour of
pretence for this mutilation of the ordinance : namely, the hypothesis
that the elements are transubstantiated, each element into the
entire substance of the Saviour.   If this hypothesis fail, the alternative remains, that the Sacrament is not as Christ ordained it,
and that (unless He, of His mercy, supplies the deficiency) it is
not such as to warrant us in the assurance that it is more than a
piece of will-worship and human invention.   We do not indeed
wish to deny that those who, in faith and ignorance, receive a
mutilated Sacrament, may receive the full blessing.   We trust
that such is the case, because we believe our gracious Lord will

give the food of everlasting life, His own blessed Body and Blood, even through imperfect means (or, it may be, without means at all) to those who come to Him in faith and penitence, not with perverse neglect, but in unwilling ignorance. But this does not prevent us from saying, that the Eucharist without the cup is not the Eucharist ordained of Christ.

[It is worthy of remark that the Councils of Constance (Sess. XIII.) and Trent (Sess. XXI. chaps. I. III.) both admit, that our Lord instituted and administered in both kinds.

Constance also admits that the Primitive Church exhibited in both kinds; while Trent (Sess. XXI. chap. II.) says, that "the use of both species has, from the beginning of the Christian religion, *not been infrequent.*"

Constance appears to justify its action on the ground that as our Lord instituted after supper, and it was afterwards the rule to receive fasting, so the Church may also change Christ's actual institution, and — *quoad recipientem* — the matter of the Sacrament. Surely, to state such reasoning is to answer it.

See Sir Humphrey Lynde's *Via Tuta,* Sec. IX. Par. 6. — *J. W.*]

ARTICLE XXXI.

Of the one Oblation of Christ finished upon the Cross.

. THE Offering of Christ once made is that perfect redemption, propitiation, and satisfaction, for all the sins of the whole world, both original and actual; and there is none other satisfaction for sin, but that alone. Wherefore the sacrifices of Masses, in the which it was commonly said, that the Priest did offer Christ for the quick and the dead, to have remission of pain or guilt, were blasphemous fables, and dangerous deceits.

De unica Christi oblatione in cruce perfecta.

OBLATIO Christi semel facta, perfecta est redemptio, propitiatio et satisfactio pro omnibus peccatis totius mundi, tam originalibus quam actualibus; neque præter illam unicam est ulla alia pro peccatis expiatio: unde missarum sacrificia, quibus vulgo dicebatur, sacerdotem offerre Christum in remissionem pœnæ, aut culpæ, pro vivis et defunctis, blasphema figmenta sunt, et perniciosæ imposturæ.

SECTION I. — HISTORY.

IT cannot be doubted that, from the very first, the fathers spoke of the Eucharist under the name of an offering or sacrifice. Clement of Rome writes of the bishops of the Church, as " unblamably and holily offering the gifts;" [1] where he is evidently alluding to the Eucharist. The gifts were the bread and wine, and the other offerings presented on the table of the Lord. The verb made use of is προσφέρειν; so that Clement calls the Eucharist by the name προσφορὰ, *offering*. Justin Martyr not only calls it προσφορὰ, *offering*, but moreover θυσία, *sacrifice*. He quotes Malachi (i. 10, 11) as prophesying, " Of the *sacrifices* to be offered by us Gentiles in every place, *i. e.* the bread of the Eucharist, and the cup of the Eucharist." [2] Irenæus cites the same prophecy, and applies it to the same Sacrament; saying that the prophet foretold " the new oblation of the new Testament, which the Church, receiving from the Apostles, offers throughout the world to God." [3] Tertullian

---

[1] ἀμέμπτως καὶ ὁσίως προσενέγκοντας τὰ ὦρα. — Clem. 1 *Ad Corinth.* c. 44.

[2] Περὶ τῶν ἐν παντὶ τόπῳ ὑφ' ἡμῶν τῶν ἐθνῶν προσφερομένων αὐτῷ θυσιῶν, τουτέστι τοῦ ἀρτοῦ τῆς Εὐχαριστίας καὶ τοῦ ποτηρίου ὁμοίως τῆς Εὐχαριστίας, προλέγει τότε εἰπῶν, καὶ τὸ ὄνομα αὐτοῦ δοξάζειν ἡμᾶς. — *Dial. c. Tryph.* p. 260; cf. pp. 344, 345.

[3] " Novi Testamenti novam docuit ob-lationem, quam Ecclesia ab Apostolis accipiens, in universo mundo offert Deo." — Lib. IV. c. 32, p. 323, Grabe.

So quoting Matt. v. 23, 24: " Cum igitur offers munus tuum ad altare," &c., he says, " Offerre igitur oportet Deo primitias ejus creaturæ " Lib IV c 34, p. 325.

constantly speaks of oblations and sacrifices, using the word *offer*
(*offerre*),[1] and so probably *oblation*[2] of the Eucharist; though the
word *sacrifice* is applied by him rather to the sacrifice of prayer or
praise.[3]

These are all authorities of the first two centuries; all witnesses within little more than a century from the Apostles. The
question which occurs concerning them is, in what sense do they
speak of offering and sacrifice?

Justin Martyr says: " The offering of fine flour, for those who
were cleansed of leprosy, was a type of the bread of the Eucharist,
which the Lord Jesus Christ commanded us to offer, in remembrance of His suffering."[4] Clemens Romanus speaks of " offering
the gifts." Justin and Irenæus both refer to the " pure offering "
of Malachi, which, though Justin after the LXX. translates it by
θυσία, *sacrifice*, is in the Hebrew מִנְחָה, *mincha*, *i. e.* an oblation.
Now the *mincha* was an offering of meal or flour baked, or of
parched corn. It is a " *meat-offering*," according to the English
version; but, as Joseph Mede observes, we might more correctly
call it a *bread-offering*.[5] Again, Tertullian speaks of the Christian
sacrifice as a sacrifice of " pure prayer; " as Justin Martyr also
had done before him.[6]

We have very similar witness from Clement of Alexandria and
Origen. The former calls the sacrifice of the Church, " Speech
exhaled from holy souls, whilst the whole understanding is laid
open before God together with the sacrifice."[7] And the holy
altar, he says, is the righteous soul.[8] Origen, in like manner, frequently spiritualizes; but specially concerning the Eucharist he
says, that " Celsus would give first-fruits to demons, so we offer
first-fruits to God."[9]

In all these fathers, then, we find no certain reference to any

---

[1] " Non permittitur mulieri in ecclesia
loqui, sed nec docere, nec tinguere, nec
offerre." — *De Veland. Virginibus*, c. 9.
[2] " Oblationes pro defunctis, pro natalitiis annua die facimus." — *De Corona
Militis*, c. 2.
[3] " *Sacrificamus* pro salute imperatoris
sed Deo nostro et ipsius, sed quo modo
præcepit Deus, *pura prece.* Non enim
eget Deus, Conditor universitatis, odoris
aut sanguinis alicujus." — *Ad Scapulam*,
c. 2. Cf. *Cont. Marc.* Lib. IV. c. 1, where
he calls Sacrificium mundum . . . . simplex oratio de conscientia pura. So *De
Orat.* 28. " Hæc (*i. e.* oratio) est hostia
spiritualis, quæ pristina sacrificia dele-
bit."
[4] ʽΗ τῆς σεμιδάλεως προσφορὰ ἡ ὑπὲρ τῶν

καθαριζομένων ἀπὸ τῆς λέπρας προσφέρεσθαι
παραδοθεῖσα, τύπος ἦν τοῦ ἄρτου τῆς εὐχαριστίας, ὃν εἰς ἀνάμνησιν τοῦ πάθους ʼΙησοῦς
Χριστὸς Κύριος ἡμῶν παρέδωκε ποιεῖν. —
Dial. pp. 256, 260.
[5] Mede, *On the Christian Sacrifice*, ch.
III.
[6] ʽΟτι μὲν οὖν καὶ εὐχαὶ καὶ εὐχαριστίαι
ὑπὸ τῶν ἀξίων γινόμεναι, τέλειαι μόναι καὶ
εὐάρεστοί εἰσι τῷ Θεῷ θυσίαι καὶ αὐτὸς φημι.
— *Dial.* p. 345.
[7] ʽΗ θυσία τῆς ἐκκλησίας, λόγος ἀπὸ τῶν
ἁγίων ψυχῶν ἀναθυμιώμενος, ἐκκαλυπτομένης
ἅμα τῆς θυσίας καὶ τῆς διανοίας ἀπάσης τῷ
Θεῷ. — Clem. *Strom.* VII. p. 848.
[8] βωμὸν δὲ ἀληθῶς ἅγιον, τὴν δικαίαν
ψυχήν. — Ibid.
[9] *Contra Celsum*, Lib. VIII. c. 33.

offering in the Eucharist, except the offering of the bread and wine in the way of gifts or oblations to the service of God ; as the fine flour and the meat or bread-offerings were presented by the Jews, and with them a sacrifice of prayer and thanksgiving. The use of the word θυσία, *sacrifice*, gives no contradiction to this statement: for besides that it is the rendering of the Hebrew *mincha* by the LXX. translators, it has been clearly proved that the word by no means of necessity implies an offering of a slain victim, though such was its primary signification ; but that it is also applicable to all other kinds of offerings and oblations, whether it be in classical or biblical Greek.[1]

Very early we have express mention of a Christian altar.[2] But we can infer no more from the use of the word *altar*, than from the use of the word *sacrifice*. A sacrifice (θυσία) implies an altar (θυσιαστήριον). If the offering of the bread and wine, as first-fruits to God, be esteemed a sacrifice, then that whereon it is offered would be esteemed an altar. If the offering of prayer and praise be a sacrifice, the soul, from which they rise up to God, would be the altar. We need not question that these early fathers, as undoubtedly those after them, believed that the bread and wine offered to the Lord were offered in remembrance of the sacrifice of Christ, and so, that the Eucharist was a commemorative sacrifice. But it is remarkable, that even this view of the Eucharistic sacrifice does not expressly appear before the time of Cyprian. If the earliest fathers really believed that Christ in the Eucharist was offered afresh for the sins of the quick and dead, it is certainly a most extraordinary example of silence and reserve, that, for two centuries after Christ, they should never once have explained the sacrifice of the Eucharist in any manner, but either as an offering of first-fruits to God, like the mincha or fine flour of the Israelites, or else as an offering of praise and thanksgiving and spiritual worship.

In Athenagoras indeed (A. D. 150) occurs, I believe, the first example of that remarkable expression, so universally adopted by later fathers, the *unbloody sacrifice*. " Of what service to me are whole burnt-offerings, of which God has no need ? Although it be

---

[1] See Johnson's *Unbloody Sacrifice*, ch. I. sect. 1. He shows, from classical authorities, that " to sacrifice is to give to the gods " (θύειν δωρεῖσθαι ἐστι τοῖς θεοῖς) ; and especially, that θυσία in the Greek, and *sacrificium* in the Latin, are the common rendering of מִנְחָה in the Hebrew. The Apostle calls Cain's offering of fruits a sacrifice, θυσία, as well as Abel's offering of cattle. Heb. xi. 4. Hence, the Christian and theological application of the term, not only to animal, but also to inanimate offerings.

[2] θυσιαστηρίου. See Ignat. *Ad Ephes.* I. 5 ; *Magnes.* 7 ; *Trall.* 7 ; *Philadelph* 4, &c.

right to offer an *unbloody sacrifice*, and to bring ,the reasonable ser-vice." [1] Mr. Johnson sees " no occasion to doubt, that he means the oblation of material bread and wine." [2] It may be so ; though we cannot with certainty say that he had the Eucharist in view at all. If he had, the very term, " unbloody sacrifice," takes us back to the distinction among the Israelites between offerings of slain beasts, *bloody sacrifices*, and offerings of bread, flour, and fruits, *un-bloody sacrifices*.   And so the very name by which the Eucharist was so constantly called afterwards, and which possibly Athenag-oras first applied to it, seems to place it, as a material offering, rather with the *mincha*, or bread-offering, than with the ὁλοκαύτωμα, the burnt-offering, or bloody sacrifice of the Jews.

From the time of Cyprian, however, it is a fact too plain and no-torious to need demonstration, that the fathers speak of the Eu-charist as a sacrifice, with special reference to the Body and Blood of Christ, commemorated and spiritually present in that holy sacra-ment. St. Cyprian, referring to the priesthood of Melchizedek as a type of Christ's priesthood, says, that " in the priest Melchizedek we see prefigured the Sacrament of the Lord's sacrifice." [3] " Who was more. a priest of the most High God, than our Lord Jesus Christ, who offered a sacrifice to God the Father ? and He offered the same which Melchizedek had offered, *i. e.* bread and wine, even His own Body and Blood." [4] He then goes on to argue for the use of wine in the Eucharist, and not of water merely, which he considers essential for the perfect following of Christ, in His first institution of the sacrament. He says, that " therefore *Christ's Blood is not offered*, if there be no wine in the cup." [5] " If Jesus Christ our Lord and God is Himself the High Priest of God the Father, and first offered Himself a sacrifice to His Father, and then commanded this to be done in remembrance of Him, then that priest truly performs the part of Christ, who imitates what Christ did, and then offers a true and full sacrifice in the Church to God the Father, if he so begin to offer, as he sees Christ to have offered before." [6]

---

[1] τί δέ μοι ὁλοκαυτωμάτων ὧν μὴ δεῖται ὁ Θεός; καί τοι προσφέρειν δέον ἀναίμακτον θυσίαν, καὶ τὴν λογικὴν προσάγειν λατρείαν. — *Legatio pro Christianis*, 12.

[2] *Unbloody Sacrifice*, ch. 11. sect. 1.

[3] " Item in sacerdote Melchisedec sac-rificii Dominici sacramentum præfigura-tum videmus." — *Epist.* 63, p. 149. Oxf. 1682.

[4] "Num quis magis sacerdos Dei Summi quam Dominus noster Jesus Christus ? qui sacrificium Deo Patri obtulit ; et obtulit hoc idem quod Mel-chisedec obtulerat, id est panem et vi-num, suum scilicet corpus et sangui-nem." — Ibid.

[5] " Unde apparet sanguinem Christi non offerri, si desit vinum calici." — Ibid. p. 151.

[6] " Nam si Jesus Christus, Dominus et Deus noster, ipse est summus sacerdos Dei Patris ; et sacrificium Patri se ip-sum primus obtulit, et hoc fieri in sui commemorationem præcepit ; utique ille

This is the first use of such language; but it was common from this time. The Roman Catholics claim it, as clearly proving that a true sacrifice and offering up anew of Christ in the Eucharist was believed in the earliest time. Protestants have, on the contrary, asserted that no material sacrifice is intended at all; that there is allusion only to a spiritual sacrifice, wherein the whole Church considered as Christ's Body is offered to God.[1] We may be so said symbolically to offer up in sacrifice *ourselves;* and that is all.[2] Time and space will not permit a full investigation of the many passages which would elucidate this question, nor a full examination of the arguments. Against the Romanist theory the following facts appear to me fatal. First, there is the already noticed silence of all the fathers, till the middle of the third century, on so essential a part, if it be a part, of the Eucharistic doctrine. That Justin, Irenæus, Clement, Tertullian, and Origen, should never have known of it, or, knowing, should never have mentioned it, seems utterly incredible, if the doctrine were from the beginning. Secondly, if there were always offered in the Church a real sacrifice of Christ Himself, then no other sacrifice could be compared with it. It must far exceed in glory and in value everything besides. Yet we find the fathers preferring spiritual sacrifices even to the oblation in the Eucharist. " Will they drive me from the altars?" says Gregory Nazianzen. " But I know there is another altar, whereof these visible altars are but the figures. . . . . To that will I present myself; there will I offer acceptable things, sacrifice and offering and holocausts, better than the one now offered as much as truth is better than a shadow. From this altar no one can debar me."[3] Is it possible that any one should prefer an altar and a sacrifice, " all," as he says, " the work of the mind " (ὅλον τοῦ νοῦ τὸ ἔργον), before the very offering up of the Saviour of the world? We may add, that the fathers too frequently speak of the sacrifice of Christians as spiritual sacrifices,[4] for us to imagine that

---

sacerdos vice Christi vere fungitur, qui id quod Christus fecit imitatur; et sacrificium verum et plenum tunc offert in Ecclesia Deo Patri, si sic incipiat offerre secundum quod ipsum Christum videat obtulisse." — Ibid. p. 155.

[1] This undoubtedly was one of the views which the fathers took of the Eucharistic Sacrifice. " Hoc est sacrificium Christianum; *multi unum Corpus in Christo.* Quod etiam sacramento altaris fidelibus nota frequentat Ecclesia, ubi ei demonstratur, quod in ea re quam offert, ipsa offeratur." — Augustin. *De Civit. Dei,* Lib. x. c. 6, Tom. vii. p. 243.

[2] This seems to be Waterland's opinion. See *On the Eucharist,* ch. xii.

[3] Θυσιαστηρίων εἴρξουσιν; ἀλλ' οἶδα καὶ ἄλλο θυσιαστήριον, οὗ τύποι τὰ νῦν ὁρώμενα. . . . τούτῳ παραστήσομαι, τούτῳ θύσω δεκτὰ, θυσίαν καὶ προσφορὰν καὶ ὁλοκαυτώματα, κρείττονα τῶν νῦν προσαγομένων, ὅσῳ κρείττον σκιᾶς ἀλήθεια. . . . τούτου μὲν οὐκ ἀπάξει με τοῦ θυσιαστηρίου πᾶς ὁ βουλόμενος.— Greg. Nazianz. *Orat.* xxviii. Tom. i. p. 484, cited by Waterland, *On the Eucharist,* ch. xii.

[4] See for instance Euseb. *Dem. Evangel.* Lib. i. c. x., cited by Waterland, as above. Cyril of Jerusalem calls the

they held a literal offering up of a literal sacrifice (that sacrifice being Christ's Body and Blood) on the altar in the Eucharist.

But, on the other hand, it seems to me that we cannot at once dismiss the whole question without farther inquiring in what sense the fathers did see in the Eucharist the sacrifice of Jesus Christ, for the propitiation of our sins. Their language, from the time of Cyprian, is both too uniform and too strong, for us to doubt that it had a pregnant significance.

The Eucharist undoubtedly succeeded to, and corresponded with the Passover. The latter was the type ; the former is the memorial of the death of Christ. One typical of the great sacrifice ; the other commemorative of the same. The one was the great federal rite of the Jews ; the other is the great federal rite of the Christians. In this view the fathers much considered it. And so, as they viewed the Passover as a typical sacrifice, they viewed the Eucharist as a commemorative sacrifice. We have already heard Chrysostom imagining and depicting, in his own fervid language, " the Lord sacrificed and lying, the priest standing by the sacrifice and praying,[1] &c." And it is admitted by most persons, that the Lord's Supper, if not a sacrifice, is yet (spiritually of course) a feast upon a sacrifice. Now the sacrifice feasted on is undoubtedly the Lord Jesus, the Lamb of God. Our ordinary idea of offering a sacrifice, when that sacrifice is a living victim, is that it must be slain when it is offered. But the early Christians appear to have understood that, although Christ was once for all slain, and so did once for all offer up Himself to God ; yet, that every time His sacrifice is commemorated, and that sacrifice spiritually fed upon, we do, as it were, present before God, plead before the Father, the efficacy of that great offering, the all-prevailing merits of His precious Blood. The same is true, more or less, in every act of devotion. No well-instructed Christian ever prays to God, without pleading the atonement and the death of Christ. So, in effect, at every prayer we present to the Father the sacrifice of His Son. But more especially, and with most peculiar significance, we may be said to plead His merits, to present His efficacious passion, and so, in a certain sense, to offer His all-prevailing sacrifice before the

---

Eucharist "a spiritual sacrifice, an unbloody service," τὴν πνευματικὴν θυσίαν, τὴν ἀναίμακτον λατρείαν. — *Cat. Mystagog.* v. c. 6. St. Augustine describes the Christian sacrifice as the Sacrament or sacred sign of the invisible sacrifice. " Sacrificium ergo visibile invisibilis sacrificii sacramentum, hoc est, sacrum

signum est." — *De Civitate Dei*, Lib. **x.** c. 5, Tom. vii. p. 241.

All such language is quite inconsistent with the notion of an actual offering up of Christ afresh for the sins of the world.

[1] Chrysost. *De Sacerdotio*, iii. quoted under Art. xxviii.

mercy-seat of God, when with the consecrated symbols of His Body and Blood before us, we approach the Table of the Lord, to be fed by Him with the food of everlasting life.

In this sense then, most especially, the fathers seem to have esteemed the Eucharist, not only a sacrificial feast, but also a sacrifice. It was indeed by a *metonymy*. The Eucharist was a remembrance (ἀνάμνησις) of the great sacrifice on the cross. And so it was called by the name of that which it recorded. But it was not only a remembrance to ourselves, it was also esteemed a special mode of pleading it before God; and therefore it was named a sacrifice. And as the sacrifice of the cross was the propitiatory sacrifice, so this too was called a sacrifice of propitiation, both because of its recalling that great propitiatory sacrifice, and because by enabling us spiritually to feed on, and to take the blessed fruit of that sacrifice to ourselves, it was the means of bringing home to our souls the pardoning efficacy of Christ's death, the propitiation for sins which He has wrought.[1]

No doubt, the other notions concerning the oblations in the Eucharist were kept in constant view. First, the fathers esteemed it an offering or presenting of the gifts of bread and wine, and of the alms of the faithful to the service of God; secondly, as an offering of the sacrifice of prayer and praise; thirdly, as a presenting of ourselves, our souls and bodies, and so of the whole mystical body of the faithful, to the Lord; but, fourthly, they esteemed it a memorial of Christ's sacrifice, a recalling of the efficacy of that sacrifice, and a pleading of its efficacy for the salvation of their souls.

This last notion it is which makes them use such solemn and awful language concerning it, which could not be applicable to the other views of it. Thus the Liturgy of St. James calls it the "tremendous and unbloody sacrifice." St. Chrysostom calls it "the fearful and tremendous sacrifice."[2] So also "most tremendous sacrifice."[3] Yet the same father, when he enters into an explanation, tells us that it is not a new sacrifice, or an offering up of Christ afresh; for he says, "There is but one sacrifice; we do not offer another sacrifice, but continually the same. Or rather we make a memorial of the sacrifice."[4] And so St. Augustine,

---

[1] Thus Cyril of Jerusalem, in the passage just cited, *Cat. Mystagog.* v. c. 6, speaks of the "spiritual Sacrifice, and the bloodless service over that *sacrifice of propitiation*," ἐπὶ τῆς θυσίας τοῦ ἱλασμοῦ.

[2] φοβερὰ καὶ φρικώδης θυσία. — *Homil.* xxxiv. *in* 1 *ad Corinth.*

[3] φρικωδεστάτη θυσία.

[4] Οὐκ ἄλλην θυσίαν, ἀλλὰ τὴν αὐτὴν ἀεὶ ποιοῦμεν· μᾶλλον δὲ ἀνάμνησιν ἐργαζόμεθα θυσίας. — *Homil.* xvii. *in Epist. ad Hebræos.* See Suicer, s. v. θυσία, ii. 2, Tom. i. p. 1421.

" Christians celebrate the memorial of the same fully finished sacrifice, by sacred oblation and participation of Christ's Body and Blood." [1]

It is easy to see that, when the doctrine of transubstantiation had once been invented and defined, the doctrine of the fathers concerning the commemoration of Christ's sacrifice in the Eucharist would be perverted into the Roman Catholic doctrine of the sacrifice of the mass. That doctrine is plainly enough expressed in the canons of the Council of Trent. Therein it is forbidden to deny, that a true and proper sacrifice is offered to God, — that Christ made His Apostles priests, on purpose that they might offer His Body and Blood, — that there is a propitiatory sacrifice for quick and dead, for sins, punishments, satisfactions, — that it profits others as well as the partakers,[2] &c.

From the belief, that in the mass there was a true offering up of Christ, not only for the benefit of the receiver, but anew for the sins of all the world, came naturally the custom, that the priest should offer the sacrifice, but the people should not communicate. Among the early Christians, all who did not communicate, left the Church. But, when the doctrine of the mass was once established, the people stayed to witness the offering up of the sacrifice, which they believed to be profitable both to them and to *all* the world, though the priest alone offered it, and the priest alone received. The Eucharist had, in fact, ceased to be a Sacrament. It had become, in the belief of the majority, a propitiatory offering, not a covenanting rite.

There was perhaps nothing against which the reformers generally were so strong in their denunciations, as against this. They deemed it derogatory to the one, full, perfect, and sufficient sacrifice, once offered on the Cross. " Christ," says Luther, " once offered Himself; nor did He will to be offered up anew by any; but He willed that a memorial of His sacrifice should be observed." [3]

---

[1] " Hebræi in victimis pecudum quas offerebant Deo . . . . prophetiam celebrabant futuræ victimæ, quam Christus obtulit. Unde jam Christiani peracti ejusdem sacrificii memoriam celebrant, sacrosancta oblatione, et participatione Corporis et Sanguinis Christi." — *Contra Faustum*, Lib. xx. c. 18, Tom. viii. p. 3.5.

[2] Sess. xxii. Can. i. " Si quis dixerit in missa non offerri Deo verum et proprium sacrificium . . . . anathema sit."

Can. ii. " Si quis dixerit . . . . . in illis verbis *Hoc facite in meam commemorationem*, Christum non instituisse Apostolos sacer-

dotes, aut non ordinasse, ut ipsi aliique sacerdotes offerrent Corpus et Sanguinem suum ; anathema sit."

Can. iii. " Si quis dixerit missæ sacrificium tantum esse laudis et gratiarum actionis, aut nudam commemorationem sacrificii in cruce peracti, non propitiatorium, vel soli prodesse sumenti, neque pro vivis et defunctis, pro peccatis, pœnis, satisfactionibus, et aliis necessitatibus offerri debere ; anathema sit."

The Creed of the Council has : " Profiteor in missa offerri Deo verum, proprium et propitiatorium sacrificium."

[3] " Christus semel seipsum obtulit, non

Calvin, after explaining the meaning of the word *sacrifice* as applied to the Eucharist by the fathers, does not blame them for the use of that term, but still regrets that they should have approached too near to Jewish notions. "Now that the sacrifice has been offered and completed," he says, "God gives us a table where we may feast, not an altar on which the victim is to be offered. He has not consecrated priests to immolate, but ministers to distribute." [1] He calls the sacrifice of the mass, the greatest abomination of all those erected against the Eucharist.[2]

The language of the English reformers is of still more interest to us. Let us hear Ridley, the most esteemed among them. "The whole substance of our sacrifice, which is frequented of the Church in the Lord's Supper, consisteth in prayers, praise, and giving of thanks, and in remembering and showing forth of that sacrifice upon the altar of the Cross; that the same might continually be had in reverence by mystery, which, once only and no more, was offered as the price of our redemption." [3] Elsewhere he acknowledges, that "the priest doth offer an unbloody sacrifice, if it be rightly understood;" which he explains by saying, that "It is called unbloody, and is offered after a certain manner and in a mystery, and as a representation of that bloody sacrifice." [4] But the mass he calls, "a new blasphemous kind of sacrifice, to satisfy and pay the price of sins, both of the dead and of the quick, to the great and intolerable contumely of Christ our Saviour, His death and passion; which was, and is the only sufficient and everlasting, available sacrifice, satisfactory for all the elect of God, from Adam the first, to the last that shall be born to the end of the World." [5]

The dread of the mass, which has prevailed generally among the reformed Churches, has made the majority of their members fear to speak at all concerning an Eucharistic sacrifice. Yet there have not been wanting, in the English Church especially, men of profound learning, deep piety, and some of them by no means attached to peculiar schools of doctrine, who have advocated the propriety of speaking of *the Christian sacrifice*, and of adopting, in some measure, the language of the primitive Church concerning it.

---

voluit denuo ab ullis offerri, sed memoriam sui sacrificii voluit fieri." — *De Abroganda Missa Privata*, Tom. II. p. 249.

1 "Mensam ergo nobis dedit in qua epulemur, non altare super quod offeratur victima; non sacerdotes consecravit, qui immolent, sed ministros qui sacrum epulum distribuant." —*Instit.* IV. xviii. 12.

2 *Inst.* IV. xviii. 1.
3 Disputations at Oxford, *Works*, Parker Society, p. 211.
4 Ibid. p. 250.
5 *A Piteous Lamentation, Works*, p. 52. Compare Cranmer, *Defence of the True and Catholic Doctrine*, Bk. V., *Works*, II. pp. 447–463.

The first who spoke strongly and clearly to this effect, was the learned Joseph Mede (A. D. 1635). His discourse was originally a Sermon on Malachi i. 11, which he maintained to be prophetic of the Eucharistic offering. And the offering in the Eucharist he defines to be an oblation of prayer and praise, of bread and wine, analogous to the *mincha* of the old Testament, and a commemoration of Christ's sacrifice on the cross.[1] Dr. Cudworth shortly after wrote his treatise on *The true notion of the Lord's Supper*, wherein he denied to the Eucharist the name of a sacrifice; but especially insisted that it was " a feast upon a Sacrifice." Grabe, in the notes on his edition of Irenæus (A. D. 1702) maintained the sentiments of Joseph Mede; for which he was attacked by Buddeus, a learned Lutheran,[2] who accused him of advocating the sacrifice of the mass, and afterwards by others, though he was defended by Pfaffius, also a Lutheran.[3] Sentiments in accordance with Mede's, and not much diverse from Grabe's, were undoubtedly adopted by a large number of our divines: *e. g.* by Hammond,[4] by Archbishop Bramhall,[5] by Bishop Patrick,[6] by Bishop Bull,[7] by Hickes,[8] by John Johnson,[9] and many others.

Bishop Bull's words may express the view which most of these divines have taken: " It is true, the Eucharist is frequently called by the ancient fathers *an oblation, a sacrifice;* but it is to be remembered that they say also, it is θυσία λογικὴ καὶ ἀναίμακτος, *a reasonable sacrifice, a sacrifice without blood:* which how can it be said to be, if therein the very Blood of Christ were offered up to God? . . . In the holy Eucharist we set before God bread and wine, ' as figures or images of the precious Blood of Christ, shed for us, and of His precious Body ' (they are the very words of the Clementine Liturgy) ;[10] and plead to God the merit of His Son's Sacrifice once offered on the cross for us sinners, and in this Sacrament represented, beseeching Him for the sake there-

---

[1] See Mede's *Works*, p. 355. London, 1677. The discourse is most valuable, and deserving of all attention.

[2] Buddeus, *De Origine Missæ Pontificiæ.*

[3] Pfaffius, *Irenæi Fragm. Anecdot.*

[4] *Practical Catechism*, p. 413. London, 1700.

[5] *Epistle to M. De la Milletière*, *Works*, I. p. 54, Edit. *Anglo-Cath. Library.* " We do readily acknowledge an Eucharistical Sacrifice of prayers and praises; we profess a commemoration of the Sacrifice of the Cross; and, in the language of Holy Church, things commemorated are related as if they were then acted . . . . We

acknowledge a representation of that action to God the Father: we acknowledge an impetration of the benefit of it: we maintain an application of its virtue. So here is a commemorative, impetrative, applicative sacrifice . . . . To make it a suppletory sacrifice, to supply the defects of the only true Sacrifice of the Cross, I hope both you and I abhor."

[6] *On the Christian Sacrifice.*

[7] *Answer to the Bishop of Meaux*, Lect. III. *Works*, II. p. 251. Oxf. 1827.

[8] *Treatise on the Christian Priesthood*, ch. II.

[9] *On the Unbloody Sacrifice.*

[10] *Constitut. Apostol.* VII. 25.

of to bestow His heavenly blessing on us. . . . The Eucharistical sacrifice thus explained is indeed λογικὴ θυσία, a reasonable sacrifice, widely different from that monstrous sacrifice of the mass taught in the Church of Rome." [1]

Section II. — SCRIPTURAL PROOF.

I. WE have seen, that in the mass the priest is said to offer up Christ afresh, as a true propitiatory sacrifice for the sins of quick and dead. That is to say, the mass is a repetition or iteration of the sacrifice of Christ on the Cross.

This is in direct contravention of a large portion of the Epistle to the Hebrews. There (from ch. v. 1 to the end of ch. x.) St. Paul is showing the superiority of Christ's priesthood to that of the Levitical priests; the superiority of the sacrifice of Christ over the sacrifices offered under the Law. Now the very line of argument which he takes, all rests upon the permanency of Christ, His priesthood, and His sacrifice. " They truly were *many* priests, because they were not suffered to continue by reason of death. But this Man, because He continueth ever, hath an unchangeable priesthood . . . . who needeth not daily, as those high priests, to offer up sacrifice first for His own sins, and then for the people's : for this He did once for all (ἐφάπαξ) when He offered up Himself " (Heb. vii. 23, 24, 27). So, again, having observed that the Jewish high-priest entered into " the Holiest of all *once every year*, not without blood " (Heb. ix. 7) : he adds, that Christ, " not by the blood of goats and calves, but by His own Blood entered in *once for all* (ἐφάπαξ) into the holy place, having obtained *eternal* redemption for us " (ver. 12). And again, " Christ is not entered into the holy places . . . . that He should offer Himself *often* . . . . but now *once for all* (ἅπαξ) in the end of the world hath He appeared to put away sin by the sacrifice of Himself. And as it is appointed unto men once to die, but after this the judgment; so Christ was *once* offered to bear the sins of many," &c. (Heb. ix. 24, 26, 27, 28).

The first twenty-two verses of the 10th Chapter are devoted to farther insisting on this truth. The repetition of the Jewish sacrifices, St. Paul tells us, resulted from their imperfection. If

---

[1] Bishop Bull, as above.

they could have made " the comers thereunto perfect . . . . would
they not have ceased to be offered ? " (vv. 1, 2). But " it is not
possible that the blood of bulls and goats should take away sin "
(v. 4). Hence, " every priest " under the Law " standeth *daily*
ministering and offering *oftentimes* the same sacrifices, which can
never take away sins. But He, after He had offered *one* sacrifice
for sins forever, sat down at the right hand of God . . . . For by
one offering He hath perfected FOREVER them that are sanctified "
(vv. 11, 12, 14). And the conclusion which is drawn is, that,
as Christ has obtained remission for our sins, and " where remission
of these is there is no more offering for sins " (v. 18); therefore
we may " draw near with a true heart with a full assurance of
faith " (v. 22); plainly, as being assured, that the one sacrifice,
once offered, has been fully sufficient for all our sins.

Now, nothing can be plainer than this argument; and if it
proves anything, surely it must prove, that to believe in the repetition of Christ's sacrifice is to believe in its imperfection. And if
it be imperfect, in what a state are we ! — we, who are lost sinners,
and who have no hope but in the efficacy of the atoning Blood of
Christ. If that atoning Blood be not of infinite value, we are of
all creatures most miserable. But if it be of infinite value, and
if the Sacrifice be perfect, and " able to make the comers thereunto
perfect," then the Apostle assures us, that it cannot need, that it
will not admit of, repetition. " The worshippers once purged shall
have no more conscience of sins " (ch. x. 2). " We are sanctified
through the offering of the Body of Jesus Christ once for all " (ver.
10). There is " a new and living way consecrated for us through
the veil, that is to say, His Flesh " (ver. 20). And not only may
we know, to our eternal comfort, that the one sacrifice has been
full, perfect, and all-sufficient; but to our warning too we are told,
that, " if we sin wilfully after we have received the knowledge of
the truth, *there remaineth no more sacrifice for sins* " (ver. 26). All
combines to assure us, that the one Sacrifice has been once offered,
that it admits no addition, that it can never be renewed. It is
once for all, as man's death is but once. It is one and forever,
as God's judgment is one and to eternity (Heb. ix. 28).

We may therefore confidently adopt the strong language of our
Article, that " the sacrifices of masses were blasphemous fables and
dangerous deceits."

II. Yet the Christian Church is said to be " an holy priesthood ; "
and is " to offer up *spiritual sacrifices* acceptable to God through

Jesus Christ " (1 Pet. ii. 5). Those spiritual sacrifices are, 1. The sacrifice of prayer and praise: " By Him let us offer the *sacrifice* of praise to God continually, that is, the fruit of the lips, giving thanks to His name " (Heb. xiii. 15). 2. The sacrifice of alms and of the first-fruits of our substance: " To do good and to communicate forget not; for with such *sacrifices* God is well pleased " (Heb. xiii. 16). 3. The sacrifice of ourselves to the Lord: " I beseech you, therefore, brethren, by the mercies of God, that ye present your bodies a living sacrifice, holy, acceptable unto God, which is your reasonable service " ($\tau\grave{\eta}\nu$ $\lambda o\gamma\iota\kappa\grave{\eta}\nu$ $\lambda a\tau\rho\epsilon\acute{\iota}a\nu$ $\acute{\upsilon}\mu\hat{\omega}\nu$), Rom. xii. 1.

Hence, though the propitiatory sacrifice of our blessed Saviour has been offered once for all, never to be repeated; it is still our privilege and duty to offer Eucharistic sacrifices or thank-offerings — " a reasonable ministration " — " acceptable to God through Jesus Christ." Such Eucharistic offerings correspond, as we have already seen, with the thank-offerings, the wave-offerings, the meat-offerings, the unbloody sacrifices of the Jews; not with the bloody sacrifices, or offerings of atonement.

It was the belief of the whole ancient Church, that the Lord's Supper consisted of two parts: one from God to us, God feeding us with the spiritual Body and Blood of His dear Son; the other from us to God, we sending up to Him the sacrifice of praise and thanksgiving, consecrating to Him of the fruits of our increase, and " presenting ourselves, our souls and bodies, to be a reasonable, holy, and lively sacrifice unto Him." Hence the whole ordinance was esteemed, not only as a feast, but also as an Eucharistic sacrifice, or thank-offering.

And moreover the Apostle has declared it to be a " showing forth ($\kappa a\tau a\gamma\gamma\epsilon\lambda\acute{\iota}a$) of the Lord's death till He come " (1 Cor. xi. 26). It was therefore, as we have seen, esteemed by the fathers a commemoration, or " continual remembrance of the sacrifice of the death of Christ." And, not only did they think of it as reminding *themselves* of God's infinite mercy to their souls, but also they believed it a proper occasion for pleading the greatness of that mercy before Him, from whom it comes down. It was a telling forth of Christ's sacrifice to man, a supplicatory representing of it to God.[1]

---

[1] There has been much questioning as to the propriety or impropriety of calling the Lord's Table an *Altar*. The word appears to have been used by the fathers, even from the time of Ignatius. See Ign. *Ad Ephes.* v.; Tertullian, *De Orat.* xix. &c. The only name by which we are certain that it is called in the new Testament, is $\tau\rho\acute{a}\pi\epsilon\zeta a$ $K\upsilon\rho\acute{\iota}o\upsilon$, " the table of the Lord," 1 Cor. x. 21. This, however, is put in opposition to the " table of demon-gods," which was probably an altar. Also in Mal. i. 7, 12, " altar " and " table of the Lord " seem to be synonymous. In Matt. v. 23, whether our Lord speaks of things as they were under the Jewish economy, or prophetically of what should be in the Christian Church, cannot certainly be re-

Lastly, they believed the prophecy in Malachi (that " among the Gentiles, in every place, incense should be offered to God's name, and a pure offering," *mincha purum*, Mal. i. 11) to have especial reference to the spiritual sacrifices thus offered in the Holy Communion. And we, in accordance with the saints of old, and with the chief lights of our own communion, adopt such language in such a sense; though the doctrine of the sacrifice of the mass, as suppletory to the sacrifice of the cross, we may reject as monstrous, and fear as profane.

solved; and therefore it cannot be concluded, whether he calls the Eucharistical table an *altar* or not. In Heb. xiii. 10, St. Paul says, " We have an altar, whereof they have no right to eat which serve the tabernacle." This is by many thought conclusive in favour of the use of the term *altar* for the Lord's table; for, though we may speak of the cross, on which the great Sacrifice was offered up, as the Christian altar, yet the Apostles could not have spoken of *eating* of the cross. The Christian feast is at the Eucharist, though the great Sacrifice was offered at the crucifixion. Hence it is contended, that the *altar*, at which Christians have a right to eat, must be the table of the Lord. The English reformers seemed, latterly at least, determined to give up the word *altar*, for fear of appearing to give sanction to the sacrifice of the mass. But the general language of Christians, both early and late, has been favourable to the use of it.

ARTICLE XXXII.

Of the Marriage of Priests.	*De Conjugio Sacerdotum.*
BISHOPS, Priests, and Deacons, are not commanded by God's Law, either to vow the estate of single life, or to abstain from marriage : therefore it is lawful for them, as for all other Christian men, to marry at their own discretion, as they shall judge the same to serve better to godliness.	EPISCOPIS, presbyteris et diaconis nullo mandato divino præceptum est, ut aut cœlibatum voveant, aut a matrimonio abstineant. Licet igitur etiam illis, ut cæteris omnibus Christianis, ubi hoc ad pietatem magis facere judicaverint, pro suo arbitratu matrimonium contrahere.

SECTION I. — HISTORY.

IT admits of evident proof, that in the earliest ages of the Church bishops, priests, and deacons, were allowed to marry. St. Polycarp speaks of Valens, a presbyter, and his wife.[1] Chæremon, Bishop of Nilus, a man of very great age, is mentioned by Eusebius [2] as flying from the Decian persecution, together with his wife. The same Eusebius, speaking of Phileas, Bishop of Thmuis, and Philoromus, says that they were urged, in the persecution under Diocletian, to have pity on their *wives* and children, and for their sakes, to save their own lives.[3] St. Clement of Alexandria, in which he is followed by Eusebius, says, that the Apostles Peter and Philip begat children, and that St. Paul also was married, but did not take his wife about with him, that he might not be hindered in his missionary journeys.[4] The same statement, namely, that St. Peter, St. Paul, and the other Apostles, were married, occurs in the interpolated epistles of St. Ignatius ;[5] a spurious work indeed, and no doubt of much later date than the real Ignatius, but not altogether valueless on that account ; as forgers always aim at verisimilitude, and would hardly express an opinion which was universally exploded and condemned at the time they wrote. Origen also appears to have believed that St. Paul was married.[6]

---

[1] *Epist.* Polyc. c. XI.
[2] *H. E.* Lib. VI. c. 42.
[3] Ib. VIII. c. 9.
[4] Πέτρος μὲν γὰρ καὶ Φίλιππος ἐπαιδοποιήσαντο . . . . καὶ ὅγε Παῦλος οὐκ ὀκνεῖ ἔν -ινι ἐπιστολῇ τὴν αὑτοῦ προσαγορεύειν σύζυ-

γον, ἣν οὐ περιεκόμιζεν, διὰ τὸ τῆς ὑπηρεσίας εὐσταλές. — *Strom.* Lib. III. p. 535 ; Potter, cf. Lib. IV. p. 607 ; Euseb. *H. E.* III. 30.

[5] Coteler. Tom. II. p. 81.
[6] " Paulus ergo (sicut quidam tradunt)

Tertullian, on the contrary, thought St. Peter was the only married Apostle.[1] Eusebius, after Hegesippus, clearly records that St. Jude was married, for he speaks of his grandchildren.[2] Epiphanius considered Peter, Andrew, Matthew, and Bartholomew, all to have been married men.[3]

There is no doubt but that in very early times *second marriages* were considered as disqualifying for ordination. Thus Origen says, that "no digamist could be a bishop, presbyter, deacon, or widow in the Church."[4] And Tertullian adduced this custom, as an argument against second marriages generally.[5] This, of course, was derived from the rule laid down by St. Paul, that a bishop should be "the husband of *one* wife" (1 Tim. iii. 2). Yet many eminent fathers did not so interpret the words of the Apostle. For instance, St. Chrysostom, Theodoret, and Theophylact understand, that the custom so common among the Jews of divorcing one wife and marrying another is that which the Apostle is forbidding, when he would have no one ordained, save those who were monogamists.[6] And it appears, that in the earliest times it was by no means universal to refuse ordination to those who had been married twice.[7]

It is not to be concealed, however, that very soon an exaggerated esteem for celibacy crept in. The ascetic views of the Essenes, of the Montanists, of the Gnostics, and of other sects external to the Church, affected more or less the Church itself. The dread of heathen vices, felt especially by those who had themselves once been heathens, made many attach some notion of impurity even to marriage. Hence, the language of our Lord (in Matt. xix.) and of St. Paul (in 1 Cor. vii.) was pressed to its utmost consequences. They had spoken of a single life as more favourable to piety, inasmuch as it separated more from worldly distractions and gave more leisure for attending to the things of the Lord. But the primitive Christians by degrees fell into the notion, that though marriage was a state permitted, it was still, if possible, to be shunned.

cum uxore vocatus est, de qua dicit ad Philippenses scribens, *Rogo te etiam, germana compar,*" &c.—Origen. *Com. in Rom.* i.

[1] "Petrum solum maritum invenio per socrum." — *De Monogamia,* 8.

[2] *H. E.* Lib. iii. c. 20.

[3] *Hæres.* lxxviii. 10. Tom. i. p. 1042. Colon. See more such authorities in Cotelerius's note 44, Tom. i. p. 80.

[4] "Ab ecclesiasticis dignitatibus non solum fornicatio, sed et nuptiæ repellunt: neque enim episcopus, nec presbyter, nec diaconus nec vidua possunt esse digami." Orig. *Hom.* xvii. *in Luc.*

[5] Tertull. *De Monogam.* c. 11.

[6] Chrysost. *Hom.* x. *in* 1 *Tim.*; *Hom.* ii. *in Tit.*; Theodoret. *Com. in* 1 *Tim.* iii. 2; Theophyl. *In* 1 *Tim.* iii. 2.

[7] So Tertullian, addressing the Catholics says, "Quot enim et digami præsident apud vos, insultantes utique apostolo." — *De Monogam.* c. 12. See also other authorities; Bingham, *E. A.* Bk. iv. ch v. sect. 4.

It was not actually unholy, but it was inconsistent with a high degree of holiness.[1]   Hence, by degrees also, the belief began to prevail, that the special ministers of God ought to choose the higher condition, and devote themselves to celibacy.   Hence, some of the clergy began to separate from their wives.   Hence, too, some laymen were disposed to withdraw themselves from the ministrations of the married clergy.

But these errors, when first they sprang up, were opposed by councils and canons.   The Canons of the Apostles order, that " A bishop, presbyter, or deacon, shall not put away his wife under pretext of religion.   If he does, he shall be separated from communion ; and, if he persevere, he shall be deposed." [2]   The Council of Ancyra (A. D. 314) decrees, that those who, at the time of ordination as deacons, declared their intention to marry, should be allowed to marry and to remain in the ministry ; but it forbids the marriage of those who professed continence at the time of ordination.[3]   The very important Council of Gangra, the canons of which were received throughout the East and West (A. D. 324), anathematizes " those who separate themselves from a married priest, as though it were not right to communicate in the oblation, when such an one ministers." [4]   But especially observable is the decision of the first and greatest of the general councils, the Council of Nice (A. D. 325).   There it was proposed, that the clergy should be obliged to abstain from the society of their wives, whom they had married before ordination.   But Paphnutius, an eminent Egyptian prelate, himself unmarried, earnestly protested against putting so heavy a burden on the clergy ; for he said, that marriage was honourable in all men, and that it ought to suffice, that the clergy should not marry after ordination, but that they should never be required to separate from their wives.   Thereupon, the whole council assented to the words of Paphnutius ; and the motion was repressed.[5]

---

[1] Two extreme views are taken of this fact. The Romanist argues that, from the very first, the Church was in favour of clerical celibacy ; therefore it must be right.   The author of *Ancient Christianity* contends, that the exaggerated esteem for a single life prevailed from the beginning ; therefore the Church was corrupt from the very days of the Apostles.   A little candour will lead us to a conclusion different from both of these.   We may admit, that an undue esteem for virginity was a natural prejudice for the first Christians to fall into ; and accordingly, before very long, they gradually slid into it.   But it was gradually.   We find nothing of the sort in Clemens Romanus, Polycarp, Ignatius, Justin Martyr, Irenæus, Clemens Alexandrinus.   Any one who will read Clem. Alexand. (*Stromat.* Lib. III.) will see, how highly that learned father esteemed matrimony, and how little he made of celibacy.   The first trace of the exaggerated notion in question is to be found in the writings of the ascetic Montanist, Tertullian.

[2] *Can. Apostol.* Can. V. ; cf. Can. LI.

[3] *Conc. Ancyr.* Can. X.

[4] *Concil. Gangr.* Can. IV.

[5] Socrat. *Hist. Eccl.* Lib. I. c. 11 ; Sozomen, Lib. I. c. 23, &c.

It is true, the Council of Illiberis (Elvira in Spain, A. D. 300) had prohibited the clergy from the use of marriage.[1] But this does not appear to have been a council of much weight; nor can its decrees, or those of such as agreed with it, be compared with the decrees of the Canons of the Apostles, the Council of Gangra, and the first great Council of Nice. It is certain, that for a long time, not only priests and deacons, but bishops also, were allowed to marry. Socrates says that, even in his day, many eminent bishops lived with their wives, and were the fathers of families.[2] In the East, the Council in Trullo (A. D. 692) laid down the rule, that though bishops must observe celibacy, yet presbyters and deacons might live with their wives;[3] and this rule has governed the custom in the Eastern Church from that day to this.

Yet this very canon of the Trullan council speaks of it as then a received rule in the Roman Church, that deacons and presbyters should profess before ordination that they would no more live with their wives. That council itself declares, that, in decreeing otherwise, it followed the ancient rule of Apostolical order.[4]

It is not easy, nor necessary, to trace exactly the progress of the principle of clerical celibacy in the West. There appears long to have been a struggle between the natural feelings of the clergy and the rigid discipline of the Church: the clergy, from time to time, in different parts of Europe, relapsing into the custom of living with their lawful wives, and the sterner disciplinarians among the bishops striving to repress it. Gregory VII. (A. D. 1073) is considered as having most effectually restrained the marriage of the clergy. He held several councils in Italy, and especially one at Rome, A. D. 1074: where the marriage of priests was condemned under the name of concubinage.

Two years afterwards (A. D. 1076), a synod of English bishops was held at Winchester, under Archbishop Lanfranc. That Synod decreed, that canons should have no wives, and forbade in future any priest to marry, or bishops to ordain such as would not declare that they were unmarried; but it permitted such priests as lived in the country, and were already married, to retain their wives.[5]

---

[1] *Concil. Illiber.* Can. xxxiii. So the Council of Carthage (A. D. 390). Can. ii. enjoins continence on all the clergy.

[2] Socrates, Lib. v. c. 22.

[3] *Concil. Trull.* Can. xiii. The Council in Trullo was held at Constantinople. It is also called *Concilium Quinisextum*, from being supplementary to the fifth and sixth councils.

[4] Ἐπειδὴ ἐν Ῥωμαίων ἐκκλησίᾳ ἐν τάξει κάνονος παραδεδόσθαι διέγνωμεν, τοὺς μέλ-

λοντας διακόνου ἢ πρεσβυτέρου χειροτονίας ἀξιοῦσθαι καθομολογεῖν ὡς οὐκέτι ταῖς αὐτῶν συνάπτονται γαμεταῖς· ἡμεῖς τῷ ἀρχαίῳ ἐξακολουθοῦντες κανόνι τῆς ἀποστολικῆς ἀκρι-βείας καὶ τάξεως τὰ τῶν ἱερῶν ἀνδρῶν κατὰ νόμους συνοικεσία καὶ ἀπὸ τοῦ νῦν ἐρρῶσθαι βουλόμεθα, κ. τ. λ. — *Concil. Trull.* Can. xiii.

[5] *Concil. Winton.* Can. i.; Wilkins's *Concil.* i. p. 367.

96

Under Anselm, the successor of Lanfranc (A. D. 1102), it was finally decreed in England, that neither priest nor deacon, nor even subdeacon, should be ordained, who did not profess chastity, *i. e.* celibacy: a decree which was further confirmed by the Council of London, A. D. 1108.[1]

In general, it may be considered that the laity in the middle ages were favourable to the celibacy of the clergy; but many of the wiser prelates of the Church considered it a doubtful, if not a dangerous restraint. It perhaps tended, in a considerable degree, to dispose many of the clergy themselves to the doctrines of the Reformation. Yet nothing could be a more effectual instrument for uniting the priestly orders together, and giving them common interests. At the same time, no doubt, it often made them more efficient, and left them more disengaged from secular employments and pursuits.

The reformers were all opposed to the vows of continence. Luther, though a monk, and therefore doubly bound to celibacy, married. It was matter of much debate, whether those who had once bound themselves to a single life did well to abandon it, even though they had discovered that such vows were undesirable and wrong. Luther's views were very peculiar. He held monastic vows to be impious and demoniacal:[2] and marriage he sometimes speaks of as a duty incumbent on all men. Indeed, though we may probably make much allowance for the vehemence of his language and the impetuosity of his character, he says many things on this subject which no well instructed Christian can approve.

Our own Cranmer not only married, but married twice. He, however, had not been, like Luther, a monk. Monastic vows were much more stringent than the mere profession of celibacy made by the priesthood. Some there were, like Bishop Ridley, who, though disapproving of restrictions on marriage, thought it not decorous to contract matrimony after they had promised celibacy, even though it were in the days of their former ignorance. Of course, those who did marry, laid themselves open to the charge of embracing the reformed doctrines for the sake of worldly indulgences.[3]

The Council of Trent has one canon condemnatory of those who would permit the clergy to marry.[4] The Confession of Augsburg has not imitated the conciseness of the Romish council, having two very long Articles, one on the marriage of the clergy, the other on monastic vows.[5]

[1] Wilkins's *Concil.* I. p. 387.
[2] *De Votis Monasticis*, Tom. II. p. 277.
[3] See Ridley's *Life of Ridley*, p. 293.
[4] Sess. XXIV. *De Sacr. Matrimon.* Can. IX.
[5] *Sylloge*, pp. 211, 219.

At this day then, the Eastern Church allows presbyters, but not bishops, to marry: the Roman Church enjoins celibacy on all: the Reformed Churches leave all to marry at their own discretion.

Section II.—SCRIPTURAL PROOF.

I. THERE are, no doubt, some strong arguments in favour of the celibacy of the clergy, which it may be well to consider before proceeding to the arguments on the other side.

Both our blessed Lord and St. Paul unquestionably give the preference to an unmarried life, as being a more favourable state for religious self-devotion than the state of matrimony. Our Lord's words are, " He that is able to receive it, let him receive it." To some it is a gift of God, and those who have the gift are advised to abstain from marriage, " for the kingdom of Heaven's sake " (Matt. xix. 12). I assume this to be the sense of the passage: first, because the whole stream of Christian antiquity so explained it ; [1] secondly, because I know no commentator of any credit in modern times, of whatever Church or sect, who has explained it differently. St. Paul's language illustrates our Lord's. He begins by saying, that it is a good thing for a man not to marry (1 Cor. vii. 1). Still, as a general rule, he recommends marriage (vv. 2–5). He recommends it, however, as a matter of permission, not as giving a command, (κατὰ συγγνώμην, οὐ κατ᾽ ἐπιταγήν, ver. 6) ; for he would prefer to see all men as he was himself; " but every man has his proper gift, one after this manner, and another after that " (ver. 7). To the unmarried he says, it is good for them, if they abide as he abode (ver. 8). Celibacy is indeed particularly to be advised " for the present distress " (ver. 26).[2] And as a general rule, he lays it down, that there is benefit in an unmarried condition, because it is less subject to the cares of this life, and causes less solicitude and anxiety, giving more time for religion and devotion to God. These are his words : " I would have you without carefulness. He that is unmarried careth for the things of the Lord, how he may please the Lord ; but he that is married careth for the things that are of

---

[1] See for instance, Tertull. *De Virginibus Velandis*, c. 10 ; *De Cultu Fœminarum*, II. 9 ; Origen *In Matt.* Tom. xv. 4, 5 ; Chrysostom, *Homil.* LXII. *in Matt.*; Epiphanius, *Hæres.* LVIII. 4, Tom. I. p. 491 ; Theophylact. *In Matt.* xix., &c.

[2] It may be a question whether " the present distress " means the state of persecution, to which the early Christians were exposed, or the distress and anxiety of the present life. — See above, p 350, note 3.

the world, how he may please his wife. There is difference also between a wife and a virgin. The unmarried woman careth for the things of the Lord, that she may be holy both in body and spirit; but she that is married careth for the things of the world, how she may please her husband. And this I speak for your profit; not that I may cast a snare upon you, but for that which is comely, and that ye may attend on the Lord without distraction" (vv. 32 –35).

Here then, though the Apostle is far from finding fault with marriage, he evidently prefers celibacy; not because there is evil in marriage, but because there is less distraction in an unmarried life.[1] Such a life, undertaken and adhered to from religious motives, involves a stricter renunciation of the world, a greater abstinence from earthly comforts and enjoyments, a more entire devotion of the soul to the one end of serving God.

We may fairly conclude from such language of the Apostle, coupled with the words of our Lord, that the tone of popular opinion, concerning marriage and celibacy, is low and unscriptural. With us marriage is ever esteemed the more honourable state; celibacy is looked on as at least inferior, if not contemptible. " But the base things of the world, and things that are despised, hath God chosen " (1 Cor. i. 28). And a true tone of Christian sentiment would make us honour those who live apart from earthly joys, that they may live more to God.[2]

Now these considerations, at first sight, seem to make for the celibacy of the clergy. God's ministers should ever seek the most excellent way. Marriage may be good and honourable; but if celibacy be a more favourable state for religious advancement, giving us leisure, like Mary, " to sit at Jesus' feet," not " careful and troubled about many things; " then must it be well for Christ's special servants to choose that good part, that they may " attend upon the Lord without distraction."

We may add to this prime argument some motives of Church policy. An unmarried clergyman is *expeditior*, more readily moved from place to place, abler to go where his duty may call him, to do what his calling may require of him. He has no children to think about, no wife to carry about with him, no interests, but those of the Church and of the Church's Head. His strength, his wealth, his intellect, he may devote all to one end; for he has no need to

---

[1] " For the evil is not in the cohabitation, but in the impediment to the strictness of life." — Chrysost. *Hom.* xx. *in Matt.*

[2] Matt. xix. and 1 Cor. vii. have been considered in another point of view under Art. xiv. pp. 348–351; which see.

have anxieties to provide for his own, or to preserve himself for their sakes. He has no temptation to heap up riches for others; none to form worldly schemes and seek worldly interest, for the advancement of his family. " He careth only for the things of the Lord, how he may please the Lord."

II. Now, I do think, we ought not to underrate such arguments as these. They have, doubtless, much weight; and accordingly long prevailed to keep the clergy in a state of single life. But no inferences from Scripture, or apparent policy and expediency, can weigh against plain declarations to the contrary; and that more especially when the question concerns a penal enactment, — a restraint upon a law of nature, and upon instincts implanted in us by the Creator, and sanctified to us by His blessing. And we assert, that Scripture does contain plain and direct evidence that God Almighty not only sanctions and blesses marriage in general, but sanctions and blesses it in the clergy, as well as in the laity. " What God hath cleansed, that call not we common."

1. If we look at the old Testament, the priests were not only allowed, but encouraged to marry. This is not, of course, a proof that the clergy under the new Covenant may marry; but the Roman Church is especially fond of comparing all things concerning the Levitical priesthood with the priesthood of the Gospel.

2. That some of the Apostles were married is admitted by all. But it is asserted by the Roman Catholics, that they did not live with their wives after they were ordained to the Apostleship. St. Paul, however, says, " Have we no power to lead about a sister, a wife, as well as other Apostles, and as the brethren of the Lord and Cephas?" (1 Cor. ix. 5). It is true, that some of the fathers understood this, not of a wife, but of those Christian women who ministered to the Apostles, as some had ministered to our Lord when on earth (Luke viii. 2, 3).[1] But the more ancient fathers understood it of carrying their own wives about with them. We have already seen that Clement of Alexandria so interpreted this passage; and his testimony is quoted with approval by Eusebius.[2] Tertullian also distinctly asserts from the same passage of Scripture, " that it was permitted to the Apostles to marry, and to lead about their wives with them."[3] The earlier interpretation, therefore, according with the more obvious sense of the words, we can-

---

[1] See Theodoret and Theophylact *ad h. l.* Isidor. Pelus. *Epist.* CLXXVI. Lib. III. The same is the opinion of Ambrose, Jerome, and Augustine.

[2] Clem. *Strom.* Lib. III. p. 535; Euseb.

H. E. III. 30, cited in the first section.

[3] " Licebat et Apostolis nubere et uxores circumducere." — *De Exhortat Castitat.* c. 8.

not but suspect that the later fathers interpreted them otherwise, from the then unduly increasing esteem for celibacy.[1]

3. But further St. Paul especially directs that bishops and deacons should be the husbands of one wife (1 Tim. iii. 2, 12 ; Tit. i. 6) ; and lays down special rules concerning their management of their children (1 Tim. iii. 4), and the conduct of their wives (ver. 11).[2] A strange interpretation has been given to this passage by some of the Roman Catholics ; namely, that the Apostle speaks figuratively, meaning that a bishop should have but one diocese. Yet I imagine that this would not be often pressed. St. Chrysostom, and after him Theodoret and Theophylact,[3] as we have seen already, understand the Apostle to forbid that any should be ordained who had divorced one wife and married another ; a custom which seems not only to have been common with Jews and heathens, but to have crept in even among Christians.[4] Some indeed among the fathers held, that second marriages after baptism were thus forbidden by St. Paul ;[5] but the ancient Church always interpreted the passage, as permitting and sanctioning at least a single marriage to the clergy, though, in some sense, forbidding a second. St. Chrysostom has even been thought to express himself as though it might be a question whether St. Paul did not *enjoin* marriage, though himself declaring that he understood it of permission, not of injunction.[6] And in another place he says, St. Paul speaks of the marriage of the clergy on purpose " to stop the mouths of heretics who condemned marriage ; showing that marriage is not unholy in itself, but so honourable, that a married man might ascend the holy throne."[7]

Thus then the words of the Apostle, as interpreted by all the ancient Church, whatever they may say about a second marriage, unquestionably sanction a single marriage to the ministers of Christ.

1 From this interpretation arose that objectionable custom in the Church, that presbyters should have female attendants instead of wives, called *mulieres subintroductæ*, συνείσακτοι, &c. This was forbidden by the Council of Ancyra, Can. XIX. It is condemned by Epiphanius, *Hæres.* LXXVIII. See Suicer, Tom. I. pp. 28, 83, 810.

2 γυναῖκας in this verse does not *certainly* mean the wives of the bishops and deacons. It is interpreted by some of the widows or deaconesses.

3 Chrysost. *Hom.* X. *in* 1 *Tim.* ; *Hom.* II. *in Tit.* ; Theodoret *In* 1 *Tim.* iii. 2; Theophylact *In* 1 *Tim.* iii.

4 See Hammond on 1 Tim. iii. 2.

5 Origen, *Hom.* XVII. *in Luc.* ; Tertull. *De Monogam.* c. 11, quoted in last Section. See also Ambros. *De Offic.* Lib. I. c. 50; Hieronym. *Ep.* II. *ad Nepotian.*

6 Δεῖ οὖν φησι τὸν ἐπίσκοπον ἀνεπίληπτον εἶναι, μιᾶς γυναικος ἀνδρα· οὐ νομοθετῶν τοῦτό φησιν, ὡς μὴ εἶναι ἄνευ τούτου γίνεσθαι, ἀλλὰ τὴν ἀμετρίαν κωλύων. — *Hom.* X. *in* 1 *Tim.* See also Erasmus on 1 Tim. iii. 2.

7 τίνος ἕνεκεν τὸν τοιοῦτον εἰς μέσον παράγει ; ἐπιστομίζει τοὺς αἱρετικοὺς τυὺς τὸν γάμον διαβάλλοντας, δεικνὺς ὅτι τὸ πρᾶγμα οὐκ ἔστιν ἐναγὲς. ἀλλ' οὕτω τίμιον ὡς μετ' αὐτοῦ δύνασθαι καὶ ἐπὶ τὸν ἅγιον ἐπιβαίνειν θρόνον. — *Hom.* II. *in Tit.*

These words alone are fully sufficient to prove the truth of the Article we have in hand, — to prove that "bishops, priests, and deacons are not commanded by God's law either to vow the estate of single life, or to abstain from marriage." And we may ask, if God has not bound us, what power in Heaven or earth has authority to bind? What can be more presumptuous than to add to the moral laws of the Creator, to forbid as sinful what He has ordained as holy?

Again, our Lord especially says, that "all men cannot receive the saying" that single life may be more profitable for the kingdom of Heaven (Matt. xix. 11). St. Paul says, that "every man has his proper gift" (1 Cor. vii. 7); and that he does not speak of the benefits of celibacy, "to cast a snare upon" us (1 Cor. vii. 35). It is therefore strangely presumptuous to impose that on whole bodies, which our Lord says some cannot receive, which St. Paul calls a peculiar gift, and which he will not *enjoin* on any, lest it be a snare to them.

4. There are some general considerations which much strengthen the above more particular arguments. " Marriage is honourable in all men " (Heb. xiii. 4). What is honourable in all, cannot surely be prohibited to any. The "forbidding to marry" is expressly spoken of by the Spirit, as a sign of the apostasy of the latter days, and as arising from " the hypocrisy of liars, whose own consciences are seared with a hot iron." [1] Above all, marriage is a type of the union of Christ and his Church (Eph. v. 23–32). It is " consecrated to such an excellent mystery, that in it is signified and represented the spiritual unity of Christ and His Church." Can we believe that to be unfit for the ministers of Christ, which Christ Himself has honoured with such high approbation and blessing?

5. Lastly, it is said that many benefits are derived to the Church from an unmarried priesthood. Such expediency, however, cannot be set up against the word of God. Romanists themselves have often admitted, that, if there were good reasons for the clergy not to marry, there were still better reasons why they should marry. And, but that such addition to our Scriptural proof seems unnecessary, we might easily bring many arguments from experience to show, that the snares of celibacy have been as great as those of matrimony; and that the charities of wedded life have been as profitable to the married, as the asceticism of single life can have been to the unmarried priesthood.

---

[1] ἐν ὑποκρίσει ψευδολόγων, κεκαυτηριασμένων τὴν ἰδίαν συνείδησιν, κωλύοντων γαμεῖν, κ. τ. λ. — 1 Tim. iv. 2, 3.

ARTICLE XXXIII.

Of Excommunicate Persons, how they are to be avoided.	*De Excommunicatis Vitandis.*
THAT person, which by open denunciation of the Church is rightly cut off from the unity of the Church, and excommunicated, ought to be taken of the whole multitude of the faithful as an Heathen and Publican, until he be openly reconciled by penance, and received into the Church by a Judge that hath authority thereunto.	QUI per publicam Ecclesiæ denunciationem rite ab unitate Ecclesiæ præcisus est, et excommunicatus, is ab universa fidelium multitudine, (donec per pœnitentiam publice reconciliatus fuerit arbitrio judicis competentis,) habendus est tanquam ethnicus et publicanus.

SECTION I.— HISTORY.

CUTTING off from the people is a punishment often denounced and commanded in the old Testament. It appears in general to have meant death by the judgment of God (1 Kings xiv. 10), or by the hand of man (Exod. xxxi. 14, 15 ; xxxv. 2 ; Levit. xvii. 4, &c.). But the later Jews understood it of excommunication, of which they had three different kinds. The first and lightest sort was called נִדּוּי (*Niddui*), separation or excommunication for a month ; to be extended to two or three months in case of impenitence. The second and more severe kind was called חֵרֶם (*Cherem*), excommunication accompanied with imprecations from Deut. xxviii. and other places of Scripture. A person so separated was not allowed to have intercourse with any of the Jews, except for the purchase of necessary food: they might not consort with him, "no, not to eat;" a custom to which St. Paul is thought to allude in 1 Cor. v. 11. The third and heaviest form of excommunication was called שַׁמַּתָא (*Shammata*), a word the derivation of which is obscure, and which some have supposed to be of the same signification with the *Maranatha* of St. Paul, namely, " the Lord cometh." [1] Whether originally the second and third form may not have been the same is still doubtful.

From the very earliest times the Christian Church exercised a

---

[1] See Buxtorf, *Lex. Chald Talm. Rabbin.* s. vv. נִדּוּי, חֵרֶם, שַׁמַּתָא, pp. 1303, 827, 2463; also Jahn's *Archæologia Biblica*, § 252.

power of the same kind.   Clemens Romanus probably alludes to it
in his First Epistle to the Corinthians.[1]   Hermas speaks of some
that have sinned and are " rejected from the tower," (which in his
vision means the Church,) and who have afterwards to do penance
for their fault.[2] Irenæus tells us of several persons of heretical
tendency, who were obliged to perform penitential acts ;[3] and of
Cerdon, as having been several times put to penance, and finally
excommunicated.[4]   Origen says, that " offenders, especially such
as offend by incontinence, are expelled from communion." [5]   Tertullian speaks of the gravity of Church censures ; and of excommunication as a kind of anticipation of the judgment of God.[6]   From
him indeed we obtain a considerable insight into the customs of
public confession, of the penance and humiliations to which offenders were put, of their absolutions and restoration to communion,
and of the utter and final excommunication from Church privileges
of obstinate and incorrigible sinners.[7]   The canons of the Apostles,
being especially directed to the ordering of discipline in the Church,
are full of sentences of separation and excommunication.[8]   It is
difficult to assign the exact date of these venerable canons ; but
Bishop Beveridge places them at the end of the second, or the
beginning of the third century.

It being thus apparent, that, from the very first, excommunication was a regular part of the discipline of the Church, it is unnecessary to continue our history through the following centuries, when
no one questions that such a punishment was in frequent use.
We may be content to notice, that among the Christians, as among
the Jews, there prevailed a distinction of greater and lesser excommunication.   The lesser excommunication, called ἀφορισμὸς or
separation, consisted in exclusion of offenders from the participation
of the Eucharist and from the prayers of the faithful, but did not
expel them wholly from the Church ; for they might be present
at the psalmody, the reading of the Scriptures, the sermon, and
the prayers of the catechumens and penitents, but might not remain to the service of the Communion.   But the greater excom-

[1] § 57; Coteler. Tom. I. p. 178, vid.
note 93.

[2] Herm. *Pastor*. Lib. I. Vis. III. § 5.

[3] Lib. I. c. 13.

[4] " Modo homologesin faciens, modo
ab aliquibus traductus in his quæ doce-
bat male, et abstentus est a religiosorum
hominum conventu." — Lib. III. c. 4.

[5] Οἷα δ' ἐστιν αὐτοῖς ἀγωγὴ καὶ περὶ
ἁμαρτανόντων καὶ μάλιστα τῶν ἀκολασται-
νόντων, οὓς ἀπελαύνουσι τοῦ κοινοῦ, κ. τ. λ.
— Origen. *Cont. Cels.* Lib. III.

[6] " Nam et judicatur magno cum pon-
dere, ut apud certos de Dei conspectu ,
summumque futuri judicii præjudicium
est, si quis ita deliquerit, ut a communicatione orationis, et omnis sancti com-
mercii relegetur." — Tertull. *Apolog.* c. 39.

[7] See Bishop Kaye's *Tertullian*, pp.
251–254, 262.

[8] See for instance Canons 5, 8, 9, 10,
12, 28, 29, 31, 36, 48.   On this subject
see Marshall's *Penitential Discipline*, ch.
II. pt. 1.

munication, called *Anathema* or *total separation* (παντελὴς ἀφορι-σμός), excluded from all Church communion whatever, from approaching to any assembly of the faithful for prayer, or sermon, or reading of the Scriptures.[1]   The former kind, it is needless to add, was used for lighter offences; the latter for grievous and deadly sins.

Something has already been said (under Art. XXV.) concerning the custom of public confession, which was a penitential discipline, enjoined on those who were sentenced either to the greater or lesser excommunication, previously to their restoration to Church fellowship; and also concerning the private confession, which gradually superseded public confession, and so loosened discipline and weakened the hands of the Church.   Yet excommunications, in cases of heresy, or of royal and national opposition to the authority of the Church, assumed a new and more formidable aspect in the Middle Ages; so that, although private offenders against morality or piety might escape more easily under the shield of private confession, the obstinate heretic, and the nation whose ruler was not submissive to the see of Rome, were handled with a severity unheard of before.   The excommunications of Huss and Wickliffe and Luther are evidence of the mode of proceedings against individual dissenters from the established faith.   The excommunication of the Emperor Henry IV. by Pope Gregory VII., and the interdict on England under John by Innocent III., exemplify the use which the successors of St. Peter made of the keys of the kingdom, when kings and nations bowed down before them.[2]

The latter part of the Article speaks of reconciliation to the Church by penance, and of reception into the Church by a competent judge.

Besides *exhomologesis* or public confession, the early Church used to impose a term of public penance on those who expressed contrition for their sins, and desired to be restored to communion. The performance of penance was anciently a matter of considerable time, in order that the sincerity of the repentance might be tested, and that full evidence of sorrow might be given to the Church. Accordingly, penitents were divided into four distinct classes, called respectively *flentes*, *audientes*, *substrati*, and *consistentes*.   The *flentes*, or *mourners*, were candidates for penance, rather than persons

---

[1] See Bingham, *E. A.* Bk. XVI. ch. II. §§ 7, 8.
[2] The primitive Church did by no means exempt princes from its discipline, as is well known in the case of Theodo-sius, whom St. Ambrose excommunicated and put to penance for the slaughter of seven thousand men in Thessalonica. — Theodoret, Lib. v c. 18; Bingham, XVI. iii. 5.

actually admitted to penitence. They used to lie prostrate at the church-door, begging the prayers of the faithful, and asking to be admitted to do penance. When they had been admitted to penance, they became *audientes* or *hearers;* because then, though not restored to communion, or the prayers of the Church, they might hear the Scriptures and the sermon. From this condition they passed into the state of *substrati* or *kneelers.* These were allowed to stay in the nave of the Church, and to join in certain prayers, specially put up for them, whilst they were on their knees. Lastly, they became *consistentes* or *co-standers,* persons allowed to stand with the faithful at the altar, and join in the common prayers, and to witness, but not partake of the Holy Communion.[1] During the term of their penance, penitents were obliged to appear in sackcloth, with ashes on their head, to cut off their hair, to abstain from all feasting and innocent amusements, to show liberality to the poor, and to make public confession of their sins.[2] How early this distinction of four orders of penitents was made, and the special rules concerning their penance were laid down, is not indisputably certain. The time of the Novatian schism, *i. e.* the middle of the third century, is the earliest period at which it is thought that mention is certainly made of these distinctions and rules of discipline.[3]

It was only for heavy offences that excommunication, and therefore penance, were ever inflicted. In general it may be said, that the crimes were reducible to three classes; namely, uncleanness, idolatry, bloodshed.[4] The duration of the term of penitence was different, according to the magnitude of the offence, the aggravation of its guilt by circumstances, and the penitence or impenitence of the offender. For the heavier crimes, ten, fifteen, twenty, thirty years, and even the whole of a life, were not thought too long. Some were not reconciled to the Church but on imminent danger of death, and some were thought to have rebelled against God too grievously ever to have communion in this world; though God's mercy might be hoped for them in the next. Moreover, we may add, that, generally speaking, public penance was allowed but once to sinners of any sort.[5]

As for the judge or officer who had power to restore to communion and give absolution, it was ordinarily the bishop. He, for just reasons, might moderate and abridge the term of penance;[6]

---

[1] Bingham, *E. A.* xviii. ch. ii.
[2] Ibid. ch. iii.
[3] Ibid. xviii. ii. 2.

[4] Marshall, *Penitential Discipline,* ch. ii. pt. ii. sect. 1.
[5] See Bingham, *E. A.* xviii. iv.
[6] Ibid. § 8.

and, as all discipline was considered to be lodged in his hands, he was esteemed both as the excommunicator, and also as the absolver of the penitent.[1] Yet, in many cases, the power of absolution was committed to presbyters; who, by authority of the bishop, or in his absence, and on great necessity, such as danger of death, might reconcile the sinner to communion, and give him the absolution of the Church.[2] Nay! as in cases of extreme necessity even deacons were allowed to give men the absolution of baptism, so, under the like circumstances, they were authorized to grant penitents the conciliatory absolution.[3]

Having thus considered the primitive customs, and spoken of some abuses in the Middle Ages of the Church, we may proceed to the time of the Reformation. The Council of Trent says, the power of excommunication is to be used " soberly and with great circumspection; " still, if an excommunicated person will not repent, it enjoins that, not only shall he be prohibited " from Sacraments, and the Communion, and intercession of the faithful; but it may even be needful to proceed against him as one suspected of heresy " (*etiam contra eum tanquam de hæresi suspectum procedi possit*).[4]

The Reformers generally insisted on the power of excommunication. The Augsburg Confession gives bishops authority " to exclude from the communion of the Church impious persons, whose impiety is notorious, by the word, not by human violence." [5] The Saxon Confession says, that " those guilty of manifest crimes ought to be excommunicated; nor is just excommunication an empty sound " (*inane fulmen*).[6] Calvin, who was himself the great legislator for all the Calvinistic communions, divides the discipline of the Church into (1) private monition; (2) reprehension before witnesses; (3) excommunication [7] (Matt. xviii. 15–17). For light offences reprehension is enough; but for heavier, exclusion from the communion of the Supper, humiliation before God, and testification of penitence before the Church, are needful.[8] No one, not even the sovereign, must be exempted from such censures; which he illustrates by the case of Theodosius.[9] The Calvinistic communions in general have been very strict observers of the discipline thus maintained by their great reformer.

---

[1] Bingham. xix. iii. 1.
[2] Ibid. § 2.
[3] Ibid. § 3. On the whole subject of primitive discipline read Bingham, *E. A.* Bks. xvi.–xix., and Marshall's *Penitential Discipline*.
[4] Sess. xxv. cap. iii.

[5] "Impios, quorum nota est impietas, excludere ex communione Ecclesiæ, sine vi humana, sed verbo." — *Sylloge*, p. 220.
[6] Ibid. p. 293.
[7] *Instit.* iv. xii. 2.
[8] Ibid. § 6.
[9] Ibid. § 7.

The Church of England is clear enough in its principles, though restrained in its practice. This Article speaks plainly her doctrine. The rubric before the Communion gives to the curate the power of repelling evil livers from the Eucharist, provided that he shall at once acquaint the bishop. The introduction to the Commination Service speaks with great regret of the relaxation of godly discipline, and with earnest desire that it may be restored. The canons of 1663 are sufficiently free in denouncing excommunication against heretics, schismatics, and dissenters of all kinds. The peculiar nature of the connection between the Church and State in England, and the prevalence of what are called Erastian opinions, have been the great causes why ecclesiastical censures have lost their power, and become a dead letter amongst us.

Section II. — SCRIPTURAL PROOF.

THERE appear two points here to be demonstrated. I. That the Church is divinely authorized to excommunicate offenders, and to restore them to communion on their repentance. II. That certain persons in the Church are judges, having authority thereto.

I. Our Lord Himself gave power to His Church to excommunicate and absolve. In Matt. xviii. 15–18, He enjoins that, if one brother or fellow Christian sin against another, and refuse to listen to private rebuke, or to the admonition of others to whom the offence may be told, then the grievance is to be communicated to the Church.[1] But if, when it is told to the Church, the erring brother still neglects to hear and to show penitence, then he is to be looked on no longer as a Christian and a brother, but it is said, " Let him be unto thee as an heathen man and a publican " (ver. 17). The meaning of this would be intelligible enough to

---

[1] τῇ ἐκκλησίᾳ. There is no sufficient reason to doubt that our Lord meant here IIis Church. It was not, indeed, then fully set up, but He was continually foretelling its establishment; why then might He not speak of it by name ? The word itself is probably a translation of the Hebrew קָהָל; but it is by no means likely, that our Lord should intend His Christian followers to tell their troubles to the Jewish congregation, or the elders thereof, who would already have excommunicated and rejected them. Whilst He was with them, He Himself would be the natural referee. Afterwards he constitutes His Church the judge; the Church, that is, acting through its elders, as the Jewish קָהָל acted through its elders. Hence Chrysostom and Theophylact explain τῇ ἐκκλησίᾳ by τοῖς προεδρεύουσι. — See Suicer, Tom. I. p. 1052.

the first disciples of Christ. They had been bred Jews, and knew that Jews had no communion with heathen men and publicans not merely not in religious ordinances, but not even to eat. This direction then Christ gives to His Church, that those who, having sinned openly against their brethren, would not listen to her godly admonitions, should be separated from the fellowship of the faithful, and treated as heathens or publicans. Then, to confirm the Church in her authority, to assure her that her censures, and her remission of censure both had a warrant from God, He adds: "Verily I say unto you, Whatsoever ye shall bind on earth shall be bound in Heaven: and whatsoever ye shall loose on earth shall be loosed in Heaven" (ver. 18). In this context there can be no reasonable question, that the binding means to place in a state of bondage or excommunication from Church privilege, that the loosing signifies to restore again to the freedom of Christian communion.

At the risk of anticipating the subject of our second division, we ought to compare with this the promise to St. Peter (Matt. xvi. 19) and to the Apostles at large (John xx. 23). To St. Peter, as to the Church, it is promised, that by means of the keys of the kingdom he shall bind, and it shall be bound in Heaven; he shall loose, and it shall be loosed in Heaven. And to all the Apostles it is promised: "Whosoever sins ye remit, they are remitted: and whosoever sins ye retain, they are retained" (ver. 23). Now to no human being, save to Christ alone, has the power of forgiving sins primarily and absolutely been committed by God. (See Matt. ix. 6. Rev. iii. 7.) But to admit to the Church (*i. e.* to the kingdom of Heaven, Christ's kingdom on earth) by baptism, to exclude from it by excommunication, to restore again by absolution and remission of censure, — these are powers which Christ commits to His people, and especially to the rulers and elders of His people.

To illustrate this, we must look at the practice of the Apostolic Church. In 1 Cor. v. 5, we find St. Paul enjoining the Corinthians to "deliver" the incestuous man "to Satan for the destruction of the flesh, that the spirit may be saved in the day of the Lord Jesus." It is true many of the ancients were of opinion that St. Paul meant here to inflict by a miracle some bodily disease upon the man. But the Apostle does not say that he himself will deliver him to Satan, but bids the Corinthian Church to do so. If it were a miraculous punishment, it is far more likely that he should have inflicted it himself. But he bids them (ver. 4) assemble together, " in the name of the Lord Jesus Christ ; " promises that, as their bishop, he will be with them in spirit; and then tells them, with the power of the Lord Jesus to deliver the offender to Satan. Now the world is Satan's kingdom ; the Church is Christ's. To expel from Christ's kingdom is to turn over into Satan's kingdom. What more fit than such language to express excommunication ? And to prove that this is what is meant, we find (in 2 Cor. ii.) that, when the incestuous man had repented, the Apostle enjoins the Corinthians to restore and forgive him ; and promises that he will forgive whomsoever they forgive. (See vv. 5–11.) All this exactly corresponds with a case of excommunication, succeeded by restoration and absolution.[1]

We may compare with these many passages, in which the Apostles enjoin upon Christians to withdraw from the company of brethren who do not live according to their Christian profession, but who are either impure in their lives, or heretical in their belief. (See Rom. xvi. 17. 1 Cor. v. 9 ; xv. 33 ; xvi. 22. 2 Cor. vi. 14, 17. 2 Thess. iii. 6, 14. 2 John 10, 11.) These, though not all directly bearing on the subject, show that Christians ought to keep themselves from all communion with ungodly men ; and therefore make it probable, that they should be enjoined to exclude them from Church-fellowship.

II.   We have next to show, that our Lord gave certain officers in His Church special authority, both to excommunicate, and to restore to communion.

The Church in the early ages must be viewed as a distinct society, separated from the world at large, held together by great and independent interests, governed by laws peculiar to itself, and ordered by its own officers. It was in the midst of the wilderness, with wolves and wild beasts all around it ; a sheepfold, and with shepherds of the sheep. The shepherds or governors were the bishops and elders. " Let the elders that rule well be counted worthy of double honour, especially they who labour in the word and doctrine " (1 Tim. v. 17). " We beseech you, brethren, to know them which labour among you, and are over you in the Lord, and admonish you ; and to esteem them very highly in love for

---

[1] See Theodoret and Theophylact *In* 1 *Cor.* v. 5 ; Balsamon and Zonaras *In Basil.* Can. vii. ; Beza *In* 1 *Cor.* v. 5 ; Estius *In* 1 *Cor.* v. 5 ; Beveridge, *Not. in Can. Apostol.* x. ; *Pandectæ*, Tom. ii. *Adnotat.* p. 20 ; Suicer, Tom. ii. p. 940. These all advocate the view taken in the text. On the opposite side see Grotius and Lightfoot on 1 Cor. v. 5 ; also Hammond, who combines both views in one, thinking both excommunication and bodily disease to have been inflicted. So, I rather think, does St. Chrysostom. See *Homil.* xv. *in* 1 *Cor.* v.

their work's sake " (1 Thess. v. 12, 13). " Remember them which
have the rule over you, who have spoken unto you the word of
God " (Heb. xiii. 7). " Obey them that have the rule over you,
and submit yourselves unto them ; for they watch for your souls,
as they that must give account," &c. (Heb. xiii. 17). Such passages show, that the primitive pastors had a pastoral *authority*, as
well as a pastoral care.

Now we have seen, that our Lord committed to His Church the
keys of discipline, the power to bind and to loose. But, as all bodies act through their officers, so, what at one time He gave to the
Church as a body, at another He specially assigned to the rulers
of that body, the Apostles and elders. To St. Peter, the first
and most honoured of the college of the Apostles, He promised,
" I will give unto thee the keys of the kingdom of Heaven : and
whatsoever thou shalt bind on earth shall be bound in Heaven :
and whatsoever thou shalt loose on earth shall be loosed in Heaven "
(Matt. xvi. 19). And the power which he thus bestowed on St.
Peter, He afterwards yet more solemnly conveyed to all the Apostles, and apparently with them to other elders of the Church (see
ver. 19), in the words, " Receive ye the Holy Ghost : whose
soever sins ye remit, they are remitted unto them ; and whose
soever sins ye retain, they are retained " (John xx. 22, 23). The
hypothesis, that this commission to the first disciples of Christ was
miraculous, and therefore temporary, is utterly untenable. If a
miraculous power were bestowed, it was no less than a power of
searching the heart, and pronouncing authoritatively a judgment
of perdition on the guilty, and pardon of sins to the penitent. But
such power is the attribute of God alone ; and He will never so give
His glory to another. The Apostles, though endued with the gift
of tongues, of prophecy, of miracles, were not endued with the
power to bestow an actual remission of offences, such as would free
the soul from all danger, when appearing before the judgment-seat
of Christ ; and as little might they hurl the thunderbolt of vengeance, and sentence transgressors to the lake that burneth with
fire and brimstone. It is plain, therefore, that the keys committed
to St. Peter were the badge of his stewardship, as " minister of
Christ, and steward of the mysteries of God." The power to bind
and to loose was the same as the Church's power to bind and to
loose. And the power to retain and to remit sins, was but the
same authority conveyed in different terms.[1]

[1] See Dr. Hammond's note on John κρατεῖν in St. John are all one with the
xx. 23. He shows that the ἀφιέναι and λύειν and δέειν in St. Matthew.

Now this power, considered as the power of admitting to, and excluding from the Church and her fellowship, as the Church exercised it, so the Apostles especially claimed it, as immediately resulting from their own commission from Christ. In the case of the incestuous man at Corinth, St. Paul enjoins the Church to excommunicate and afterwards to restore him; but, in both instances, he himself is to be considered as judging with them and ratifying their sentence, by virtue of his own special authority as an Apostle of Christ; in which office he claims to be exercising Christ's own authority. Thus (in 1 Cor. v. 3, 4, 5), he says, "I verily, as absent in body, but present in spirit, have judged already .... In the name of our Lord Jesus Christ, when ye are gathered together, and my spirit, with the power of our Lord Jesus Christ, to deliver such an one to Satan." Here is a solemn excommunication, performed by the Church, ratified by the Apostle, and so confirmed by Christ Himself. And, in 2 Cor. ii. 10, when enjoining that the penitent sinner should be restored to communion, he writes, "To whom ye forgive anything, I forgive also: for if I forgave anything, to whom I forgave it, for your sakes forgave I it, in the person of Christ." What can be plainer than that, in both these cases, St. Paul considered that he had himself, as a chief governor in the Church, an especial power, coupled with the general assent of the Church, to judge, to expel, and to restore? So (in 1 Tim. i. 20) he says that he had himself excommunicated Hymenæus and Alexander. Whether we must infer that he did so of his own authority alone, or calling in other members of the Church, as assessors to him, we cannot say. Again, in 2 Cor. xiii. 1, 2, 10, we find him threatening to hold a regular judicial inquiry, summoning witnesses, not sparing those who should be proved to have sinned, but using sharpness, "according to the power which the Lord had given him, to edification, not to destruction."

To pass to other chief pastors, besides the Apostles themselves, we find that to Timothy and Titus, appointed bishops in the Church, St. Paul lays down rules, how they should judge, rebuke, and reject (1 Tim. v. 19–21. Tit. iii. 10, 11). Moreover, we have at least one case of the abuse of this power recorded in the new Testament. Diotrephes, who aimed at a primacy (φιλοπρωτεύει), cast the brethren out of the Church (3 John 10). And herein we may recognize that Divine wisdom which ordained that, though the chief officers of the Church should be the principal executors of its authority, yet the authority should not be vested in them alone, but, with them, in the whole body of the faithful. (See again

98

Matt. xviii. 17, 18.)   And it may appear that, as our Lord, in immediate context with the promise of ratifying Church censures and Church absolutions, promised that " where two or three were gathered together in His name, He would be in the midst of them " (ver. 20) ; so it was with a kind of synodical authority that the Apostles ordinarily armed themselves, when they administered discipline (compare again 1 Cor. v. and 2 Cor. ii), that so they might not seem to lord it over the heritage of God, and that their power might be obviously for edification, not for destruction.[1]

[1] If we pass from the early to the present times, we may observe, that our Ecclesiastical Courts are, in theory, formed upon the primitive principle. They are, indeed, lay tribunals. Yet their judges represent, first, the authority of the primate, whose delegates they are; and secondly, as being themselves laymen, and as holding power from our civil, as well as our ecclesiastical rulers, they represent not only the hierarchy, but also the laity of the Church.

ARTICLE XXXIV.

It is not necessary that Traditions and Ceremonies be in all places one, and utterly like; for at all times they have been divers, and may be changed according to the diversities of countries, times, and men's manners, so that nothing be ordained against God's Word. Whosoever through his private judgment, willingly and purposely, doth openly break the traditions and ceremonies of the Church, which be not repugnant to the Word of God, and be ordained and approved by common authority, ought to be rebuked openly, (that others may fear to do the like,) as he that offendeth against the common order of the Church, and hurteth the authority of the Magistrate, and woundeth the consciences of the weak brethren.

Every particular or national Church hath authority to ordain, change, and abolish, ceremonies or rites of the Church, ordained only by man's authority, so that all things be done to edifying.

Traditiones atque cæremonias easdem non omnino necessarium est esse ubique aut prorsus consimiles. Nam et variæ semper fuerunt et mutari possunt, pro regionum, temporum, et morum diversitate, modo nihil contra verbum Dei instituatur.

Traditiones, et cæremonias Ecclesiasticas, quæ cum verbo Dei non pugnant, et sunt autoritate publica institutæ atque probatæ, quisquis privato consilio volens, et data opera, publice violaverit, is, ut qui peccat in publicum ordinem Ecclesiæ, quique lædit autoritatem Magistratus, et qui infirmorum fratrum conscientias vulnerat, publice, ut cæteri timeant, arguendus est.

Quælibet Ecclesia particularis, sive nationalis, autoritatem habet instituendi, mutandi, aut abrogandi cæremonias, aut ritus Ecclesiasticos humana tantum autoritate institutos, modo omnia ad ædificationem fiant.

THE Reformation was in a great measure a national movement. The power and authority of the see of Rome had annihilated the distinctions of national Churches, and produced an uniformity, not only of doctrine, but also of ceremonial and discipline, throughout the West. This Article, like the XVth of the Confession of Augsburg, is an assertion of the right of particular Churches to retain or adopt, in things indifferent, local and peculiar usages. The Preface to the Book of Common Prayer, headed "Of Ceremonies, why some be abolished and some retained," is a farther and fuller exposition of the sentiments of our Reformers on this head. It should be read in connection with the Article.

The two points insisted on, and which we have to consider, are

I. That traditions and ceremonies were not to be everywhere alike, but that particular or national Churches may ordain, change, and abolish ceremonies of mere human authority, so all be done to edifying.

II. That private persons, of their private judgment, are not justified in openly breaking the traditions and ceremonies of the Church, which be not repugnant to God's word.

I. There is little direct proof, either for or against our first position, to be drawn from holy Scripture itself. The Apostolic rule was, that all things should "be done to edifying" (1 Cor. xiv. 26); "all decently and in order" (ver. 40). This certainly leaves a great liberty, and a great latitude, to order the ceremonies and offices of the Church.

But, if we come to Christian history, we shall find that the different Churches, in early times, though having wonderful concord in doctrine, and in Apostolical government, had yet great variety in discipline and ritual. The well-known controversy concerning Easter very early divided the East and West. The Church of Rome kept Easter, as we keep it now, so that it always falls on a Sunday; whilst the Churches of Asia Minor observed it on the fourteenth day of the month Abib, after the manner of the Jewish Passover, let it fall on whatever day of the week it might. The Apostolical Polycarp, Bishop of Smyrna, paid Rome a visit, to endeavour to arrange with Anicetus an uniformity of custom on this head; but though they could come to no agreement here, they agreed that the unity and harmony of the Churches should not be broken on such a point of tradition and ceremony.[1] Later indeed, Victor, Bishop of Rome, was disposed to excommunicate the Asiatic Churches, because they did not follow the Roman custom; for which uncharitableness Irenæus sent him a letter of reproof.[2]

The still more important controversy concerning the rebaptizing of heretics arose in the next century; Cyprian and the African bishops maintaining the propriety of baptizing anew those who had received baptism from heretics; whilst Stephen and the Roman Church maintained, that such baptism was valid, and therefore that it could not be repeated. The controversy indeed ran high; but for a length of time each branch of the Church followed its own views.[3]

Another instance of diversity of custom was the mode in which the Jewish Sabbath was treated. Some Churches, those of the Patriarchate of Antioch especially, not only observed the Christian Lord's day, but also the Jewish Sabbath. On the other hand, some Churches used to fast on the Saturday, or Sabbath, as well as on the Friday; because on the former our Lord lay in the grave, as

[1] Euseb. *H. E.* iv. 14, v. 24.
[2] Ibid.
[3] See Mosheim, *De Rebus ante Constan-* *tinum*, sæc. iii. § xviii. Also Mosheim, *Eccles. Hist.* Cent. iii. Pt ii. ch. iii. § 13.

on the latter he was crucified. St. Augustine mentions, that St. Ambrose wisely determined to fast on the Saturday, when he was in those places where it was customary; but not to fast on that day, where the custom was against it.[1]

Another observable thing in the early ages is, that the different bishops were so far independent of each other, that they were allowed to frame their own Liturgies, and even to express the Creed in different forms.[2] Accordingly, we hear of the Liturgies of Antioch, and Constantinople, of Alexandria, of Rome, of Gaul, of Spain,[3] &c. &c.

Now, all these facts prove the right of particular Churches to some degree of independence one of another, as regards bare ceremonies and traditional rites and customs.

II. That private persons should not wantonly break or neglect the traditions of the Church to which they belong, may be said to result from the very nature of a Christian society, and indeed of society altogether.

The scriptural authority is strong in favour of obedience to both civil and ecclesiastical authorities; even when both are corrupt. Of the former see Rom. xiii. 1; Tit. iii. 1; 1 Pet. ii. 13, 17. Of the latter, we have our Lord's injunction to His disciples to obey the Pharisees, because they sat in Moses' seat, Matt. xxiii. 2, 3; and the example of the Apostles, who, in all things not unlawful, adhered to Jewish observances and the customs of their own nation, even after the Church of Christ had been set up in the world. See Acts ii. 46; xxi. 20, 26; xxviii. 17. The Apostles indeed denounce severely those who cause divisions and schisms in the Church (Rom. xvi. 17. 1 Cor. iii. 3, &c.); and enjoin all Christians to obey their spiritual rulers, and to submit themselves to them (1 Cor. xvi. 16. 1 Thess. v. 12. Heb. xiii. 17).

It seems unnecessary to add authority from the primitive ages. The whole system of discipline and order, then so strictly observed, of necessity involves the principle, that laws and regulations made by the body of the Church were binding on, and to be observed by, every individual Christian who belonged to the Church. The decrees of Councils and Synods, often relating to discipline and ceremony, of course proceeded on the same understanding and principle.

---

[1] " Cum Romam venio, jejuno Sabbato; cum hic, non jejuno; Sic etiam tu ad quam forte Ecclesiam veneris, ejus morem serva, si cuiquam non vis esse scandalo, nec quemquam tibi." *Epist.* LIV. *ad Januariam*, Tom. II. p. 154, quoted by Beveridge on this Article.
[2] See Bingham, *E. A.* Bk. II. ch. VI.
[3] See Palmer, *Origines Liturgicæ,* " Dissertation on Primitive Liturgies."

ARTICLE XXXV.

Of the Homilies.	*De Homiliis.*

The second Book of Homilies, the several titles whereof we have joined under this Article, doth contain a godly and wholesome doctrine, and necessary for these times, as doth the former Book of Homilies, which were set forth in the time of *Edward* the Sixth ; and therefore we judge them to be read in Churches by the Ministers diligently and distinctly, that they may be understood of the people.

Tomus secundus homiliarum, quarum singulos titulos huic articulo subjunximus, continet piam et salutarem doctrinam, et his temporibus necessariam, non minus quam prior tomus homiliarum, quæ editæ sunt tempore Edwardi Sexti. Itaque eas in Ecclesiis per ministros diligenter et clare, ut a populo intelligi possint, recitandas esse judicavimus.

Of the names of the Homilies.

1 *Of the right Use of the Church.*
2 *Against Peril of Idolatry.*
3 *Of repairing and keeping clean of Churches.*
4 *Of good Works: first of Fasting.*
5 *Against Gluttony and Drunkenness.*
6 *Against Excess of Apparel.*
7 *Of Prayer.*
8 *Of the Place and Time of Prayer.*
9 *That Common Prayers and Sacraments ought, to be ministered in a known tongue.*
10 *Of the reverend estimation of God's Word.*
11 *Of Alms-doing.*
12 *Of the Nativity of Christ.*
13 *Of the Passion of Christ.*
14 *Of the Resurrection of Christ.*
15 *Of the worthy receiving of the Sacrament of the Body and Blood of Christ.*
16 *Of the Gifts of the Holy Ghost.*
17 *For the Rogation-days.*
18 *Of the State of Matrimony.*
19 *Of Repentance.*
20 *Against Idleness.*
21 *Against Rebellion.*

De Nominibus Homiliarum.

Of the right Use of the Church.
Against Peril of Idolatry.
Of repairing and keeping clean of Churches.
Of good Works: first of Fasting.
Against Gluttony and Drunkenness.
Against Excess of Apparel.
Of Prayer.
Of the Place and Time of Prayer.
That Common Prayers and Sacraments ought to be ministered in a known tongue.
Of the reverend estimation of God's Word.
Of Alms-doing.
Of the Nativity of Christ.
Of the Passion of Christ.
Of the Resurrection of Christ.
Of the worthy receiving of the Sacrament of the Body and Blood of Christ.
Of the Gifts of the Holy Ghost.
For the Rogation-days.
Of the State of Matrimony.
Of Repentance.
Against Idleness.
Against Rebellion.

[The American revision adds, " This Article is received in this Church, so far as it declares the Books of Homilies to be an explication of Christian doctrine, and instructive in piety and morals. But all references to the constitution and laws of England are considered as inapplicable to the circumstances of this Church: which also suspends the order for the reading of said Homilies in churches, until a revision of them may be conveniently made, for the clearing of them, as well from obsolete words and phrases, as from the local references." It is needless to add that the revision has never been made. — *J. W.*]

THERE is not much to be said concerning this Article. At the time of the Reformation there was great need of simple and sound instruction for the people, and but few were competent to give it. Many of the clergy were but partially affected to the so-called new learning. Many were very illiterate. In many parishes, therefore, the clergy were not licensed to preach, and hence the reformers put forth these popular discourses, to meet the exigencies of the times.

The First Book of Homilies, which was published in the reign of Edward VI., is attributed to the pens of Cranmer, Ridley, Latimer, and others. The second, published in Elizabeth's reign, is supposed to be due in great part to Jewel. The former seems to be written with much greater care and accuracy than the latter, and is indeed most full of sound and valuable teaching.

It is not possible to prove the assertion, that they " contain a godly and wholesome doctrine," without going through the whole book of Homilies, and commenting on them all. All writers on the subject have agreed, that the kind of assent, which we are here called on to give to them, is general, not specific. We are not expected to express full concurrence with every statement, or every exposition of Holy Scripture contained in them, but merely in the general to approve of them, as a body of sound and orthodox discourses, and well adapted for the times for which they were composed. For instance, we cannot be required to call the Apocrypha by the name of Holy Scripture, or to quote it as of Divine authority, because we find it so in the Homilies. We cannot be expected to think it a very cogent argument for the duty of fasting, that thereby we may encourage the fisheries and strengthen the seaport towns against foreign invasion.[1]   And perhaps we may agree with Dr. Hey, rather than with Bishop Burnet,[2] and hold, that a person may fairly consider the Homilies to be a sound collection of religious instruction, who might yet shrink from calling the Roman Catholics idolaters. The Homilies are, in fact, semi-authoritative documents. The First Book is especially valuable, as having been composed by those who reformed our services and drew up our Articles. The second also shows popularly the general tone of instruction, which the divines of the reign of Elizabeth thought wholesome for the people. They are therefore of much

[1] See Homily *On Good Works; and first, Of Fasting.*

[2] See Burnet on Art. xxx r.; Hey, iv. p. 466.

value in throwing light on documents more authoritative than themselves; and may be useful for the instruction of our clergy and people in the doctrines of the Reformation. The higher education of our parish priests, and the now somewhat antiquated style of the discourses in question, render it not very likely that they will ever again be much read in Churches.

Something has been said before of the "Homily of Salvation," [1] which is of greater 'authority than the rest, being referred to in Article XI. as a fuller exposition of the doctrine there delivered. It was written by Cranmer, and is indeed of great value, sound, simple, and eloquent.

It has been apparently thought doubtful by some, whether anything uninspired ought to be read in Churches. The Bible should be read there, prayers offered up, and sermons preached; but to read ancient writings which are not inspired, is to put them on the same level with the inspired Scriptures. This objection has been considered, with reference to the reading of the Apocrypha, under Article VI.[2] What was said of that will fully apply to the reading of homilies. There can be no danger that the Homilies, or any such things, should ever be esteemed by the people as of like authority with the Scriptures. The same objection would apply to sermons and hymns, at least as strongly as to homilies. It is not possible, in any ordinary state of the Church, that all sermons should be, not only extempore effusions, but uttered by direct inspiration of the Spirit. We must therefore esteem them as merely human compositions. And, though special blessing may be expected on the teaching of faithful ministers of Christ; yet it is difficult to see what there is to raise their written or precomposed discourses to an eminence above the writings of martyred bishops, such as Cranmer and his fellows. The lawfulness therefore of the putting forth of the Homilies seems unquestionable.

[1] See above, p. 299.   [2] Art VI. sect. III. No. II. p. 188.

ARTICLE XXXVI.

Of Consecration of Bishops and Ministers.

THE Book of Consecration of Archbishops and Bishops, and Ordering of Priests and Deacons, lately set forth in the time of *Edward* the Sixth, and confirmed at the same time by authority of Parliament, doth contain all things necessary to such Consecration and Ordering: neither hath it anything, that of itself is superstitious and ungodly. And therefore whosoever are consecrated or ordered according to the Rites of that Book, since the second year of the forenamed King *Edward* unto this time, or hereafter shall be consecrated or ordered according to the same Rites; we decree all such to be rightly, orderly, and lawfully consecrated and ordered.

De Episcoporum et Ministrorum Consecratione.

LIBELLUS de consecratione Archi-episcoporum, et Episcoporum, et de ordinatione Presbyterorum et Diaconorum, editus nuper temporibus Edwardi VI. et authoritate Parliamenti illis ipsis temporibus confirmatus, omnia ad ejusmodi consecrationem, et ordinationem necessaria continet, et nihil habet, quod ex se sit, aut superstitiosum, aut impium : itaque quicunque juxta ritus illius libri consecrati, aut ordinati sunt, ab anno secundo prædicti regis Edwardi, usque ad hoc tempus, aut ordinabuntur, rite, atque ordine, atque legitime statuimus esse et fore consecratos et ordinatos.

[The only change, in the American revision, is the omission of the references to the time of Edward the Sixth, and the insertion of a reference to the General Convention of 1792, by which the Ordinal was set forth. One change was, however, made in the Ordinal itself, of which something must be said ; since the alteration of the age requisite for the Diaconate, — which only recurs to the provisions of the period antecedent to 1662, — and the local adaptations of promises and oaths, require no special consideration.

In the PROPOSED BOOK, the English Ordinal was accepted, with a proviso omitting "any oaths inconsistent with the American Revolution."

Bishop White says, that "the alterations of the Ordinal were prepared by the Bishops ; " and adds, "there was no material difference of opinion, except in regard to the words used by the Bishop at the ordination of Priests." Bishop Seabury was urgent for retaining the words in the English Ordinal, though he finally consented to the insertion of the alternative form. Bishops White, Provoost, and Madison appear to have been disposed to omit the words, though they also agreed to the alternative. Indeed, it is believed that Bishop White proposed it.

Some, doubtless, may object to the alternative form as insufficient. To such persons it is quite enough to reply that no special form of words has ever been considered requisite, as accompanying the imposition of hands. Others will fault the first form, as savouring of Romish superstition. Let such remember that the words objected to are the very words used by our Lord in commissioning His Apostles ; that unless they involved Romish superstition in His using, they need not in ours ; that to give up all Scripture which the Roman Church has corrupted is something worse than folly ; and that the retention and use of our Lord's words in the Ordinal is, when rightly viewed, the strongest possible protest against such corruption.
— *J. W.*]

99

WHEN the Liturgy of the Church was undergoing a revision in the reign of Edward VI., it was obviously desirable that the Ordinal should be revised too. Accordingly, A. D. 1549, an act of Parliament was passed to appoint six prelates and six other learned men, to devise a form of making and consecrating archbishops, bishops, priests, deacons, and other ministers.[1] The Ordinal, drawn up by these divines, was in use till 1552 ; and six bishops were consecrated by means of it.

According to the forms in the Ancient Roman Pontificals, those who were ordained priests had their hands anointed, the vessels of the Eucharist were delivered to them, and authority was given them to offer sacrifice. The new Ordinal omitted the Chrism, and all mention of offering sacrifices, but retained the custom of delivering " the chalice or cup with the bread." [2]

In the year 1552, the Second Service Book of Edward VI. came forth ; and with it a still further revision of the Ordinal. In the latter, the porrection of the chalice and paten was omitted. The form of ordination was nearly as in our present services ; except that in the prayer of ordination of priests it was only said, " Receive thou the Holy Ghost," without adding, " for the office of a priest," &c. ; and in the prayer of consecration of bishops, it was said, " Take the Holy Ghost," without the words, " for the office and work of a bishop," &c.

On the accession of Queen Mary, the new Ordinal was immediately suppressed. The orders conferred in the late reign, and with the use of the reformed Ordinal, were not declared invalid ; but those who had been so ordained, were to be reconciled, and the deficiencies supplied, such as unction, porrection of the chalice,[3] &c.

In the reign of Elizabeth the reformed Ordinal was again restored, and in its use were consecrated Parker, the primate, and other bishops of the reformed Church. In confirmation of its authority, the Convocation of 1562 inserted this present Article among the XXXIX., in place of the XXXVth Article of 1552, which was more general, and concerned the whole Prayer Book, this being restricted to the Ordination Services. It was farther enforced by Act of Parliament, A. D. 1566 ; and the Article of 1562 was confirmed in 1571. On the accession of Charles II. and

---

[1] Heylyn, *History of Reformation*, p. 82.
[2] *Liturgies of Edward VI.* Parker Society, p. 179.
[3] Heylyn, *Hist. Ref.* History of Queen Mary, p. 36.

the restoration of Episcopacy, which had been abolished during the Commonwealth, the ordination services, being restored, were, however, subjected to a review, and reduced to their present form. The most important additions were the insertion, in the prayer of ordination of priests, after the words "Receive thou the Holy Ghost," of the words "for the office and work of a priest in the Church of God, now committed unto thee by the imposition of our hands;" and a like change in the prayer of consecration of bishops; so that the office of a bishop is distinctly expressed, whereas at first the words were general, and as applicable to a priest as to a bishop.

The Preface, which is assigned to Cranmer, was the same in the first reformed Ordinal as it is in the present Ordination Service in our Prayer Books.[1]

The object of this Article is to meet objections to the validity and propriety of ordinations conferred in the use of this Ordinal. The objections are of two kinds: I. That the Ordinal lacks some essential ceremonies. II. That it has some superstitious forms and expressions.

I. The first objection comes from the Romanists.

1. It is urged, that our bishops do not confer the chrism, nor offer the sacred vessels, nor more especially give the power of sacrificing; therefore none can be truly ordained by them to the Christian priesthood.

To this we answer, first, that Scripture gives no authority for all these forms. All that we read of there, is laying on of hands with prayer. Secondly, we say that we find no authority for such forms in the customs of the primitive Church. Gregory Nazianzen[2] indeed speaks of unction, but he means the unction of the Holy Ghost. The earliest specimen we have of a form of ordination is in the VIIIth book of the Apostolical Constitutions, c. 16, which is as follows.

"When thou ordainest a presbyter, O bishop, place thy hand on his head, the presbytery standing with thee, and also the dea-

---

[1] The question concerning the unbroken succession of our Bishops might naturally occur to us here. But it does not properly come under consideration in this or any other of the XXXIX. Articles. The student may consult Courayer, *Defence of English Ordinations*; Bramhall, *Protestants' Ordinations Defended*; Mason's *Vindiciæ Ecclesiæ Anglicanæ*. See also Palmer, *Origines Liturgicæ*, II. ch.

XII.; *On the Church*, part VI. ch. X.; Harington's *Succession of Bishops in the English Church*.

[The student may profitably read Dr. Evan's excellent *Essay* on *Anglican Ordinations*, and Dr. Oldknow's small, but very useful tract on the same subject. — J. W.]

[2] *Orat.* v. Tom. I p. 136.

cons; and pray thus: O Lord, Almighty, our God, who hast created all things by Jesus Christ, and by Him providest for all, in
whom is the power of providing in various ways. Now therefore,
O God, Thou providest for immortals by preservation, for mortals
by succession, for the soul by care of laws, for the body by supply
of necessity. Do thou, therefore, now look upon Thy holy Church,
increase it, and multiply those who preside over it; and give power
that they may labour in word and work to the edification of Thy
people. Do thou also look now upon this Thy servant, who, by
suffrage and judgment of all the clergy, is chosen into the presbytery; and fill him with the Spirit of grace and counsel, that he
may aid and govern Thy people with a pure mind; in like manner
as Thou hadst respect to Thine elect people, and as Thou com-
mandest Moses to choose elders whom Thou filledst with Thy
Spirit. And now, O Lord, make good this, preserving in us an unfailing Spirit of Thy grace, that he, being filled with healing powers,
and instructive discourse, may with meekness teach Thy people,
and serve Thee sincerely with a pure mind and willing soul, and
may perform the blameless sacred rites for Thy people.[1] Through
Thy Christ, with whom to Thee and the Holy Ghost, be glory,
honour, and reverence forever. Amen."

This is the whole form of ordaining priests given in the Apostolical Constitutions. The words in Italics are the only words which
can refer to sacrifice or Sacraments; and they are certainly as general as those in our own Ordinal, " Be thou a faithful dispenser of
the word of God and of His holy Sacraments." The words in the
Roman Pontifical, " Receive thou power to offer sacrifices to God,
and to celebrate the mass for the quick and the dead," were not
in any ancient form of consecration. Morinus, as cited by Bishop
Burnet, acknowledges that he could not find any such words for
the first 900 years.[2] The Greek Church merely prays God to
grant to the newly ordained presbyter, " that he may stand blameless at Thy altar, may preach the gospel of Thy Salvation, offer to
Thee gifts and spiritual sacrifices, and renew Thy people by the
laver of regeneration."[3] This again is perfectly general; and the
earlier we go, the simpler we find all the forms of ordination, in all
parts of the world. " Not a father, not a council, not one ancient
author at any time mentions the delivery of the paten or chalice,
or the formal words used by the Church of Rome, even when they

---

[1] τὰς ὑπὲρ τοῦ λαοῦ ἱερουργίας ἀμώμους   [3] Morinus, *De Sacr. Ordin.* pt. ii. p.
ἐκτελῇ.   55; Walcott's *English Ordinal,* p. 260.
[2] Burnet, *Vindication of English Orders,*
p. 24; Bingham, ii. xix. 17.

describe the ordination of their days, and where this could not have been omitted, if it had been essential."[1] This is surely proof enough that the omissions complained of are not sufficient to invalidate all the orders of the Church.

2. It has also been objected, that the bishops consecrated according to the Ordinal of Edward VI. and Elizabeth, could not have been rightly consecrated, because the words of consecration were only, "Take the Holy Ghost, and remember that thou stir up the grace of God which is in thee by imposition of hands : for God hath not given us the spirit of fear, but of power, and love and soberness." Here is nothing which might not apply to a priest or deacon, as well as to a bishop.

But we may reply, that the whole service concerns bishops, not priests and deacons ; and that, if the words, "for the office of a bishop," &c. afterwards inserted, were not at first added, it is quite evident that they were sufficiently implied. Everybody must have felt that it was episcopal consecration which was conferred. The form of ordination does not consist merely in the prayer of consecration. The whole service forms part of it. And, moreover, even in the Roman Pontifical, the words which accompany the imposition of hands are simply, "Receive the Holy Ghost ; " and the prayer, which follows, does not directly mention the office of a bishop.[2]

II. Another objection proceeds from a very different quarter. The Puritans, and many well-meaning Christians since them, have much stumbled at our using those memorable words of our Lord and Saviour Christ, "Receive the Holy Ghost . . . . Whose sins thou dost forgive, they are forgiven ; and whose sins thou dost retain, they are retained." The objection is of this nature.

1. The power of remitting and retaining sins was miraculous, and confined to the Apostles, and so not to be expected by other ministers.

2. Man cannot bestow God's Spirit, and it is profane to claim the power to do so.

It is remarkable, that the reformers who rejected as superstitious some mere ceremonies, such as delivering the paten and chalice,

---

[1] Bramhall, *Protestants' Ordinations Defended, Works, Anglo-Cath. Library,* v. p. 216. Several ancient forms, and much useful information, may be found in Walcott, *On the English Ordinal,* ch. vi.

[2] Palmer, *On the Church,* pt. vi. ch. x. Vol. ii. p. 460.

and the anointing of the hands, should yet have retained this form of words, which to many seems nothing short of blasphemy. Was it that the reformers had a deeper insight into Scripture than those who now object to their proceedings?

1. Under Art. XXXIII. I have already considered at length the question concerning the remitting and retaining sins. There it has been shown that such power was not miraculous, nor peculiar to the Apostles. A power of that higher kind never was given to mere man. The only authority which our blessed Lord thus conveyed to His first ministers was, more solemnly than before, authority to bind and to loose, — that which is elsewhere called the power of the keys, — so that ministerially they had the keys of the Church or kingdom, to admit men to it by preaching and baptism, to exclude men from it by excommunication, to restore them to it again by absolution. The assurance given them is, that their acts, as Christ's ministers in all these respects, shall be ratified in Heaven. It has been shown moreover, that this power of the keys is a portion of the Church's birthright. It is committed to the Church as a body, and more particularly to her bishops and presbyters. Hence every bishop, having authority to ordain, has also authority to declare that the power of the keys is committed to the person ordained by him. And no more is meant by these solemn words in our ordination service, than that, as Christ has left to the presbytery the right of ministering His Sacraments, and of excluding from His Sacraments ; so the newly ordered presbyter now receives by Christ's own ordinance that right, — a divine commission to minister, and at the same time a divine commission duly to exercise the authority of excluding the unworthy, and admitting again the penitent sinner.[1]

2. On the words, " Receive thou the Holy Ghost," we may observe, that, as the power to remit and retain sins was not a personal and miraculous power conferred on the Apostles, so neither was the gift of the Spirit then breathed upon them the personally sanctify-

---

[1] I have not fully entered into the question of the efficacy of absolution, when pronounced on a repenting sinner. That it may restore to Church communion, none can doubt. But many, in our day, question, or rather deny, that it can be accompanied with any spiritual grace. The whole subject of ministerial blessing and absolution seems to be explained by the words of our Lord (Luke x. 5, 6): "Into whatsoever house ye enter, first say, Peace be to this house. And if the son of peace be there, your peace shall rest upon it ; if not, it shall turn to you again." Here the blessing of the minister was to be accompanied by blessing from above, if the recipient was rightly disposed for blessing. But if the recipient was unbelieving and impenitent, the blessing could not reach his heart ; but yet the minister would himself have comfort from having acted on his commission, and having sought to convey comfort to others.

ing influence, nor yet the miraculous gifts of the Holy Ghost. We cannot doubt that they had long ago received the sanctifying grace of God in their hearts, and so the ordinary operations of the Third Person of the Blessed Trinity. And the miraculous baptism of the Spirit, which gave them powers peculiar to the Apostolic age, they did not receive until the day of Pentecost. Hence, this bestowal of the Spirit in the twentieth chapter of St. John was neither the one nor the other of these. What then must it have been? Evidently the ordaining grace of God. All ministerial authority has ever been believed to proceed from the Holy Ghost. Ministry, the right to minister, is one of the *charismata* of the Spirit. That *charisma* our Lord then for the first time fully bestowed upon His Church. But the same *charisma* was afterwards given " by the laying on of the Apostle's hands (2 Tim. i. 6), and, " with the laying on of the hands of the presbytery " (1 Tim. iv. 14). Not that the Apostles or their successors could from themselves send forth the Spirit of God, or the gifts of the Spirit; but that, as our Lord had appointed ordination to be the means of receiving the grace of ordination, so the Church in undoubting faith believes, that, whensoever ordination is rightly ministered, the proper gift of orders flows down direct from the ordaining Spirit; not to sanctify the individual personally, but to constitute him truly a minister of Christ, and to make his ministry acceptable to God. Hence, when the bishop's hand is laid on the head of him whom he ordains, we doubt not that the *charisma* of God's Spirit is given, " for the office and work of a priest in the Church of God." The difference between such an ordination and our Lord's ordaining of His first ministers recorded in St. John chap. xx. is this. In the latter case, Christ Himself, to whom the Spirit is given without measure, gave of that Spirit authoritatively to His disciples; and so, in giving, He breathed on them, as showing that the Spirit proceeded from Him. But in the other case, our bishops presume not to breathe, nor did the Apostles before them, for they know that ordaining grace comes not from them, but from Christ, whose ministers they are; and so they simply, according to all Scriptural authority, use the outward rite of laying on of hands, in use of which they believe a blessing will assuredly come down from above.[1] That blessing is the gift of the Spirit of God, for the office and work of a priest.

And thus we conclude, that, as the Ordinal lacks nothing essential to the due administering of orders in the Church, so does it not contain anything that of itself is superstitious and ungodly.

[1] See Hooker, Bk. v. 77, 78.

ARTICLE XXXVII.

Of the Civil Magistrates.

THE Queen's Majesty hath the chief power in this Realm of *England*, and other her Dominions, unto whom the chief Government of all Estates of this Realm, whether they be Ecclesiastical or Civil, in all causes doth appertain, and is not, nor ought to be, subject to any foreign Jurisdiction.

Where we attribute to the Queen's Majesty the chief government, by which Titles we understand the minds of some slanderous folks to be offended; we give not to our Princes the ministering either of God's Word, or of the Sacraments, the which thing the injunctions also lately set forth by *Elizabeth* our Queen do most plainly testify; but that only prerogative, which we see to have been given always to all godly Princes in Holy Scriptures by God himself; that is, that they should rule all states and degrees committed to their charge by God, whether they be Ecclesiastical or Temporal, and restrain with the civil sword the stubborn and evil-doers.

The Bishop of *Rome* hath no jurisdiction in this Realm of *England*.

The Laws of the Realm may punish Christian men with death, for heinous and grievous offences.

It is lawful for Christian men, at the commandment of the Magistrate, to wear weapons and serve in the wars.

De Civilibus Magistratibus.

REGIA Majestas in hoc Angliæ regno, ac cæteris ejus dominiis, summam habet potestatem, ad quam, omnium statuum hujus regni, sive illi ecclesiastici sint, sive civiles, in omnibus causis, suprema gubernatio pertinet, et nulli externæ jurisdictioni est subjecta, nec esse debet.

Cum Regiæ Majestati summam gubernationem tribuimus, quibus titulis intelligimus, animos quorundam calumniatorum offendi, non damus regibus nostris, aut verbi Dei, aut Sacramentorum administrationem, quod etiam injunctiones ab Elizabetha Regina nostra, nuper editæ, apertissime testantur. Sed eam tantum prærogativam, quam in sacris Scripturis a Deo ipso, omnibus piis Principibus, videmus semper fuisse attributam, hoc est, ut omnes status, atque ordines fidei suæ à Deo commissos, sive illi ecclesiastici sint, sive civiles, in officio contineant, et contumaces ac delinquentes, gladio civili coerceant.

Romanus pontifex nullam habet jurisdictionem in hoc regno Angliæ.

Leges Regni possunt Christianos propter capitalia, et gravia crimina, morte punire.

Christianis licet, ex mandato magistratus, arma portare, et justa bella administrare.

[The American Article reads : —

"ART. XXXVII. *Of the Power of the Civil Magistrate.*

" The Power of the Civil Magistrate extendeth to all men, as well Clergy as Laity, in all things temporal ; but hath no authority in things purely spiritual. And we hold it to be the duty of all men who are professors of the Gospel, to pay respectful obedience to the Civil Authority, regularly and legitimately constituted."

The writer ventures to consider it unfortunate that the two declarations concerning "capital punishment," and the propriety of Christians bearing arms, were omitted. The reasons for the omission, though he can conjecture what they were, he does not feel sufficiently sure of, to state. — *J. W.*]

Section I. — THE SUPREMACY OF THE CROWN.

THE present Article concerns one of the most involved and difficult questions that have agitated Christian men: the question,
namely, of the due proportions and proper relation between the
civil and ecclesiastical powers in a Christian Commonwealth. The
whole course of Church History, from the time of Constantine to
the present, seems to have been striving to unravel the difficulty
and solve the problem. Perhaps it never will be solved, until
the coming of the Son of Man, when there shall be no king but
Christ, and all nations, peoples, and languages, shall bow down
before Him.

Without pretending then to clear up all that is dark in such a
question, we may by a hasty survey of past events be enabled to
place ourselves in such a position, that the mists of prejudice,
whether religious or political, may not blind us to the perception of
that light which Providence has given to guide us.

For the first three hundred years, the spiritual kingdom of Christ
was on earth, having no relation to any earthly kingdom. The
kingdoms of this world, instead of fostering, persecuted it. There
was a direct antagonism between the Church and the world; and
the external development of that antagonism was plainly visible
in the opposing organization of Church and State. Christians
indeed were from the first obedient subjects, wherever obedience
was not incompatible with religion. They even marched in the
armies of the heathen emperors, prayed for them in their public
liturgies, and in persecution took joyfully the spoiling of their goods,
resisting none but those commands which could be obeyed only by
disobedience to God. But the whole Christian Church, as far as
possible, shrank within itself from the polluting atmosphere of heathenism and heathen morality. The Apostle had condemned the
Corinthians for going to law before the unbelievers (1 Cor. vi. 1),
and had encouraged them to erect private tribunals among themselves, for the decision of disputes, which would inevitably arise.[1]
The result was naturally, that the courts of the bishop became the
ordinary courts of judicature, when Christians impleaded Christians. The rulers of the Church were looked up to with that kind
of veneration which we call loyalty; whilst obedience to the em-

[1] 1 Cor. vi. 4. Some consider the word ἐξουθενημένους, used in this verse, to mean persons destitute of any public authority in the state.

100

peror was the result of no natural enthusiasm, but of a principle of
self-denying, self-sacrificing obligation.

The accession of Constantine to the throne of Augustus, his
conversion to Christianity, and his removal of the seat of empire
to Byzantium, produced a remarkable revolution. Christians fondly
hoped, that the kingdoms of this world had become the kingdoms
of our God and of His Christ. They naturally recognized the
duty of Christian princes to protect the faith of the Gospel. They
joyfully embraced the newly opened course for the progress of the
Gospel. They reasonably were thankful for the promised freedom
to worship God according to their consciences; and alas! it is to
be feared, that they were not averse to using the civil authority to
put down the pride of the now fast increasing heresy of Arius. Constantine, on his part, whether sincere or politic in his adoption of
the Gospel, could not be ignorant of the vast machinery which his
connection with the Church might put into his hands. In heathen
times, the supreme ruler at Rome was also the supreme adminis-
trator of the affairs of religion. There was a sacredness attached
to him, however vile his personal character. The Roman Emperor
even became the Pontifex Maximus.[1] And, although Constantine
found it not possible to assume a sacerdotal function in the Christian Church, he yet claimed a peculiar supremacy; which was
sufficiently undefined to be inoffensive to others, and yet satisfactory to himself. " You," said he to the Christian prelates, " are
bishops of the things within the Church; but I am constituted by
God bishop of those which are without." [2] The words were perhaps originally spoken in jest, but time led him to apply them in
earnest.

From this period the Church, though never endowed by the
State, received a full and ample protection for the revenues which
it might acquire. The Christian princes ever considered themselves as its protectors, and in some sense as its governors. There
is good reason to think, that the power, which they so exercised,
was often by no means paternal, but as tyrannical and arbitrary as
was their more secular administration. The bishops indeed maintained the exclusive right of the clergy to minister in sacred things ;
and the emperors readily admitted that to the clergy alone such
functions appertained.[3] Moreover, the ecclesiastical jurisdiction
of bishops and patriarchs was carefully preserved to them. Patri-

[1] Gibbon, ch. xx.
[2] Euseb. *Vit. Constant.* iv. 24.
[3] The story of St. Ambrose forbidding

Theodosius to enter the chancel (Theodoret, l. v. c. 18) is well known.

archs were permitted to call provincial, and bishops to call diocesan synods; but a synod of the universal Church was never called but by the Emperor himself. Though the decrees of the councils were made by the bishops, yet the Emperor thought himself justified in enforcing them by his own temporal power. Thus Arius, condemned at Nice, was banished by Constantine; and there is too good reason to fear that court influence was unsparingly used to intimidate the members of a synod into voting with the Emperor, or absenting themselves altogether. Eusebius assigns to Constantine a principle, which was probably never admitted by the Church at large, but which may have materially influenced him in his own conduct; namely, that as a kind of universal bishop, he assembled councils of the ministers of God.[1]

From this time, then, the Church and the State were no longer in the position of a persecuting power and a patient victim. They no longer represented, respectively, the principle of good and the principle of evil. The good of the one had penetrated the other; and it may be feared, that there was something of reciprocal interchange. They had, however, entered into an alliance; but still, more or less, the Christianized state was sure to retain some of the worldly elements which characterized it when heathen; and there was still a struggle, though less conspicuous, between the Church in the Church and the world in the State. In the East, the power of the Emperor over the Church was the greater, because the East had become the seat of empire; and there is little doubt, that the degeneracy of the Eastern Church had much connection with the influence of the court. Nay! the power of that court became at once apparent, when, on the adoption of heresy by the Emperor, the whole East seemed suddenly overspread with Arianism.

There was a different state of things in the West; the result, it may be, in part, of the greater vigour of the Western bishops, but still more of the absence of the seat of government from Rome. The Church was no longer the same isolated, distinct body that it had been when the empire was heathen; and had it not been for the nucleus formed for it by the clergy, it might have been all dissipated in the midst of the half Christianized people that were around it. But the clergy were still a substantive, tangible body; and, irrespective of any ambition of their own, it was almost essential to the existence of the Church, that they should form them-

---

[1] Οἴά τις κοινὸς ἐπίσκοπος ἐκ Θεοῦ καθι- συνεκρότει. — De Vit. Constantin. Lib. I. c. στάμενος, συνόδους τῶν τοῦ Θεοῦ λειτουργῶν　44.

selves into that kind of close corporation which had before embraced the whole society of Christians. Besides which, as their sacred character brought them respect even in the eyes of their tyrants, as they had a prescriptive right to hold private tribunals for the settlement of their private differences, as their sacred buildings had conceded to them the right of sanctuary possessed of old by heathen temples; they had in their hands the power, not only of supporting religion, but also of evading, or at least limiting, both for themselves and their fellow-Christians, the tyrannical domination of the emperor. The subject has been so clearly and liberally set forth by an accomplished writer of the day, that we may well use his own words. "If it be right to condemn the fiscal tyranny of the Roman rulers, it can hardly be also right to condemn those sacerdotal claims, and those imperial concessions, by which the range of that tyranny was narrowed . . . The Church is arraigned as selfish and ambitious, because it formed itself into a vast clerical corporation, living under laws and usages peculiar to itself, and not acknowledging the jurisdiction of the temporal tribunals. That the Churchmen of the fourth century lived beneath a ruthless despotism no one attempts to deny. That they opposed to it the only barrier by which the imperial tyranny could, in that age, be arrested in its course, is equally indisputable. If they had been laymen, they would have been celebrated as patriots by the very persons who, because they were priests, have denounced them as usurpers. If the bishops of the fourth century had lived under the republic, they would have been illustrious as tribunes of the people. If the Gracchi had been contemporaries of Theodosius, their names would have taken the place which Ambrose and Martin of Tours at present hold in ecclesiastical history. A brave resistance to despotic authority has surely no less title to our sympathy, if it proceeds from the episcopal throne, than if it be made amidst the tumults of the forum." [1]

If this was true of the relation of the Church to the empire, it was certainly not less true as regards its condition under the several kingdoms which were formed by the Gothic barbarians out of the ruins of the empire. The feudal monarchies, whether in their earlier condition or in their more matured and full-grown despotism, were amongst the most lawless, oppressive, and tyrannical forms of government that an unhappy people have ever groaned under. In those days when might was the only right, " we may rejoice to know," says the just-cited authority, " that the

---

[1] *Lectures on the History of France*, by the Rt. Hon. Sir James Stephen i. p. 38.

early Church was the one great antagonist of the wrongs which were then done upon the earth, that she narrowed the range of fiscal tyranny, — that she mitigated the overwhelming poverty of the people, — that she promoted the accumulation of capital, — that she contributed to the restoration of agriculture, — that she balanced and held in check the imperial despotism, — that she revived within herself the remembrance and the use of the franchise of popular election, — and that the gloomy portraits which have been drawn of her internal or moral state, are the mere exaggerations of those who would render the Church responsible for the crimes with which it is her office to contend, and for the miseries which it is her high commission effectually, though gradually, to relieve." [1]

The same may be said of much later times. The struggle between the crown and the clergy was, in fact, often a struggle of religion against lawlessness, avarice, licentiousness, and tyranny. The clergy were the guardians not only of the Church, but of the people ; and one great secret of their increasing power was the conviction, even among their opponents, of the righteousness of their cause, and, among those whom they defended, of the bless-ings of their protection.

But there was one important element at work, which we have now to take into account. From the earliest times, the Bishop of Rome was the most important prelate in the West. His see was in the imperial city. It claimed the chief of the Apostles as its founder. The Apostolic sees were everywhere respected ; and Rome was the only Church in Europe certainly Apostolic. So early as the third century, St. Cyprian had urged the priority of St. Peter, and the precedence of the Bishops of Rome, as an argu-ment for the unity of the Church. To all Europe Rome was, on every account, a centre ; and the ambition of its prelates never ceased to turn such advantage to their own account. There were few Churches which owed not some obligation to the Roman Church ; if not as founding, yet as strengthening and enlightening them. There were a thousand causes tending to give additional importance to the Popes. The emperors found it politic to court them. The patriarchs of Alexandria and Antioch sought defence from them against the overwhelming power of Constantinople in the East. The kings of distant nations asked for missionaries from them, to instruct their people more perfectly in the Gospel. The removal of the seat of empire to Constantinople, whilst it raised the see of that city to the position of eminence next to that

[1] *Lectures on the History of France*, by the Rt. Hon Sir James Stephen, I. p. 37

of Rome, yet rather favoured the increase of the power of the
latter.   When there was an emperor at Rome, the Pope was con-
trolled by a superior ; but when the emperor was at a distance, the
Christian bishop became the most important person in the imperial
city.   By degrees a *primacy*, which might have been reasonable,
became a *supremacy* which was pernicious.   The whole constitution
of Europe favoured such an arrangement.   As all Europe looked
to Rome as its civil centre, so Christian Europe looked to Rome
as its ecclesiastical centre.   Then, the power of the Pope was a
happy counterpoise for the power of the sovereign.   In the Middle
Ages the barons owed fealty to their feudal suzerain ; and the
bishops and clergy owed a spiritual fealty to their ecclesiastical
head.   The Church, as an united body, was disposed to look to
one visible centre, one visible head.   Evil as its consequences have
been, still in these dark and troubled times such union and sub-
mission on the one hand, and a corresponding aid and protection
on the other, may possibly have been the means of keeping the
Church from utter disintegration, by protecting it from that lawless and arbitrary feudalism which might otherwise have swept
away both Church and religion from the earth.

But the authority, thus fostered and matured, now overtopped
all other authorities, and grew into a tyranny as intolerable as
that against which it once promised to be a bulwark.   Like a dic-
tatorship after a republic, it was more absolute than legitimate
monarchy.   The power of the Pope was not merely spiritual, but
political.[1]   In the first place, the clergy were not esteemed as
subjects of the crown, in the country in which they lived.   The
Pope was their virtual sovereign ; to him they owed a supreme
allegiance.   All causes concerning them were referred to spiritual
tribunals, and there was a final appeal to the jurisdiction of Rome
tself.   Bishops felt the grievance of such a power, when the Pope
at his pleasure exempted monasteries from their control, and
claimed all benefices, as of right vested in the supreme pontiff, and
not held legally without his permission.   But kings felt it still
more ; when a large portion of their subjects were withdrawn
from their authority ; when a large number of causes, under the

---

[1] Bellarmine calls it a heresy not to
allow to the Pope power over sovereign
princes in temporal affairs.   And Baronius says, " They are branded as heretics, who take from the Church of Rome
and the see of St. Peter one of the two
swords, and allow only the spiritual."
This heresy Baronius calls the " Heresy
of the Politici."   Bellarmin. *De Rom.*
Pont. v. 1 ; Baronius, Anno 1053, § 14 ;
Anno 1073, § 13, quoted by Barrow, *On*
the Pope's Supremacy, p. 17.   Bellarmine
states it as the general Catholic sentiment, that popes have not *directly* temporal authority, but that *indirectly*, by virtue of their spiritual authority, they have
temporal authority.

name of ecclesiastical, were withdrawn from their courts; when taxes were levied in the name of Peter's pence upon their kingdoms; when their clergy and many of their people could be armed against them by a foreign influence; and, worst of all, when the right was asserted of putting their whole country under an interdict, nay, even of either granting to them new kingdoms,[1] or of deposing them from their thrones, and releasing their people from their oaths of allegiance.[2]

The Reformation was a reaction from this state of things, as well as a throwing off of internal corruption of faith. It was viewed indeed by different persons according to their respective feelings and interests. The prince desired it, for the sake of regaining his former, and more than his former authority. The nobles desired it, that they might fatten on the spoils of the Church. The reforming prelates and clergy desired it, that they might be freed from the power of Rome, and have liberty to order God's worship aright. The people desired it, that they might have freedom of conscience and purity of faith. As the fathers had hailed the conversion of an emperor, to free them from heathen tyranny; as clergy and people in the Middle Ages had sought a refuge at Rome from the exactions of their domestic oppressors; so now the reformers hoped that the throne would prove to them a protection from the tyranny of the Vatican. We must plead this in excuse for what is the foulest stain on the Reformation, namely, the undue servility of the ecclesiastical leaders of it to the vicious and tyrannical princes that sided with it.

In England, Henry, whose love for reformation was love only for his own power, passions, and interests, wished not to free religion from restraint, but to transfer to himself the power formerly wielded by the Pope. And we may partly account for the opposition to reform among the commonalty, who had originally sighed for it, by remembering that they discovered now a prospect for themselves of the same tyranny here in England which had heretofore been as distant as Rome. Their desire for a restoration to a simpler worship and a purer faith had been met by a rapacious seizing of those ecclesiastical revenues from which so much benefit had

---

[1] As Alexander III. gave Henry II. a grant of Ireland.

[2] As Gregory VII. did to the Emperor Henry IV. a. d. 1076; Alexander III. did to the Emperor Frederick I. a. d. 1168; Innocent III. did to the Emperor Otho IV. a. d. 1210; and to our own King John, a. d. 1212. Thomas Aquinas, the great school authority, lays it down as a principle, that the subjects of excommunicate princes are released from their allegiance. "Quum quis per sententiam denunciatur propter apostasiam, excommunicatus, ipso facto ejus subditi a dominio et juramento fidelitatis ejus liberati sunt." — Tom. ii. Secund. qu. 12, Art. ii.; Barrow, On the Pope's Supremacy, p. 3.

ever been derived to the poor and to the oppressed; and by a transference of a power over their consciences from one whom they did look up to as a Christian prelate, to an avaricious and blood-stained sovereign.

However, notwithstanding the difficulties of the case, and the evil passions of some, the problem was working itself out. The Pope's power was happily abolished. Appeals to Rome were no longer legal. Ecclesiastical as well as civil causes were heard in the king's name. The acts of Convocation in the reforming of the doctrines and formularies were sanctioned by the crown. The clergy were all made amenable to the civil tribunals, and became in fact subjects of the throne of England, not of the throne of St. Peter.

But in what sense had the king thus become the head or chief governor of the Church? The very principle of the Reformation may be said to have been, that there is no Supreme Head of Christ's Church but Christ Himself. Yet by the acts 26 Henry VIII. c. 1, and 35 Henry VIII. c. 3, the king is declared in express terms, "the only supreme head in earth of the Church of England." And in the following reign, the Article of 1552 is worded in accordance with such acts, " The King of England is supreme head in earth, next under Christ, of the Church of England and Ireland." [1]

Many thoughtful men, not disinclined to the Reformation, were much offended at this apparent assumption of spiritual authority over Christ's flock by a temporal sovereign. Bishop Fisher and Sir Thomas More went to the scaffold, rather than acknowledge it. But among those who submitted to the authority, there was a diversity of feeling as to the sense attached to it. Henry himself doubtless wished to be both pope and king. The Parliament prob-ably accepted the title in no very definite signification ; but re-joiced in any advance of the lay power to preëminence over the clergy. The Convocation thought it doubtfully consistent with their allegiance to God, and recognized the title only " so far as by the law of Christ they could." [2]

What was the opinion of the leading divines of the Reformation on this subject, and especially of the Archbishop, must be an in-teresting question. I have been surprised to find so little about it in the writings of Cranmer, Ridley, and Latimer. Cranmer had

---

[1] " Rex Angliæ est supremum caput in terris, post Christum, Ecclesiæ Angli-canæ et Hiberniæ."

[2] "Ecclesiæ et cleri Anglicani, cujus singularem protectorem et supremum Dominum, et, quantum per Christi legem licet, etiam supremum caput ipsius maj estatem recognoscimus."

evidently, at one time, a very extravagant notion of the sacredness of kings, as he had a very low view of the office of the ministry; so that he even ventured a statement, that the royal power might make a priest.[1] But this sentiment he afterwards entirely abandoned. We may remark then, that he ever constantly affirmed that in all countries the king's power is the highest power under God, to whom all men by God's laws owe most loyalty and obedience; and that he hath power and charge over all, as well bishops and priests as others.[2] But the occasion on which he gave the fullest exposition of the meaning which he and his fellows attached to the supremacy, was in his examination before Brokes, just before his death. Then he declared, that " every king in his own realm is supreme head, and therefore that the king of England is supreme head of the Church of Christ in England." He admits that on this principle, " Nero was Peter's head," and " head of the Church;" and that " the Turk is the head of the Church in Turkey." [3] " After this, Dr. Martin demanded of him, who was supreme head of the Church of England? Marry, quoth my Lord of Canterbury, Christ is head of this member, as He is of the whole body of the universal Church. Why, quoth Dr. Martin, you made King Henry the Eighth supreme head of the Church. Yea, said the Archbishop, of all the people of England, as well ecclesiastical as temporal. And not of the Church, said Martin. No, said He, for Christ is the only head of His Church, and of the faith and religion of the same. The king is head and governor of his people, which are the visible Church. What! quoth Martin, you never durst tell the king so. Yes, that I durst, quoth he, and did. In the publication of his style, wherein he was named supreme head of the Church, there was never other thing meant." [4]

Whether Cranmer durst or durst not tell the king thus, the king probably took it differently; and indeed it is pretty clear, that something more than the power of Nero, or of " the Turk," over Christians in their dominions, was intended to be assigned to Christian kings over their Christian subjects. Whatever too was meant by the publication of the style, " Supreme head of the Church," it caused offence to many besides those who were sure to take offence. Accordingly, when the Acts of Henry VIII. and Edw. VI. had been repealed by the Statute 1 Philip and Mary, c. 8, the title, " Supreme head," was never revived by authority, but was rejected by

---

[1] *Answers to Questions on the Sacraments,* A. D. 1540. See this subject considered under Article XXIII.

[2] See Cranmer's *Works,* IV. Appendix, pp. 266, 308, 328, &c.

[3] *Works,* IV. p. 98.

[4] Cranmer's *Works,* IV. pp. 116, 117.

Elizabeth, and "Supreme governor" substituted in its place.[1]
The Statute 1 Eliz. c. 1, is an "act for restoring to the crown the
ancient jurisdiction over the state ecclesiastical and spiritual, and
abolishing all foreign power repugnant to the same." In this act
all foreign jurisdiction is abolished, and the power of visiting and
correcting ecclesiastical abuses is, by the authority of Parliament,
annexed to the imperial crown of the realm. But the acts conferring the title of "Head of the Church" (26 Henry VIII. c. 1, 35
Henry VIII. c. 3) are not revived, and thenceforward "government" is substituted for "headship." [2]

In Elizabeth's reign, the authorized formularies explain, to a
considerable extent, the meaning attached at that time to the
authority in question. First comes this article, the words of which
should be carefully considered. It excludes all foreign domination,
assigns to the sovereign the only supreme authority over all sorts
of men, whether civil or ecclesiastical, but especially denies that
sovereigns have any ministerial function in the Church, whether as
regards the Sacraments or the word of God; but the power which
they have is such as godly princes in Scripture had, — "to rule
all estates and degrees, whether ecclesiastical or temporal, and restrain with the *civil* sword the stubborn and evil-doers."

The Injunctions of Elizabeth, to which the Article refers, enjoin
all ecclesiastics to observe the laws made for restoring to the crown
the ancient jurisdiction over the state ecclesiastical, and abolishing
all foreign authority. The queen's power is declared to be "the
highest under God, to whom all men within the same realms
and dominions by God's law owe most loyalty and obedience." [3]

In the reign of James I. the Convocation agreed on the Canons
of 1603. The second canon expressly affirms, that the "king's
majesty hath the same authority in causes ecclesiastical that the
godly kings had among the Jews, and Christian emperors of the
Primitive Church;" and both the first and second canon speak of
the laws, as having "restored to the crown of this kingdom the
ancient jurisdiction over the state ecclesiastical." The XXXVIth
Canon contains three articles, which are subscribed by all ministers
at their ordination. The first is, I. "That the king's majesty,

[1] Jewel mentions the Queen's refusal
of the title of Head of the Church in a
letter to Bullinger, May 22, 1559: "The
Queen is unwilling to be addressed,
either by word of mouth, or in writing, as the Head of the Church of England. For she seriously maintains, that
this honour is due to Christ alone, and
cannot belong to any human being whatever." — Collier, *Church History*, pt. II.
Bk. VI.

[2] See a very learned pamphlet entitled
The Papal Brief Considered, by Ralph
Barnes, Esq. Rivingtons, 1850. Note,
page 90.

[3] Sparrow's *Collection of Articles*, **p. 67**.
See also p. 83.

under God, is the only supreme governor of this realm, and of all other his highness's dominions and countries, as well in all spiritual or ecclesiastical things or causes as temporal; and that no foreign prince, person, prelate, or potentate hath, or ought to have any jurisdiction, power, superiority, preëminence, or authority, ecclesiastical or spiritual, within his majesty's said realms, dominions, and countries."

These documents, then, which at present form the charter of union between Church and State, evidently assign to the sovereign no *new·* functions. The principle enunciated by them is, that the sovereign is entitled to those ancient privileges which belonged, 1, to devout princes in Scripture; 2, to Christian emperors in primitive times; 3, to the ancient sovereigns of England before the times of Papal domination. The very reference to Scriptural and primitive examples seems to be a demonstration of the justice of the claims; for, if nothing is claimed beyond what Scripture warrants and the Catholic fathers allowed, the claim should seem to be both Scriptural and Catholic. Yet some important objections may be urged, which we must not neglect to consider.

1. It is said that " godly princes in Scripture " must mean " godly kings among the Jews." Now the Jewish dispensation was utterly dissimilar from the Christian; for the Jewish Church was national, the Christian Church is not national, but Catholic. Hence naturally among the Jews the king, as head of the nation, was supreme over the Church. But the Catholic Church acknowledges no local distinctions; and to assign a national supremacy is to rend the Church of Christ into separate societies. Kings, as well as others, are but members of the one spiritual body, which meddles not with temporal distinctions, but holds all alike as subjects and servants of Christ.

To this we reply, that our kings, since at least the time of Elizabeth, have not an authority such as should separate one portion of the Church from the other. It is not our national distinctions, but our doctrinal differences, which divide us from our fellow-Christians. Our sovereigns claim only those powers which were exercised by their predecessors, in times which Romanists must acknowledge to have been Catholic, but before the full-grown authority of the see of Rome. Gregory VII. was the original founder of that great authority, and it culminated under Innocent III. But we see not that the Church was less Catholic in the days of Alfred and Edward the Confessor, than in the reigns of the Plantagenets. If then we concede to our princes the influence of the Saxon monarchs, we shall not have destroyed the Catholicity of the Church, more than it was destroyed centuries before the Reformation.

2. It is said again that the Jewish princes can be no examples for us, because, from the theocratic nature of the Jewish kingdom, there was a sacredness attaching to their office, as that of God's special vicegerents, which cannot attach to ordinary rulers. Israel, as a theocracy, was a type of the Church; and its kings were types of Christ. As the high priests foreshadowed His priestly office in His Church, so the kings foreshadowed His regal authority over His spiritual kingdom. But there is no vicegerent of Christ on earth; no type now of His spiritual sovereignty. Hence earthly kings now cannot claim the position and privileges of the ancient Jewish kings.

This is doubtless a very weighty argument, and is a just reply to some who would unduly magnify the royal authority in things ecclesiastical. But it has been observed in a former Article,[1] that the Jewish state may be considered in some respects as a model republic; and that, notwithstanding the peculiar circumstances and special object of its institution, we may still derive lessons of political wisdom from the ordinances appointed by the All-wise for the government of His own chosen race. Now, in that government, He was pleased to conjoin the spiritual and secular elements, in such a manner that the king was to show a fatherly care for religion, yet not to intrude upon its sacred offices (see 1 Sam. xiii. 8–14; 2 Chron. xix. 11, &c.); and we may humbly conclude, that what was ordained by heavenly wisdom then, cannot be wholly evil now.[2] Besides which, we see throughout Scripture that there is a sacredness in civil government. Kings are always said to hold their power of God, and to be especially under His protection and guidance. They are His ministers for good; and therefore to be esteemed by God's people, as exercising in some degree God's authority (see Prov. viii. 15; Dan. ii. 21, 37; Rom. xiii. 1–5; 1 Pet. ii. 13, 17; 1 Tim. ii. 1, 2, &c.).[3]

---

[1] Art. VII. See above, p. 214.

[2] The way in which kings and rulers among the Jews interfered in the affairs of religion may be seen from the following passages: Josh. xxiv. 25, 26; 1 Chron. xv. 12; xxiii. 6; 2 Chron. viii. 14, 15; xv. 8, 9; xvii. 9; xx. 3, 4; xxix. 3–5, 25; xxxiv. 31, 32.

[3] Rom. xiii. 1: "Let every soul be subject to the higher powers." Archbishop Laud thus sums up the consent of the ancient fathers, that "*omnis anima, every soul*, comprehends all without exception, all spiritual men, even the highest bishop; Πᾶσι ταῦτα διατάττεται, καὶ ἱερεῦσι. ... Omnibus ista imperantur et sacerdotibus et monachis .... Et postea: Etiamsi Apostolus sis, si evangelista, si propheta, sive quisquis tandem fueris. — St. Chrysost. *Hom.* xxiii. *in Rom.* Sive est sacerdos, sive antistes. — Theodoret. *In Rom.* xiii. Si omnis anima est vestra.

3. Another objection to the precedents claimed by the English monarchs is, that the influence of the Christian emperors, and the connection of religion with the state, which sprang up after the time of Constantine, were the very origin of evil and corruption in the Church. It was an unhallowed alliance between the Church and the world, and never had God's blessing on it.

It perhaps cannot be denied that the sunshine of worldly prosperity has never been the most favourable condition for the development of Christian graces. When the Church could no longer say, " Silver and gold have I none," it could no longer command the impotent man to "arise and walk." Yet we cannot thence conclude, that the Church is ever to seek persecution, or to refuse such vantage-ground as God's providence permits it to stand upon. To court or fawn upon the great is indeed most earnestly to be shunned. The minister of God must reason before the governor, of "righteousness, temperance, and judgment to come ; " and, if possible, make the ungodly ruler " tremble," as much as the meanest of the people. Yet St. Paul rejoiced to gain converts in Cæsar's household (Phil. i. 13 ; iv. 22). And, as there seems no more probable way to Christianize a people than to Christianize their rulers, it is obviously desirable that the government of a country should be induced to support religion in it. And again, on the other hand, it is the plain duty of sovereigns and constituted authorities to maintain true religion in the land. Nations and rulers are as much responsible to God's judgment as private individuals. Scripture condemns ungodly rulers and ungodly nations, as much as ungodly individuals ; and praise is given to such sovereigns as fear God and honour His name. (See Psalm ii. 10. Jer. xviii. 7–10. Jonah *passim*.) National, as well as individual, mercies and judgments come from Him. Now, nations and their rulers can only show their piety to God in a public and national manner, by maintaining true religion and the public service of religion. Moreover, it was prophesied concerning the Christian Church, that "kings should be her nursing fathers and queens her nursing mothers " (Isai. xlix. 23) ; and it is difficult to know how they can be nurses to the Church, if it be forbidden her to have any connection with them.[1]

Quis vos excipit ex universitate ? . . . . Ipsi sunt qui vobis dicere solent, servatis vestræ sedis honorem. . . . . Sed Christus aliter et jussit et gessit, &c. — S. Bernard. *Epist.* 42 *ad Henricum Senonensem Archiepiscopum.* Et Theophylact. *In Rom.* xiii., where it is very observable that Theoph-

ylact lived in the time of Pope Gregory VII., and St. Bernard after it ; and yet this truth obtained then : and this was about the year 1130." — Laud, *Conference with Fisher,* p. 170, note. Oxford, 1839.

[1] The Eastern Church admits the supremacy of the Crown, probably in a

If we once admit the propriety of a connection between the Church and the State, and at the same time deny the supremacy of the Pope, it seems almost to follow of necessity, that we should admit a supremacy of the sovereign. The sovereign must in that case hold some position in the Church; and it can only be the highest. It is not consistent with his sovereignty that he should have a superior in his own kingdom. But, in considering the sovereign as chief ruler over all persons in all causes, ecclesiastical as well as civil, we must remember one or two particulars. "It may be, that two or three of our princes at the most (the greater part whereof were Roman Catholics) did style themselves, or gave others leave to style them, 'the Heads of the Church within their dominions.' But no man can be so simple as to conceive, that they intended a spiritual headship, — to infuse the life and motion of grace into the hearts of the faithful; such an Head is Christ alone; no, nor yet an ecclesiastical headship. We did never believe that our kings, in their own persons, could exercise any act pertaining either to order or jurisdiction; nothing can give that to another which it hath not itself. They meant only a civil or political head, as Saul is called 'the head of the tribes of Israel;' to see that public peace is preserved; to see that all subjects, as well ecclesiastics as others, do their duties in their several places; to see that all things be managed for that great and architectonical end, that is, the weal and benefit of the whole body politic, both for soul and body." [1]

The sovereign "assumes not the office of teaching or of explaining the doubtful points of the law, nor of preaching or of minister-

---

more unrestricted sense than the Anglican Church. Yet they maintain the sole spiritual Headship of Jesus Christ, as opposed to the supremacy of the Pope.

"In 1590 certain prelates of the Russian Church joined the Roman communion on some concessions being made to them. Thus Rome raised the *Unia;* and it continued nearly 250 years. At the first partition of Poland, between two and three million uniats returned to the Eastern Church; and in 1839 the remaining Russian uniats were received into the unity of the Eastern Church, the only act of profession required being, that 'Our Lord Jesus Christ is the only true Head of the one true Church.'" — Neale's *History of the Eastern Church,* i. pp. 56, 57.

"In 1833 a Synod met at Nauplia for the regeneration of the Greek Church. The two following propositions were approved by thirty-six prelates: —

"1. The Eastern Orthodox and Apostolic Church of Greece, which spiritually owns no head but the Head of the Christian faith, Jesus Christ our Lord, is dependent on no external authority, while she preserves unshaken dogmatic unity with all the Eastern orthodox churches . . . . with respect to the administration of the Church, which belongs to the Crown, she acknowledges the King of Greece to be her supreme head as is in nothing contrary to the holy Canons.

"2. A permanent synod shall be established, consisting entirely of archbishops and bishops appointed by the king, to be highest ecclesiastical authority, after the model of the Russian Church." — Ibid. p. 60.

[1] Archbishop Bramhall, *Answer to M. de Milletière, Works,* i. pp. 29, 30.

ing Sacraments, of consecrating persons or things, of exercising the power of the keys, or of ecclesiastical censures. In short, he undertakes not anything which belongs to the office of the ministers of Christ. But in matters of external polity he claims the right of legislating; and we gladly give it him. The care of religion is an affair of the sovereign and the nation, not merely of the clergy." [1]

Again, the supremacy of the crown must not (according to our constitution in Church and state) be considered as an arbitrary and unlimited supremacy. Everything in England is limited by law: and nothing more than the power of the sovereign. In matters of state, the power of the crown is limited by the two houses of Parliament; in the affairs of the Church, it is limited also by the two houses of Convocation. Legally and constitutionally, the sovereign or the sovereign's government can do nothing concerning the state of the Church, her doctrine and discipline, without first consulting the clergy in Convocation, and the laity in Parliament; so that, when we acknowledge the supremacy of the crown, we do not put our consciences under the arbitrary guidance of the sovereign or the ministry; for we know, that legally nothing can be imposed upon us, but what has received the consent of our clergy and laity, as represented respectively.

Indeed, of late, no small difficulty has arisen. The supremacy of the crown is now wielded, not by the sovereign personally, but by the minister; that minister is the choice of the House of Commons: that House of Commons is elected by the three kingdoms; and, in two out of those three kingdoms, the vast majority of electors are not members of the Church of this kingdom of England. In short, the supremacy of the crown has insensibly passed, or at least is rapidly passing, into a virtual supremacy of Parliament. This unhappily is not a supremacy of the laity of the Church of England; because Parliament is composed of representatives from England, Ireland, and Scotland; and in the two last the majority are Roman Catholics and Presbyterians. This difficulty existed not at the period of the Reformation; but is steadily increasing on us

---

[1] The words are those of Bishop Andrewes, selected by James I. to defend his supremacy against Bellarmine. "Docendi munus vel dubia legis explicandi non assumit, vel conciones habendi, vel rei sacræ præeundi, vel sacramenta celebrandi; non vel personas sacrandi vel res; non vel clavium jus, vel censuræ. Verbo dicam, nihil ille sibi, nihil nos illi fas putamus attingere, quæ ad sacerdotale munus spectant, seu potestatem ordinis consequuntur. Procul hæc habet Rex; procul a se abdicat.

"Atqui in his quæ exterioris politiæ sunt, ut præcipiat, suo sibi jure vendicat; suosque adeo illi lubentes merito deferimus. Religionis enim curam rem regiam esse, non modo pontificiam," &c.—Andrewes, *Tortura Torti*, p. 380, p. 467, *Anglo-Catholic Library*.

at present. Up to the time of the Reformation, the whole nation
was of one faith, and united as one Church. The Reformation did
not introduce a new faith, but restored purity to the old, and r---
moved the abuses which time had permitted. It was the work of
prince, prelates, and people ; and the Church, which had from the
beginning been protected by the state, was protected by it still.[1]

It has been reasonably thought, that the supremacy of the Pope,
which was suffered before the Reformation, was (to use a term
growing into use) the extreme *expression* for the superiority of the
clergy and their dominance over the laity ; whereas the supremacy
of the crown was the counter expression for the independence and
power of the laity.

The same principle only would be expressed by the supremacy
of Parliament, and so of the minister, if Parliament represented
only the laity of the English Church. But, as at present constituted, it in part represents, not only the laity, but the clergy
also of other communions, which we must, alas ! almost call hostile
to us.

It is utterly vain to speculate on the future. We cannot question, that the relation between Church and state is now widely
different from that which once existed, and that it is fraught with
new dangers. Yet perhaps it may also bring new advantages.
And the Rock of the Church still stands unshaken ; and shall forever stand. There is our hope ; not in the favour of princes, nor
of multitudes of the people. Nor need our fear be of their frown.
Our real danger is, lest the lukewarmness of the Church lead to
Erastian indifference, or her zeal degenerate into impatience, faction, or intemperance.

|Note. A few words may be added, on a point which, it is believed, is not gen-
erally understood.

It is matter of history, that Cranmer and other Bishops took out commissions
from Edward VI. for the exercise of their Episcopal functions. This has been insisted on, especially by the late Lord Macaulay, as proof positive that they regarded
the Sovereign as the source of their spiritual authority. The truth however is,
that the act was the natural result of a distinction which was made between *spiritual power*, and the *right to exercise that power, after a coercive manner*, in any country
or state.

There is contemporaneous evidence. in the book called the *Institution of a Christian man*, published in 1537, that this distinction was made. It is therein asserted,

---

[1] The remarks in the text are abundant answer to the cavil, that the Church
of England is an Act of Parliament
Church. At the time of the Reformation,
and at the various reviews of our Services, the Church was, to a very great extent, truly represented as to its clergy in
Convocation, as to its laity in Parliament.
The acts of Convocation and Parliament,
ratified by the Crown, were therefore the
true acts of the Church of England, king,
priests, and people.

that " *God's* law committed to bishops or priests the power of jurisdiction .n excommunicating or absolving offenders, *but without corporeal restraint or violence.*" This
last is something which it clearly contemplates as coming from the State, and which,
therefore, the State can revoke.

So too Bramhall, in his first *Vindication*, says, " It is true the *habitual* jurisdiction
of bishops flows from their ordination ; but the actual exercise of it, *in public courts,*
after a coercive manner, is from the gracious concessions of Sovereign Princes." And
again, " *Habitual* jurisdiction is derived only by ordination. *Actual* jurisdiction is a
right to exercise that habit, arising from the lawful application of the matter or the
subject." And yet again, " We must distinguish between the interior and the ex-
terior courts, — between the court of conscience and the court of the Church. . . .
The power which is exercised in the court of conscience is *solely* from *ordination*.
But that power which is exercised in the court of the Church [*i. e.* as he explains
it, coercive power imposing other than spiritual penalties] is partly from the Sovereign Magistrate."

The commissions, then, which Cranmer and his brethren in the Episcopate received from the Sovereign, were not considered to convey *habitual jurisdiction*. That
had been received in ordination. But they gave them the right to exercise that
habitual jurisdiction, in recognized courts, and after a coercive manner. The idea
of course grows out of the union of Church and State ; and however little it may
approve itself to us, however undesirable it may seem to add temporal penalties to
spiritual censures, it at least proves that no such theory was entertained as the taking out of the commissions has been supposed to indicate. — *J. W.*]

Section II. — THE SUPREMACY OF THE BISHOP OF ROME.

THIS is a most extensive subject, and of primary importance in the
controversy between the Churches of Rome and England.
For, if once the supreme authority of the Roman Patriarch is conceded, all other Roman doctrines seem to follow as of course.
And so it will probably be found, that all converts to the Roman
Church have been led to it from a conviction of the necessity of being in communion with the Supreme Pontiff, not from persuasion
of the truth of particular dogmas.

The grounds on which the claim rests, are as follows : I. That
St. Peter had a supremacy given him over the universal Church.
II. That St. Peter was Bishop of Rome. III. That this supremacy
is inherited by his successors; those successors being the Bishops
of Rome.

I. It is said, that St. Peter had a supremacy given him over the
rest of the Apostles, and over the universal Church.

1. We may readily admit that St. Peter had a certain priority
among his brother Apostles assigned to him by our blessed Lord.

It is constantly the case that, in a company of equals, one, from greater age, greater energy and zeal, greater ability, or greater moral goodness, takes a lead, and acquires a superiority. This may have been the case with St. Peter. Our Lord certainly appears to have honoured him and St. John, and St. James, with His peculiar love and favour. And, both during our Lord's ministry and after His resurrection, St. Peter appears to have been signally forward in the service of Christ. The fathers observe much this quickness, boldness, activity, and energy of St. Peter; which naturally brought him into the foremost position, and also qualified him to take the lead among the disciples.[1]

Accordingly, a kind of priority of position or rank was apparently conceded by the other Apostles to St. Peter. This is what St. Augustine observes, that "St. Peter being the first in the order of the Apostles, the most forward in the love of Christ, often alone answers for the rest."[2] The fathers account for this on the grounds: 1, that he was the first called of the Apostles;[3] 2, that he was the eldest; for which cause St. Jerome supposed that he was preferred to St. John, lest a youth should take precedence of an elderly man;[4] 3, that he outstripped his brethren in a ready confession of faith in Christ.[5] So, St. Peter's name is ever first in the catalogue; and he seems to take the lead in speaking and writing.

2. But this priority of order involved not a primacy of power, or preëminence of jurisdiction.

(1) If it had done so, we should have found some commission of this kind given to him in Scripture. There is plain enough commission to the Apostleship; but none to a hyper-apostleship, nor any mention of the existence of such an office in the history of the Gospels and Acts, or in the Epistles of the Apostles. (2) There is no title of preëminence given to St. Peter, such as Vicar of Christ, Sovereign Pontiff, or Arch-apostle. (3) There was no office known to the Apostles or the primitive Church higher than that of Apostleship. This, St. Chrysostom tells us, is "the greatest authority, the very summit of authorities."[6] (4) Our Lord distinctly declared against any such superiority; and said that if any of the Apostles coveted it, he should be counted least of all (Matt.

---

[1] θερμότερος τῶν ἄλλων εἰς ἐπίγνωσιν Χριστοῦ. — Greg. Naz. Orat. 34. Tom. I. p. 549. Colon. See several passages to a like effect in Barrow, On the Pope's Supremacy, pp. 30, 31.

[2] "Ipse enim Petrus in Apostolorum ordine primus, in Christi amore promptissimus, sæpe unus respondet pro omnibus." — August. De Verbis Evangelii, Matt. xiv. Serm. 76, Tom. v. p. 415.

[3] "Quem primum Dominus elegit." — Cypr. Ep. 71.

[4] Hier. In Jovin. I. Tom. IV. part II. p. 168.

[5] "Supereminentem beatæ fidei suæ confessione gloriam promeruit." — Hilar. De Trin. Lib. VI.

[6] ἀρχὴ μεγίστη . . . κορυφὴ ἀρχῶν. Chrys. De Utilit. Lect. Script. in Princip. Actorum iii. Tom. III. p. 75. Edit. Benedict.

xx. 27; xxiii. 8. Mark ix. 34, 35; x. 44. Luke ix. 46; xxii. 14, 24, 26). (5) St. Peter, in his Epistles, claims no peculiar authority (see 1 Pet. v. 1; 2 Pet. iii. 2); and in the history, there is no appearance of his taking it. The appeal in Acts xv. is not to St. Peter, but to the Apostles and elders; and the decree runs in their names, ver. 22. If any one presided there, it was not he, but St. James. Nay! the other Apostles took upon themselves to *send* Peter and John into Samaria (Acts viii. 14); and " he that is sent is not greater than he that sends him " (John xiii. 16). (6) If St. Peter had been the visible head of the Church, those who were of Paul or of Apollos might indeed have been factious; but St. Paul as severely reproves for a schismatical spirit those who say, " I am of Cephas " (1 Cor. i. 12; iii. 21). (7) The complete independence of the Apostles in all their proceedings, in their missionary journeys, their founding of Churches, &c. shows the same thing (see 1 Cor. iv. 14, 15; ix. 2; Gal. iv. 19, &c.). (8) St. Paul's conduct especially proves that he owned no dependence on St. Peter, nor subjection to him. He declares himself, " in nothing behind the very chiefest Apostles " (2 Cor. xii. 11). On his conversion, he took no counsel with men, not even with the Apostles (Gal. i. 16, 17); but acted on his independent commission derived direct from Christ (Gal. i. 1). James, Cephas, and John gave him the right hand of fellowship, as their equal and co-Apostle (Gal. ii. 9). He hesitated not to " withstand St. Peter to the face, because he was to be blamed " (Gal. ii. 11). And St. Chrysostom observes, that thus St. Paul showed himself equal to St. Peter, St. John, and St. James, and that by comparing himself, not to the others, but to their leader, he proved that each enjoyed equal dignity and importance." [1]

Lastly, all these arguments from Scripture, against a supreme authority of St. Peter over the rest of the Apostles, are fully borne out by the statements of the fathers, who, though they speak much of the high honour of the former, yet declare that the other Apostles were all equal and coördinate with him in power and authority. Thus St. Cyprian: " The other Apostles were what Peter was, endowed with an equal share of honour and power; but the beginning proceeds from unity, that the Church might be shown to be one." [2] " His was," says St. Ambrose, " a precedence

---

[1] δείκνυσιν αὐτοῖς ὁμότιμον ὄντα λοιπὸν, καὶ οὐ τοῖς ἄλλοις ἑαυτὸν, ἀλλὰ τῷ κορυφαίῳ συγκρίνει, δεικνὺς ὅτι τῆς αὐτῆς ἕκαστος ἀπέλαυσεν ἀξίας. — Chrys. *In Gal.* ii. 8.

[2] " Hoc erant utique et cæteri Apostoli

quod fuit Petrus, pari consortio præditi et honoris et potestatis; sed exordium ab unitate proficiscitur, ut Ecclesia una monstretur." — Cyp. *De Unit. Eccles.* p. 107.

of confession, not of honour ; of faith, not of order."[1]   St. Jerome says that, though the Church were founded on St. Peter, yet it was equally on the other Apostles.[2] So Isidore: "The other Apostles received equal share of honour and power with St. Peter, and dispersed throughout the world preached the Gospel; to whom, on their departure, succeeded the bishops, who are constituted through the world in the sees of the Apostles."[3]

Let us now, on the other side, consider those passages of Scripture, on which it is contended that a distinct supremacy over the universal Church was granted to St. Peter.

1. The first is Matt. xvi. 18: "I say also unto thee, that thou art Peter, and upon this Rock I will build My Church; and the gates of hell shall not prevail against it."   Here, say the Roman divines, St. Peter is called the foundation of the Church; and foundation implies government and superiority.

It is observable, that our Lord called St. Peter Πέτρος, in the masculine, which properly signifies *a stone*, or *fragment of a rock;* and that He said He would build His Church, ἐπὶ ταύτῃ τῇ πέτρᾳ, using the feminine noun, which more expressly denotes *an entire rock.*   This has led many commentators, ancient and modern, to believe that the Rock on which the Church should be built, was not St. Peter; since in that case, the Lord would have used the masculine word πέτρῳ.[4]

Accordingly, a large number of the fathers were of opinion that the Rock, on which the Church was to be built, was either Christ Himself, or, which is much the same thing, the faith of Christ thus confessed by St. Peter.   Thus, St. Chrysostom interprets " On this Rock," by " On the faith of this confession."[5]   So

[1] " Primatum confessionis utique, non honoris ; primatum fidei, non ordinis." — *Lib. de Incarn.* T. iv.

[2] " At dicis super Petrum fundatur Ecclesia, licet id ipsum alio loco super omnes apostolos fiat, et ex æquo super eos Ecclesiæ fortitudo solidetur." — Hier. *In Jovin.* i. Tom. iv. part. ii. p. 168.

[3] " Cæteri Apostoli cum Petro par consortium honoris et potestatis acceperunt, qui etiam in toto orbe dispersi evangelium prædicaverunt, quibusque decedentibus successerunt episcopi, qui sunt constituti per totum mundum in sedibus Apostolorum." — Isidor. Hispal. *De Offic.* Lib. ii. c. 5.

[4] It is thought that the Syriac version refutes this opinion; since our Lord spoke Syriac, and in that version the words are the same, both being ܟܺܦܳܐ. It is, however, justly observed by Bp. Beveridge on this Article, that the second ܟܺܦܳܐ, where it means *a rock,* is shown to be feminine, by the use of the feminine pronoun ܗܳܕܶܐ ; whereas the first must be masculine, since it is a man's name. Hence the difference between Πέτρος and Πέτρα is not quite lost in the Syriac; though that language does not admit of the same changes of termination as the Greek has.

[5] ἐπὶ ταύτῃ τῇ πέτρᾳ . . . τουτέστι ἐπὶ τῇ πίστει τῆς ὁμολογίας. — *Hom.* lvi. *in Matt.* xvi.

St. Augustine says that our Lord meant, " On this Rock, which thou hast confessed, will I build My Church." [1] And, in his *Retractations*, he tells us that he had formerly interpreted the passage of St. Peter, but that he afterwards thought it more correct to understand it of Him whom St. Peter confessed. *Non enim dictum est illi, Tu es Petra, sed Tu es Petrus. Petra enim est Christus, quem confessus Simon, sicut tota ecclesia confitetur, dictus est Petrus.* Yet he leaves to the reader to choose which is the more probable interpretation.[2] In like manner St. Ambrose had said, that not Peter, but the faith of Peter, was the foundation of the Church ; [3] and in another place the same father writes, that " The Rock is Christ, who granted to His disciple that he should be called *Petrus*, as having from the Rock the solidity of constancy and firmness of faith." [4]

To the same effect write Hilary,[5] Cyril of Alexandria,[6] Basil of Seleucia,[7] Theodoret,[8] Isidore of Pelusium,[9] Theophylact,[10] and others.

On the other hand, no doubt, a great many of the ancients understood Peter himself to be the rock. Tertullian is the first who so applies the passage ; but we shall see hereafter, that he understood no supremacy to be implied in it, and certainly did not consider it to be transmitted to the Bishop of Rome.[11] Origen too applies it to St. Peter, but evidently understood all the other Apostles to have a similar promise.[12] Nay ! he declares that every disciple of Christ is a rock, as having drunk from the Spiritual Rock ; and on every such rock as this the word of the Church is founded.[13] Next comes St. Cyprian, who also calls St. Peter the rock ; and he says : " Though He committed an equal power to all the Apostles, saying, *As My Father hath sent Me, so send I*

[1] " Super hanc Petram, quam confessus es, ædificabo ecclesiam meam." — August. *In Johan.* tr. 124, Tom. III. par. II. p. 822, and *De Verbo Evangelii, Matt.* xiv. ; *Serm.* 76, Tom. v. p. 415.

[2] *Retractat.* I. 21, Tom. I. p. 32.

[3] " Fides ergo est Ecclesiæ fundamentum. Non enim de carne Petri, sed de fide dictum est, quia portæ mortis ei non prævalebunt, sed confessio vincit infernum." — Ambros. *De Incarnat. Domin. Sacrament.* c. 5.

[4] " Petra est Christus ; qui etiam discipulo suo hujus vocabuli gratiam non negavit, ut et ipse sit Petrus, quod de Petra habeat soliditatem constantiæ, fidei firmitatem." — Ambros. Lib. vi. *In Evangel. Lucæ.*

[5] " Super hanc confessionis Petram

Ecclesiæ ædificatio est." — Hil. *De Trin.* Lib. vi.

[6] *In cap.* xliv. *Jesaiæ,* p. 598 ; Id. *Dial.* iv. *De SS. Trinit.* p. 507.

[7] *Orat.* xxv. p. 142.

[8] *Epist.* 77.

[9] *Epist.* 235, Lib. I.

[10] *In Matt.* xvi. 18.

[11] *De Pudicit.* c. 21 ; *De Præscript. Hæret.* c. 22.

[12] εἰ δὲ ἐπὶ τὸν ἕνα ἐκεῖνον Πέτρον νομίζεις οἰκοδομεῖσθαι τὴν ἐκκλησίαν μόνον, τὶ ἂν φήσαις περὶ Ἰωάννου τοῦ τῆς βροντῆς υἱοῦ καὶ ἑκάστου τῶν Ἀποστόλων. — Origen. *In Matt.* Tom. XII. 11.

[13] Πέτρα γὰρ πᾶς ὁ Χριστοῦ μαθήτης, ἀφ' οὗ ἐπίνον οἱ ἐκ πνευματικῆς ἀκολουθούσης πέτρας, κ. τ. λ. — Ibid.

you. Receive ye the Holy Ghost; Whose soever sins ye remit, they are remitted unto him; and whose soever sins ye retain, they shall be retained; yet, that He might manifest unity, He disposed by His authority the origin of that unity, so that it might take its rise from one. The rest of the Apostles indeed were what Peter was; endowed with an equal share of honour and power; but the beginning proceeds from unity, that the Church may be shown to be but one."[1]

So Gregory Nazianzen,[2] Epiphanius,[3] Basil the Great,[4] Jerome,[5] and others understand, that St. Peter was the rock.

But supposing this latter to be the true interpretation; does it follow thence, that St. Peter had a supreme government over the other Apostles? Foundation does not, of necessity, imply government. Our Lord may have promised to St. Peter, that he should be the first to found His Church; which was fulfilled on the great day of Pentecost, when St. Peter's noted sermon brought the first-fruits of the Church of Christ.[6] But the fathers say, that the other Apostles were rocks as well as St. Peter, and that the Church was built on them also.[7] The Fathers, in no instance, suppose the other Apostles to have any dependence on, or subjection to St. Peter; and Dr. Barrow justly observes, that the Apostleship itself could not be built on St. Peter, for that had been founded by Christ Himself before this promise was given; and hence the Apostles were all clearly independent of St. Peter, and therefore their successors, the bishops, must be independent of his successors.[8] A passage so doubtful in its interpretation can never be sufficient to the purpose for which it is adduced; especially seeing that none of the most ancient fathers, however they may interpret it, have discovered in it that supremacy of St. Peter which has since been asserted. If St. Peter be called a

---

[1] "Super unum ædificat ecclesiam suam. Et quamvis Apostolis omnibus parem potestatem tribuat et dicat; *Sicut misit Me Pater, et Ego mitto vos, accipite Spiritum Sanctum; si cui remiseritis peccata, remittentur illis, si cui tenueritis, tenebuntur:* tamen ut unitatem manifestaret, unitatis ejus originem ab uno incipientem sua auctoritate disposuit. Hoc erant utique et cæteri Apostoli quod fuit Petrus, pari consortio præditi et honoris et potestatis; sed exordium ab unitate proficiscitur, ut una ecclesia monstretur."—Cypr. *De Unitate*, p. 106. Fell.
[2] *Orat.* XXVI. Tom. I. p. 418.
[3] *Hæres.* LIX. Tom. I. p. 500.
[4] *In Cap.* ii. *Jesaiæ*, Tom. II. p. 869.

[5] Hieronym. *Ad Marcellam adv. Montanum*, Epist. 27. Tom. IV. part II. p. 64.
[6] "Petrus dicitur, eo quod primus in nationibus fidei fundamenta posuerit."—Pseudo-Ambros. *De Sanctis, Serm* 2.
[7] See Origen, as above. So Jerome: "Dicis super Petrum fundatur Ecclesia, licet id ipsum in alio loco super omnes Apostolos fiat." — Hieron. *In Jovin.* Tom. IV. par. II. p. 168. So Basil. M.: ἐκκλησία ᾠκοδόμηται ἐπὶ τῷ θεμελίῳ τῶν ἀποστόλων καὶ προφητῶν· ἐν τῶν ὀρέων ἦν καὶ Πέτρος, ἐφ' ἧς καὶ Πέτρας ἐπηγγείλατι ὁ Κύριος οἰκοδομήσειν αὐτοῦ τὴν ἐκκλησίαν. — Basil. *In Isai.* ii. p. 869.
[8] Barrow, *Supremacy*, p. 62.

rock and a foundation, still all the Apostles were foundations, as well as he. " In the twelve foundations of the city are the names of the twelve Apostles of the Lamb" (Rev. xxi. 14). It is "built on the foundation of the Apostles and prophets" (Ephes. ii. 20). In the highest sense, which indeed points out supremacy, "other foundation can no man lay, than that is laid, which is Jesus Christ" (1 Cor. iii. 11). And, as St. Ambrose says that the Apostle was a rock, as deriving firmness from the Rock; so the Apostles were foundations, as themselves built on the One Foundation ; and their qualification, as rocks or as foundations, they received, not from Peter, but from Christ.

2. The next argument for St. Peter's supremacy is the verse immediately following the last ; namely, " And I will give unto thee the keys of the kingdom of Heaven ; and whatsoever thou shalt bind on earth shall be bound in Heaven" (Matt. xvi. 19). Here it is said that the power of the keys was given to St. Peter alone, and that the rest of the Church therefore derives that power through him.

We may admit, that the promise being first given to St. Peter was a mark of special honour to him. But the same power was conferred upon the *Church* as a body; to which our Lord said, " Verily I say unto you, Whatsoever ye shall bind on earth shall be bound in Heaven" (Matt. xviii. 18). And again, after the resurrection, the same power was given to all the Apostles, when the risen Saviour "breathed on them, and saith unto them, Receive ye the Holy Ghost ; whose soever sins ye remit, they are remitted unto them ; and whose soever sins ye retain, they are retained" (John xx. 22). It is evident therefore, that neither the Church nor the Apostles received this power through St. Peter, but directly from Christ Himself ; and though the *promise* was first to St. Peter, yet the *gift* appears to have been simultaneous to all. So then, though St. Peter is honoured by a priority, the whole College of the Apostles is endowed with an equality of power.

The fathers unanimously consent to this view of the case. "Are the keys of the kingdom of Heaven given to St. Peter alone, and shall not all the saints receive them? And if this be common, how are not all the things common which were spoken to St. Peter?" So writes Origen.[1] And St. Cyprian, "Christ, after His resurrection, gave an equal power to all His Apostles, and

---

[1] Ἆρα οὖν τῷ Πέτρῳ μόνῳ δίδονται ἀπὸ τοῦ Κυρίου αἱ κλεῖδες τῶν οὐρανῶν βασιλείας, καὶ οὐδεὶς ἕτερος τῶν μακαρίων αὐτὰς λήψεται; εἰ δὲ κοινόν ἐστι καὶ πρὸς ἑτέρους τὸ δώσω σοι τὰς κλεῖδας τῆς βασιλείας τῶν οὐρανῶν, πῶς οὐχὶ καὶ πάντα τὰ τε προειρημένα καὶ τὰ ἐπιφερόμενα ὡς πρὸς Πέτρον λελεγμένα.—Origen. *In Matt.* Tom. xii. 11.

said, *As the Father hath sent Me, so send I you. Receive ye the Holy Ghost : whose soever sins ye remit, they are remitted ; and whose soever sins ye retain, they are retained."* [1] " On all," says St. Jerome, "the strength of the Church is equally founded. You will say, the Church is founded on Peter; but in another place this is said to be on all the Apostles; and all receive the keys of the kingdom of Heaven." [2] St. Ambrose, " What is said to Peter, is said to all." [3] St. Augustine, " Did Peter receive the keys, and not Paul ? Peter, and not John and James and the rest of the Apostles ? " [4] Theophylact, " Though it be spoken to Peter alone, *I will give thee*, yet it is given to all the Apostles. When ? Why, when He said, *Whose soever sins ye remit they are remitted.*" [5] And so St. Leo, himself a famous Bishop of Rome, says, that " This power of the keys is translated to all Apostles and bishops. It was commended singly to St. Peter, because the example of St. Peter was propounded to all pastors of the Church." [6]

Some indeed considered, that the whole Church received the keys with St. Peter. St. Peter they esteemed as a kind of figure of the Church, and an emblem of its unity; and so that all received the power, even when it was ostensibly given to but one.[7]

And if, notwithstanding this testimony of the fathers, we still esteem some special authority to be implied in the promise, we can only understand it of his being appointed to be the first, who, by preaching of the word and admitting converts to baptism, should unlock the gates of the kingdom, and open them to believers. " So," says Tertullian, " the event teaches. The Church was built on him, *i. e.* by him. He first put in the key, when he said,

---

[1] " Christus Apostolis omnibus post resurrectionem suam parem potestatem tribuit et dicit : Sicut misit me Pater, et Ego mitto vos, accipite Spiritum S. Si cui remiiseritis peccata, remittentur ei, si cui retinueritis, tenebuntur." — Cyprian. *De Unitate*, p. 107. Fell.

[2] " Dicis, super Petrum fundatur Ecclesia ; licet id ipsum in alio loco super omnes Apostolos fiat, et cuncti claves cœlorum accipiant; et ex æquo super eos ecclesiæ fortitudo solidetur."—Hieron. *C. Jovinian.* Lib. i. Tom. iv. part ii. p. 168.

[3] " Quod Petro dicitur, cæteris Apostolis dicitur." — Ambros. *In Ps.* xxxviii.

[4] " Numquid istas claves accepit Petrus, et Paulus non accepit ? Petrus accepit, et Joannes, et Jacobus non accepit, et cæteri apostoli ? " — August. *Serm.* cxlix. Tom. v. p. 704.

So, again, " Ecclesia quæ fundatur in Christo, claves ab eo regni cœlorum accepit, i. e. potestatem ligandi, solvendique

peccata." — Aug. *Tract.* 124, *in Joh.* Tom. iii. par. ii. p. 822.

[5] εἰ γὰρ καὶ πρὸς Πέτρον μόνον εἴρηται τὸ δώσω σοι, ἀλλὰ καὶ πᾶσι ἀποστόλοις δέδοται · πότε ; ὅτε εἶπεν ἂν τινῶν ἀφῆτε τὰς ἁμαρτίας ἀφίενται. — Theophyl. *in loc.*

[6] " Hæc clavium potestas ad omnes etiam apostolos et Ecclesiæ præsules est translata. Quod autem sigillatim Petro sit commendata, ideo factum est, quod Petri exemplum universis Ecclesiæ pastoribus fuit propositum." — Leo. I. *Serm. de Natio.*

[7] " In typo unitatis Petro Dominus dedit potestatem." — August. *De Bapt.* iii. 17. Tom. ix. p. 117.

" Quando ei dictum est, *Tibi dabo claves* . . . . universam significavit ecclesiam." — *Tract.* 124 *in Johan.* Tom. iii. pt. ii. p. 822.

" Ecclesiæ claves regni cœlorum datæ sunt, cum Petro datæ sunt." — *De Agone Christi* 30, Tom. vi. p. 260.

Ye men of Israel, hear these words; Jesus of Nazareth, &c. Acts ii. 22. He first opened the entrance to the kingdom of Heaven by baptism, whereby the sins were loosed by which they had been bound; and he too bound Ananias with the bond of death," [1] &c.

3. The last argument of any weight, for St. Peter's supremacy, is the command, " Feed My sheep " (John xxi. 16).

This, however, is an injunction and command, not the bestowal of a privilege. Dr. Barrow has observed, that, as well might the elders of Ephesus, whom St. Paul exhorts to " feed the Church of God " (Acts xx. 28), have esteemed, that St. Paul thereby constituted each of them an universal governor of the Church, as St. Peter, that he was made by this command an universal bishop. And so the fathers understood, that what was here enjoined on St. Peter was equally enjoined on all pastors. " When it is said to Peter, it is said to all," says St. Augustine.[2] " These sheep and this flock," says St. Ambrose, " not only St. Peter did then receive, but all we pastors received with him." [3] And so St. Cyprian, " All of them were shepherds; but the flock was shown to be one, which was fed by all the Apostles, with unanimous consent." [4] The command, too, is to feed the flock, not to feed the shepherds. Hence, whatever authority may be supposed to be given over the people by these words, plainly none is given over the other Apostles. Every pastor is, in some sense, a pastor of the whole flock of Christ; the Church of God is committed unto him. But every pastor has not therefore authority over his brethren, neither can it be shown, that, in thus committing a duty to St. Peter as regards the laity, our blessed Lord assigned him a supremacy over the clergy.

The most then that can be fairly made of the case is, that St. Peter had a priority of honour among the Apostles; that he was *primus inter pares.* More than this our Lord did not bestow on him; more the Apostles did not concede to him; more the earliest fathers never assigned to him; and especially, more he never claimed or exercised himself. Eusebius quotes, from Clement of Alexan-

---

[1] " Sic enim et exitus docet. In ipso Ecclesia extructa est, id est, per ipsum: ipse clavem imbuit; vides quam — *Viri Israelitæ, auribus mandate quæ dico; Jesum Nazarenum, virum a Deo destinatum* et reliqua. Ipse denique primus in Christi baptismo reseravit aditum cœlestis regni, quo solvuntur alligata retro delicta, et alligantur quæ non fuerint soluta secundum veram salutem, et Ananiam vinxit vinculo mortis." — Tertull. *De Pudicitia,* c. 21.

[2] " Cum ei dicitur, ad omnes dicitur, *Amas me? Pasce oves meas.*" — August. *De Agone Christi,* 30, Tom. vi. p. 260.

[3] " Quas oves et quem gregem non solum tum B. suscepit Petrus, sed et cum eo nos suscepimus omnes." — Ambros. *De Dignitat. Sacerd.* 2.

[4] " Pastores sunt omnes, sed grex unus ostenditur, qui ab apostolis omnibus unanimi consensione pascitur." — Cypr. *De Unitate Eccles.*

dria, a passage markedly illustrative of all these statements. " Peter
and James and John," says he, " after the ascension of the Saviour,
contended not for glory, as having been most highly honoured by
the Lord, but chose James the Just to be Bishop of Jerusalem." [1]
The writer of this passage could not have believed that St. Peter
had, or claimed a supremacy over his brethren ; nor, we may observe
by the way, could he have thought any bishopric in the Church
more honourable than that of Jerusalem.

II. The next position of the Roman Church is, that St. Peter
was bishop of Rome.

It is not to be doubted, that a tradition did exist in early times
that St. Peter was Bishop of Rome.   But, if that tradition be submitted, like others of the same kind, to the test of historical investigation, it will be found to rest on very slender foundation.   In the
first place, Scripture is silent about his having been at Rome, — a
remarkable silence, if his having been Bishop there was a fact of
such vital importance to the Church, as the Roman divines have
made it to be.   Then, the first tradition of his having been at Rome
at all does not appear for more than a century after his death.   It
is nearly two centuries after that event that we meet with anything like the opinion that the Roman bishops were his successors.
It is three centuries before we find him spoken of as Bishop of
Rome.   But when we reach three centuries and a half, we are told,
that he not only was Bishop of Rome, but that he resided five and
twenty years at Rome ; a statement utterly irreconcilable with the
history of the New Testament.

To begin with the new Testament, the only evidence that can
be thence adduced for St. Peter's having been at *Rome*, is that he
seems to have written his first Epistle from *Babylon* (1 Pet. v.
13).   Eusebius [2] says this meant Rome.   He appears to say it on
the authority of Papias; though some learned men deny, that he
ascribes the tradition to Papias.   Jerome follows Eusebius in this
statement.[3]   The Roman divines generally adopt it.   Yet a learned
writer of their communion truly observes, that the use of such a
metonymy may be very proper in a symbolical book, like the
Apocalypse, " but would only be credible in the subscription of an
epistle, if *arcana nomina Ecclesiarum* had existed among Christians." [4]   If the tradition be due to Papias, he is doubtless a very

---

[1] "Euseb. *II. E.* ii. 1, quoting Clement
from the sixth book of the *Hypotyposes*.
[2] *H. E.* Lib. ii c. 15.

[3] *De Viris Ill.* c. 8.
[4] Hug, *Introduction to the New Testament*, part ii. sect. 165.

early authority (A. D. *circ.* 110) ; but Eusebius himself has given us to understand, that he was a person whose judgment was not to be depended on, and particularly that he was an enthusiast about the Apocalypse. Hence his interpreting St. Peter by the language of the Apocalypse is not of much weight.

Farther than this, the Acts of the Apostles, St. Paul's Epistle to the Romans, St. Paul's four Epistles written from Rome, St. Peter's two Epistles, are all profoundly silent about St. Peter ever having been at Rome. Indeed, it seems almost certain that, when St. Paul went to Rome, St. Peter had not been there. Not only is there no mention of such a thing, but St. Paul, when writing to the Romans, writes much as if no Apostle had ever been amongst them. (Comp. Rom. i. 10–15 ; xv. 15–24). And, when he was at Rome, it seems clear from the narrative, that the Jews of Rome had had no communication with any chief teacher among the Christians, at least with any who had been converted from Judaism ; they were therefore desirous to hear of him what *he* thought, knowing only that the sect of Christians was everywhere spoken against (Acts xxviii. 22). Now how is this compatible with the alleged fact, that St. Peter, the Apostle of the circumcision, to whom the conversion of the Jews had been peculiarly intrusted, had been the founder of the Church of Rome, and had been resident there for some time ? Again, if St. Peter had been at Rome, when St. Paul wrote to the Romans, St. Paul would surely have saluted him. If he had been there when St. Paul was there, it would surely have been mentioned in the Acts. If he had previously been there, and had been established as bishop of the city, it is utterly incredible that St. Paul should have assumed such authority over St. Peter's flock, as he does assume over the Romans, and that the Jews of Rome should have been utterly uninstructed in the Gospel.

Of the fathers, the first who speaks to the purpose is Irenæus. He says, that the blessed Apostles, Peter and Paul, founded and established the Church of Rome, and delivered the bishopric to Linus, to whom succeeded Anacletus, and to him Clement.[1] Clement of Alexandria says that St. Peter preached at Rome, and that St. Mark wrote his Gospel at the request of St. Peter's hearers.[2] Tertullian says, Clement was ordained by St. Peter to be Bishop of Rome.[3] Origen tells us, that St. Peter, having preached to the Jews in Pontus, Galatia, Bithynia, Cappadocia,

[1] Iren. III. 3.   [2] *Hypotyp.* Lib. VI. apud Euseb. *H. E.* II. 14.
[3] *De Præscript.* c. 32.

and Asia, *at last* ($\epsilon\pi\iota$ $\tau\epsilon\lambda\epsilon\iota$) came to Rome, and was crucified with his head downwards.[1]   The Apostolical Constitutions say, that Linus was made first Bishop of Rome by St. Paul, and that after his death Clement was ordained to the same office, by St. Peter.[2] Lactantius tells us that the time of St. Peter's going to Rome was the reign of Nero.[3]   Eusebius speaks of Linus as the first Bishop of Rome, after St. Paul and St. Peter; [4] and elsewhere, that Linus was first Bishop of Rome after St. Peter, and that Clement was the third.[5]   Also he assigns the date of St. Peter's first going to Rome to the reign of Claudius.[6]

Now here we have a collection of the earliest and best authorities, concerning St. Peter's connection with Rome, and concerning the bishops that first presided there.   Origen says, he went there *at last;* Lactantius says, in the reign of Nero.   Eusebius, later than either of them, and much later than Origen, assigns as a date the reign of Claudius.   None of them say, that he was Bishop of Rome.   On the contrary, all agree in saying that the first bishop of that see was Linus.   All place Linus there during the Apostles' lifetime.   Some say that St. Paul, others that St. Peter and St. Paul, ordained him; whilst some say that Clement, the third bishop, was ordained by St. Peter.   The inference is plainly this.   At whatever time St. Peter came to Rome, (which most probably was in Nero's reign, and very shortly before that tyrant put him to death,) there was some one else Bishop of Rome then, and therefore St. Peter was not Bishop of Rome.   Linus was bishop first, then Anacletus, then Clement.   Very probably all three, one after the other, were bishops before St. Peter's death.   But, whether one or three, some one else, not St. Peter, was Bishop of Rome, in St. Peter's lifetime.   Two bishops were never permitted to preside over one see; and therefore it is quite clear that St. Peter was not Bishop of the see of Rome.

It is very true that St. Cyprian and Firmilian, in the middle of the third century, speak of Stephen, Bishop of Rome, as claiming to be successor to St. Peter; and, though not submitting to his authority, they still appear to acknowledge his claim.   Yet they never said that St. Peter was Bishop of Rome; but they acknowledged Stephen's succession from him, because they considered that St. Peter founded the Church of Rome, ordained the first

---

[1] Ap. Euseb. *H. E.* III. 1.
[2] *Constitut. Apostol.* VII. 46.   Here Clement is made the second bishop of Rome; Anacletus, whom Irenæus mentions as second, being omitted.

[3] *De Mortibus Persecutorum*, c. 2.
[4] III. 2.
[5] III. 4.
[6] II. 14.

bishop there, and that therefore the apostolical succession came, through the Bishops of Rome, from that Apostle.

The circumstances of the Roman Church were very remarkable. It was the only Church in the West that could *certainly* trace its origin to Apostles. The Apostles who were at Rome, were the greatest of all; for there St. Paul undoubtedly taught, there probably both St. Paul and St. Peter ordered the Church, ordained its first bishops, and finally watered it with their blood. There, if the tradition speak truly, St. John too was thrown into boiling oil, and escaped unhurt. The three greatest Apostles then had probably taught and suffered at Rome. St. Peter and St. Paul had ordered the Church, and ordained very probably the first three bishops. No Church but Jerusalem could claim such privileges as this. No wonder then, that throughout the West the Church of Rome and her bishop should be had in high honour. No wonder that St. Cyprian, himself a Western bishop, should have looked up to the see of Rome as the centre of Christian unity, and the depository of sound doctrine. But all this does not make St. Peter the first diocesan bishop there, nor does it prove that Cyprian thought him so.

The explanation of Rufinus is evidently the true, namely, that Linus, Cletus, and Clement were the Bishops of Rome; but that St. Peter, whilst he was there, exercised apostolical authority, which was above every episcopate, and therefore not interfering with it.[1]

And so it is observed, that many churches took their names from the Apostles, and were called Apostolical sees; not because Apostles were Bishops in them, but because Apostles taught and appointed bishops there. Thus Ephesus was so called, because St. Paul founded it, and St. John resided and ordained there. Smyrna, because Polycarp was placed there by St. John or other Apostles. Alexandria, because St. Mark was placed there by St. Peter. Corinth, Thessalonica, Philippi, because founded by St. Paul. Antioch, because St. Peter is said to have resided there, and to have constituted its first bishops.

It is true that, when we get to the later fathers, we find that the story of St. Peter's Roman episcopate (a fiction eagerly cherished by the prelates of that see) was gaining ground and attracting credit. Epiphanius therefore speaks of St. Peter and St. Paul as

---

[1] " Linus et Cletus fuerunt quidem ante Clementem episcopi in urbe Roma, sed superstite Petro ; videlicet ut illi Episco- patus curam gererent, ipse vero Apostolatus ir pleret officium." — Rufin. *in Præf. Clem. Recog.*

the first Apostles, and also bishops of Rome ; [1] no very definite
statement after all. But Jerome (a. d. *circ.* 400) positively asserts,
that St. Peter, after having been Bishop of Antioch, went to Rome,
where he was bishop for five and twenty years. He says this, both
in his treatise *De Viris Illustribus*,[2] and also in his Latin translation
of Eusebius's *Chronical Canon ;* [3] which, however, contains many
things not said by Eusebius, and this amongst the rest.[4]   The fact,
thus stated by Jerome, is simply impossible ; and the origin of it is
probably to be attributed to a perversion of the account of Lactantius ; which account is, that, after preaching five and twenty
years in divers provinces, Peter came, in Nero's reign, to Rome.[5]
Thus the tradition was like Homer's Ἔρις : —

Ἡ τ' ὀλίγη μὲν πρῶτα κορύσσεται, αὐτὰρ ἔπειτα
Οὐρανῷ ἐστήριξε κάρη, καὶ ἐπὶ χθονὶ βαίνει.[6]

At first, it was but that St. Peter and St. Paul had constituted
the Church in Rome, ordained Linus as its bishop, and there suffered for their testimony.   Then they are spoken of as if they
might have been bishops themselves ; the Roman bishops are then
said to be St. Peter's successors ; and lastly, it is roundly asserted
that St. Peter was actually Bishop of Rome for five and twenty
years.   That to fan the spark into a flame was the interest and
the wish of such prelates as Victor and Stephen, even charity
cannot make us doubt.   But, after such a plain history of the rise
and progress of the tradition, it is impossible not to see that it has
no firm foundation.

There is indeed no good reason to doubt, that St. Peter was at
Rome ; that he assisted St. Paul to order and establish the Church
there ; that, in conjunction with St. Paul, he ordained one or more
of its earliest bishops, and that there he suffered death for the sake
of Christ.   But there is no reason to believe, that he was ever, in
any proper or local sense, Bishop of Rome ; or indeed that, in that
sense, any one of the Apostles had a fixed episcopate ; with the
single exception of St. James (if he were an Apostle), who was
appointed to preside over Jerusalem, lest that city, where Jesus died,

---

[1] Ἐν Ῥώμῃ γὰρ γεγόνασι πρῶτοι Πέτρος
καὶ Παῦλος οἱ ἀπόστολοι αὐτοὶ καὶ ἐπίσκοποι,
εἶτα Λῖνος. — Epiph. *Hær.* xxvii. num. 6.

[2] " Post episcopatum Antiochensis Ecclesiæ . . . Romam pergit, ibique viginti
quinque annis cathedram sacerdotalem
tenuit." — *De V. I.* c. 1.

[3] *Chron.* p. 160.

[4] The Greek of Eusebius is, Πέτρος ὁ
κορυφαῖος τὴν ἐν Ἀντιοχείᾳ πρώτην θεμε-
λιώσας ἐκκλησίαν εἰς Ῥώμην ἄπεισι κηρύττων
τὸ εὐαγγέλιον. — *Χρον. Καν. ad Nun.* M. Γ.

[5] " Apostoli per annos xxv usque ad
principium Neroniani imperii per omnes
provincias et civitates Ecclesiæ fundamenta miserunt. Cumque jam Nero impe-
raret, Petrus Romam advenit," &c. — *De
Mortibus Persecutorum,* c. 2. Pagi gives
this explanation, *Critic. in Baron. Ann.* 43,
num. iii. quoted by Lardner, *Works,* vi.
p. 547.

[6] *Il.* Δ. 442.

and rose from the dead, and from whence the Church first took its origin, and thence spread through the world, should lack an Apostle, and witness of the resurrection, to be constantly present there, and to form a kind of centre and home for the first preachers of the faith. All the other Apostles had the world for their diocese; and wheresoever they came, they, as a thing of course, exercised supreme and hyper-episcopal control, discipline, and government. Indeed, if any Apostle could be called Bishop of Rome, St. Paul has more claim to that title than St. Peter. For St. Paul was the Apostle of the Gentiles; whereas St. Peter's mission was to the Jews. St. Paul wrote an Epistle to the Romans, which St. Peter did not. St. Paul lived two years at Rome, before there is any good ground for believing that St. Peter had been there at all. St. Paul is said to have constituted the first bishop there.[1] More-over, St. Paul himself speaks of having "the care of all the Churches," *i. e.* the Gentile Churches (2 Cor. xi. 28). All this will constitute a better case for St. Paul's Roman episcopacy, and for his supremacy over the Gentile Churches, than can possibly be made out for St. Peter's.

III. The third position of the Roman divines is, that St. Peter's supremacy is inherited by his successors, the Bishops of Rome.

If we have seen that St. Peter had no proper supremacy, and that he was not Bishop of Rome; then, the premises being gone, the consequence must fall with them. If St. Peter had no suprem-acy, it could not be inherited. If he was not Bishop of Rome, the Popes could not inherit from him.

But farther, whatever priority St. Peter had among his brother Apostles was personal, not official. He held no office, which they did not hold equally. There is no mention of an Arch-Apostle; and though St. Paul speaks of the chiefest Apostles (οἱ ὑπὲρ λίαν ἀπόστολοι), he speaks of them in the plural, not as if there were but one of supreme authority; and he says that he himself was "not a whit behind them" (2 Cor. xi. 5). As then St. Peter's prior-ity was personal, not official, it could not be inherited. It was grounded on personal acts, especially his faithful confession of Christ. It contained some personal privileges; *e. g.* the first found-ing of the Church, which, being that on which much stress is laid, is yet incommunicable to his successors, who cannot now be the first founders of the Christian temple or commonwealth. And so Tertullian observes, that the manifest intention of the Lord was to

---

[1] *Constitut. Apostol.* vii. 46, *as above.*

confer this privilege personally on St. Peter, and that the presuming to derive that power to the bishop of a particular see was a subverting of that intention.[1]

Again, we can trace the rise and progress of this supremacy of Rome, and easily perceive the grounds of it. It was not admitted at the first, but crept in by degrees, till it reached its perfect stature. St. Clement, who was Bishop of Rome, writes to the Corinthians in a brotherly tone, and with less appearance of authority than St. Ignatius, Bishop of Antioch, seems to assume when writing to the Romans. St. Polycarp knew nothing of the supremacy of Anicetus, when he went to consult with him about the keeping of Easter. He yielded in no degree to the Roman Bishop's authority ; but both determined to retain their own customs and sentiments, yet not on that account to divide the Catholic Church.[2] Not very long after this, we find Polycrates, a successor to Polycarp in the see of Smyrna, again at issue with Victor, Bishop of Rome, on the Easter controversy. Victor indeed showed much of the spirit which has since prevailed at the Vatican, and excommunicated Polycrates. But Polycrates and the Synod of Asiatic bishops refused to acknowledge the authority of that prelate.[3] Several bishops, though agreeing in Victor's opinion, were much displeased at his violence ; and letters were written by them severely reproving him for such conduct. Especially St. Irenæus, Bishop of Lyons, in the name of the Christians of Gaul, over whom he presided, wrote a dignified remonstrance, warning Victor not to break the unity of the Catholic Church.[4]

At the end of the second century, we find from Tertullian that the Bishop of Rome claimed that he, *and all other Churches founded by St. Peter*, derived through St. Peter the power to bind and to loose.[5] This claim Tertullian disallows ; but it is a claim very different from that of universal dominion ; for it must have admitted the Bishops of Antioch and others to the like privilege.

---

[1] " Qualis es evertens atque commutans manifestam Domini intentionem personaliter hoc Petro conferentem." — *De Pudicit.* c. 21. See also Bishop Kaye's *Tertullian*, pp. 236, 237.

[2] Euseb. *H. E.* iv. 14, v. 24.

[3] " Si qui discrepabant ab illis Victori non dederunt manus." — Hieronym. *De V. I.* s. v. Irenæus.

[4] Euseb. *H. E.* v. 24 ; Hieronym. *De V. I.* Irenæus indeed in one place says, that, " in the Church of Rome, on account of her more powerful principality, the faithful everywhere must meet, in which,

by the resort of so many, Apostolical tradition is preserved." — *Adv. Hær.* iii. 3. All that we can gather from this is, that the city and the Church of Rome had a great preëminence, that it was the great centre or focus of the Christian world, and so the truth was best preserved there.

[5] " Idcirco præsumis et ad te derivasse solvendi et alligandi potestatem, id est, *ad omnem ecclesiam Petri propinquam*." — *De Pudicit.* c. 21. The *De Pudicitia* is a Montanist tract, but its evidence as to the claims of Rome is as good as if it were Catholic.

In the third century, we have the famous controversy about heretical baptism, dividing the Western Church.   It had first begun
amongst the Asiatics.   Afterwards, Cyprian, Bishop of Carthage,
being consulted by the Numidian bishops, called several councils at
Carthage, A. D. 255, which were attended by large numbers of African bishops.[1]   They unanimously decreed the rebaptizing of heretics.   This brought them into collision with Stephen, Bishop of
Rome ; as the Roman Church took the opposite view.   Stephen
refused to listen to the deputies from the Council, and renounced
communion with the African Churches.   They, on the other hand,
maintained their own views, and expressed their disapproval of
Stephen's attempt to make himself a " bishop of bishops." [2]   A correspondence took place between Cyprian and Firmilian, Bishop of
Cæsarea in Cappadocia ; in which both express extreme disappro-
bation of Stephen's conduct, and accuse him of schismatically introducing differences throughout the Church.   Firmilian says, the power
of binding and loosing was given by Christ to the Apostles and the
bishops who succeeded them ; and blames the manifest folly of
Stephen, who gloried in the place of his episcopate, and contended
that he was a successor of St. Peter, on whom the Church's foundation was laid, and yet himself introduced new rocks and new
foundations.[3]   Again on another occasion, the bishops of Africa,
among whom was St. Augustine, not only submitted not, in the
case of Apiarius, to the authority of the Bishops of Rome, Zosimus,
Boniface, and Celestine, but in the Council of Africa, A. D. 424,
wrote strongly to Pope Celestinus, denying his right to interfere
with their jurisdiction, complaining that he violated the canon of
the Council of Nice, which directed, that causes of the bishops and
clergy should be heard by their own metropolitan, and not carried
elsewhere.[4]   They had even in a previous Council at Milevis, A. D.
416, forbidden appeals to be carried beyond the seas, on pain of
separation from all communion with the African Churches.[5]

But above all, Pope Gregory the Great, himself an illustrious
Bishop of Rome, so vehemently protested against John Nesteuta,

[1] Seventy-one were present at the second, and eighty-seven at the third Council.

[2] " Neque enim quisquam nostrum
episcopum se episcoporum constituit ; aut
tyrannico terrore, ad obsequendi necessitatem collegas suos adegit ; quando habeat omnis episcopus pro licentia libertatis et potestatis suæ, arbitrium proprium,
tamque judicari ab alio non possit, quam
nec ipse potest judicare." — Cyprianus In
Concil. Carthag.

[3] Epistol. Firmilian. Oper. Cyprian
Epist. LXXV. p. 225, E.

[4] Concil. Tom. II. p. 1674 ; Justelli,
Cod. Can. Eccle. Afric. p. 408.

[5] " Non provocent nisi ad Africana
concilia, vel ad primatas provinciarum
ad transmarina autem qui putaverit ap
pellandum, a nullo intra Africam in com
munionem suscipiatur." — Concil. Milev
Can. 22 ; Barrow, On the Supremacy, p
248.   See also Bingham, IX. i. 11 ; Hus
sey's Rise of the Papacy, pp. 40–46.

the Bishop of Constantinople, for desiring to have the name of universal bishop, that he pronounced such an assumption a proof that he who made it was the *forerunner of Antichrist*.[1] " None," says he, " of my predecessors ever consented to use so profane a word; because if one patriarch is called universal, the name of patriarch is taken away from the rest."

If we look to the canons of the general councils, we find that they acknowledge the great Patriarchs; that they give them authority according to ancient custom within their own patriarchates; that they put Rome first, not because of St. Peter's primacy, but because Rome is the imperial city; Constantinople next, because it is new Rome; and afterwards elevate Constantinople to an equality with Rome; and that they specially forbid bishops to interfere with the dioceses of other bishops. Thus, the vɪth Canon of the Council of Nice says: " Let those ancient customs be in force which concerned Egypt, Lybia, and Pentapolis, that the Bishop of Alexandria should have authority over them, since the like is customary with the Bishop of Rome. So also in Antioch, and the other provinces, let the dignities be preserved to the Churches."[2] Balsamon's gloss on this is, that they confirmed the authority of the four Patriarchs, namely, of Rome, Alexandria, Antioch, and Jerusalem, over their respective patriarchates.[3] So that this great Council placed the Roman Bishop only on a level with those of Antioch, Alexandria, and Jerusalem; and this too, as a matter of ancient custom, not of divine right.

The second canon of the Council of Constantinople (A. D. 381) especially forbids that bishops should go beyond their dioceses, restrains the Bishop of Alexandria to Egypt, the eastern bishops to the East, and so on; and forbids, that any bishop should go out of his own diocese for ordination, or any other ecclesiastical ministrations.[4] The third canon of the same council decrees, that the Bishop of Constantinople shall take rank immediately after the Bishop of Rome, because Constantinople is new Rome.[5]

The eighth canon of the Council of Ephesus (A. D. 431) forbids

---

[1] " Ego autem fidenter dico quia quisquis se universalem sacerdotem vocat, seu vocari desiderat, in elatione sua Antichristum præcurrit, quia superbiendo se cæteris præponit." — Gregor. Magn. *Epist.* vɪɪ. 33.

So again, " Nullus unquam decessorum meorum hoc tam profano vocabulo uti consensit, quia videlicet si unus Patriarcha universalis dicitur, patriarcharum nomer cæteris derogatur." — Ibid. v. 43.

" Indignant as Gregory was at the Bishop of Constantinople calling himself Œcumenical Patriarch, that title had been given him by law from the time of Justinian, and was therefore no new thing in Gregory's time." — See Bingham, *E. A.* xvɪɪ. 21.

[2] Bevereg. *Synodic.* Tom. ɪ. p. 66.

[3] Ibid.

[4] Ibid. p. 87.

[5] διὰ τὸ εἶναι αὐτὴν νέαν Ῥώμην. — Ibid. p. 89.

any bishop to invade another province, which has not from the beginning been under his own authority.[1]

The twenty-eighth canon of the Council of Chalcedon declares, that the fathers of the Council of Constantinople gave privileges to the see of Rome, because that city was the seat of empire. Wherefore also, moved by the same reason, the fathers assigned the like privileges to the see of new Rome, *i. e.* Constantinople, seeing that Constantinople was now honoured with the empire and the senate.[2] These decrees of the Council of Constantinople the Council of Chalcedon accordingly confirms.

From all this we plainly learn, that the Roman Patriarch had no more authority given him than the other Patriarchs, of Constantinople, Antioch, and Alexandria; that the first place was assigned to Rome, because Rome was the imperial city, not because her bishop had a divine right to preëminence; that, however, the Bishop of Constantinople had a like honour bestowed upon him, when his city rose to the like position with that of his brother Patriarch; and, above all, that no bishop was ever to invade any diocese, which had not from old times been subject to him or to his predecessors. How any of these considerations will agree with the later claims of the Roman Pontiff, it is hard to say.

The first great step towards supremacy was given to the Pope by the Council of Sardica (A. D. 347). Before this time, when bishops had been deposed and had reason to complain, they appealed to the Emperors to summon a larger synod to review their cause. The great Athanasius had thus appealed to the Emperor, and had been restored, after he was deposed by the Tyrian Synod. The xiith Canon of the Council of Antioch, supposed to be directed against him, forbade such an appeal. Subsequently Athanasius, ill-used by the Eastern bishops and by Constantius the Arian Emperor, had fled for assistance and support to the Western bishops, especially to the Patriarch of Rome. As there was an Arian Emperor, and there had at all times been a difficulty connected with the imperial interference in doctrinal questions, it was not unnatural for the orthodox bishops to look for some other

---

[1] ὥστε μηδένα τῶν θεοφιλεστάτων ἐπισκόπων ἐπαρχίαν ἑτέραν, οὐκ οὖσαν ἄνωθεν καὶ ἐξ ἀρχῆς ὑπὸ τὴν αὐτοῦ ἡγοῦν τῶν πρὸ αὐτοῦ χεῖρα, καταλαμβάνειν. — Bevereg. *Synodic.* Tom. I. p. 104.

[2] Καὶ γὰρ τῳ θρόνῳ τῆς πρεσβυτέρας Ῥώμης διὰ τὸ βασιλεύειν τὴν πόλιν ἐκείνην οἱ πτέρες εἰκότως ἀποδεδώκασι τὰ πρεσβεῖα. Καὶ τῷ αὐτῷ σκοπῷ κινούμενοι οἱ ἑκατὸν πεντήκοντα θεοφιλέστατοι ἐπίσκοποι τὰ ἴσα πρεσβεῖα ἀπένειμαν τῷ τῆς νέας Ῥώμης ἁγιωτάτῳ θρόνῳ εὐλόγως κρίναντες τὴν βασιλείᾳ καὶ συγκλήτῳ τιμηθεῖσαν πόλιν, καὶ τῶν ἴσων ἀπολαύουσαν πρεσβείων τῇ πρεσβυτέρᾳ βασιλίδι Ῥώμῃ, καὶ ἐν τοῖς ἐκκλησιαστικοῖς, ὡς ἐκείνην, μεγαλύνεσθαι πράγμασι, δευτέραν μετ' ἐκείνην ὑπάρχουσαν — Ibid. p. 145.

centre, where appeals might be made; and the see of Rome most
naturally presented itself. The bishop there was the most important on every account. Rome was the head of the world, the
centre of civilization, the centre of orthodoxy; and the greatest
number of bishops and clergy looked up to its Patriarch as their
leader and chief. Accordingly, in an unhappy moment, the Synod
of Sardica, in its third canon, gave to Julius, Bishop of Rome,
"honouring the memory of St. Peter," the power, if he thought fit,
"to appoint the neighbouring bishops of a province to hear" an
appeal, "and to send assessors," such as the emperor used to send.[1]
It is added, by the fourth canon, that if a deposed bishop appeal
to Rome, his place shall not be filled till the Bishop of Rome has
heard the case.[2] And by the fifth canon it is decreed, that, when
an appeal has been made to the Bishop of Rome, he may appoint
the provincial bishops to try the case, or send legates himself.[3]
The whole wording of the canons shows that all this was new.
Moreover, the council was not general. But the effect of its
decrees was very evil. Pope Zosimus afterwards quoted them as
decrees of the Council of Nice, in the case of Apiarius mentioned
above; and the African bishops were obliged to investigate the
question, as to whether they did really issue from that great
synod; and finding that they did not, they utterly rejected their
authority.[4] Yet these canons laid the foundation of appeal to
Rome, and so of Roman supremacy. And Dr. Barrow calls them
"the most unhappy ever made in the Church." [5]

From this time, the power of the see of Rome rapidly gained
ground. It would be long to trace its progress, and the opposition which was raised to it by wise and far-seeing men, as it
advanced towards its zenith.[6] Such a survey of history would
indeed be instructive, as showing how different were the pretensions
of Gregory VII. and Innocent III. from those of such prelates as
even Victor or Stephen; though the latter were amongst the most
imperious of the early "successors of the fisherman." .Suffice it to
have given some proof, that St. Peter had no proper supremacy;
that he was never Bishop of Rome; and that the Roman Patriarchs had not *jure divino*, nor from the earliest ages, a jurisdiction
over the universal Church.

---

[1] Bevereg *Synodic.* Tom. I. p. 485.
[2] Ibid. p. 487.
[3] Ibid. p. 488.
[4] See Hussey's *Rise of the Papacy*, pp.
44–47.
[5] See Barrow, p. 250; Stillingfleet's

Origines Britan. ch. III., near the end;
Palmer, *On the Church,* II. pp. 520, 548.
[6] The progress is well traced by Professor Hussey in the small volume al
ready referred to.

IV. There is one other ground, besides that of universal Primacy, on which the Pope claims jurisdiction in England ; namely, that England was in the Patriarchate of Rome.

When patriarchates first arose is uncertain. The name is first used by Socrates (about A. D. 440 [1]). But the office was evidently more ancient. It probably arose from the gradually apparent usefulness of such an order in the government of the Church. Their authority was confirmed, as we have seen, to the great patriarchs, by the Council of Constantinople, and afterwards by those of Ephesus and Chalcedon.[2] All bishops indeed were esteemed equal, as bishops, by the primitive fathers ; *i. e.* they were of equal authority, *jure divino ;* [3] but, for the sake of a more orderly Church-government, metropolitans were placed over provinces, and patriarchs over those still larger divisions which were then called dioceses, corresponding with the civil divisions of the Empire.[4]

As to the limits of the Roman Patriarchate, much depends on what is meant by the term *Suburbicary Churches.* Rufinus, in his translation of the Nicene Canons, gives us the sixth of these in the words : " The custom of Alexandria and of Rome shall still be observed, that the one shall have the care of the Egyptian, the other of the suburbicarian Churches." [5] The very word *suburbicarian* clearly points to churches not far distant from Rome ; and it has been proved, that the suburbicarian Churches meant those within the district, which belonged to the *Vicarius Urbis ; i. e.* the

---

[1] Socr. *H. E.* v. 8. Conc. Chalced.

[2] Bing. *E. A.* ii. xvii. 1, 9.

[3] " Episcopatus unus est, cujus a singulis in solidum pars tenetur." — Cyprian. *De Unitate*, p. 108.

" Ubicunque est episcopus, sive Romæ, sive Eugubii, ejusdem est meriti, ejusdem sacerdotii ; potentia divitiarum et paupertatis humilitas sublimiorem vel inferiorem episcopum non facit." — Hieronym. *Ad Evagrium*, Epist. 85.

[4] A bishop's jurisdiction was over a παροικία, a metropolitan's over an ἐπαρχία, a patriarch's over a διοίκησις, corresponding with the civil jurisdiction of imperial officers. In the Empire there were seven dioceses in the East, and six in the West, besides the Prefecture of Rome. Hence, in the Church there were fourteen dioceses or patriarchates. In the East, 1. Egypt, under the Patriarch of Alexandria. 2. The East, under the Patriarch of Antioch. 3. Asia, under the Patriarch of Ephesus first, — afterwards under Constantinople. 4. Pontus, under Cæsarea. 5. Thrace, under Thessalonica, — afterwards under Constantinople. 6. Macedonia. 7. Dacia. In the West, 1.

Rome, containing the suburbicarian provinces, under the Patriarch of Rome. 2. Italy, under Milan. 3. Africa, under Carthage. 4. Illyria, which afterwards fell under Constantinople. 5. Gaul, under Treves, — afterwards under Arles 6. Spain, under Seville, — afterwards under Toledo. 7. Britain, under York. In the fourteen dioceses of the empire there were 118 provinces ; and there was the like number in the Church. But, as in the civil government there were three chief cities, Rome, Alexandria, Antioch, so the bishops of these were called Patriarchs by preëminence (as was afterwards the Bishop of Constantinople) ; the bishops of the other great dioceses being called Primates, though with patriarchal powers, — *Primates of dioceses*, not merely metropolitans of provinces. See Crackanthorp, *Defensio Eccles. Anglican.* cap. xxii. §§ 64, 65.

[5] " Ut apud Alexandriam, et in urbe Roma, vetusta consuetudo servetur, ut vel ille Ægypti, vel hic suburbicarium ecclesiarum sollicitudinem gerat." — Rufin. *Hist.* Lib. i. c. 6.

greater part of middle Italy, all lower Italy, Sicily, Sardinia, and
Corsica.[1] It has been shown that the Bishop of Rome did not in
early ages exercise authority in Spain, or Gaul, or Africa, nor even
over the Bishops of Milan and Aquileia.[2] Far less could he have
had patriarchal rights in the more distant isles of Britain. And,
though the Synod of Arles, A. D. 314, speaks of the Bishop of
Rome as "holding the larger dioceses,"[3] which Roman divines
have construed to mean all the great divisions of the Western
Empire, yet there is good proof, that the word *diocese* had before
this time been assigned to the ordinary provinces of the empire,
and that it was even used of single episcopal Churches; so that it
must by no means be inferred that the Synod of Arles meant to
speak of the Roman patriarchate as including all the West.[4]

Again, it has been proved, beyond a question, that the British
Church was of very early origin: founded as early as, perhaps earlier than, the Church of Rome.[5] It clearly acknowledged no obedience to the Pope; for, when Augustine met the British bishops,
and pleaded with them for subjection to Rome, they replied, "that
they owed no obedience to the Bishop of Rome, but were under
the government of the Bishop of Caerleon upon Uske, who was
their overseer under God."[6] They refused too to alter their time
for keeping Easter, to suit the Roman custom;[7] and show no
intention whatever of submitting to papal authority. Indeed, the
only reasonable claim which the Roman Pontiff can put in, to a
superiority over our English bishops, is derived from the mission
of Augustine, A. D. 599. But it is to be observed that, as there
was already a Church and several bishops in Britain, so there were
Christians, before his arrival, even among the Saxons; that he
converted only a small portion of England, namely, Kent, and a few
adjacent counties; other parts being converted by Irish and Scots
missionaries, not sent from Rome;[8] that he did not receive his
appointment to the see of Canterbury from Gregory the Pope, but
from Ethelbert the King.[9] Besides all this, the benefit conferred,

---

[1] Bevereg. *Synodicon. Annotat. in Can.
Concil. Nic. Prim.*; Stillingfleet, as above;
Bingham, IX. i. 9, 10.

[2] Stillingfleet, *Origines Britan.* ch. III.;
Bingham, IX. i. 11; Dr. Allix (*Churches
of Piedmont*, ch. XIII.) shows, that the diocese of Milan was independent of Rome
to the middle of the 11th century.

[3] "Qui majores dioceses tenes." —
Conc. Arelatens. I.; *Epist. Synod. Concil.*
Tom. I. p. 1426.

[4] Bingham, IX. i. 12; Palmer, *On the
Church*, II. p. 543.

[5] Stillingfleet, *Orig. Britann.* ch. I. See

the Introduction to Soames's *Anglo-Saxon
Church*, where in two pages a summary
of the evidence for Britain's early conversion is given.

[6] Spelman, *Concil. Britan.* An. 601,
Tom. I. p. 108; Bingham, IX. i. 11; Still-
ingfleet, ch. V., near the end; Bramhall,
I. p. 160.

[7] Bede, *Hist.* Lib. II. c. 2, 19; III. 25;
v. 16, 22; Bingham, Ibid.

[8] See Bramhall, *Works*, I. 266, 267·
II. 94, 133, 300.

[9] Ibid. I. 132; Bed. *H. E.* I. 25.

of converting a nation, does not necessarily involve a supreme jurisdiction over it. Such a jurisdiction was not conceded by the earlier Saxon kings; and if it had been so, a power, which did not originate till the seventh century, whereas there had been a Church in Great Britain in the first century, cannot be a power of that inviolable character, that to throw it off is to separate from Christ, and from the communion of Christ's holy Church. We maintain, that Britain and British Churches were not within the patriarchal rule of Rome in the earliest ages, nor at the times of the four great general Councils. And we deny that, by right of conquest, the Bishop of Rome could obtain authority over them, since it was to Christ, and not to Gregory, that Augustine was sent to conquer the Saxons. We assert therefore that, by claiming patriarchal jurisdiction in England, the Roman Patriarch violates the eighth Canon of the third general Council, 'which forbids a bishop to intrude into any province which was not under his authority from the very beginning (ἄνωθεν καὶ ἐξ ἀρχῆς).

If the Pope had been contented to exercise jurisdiction within his own patriarchate, and to take precedence of rank over all the other bishops of Christendom, without attempting to exercise an unwarranted control over bishops and Churches not within the limits of his own lawful government; it is probable that his privileges would never have been objected against, nor his precedence denied him. But when he wishes to be sole Vicar of Christ on earth, the head of the whole Church, and to be above all earthly power and dominion, we believe that he arrogates to himself a title which belongs not to any human being, and claims a power which is only Christ's.[1]

Section III.

IT will be necessary to give but a small space to the concluding paragraphs of this Article. The first is, —

---

[1] Dr. Barrow, *On the Supremacy of the Pope*, is a complete storehouse of information and argument on this subject.

Crackanthorp, *Defensio Eccl. Anglic.* ch. XXII. contains an excellent summary of arguments. Palmer, *On the Church*, Part VII. has also much information in a small compass. For the antiquity and independence of the British Churches see Usher, *De Primord. Eccl. Britan.*; Stillingfleet, *Origines Britannicæ*; Bramhall and Bingham, as referred to above; Beveridge, Note on VI. Can. of the Nicene Synod, Tom. II. *Annotat.* pp. 51-60; Hales, *Origin and Purity of the British Church*; Burgess's *Tracts*; Williams's *Antiquities of the Cymry* &c.

I. " The laws of the realm may punish Christian men with death for heinous and grievous offences."

The chief arguments against capital punishments in a Christian state, must be drawn from general considerations of benevolence, and from the evil of taking away from the sinner the time for re-pentance. To these may be added our Lord's cautions against revenging ourselves, and His injunctions that we should not resist evil (Matt. v. 38, 45, &c.).

On the other side, it is truly said, that punishments inflicted by public authority are not for revenge, but for the suppression of evil. More benevolence is shown in punishing violence, and so repressing it, than in suffering it to prevail. We may not indeed altogether reason from Jewish precedent; because the character of the Jewish commonwealth was peculiar : and some crimes were then visited with capital punishment, which in any other common-wealth must be left almost without public condemnation. But, before the Law, God gave to Noah a command, which seems appli-cable to the whole human race : " Whoso sheddeth man's blood, by man shall his blood be shed ; for in the image of God made He man " (Gen. ix. 6). And under the Gospel, St. Paul maintains the authority of the civil sword. He speaks of the higher powers as ordinances of God, forbids Christians to resist them, and, speak-ing of the magistrate, says : " He beareth not the sword in vain ; for he is the minister of God ; a revenger to execute wrath upon him that doeth evil " (Rom. xiii. 1–4).

So then in the patriarchal ages, and under the Gospel, we have authority for capital punishments. Whether such sentence should be pronounced on any but murderers, or virtual murderers, is an-other question. But for murder, at least, there seems full Scrip-ture authority, that nations should inflict the punishment of death.

II. The last paragraph in the Article is : " It is lawful for Christian men, at the commandment of the magistrate, to wear weapons and serve in the wars."

Tertullian, in his treatise, *De Corona Militis*, argues against the lawfulness of a Christian's engaging in the military profession.[1] But in his *Apology*, he says, that Christians were in the habit of enlisting both in the Roman armies and the Roman navies.[2] The well-known story of " The Thundering Legion " proves, that, in the year 174, in the reign of Marcus Aurelius, there were many

[1] *De Coronâ*, c. 11.
[2] *Apol.* c. 42.   See Bp. Kaye's *Tertullian*, p. 364.

Christians among the imperial troops, even if we hesitate to believe that there was a whole Christian legion, or that their prayers brought down thunder and rain.[1]

When we come to Scripture, we find one or two passages in the new Testament which' seem to some persons decisive against the lawfulness of war altogether, and therefore against the lawfulness of serving in war. They are especially, Matt. v. 38–41, where our Lord forbids us to " resist evil," bidding us turn the left cheek to one who smites us on the right ; and Matt. xxvi. 52, " All they that take the sword shall perish with the sword." What applies to individuals may be thought equally applicable to societies of individuals, and therefore to whole nations. Indeed we may justly apply the argument, so far as to say that no Christian nation or governor is justified in making war upon a principle of revenge. Revenge is an unchristian feeling, and therefore forbidden to nations as well as to individuals. Therefore, not only are wars for mere glory unquestionably wholesale murder, but wars for any end save necessary preservation, and protection of life, liberties, and independence, are clearly against the will of God, and the spirit of the Gospel of Christ. Yet we may press doctrines and passages of Scripture so far as to overturn the whole fabric of society. If Christian nations may never resist aggression, or defend the weak, civilization and religion would be hourly exposed to destruction from the invasion of barbarians and unbelievers. In such a case, the Gospel would have established the supremacy of the violent and the ungodly.

But He, who in the old Testament repeatedly calls Himself " the Lord of Hosts, the God of the armies of Israel," can hardly have altogether forbidden just war. John the Baptist, when the soldiers inquired of him what they should do to prepare for the kingdom of Christ, did not bid them give up serving in the armies, but required them to do no violence, and to be content with their wages (Luke iii. 14). Nowhere in the new Testament is there any injunction against the military profession, although our blessed Lord and His Apostles are frequently brought into contact with soldiers, and are led to speak of war. Thus the centurion, whose servant our Lord healed, received high commendation for his faith,

---

[1] Concerning the Thundering Legion, see Mosheim, *De Rebus ante Constant. Mag.* sec. ii. § 17; Lardner, vii. p. 438.

Many later sects, whose doctrines and practices were very rigid, seem to have opposed capital punishments and the lawfulness of war ; as the Waldenses (see Mosheim, Cent. xii. part ii. sect. v. 12) and the Anabaptists. Mosh. Cent. xvi. sect. iii. pt. ii. ch. iii. 16.

but no rebuke for his vocation (Matt. viii. 5–13).   Cornelius, another centurion, has visions and miracles vouchsafed to him, and
an Apostle is sent to instruct and baptize him ; but no hint is
given, that he ought to give up serving in the Roman armies after his
baptism and adoption of the faith (Acts x.).   Our Lord and St.
Paul both refer to the customs of war, as illustrations of the Christian's warfare, and commend the prudence and wisdom of the
worldly warrior to the imitation of the soldier of the Cross, without
any reservation or intimation that this world's warrior is to be condemned for following his calling.   (See Luke xiv. 31, 32. 2 Tim.
ii. 4.)   The rebuke to St. Peter, " They that take the sword shall
perish with the sword," was evidently directed against an individual's voluntarily taking on himself to fight ; and also against using
carnal weapons in a spiritual cause.   It is not therefore applicable
to serving as a soldier, in defence of our country, and at the command of the magistrate, who, by God's own ordinance " beareth
the sword," and " is a revenger to execute wrath upon him that
doeth evil " (Rom. xiii. 4).

ARTICLE XXXVIII.

———◆———

Of Christian men's Goods, which are not common.

THE Riches and Goods of Christians are not common, as touching the right, title, and possession of the same, as certain Anabaptists do falsely boast. Notwithstanding, every man ought, of such things as he possesseth, liberally to give alms to the poor, according to his ability.

De illicita bonorum communicatione.

FACULTATES et bona Christianorum non sunt communia, quoad jus et possessionem (ut quidam Anabaptistæ falso jactant) debet tamen quisque de his quæ possidet, pro facultatum ratione, pauperibus eleemosynas benigne distribuere.

SECTION I. — HISTORY.

THERE is no doubt, that the early Christians practised almsgiving and sacrifice of their own wealth for the Church and the poor, to an extent unknown in our days. There are indeed passages in the *Apologies* of Justin Martyr and Tertullian, which appear at first sight as if there were in the early ages a complete community of goods. The former speaks of Christians as having formerly placed their greatest pleasure in acquiring wealth and possessions, " but now bringing all that they have into a common stock, and imparting to every one in need." [1] The latter says, " We, who are united in mind and soul, hesitate not to have our possessions in common. With us all things are in common but our wives." [2] But, that they did not mean a real community of goods, appears from an earlier passage in the same chapter : " Even if there be with us a sort of treasury, no sum is therein collected discreditable to religion, as though she were bought. Every man places there a small gift on one day of the month, or whenever he wills, so he be but willing and able ; for no man is constrained, but contributes willingly." [3] It is plain that, where there were collections, according as men were able and willing, there could be no true community of goods. Clement of Alexandria wrote his tract, *Quis Dives Salvetur*, to prove, that it was not the design of the Gospel that all men should reject the possessions with which Providence had blessed them. It was one of the errors attributed

[1] Justin M. *Apol.* I. p. 61, B.   [2] Tertull. *Apol.* 39.   [3] Ibid.

to the Pelagians, " that a rich man must sell all that he has, or
he cannot enter into the kingdom of God." [1]   But, that this was
not a precept of universal obligation, St. Augustine argues against
them at great length.[2]   Several early sects are mentioned, as having forbidden possessions, and denied salvation to those who had
wealth,— as the Apostolici ; [3] and the Eustathians, who for this and
other errors were condemned by the Council of Gangra.[4] Persons,
who adopted such opinions, were called by the fathers *Apotactitæ*.[5]
The fact, that they were esteemed heretics, shows that the Church
repudiated and condemned their peculiarities.

Some very zealous Christians in all ages have felt personally
bound to relinquish their wealth, and devote themselves to a voluntary poverty ; and with them may be classed the mendicant orders,
and indeed all those religious communities which have required
vows of poverty from their numbers. This, however, is a different
view of things from that condemned in the Article. The Article
refers to the belief that all property is unlawful, and that goods in
a Christian society must be common. This is a tenet which has
only been adopted, whether in primitive or later ages, by certain
fanatical sects ; and it is here especially spoken of as an error of
the Anabaptists. With them the doctrine was a source, not so
much of personal self-denial, as of efforts to subvert civil government and the whole framework of society ; and it was not therefore
to be treated as an innocent enthusiasm, but to be denounced as
a dangerous error.[6]

Section II.—SCRIPTURAL PROOF.

A GREAT many passages from the new Testament might be
brought to prove the danger of riches ; and some few of our
Lord's own sayings seem even to enjoin on His followers a renunciation of worldly wealth. Such are Matt. v. 42 ; vi. 19 ;
Luke xvi. 19–25 ; 1 Tim. vi. 9, 10 ; James v. 1. The two most
remarkable, however, are Matt. xix. 21, where the young man is
bidden to sell all that he has, and give to the poor ; and Luke xii.
33, where our Saviour, addressing His disciples generally, says,

---

[1] Augustin. *Ep.* 156, Tom. ii. p. 542.
[2] *Ep.* 157, Tom. ii. pp. 553–559. See
also Wall, *On Infant Baptism,* pt. i. ch.
xix. Vol. i. p. 396. Oxf. 1836.
[3] August. *Hær.* 40 ; Epiphan. *Hær.*
lxi, *Apostol.*

[4] Bevereg. *Synod.* Tom. i. p. 415.
[5] See Bingham, xvi. xii. 1.
[6] See an account of their doctrines
and proceedings, Mosheim, *E. H.* Cent.
xvi. sect. iii. pt. ii. ch. iii. 5, &c.

" Sell that ye have, and give alms; provide yourselves bags which wax not old, a treasure in the heavens that faileth not," &c. The former passage (Matt. xix. 21) has been considered at some length under Art. XIV.[1] The other (Luke xii. 33) appears to me the strongest argument from Scripture in favour of their opinion who think that every sincere follower of Jesus Christ should divest himself of all his personal possessions, and embrace a voluntary and strict poverty. We must take heed how we weaken and dilute injunctions of our Saviour, especially when they cross our natural propensities. Yet we must not explain one passage of Scripture so as to make it contrary to other passages of Scripture. Our Lord tells us in another place, that, if a man " hate not his father and mother, and wife and children, and his own life also, he cannot be His disciple " (Luke xiv. 26). Such a declaration, pressed to its utmost limits, would make us " without natural affection," (a mark of heathen reprobation, Rom. i. 31,) and would even lead us to break the fifth commandment. And so of the passage in question; though in its most literal and general application it would not lead to consequences so serious as this, yet it would, so interpreted, make it impossible for us to provide for those of our own house, which St. Paul tells us would be a proof that we had denied the faith and had become worse than infidels (1 Tim. v. 8). It is probable therefore, that we must consider our blessed Saviour's exhortation as rather addressed to His immediate followers, who could only follow Him in His wanderings, and preach His Gospel in the world, by utter abandonment of houses and possessions, than as applicable to all His disciples through all ages of the Church. And, even if we pressed His words to their utmost length, they would merely be an injunction to individuals to renounce their wealth, not a rule binding on society, that private wealth should be confiscated, and only a public fund permitted to exist.

In favour of that view, the only tenable argument is drawn from the early chapters of the Acts; where we read that the first believers " had all things in common, and sold their possessions and goods, and parted them to all men as every man had need " (Acts ii. 44, 45); that the multitudes of them that believed were of one heart and one soul, neither said any of them that ought of the things which he possessed was his own; but they had all things common (Acts iv. 32; compare 34–37). This self-devotion of the primitive Christians affords indeed a most instructive example for

---

[1] See above, p. 344.

all succeeding generations. It sprang from an intense feeling of love and gratitude to the Saviour; and whilst it was fervent and enthusiastic, it was reasonable and necessary. Had there not been self-sacrifice among the rich, what would have become of the poor of the flock, whose name was, for Christ's sake, cast out as evil? But even at this very time we find the right of the owners to their property fully recognized in the Scriptures and by the Apostles, so as abundantly to show that no absolute community of goods had been exacted. The very fact that it is written, "No man said that ought of the things which he possessed was his own," shows that the possessions were acknowledged to be theirs by others, though voluntarily renounced by themselves; and that therefore it was a voluntary renunciation, and not made according to an obligation imposed on them by the Church. Also, St. Peter said to Ananias: "Whilst it remained, was it not thine own? and after it was sold, was it not in thine own power?" (Acts v. 4). So that, before the property was sold, the Apostle acknowledged that it was of right the property of Ananias; and even after it was sold, there was no necessity upon him to give it up to the Apostles. His sin was, not in the retaining of his goods, but in pretending to give all, and yet keeping back a part.

There are numerous injunctions to provide for our families (Acts xx. 35. 2 Cor. xii. 14. 1 Tim. v. 8), — to give alms (Matt. vi. 1; x. 42), — to make friends of the mammon of unrighteousness (Luke xvi. 9), — to lay by in store as God prospers us, and then to give (1 Cor. xvi. 2), — to feed the hungry and clothe the naked (Matt. xxv. 35, &c.), — to call the maimed, the lame, and the blind to our feasts (Luke xiv. 13), — to do good as we have opportunity (Gal. vi. 10), — to distribute to the necessity of the saints (Rom. xii. 13), — to give with a willing mind (2 Cor. viii. 12), not grudgingly or of necessity, as knowing that God loveth a cheerful giver (2 Cor. ix. 7), — to be given to hospitality (Rom. xii. 13) — to use hospitality one to another without grudging (1 Pet. iv. 9). All these precepts, whilst they impose the strongest obligations to abundant and most liberal almsgiving, yet presuppose the existence of distinct possessions, and of different ability to give in the different members of the Church. If all things were common, the grace and duty of giving from our own private means would thereby have become impossible. So again, the recognized distinction between master and servant, the one being enjoined to be just and liberal, the other honest and obedient, proves the difference of condition and the possession of property (Eph. vi. 5–9. Col. iv. 1. Philem. 10–20).

Especially, where the Apostles address the rich, and bid them to be rich in good works and bountiful to others, they clearly show, that there may be rich men in the Christian community, and that such may fulfil their Christian obligations, and lay up a good foundation for the future by giving liberally, though they do not sell all that they have. For example: " *Charge them that are rich in this world,* that they be not high-minded, nor trust in uncertain riches . . . that they do good, that they be rich in good works, ready to distribute, willing to communicate; laying up in store for themselves a good foundation against the time to come " (1 Tim. vi. 17–19). " Whoso *hath this world's goods,* and seeth his brother have need, and shutteth up his bowels of compassion from him, how dwelleth the love of God in him?" (1 John iii. 17). " To do good and to communicate forget not: for with such sacrifices God is well pleased " (Heb. xiii. 16).

Thus then Scripture plainly confirms the teaching of the Church, that " the goods of Christian men are not common as touching the right, title, and possession of the same : " but yet that every man, as a follower of Christ, has the most cogent and inevitable obligation, " liberally to give alms to the poor, according to his ability."

ARTICLE XXXIX.

—◆—

Of a Christian man's Oath.	*De Jurejurando.*
As we confess that vain and rash Swearing is forbidden Christian men by our Lord Jesus Christ, and *James* his Apostle, so we judge, that Christian Religion doth not prohibit, but that a man may swear when the Magistrate requireth, in a cause of faith and charity, so it be done according to the Prophet's teaching, in justice, judgment, and truth.	QUEMADMODUM juramentum vanum et temerarium a Domino nostro Jesu Christo, et Apostolo ejus Jacobo, Christianis hominibus interdictum esse, fatemur : ita Christianorum religionem minime prohibere censemus, quin jubente magistratu in causa fidei et charitatis jurare liceat, modo id fiat juxta Prophetæ doctrinam, in justitia, in judicio et veritate.

Section I. — HISTORY.

WHEN the early Christians were called on to swear before heathen magistrates, they were mostly required to use idolatrous oaths. These were naturally abhorred by them, and perhaps inclined them to a dread of swearing altogether, even more than Scripture would inculcate. Thus Tertullian says, " I say nothing of perjury, since it is unlawful even to swear."[1] Yet from a passage in his *Apology* we find that Christians did not refuse to take lawful oaths ; though idolatrous oaths they, of necessity, rejected. Christians, he says, would not swear by the Emperor's genii ; for the genii were dæmons ; but by the safety of the Emperor they were willing to swear.[2] The same swearing by the safety of the Emperor (ὑπὲρ τῆς σωτηρίας τοῦ εὐσεβεστάτου Αὐγούστου Κωνσταντίου) is mentioned by Athanasius.[3] Vegetius, who lived about A. D. 390, says, the Christian soldiers " swore by God, and Christ, and the Holy Spirit, and the majesty of the Emperor."[4] Nay ! Athanasius required of Constantius that his accusers should be put upon their oath.[5] And much more has been alleged, in

[1] " Taceo de perjurio, quando ne jurare quidem liceat." — *De Idol.* c. 11.

[2] " Sed et juramus, sicut non per genios Cæsarum, ita per salutem eorum, quæ est augustior omnibus geniis. Nescitis genios dæmonas dici ? &c." — *Apol.* c. 32. See other examples of the like objection, *ap.* Bingham, XVI. vii. 7.

[3] *Epist. ad Monach.* Tom. I. p. 866. Colon.

[4] " Jurant autem per Deum, et per Christum, et per Spiritum Sanctum, et per majestatem imperatoris." — Veget. *Institutio Rei Militaris.* See Lardner, VIII. p. 479 ; Cave, *Prim. Christ,* pt. III. ch. I. p. 214.

[5] Athanas. *Apol. ad Constantium,* Tom. I. p. 678.

proof that the early Christians did not refuse legitimate oaths in legal inquiries.

There was, however, doubtless, much scruple on the subject of swearing among the ancients generally. Clement of Alexandria says, the enlightened Christian will never perjure himself. And so he considers it an indignity for a Christian to be put upon oath, as disparaging his fidelity ; and that he will avoid swearing, saying only Yea and Nay.[1] And Lactantius says, that a Christian will never perjure himself, lest he mock God ; nor indeed will he swear at all, lest he fall by accident, or carelessly, into perjury.[2]

Against idle swearing, swearing by the creatures, and perjury, the primitive Church was very severe.[3] And it does indeed appear, that some of the fathers, led by the strong language of Matt. v. 34, and James v. 12, doubted even the lawfulness of oaths at all ; thinking that they may have been permitted to Jews, but forbidden to Christians.[4] The Pelagians took up, as one of their positions, that a man must not swear at all.[5] But Augustine replied, in an epistle cited in the last Article. There he enjoins to avoid swearing as much as possible ; but shows that, in cases of necessity, there was Scriptural ground for it.[6]

In later ages, the Waldenses,[7] the Anabaptists,[8] the Quakers, and some other sects, have held all oaths unlawful. It is against the Anabaptists probably, that this Article, as well as the last, is specially directed.

SECTION II. — SCRIPTURAL PROOF.

IT is probably an admitted fact that oaths were lawful under the old Testament. This Article refers to a passage in the Prophet Jeremiah (iv. 2) : " Thou shalt swear, The LORD liveth, in truth, in judgment, and in righteousness." The only prohibition was against false swearing, or swearing by false gods.[9] It seems likely

---

[1] *Stromat.* VII. 8, p. 861. Potter.

[2] " Hic non pejerabit, ne Deum ludibrio habeat; sed ne jurabit quidem ; ne quando, vel necessitate, vel consuetudine, in perjurium cadat." — Lactant. *Epitome*, c. 6.

[3] Bingham, XVI. vii. 5–8.

[4] So Chrysostom, *Homil.* XV. *in Genesin: Homil.* VIII. *in Act.* ; Theodoret. *In cap.* iv. *Jeremiæ* ; Theophyl. *In cap.* v. *Matth.*, &c. See Suicer, s. v. ὅρκος, Tom. II. p. 510.

[5] Augustin. *Opp.* Tom. II. p. 542.

[6] *Epist.* 157, Tom. II. p. 559. The opinions of the primitive Christians on swearing are fully discussed by Cave, *Prim. Christianity*, pt. III. ch. I. p. 212 ; and Bingham, XVI. vii. See also Suicer, as above.

[7] Mosheim, Cent. XII. pt. II. ch. V. 12.

[8] Ibid. Cent. XVI. sect. III. pt. II. ch. III. 16.

[9] The Third Commandment is probably a prohibition of perjury. " Thou

that the Jews somewhat abused this permission, and were rather free in their use of oaths, and of the name of the Almighty on trivial occasions. Accordingly some strict and ascetic sects among them were led to the opposite extent of refusing to take an oath under any circumstances.[1] If the Jews were thus profane and careless in swearing, we can readily see the object of our Saviour's denunciation of rash oaths. There are obvious and very great dangers in a habit of this kind. If, on every trivial occasion, we have recourse to an oath for attestation, it will almost necessarily follow, that we shall lightly regard an ordinary assertion, and that the sanctity of an oath itself will be less revered. Hence such swearing must foster a spirit of untruthfulness. And again, the readily bringing into common conversation the most sacred name of God, must necessarily lead to irreverence and impiety. What can be more alien from the spirit of the Gospel, than these two habits of falsehood and irreverence ?

Now it seems very apparent, that it is this evil habit which our Lord condemns. The Jews appear to have satisfied themselves, that they might swear as much as they chose, if they did not forswear themselves. But our Lord, enforcing the spirit, not merely the letter, of the commandment, tells them not to swear at all ; and enjoins that, in their common discourse, they should only say yea and nay ; as more than this can come only from the evil one ; Ἔστω δὲ ὁ λόγος ὑμῶν ναὶ ναὶ, οὒ οὔ· τὸ δὲ περισσὸν τούτων ἐκ τοῦ πονηροῦ ἐστιν (Matt. v. 37). The very words used, and the whole tenor of the passage, show that it is to common conversation that the precept applies. St. James's words (James v. 12) are so nearly a repetition of our Lord's, that the former must be interpreted by the latter.

So far then we see the great evil of profane swearing, and of solemn asseverations on unimportant occasions. All such are strictly forbidden by, and thoroughly opposed to, the Gospel of Christ.

But, on solemn and important occasions, and especially in courts of justice, we have new Testament authority for believing that oaths are lawful to Christians as well as to Jews. Our Lord Himself was adjured by the High Priest, and, instead of refusing to plead

---

shalt not lift up the name of the LORD thy God 'to falsehood," *i. e.* Thou shalt not swear falsely by Him. " To take or lift up the name of God " is unquestionably to swear by His name. The word לַשָּׁוְא ? " to vanity," most probably means "for a falsehood." Some interpret it as the LXX., ἐπὶ ματαίῳ, *for a light and vain purpose.* But שָׁוְא is constantly used of *falsehood.* See Exod. xxiii. 1. Deut. v. 17. Psalm xii. 3. &c.

[1] Joseph. *De B. J.* Lib. ii. c. 12.

to such an adjuration, He answered immediately.[1]   This one argument seems a host in itself.   Our Lord consented to be put upon
His oath.   Oaths therefore before a civil tribunal cannot be forbidden to His disciples.   St Paul frequently, in very weighty matters,
calls God to witness, which is essentially taking an oath.   See
Rom. ix. 1.   1 Cor. xv. 31.   2 Cor. i. 18, 23 ; xi. 10, 31; xii. 19.
Gal. i. 20.   Phil. i. 8.   This is St. Augustine's argument against
the Pelagians ; though he says truly, that we must not swear carelessly, because St. Paul swore when there was good reason for
swearing.   Again, in the Epistle to the Hebrews (iii. 11 ; vi. 16,
17), the Almighty is represented as swearing ; and, in the latter
passage, the Apostle compares God's swearing with the swearing
common among men, saying, " Men verily swear by the greater ;
and an oath for confirmation is the end of all strife " (Heb. vi. 16).
With this we ought to compare Matt. xxiii. 16–22.   See also
Rev. x. 6.

Weighing then, all that has been said above, very strong as our
Lord's and St. James's language against oaths may be, it yet
seems impossible to doubt, that it is directed against vain, trivial,
and thoughtless swearing, but not against that legal confirming of
the truth by a solemn attestation in the sight of God, which was
commanded in the Law of Moses, which our blessed Saviour Himself submitted to before Caiaphas, and which the example of the
Apostles, and their general language on the subject, seem not only
to permit, but to sanction also, if not to enjoin.   In short, profane
swearing is altogether forbidden to Christians ; but religious attestation upon oath seems to be acquiesced in as necessary, and admitted as lawful.

---

[1] The high-priest (Matt. xxvi. 63, 64)   on his oath, in the most solemn possible
said ἐξορκίζω σε κατὰ τοῦ Θεοῦ τοῦ ζῶντος :   manner.
a form equivalent to putting a witness

CATALOGUE

OF A

FEW PRINCIPAL FATHERS, COUNCILS, ETC.
WITH THEIR PROBABLE DATES.

	A. D.
Clemens Romanus	70 al. 96
Ignatius	107
Polycarp	108
Papias	116
Justin Martyr	147
Irenæus	180
Clemens Alexandrinus	194
Tertullian	200
Origen	230
Cyprian	250
Lactantius	306
Eusebius of Cæsarea	315
Council of Nice. I.	325
Athanasius	350
Cyril of Jerusalem	350
Hilary of Poictiers	350
Basil of Cæsarea	370
Gregory Nazianzen	370
Gregory Nyssen	370
Epiphanius	370
Ambrose	374
First Council of Constantinople. II.	381
Jerome	390
John Chrysostom	398
Augustine	398
Cyril of Alexandria	412
Isidore of Pelusium	412
Theodoret	423
Hilary of Arles	424
Council of Ephesus. III.	431
Vincentius Lirinensis	434

A. D.

Prosper of Aquitaine 440
Socrates 440
Sozomen 440
Leo I. Pope 440
Council of Chalcedon. IV. 451
Gelasius. Pope 492
Second Council of Constantinople. V. 553
Gregory the Great. Pope 590
Third Council of Constantinople. VI. 681
Venerable Bede 701
Joannes Damascenus 736
Paschasius Radbert 840
Ratramn or Bertram 840
Ælfric, Archbishop of Canterbury 980
Berengarius 1050
Theophylact 1077
Bernard of Clairvaux 1115
Peter Lombard 1141
Thomas Aquinas 1255
Council of Constance . . . . 1414 to 1418
Council of Basil . . . . 1431 to 1443
Council of Florence 1439
Martin Luther 1517
Council of Trent . . . . 1545 to 1563

INDEX OF SUBJECTS.

107

Church and State, and prevalence of Erastian opinions : 772, 773.

Scriptural proof that the Church is divinely authorized to excommunicate offenders, and to restore them on repentance to communion, 773–775 . . . that certain persons in the Church have received from Christ authority to excommunicate and to restore — The chief officers of the Church the principal executors of its authority, yet that authority vested by Divine wisdom not in them alone, but, with them, in the whole body of the faithful : (Ecclesiastical Courts, 778, n.) 775–778.

Extreme Unction, see *Sacraments*, 596, &c.

Faith, see *Justification*, 307, &c.

Final Perseverance, see *Sin after Baptism*, 372, &c., 393, &c., and *Predestination*.

Free Will, Art. x. 261 — sentiments of Apostolical Fathers on, not distinctly expressed — Justin Martyr — Heretics —Origen—Augustine : 261-265 : Goteschalc—Peter Lombard — Schoolmen ; Thomas Aquinas and Duns Scotus, heads of opposing parties : 265, 266, (416.)

Luther ; Melancthon — Council of Trent — Calvin and his followers — Arminius — Synod of Dort : (417–419,) 267–269. Controversies in the Church of Rome on the subject after the Council of Trent; Jansenists ; Jesuits : 269. Socinians, 270. Statements of, and controversies on, doctrine of Free Will in the Church of England — Carefully guarded language of the Art. : 270–273. Scriptural proof of inability of man since the fall to turn himself to faith and godliness, or to do good works acceptable to God — Pelagian arguments refuted : 273–276. Scripture proof of necessity for grace of God, 276–281 . . . for *preventing* grace, 278 — for *coöperating* grace, (language of Art. vindicated,) 279–281.

God, Nature and essential attributes of, 19. Scripturally shown to be Spiritual ; A Personal Being of infinite excellence ; One : 34, 35.

Good Works, present Art., xii., on, added in 1562 . . . supplementary to Art. xi. lest that should be supposed to teach Solifidianism . . . opposed to Antinomian errors . . . to doctrine of schoolmen of good works meriting grace *de congruo*, and *de condigno :* 324, 325. Scriptural proofs that the good works of justified men cannot put away sin and endure God's judgment . . . yet that they are pleasing to God in Christ . . . that they necessarily spring out of a true and living faith : 325–330.

Goods of Christians not common, Art. xxxviii. 835. Almsgiving and sacrifice of wealth for the Church and poor practised by the early Christians to an extent now unknown — Language of Justin Martyr and Tertullian which might seem at first sight to affirm community of goods, shown not really and strictly to mean it — Clement of Alexandria and Augustine argue against necessity of resignation of all property — Erroneous views on this subject condemned by the Church — Voluntary poverty not condemned in the Art., but only the fanatical belief that all property is unlawful : 835, 836. The right of owners to their property recognized by the New Testament — passages which might seem inconsistent with this view explained — Most cogent obligation on every follower of Christ liberally to give alms according to his ability : 836–839.

Heresies and Sects, sundry, notices of : — *Anabaptists ;* 195, 369., 377, 555, 613, 646, 664, 836, 841. — *Antinomians ;* 194, 195, 297. — *Apollinarianism ;* 67, 94, 96, 230, 234, 235. — *Arianism :* 30–32, 47, 50, 53, 66–68, 93, 119, 223–227, 232–234, 368. — *Donatists ;* 371, 611–614. — *Eutychianism ;* 69, 105, 230, 232, 234. — *Gnosticism ;* 20, 28, 46, 60, 61, 67, 70, 105, 107, 119, 177, 194, 234, 241, 262, 364, 600, 651, 692, 759. — *Macedonianism ;* 32, 50, 120, 226. — *Manichæanism ;* 20, 31, 67, 105, 107, 177, 194, 241, 264, 357, 371, 600. — *Marcionitism ;* 105, 107, 194, 241, 262. — *Monothelites ;* 70. — *Montanism ;* 26, 121, 365, 613, 759. — *Nestorianism ;* 68, 74, 230, 232, 235. — *Novatians ;* 26, 366, 388. — *Pelagianism :* 242, 243, 252, 264, 274, 332, 333, 354, 415, 444, 645, 841. — *Quakers ;* 555, 841. — *Sabellianism ;* 29, 30, 54–62, 119, 232, 233, 371. — *Socinianism ;* 56, 67, 70, 80, 121, 247, 270. — *Swedenborgians ;* 70, 107.

Holy Ghost, the, Divinity of; early heretics who denied it generally disbelievers of His Personality — Gnostics ; Sabellians : 119. His Divinity, though not Personality, denied by Arians and Macedonians, 119, 120.

Unsound doctrines concerning the Holy Ghost imputed to Origen (probably without sufficient reason), and to Lactantius, 120. Strange heresy attributed to Montanus, 121. Personality of the Holy Ghost generally denied by the Socinians, 121. Procession of the Holy Ghost, see *Procession*. Holy Ghost, Sin against the, see *Sin after Baptism*.

Holy Ghost, the other particulars concerning, see *Trinity*.

Homilies, the, Art. xxxv. Great need

ing with Luther in. statement on justification, 295–298.

Doctrine of Luther (modified) embraced by English Reformers — Judgment of Cranmer and his companions expressed by Homily of Justification (or Salvation) and xith Art. of 1552 — Language of present Art. very similar to that of Melancthon and the Augsburg Confession — Doctrine of Homily of Salvation, and Liturgy, &c. — Differences among later English Divines rather logical than practical — Hooker — Bp. Bull — Barrow — Waterland, &c. — Certain practical truths of importance allowed by all parties, Romanist and Protestant: 298–303. "Justification," Scriptural meaning of, investigated, 304–307.

"*Faith*," investigation of usages of the term in Scripture, especially in St. Paul's writings, 307–312. Faith in general, 308–310. Justifying Faith, 310–312. Justification, general Scriptural view of doctrine of, 313, 314. Justification by faith, investigation of peculiar signification attached by St. Paul to this his favourite formula, 314–318. Justification, certain questions on — An *act* or a *state* ? — Faith ? or Faith and good works ? or Faith and holiness ? to be called the *condition* or *conditions* of justification ? — Justification by faith, how consistent with judgment according to works ? (see 115) — Baptism and Faith being the ordinary instruments of justification, whether necessary for it without exception ? — Whether the language of St. James is opposed to the doctrine of St. Paul ? 318–323.

Lambeth Articles, see *Sin after Baptism*, 379, 380, and *Predestination*, 426, n.

Lord's Supper, the, Art. xxviii. 683. Presence of Christ in that Sacrament, four principal opinions on: Transubstantiation, doctrine of Church of Rome ; Consubstantiation, of Luther ; Real Spiritual Presence, of Church of England and of Calvin ; no presence, mere commemoration of Christ's death, doctrine of Zuingle : 683, 684. Doctrine of the early ages concluded, on weighing all considerations, and notwithstanding some remarkable phrases, (the language of the fathers is often rhetorical, and not so guarded as ours has necessarily become, 685,) to be not in favour of a miraculous change in the consecrated elements, nor of a carnal presence of the natural body of Christ, but in favour of a real, effectual, life-giving presence of Christ's spiritual Body, communicated to the faithful, and feeding the souls of His disciples, (701.) (Perhaps *possible* alternative of consubstantiation being contemplated by some of the fathers, 701, 702.) Subject discussed ; and quotations adduced, from Ignatius to Theodoret : 684–701. Controversies of the Middle Ages — Growth of transubstantiation — the doctrine nearly, if not quite, expressed in language of Radbert, about A. D. 830 — the *term* said to have been invented about A. D. 1100 — the doctrine declared an article of faith by Council of Lateran, A. D 1216 — and decreed by Council of Trent, and professed in creed of Pius IV. — Established doctrine of the Roman Church — differences of statement and of thought, however, still admitted on the subject : 702–707. Doctrines of the Reformation — Luther ; Zuingle ; Calvin — English Reformers — Cranmer and Ridley — Formularies and Views of the Church of England : 707–715 (and 683, 684). Scriptural proof of the true doctrine of the Lord's Supper . . . from *The Words of Institution*, 715–723 . . . from *Our Lord's Discourse at Capernaum*, John vi. 723–727 . . . from *The Statements of St. Paul*, 727–731. Elevation, &c. of the Host founded on belief in Transubstantiation, consequently rejected with that doctrine, 731, n. See *Sacraments*.

Marriage of Priests, Art. xxxii. 758. Marriage of clergy evidently allowed in the earliest ages of the Church — *Second* marriages considered in very early times as disqualifying for ordination, though not universally so held ; St. Paul's words on monogamy of a Bishop being interpreted by many eminent fathers of divorce and subsequent marriage : 758, 759. Early creeping in, however, of exaggerated esteem for celibacy — Ascetic views of Essenes, Montanists, Gnostics, and others — Language of our Lord and of St. Paul, speaking of a single life as more favourable to piety, because freer from worldly distractions, pressed to its utmost consequences — Some clergy began to separate from their wives, and laymen to refuse the ministration of a married priest — these errors at first opposed by Councils and Canons — Proposal made at the Council of Nice that the clergy should be obliged to abstain from the society of their wives married before ordination, but opposed by Paphnutius, who urges that it should suffice that the clergy should not marry after ordination ; the whole council assent to his words — Notices of other Councils — Gradual progress of principle of clerical celibacy in the West — Clerical celibacy

ural declarations of the perfect dominion, &c. enjoyed by Christ on His final exaltation to be seated at the right hand of the Father, 110, 111.   See *Resurrection*.

Sin after Baptism; Art. xvi. very nearly same as Art. xv. of 1552, which was followed by an express Art. on Blasphemy against the Holy Ghost, 364.

Possibility of repentance and forgiveness for sins committed after Baptism, some stir on, even in early ages of the Church—opinions of fathers; heretics; sects: 364–368. Views on the subject at the time of the Reformation—Anabaptists—Council of Trent—Continental and English Reformers: 369, 370. Holy Ghost, sin against the; language of the Art. directed against opinion first broached by Origen, that blasphemy against the Holy Ghost is when baptized Christians sin . . . opposed by Athanasius—Observations of Augustine—Origen's theory rejected by the Church at large, but adopted by the Novatians: 370–372. Sin against the Holy Ghost, nature of, investigated from Scripture—Statements of Athanasius and of Augustine: 391–393. Possibility of falling from grace; closely connected with Predestination—Meaning attached by early fathers to Scripture language used by them respecting predestination to grace, not immediately certain—Augustine; his doctrine of perseverance—Greater precision of terms induced by controversies on Pelagianism, and on the predestinarian doctrines of Augustine—Augustine's doctrine of perseverance: 372–376.

Final Perseverance discussed at time of the Reformation—Council of Trent—Luther; Zuingle; Confession of Augsburg; Calvinistic divines—English Reformers; this Art., Homilies, Liturgy, etc.: 376–378. Lambeth Articles; Hampton Court Conference: 379, 380 (and 425).

Scriptural proof that sins after baptism are not, generally, unpardonable, 380–383. Scripture passages which have led to belief that deadly sin after baptism is unpardonable, considered, and concluded, although so severe against wilful offenders against light and grace, (and strict as the discipline of the early Church was against all such offenders,) yet not to afford any proof that heinous sin after baptism cannot be pardoned on repentance; strongest and severest texts seem to apply to apostates hardened in sin: 384–391.

Final Perseverance, or Indefectibility of Grace, doctrine of, rejected in Art. xvi.—Views of Zuinglians and high Calvinists—Augustine—Lutherans—English Reformers: 393, 394. Arguments alleged from Scripture in favour of doctrine of Final Perseverance; shown to be invalid: 394–397. Scripture proof of possibility of falling from a state of grace—doctrine of Indefectibility of grace introduced (it is contended) by Calvin as seeming necessary to the harmony and completeness of his predestinarian scheme; 397–400.

Sin, Christ alone without; Art. xv. (connected with some preceding Artt. and probably supplementary to preceding Art.)—Pelagianism—Sinfulness of the Virgin Mary made a question . . . not decided in Council of Trent: 354, 355. Scriptural proof of sinlessness of our Saviour; who took our *perfect* nature, which includes *liability* to sin, though He took not sin, a *fault* of it: 356–358. Scriptural proof of sinfulness of all other men, even though baptized and born again—*Blameless* perfection attributed to persons in Scripture in a popular, not absolute sense: 359–361. The Blessed Virgin scripturally shown to be, though most singularly holy, not exempt from sin, 361–363.

Sin, Original, Art. ix. 239. Origin of evil a very early subject of speculation among philosophers and divines—Original Sin; doctrine of, appears to have been held by the Jews: 239 . . . Belief of, by the Christian fathers, 240 . . . Early heresies on, 241. Origen's theory, 241. Pelagianism; Semi-Pelagians: 242, 243. Views of the mediæval Schoolmen on Original Sin, 243, 244. Decrees of Council of Trent on this subject, 244 . . . differing from doctrine of Anglican Church in affirming the entire cancelling of original sin in baptism, 245. Lutheran views; our ix. Art. derived from iid of Augsburg Confession: 245. Calvin—Difference among Calvinists on first introduction of original sin—Difference between Calvinists and Arminians on *extent* of vitiation of our nature by the fall: 246, 247. (See also 253–256.) Anabaptists—Socinians: 247. Guarded language of the Church of England—Homilies: 247, 248. Scriptural proof that Original Sin infects all men, 248–251 . . . is not derived from imitation, but inherited by birth, 251–253. Scriptural views considered relating to the *extent* of this naturally inherited corruption, 253–256 . . . of the doctrine that original sin deserves God's wrath and damnation, 256–258. Scripture proof that infection of original sin is not wholly removed by baptism, 258–260

the Arian finally, by Council of Constantinople — Philoponus : 32. Nominalists charged with Tritheism, 32, 33. Unitarians — Lælius and Faustus Socinus — Whiston and Clarke — Priestley — Tendency of Presbyterians, with exception of Kirk of Scotland, to Socinianism — Foreign Protestant Rationalism favourable to Unitarian views : 33. Trinity of distinct Persons in the Godhead Scripturally proved, 37–64. Doctrine not so expressly declared in Scripture as some others ; not therefore less true — Manner of Scripture teaching — Means for instruction provided in the Church : 37.

Scripture teaches Unity of God . . . Plurality in the Godhead . . . yet not plurality of Gods . . . Distinct personality of the Father, Son, and Holy Ghost : 38. Intimations of Plurality in the Godhead in Old Testament, 39, 40.

Distinct declarations of such Plurality, and of the Godhead of the Father, Son, and Holy Ghost, in New Testament, 41. Godhead of the Son taught in New Testament, by *reasonable inference*, 41–43 . . . by *direct statement*, 44–49. Godhead of the Holy Ghost taught in Scripture, 49–51.

Unity of Godhead in Trinity of Persons scripturally proved, 51–54. Distinct Personality of the Father, Son, and Holy Ghost, scripturally proved, 54, 55 . . . of the Son, 51–62. (Sabellian views of first chap. of St. John confuted, 59–62.) . . . of the Holy Ghost, 62, 63. The whole subject, though above our understanding, yet not contrary to our reason, 64. Language of the fathers in relation to three Persons in one God, 64, 65.

Unworthiness of Ministers, Art. xxvi. 610. Heretical Baptism, question concerning, in the primitive Church . . . connected with, though quite different from, the question treated of in this Art. — Necessity of personal holiness of ministers to validity of ministrations, held by Donatists ; by Anabaptists ; (evil living of lower class of friars in Middle Ages a principal ground for cry of reform, 613 ;) not held by the fathers ; not by Church of Rome ; not by foreign nor English Reformers : 610–614.

"*Intention*" of ministers necessary to validity of ministration, Roman Catholic doctrine of, not originally aimed at, but in effect met, by this Art., 614, 615. Evil ministers, inquiry to be made concerning, and they when found guilty to be deposed, 616. Scriptural proof that "in the Visible

Church the evil are ever mingled with the good " . . . and that the ministration of evil ministers is valid . . . yet that obviously ministers ought to be holy, and ought, if proved to be ungodly, to be deposed : 616–618.

War not necessarily unlawful, see *Civil Magistrates*, 832–834.

Wicked, the, do not eat the Body of Christ in the Lord's Supper, Art xxix. (expunged for a time by Queen Elizabeth, probably as not agreeable to the members of the Church holding Lutheran views, 735), 732. The Body and Blood of Christ either not eaten at all, or eaten, but only to condemnation, the two only alternatives ; the former generally held, in latter times, by advocates of a spiritual feeding, the latter by believers in transubstantiation, and (it is supposed) though not necessarily, by most believers in consubstantiation — Teaching of the fathers obscure, yet some plain passages in them strongly in favour of the view taken in this Art. — Quotations — Prayer in ancient Liturgies for descent of the Holy Ghost on the elements no proof of necessary belief that communicants, unworthy as well as worthy, must necessarily partake of Christ's Body and Blood if partaking of the elements after that descent — Similar invocation of the Spirit made in Baptism known to involve neither change of the water (nor admixture of the Holy Spirit with it) nor obtaining of sanctification by an unworthy recipient — Sanctification of the elements, to a new relation, not to a new nature — Belief of reception of the very Body and Blood of Christ naturally held with belief in the *opus operatum*, and in transubstantiation : 732–735. Scriptural proof of the doctrine of this Art. 735–737.

Works before justification, Art. xiii. (*title* of Art. probably adopted because the question discussed in it went by that name at the time of the Reformation, 335), 331. Nature of heathen virtue a question of great difficulty, touched on by the fathers before and after Pelagian controversy — Augustine's answer to Pelagian arguments — Doctrine of schoolmen concerning grace *de congruo* like that of Semi-Pelagians . . . opposed by Luther (see also 289). 331–333. On subject of this Art. decision of Council of Trent . . . views of Lutherans . . . of our own Reformers : 333, 334. Arguments alleged from Scripture against the positions of this Art. that works before grace are not pleasing to God, but rather have the nature of sin . . . and refuted

INDEX OF TEXTS

EXPLAINED, ILLUSTRATED, OR REFERRED TO.

———◆———

109

THE END.